Collins
Shorter Contemporary Dictionary

COLLINS SHORTER CONTEMPORARY DICTIONARY

26,000 words and phrases
clearly and simply explained

edited by
F. R. WITTY, M.Ed., B.Sc.
HEADMASTER, STANLEY SECONDARY SCHOOL, SOUTHPORT.

COLLINS: LONDON AND GLASGOW

This edition first published 1972

PRINTED IN GREAT BRITAIN
COLLINS CLEAR-TYPE PRESS

CONTENTS

ABBREVIATIONS
USED IN THIS BOOK

adj.	adjective
adv.	adverb
comp.	comparative
conj.	conjunction
e.g.	for example
esp.	especially
fem.	feminine
i.e.	that is to say
interj.	interjection
masc.	masculine
n.	noun
p. part.	past participle
p.t.	past tense
pers.	person
pl.	plural
prep.	preposition
pres. part.	present participle
pron.	pronoun
sing.	singular
sup.	superlative
v.	verb

USING THE DICTIONARY

This addition to the family of CONTEMPORARY DICTIONARIES is intended for students who are at an intermediate stage in their study of English. It contains about 26,000 words and phrases and so presents sufficient material to meet their needs with something to spare.

A notable feature of the book is the inclusion of local words from a variety of English-speaking countries. This means that the student is likely to find in A SHORTER CONTEMPORARY DICTIONARY those words he meets and needs in his everyday life as well as those in his literary studies.

HEADWORDS AND GUIDEWORDS

Under each headword the user will find closely related *derived* words and compounds. This, however, is done only when the derived words are so close to the headword in spelling and sound that no difficulty can arise. When there is any doubt the derived word is given an entry of its own at its proper alphabetical place.

EXAMPLES

admin'ister *v.* 1. to manage. 2. to dispense, as justice. 3. to give, as medicine or First Aid.—**administra'tion** *n.* 1. management, esp. Government. 2. those who administer. 3. application.—**admin'istrative** *adj.*—**admin'istrator** *n.*

ad'miral *n.* a naval officer of the highest rank.—**Ad'miralty** *n.* the government department which controls naval affairs

admire' *v.* 1. to wonder at. 2. to love. 3. to respect.—**admir'ing** *pres. part.*—**admir'er** *n.*—**ad'mirable** *adj.* excellent.—**admira'tion** *n.*

admis'sible *adj.* allowable, acceptable.—**admis'sibly** *adv.*

admis'sion (ad-mish'un) *n.* 1. entrance. 2. entrance fee. 3. confession, as *The prisoner's admission of his guilt was a surprise*

In this extract derived words can be seen under the headwords **administer, admiral, admire.** But **admissible** is given an entry to itself. It is not put under **admission,** because although the words are related the meanings are different.

The guidewords at the top of each page show the first and last words on that page and so guide the reader more quickly to the word he wants.

PRONUNCIATION

There are two main difficulties about pronouncing unfamiliar words. One is the question of accent or stress—which syllable should be accented. The other is the pronunciation of the syllables themselves, with their vowels and consonants. Both difficulties are dealt with in this dictionary.

First, the stress mark (′) is placed *immediately after the stressed or accented syllable of the word.* It should thus be quite clear that the stress falls on the second syllable of **aback′** and **abhor′** and on the fourth syllable of **impossibil′ity.**

The pronunciation of the sounds in the syllables has been dealt with as follows:

1. When the vowel in a stressed syllable is *long*, the stress mark comes immediately after the vowel and before the next consonant. When the vowel is *short*, the stress mark follows the consonant. Thus, **sa′vour** has a long ā, but **sav′age** has a short ă.

2. Where there is any doubt or difficulty about the pronunciation of a word, it is given in brackets in ordinary type, immediately after the head-word thus: **coun′try** (kun′tri). To make the pronunciation clear only certain letters have been used. Here is a list. Note that any one letter *always* has the same sound as in the pronunciation guide.

SOUND	EXAMPLES
ā *in* pay	rate (rāt), break (brāk), weigh (wā)
a *in* pat	after (after), adjacent (a-jā′sent), bargain (bar′gan)
ah *in* calm	father (fah′THer), castle (kahs′l), laugh (lahf)
aw *in* law	auction (awk′shun), alter (awl′ter), bought (bawt)
ee *in* freeze	chief (cheef), eat (eet), quay (kee)
e *in* get	echo (ek′ō), enrage (en-rāj′), bereft (bee-reft′)
i *in* hit	squint (skwint), initial (in-ish′al), mix (miks)
ī *in* bite	night (nīt), tire (tīr), bicycle (bī′sikl)
o *in* lot	block (blok), knot (not), cross (kros)
ō *in* rope	open (ō′pen), groan (grōn), blow (blō)
oo *in* book	look (look), would (wood), fool (fool)
ōō *in* food	ooze (ōōz), boot (bōōt), groove (grōōv)
ū *in* tune	due (dū), cure (kūr), view (vū)
u *in* hut	butter (but′er), numb (num), some (sum)
oi *in* boil	oily (oi′li), enjoy (en-joi′), buoy (boi)
ow *in* how	mouse (mows), brown (brown), aloud (a-lowd′)
ch *in* church	chief (cheef), match (mach), achieve (a-cheev′)
f *in* film	faint (fānt), phrase (frāz), rough (ruf)
g *in* got	agree (a-gree′), guest (gest), ghost (gōst)
gw *in* language	anguish (ang′gwish)
gz *in* example	exact (egz-akt′), examine (egz-am′in), exert (egz-ert′)
hw *in* what	why (hwī), which (hwich), whether (hweTH′er)
j *in* jam	jolly (jol′i), agile (aj′īl), judge (juj)
k *in* kill	kitchen (kich′en), comb (kōm), chorus (kō′rus)
ks *in* box	expose (eks-poz′), tax (taks), quixotic (kwiks-ot′ik)
kw *in* quick	quiet (kwī′et), inquire (in-kwīr′), qualify (kwol′i-fī)
n *in* not	nail (nāl), knot (not), pneumatic (nū-mat′ik)
ng *in* ring	single (sing′l), monkey (mung′ki), banquet (bang′kwet)
s *in* hiss	sister (sis′ter), cigar (si-gar′), science (sī′ens)
sh *in* shut	shoulder (shol′der), sure (shoor), action (ak′shun)
th *in* think	thought (thawt), breath (breth), bath (bath)
TH *in* this	though (THō), breathe (breeTH), bathe (bāTH)
y *in* yes	yacht (yot), yesterday (yes′ter-dā), you (yōō)
z *in* zest	Zulu (Zoo′loo), was (woz), fuse (fūz)
zh *in* pleasure	āzure (a′zher), measure (mezh′ur)

GRAMMATICAL LABELS

It is often necessary to know what part of speech a word usually is. This is indicated after every headword and derived word as follows: *n.* (noun), *v.* (verb), *adj.* (adjective), *adv.* (adverb), *prep.* (preposition), *conj.* (conjunction), *int.* (interjection). It is important, however, to remember that 'parts of speech' are not fixed things. Almost every word can be used as more than one part of speech, depending on its function in the sentence. It is *function* that is important, not the label in the dictionary. If you are not sure what this means, ask your teacher to explain.

In addition, the dictionary spells out plurals of nouns and the participles and past tenses of verbs wherever these are in any way irregular (for example, see **tooth, appendix, eat, carry**). Masculine and feminine forms and collective (or group) nouns are also listed (see **sheep, partridge**).

MEANINGS

Meanings are given in simple words to avoid as far as possible the need for further 'looking up' of unfamiliar words. Where a word has different meanings, these are numbered 1, 2, 3, and so on. Be sure to read *all* of the meanings before picking the one that fits the sentence you are reading.

EXAMPLE

> **age** *n.* **1.** length of time a person or thing has existed. **2.** period of history, as *the Elizabethan age.* **3.** a long time—*v.* to make or grow old.—**ageing** or **ag'ing** (ā'jing) *pres. part.*—**aged** (ājd) *p.t., p. part.* and *adj.* **1.** grown old. **2.** of the age of, as *a girl aged six.* **3.** (ā'jed) elderly.—**the aged** (ā'jed) *n. pl.* old people.—**age'less** *adj.* not growing old.—**age'long** *adj.* lasting for a long time.—**of age,** recognised by law as grown up, usually at age of 21 years

EXAMPLES

Where it helps to make things clear, sample sentences or phrases showing the word in use are given in italic type. These are particularly useful when a word has several meanings.

EXAMPLE

> **car'ry** *v.* **1.** to take from one place to another, as *to carry a parcel.* **2.** to reach, as *The shot did not carry far enough.* **3.** to hold, behave, as *She carries herself well.* **4.** to maintain, support, as *to carry heavy responsibilities*

See also under **care** and **make.**

When examples of this kind are given, please read them carefully as they help you to see *how* the word is used.

SYNONYMS AND ANTONYMS

For certain words a selection of synonyms and antonyms is given, introduced by the words *Compare* or *Contrast*. Where necessary, notes are added on how the different words are used.

EXAMPLES

At the end of the entry **merciful** you will find:

> *Compare:* gentle, forgiving, humane, compassionate, clement, pitiful, pitying, tender-hearted. *Contrast:* cruel, brutal, fierce, inhuman, merciless, pitiless, ruthless, savage, unmerciful

Under **clever** you will find:

> *Compare:* intellectual, intelligent, bright, quick-witted, sharp, smart, talented, gifted. *Contrast:* silly, stupid, foolish, dull, thick-headed, unintelligent, slow, backward
>
> *Note: Clever* is a general term covering many kinds of mental ability and should not be over-worked. *Intellectual* means possessing the higher qualities of the mind. *Intelligent* means mentally alert, *bright* or *quick-witted*; but the meaning of the latter shades off into *sharp* and *smart*, which are sometimes used to describe rather unpleasant qualities. *Talented* and *gifted* mean having natural abilities

See also **habitual, honest, house.** Almost every page of the dictionary contains examples of this aid to understanding.

NOTES ON USAGE

One of the aims of this dictionary is to help the student in the correct use of words. Therefore, notes have been included on special usages and attention is drawn to common errors in usage. These notes occur at the end of the main entry.

EXAMPLES

Under **both** you will find:

> *Note:* The various uses of *both* may be shown as follows—Adjective, *Both men were there.* Pronoun. *Both are here.* Adverb. *He is both tired and hungry.* Conjunction. *Both boys and girls came to the party*

Under **neither** you will find:

> *Note:* 1. *neither* may be followed by *nor*, but not by *or* (*either* is followed by *or*). 2. *neither* is followed by a singular verb after singular nouns. *Neither* is followed by a plural verb only after plural nouns. Thus,

> *neither Jack nor Jill was hurt. Neither knives nor forks were on the table.* Note also, *neither of them was hurt*

Under **awful** you will find:

> *Note:* In common speech the word *awful* is often used to mean troublesome, bad, horrid, etc., as *an awful nuisance*

Under **lot** you will find:

> *Note:* The expressions *a lot of, lots of,* are vague and should be avoided before words of quality. Use instead *much, many, several, numerous,* etc. before words expressing number

In this connection, special care has been taken to show how the meaning of a word may be changed by the preposition that follows it. For example, under **call** you will find:

> *Note:* The meaning of this word is altered by the prepositions used with it. Thus **call for** means to require, as *This calls for an answer*; *call forth*, produce; *call off*, cancel; *call on*, visit; invite, as *He called on me for help*; *call up*, to summon for service esp. military; recall

See also **break.**

COMPOUND WORDS

More compound words are given than is usual in small dictionaries. This is because it is felt that these are the words that students often find difficulty with. Sometimes the meaning of the original word is changed, and often it is impossible to guess the meaning of a compound word if you know only the original word. The ordinary meaning of **set** does not tell you that a **setback** is a check or **set-to** a fight; nor does **short** tell us that **shortcake** is a biscuit and a **short circuit** an electrical fault, nor **blue** that a **bluebottle** is a kind of fly, or a **bluejacket** a sailor, or a **blueprint** a plan, or a **blue-book** a government report.

PHRASES AND IDIOMS

A special feature of the dictionary is the large number of *phrases* and *idioms* that are explained. These usages are a constant source of difficulty to students of English and this dictionary will be more than usually valuable because of the help it gives in mastering them. Examples can be found on every page. Here are a few chosen at random: sail near the wind, up to scratch, see something through, see through something, up to the eyes, fall back, fall off, fall on, fall out, fall in, fall to, fall through, fall short. Prepositions following verbs are especially troublesome. It is important, for example, to be clear about the difference between play down, play up, play up to, and between take after, take down, take in, take off, take on, take out, take over, take to, take up, not to speak of take in hand, take the chair, take it out of, and so on.

The phrases are arranged in alphabetical order, after the headword and derived words have been defined, like this:

EXAMPLES

blow (blō) *n.* a stroke.—**at one blow** all at once
Compare: stroke, box, buffet, thump, misfortune, disaster, shock
A *blow* is delivered suddenly by the hand or a weapon. A *box* on the ears or a *buffet* or *thump* are usually given with the hand. A *stroke* is a sweeping kind of *blow*, given py a sword, for example. A *blow* delivered by fate is a *disaster* or *misfortune*. A *shock* is rather what results from a *blow* than the *blow* itself

blow (blō) *v.* to make a current of air; puff, pant, as *The wind blows, He blows a bugle.* —**blew** *p.t.*—**blown** *p. part.*—**to blow hot and cold** to be irresolute.—**to blow one's own trumpet** to boast.—**to blow one's top** (slang) to be furiously angry.—**to blow over** to pass off.—**to blow up** to explode

make *v.* 1. to build, shape, produce, put together, as *to make a ship, a cake.* 2. to appoint, as *He was made a bishop.* 3. to cause to do something, as *We were made to get up.* 4. to reach, as *The ship made port in safety.* 5. to earn, as *He makes £20 a week.* 6. to perform, do, as *to make a mistake, a journey.* 7. to amount to, as *Two and two make four.* 8. to prepare, as *to make a bed.*—**ma'king** *pres. part.*—**made** *p.t.* and *p. part.*—*n.* 1. style, form, as *A good make of shoe.* 2. kind, as *What make of car is that?*—**ma'ker** *n.*—**make'shift** *n.* something used instead of the right thing. —**ma'king** *n.* make, structure.—*pl.* essential qualities, as *He has the makings of a good bowler.*—**make away with** to get rid of, kill.—**make believe** to pretend.—**make for** to go towards with purpose.—**make fun of** to laugh at.—**make good** to pay for, fulfil.—**make a little of** to treat lightly.—**make much of** to treat as being important.—**make out** 1. to write out, e.g. a cheque. 2. to pretend. 3. to understand. 4. to succeed, get on, as *How did you make out?*—**make over** to hand over.—**make sail** to start out.—**make up** 1. to put together. 2. to invent. 3. to put powder, lipstick, etc. on a face. 4. to settle a quarrel.—**make up to** to make friendly approaches to

These two examples show many of the features discussed above—pronunciation, meanings simply explained, irregular parts fully given, sample sentences showing usage, synonyms, notes on usage, compounds, phrases and idioms.

ABBREVIATIONS

A.1 first-rate
A.A. Automobile Association
A.B. able-bodied seaman
A.B.C. Australian Broadcasting Corporation
A.C. alternating current
acc., a/c account
A.C.T. Australian Capital Territory
A.D. *Anno Domini*, in the year of Our Lord
ad. lib. *ad libitum*, as much as you please
advt. advertisement
A.I.F. Australian Infantry Forces
Ala. Alabama
Alta. Alberta
a.m. *ante meridiem*, before noon
anon. anonymous
Ariz. Arizona
Ark. Arkansas
Atty. Gen. Attorney General
B.A. Bachelor of Arts
Bart., Bt. Baronet
B.B. Boys' Brigade
B.B.C. British Broadcasting Corporation
B.C. before Christ; British Columbia
B.D. Bachelor of Divinity
B.Ed. Bachelor of Education
Beds. Bedfordshire
Berks. Berkshire
Bib. Bible; biblical
B.M.A. British Medical Association
Bros. Brothers (commercial)
B.Sc. Bachelor of Science
Bucks. Buckinghamshire
C. centigrade, Celsius
Cal. California
Cambs. Cambridgeshire
Cantab. Cambridge
Capt. Captain
C.B.C. Canadian Broadcasting Corporation
cf. compare
C.I.D. Criminal Investigation Department
Co. Company; county
c/o care of (on letters)
C.O.D. cash on delivery
Col. Colonel
Colo. Colorado
Conn. Connecticut
Co-op. Co-operative Society
Cr. credit
C.S.I.R.O. Commonwealth Scientific and Industrial Research Organisation
D.C. District of Columbia; direct current
D.C.M. Distinguished Conduct Medal
D.D. Doctor of Divinity
Del. Delaware
dept. department
D.F.C., D.F.M. Distinguished Flying Cross, Medal
do. *ditto*, the same again
Dr. Doctor
D.Sc. Doctor of Science
D.S.C., D.S.M., D.S.O. Distinguished Service Cross, Medal, Order
E.E.C. European Economic Community
e.g. *exempli gratia*, for example
E.R. *Elizabeth Regina*, Elizabeth Queen
esq. esquire
etc. *et cetera*, and so on
f, ff (in music) *forte*, *fortissimo*, loud, very loud
F.B.I. Federation of British Industries; (U.S.A.) Federal Bureau of Investigation
Fla. Florida
F.P. fire plug (hydrant)
Fr. Father (used before a priest's name)
F.R.C.P., F.R.C.S. Fellow of the Royal College of Physicians, Surgeons
F.R.S. Fellow of the Royal Society
ft. foot
Ga. Georgia
gal. gallon
G.C. George Cross
Glos. Gloucestershire
G.M.T. Greenwich Mean Time
G.P.O. General Post Office
Hants. Hampshire
Herts. Hertfordshire
H.M. Her (or His) Majesty
H.M.A.S. Her (or His) Majesty's Australian Ship
H.M.C.S. Her (or His) Majesty's Canadian Ship
H.M.S. Her (or His) Majesty's Ship
H.M.S.O. Her (or His) Majesty's Stationery Office
Hon. Honorary; Honourable
H.P. Houses of Parliament
h.p. horse power
H.R.H. Her (or His) Royal Highness
i.e. *id est*, that is
Ill. Illinois
inc. incorporated
Ind. Indiana
inst. instant; this month
I.O.U. I owe you
I.Q. Intelligence Quotient
I.R.A. Irish Republican Army
J.P. Justice of the Peace
jun., jr. junior
Kan. Kansas
km. kilometre(s)
Ky. Kentucky
La. Louisiana
Lancs. Lancashire
lat. latitude
l.b.w. leg before wicket (in cricket)
Leics. Leicestershire
Lieut. Lieutenant
Lincs. Lincolnshire
Ll. B. Bachelor of Laws
lon(g). longitude

Ltd. Limited (after the name of a firm)
Lt.-Gov. Lieutenant-Governor
M.A. Master of Arts
Maj. Major
Man. Manitoba
Mass. Massachusetts
M.B. Bachelor of Medicine
Md. Maryland
Me. Maine
Messrs. *messieurs*, gentlemen
Mich. Michigan
Minn. Minnesota
Miss. Mississippi
M.L.A. Member of the Legislative Assembly
Mo. Missouri
Mont. Montana
M.P. Member of Parliament
MS(s) manuscripts
Mus. Bac. Bachelor of Music
N.A.T.O. North Atlantic Treaty Organisation
N.B. *nota bene*, note well
N.B. North Britain; New Brunswick
N.C. North Carolina
N.C.O. non-commissioned officer
N. Dak. North Dakota
Nebr. Nebraska
Nev. Nevada
N'f'ld Newfoundland
N.H. New Hampshire
N.J. New Jersey
N. Mex. New Mexico
no. *numero*, number
Northants. Northamptonshire
Notts. Nottinghamshire
N.S. Nova Scotia
N.S.W. New South Wales
N.T. Northern Territory
N.W.T. Northwest Territories
N.Y. New York
O.B.E. Officer of the British Empire
O.H.M.S. On Her (or His) Majesty's Service
O.K. all right
Okla. Oklahoma
Ont. Ontario
Oreg. Oregon
Oxon. Oxford
Penn. Pennsylvania
p, pp (in music) *piano*, *pianissimo*, soft, very soft
P.C. Privy Councillor; Police Constable; post card
P.E. Physical Education
P.E.I. Prince Edward Island
per cent *per centum*, out of each hundred
p.m. *post meridiem*, after noon
P.O. post office; postal order
p.p. *per pro*, on behalf of (used when signing a letter for someone else)
P.Q. (province of) Quebec
P.S. *post scriptum*, written after
P.T.O. please turn over
Pty. Proprietary (in names of firms)
Q., Qld. Queensland
q.e.d. *quod erat demonstrandum*, which was to be shown
Que. Quebec
q.v. *quod vide*, which see
R.A. Royal Academy; Royal Artillery
R.A.A.F. Royal Australian Air Force
R.A.C. Royal Automobile Club
R.A.F. Royal Air Force
R.A.N. Royal Australian Navy
R.C. Roman Catholic
R.C.A.F. Royal Canadian Air Force
R.C.M.P. Royal Canadian Mounted Police
R.C.N. Royal Canadian Navy
Rev. (before the name of a clergyman) Reverend
R.I. Rhode Island
R.I.P. (on tombstones) *requiescat in pace*, rest in peace
R.N. Royal Navy
R.N.V.R. Royal Naval Volunteer Reserve
R.S.V.P. *Répondez s'il vous plaît*, please reply
Rt. Hon. Right Honourable
S.A. South Australia
Salop. Shropshire
Sask. Saskatchewan
S.C. South Carolina
S. Dak. South Dakota
S.E.A.T.O. South East Asia Treaty Organisation
S.S. steamship
St. Saint; street
Staffs. Staffordshire
Tas. Tasmania
Tenn. Tennessee
Tex. Texas
tp. township
U.K. United Kingdom
ult. last (month)
U.N. United Nations
U.N.E.S.C.O. United Nations Educational, Scientific and Cultural Organisation
U.N.O. United Nations Organisation
U.S.A. United States of America
U.S.S.R. Union of Soviet Socialist Republics
v. versus
Va. Virginia
V.C. Victoria Cross
Vic. Victoria
Vt. Vermont
W.A. Western Australia
Warwicks. Warwickshire
Wash. Washington
W.C. water closet
W.H.O. World Health Organisation
Wilts. Wiltshire
Wis. Wisconsin
Worcs. Worcestershire
W.Va. West Virginia
Wyo. Wyoming
Y.H.A. Youth Hostel Association
Y.M.C.A., Y.W.C.A. Young Men's (Women's) Christian Association
Yorks. Yorkshire
Y.T. Yukon Territory

FOREIGN WORDS AND PHRASES

L.=Latin Fr.=French Gr.=Greek It.=Italian Ger.=German

ad infinitum (L.) to infinity
ad libitum (L.) as much as you please
ad nauseam (L.) to the point of disgust
aide-de-camp (Fr.) an officer who helps a general (*abb.* A.D.C.)
à la carte (Fr.) (of a meal) ordered course by course as you wish
al fresco (It.) in the open air
alma mater (L.) your university or school
amour propre (Fr.) "self love", vanity
Anno Domini (L.) in the year of Our Lord (*abb.* A.D.)
au fait (Fr.) well acquainted with
au revoir (Fr.) goodbye, till we meet again
autobahn (Ger.) a highway for motor traffic
bête noir (Fr.) something you dislike much
billet doux (Fr.) a little note
blasé (Fr.) bored
bona fide (L.) in good faith
bon mot (Fr.) a witty remark
bon voyage (Fr.) happy journey
carte blanche (Fr.) freedom to do as you like
chef-d'oeuvre (Fr.) chief work
chic (Fr.) smart
cliché (Fr.) a well-known and well-worn phrase
cordon bleu (Fr.) a cook of the highest excellence
coup de grâce (Fr.) a finishing stroke
début (Fr.) a first appearance
Dieu et mon droit (Fr.) God and my right
dramatis personae (L.) the characters in a play
élan (Fr.) force, dash, driving power
en bloc (Fr.) all together
en masse (Fr.) all together, in a mass
en route (Fr.) on the way; while travelling
entre nous (Fr.) between ourselves
esprit de corps (Fr.) team spirit
et cetera (L.) and so forth (*abb.* etc.)
eureka! (Gr.) I have found it! Here it is!
ex officio (L.) by virtue of your position
fait accompli (Fr.) something already done
faux pas (Fr.) a slip in behaviour
finis (L.) the end
grand prix (Fr.) the great event
honi soit qui mal y pense (Fr.) shame to him who evil thinks
hors de combat (Fr.) out of condition to fight; disabled
hors d'oeuvre (Fr.) a light course served at the beginning of a meal
locum tenens (L.) a doctor or clergyman who acts as deputy for a short time while another is away
maître d'hôtel (Fr.) a restaurant manager: a head waiter
mêlée (Fr.) a skirmish; a small fight
modus operandi (L.) a way of working
multum in parvo (L.) much in a small space
née (Fr.) born. Used to show a woman's name before marriage, as *Mrs. Brown née Cameron*
noblesse oblige (Fr.) much is expected of anyone in a high position; a person in a high position should give a good lead
nom de plume (Fr.) a writer's "pen-name" or assumed name
par excellence (Fr.) to the highest degree
pièce de résistance (Fr.) the chief item on the programme
potage (Fr.) soup
pot-pourri (Fr.) a mixture
précis (Fr.) a short summing-up
prima donna (It.) the leading woman singer in an opera
prima facie (L.) at first sight
pro patria (L.) for your country
protégé(e) (Fr.) a person under the protection of another (ends in double "e" if a female)
quo vadis? (L.) whither goest thou?
reductio ad absurdum (L.) taking an argument to the point where it becomes foolish
résumé (Fr.) a summary
sang froid (Fr.) coolness in an emergency; freedom from excitement
savoir faire (Fr.) knowing how to behave in society; having an easy, pleasant manner
sine qua non (L.) an absolute necessity
sotto voce (It.) in a low voice
status quo (L.) the existing state of affairs
sub judice (L.) in process of being judged
table d'hôte (Fr.) in a restaurant, a meal of several courses at a fixed price with little or no choice
tête-à-tête (Fr.) a conversation between two people only
vice versa (L.) the other way round
vox populi (L.) the voice of the people

A

A *n.* the first letter of the alphabet.—**A1** very good

a *adj.* or *indefinite article.* 1. one. 2. any, as *A man needs food*

Note: Used before a word beginning with a vowel or with a silent *h*, this word becomes *an.* Thus *a book, a holiday,* but *an apple, an hour*

aback' *adv.* backwards.—**taken aback** surprised

ab'acus *n.* counting frame with balls sliding along wires

aban'don *v.* 1. to give up. 2. to desert.—*n.* as *He danced with abandon.*—**aban'doned** *adj.* 1. given up to too wild enthusiasm (as to a vice). 2. wicked.—**aban'donment** *n.*

Compare: leave, forsake, *Contrast:* keep, defend, cherish

abase' *v.* to bring low, humble.—**abase'ment** *n.*—**abas'ing** *pres. part.*

Compare: degrade, depress, humiliate. *Contrast:* raise, honour, exalt

abash' *v.* to make confused and ashamed

Compare: embarrass, humiliate, shame. *Contrast:* put at ease, encourage

abate' *v.* 1. to lessen, slow down. 2. to reduce, as a debt.—**abat'ing** *pres. part.*—**abate'ment** *n.* reduction

Compare: diminish, decrease, subside. *Contrast:* intensify, increase, continue

ab'attoir (ab'atwar) *n.* slaughter-house

ab'bé (a'bā) *n.* a French priest or clergyman

abb'ess *n. fem.* of **abbot**, the head of a convent, or abbey.—**abb'ey** *n.* 1. where monks or nuns live. 2. a church once forming part of a monastery.—**abb'eys** *pl.*—**abb'ot** *n.* head of a monastery. —**abb'ess** *fem.*

abbre'viate (a-bree'vi-āt) *v.* to shorten.—**abbre'viating** *pres. part.*—**abbrevia'tion** (-shun) *n.* a shortened form, as *exam.* for *examination,* or *R.A.F.* for *Royal Air Force*

Compare: abridge, curtail, condense. *Contrast:* enlarge, lengthen, expand

ABC *n.* 1. first three letters of the alphabet. 2. the alphabet. 3. the first facts, as the *A B C of mathematics*

ab'dicate (-kāt) *v.* to give up power or position, esp. royal power, as *King Edward VIII abdicated in* 1936.—**ab'dicating** *pres. part.*—**abdica'tion** *n.*

abdo'men *n.* 1. the belly. 2. in insects, the last third of the body.—**abdom'inal** *adj.*

abduct' *v.* to take away by stealth or force.—**abduc'tion** *n.* kidnapping

aberr'ant *adj.* 1. wandering from the right way. 2. (biol.) abnormal

aberra'tion (-shun) *n.* 1. wandering, esp. of the mind, as *His extreme forgetfulness was a form of mental aberration.* 2. (optics) failure of rays to come to a focus

abet' *v.* to encourage, to help, esp. to do wrong.—**abet'ting** *pres. part.*—**abet'ted** *p.t.* and *p. part.*—**abet'tor** *n.*

abey'ance (a-bā'ans) *n.* 1. suspension, as *The matter must remain in abeyance until the committee decides.* 2. disuse, as *That rule is in abeyance at the present time*

abhor' *v.* to hate deeply, to detest.—**abhorr'ing** *pres. part.*—**abhorred'** *p.t.* and *p. part.* —**abhor'rence** *n.* deep hatred.—**abhor'rent** *adj.* hateful

abide' *v.* 1. to dwell. 2. to last, as *Love abides always.* 3. to endure, as *He can't abide teasing.* 4. to wait for, as *I abide your coming.*—**abi'ding** *pres. part.*—*adj.* lasting.—**abi'ded** or **abode'** *p.t.* and *p. part.* —**to abide by** submit to, obey, as *I will abide by your decision*

abil'ity *n.* 1. power. 2. skill.—**abil'ities** *pl.*

ab'ject *adj.* low, contemptible, miserable, as *an abject failure.*—**ab'jectly** *adv.*

ablaze' *adj.* 1. on fire. 2. glowing, as *The woods were ablaze with autumn colours*

a'ble *adj.* 1. having means or power, as *He is able to swim.* 2. skilful, clever, as *An able physician.*—**a'bly** *adv.* capably, as *The work was ably performed.*—**able-bod'ied** *adj.* physically sound and fit

ablu'tion (a-bloo'shun) *n.* washing, cleansing the body

abnor'mal *adj.* not according to rule, unusual. —**abnormal'ity** *n.* anything out of the ordinary.—**abnor'mally** *adv.*

ab'o (ab'ō) *n.* (slang) Australian aboriginal

aboard' *adv.* and *prep.* on board, on a ship or train, as *We went aboard ship at noon* and *The men eat well aboard*

abode' *p.t.* and *p. part.* of **abide**.—*n.* home, dwelling

abol'ish *v.* to do away with, to end.—**abolit'ion** (ab-ol-ish'un) *n.*—**abolit'ionist** *n.* in America, one who wished to do away with Negro slavery

A-bomb *n.* atomic bomb. See **atom**

abom'inate *v.* to hate or loathe.—**abom'inating** *pres. part.*—**abom'inable** *adj.*—**abom'inably** *adv.*—**abomina'tion** *n.* 1. strong dislike. 2. a disgusting thing

aborig'inal (-ij'-) *n.* (esp.) a native of Australia.—*adj.*

abor'tive *adj.* unsuccessful, fruitless.—**abor'tion** *n.* failure to develop, miscarriage

abound' *v.* to be plentiful, as "*Blessings abound where'er He reigns*" (hymn).—**to abound in,** to contain many or plenty, as *The forest abounds in wild animals*

about' *adv.* 1. on all sides, as *to stand about.* 2. out, astir, as *to be out and about.* 3. in a reverse direction, as *to put the ship* *about.* 4. nearly, as *I have had about enough of this.* 5. approximately, as *It is about a mile away.* 6. on the point of doing, as *They were about to sit down to dinner.* 7. in rotation, as *They took turn about to keep watch.—prep.* 1. dealing with, relating to, as *to talk about something.* 2. around, as *There were not many people about the streets.* 3. on the person, as *I haven't a box of matches about me*

above' (a-buv') *adv.* 1. in a higher place, as *The house stood above, on a hill.* 2. overhead, *The sky is above.* 3. in or to heaven, as *He has gone up above.* 4. earlier, in a book or letter, as *stated in the paragraph above.* *—prep.* 1. on top of. 2. higher in rank or position. 3. more than, as *The price was above a shilling.—adj.* mentioned earlier, as *Note the above instructions.*—**above'-board** *adj.* honest, with nothing hidden.—**above deceit** too honest to be capable of deceit.—**above reproach** too good to be open to blame

abracadab'ra *n.* a word used in magic

abrade' *v.* to wear or rub off.—**abra'ding** *pres. part.*

abra'sion (a-brā'zhun) *n.* a place worn or rubbed, as a grazed knee.—**abra'sive** *n.* substance, as used for polishing, that rubs away.*—adj.*

abreast' *adv.* 1. side by side. 2. up or level with, as *to keep abreast with one's work*

abridge' (a-brij') *v.* to shorten, curtail.—**abridge'able** *adj.*—**abridg'ing** *pres. part.* —**abridg'ment, abridge'ment** *n.* a shortened form, esp. of a book; a summary

abroad' (a-brawd') *adv.* 1. in or to foreign lands. 2. out of doors, as *To walk abroad.*—**to spread abroad** to spread far and wide

abrupt' *adj.* 1. sudden, as *an abrupt ending.* 2. curt, as *an abrupt manner of speaking.* 3. steep.—**abrupt'ness** *n.* gruffness. shortness, esp. in manner or speech.—**abrupt'ly** *adv.*

ab'scess (ab'ses) *n.* a gathering of diseased matter in the body; a boil

abscond' *v.* to go away secretly, esp. in order to escape the law

ab'sence *n.* 1. being away. 2. period when one is away, as *It happened during my absence.* 3. inattention, as *in a moment of absence.* **ab'sent** *adj.* 1. not present. 2. not attending. —**absent' oneself** *v.* to stay away, withdraw.—**absentee'** *n.* 1. one who is away. 2. one who habitually stays away.—**ab'sent-mind'ed** *adj.* 1. inattentive. 2. forgetful.—**ab'sent-mind'edly** *adv.*

ab'solute *adj.* 1. certain. 2. complete, as *absolute freedom.* 3. not obliged to obey the laws, as *an absolute monarch.*—**absolu'tely** *adv.* entirely.—**absolu'tion** *n.* freedom from punishment, forgiveness of sins.—**absolute zero** (phys.) the lowest temperature possible (—273°C.)

absolve' *v* .1. to set free from. 2. to pardon. —**absol'ving** *pres. part.*

absorb' *v.* 1. to drink in. 2. to claim one's attention.—**absorb'ed** *adj.* deeply interested.—**absor'bent** *n.* anything that absorbs. —**absor'bing** *adj.*—**absorp'tion** *n.*

abstain' *v.* to keep from, as *to abstain from smoking.*—**abstain'er** *n.* a person keeping from strong drink.—**absten'tion** *n.*—**ab'stinence** *n.* doing without pleasures such as food, drink, etc.

abste'mious *adj.* sparing in use of anything, esp. food and drink

abstract' *v.* to remove, draw away from.—**abstract'ed** *adj.* 1. taken away. 2. absent-minded.—**abstrac'tion** *n.*

ab'stract *adj.* 1. considered as an idea, as *abstract justice.* 2. hard to understand.*—n.* a summary.—**abstrac'tion** *n.* an idea.—**ab'stract noun** a noun denoting a quality, e.g. *truth.* A concrete noun denotes a thing, e.g. *chair*

abstruse' (ab-stroos') *adj.* hard to understand.—**abstruse'ly** *adv.*

absurd' *adj.* 1. unreasonable. 2. ridiculous or silly.—**absurd'ity** *n.* something absurd.—**absurd'ities** *pl.*—**absurd'ly** *adv.*

abun'dance *n.* great plenty.—**abun'dant** *adj.* in great quantity.—**abundantly** *adv.*

abuse' (a-būz') *v.* 1. to misuse. 2. to speak harshly to.—**abu'sing** *pres. part.*—**abuse'** (a-būs') *n.* 1. ill usage. 2. rude language. 3. a bad practice.—**abu'sive** *adj.* full of abuse.—**abu'sively** *adv.*

abut' (on, against) *v.* 1. to end on, border on. 2. to touch, be against.—**abutt'ing** *pres. part.*—**abutt'ed** *p.t.* and *p. part.*

abyss' (abis') *n.* a bottomless depth or hole.—**abys'mal** (a-biz'mal) *adj.* bottomless. 2. deep, as *abysmal ignorance*

Abyssin'ia *n.* kingdom in north-east Africa, Ethiopia.—**Abyssin'ian** *n.* native of Abyssinia

aca'cia (a-kā'sha) *n.* a family of trees and shrubs yielding gum

acad'emy *n.* 1. a higher school. 2. a school for special study. 3. a society to support art or science.—**acad'emies** *pl.*—**academ'ic** *adj.* 1. learned. 2. theoretical, unpractical. —**academic'ian** *n.* member of the Royal Academy

accede' (ak-seed') *v.* 1. to agree, as *He acceded to my request.* 2. to come to the throne.—**acced'ing** *pres. part.*—**acced'ed** *p.t.* and *p. part.*

Compare: consent, comply. *Contrast:* disagree, decline, refuse

accel'erate (ak-sel'e-rāt) *v.* to increase speed.—**accel'erating** *pres. part.*—**acceler-a'tion** (-shun) *n.* increase of speed.—**accel'erator** *n.* mechanism to increase speed, esp. in a motor-car

ac'cent (ak'sent) *n.* 1. stress, emphasis, esp. in speaking and in music. In the word *father*, the accent falls on the first syllable. 2. a mark to show where the stress should fall or the pronunciation of certain letters. 3. mannerisms of speech, as *He spoke with a Welsh accent.*—**accent'** *v.* to give stress, esp. to a syllable of a word. —**accen'tuate** *v.* to stress.—**accen'tuating** *pres. part.*—**accentua'tion** *n.*

accept' (ak-sept') *v.* 1. to take, as a gift, invitation, etc. 2. to agree to, as *I accept your decision.*—**accept'able** *adj.* welcome. —**ac-cept'ance.**—**accepta'tion** *n.* 1. reception. 2. the agreed meaning of a word

ac'cess (ak'ses) *n.* 1. admission, entrance. 2. increase, as *a sudden access of wealth.* 3. attack, as *an access of coughing.*—**access'ible** *adj.* 1. easy to approach. 2. within reach.—**accessibil'ity** *n.*—**access'ibly** *adv.*

access'ary *n.* a helper, esp. in wrong-doing. —**access'aries** *pl.*

access'ible *adj.* See **access**

access'ion (-shun) *n.* 1. coming to, as *accession to the throne, to office, etc.* 2. increase

access'ory *adj.* helping, additional.—*n.* 1. an additional detail or part. 2. used in error for **accessary.**—**access'ories** *pl.*

ac'cident (ak'si-dent) *n.* 1. something happening by chance, as *I found it by accident.* 2. a mishap, as *a motor accident.* 3. an unexpected event.—**accident'al** *adj.*—**accident'ally** *adv.*—**by accident** by chance

Compare: chance, mishap. *Contrast:* design, certainty

acclaim' *v.* to welcome or hail, with a shout of joy, as *They acclaimed him king.*—**acclama'tion** *n.* shout of applause

accli'matise *v.* to accustom to a new climate. —**accli'matising** *pres. part.*

ac'colade *n.* ceremony of conferring knighthood

accom'modate *v.* 1. to be or make suitable for. 2. to lodge, as *The inn could accommodate ten guests.* 3. to fit. 4. to supply with, as money.—**accomm'odating** *pres. part.* and *adj.* obliging.—**accommoda'tion** *n.* 1. lodging. 2. a loan. 3. adjustment

accom'pany (-kum) *v.* 1. to go with, join with. 2. to provide a musical background for.—he **accom'panies.**—**accom'panying** *pres. part.*—**accom'panied** *p.t.* and *p. part.*—**accom'paniment** *n.* something that goes with, esp. music played on the piano while another person sings, or plays a stringed instrument.—**accom'panist** *n.*

accom'plice *n.* a partner, esp. in crime

accom'plish *v.* 1. to finish completely. 2. fulfil.—he **accom'plishes.**—**accom'plished** *adj.* 1. complete. 2. skilled.—**accom'plishment** *n.* 1. completion. 2. something one has learned to do, as *Her accomplishments included playing the piano, and singing in Italian*

Compare: fulfil, achieve, execute. *Contrast:* leave unfinished, fail in

accord' *n.* harmony, agreement.—*v.* 1. to grant, as *The speaker was accorded a vote of thanks.* 2. agree with.—**accord'ance** *n.*—**accord'ing to** *adv.* 1. in agreement with. 2. as told by.—**accord'ingly** *adv.* 1. therefore. 2. as required by something previously stated. *You are a soldier and must behave accordingly.*—**in accordance with** in agreement with.—**on, of one's own accord** on one's own initiative, without being told.—**with one accord** by general agreement

accord'ion *n.* musical wind-instrument with bellows and keyboard

accost' *v.* to speak first to, as *Beggars accost passers-by*

account' *v.* 1. to judge, as *He is accounted brave.* 2. to answer for, explain.—*n.* 1. a bill. 2. a story or narrative. 3. a report, esp. of money spent and received. 4. credit, as at a shop. 5. importance, as *a person of some account.*—**account'able** *adj.* responsible.—**account'ant** *n.* one trained to make and read money accounts.—**on account** on credit; in part payment.—**on my account** for my sake, for me, as *He'll never go on my account.*—**on account of** because of.—**take into account** remember, consider.—**on no account** certainly not.—**person of no account** person of no importance.—**to give a good account of oneself** to fight well.—**to take into account** to allow for.—**to turn to account** to make use of

accou'trements (a-kōō'tre-ments) *n.pl.* military equipment

accred'ited *adj.* vouched for, guaranteed

accrue' (ak-roo') *v.* to be added to, to grow from, as *Interest accrues on money invested.*—**accru'ing** *pres. part.*—**accrued'** *p.t.* and *p. part.*

accu'mulate *v.* to amass, collect together.—**accu'mulating** *pres. part.*—**accumula'tion** *n.* a heap.—**accu'mulator** *n.* 1. one who amasses. 2. battery for storing electric power

Compare: gather, store, hoard, collect. *Contrast:* scatter, disperse, squander

ac'curacy (ak'u-ra-si) *n.* exactness.—**ac'curate** *adj.* correct, precise.—**ac'curately** *adv.*

Compare: exact, precise. *Contrast:* inaccurate, careless, loose

accurs'ed *adj.* under a curse, hateful

accu'sative *adj.* in grammar, objective. The **accusative case** is another name for the objective case. In the sentence, *I see him, him* is in the accusative or objective case, because it is the object of *see*

accuse' *v.* to blame, charge, esp. with doing wrong.—**accus'ing** *pres. part.*—**accused'** *p.t.* and *p. part.*—*n.* the person charged with wrong-doing.—**ac'cusation** *n.* a charge

accus'tom *v.* to make or be used to.—**accus'tomed** *adj.* familiar, usual

ace *n.* 1. a card, domino, etc., with only one spot. 2. a very successful fighting airman.

3. one who far excels others.—**within an ace of** very near

ac'etate (as'itāt) *n.* 1. salt of acetic acid. 2. cellulose acetate film, or rayon

ace'tic (asee'tik) *adj.* relating to **ace'tic acid** present in vinegar

acet'ylene (a-set'i-leen) *n.* a gas used, esp. for lighting purposes, made by pouring water on calcium carbide

ache (āk) *n.* a continuous pain.—*v.* 1. to be in pain. 2. to long for.—**ach'ing** *pres. part.*—**ached** *p.t.* and *p. part.*

achieve' (a-cheev') *v.* to perform, to win.—**achiev'ing** *pres. part.*—**achieve'ment** *n.* 1. a deed performed. 2. a great deed

Achil'les' heel *n.* fatal weakness

achromat'ic (ak-rō-mat'ik) *adj.* (optics) colourless, not showing colour

a'cid (a'sid) *n.* 1. a sour substance. 2. in chemistry, substance used with a base to make a salt.—*adj.* sour.—**acid'ity** *n.* sourness.—**acid test** final test of value

ack-ack *adj.* anti-aircraft

acknowl'edge (ak-nol'ij) *v.* 1. to own, admit. 2. to thank, to say one has received something, as a letter.—**acknowl'edging** *pres. part.*—**acknowl'edgment** *n.* something showing or expressing thanks

ac'me *n.* the highest point; point of perfection

ac'onite *n.* 1. a poisonous plant. 2. drug from this.—wolf's bane, or monkshood

a'corn *n.* the fruit of the oak

acous'tic *adj.* relating to hearing.—**acous'tics** *n.pl.* 1. the science of sounds 2. quality of sound in a room, as *The acoustics of the concert hall were excellent*

acquaint' *v.* to inform, to make familiar with.—**acquaint'ance** *n.* 1. a person one knows. 2. knowledge.—**acquaint'anceship** *n.*

acquiesce' (ak-wee-es') *v.* to accept. submit, esp. without protest. Often followed by *in*.—**acquiesc'ing** *pres. part.*—**acquiesc'ence** *n.*—**acquiesc'ent** *adj.*

acquire' *v.* to gain, to obtain.—**acquir'ing** *pres. part.*—**acquire'ment** *n.* something gained or learned.—**acquisi'tion** (a-kwi-zi'shun) *n.* the act of getting, a gain.—**acquis'itive** *adj.* fond of gaining, esp. money

acquit' *v.* 1. to free, esp. from an accusation. 2. to settle, as a debt. 3. to conduct oneself, as *He acquitted himself manfully in the battle.*—**acquit'ting** *pres. part.*—**acquit'ted** *p.t.* and *p. part.*—**acquit'tal** *n.*

a'cre (ā'ker) *n.* a measure of land amounting to 4840 square yards.—*pl.* estate lands, as *his broad acres.*—**a'creage** (ā'ker-ij) *n.* number of acres in any plot of ground

ac'rid *adj.* bitter, stinging

ac'rimony *n.* bitter feeling or speech.—**acrimo'nious** *adj.* sharp

ac'robat *n.* one who does skilled or unusual bodily feats, as rope-dancing, etc.—**acrobat'ic** *adj.*

acrop'olis *n.* a fortress in a Greek city, esp. the Acropolis of Athens

across' *adv,* and *prep.* 1. crosswise. 2. from one side to the other, as *to walk across the road.* 3. on the other side of, as *She lives across the road.*—**to come across** to find or meet by chance

acros'tic *n.* puzzle in which the first letters of the answers spell out a word

Ac'rylan *n.* a man-made fibre

act *n.* 1. a thing done or being done, a deed. 2. law or decree. 3. a division of a play.—*v.* 1. to take action, as *He acted promptly.* 2. to behave. 3. to pretend. 4. to take part in a play.—**Act of Parliament** law passed by Parliament

act'ing *n.* performance of a part, esp. in a play.—*adj.* doing another's work, as *The acting headmaster*

Compare: deed, feat, exploit, achievement, action, performance, execution. While *act* usually means the doing of something, *deed* means what has been done. *Execution* and *performance* mean the carrying out of some undertaking. *Feat* and *exploit* generally mean some remarkable act. *Action* means a series of acts or a continuous act. *Achievement* means a completed act

ac'tion (ak'shun) *n.* 1. deed. 2. motion. 3. battle. 4. effect, way of working, as *the action of a sewing-machine.* 5. law-suit.—**action stations** positions in readiness for battle.—**out of action** disabled.—**take action** to do what needs to be done

Compare: act

ac'tivate *v.* cause to act

ac'tive *adj.* 1. brisk, lively, busy. 2. working, as *an active partner.* 3. in grammar, used to describe a verb the subject of which is the doer of the action.—**activ'ity** *n.* 1. the doing of things. 2. occupation.—**activ'ities** *pl.*

Note: In the sentence *Cats catch birds* the verb *catch* is said to be active because *cats* (subject of the verb) do the catching. If we say *Birds are caught by cats* the verb *are caught* is said to be passive, because *birds* (subject of the sentence) do not do the catching, but have it done to them

Contrast: passive

ac'tor *n.* one who acts or performs, esp. a stage or film player.—**ac'tress** *fem.*

ac'tual *adj.* real.—**ac'tually** *adv.* in fact

ac'tuate *v.* to cause to act, to urge on, as *Gamblers are actuated by a desire for money.*—**ac'tuating** *pres. part.*

acu'men *n.* sharpness and quickness of mind, shrewdness

acute' *adj.* 1. sharp-pointed. 2. keen, penetrating. 3. severe, as *an acute pain.*—**acute'ly** *adv.*—**acute'ness** *n.* 1. sharpness. 2. quickness of mind.—**acute accent** an accent as used in the French word *abbé.*

—**acute angle** one less than a right angle
Compare: sharp, intense, sensitive. *Contrast:* blunt, obtuse, slow-witted

ad'age *n.* a proverb, an old saying, as "*A stitch in time saves nine*"

ada'gio (ada'jiō) *adv.* (in music) slowly.—*n.* a slow movement.—*adj.*

Ad'am *n.* the first man.—**Adam's apple** the part of a man's throat that sticks out.—**son of Adam** man

ad'amant *n.* a very hard stone, a diamond.—*adj.* 1. very hard. 2. unshakable in a decision

adapt' *v.* to alter for a new use, to fit.—**adapt'able** *adj.*—**adaptabil'ity** *n.*—**adapta'tion** *n.* 1. adjustment. 2. an altered version of a poem, play, etc.

add *v.* 1. to join on. 2. to put to or with. 3. to count together, esp. numbers. 4. to say further

Compare: cast up, increase, augment, attach, join on, enlarge. *To cast up* a column of figures is to add them together. *To attach* and to *join on* are other ways of adding things together. To *increase, augment* and *enlarge* mean to make greater or bigger, usually by adding something

adden'dum *n.* something added, *esp.* in a book

ad'der *n.* 1. a small, poisonous European snake, the viper. 2. a harmless American snake

ad'dict *n.* one given up to a habit, as *a drug addict.*—**addict'ed** (to) *adj.* given over to —**addic'tion** *n.*

addi'tion (ad-ish'un) *n.* 1. the act of adding. 2. anything added.—**addi'tional** *adj.* extra. —**addi'tionally** *adv.*—**in addition** also, as well

ad'dled *adj.* 1. bad, esp. of eggs. 2. confused. —**ad'dle-head'ed**, muddled in mind

address' *n.* 1. name of house, street, etc., where a person lives. 2. a speech or formal communication. 3. skill. 4. manners.—*v.* 1. to direct, as an envelope. 2. to speak or write to.—he **address'es.**—**To address oneself to a task** to get on with it

adduce' *v.* to bring forward as proof

ad'enoids *n.pl.* growths at the back of the nose, making breathing difficult

a'dept *n.* an expert.—**adept'** *adj.* skilful

ad'equate (-kwāt) *adj.* sufficient, enough, as *This quantity of food is adequate for four persons.*—**ad'equacy** *n.*—**ad'equately** *adv.* as required

Contrast: inadequacy, lack, insufficiency

adhere' 1. (to) *v.* to stick to, as *Glue adheres to the fingers.* 2. to support.—**adher'ing** *pres. part.*—**adher'ence** *n.* support.—**adher'ent** *n.* a supporter.—*adj.*

adhe'sion (ad-hee'zhun) *n.* the act of sticking. —**adhe'sive** *adj.* sticky.—*n.* something sticky, as glue.—**adhe'siveness** *n.*

adieu' *interj.* French for good-bye.—*n.* a farewell

ad'ipose *adj.* fatty

adja'cent (a-jā'sent) *adj.* 1. near to 2. neighbouring, as *Norway and Sweden are adjacent countries*

ad'jective *n.* a word (part of speech) which describes a noun or pronoun. In the following sentences the word *dark* is an adjective. *It is a dark night. The night is dark.* Some adjectives can be used only in this second way.—**adjecti'val** *adj.* used as an adjective

adjoin' *v.* to be next to, as *The park adjoins the sports ground.*—**adjoin'ing** *adj.* neighbouring, next to

adjourn' (a-jurn') *v.* 1. to put off till later. 2. to stop for the time being, as *After an hour the discussion was adjourned for a week.*—**adjourn'ment** *n.*

adjudge' *v.* 1. to decide. 2. to give an award.—**adjudg'ing** *pres. part.*

adju'dicate (a-jōō'dik-āt) *v.* to act as judge

ad'junct *n.* and *adj.* something added, as *A trailer is an adjunct of a motor-car*

adjust' *v.* 1. to put right, as a clock. 2. alter to fit.—**adjus'table** *adj.*—**adjust'ment** *n.* 1. rearrangement. 2. settlement

Compare: arrange, rectify, regulate, adapt. *Contrast:* disarrange, dislocate

ad'jutant *n.* 1. an army officer, an assistant, esp. who assists a superior officer. 2. a large Indian stork.—**ad'jutant-general** *n.* adjutant to a general

adlib' *adv.* freely, as it pleases one.—**ad-lib** *v.* to speak without a prepared script

admin'ister *v.* 1. to manage. 2. to dispense, as justice. 3. to give, as medicine or First Aid.— **administra'tion** *n.* 1. management, esp. Government. 2. those who administer. 3. application.—**admin'istrative** *adj.*—**admin'istrator** *n.*

ad'miral *n.* a naval officer of the highest rank.—**Ad'miralty** *n.* the government department which controls naval affairs

admire' *v.* 1. to wonder at. 2. to love. 3. to respect.—**admir'ing** *pres. part.*—**admir'er** *n.*—**ad'mirable** *adj.* excellent.—**admira'tion** *n.*

admis'sible *adj.* allowable, acceptable.—**admis'sibly** *adv.*

admis'sion (ad-mish'un) *n.* 1. entrance. 2. entrance fee. 3. confession, as *The prisoner's admission of his guilt was a surprise*

admit' *v.* 1. to let in. 2. to confess. 3. to receive as true.—**admitt'ing** *pres. part.*—**admitt'ed** *p.t.* and *p. part.*—**admitt'ance** *n.* permission to enter

admix'ture *n.* 1. mixture. 2. added ingredient

admon'ish *v.* 1. to warn. 2. to reprove gently. 3. to advise.—**admoni'tion** (-ish'un) *n.* 1. reproof. 2. advice.—**admon'itory** *adj.*

ado' (a-dōō') *n.* fuss, as Shakespeare's *Much Ado about Nothing*

ado'be (adō'bi) *n.* house of sun-dried clay

adoles'cence (ad-o-les'ens) *n.* the period of life between childhood and maturity.—**adoles'cent** *adj.* growing up.—*n.* young person not quite grown up

adopt' *v.* to take as one's own, as *Many of the Britons adopted Roman ways. Having no children of their own, they adopted an orphan.*—**adopt'er** *n.*—**adop'tion** *n.*

adore' *v.* to worship, to love deeply.—**ado'ring** *pres. part.*—**ado'rable** *adj.*—**adora'tion** *n.* love, worship.—**ado'rer** *n.*

Compare: reverence, honour, venerate. *Contrast:* abhor, despise, hate

adorn' *v.* to decorate, to dress.—**adorn'ment** *n.* ornament

Compare: deck, beautify, embellish. *Contrast:* mar, spoil, disfigure

adrift' *adj.* or *adv.* floating free, loose

adroit' *adj.* skilful, clever.—**adroit'ly** *adv.*—**adroit'ness** *n.*

Compare: dexterous, nimble, expert. *Contrast:* unskilled, clumsy, inept

ad'ulate *v.* to flatter, praise too highly.—**adula'tion** *n.* flattery.—**adula'tory** *adj.*

adult' (or **ad'ult**) *adj.* grown-up, mature.—*n.* a grown-up person

adul'terate *v.* to make impure by mixture, as to *adulterate milk with water.*—**adul'terating** *pres. part.*—**adul'terated** *adj.*—**adultera'tion** (-shun) *n.*

advance' *v.* 1. to go or move forward. 2. to put forward, as *to advance arguments.* 3. to lend money or pay it before it is due. 4. to increase in price.—*n.* 1. progress. 2. a rise, esp. in wages or price. 3. a loan.—**advanced'** *adj.* 1. ahead. 2. very modern, as *advanced ideas.*—**advance'ment** *n.* progress, improvement, promotion.—**advanc'ing** *pres. part.*—**to make advances to** to approach, as in friendship

Compare: progress, proceed, improve, promote, raise. *Contrast:* retreat, retire, deteriorate, retard

advan'tage *n.* 1. benefit. 2. better position. 3. chance. 4. (at tennis) next point won after both sides have 40.—*v.* to benefit.—**advan'taging** *pres. part.*—**advanta'geous** (ad-van-tā'jus) *adj.* profitable.—**advanta'geously** *adv.*—**to have the advantage of** someone to address by name someone who does not know your name.—**to take advantage of,** to profit by

ad'vent *n.* arrival.—**Ad'vent** 1. the coming of Christ. 2. the four weeks before Christmas

adven'ture *n.* 1. a bold undertaking. 2. an exciting experience. 3. a risk.—*v.* to dare.—**adven'turing** *pres. part.*—**adven'turer** *n.* one who seeks adventure.—**adven'turess** *n. fem.*—**adven'turesome** *adj.* bold, daring.—**adven'turous** *adj.* perilous

ad'verb *n.* a word used with verbs, adjectives, or other adverbs to tell more about (modify) their meanings. *Shortly, quickly, never, soon, very* are adverbs. In the sentence, *He ran quickly,* the adverb *quickly* tells more about the verb *ran.* In the sentence *He ran very quickly,* the adverb *very* tells more about the other adverb *quickly.* In the sentence *His manner is extremely curt,* the adverb *extremely* modifies the adjective *curt*

ad'versary *n.* an enemy.—**ad'versaries** *pl.*

ad'verse *adj.* contrary, opposed, as *adverse weather conditions.*—**adver'sity** *n.* misfortune

Compare: unfavourable, hostile, harmful. *Contrast:* favourable, friendly, advantageous

ad'vert *n.* shortened form of **advertisement**

ad'vertise (ad'ver-tīz) *v.* to give notice, to make public.—**ad'vertising** *pres. part.*—**adver'tisement** (tiz-) *n.* a public notice.—**ad'vertiser** *n.*

advice' *n.* counsel, instruction, information

advise' (ad-vīz') *v.* to give advice, to inform.—**advi'sing** *pres. part.*—**advi'sable** *adj.* wise, recommended, as *It is advisable to be early.*—**advisabil'ity** *n.*—**advi'ser** *n.* one who gives advice.—**advi'sedly** *adv.* purposely.—**advi'sory** *adj.* having power to advise

ad'vocate *n.* one who speaks in favour of a person or cause.—*v.* to plead in favour of.—**ad'vocating** *pres. part.*—**ad'vocacy** (ad'-vo-ka-si) *n.* a pleading for

adze, adz *n.* a carpenter's tool for chipping

ae'gis (ee'jis) *n.* originally the shield of Zeus, king of the gods, protection.—**under the aegis of** under the protection of

ae'on, e'on (ee'on) *n.* a very long time, an age

ae'rate (ayer'āt) *v.* to bubble air through water, as in an aquarium, to dissolve gas in a liquid, carbon dioxide in lemonade.—**aera'tion** *n.*—**aerated water** water with gas dissolved in it, soda water, etc.

aer'ial (ār'i-al) *adj.* belonging to the air.—**aerial photograph** one taken from an aircraft.—*n.* wire that receives or transmits radio signals

ae'rie, ae'ry (ā'ri, ī'r'i) **eyrie, eyry** *n.* the nest of a bird of prey

aerobat'ics *n.* acrobatic flying by aircraft

ae'rodrome *n.* an aircraft station

aerodynam'ics *n.* study of the effects of air or other gases in motion

ae'ronaut (ā'ro-nawt) *n.* an air-navigator, airman.—**aeronau'tic** *adj.*—**aeronau'tics** *n. pl.* the science of aviation

ae'roplane *n.* a heavier-than-air flying-machine

ae'rosol *n.* spray of particles suspended in a gas

aesthet'ic *adj.* 1. concerning beauty. 2. pleasing, artistic.—*n.* **aesthet'ics**

afar' *adv.* at a distance, far away

af'fable *adj.* easy to talk to, pleasant.—**affabil'ity** *n.* pleasant manner.—**af'fably** *adv.*

affair' *n.* 1. business, concern, as *That is my*

affair. 2. happening, as *The flood was a terrible affair*

affect' *v*. 1. to act upon, influence, as *The change in the weather will affect our plans.* 2. to pretend, as *He affected not to hear me.* 3. to move the feelings, as *Her distress affected me deeply*. 4. to have a taste for, as *She affects bright colours.*—**affecta'tion** (-shun) *n*. pretence.—**affec'ted** *adj*. not natural, as *He spoke in an affected manner.* —**affec'ting** *adj*. moving

Note: This word must not be confused with *effect*

affec'tion (-shun) *n*. 1. fondness, love. 2. disease, as *Owing to an affection of the eyes he had to wear blue spectacles.*—**affec'tionate** *adj*. showing love.—**affec'tionately** *adv*.

Compare: tender, kind, loving. *Contrast:* cold, distant, undemonstrative

affi'ance (a-fī'ans) *v*. to promise to marry

affida'vit *n*. written statement of evidence on oath

affil'iate *v*. to associate, to join—*n*. **affilia'tion**

affin'ity *n*. relationship, attraction.—**affin'ities** *pl*.—**affin'itive** *adj*.

affirm' *v*. to declare as true.—**affirma'tion** (-shun) *n*.—**affir'mative** *adj*. affirming, asserting.—*n*. a word or statement meaning yes.—**to answer in the affirmative** to answer "yes"

Note: The opposite of *affirmative is negative*

affix' *v*. to add to, to attach.—*n*. (aff'iks) 1. an addition. 2. a syllable or letter joined to the beginning or end of a word to show a change in its meaning or use. In the words *untrue*, *unable*, *unwilling*, the affix *un-* changes the meaning so that *true* becomes *not true*, *able* becomes *not able*, etc. In the words *shortly*, *slowly*, the affix *-ly* changes the adjectives *short* and *slow* into adverbs

afflict' *v*. to give pain or grief.—**afflic'tion** (a-flik'shun) *n*.

af'fluence (af'loo-ens) *n*. abundance, wealth. —**af'fluent** *adj*. wealthy.—*n*. a tributary of a river

afford' *v*. 1. to be able to spend (time, money, etc.) as *He could afford to buy a new suit*. 2. produce, yield, as *Daily life affords us many opportunities of helping others*

affores'ta'tion *n*. planting of trees to make forests

affray' *n*. a fight in public, a brawl

affright' *v*. to frighten.—*n*. fear, terror

affront' *v*. to insult.—*n*. an insult.—**affront'ed** *adj*.

Afghan'istan *n*. country north-west of India. —**Af'ghan** *n*. native of Afghanistan

afield' *adv*. abroad, away from home, as *He wandered far afield*

afire' *adv*. on fire

aflame' *adj*. or *adv*. 1. flaming, ablaze, as *a burning house*. 2. ardent, passionate, as *aflame with indignation*

afloat' *adj* or *adv*. 1. borne along on air or liquid. 2. flooded. 3. going about, as *There is a story afloat that the shop will close down*

afoot' *adv*. 1. on foot, walking. 2. astir, in preparation, as *A scheme is afoot*

afore' *adv*. and *prep*. before

afore —meaning before, is often put at the beginning of a word, as **afore'said** said before, **afore'thought** thought before.—**afore'time** before this time

afraid' *adj*. timid, frightened

afresh' *adv*. anew, over again

Af'rica *n*. one of the five continents.—**Af'rican** *n*. native of Africa.—*adj*.

African'der, Afrikan'der *n*. South African of white parentage

Afrikaans' *n*. one of the official languages of South Africa, derived from 17th century spoken Dutch

aft *adj*. or *adv*. toward, or at, the back of a ship

af'ter *prep*. 1. behind, below in rank. 2. later, as *after dinner*. 3. following, as *the dog came after me*. 4. in imitation of, as *a painting after Constable* or *named after her aunt*. 5. seeking, as *What are you after?* 6. in spite of, as *After all I did, she treated me badly.*—*adv*. behind in time and place, as "*We look before and after and pine for what is not*" (*Shelley*).—*adj*. as *in after times.*—**after all**, in the end

af'ter—meaning second or later, is often put at the beginning or end of another word to make a compound word, as **afterthought** a thought that comes later. **afterglow** second glow. **after-effects** effects coming later. **hereafter** later

af'termath *n*. 1. a second crop of grass after first cutting. 2. results, consequences

af'ternoon *n*. the time from noon to evening

af'terwards *adv*. later

again' *adv*. 1. once more. 2. in return. 3. besides.—**again and again** frequently

against' *prep*. 1. in opposition to, as *They fought against each other*. 2. in contact with, as *He fell against the ropes*. 3. in preparation for, as *to save against a rainy day*

agape' *adj*. with mouth or jaws wide open

ag'ate *n*. a semi-precious stone

age *n*. 1. length of time a person or thing has existed. 2. period of history, as *the Elizabethan age*. 3. a long time.—*v*. to make or grow old—**ageing** or **ag'ing** (ā'jing) *pres. part*.—**aged** (ājd) *p.t., p. part*. and *adj*. 1. grown old. 2. of the age of, as *a girl aged six*. 3. (ā'jed) elderly.—**the aged** (ā'jed) *n.pl*. old people.—**age'less** *adj*. not growing old.—**age'long** *adj*. lasting for a long time.—**of age** recognised by law as grown up, usually at age of 21 years

a'gency (ā'jen-si) *n*. 1. help, means of bringing about, as *Rocks are worn smooth by the agency of the sea.* 2. the business or place of business of an agent.—**a'gencies** *pl.*

agen'da (a-jen'da) *n.pl.* items of business to be discussed at a meeting

a'gent (ā'jent) *n.* one who does business for another person or for a firm

agglom'erate *n.* (geol.) fused mass of rock.—**agglomera'tion** *n.* 1. a heaping up. 2. untidy heap

ag'grandise *v.* to make greater.—**ag'grandising** *pres. part.*—**aggran'disement** (agran'-disment) *n.* being made greater

ag'gravate *v.* 1. to make worse. 2. to provoke, irritate.—**ag'gravating** *pres. part.*—**ag'grava'tion** (-shun) *n.*

ag'gregate (-gat) *n.* and *adj.* total.—*v.* (-gāte) to collect together into a whole.—**ag'gregating** *pres. part.*—**aggrega'tion** (-shun) *n.*

aggres'sion (a-gresh'un) *n.* an unprovoked attack.—**aggress'ive** *adj.* quarrelsome.—**aggres'siveness** *n.* quarrelsomeness.—**aggres'sor** *n.* the one who attacks first

aggrieve' (a-greev') *v.* to pain or vex.—**aggriev'ing** *pres. part.*—**aggrieved'** *adj.* hurt in the feelings or annoyed

aghast' (a-gast') *adj.* amazed or horrified

ag'ile (aj'īl) *adj.* quick, nimble, active.—**agil'ity** (a-jil'-iti) *n.*

ag'itate (aj'i-tāt) *v.* 1. to set in motion, as *He agitated the surface of the pond with a stick.* 2. to excite, disturb, as *He was very agitated when he heard of his loss.* 3. to argue publicly in favour of a cause, as *Bright and Cobden agitated for the repeal of the Corn Laws.*—**agi'tating** *pres. part.*—**agita'tion** (-shun) *n.*—**ag'itator** *n.* one who stirs up others, esp. about politics

aglow' *adj.* or *adv.* bright, rosy

agnos'tic *n.* one who does not believe that we have any knowledge of God or things outside the material world.—*adj.*—**agnos'ticism** *n.*

ago' *adj.* and *adv.* past, gone by

agog' *adj.* or *adv.* eager, excited

ag'ony *n.* very severe pain of body or mind.—**ag'onies** *pl.*—**ag'onise** *v.* 1. to suffer severely. 2. to give great pain.—**ag'onising** *pres. part.*

Compare: anguish, pang, torment, throe

agra'rian *adj.* relating to land or farming

agree' *v.* 1. to be of the same opinion, as *We all agree that the party was enjoyable.* 2. to consent, as *His father agrees to his having a bicycle.* 3. to be in harmony, as *My neighbour and I agree very well.* 4. to correspond, as *We both added the figures, and my total agreed with hers.* In grammar, to correspond in number, gender, case or person, as a verb *agrees* with its subject.—**agree'able** *adj.* 1. pleasing. 2. willing to consent.—**agree'ableness** *n.*—**agree'ment** *n.* 1. the act of agreeing. 2. a contract, as *The tenant of the house signed an agreement with the landlord.*—**agree with** to suit, as *The sea air agrees with me*

Note: One person *agrees with* another. People *agree on* or *upon* certain ideas. They *agree to* suggestions. They *agree among* themselves. People are *in agreement* when they agree, and *enter into an agreement* when they make a contract

ag'riculture *n.* cultivation of the soil, farming.—**agricul'tural** *adj.*—**agricul'turist** *n.* a farmer

aground' *adj.* or *adv.* run ashore, touching bottom (of a ship)

a'gue (ā'gew) *n.* 1. a disease marked by fever and shivering fits. 2. a shivering fit

ah *int.* an exclamation showing surprise, understanding, etc.

aha' *int.* an exclamation showing satisfaction (at a discovery, etc.) or mockery

ahead' *adv.* forward, in advance

ahoy' (a-hoi') *int.* cry used by seamen in hailing a ship

aid *v.* to help.—*n.* 1. assistance. 2. person or thing that helps.—**first aid** help given to an injured person before the doctor comes

Compare: succour, relieve, subsidise.
Contrast: impede, thwart, hinder

aide-de-camp (ād'di-kohng) *n.*—**aides-de-camp** (*pl.*) French term for an officer who attends Royalty or a general

ail *v.* 1. to trouble. 2. to be ill.—**ail'ment** *n.* disease, sickness.—**ail'ing** *pres. part.* and *adj.* sickly

ai'leron *n.* part of the wing of an aeroplane that helps to balance and steer the machine

aim *v.* 1. to direct or point a weapon. 2. to endeavour.—*n.* 1. act of pointing or directing. 2. intention.—**aim'less** *adj.* without object

air *n.* 1. the mixture of gases we breathe, the atmosphere. 2. a breeze. 3. a tune. 4. a manner.—*v.* 1. to expose to air or warmth, as *to air clothes.* 2. to make known, as *She aired her views.*—**air'ily** *adv.* gaily, light-heartedly.—**air'iness** *n.* 1. openness to the air. 2. lightness of manner.—**air'less** *adj.*—**air'y** *adj.*—**air-tight** *adj.* sealed to prevent air getting in.—**in the air** not certain, as *My plans at the moment are in the air.*—**to put on airs** to behave in an affected manner

air-base *n.* headquarters for aeroplanes

air-borne *adj.* carried by the air

air-compressor *n.* machine compressing air to a higher pressure to make it do work

air-conditioning *n.* system for filtering and cooling air and passing it into a building

air-cooled *adj.* (of an engine) cooled by air instead of water

air'craft *n.* and *n.pl.* flying machines

aircraft car'rier *n.* a ship that acts as a base for aircraft

Aire'dale *n.* large wiry-haired terrier dog,

originally bred in Airedale in Yorkshire

air'field *n.* station used for the taking off and landing of aeroplanes (*esp.* military ones) and for their maintenance

air-force *n.* the strength of a country in aircraft

air-gun *n.* a gun discharged by force of air

air'-hostess *n.* woman who looks after the needs of passengers in an airliner

air'-letter *n.* sheet of special paper to be written on and sent by air without being put in an envelope

air'ing cupboard *n.* heated cupboard for airing clothes

air'line *n.* company providing regular air services for passengers and goods

air'liner *n.* large passenger-carrying aircraft

air'-lock *n.* stoppage caused by a bubble of air blocking a pipe

air'mail *n.* letters sent by air

air'man *n.* one of the crew of an aircraft

air-mind'ed *adj.* regarding aviation as normal, safe, and necessary

air'plane *n.* a flying machine

air-pock'et *n.* a vacuum in the air which makes an aeroplane drop suddenly

air-port *n.* a station for passenger aircraft

air-raid *n.* an attack by aircraft.—**air-raid-precautions** *n.pl.* (A.R.P.) measures taken to protect people against air-attack.—**air-raid-shelter** *n.* a place made to resist attack from the air.—**air-raid-warden** *n.* a person in charge of air-raid-precautions.—**air-raid-warning** *n.* a signal given when an air-raid is expected

air'ship *n.* a flying machine in the form of a long, cigar-shaped balloon.—**air'sickness** *n.* illness caused by the motion of aircraft.—**air'tight** *adj.* not allowing air to pass in or out.—**air'way** *n.* regular aircraft route.—**airworthy** *adj.* fit to fly (of a machine)

air'strip *n.* (temporary) landing ground for aircraft

aisle (īl) *n.* a passage in a church

ajar' *adv.* partly open, as a door

akim'bo *adj.* or *adv.* with hands on hips and elbows bent

akin' *adj.* 1. related as members of the same family. 2. alike, as *Their tastes were akin*

al'abaster (al'a-bahs-ter) or **alabas'ter** *n.* a soft, white stone resembling marble in appearance.—*adj.* made of, or white like alabaster

alack' *interj.* a cry of sorrow

alac'rity *n.* cheerful readiness to do a thing

alarm' *n.* 1. a warning of danger, as an air-raid alarm, fire-alarm. 2. device to give warning. 3. call to arms. 4. fright.—*v.* to frighten.—**alarm'ist** one who raises alarms with little cause.—**alarm-clock** clock that can be set to ring at a certain time

alas' (or a-lahs') *interj.* a cry of grief

al'batross *n.* a large white, web-footed bird, common in the South Seas

albi'no (al-bee'no) *n.* animal or person with white hair and pink eyes through absence of colouring pigment

al'bum *n.* a book of blank leaves for photographs, stamps, autographs, etc.

albu'men *n.* 1. the white of an egg. 2. substance found in animal and vegetable matter as, for instance, in the white of egg.—**albu'minous** *adj.*

al'chemy (al'kemi) *n.* chemistry of early times, in which chemists tried to turn base metals into gold.—**al'chemist** *n.*

al'cohol *n.* 1. pure spirit (ethyl alcohol) which intoxicates. 2. beer, wine, spirits, etc.—**alcohol'ic** *adj.*—*n.* one suffering from alcoholism, as *Alcoholics Anonymous.*—**alcoholism** *n.* a craving for alcohol, habitual drunkenness

al'cove *n.* recess in the wall of a room, garden, or outer wall of a building

al'der (awl'der) *n.* a tree of the birch family, which grows in marshy soils

al'derman (awl'der-man) *n.* a member of town or city council next in rank to the mayor

ale *n.* a light-coloured beer, made from malt and hops

alert' *adj.* watchful, brisk.—*n.* a warning given by watchers, as an air-raid warning.—**on the alert** ready, on the watch.—**alert'ness** *n.*

alfres'co *adv.* or *adj.* (of a meal) in the open air

al'gebra (al'je-bra) *n.* a branch of mathematics in which letters are used to represent numbers.—**algebra'ic** *adj.*

a'lias (ā'li-as) *adv.* otherwise called, as *Smith, alias Thomson.*—*n.* a false name, as *The criminal had several aliases*

al'ibi (al'ib-ī) *n.* a plea that a person charged with a crime was somewhere else when it was committed.—**al'ibis** *pl.*

a'lien (ā'li-en) *n.* a foreigner.—*adj.* 1. foreign. 2. strange, unnatural.—**a'lienate** *v.* to turn away (affection, friendship, etc.) as *His friends were soon alienated by his disagreeable manner.*—**a'lienating** *pres. part.*

alight' *adj.* or *adv.* 1. on fire. 2. lighted up. 3. radiant

alight' *v.* 1. to descend, as from a vehicle. 2. to come down from the air and settle, as a bird

align' aline' (a-līn') *v.* to put or come into a straight line.—**align'ment, aline'ment** *n.* arrangement in a straight line

alike' *adj.* and *adv.* similar, in the same manner

alimen'tary *adj.* concerning food.—**alimentary canal** parts of the body through which food passes

aline see align

alive' *adj.* 1. living. 2. lively. 3. full of moving people or things.—**alive to** aware of

al'kali (or al'ka-lī) *n.* a substance such as soda, which combines with acids to form salts.—**al'kalis, al'kalies** *pl.*—**al'kaline** *adj.*

all *n.* and *pron.* 1. the whole as *He has lost*

all. 2. *adj*. every one of, the whole, as "*All people that on earth do dwell.*" 3. *adv*. entirely, as *all too soon*.—**all and sundry** everybody.—**all in all** altogether.—**all over** finished

Note: All is used in many phrases as *at all*, in any way, *all but*, nearly, *all right* (not *alright*), correct, pleasing, *all along*, all the time, *all the same*, nevertheless, *all told*, everything considered or counted

Al'lah *n*. the Mohammedan name for God

allay' *v*. 1. to quieten, to soothe. 2. to lessen

Compare: calm, check, alleviate, compose. lull. *Contrast:* arouse, inflame, irritate

All Black *n*. member of New Zealand international rugby team.—*adj*.

allega'tion (-shun) see **allege**

allege' (a-lej') *v*. 1. to bring forward as argument or excuse. 2. to declare. 3. to state without proof as, *The police allege that the prisoner committed a burglary*.—**alleg'ing** *pres. part*.

alle'giance (a-lee'jans) *n*. loyalty

Compare: homage, fealty, obedience. *Contrast:* disloyalty, treason, rebellion

all'egory *n*. a story with another meaning beyond the one first seen, as a Parable in the Bible and Bunyan's *Pilgrim's Progress*.—**al'legories** *pl*.—**allegor'ical** *adj*. figurative

alleg'ro *adv*. (in music) lively.—*n*. a lively movement.—*adj*.

allelu'ia (al-e-loo'ya) *n*. song of praise.—*interj*. praise the Lord: See also **halleluiah, hallelujah**

all'ergy (-ji) *n*. unusual sensitivity to some particular substance (*esp*. food and flower pollen) which can make a person ill.—**aller'gic** (-jik) *adj*. usually in the phrase *allergic to*, suffering from this kind of sensitivity to (a particular substance)

alle'viate (a-lee'veeāt) *v*. to ease, to lessen, as *the doctor tried to alleviate the sufferings of the injured*.—**alle'viating** *pres. part*.—**allevia'tion** (-shun) *n*. relief

Compare: mitigate, assuage, relieve. *Contrast:* aggravate, increase

al'ley *n*. 1. a narrow lane or passage. 2. a long enclosed space for playing bowls or skittles.—a **blind alley** a path which leads nowhere

All Hall'ows *n*. All Saints' Day, Nov. 1st

alli'ance *n*. union, esp. between countries by treaty, or families by marriage

al'ligator (al'i-gā-ter) *n*. a large, tough-skinned animal related to the crocodile. It has a long body, short legs, a snout and a tail, and is found in the rivers and marshes of parts of America

allitera'tion (a-lit-er-a'shun) *n*. the beginning of two or more words close together in a group with the same letter or sounds, as *Sing a song of sixpence*.—**allit'erate** *v*.—**allit'erative** *adj*.

al'locate *v*. 1. to give as a share. 2. to assign to a special purpose or person.—**alloca'tion** *n*.—**al'locating** *pres. part*.

allot' (a-lot') *v*. to give out as shares.—**allott'ing** *pres. part*.—**allott'ed** *p.t*. and *p. part*.—**allot'ment** *n*. 1. a share. 2. a plot of land for gardening

allow' *v*. 1. to permit, as *The sentry allowed him to pass the barrier*. 2. to grant, as *Jane is allowed sixpence a week pocket money*. 3. to acknowledge, as *I allow that you know best about that*. 4. to deduct, as *The shopkeeper allowed me a shilling off the original price*. 5. to set aside, as *I have allowed* £10 *for my holiday*.—**allow'able** *adj*. that which is permitted.—**allow'ance** *n*. a sum of money allowed.—**to make allowance** to take into consideration, as *The teacher made allowance for the pupil's age*

al'loy *n*. 1. a mixture of different metals. 2. a base metal mixed with a more valuable one, as lead is said to be an *alloy* when mixed with silver. 3. anything which lowers the quality of that with which it is mixed, as *Their pleasure at meeting was alloyed with the thought of parting again*.—*v*. 1. to mix, as to melt two metals together. 2. to lessen, by adding something baser

allude' (alood') *v*. to mention, to refer to indirectly.—**allu'ding** *pres. part*.

allure' *v*. 1. to tempt, to entice. 2. to attract.—**allur'ing** *pres. part*.—**allure'ment** *n*.

allusion (aloo'zhun) *n*. passing or indirect reference to something in speech or writing (do not confuse with **illusion**).—**allu'sive** (aloo'sive) *adj*. referring to something indirectly; (of a piece of writing) full of such references (do not confuse with **illusive**)

allu'vial (a-loo'vi-al) *adj*. consisting of earth, gravel, mud, etc., deposited by river or flood.—**allu'vium** *n*.

ally' (a-lī') *v*. to unite by treaty, marriage, or in friendship.—**ally'ing** *pres. part*.—**allied'** *p.t*. and *p. part*.—*n*. (al-ī', al'ī) a nation or a person united to another in friendship

al'manac *n*. a calendar of days, weeks and months

almight'y *adj*. all-powerful.—**The Almighty** God

almo'nd (ahm'ond) *n*. 1. the kernel of the fruit of a small tree belonging to the peach-tree family. 2. the tree itself

al'moner *n*. formerly an official who distributed money and other help to needy persons, now a hospital official who attends to social services for patients

al'most (awl'most) *adv*. very nearly, all but

alms (ahmz) *n. sing*. and *pl*. gifts to the poor.—**alms-house** *n*. a house in which a poor person may live rent-free

al'oe *n*. a plant with a bitter juice.—**al'oes**, medicine made from the aloe plant

aloft′ *adv.* 1. on high. 2. far above the earth. 3. at the masthead of a ship

alone′ *adj.* solitary, single.—*adv.* by itself, singly

along′ *prep.* 1. through the length of, as *The books were arranged along the shelves. adv.* 1. onward, as *Do come along.* 2. in company (with), as *He is walking along with me.*—**along′side** *adv.* and *prep.* 1. by the side of. 2. near a ship's side.—**all along,** all the time

aloof′ *adj.* and *adv.* at a distance, apart, as (*adv.*) *She held herself aloof from the other children.*—**aloof′ness** *n.*

aloud′ *adv.* in a voice loud enough to be heard

alp *n.* a mountain pasture, a high mountain. —**al′pine** *adj.* relating to the Alps.—*n.* a plant that grows wild on high mountains. —**al′pinist** *n.* a mountain climber.—**The Alps** a mountain range in Southern Europe

alpac′a *n.* 1. a sheep-like animal of Peru. 2. cloth containing wool of the alpaca

al′penstock *n.* iron-tipped stick used by mountain climbers

al′pha *n.* 1. the first letter of the Greek alphabet. 2. the first.—**Alpha and Omega** the beginning and end.—**alpha particle** (α-particle) a high speed helium nucleus, given out in the decay of certain elements like uranium and radium

al′phabet *n.* the letters of a language arranged in order; the a b c.—**alphabet′ical** *adj.* in the order of the alphabet

alread′y (awl-red′i) *adv.* before this, even now, as *The train is in already*

alright′ a common but incorrect way of writing *all right*

Alsa′tian (al-sā′-shun) *n.* 1. a native of Alsace. 2. a large breed of dog, resembling a wolf.—*adj.* of or belonging to Alsace

al′so (awl′so) *adv.* further, too, as *They came also.*—**an also ran** in common talk, someone who has failed to achieve what others have done

Compare: besides, in addition, likewise, as well

al′tar (awl′ter) *n.* 1. a table or raised place on which sacrifices are offered. 2. the communion table in a Christian church

al′ter (awl′ter) *v.* to change, as *The town has altered much since I was last there.*—**altera′tion** *n.*

al′tercate (awl′ter-kāt) *v.* to dispute, wrangle. —**al′tercating** *pres. part.*—**alterca′tion** (-shun) *n.* angry exchange of words

alter′nate (awl-ter′nāt) *adj.* by turns, one following the other, as *Day and night are alternate*

al′ternate (awl′ter-nāt) *v.* to happen or cause to happen by turns, as *Day alternates with night.*—**al′ternating** *pres. part.*—**alter′native** *n.* 1. a choice of two things, as *You have the alternative of going to the country instead of the seaside.* 2. one of two choices.—*adj.* as *An alternative arrangement would be to go by train instead of by car.*—**alternating current** (*abbrev.* A.C.) electrical current which flows rapidly backwards and forwards

although′ (awl-thō′) *conj.* though, notwithstanding

al′timeter *n.* an instrument which shows the height above sea level

al′titude *n.* 1. height. 2. distance above sea level. —*pl.* high regions

Compare: elevation, loftiness, eminence. *Contrast:* lowness, depth, depression

al′to *n.* 1. the highest man's voice, i.e. counter-tenor; a boy's voice lower than treble; (short for **contralto**) a woman's voice below soprano. 2. a person who sings in such a voice. 3. the musical part sung by this voice.—**al′tos** *pl.*

altogeth′er (awl-to-geth′er) *adv.* 1. entirely. 2. on the whole, as *Altogether the pageant was a grand sight*

Note: This word must not be used instead of *all together*

al′truism *n.* unselfishness.—**al′truist** *n.*—**altruis′tic** *adj.*

al′um *n.* a white mineral salt, double sulphate of aluminium and potassium

alu′mina *n.* oxide of aluminium, extracted from bauxite as a stage in making aluminium

alumin′ium *n.* a white metal. It is very light and does not tarnish

alu′minum *n.* (N.Amer.) commercial name for *aluminium*

al′ways (awl′wāz) *adv.* 1. at all times. 2. for ever

Compare: ceaselessly, continuously, perpetually, invariably. *Contrast:* never, sometimes, occasionally

am first pers. sing. *pres.* of the verb to be

Note: The negative of *I am* is *I am not* or (spoken) *I'm not*

amain′ *adv.* 1. with all strength or force. 2. rapidly

amal′gam *n.* 1. a mixture of mercury with another metal. 2. any soft mixture.—**amal′gamate** *v.* 1. to mix. 2. to combine, as *The two firms have amalgamated.*—**amal′gamating** *pres. part.*—**amalgama′tion** (-shun) *n.*

amanuen′sis *n.* a person who writes what another dictates, or copies what another has written.—**amanuen′ses** *pl.*

amass′ *v.* to heap together, to collect

am′ateur (am′ater or am′atūr) *n.* 1. one who practises art, sport, etc., for enjoyment, without payment. 2. one who does something rather badly.—*adj.* non-professional. —**amateur′ish** *adj.* imperfect

amaze′ *v.* to astonish.—**ama′zing** *pres. part.* and *adj.*—**amaze′ment** *n.* great astonishment

Am′azon *n.* 1. a female warrior. 2. a strong, manlike woman

ambas'sador *n.* 1. minister living in a foreign country to represent his own government's interests there. 2. a messenger with a special mission.—**ambas'sadress** *fem.*

am'ber *n.* a yellowish-brown fossil resin, used for beads, cigarette holders, etc.—*adj.*, made of, or coloured like amber

am'bergris (am'ber-grees) *n.* waxy substance produced by some whales, found floating in the sea, and used in making perfumes

ambidex'trous, ambidex'terous (am-bi-dex'-trus) *adj.* able to use both hands equally well.—**ambidexter'it-y** *n.*

ambigu'ity see **ambiguous**

ambig'uous (-us) *adj.* having more than one meaning, uncertain. *When the cat climbed on the book it fell down* is an *ambiguous* remark, because it may mean either that the cat or the book fell down.—**ambigu'ity** *n.* lack of clarity.—**ambigu'ities** *pl.*

ambi'ti.n (-shun) *n.* 1. desire for power, fame, honour. 2. the object of that desire, as *to achieve one's ambition.*—**ambi'tious** (am-bi'shus) *adj.* eager to attain success

am'ble *v.* 1. (of a horse) to move by lifting both feet on one side together, then both the other side. 2. to move at an easy pace. —*n.* 1. the movement of a horse. 2. an easy gait.—**am'bling** *pres. part.*

ambro'sia *n.* 1. food of the gods. 2. anything delicious.—**ambro'sial** *adj.* delicious

am'bulance *n.* a van for carrying the sick or wounded

am'bush *n.* 1. a lying in wait to attack. 2. hidden troops waiting to attack.—*v.* to attack from hiding-place

ame'liorate (a-meel'yor-ate) *v.* to improve, as *Lord Shaftesbury worked to ameliorate the lot of children working in factories.* —**ameliora'tion** *n.* improvement

Compare: alleviate, assuage, amend, relieve

amen' (ah-men', ā-men') *adv.* or *interj.* so be it.—**say amen to that** to agree

ame'nable (a-mee'na-bl) *adj.* willing to be led or controlled, as *amenable to reason*

amend' *v.* 1. to change for the better. 2. to alter a law, document, or any official decision.—**amend'ment** *n.* a change.—**amendst** *n.pl.* compensation.—**to make amends,** to atone

ame'nity (-meen-' or -men'-) *n.* pleasantness. —**ame'nities** (or a-men'i-ties) *n.pl.* pleasant or convenient features, as *The amenities of the district included a park and a recreation ground*

Amer'ica *n.* 1. The two continents of North and South America, which comprise most of the Western hemisphere. 2. North America. 3. the United States.—**Amer'ican** *adj.*

am'ethyst *n.* 1. a precious stone of violet colour. 2. the colour of the stone

a'miable (ām') *adj.* friendly, kindly.—**amiabil'ity** *n.* pleasantness of disposition.—**a'miably** *adv.*

Compare: lovable, pleasant, sweet, engaging. *Contrast:* unamiable, hateful, disagreeable, sour

am'icable *adj.* friendly, peaceable.—**amicabil'ity** *n.*—**am'icably** *adv.*

amid', amidst' *prep.* in the middle of

Compare: among, amongst, between, midst

amid'ships *adv.* half-way between stem and stern of a ship

amiss' *adj.* wrong.—*adv.* wrongly.—**nothing comes amiss to him** he takes and uses anything.—**to take something amiss** to be offended by something

am'ity *n.* friendship

am'meter *n.* instrument that measures electric current, in ampères

ammo'nia *n.* 1. a strong-smelling gas which will dissolve in water. 2. the liquid produced by dissolving the gas in water.—**ammoni'acal** *adj.* containing ammonia in chemical combination.—**ammo'niated** *adj.* mixed with ammonia

ammuni'tion (am-u-ni'shun) *n.* bullets, shells, powder, etc., for firearms

amne'sia (am-nee'zya) *n.* loss of memory

am'nesty *n.* a general pardon, esp. for offences against the State

amoe'ba (amee'ba) *n.* a tiny, shapeless water-animal, one of the simplest forms of life.—**amoe'bas, amoe'bae** *pl.*

amok see **amuck**

among', amongst' *prep.* 1. mixed with, making part of, as *The mayor was among those present.* 2. between more than two, as *The presents were divided amongst the children*

amor'al *adj.* not concerned with morals, not recognising right and wrong

Note: *immoral* **means recognising right and wrong, but still doing wrong**

am'orous *adj.* falling in love easily

amor'phous (a-mor'fus) *adj.* 1. shapeless. 2. (chemistry) non-crystalline

amount' *n.* the sum total, the whole.—*v.* to come to, be equal to

am'pere *n.* unit of electric current, the current that one volt sends through one ohm

amphib'ian (am-fib'ian) *n.* 1. animal or plant that lives both on land and in water. 2. an aeroplane that can rise and alight on both land and water. 3. a vehicle that can travel over both land and water.—**amphib'ious, amphib'ia** *pl.*—**amphib'ian, amphib'ious** *adj.* capable of living or being used on land or in water

amphithe'atre (am-fi-thee'a-ter) *n.* 1. an unroofed building used for public sports. 2. the gallery of a theatre

am'ple *adj.* 1. enough. 2. big. 3. abundant.—**am'plitude** *n.* largeness, abundance.—**am'ply** *adv.*

Compare: capacious, plenty, plenteous,

spacious. *Contrast:* scanty, inadequate, insufficient, cramped

am'plify *v.* to make greater, louder, or fuller, as *He was asked to amplify his account of the affair.*—**am'plifies.**—**am'plified** *p.t.* and *p. part.*—**amplifica'tion** (-shun) *n.*—**am'plifier** *n.* a device for increasing volume of sound, as in radio reception

am'poule (am'pool) *n.* a small sealed glass container for medicine

am'putate *v.* to cut off, as a limb.—**am'-putating** *pres. part.*—**amputa'tion** (-shun) *n.*

amuck', amok' *adj.* or *adv.* used only in the phrase **to run amock or amok,** i.e. to rush about attacking at random

am'ulet *n.* something worn as a charm against evil

amuse' *v.* 1. to occupy pleasantly. 2. to make smile.—**amu'sing** *pres. part.*—*adj.* funny.—**amuse'ment** *n.* 1. feeling caused by something funny. 2. recreation

Compare: divert, enliven, entertain. *Contrast:* bore, weary, tire

an *adj.* or *indefinite article* used before a vowel or silent *h*, as *an honourable man*

an'abranch *n.* (Aus.) a tributary of a river which rejoins the main stream forming an island between the two water-courses

anach'ronism (a-nak'ron-izm) *n.* 1. the placing of some person or thing in a period of history, to which it could not have belonged. It would be an anachronism to say that *King John of England sent a telegram,* since the telegraph system had not been invented in his time. 2. anything put out of its proper place in time

anacon'da *n.* a large snake that crushes its prey

anae'mia (an-ee'mi-a) *n.* illness resulting from lack of blood or of red blood corpuscles.—**anae'mic** *adj.* suffering from anaemia

anaesthe'sia, anesthe'sia *n.* loss of feeling of pain, heat, cold, etc.

anaesthet'ic, anesthet'ic (an-es-thet'ik) *n.* a drug or gas (such as chloroform), which prevents pain being felt.—*adj.* having the effect of deadening pain.—**anaes'thetise** *v.* to treat a person so as to make him unconscious of pain.—**anaes'thetist** *n.* one who gives an anaesthetic

an'agram *n.* a word or sentence made by rearranging in a different order the letters of another word or sentence, as the word *ant* made from *tan*

analge'sic (-jeez'ik) *n.* any drug which relieves pain

an'alogue comput'er (an'alog) *n.* a computer specially designed for mathematical and scientific problems

anal'ogy (a-nal'o-ji) *n.* similarity, comparison as *The teacher drew an analogy between ripples of a stone thrown in a pond, and radio waves.*—**anal'ogies** *pl.*—**anal'ogous** (a-nal'ogus) *adj.* resembling

an'alyse (an'a-līz) *v.* to split up into separate parts in order to study and compare them. —**an'alysing** *pres. part.*—**anal'ysis** *n.* the separation of anything into its parts.—**anal'yses** *pl.*—**an'alyst** *n.* one skilled in analysis.—**analyt'ic, analyt'ical** *adj.*

Note: 1. In grammar *analysis* is an exercise which consists of dividing a sentence into its parts of subject, predicate, object, etc. Sentences containing more than one finite verb have to be *analysed* into clauses, and the clauses *analysed* into their parts 2. In the U.S.A. *analysis, analyst* and *analyse* are used as short forms for *psycho-analysis* etc.

an'archist (an'ar-kist) *n.* one who believes there should be no government or laws.—**an'archy** (an'ar-ki) *n.* lawless disorder

anath'ema *n.* 1. a solemn curse. 2. something hateful.—**anath'ematise** *v.* to curse

anat'omy *n.* 1. the structure of an animal or plant. 2. the study of the parts of an animal or plant. 3. the separation of the parts of an animal or plant to study their arrangement.—**anatom'ical** *adj.*—**anat'omist** *n.*

an'cestor (an'ses-tor) *n.* a relative from whom one is descended, as a parent, grandparent, etc.—**an'cestress** *fem.*—**ances'tral** *adj.*—**an'cestry** *n.* line of ancestors. —**an'cestries** *pl.*

an'chor (ang'ker) *n.* a heavy iron instrument attached to a ship by a chain, that hooks into the ground below water and so holds the vessel fast.—*v.* 1. secure a vessel with an anchor. 2. fix securely.—**an'chorage** 1. the act of anchoring. 2. a place in which to anchor.—**to cast (or to drop) anchor** to let the anchor into the water.—**to weigh anchor** to raise the anchor and set sail

ancho'vy (or **an'cho-vy**) *n.* a small fish of the herring family. It has a strong flavour and is used for sauces, etc.—**ancho'vies** *pl.*

an'cient (ān'shent) *adj.* 1. old. 2. belonging to olden times.—*n.* an old person.—**the ancients** those who lived in olden times.—**an'ciently** *adv.*

ancill'ary (ansil'ari) *adj.* subordinate to, auxiliary

and *conj.* a connecting word, used to join words, phrases and sentences

andan'te *adv.* in music, moderately slow

and'iron (and'ī-ron) *n.* iron bar or bracket for holding logs in a fire

an'ecdote *n.* a little story told of some person or happening

anemom'eter *n.* an instrument for measuring wind-speed

anem'one *n.* a woodland flower, the wind-flower

an'eroid *n.* and *adj.* (barometer) that measures air-pressure without using liquids

anew' *adv.* afresh, again

an'gel (ān'jel) *n.* 1. a Divine messenger. 2. a ministering spirit. 3. a person having the qualities of a good spirit. 4. ancient English coin.—**angel'ic, angel'ical** *adj.*

an'ger (ang'ger) *n.* wrath, strong displeasure. —*v.* to rouse wrath

an'gle (ang'gil) *n.* 1. a corner. 2. space between two lines meeting at a point. 3. space between two flat surfaces which meet at one edge. 4. a point of view.—**an'gular** *adj.* having angles, pointed.—**angular'ity** *n.*—**at an angle** tilted

an'gle *v.* 1. to fish with line and hook. 2. to use hints and ruses to obtain something, as *She angled for an invitation.*—**an'gling** *pres. part.*—**an'gler** *n.*

An'glican *n.* and *adj.* belonging to the Church of England.—**an'glicise** *v.* to make English the speech, manners, customs, etc. of another country, as *adieu* is a French expression which has become *anglicised.*—**an'glicising** *pres. part.*

An'glo'- English, added at the beginning of other words to form compounds.—**Anglo-In'dian** *n.* a person of mixed English and Indian parentage.—**Anglo-Cath'olic** *n.* an Anglican who rejects the term *Protestant* and sees an unbroken connection between the Anglican and early Catholic churches.——**Anglo-Sax'on** *n.* 1. one who lived in England before the Norman Conquest. 2. the language of England before the Conquest.—*adj.* concerning the English or their language before the Conquest

angor'a *n.* 1. a long-haired cat, goat, or rabbit. 2. fur, cloth, or wool made from goat or rabbit

ang'ry *adj.* 1. enraged, in the grip of anger. 2. (of a cut) inflamed.—**ang'rier** *comp.*—**ang'riest** *sup.*—**ang'rily** *adv.*

an'guish (ang'gwish) *n.* extreme pain, or body or mind. See **agony**

ang'ular (ang'gū-lar) *adj.* see angle

an'iline *n.* a product of coal-tar, from which dyes are obtained

an'imal *n.* 1. a being having life, feeling and the power to move, as a man, a horse, a bird, a fish. 2. a mammal other than a human being, as a lion, cat, rabbit, etc.—*adj.* concerning, or like, an animal.—**animal'cule** *n.* a very minute animal.—**animal Kingdom** that part of the living world which consists of animals with power of movement, as distinct from the Vegetable Kingdom.—**animal spirits** noisy high spirits

an'imate *v.* to give life to, enliven.—*adj.* living.—**an'imating** *pres. part.*—**an'imated** *adj.* alive, spirited.—**animated cartoon** *n.* motion picture made from a series of drawings.—**anima'tion** (-shun) *n.*—**an'imator** *n.*

Compare: stimulate, invigorate, quicken. *Contrast:* deaden, depress, dispirit

animos'ity *n.* hatred, as a cat and a dog *usually regard one another with feelings of animosity.*—**animos'ities** *pl.*

an'ion (an'ī-on) *n.* in an electrolytic solution, the negatively charged ion moving towards the cathode

an'iseed *n.* plant giving seeds used for flavouring cakes, etc., and in medicines

an'kle (ang'kl) *n.* the joint between the foot and the leg.—**ank'let** *n.* an ornament for the ankle

an'nals *n.pl.* 1. a yearly record of events. 2. a history.—**an'nalist** *n.* a writer of annals

anneal' *v.* 1. to heat, and then cool slowly. 2. to heat in order to fix colours

annex' *v.* to unite at the end, to add, take possession of, esp. territory.—**annexa'tion** *n.* the act of uniting.—**ann'exe** *n.* an addition, especially an additional building, as to an hotel

anni'hilate (an-ī-il-āt) *v.* to destroy utterly.—**anni'hilating** *pres. part.*—**anni'hilated** *p.t.* and *p. part.*—**annihila'tion** *n.* total destruction

anniver'sary *n.* a day celebrated as it returns each year.—*adj.* yearly.—**anniver'saries** *pl.*

An'no Dom'ini (dom'in-ī) Latin for "in the year of our Lord" used with dates in the Christian era, as A.D. 1066

ann'otate *v.* to make comments or notes upon.—**ann'otating** *pres. part.*—**ann'otated** *p.t.* and *p. part.* as *an annotated edition of Shakespeare's plays.*—**annota'tion** *n,* a note or comment.—**annota'tor** *n.*

announce' *v.* to make known.—**announ'cing** *pres. part.*—**announ'ced** *p.t.* and *p. part.*—**announ'cement** *n.* proclamation, declaration.—**announ'cer** *n.* in radio or television, one who announces items in a programme

Compare: declare, publish, advertise, disclose. *Contrast:* conceal, suppress

annoy' *v.* to worry, vex, as *Noise annoys elderly people.*—**annoy'ance** *n.*

ann'ual *adj.* 1. returning or happening every year 2. yearly 3. lasting only one year.—*n.* 1. a plant that only lives one year or season. 2. a children's book published once a year.—**annually** *adv.* each year

annu'ity *n.* a sum of money payable yearly.—**annu'ities** *pl.*

annul' *v.* to make of no effect, as a law, agreement, contract or marriage may be annulled.—**annulling** *pres. part.*—**annulled'** *p.t.* and *p. part.*—**annul'ment** *n.*

Compare: repeal, abolish, rescind, cancel

the Annuncia'tion *n.* the angel's announcement to the Virgin Mary that she was to be the Mother of Jesus

an'ode *n.* the positive electrode of a cell, or plate in a valve

an'odyne *n.* a drug which allays pain.—*adj.* relieving pain

anoint' *v.* to pour oil upon; to consecrate with oil.—**anoin'ted** *adj.* consecrated.—**anoint'ment** *n.*

anom'aly *n.* departure from the common rule, as *Snow in summer is an anomaly.*—**anom'alies** *pl.*—**anom'alous** *adj.* irregular

anon' *adv.* quickly, immediately

anon'ymous *adj.* without a writer's name (often written **anon**), as *He received an anonymous letter.*—**anony'mity** *n.*

an'orak *n.* hooded windproof jacket

anoth'er (an-uTH'er) *adj.* different.—*pron.* an additional one

an'swer (an'ser) *n.* 1. something said or written in return to a question. 2. the solution of a problem.—*v.* 1. to speak or write in return. 2. to reply. 3. to suit.—**to answer for** to be responsible for.—**to answer to** to correspond.—**an'swerable** *adj.* liable, responsible, as *He was held answerable for his wife's debts*

Compare: reply, response, rejoinder, retort. *Contrast:* question, interrogation, query, enquiry. An *answer* may be an action, as *His answer to the insult was to knock the man down.* An *answer* deals with the points raised by the question, but a reply does not necessarily do so. *Rejoinder, response* and *retort* are special kinds of *answers.* See definition of them

ant *n.* a small insect. A large number of ants is called a *swarm.*—**ant'eater** *n.* an animal which feeds on ants by means of a long, sticky tongue.—**ant-eggs** the larvae (grubs) of ants.—**ant'hill** *n.* the mound raised by ants.—**white ant** not an ant, but a termite

antag'onise *v.* to arouse hostility.—**antag'onism** *n.* opposition, hostility.—**antag'onist** *n.* opponent.—**antagonist'ic** *adj.*

antar'ctic *n.* region between the South Pole and the Antarctic Circle

an'te- *prefix* before, as *antedate* means to mark or stamp a date before the true time

Note: Ante- at the beginning of a word usually means before. This must not be confused with *anti-* meaning *against*

antece'dent (an-te-see'dent) *adj.* going before in time.—*n.* that which goes before.—*n.pl.* the previous life and character of a person

an'techamber *n.* a room leading to a more important apartment

antedate' *v.* to date before the true time

antedilu'vian *adj.* 1. before the Flood. 2. antiquated.—*n.* one that lived before the Flood

an'telope *n.* an animal partly like a deer and partly like a goat

antemerid'iem (latin) or **antemerid'ian** *adj.* before noon (written "*a.m.*")

antena'tal *adj.* happening before birth

antenn'a *n.* 1. an insect's feeler. 2. in radio, an aerial.—**antennae** (an-ten'i) *pl.*

ante'rior *adj.* before or previous

Compare: earlier, former, foregoing. *Contrast:* posterior, later, following

an'them *n.* a hymn sung in parts.—**National Anthem** a song expressing national identity and sung at public gatherings

an'ther *n.* the little sac on the stamen of a flower, containing the pollen

anthol'ogy (an-thol'o-ji) *n.* a collection of poems or gems of writing.—**anthol'ogies** *pl.*

an'thracite (an'thra-sīt) *n.* very hard coal, that burns with little smoke

an'thrax *n.* a disease of sheep and cattle, also affecting man

an'thropoid *n.* an ape resembling man—*adj.* like man

anthropol'ogy (an-thro-pol'o-ji) *n.* the scientific study of mankind esp. of early man

anthropolog'ical *adj.* concerning the study of early man.—**anthropol'ogist** *n.*

an'ti- *prefix* against, as *anti-aircraft gun* means a gun used against aircraft

Note: anti- at the beginning of a word usually means against. This must not be confused with *ante-*

an'ti-air'craft *adj.* employed against aircraft

antibiot'ic (an-ti-bī-ot'ik) *n.* substance such as penicillin which kills bacteria.—*adj.*

anti'cipate (an-ti'si-pāt) *v.* to be beforehand; to foresee; enjoy in advance.—**anticipa'tion** *n.* (an-ti-si-pā'shun) expectation

Compare: expect, forecast, count upon, prepare for

anticli'max *n.* something trivial which destroys a magnificent effect. See **climax**

an'tics *n.pl.* odd, fanciful or foolish actions

anti-cy'clone (an-ti-sī'klōn) *n.* an outflow of weak, spiral winds from an area of high pressure. It is usually accompanied by bright, dry weather in summer, and cold dry weather in winter

an'tidote *n.* a medicine to make poison ineffective

an'tifreeze *n.* substance added to water in motor-car radiators to prevent freezing

antimacass'ar *n.* an ornamental covering for chair-backs to prevent them from being soiled

an'timony *n.* a metal, used in alloys and in medicine

anti'pathy *n.* dislike.—**antipathet'ic** *adj.*

Compare: aversion, dislike, disgust, hatred. *Contrasts* sympathy, love, affection, attraction

anti'podes (an-tip'o-deez) *n.pl.* the regions on the opposite side of the globe (Australasia)

an'tiquary *n.* a collector of old things.—**antiqua'rian** *n.* and *adj.*

an'tiquated *adj.* grown old or out of fashion

antique' (anteek') *n.* something belonging to ancient times.—*adj.* ancient, old-fashioned.—**anti'quity** *n.* ancient times.—**anti'quities** *pl.* the remains of ancient times

antisem'itism *n.* dislike or persecution of Jewish people

antisep'tic *n.* a substance that prevents festering or decay.—*adj.*

antith'esis *n.* 1. a sharp contrast, as *War is the antithesis of peace.* 2. a figure of speech involving a contrast, as "*To err is human, to forgive divine.*"—**antith'eses** *pl.*—**antithet'ical** *adj.*

ant'ler *n.* a branch of the horn of a stag

an'tonym (-nim) *n.* a word of opposite meaning, as *Good and bad are antonyms* of *each other*

a'nus (ā'nus) *n.* the opening through which solid waste is passed from the body

an'vil *n.* 1. an iron block on which metals are shaped by the smith. 2. one of the bones of the middle ear

anxi'ety (ang-zī'e-ti) *n.* trouble, worry, esp. about the future.—**anxi'eties** *pl.*—**an'xious** (angk'shus) *adj.* troubled, worried

Compare: uneasy, disquieted, restless. *Contrast:* easy, carefree, untroubled, undisturbed

an'y (en'i) *adj.* and *pron.* one, some.—**an'ybody** *n.*—**an'yhow** *adv.* in some way or another.—**an'yone** *n.*—**an'ything** *n.*—**an'yway** *adv.* at any rate.—**an'ywhere** *adv.* in any place

Note: Some authorities deny that **any** can be used as a pronoun, except in compounds such as *anyone*. It is seen as an adjective in such expressions as *any money*, and as an adverb in *any more*

An'zac *n.* a soldier of the Australian-New Zealand Army Corps in the war of 1914-1918 (from the initial letters)

aor'ta *n.* the great artery which rises from the left ventricle of the heart

Aotearo'a (ā-o-tee-a-ro'a) *n.* traditional Maori name for New Zealand

apach'e (apach'ā) *n.* 1. a Red Indian tribe. 2. (apash') a desperado, esp. a Parisian one

apart' *adv.* separately, aside, at a distance

apart'heid (apart'hāt, hīt) *n.* (in South Africa) the policy of separate development of the whites and different racial groups in South Africa

apart'ment *n.* 1. a room. 2. U.S., a flat.—*pl.* lodgings, rooms rented

ap'athy *n.* indifference.—**apathet'ic** *adj.* without feeling

Compare: unconcern, calmness, stolidity. *Contrast:* enthusiasm, agitation, zeal

ape *n.* 1. a tailless monkey, chimpanzee, gorilla, etc. 2. a silly imitator.—*v.* to try to imitate

aper'itif (ap-ā'reet-eef) *n.* a drink taken before a meal to whet one's appetite

ap'erture *n.* an opening; a gap; in a camera, the opening letting light through the lens

a'pex (ā'pex) *n.* the top, tip, or summit of anything.—**a'pices** *pl.*

a'phis (ā'fis) *n.* a family of small insects found as parasites on roots, leaves. The greenfly is an aphis.—*pl.* **a'phides**

aph'orism *n.* a maxim expressed in a few words, as *Better late than never*

a'piary (ā'pi-ar-i) *n.* a place where bees are kept.—**a'piculture** *n.* bee-keeping

apiece' *adv.* for each, to each, to the share of each, as *The boys were given an orange apiece*

apoc'alypse (-lips) *n.* the Revelation of St. John; any revelation.—**apocalyp'tic** *adj.*

Apoc'rypha (a-pok'ri-fa) *n.* books of the Old Testament accepted by Roman Catholics but not by Protestants or Jews.—**apoc'ryphal** *adj.* of doubtful authority

ap'ogee (-jee) *n.* the point of orbit of a planet or the moon, farthest from the earth

apol'ogise (-jīz) *v.* to offer an excuse, as *He apologised to the teacher for being late.*—**apologet'ic** (a-po-lo-jet'ic) *adj.* admitting or excusing a fault.—**apol'ogy** *n.* 1. an excuse. 2. a defence.—**apol'ogies** *pl.*

apoplec'tic *adj.* concerning apoplexy, as *an apoplectic fit*

ap'oplexy *n.* a sudden stroke, causing loss of the power to feel and move

apos'tle (a-pos'el) *n.* 1. one sent to preach the Gospel, esp. one of the first disciples of Christ. 2. the chief champion of any new system.—**apost'leship** *n.* the office of an apostle.—**apostol'ic** *adj.*

apos'trophe (ap-os'trof-i) *n.* a mark (') indicating the possessive case, as *Tom's book*, or the omission of one or more letters of a word, as *don't*, *e'er*

apoth'ecary *n.* one who sells drugs and medicines

apotheos'is (ap-oth-ee-ō'sis) *n.* raising to the ranks of the gods, exaltation

appal' (ap-awl') *v.* to dismay, terrify.—**appall'ing** *pres. part.*—**appalled'** (ap-awld') *p.t.* and *p. part.*—**appall'ing** *adj.* terrifying

appara'tus (ap-par-ā'tus) *n.* a set of implements for performing a particular purpose

appar'el *n.* clothing.—*v.* to clothe, to adorn

appar'ent *adj.* visible, plain; seeming.—**appar'ently** *adv.*

Compare: evident, obvious, certain. *Contrast:* obscure, concealed, improbable

appari'tion *n.* 1. appearance. 2. a ghost

appeal' *v.* 1. to ask earnestly. This verb may also stand alone with the meaning: to reopen a case before a higher court. 2. to be attractive.—*n.* act of appealing

Note: We say *appeal for* help or subscriptions. *Appeal to* has several meanings, as *I appeal to you to think again*; *It does not appeal to me*

appear' *v.* 1. to come in sight. 2. to be seen. 3. to seem.—**appear'ance** *n.* 1. a coming in sight. 2. outward show.—**to keep up appearances** to make a good outward show.—**to put in an appearance** to appear

appease' *v.* to quieten down.—**appeas'ing** *pres. part.*—**appeased'** *p.t.* and *p. part.*—**appease'ment** *n.*

Compare: pacify, soothe, placate. *Contrast:* enrage, incense, irritate

appela'tion (a-pel-a'shun) *n.* a name, title

append' *v.* to hang, or attach to; to add to, as *The mayor appended his seal to the document.*—**appen'dage** *n.* something accompanying

appendici'tis (ap-en-di-sī'tis) *n.* inflammation of the appendix of the larger intestine
appen'dix *n.* 1. something added, as at the end of a book. 2. a little tube attached to the large intestine.—**(appen'dixes, appen'dices** *pl.*)
appertain' (to) *v.* to belong to; relate to
app'etite *n.* a desire or hunger, esp. for food or drink.—**app'etise** *v.* to create an appetite.—**app'etiser** *n.* something stimulating to the appetite.—**app'etising** *adj.*
applaud' *v.* to praise, esp. by clapping the hands.—**applause'** (ap-plaws') *n.* approval publicly expressed
ap'ple *n.* a round, firm, fleshy fruit.—**apple-cheeked'** *adj.* rosy as an apple.—**in apple-pie order** in perfect order.—**the apple of one's eye** a great favourite
appli'ance *n.* instrument, device
app'licable *adj.* suitable
app'licant *n.* one who applies.—**applica'tion** *n.* 1. a request. 2. hard work. 3. a putting into practice
apply' *v.* 1. to place on, as *to apply a poultice.* 2. to put into practice, as *He applied the principles of First Aid.* 3. to devote, employ, as *He applied himself to learning shorthand.* —**applied'** *p.t.* and *p. part.*
Note: The argument does not apply: that is, does not refer to or *apply to* this case. You *apply to* someone for assistance, but you *apply for* a job
appoint' *v.* 1. to settle. 2. to choose for a post. —**appoint'ment** *n.* 1. choice for a position. 2. promise to be somewhere to meet someone
appor'tion *v.* to divide out fairly
app'osite (app'ōz-it) *adj.* well put, well adapted to the situation, as *an apposite quotation*
apposi'tion (app-ōz-i'shun) *n.* 1. placing side by side. 2. in Grammar when one noun is put next to another and they extend each other's meaning, they are *in apposition* to each other, as *my brother John, William the Conqueror*
appraise' *v.* to put a price on, to fix the value of.—**apprais'al** *n.*
appre'ciate (a-pree'shi-āt) *v.* 1. to value, as *We appreciated their kindness.* 2. to rise in value, as *The value of the land appreciated* —**apprecia'tion** (a-pree-shi-ā'shun) *n.*—**appreci'ative** *adj.*—**apprec'iable** *adj.* 1. able to be estimated. 2. perceptible as *an appreciable change*
apprehend' *v.* 1. to lay hold of, as *apprehended by the police.* 2. to understand, as *to apprehend the difference between two things.* 3. to fear.—**apprehen'sion** *n.* 1. understanding. 2. fear for the future.—**apprehen'sive** *adj.* fearful, regarding with apprehension, having feelings of apprehension
appren'tice (-tis) *n.* one bound to a master to learn an art or trade.—**appren'ticeship** *n.* 1. the condition of an apprentice. 2. the time for which he serves
apprise' *v.* to inform, to give notice, as *He was apprised of our intentions*
approach' *v.* 1. to draw near. 2. to make advances to anyone, as *The secretary has approached Mr. Jones with a view to his becoming a vice-president of the club.*—*n.* 1. drawing near. 2. a path or avenue. 3. a golf stroke which places the ball on the green.—**approach'able** *adj.*
approba'tion (a-pro-bā'shun) *n.* approval
appro'priate *adj.* suitable.—*v.* 1. to set apart for a special purpose. 2. to take for oneself. —**appro'priately** *adv.*—**appropria'tion** *n.* the act of setting apart for a purpose
Note: There is a slight difference in the pronunciation of the adjective *appropriate* and the verb. The adjective (as *Appropriate hymns were chosen for the occasion*) is pronounced ap-prō'pri-at. The verb (as *The dishonest servant appropriated her mistress's stockings*) is pronounced ap-prō'pri-āt
approve' (a-proov') *v.* to be pleased with, as *Do you approve of the scheme? Yes, I approve. Note: approve of.*—**appro'val** *n.* act of approving, trial, as *to take goods on approval,* sanction—**approv'ing** *pres. part.*—**approv'ed** *p.t.* and *p. part.*
approx'imate *v.* to come near to.—*adj.* near to, nearly correct.—**approx'imately** *adv.*—**approxima'tion** *n.*
Note: The verb (as *Your answer approximates to the correct one*) is pronounced ap-prox'i-māt. The adjective (as *the approximate number*) is pronounced ap-prox'i-mat
appur'tenances *n.pl.* belongings, as, *He sold the farm and all its appurtenances*
a'pricot *n.* an orange-coloured stone-fruit of the plum kind.—*adj.*
A'pril (ā'pril) *n.* the fourth month of the year
a'pron (ā'pron) *n.* a garment worn in front to protect the clothes.—**apron stage** a stage at least part of which has the audience on three sides
apse *n.* an arched recess at the eastern end of a church
apt *adj.* suitable, ready, prompt.—**apt to do** likely to do, or in the habit of doing. —**ap'titude** *n.* fitness for something. —**apt'ly** *adv.* properly, fitly.—**apt'ness** *n.* fitness, readiness
aqu'alung *n.* an under-water breathing apparatus
aqua'rium (a-kwā'ri-um) *n.* a vessel or tank for keeping fish or other water animals or plants
aquat'ic *adj.* 1. growing or living in water. 2. practised on or in water (swimming is an *aquatic* sport)
aque'duct *n.* a course or channel for conveying water

a'queous (ā'kweeus) *adj.* watery

a'quiline *adj.* belonging to the eagle, hooked like the beak of an eagle, as *An aquiline nose*

Ara'bia *n.* a large peninsula in south-west Asia.—**A'rab** *n.* a person belonging to Arabia or nearby countries.—**Ar'abic** *n.* the language of the Arabs.—*adj.* **Arabic numerals** the numerals 1, 2, 3 . . .

arabesque' (a-ra-besk') *n.* 1. a painted or carved ornament with a design of leaves and scrolls. 2. a pose in ballet in which the dancer stands on one leg with the other stretched horizontally backwards

ar'able *adj.* fit for tillage or ploughing

Ar'awak *n.* one of an Amerindian tribe

ar'biter *n.* one who decides some question

Compare: judge, referee, umpire, arbitrator

Note: An *arbiter* differs from these others in that he decides absolutely and there is no appeal from his decision

ar'bitrary *adj.* not bound by rules, as *an arbitrary form of government.*—**ar'bitrarily** *adv.*

Compare: despotic, absolute, dictorial, tyrannical, unrestrained, *Contrast:* constitutional, limited, restrained

ar'bitrate *v.* to decide a dispute.—**arbitra'tion** *n.*—**ar'bitrator** *n.* one chosen to decide a dispute

arbor'eal *adj.* relating to trees

ar'bour *n.* a bower shaded by trees

arc *n.* part of the circumference of a circle. A stone thrown into the air describes an arc as it goes up and then down, in a curve. —**arc'light** *n.* a light from an electric current passing between carbon electrodes

arcade' *n.* a covered walk or avenue

arch *n.* any construction forming a bridge, in a curve.—*v.* to make into an arch, as *The cat arched its back*

arch *adj.* roguish or sly, mischievous

arch *adj.* chief. This is usually added to the beginning of a word, as in *archbishop, arch-enemy.* It is sometimes pronounced *ark.* See **archangel**

archaeo'logy (ar-ki-ol'o-ji) *n.* the study of ancient monuments and arts

archa'ic (ar-kā'ic) *adj.* ancient.—**ar'chaism** (ar'kā-ism) *n.* an oldfashioned word or phrase or one no longer used, as *afeard, prithee*

arc'hangel (ark'ān-jel) *n.* an angel of the highest order

archbish'op *n.* chief bishop in a Church province.—**archbish'opric** *n.* the office of an archbishop

archdea'con *n.* a chief deacon, the clergyman next in rank to a bishop.—**archidia'conal** (ar-ki-dī-a'kon-al) *adj.*

arch'duke *n.* a grand duke.—**arch'duch'ess** *fem.*

arch'er *n.* a bowman.—**arch'ery** *n.* the art of shooting with a bow and arrow

archipel'ago (ark-i-pel'a-go) *n.* 1. a group of islands. 2. a sea full of small islands

ar'chitect (ark'i-tekt) *n.* one who plans buildings.—**ar'chitec'tural** *adj.*—**ar'chitecture** *n.* the art of building, style of building

ar'chives (ar'kīvz) *n.pl.* 1. documents and records. 2. place where they are stored.—**ar'chivist** *n.* person who looks after them

arch'way *n.* an entrance under an arch

arc'tic *n.* region between the North pole and the arctic circle.—**arctic circle** *n.* the line of latitude 66° 33′ N

ar'dent *adj.* enthusiastic, zealous, as *An ardent reformer.*—**ar'dour** *n.* enthusiasm, eagerness, zeal

Compare: eager, fervent, fervid, keen. *Contrast:* indifferent, lukewarm, apathetic, cool

ar'duous *adj.* difficult to do, hard

are (ar) first, second and third person plural of the present tense of the verb **be**

Note: The negative of *are* is *are not* or (in speech) *aren't.* It is incorrect to say *ain't*

a'rea *n.* 1. any plane surface, as the floor-space of a room. 2. amount of surface, as *He multiplied the length of the field by its breadth to find its area.* 3. a sunken space round a building

are'na (ee) *n.* the sand-strewn space of a Roman amphitheatre

Argenti'na *n.* a South American country.—**Argentin'ian** *n.* a native of Argentina.—*adj.*

ar'gon *n.* a rare inert gas

ar'gosy *n.* a large merchant ship.—**ar'gosies** *pl.*

ar'gue *v.* to debate.—**ar'guing** *pres. part.*—**ar'gument** *n.* 1. debate. 2. an outline of a play or poem.—**argumen'tative** *adj.* fond of arguing

Note: You *argue with* a person when disputing or discussing some matter with him. You *argue in favour of* your own point of view; you *argue that* your opinions are correct. When you do this you are *arguing* your case

ar'ia (ah'ree-a) *n.* an air or song in a cantata or opera

ar'id *adj.* dry, as *an arid desert, an arid subject.*—**arid'ity** *n.*

aright' *adv.* rightly, correctly

arise' *v.* to come up, spring up.—**ari'sing** *pres. part.*—**arose'** *p.t.*—**aris'en** *p. part.*

aristoc'racy *n.* 1. government by nobles. 2. the nobility.—**ar'istocrat** *n.*—**aristocrat'ic** *adj.*

arith'metic *n.* the art of reckoning by figures. —**arithmet'ical** *adj.*—**arithmetical progression** series of numbers which increase or decrease by a uniform difference.—**arithmeti'cian** *n.* one skilled in arithmetic

ark *n.* 1. the vessel in which Noah and his

family were saved from the Flood. 2. a box, chest. 3. a ship

arm *n.* 1. the part of the body between the shoulder and the hand. 2. something resembling this, like the arm of a chair, a branch of the sea.—**arm'ful** *n.* as much as can be held in the arms.—**with open arms** in a friendly way

arm *n.* 1. a branch of the military service. 2. a weapon.—*v.* to supply with weapons. This verb may also stand alone with the meaning of to take up arms.—**a call to arms** a call to fight.—**a coat of arms** a badge of rank and family, used in heraldry. —**Armed Services** a nation's army, navy and air force.—**armed to the teeth** well armed

armad'a (ar-mah'da or ar-mā'da) *n.* a fleet of armed ships (e.g. the **Spanish Armada** of 1588)

armadill'o *n.* an animal living in South America (the body is encased in an armour of small bony plates)

ar'mament *n.* land or naval forces equipped for war

arm'ature *n.* in electricity, the rotating coil of a dynamo or electric motor

arm'istice *n.* a truce, an end of fighting (e.g. in the First World War, Nov. 11th, 1918)

arm'let *n.* a band worn round the arm

ar'mour (ar'mer) *n.* 1. anything worn to protect in battle. 2. the steel covering of warships.—**ar'mourer, ar'morer** *n.* a maker of arms.—**ar'moury, ar'mory** *n.* arms store. —**armour-plate** steel plating to protect from shells and mines

ar'my *n.* 1. a large body of men armed for warfare and under military command. 2. a host, a great number.—**ar'mies** *pl.*

aro'ma *n.* an odour, smell, flavour.—**aromat'ic** *adj.* sweet-smelling

around *adv.* on every side, in a circle, as *They sat around talking.*—*prep.* on all sides of, as *They walked around the town*

arouse' *v.* to awaken, as *to arouse interest, to arouse from slumber.*—**arous'ing** *pres. part.*—**aroused'** *p.t.* and *p. part.*

Compare: excite, disturb, stir up. *Contrast:* allay, quieten, lull, soothe

arpegg'io (arpej'iō) *n.* in music, notes of a chord played one after another instead of together

arraign' (a-rān') *v.* to accuse publicly

Note: The prisoner is *arraigned of* or *for* the crime or *on* a charge, *at* the bar or *before* the court

arrange' *v.* 1. to put into order. 2. plan.—**arrang'ing** *pres. part.*—**arranged'** *p.t.* and *p. part.*—**arrange'ment** *n.* adjustment, plan

ar'rant *adj.* very bad, as *an arrant rascal*

ar'ras *n.* tapestry, made first at Arras

array' *n.* 1. arrangement in regular lines, as *an array of troops, of jewels.* 2. apparel. —*v.* 1. to draw up, as troops for battle. 2. to deck

arrears *n.pl.* 1 unpaid debts 2 unfinished work which is overdue —**in arrears** means to owe or to be owed, as *He was in arrears with his payments; The rent was in arrears*

arrest' *n* making prisoner.—*v.* 1. to stop, as *to arrest bleeding.* 2. to take prisoner by authority of law, as *The policeman arrested the thief*

arrive' *v.* to reach a place, a conclusion or a decision.—**arri'ving** *pres. part.*—**arrived'** *p.t.* and *p. part.*—**arri'val** *n.* act of arriving

Note: Sometimes used with *at*, as *They arrived at their destination;* sometimes without, as *The visitors have arrived*

ar'rogance *n.* insolent pride.—**ar'rogant** *adj.* overbearing

ar'row *n.* a pointed weapon to be shot with a bow.—**broad arrow** mark placed on British government stores, convicts' clothes

ar'rowroot *n.* a West Indian plant, giving a starchy food

ar'senal *n.* a depot for naval or military arms and stores

ar'senic *n.* poisonous semi-metallic element

ar'son *n.* the crime of deliberately setting property on fire

art *n.* 1. skill. 2. human skill as opposed to nature. 3. a profession or craft.—*pl.* 4. certain branches of learning, such as languages and history, as distinct from science.—**the fine arts** include painting, sculpture, music, dancing.—**art'ful** *adj.* cunning.—**art'less** *adj.* guileless, natural.—**art gallery** rooms in which works of art are exhibited

Compare: guileless, innocent, simple

art 2nd person sing. present of **be**, as *Our Father which art in heaven*

art'ery *n.* a vessel that carries the blood from the heart.—**ar'teries** *pl.*—**arte'rial** (ar-tee'-ri-al) *adj.* 1. pertaining to an artery. 2. main, important, as *arterial road*

arte'sian wells (ar-tee'zi-an) *n.pl.* wells bored down until water is forced up by internal pressure

arthri'tis (-rī-) *n.* inflammation of a joint.—**arthrit'ic** *adj.*

ar'tichoke *n.* a vegetable akin to the thistle.—**Jerusalem ar'tichoke,** an edible root

ar'ticle *n.* 1. a prose composition in a magazine or newspaper. 2. a particular thing. 3. a clause, section.—*v.* to bind as an apprentice.—**ar'ticled** *p.t.* and *p. part.* as *He was articled to a solicitor*

Note: In Grammar we speak of the *indefinite article,* which means *a* or *an,* and the *definite article,* which means *the*

artic'ulate *adj.* 1. speaking clearly. 2. able to express oneself clearly. *v.* 1. to connect by a joint. 2. to utter distinctly.—**artic'ulating** *pres. part.*—**artic'ulated** *p.t.* and *p. part.*—*adj.* 1. jointed. 2. pronounced distinctly.—**articula'tion** *n.* distinct pronunciation.—**articulated vehicle** one whose

driver's cab is connected to the body by a swivelling joint
ar'tifice (ar'ti-fis) *n.* 1. skill. 2. a trick.—**artif'icer** *n.* a skilful workman
artifi'cial (ar-ti-fish'al) *adj.* made by art, manufactured
Compare: false, unnatural, sham, conventional, fictitious
artill'ery *n.* 1. cannon or great guns. 2. the troops employed about the guns
ar'tisan (ar'-ti-zan) *n.* a workman, mechanic, craftsman
art'ist *n.* one who practises a fine art, e.g. painting.—**artis'tic** *adj.*—**art'istry** *n.* artistic effect or ability
artiste' (arteest') *n.* a professional entertainer
A'ryan (ā'ri-an) *adj.* Indo-European, applied to one of the great families of mankind.—*n.* an Indo-European
as *adv., conj.* and *pron.* in that degree, so far, since, because
Note: In the following sentences as is a conjunctive adverb. *He whistled as* (=while) *he worked, Do as* (=how) *you please, They decided to go home as* (=because) *it was late.* It is a relative pronoun in the sentence, *Her hair is the same colour as* (=which, that) *yours* (*is*), but beware of the wrong use of *as* as a relative pronoun instead of who, whom, or which (e.g. *This is the man as I told you about*). *As* is often used to make up useful common phrases, for example, *as yet* (=up to now), *as well* (=also), *as though* (=in such a manner), *as to* (=concerning, but only to be used at the beginning of sentences), *as it were* (=so to speak), *as regards* (=with reference to)
asbes'tos *n.* a fireproof fibrous mineral
ascend' (a-send') *v.* to move upward, to climb.—**ascend'ant** *adj.* above the horizon, surpassing.—**ascen'dancy** *n.* controlling influence
ascen'sion *n.* going up, as *Christ's Ascension* to heaven after his crucifixion and resurrection
ascent' *n.* 1. rising, climbing. 2. a slope
ascertain' (a-ser-tān') *v.* to make certain, to find out.—**ascertain'able** *adj.*
Compare: discover, learn, verify, enquire
ascet'ic (a-set'ik) *n.* one who practises self-denial.—*adj.* as *A hermit leads an ascetic life.*—**asceti'cism** (a-set'-isizm) *n.*
ascribe' (to) *v.* to give to, to regard as caused by something else, as *He ascribed his success to hard work.*—**ascri'bing** *pres. part.*—**ascribed'** *p.t.* and *p. part.*
asep'tic *adj.* not liable to decay, or to blood-poisoning
ash *n.* a familiar timber-tree.—**ash'es** *pl.*—**ash'en** of the ash-tree
ash *n.* the dust or remains of anything burnt.—**ash'en** pale, like ashes, as *ashen cheeks.*—**ash'y** *adj.*—**ash can** *n.* dustbin.—**Ash Wednesday** first day of Lent.—**The Ashes** imaginary symbol of victory in cricket test-match series between England and Australia
ashamed' *adj.* filled with shame
ashore' *adv.* on shore
A'sia *n.* one of the five continents, lying eastwards of the Suez Canal.—**Asiat'ic** *n.* a native of Asia.—*adj.*
aside' *n.* words spoken softly, esp. by actors.—*adv.* 1. to, or on one side. 2. privately
as'inine *adj.* like an ass; stupid
ask *v.* to request, question, invite
Compare: crave, solicit, beg, implore, beseech, demand
Note: These are special kinds of asking. All but *demand* suggest making an appeal. *Demand* carries the suggestion of a threat. We *ask* a question; we *ask* someone to dinner; we *ask* for reasons, an explanation, etc.
askance', askant' *adv.* with a side look, sideways.—**to look askance** to look at with suspicion
askew' *adv.* sideways, crookedly
aslant' *adv.* in a slanting direction
asleep' *adj.* and *adv.* sleeping, at rest
asp *n.* a small, poisonous serpent
aspar'agus *n.* a garden plant whose shoots are edible
as'pect *n.* 1. look, appearance, as *The situation assumed a serious aspect*; view, as *There are several aspects to the problem*; position, outlook, as *The house had a southerly aspect*
as'pen *n.* the trembling poplar-tree so known because of its quivering leaves
asper'ity *n.* 1. roughness, harshness of temper or manner. 2. difficulty.—**asper'ities** *pl.*
asper'sion *n.* accusation or false report, as *to cast aspersions on anyone's character*
as'phalt *n.* hard bitumen or pitch, mixed with chips used in roadmaking
asphyx'ia (as-fiks'i-a) *n.* suffocation.—**asphyx'iate** *v.* to suffocate.—**asphyx'iating** *pres. part.*—**asphyx'iated** *p.t.* and *p. part.*
as'pic *n.* 1. the asp. 2. a jelly containing meat, eggs, or fish
aspidis'tra *n.* a plant with broad tapering leaves, often grown in pots
as'pirate *v.* to pronounce with a breathing, to add an *h* sound
aspire' (to) *v.* to long for; aim at, as an ambition, as *Macbeth aspired to the title of King.*—**aspir'ing** *pres. part.*—**aspired'** *p.t.* and *p. part.*—**aspi'rant** *n.*—**aspira'tion** *n.* seeking for what is better
As'pirin *n.* a drug used to relieve headache and other pains
ass *n.* 1. a donkey. 2. a stupid fellow
assail' *v.* to attack.—**assail'ant** *n.* attacker
assass'in *n.* a treacherous murderer *esp.* a hired murderer.—**assass'inate** *v.* to murder by sudden and cunning attack.—**assass'inating** *pres. part.*—**assass'inated** *p.t.* and *p. part.*—**assassina'tion** *n.*

assault′ (a-sawlt′) *n.* a violent attack.—*v.* to attack with violence, to storm
assay′ *n.* a test of the quantity of metal in ores, coin.—*v.* to test.—**assay′er** *n.*
ass′egai, ass′agai (as′egī) *n.* African wooden spear tipped with iron
assem′blage *n.* a putting together
assem′ble *v.* 1. to bring or call together. 2. to meet together.—**assem′bling** *pres. part.*—**assem′bled** *p.t.* and *p. part.*—**assem′bly** *n.* a meeting.—**assembly line** workers and machines building the final product by adding separate parts one at a time.—**assembly rooms** rooms hired for meetings, dances, etc.—**assem′blies** *pl.*
assent′ *v.* 1. to agree. 2. to admit a statement.—*n.* agreement.—**The Royal Assent** the king's or queen's agreement to an Act of Parliament
Compare: acquiesce, concur, consent. *Contrast:* dissent, disagree, demur
assert′ *v.* to declare, as *He asserted that he was innocent*; to lay claim to, as *They asserted their rights as citizens.*—**asser′tion** *n.* a declaration.—**asser′tive** *adj.* too self-confident
Compare: say, affirm, allege, maintain. *Contrast:* deny, dispute, oppose, contradict
assess′ *v.* to fix the value of, as *It is difficult to assess the damage.*—he **assess′es.**—**assess′ment** *n.* valuation for the purpose of taxation.—**assess′or** *n.* person who fixes valuation
as′set *n.* a thing of value, as *A sense of humour is a great asset in meeting life's troubles.*—*pl.* property available for payment of debt
assid′uous *adj.* constant in attention, as *an assiduous reader of the newspapers.*—**assidu′ity** *n.* close attention (as to work)
assign′ *v.* to make over to another, allot.—**assign′ment** *n.* 1. a transfer of title or interest. 2. an allotted task
assigna′tion (a-sig-nā′shun) *n.* an appointment
assim′ilate *v.* to make or become similar; to absorb, as knowledge.—**assim′ilating** *pres. part.*—**assim′ilated** *p.t.* and *p. part.*—**assimila′tion** *n.* absorbing (as food into the system)
assist′ *v.* to help.—**assis′tance** *n.* help, aid.—**assis′tant** *n.* and *adj.*
assi′zes *n.pl.* circuit sittings of judges of the criminal courts of England
asso′ciate (with) (a-so′shi-āt) *v.* 1. to class together, as *We associate sunshine with summer.* 2. to keep company, as *He associates with boys of his own age.*—**asso′ciating** *pres. part.*—**asso′ciated** *p.t.* and *p. part.*—*n.* 1. a companion, a partner. 2. a member of an association
associa′tion *n.* 1. combining together. 2. a society.—**Association football** eleven-a-side football played with a round ball
assort′ *v.* 1. to arrange. 2. to match.—**assort′ed** *adj.*—**assort′ment** *n.* a collection of things arranged
assuage′ (a-swāj′) *v.* to soften, to abate, to calm, e.g. grief, sorrow.—**assuag′ing** *pres. part.*—**assuaged′** *p.t.* and *p.part.*—**assuage′ment** *n.*
assume′ *v.* 1. to take for granted. 2. to put on, as *To assume a look of surprise.*—**assu′ming** *pres. part.*—**assumed′** *p.t.* and *p. part.*—**assump′tion** *n.* 1. a taking upon oneself (e.g. authority). 2. a supposition
assur′ance (a-shoor′ans) *n.* 1. certainty. 2. confidence. 3. insurance (of life)
assure′ (a-shoor′) *v.* 1. to make sure, as *I wish to assure success*; to convince, as *I assure you that it is so.* 2. to insure against loss.—**assu′ring** *pres. part.*—**assured′** *p.t.* and *p. part.*—**assur′edly** *adv.*—**assur′edness** *n.*
as′ter *n.* a plant with star-like flowers
as′terisk *n.* the mark (*), a small star used to call attention to a note
astern′ *adv.* towards the rear part of a ship
as′teroid *n.* a small planet.—*adj.* star-shaped
asth′ma (as′ma) *n.* a disease making breathing difficult.—**asthma′tic, asthma′tical** *adj.*
astig′matism *n.* a defect of vision due to the bad shape of the lens of the eye
astir′ *adv.* on the move
aston′ish *v.* surprise greatly.—**he aston′ishes.**—**aston′ishing** *adj.*—**aston′ishment** *n.*
Compare: amaze, bewilder, dumbfound
astound′ *v.* to amaze, to stun
astrakhan′ *n.* lamb-skin with curled wool, obtained from Astrakhan
as′tral *adj.* star-like, of the stars
astray′ *adj.* and *adv.* out of the right way
astride′ *adv.* and *prep.* with one foot on each side of
astrin′gent (a-strin′jent) *adj.* binding, shrinking.—*n.* a medicine to stop bleeding from cuts.—**astrin′gency** *n.*
astrol′ogy (as-trol′o-ji) *n.* foretelling events by studying the stars.—**astrol′oger** *n.*—**astrolog′ical** *adj.*
as′tronaut *n.* a traveller in space
astron′omy *n.* the science of the heavenly bodies.—**astron′omer** *n.*—concerning astronomy, immense.—**astronomic** *adj.* (loosely) immense
astute′ *adj.* cunning, crafty.—**astute′ness** *n.*
Compare: sharp, acute, quick-witted, clever, shrewd, wily. *Contrast:* stupid, slow, dull
asun′der *adv.* apart, separately, into pieces
asy′lum *n.* 1. a refuge, sanctuary. 2. a home for the insane, etc.
asymmet′rical *adj.* out of symmetry, unbalanced
at *prep.* near to, by, in; engaged on; in the direction of
ate *p.t.* of eat
a′theism *n.* believing there is no God.—**a′theist** *n.*—**atheis′tic, atheis′tical** *adj.*
ath′lete *n.* a man strong and active by

training, good at games.—**athlet'ic** *adj.*.—**athletics** *n.pl.* sports

athwart' *adv.* and *prep.* across, from side to side of

at'las *n.* a volume of maps

at'mosphere *n.* 1. the mass of air, clouds and vapour surrounding the earth. 2. the feeling which a place, novel or play may seem to have or convey.—**atmospher'ic, atmospher'ical** *adj.* relating to the earth's atmosphere. —**atmospher'ics** *n.pl.* noises in wireless reception due to electrical disturbances from the atmosphere

at'oll *n.* a ring-shaped coral island

at'om *n.* 1. the smallest particle of matter which enters into chemical combination. 2. anything very small.—**atom'ic, atom'ical** *adj.*—**atomic bomb'** *n.* a very powerful bomb whose power comes from energy stored in atoms of uranium and plutonium.—**atomic en'ergy** *n.* energy stored in atoms.—**atomic num'ber** *n.* the number of positive charges carried by the nucleus of an atom, which decides its position in the periodic table.—**atomic pile', atomic reac'tor** *ns.* devices for releasing atomic energy.—**atomic weight'** *n.* the weight of any atom compared with the weight of an atom of hydrogen

at'omiser *n.* device for making a fine spray

atone' *v.* to make up for doing wrong, as *Scrooge tried to atone for his former miserliness by acts of generosity.*—**ato'ning** *pres. part.*—**atones'** *p.t.* and *p. part.*—**atone'ment** *n.* satisfaction, amends. —**The Atonement** Christ's crucifixion. —**Day of Atonement** Jewish fast

atro'cious (a-trō'shus) *adj.* very wicked, extremely cruel; as *atrocious crimes.*—**atro'city** (a-tro'si-ti) *n.* cruel wickedness.—**atro'cities** *pl.*

at'rophy *n.* a wasting away.—**at'rophied** *adj.*

attach' *v.* to bind, fasten or tie.—he **attach'es.** —**attach'able** *adj.*

Compare: connect, join link. *Contrast:* detach, separate, untie

attaché (a-tash'ā) *n.* a member of an ambassador's staff.—**attach'é-case** *n.* a small hand-case for carrying papers, etc.

attack' *v.* to set upon with force, damage, criticise harshly.—*n.*

Compare: aggression, onslaught, onset, assault, assail, combat, damage. *Contrast:* defend, protect, shelter, aid

Note: An attack of measles etc.

attain' *v.* to reach, to accomplish, to arrive at.—**attain'able** *adj.*—**attain'ment** *n.*—*pl.* abilities acquired by effort, as *A person of considerable attainments, speaking four languages*

att'ar *n.* the fragrant oil made from rose-petals

attempt' *n.* an effort, as *He made one last attempt to catch the fish.* —*v.* 1. to try. 2. to make an attack on

attend' *v.* 1. to go with, as companion or servant. 2. to wait on. 3. to give the mind to.—**attend'ance** *n.* 1. presence, as *Your attendance is requested.* 2. people present, as *There was a large attendance.*—**attend'ant** *n.* and *adj.*

atten'tion (a-ten'shun) *n.* 1. the act of attending; as *Please give me your attention.* 2. notice, care, as *to receive every attention.* —**atten'tive** *adj.*—**atten'tively** *adv.*

atten'uate *v.* to make thin or fine.—**atten'uating** *pres. part.*—**atten'uated** *p.t.* and *p. part.*—**attenua'tion** *n.* in wireless, loss of energy in ether waves with obstruction or distance

attest' *v.* to bear witness to.—**attesta'tion** *n.* testimony, signing a writing to show that it is true

att'ic *n.* room at the top of a house

attire' *n.* dress, apparel.—*v.* to dress.—**atti'ring** *pres. part.*—**attired'** *p.t.* and *p. part.*

att'itude *n.* 1. position. 2. behaviour

attor'ney (a-ter'ni) *n.* 1. (in the U.S.) a solicitor a lawyer. 2. one appointed to act for another.—**attor'ney-gen'eral** *n.* the official whose duty it is to manage legal business for the State.—**attor'ney-generals** *pl.*—**power of attorney** authorization to act for another

attract' *v.* to cause to approach.—**attrac'tion** *n.* 1. the power of drawing. 2. the thing that draws, as *a popular attraction.*—**attrac'tive** *adj.*

Compare: (with *n.*) enticement, allurement, fascination, interest. *Contrast:* repulsion, revulsion, indifference

att'ribute *n.* a quality belonging to, as *Darkness is an attribute of night.*—**attrib'ute** (to) *v.* to consider as belonging to or being due to.—**attribu'tion** *n.*—**attrib'utable** *adj.*—**attri'buting** *pres. part.*—**attrib'uted** *p.t.* and *p. part.*

Compare: ascribe, assign, impute

attri'tion (a-trish'un) *n.* rubbing away, wearing down

attune' *v.* to put in tune, to make musical.—**attu'ning** *pres. part.*—**attuned'** *p.t.* and *p. part.*

au'burn *adj.* (hair) reddish brown

auc'tion (awk'shun) *n.* a public sale of property to the highest bidder.—**auctioneer'** *n.* one who sells goods by auction

auda'cious (aw-dā'shus) *adj.* 1. daring. 2. shameless, insolent.—**audac'ity** *n.* boldness, impudence

au'dible *adj.* able to be heard.—**au'dibly** *adv.*

Contrast: inaudible

au'dience 1. a gathering of hearers. 2. a formal interview, as *to have audience with the king.* 3. a hearing

au'dio- *prefix* related to hearing

audio-fre'quency *adj.* (of radio signals) in the band of frequencies that can be heard

audio-vis'ual *adi.* that can be seen and heard,

as *sound-films are audio-visual aids to education*

au'dit *n.* an examination of accounts.—*v.* to examine accounts.—**au'ditor** *n.*

audi'tion (aw-dish'un) *n.* 1. sense of hearing. 2. a test for a stage, musical or television performer

auditor'ium *n.* a hall designed for an audience

au'ditory *adj.* related to hearing

au'ger *n.* a drilling tool

aught (awt) *n.* anything

Contrast: naught

aug'ment *v.* to increase, to grow larger.—**augmen'table** *adj.*—**augmenta'tion** *n.*

Compare: expand, amplify, magnify. *Contrast:* decrease, diminish, lessen

au'gur *n.* among the Romans, one who predicted the future.—*v.* to foretell.—**au'gury** *n.* an omen, or sign of the future

Au'gust *n.* eighth month of the year

august' *adj.* majestic

auk *n.* a diving bird of northern waters

aunt (ahnt) **aunty, auntie** *n.* sister of one's father or mother; wife of one's uncle

au pair (ōpayr) *adj.* undertaking housework in return for board and lodging as, *she came to Mrs. Smith as an au pair girl*

au'ra *n.* atmosphere or personality around a person

au'ral *adj.* belonging to the ear

au'ricle *n.* 1. the outer ear. 2. one of two cavities of the heart.—**auric'ular** *adj.*

auror'a *n.* the dawn.—**auror'al** *adj.*—**auror'a borea'lis** *n.* the northern lights.—**auror'a austra'lis** *n.* the southern lights

aus'pices (-ses) *n.pl.* 1. omens. 2. patronage (*under the auspices of*).—**auspi'cious** (aws-pi'shus) *adj.* favourable, lucky

Contrast: inauspicious, unlucky, unfortunate, ill-starred

austere' *adj.* severe.—**auster'ity** *n.*

Compare: ascetic, severe, strict. *Contrast:* self-indulged, easy-going, genial

aus'tral *adj.* southern

Austra'lia *n.* island continent of the southern hemisphere.—**Austra'lian** *n.* a native of Australia.—*adj.*—**Australa'sia** *n.* Australia and the islands around.—**Australian' rules** *n.* a type of rugby football developed in Australia.—**Austra'lian'a** *n.* books, pictures, documents and charts relating to Australia.—**Austra'lianism** *n.* word or phrase originating in Australia

aus'traloid *adj.* describing the Australian aborigine race

Aus'tria *n.* a country in central Europe.—**Aus'trian** *n.* a native of Austria.—*adj.*

authen'tic *adj.* genuine, true.—**authen'ticate** *v.* confirm as true.—**authen'ticating** *pres. part.*—**authen'ticated** *p.t.* and *p. part.*—**authenti'city** (aw-then-ti'si-ti) *n.* genuineness

au'thor *n.* 1. person who writes. 2. the beginner of anything.—**au'thorship** *n.*

author'ity *n.* 1. power. 2. an expert, as *an authority on foreign stamps.* 3. a person who has power (esp. in print.—*the authorities*).—**author'itative** *adj.*—**author'itatively** *adv.*

auth'orise *v.* to empower, give authority.—**auth'orising** *pres. part.*—**auth'orised** *p.t.* and *p. part.*, as *The Authorised Version of the Bible, issued in* 1611

au'to- *prefix*, self.—**au'to** *n.* shortened form of **au'tomobile**, motor car.—**au'to-changer** *n.* record-player that changes records by itself as required

autobiog'raphy *n.* a life of a person written by himself.—**autobiog'raphies** *pl.*—**autobiograph'ical** *adj.*

autoc'racy (aw-tok'ra-si) *n.* absolute rule.—**autoc'racies** *pl.*—**aut'ocrat** *n.* a ruler with unlimited power.—**autocrat'ic** *adj.*

aut'ograph *n.* someone's own handwriting or signature.—**autograph'ic** *adj.*

automat'ic *adj.* self-acting, mechanical.—*n.* a self-loading revolver.—**automat'ically** *adv.*

automa'tion *n.* the wide use of automatic machines in industry

autom'aton 1. a machine which imitates the actions of a living body. 2. a person who acts mechanically, without thinking.—**autom'ata** *pl.*

automobile' (aw-to-mo-beel') *n.* a motor-car

auton'omy *n.* right of self-government.—**auton'omous** *adj.*

autop'sy *n.* examination of a dead body to see how death occurred

au'tumn (aw'tum) *n.* the third season of the year.—**autum'nal** *adj.*

auxil'iary *adj.* helping.—*n.* a helper.—**auxil'iaries** *pl.*, as *There were many auxiliaries in support of the regular troops*

Note: In Grammar, an auxiliary verb is one used to form tenses of other verbs. Thus in *I have eaten, have* is an auxiliary verb, having given up its usual meaning to help to form the present perfect tense of *to eat*

avail' *v.* to profit, to assist, to be of use.—**avail'able** *adj.* usable.—**of no avail** in vain

av'alanche (-lanch or -lahnsh) *n.* snow and ice moving down a mountainside

av'arice *n.* greed for riches.—**avarici'ous** (a-va-ri'shus) *adj.* covetous, grasping

Compare: covetousness, cupidity, miserliness. *Contrast:* liberality, generosity, bounty

avenge' *v.* to have vengeance for, as *He avenged his wrongs on his enemy.*—**to be avenged.**—**aven'ging** *pres. part.*—**avenged'** *p.t.* and *p. part.*—**aven'ger** *n.*

Compare: revenge, retaliate, requite. *Contrast:* forgive, pardon

av'enue *n.* a walk bordered with trees

aver' *v.* to declare positively, assert.—**aver'ring** *pres. part.*—**averred'** *p.t.* and *p. part.*

av'erage *n.* 1. the ordinary standard, as

His abilities are above the average. 2. the mean value of a number of values, as the *average* of 9, 5, 6, 11 and 9 is 8, i.e. the terms added together and divided by the number of terms—40÷5=8.—*adj.*, as *the average person, the average number.* —*v.*, as *His wages averaged (so much) per week*

averse' (to) *adj.* opposed, reluctant.—**aver'sion** *n.* dislike

avert' *v.* 1. to turn one's eyes or mind from. 2. to prevent

a'viary *n.* a place for keeping birds

avia'tion (ā-vi-ā'shun) *n.* flying in aircraft

a'viator (ā'vi-ā-tor) *n.* one who flies aircraft

a'vid (for) *adj.* eager, greedy.—**avid'ity** *n.*

avocad'o *n.* a sub-tropical, pear-shaped fruit. —**avocad'os** *pl.*

avoca'tion ('shun) *n.* business, profession

avoid' *v.* to shun, as *to avoid anyone's company*; to evade, as *to avoid trouble.*—**avoid'able** *adj.*—**avoid'ance** *n.*

avoirdupois' (aver-di-poiz') *n.* the British system of weights

avow' *v.* to declare openly, to confess as *an avowed enemy*, meaning an open or unconcealed enemy.—**avow'able** *adj.*—**avow'al** *n.*

avun'cular *adj.* pertaining to an uncle

await' *v.* to wait, or stay for

awake', awa'ken *v.* to rouse from sleep, stir up.—*adj.* alert, not asleep, as *wide-awake.*—**awa'king** *pres. part.*—**awoke'** or **awaked'** *p. t.* and *p. part.*—**awa'kening** *n.* an arousing

Note: We say, *I awoke*, but *He awaked me*

award' *n.* a judge's decision, a prize.—*v.* to adjudge, to give as a prize, as *He was awarded a medal for his bravery*

aware' *adj.* informed, conscious.—**aware'ness** *n.*

awash' *adj.* washed over by waves, or level with the surface of water

away' *adv.* absent, apart, at a distance

awe *n.* fear, reverence, dread.—*v.* to strike with fear.—**awesome** *adj.* causing awe.—**awe'struck** *adj.* filled with awe

aw'ful *adj.* very impressive, dreadful.—**aw'fully** *adv.*

Note: In common speech the word *awful* is often used to mean troublesome, bad, horrid, etc., as *an awful nuisance*

awhile' *adv.* for a short time

awk'ward *adj.* 1. clumsy, ungraceful. 2. embarrassing, inconvenient, as *an awkward situation.*—**awk'wardness** *n.*

awl *n.* a pointed instrument for making small holes

aw'ning *n.* a shade from the sun

awry' (a-rī') *adj.* and *adv.* twisted to one side crooked

axe (U.S. ax) *n.* a tool for hewing or chopping.—**to have an axe to grind** to have an ulterior motive, esp. a grievance to settle, for one's actions

ax'iom *n.* a self-evident truth, as *A straight line is the shortest distance between two points.*—**axiomat'ic** *adj.* self evident

ax'is *n.* a straight line round which a body revolves.—**ax'es** (aks'eez) *pl.*

ax'le (ak'sl), **ax'le-tree** *n.* the rod on which a wheel turns

ay, aye (ā) always

aye, ay (ī) yes.—**ayes** *pl.* those for a motion

a'zure (a'zher or ā'zher) *adj.* sky blue

B

bab'ble *n.* to chatter.—*v.* to talk idly.—**babbler** *n.*

babe *n.* baby

ba'bel (bā-) *n.* a confusion of sounds

baboon' *n.* a big, long-faced moneky

ba'by *n.* a very young child.—**ba'bies** *pl.*—**ba'byish** *adj.*—**ba'byhood** *n.*—**ba'bysitter**-*n.* someone who looks after a baby temporarily while its parents are out

bach'elor *n.* 1. an unmarried man.—**spinster** *fem.* 2. one having first degree at a university, as *Bachelor of Arts*

bacill'us (ba-sil'us) *n.* rod-like organism causing disease.—**bacill'i** *pl.*

back *n.* 1. a hind part. 2. a player to the rear of the team in football, hockey, etc.—*v.* 1. to support, as *to back someone's application.* 2. to cause to go backwards, as a boat or car. 3. to wager on, as *to back a horse to win a race.*—*adj.* situated behind.—*adv.* 1. to the rear. 2. in return.—**backer** *n.* supporter.—**back bench'er** *n.* a member of Parliament in a back seat.—**backbone** *n.* the spine.—**back cloth** *n.* the painted cloth at the back of a stage.—**back number** *n.* 1. an earlier issue of a periodical than the present one. 2. someone or something past its prime.—**behind one's back** secretly, unknown to one.—**to back-bite** to speak ill of someone in his absence.—**to back down** to give way.—**to back out** to withdraw.—**to go back on one's word** to break a promise.—**to put one's back into** to do one's best at.—**to take a back seat** to retire to a more modest position.—**with backs to the wall** in a desperate plight

back'-blocks *n.pl.* the interior of Australia

back'bone *n.* 1. spine. 2. firmness

back'-fire *n.* explosion in cylinder of internal combustion engine, before the piston has reached the top of its stroke.—*v.*

backgam'mon *n.* game played with a die and fifteen pieces on a special board

back'ground *n.* 1. further away part of a scene. 2. setting. 3. general information on a subject. 4. experience and education of a person

Contrast: foreground

Note: To be *in the background* may mean either to be in an obscure or subordinate position, or to be present but not noticed, or having any effect immediately

back'hand *n.* 1. writing that slopes to the left. 2. a backhand stroke.—*adj.* delivered with the back of the hand or the hand turned backwards.—**backhanded** *adj.* 1. backhand. 2. doubtful, as *a backhanded compliment*

back'ing *n.* 1. support. 2. act of going backwards

backslide' *v.* to slip back into bad ways.—**backsli'der** *n.*

back'ward *adj.* 1. slow. 2. primitive, as *backward races*. 3. less developed mentally or physically than people of the same age —*adv.* behind.—**back'wards** 1. in reverse. 2. towards the past. 3. towards a worse state

Compare: 1. retarded, dull, shy. 2. uncivilised. *Contrast:* 1. advanced, precocious, forward. 2. civilised

back'water *n.* 1. water thrown back. 2. a creek, away from the main stream, a quiet, undisturbed place

back'woods *n.pl.* outlying, uncleared forests. —**backwoods'-man** *n.* 1. man from the wilds. 2. uncivilised fellow

ba'con (bā-) *n.* cured pig's flesh

bacteriol'ogy (bak-tee-ri-ol'oj-i) *n.* the study of bacteria

bacte'rium *n.* simplest form of life, a microbe, a disease-germ.—**bacte'ria** *pl.*

bad *adj.* not good (*worse, comp.*—*worst sup.*).—**bad'ly** *adv.*—**a bad egg** a bad person.—**bad blood** ill feeling.—**bad debt** a debt that cannot be paid off.—**bad language** foul language, swearing.—**badly off** poor, in a bad position.—**with a bad grace** sulkily

Compare: evil, wicked, noxious, harmful, ill. See **good**

The word *bad* may be used in the moral sense, when it means the same as wicked and evil, as *a bad man.* In the material sense it means harmful, hurtful, unpleasant, as *to have a bad cold.* Again, it may mean rotten or corrupt, as *This is egg bad.* It is also used in such common expressions as *to feel bad, to go bad.* It is used as a *noun* in the expression *to go to the bad*

Note: The use of *badly* in common speech to mean very much or extremely, as *The door badly needs painting.* Putting the adverb *badly* in the wrong place would alter the meaning here

bade (bad, bād in poetry) *p.t.* of **bid**

badge (baj) *n.* a mark or sign

badg'er *n.* a grey hairy nocturnal burrowing animal.—*v.* to worry

Compare: pester, torment, plague, harass

bad'inage (bad'ee-nazh) *n.* light good-humoured talk or banter

bad'minton *n.* a game played with rackets and shuttlecocks

baf'fle *v.* to check, to puzzle.—*n.* a plate to regulate the flow of a liquid or gas.—**baf'fling** *pres. part.*—**baf'fled** *p.t.* and *p. part.*—**baf'fling** *adj.*

Compare: thwart, frustrate, balk, hinder, foil. *Contrast:* aid, assist, advance

bag *n.* 1. a sack, pouch. 2. booty, as *The sportsmen had a good bag of game.*—*v.* 1. to bulge. 2. to put in a bag. 3. (in sport) to catch, shoot, etc.—**bag'ging** *pres. part.*—**bag'ged** *p.t.* and *p. part.*—**bag'gy** *adj.* bulging, loose.—**bag'ful** *n.* as much as a bag will hold.—**the whole bag of tricks** everything possible.—**to let the cat out of the bag** to let out a secret

bagatelle' *n.* 1. a game played with balls and cue on a board. 2. a mere trifle

bag'gage *n.* 1. tents and stores of an army. 2. luggage. 3. a shameless female

bag'pipe *n.* a musical wind-instrument

bail *n.* 1. a security for a prisoner's reappearance. 2. a person giving security.—*v.* to secure release.—**to stand bail for** to guarantee someone's appearance in court

bail *n.* in cricket one of the small pieces of wood lodged across the top of the stumps

bail (out) *v.* to empty water from a boat. **bale, bail** (out) *v.* to drop from aircraft by parachute

Bail'ey bridge *n.* a kind of temporary bridge quickly set up

bail'iff *n.* 1. a sheriff's officer. 2. a manager of an estate

bairn *n.* a child

bait *n.* food put on hook to entice fish.—*v.* 1. to set a trap. 2. to annoy, as in **bear-baiting.** 3. to feed, as a horse

baize *n.* coarse woollen cloth

bake *v.* 1. to cook or harden by dry heat. 2. to make bread.—**ba'king** *pres. part.*—**baked** *p.t.* and *p. part.*—**bake'house** *n.*—**ba'ker** *n.*—**ba'kery** *n.*—**a baker's dozen** thirteen.—**baking powder** a mixture of tartaric acid and bicarbonate of soda added to dough to make it rise

bak'elite (bāk'-e-līt) *n.* a hard strong synthetic resin, used for insulating and for coloured ware

bal'ance *n.* 1. a pair of scales. 2. equilibrium. 3. a surplus. 4. a sum due on an account.—*v.* 1. to weigh. 2. to make equal.—**bal'ancing** *pres. part.*—**bal'anced** *p.t.* and *p. part.* —**bal'ance sheet** *n.* a statement of money received and paid out

bal'cony *n.* a platform or gallery projecting from a building.—**bal'conies** *pl.*

bald (bawld) *adj.* 1. hairless. 2. plain. 3. meagre, as *He gave a bald statement of the facts, but no explanation of them.*—**bald'ly** *adv.*—**bald'ness** *n.*

bal'derdash (bawl'der-dash) *n.* senseless talk

bale *n.* a bundle of goods

bale *n.* evil, woe.—**bale'ful** *adj.*—**bale'fully** *adv.*

balk (bawk) *n.* 1. a squared timber beam. 2. hindrance.—*v.* 1. to hinder, disappoint. 2.

(at) to stop abruptly in order to avoid

ball (bawl) *n.* 1. anything round. 2. a globe, sphere. 3. a bullet.—**no ball** in cricket, a ball bowled unfairly and not to be counted.—**ball bear'ings** *n.* small steel balls placed in grooves between revolving parts of a machine to reduce friction.—**ball-cock** *n.* a valve in a cistern operated by a floating ball, which automatically regulates the flow of water

Note: Besides the common kind of *balls* such as *footballs, tennis balls*, etc., we speak of *snowball*, a *ball* of fire, or a *ball* of wool, meaning a spherically-shaped collection of material or articles

ball (bawl) *n.* an assembly for dancing.—**ball'room** *n.* a large room for dancing

ball'ad *n.* 1. a simple song. 2. a narrative poem in a traditional style, such as *Sir Patrick Spens, Chevy Chase*

ballade' (bal-lahd') *n.* a poem with a refrain such as *Ballade of Dead Ladies* (*Rossetti*)

bal'last *n.* heavy material placed in ship to steady it.—*v.* to steady

balleri'na (baleree'na) *n.* a female ballet dancer

ball'et (bal'ā) *n.* a theatrical dance

balloon' *n.* a large bag filled with gas to make it rise.—**balloon-barrage** a formation of captive balloons to protect from low attack by aircraft.—**balloon-tyre** big air-filled tyre

ball'ot *n.* a method of voting secretly.—*v.* to vote secretly

ball'point *n.* a pen with a tiny ball to serve as a nib and its own ink reservoir

balm (bahm) *n.* 1. a fragrant plant. 2. a healing ointment. 3. anything soothing.—**bal'my** *adj.* mild

bal'sa (bawl'sa) *n.* the very light wood of a West Indian tree, used for aeroplane models

bal'sam (bawl'sam) *n.* an ointment.—**Can'ada bal'sam** *n.* a kind of turpentine

bal'uster, ban'ister *n.* 1. a short pillar supporting rail of stair-case. 2. a stair-rail.—**balustrade'** *n.* a row of short pillars surmounted by rail

bamboo' *n.* tropical jointed reed.—**bamboos'** *pl.*

bamboo'zle *v.* to trick, to deceive

ban *n.* 1. a forbidding, as *a ban on trade*. 2. outlawry, excommunication.—*v.* to forbid.—**bann'ing** *pres. part.*—**banned'** *p.t.* and *p. part.*

ban'al (bā'nal or ban-ahl') *adj.* commonplace.—**banal'ity** *n.*

bana'na *n.* a sub-tropical fruit

band *n.* 1. a strip of material. 2. a group of people. 3. a group of musicians.—*v.* (together) to join into a company.—**band'age** *n.* strip of cloth used for binding up wounds

ban'dicoot *n.* 1. an Indian rat. 2. an Australian pouched animal

ban'dit *n.* an outlaw, robber.—**ban'dits, banditt'i** *pl.*

Compare: highwayman, brigand, foot-pad

ban'dy *adj.* bent outwards, as *bandy-legged*—*v.* to pass to and fro, exchange, as *to bandy words, to bandy insults.*—**ban'dying** *pres. part.*—**ban'died** *p.t.* and *p. part.*

bane *n.* 1. poison. 2. ruin.—**bane'ful** *adj.*—**bane'fully** *adv.*

bang *n.* 1. a heavy blow. 2. a loud noise, explosion.—*v.* to slam, beat, make a loud noise

ban'gle (bang'gil) *n.* a ring worn on arm or leg

ban'ish *v.* 1. to exile, as *The Emperor Napoleon was banished to St. Helena*. 2. to drive away, as *to banish care.*—**ban'ishment** *n.*

ban'ister *n.* see **baluster**

banjo' *n.* a musical instrument with strings.—**banjos'** *pl.*

bank *n.* 1. raised ground. 2. edge of a river or lake.—*v.* 1. to pile up. 2. to tilt sharply in turning aircraft

bank *n.* an establishment for keeping, lending and exchanging money.—*v.* to put in a bank.—**bank'er** *n.* director of a bank

bank'rupt *n.* one who cannot meet his debts.—*v.* to force into that state.—*adj.* as *to go bankrupt.*—**bank'ruptcy** *n.*

Compare: insolvent, ruined

bann'er *n.* flag.—*adj.* (U.S.), very good as *a banner year.*—**banner headline** a prominent newspaper headline

banns *n.pl.* notice of a coming marriage read out in church

ban'quet (bang'kwet) *n.* a feast.—*v.*

ban'shee *n.* a spirit whose wail announces death

ban'tam *n.* 1. a small variety of fowl. 2. a very light boxing weight of less than 8st. 6 lbs.

ban'ter *n.* joking.—*v.* to joke with.—**ban'tering** *adj.*—**ban'teringly** *adv.*

baptise' (bap-tīz) *v.* to give baptism, christen, name.—**bap'tism** *n.* admission into the Church of Christ by a sacrament.—**bap'tist** *n.* as *John the Baptist.*—**baptis'mal** *adj.* as *His baptismal name was Henry.*—**bap'tistery** *n.* part of church where baptisms take place.—**baptism by fire** a trying first experience of something

bar *n.* 1. a rod of any substance. 2. an obstacle. 3. a bank of sand at the mouth of a river. 4. a counter in a public-house. 5. where prisoners stand in court. 6. a division in music.—**to be called to the Bar** to become a barrister.—*v.* 1. to fasten. 2. hinder. 3. exclude.—**bar'ring** *pres. part.*—**barred'** *p.t.* and *p. part.*—*prep.* except.—**bar'ring** excepting.—**bar none** with no exception

barb *n.* a spike on a fish-hook, etc.—*v.* fit with barbs.—**barbed wire** *n.* used for fences

barba'rian *n.* a savage.—*adj.* uncivilised.—

bar'bar'ic *adj.* uncultured, primitive.—**bar'barism** 1. savagery. 2. lack of culture. 3. an uncouth expression.—**barbarousness** *n.*—**barbar'ity** *n.* savage cruelty

bar'ber *n.* one who cuts hair and shaves, a hairdresser

bard *n.* a poet and minstrel, as *Shakespeare is sometimes called The Bard of Avon.*—**bar'dic** *adj.* concerning bards and their poetry

bare *v.* to uncover.—**ba'ring** *pres. part.*—**bared** *p.t.* and *p. part.*—*adj.* 1. uncovered, naked. 2. scanty, mere, as *A bare handful of soldiers was defending the fort.*—**bare'ly** *adv.* scarcely, hardly.—**bare-back'** *adv.* without a saddle.—**bare-faced'** *adj.* impudent.—**bare-foot'** *adj.*—**bare-head'ed** *adj.*—**bare'ly** *adv.* hardly.—**bare'ness** *n.*

bar'gain (bar'gan) *n.* 1. agreement between buyer and seller. 2. something bought cheaply.—*v.* to make a bargain. **to bargain for** to expect.—**into the bargain** as well.—**bargain basement** lowest floor of a large store in which cheap goods are sold.—**to strike a bargain** to agree to terms in a deal
Compare: deal, contract, transaction

barge (barj) *n.* a large flat-bottomed boat.—**bargee'** *n.* bargeman.—**barge in** to intrude

bar'itone *n.* the male voice between tenor and bass

ba'rium *n*, a white metal element

bark, barque *n.* 1. a vessel with three masts. 2. in poetry, a small ship

bark *n.* covering of a tree.—*v.* 1. to strip the bark from. 2. to rub off (skin)

bark *n.* short, sharp cry of a dog, etc.—*v.* to make this sound

bar'ley *n.* grain used as food or in making malt.—**bar'ley-water** *n.* a drink made from barley and water

barn *n.* store-house.—**barn'dance** *n.* a lively dance danced by couples in a circle
Compare: outhouse, garner, granary, shed, byre, stable
Note: Outhouse and *shed* mean any kind of outside store-house. *Garner* and *granary* means barns used for grain. *Byre* and *stable* mean barns used for cattle and horses respectively. A *Dutch barn* has a roof, but no sides

bar'nacle *n.* a shell-fish which sticks to rocks and bottoms of ships

barom'eter *n.* an instrument for measuring air pressure.—**baromet'ric** *adj.*

bar'on *n.* a nobleman, lord.—**baroness'** *fem.*—**baro'nial** *adj.*—**a baron of beef** *n.* a joint of two sirloins

bar'onet *n.* a person holding hereditary title of "Sir"—**bar'onetcy** *n.*
Compare: knight

baroque' (bar-ok') *adj.* highly ornamented style (in art and architecture)

bar'rack *v.* 1. to jeer at, esp. on cricket field. 2. (N.Z.) to encourage

bar'racks *n.pl.* a building for lodging soldiers

barracu'da *n.* a large W. Indian fish

bar'rage (bar'azh) *n.* 1. a dam across a river. 2. a curtain of gunfire to cover attack

bar'rel *n.* 1. a round wooden vessel. 2. quantity held by barrel. 3. the tube of a gun

bar'ren *adj.* unable to bear young, not fertile, as a *barren field.*—**bar'renness** *n.*

barricade' *n.* a barrier to hold up the enemy.—*v.*—**barrica'ding** *pres. part.*—**barrica'ded** *p.t.* and *p. part.*

bar'rier *n.* 1. an obstruction. 2. a fence.—**bar'rier-reef** *n.* a coral reef in the sea parallel to the coast

bar'rister *n.* a lawyer who pleads in the higher courts. See **solicitor**

bar'row *n.* a one-wheeled hand-cart

bar'row *n.* a burial mound

bar'ter *n.* exchange of goods, as *Before the invention of money trade was carried on by means of barter.*—*v.*

bas'alt (bas'awlt) *n.* a dark, hard rock

base *n.* 1. bottom, foundation. 2. headquarters of army, navy, or airforce. 3. starting-point in a game.—**baseless** *adj.* without foundation, as *a baseless accusation.*—*v.* to found, establish as *He based his argument on lies*

base *adj.* 1. low, mean. 2. inferior in quality, as *Lead is a base metal, whereas gold is a precious one.*—*v.* to found, to establish.—**base'ly** *adv.*—**base'ness** *n.*
Compare: dishonourable, ignoble, vile.
Contrast: honourable, noble, worthy

base'ball *n.* a team-game played with bat and ball

base'ment *n.* the lowest floor of building

ba'ses *pl.* of **basis** and **base**

bash *v.* to smash in.—**he bash'es**

bash'ful *adj.* shy, modest
Compare: retiring, coy, diffident, timid.
Contrast: bold, forward, daring, shameless

ba'sic (bā'sik) *adj.* forming the base.—**basic English** a form of English with a simple vocabulary, for the use of foreigners.—**basic slag** a by-product in the manufacture of steel, used in road-making and in fertilisers

basil'ica *n.* a church built with double colonnade and apse

ba'sin (bās'n) *n.* 1. a deep round dish. 2. a dock for ships. 3. the land drained by a river (*the Nile Basin*)

ba'sis (bā'sis) *n.* foundation.—**ba'ses** *pl.*

bask *v.* to lie in warmth, or sunlight

bas'ket *n.* a container made of plaited cane, etc.—**bas'ket-ball** *n.* team-game played with large leather ball

Basque *n.* 1. a native of the Basque country (on the western mountainous border between France and Spain). 2. the language of this area.—*adj.*

bass (bās) 1. lowest part in music. 2. a low man's voice or musical instrument

bass *n.* a fish of the perch family

bassoon' *n.* wood-wind instrument
bas'tard *n.* a child of unmarried parents.—*adj.* born of unmarried parents
baste *v.* 1. to beat with a stick. 2. to pour fat over roasting meat.—**bas'ting** *pres. part.* —**bas'ted** *p.t.* and *p. part.*
baste *v.* to sew loosely. —**bas'ting***pres. part.*—**bas'ted** *p.t.* and *p. part.*
bas'tion *n.* projecting part of a fortification
Ba'suto *n.* a branch of the Bantu people, particularly the inhabitants of Lesotho, formerly Basutoland
bat *n.* an implement used for hitting ball in cricket, etc.—*v.* to strike with a bat.—**bat'ting** *pres. part.*—**bat'ted** *p.t.* and *p. part.* —**bat'ting** *n.*—**bats'man** *n.*—**off one's own bat** (done) by oneself, without help
bat *n.* a mouse-like flying animal.—**to have bats in the belfry** to have crazy ideas
batch *n.* 1. quantity of bread made at one baking. 2. a set
bath *n.* 1. all-over wash. 2. a container for bath-water.—*v.* to wash all over.—**bath'-chair** *n.* a wheeled chair for invalids.—**bath'room** *n.* a room in a house for bathing. —**baths** *n.pl.* a building for public bathing. —**Turkish bath** *n.* a very hot air-bath in which the bather is sweated, massaged, and cooled
bathe (bāthe) *v.* 1. to wash. 2. to go swimming.—**ba'thing** *pres. part.*—**ba'thed** *p.t.* and *p. part.*—**ba'thing** *n.*
ba'thos (bā-) *n.* a sudden descent from the lofty to the commonplace
bath'ysphere *n.* a deep-water diving bell
bat'man *n.* (*mil.*) an officer's servant
bat'on *n.* a policeman's stick or band conductor's staff
battal'ion *n.* a body of about 1000 foot soldiers
bat'ten *n.* a narrow piece of wood.—*v.* to nail down the hatches of a ship, as during a storm
bat'ten (on) *v.* 1. to fatten. 2. to live in luxury, as *The invading army battened on the country and ate up all the food*
bat'ter *n.* a mixture of flour, eggs, milk, etc. —*v.* to strike repeatedly.—**bat'tering-ram** *n.* a beam formerly used to break down gates and walls
bat'tery *n.* 1. a number of cannon. 2. a set of electric cells.—**bat'teries** *pl.*—**bat'tery hens** hens kept in a series of boxes for intensive egg-laying
bat'tle *n.* a fight between armed forces.—*v.* fight.—**bat'tling** *pres. part.*—**bat'tled** *p.t.* and *p. part.*—**bat'tle-axe** *n.* an axe used as a weapon.—**bat'tle-cruiser** *n.* a fast warship.—**bat'tlecry** *n.* a shout to rally soldiers in battle.—**pitched battle** a battle planned by both sides beforehand

Compare: engagement, skirmish, war

A *battle* is an engagement of importance. A small engagement is a *skirmish.* A *war* usually consists of a number of *battles*

batt'ledore *n.* a bat used with a shuttlecock
bat'tlement *n.* a wall on a fortification with openings
bau'ble (baw'bl) *n.* trinket, trifle
bawl *v.* to shout
bay *adj.* reddish brown, reddish brown, as *a bay horse*
bay *n.* a wide inlet of the sea, a recess.—**bay-win'dow** *n.* window built out
bay *n.* laurel-tree
bay *n.* cry of hounds.—*v.* 1. to bark at. 2. to bark.—**at bay** cornered.—**to keep at bay** to ward off
bay'onet *n.* a blade fixed to the end of a rifle-barrel
bazaar' *n.* 1. an Eastern market. 2. a shop, sale, esp. for charity
be *v.* 1. to exist. 2. live. 3. to stay, as *Don't be long.* 4. to cost, as *these cakes are* 6d. *each.* 5. to be situated, as *Where is London?* 6. to visit, as *She has been to France.* 7. to take place, as *When will the wedding be?*

Be is also an auxiliary verb, to show the tenses or form the passive, as *he will be going* or *he was hurt.*—**be'ing** *pres. part.*—**was** *p.t.* **were** *p.t.*—**been** *p. part.*—**be-all and end-all** the most important thing

Note: I am, thou art, he is; we, you, they, are—present, I was, thou wast, wert, he was; we, you, they, were—past. I shall be, thou wilt be, he will be; we shall be, you, they will be—future. Note also the imperative (*Be a good boy*)

beach *n.* sea-shore.—*v.* to run a boat ashore. —**beach'-comber** *n.* 1. one who makes a living from what he finds on beaches. 2. an idle vagrant. 3. a long curling wave
beac'on (bee'kon) *n.* 1. a signal fire on a hill. 2. traffic sign.—**Belisha beacon** *n.* a yellow globe on a pole to mark a pedestrian crossing
bead *n.* 1. bit of wood, glass or metal pierced for threading. 2. a drop, as *beads of perspiration.*—**bead'ing** *n.* pattern on wood-work.—**bea'dy** *adj.*
bea'dle (bee'dl) *n.* 1. a mace-bearer. 2. a parish-officer
bea'gle (bee'gl) *n.* a small hound
beak *n.* the bill of a bird
bea'ker *n.* 1. a drinking-cup. 2. a glass with lip used for experiments
beal *n.* in Australia, a sweet drink made from honey-bearing flowers
beam (beem) *n.* 1. a long squared piece of wood. 2. the bar of a balance. 3. a ray or shaft, as of light. 4. a bright smile.—*v.* to shine, smile brightly, as *Mr. Pickwick's face beamed with benevolence.*—**on her beam ends** (of a ship) lying over on one side.—**on one's beam ends** (slang) without money
bean (been) *n.* a seed of plants with long pods
bear *v.* 1. to carry, as *When Tom bears logs*

into the hall (Shakespeare). 2. to support, put up with, as *to bear a weight*, *to bear pain*. 3. to produce, as crops or young. 4. to press (upon).—**bore** *p.t.*—**born** *p. part.* meaning produced.—**borne** *p. part.* meaning carried.—**to bear a hand** to help

bear *n.* a heavy, thick-furred animal.—**bear'skin** *n.* tall fur cap worn by Guards.—**the Great Bear** a groups of stars in the northern sky

beard (beerd) *n.* hair on the chin.—*v.* to defy, as *to beard the lion in its den*

bear'ing *n.* 1. behaviour, as *Every one admired his manly bearing*. 2. relation, as *What say you has no bearing on the matter*. 3. part of a machine (see **ball-bearing**).—*pl.* direction, as *He lost his bearings in the fog*

beast (beest) *n.* 1. a four-footed animal. 2. a brutal person.—**beast'ly** *adj.* horrid, disgusting.—**beast'liness** *n.*

Compare: creature, brute, ox. *Contrast:* man, bird, insect

In general all animals or creatures other than human beings, birds or insects, are *beasts*, but the word is especially applied to oxen and horses. These are *beasts of burden*. A farmer always means an ox or cow by *beast*. The word is sometimes used in a pitying or contemptuous way (*the poor beast was suffering*, *the beasts that perish*), and then it is akin to *brute*. In this sense it is figuratively applied to a brutal or brutish person

beat (beet) *n.* 1. a stroke. 2. a pulsation, e.g. **heart-beat**. 3. a policeman's round. 4. accent, in music.—*v.* 1. to keep striking. 2. to defeat.—**beat** *p.t.*—**bea'ten** or **beat** *p. part.*—**beat about the bush** to skirt round a subject instead of dealing with it. —**beat a retreat** to retire, or give order to do so.—**to beat down** to force a price down. —**beat off** to drive back.—**to beat one's brains** to think very hard.—**to beat out** to flatten by hammering.—**beat time** mark the rhythm of music with a baton or the hand.—**to beat up** to treat brutally.—**beaten path** usual way

beatif'ic *adj.* making blessed, happy, as *a beatific smile*.—**beat'ify** *v.* make blessed

beat'itude *n.* blessedness.—**The beatitudes** St. Matthew v. 3-12

beat'nik *n.* a young person who wears unconventional clothes and has modern views.—**beat** *adj.*

beau (bō) *n.* a dandy, an admirer (of a lady). —**beaux** (bōz) *pl.*

beau'teous (bū'-ti-us) *adj.* beautiful

beau'tiful (bū'-ti-ful) *adj.* pleasing, delightful. —**beau'tifully** *adv.*—**beau'tify** (bū'ti-fī) *v.* to make beautiful.—**beau'tifying** *pres. part.*—**beau'tified** *p.t.* and *p. part.*—**beau'ty** (bū'ti) *n.* 1. loveliness. 2. a beautiful person.—**beau'ties** *pl.*—**beautic'ian** *n.* someone who sells and applies aids to beauty

Compare: handsome, pretty, comely, fair. *Contrast:* ugly, hideous, repulsive

Beautiful is applied to people, landscapes works of art, actions and thoughts. *Handsome* is applied to males rather than females. *Pretty* is a weaker word than *beautiful* and cannot be applied to majestic or serious things. *Comely* refers to the figure as well as the face of a person, while *fair* is used in much the same way

bea'ver (bee'ver) *n.* 1. a soft-furred animal living both on land and in water. 2. its fur. 3. lower part of the face guard of a helmet. —**eager beaver** an active person who enjoys hard work

becalm' (be-kahm') *v.* (of a ship) to keep from moving by lack of wind.—**becalmed** *adj.*

because' (be-koz') *adv.* and *conj.* by reason of

Bechu'ana *n.* an inhabitant of Botswana

beck *n.* 1. a sign, nod, as *to be at anyone's beck and call*. 2. a brook

beck'on *v.* to call by nod or sign

become' (be-kum') *v.* 1. to suit, fit, as *That dress becomes you*. 2. to come to be, as *She intends to become a nurse*.—**becom'ing** *pres. part.*—**became'** *p.t.*—**become'** *p. part.* —**becom'ing** *adj.* 1. suitable. 2. (clothes etc.) looking well

bed *n.* 1. a place to sleep on. 2. the bottom of a river. 3. foundation. 4. a garden-plot.—*v.* to plant.—**bed'ding** *pres. part.*—**bed'ded** *p.t.* and *p. part.*—**bed'ding** *n.* bed-clothes, mattress, etc.—**bedrid'den** *adj.* kept in bed by age or sickness.—**bed'rock** *n.* 1. solid rock. 2. foundation.—**bed'spread** *n.* top cover on bed.—**bed'stead** *n.* framework of bed.—**bed and board** lodging and food.—**to get out of bed on the wrong side** to be bad-tempered all day

bedaub' *v.* to smear

bedeck' *v.* to adorn, decorate

bed'lam *n.* 1. a mad-house. 2. an uproar

bed'ouin (bed'oo-in) *n.* a desert Arab

bedrag'gled *adj.* soiled and muddy

bee *n.* 1. an insect that makes honey. A large number of bees makes up a **swarm**. 2. meeting for some definite object, as *Spelling-bee*, *sewing-bee*.—**bee'hive** *n.* a house for bees.—**bee'-line** *n.* the shortest route.—**bees'wax** *n.* wax used for polishing. —**a bee in one's bonnet** a crazy idea

beech *n.* a tree with smooth grey bark

beef *n.* the flesh of ox or cow.—**beeves** *pl.* cattle intended for slaughter.—**beef'eater** *n.* a Yeoman of the Guard.—**beef'-steak** (-stāk) *n.* a cut of beef.—**beef'y** *adj.* fleshy, heavy

beer *n.* a drink made from hops and malt

beet *n.* a vegetable with red or white root. The white-rooted **sugar beet** is used for making sugar

bee'tle *n.* an insect with hard cases covering folded wings.—*v.* to overhang.—**beet'ling** *adj.* overhanging, shaggy, as *beetling brows*, *cliffs*

beet'root *n.* the red root of the beet, used as a vegetable

befall' *v.* to happen.—**befell'** *p.t.*—**befall'en** *p. part.*

Compare: occur, bechance, betide

be'fit *v.* to be suitable to.—**befit'ting** *pres. part.*—**befit'ted** *p.t.* and *p. part.*—**befit'ting** *adj.*

Compare: becoming, appropriate, proper

before' *adv.* 1. in front. 2. earlier.—*conj.* sooner than, as *Have a drink before we go; he left before it rained.*—*prep.* 1. in front of. 2. earlier than, as *before daybreak.*—**before'hand** *adv.* in advance, in readiness

Compare: after, afterwards. *Contrast:* behind

befriend' (be-frend') *v.* to help

beg *v.* to ask earnestly. This verb may also stand alone with the meaning of ask for alms.—**beg'ging** *pres. part.*—**beg'ged** *p.t.* and *p. part.*—**beg'gar** *n.*

Compare: beseech, implore, pray

beget *v.* to be father of, to produce as *kindness begets gratitude.*—**begot** *p.t.*.—**begot** or **begot'ten** *p. part.*

begin' *v.* to commence.—**begin'ning** *pres. part.*—**began'** *p.t.*—**begun'** *p. part.*—**begin'ning** *n.* start.—**begin'ner** *n.* someone beginning to learn a skill.—**to begin with** in the first place

Compare: commencement, inception, origin, outset, inauguration

begone' *interj.* away! depart!

begrudge' *v.* 1. to envy someone, the possession of something, as *Her ugly sisters begrudged Cinderella her good looks.* 2. to give unwillingly, as *He put some money into the collecting-box but we could see that he begrudged it.*—**begrudg'ing** *pres. part.*—**begrudged'** *p.t.* and *p. part.*

beguile' (be-gīl') *v.* 1. to cheat, deceive. 2. to while away (time). 3. amuse

be'gum (bee'gum) *n.* a Muslim princess or lady of high rank, a princess

behalf' (be-half') *n.* someone's place, part, advantage or protection, as *I thank you on behalf of my friends. He made a plea on the prisoner's behalf.*—**behalves'** *pl.*

behave' (be-hāv') *v.* to conduct (oneself), to act.—**beha'ving** *pres. part.*—**behaved'** *p.t.* and *p. part.*—**beha'viour** *n.*

behead (be-hed') *v.* to cut off the head

behest' *n.* a command

behind' *adv.* late, in the rear.—*prep.*—**behind'hand** *adj.*—**behind one's back** deceitfully.—**behind the scenes** privately, unobstrusively

behold' *v.* to see.—**beheld'** *p.t.* and *p. part.*—**behold'er** *n.*

behold'en *adj.* indebted (to)

be'ing *n.* 1. existence. 2. a person.—*pres. part.* of be

bela'bour (-lā') *v.* to beat soundly

bela'ted (-lā') *adj.* late, overtaken by night

belay' *v.* to fasten a rope by winding it round something

belch *v.* to throw up from within

belea'guer (be-lee'ger) *v.* to besiege

bel'fry (bel'fri) *n.* a bell-tower.—**bel'fries** *pl.*

Belgium (bel'jum) *n.* a country in Europe.—**Bel'gian** (bel'jan) *n.* a native of Belgium.—*adj.*

belie' *v.* 1. to give a wrong impression, as *His appearance belies his character.* 2. disappoint (hopes, promises, etc.).—**bely'ing** *pres. part.*—**belied'** *p.t.* and *p. part.*

belief' *n.* 1. trust. 2. what one accepts as true

Compare: conviction, credence, opinion. *Contrast:* disbelief, scepticism, unbelief, doubt

believe' *v.* 1. to regard as true. 2. to have faith.—**believ'ing** *pres. part.*—**believed'** *p.t.* and *p. part.*—**believ'er** *n.*

belit'tle *v.* to under-value, disparage.—**belitt'ling** *pres. part.*—**belit'tled** *p.t.* and *p. part.*

bell *n.* a metal cup which rings when struck.—**bell'boy** *n.* in America, pageboy in an hotel.—**bell'-ringer** *n.* someone who rings church bells.—**bell'-tent** *n.* a tent shaped like a cone or bell.—**sound as a bell** in perfect condition.—**to bell the cat** to undertake a dangerous task for others

belladon'na *n.* the deadly nightshade, a poisonous plant with red berries

bel'licose (bel'i-kōs) *adj.* warlike.—**bellicos'ity** (bel-i-kos'i-ti) *n.*

bellig'erent (bel-ij'er-ent) *adj.* waging war.—*n.* a nation at war

bell'ow (bel'ō) *v.* to roar.—*n.*

bell'ows (bel'ōz) *n.pl.* instrument for making a current of air

bell'y *n.* the part of the body containing the stomach, etc.—**bell'ies** *pl.*—*v.* to swell, as *The sails bellied with the wind.*—**bell'ied** *p.t.* and *p. part.*

belong' *v.* 1. to be the property of. 2. to be connected with.—**belong'ings** *n.pl.* possessions

belov'ed *adj.* much loved.—*n.*

below' (be-lō') *adv.* beneath.—*prep.* lower than, under

belt *n.* 1. a band. 2. a girdle.—*v.* 1. to fasten with a belt. 2. to beat with a belt, to hit. 3. to rush, run fast.—**green belt** undeveloped land round a town.—**conveyor belt** long moving platform for transporting goods.—**to hit below the belt** to take an unfair advantage.—**to tighten one's belt** to economise, take economical measures

bemoan *v.* to show deep grief for

Compare: bewail, mourn, grieve, lament. *Contrast:* rejoice, exult

bench *n.* 1. a long seat. 2. a table in a workshop. 3. a judge's seat in court. 4. body of judges

bend *v.* 1. to curve, 2. to stoop. 3. to tie (a rope).—**bent** *p.t.* and *p. part.*—**bend'ed**

p. part., as *on bended knee.*—*n.* a curve.—**to be bent on** to be determined to do

beneath' (-neeth) *adv.* in a lower place.—*prep.* under

benedic'tion (-shun) *n.* a blessing
Contrast: malediction, curse, anathema

benefac'tion (-shun) *n.* 1. doing good, charity. 2. a gift for charity.—**benefac'tor** *n.* one who helps another, charitable person.—**benefac'tress** *fem.*

ben'efice (ben'e-fis) *n.* a church living

benef'icence (ben-ef'i-sens) *n.* kindness, charity.—**benef'icent** *adj.*

benefi'cial (ben-e-fish'al) *adj.* helpful, useful.—**benefic'iary** *n.* someone who receives a benefit

ben'efit *n.* 1. an advantage. 2. an act of kindness.—*v.* 1. do good to. 2. receive good.—**ben'efiting** *pres. part.*—**ben'efited** *p.t.* and *p. part.*

benev'olence *n.* goodwill.—**benev'olent** *adj.*
Compare: kindliness, generosity, charity.
Contrast: malevolence, illwill, unkindness, meanness

benight'ed (be-nīt'ed) 1. in darkness. 2. ignorant, as *benighted heathen*

benign' (be-nīn') *adj.* kind, mild.—**benig'nant** *adj.* gracious, kind.—**benig'nancy, benig'nity** *n.*
Contrast: malign, malignant, malignancy, malignity

ben'ison (ben'i-zon) *n.* a blessing

bent *n.* inclination, turn of mind

bent *n.* coarse grass, heathy land

ben'zene *n.* a by-product of coal tar

ben'zine (ben'zeen) *n.* a liquid made from petroleum

bequeath' (be-kweeth') *v.* to leave by will.—**bequest'** (be-kwest') *n.* something left by will

bereave' *v.* to rob of, leave desolate, usually by death.—**bereaved', bereft'** *p.t.* and *p. part.*—**bereave'ment** *n.* loss
Note: One is *bereaved* by the death of relatives and friends. One is *bereft* of possessions

ber'et (ber'ā) *n.* a round, flat cap without a peak or brim

berg *n.* 1. a large mass of ice. 2. in South Africa, a mountain

ber'ry *n.* a juicy, stoneless fruit.—**ber'ries** *pl.*—**ber'ried** *adj.* covered with berries

ber'serk *adj.* fighting mad

berth *n.* 1. ship's anchoring place. 2. sleeping-place on a ship or train. 3. post or situation.—*v.* to moor, as a ship.—**to give a wide berth to** to avoid

ber'yl *n.* a precious stone

beseech' *v.* to beg, implore.—**besought'** (be-sawt') *p.t.* and *p. part.*

beset' *v.* attack on all sides.—**beset'ting** *pres. part.*—**beset'** *p.t.* and *p. part.* as *beset by so many and great dangers.*—**beset'ting sin** a sin which is always tempting one

beside' *prep.* by the side of, near.—**beside oneself,** out of one's senses

besides' *adv.* also.—*prep.* as well as

besiege' (be-seej') *v.* 1. to surround with armed forces. 2. to crowd round.—**besieg'ing** *pres. part.*—**besieged'** *p.t.* and *p. part.*

be'som (bee'zum) *n.* broom made of twigs

besot'ted *adj.* stupefied

besought (be-sawt') *p.t.* and *p. part.*of **beseech**

bespat'ter *v.* to throw mud on

bespeak' *v.* to order in advance.—**bespo'ken** *p. part.*—**bespoke'** *p.t.*—**bespoke tailor** tailor who makes clothes to order

best 1. *sup.* of *good.* 2. *sup.* of *well.*—*v.* to defeat.—**at best** at the most.—**best man** the bridegroom's man.—**best-seller** a book that sells exceptionally well.—**have the best of it** to win.—**to make the best of it** to put up with and make the most of it

best'ial *adj.* beastly.—**bestial'ity** *n.*

bestir' *v.* to rouse.—**bestir'ring** *pres. part.*—**bestir'red** *p.t.* and *p. part.*
Compare: awaken, arouse, stimulate, incite

bestow' (be-stō') *v.* 1. to give, as *Queen Elizabeth bestowed a knighthood on Francis Drake.* 2. to put away

bestride' *v.* to stride over, as *He doth bestride the narrow world like a Colossus* (Shakespeare).—**bestri'ding** *pres. part.*—**bestrode'** *p.t.* and *p. part.*

bet *v.* to lay money on, wager.—**bet'ting** *pres. part.*—**bet'ted** *p.t.* and *p. part.*—*n.*

be'ta (bee'ta) *n.* the second letter of the Greek alphabet.—**be'ta rays** a stream of fast electrons thrown off by radioactive substances

betide' *v.* to happen, as *I will be there, whatever betide*

betimes' *adv.* in good time

beto'ken *v.* to show by some sign
Compare: augur, portend, import

betray' *v.* 1. to give away, as *to betray a secret or his looks betrayed his thoughts*; deceive. 2. to be false to.—**betray'al** *n.*

betroth' *v.* to engage to marry.—**betro'thal** *n.* engagement

bet'ter *comp.* of *good* and of *well.*—*v.* to improve.—**get the better of** overcome.—**think better of** to change one's mind.—**better off** in a better position

between', betwixt' *adv.* midway.—*prep.* 1. in the middle of. 2. among.—**betwixt and between** neither one thing nor the other
Note: Between usually means in the middle of two and *among* means in the midst of more than two. Avoid the common error of saying *between you and I.* It should be *between you and me*

bev'el *n.* a sloping edge.—*v.* to make a sloping edge.—**bev'elling** *pres. part.*—**bev'elled** *p.t.* and *p. part.*—**bev'elled** *adj.*

bev'erage *n.* a drink

bev'y *n.* 1. a flock of birds. 2. a group (of ladies, girls).—**bev'ies** *pl.*

bewail' *v.* to mourn for, weep for

beware' *v.* to be careful

bewil'der *v.* to puzzle, confuse.—**bewil'dering** *adj.*—**bewil'derment** *n.*

Compare: amaze, perplex, confuse, astonish, *Contrast:* explain, simplify, elucidate

bewitch' *v.* to put a spell on, charm.—**bewitch'ing** *adj.* charming

beyond' *adv.* farther away.—*prep.* 1. on the farther side of. 2. later than. 3. out of reach of

bi'as *n.* 1. a slant. 2. a leaning towards. 3. (in bowls) a weight on one side of the bowl, making it swerve.—*v.* to influence, prejudice.—**bi'asing** or **bi'assing** *pres. part.*—**bi'ased** or **bi'assed** *p.t.* and *p. part.*

bib *n.* a cloth put under a child's chin

Bi'ble *n.* the sacred writings of the Christian Church.—**bib'lical** *adj.*

bibliog'raphy (bib-li-og'ra-fy) *n.* a list of books

bib'liophile *n.* a book-lover

bicente'nary *n.* a two-hundredth anniversary

bi'ceps (bī'seps) *n.* a muscle in the upper arm

bi'cimal *n.* any number in the binary system of numbers

bick'er *v.* to quarrel

bi'cycle (bī'si-kl) *n.* a vehicle with two wheels, one in front of the other.—**moulton bicycle** a modern safety bicycle

bid *v.* 1. to command. 2. to offer (a price). 3. to say, as *to bid anyone goodbye*.—*n.* 1. offer (of a price). 2. an attempt.—**bid'ding** *pres. part.*—**bid** or **bade** *p.t.*—**bid'den** *p. part.*—**bid'der** *n.*—**bid'ding** *n.* command, order

bienn'ial (bī-en'i-al) *adj.* 1. happening every two years. 2. lasting two years.—*n.* a plant which lives two years

bier (beer) *n.* a wooden frame for bearing the dead to the grave

big *adj.* of great size.—**big'ger** *comp.*—**big'gest** *sup.*—**big game** the larger animals shot for sport.—**to talk big** to boast.—**too big for one's boots** conceited

Compare: large, bulky, vast, considerable. *Contrast:* small, tiny, minute, little

The word *big* is of more general application than any of the words with which we can compare it. It is apt to be overworked by people who do not know how to say, or do not trouble to think, which kind of bigness they mean

big'amy *n.* the crime of having two husbands or wives at once.—**big'amist** *n.*—**big'amous** *adj.*

bight (bīt) *n.* 1. a wide bay. 2. the loop of a rope

big'ot *n.* a narrow-minded person.—**big'oted** *adj.*—**big'otry** *n.*

Compare: fanatic, zealot, dogmatist

bike *n.* a short name for bicycle

biki'ni (bik-ee'ni) *n.* a woman's two-piece swim suit

bilat'eral (bī-lat-er-al) *adj.* two-sided

Contrast: unilateral, multilateral

Note: bi- at the beginning of a word often means "two" or "double," as in *bicycle, bilingual*, etc.

bil'berry *n.* a plant with blue berries

bile *n.* 1. a bitter fluid secreted by the liver. 2. ill-humour

bilge (bilj) *n.* 1. the bottom of a ship's hull. 2. the dirt found there

biling'ual (bī-ling-wal) *adj.* speaking or expressed in two languages, as *Many Welsh people are bilingual, speaking both Welsh and English*

bil'ious *adj.* 1. sick with bile. 2. peevish

bill *n.* 1. a bird's beak. 2. a tool for pruning.—*v.* to touch bills (of birds).—**bill and coo** to behave affectionately

bill *n.* 1. a public notice. 2. an account. 3. a measure proposed to become law. 4. in America, a paper money note.—**to fill the bill** to be what is required.—**to foot the bill** to pay the expenses

bill'abong *n.* (Aus.) a backwater, creek

bill'et *n.* 1. lodging (usually for a soldier). 2. a job. 3. a piece of wood.—*v.* to place soldiers in houses

bill'iards *n.pl.* a game played on a table with balls and cues

bill'ion *n.* a million millions; (in America and France) a thousand millions

bill'ow (bil'ō) *n.* a great swelling wave.—*v.* to rise in waves.—**bill'owy** *adj.*

billy (-can) *n.* (Aus.) a round tin can with a lid, used as a kettle

bill'y-goat *n.* a he-goat.—**nanny-goat** *fem.*

bil'tong *n.* in South Africa, strips of dried meat

bin *n.* a large box for holding corn, rubbish, etc.

bi'nary numbers *n.pl.* a system of numbers in which no digit can be greater than one

bind *v.* 1. to tie. 2. to tie together. 3. put a book into a cover. 4. to oblige, compel.—**bound** *p.t.* and *p. part.*—**bound'en** *p. part.* as *our bounden duty*.—**bind'ing** *n.* book-cover.—**bound up in** entirely absorbed in

Compare: bandage, fix, fasten. *Contrast:* loose, undo, relax

bin'go *n.* a game of chance in which numbers on a card are covered as they are drawn at random, until every number on the card is accounted for

binn'acle *n.* a box holding a ship's compass

binoc'ulars (bī-nok'ū-larz) *n.pl.* two-eyed field-glasses

biochem'istry *n.* the chemistry of living things

biog'raphy *n.* the written life of a person.—**biog'raphies** *pl.*—**biog'rapher** *n.*—**biograph'ical** *adj.*

Note: bio- at the beginning of a word often means "life"

biol'ogy (bī-ol'o-ji) *n.* the study of living

things.—**biolog'ical** (bī-o-loj'i-kal) *adj.*—**biol'ogist** *n.*

bi'ped (bī'ped) *n.* a two-footed animal

bi'plane *n.* an aircraft with two planes in each wing

birch *n.* 1. a slender tree with smooth white bark. 2. a rod for whipping.—*v.* to cane

bird *n.* a feathered animal.—**bird of passage** moves with the changing seasons.—**bird of prey** one that eats flesh.—**birds of a feather** people of the same type.—**a bird in the hand is worth two in the bush** a certainty is worth more than a promise.—**a bird's eye view** a general view of a situation

birth *n.* 1. a coming to life. 2. beginning.—**of good birth** of good family.—**birth'day** *n.* 1. day on which one was born. 2. its anniversary.—**birth'place** *n.* where one is born.—**birth'rate** *n.* the proportion of births to the population

birth'right *n.* anything to which one has a right by birth, as *Esau sold his birthright to Jacob for a mess of pottage*

bis'cuit (bis'kit) *n.* 1. a thin dry cake. 2. unglazed pottery.—*adj.* light brown.—**to take the biscuit** to be the worst or best at something

bisect' (bī-sekt') *v.* to divide into two equal parts.—**bisec'tion** *n.*—**bisec'tor** *n.* a line which bisects

bish'op *n.* a clergyman in charge of a diocese.—**bish'opric** *n.* bishop's position or diocese

bis'muth (biz'muth) *n.* a reddish-white metal

bi'son (bī'son) *n.* the American buffalo, or European wild ox

bit 1. a small piece. 2. the biting part of a tool. 3. the mouth-piece of a horse's bridle.—**to take the bit between one's teeth** to act on one's own

bitch *n.* a female dog. (*dog* or *hound masc.*)

bite *v.* 1. to cut into, *esp.* with the teeth. 2. to cause pain.—**bi'ting** *pres. part.*, as *a biting remark.*—**bit** *p.t.*—**bit, bit'ten,** *p. part.*—*n.* 1. cut from biting. 2. mouthful.—**the biter bit** the attacker is attacked.—**to bite the dust** to fall in combat

bitt'er *adj.* 1. biting to the taste. 2. wounding to the feelings, as *They had bitter memories of their defeat.*—**bitt'erness** *n.*—**bitt'erly** *adv.*—**to the bitter end** to the very end

Compare: acrid, pungent, caustic. *Contrast:* sweet, honeyed, soothing, agreeable

bitt'ern *n.* a bird of the heron family

bit'umen *n.* a mineral pitch, e.g. petroleum, asphalt, etc.—**bitu'minous** *adj.*

biva'lent *adj.* (chemistry) able to combine with or replace two hydrogen atoms

bi'valve *n.* a mollusc, such as an oyster or mussel, with two hinged shells

bi'vouac (bi'voo-ak) *n.* an open-air encampment.—*v.* to camp without tents

bizarre' *adj.* odd, fantastic

Compare: grotesque, peculiar, extraordinary

blab *v.* to tell tales.—*pres. part.*—**blabbed** *p.t.* and *p. part.*

black *adj.* 1. of the darkest colour. 2. without light.—*n.* a negro.—*v.* as *to black shoes, to black someone's eye.*—**black'en** *v.* to make black.—**blackness** *n.*—**black'fellow** *n.* (Aus.) aborigine.—**the black sheep of the family** a disgraceful member.—**Black maria** a police van.—**black market** unlawful dealing in scarce goods.—**black and blue** badly bruised

black'ball *v.* to vote against (by putting black balls into ballot-box)

black'berry *n.* the bramble and its fruit.—**black'berrying** *n.* picking blackberries

black'bird *n.* a song-bird

black'board *n.* a dark surface prepared for writing with chalk

blackcur'rant *n.* 1. a shrub bearing small edible black berries. 2. the berries

black'guard (blag'ard) *n.* a scoundrel

Compare: rascal, scoundrel, cad

black'ing *n.* a polish used for stoves, shoes, etc.—**black lead** *n.* a mineral used for cleaning grates

black'leg *n.* a workman who continues to work when his mates are on strike

black'mail *n.* money obtained by threats.—*v.*—**blackmail'er** *n.*

black'-out *n.* 1. a fainting fit. 2. the failure of a town's electric power. 3. a sudden darkening of a theatre stage. 4. the screening of all lights in wartime.—*v.*

black'smith *n.* a man working in iron, who shoes horses, etc.

black'thorn *n.* the sloe tree

blad'der *n.* a bag to contain liquid in human and other bodies

blade *n.* 1. a flat edge, e.g. of an oar, leaf. 2. (poetically) swaggering fellow. 3. cutting edge of a tool or weapon

blame *n.* disapproval, fault.—*v.* to find fault with.—**blam'ing** *pres. part.*—**blamed** *p.t.* and *p. part.*—**blam'able** *adj.*—**blame'worthy** *adj.*—**blame'less** *adj.*

Compare: accuse, censure, reproach, rebuke, *Contrast:* praise, commend, exonerate, acquit

blanch *v.* 1. to put in hot water (to remove skins), as *to blanch almonds.* 2. to become white, as *His face blanched with terror.*—he **blanch'es**

blancmange' (bla-mongzh') *n.* opaque jelly pudding

bland *adj.* mild, smooth.—**bland'ish** *v.* to coax with smooth words.—**blan'dishment** *n.* flattery

blank *adj.* 1. without writing or printing, as *a blank page.* 2. vacant, confused, as *When asked a question he looked blank.*—**blank verse** verse without rhyme.—*n.* 1. an empty space. 2. bull's-eye of a target.—**draw a blank** fail to achieve success.—**a blank cartridge** a cartridge with the bullet removed.—**a blank cheque** a cheque payable for the amount the receiver writes on it

blan'ket *n.* a woollen covering for a bed.—*v.* to cover.—**a wet blanket** someone who lessens the enthusiasm or enjoyment of others

blare *v.* to roar, to trumpet.—*n.*—**blar'ing** *pres. part.*—**blared** *p.t.* and *p. part.*

blar'ney *n.* coaxing, flattery

blaspheme' (blas-feem') *v.* to speak irreverently of God.—**blasphem'ing** *pres. part.*—**blasphemed'** *p.t.* and *p. part.*—**blasphem'er** *n.*—**blas'phemy** (blas'fem-i) *n.*—**blas'phemous** *adj.*

Compare: profanity, impiety, swearing

blast *n.* 1. a gust of air, wind or sound, as *a blast of wind, the blast of a trumper.* 2. an explosion.—*v.* 1. to blow up. 2. to ruin, as *to blast one's hopes.*—**blas'ted** *adj.* blighted

blast'-fur'nace *n.* a smelting-furnace worked by a strong draught

blast'-off *n.* the launching of a rocket or missile

bla'tant (blā'tant) *adj.* noisy, vulgar

blaze *n.* 1. a flame. 2. an outburst.—*v.* to burn, esp. with passions, as *His eyes were blazing with anger.*—**bla'zing** *pres. part.*—**blazed** *p.t.* and *p. part.*

Compare: flare, gleam, glare

blaze *n.* a white mark. 1. on a horse. 2. on a tree made by stripping bark.—*v.* as *to blaze a trail*

bla'zer (blā'zer) *n.* a coloured sports coat with a badge on the breast pocket

bla'zon (blā'zon) *n.* a coat of arms.—*v.* 1. to describe a coat of arms. 2. to make public

bleach *v.* 1. to whiten. 2. to grow white.—he **bleach'es**

bleak *adj.* cold, cheerless.—**bleak'ness** *n.*

Compare: dreary, dismal, forbidding. *Contrast:* cosy, cheerful, genial

blear *adj.* dim and watery, as in **blear-eyed.**—**blear'y** *adj.*

bleat *n.* the cry of sheep or goat.—*v.*

bleed *v.* 1. to lose blood. 2. to draw blood from.—**bled** *p.t.* and *p. part.*

bleep *n.* a high-pitched radio signal

blem'ish *n.* a stain, fault.—*v.*

blench *v.* to shrink back.—he **blench'es**

blend *v.* to mix, as different kinds of tea or tobacco.—*n.* a mixture.—**blend'ed** or **blent** *p.t.* and *p. part.*

bless *v.* 1. to make holy, consecrate. 2. to give thanks to. 3. to make happy.—he **bless'es.**—**bless'ing** *n.* 1. a benediction. 2. happiness. 3. a good wish.—**bless'ed** *adj.*—**bless'edness** *n.*—**blessing in disguise** a benefit hidden in apparent misfortune

blight (blīt) *n.* 1. plant disease. 2. any evil which destroys hope.—*v.* to ruin

blind (blīnd) *adj.* 1. without sight. 2. closed at one end.—*n.* 1. screen for a window. 2. something serving as an excuse.—*v.* to make blind.—**blind'ly** *adv.*—**blind'ness** *n.*—**blind alley** *n.* a dead-end, a job with no prospects of promotion.—**blind-worm** *n.* a slow-worm.—**to turn a blind eye to** to pretend not to see.—**Venetian blind** a window blind with horizontal slats

Compare: subterfuge, artifice, ruse

blind'fold *adj.* with the eyes covered.—*v.* to bandage the eyes

blind-man's-buff *n.* a game in which a blindfold person tries to catch one of the others

blink *v.* to open and shut the eyes.—**blink'ers** *n.pl.* screens for horses' eyes

Note: To blink the facts, meaning to refuse to notice unpleasant facts

bliss *n.* complete happiness.—**bliss'ful** *adj.*—**bliss'fully** *adv.*

Compare: felicity, blessedness, rapture. *Contrast:* woe, sorrow, misery

blis'ter *n.* 1. a bubble on the skin. 2. a similar bubble on metal or painted surface.—*v.* to raise a blister

blithe, blithe'some *adj.* gay.—**blithe'ly** *adv.*

bliz'zard *n.* a blinding storm of wind and snow

bloa'ted (blō'ted) *adj.* puffy.—**bloa'ter** *n.* dried herring

block *n.* 1. a solid piece of wood, etc. 2. an obstacle, as a **traffic-block.** 3. a group of houses.—*v.* to stop up, prevent.—**to be a chip off the old block** to resemble one's father

blockade' *n.* shutting off a place or country from supplies.—*v.*

block'head *n.* a stupid fellow

block'house *n.* a small fort

blonde *adj.* fair-haired.—*n.* a fair-haired woman

blood (blud) *n.* 1. the red fluid in the veins of men and animals. 2. race, descent, as *to have foreign blood.*—**blue blood** aristocratic descent. 3. temper.—**blood'y** *adj.*, as *a bloody battle.*—**blood'ily** *adv.*—**bad blood** bitterness.—**blood-curdling** frightening.—**in cold blood** in a cool deliberate way

blood bank *n.* a place where blood is stored ready for transfusion

blood'hound *n.* a dog used to track people by scent

blood'shed *n.* slaughter

blood'shot *adj.* red with inflamed blood-vessels (referring to the eyes)

blood'thirsty *adj.* liking bloodshed

blood'transfusion *n.* passing blood from the body of one person to another

blood'vessel *n.* a vein or artery

bloom *n.* 1. a flower. 2. freshness, perfection. 3. powdery coating on fruit.—*v.* to flower, to flourish.—**bloo'ming** *adj.*

bloss'om *n.* a flower.—*v.* to flower

blot *n.* 1. a spot, stain. 2. disgrace.—*v.* 1. to stain. 2. (out) destroy. 3. to dry ink with **blot'ting-paper.**—**blot'ting** *pres. part.*—**blot'ted** *p.t.* and *p. part.*

blotch *n.* a spot on the skin.—**blotch'y** *adj.*

blouse (blouz) *n.* a loose upper garment

blow (blō) *n.* a stroke.—**at one blow** all at once

Compare: stroke, box, buffet, thump, misfortune, disaster, shock

A *blow* is delivered suddenly by the hand or a weapon. A *box* on the ears or a *buffet* or *thump* are usually given with the hand. A *stroke* is a sweeping kind of *blow*, given by a sword, for example. A *blow* delivered by fate is a *disaster* or *misfortune*. A *shock* is rather what results from a *blow* than the *blow* itself

blow (blō) *v.* to make a current of air; puff, pant, as *The wind blows, He blows a bugle.* —**blew** *p.t.*—**blown** *p. part.*—**to blow hot and cold** to be irresolute.—**to blow one's own trumpet** to boast.—**to blow one's top** (slang) to be furiously angry.—**to blow over** to pass off.—**to blow up** to explode

blow'-fly *n.* the bluebottle, a fly which lays its eggs in meat

blow'hole *n.* a breathing-hole for whales, seals, etc.

blow'-lamp *n.* a lamp giving a hot flame for soldering metals or burning off paint

blow'pipe *n.* 1. an instrument for increasing heat or flame by blowing. 2. a tube through which some tribes blow poisoned darts

blow'zy *adj.* untidy, sluttish

blub'ber *n.* the fat of whales, etc.—*v.* to weep

blud'geon (bluj'on) *n.* a short, thick club.—*v.*

blue *adj.* 1. of the colour of the sky. 2. (figuratively) depressed, unhappy.—**blu'ish** *adj.*—**blue'bell** *n.* a wild hyacinth.—**blue'-book** *n.* a government report.—**blue'bottle** *n.* a blowfly.—**blue'jack'et** *n.* a sailor in the navy.—**blue'pencil** *v.* to correct.—**Blue Peter**, a blue flag with a white centre, hoisted by a ship about to sail.—**blue'print** *n.* a copy of a drawing or plan.—**blue** *n.* one chosen to represent his university at games or sports.—**blue-rib'bon** *n.* the highest honour.—**blue'-stocking** *n.* a woman having or pretending to great learning.—**blues** *n.* kind of dance, melancholy dance music.—**to have the blues** to feel miserable.—**once in a blue moon** very rarely.—**out of the blue** unexpectedly

bluff *n.* a high steep bank.—*adj.* rough and hearty.—*v.* to deceive by a pretence

blun'der *n.* a clumsy mistake.—*v.*—**blun'derer** *n.*

blun'derbuss *n.* an old-fashioned hand-gun with a wide muzzle

blunt *adj.* 1. having dull edge or point. 2. plain-spoken.—*v.* to make blunt.—**blunt'ly** *adv.*

Contrast: subtle, ceremonious, diplomatic

blur *n.* a smear, stain.—*v.* to smear, make dim.—**blu'rring** *pres. part.*—**blurred** *p.t.* and *p. part.*

blurt *v.* to speak without thinking, as *He blurted out the bad news in front of the whole family*

blush *v.* to become red in the face.—*n.*—he **blush'es**

blus'ter *v.* 1. to blow noisily (of wind). 2. to swagger and talk noisily.—**blus'terer** *n.*

bo'a (bō'a) *n.* 1. a large non-poisonous snake. 2. a long fur for the neck

boar (bōr) *n.* male pig.—**sow** *fem.*

board (bōrd) *n.* 1. a flat sheet of wood, paper. 2. meals, as in **board and lodging**. 3. a body of men, as *a board of directors.*—*v.* 1. to supply food daily. 2. to enter ship, train, etc. 3. to cover with planks.—**to go by the board**, to be swept away, to be counted as a loss.—**to sweep the board** to win everything

boar'der *n.* lodger.—**boar'ding-house** *n.*—**boar'ding-school** *n.* residential school

boast (bōst) *v.* to brag,—*n.*—**boast'ful** *adj.*—**boast'fulness** *n.*—**boast'ful ly** *adv.*

boat (bōt) *n.* 1. a small open vessel. 2. a ship. —*v.* to sail in a boat.—**boat'-hook** *n.*—**boat'-house** *n.*—**boat'ing** *n.* sailing in a boat.—**boat'swain** (bōsn) *n.* a ship's officer. —**to burn one's boats** to act so that there is no turning back

bob *v.* 1. to move up and down. 2. to cut short (hair, tail).—**bob'bing** *pres. part.*—**bobbed** *p.t.* and *p. part.*—*n.*

bo'blink *n.* an American songbird

bob'bin *n.* a reel or spool

bob'olink *n.* a North American song-bird, the *reed-bird* or *rice-bird*

bode *v.* to portend, as *To begin the enterprise on Friday the* 13*th bodes ill for its success*

Compare: foretell, augur, presage

bod'ice (bod'is) *n.* the part of a dress from the waist up

bod'kin *n.* a tool for piercing or threading

bod'y *n.* 1. the whole mass or substance, esp. of a person or animal. 2. the trunk as distinguished from the limbs. 3. a collection of persons or things, as *The soldiers were a fine body of men.* 4. the containing part of a vehicle.—**bod'ies** *pl.*—**bod'iless** *adj.*—**bod'ily** *a.* in the flesh.—*adv.* in a body.—**bod'y-builder** *n.* 1. nourishing food 2. apparatus for developing muscles by exercise.—**bod'yguard** *n.* a man employed to protect another.—**bod'y-line** (cricket) bowling aimed, at the batsman to frighten him.—**bod'y serv'ant** *n.* personal servant, valet.—**bod'y snatch'er** *n.* a grave-robber. —**bod'y-work** *n.* the body of vehicles

Compare: form, frame, corpse, carcass.

Contrast: soul, mind, spirit

Bo'er *n.* old name for an inhabitant of South Africa of Dutch descent

bog *n.* wet, soft ground.—*v.* as *The cart was bogged up to the axles.*—**bog'gy.**—*adj.*

bo'gey *n.* a goblin, evil spirit

bog'gle *v.* to hesitate, fumble.—**bogg'ling** *pres. part.*—**bogg'led** *p.t.* and *p. part.*

bo'gie *n.* 1. wheeled truck or undercarriage. 2. (golf) a score for a hole which a good player would make

bo'gus (bō'gus) *adj.* sham

Compare: fraudulent, spurious, counterfeit

bohe'mian *n.* a person living an unconventional life.—*adj.*

boil *v.* 1. to heat a liquid to its **boiling-point** at which it bubbles, as *She boils water.* 2. to come to the **boil**—*n.*, as *The water boils.* 3. to be excited, as *She boiled with indignation.*—**boiler** *n.* a vessel for boiling, esp. in an engine.—**boil'er suit** *n.* overalls to protect clothing.—**boil'ing-point** *n.* the temperature at which a liquid changes into vapour.—**boil down** to summarise

boil *n.* an inflamed swelling on the body, containing pus, or matter

bois'terous *adj.* rough, noisy

bold *adj.* 1. fearless. 2. clear, outstanding, as *to sketch with bold strokes.*—**bold'ly** *adv.*—**bold'ness** *n.*

Compare: brave, daring, heroic, audacious. *Contrast:* cowardly, timid, shrinking, fearful

bole *n.* the trunk of a tree

Boliv'ia *n.* a country in South America.—**Boliv'ian** *n.* a native of Bolivia.—*adj.*

bol'lard *n.* 1. a post on a jetty to which vessels are moored. 2. a short post in a roadway to divert traffic

bol'shevik *n.* a member of the Russian Communist Party, which took power in Russia in 1917.—**bol'shevist** *adj.*

bol'ster (bōl'ster) *n.* a long pillow.—*v.* (up) to support

bolt (bōlt) *n.* 1. a bar or pin. 2. a rushing away. 3. a short heavy arrow for a cross-bow.—*v.* 1. to fasten with a bolt. 2. to rush away. 3. to swallow hurriedly, as *Dogs bolt their food.*—**bolt from the blue** a great surprise

bomb (bom) *n.* a metal shell filled with explosives.—*v.* to attack with bombs.—**bombard'** *v.* 1. to shell. 2. to hurl at, as *He was bombarded with questions.*—**bombardier'** (-deer') *n.* an artillery non-commissioned officer.—**bombard'ment** *n.*—**bom'ber** (bom'er) *n.* an aircraft that drops bombs

bom'bast *n.* big talk.—**bombast'ic** *adj.*

bond *n.* 1. a link. 2. a promise.—*pl.* chains

bon'dage (bon'dāj) *n.* slavery, imprisonment.—**bond'man, bonds'man** *n.* slave

bone *n.* 1. a hard substance forming the skeleton. 2. a piece of this.—*v.* to remove bone.—**bo'ny** *adj.*—**a bone of contention** a cause of strife.—**bone-dry'** *adj.* completely dry.—**to have a bone to pick with someone** to have a complaint to talk over with someone.—**to make no bones about** to have no hesitation about

bon'fire *n.* a large open-air fire

bon'net *n.* 1. a hat with strings. 2. a cap

bon'ny *adj.* rosy, healthy.—**bon'nier** *comp.*—**bon'niest** *sup.*

bo'nus (bō'nus) *n.* an extra payment

boo'by *n.* a stupid person.—**boo'bies** *pl.*—**boo'by-prize** *n.*

book *n.* sheets of paper bound together.—*v.* to enter in a book, reserve, as *to book a passage on a ship*—**book'keeping** *n.* accounts.—**book'let** *n.* a small book.—**book'maker** *n.* a professional betting man.—**book'-token** *n.* a voucher enabling one to buy books to the value shown on the voucher.—**book'worm** *n.* a great reader.—**to bring to book** to bring to justice to call to account

Note: To be in anyone's *good books* or *bad books* means to be in, or out of, favour with them

boom *n.* a deep roar.—*v.* sudden prosperity in business

boom *n.* 1. a long spar. 2. a barrier

boom'erang *n.* a bent, flattish club of wood used by natives in Australia which, when thrown, returns to the thrower

boon *n.* 1. a favour, as *He asked the king a boon.* 2. a blessing, as *Radio is a boon to blind people.*—*adj.* gay, as *a boon companion*

boor *n.* a rude person.—**boor'ish** *adj.*

boost *v.* 1. to push up. 2. to advertise

boot *n.* 1. a covering for foot and leg. 2. the luggage-box in a coach or car.—**boot'ed** *adj.*—**boot'jack** *n.* a tool for taking off boots.—**boot'lace** *n.* a lace for fastening shoes or boots.—**boot'-legger** *n.* a smuggler of liquor.—**boots** *n.* a hotel-servant

boot *v.* to benefit, be of use.—**boot'less** *adj.* useless.—**to boot** in addition.—**the boot is on the other foot** the one who was at a disadvantage now has the advantage

booth *n.* 1. a stall at a fair. 2. a polling-place

boo'ty *n.* plunder, spoil

bo'rax *n.* a salt used to destroy germs and for soldering

bor'der *n.* 1. a boundary, limit. 2. an edge. 3. a strip of garden.—*v.*

Compare: margin, frontier, verge

bore *v.* 1. to make a hole. 2. to weary.—**bo'ring** *pres. part.*—**bored** *p.t.* and *p. part.*—*n.* 1. a hole. 2. the internal diameter of a tube or gun. 3. a tiresome person.—**bore'dom** *n.*

bore *n.* a tidal wave in a river

bor'ic acid, borac'ic acid *n.* white crystals used as a mild antiseptic

bo'ron *n.* a chemical element present in borax and boric acid

borough (bur'a) *n.* a town with a corporation

bor'row (bor'ō) *v.* to take on loan

bo'som (boo'zum) *n.* the breast.—*adj.* close, as a *bosom friend*

boss *n.* a knob, or raised ornament

boss *n.* a master, manager, gang-leader.—*v.* to give orders.—he **boss'es**

bot'any *n.* the science of plants.—**botan'ical** *adj.*—**bot'anist** *n.*

botch 1. to patch clumsily. 2. to bungle.—*n.*

both (bōth) *adj.* and *pron.* the two.—*adv.* and *conj.* as well
Note: The various uses of *both* may be shown as follows—Adjective, *Both men were there.* Pronoun, *Both are here.* Adverb, *He is both tired and hungry.* Conjunction, *Both boys and girls came to the party*

both'er (boTH'er) *v.* 1. to fuss. 2. to take trouble. 3. to pester.—*n.* a nuisance

Botswan'a *n.* Bantu republic, formerly Bechuanaland

bot'tle *n.* a narrow-necked container for liquids.—*v.* to put into a bottle.—**bott'ling** *pres. part.*—**bott'led** *p.t.* and *p. part.*—**bottle-neck** 1. a narrow part of a road that obstructs the flow of traffic. 2. anything that obstructs a flow of production

bot'tom *n.* 1. the lowest part. 2. the seat. 3. the bed of a sea, river, ship.—*adj.* as *the bottom boy in the class.*—**bot'tomless** *adj.*—**bot'tom drawer** *n.* the accumulation of a bride's trousseau.—**to get to the bottom of** to investigate thoroughly
Compare: base, foundation. *Contrast:* top, summit, apex

bough (bow) *n.* a branch of a tree

boul'der (bōl'der) *n.* a large rock

boul'evard (bool'vahr) *n.* a broad street or promenade planted with trees

bounce (bowns) *v.* 1. to bound, as a ball. 2. to throw oneself about.—**boun'cing** *pres. part.*—**bounced** *p.t.* and *p. part.*—*n.* a leap, rebound, boasting.—**boun'cing** *adj.*

bound *n.* 1. limit, boundary of land. 2. restriction, as *Her joy knew no bounds.*—*v.* to limit, close in.—**boun'dary** *n.*—**boun'daries** *pl.*—**bound'less** *adj.*—**out of bounds** forbidden ground

bound *v.* to spring, leap.—*n.* a leap.—**by leaps and bounds** (progress) in great strides

bound *adj.* 1. compelled. 2. ready to go, as **outward bound**

bounded see **bind**

boun'ty (bown'ti) *n.* 1. liberality. 2. reward.—**boun'ties** *pl.*—**boun'teous** *adj.*—**boun'tiful** generous

bouquet' (boo-kay') *n.* a bunch of flowers

bour'geois (boor'zhwah) *adj.* middle-class, ordinary

bout (bowt) *n.* 1. a contest, as *a boxing bout.* 2. fit, as *bout of illness, drinking-bout*

bo'vine *adj.* 1. relating to oxen. 2. dull, stupid, as *The peasant had a bovine look*

bow (bō) *n.* 1. something bent in the shape of an arch, as a *rainbow* or *bow-window.* 2. a knot of ribbon. 3. weapon for shooting arrows.—**bow'man** *n.* implement for playing the violin.—**bow-legged'** *adj.* bandy.—**bow-win'dow** *n.* See **bay-window.**—**to draw the long bow** to exaggerate.—**to have two strings to one's bow** to have the choice of two plans

bow (bou) *v.* 1. to bend the body in respect or greeting. 2. to submit, as *I bow to your superior knowledge*
Compare: salutation, obeisance, salute, curtsey

bow (bou) *n.* the fore end of a ship (usually used in *pl.*)—**bow'sprit** (bō'sprit) *n.* a spar projecting from the bow

bow'els *n.pl.* 1. intestines, guts. 2. inward parts, as *the bowels of the earth.* 3. feelings, as *bowels of compassion*

bow'er *n.* 1. a shady nook. 2. a lady's room

bow'ie-knife (bō'i-nīf) *n.* a long hunting-knife.—**bow'ie-knives** *pl.*

bowl (bōl) 1. a basin. 2. a hollow part, as *bowl of a pipe*

bowl (bōl) *n.* a wooden ball.—*v.* to roll or pitch a ball.—**bow'ler** *n.* 1. person who bowls. 2. stiff felt hat (called a derby in U.S.)—**bowls** *n.pl.* game played on a covered *bowling-alley* in which skittles are knocked down, or with wooden balls on a grass *bowling-green*
Compare: throw, toss, hurl, sling

box *n.* 1. a case. 2. a tree giving hard wood. 3. a small country-house, as *shooting-box.* 4. a driver's seat. 5. seat overlooking stage. —*v.* to put in a box.—**box' of'fice** *n.* place for booking seats.—**box-car** *n.* (N. Amer.) a closed railway truck.—**to box the compass** to name the 32 points of the compass in order

box *n.* 1. a blow (see **blow**). 2. a present, gift, as in *Christmas-box, Boxing-Day.*—*v.* to fight with fists, esp. with padded gloves. —**box'er** *n.*—**boxing** *n.*—**box'ing ring** square area bounded by ropes in which boxing matches take place

boy *n.* 1. a male child, lad. 2. a native servant. —**girl** *fem.*—**boy'hood** *n.*—**boy'ish** *adj.*—**boy'ishly** *adv.*—**Boys' Brigade** an organisation founded by Sir Wm. A. Smith in 1883 for furthering good citizenship among boys

boy'cott *v.* to join in refusing to have anything to do with a person.—**boy'cotting** *pres. part.*—**boy'cotted** *p.t.* and *p. part.*—*n.*

brace (brās) *n.* 1. a clasp, clamp. 2. a pair, as *a brace of pheasants.* 3. a support. 4. a carpenter's tool.—*pl.* trouser-suspenders. —*v.* to support, make firm, as *He braced himself up to meet the attack.*—**bra'cing** *pres. part.*—**braced** *p.t.* and *p. part.*—**bra'cing** *adj.* invigorating

brace'let (brā'slet) *n.* an ornament for the arm

brack'en *n.* fern

brack'et *n.* 1. a support for a shelf. 2. the marks ( ) used to enclose words.—*v.* 1. to enclose in brackets. 2. couple together

brack'ish *adj.* rather salty (usually referring to water)

bract *n.* a small leaf

brad *n.* small nail.—**brad'awl** *n.* a tool to pierce holes

brag *v.* to talk in a conceited or blustering

way, vaunt oneself, boast.—**brag'ging** *pres. part.*—**bragged** *p.t.* and *p. part.*—**brag'gart** *n.* a boaster

Brah'min *n.* a high-caste Hindu or Hindu priest

braid *v.* 1. to plait. 2. to trim with braid.—*n.*

braille (brāl) *n.* a system of printing books for the blind, with raised dots instead of letters

brain *n.* 1. a nerve-tissue in the skull. 2. intellect.—**brain'y** *adj.*—**brain'less** *adj.*—*v.* to knock out the brains of.—**brain'storm** *n.* a disturbance of the mind.—**Brains Trust** *n.* a panel of experts who answer questions before an audience.—**brain'wave** *n.* a bright idea.—**to brain-wash** to clear the mind of ideas and beliefs and replace them with others by psychological pressure

braise (brāz) *v.* to cook slowly in a covered pan.—**brais'ing** *pres. part.*—**braised** *p.t.* and *p. part.*

brake *n.* a thick growth of bushes, thicket

brake *n.* an instrument for checking speed of a vehicle.—*v.* to apply a brake.—**bra'king** *pres. part.*—**braked** *p.t.* and *p. part.*

bram'ble *n.* the blackberry

bran *n.* sifted husk of corn

branch *n.* 1. a limb of a tree. 2. a division, department, as *Chemistry is a branch of science; He is manager of our London branch.*—**branch'es** *pl.*—*v.* to divide

brand *n.* 1. a burning piece of wood. 2. a mark made by hot iron. 3. a class of goods, trade-mark.—*v.* to mark, as cattle.—**brand-new'** *adj.* completely new.—**fire-brand** *n.* figuratively, stirrer-up of trouble, extremist

bran'dish *v.* to wave about, as *He brandished a sword.*—he **bran'dishes**

bran'dy *n.* a strong drink made from wine.—**bran'dies** *pl.*

brash *adj.* rash, impudent, tactless

brass *n.* a mixture of copper and zinc.—**brass'y** *adj.* vulgarly showy in dress and behaviour.—**brass'y** *n.* a golf club.—**brass-band** a group of musicians playing brass instruments.—**brass tacks** fundamentals

brat *n.* a child, used contemptuously

brava'do (bra-vah'dō) *n.* a show of boldness

Compare: arrogance, swagger, boastfulness

brave *adj.* 1. bold, fearless. 2. splendid, as *The Guards made a brave show in their gold-laced coats.*—*n.* Red Indian warrior.—*v.* to defy.—**brave'ly** *adv.*—**bra'very** *n.*

Compare: adventurous, bold, courageous, daring, fearless, valiant, gallant, heroic, intrepid, stout-hearted. *Contrast:* cowardly, craven, fearful, frightened, timid, timorous, faint-hearted

The *adventurous* and *daring* seek danger. The *bold* and *fearless* disregard it. The *intrepid* man does not know of the existence of fear. The *stout-hearted* man and the *bold* run risks for the sake of their duty or principles. *Valiant* is usually applied to warriors. The bravery of the *gallant* man is of the dashing kind, that of the *courageous* man steady and lasting. *Heroic* is a term of high praise

bravo' *interj.* well done.—*n.* a ruffian

brawl *n.* a noisy quarrel.—*v.*

brawn *n.* 1. muscle, strength. 2. potted meat.—**brawn'y** *adj.* strong

bray *n.* the donkey's cry.—*v.*

braze *v.* to solder with alloy of brass

bra'zen *adj.* 1. like brass. 2. shameless, as *a brazen hussy.*—*v.* as *He tried to brazen it out by the most bare-faced lies*

bra'zier *n.* a pan for burning charcoal

Brazil' *n.* a country of South America.—**Brazil'ian** *n.* an inhabitant of Brazil.—*adj.*

breach (breech) 1. a gap, as *a breach in our defences.* 2. a breaking, as *breach of discipline, breach of promise.* 3. neglect, as *a breach of duty.* 4. a quarrel.—*v.* to make a gap

bread *n.* 1. food made of flour or meal baked. 2. food, living.—**bread-winner** *n.* the member of a family who earns money.—**to know on which side one's bread is buttered** to know where one's own interest lies.—**on the breadline** very poor

breadth *n.* width

break (brāk) *v.* 1. to fall apart. 2. to crush, destroy. 3. to fail to keep, as *to break a promise.* 4. to collapse. 5. to appear.—**broke** *p.t.*—**bro'ken** *p. part.*—*n.* gap, interruption.—**break'able** *adj.*—**break'age** *n.*—**break'down** *n.* collapse.—**break'fast** (brek-) *n.* the first meal of the day.—**break'er** *n.* large wave.—**break of day** dawn.—**to break cover** to come out into the open.—**to break in** to train.—**to break into** to enter by force.—**to break loose** to escape from captivity.—**to break off** to end abruptly.—**to break out** to force a way out; to spread.—**to break up** to destroy, to end.—**to break the back of a task** to get through most of it.—**to break the ice** to overcome first shyness.—**to break with** to quarrel with, to separate from

Compare: smash, shatter, split, fracture. *Contrast:* mend, join, repair

Smash and *shatter* denote very severe breakage, whereas *fracture* is usually applied to the breaking of a bone. *Split* means break from the top downwards

Note: The noun *break* has several meanings peculiar to sport. In pool the *break* is the first shot; in billiards it means the number of points scored by a player in one turn; in cricket or baseball it means the ball turning when bowled. In U.S. *break* means chance or opportunity, as *a lucky break*, and it may mean a blunder, as *to make a bad break*

break'water *n.* a barrier to break the force of the waves

bream (breem) *n.* a fresh-water fish

breast (brest) *n.* the front top part of the body.—*v.* to face, mount.—**breast'-plate** *n.* a metal covering to defend the breast.—**breast'work** *n.* fortification.—**to make a clean breast of it** to confess everything

breath (breth) *n.* 1. air taken into and expelled from lungs. 2. life.—**breath'less** *adj.* out of breath.—**to take one's breath away** to startle one

breathe (breTHe) *v.* 1. to take in and expel air from the lungs. 2. to speak softly.—**breath'ing** *pres. part.*—**breathed** *p.t.* and *p. part.*—**breath'ing** *n.*—**breath'ing-space** *n.* a short pause.—**breath'er** *n.* a short period of rest.—**to breath again** to feel relief.—**to breathe freely** to feel safe from danger

breech *n.* the back end of a gun.—**breech'es** *n.pl.* trousers.—**breech'es-buoy** *n.* a life-buoy with canvas breeches

breed *v.* 1. to produce young, as *Penguins breed on the island.* 2. to rear, as *He breeds prize rabbits.*—**bred,** *p.t.* and *p. part.*—*n.* 1. young. 2. race, kind.—**breed'ing** *n.*—**well-bred** *adj.* well-mannered.—**breed'er** *n.* an apparatus for producing quantities of radioactive material

breeze *n.* a gentle wind.—**breez'y** *adj.*—**breez'ily** *adv.*

bren'-gun *n.* a light machine gun

brethren (breTH'ren) *pl.* of **brother**

brev'iary *n.* a Roman Catholic prayer book.—**brev'iaries** *pl.*

brev'ity *n.* shortness

brew (broo) *v.* 1. to make a drink. 2. to plot. 3. to be gathering, as *a storm is brewing.*—**brew'er** *n.*—**brew'ery** *n.* where liquor is made

bri'ar, brier *n.* a wild rose-bush

bribe *n.* something promised or given to persuade someone to do wrong or what they would not do otherwise.—*v.*—**bri'bing** *pres. part.*—**bribed** *p.t.* and *p. part.*—**bri'bery** *n.*

brick *n.* a long block of hardened clay.—*v.* to pave with bricks.—**brick'kiln** *n.* where bricks are baked.—**brick'-layer** *n.*—**to drop a brick** to make a tactless mistake

bri'dal (brī'dal) *n.* a wedding.—*adj.*—**bride** *n.* a woman on her wedding-day.—**bride'-groom** *n.* a man on his wedding-day.—**brides'maid** *n.* an attendant on a bride

bridge (brij) *n.* 1. a way built over a river, etc. 2. an officer's platform on a ship. 3. an upper part of nose. 4. a card game.—*v.* to build a bridge, span.—**bridge'head** (in war) an advanced position from which further attacks can be made

bri'dle (brī'del) *n.* a rein and bit to control a horse.—*v.* 1. to put bridle on. 2. to control, check, as *You must learn to bridle your passions.*—**bri'dle-path** *n.* a path just wide enough for a horse to be led

brief (breef) *adj.* short.—*n.* a summary of a law case.—*v.* (military and legal) to give detailed instructions to.—**brief'-case** *n.* a leather case for holding documents.—**in brief** in a few words

Compare: concise, terse, compact. *Contrast:* long, lengthy, protracted

briefs *n.pl.* very short underpants

brig *n.* a two-masted square-rigged ship.—**brig'antine** (-tin or -teen) *n.* same as a brig, but with square sails only on the foremast

brigade' *n.* two or more regiments under a general.—**brigadier'** *n.* a brigade-commander

bri'gand *n.* a robber. See **bandit.**—**brig'andage** *n.*

bright (brīt) *adj.* 1. shining, as *a bright light.* 2. cheerful, as *bright weather, a bright church service.* 3. clever, as *a bright pupil.* 4. vivid, as *bright blue in colour.*—**bright'en** *v.* to grow or make brighter.—**bright'ly** *adv.*—**bright'ness** *n.*

brill'iant *adj.* 1. very bright. 2. very clever, as *a brilliant scholar.* 3. splendid, as *a brilliant victory.*—**brill'iance** *n.*

brim *n.* a margin, edge.—*v.* to be full.—**brim'ming** *pres. part.*—**brim'ming** *adj.*—**brim'ful** *adj.*

brim'stone *n.* sulphur

brin'dled *adj.* spotted and streaked, as *a brindled bulldog*

brine *n.* salt water.—**bri'ny** *adj.*

bring *v.* to fetch, convey.—**brought** *p.t.* and *p. part.*—**bring about** cause.—**bring forth** produce.—**bring off** carry out with success.—**bring round, bring to** bring back to consciousness.—**bring up** 1. to raise, educate. 2. to be sick. 3. to introduce a matter for discussion.—**bring to book** to bring to justice

brink (bringk) *n.* the edge of a steep place

Bri-ny'lon *n.* (trade-name) an artificial man-made fibre

brisk *adj.* quick, active. See **active, alert.**—**brisk'ly** *adv.*

bris'tle (bris'l) *n.* short, stiff hair.—*v.* to stand on end (of hair).—**brist'ling** (bris'ling) *pres. part.*—**brist'led** *p.t.* and *p. part.*

Brit'ain *n.* Great Britain, including England, Scotland and Wales.—**Brit'ish** *adj.* concerning Britain or the Commonwealth.—**Brit'on** *n.* a native of Great Britain

brit'tle *adj.* easily broken, as *Dry twigs are brittle*

Compare: fragile, delicate, frail. *Contrast:* tough, flexible, supple

broach *n.* a spit for roasting.—*v.* to pierce, open, as *to broach a barrel, to broach a subject*

broad (brawd) *adj.* 1. wide, ample, as *a broad highway.* 2. open, plain, as *broad daylight, a broad hint.* 3. general, as *The broad facts are as follows.* 4. with a marked local dialect, as *His accent is very broad.*—**broad'ly**

adv.—**broad-ar'row** *n.* government mark.—**broad'cast** *n.* the sending out by radio of messages and entertainment.—*v.* to send out by radio.—**broad'en** *v.* to grow broad.—**broad'cloth** *n.* cloth with smooth finish.—**broad'mind'ed** *adj.* tolerant.—**broad'side** *n.* discharge of all guns on one side of ship.—**broad'sword** *n.* sword with broad blade.—**broad-min'ded** *adj* understanding, liberal.—**as broad as it is long** as much can be said for it as against it

brocade' *n.* figured silk or velvet

broc'coli *n.* kind of cabbage

brogue (brōg) *n.* stout shoe

brogue (brōg) *n.* broad accent (usually Irish)

broil *v.* to cook over a hot fire.—**broil'er** *n.* a small chicken reared in a confined space for eating

broke *p.t.* of **break**—without money.—**bro'ken** *p. part.* of **break.**—**brok'en-heart'ed** grief-stricken

bro'ker *n.* person who buys and sells for others, as *stockbroker, insurance-broker, metal-broker*.—**bro'kerage** *n.* payment to a broker

bro'mide *n.* (chemistry) a compound of bromine

bro'mine (brō'meen) *n.* a poisonous liquid element

bronchi'tis (bron-kī'tis) *n.* inflammation in the tubes of the wind-pipe

bron'co, bron'cho *n.* (N. Amer.) a half-tamed horse.—**bron'cos** *pl.*—**bron'co-buster** *n.* one who breaks in broncos

bronze *n.* alloy of copper and tin.—**bronzed** *adj.* 1. coated with bronze. 2. sunburnt.—**Bronze Age** the prehistoric period when bronze was used for weapons and tools

brooch (brōch) *n.* ornamental pin

brood (brōōd) *n.* a family of young.—*v.* 1. to sit, as a bird on its nest. 2. to meditate in a worried way, as *He brooded over his troubles*.—**broo'dy** *adj.*

brook *n.* small stream.—**brook'let** *n.* a very small stream

brook *v.* to endure, as *I will not brook such insults*

broom *n.* 1. yellow-flowering shrub. 2. brush for sweeping.—**broom'stick** *n.*

broth *n.* soup of meat and vegetables

broth'er (bru'THer) *n.* son of the same parents.—**broth'ers** or **breth'ren,** *pl.*—**sister,** *fem.*—**broth'erhood** *n.* a society of men—*sisterhood fem.*—**broth'er-in-law** *n.* wife's or husband's brother, sister's or **sister-in-law's** husband

brought (brawt) *p.t.* and *p. part.* of bring

brow *n.* 1. forehead, eyebrow. 2. the edge of a hill.—**brow'beat** *v.* to bully

brown *adj.* of the colour of toast, etc.—*n.* the colour.—*v.* to make or become brown.—**brow'nie** *n.* 1. elf, fairy. 2. junior Girl Guide.—**brown-stud'y** *n.* a day-dream

browse *v.* to feed on grass or leaves

bruise (brōōz) *v.* to hurt without breaking the skin.—**brui'sing** *pres. part.*—**bruised** *p.t.* and *p. part.*

brunette' (brōō-net') *n.* a woman with a dark skin, hair, etc.

Contrast: blonde

brunt *n.* the hardest part, chief strain, as *The rearguard bore the brunt of the enemy's onslaught*

brush' *n.* 1. bristle or hair attached to a handle and used for sweeping, painting, etc. 2. a short fight (see **skirmish**). 3. a bushy tail, as *a fox's brush*.—*v.* 1. to sweep or clean. 2. to touch lightly.—**to brush aside** to ignore, to set aside angrily.—**to brush up** to clean up, to renew knowledge of

brush'wood *n.* undergrowth

brusque (brusk or brōōsk) *adj.* curt

Compare: blunt, offhand, rude. *Contrast:* polite, gracious, ingratiating

brussels sprouts' *n.pl.* vegetables like very small cabbages growing several on one stalk

brute (brōōt) *n.* 1. one of the lower animals. 2. stupid, cruel person. See **beast.**—**bru'tal** *adj.* cruel.—**bru'tally** *adv.*—**brutal'ity** *n.*

bub'ble *n.* a globe of liquid full of air.—*v.* 1. to form a bubble. 2. to be **bubbling with joy.**—**bub'bling** *pres. part.*

buccaneer' *n.* pirate

buck *n.* male rabbit, hare, deer, etc.—*doe, fem.* 2. (S.A.) any one of various kinds of antelope.—**buck'skin** *n.* leather from deer.—**buck'wagon** *n.* in South Africa, cart drawn by oxen.—**buck** *v.* to try to throw the rider by springing in the air, as a horse or bronco.—**buck'jumper** *n.* (Aus.) 1. a horse that bucks. 2. a person who can ride a bucking horse

buck'et *n.* a large metal vessel for water, a pail

buck'le *n.* a metal clasp.—*v.* 1. to fasten; 2. to bend, as *The wheel of the bicycle was buckled*.—**buck'ler** *n.* a shield

buck'ram *n.* a coarse stiffened cloth

buck'shot *n.* large shot for hunting game

buck'wheat *n.* (N. Amer.) 1. a cereal. 2. meal or flour made from buckwheat

bud *n.* an undeveloped shoot.—*v.* 1. to show buds. 2. to graft.—**bud'ding** *pres. part.*—**bud'ded** *p.t.* and *p. part.*

Bud'dhism *n.* the religion founded in India by Buddha.—**Bud'dhist** *n.* a follower of Buddha.—*adj.*

budge (buj) *v.* to move.—**bud'ging** *pres. part.*—**budged** *p.t.* and *p. part.*

budg'erigar *n.* a small Australian parakeet

budget (buj'et) *n.* 1. a yearly estimate of expenditure. 2. a collection, mass, as of news or letters

buff *n.* a dull yellow

buff'alo *n.* a kind of wild ox, the American bison.—**buff'aloes,** or **buffalo** *pl.*

buff'er *n.* a device to lessen shock of collision

buff'et *n.* a blow, slap.—*v.* to strike, as *The ship was buffeted by the winds and waves*

buff'et (boo'fā) *n.* 1. a refreshment bar. 2. table laid with food from which people can help themselves
buffoon' *n.* a clown, fool.—**buffoon'ery** *n.* jesting
bug *n.* a small blood-sucking insect.—**bug'-bear** *n.* object of dislike
bug'gy *n.* a light four-wheeled carriage drawn by a horse, once used in the United States
bu'gle (bū'gl) *n.* 1. an instrument blown by a person. 2. a glass bead used as ornament on a dress.—**bu'gler** *n.*
build (bild) *v.* to construct, as a house, etc.—**built** *p.t.* and *p. part.*—*n.* make, form.—**build'er** *n.*—**build'ing** *n.*—**buil'ding society** *n.* a firm which lends money for people to buy or build houses
Compare: erect, compose. *Contrast:* destroy, wreck, smash
bulb *n.* 1. a rounded underground bud for storing food. 2. an onion-shaped globe.—**bulbous** *adj.* bulb-shaped
bulge (bulj) *v.* to swell out.—**bulg'ing** *pres. part.*—**bulged** *p.t.* and *p. part.*—*n.*—**bul'gy** *adj.*
bulk *n.* 1. size, as *The first thing that strikes us about an elephant is its great bulk* 2. the greater part, as *He left the bulk of his money to his children.*—**bul'ky** *adj.*
bull *n.* 1. a male ox, elephant or other large animal (*cow, fem.*).—**bull'ock** *n.* a young bull.—**like a bull in a china shop** clumsy, tactless.—**to take the bull by the horns** to attack fearlessly.—**bull'-dog** *n.* heavy breed of dog
bull *n.* an order from the Pope
bull'dozer *n.* a powerful machine for levelling rough ground
bull'et *n.* a piece of lead to be shot from a gun
bull'etin *n.* an official report
bull'ion *n.* gold or silver in bars
bull's-eye *n.* 1. the centre of a target. 2. a small portable lantern. 3. a sweet
bul'ly *n.* a person who frightens and threatens the weaker ones.—**bullies** *pl.*—**bully-off** *n.* starting a hockey match by crossing sticks three times over the ball
bul'ly beef *n* tinned corned beef
bul'rush *n.* a rush growing in water
bul'wark *n.* 1. the raised side of a ship. 2. a rampart
bum'ble-bee *n.* a large bee
bump *n.* 1. a dull, heavy blow. 2. a bruise or swelling.—*v.* to strike against
Compare: thump, bang, crash
bum'per *n.* 1. a full glass. 2. a device to protect a car in collisions.—*adj.* specially good, as *There was a bumper crop of apples that year*
bump'kin *n.* a clumsy country fellow
Compare: yokel, rustic, clown
bump'tious (bump'shus) *adj.* conceited.—**bump'tiousness** *n.*
bun *n.* a small sweet cake
bunch *n.* a number of things tied, growing, or collected together, as *a bunch of flowers, bunch of keys.*—**bunch'es** *pl.*—*v.* to put together, huddle
bun'dle *n.* a number of things tied up together.—*v.* 1. to tie together. 2. to send away hurriedly, as *He was bundled out of the house and into the waiting carriage.*—**bund'ling** *pres. part.*—**bund'led** *p.t.* and *p. part.*
bung *n.* a large cork to plug a hole in a cask.—**bung'hole** *n.*
bung'alow (bung'ga-lo) a one-storied house
bung'le *v.* to blunder, to manage awkwardly, as *He was nervous and bungled the job.*—*n.* something clumsily done.—**bung'ling** *pres. part.*—**bung'led** *p.t.* and *p. part.*—**bung'ler** *n.*
bun'ion *n.* the swelling on the foot
bunk (bungk) *n.* a narrow sleeping place, usually on the wall of a ship or train
bunk'er (bungk'er) *n.* 1. a coal-bin on a ship. 2. a sandy hollow on a golf-course
bun'sen burner *n.* a gas burner with a variable flame, widely used in science
bun'ting *n.* 1. material for flags. 2. a bird
buoy (boi) *n.* 1. a floating mark to guide ships. 2. something to keep a person afloat (life-buoy).—*v.* to keep from sinking, support.—**buoy'ancy** *n.*—**buoy'ant** *adj.* floating; light-hearted
bur, burr *n.* prickly head of a plant
bur'den, bur'then (-TH') *n.* 1. a load, weight, as *a heavy burden, a ship of* 1000 *tons burden.* 2. the theme of a song. 3. something hard to bear.—*v.* to load.—**bur'densome** *adj.*
bureau' (bū-rō') 1. a writing-desk. 2. a business office.—**bureaux** *pl.*—**bureau'cracy** (bū-rok'rasi) *n.* government by officials.—**bur'eaucrat** *n.*
burette' *n.* a tall thin glass vessel, marked with a scale, for measuring liquids
bur'gess (bur'jes) *n.* a citizen or freeman.—**bur'gesses** *pl.*
burgh (bur'ah) *n.* a Scottish town having a charter
bur'gher (bur'ger) *n.* a citizen of a burgh or borough
bur'glar *n.* a person who breaks into a house.—**burgla'rious** (bur-glā'ri-ous) *adj.*—**bur'glary** *n.*
bur'gomaster *n.* a mayor in the Netherlands
bur'ial (ber'i-el) *n.* putting into the earth, esp. a grave.—*adj.*—**bur'ial-ground** *n.* a cemetery
burlesque' (burlesk') *n.* a laughable imitation.—*v.*
Compare: parody, caricature. A *burlesque* is usually a stage performance, whereas a parody is usually an exaggerated imitation of someone else's work in literature, and a caricature is usually a comic drawing which exaggerates a person's chief characteristics

bur'ly *adj.* big and strong.—**bur'lier** *comp.*—**bur'liest** *sup.*
Compare: sturdy, stalwart, bulky, massive. *Contrast:* puny, undersized, feeble, slight

Bur'ma *n.* a country of South-east Asia.—**Bur'mese** *n.* a native of Burma.—*adj.*

burn *v.* 1. to destroy or injure by fire. 2. to be on fire; figuratively, as *to burn with indignation.*—**burned** or **burnt** *p.t.* and *p. part.*—*n.* injury by fire.—**a burning question** a matter of urgency and interest.—**money burns a hole in one's pocket** one cannot resist spending.—**to burn the candle at both ends** to work night and day.—**to burn one's fingers** to harm oneself by meddling.—**to burn one's boats** to cut off one's retreat and venture everything on success
Note: We *burn* rubbish *with* fire and a house is *burned by* fire. The premises are *burned down.* The coal on the fire *burns away*

burn *n.* in Scotland, a brook

bur'nish *v.* to polish

bur'row *n.* a hole of rabbits, etc.—*v.* to dig down

bur'sar *n.* 1. the treasurer of a college. 2. a scholar receiving a grant or **bur'sary**

burst *v.* 1. to fall apart. 2. to break into pieces. 3. to break out.—**burst** *p.t.* and *p. part.*—*n.* an explosion, outbreak

bur'y (ber'i) *v.* 1. to put underground. 2. to hide, as *She buried her face in her hands.* 3. to put in a grave.—**he buries.**—**bur'ying** *pres. part.*—**bur'ied** *p.t.* and *p. part.*—**to bury the hatchet** to make peace

bus *n.* a motor-vehicle carrying passengers.—**a busman's holiday** a holiday spent in or near one's work.—**to miss the bus** to miss an opportunity

bus'by (buz'bi) *n.* fur hat worn by hussars.—**bus'bies** *pl.*

bush (boosh) *n.* 1. a small shrub. 2. uncleared land, outback as opposed to city in Australia and Africa. 3. (N.Z.) forestland.—**bush'y** *adj.* growing densely, as *a bushy beard.*—**bush'ranger** *n.* Australian highwayman.—**bush-telegraph** a rapid spread of news.—**to beat about the bush** to talk round a matter without touching the main point

bush'el *n.* a dry measure of 8 gallons

bush'man *n.* 1. a native of S. Africa, almost extinct. 2. an Australian who lives in the bush

bus'iness (biz'ness) *n.* 1. an occupation, trade, affairs, as *He had a good business.* 2. concern, as *It is no business of yours.*—**bus'iness-like**, efficient, practical
Compare: calling, avocation, commerce, industry, pursuit, occupation. *Contrast:* leisure, pleasure, idleness, relaxation

bus'kin *n.* a high boot, esp. that worn by tragic actors in Ancient Greece

bust *n.* 1. the upper part of the body. 2. a statue of person's head and shoulders

bus'tard *n.* a large water-bird

bus'tle (busl) *n.* hurry, stir.—*v.* to move busily.—**bus'tling** *pres. part.*—**bus'tled** *p.t.* and *p. part.*

bus'y (biz'i) *adj.* active, having much to do.—**bus'ier** *comp.*—**bus'iest** *sup.*—*v.* to occupy.—**bus'ied** *p.t.* and *p. part.*—**bus'ily** *adv.*—**bus'ybody** *n.* meddler
Compare: industrious, occupied, engaged. *Contrast:* idle, leisured, inactive, disengaged

but 1. *conj.* still, yet, besides, as *She came but did not stay. He is poor but honest.* 2. *adv.* only, except, as *He is but five years old. She does nothing but play all day long.* 3. *prep.* except, as *The teacher asked everyone but me*

bu'tane *n.* an inflammable gas used in some cigarette lighters

but'cher (boo'cher) *n.* 1. one who sells meat. 2. a savage man.—*v.* to slaughter.—**but'chery** *n.*

but'ler *n.* a head manservant, in charge of wine-cellar and silver

butt *n.* a large cask

butt *n.* 1. a target. 2. an object of ridicule

butt *n.* the thick end

butt *v.* to push with the head.—*n.*

but'ter *n.* fat obtained from cream by churning.—*v.* to spread with butter.—**but'tercup** *n.* a bright yellow field-flower.—**but'ter-milk** *n.* milk left after churning.—**but'tery** *n.* a place (usually in a college) where food and drink are stored or served.—**but'ter-fingered** *adj.* liable to miss a catch

but'terfly *n.* an insect with brightly-coloured wings.—**but'terflies** *pl.*

but'tock *n.* the rump

but'ton *n.* a knob or stud esp. for fastening dress.—*v.* to fasten with buttons.—**but'tonhole** *n.*—**but'tonhook** *n.*—**to buttonhole someone** to hold him in conversation against his will

but'tress *n.* a prop to support a wall.—*v.*

bux'om *adj.* plump

buy (bī) *v.* to obtain by payment.—**bought** (bawt) *p.t.* and *p. part.*—**buy'er** *n.*—**to buy off** to pay someone to be rid of a claim of his.—**to buy out** to buy all of someone's goods.—**to buy over** to bribe.—**to buy up** to buy all
Compare: purchase, procure, acquire. *Contrast:* sell, dispose of

buzz *n.* a humming sound.—*v.* to hum.—**buz'zer** *n.* a factory steam-whistle

buz'zard *n.* a bird of prey

by 1. *prep.* near, beside, with, through, as *We learn by our mistakes. He stood by me.* 2. *adv.* near, beside, as *to stand by*, to *pass by.* 3. at the beginning of a word, *by* often means not so important, as in **by-way**; at the side, as in **by-stander**; subordinate, not principal, as in **by-product, by-play.**—**by-and-by** soon.—**by and large** on the whole

by, bye *n.* 1. in cricket, a run scored off a ball which passes the bat untouched. 2. in sport, the state of not having an opponent, as *He drew a bye in the first round*

by'election (bī'el-ek'-shun) *n.* a parliamentary election between general elections
Contrast: general election

by'gone *adj.* past.—**let bygones be bygones** forget all that has happened

by'law, bye'law *n.* a law made by a city, etc.

by'-pass *n.* a road for diversion of traffic

by'-product *n.* a secondary product in the manufacture of a main article

byre *n.* a cow-house

by'word *n.* 1. a common saying. 2. an object of ridicule

C

cab *n.* 1. a carriage for hire. 2. a driver's place on a locomotive, etc.

cabal' *n.* 1. a secret plot. 2. a group of plotters
Compare: conspiracy, faction, intrigue, clique, junto

cab'aret (kab'a-rā) *n.* variety entertainment in a restaurant

cab'bage *n.* a vegetable having a round head of leaves, usually green

ca'ber (kā'ber) *n.* a pole tossed by competitors in highland games

cab'in *n.* 1. a small hut. 2. a small room in a ship or aeroplane.—**cab'ined** *adj.* shut up in a small space.—**cab'in-boy** *n.* one waiting on ship's officers or passengers

cab'inet *n.* 1. a case of drawers, as a *filing-cabinet.* 2. a cupboard with shelves, as *a china-cabinet.* 3. a small room. 4. a committee of chief ministers of Government.—**cab'inet-maker** *n.* a craftsman who makes furniture

ca'ble *n.* 1. a strong rope, often of wire. 2. a telegraph line under the sea. 3. message sent by this line.—*v.* to send a message by cable.—**ca'bling** *p. part.*—**ca'blegram** *n.* a cabled message

caboose' *n.* 1. a ship's kitchen or galley. 2. a workmen's van at the end of a North American freight train

caca'o (kakā'ō) *n.* a C. American tree from whose seeds cocoa and chocolate are made

cache (kash) *n.* 1. a hiding-place. 2. the material hidden

cack'le *v.* and *n.* to chatter, as a hen, cluck, chuckle.—**cack'ling** *pres. part.*

cad'die *n.* a golfer's club-carrier.—*v.* act as a caddie.—**cad'dying** *pres. part.*—**cad'die-car** *n.* a small wheeled golf-club carrier

cad'dy *n.* a small tea-box.—**cad'dies** *pl.*

cadet' *n.* 1. a student in naval or military college. 2. a younger son or brother

cadge (kaj) *v.* 1. to hawk goods. 2. to beg or sponge.—**cadg'ing** *pres. part.*—**cadg'er** *n.*

cad'mium *n.* a silvery metallic element

café' (kaf'ā) *n.* a tea-shop, restaurant.—**cafete'ria** *n.* a restaurant where customers wait on themselves

caff'eine (kaf'een) *n.* a chemical present in tea and coffee, which acts as a stimulant

cage (kāj) *n.* 1. a prison made of wire and bars, for birds or animals. 2. a lift in a mine.—*v.* put or keep in a cage.—**ca'ging** *pres. part.*—**ca'gey** *adj.* cautious

cairn *n.* a pile of stones used as a landmark

cajole' (kaj-ōl') *v.* to persuade by flattery.—**cajol'ing** *pres. part.*—**cajol'ery** *n.*—**cajol'eries** *pl.*

cake *n.* 1. a mixture of flour, eggs, etc., baked or fried. 2. a flat, hard mass, as *a cake of soap.*—*v.* to form into a mass, as *His clothes were caked with mud*

calam'ity *n.* disaster.—**calam'ities** *pl.*—**calam'itous** *adj.*
Compare: misfortune, catastrophe, accident. An *accident* is a calamity if its results are very serious. A motor accident in which the Prime Minister was killed would be a calamity. A *catastrophe* is a very great calamity with results which cannot be mended. The burning of the Guildhall, London, was a catastrophe, of war. Sudden and great *misfortune,* such as the loss of a limb, is also a calamity

calca'reous (kal-kā'ri-us) *adj.* made of lime

cal'cium (kal'si-um) *n.* a soft metal, found in chalk, marble, bone and lime

cal'culate (kal'ku-lāt) *v.* to reckon up, count.—**cal'culating** *adj.* scheming.—**calcula'tion** *n,*—**cal'culable** *adj.* capable of being estimated or measured

cal'culus *n.* a branch of mathematics

cal'endar *n.* 1. a table of months, weeks and days in a year. 2. a register

calf (kahf) *n.* 1. the young of cow, elephant, whale, etc. 2. calf-skin.—**calves** *pl.*

calf (kahf) *n.* the fleshy back part of the human leg below the knee.—**calves** *pl.*

cal'ibrate *n.* to mark the scale on a measuring instrument

cal'ibre (kal'iber) *n.* 1. the inside diameter of a gun-barrel. 2. ability, as *a man of great calibre*

cal'ico *n.* and *adj.* cotton cloth.—**cal'icoes cal'icos** *pl.*

ca'liph, ca'lif (ka'lif, kā'lif) *n.* a title of rulers who succeeded Mohammed, esp. in Turkey

call (kawl) *v.* and *n.* 1. to shout, cry out, as *He called for help.* 2. to awaken, as *Call me early.* 3. to summon, as *He called his dog.* 4. to visit, as *to pay a call on someone.* 5. to name, as *a boy called Tom.*—**call'er** *n.* one who calls.—**call'ing** *n.* a trade, profession.—**a close call** a narrow escape.—**call-box** a telephone booth.—**to call in question** to cast doubt on.—**to call off** to cancel.—**to call to mind** to remember.—**to call to the bar** to admit as a barrister

Note: The meaning of this word is altered by the prepositions used with it. Thus **call for** means to require, as *This calls for an answer*; *call forth*, produce; *call off*, cancel; *call on*, visit; invite as *He called on me for help*; *call up*, to summon for service esp. military; recall

call'ipers, cal'ipers *n.pl.* an instrument for measuring the width or thickness of something

cal'lous (kal'us) *adj.* hard, unfeeling

Compare: cruel, unsympathetic, insensitive. *Contrast:* tender, sympathetic, considerate

calm (kahm) *n.* 1. stillness. 2. absence of wind. 3. composure.—*v.* to make calm, become calm.—*adj.* still, composed.—**calm'ly** *adv.*—**calm'ness** *n.*—**to calm down** to make, or become calm

Compare with adj.: unruffled, smooth, placid. *Contrast:* excited, turbulent, stormy

cal'orie, cal'ory *n.* 1. one unit of heat. The amount of heat required to raise the temperature of one gramme of water one degree Centigrade. 2. a large calorie, a unit of one thousand calories, used as a unit of the energy value of foods.—**calorif'ic** *adj.* heat-making

calorim'eter *n.* a copper vessel used in experiments concerning the measurement of heat

cal'umny (kal'umi) *n.* malicious slander

calve (kahv) *v.* to give birth to a calf.—**calves** (kahvz) *n.pl.* the plural of calf

calyp'so *n.* type of song popular in the W. Indies, topical and improvised, with a characteristic rhythm

ca'lyx (kā'liks) *n.* the outermost green cup of a flower.—**ca'lyces** (kā'li-seez) *pl.*

camara'derie (kam-ar-ah'dir-ee) *n.* good-fellowship

cam'ber *n.* a curvature of an upper surface, as of a road or aeroplane wing

cam'bium *n.* (botany) soft woody plant tissue

cam'el *n.* an animal used as beast of burden in deserts. The *Bactrian camel* has two humps; the *Arabian camel* or *dromedary*, one

cam'era *n.* apparatus for taking photographs.—**in cam'era** in private, in secret

cam'ouflage (kam'ōō-flahzh) *v.* 1. to disguise. 2. to protect guns, buildings, etc., from enemy observation.—*n.*

camp *n.* 1. ground where soldiers, scouts, etc., pitch their tents. 2. the tents of an army. 3. permanent military quarters, as at Aldershot. 4. temporary resting place for hikers, explorers, etc. 5. side, as *He belongs to the opposite camp.*—*v.* to make or live in a camp.—**camp'-bed, camp'-stool** a bed or stool that folds up

campaign' (kam-pān') *n.* 1. a series of war operations. 2. a planned attempt to gain public support, as *a publicity campaign.*—*v.* to serve in a war.—**campaign'er** (kam-pā'ner) *n.* a tried soldier

cam'phor (kam'fer) *n.* a white strong-smelling substance used in medicine.—**cam'phorated** *adj.* containing camphor

can *v.* 1. be able, as *I can spell.* 2. be allowed, as *You can go.*—thou **canst.**—**could** *p.t.*—thou **couldst**

Note: This verb has no infinitives, participles, or future tense

can *n.* a metal container.—*v.* to put or preserve in a tin.—**can'ning** *pres. part.*—**canned'** *p.t.* and *p. part.*

canal' *n.* 1. a waterway made by man. 2. a tube-like part of plant or animal body, carrying food, air, or liquid

cana'ry (kan-ā'ri) *n.* 1. a yellow singing bird. 2. a sweet wine from the Canary Islands.—**cana'ries** *pl.*—*adj.* light yellow in colour

can'cel (kan'sel) *v.* 1. to cross out, esp. by putting a line through. 2. do away with. 3. in arithmetic, to cross out a common factor from the numerator and denominator of a fraction.—**can'celling** *pres. part.*—**can'celled** *p.t.* and *p. part.*—**cancella'tion** *n.*

Compare: annul, obliterate, abolish, destroy

can'cer (kan'ser) *n.* a dangerous growth in the body.—**can'cerous** *adj.* spreading and harmful, like a cancer.—**Tropic of Cancer** the line of latitude 23½°N, which marks the sun's furthest travel north

can'did *adj.* frank, open, sincere.—**can'didly** *adv.*

Contrast: deceitful, secretive, insincere

can'didate *n.* one who seeks an appointment or privilege, as *a candidate for a scholarship.*—**can'didature** *n.* being a candidate

can'died *adj.* preserved with sugar, as **candied peel.**—*p. part.* of **candy**

can'dle *n.* 1. a stick of wax with a wick, burnt to give light. 2. anything like a candle.—**can'dle-power** *n.* a unit of light.—**can'dle-stick** *n.* a holder for a candle.—**Can'dle-mas** a Festival in the Roman Catholic Church, Feb. 2nd.—**the game is not worth the candle** the result is not worth the labour

can'dour *n.* outspokenness, honesty

can'dy *n.* crystallised sugar, sweetmeats.—**can'dies** *pl.*—*v.* to cook or coat in sugar.—**can'died** *p.t.* and *p. part.*—**can'dying** *pres. part.*

can'dytuft *n.* a plant with blue, white, or pink flowers

cane *n.* 1. stem of bamboo, etc. 2. walking-stick.—*v.* to beat.—**ca'ning** *n.* a beating with a cane.—**cane-sugar** *n.* sugar from sugar-cane

ca'nine (kā'nīn, ka'nīn) *adj.* relating to a dog.—*n.* one of the four pointed teeth

can'ister *n.* a box for holding tea, etc.

can'ker *n.* 1. disease that eats away. 2. a sore in the mouth

can'nibal *n.* 1. a person who eats human flesh. 2. an animal that eats its own kind.—**can'nibalism** *n.*

can'non *n.* a big, mounted gun.—**cannons, cannon** *pl.*.—**can'nonball** *n.* round shot.—**can'nonade** *n.* an attack with cannon

Note: The plural of *cannon* is *cannons* or *cannon,* according to the sense, as *two cannons,* but *The general believed in using cannon*

can'non *n.* a billiard stroke where one's ball hits two others successively.—*v.* 1. to make this stroke. 2. to rush into or against, as *Running out, he cannoned into his father*

can'not *v.* negative form of **can**

can'ny *adj.* 1. cautious. 2. shrewd, wise.—**can'nier** *comp.*—**can'niest** *sup.*—**can'nily** *adv.*

can'oe (kan-ōō') *n.* light boat rowed with a paddle.—**canoes'** *pl.*—**canoe'ist** *n.* one who can manage a canoe

can'on *n.* 1. clergyman attached to a cathedral. 2. a church law, rule

ca'ñon, can'yon *n.* a deep gorge

can'onise *v.* to place on the list of saints.—**can'onising** *pres. part.*—**can'onised** *p.t.* and *p. part.*—**canonisa'tion** *n.*

can'opy *n.* a roof-like cover.—**can'opies** *pl.*

cant *n.* 1. insincere talk. 2. a special kind of slang

Compare: hypocrisy, humbug, pretence

cantan'kerous *adj.* quarrelsome

canta'ta (kan-tah'ta) *n.* music for a chorus

canteen' *n.* 1. a soldier's water and food tin. 2. a shop in camp or town for soldiers. 3. a restaurant attached to a works or factory. 4. case of cutlery, etc.

can'ter *n.* an easy gallop.—*v.*

Canterbury pilgrims *n.* the first English settlers of Canterbury province, South Island, New Zealand

can'tilever *n.* a girder fixed at one end only.—**can'tilever bridge** a bridge fixed at either end, and made of cantilever girders

can'ting *adj.* whining

can'to *n.* a division of a poem.—**can'tos** *pl.*

can'ton *n.* a small division of a country

can'vas *n.* 1. coarse linen cloth. 2. the sails of a ship. 3. a painting on canvas.—**under canvas** 1. living in tents. 2. (of a boat) under sail

can'vass *v.* 1. to invite votes or custom. 2. to discuss thoroughly.—he **can'vasses**

can'yon. See **cañon**

cap *n.* 1. a close-fitting covering for the head. 2. a lid or top. 3. a cap showing that wearer has been chosen to play in a special team.—*v.* 1. to put a cap on. 2. to outdo. 3. to award a player with a cap.—**cap'ping** *pres. part.*—**capped'** *p.t.* and *p. part.*—**a feather in one's cap** something to be proud of.—**black cap** a cap worn by a judge when passing the death sentence.—**cap in hand** humbly (asking a favour).—**if the cap fits** if the remark applies

ca'pable (kā'pa-bl) *adj.* able.—**capabil'ity** *n.*—**capabil'ities** *pl.*—**capable of** as *He is quite capable of doing it,* meaning he is likely to do it, good enough or wicked enough to do it

Compare: competent, efficient, adequate. *Contrast:* incapable, inefficient, incompetent

capa'cious (kap-ā'shus) *adj.* roomy.—**capac'ity** (kap-a'si-ti) *n.* 1. room, space, as *The capacity of the tank was* 500 *gallons.* 2. ability, as *man of great capacity.* 3. position, as *He was acting in the capacity of manager.*—**capac'ities** *pl.*

Compare: spacious, wide, ample. *Contrast:* limited, narrow, restricted

cape *n.* a loose, sleeveless garment

cape *n.* land jutting out into the sea.—**cape-boy** in S. Africa, a half-caste.—**cape-cart** in S. Africa, a two-wheeled, hooded cart

capar'ison *n.* a rich covering for a horse.—*v.*

ca'per (kā'per) *v.* 1. to skip about. 2. to play the fool.—*n.* as *to cut a caper*

ca'per (kā'per) *n.* a pickled flower-bud of Sicilian shrub.—**caper-sauce'** *n.*

capill'ary *adj.* fine as a hair.—*n.* a blood vessel.—**capill'ary tube** *n.* a tube with a bore as fine as a hair.—**capillar'ity** *n.* the rise or fall of liquids in fine, hair-like tubes.—**capillar'ities**

cap'ital *adj.* 1. chief. 2. excellent.—*n.* 1. chief town. 2. head of a pillar. 3. money used for business. 4. large-sized letter.—**capital pun'ishment** punishment by death.—**cap'italist** *n.* a rich man.—**cap'italism** *n.* power and influence of the capitalist.—**to make capital out of** to take advantage of

capit'ulate *v.* to surrender on terms.—**capitula'tion** (shun) *n.*

ca'pon (kā'pon) *n.* a cock fed for the table

caprice' (kap-rees') *n.* a sudden change of mind.—**capric'ious** (kap-ri'shus) *adj.* fickle

Compare: whim, fancy, vagary, freak

Cap'ricorn *n.* the tropic, or latitude $23\frac{1}{2}$°S, which marks the sun's furthest travel south

capsize' *v.* to upset, as *A sudden squall of wind made the boat capsize.*—**capsi'zing** *pres. part.*—**capsized'** *p.t.* and *p. part.*

cap'stan *n.* a windlass, or wheel used for winding up ship's cable

cap'sule *n.* 1. a seed-case in plants. 2. a gelatine case for dose of medicine. 3. the part of a spaceship in which the astronaut is placed

cap'tain (kap'tin) *n.* 1. a leader. 2. the commander of a vessel, or of a company of soldiers.—*v.* as *to captain a team.*—**cap'taincy** *n.*

cap'tion (-shun) *n.* the title of an article, picture, etc.

cap'tious (kap'shus) *adj.* hard to please, as *a captious critic*

cap'tivate *v.* to fascinate.—**cap'tivating** *adj.*

cap'tive *n.* a prisoner.—*adj.* imprisoned.—**captiv'ity** *n.*—**cap'tor** *n.* one who holds a prisoner

cap'ture *v.* to seize, to arrest.—*n.* seizing

car *n.* 1. a wheeled vehicle. 2. a motor-car or automobile

car'amel *n.* 1. burnt sugar. 2. a kind of toffee

car'at *n.* 1. a jeweller's weight. 2. a measure used to state purity of gold

car'avan *n.* 1. a company of merchants travelling together across the desert. 2. a movable living accomodation to be drawn by horse or car.—**caravan'serai** *n.* an inn where caravans halt at night

car'away *n.* a plant with highly flavoured seeds

car'bine *n.* a short rifle.—**carabineer'** *n.* a soldier armed, with a carbine

carbohy'drate (kar-bō-hī'drāt) *n.* 1. a chemical compound of carbon, hydrogen and oxygen. 2. a foodstuff made up of these elements, such as starch or sugar

carbol'ic acid *n.* an acid made from coaltar, used for killing germs

car'bon *n.* 1. a chemical element found pure in graphite, charcoal and diamond. 2. carbon paper for copying

car'buncle *n.* 1. a red gem. 2. a large boil

carburett'or *n.* a device for mixing petrol vapour and air in an engine

car'case, car'cass *n.* a dead body

card *n.* a piece of stiff paper used as a **playing-card,** a **post-card** or a **visiting-card** etc.—**card'board** *n.* thick, stiff card.—**card-index** an index or file with each entry on a separate card.—**to put one's cards on the table** to reveal one's plans

card *n.* an instrument for combing wool.—*v.* to comb.—**car'der** *n.*

car'diac *adj.* relating to the heart

car'digan *n.* a knitted woollen jacket

car'dinal *adj.* chief.—*n.* member of the Pope's council.—**car'dinal num'bers** 1, 2, 3, etc.—**car'dinal points,** north, south, east, west

care *n.* worry, attention, having charge of.—*v.* 1. to worry about, as *He does his work badly because he does not care.* 2. to be disposed to, as *I do not care to do it.* 3. to mind or look after, as *Nurses care for the sick.* 4. to be fond of, as *We do not care for wet weather.*—**cared** *p.t.* and *p. part.*—**car'ing** *pres. part.*—**care'free** *adj.*—**care'less** *adj.*—**care'ful** *adj.*—**care'taker** *n.* a person who takes care of premises.—**care'worn** *adj.*—**to take care** to be cautious.—**to take care of** to look after.—**to care for** 1. to be fond of. 2. to tend, to look after

Compare: anxiety, solicitude, oversight, heed, caution, wariness. *Contrast:* negligence, heedlessness, disregard

Note: anxiety and *solicitude* mean *care* in the sense of worrying about someone or something. *Oversight* in this sense means the kind of *care* which involves management or control of something. *Heed* and *caution* contain the idea of looking before you leap or taking *care. Wariness* is the habit of taking *care*

careen' *v.* to turn a ship over

career' *n.* 1. a course through life. 2. a profession.—*v.* to move rapidly

caress' *v.* to touch lovingly, fondle.—*n.*

car'go *n.* a ship's load.—**car'goes** *pl.*

car'ib *n.* one of the native race found in the West Indies

car'ibou (kar'ib-oo) *n.* a North American reindeer.—**car'ibou** *pl.*

car'icature *n.* a likeness exaggerated or distorted to appear ridiculous. See **burlesque**

car'illon *n.* a peal of bells

car'mine *n.* bright crimson

car'nage *n.* slaughter

car'nal *adj.* fleshy, worldly

Compare: sensual, bodily, sinful, gross. *Contrast:* spiritual, ethereal, refined

car-na'tion (-shun) *n.* 1. a double-flowering pink. 2. rosy colour

car'nival *n.* 1. a festival just before Lent. 2. a revel

carniv'ora *n.pl.* flesh-eating animals.—**carniv'orous** *adj.*

car'ol *n.* song of joy or praise esp. about the birth of Christ.—*v.* to sing.—**car'olling** *pres. part.*—**car'olled** *p.t.* and *p. part.*—**car'oller** *n.*

carouse' (karowz') *n.* a drinking-party.—*v.*

carp *n.* a fresh-water fish

carp (at) *v.* to find fault (with).—**carp'ing** *adj.*

car'penter *n.* a man who works on timber for buildings.—**car'pentry** *n.*

Note: a carpenter works on large wooden structures, *a joiner* does lighter woodwork

car'pet *n.* a thick cloth for covering floors.—**on the carpet** 1. under consideration. 2. under reprimand.—*v.* to cover with a carpet

carpet-bag *n.* a bag made of carpet material

car'peting *n* carpet material

car'port *n.* an open-sided shelter for a motor-car, attached to a building

car'riage (kar'ij) *n.* 1. act or cost of carrying. 2. a vehicle. 3. bearing, conduct, as *He had an upright carriage.*—**carriage forward** with the cost of carriage on goods to be paid by the receiver.—**carriage paid** with the cost of carriage paid by the sender

car'rier *n.* 1. one who carries goods. 2. a kind of pigeon

car'rion *n.* dead, decaying flesh

car'rot *n.* a vegetable with a red root

car'ry *v.* 1. to take from one place to another, as *to carry a parcel.* 2. to reach, as *The shot did not carry far enough.* 3. to hold, behave, as *She carries herself well.* 4. to maintain, support, as *to carry heavy* *responsibilities.*—he **carries.**—**car'ried** *p.t.* and *p. part.*—**to carry on** to continue.—**to carry out** to continue to the end.—**to be carried away** to be full of enthusiasm

Compare: bear, uphold, transport, move, fetch, take, convey

Note: The word *carry* is used in a number of phrases such as *to be carried away* with emotion; *to carry out* a plan or design; *to carry on*, meaning to continue, or (in common speech) to behave outrageously or to complain violently. We also speak of *carrying* (that is, capturing) the enemy's position and *carrying one's* point (that is, getting it accepted) in an argument

cart *n.* a vehicle.—*v.* to convey, as in a cart.—**cart'er** *n.*—**cart'horse** *n.*—**to put the cart before the horse** to put things in reverse order

car'tilage (kar'til-ij) *n.* gristle

car'ton *n.* a cardboard box

cartoon' *n.* an illustration in a journal, relating to current events.—**cartoon'ist** *n.* an artist who draws cartoons

cart'ridge *n.* a case containing charge for a gun.—**blank cartridge** a cartridge with the bullet or shot removed

carve *v.* to cut meat, stone, wood, etc.—**car'ving** *pres. part.*—and *n.*—**carved** *p.t.* and *p. part.*

cascade' *n.* a small waterfall.—*v.*

case *n.* a box, sheath, covering

case *n.* 1. an instance. 2. a state of affairs. condition. 3. law-suit.—**in any case** whatever happens.—**in case** if it should happen that

Note: Some examples of the many uses of *case* are—*It was a sad case* (affair). *This is not the case* (state of affairs). *He was in good case* (state). *The doctor took a serious view of the case* (condition of the patient). *The case is to be tried to-morrow* (law-suit). The expression *in the case of* is apt to be misused. *In case* he comes means if he comes. *In case of fire* means in the event of fire

case'book *n.* a doctor's records of his patients

case'ment *n.* a window-frame, window

cash *n.* money.—*v.* to exchange for, or turn into money, as *to cash a cheque.*—**cashier'** (kash-ēr') *n.* one in charge of money.—**cash on delivery** (C.O.D.) payment to be made to the carrier of goods.—**cash register** a till that records money payments.—**hard cash** ready money

cashier' (kashēr') *v.* to dismiss, as *The officer was cashiered for neglect of duty*

cashmere' *n.* fine woollen stuff

cas'ino (kas-ee'nō) *n.* a dancing or gambling-hall.—**casi'nos** *pl.*

cask *n.* a barrel

cas'ket *n.* small case or jewel-box

cassav'a *n.* 1. a tropical plant with tuberous roots. 2. flour obtained from the roots. 3. bread made from the flour

cass'erole (kas'erōl) *n.* 1. a baking dish with a lid for stewing meat. 2. a meat stew cooked in such a dish

cas'sock *n.* long tunic worn by priest

cass'owary (kas'ō-wāir-i) *n.* a large Australian running bird, like an ostrich but smaller

cast *v.* 1. to throw. 2. to shed, as *The horse cast a shoe.* 3. to allot parts in a play. 4. to found (metal).—**cast** *p.t.* and *p. part.*—*n.* 1. a throw. 2. quality, type, colour, as *He had a peculiar cast of features.* 3. squint. 4. set of actors.—**cast down** sad.—**cast iron** moulded iron.—**to cast off** 1. to throw aside. 2. (knitting) to remove the last row of stitches.—**to cast up** to add

castanets' *n. pl.* two hollowed-out pieces of wood for clicking together rhythmically with the fingers of one hand

cast'away *n.* shipwrecked person

caste *n.* class of people, esp. in India

cas'tigate *v.* to punish

casting *n.* 1. the act of throwing. 2. the placing of molten metals or plastics in moulds. 3. the object moulded. 4. the choosing of actors for a play or film.—**casting vote** a chairman's deciding vote

cas'tle (kahs'l or kas'l) *n.* 1. fortress. 2. country mansion

cas'tor *n.* a small wheel under furniture

cas'tor *n.* a container for sugar, salt, etc.—**castor sugar** sugar finely ground

cas'tor-oil *n.* a medicine made from seeds of **castor-oil plant**

cas'ual (kazh'ool) *adj.* 1. accidental. 2. occasional. 3. careless, negligent.—**cas'ually** *adv.*

cas'ualty *n.* victim of an accident.—**cas'ualties** *pl.* soldier killed or injured in war or disaster.—**casualty ward** hospital ward for accident cases

cat *n.* a common animal.—**cat'like** *adj.*—**cat'ty** *adj.* spiteful.—**cat'gut** *n.* tough fine cord used for violin strings, etc.—**cats'paw** *n.* person made use of by another.—**cat'-o'-nine'tails** *n.* whip with nine lashes

cat'aclysm (-klizm) *n.* an upheaval. See **catastrophe**

cat'acomb (kat'a-kōm) *n.* an underground cave for burial

cat'alogue (kat'a-log) *n.* a descriptive list.—*v.*

cat'apult *n.* a device for throwing stones, nowadays made of a small forked stick and elastic. but in ancient times a large engine of war.—*v.*

cat'aract *n.* 1. waterfall. 2. eye-disease

catas'trophe (kat-as'tro-fi) *n.* disaster.—**catastroph'ic** *adj.*

Compare: calamity, cataclysm, mishap

catch *v.* 1. to take, seize, as *to catch measles, to catch fish, to catch a ball.* 2. to surprise, as *to catch someone napping.* 3. to understand, as *to catch a person's meaning.*—**caught** (kawt) *p.t.* and *p. part.*—*n.* 1. anything that holds or stops, as *a safety-catch.*

2. amount caught, as *a good catch of fish.* 3. a song.—**catch'word** popular saying, slogan
Compare: capture, grasp, hold, apprehend, entrap
cat'echise (kat'i-kīz) *v.* to instruct by question and answer.—**cat'echism** (kat'i-kism) *n.*
cat'egory *n.* a class, order, type.—**cat'egories** *pl.*—**categor'ical** *adj.* precise
ca'ter (kā'ter) *v.* to provide food.—**ca'terer** *n.*
cat'erpillar *n.* the hairy grub of a moth or butterfly.—**cat'erpillar-wheel** *n.* an endless band instead of a wheel for tanks, etc.
cathe'dral (kath-ee'dral) *n.* the principal church in the diocese
cath'ode *n.* a negative electrode.—**cathode rays** electrons from the negative electrode in a vacuum tube
Cath'olic *n.* member of the Roman Catholic Church.—*adj.* universal (not beginning with a capital letter), as *He had a catholic taste in literature, enjoying books of all kinds.* Beginning with a capital letter *Catholic* means pertaining to the Roman Catholic Church
cat'kin *n.* flower of willow, hazel, etc.
cat'tle *n.pl.* farm-animals, esp. oxen, cows
caul'dron, cal'dron *n.* a large kettle or boiler
caul'iflower (kol'i-flower) *n.* a vegetable with white flower-head
cause (kawz) *n.* 1. what makes a thing happen. 2. an object for which one fights, as *Lord Shaftesbury took up the cause of factory reform.* 3. a law-suit.—*v.* to bring about.—**cau'sing** *pres. part.*—**caused** *p.t.* and *p. part.*
Contrast: effect, result, outcome, consequence, issue
cause'way *n.* 1. a raised road. 2. a paved street
caus'tic (kaw'stik) *adj.* 1. burning, as *caustic soda.* 2. cutting, sarcastic, as *He made caustic remarks about his opponents.*—*n.* a solid which corrodes organic matters.—**caustic potash** potassium hydroxide, a corrosive white solid.—**caustic soda** corrosive sodium hydroxide.—*n.*
cau'terise *v.* to burn with a hot iron or caustic.—**cauterisa'tion** *n.*
cau'tion (kaw'shun) *n*, 1. care, as *As it was foggy we proceeded with caution.* 2. a warning, as *Let this be a caution to you never to be so careless again.*—*v.* to warn.—**cau'tious** (kaw'shus) *adj.*—**cau'tiously** *adv.*
cavalcade' *n.* procession of people on horseback
cavalier' (kav-a-leer') *n.* 1. a knight, horseman. 2. a supporter of Charles 1.—*adj.* gay, off-hand
cav'alry *n.* horse-soldiers
cave *n.* a hollow place underground.—**cav'ern** *n.* a deep cave.—**cav'ernous** *adj.*—**cave in** to fall in, give way
cav'iar, cav'iare *n.* salted sturgeon roe
ca'vil (at) *v.* to find fault without good reason. See **carp.**—**ca'villing** *pres. part.*—**ca'villed** *p.t.* and *p. part.*
cav'ity *n.* a hollow place.—**cav'ities** *pl.*
caw *n.* the crow's cry.—*v.*
cayenne' (kā-en') *n.* hot red pepper
cay'man *n.* a South American alligator
cease (sees) *v.* to stop.—**ceas'ing** *pres. part.*—**ceased** *p.t.* and *p. part.*—**cease'less** *adj.* never stopping.—**cease'lessly** *adv.*
ce'dar (see'dar) *n.* a large evergreen tree
cede (seed) *v.* to give up, as *Germany had to cede South-west Africa to the United Nations.*—**ce'ding** *pres. part.*—**ce'ded** *p.t.* and *p. part.*—**cess'ion** (sesh'un) *n.*
Contrast: annex
ceil'ing (see'ling) *n.* the roof of a room
Celanese (sel-an-ez') *n.* the trade name for a silky man-made fibre
cel'ebrate (sel'e-brāt) *v.* 1. to perform, as *The wedding ceremony was celebrated in the cathedral.* 2. to observe. honour, as *to celebrate an anniversary.*—**cel'ebra'ted** *adj.* famous.—**celebra'tion** *n.*—**celeb'rity** *n.* 1. fame. 2. a famous person.—**celeb'rities** *pl.*
cel'ery (sel'e-ri) *n.* a vegetable with long edible stalk
celes'tial (se-les'ti-al) *adj.* heavenly
Contrast: terrestrial, earthly, worldly
cel'ibacy (sel'i-ba-si) *n.* unmarried state.—**cel'ibate** (sel'i-bat) *n.* one who has chosen to stay unmarried
cell (sel) *n.* 1. a small room. 2. a small hollow. 3. a unit of living matter. 4. a division of an electric battery.—**cell'ular** *adj.*
cel'lar (sel'ar) *n.* underground room for storing
cel'lo (chel'o) *n.* violoncello, musical instrument like a large violin.—**cel'los** *pl.*
Cel'lophane (sel'ōfān) *n.* the trade name for a thin transparent material used for wrappings
cell'uloid (sel'ū-loid) *n.* substance used to imitate ivory, tortoise-shell, etc. make photographic film
cell'ulose (sel'ū-lōs) *n.* substance of vegetable cell-wall (used in manufacture of artificial silk)
cement' (se-ment') *n.* a fine mortar.—*v.* to join together
cem'etery (sem'i-ter-i) *n.* a graveyard
cen'otaph (sen'o-taf) *n.* a monument to someone buried elsewhere
cen'ser (sen'ser) *n.* pan for burning incense
cen'sor (sen'sor) *n.* one who examines plays, books, news, etc., before publication.—*v.*—**censor'ious** (sen-sō'ri-us) *adj.* fault finding.—**cen'sorship** *n.*
cen'sure (sen'shur) *n.* blame.—*v.* to blame, rebuke, as *He was censured for his neglect of duty*
cen'sus (sen'sus) *n.* an official counting of the people of a country

cent (sent) *n.* a copper coin, a hundredth part of a dollar.—**per cent** in, to each hundred, as *Ten per cent of two hundred is twenty*

cen'taur (sen'tor) *n.* a legendary being, half-man, half-horse

centenar'ian (sen-ten-ā'ri-an) *n.* a person 100 years old

cente'nary (sen-tee'na-ri) *n.* 1. a hundred years. 2. the celebration of hundredth anniversary.—*adj.*

cent'igrade (sent'i-grād) *adj.* divided into 100 degrees, esp. of **cent'igrade thermom'eter**

cent'igramme *n.* one hundredth part of a gramme

cent'ilitre *n.* one hundredth part of a litre

cent'imetre *n.* one hundredth part of a metre

cent'ipede (sent'i-peed) *n.* small animal with many legs

cen'tral (sen'tral) *adj.* 1. at the middle point.—**cen'tralise** *v.* 1. to bring to a centre. 2. to concentrate under one control.—**centralisa'tion** *n.*—**cen'trally** *adv.*

cen'tre *n.* middle point.—**the Centre** *n.* Central Australia

centrifu'gal *adj.* moving away from the centre

centripe'tal (sen-tri-pēt'al) *adj.* moving towards a centre

centu'rion (sen-tū'ri-on) *n.* a Roman officer commanding 100 men

cen'tury (sen'tū-ri) *n.* 1. a hundred. 2. a hundred years.—**cen'turies** *pl.*

cera'mic (ser-am'ik) *adj.* relating to pottery

ce'real (see're-al) *adj.* relating to corn or grain.—**ce'reals** *n.pl.* grain used as food

cer'ebral (ser'i-bral) *adj.* belonging to the brain

ceremo'nial (ser-e-mō'ni-al) *n.* outward form, show or pomp, as *The coronation was accompanied with stately ceremonial*

cer'emony (ser'e-mo-ni) *n.* 1. a religious rite, as *a wedding ceremony*. 2. special formal observance, as *The ceremony of inaugurating the President of the U.S.A.*—**cer'emonies** *pl.*—**ceremo'nial** *adj.*—**ceremo'nious** *adj.* very polite, using ceremonial or ceremony

cerise' (ser-ēz') *adj.* of a cherry red colour

cer'tain (ser'tin) *adj.* 1. sure. 2. some, one, as *A certain man went down from Jerusalem to Jericho* (St. Luke x., 30).—**cer'tainly** *adv.* without doubt.—**cer'tainty** *n.*

Compare: positive, definite, incontestable. *Contrast:* uncertain, vague, indefinite

certif'icate (ser-tif'i-kāt) *n.* a written declaration.—**cer'tify** *v.* to declare that a thing is true.—**he cert'ifies.**—**cer'tified** *p.t.* and *p. part.*

cer'titude (ser'ti-tūd) *n.* feeling certain

Compare: conviction, assurance, confidence

cessa'tion (ses-ā'shun) *n.* stopping

cess'ion (sesh'un) *n.* See cede

cess'pool (ses'pōōl) *n.* pool or pit for sewage

chafe *v.* 1. to warm by rubbing. 2. to wear or irritate by rubbing.—**cha'fing** *pres. part.*—**chafed** *p.t.* and *p. part.*

chaff *n.* 1. husks of corn. 2. chopped hay and straw. 3. banter—*v.* to make fun of

chaf'finch *n.* a small song-bird

chagrin' (sha-grin') *n.* vexation

Compare: disappointment, humiliation, mortification

chain *n.* 1. a string of links. 2. a mountain range. 3. land measure (66 feet).—**chain reac'tion** *n.* a series of actions building up in power.—**chain' store** *n.* one of a series of shops owned by one firm.—**in chains** bound a prisoner

chair *n.* 1. a movable seat. 2. a position of authority, esp. of a professor.—*v.* 1. to carry in triumph. 2. to preside over a meeting.—**chair'man** *n.* 1. one who presides over a meeting. 2. principal director of firm etc.—**chair'manship** *n.*

cha'let (sha'lā) *n.* 1. a Swiss cottage. 2. a wooden house

cha'lice (cha'lis) *n.* 1. a cup. 2. Communion-cup

chalk (chawk) *n.* 1. a white substance, carbonate of lime. 2. crayon used for writing. etc.—*v.* to mark with chalk.—**chal'ky** (chaw'ki) *adj.*—**not by a long chalk** not at all.—**not to know chalk from cheese** not to know anything about a matter

chall'enge *v.* 1. to call to fight, or invite to a game. 2. to dispute, as *I challenge the truth of that statement*. 3. to stop and question, as *challenged by a sentry*.—**chall'enging** *pres. part.*—**challenged** *p.t.* and *p. part.*—*n.*

cham'ber *n.* 1. a room or office. 2. an assembly, as *Parliament has two chambers, the Lords and the Commons*. 3. a compartment, division, vessel, as *a cold-storage chamber, a revolver with six chambers*.—**cham'berlain** *n.* an officer in a royal household.—**cham'ber-mus'ic** *n.* music for a small orchestra

chame'leon (ka-mē'le-on) *n.* a lizard which changes its colour to match its surroundings

cham'fer *n.* a right-angled corner cut across at 45 degrees

cham'ois (sham'wa) *n.* 1. a kind of antelope. 2. its skin.—**chamois leather** (sham'i leTH'er) *n.* chamois skin used for cleaning

champ *v.* to bite and chew

champagne' (sham-pān') *n.* a sparkling white wine

cham'pion *n.* 1. one who fights for another. 2. one who defends a cause, as *George Washington was the champion of American Independence*. 3. in sport, one who takes first place.—*v.* to fight for.—**cham'pionship** *n.*

chance *n.* 1. happening. 2. opportunity. 3. fate, luck, as *a game of chance*.—*v.* 1. **to**

happen, as *it chanced that* . . . 2. to risk, as *to chance it.—adj.* unexpected.—**chan'cing** *pres. part.*—**chanced** *p.t.* and *p. part.*—**on the off chance** with the slight possibility of.—**to chance upon** to find unexpectedly.—**to stand a good chance** to have a reasonable expectation.—**to take a chance** to take a risk

chan'cel *n.* the part of a church where the altar is placed

chan'cellor *n.* 1. high officer of state. 2. head of a university.—**chan'cellery** *n.*—**chancellor of the Exchequer** the British minister of finance

chan'cery *n.* a division of the High Court of Justice

chandelier' (shan-de-leer') *n.* a frame with branches to hold lights

chand'ler *n.* a dealer, as *ship's chandler*

change (chānj) *v.* 1. to alter, make different. 2. to become different. 3. to exchange.—**chan'ging** *pres. part.*—**changed** *p.t.* and *p. part.*—*n.* 1. alteration. 2. coins of small value. 3. balance received on payment.—**change'able** *adj.* variable.—**change'ful** *adj.* —**change'less** *adj.* unchanging.—**change'-ling** *n.* a child substituted for another.—**small change** small coins.—**to change colour** to turn pale, or blush.—**to change one's mind** to alter a decision.—**to change one's tone** to alter one's manner of speaking.—**to get no change out of someone** to get no advantage or information.—**to ring the changes** to try all ways

Compare: alter, convert, transform

Note: We *change* one thing *for* another. We may *change* clothes *with* someone. In a fairy story the hero was *changed from* a prince *into* a frog. In the evening day *changes to* night

chan'nel *n.* 1. the bed of a stream. 2. the deeper part of a strait, bay, etc. 3. a strait. 4. means of communication, as *I heard the news through a reliable channel.* 5. a band of frequencies wide enough for radio or television transmission.—*v.* to form a channel

chant *n.* 1. a song. 2. a kind of church melody.—*v.* to sing

chant'icleer *n.* a cock

cha'os (kā'os) *n.* 1. utter confusion, disorder. 2. the state of the universe before the Creation.—**chaot'ic** (kā-ot'ik) *adj.*

chap *v.* (of skin) to split.—**chap'ping** *pres. part.*—**chapped** *p.t.* and *p. part.*

chap *n.* (in common speech) a lad, a fellow

chap'el *n.* 1. a place of worship. 2. part of a church. 3. an association of printers

chap'eron (shap'er-ōn) *n.* a lady in charge of a girl on public occasions.—*v.*

chap'lain (chap'lin) *n.* a clergyman attached to a regiment, warship, private chapel, etc.

chap'let *n.* a wreath for the head

chaps *n.pl.* 1. jaws. 2. wide leather leggings worn by cowboys

chap'ter *n.* 1. a division of a book. 2. clergymen belonging to a cathedral.—**a chapter of accidents** a series of misfortunes.—**chapter and verse** exact source of information

char *v.* to scorch, burn.—**char'ring** *pres. part.* —**char'ring** *p.t.* and *p. part.*—

char *v.* to do housework for payment.—**char'woman** *n.* a woman who chars

char *n.* small fish of the salmon family

char'-a-banc (shar'-a-bang) *n.* a motor coach used for pleasure trips

char'acter (kar'ak-ter) *n.* 1. a letter, sign, mark. 2. a person's qualities counted together. 3. a person in a play or book. 4. a peculiar person.—**characteris'tic** *n.* a distinctive feature, as *A characteristic of the pig is greed.—adj.* peculiar, distinguishing, as *With characteristic generosity he gave a large subscription*

char'acterise (kar'ak-terīz) *v.* to mark out, to distinguish.—**characterisa'tion** *n.*

charade' (shah-rahd') *n.* a game, in which a riddle on the syllables of a word is acted

char'coal *n.* a kind of carbon made by charring wood used as fuel, pencils, etc.

charge *n.* 1. cost, price. 2. a load for a gun. 3. command. 4. an accusation.—*pl.* 5. expenses.—*v.* 1. to fill, load. 2. to attack. 3. to ask a price. 4. to accuse.—**char'ging** *pres. part.*—**charged** *p.t.* and *p. part.*—**charge'able** *adj.*—**in charge of** responsible for.—**to give in charge** to hand over to the police.—**to take charge** to assume responsibility for

Note: A battery is *charged with* electricity. A prisoner is *charged with a crime.* An official is *charged with* his duties by his superiors. A shopkeeper *charges for* his goods

char'ger (char'jer) *n.* a war-horse

cha'rily (chā'ri-li) *adv.* cautiously. See **cha'ry**

char'iot *n.* 1. a war-car. 2. a state carriage.—**charioteer'** *n.* a driver of a chariot

char'itable *adj.* kind, generous

char'ity *n.* 1. love, kindness. 2. giving to the poor.—**char'ities** *pl.* institutions or funds to care for the poor, the sick, etc.

Compare: benevolence, liberality, bounty

char'latan (shar-) *n.* a quack doctor, impostor

charm *n.* 1. a magic spell. 2. a thing worn for luck. 3. attractiveness.—*v.* to delight, attract.—**char'ming** *adj.*

Compare: fascinate, captivate, enchant.

Contrast: disgust, revolt, offend

chart *n.* 1. a map of the sea. 2. a sheet of information with diagrams

char'ter *n.* a writing granting privileges, etc. —*v.* to hire, as *to charter a boat, or a taxi*

cha'ry (chār'i) *adj.* cautious, sparing.—**cha'rily** *adv.*—**cha'riness** *n.*

Note: Often followed by *of*, as *The teacher was unpopular because she was chary of giving praise for good work*

chase *v.* to pursue, to hunt.—**cha'sing** *pres. part.*—**chased** *p.t.* and *p. part.*—*n.* hunting

chase *v.* to engrave metal

chasm (kazm) *n.* a deep opening, an abyss

chas'sis (shas'i) *n.* 1. the frame-work, wheels and mechanism of a motor-car. 2. the underframe of an aircraft

chaste *adj.* 1. pure. 2. simple in style

chas'ten (chā'sn) *v.* to correct faults by punishment.—**chas'tened** *adj.*

chastise' *v.* to punish, esp. with the cane, etc. —**chasti'sing** *pres. part.*—**chastised'** *p.t.* and *p. part.*—**chas'tisement** (chas'tiz-ment) *n.*

chas'tity *n.* purity

chat *v.* to talk idly.—**chat'ting** *pres. part.*—**chat'ted** *p.t.* and *p. part.*—*n.* idle talk.—**chat'ty** *adj.*

chattels *n.pl.* movable belongings

chat'ter *v.* 1. to talk idly or rapidly. 2. to jabber, as a monkey. 3. to click together, as *His teeth chattered with the cold.*—**chat'terer** *n.*—**chat'terbox** *n.* one who talks a great deal

chauf'feur (shō'fer) *n.* a paid motor-car driver

cheap *adj.* 1. costing little. 2. easily obtained. 3. of little value, as *to hold something cheap, to make oneself cheap.*—**cheap'ly** *adv.*—**cheap'ness** *n.*—**cheap'en** *v.* to make or become cheap

cheat *v.* to deceive, to play unfairly.—*n.* dishonest person, player

check *v.* 1. to stop. 2. to control, as *This bad habit must be checked.* 3. to examine, verify, as *to check accounts, additions, etc.* —*n.* 1. restraint. 2. a ticket.—**check'mate** *n.* the situation in chess, where one player cannot move his king and so loses.—**check'point** a point on a road where traffic is stopped for inquiry

check'ers *n.* the game of draughts

cheek *n.* 1. side of the face below the eye. 2. impudence.—*v.* to talk impudently to.—**cheek'y** *adv.*—**cheek'ily** *adv.*

cheep *n.* the noise of a young chick or a mouse

cheer *n.* 1. joy. 2. food, as *Christmas is a time of good cheer.* 3. shout of joy, approval, encouragement.—*v.* 1. to comfort, encourage. 2. to shout for joy, or to encourage someone.—**cheer'ful** *adj.*—**cheer'fully** *adv.*—**cheer'y** *adj.*—**cheer'ily** *adv.*—**cheer'less** *adj.*—**cheer'-leader** *n.* one who leads the cheering

cheese (cheez) *n.* food made from milk by pressing curds.—**cheese'-paring** *adj.* stingy, mean

chee'tah *n.* a fast-running wild animal like a leopard

chef (shef) *n.* the head cook

chem'ist (kem'ist) *n.* 1. one who studies chemistry. 2. one who sells medicines, etc.—**chem'istry** (kem'ist-ri) *n.* the science dealing with the elements and their compounds, and their reactions.—**chem'ical** *adj.*

cheque *n.* an order for money from a bank.—**cheque'-book** *n.*—**blank cheque** a signed cheque with the amount left blank

che'quer (check'er) *v.* to mark in squares.—**che'quered** *adj.* patterned in squares; varied, as *a chequered career*

cher'ish *v.* 1. to treat with affection. 2. to protect. 3. to believe fondly, as *to cherish an opinion.*—he **cher'ishes**

che'root (shi-) *n.* a kind of cigar

cher'ry *n.* a small stone-fruit.—**cher'ries** *pl.*

cher'ub *n.* 1. a kind of angel. 2. an angelic child.—**cher'ubs** and **cher'ubim** *pl.*—**cheru'bic** *adj.*

chess *n.* a game of skill played by two persons on a checkered board with 32 **chess'men**

chest *n.* 1. a large, strong box. 2. the upper part of the body.—**to get something off one's chest** to speak freely about a worry

Compare: coffer, case, trunk

chest'nut (ches'nut) *n.* 1. a large reddish-brown nut. 2. the tree

chev'ron (shev-) *n.* a V-shaped band of braid used as a badge in the Forces

chew *v.* to grind with the teeth.—**chew'ing-gum** *n.* a sweetened gum for chewing

chic (sheek) *n.* stylish, smart

chica'nery (shi-kā'ne-ri) *n.* trickery.—**chic'-ane** *v.*

chick, chick'en *n.* the young of birds, esp. of the hen.—**chicks, chickens** *pl.*—**chick'en-pox** *n.* a fever.—**chicken-heart'ed** *adj.* timid

chick'adee *n.* the blackcap titmouse, a small North American bird

chic'ory *n.* a salad plant, the root of which is ground and mixed with coffee

chide *v.* to scold.—**chi'ding** *pres. part.*—**chid** *p.t.*—**chid'den, chid** *p. part.*

chief (cheef) *n.* a leader, head.—**chiefs** *pl.* —*adj.* foremost, leading.—**chief'ly** *adv.*—**chief'tain** *n.* the leader of a clan or tribe

chif'fon (shif'on) *n.* a thin gauze-like fabric

chil'blain *n.* a sore on feet, hands or ears due to cold

child (chīld) *n.* 1. a young boy or girl. 2. son or daughter.—**chil'dren** *pl.*—**child'hood** *n.*—**chil'dish** (chīl'dish) *adj.*—**child'like** *adj.*

Note: childish means "like a child" in a bad sense, *childlike* means "like a child" in a good sense

Compare: childish with petty, puerile, infantile, trifling, silly. *Compare: childlike* with innocent, artless, simple

Chil'e (chil'i) *n.* a country on the west of South America.—**Chil'ean** *n.* a native of Chile

chill *n.* 1. coldness. 2. a cold.—*adj.* cold.—**chill'iness** *n.*—**chil'ly** *adj.*

chime *n.* 1. the sound of bells. 2. a peal of bells.—*v.* to ring in harmony.—**chim'ing** *pres. part.*—**chimed** *p.t.* and *p. part.*—**chime in** to join in a conversation

chim'ney (chim'ni) *n.* a passage for smoke.—**chim'neys** *pl.*—**chim'ney-sweep** *n.* a cleaner of chimneys

chimpanzee' *n.* a large ape

chin *n.* the part of the face below the mouth

Chi'na *n.* a large country in Asia.—**Chi'nese** *adj.* relating to China.—**Chinese lantern** a paper lantern

chi'na (chī'na) *n.* 1. fine white earthenware. 2. cups, dishes, etc., made of china

chinchil'la *n.* a small animal with valuable fur

chink *n.* a narrow opening

chink *n.* the sound of metal pieces knocking together.—*v.*

chintz *n.* a kind of printed cloth

chip *v.* 1. to cut into small pieces. 2. to break off.—**chip'ping** *pres. part.*—**chipped'** *p.t.* and *p. part.*—*n.* a small slice, *esp.* of fried potato.—**a chip of the old block** a child like his parents.—**to have a chip on one's shoulder** to have a grievance

chip'munk *n.* the small striped North American ground squirrel

chirop'ody (ki-rop'o-di) *n,* the treatment of foot ailments.—**chirop'odist** *n.*

chirp *n.* short, sharp cry of a bird.—*v.*

chis'el (chizl) *n.* 1. a carpenter's tool with cutting edge.—*v.* to cut or carve.—**chiselling** *pres. part.*—**chis'elled** *p.t.* and *p. part.*

chit *n.* 1. a child, little girl. 2. a note, permit or pass

chiv'alry (shiv'al-ri) *n.* 1. knighthood, knights, as *The Order of the Garter is an Order of Chivalry.* "*Charlemagne and all his chivalry.*" 2. valour, gallantry. 3. courtesy, esp. towards ladies.—**chiv'alrous** *adj.*

chlor'ine (klor'in, klor'een) *n.* a heavy green gas with a suffocating smell.—**chlor'ate** *n.* a salt containing chlorine and oxygen.—**chlor'ide** *n.* a compound of chlorine and another element

chlor'oform (klor'o-form) *n.* a liquid whose smell puts one to sleep.—*v.*

chlor'ophyll (klor'o-fil) *n.* the green colouring matter in plants

chock *n.* a wooden wedge.—**chock-a-block, chock-full** completely full

choc'olate *n.* a sweet, or drink made from seeds of cacao-tree, sugar, etc.

choice *n.* 1. choosing, as *Portia's suitors were offered the choice of three caskets.* 2. thing chosen, as *Bassanio's choice was the leaden casket.*—*adj.* of good quality, as *choice wines and cigars.*—**Hobson's choice** a compulsory choice, with no alternative

choir (kwīr) *n.* a band of singers, esp. in a church.—**cho'ral** (kō'ral) *adj.* belonging to a choir

choke *v.* 1. to stop up. 2. to smother, stifle, suffocate; to suffer or cause to suffer these.—**cho'king** *pres. part.*—**choked** *p.t.* and *p. part.*—*n.* act or noise of choking

cho'ler (ko'ler) *n.* anger.—**chol'eric** (kol'er-ik) *adj.* hot-tempered

chol'era (kol'er-a) *n.* a dangerous infectious disease

choose (chōōz) *v.* 1. to select, pick out. 2. to think fit, as *He did not choose to go.*—**choo'sing** *pres. part.*—**chose** *p.t.*—**cho'sen** *p. part.*

chop *v.* 1. to cut with a blow. 2. to cut in pieces.—**chop'ping** *pres. part.*—**chopped** *p.t.* and *p. part.*—*n.* 1. a blow. 2. a slice of meat cut with a **chop'per** *n.*—**chop'py** *adj.* (of the sea) rough

chop'sticks *n.pl.* two thin sticks held in the right hand used by Chinese instead of knife and fork

cho'ral see **choir**

chord (kord) *n.* 1. string of a musical instrument. 2. combination of musical notes. 3. a straight line joining the ends of an arc

chores *n.pl.* odd jobs

chor'ister (kor'is-ter) *n.* a choir singer

chor'us (kō'rus) *n.* 1. a band of singers, choir. 2. music sung by many voices

chow *n.* a kind of small dog

chris'ten (kris'n) *v.* to baptise a child.—**christ'ening** *n.*

Christ'endom (kris'n-dom) *n.* all Christian countries

Christian'ity (kris-ti-an'i-ti) *n.* religion of the followers of Christ.—**Chris'tian** *n.* and *adj.*—**Chris'tian name** one's first name given when christened

Christ'mas, Xmas (Kris'mas) *n.* the festival of the birth of Christ

chromat'ic (krō-mat'ik) *adj.* 1. relating to colours. 2. in music, describes a scale proceeding by semi-tones

chro'mium (krō'mi-um) *n.* a hard white metal

chron'ic (kro'nik) *adj.* lasting a long time, as *a chronic disease*

chronolog'ical (kron-ō-loj'i-kal) *adj.* arranged in order of time

chronom'eter (kro-nom'e-ter) *n.* a very accurate clock, used especially for fixing positions of ships at sea

chrys'alis (kris'a-lis) *n.* 1. the stage of an insect's life between grub and fly. 2. the case from which an insect emerges

chub *n.* a fresh-water dish

chub'by *adj.* round and plump

chuck *v.* 1. to pat, as *to chuck someone under the chin.* 2. to throw.—*n.* an arrangement for holding wood or metal in a lathe

chuck'le *v.* to laugh quietly.—*n.*

chum *n.* a close friend

chunk (chungk) *n.* a thick lump or piece

church *n.* 1. a building for Christian worship. 2. all Christians. 3. the clergy. 4. a body or sect of Christians.—**church war'den** *n.* an officer in charge of church property, etc.—**church'yard** *n.* ground round a church

churl *n.* a rude surly person.—**churl'ish** *adj.* surly

Compare: boor, rustic, curmudgeon

churn (chern) *n.* a machine for beating milk into butter.—*v.*

chute (shoot) *n.* 1. a slide for sending timber, etc., to a lower level. 2. a water-fall. 3. a toboggan-run

chut'ney *n.* a pickle

cica'da (si-ka'da) *n.* a tree cricket, the male of which emits a shrill chirping sound

ci'der, cy'der (sī'der) *n.* a drink made from apples

cigar' (si-gar') *n.* a roll of tobacco-leaves for smoking.—**cigarette'** *n.* finely-cut tobacco rolled in paper

cin'der (sin'der) *n.* partly-burnt coal or wood.—**cin'der-path** *n.* a running or racing-track laid with small cinders

cin'ema (sin'e-ma) *n.* 1. motion pictures. 2. art of making or acting in motion pictures. 3. a theatre for showing motion pictures.—**cine'mascope** *n.* method of motion picture projection upon a wide screen

ci'ne-photography (sin'e-) *n.* photography with moving pictures

cin'namon (sin'a-mon) *n.* the bark of a tree used in medicine and as spice

ci'pher (si'fer) *n.* 1. zero, nought. 2. a secret way of writing. 3. a person of no importance

cir'cle (sir'kel) *n.* 1. a ring. 2. a round plane figure. 3. the line enclosing it. 4. a set of people, as *the family circle.*—*v.* 1. to surround. 2. to move in a circle.—**cir'clet** *n.* small circle

cir'cuit (sir'kit) *n.* 1. moving around. 2. a tour made by judges during Assizes. 3. the path of an electric current.—**circu'itous** (sir-kū'itus) *adj.* roundabout

cir'cular (sir'kū-lar) *adj.* 1. like a circle. 2. moving in a circle.—*n.* a letter sent to a number of people.—**cir'cularise** *v.* to send notices

cir'culate (sir'kū-lāt) *v.* to spread, to pass around.—**circula'tion** (sir-kū-lā'shun) *n.* 1. a passing around. 2. movement of the blood to and from the heart. 3. the number of newspapers, etc., sold in a given time

circum'ference (sir-kum'fer-ens) *n.* the line bounding a circle

Note: Circum at the beginning of a word usually conveys the meaning of *around*

circumnav'igate *v.* to sail around, as *Drake circumnavigated the World.*—**circumnaviga'tion** *n.*

cir'cumscribe (sir'kum-skrīb) *v.* 1. to draw a line around. 2. to lay down limits

Compare: bound, limit, hamper

cir'cumspect (sir'kum-spekt) *adj.* careful. discreet.—**circumspec'tion** *n.*

cir'cumstance (sir'kum-stans) *n.* an event, incident, fact.—*n.pl.* condition of affairs.—**circumstan'tial** (sir-kumstan'shal) *adj.* detailed, as *a circumstantial account of what happened.*—**circumstantial evidence** evidence pointing to the guilt or innocence of an accused person, but not actually proving it

circumvent' (sir-kum-vent') *v.* to outwit.—**circumven'tion** *n.*

cir'cus (sir'kus) *n.* 1. an enclosure for games, etc. 2. a travelling show of trained animals

cis'tern (sis'tern) *n.* a water-tank

cit'adel (sit-a'del) *n.* a fortress in a city

cite (sīt) *v.* 1. to summon (to court of law). 2. to mention, quote.—**ci'ting** *pres. part.*—**ci'ted** *p.t.* and *p. part.*—**cita'tion** (sī-tā'-shun) *n.*

cit'izen (sit'izen) *n.* 1. one who lives in a city. 2. a member of a nation.—**cit'izenship** *n.*

ci'trus *n.* kind of tree including lemon, lime, orange, grapefruit.—*adj.*—**cit'ron** *n.* fruit like a lemon but larger.—**cit'ric** *adj.* obtained from citrus fruits, as *citric acid*

ci'ty (sit'i) *n.* large town.—**ci'ties** *pl.*

ci'vic (siv'ik) *adj.* relating to a city or citizen

ci'vil (siv'il) *adj.* 1. polite. 2. relating to a city or state.—**civil'ian** *n.* a person not in the Forces.—*adj.*—**civil'ity** *n.* politeness.—**civil'ities** *pl.*—**ci'vil ser'vice** *n.* public service other than military, naval or political.—**civil war** war between citizens of the same country

Contrast: 1. uncivil, rude, discourteous, incivility. 2. military, ecclesiastical

civilisa'tion (si-vil-ī-zā'shun) *n.* an advanced state of social progress.—**ci'vilise** *v.* to bring out of savagery into a better state.—**ci'vilising** *pres. part.*—**ci'vilised** *p.t.* and *p. part.*

Contrast: uncivilised, barbarous, savage, primitive

clack *n.* 1. a short sharp sound. 2. chatter.—*v.*

Note: In this word, the sound echoes the sense. Compare it in this respect with *clang, clash, clank, clatter, click, clink.* See **onomatopoeia**

claim *v.* to demand as a right.—*n.*—a demand, an assertion.—**claim'ant** *n.* person claiming

clam *n.* 1. shell-fish with hinged shell. 2. a silent secretive person

clam'ber *v.* to climb, using hands and feet

clam'my *adj.* sticky, moist.—**clam'mier** *comp.* —**clam'miest** *sup*

clam'our *n.* a loud confused noise.—**clam'our** *v.* (for) to demand.—**clam'orous** *adj.*

clamp *n.* 1. an iron band for holding things together. 2. a tool for this purpose.—*v.* 1. to hold firm with a clamp. 2. to tread heavily

clan *n.* a group of families with common ancestor, esp. in Scotland.—**clan'nish** *adj.*

clandes'tine (-tin) *adj.* secret

clang *n.* a loud, metallic sound.—*v.*—**clan'gour** *n.* continued clanging

clank *n.* a rattling metallic sound.—*v.*

clap *n.* sudden sharp noise.—*v.*—1. to strike one's palms together. 2. to strike quickly. —**clap'ping** *pres, part.*—**clapped** *p.t.* and *p. part.*—**clap'per** *n.* tongue of bell.—**clap'trap** *n.* empty talk

clap'board *n.* (N. Amer.) weather-boarding

clar'et *n.* a light red wine

clarifica'tion *n.* a clearing-up, being made clear

clar'ify *v.* to make clear.—he **clar'ifies.**—**clar'ified** *p.t.* and *p. part.*

clarinet' *n.* a wood-wind instrument

clar'ion *n.* a shrill-noted trumpet

clar'ity *n.* clearness

clash *n.* 1. a harsh metallic sound. 2. conflict, collision.—*v.*—1. to strike together. 2. to come into conflict

clasp *n.* 1. hook or other fastening. 2. an embrace or hold.—*v.*—1. to fasten. 2. to hold.—**clasp'-knife** *n.* a pocket knife with a folding handle

class *n.* 1. any sort or division. 2. a rank of society, as *working-class, middle-class, upper-class.* 3. group of pupils.—*v.*—to put in a class.—he **classes**

clas'sic *n.* 1. a work of the highest order, esp. of literature, e.g. *The Iliad, Paradise Lost.* 2. author of highest rank, e.g. Shakespeare.—*adj.* perfect, beautiful, as *classic grace, classic style.*—**class'ical** *adj.* 1. belonging to Greek and Roman culture. 2. first-class. 3. handsome and regular, as *he had classical features.*—**class'ics** *n.pl.* ancient Latin and Greek literature

classifica'tion (-shun) *n.* an arrangement in classes.—**class'ify** *v.*—he **class'ifies.**—**class'ified** *p.t.* and *p. part.*

clat'ter *n.* 1. a rattling noise. 2. noisy talk.—*v.*

clause (klawz) *n.* 1. a section, article, or paragraph in a document. 2. (Grammar) a part of a sentence containing a finite verb and making sense, but not necessarily complete sense, in itself

Note: When the clauses of a sentence are of equal importance they are *co-ordinate* (e.g. *He opened the door and went out*). Here the two co-ordinate clauses are joined together by *and.* When one clause is more important than the other or others, which depend on it, it is called the *Principal* or *Main* clause of the sentence. The others are called *Subordinate* or *Dependent* clauses and they may be either. 1. *Adjectival,* 2. *Adverbial* or 3. *Noun.* Examples of a Principal Clause with 1, 2 and 3, respectively are as follows.—1. *That is the man who called here yesterday.* 2. *He called because he wanted to see father.* 3. *I said that father was not at home*

clav'icle *n.* the collar-bone

claw *n.* 1. the hooked nail of bird or beast. 2. anything resembling this.—*v.*—to tear with claws.—**claw'-hammer** *n.* a hammer split at one end for drawing nails

clay *n.* 1. sticky earth. 2. figuratively, the human body.—**clay'ey** *adj.*

clay'more *n.* a Highland sword

clean (kleen) *adj.* 1. free from dirt. 2. guiltless. 3. well cut, with clear lines.—*v.*—to free from dirt.—**clean'er** *n.*—**clean'ly** *adv.*—**clean'liness** (klen'li-nes) *n.*—**cleanse** (klenz) *v.* to make clean

Compare: pure, unsoiled, spotless, unstained. *Contrast:* dirty, soiled, sullied, stained

clear (kleer) *adj.* 1. bright. 2. open. 3. plain, distinct.—*v.*—1. to make bright. 2. to free from hindrance.—**clear'ance** *n.* removal of obstruction.—**clear'ness** *n.*—**clear'ing** *n.* open space.—**clear-sight'ed** *adj.*—**clear-cut'** *adj.* sharp.—**clear-head'ed** *adj.* not easily confused.—**to clear up** 1. to tidy. 2. (of weather) to become fine. 3. (of a mystery) to solve

Contrast: thick, dense, dim, doubtful, indistinct, vague

clear'ing *n.* land cleared for cultivation

clear'way *n.* a road on which vehicles may not stop

cleave (to) (kleev) *v.* to stick closely to, to be faithful to.—**cleav'ing** *pres. part.*—**cleaved,** *clave* (old form) *p.t.*—**cleaved** *p. part.*

cleave (kleev) *v.* 1. to split asunder. 2. to crack.—**cleav'ing** *pres. part.*—**clove, cleft** *p.t.*—**cloven, cleft** *p. part.* **cleav'er** *n.* butcher's chopper

clef *n.* mark in music showing pitch

cleft *n.* a crack

clem'ency *n.* 1. mercy. 2. mildness, e.g. of the weather.—**clem'ent** *adj.*

Contrast: inclement

clench *v.* 1. grasp. 2. set tightly together, esp. the teeth.—he **clen'ches**

cler'gy (kler'ji) *n.* ministers of the church.—**cler'gyman** *n.*

cler'ic *n.* clergyman.—**cler'ical** *adj.* 1. relating to a clergyman, as *a clerical collar.* 2. relating to an office clerk

Compare: priestly, ecclesiastical. *Contrast:* lay, temporal, civil

clerk (klark) *n.* 1. an office-worker. 2. a clergyman

clev'er *adj.* able, skilful.—**clev'erly** *adv.*—**clev'erness** *n.*

Compare: intellectual, intelligent, bright, quick-witted, sharp, smart, talented, gifted. *Contrast:* silly, stupid, foolish, dull, thick-headed, unintelligent, slow, backward

Note: Clever is a general term covering many kinds of mental ability, and should not be over-worked. *Intellectual* means possessing the higher qualities of the mind. *Intelligent* means mentally alert, *bright* or *quick-witted;* but the meaning of the latter shades off into *sharp* and *smart,* which are sometimes used to describe rather unpleasant qualities. *Talented* and *gifted* mean having natural abilities

cli'ché (klee'shā) *n.* an over-worked expression, e.g. *sleep the sleep of the just, long time no see*

click *n.* a short, sharp sound.—*v.*

cli'ent (klī'ent) *n.* customer.—**clientele'** (klee-on-tel') *n.* body of customers

cliff *n.* a steep rock face

cli'mate *n.* weather conditions of a place.—**climat'ic** *adj.*

cli'max (klī'maks) *n.* 1. the highest point. 2. the most exciting part of a story, play, etc. 3. a figure of speech depending on the piling up of the effect

climb (klīm) *v.* to go up.—*n.*—**clim'ber** (klī'-mer) *n.*—**clim'bing** *n.*
Compare: mount, ascend, clamber

clime *n.* (poetical) region, climate

clinch *n.* 1. a firm grip. 2. a hold in boxing

cling *v.* to stick to or hang on to.—**clung** *p.t.* and *p. part.*

clin'ic *n.* a place where medical advice and treatment are given.—**clin'ical** *adj.* medical

clink (klingk) *n.* a sharp metallic sound

clink'er (kling'ker) *n.* cinder from a furnace

clip *v.* to grip tightly or closely.—*n.* device for gripping.—**clip'ping** *pres. part.*—**clipped** *p.t.* and *p. part.*

clip *v.* 1. to cut with scissors or shears. 2. to cut short.—**clip'ping** *pres. part.*—**clipped** *p.t.* and *p. part.*

clip'per *n.* a fast sailing ship

clique (kleek) *n.* a small set of people

cloak (klōk) *n.* 1. loose outer garment. 2. a disguise.—*v.* to hide or disguise.—**cloak'-room** *n.* a place for keeping luggage, etc.
Compare: robe, mantle, cape

cloche (klosh) *n.* a bell-shaped glass cover to protect plants

clock *n.* an instrument for measuring time.—**clock'-golf** *n.* a game of putting from positions forming a circle round the hole.—**clock'wise** *adv.* moving in the same direction as the hands of a clock.—**clock'work** *n.* machinery which works by means of spring, wound up like that of a clock

clod *n.* a lump of earth.—**clod'hopper** *n.* a lout

clog *n.* 1. a hindrance. 2. a wooden-soled shoe.—*v.* to choke up.—**clog'ging** *pres. part.*—**clogged** *p.t.* and *p. part.*

clois'ter *n.* a covered walk in a monastery or nunnery.—**clois'tered** *adj.* shut up, sheltered

close (klōs) *adj.* 1. near, as *at close quarters, close on a hundred poeple*. 2. restricted, not open, as *a close scholarship, the close season* 3. dense, thick, stuffy, as *a close atmosphere, to advance in close order*. 4. secret, secretive. 5. mean, as *close-fisted*.—*n.* a shut-in place.—*adv.* near.—**close'ly** *adv.*—**close call, close shave** a narrow escape.—**close-up** a cinema shot taken very near the subject

close (klōz) *v.* 1. to shut. 2. to end. 3. (with) to grapple with

clos'et *n*, a small room

clot *n.* mass, lump.—*v.* **clot'ting** *pres. part.*—**clot'ted** *p.t.* and *p. part.*

cloth *n.* woven material

clothes (klōthz) *n.pl.* 1. garments. 2. bed coverings.—**clothe** *v.* to dress.—**clo'thing** *pres. part.* of *clothe*.—*n.* clothes.—**clothed, clad** *p.t.* and *p. part.* of *clothe*.—**clo'thier** *n.* one who sells or makes cloth or clothes.—**clothes'-horse** *n.* a wooden frame on which clothes are aired.—**clothes'-line** *n.* a cord on which clothes are hung to dry

cloud (klowd) *n.* 1. condensed water-vapour floating in the air. 2. gloom. 3. a great number.—*v.* to darken.—**clou'dy** *adj.*—**cloud'iness** *n.*

clout *n.* 1. a piece of cloth. 2. a blow.—*v.* 1. to patch. 2. to strike

clove *n.* a spice, bud of clove-tree

clo'ven *p. part.* of cleave

clo'ver (klō'ver) *n.* a trefoil used as fodder.—**cloverleaf junc'tion** *n.* a road crossing with one road above another and curved approaches

clown *n.* 1. a jester. 2. a lout.—*v.*

cloy *v.* to weary by excess, esp. of sweetness
Compare: sate, satiate, surfeit

club *n.* 1. a thick stick. 2. a stick for hitting a golf-ball. 3. one of the suits at cards. 4. a society.—*v.* 1. to strike with a club. 2. (together) to join for a common object.—**club'bing** *pres. part.*—**clubbed** *p.t.* and *p. part.*

cluck *n.* the noise of a hen.—*v.*

clue (kloo͞) *n.* something helping to solve a mystery or puzzle

clump *n.* a cluster of trees

clum'sy 1. awkward. 2. badly made.—**clum'-sier** *comp.*—**clum'siest** *sup.*—**clum'sily** *adv.*—**clum'siness** *n.*
Compare: bungling, ungainly, unwieldy. *Contrast:* deft, graceful, delicate

clung *p.t.* and *p. part.* of cling

clus'ter *n.* a bunch.—*v.*—**clus'tered** *adj.* in clusters

clutch *v.* to seize, grip, grasp.—*n.* 1. grip, grasp. 2. a device in machinery for connecting and disconnecting

clutch *n.* 1. a brood of chickens. 2. a group of eggs laid together

clut'ter *v.* to litter, to pile up untidily

coach *n.* 1. a large carriage. 2. a tutor.—**coach'man** *n.*—*v.* to train a sports team, or candidate for an examination

coag'ulate *v.* to curdle, to clot.—**coagula'-tion** *n.*

coal (kōl) *n.* 1. a mineral used as fuel. 2. a piece of this mineral. 3. a glowing ember.—*v.* to take in coal.—**coal'field** *n.* an area where coal is found.—**coal'-mine** *n.* an underground mine for coal.—**to heap coals of fire one someone's head** to return good for evil.—**to carry coals to Newcastle** to do something unnecessary

coalesce' (kō-al-es') *v.* to unite, grow together.—**coales'cence** *n.*—**coali'tion** (kō-

al-ish'un) *n.* an alliance, esp. of two political parties
Note: Two things may *coalesce together* or *coalesce with* one another

coarse (kōrs) *adj.* rough.—**coars'er** *comp.*—**coars'est** *sup.*—**coarse'ly** *adv.*—**coarse'ness** *n.*—**coars'en** *v.* to make or become coarse
Compare: common, crude, indelicate, vulgar. *Contrast:* fine, delicate, smooth, refined

coast (kōst) *n.* 1. the sea-shore.—*v.* 1. to sail along the coast, as a coaster does. 2. to go downhill by force of gravity.—**coast'guard** *n.* a man who watches the coast for smugglers and wrecks.—**the coast is clear** all is safe

coat (kōt) *n.* 1. an outer garment. 2. an animal's fur or feathers. 3. a layer, e.g. of paint.—*v.* to cover.—**coat'ing** *n.* a covering of paint, etc.—**coat of arms** the emblems of a man of high rank

coax (kōks) *v.* to wheedle, persuade.—he **coax'es**

cob *n.* 1. a short-legged strong horse. 2. in America, the central part of an ear of Indian corn (maize), as *corn on the cob*

co'balt (kō'bawlt) *n.* 1. a mineral. 2. a bright blue

cob'ber *n.* (Aus.) friend, mate, companion

cob'ble *n.* a round stone.—*v.*1. to mend roughly. 2. to patch shoes.—**cob'bler** *n.* a shoe-mender

co'bra (kō'bra) *n.* a poisonous hooded Indian snake

cob'web *n.* a spider's web

cock *n.* 1. the male bird—hen *fem.* 2. the hammer of a gun.—*v.* 1. to draw back gun-hammer. 2. raise or lift, as *The dog cocked his ears.*—**cocked'-hat** *n.* hat with sides turned (*cocked*) up.—**cock'eyed** *adj.* with a cast or squint in the eye.—**cock'erel** *n.* a young cock.—**a cock and bull story** a made-up tale, a lie.—**cock of the walk** a swaggering champion

cockade' *n.* a rosette, badge

cockatoo' *n.* a crested parrot

cock'chafer *n.* a flying beetle

cock'le *n.* a shell-fish

cock'ney *n.* a native of London.—**cock'neys** *pl.*

cock'pit *n.* 1. a place for cock-fights. 2. an enclosed pilot's seat in aircraft. 3. the scene of frequent battles

cock'roach *n.* a black beetle

cock'sure *adj.* very self-confident

cock'tail *n.* a short mixed drink

co'coa (kō'kō) *n.* 1. a powder made from seed of the cacao, a tropical tree. 2. a drink made from the powder

co'conut *n.* a large nut from the coco palm

cocoon' *n.* the sheath of an insect in chrysalis stage

cod *n.* a large sea-fish.—**cod** *pl.*

cod'dle *v.* to treat as an invalid, pamper

code *n.* 1. a collection of laws. 2. a system of signals.—**cod'ify** *v.*—**morse code** a system of signalling with dots and dashes

co'dicil (ko'dis-il) *n.* something added, esp. to a will

co-educa'tion *n.* education of boys and girls together.—**co-ed'**, **co-educa'tional** *adj.*

coeffic'ient (kō-efish'ent) *n.* a number serving as an index or factor

coerce' (kō-ers') *v.* to compel.—**coer'cion** (kō-er'shun) *n.*
Compare: force, constrain, make

coe'val (kō-ee'val) *adj.* of the same age, date or time.—*n.*

co-exist' *v.* to exist at the same time or place.—**co-exist'ence** *n.*

cof'fee (ko'fi) *n.* 1. seeds of a South American shrub. 2. a drink made from these

cof'fer *n.* a chest for valuables

cof'fin *n.* a burial-chest

cog *n.* a tooth on a wheel

co'gent (kō'jent) *adj.* convincing, as *He advanced many cogent arguments*

cog'itate (koj'i-tāt) *v.* to think over.—**cogita'tion** *n.*

cogn'ac (kon'yak) *n.* French brandy

cog'nate *adj.* related to, similar, as *Arithmetic and Algebra are cognate subjects*
Note: Cognate is often followed by *with*, as *Algebra is cognate with Arithmetic*

cog'nizance *n.* awareness, perception.—**cog'nizant** (of) *adj.* aware (of)
Note: to take cognizance of means to take note of

cohere' *v.* 1. to stick or hold together. 2. to be consistent or clear.—**cohe'rence** (kō-heer'ens) *n.*—**cohe'rent** *adj.*, as *His reasoning was coherent and therefore convincing.*—**cohe'rently** *adv.*—**cohe'sion** (kō-hee'zhun) *n.* connection
Contrast: incoherence

co'hort *n.* the tenth of a Roman legion—300 to 600 men

coiffure' (kwaf-ūr') *n.* 1. head-dress. 2. way of dressing hair.—**coiffeur'** (kwa-fihr') *n.* male hairdresser—*fem.* **coiffeuse'** (kwa-fihz')

coil *v.* 1. to twist, lay in rings.—*n.* a series of connected rings

coin *n.* a piece of money.—*v.* 1. to make into money. 2. to invent, esp. a phrase or expression.—**coin'age** *n.* system of coins.—**coin'er** *n.* one who coins, esp. false money

coincide' (kō-in-sīd') *v.* 1. to happen together, as *I am glad that your holiday coincides with mine.* 2. to agree, as *My opinion coincides with yours.*—**coin'cidence** (kō-in'si-dens) *n.* a chance happening together.—**coin'cident** *adj.*

coke *n.* a solid fuel made from the distillation of coal, used in stoves and furnaces

col'ander, cul'lender *n.* a sieve, a strainer

cold *adj.* 1. without heat. 2. without feeling.—*n.* 1. lack of heat. 2. illness marked by running nose, etc.—**cold'ly** *adv.*—**cold'ness.** —**cold-blood'ed** 1. with a temperature the same as that of the surroundings, as *Fish are cold-blooded.* 2. deliberately cruel.—**cold-frame** an unheated glass covered box in which plants and seedlings are reared.—**cold war** enmity stopping short of actual war.—**cold-storage** the preserving of food in large refrigerators.—**to give the cold shoulder to** to treat in an unfriendly way.—**to have cold feet** to be afraid.—**to throw cold water on** to belittle

Compare: 1. chilly, frigid, bleak, icy. 2. distant, haughty, unemotional, unsympathetic. *Contrast:* 1. hot, warm, sultry, mild, balmy, genial. 2. emotional, sensitive, affable, genial, friendly

col'ic *n.* a disorder in the bowels

collab'orate *v.* to work together, as *Charles and Mary Lamb collaborated in writing "Tales from Shakespeare."*—**collab'orating** *pres. part.*—**collab'orated** *p.t.* and *p. part.* **collabora'tion** *n.*—**collab'orator** *n.*

collapse' *v.* to fall in, to break down.—**collap'sing** *pres. part.*—**collapsed'** *p.t.* and *p. part.*—*n.* sudden failure.—**collap'sible** *adj.*

col'lar *n.* a band worn round the neck.—*v.* to seize

collate' *v.* to compare carefully.—**colla'tion** *n.* 1. comparison. 2. a meal

collat'eral *adj.* 1. parallel. 2. secondary

col'league (kol'eeg) *n.* an associate, a partner

collect' *v.* to gather, bring or come together. —**col'lect** *n.* a short prayer.—**collec'ted** *adj.* calm.—**collec'tion** *n.* 1. a group, heap. 2. money collected

collec'tive *adj.* forming a whole.—**collective noun**—a noun naming a group or collection, e.g. *flock, herd*

col'leen *n.* an Irish girl

col'lege (kol'ej) *n.* 1. part of a university. 2. a school. 3. an association.—**colle'gian** (kol-ee'jan) *n.* a student.—**colle'giate** *adj.*

collide' *v.* to dash together—**colli'ding** *pres. part.*—**colli'ded** *p.t.* and *p. part.*

col'lie *n.* a sheep-dog

col'lier *n.* 1. a coal-miner. 2. a coal-carrying ship.—**col'liery** *n.* coal-mine

collis'ion (kol-izh'un) *n.* 1. a violent dashing together. 2. conflict, as of opinions, wills, etc.

col'loid *n.* a solution made up of a substance suspended in a liquid in very fine particles. —**colloid'al** *adj.*

collo'quial (kol-ō'kwi-al) *adj.* belonging to familiar speech.—**collo'quialism** *n.* e.g. *kids*, meaning children

collu'sion (kol-ōō'zhun) *n.* secret agreement for a wrong purpose

co'lon (kō'lon) *n.* a mark (:) indicating a break in a sentence

colonel (kur'nel) *n.* the commander of a regiment

colonnade' *n.* a row of columns or pillars

col'ony *n.* 1. a body of people settled in a new land. 2. an overseas possession. 3. a community of animals, esp, bees.—**col'onies** *pl.*—**colo'nial** (kol-ō'ni-al) *n.* and *adj.*—**col'onist** *n.* a settler.—**colonisa'tion** *n.* —**col'onise** *v.* to make a colony

colos'sus *n.* a gigantic statue.—**colo'ssuses, colo'ssi** *pl.*—**colos'sal** *adj.*

Compare: huge, titanic, enormous, gigantic

co'lour *n.* 1. a hue such as green, blue, etc. 2. paint, stain. 3. complexion.—*pl.* the flag.—*v.* 1. to paint. 2. to disguise. 3. to blush.—**col'oured** *adj.* belonging to a dark-skinned race.—**co'lour-blind** *adj.* unable to distinguish colours.—**co'lourful** *adj.* brightly coloured.—**to lend colour to** to give an appearance of truth or likelihood to.—**to join the colours** to enlist as a soldier, sailor or airman.—**with flying colours** in triumph. —**colour bar** state of affairs in which white people behave as if coloured people were inferior

colt (kōlt) *n.* a young horse

col'umn (kol'um) *n.* 1. a tall pillar, 2. a line of soldiers. 3. a division of a page.—**fifth column** body of traitors

co'ma (kō'ma) *n.* stupor, a deep sleep—**com'atose** *adj.* drowsy

comb (kōm) *n.* 1. an instrument with teeth, for arranging hair. 2. a cock's crest. 3. a mass of honey-cells.—*v.* to use a comb for the hair, etc.

com'bat (kom', kum'bat) *n.* a fight.—*v.*—**com'bating** *pres. part.*—**com'bated** *p.t.* and *p· part.*—**com'batant** *n.*—**com'bative** *adj.* ready to fight

combe (kōōm) *n.* a hollow among hills

combine' *v.* to join together.—**combina'tion** (kom-bin-ā'shun) *n.*—*pl.* underwear made in one piece.—**com'bine** *n.* 1. business combination. 2. agricultural machine which cuts and threshes corn, a **combine harvester**

combus'tion *n.* burning.—**combus'tible** *adj.* easily burned

come (kum) *v.* 1. to approach, as *Christmas is coming.* 2. to reach, as *The speech came to an end. The expenses came to a large sum.* 3. to become, as *The parcel came undone.* 4. to result, originate, as *This is what comes of getting your feet wet. He comes from Scotland. He comes of an old Scottish family.* 5. to appear, emerge, as *The newspaper comes out each week.*—**com'ing** *pres. part.*—**came** *p.t.*—**come** *p. part.*—**a come down** a humiliation.—**to come about** to happen.—**to come across** to meet by chance.—**to come by** to obtain.—**to come down on** to be severe to.—**to come in for** to receive.—**to come into** to inherit.—**to come of age** to be 21 years old.—**to come off** to happen.—**to come out with** to utter.—**to come round, to come to** to recover from a faint.—**to come through** to survive.—

to come to pass to happen.—**to come up to** to equal.—**to come up with** 1. to meet and overtake. 2. to suggest

come'dian (kom-ee'di-an) *n.*—**comedienne'** *fem.* a comic performer, esp. in—**com'edy** *n.* 1. a play dealing with the lighter side of life. 2. an amusing story or happening.—**com'edies** *pl.*

come'ly (kum'li) *adj.* pleasant to look at.—**come'lier** *comp.*—**come'liest** *sup.*—**come'liness** *n.*

com'et *n.* a heavenly body with a tail of light

com'fort (kum'firt) *n.* ease of body or mind. —*pl.* things which make life pleasanter.—*v.* to console.—**com'fortable** *adj.* **com'fortably** *adv.*—**com'forter** *n.* 1. one who comforts. 2. baby's dummy. 3. woollen scarf.—**Job's comforter** someone who tries to console, but only discourages

com'ic, com'ical *adj.* funny.—**com'ically** *adv.* —**com'ic** *n.* 1. a paper consisting mainly of strip cartoon stories. 2. a comedian.—**comic strip** a picture serial in a paper

Compare: ludicrous, ridiculous, absurd, laughable, humorous, droll

com'ma *n.* a mark (,) separating short parts of a sentence.—**inverted commas** punctuation marks (" ") enclosing words actually spoken

command' *v.* 1. to order. 2. to be in charge. 3. to be able to get, as *to command a large salary.* 4. to overlook, dominate, as *The fort commands the entrance to the harbour.*—*n.* 1. an order. 2. control. 3. troops under a commander.—**comman'der** *n.* a naval or military leader

commandant' *n.* a commanding officer

commandeer' *v.* to seize esp. for the use of the army

command'ment *n.* a law. (See esp. Exodus 20:1-17)

comman'do *n.* specially trained soldier for dangerous duties.—*pl.* **comman'dos**

commem'orate *v.* 1. to celebrate, as *their anniversary was commemorated.* 2. to preserve the memory of, as *a monument commemorates the battle.*—**commemora'tion** *n.*

commence (kom-ens') *v.* to begin.—**commen'cing** *pres. part.*—**commen'ced** *p.t.* and *p. part.*—**commence'ment** *n.*

commend' *v.* to praise, recommend.—**commend'able** *adj.* praiseworthy.—**commend'atory** *adj.* praising.—**commenda'tion** *n.*

commen'surate *adj.* proportionate (to, with) equal in size or length of time (with)

com'ment *n.* a note, explanation, remark.—*v.* to make notes.—**com'mentary** *n.* 1. series of notes. 2. a running description of a game, etc.—**com'mentator** *n.*

com'merce (kom'ers) *n.* trade, business.—**commer'cial** (komer'shal) *adj.*—**commercial trav'eller** *n.* a manufacturer's representative

commis'erate *v.* to show or express pity, as *I commiserated with him on his bad luck.*—**commisera'tion** *n.*

Com'missar *n.* one of the heads of a Soviet government department

commissar'iat (-sār-) *n.* an army department dealing with food supplies.—**com'missary** *n.* a deputy.—**com'missaries** *pl.*

commission (kom-ish'un) *n.* 1. a doing, e.g. of a sin. 2. a duty entrusted. 3. fee allowed to an agent. 4. officer's rank. 5. authorisation.—*v.* to authorise.—**commis'sioner** *n.* one empowered to act for government.—**in commission** in active service

commissionare' (kom-ish-on-ār') *n.* messenger or door-keeper

commit' *v.* 1. to entrust, deliver, as *to commit something to someone's care; to commit to the flames, to writing.* 2. to undertake, promise, as *to commit oneself to do something.* 3. to send to prison. 4. to be guilty of, as *to commit a crime.*—**commit'ting** *pres. part.*—**commit'ted** *p.t.* and *p. part.*—**commit'tal** *n.* imprisonment.—**commit'ment** *n.* obligation, undertaking, promise

commit'tee *n.* a group of persons for some special work

commo'dious *adj.* 1. convenient. 2. roomy

commod'ity *n.* 1. an article of trade. 2. something useful.—**commod'ities** *pl.*

com'modore *n.* 1. the commander of a squadron of ships. 2. a senior captain

com'mon (kom'un) *adj.* 1. shared by, or belonging to both or all, as *We must all help the common cause, x is common to both of the expressions x+y and x+z.* 2. general, public, as *It is common knowledge.* 3. ordinary, usual, as *common sense, a common experience.* 4. mean, low. 5. widespread, frequent.—*n.* public or unenclosed land.—**commons** *n.pl.* 1. ordinary people. 2. **the House of Commons** an assembly elected by the people of Britain. 3. rations, as *to be on short commons.*—**com'monly** *adv.*—**common noun** a noun which refers to a thing which is one of a number of such things, e.g. man, house, river. See **abstract, collective, proper.**—**com'moner** *n.* 1. person not of noble rank. 2. University student not holding a college scholarship or exhibition. 3. one who has rights in common land.—**Com'monplace** *adj.* ordinary, trivial.—**common sense** ordinary everyday wisdom.—**Common Market** (European) a free-trading agreement between certain European countries

com'monwealth *n.* 1. a democratic state. 2. Cromwell's protectorate. 3. a group of British self-governing nations

commo'tion (kom-ō'shun) *n.* a stir, disturbance

com'munal *adj.* public, shared by all

commune' (with) *v.* to talk intimately with

com'mune *n.* 1. a small administrative district. 2. a revolutionary government (e.g. in Paris during the Reign of Terror)
commu'nicant *n.* one who receives Communion
commu'nicate *v.* 1. to tell, inform. 2. to impart, transmit. 3. to connect. 4. to receive Holy Communion.—**commu'nicating** *pres. part.*—**commu'nicated** *p.t.* and *p. part.*—**communica'tion** *n.* 1. a message. 2. a passage. 3. means of exchanging messages. —**commu'nicative** *adj.* free with information
commu'nion *n.* 1. fellowship. 2. union in religion.—**Commu'nion** *n.* the sacrament of the Lord's Supper
com'munism *n.* 1. the doctrine that all goods, means of production, etc. should be the property of the community. 2. the political system of U.S.S.R., China, etc..—**com'munist** *n.* person believing in communism
Compare: socialism. *Contrast:* capitalism, individualism
commu'nity *n.* 1. the public. 2. body of people with something in common.—**commu'nities** *pl.*
com'mutator *n.* an apparatus for reversing the direction of an electric current
commute' *v.* 1. to exchange, esp. one obligation for another. 2. to lighten a punishment, as *The sentence of death was commuted to one of life imprisonment.* 3. to travel daily by train or bus.—**commu'ter** *n.* someone who travels daily by train to work.—**commuta'tion** *n.*
com'pact *n.* 1. an agreement. 2. a lady's small powder-case
compact' *adj.* 1. neatly arranged. 2. solid, concentrated.— **compact'ly** *adv.* —**compact'ness** *n.*
compan'ion *n.* 1. person accompanying. 2. mate, comrade. 3. staircase leading below from ship's deck. 4. one article of a pair.—**compan'ionable** *adj.* friendly.—**compan'ionship** *n.*
com'pany (kum'pan-i) *n.* 1. a gathering of people. 2. association for business. 3. a troop under a captain.—**com'panies** *pl.*—**to keep someone company** to stay with someone so that he will not be alone—**to part company with** to leave, to disagree
com'parable *adj.* that can be compared
Note: one thing is said to be *comparable to* or *with* another
compar'ative *adj.* 1. able to be compared, relative, partial. 2. in Grammar, applied to an adverb or adjective which expresses a higher degree than the positive degree of the word, e.g. *smaller* is the comparative of *small, more slowly* of *slowly.* See **positive, superlative.**—**compar'atively** *adv.*
compare' (kum-pār') *v.* 1. to notice likenesses and differences. 2. to liken or contrast.—**compar'ing** *pres. part.*—**compared'** *p.t.* and *p. part.*
Note: one can *compare* two things or *compare* one thing *to* or *with* the other
compar'ison *n.* 1. the act of comparing. 2. a thing which is compared with another
compart'ment *n.* a division, section
com'pass (kum'pas) *n.* 1. extent, area, scope. 2. an instrument for showing the North.—*v.* 1. to contrive. 2. surround.—**com'passes** *pl.* instrument for drawing circles
compas'sion (kom-pash'un) *n.* pity, sympathy.—**compas'sionate** *adj.*—**compas'sionately** *adv.*
compat'ible *adj.* agreeable, consistent.—**compatibil'ity** *n.*
compa'triot *n.* a fellow-countryman
compel' *v.* to force.—**compel'ling** *pres. part.*—**compel'led** *p.t.* and *p. part.*
Compare: make, oblige, coerce
compen'dium *n.* a summary.—**compen'dious** *adj.*
com'pensate *v.* to make up for, pay, as *He was compensated for his trouble by* (or *by means of* or *with*) *a sum of money.*—**com'pensating** *pres. part.*—**com'pensated** *p.t.* and *p. part.*
compensa'tion *n.* 1. the act of compensating. 2. money etc. paid for causing an injury. 3. something which makes up for a defect or setback
com'père (kom'pār) *n.* a man who explains a theatrical show
compete (kom-peet') *v.* 1. to take part in a competition. 2. to try to be first.—**compe'ting** *pres. part.*—**compe'ted** *p.t.* and *p. part.*—**competi'tion** *n.* 1. a contest. 2. rivalry.—**compet'itive** *adj.*—**compet'i-tor** *n.*
com'petence *n.* 1. ability. 2. sufficient money to live on.—**com'petent** *adj.* capable
compile' *v.* to collect, to make up from various sources.—**compi'ling** *pres. part.*—**compiled'** *p.t.* and *p. part.*—**compi'ler** *n.*—**compila'tion** *n.*
compla'cence compla'cency (komplā'sens) *n.* self-satisfaction.—**compla'cent** (kom-plā'sent) *adj.*
complain' *v.* 1. to find fault with. 2. to talk about one's troubles.—**complain'ant** *n.*—**complaint'** *n.* 1. a grievance. 2. an illness
Compare: protest, grumble, remonstrate. *Contrast:* approve, commend, praise, rejoice
complai'sance (kom-plā'zans) *n.* a desire to please.—**complai'sant** *adj.*, obliging
com'plement *n.* 1. something making up a whole. 2. a full allowance.—*v.* to complete. —**complement'ary** *adj.*
Note: Do not confuse the spelling with *compliment.* In Grammar the *complement* is the part of the sentence which completes its meaning, but is not the object of the verb, e.g. in *He is old, old* is the *complement.* In *Work makes us tired, tired* is the *complement*
complete *adj.* full, finished, perfect.—*v.* to make whole, to finish.—**comple'ting** *pres.*

part.—**comple'ted** *p.t.* and *p. part.*—**complete'ly** *adv.* wholly.—**complete'ness** *n.*—**comple'tion** *n.* finishing

com'plex *adj.* 1. having many parts. 2. difficult.—*n.* mental abnormality, obsession, as *an inferiority complex.*—**complex'ity** *n.*

complex'ion (kom-plek'shun) *n.* 1. colour and quality (of the skin of the face). 2. appearance, as *to put a different complexion on matters*

compli'ance (kom-plī'ans) *n.* giving in to a request.—**compli'ant** *adj.* obliging.—**in compliance with** in obedience to

com'plicate *v.* to make difficult.—**com'plicating** *pres. part.*—**com'plicated** *p.t.* and *p. part.*—**complica'tion** *n.* difficulty

complic'ity (kom-plis'i-ti) *n.* partnership in wrong-doing, as *He was accused of complicity in the crime*

com'pliment *n.* expression of admiration.—*pl.* greetings.—*v.* to congratulate.—**complimentary'** *adj.*

Note: Do not confuse the spelling with *complement*

comply' (with) *v.* to consent, agree, as *to comply with the regulations*—he **complies'**—**complied'** *p.t.* and *p. part.*

compo'nent (-pō') *adj.* helping to make a whole.—*n.* a part

compose' *v.* 1. to arrange, put in order. 2. to write books or music. 3. to calm.—**compo'sing** *pres. part.*—**composed'** *p.t.* and *p. part.*—*adj.* calm, peaceful.—**compo'ser** *n.* one who writes music or books.—**com'posite** *adj.* made up of different parts.—**composit'ion** *n.* 1. composing. 2. something composed.—**compos'itor** (kom-poz'itor) *n.* one who arranges type for printing

com'post *n.* rotted vegetation and soil used as a fertilising mixture

compo'sure (kom-pō'zhur) *n.* calmness

com'pound *n.* in the East, an enclosure containing houses

com'pound *adj.* having several parts.—*n.* 1. a mixture. 2. (chemistry) a new substance different from the elements of which it is made. 3. (S.A.) an enclosed housing area for natives employed in industry and mining.—**compound fracture** a broken bone, with a flesh wound.—**compound interest** interest on the interest obtained from capital.—**compound sentence** a sentence containing two or more co-ordinate clauses, i..e clauses of equal grammatical importance, as *I came downstairs and had my breakfast.*—**compound'** *v.* 1. to mix, put together. 2. to make terms (with)

comprehend' *v.* 1. to understand. 2. to include.—**comprehen'sible** *adj.* understandable.—**comprehen'sion** *n.* power of understanding.—**comprehen'sive** *adj.* including much.—**comprehen'sive school** *n.* a large school providing secondary education of all kinds

compress' *v.* to press together, make smaller.—he **compress'es.**—**com'press** *n.* pad of wet lint, etc., applied to a wound.—**compres'sion** (kom-presh'un) *n.*—**compress'or** *n.* a pump for compressing a gas

comprise' (kom-prīz') *v.* to include, as *The school comprised six class-rooms, an assembly hall and a laboratory.*—**compri'sing** *pres. part.*—**compri'sed** *p.t.* and *p. part.*

com'promise (kom'prō-mīz) *n.* an agreement made by both sides giving up part of a claim.—*v.* 1. to come to terms. 2. to expose to suspicion.—**com'promising** *pres. part.*—**com'promised** *p.t.* and *p. part.*

comptom'eter *n.* a calculating machine

compul'sion (kom-pul'shun) *n.* force.—**compul'sory** *adj.* compelling

compunc'tion (-shun) *n.* regret, a pricking of conscience, as *He felt no compunction at killing the snake*

computa'tion (com-pū-tā'shun) *n.* reckoning.—**compute'** *v.* to reckon, estimate.—**compu'ting** *pres. part.*—**compu'ted** *p.t.* and *p. part.*—**compu'ter** *n.* a machine which answers problems from facts supplied to it

com'rade *n.* companion, friend.—**com'radeship** *n.*

Compare: associate, mate, chum, colleague, fellow

con *v.* 1. to study. 2. to steer (a ship).—**con'ning** *pres. part.*—**conned** *p.t.* and *p. part.*—**con'ning-tower** *n.* the observation tower of a ship or submarine

Note: Con is sometimes used as an abbreviation for *contra,* which means "against," as in the expression *pros and cons,* meaning arguments or reasons for and against anything

concave' *adj.* hollow, curved, inwards.—**concav'ity** *n.*—**concave lens** a lens thicker at the edge than at the centre

Contrast: convex

conceal (kon-seel') *v.* to hide.—**conceal'ment** *n.*

concede' (kon-seed') *v.* 1. to admit. 2. to grant, yield.—**conce'ding** *pres. part.*—**conce'ded** *p.t.* and *p. part.*

conceit' (kon-seet') *n.* 1. vanity. 2. fanciful notion, comparison or expression.—**conceit'ed** *adj.* vain

conceiv'able *adj.* imaginable.—**conceive** (kon-seev') *v.* 1. to imagine. 2. to have an idea.—**conceiv'ing** *pres. part.*—**conceived'** *p.t.* and *p. part.*

Note: This verb is often followed by *of,* as *I cannot conceive of his doing such a thing*

con'centrate (kon'sen-trāt) *v.* 1. to gather in one place. 2. to make stronger, as *a concentrated essence.* 3. to attend closely.—**con'centrating** *pres. part.*—**con'centrated** *p.t.* and *p. part.*—**concentra'tion** *n.*—**concentra'tion camp** *n.* a camp for military or political prisoners

Note: This verb is often followed by **on,**

as *The master advised the boy to concentrate on his weaker subjects*

concen'tric (kon-sen'trik) *adj.* having the same centre

con'cept (kon'sept) *n.* a general or abstract idea

concep'tion (kon-sep'shun) *n.* an idea, notion

concern' (kon-sern') *n.* 1. affair, as *It is no concern of ours.* 2. business, as *He bought the shop as a going concern.* 3. anxiety, as *The owners feel grave concern about the fate of the ship.*—*v.* 1. to interest, affect. 2. to make anxious.—**concer'ning** *prep.* about

con'cert (kon'sert) *n.* 1. musical entertainment. 2. agreement, harmony.—**concert'** (kon-sert') *v.* to plan together.—**concert'ed** *adj.* planned jointly

concerti'na (kon-ser-tee'na) *n.* a small musical instrument with bellows and keys

concer'to (kon-cher'tō) *n.* a musical composition for solo instrument and orchestra.—**concer'tos** *pl.*

concess'ion (kon-sesh'un) *n.* a grant, a yielding

conch *n.* a large sea-shell.—**conchol'ogy** *n.* the study of sea-shells

con'cierge (kon'si-ārzh) *n.* (France) a caretaker or janitor

concil'iate (kon-sil'i-āt) *v.* to win over, make friendly.—**concilia'tion** *n.*—**concilia'tory** *adj.* friendly

concise' (kon-sīs') *adj.* brief, in few words.—**concise'ly** *adv.* briefly.—**concise'ness** *n.*

con'clave *n.* 1. a private meeting. 2. a meeting of cardinals to elect a Pope

conclude' (kon-kloŏd') *v.* 1. to end. 2. to settle, as *Peace was concluded.* 3. to decide, reason, as *I concluded that no one was at home because the house was in darkness.*—**conclu'ding** *pres. part.*—**conclu'ded** *p.t.* and *p. part.*—**conclu'sion** (kon-kloŏ'zhun) *n.* an end, result, opinion, decision.—**conclu'sive** *adj.* final.—**conclu'sively** *adv.*—**a foregone conclusion** a conclusion which can be predicted beforehand

concoct' *v.* to plan, make up a mixture.—**concoc'tion** (-shun) *n.*

concom'itant *adj.* accompanying

con'cord *n.* agreement.—**concord'ance** *n.* 1. agreement. 2. an index to the words of a book.—**concor'dant** *adj.*

con'course *n.* a crowd

con'crete *adj.* real, existing as a material thing, not only as an idea.—*n.* a mixture of sand, cement, stones and water, used in building

Contrast: abstract

concur' *v.* 1. to agree. 2. to happen together.—**concur'ring** *pres. part.*—**concurred'** *p.t.* and *p. part.*—**concur'rence** *n.* coincidence, agreement.—**concur'rent** *adj.* acting together, happening at the same time.—**concur'rently** *adv.*

Note: My opinions *concur with* yours, but I *concur in* your decision

concus'sion (kon-kush'on) *n.* 1. a violent shock. 2. injury by blow

condemn' (kon-dem') *v.* 1. to blame. 2. to find guilty. 3. to sentence to a punishment. 4. to find unfit for use.—**condemna'tion** (-shun) *n.*

condensa'tion (-shun) *n.* condensing.—**condense'** *v.* 1. to make closer or more solid. 2. to turn from gas to liquid. 3. to pack into few words.—**conden'sing** *pres. part.*—**condensed'** *p.t.* and *p. part.*

condens'er *n.* 1. an apparatus for storing electrical energy. 2. an apparatus for cooling a vapour to obtain a liquid. 3. a large convex lens that concentrates light in a slide or film projector

condescend' (kon-de-send') *v.* 1. to do something involving coming down from one's superior position. 2. to be gracious to inferiors.—**condescen'sion** (-shun) *n.*

Compare: deign, stoop, patronise

con'diment *n.* a seasoning for food

condit'ion (-shun) *n.* 1. that on which something depends. 2. state, quality.—*v.* to make healthy, to regulate.—**condit'ional** *adj.* depending on something

condole' (with) *v.* to offer sympathy.—**condo'lence** (kon-dō'lens) *n.*—an expression of sympathy

condone' *v.* to forgive, overlook.—**condo'ning** *pres. part.*—**condoned'** *p.t.* and *p. part.*—**condona'tion** *n.*

con'dor *n.* a large South American vulture

conduce' (kon-dūs') *v.* to lead to, to be favourable for.—**condu'cing** *pres. part.*—**conduced'** *p.t.* and *p. part.*—**condu'cive** (to) *adj.* helpful, favourable

con'duct *n.* 1. behaviour. 2. management.—**conduct'** *v.* 1. to lead, direct. 2. to manage. 3. (science) to allow heat or electricity to pass along a substance.—**conduc'tor** *n.* 1. a leader of a band or group. 2. a person in charge of a bus.—**conduc'tress** *fem.* 3. (science) a substance, such as a metal, which conducts heat or electricity.—**conduc'tion** *n.* 1. act of leading or directing. 2. (science) transmission of heat or electricity.—**conductiv'ity** *n.* (science) the extent to which a substance is able to transmit heat or electricity

con'duit (kon'dit) *n.* 1. a pipe or channel to convey water. 2. the pipe enclosing an electric cable

cone *n.* 1. a solid body with a circular base and tapering to a point. 2. edible container of this shape for ice cream. 3. fruit of the pine, fir, etc.—**con'ic, con'ical** *adj.*

confec'tion (-shun) *n.* 1. a sweet-meat. 2. fruit prepared with sugar.—**confec'tioner** *n.* one who sells cakes, sweets.—**confec'tionery** *n.* 1. sweets, cakes, etc. 2. place where they are sold

confed'eracy *n.* a union of countries.—**confed'erate** *n.* 1. an ally. 2. an accomplice.—**confedera'tion** (-shun) *n.* a union, alliance.—**Confederate States of America** the eleven Southern states of the American Civil War of 1860-65

confer' *v.* 1. to give, grant. 2. to talk with, to consult.—**confer'ring** *pres. part.*—**conferred'** *p.t.* and *p. part.*—**con'ference** *n.* a meeting for discussion.—**confer'ment** *n.* the act of giving, granting

Note: People *confer with* one another *about* matters. Honours, benefits, etc. are *conferred on* people

confess' *v.* 1. to admit, own up. 2. to declare one's sins to a priest.—he **confess'es.**—**confes'sion** (kon-fesh'un) *n.* owning up.—**confess'ional** (kon-fesh'on-al) *n.* place where priest hears confessions.—**confes'sor** *n.* priest who hears confessions

confet'ti *n.pl.* small bits of coloured paper thrown at weddings, carnivals, etc.

confidant' *n.* a person entrusted with secrets.—**confidante'** *fem.*

confide' (kon-fīd) *v.* 1. to trust in, as *to confide in the strength of the Navy.* 2. to entrust, as *to confide money to someone's care.* 3. to tell someone your secrets, as *You may confide in your mother.*—**confi'ding** *pres. part.*—**confi'ded** *p.t.* and *p. part.*—**con'fidence** (kon'fi-dens) *n.* 1. trust. 2. boldness, assurance.—**con'fident** *adj.* trustful, bold.—**confiden'tial** (kon-fid-en'shal) *adj.* 1. secret. 2. trusted

configura'tion (-shun) *n.* 1. shape. 2. appearance

confine' *v.* 1. to shut up. 2. to keep within bounds.—**confi'ning** *pres. part.*—**confined'** *p.t.* and *p. part.*—**con'fines** *pl.* boundaries.—**confine'ment** *n.* 1. being confined. 2. giving birth to a child

confirm' *v.* 1. to establish strongly. 2. to make certain. 3. to admit to full communion in the church. —**confirma'tion** (-shun) *n.*—**confirmed'** *adj.* habitual

con'fiscate *v.* to seize by authority.—**con'fiscating** *pres. part.*—**con'fiscated** *p.t.* and *p. part.*—**confisca'tion** (-shun) *n.*

conflagra'tion (-shun) *n.* a great fire

con'flict *n.* a struggle.—**conflict'** *v.* to clash

con'fluence (kon'flu-ens) *n.* a meeting-place esp. of streams.—**con'fluent** *adj.* flowing together.—**con'flux** *n.* a crowd

conform' *v.* 1. to become or make similar. 2. to follow (custom).—**conform'able** *adj.*—**conforma'tion** *n.* 1. conforming. 2. form, structure.—**conform'ity** *n.* agreement with accepted standards

confound' *v.* 1. to mix up, confuse. 2. to astound. 3. to defeat.—**confoun'ded** *adj.*

confront' *v.* 1. to bring face to face, as *The villain was confronted with his victim.* 2. to oppose, as *to confront one's opponents.*—**confronta'tion** (-shun) *n.*

Confu'cian (kon-fū'shan) *n.* a follower of the Chinese teacher Confucius

confuse' *v.* 1. to mix up, esp. in the mind. 2. to embarrass.—**confu'sing** *pres. part.*—**confused'** *p.t.* and *p. part.*—**confu'sion** (kon-fū'zhon) *n.* 1. disorder. 2. tumult. 3. embarrassment

confute' *v.* to prove wrong.—**confu'ting** *pres. part.*—**confu'ted** *p.t.* and *p. part.*—**confuta'tion** (-shun) *n.*

congeal' (kon-jeel') *v.* to freeze, thicken, clot

conge'nial (kon-jee'ni-al) *adj.* agreeable, as *a congenial companion*

congen'ital (kon-jen'i-tal) *adj.* dating from birth

con'ger (kong'ger) *n.* a large sea-eel

congest' (kon-jest') *v.* to overcrowd, overfill.—**conges'tion** *n.* an accumulation (of blood, traffic, etc.)

conglom'erate *adj.* gathered into a mass.—**conglomera'tion** (-shun) *n.* a collection, mass

congrat'ulate *v.* 1. to wish joy to. 2. to compliment.—**congrat'ulating** *pres. part.*—**congrat'ulated** *p.t.* and *p. part.*—**congratula'tion** *n.* expression of good wishes.—**congratula'tory** *adj.*

con'gregate *v.* to flock together.—**con'gregating** *pres. part.*—**con'gregated** *p.t.* and *p. part.*—**congrega'tion** (-shun) *n.* 1. a crowd. 2. a gathering for worship.—**congrega'tional** *adj.* —**Congregational Church** a Nonconformist Church in which each congregation is self-governing

con'gress (kong'gres) *n.* 1. an assembly. 2. the Senate and House of Representatives of the United States.—**congress'ional** (kon-gresh'on-al) *adj.*—**con'gressman** *n.* member of Congress

con'gruence (kon'grōō-ens) *n.* harmony, agreement.—**congru'ity** *n.*—**con'gruent** *adj.* 1. corresponding (with). 2. (geometry) of figures, such that one laid upon another will fit exactly.—**con'gruous** (kong'grōō-us) *adj.* suitable, fitting

con'ic, con'ical *adj.* cone-shaped

co'nifer (kō'ni-fer or kon'i-fer) *n.* a cone-bearing tree.—**coni'ferous** *adj.*

conjec'ture *n.* a guess.—*v.* to guess.—**conjec'tural** *adj.*

conjoint' *adj.* concerted.—**conjoint'ly** *adv.* together

con'jugal *adj.* relating to marriage

con'jugate *v.* (Grammar) to name a verb in its various forms.—for tense, number, person, voice, mood.—**conjuga'tion** *n.*

conjunc'tion (-shun) *n.* 1. a union. 2. (Grammar) a part of speech joining words, phrases, etc., as *and, but, for, because,* etc.—**conjunc'tive** *adj.* 1. joining. 2. joint

con'jure (kun'jer) *v.* to juggle, perform tricks.—**con'juring** *pres. part.*—**con'jured** *p.t.* and *p. part.*—**con'jurer, con'juror** *n.* magician, juggler

con'ker *n.* a nut of the horse-chestnut tree, used in the game of **conkers**

connect' *v.* 1. to join together. 2. to think of together.—**connec'ting-link** anything which joins together other things or ideas. —**connec'ting-rod** a rod connecting the crank to the piston.—**connec'tive** *adj.* and *n.*—**connec'tion, connex'ion** *n.* 1. a joining. 2. relation with another thing

conni'vance (kon-ī'vans) *n.* knowing of some crime or fault and doing nothing to prevent it.—**connive'** (at) *v.* to pretend not to see a fault.—**conni'ving** *pres. part.*—**connived'** *p.t.* and *p. part.*

connoisseur' (kon-i-ser') *n.* an expert in art and in matters of taste

connota'tion (-shun) *n.* a meaning suggested in addition to the chief meaning.—**connote'** *v.* to imply, suggest, as *The word "Summer" connotes flowers and sunshine*

connu'bial *adj.* connected with marriage

con'quer (kong'ker) *v.* 1. to overcome. 2. to win by war.—**con'queror** *n.*—**con'quest** (kon'kwest) *n.*

con'science (kon'shens) *n.* a sense of right and wrong.—**conscien'tious** (kon-shi-en'-shus) *adj.* 1. painstaking. 2. ruled by conscience.—**conscien'tiously** *adv.*—**conscience-stricken** full of remorse

con'scious (kon'shus) *adj.* 1. aware. 2. awake.—**con'sciously** *adv.*—**con'sciousness** (kon'shus-nes) *n.* awareness

con'script *n.* one compelled to serve in the army.—**conscript'** *v.* to enrol.—**conscrip'-tion** (-shun) *n.*

con'secrate *v.* 1. to declare sacred. 2. to devote.—**con'secrating** *pres. part.*—**con'secrated** *p.t.* and *p. part.*—**consecra'tion** *n.*

consec'utive *adj.* following in unbroken order.—**consec'utively** *adv.*

consen'sus *n.* general agreement

consent' *v.* to agree.—*n.* agreement, permission.—**with one consent** by general agreement

Compare: approve, permit, acquiesce, assent, yield. *Contrast:* refuse, disagree, demur, dissent

con'sequence *n.* a result, effect.—**con'sequent** *adj.* following.—**consequen'tial** (kon-se-kwen'shal) *adj.* 1. as a consequence of. 2. self-important.—**con'sequently** *adv.* as a result

conserva'tion (-shun) *n.* preservation.—**conser'vatism** *n.* dislike of change or progress.—**conser'vative** *adj.* 1. having to preserve. 2. disliking change.—**Conservative** *n.* a member of a political party which opposes great changes

conser'vatory *n.* 1. a greenhouse for tender plants. 2. (and **conservatoire'**, kon-sār-va-twar') a school of music.—**conser'vatories** *pl.*

conserve' *v.* to preserve, keep from harm.—**conser'ving** *pres. part.*—**conserved'** *p.t.* and *p. part.*—*n.* 1. fruit preserved in sugar. 2. jam

consid'er *v.* 1. to think over, as *We must consider what to do.* 2. to regard as, as *He is considered to be very clever.*—**consid'erable** *adj.* important, large.—**consid'erably** *adv.*

consid'erate *adj.* thoughtful for others.—**considera'tion** *n.* 1. serious thought. 2. thoughtfulness. 3. reason as *On no consideration will I do it.* 4. reward, as *I will do it for a consideration.*—**consid'ering** *presp.* in view of

con'sign *v.* to deliver, hand over.—**consign'-ment** *n.* 1. delivering. 2. the things delivered. —**consignee'** *n.* the person to whom goods are consigned

consist' *v.* to be composed of.—**consis'tence, consis'tency** *n.* 1. degree of density. 2. firmness. 3. regularity, reliability. 4. agreement.—**consis'tent** *adj.* 1. firm. 2. not contradictory, remaining the same.—**consis'tently** *adv.*

Note: This verb is usually followed by *of* or *in*

consola'tion (-shun) *n.* comfort.—**consol'a-tory** *adj.*—**console'** (kon-sōl') *v.* to comfort.—**conso'ling** *pres. part.*—**consoled** *p.t.* and *p. part.*—**consola'tion prize** a prize for the runner-up

con'sole (kon'sōl) *n.* 1. bracket. 2. keyboard, etc., of an organ. 3. a cabinet television set or radiogram

consol'idate *v.* to make firm, solid or secure. —**consol'idating** *pres. part.*—**consol'idated** *p.t.* and *p. part.*—**consolida'tion** *n.*

consommé (kon-so-mā') *n.* clear meat soup

con'sonant (with) *adj.* agreeing with, consistent.—*n.* a sound making a syllable only with a vowel (in the alphabet, the letters a, e, i, o, u are vowels; the rest are consonants)

con'sort *n.* 1. a wife or husband, esp. of a king or queen. 2. a ship sailing with another.—**consort'** (with) *v.* to associate with

conspic'uous *adj.* 1. easily seen. 2. prominent. —**conspic'uously** *adv.*

conspir'acy (kon-spir'a-si) *n.* a combination, usually for an evil purpose, a plot.—**conspir'acies** *pl.*—**conspir'ator** *n.* a plotter. —**conspire'** (kon-spīr') *v.* to plot.—**conspi'ring** *pres. part.*—**conspired'** *p.t.* and *p. part.*

con'stable (kun'sta-bl) *n.* a policeman.—**constab'ulary** *n.* a police force.—**special con'stable** *n.* person sworn in as a constable in an emergency

con'stancy (kon'stan-si) *n.* firmness, faithfulness.—**con'stant** *adj.* unchanging.—**con'-stantly** *adv.* 1. faithfully. 2. continually

constella'tion *n.* a group of stars

consterna'tion (-shun) *n.* dismay, terror

constipa'tion (-shun) *n.* difficulty in emptying the bowels

constit'uency *n.* 1. a body of electors. 2. a parliamentary division.—**constit'uent** *n.* 1. an essential part. 2. an elector.—*adj.*

con'stitute *v.* to set up, establish, found, compose, as *A new government was constituted. His performance constitutes a* *record.*—**con'stituting** *pres. part.*—**constituted** *p.t.* and *p. part.*—**constitu'tion** (-shun) *n.* 1. composition. 2. health, as *a strong constitution, a weak constitution.* 3. the principles or laws by which a state is governed.—**constitu'tional** *n.* a walk taken for health's sake.—*adj.* 1. belonging to a person's constitution or character, habitual. 2. ruling according to law, as *The Queen of England is a constitutional monarch*

constrain' *v.* to force, compel.—**constraint'** *n.* 1. compulsion. 2. holding back one's feelings

constrict' *v.* to draw together, compress, cramp.—**constric'tion** (-shun) *n.* compression.—**constric'tor** *n.* a snake that kills by crushing its prey

construct' *v.* to build, put together.—**construc'tion** (-shun) *n.* building.—**construc'tive** *adj.* helpful

construe' (con-strōō') *v.* 1. to interpret, as *Your presence at the meeting was construed as a sign of sympathy with our proposals.* 2. to translate. 3. to analyse grammatically.—**constru'ing** *pres. part.*—**construed'** *p.t.* and *p. part.*

con'sul *n.* 1. an official representing his government abroad. 2. one of two Heads of State in ancient Rome, or one of three chief magistrates in revolutionary France between 1799 and 1804.—**con'sular** *adj.* —**con'sulate** *n.* 1. being a consul (also **consulship**). 2. government by consuls. 3. a consul's official residence

consult' *v.* 1. to ask advice. 2. to seek information, as *to consult a doctor.*—**consulta'tion** (-shun) *n.* meeting to consider something.—**consul'tative** *adj.* advisory.—**consul'tant** *n.* a specialist doctor

consume' *v.* 1. to use up. 2. to eat or drink up. 3. to destroy, as by fire.—**consu'ming** *pres. part.*—**consumed'** *p.t.* and *p. part.*—**consu'mable** *n.* and *adj.*—**consu'mer** *n.* person who uses what the producer makes

con'summate (kon'sū-māt) *v.* to complete.—**consum'mate** (kon-sum'āt) *adj.* perfect, supreme, utter.—**consumma'tion** (-shun) *n.* completion

consump'tion (-shun) *n.* 1. using up. 2. destruction. 3. wasting disease of the lungs, tuberculosis.—**consump'tive** *adj.*

con'tact *n.* 1. touch. 2. connection.—*v.*—**con'tact lens** a thin plastic or glass lens fitted over the eyeball.—**to make (break) contact** to complete (interrupt) an electric circuit

conta'gion (kon-tā'jon) *n.* 1. spreading of disease by touch. 2. a plague or pestilence, either moral or physical.—**conta'gious** (kon-tā'jus) *adj.*

contain' *v*, 1. to hold inside. 2. to include. 3. to restrain (oneself).—**contain'er** *n.* anything which holds something, e.g. a tin or box

contam'inate *v.* to defile, stain, corrupt.—**contam'inating** *pres. part.*—**contam'inated** *p.t.* and *p. part.*—**contamina'tion** *n.*

con'template *v.* 1. to look at. 2. to think about, meditate. 3. to intend, as *He contemplates taking a holiday.*—**con'templating** *pres. part.*—**con'templated** *p.t.* and *p. part.* —**contempla'tion** *n.*—**contem'plative** *adj.* thoughtful

contempora'neous *adj.* belonging to the same period.—**contem'porary** *adj.* living or happening at the same time.—*n.*—**contem'poraries** *pl.*

contempt' *n.* scorn.—**contemp'tible** *adj.* mean, deserving contempt.—**contemp'tuous** *adj.* scornful

contend' *v.* 1. to strive, dispute, as *to contend for a prize.* 2. to argue, as *He contended that the other motorist was to blame for the accident*

content' *adj.* satisfied, happy, comfortable.—*v.* to satisfy, please.—*n.* satisfaction.—**conten'ted** *adj.*

con'tent *n.* holding capacity.—*pl.* what is contained

conten'tion (-shun) *n.* 1. dispute. 2. an opinion, argument.—**conten'tious** (kon-ten'-shus) *adj.* quarrelsome

content'ment *n.* satisfaction, happiness

con'test *n.* 1. struggle, fight. 2. competition.—**contest'** *v.* to dispute, debate, struggle for. —**contest'ant** *n.*

con'text *n.* what comes before and after a passage or words

contigu'ity *n.* nearness.—**contig'uous** *adj.* touching, neighbouring, as *Norway and Sweden are contiguous*

con'tinence *n.* self-restraint.—**con'tinent** *adj.* restrained, self-disciplined

con'tinent *n.* one of the main land-masses of the earth.—**the Continent** Europe.—**continen'tal** *adj.*

contin'gency (kon-tin'jen-si) *n.* 1. chance. 2. possibility.—**contin'gencies** *pl.*—**contin'gent** *adj.* 1. dependent on something uncertain (usually followed by *on* or *upon*). 2. accidental.—*n.* a body of troops

contin'ual *adj.* 1. endless. 2. often repeated.—**contin'ually** *adv.* very often.—**contin'uance** *n.* 1. lasting. 2. remaining.—**continua'tion** *n.* 1. extra part. 2. starting again

contin'ue *v.* 1. to go on, carry on. 2. to last remain. 3. to start again, resume.—**contin'uing** *pres. part.*—**contin'ued** *p.t.* and *p. part.*—**continu'ity** *n.* 1. being uninterrupted. 2. a connected whole.—**contin'uous** *adj.* uninterrupted.—**continu'ity-girl** one who sees to it that the clothes etc. in the different parts of a cinema film are consistent

contort' *v.* to twist out of shape.—**contor'tion** (-shun) *n.*—**contor'tionist** *n.* an acrobat who can twist himself into peculiar shapes

con'tour *n.* outline, esp. of mountains, coast,

etc.—**con'tour-line** line on a map showing places of the same height

con'traband *n.* 1. prohibited goods. 2. smuggling.—*adj.* prohibited

con'tract *n.* 1. a bargain. 2. a business agreement.—**contract'** *v.* to agree upon, as *He contracted to complete the work within a month.*—**contrac'tor** *n.* a builder working to a contract.—**contract bridge** a card game

contract' *v.* to become smaller.—**contract'ion** *n.* a shortening.—**contract'ible** *adj.*

contradict' *v.* 1. to deny. 2. to say the opposite.—**contradic'tory** *adj.* inconsistent—**contradic'tion** *n.* disagreement

contral'to *n.* lowest female singing-part.—**contral'tos** *pl.*

con'trary *adj.* 1. opposite, other. 2. perverse (often pronounced kontrār'-i), as *Mary, Mary, quite contrary.* 3. unfavourable, as *The wind was contrary.*—*n.* the exact opposite.—**on the contrary** not at all.—**to the contrary** to the opposite effect.—**by contraries** in an opposite sense or manner

con'trast *n.* a striking difference.—**contrast'** *v.* to compare by showing differences

contravene' *v.* 1. to break (a rule). 2. to conflict with, infringe.—**contraven'tion** (-shun) *n.*

contrib'ute *v.* 1. to pay to a common fund, subscribe. 2. to help, as *Your assistance contributed greatly to my success.* 3. to write articles, etc. for a paper.—**contrib'uting** *pres. part.*—**contrib'uted** *p.t.* and *p. part.*—**contribu'tion** *n.* help or money given.—**contrib'utive** *adj.*—**contrib'utor** *n.* used esp. of one who contributes articles to a paper.—**contrib'utory** *adj.* helping towards

con'trite (kon'trīt) *adj.* deeply sorry for wrong-doing.—**contrit'ion** (kon-tri'shun) *n.* penitence

Compare: repentant, penitent

contri'vance (kon-trī'vans) *n.* 1. scheme, plan. 2. device.—**contrive'** *v.* 1. to invent. 2. to succeed in bringing about, manage.—**contri'ver** *n.* schemer.—**contri'ving** *pres. part.*—**contrived'** *p.t.* and *p. part.*—*adj.* artificial, unspontaneous

control' (kon-trōl') *n.* 1. check, as *The government decided to impose a strict control of prices.* 2. authority, restraint, as *He has complete control of all that goes on in the factory.*—*pl.* levers, etc. regulating the working of a machine, aeroplane, etc. —*v.* 1. to direct, manage, restrain. 2. to check, test.—**control'ling** *pres. part.*—**controlled'** *p.t.* and *p. part.*—**control'lable** *adj.*—**control'ler** *n.* person controlling (expenditure).—**self-control** being able to control one's own behaviour.—**out of control** not controllable.—**under control** in working order, able to be controlled

controver'sial (kon-trō-ver'shal) *adj.* liable to raise a difference of opinion.—**con'troversy, controv'ersy** *n.* dispute, argument.—**con'troversies** *pl.*

con'trovert *v.* to deny, oppose.—**controvert'ible** *adj.* capable of being denied

con'tumely (kon'tūm-li) *n.* disgrace, scornful behaviour, insolence

contuse' *v.* to bruise.—**contu'sion** (kon-tū'-zhun) *n.*

conun'drum *n.* a riddle

convalesce' (konvales') *v.* to recover from illness.—**convales'cence** *n.* period of recovery.—**convales'cent** *adj.* and *n.*—**convales'cent home** a nursing home where patients convalesce

convec'tion (-shun) *n.* transmission of heat by currents in liquids or gases

convect'or *n.* a space heater convecting warm air

convene' *v.* to call together.—**conven'ing** *pres. part.*—**convened'** *p.t.* and *p. part.*—**conve'ner** *n.*

conve'nience (kon-vee'ni-ens) *n.* something useful or helpful.—**conve'nient** *adj.* handy, suitable.—**conve'niently** *adv.*

Compare: (*adj.*) helpful, opportune, comfortable, favourable, timely, proper, fit. *Contrast:* (*adj.*) inconvenient, awkward, useless, unsuitable, unfit

con'vent *n.* 1. a community of nuns. 2. their building

conven'tion (-shun) *n.* 1. assembly. 2. a treaty. 3. an accepted custom or form.—**conven'tional** *adj.* 1. customary. 2. formal. —**conven'tionally** *adv.*—**conventional'ity** *n.* —**conventional'ities** *pl.*

converge' (kon-verj') *v.* to tend to meet, as *Railway lines appear to converge in the distance.*—**conver'ging** *pres. part.*—**converged'** *p.t.* and *p. part.*—**conver'gence** *n.*—**conver'gent** *adj.* tending to meet

conver'sant (with) *adj.* familiar with

conversa'tion (-shun) *n.* talk.—**conversa'tional** *adj.*—**conversa'tionalist** *n.* a person who is fond of, or good at, conversation.—**converse'** (with) *v.* to talk.—**conver'sing** *pres. part.*—**conversed'** *p.t.* and *p. part.*—**con'verse** *n.* talk

con'verse *adj.* opposite.—*n.* the opposite

conver'sion (-shun) *n.* 1. change. 2. change of belief

convert' *v.* 1. to change. 2. to cause to change an opinion or belief esp. to Christianity. 3. (N.Z.) to take possession of an article (esp. a motor car) without authority.—**con'vert** *n.* a converted person.—**convert'ible** *adj.*

con'vex *adj.* curved outwards.—**convex'ity** *n.* —**con'vex lens** a lens thicker at the centre than the edges

Contrast: concave

convey' *v*, 1. to carry. 2. to communicate, as *Words fail to convey my feelings.* 3. (legal term) to transfer property from one owner to another.—**convey'ance** *n.* 1. communication. 2. a vehicle. 3. transfer of property. —**convey'er** *n.* 1. one who conveys. 2. an endless belt for moving goods.—**convey'er-belt** *n.* a continuous moving belt carrying goods and machines for assembly

con'vict *n.* a criminal serving his term of imprisonment.—**convict'** *v.* to prove guilty, as *The man was convicted of theft.*—**convic'tion** (-shun) *n.* 1. verdict of guilty. 2. firm belief

Compare: faith, certainty, doctrine

convince' (kon-vins') *v.* to persuade strongly, to satisfy by proof.—**convin'cing** *pres. part.* —**convinced'** *p.t.* and *p. part.*—**convin'cing** *adj.* effective

conviv'ial *adj.* festive, jolly.—**convivial'ity** *n.*

convoca'tion *n.* 1. an assembly. 2. an assembly of clergy. etc.—**convoke'** *v.* to call together. —**convo'king** *pres. part.*—**convoked'** *p.t.* and *p. part.*

convolu'tion (-shun) *n.* 1. being coiled. 2. coil or spiral

convol'vulus *n.* a plant with twining stem

con'voy *n.* ships, troops, etc., accompanied by, or accompanying others for protection. —**convoy'** *v.* to escort for protection

convulse' *v.* 1. to shake violently. 2. to agitate.—**convul'sing** *pres. part.*—**convulsed'** *p.t.* and *p. part.*—**convul'sion** (-shun) *n.* violent disturbance.—**convul'sive** *adj.*

co'ny, co'ney (kō'ni) *n.* 1. rabbit. 2. rabbit fur. —**co'nies** *pl.*

coo *v.* to make a soft noise like a dove or a baby.—**cooed** *p.t.* and *p. part.*

cooee' *interjection* a cry to attract notice

cook *v.* 1. to prepare food for the table esp. by heat. 2. to be cooked. 3. to tamper with (accounts, etc.).—*n.* a person who cooks.—**coo'ker** *n.* apparatus for cooking.—**coo'kery** *n.*—**coo'kie** *n.* a small flat sweetened cake or biscuit.—**to cook someone's goose** to spoil someone's plans

cool *adj.* 1. fairly cold. 2. calm, as *He was quite cool and collected.* 3. unfriendly, as *a cool reception.* 4. impudent, audacious.—*v.* to make cool.—**coo'ler** *n.*—**cool'ness** *n.*

coo'lie *n.* native labourer in India or China

coop *n.* a cage or pen for fowls.—*v.* to shut up in a coop, to confine

coo'per *n.* a maker of barrels

co-op'erate (kō-op'er-āt) *v.* to work together. —**co-op'erating** *pres. part.*—**co-op'erated** *p.t.* and *p. part.*—**co-opera'tion** (-shun) *n.*—**co-op'erative** *adj.* ready to work together

coor'dinate (kōord'ināt) *v.* 1. to place in the same rank. 2. to bring into order as parts of a whole.—*adj.* equal in importance.—**co-ordina'tion** *n.*

Note: In Grammar a co-ordinate clause is one joined to another, with which it is of equal importance, by a conjunction, as *He came downstairs and had his breakfast*

coot *n.* a small black water-fowl

co'pal (kō'pal) *n.* a resin used in varnish

cope *n.* a cloak worn by priests

cope (with) *v.* to deal with.—**co'ping** *pres. part.*—**coped'** *p.t.* and *p. part.*

co'-pilot *n.* an assistant pilot

co'ping *n.* top course of a wall

co'pious (kō'pi-us) *adj.* abundant, plentiful. —**co'piously** *adv.*

cop'per *n.* 1. a reddish-brown metal. 2. a copper coin.—**cop'per head** *n.* a poisonous North American snake.—**copperplate** *n.* 1. a plate for engraving or etching. 2. very neat writing.—**cop'persmith** *n.* craftsman who works in copper

cop'pice, copse *n.* a wood of small growth for cutting

Compare: spinney, covert, brake, thicket

cop'ra *n.* the dried kernel of coconuts

Copt *n.* a Christian Egyptian.—**Cop'tic** *n.* the language of the Copts

cop'y *n.* 1. an imitation. 2. one of a set of books, etc. 3. matter for printing.—*v.* to make a copy of.—he **cop'ies.**—**cop'ying** *pres. part.*—**cop'ied** *p.t.* and *p. part.*—**cop'yhold** *n.* and *adj.* old form of land holding with *copy* of the manor court-roll as title.—**cop'yist** *n.*—**cop'yright** *n.* the sole right to publish anything.—**cop'y-book** *n.* a book for learners to copy writing

coquette' *n.* a flirt.—**coqu'etry** *n.*

cor'acle *n.* a boat of wicker covered with skins

cor'al *n.* a hard pink or white substance built up in tropical seas by tiny animals.—**cor'al line** *adj.*—**coral-reef'** *n.* a ridge of coral in a tropical sea

cor ang'lais (kawr-ong'lā) *n.* a wood-wind instrument

cord *n.* 1. a thin rope or thick string. 2. a measure of cut wood (128 cubic feet).—*v.* to fasten with cord.—**cord'age** *n.* cords, ropes

cor'dial *adj.* hearty, warm.—*n.* a stimulating drink.—**cordial'ity** *n.*—**cor'dially** *adv.*

cor'don *n.* 1. a chain of troops or police. 2. an ornamental cord or badge

corduroy' (kor-dū-roi') *n.* 1. corded or ribbed cotton velvet. 2. (in Canada) a road made of logs laid across

core *n.* the heart or centre of anything.—*v.* to take out the core

cor'gi *n.* a kind of small Welsh dog

cork *n.* 1. bark of the cork-tree. 2. a stopper made of this.—*v.* to stop up.—**cork'screw** *n.* tool for pulling out corks

corm *n.* an underground stem resembling a bulb

corm'orant *n.* a large, greedy sea-bird

corn *n.* 1. grain, wheat. 2. (U.S.) maize (Indian corn).—*v.* to preserve (meat) with salt, as *corned beef.*—**corn'flour** *n.* flour made from Indian corn.—**Corn in Egypt** plenty

corn *n.* a horny growth on foot or toe.—to **tread on someone's corns** to annoy someone, to hurt his feelings

cor'nea *n.* a thin skin over the eyeball

cor'ner *n.* 1. point where two lines, walls,

streets, etc. meet. 2. a nook. 3. buying up all the stocks of a commodity.—*v.* 1. to drive into an awkward position. 2. to make a corner (see 3 above) in some commodity, as *to corner the market.* 3. to turn a corner (in a car.)—**a tight corner** a desperate situation.—**to turn the corner** to recover from a bad situation

cor'nerstone *n.* 1. a principal stone that forms the corner of the foundation of a building. 2. a principal factor, as *confidence was the cornerstone of his success*

cor'net *n.* a kind of trumpet

cor'nice (kor'nis) *n.* a moulding along the top of a wall or pillar

corol'la *n.* petals of a flower

corol'lary *n.* 1. a natural consequence. 2. something understood from what has been said. 3. in geometry, a proposition that follows from one already proved.—**corol'laries** *pl.*

coro'na *n.* a halo round a heavenly body.—**coro'nas, coro'nae** *pl.*

corona'tion (-shun) *n.* the ceremony of crowning a sovereign

cor'oner *n.* an official who holds inquests into the cause of sudden death

cor'onet *n.* a small crown worn by nobles

cor'poral *n.* a non-commissioned officer below a sergeant

cor'poral *adj.* bodily.—**cor'porate** *adj.* acting as one united body.—**cor'poral punishment** caning, flogging

Contrast: spiritual

corpora'tion (-shun) *n.* 1. a society acting as one person. 2. the authorities of a town or city.—**corpor'eal** *adj.* material, of the body

corps (kor) *n.* a body of soldiers or trained nurses.—**corps de ballet** (French) a company of ballet dancers.—**corps** (kōrz) *pl.*

corpse *n.* a dead body

cor'pulence *n.* fatness.—**cor'pulent** *adj.* very stout

cor'puscle (kor'-pus-l) *n.* a minute particle, *esp.* the red and white corpuscles of the blood

corral' *n.* 1. a pen or enclosure for horses or cattle. 2. a circle of wagons to form an enclosure.—*v.* to make an enclosure

correct' *adj.* right, accurate.—*v.* 1. to reprove or punish, as *The teacher corrected the pupils.* 2. to put or make right, as *The teacher told the children to correct their mistakes in spelling.*—**correc'tion** (-shun) *n.* putting right.—**correct'ly** *adv.*

cor'relate *v.* to bring into mutual relation, as *Teachers try to correlate the various subjects they teach.*—**correla'tion** *n.*

correspond' *v.* 1. to exchange letters. 2. to agree with, as *Your impression of what happened corresponds with mine.*—**correspond'ence** *n.* 1. letters. 2. similarity.—**correspond'ent** *n.* 1. an agent employed by newspaper to send news. 2. a writer of letters

cor'ridor *n.* a passage in a building, railway-train, etc.

corrob'orate *v.* to confirm, as *The second witness corroborated the evidence of the first.*—**corrob'orating** *pres. part.*—**corrob'orated** *p.t.* and *p. part.*—**corrobora'tion** *n.* confirmation.—**corrob'orative** *adj.*

corroboree' *n.* an Australian aboriginal festival of tribal dances

corrode' *v.* to eat or wear away by degrees, as *Rust and acids corrode metals.*—**corro'sion** (kor-ō'zhun) *n.*—**corro'sive** *adj.* and *n.*

cor'rugated *adj.* bent into ridges and grooves, as *corrugated iron*

corrupt' *v.* 1. to make rotten. 2. to make evil, bribe.—*adj.* 1. rotten, dishonest. 2. spoilt by mistakes.—**corrup'tible** *adj.*—**corrup'tion** (-shun) *n.*—**corrup'tly** *adv.*

cor'sair *n.* pirate

corse'let *n.* body armour.—**cor'set** *n.* stiffened inner bodice

cor'tex *n.* bark.—**cor'tices** *pl.*—**cor'tical** *adj.*

corvette' *n.* a small fast-moving warship

cosmet'ic *n.* a preparation for the skin.—**cosmetic surgery** surgery to improve facial features

cos'mic (koz-mik) *adj.* relating to the universe.—**cos'mos** *n.* the universe.—**cos'monaut** (-not) *n.* an astronaut, esp. Russian.—**cosmopol'itan** *n.* a citizen of the world.—*adj.* free from national prejudice.—**cosmic rays** radiation reaching the earth from outer space

Coss'ack *n.* one of a group of people in South Russia, famous as horsemen

cost *n.* price in money, time or labour.—*v.* to have as price.—**cost** *p.t.*—**at all costs** at any price.—**cost price** the price paid

Note: This verb may also mean to put a price on an article or job. When it is used in this sense the *p.t.* and *p. part.* are *costed*, as *Those goods have not been costed yet*

cos'ter, cos'termonger *n.* a hawker of fruit, fish, etc.

cost'liness *n.* great cost.—**cost'ly** *adj.* expensive

cos'tume *n.* 1. a style of dress. 2. a woman's outer clothes. 3. fancy dress *adj.*, as *a costume ball, a costume play.*—**costu'mier** *n.* lady's tailor.—**costume jewellery** artificial jewellery worn as a part of an ensemble

co'sy (kō'zi) *adj.* snug, comfortable.—**co'sier** *comp.*—**co'siest** *sup.*—*n.* a cover for a tea-pot.—**co'siness** *n.*

cot *n.* a small house

cot *n.* a child's bed

cote *n.* a shelter for animals esp. sheep or doves. Hence **sheep-cote, dove-cote**

co'terie (kō'ter-i) *n.* a circle of persons with similar interests and views, a clique

cot'tage *n.* a small house.—**cot'tager** *n.*

Compare: house, cot, cabin, hut

cot'ton *n.* 1. a plant. 2. the white downy covering from its seeds. 3. cloth or thread made from this.—**cotton-wool'** *n.* a fluffy mass of cotton hairs.—**to wrap in cotton-wool** to pamper

cotyle'don (kot-i-lē'don) *n.* the seed-leaf of a plant.—**cotyle'donous** (kot-i-lē'don-us) *adj.*

couch (kowch) *n.* 1. a bed or sofa. 2. any resting place.—**couch'es** *pl.*—*v.* 1. to express, as *The message was couched in polite language.* 2. to lie down, as "*Here I couch when owls do cry.*" (*Midsummer Night's Dream*). 3. to lower (a spear)

cou'gar (koo'gar) *n.* a wild catlike animal, a puma

cough (kof) *v.* to expel air from the lungs with effort and noise.—*n.*

coun'cil (kown'sil) *n.* 1. assembly called together for discussion. 2. governing body of a city, town, etc.—**coun'cillor** *n.* member of council.—**Privy Council** a council appointed to advise the Sovereign

Note: These words should not be confused with *counsel* and *counsellor*

coun'sel (kown'sel) *n.* 1. advice, opinion. 2. a barrister.—*v.* to advise.—**coun'selling** *pres. part.*—**coun'selled** *p.t.* and *p. part.*—**coun'sellor** *n.* person who gives advice.—**counsel of perfection** good advice not easy to carry out

count (kownt) *v.* 1. to add up, reckon, as *He was counting his money.* 2. to include, as *There are six here, counting myself.* 3. to depend on, as *I count on your help.* 4. to be of importance, as *He is a man who counts in this city.*—*n.* a reckoning.—**count for** to be worth, as *That does not count for much.*—**count'less** *adj.* more than can be counted.—**on all counts** in every way.—**to count down** to count back to zero in sending off a missile.—**to count on** to rely on.—**to take no count off** to take no notice of.—**to take the count** (boxing) to be counted out

count (kownt) *n.* a nobleman.—**count'ess** *fem.*

coun'tenance (kown'te-nans) *n.* 1. the face. 2. its expression. 3. support.—*v.* to support, allow, permit, as *I cannot countenance such an action.*—**keep one's countenance** keep one's composure, or a straight face.—**keep in countenance** support a person (often by doing the same thing oneself).—**put out of countenance** disconcert a person

coun'ter (kown'ter) *n.* 1. piece of wood, metal, etc. used in reckoning. 2. table in bank or shop on which money is paid.—**Geiger counter** instrument for measuring radioactivity

coun'ter (kown'ter) *v.* to oppose.—*adj.* contrary.—*adv.* in the opposite direction.—**counteract'** *v.* to act contrary to, to hinder, neutralise

Note: Counter at the beginning of compound words means *against* or *opposite.* To find the meaning of such words as *counter-attack* look up the second half of the word

counterbalance *v.* to balance one weight with an equal one

coun'terfeit (-feet or -fit) *n.* a forgery, sham.—*v.* 1. to imitate with intent to deceive. 2. to forge.—*adj.* sham

coun'terfoil *n.* the part of a cheque, receipt, etc. kept as a record

countermand' *v.* to cancel (an order)—*n.*

coun'terpane *n.* a bed-covering, quilt

coun'terpart *n.* 1. a copy. 2. persons or things with close resemblance

coun'terpoint *n.* 1. a melody added as an accompaniment to another. 2. the act of doing so

coun'terpoise *n.* a weight which balances another

coun'tersign (sīn) *n.* 1. in the army a password. 2. a secret sign made in reply—*v.* to sign a document etc. already signed by someone else

coun'try (kun'tri) *n.* 1. a region. 2. land belonging to a nation. 3. land of one's birth. 4. inhabitants of a country, as *The country is tired of the present government.* 5. rural district (not town).—**a country cousin** someone bewildered by city life—**coun'tries** *pl.*—**coun'tryside** *n.*—**coun'trified** *adj.*

Compare: region, land, territory, district, area, neighbourhood

A *region* usually means a geographical or climatic division of the earth's surface, whereas *country* means a political division, e.g. France. A *territory* is usually part of a country, and we speak of British *territory* (i.e. possessions) in contrast with foreign *territory.* The terms *district* and *neighbourhood* all refer to smaller *areas* of land than does country. The word *land* is of general application, and may mean a *country* or a smaller or larger *area*

coun'ty (kown'ti) *n.* a division of a country or state.—**coun'ties** *pl.*

coup (kōō) *n.* a successful stroke

cou'pé (koo'pā) *n.* two-seater saloon motor-car

couple (kupl) *n.* a pair.—*v.* to connect.—**coup'ling** *n.* a device for connecting parts.—**coup'let** *n.* two lines of verse, rhyming and of equal length

cou'pon (kōō'pon) *n.* a ticket, entitling the holder to something

cour'age (kur'ij) *n.* bravery.—**coura'geous** (kur-ā'jus) *adj.* See **brave.**—**coura'geously** *adv.*

cou'rier (kōō'ri-er) *n.* 1. messenger. 2. attendant on travellers

course (kōrs) *n.* 1. way, path, track, as *race-course, course of a stream, golf-course, etc.* 2. line of action or behaviour, as *We decided what course to adopt.* 3. series, procedure, as *course of lectures, course of study.* 4. career, journey, as *a ship's course.* 5. part of a meal. 6. layer of stone in building. 7. a sail.—*v.* to run, to hunt.—**cours'ing** *pres. part.*—**coursed** *p.t.* and *p. part.*—**cour'ser** *n.* a swift horse.—**cours'ing** *n.* hunting hares.—**of course** naturally.—**a matter of course** usual thing.—**in the course of** during.—**in due course** at the right time

court (kōrt) *n.* 1. a yard. 2. residence of a sovereign. 3. attendants on a sovereign. 4. a seat of justice. 5. attention, flattery, as *to pay court to someone.*—*v.* to woo, to attract.—**cour'tier** (ti-er) *n.* a court-attendant.—**court'ship** *n.* wooing.—**court'ly** *adj.* very polite

Courtelle' (trade name) *n.* a man-made fibre

cour'teous (kur'te-us) *adj.* polite.—**cour'teously** *adv.*—**cour'tesy** *n.* politeness

court-house *n.* (N. Amer.) a building in which law cases are heard

court-mar'tial (kōrt-mar'shal) *n.* a naval or military court for trying offences.—**courts-mar'tial** *pl.*

court'yard *n.* a space enclosed by buildings

cousin (kuz'n) *n.* a son or daughter of an uncle or aunt

cove (kōv) *n.* a small inlet, bay

cov'enant (kuv'e-nant) *n.* 1. a contract. 2. an agreement.—*v.* to agree to.—**covenant'er** *n.* 1. one who covenants. 2. one who adhered to the Solemn League and Covenant in 1643, or Scottish National Covenant, in 1638

cov'er (kuv'er) *v.* 1. to place or spread over. 2. to protect, as *The rearguard covered the army's retreat.* 3. to shield, screen. 4. to deal with, include, as *His speech covered the whole subject.*—*n.* anything that hides or protects, lid.—**cov'ering** *n.* something that covers.—**cov'erlet** *n.* top covering of a bed.—**cover-point** (cricket) a fielder's position right of point.—**to break cover** to come out of hiding.—**to remain covered** to keep one's hat on.—**take cover** hide oneself

cov'ert (kuv'er or kuv'ert) *n.* a thicket, hiding-place.—*adj.* (kuv'ert) secret.—**cov'ertly** *adv.*

cov'et (kuv'et) *v.* to want eagerly what belongs to another.—**cov'etous** *adj.*—**cov'etousness** *n.*

Compare: envy, desire, greed, avarice

cov'ey (ku-vi) *n.* a small flock of birds

cow *n.* 1. a female ox. See **bull.** 2. female of elephant, whale, etc.—*v.* to fill with fear. —**cows, kine** *pl.*—**cow'herd** *n.* a man who tends cows.

cow'ard *n.* a person without courage.—**cow'ardice** (kow'ar-dis) *n.* want of courage. See **bravery.**—**cow'ardly** *adj.*

cow'boy *n.* herdsman on a ranch working usually on horseback

cow'er *v.* to crouch (in fear or cold)

cowl *n.* 1. a monk's hood. 2. a chimney cover. —**cow'ling** *n.* casing round an aero-engine

cow'slip *n.* a yellow field-flower

cox'comb (coks'kōm) *n.* a vain fellow

cox'swain, cox (kok'sn) *n.* one who has charge of, or steers a boat

coy *adj.* shy, or pretending to be shy.—**coy'ly** *adv.*—**coy'ness** *n.*

coyo'te (koi-ō'ti) *n.* a small North American prairie wolf

crab *n.* 1. water-animal with ten legs and broad hard shell. 2. sour person. 3. wild sour apple.—**catch a crab** in rowing to miss the water or strike it too deeply with the oar and therefore fall backwards.—**crabbed'** *adj.* 1. bad-tempered. 2. (of writing) hard to read, cramped.—**walk crabwise** walk sideways

crack *v.* 1. to break, split. 2. to make a sharp noise.—*n.* 1. a sharp noise. 2. a flaw, fissure.—*adj.* expert, as *a crack cyclist.*—**cracks'man** *n.* a burglar.—**at the crack of dawn** at daybreak

crack'er *n.* 1. a kind of firework. 2. a biscuit

crack'le *n.* sound of small cracks.—*v.*—**crack'ling** *n.* 1. crackle. 2. the rind of roast pork

cra'dle *n.* 1. rocking-cot for babies. 2. supporting frame. 3. S.A. and (Aus.) a box used by alluvial miners in final gold wash.—*v.* to lay as in a cradle

craft *n.* 1. skill, skilled trade.—**crafts** *pl.* 2. cunning. 3. ship, boat, vessel (also, collectively, ships, etc.)—**craft** *pl.*—**crafts'man** *n.*—**craft'y** *adj.* cunning.—**craf'tily** *adv.*

crag *n.* a steep, rugged rock.—**crag'gy** *adj.*

cram *v.* 1. to stuff, force into. 2. to learn too quickly.—**cram'ming** *pres. part.*—**crammed** *p.t.* and *p. part.*—**cram-full'** *adj.* full to overflowing

cramp *n.* painful contraction of muscles.—*v.* to hinder, limit

cran'berry *n.* a sour red berry.—**cran'berries** *pl.*

crane *n.* 1. a tall wading-bird. 2. a machine for raising heavy weights.—*v.* to stretch the neck.—**cra'ning** *pres. part.*—**craned** *p.t.* and *p. part.*—**crane'-fly** *n.* a daddy-long-legs

cra'nium (krā'ni-um) *n.* the skull

crank *n.* 1. lever. 2. a faddist.—*v.* to turn, wind.—**crank'shaft** *n.* the chief shaft of an engine

cran'ny *n.* a chink, open crack.—**cran'nies** *pl.*—**cran'nied** *adj.*

crash *n.* 1. a loud noise of breaking. 2. collapse or downfall.—*v.* to fall violently, to collapse.—he **crash'es.**—**crash'-dive** *n.* a sudden dive of an aeroplane or submarine. —*v.*—**crash'-helmet** *n.* a helmet worn by motor-cyclists.—**crash-land'ing** a forced landing of an aeroplane

crash *n.* coarse linen

crass *adj.* thick, stupid

crate *n.* a large packing case

cra'ter *n.* a cavity in the earth caused by a volcano, bomb, shell, etc.

cravat' *n.* a neck tie

crave *v.* 1. to long for, as *He craved for a*

cigarette. 2. to ask earnestly for, as *I crave your pardon*.—**cra'ving** *pres. part.*—**craved** *p.t.* and *p. part.*—**cra'ving** *n.*

cra'ven *adj.* cowardly.—*n.*

crawl *v.* 1. to move on hands and knees. 2. to move very slowly.—*n.* 1. a crawling or slow motion. 2. an overarm swimming stroke with the head kept low

cray'fish, craw'fish *n.* kind of fresh-water lobster

cray'on (krā'on) *n.* pencil of coloured chalk

craze *n.* 1. madness, mania. 2. a current popular fashion.—**cra'zy** *adj.* 1. falling to pieces. 2. made of pieces, as *crazy-paving*. 3. insane. 4. madly eager (for) as *crazy for pleasure*. 5. foolish

creak (kreek) *n.* a squeaking sound.—*v.*

cream (kreem) *n.* 1. the oily part of milk. 2. the best part of anything.—**cream'ery** *n.* dairy.—**cream'y** *adj.*—**cream-cheese'** *n.* soft cheese

crease (krees) *n.* 1. line made by folding. 2. (cricket) line showing bowler's and batsman's positions.—*v.*—**creas'ing** *pres. part.*—**creased** *p.t.* and *p. part.*

create' (kree-āt') *v.* 1. to make, cause. 2. to bring into being.—**crea'ting** *pres. part.*—**crea'ted** *p.t.* and *p. part.*—**crea'tion** (-shun) *n.* what is created.—**crea'tive** *adj.* inventive.—**Crea'tor** *n.* God.—**crea'ture** (kree'-chur) *n.* a living being

crèche (kresh) *n.* a public day-nursery where mothers at work can leave their babies

cre'dence (kree'dens) *n.* belief

creden'tials (kre-den'shals) *n.pl.* letters of introduction

cred'ible *adj.* believable

cred'it *n.* 1. belief. 2. good name, reputation. 3. confidence that goods bought will be paid for at a later date.—**cred'its** *pl.* the list of names appearing at the beginning or end of a film or television programme of those responsible for making it.—*v.* to believe.—**cred'itable** *adj.* bringing honour.—**cred'itor** *n.* one to whom a debt is due

credu'lity *n.* readiness to believe without proof.—**cred'ulous** *adj.*—**cred'ulousness** *n.*

creed *n.* a belief, doctrine

creek *n.* 1. a narrow inlet. 2. (Aus.) a small river

creep *v.* 1. to move like a snake. 2. to grow by clinging.—**crept** *p.t.* and *p. part.*—**cree'per** *n.* a climbing plant.—**cree'py** *adj.* uncanny, unpleasant

cremate' *v.* to burn, esp. a corpse.—**crema'ting** *pres. part.*—**cre'mated** *p.t.* and *p. part.*—**crema'tion** *n.*—**cremator'ium** *n.* place for cremation

cre'osote (kree'ō-sōt) *n.* oil from coal tar, used to preserve wood

crêpe (krāp) *n.* fabric with rough surface. When black, often used as mourning.—**crêpe-de-chine'** (sheen) *n.* a silk fabric.—**crêpe-rub'ber** *n.* rough-surfaced rubber

crescen'do (kre-shen'do) *n.* increase of loudness, esp. in music.—*adv.*

cres'cent (kres'ent) *n.* 1. the moon in her first quarter. 2. anything of this shape.—*adj.* growing, increasing

cress *n.* a plant with edible leaves

crest *n.* 1. a comb or tuft on an animal's head. 2. a plume on a helmet. 3. the top of a wave. 4. the badge above the shield of a coat-of-arms.—**crest'fallen** *adj.* discouraged by defeat or failure

cret'in *n.* an idiot

cretonne' *n.* a strong cotton cloth printed in colours, used for curtains, etc.

crevasse' *n.* a chasm in an icefield.—**crev'ice** (krev-is) *n.* a cleft, a crack

crew (krōō) *n.* 1. a ship or boat's company. 2. a gang, set

crib *n.* 1. a rack for fodder. 2. a child's bed. 3. a translation.—*v.* to copy, cheat.—**cribbing** *pres. part.*—**cribbed** *p.t.* and *p. part.*—**crib'bage** *n.* a card game

crick'et *n.* a kind of grasshopper

crick'et *n.* a team-game played with bats, ball and stumps

crime *n.* 1. a wicked act. 2. lawbreaking.—**crim'inal** *n.* and *adj.*—**criminol'ogy** *n.* the study of crime

crim'son (krim'zon) *n.* a deep red

cringe (krinj) *v.* to shrink, cower.—**cring'ing** *pres. part.*—**cringes** *p.t.* and *p. part,*

crin'kle (kring'kl) *v.* 1. to form into wrinkles. 2. to rustle

crin'oline (krin'o-leen) *n.* a hooped petticoat

crip'ple *n.* a lame person.—*v.* to disable, weaken.—**crip'pling** *pres. part.*—**crip'pled** *p.t.* and *p. part.*

cri'sis (krī'sis) *n.* a turning point, decisive moment.—**cri'ses** (krī'seez) *pl.*

crisp *adj.* brittle and firm.—*n.* a wafer of fried potato

criss-cross *n.* a pattern of crossing lines

crite'rion (krī-tee'ri-on) *n.* a standard of judgment, test.—**crite'ria** *pl.*

crit'ic *n.* 1. one who judges books, plays, films, etc. 2. a person who finds fault.—**crit'ical** *adj.* 1. like a critic, judging, fault-finding. 2. at a turning point, in danger, as *He is in hospital in a critical condition*.—**crit'ically** *adv.*—**crit'icise** (krit'i-sīz) *v.* to examine and judge.—**crit'icising** *pres. part.*—**crit'icised** *p.t.* and *p. part.*—**crit'icism** *n.* 1. judgment. 2. fault-finding

croak (krōk) *n.* a hoarse cry.—*v.*

cro'chet (krō'shā) *n.* a kind of fine netting, done with a **crochet hook**.—*v.*

crock *n.* a jar or pot.—**crock'ery** *n.* earthenware

croc'odile (krok'ō-dīl) *n.* a large reptile.—**croc'odile tears** sham tears

cro'cus *n.* a spring flower

croft *n.* a small farm.—**crof'ter**

crook *n.* 1. a shepherd's hooked staff. 2. any hook. 3. a criminal, swindler.—*v.* to bend.—**crook'ed** *adj.* twisted

croon *v.* to sing or hum a soft sentimental song

crop *n.* 1. the produce of a field, harvest. 2. a bird's food-pouch. 3. a close hair-cut. 4. a hunting whip.—*v.* 1. to cut short, as hair, etc. 2. to eat down, as *The horse was cropping the grass.*—**crop'ping** *pres. part.*—**cropped** *p.t.* and *p. part.*—**crop up** to happen, occur.—**come a cropper** to fall heavily

cro'quet (krō'kā) *n.* a garden game played with hoops, mallets and ball

cross *n.* 1. post with cross-bar. 2. **the Cross** that on which Christ died. 3. a misfortune, an affliction. 4. animal or plant of mixed breed. 5. mark made by crossing two lines (× or +)—*v.* 1. to pass across or over, as *to cross the road.* 2. to place across, draw across, as *to cross one's legs, to cross a "t."* 3. to mix breeds. 4. to oppose.—he **cross'es.**—*adj.* annoyed.—**cross'ly** *adv.*—**to cross a cheque** to draw two lines across so that it can only be paid into a bank.—**to cross one's mind** to occur to one.—**to cross someone's path** to interfere with his plans

Note: The word *cross* is often used in compound words such as *cross-country, cross-stitch,* in which the meaning can be inferred by adding *across* to the meaning of the second part of the word

cross'bow *n.* a bow on long stock

cross'breed *n.* a plant or animal produced by crossing two breeds.—**cross'bred** *adj.*

cross-exam'ine *v.* to question a witness after he had given evidence for the other side

cross'ing *n.* 1. a place where roads cross. 2. a sea-passage. 3. a place where one may cross the road, as *a pedestrian crossing*

cross'roads *n.* a road junction

cross'word *n.* a puzzle made up of squares to be filled in with letters

crot'chet *n.* a musical note (♩)

crouch (krowch) *v.* to bend low with legs bent.—he **crouch'es**

croup (krōōp) *n.* a throat complaint with cough

croup (krōōp) *n.* a horse's hind-quarters

crow (krō) *n.* a large, black bird

crow (krō) *n.* a cock's cry.—*v.* **crowed, crew** *p.t.*—**crow over a person, or about something,** to exult, boast

crow'bar (krō'bar) *n.* an iron bar used as lever

crowd *n.* a mass of people.—*v.* 1. to flock together. 2. to fill.—**crowd'ed** *adj.* full of people

Compare: (with *n.*) multitude, mob, company, assemblage, throng, mass. (with *adj.*) thronged, assembled, massed

crown *n.* 1. a monarch's head-dress. 2. a wreath. 3. a coin. 4. top of head, hat, hill. —*v.* 1. to put a crown on. 2. to be at the top of, as *A monument crowned the summit of the hill.*—**crown prince** the heir to a throne

cru'cial (krōō'shal) *adj.* decisive

cru'cible (krōō'si-bl) *n.* a melting-pot

cru'cifix (krōō'si-fiks) *n.* a figure of Christ on the Cross.—**crucifix'ion** *n.* (-fik'-shun) being crucified.—**cru'cify** *v.* to put to death on a cross.—**cru'cified** *p.t.* and *p. part.*

crude *adj.* 1. raw, unfinished. 2. harsh, rough.—**cru'dity** *n.*

cru'el *adj.* 1. delighting in causing pain. 2. hard-hearted. 3. severe, distressing, as *to suffer a cruel blow.*—**cru'elly** *adv.*—**cru'elty** *n.* 1. fondness for being cruel. 2. cruel action

cru'et *n.* a set of containers for salt, pepper, etc.

cruise (krōōz) *v.* to sail about.—**crui'sing** *pres. part.*—**cruised** *p.t.* and *p. part.*—*n.* a cruising voyage.—**crui'ser** (krōō'zer) *n.* warship.—**cruis'er-weight** *n.* (boxing) a light heavyweight

crumb (krum) *n.* 1. a small bit of bread, cake etc. 2. soft part of bread. 3. a tiny portion. —*v.*

crum'ble *v.* to break into small fragments.—**crum'bling** *pres. part.*—**crum'bled** *p.t.* and *p. part.*

crum'pet *n.* a flat, soft, unsweetened cake, eaten toasted

crum'ple *v.* to crush, crease.—**crum'pling** *pres. part.*—**crum'pled** *p.t.* and *p. part.*

crunch *n.* a crisp sound.—*v.* to chew, tread, etc. making this sound

crusade' *n.* 1. a war to win the Holy Land from the Turks. 2. a campaign against evil.—**crusa'der** *n.*

crush *v.* 1. to break or crumple by pressing. 2. to defeat as *The rebellion was crushed.*—he **crush'es.**—*n.* a crowd.—**crush'-barrier** *n.* a steel barrier to control crowds

Compare: break, smash, conquer, subdue, repress

crust *n.* 1. the hard surface of bread. 2. a hard outer surface.—**crust'y** *adj.* 1. hard. 2. bad-tempered.—**crusta'cean** (krus-tā'-shan) *n.* a hard-shelled animal.—**crusta'cea** (shi-a) *pl.*

crutch *n.* a support for cripples.—**crut'ches** *pl.*

cry (krī) *v.* 1. to utter a call esp. announcing that you have something to sell. 2. to shout. 3. to weep.—he **cries.**—**cry'ing** *pres. part.*—**cried** *p.t.* and *p. part.*—*n.* 1. a call, shout, wail. 2. popular saying or demand, catch-word.—**cry'ing** *adj.* flagrant, notorious, as *a crying shame.*—**cry quits** to say that neither party has an advantage.—**a far cry** a long way.—**in full cry** in full pursuit.—**cry up** to praise.—**cry down** to disparage.—**to cry over spilt milk** to make a fuss over something which cannot be altered

crypt (kript) *n.* a vault esp. under a church.—**crypt'ic** *adj.* secret, mysterious

crypt'ogam *n.* a plant like a fungus reproducing by spores

crypt'ogram *n.* a secret writing

crys'tal (kris'tal) *n.* 1. a clear, transparent mineral. 2. very clear glass. 3. a natural form assumed by certain minerals, glassy and regular.—**crys'talline** *adj.*—**crys'tallise** *v.* to form into crystals

cub *n.* the young of a fox, etc.

Cu'ba *n.* a large island between Mexico and Florida.—**Cu'ban** *n.* a native of Cuba

cub'by-hole *n.* a very small room, snug place

cube (kūb) *n.* 1. a regular solid body contained by six equal squares. 2. the product of a number multiplied by itself twice, as *The cube of two is eight.*—**cu'bic, cu'bical** *adj.*—**cube root** a number which when multiplied by itself twice gives the cube, as 2 *is the cube root of* 8

cu'bicle (kū'bi-kl) *n.* small compartment in a larger room

cu'bit (kū'bit) *n.* a measure of 18 inches

cuck'oo (kōō'kōō) *n.* a bird named from its call

cu'cumber (kū'kum-ber) *n.* a plant with long, fleshy green fruit

cud *n.* food chewed again by cows, etc.

cud'dle *v.* to hug, to fondle

cud'gel (ku'jel) *n.* a short thick stick.—*v.* to beat.—**cud'gelling** *pres. part.*—**cud'gelled** *p.t.* and *p. part.*—to take **up the cudgels** (on behalf of someone or something) to stand up for, take the part of

cue (kū) *n.* 1. a signal, hint. 2. billiards player's long rod

cuff *n.* wrist-band, end of sleeve.—**cuff'-link** *n.* a metal fastening for a cuff

cuff *n.* blow with the hand.—*v.*

cuirass' (kwi-ras') *n.* a breast-plate

cuisine' (kwee-zeen') *n.* a style of cooking

cul-de-sac *n.* a blind alley.—**culs-de-sac** *pl.*

cul'inary *adj.* relating to cooking

cull *v.* to gather, select, pick

cull'ender *n.* see **col'ander**

cul'minate *v.* 1. to reach the top. 2. to end in, reach a result.—**cul'minating** *adj.* final.—**culmin-ation** (-shun) *n.* the highest point, climax

cul'pable *adj.* deserving blame

cul'prit *n.* an offender

cult *n.* 1. a system of religious belief. 2. worship. 3. popular admiration for someone in which the dress and mannerisms of that person are imitated by a great number, as *the Beatles cult*

cul'tivate *v.* 1. to prepare soil and grow crops. 2. to improve. 3. to cherish, seek after, as *to cultivate someone's company.*—**cul'tivated** *adj.* 1. planted with crops. 2. cultured.—**cultiva'tion** (-shun) *n.*—**cul'tivator** *n.* a machine for tilling land

cul'ture *n.* 1. farming. 2. careful raising, as of bees, etc. 3. mind-training, refinement. 4. the particular form of intellectual development of a community.—**cul'tured** *adj.* educated, having refined tastes.—**cul'tural** *adj.*

cul'vert *n.* an underground water-channel

cum'ber *v.* to hinder.—**cum'bersome, cum'brous** *adj.* clumsy, awkward

cum'ulative *adj.* increasing

cun'ning *n.* 1. skill. 2. skill in deceit. See **craft.**—*adj.* skilful, sly

cup *n.* 1. a drinking-vessel with handle. 2. anything of that shape.—**cup'ful** *n.*—**cup'fuls** *pl.*—**cup'board** (kub'erd) *n.* a closed case with shelves.—**cup'pa** *n.* a cup of tea.—**cup'-tie** *n.* a football match in a knockout competition for a cup

cupid'ity (kū-) *n.* greed

cupr'ic, cupr'ous (kū) *adj.* (chemistry) containing copper

cur *n.* 1. a mongrel dog. 2. an ill-bred person

cu'rate (kū'rāt) *n.* an assistant clergyman.—**cu'racy** (kū'ra-si) *n.*

cura'tor (kū-rā'tor) *n.* a person in charge, esp. of a museum, art-gallery, etc.

curb *n.* 1. a chain on horse's bit. 2. a check. 3. edging of path, fire-place, etc., same as *kerb.*—*v.* to hold back, as *You must learn to curb your impatience*

curd *n.* milk turned thick and sour.—**cur'dle** *v.* to turn thick

cure (kūr) *v.* 1. to make well. 2. to preserve (skins, meat, etc.). 3. spiritual care, as *A clergyman has the cure of souls.*—*n.* successful treatment.—**cur'able** *adj.* able to be cured.—**cur'ative** able to cure

cur'few (kur'few) *n.* a bell rung at fixed hour, formerly as signal to put out fires, now to mark time when inhabitants must be indoors

cu'rio (kū'ri-o) *n.* something odd and rare.—**cu'ri-os** *pl.*

curios'ity (kū-ri-os'it-i) *n.* 1. eagerness to know. 2. something strange.—**cu'rious** *adj.* 1. eager to know, as *The villagers threw curious glances at the strangers.* See **inquisitive.** 2. strange, as *The explorer brought back many curious objects.*—**cu'riously** *adv.*

curl *v.* to twist into rings or loops.—*n.* a lock of hair.—**curl'y** *adj.*—**cur'ling** *n.* a game played on ice with flat heavy stones.—**cur'ler** *n.* a roller for curling hair

cur'lew (kur-lū) *n.* a long-billed waterbird

cur'rant *n.* 1. a small dried grape. 2. a small sour red or black berry

cur'rawong *n.* a common Australian bird

cur'rency (kur'en-si) *n.* 1. money in use. 2. circulation

cur'rent *n.* a flow of air, water, etc.—*adj.* in general or present use, as *a current expression a current issue of a magazine.*—**current events** present day affairs

curric'ulum (kur-i'kū-lum) *n.* a course of study.—**curric'ula** *pl.*

cur'ry *v.* 1. to rub down (a horse). 2. to dress (leather).—he **cur'ries.**—**cur'ried** *p.t.*

and *part. p.*—**curry favour** to seek for favours by flattery

cur'ry *n.* 1. hot seasoning. 2. a dish of stewed meat or fish with hot seasoning

curse *v.* 1. to swear. 2. to call down evil on.—*n.* 1. bad language. 2. evil called down on someone. 3. a scourge, affliction.—**cursed** (kurst) *adj.* under a curse

cur'sive *adj.* (handwriting) with linked letters

cur'sory *adj.* short, hasty, as *He gave a cursory glance at the letter before turning to other matters*

curt *adj.* short, rudely brief.—**curt'ly** *adv.*

curtail' *v.* to cut short.—**curtail'ment** *n.*

cur'tain (kur'tin) *n.* 1. a cloth hung as a screen. 2. screen between audience and stage.—**cur'tain-raiser** *n.* short play before the main one.—**to draw a curtain over** to say no more about it

curt'sy *n.* a woman's bow.—**curt'sies** *pl.*—*v.* to bow low.—she **curt'sies.**—**curt'sying** *pres. part.*—**curt'sied** *p.t.* and *p. part.*

curve *n.* a bent line.—*v.* to bend into a curve.—**cur'ving** *pres. part.*——**curved** *p.t.* and *p. part.*—**cur'vature** *n.* amount of curve

cush'ion (kōōsh'in) *n.* a bag filled with stuffing of air

cus'tard *n.* cooked eggs and milk

cus'tody *n.* 1. safe keeping. 2. imprisonment.—**custo'dian** *n.* keeper

cus'tom *n.* 1. a fashion, habit. 2. a tax on goods entering or leaving a country. 3. regular business dealing.—**cus'tomary** *adj.* usual.—**cus'tomarily** *adv.*—**cus'tomer** *n.* one who buys.—**cus'tom-house** *n.* place where dues are paid at a sea-por t

cut *n.* 1. a sharp stroke with a knife, tool, bat, etc. 2. a blow. 3. a wound. 4. an omission or abbreviation.—*v.* 1. to divide with, e.g. a knife. 2. to wound. 3. reduce, as wages, prices, etc.—**cut'ting** *pres. part.*—**cut** *p.t.* and *p. part.*—*adj.* as *cut glass.*—**a cut above** something better.—**cut and dried** decided beforehand.—**cut glass** glass in which the pattern is cut and not stamped.—**to cut both ways** to produce two effects.—**to be cut out for** to be fitted for.—**to cut dead** to snub.—**to cut it fine** to leave little margin.—**to cut no ice** to make no difference.—**to cut off with a shilling** to disinherit.—**to cut one's coat according to one's cloth** to spend only what one has.—**to cut someone dead** deliberately to ignore him.—**to cut up rough** to cause a commotion

cute *adj.* charming, quick-witted

cu'ticle (kū'tikl) *n.* an outer skin

cut'lass *n.* a sailor's short sword

cut'ler *n.* one who makes, repairs and sells knives, etc.—**cut'lery** *n.* knives, etc.

cut'let *n.* a slice of meat

cut'ter *n.* 1. a person or machine that cuts. 2. a warship's boat

cut'tlefish *n.* a sea-animal which squirts out inky fluid when attacked

cy'anide (sī'a-nīd) *n.* a poisonous chemical, a salt of prussic acid

cy'cle (sī'kl) *n.* 1. a series. 2. a period of time. 3. a group of poems or songs. 4. a bicycle.—*v.* to ride a bicycle.—**cy'cling** *pres. part.*—**cy'cled** *p.t.* and *p. part.*—**cy'clist** *n.*

cy'clone (sī'klōn) *n.* a circular storm around a region of low air-pressure.—**cyclon'ic** (sī-klon'ik) *adj.*

cy'clops *n.* a water creature with one eye

cyg'net (sig'net) *n.* a young swan

cyl'inder (sil'in-der) *n.* 1. a roller-shaped body, roll. 2. the piston-chamber of an engine.—**cylin'drical** *adj.*

cym'bals (sim'balz) *n.pl.* saucer-shaped brass clappers used in orchestras

Cym'ric *adj.* Welsh

cyn'ic (sin'ik) *n.* a sneering person who doubts human goodness.—**cy'nical** *adj.*—**cy'nicism** (sin'i-sizm) *n.*

cy'nosure (sī'nō-shoor) *n.* centre of attraction

cy'press (sī'pres) *n.* a cone-bearing tree

cyst (sist) *n.* a kind of deep blister containing fluid

czar, tsar (zar) *n.* a former emperor of Russia.—**czari'na** (-ee') *fem.*

Czechoslovak'ia (chek-ō-slōv-ak'i-a) *n.* a country in central Europe.—**Czechoslovak'ian** *n.* a native of Czechoslovakia

D

dab *n.* 1. a slight tap. 2. a smear. 3. a small flat fish.—*v.* to strike or touch feebly.—**dab'bing** *pres. part.*—**dabbed** *p.t., p. part.*

dab'ble *v.* 1. to splash about. 2. to trifle, to do with no serious interest (followed by *with* or *in*)

dace *n.* a small fresh-water fish

dachs'hund (daks'hoont) *n.* a short-legged dog with long body

dad, dad'dy *n.* father.—**dad'dy-long'legs** *n.* a crane fly

da'do *n.* moulding or skirting round lower part of room wall.—**da'does** *pl.*

daff'odil *n.* a yellow type of narcissus

dagg'er *n.* a short sword.—**at daggers drawn** full of hate

dahl'ia (dā'li-a) *n.* a garden flower grown from a tuber

dai'ly *adj.* happening, or published every day.—*n.* a daily newspaper.—**dai'lies** *pl.*—*adv.* every day

dain'ty *adj.* 1. pretty, delicate. 2. hard to please.—**dain'tily** *adv.*—**dain'tiness** *n.*

dai'ry (dā'ri) *n.* a place where milk, butter, etc., are kept or sold.—**dai'ries** *pl.*

dais (dās) *n.* a low platform

dale *n.* a valley, glen

dal'ly *v.* to trifle with, to waste time.—he **dal'lies.**—**dal'lying** *pres. part.*—**dal'lied** *p.t.* and *p. part.*—**dal'liance** *n.*

Dalma'tian *n.* a type of dog, white with black spots

dam *n.* a mother (of animals).—**sire** *masc.*

dam *n.* 1. a bank to stop water. 2. water so collected.—*v.* to hold with a dam (often followed by *up*).—**dam'ming** *pres. part.*—**dammed** *p.t.* and *p. part.*

dam'age (dam'ij) *n.* injury, harm. *pl.* money in compensation for harm, or injury

dam'ask *n.* flowered silk or linen. *adj.* rose-coloured

dame *n.* a lady (often elderly).—**squire** *masc.*

damn (dam) *v.* to condemn.—**damna'tion** (-shun) *n.* 1. doom, curse, condemnation. 2. an impatient interjection

damp *n.* 1. moisture. 2. a dangerous gas in coal-mines.—*v.* 1. to moisten. 2. to discourage, as *Our enthusiasm has been damped by your gloomy warnings.*—*adj.* **dam'per** *n.* plate in a flue.—**damp'ness** *n.*—**damp'en** *v*, to moisten

dam'sel (dam'zel) *n.* a girl

dam'son *n.* a small plum

dance *n.* 1. a movement in time with music. 2. a dancing-party.—*v.* 1. to move with rhythmic steps esp. to music. 2. to move, or cause to move, up and down.—**dan'cing** *pres. part.*—**danced** *p.t.* and *p. part.*—**dan'cer** *n.*—**to lead someone a dance**

dan'dle *v.* to move (a child) up and down

dan'druff *n.* scurf on the head

dan'dy *n.* a man very attentive to dress.—**dan'dies** *pl.*

dan'ger (dān'jer) *n.* risk, exposure to injury. —**dan'gerous** (dān'jer-us) *adj.*—**dan'gerously** *adv.*—**dan'ger-money** *n.* extra money paid for dangerous work

Compare: peril, insecurity, jeopardy, hazard. *Contrast:* safety, security, protection, shelter

dan'gle (dang'gl) *v.* to hang loosely.—**dan'gling** *pres. part.*—**dan'gled** *p.t.* and *p. part.*

Dan'ish *adj.* belonging to Denmark

dank *adj.* unpleasantly or unhealthily moist, as *a dank cellar*

dap'per *adj.* 1. neat. 2. little and active

dap'ple *n.* a spot.—*v.* to mark with rounded spots.—**dap'pled** *adj.* spotted

dare *v.* 1. to have the courage, as *Dare you do it?* 2. to challenge, defy, as *He dared me to do it.*—he **dares**, he **dare not**, we, you, they **dare.**—**da'ring** *pres. part.*—**durst, dared,** *p.t.*—**dared** *p. part.*—**da'ring** *adj.* 1. bold, brave. 2. audacious.—**dare'-devil** *n.* a reckless person

darg *n.* (Aus.) quantity of work a coalminer is allowed to do in a given time by agreement or award

dark *adj.* 1. dim, without light. 2. gloomy, as *The outlook is dark.* 3. secret, wicked, as *The criminal had dark designs.* 4. of a deep colour, as *dark blue.*—*n.* blackness, ignorance.—**dark'en** *v.*—**dark'ling** *adj.* and *adv.* in the dark.—**dark'ly** *adv.*—**dark'ness** *n.* lack of light.—**Dark Ages** the 5th to the 12th centuries in Europe when little progress was made.—**dark horse** someone mysterious, not well known.—**dark'room** a darkened room used for photography.—**to keep it dark** to say nothing

Compare: black, dusky, murky, dim, obscure, shadowy, swarthy. *Contrast:* light, bright, brilliant, clear, gleaming, illuminated

dar'ling *n.* and *adj.* beloved

darn *v.* to mend.—*n.* a mend.—**darn'ing** *n.*

dart *n.* 1. a light, pointed weapon. 2. a quick move, as *He made a dart for the door.* 3. *pl.* indoor game with target.—*v.* to throw or move rapidly.—**dart'board** *n.* a circular board used in the game of darts

dash *n.* 1. a rush, as *He made a dash for the door.* 2. energy, as *The team played with great dash.* 3. a mark.—*v.* 1. to throw violently. 2. to rush.—he **dash'es.**—**dash'ing** *adj.* showy.—**dash'board** a panel near car-driver with indicators, etc.

das'tard *n.* a coward.—**das'tardly** *adj.* cowardly

da'ta (dā'ta) *n.pl.* facts given or accepted.—**da'tum** *sing.*

date *n.* the fruit of the palm

date *n.* 1. time. 2. stating of time.—*v.* to write the date.—**out of date'** *adj.* old-fashioned.—**up to date** *adj.* 1. modern. 2. up to now.—**date'-line** *n.* the line of longitude 180° from Greenwich, on either side of which the date changes

daub *v.* 1. to smear, splash on. 2. to paint badly.—*n.*—**wattle and daub** (of a house) wood and clay

daugh'ter (daw'ter) *n.* a girl-child.—**son** *masc.*—**daugh'ter-in-law** *n.* a son's wife

daunt (dawnt) *v.* to frighten, put off.—**daunt'-less** *adj.* fearless

dau'phin (daw'fin) *n.* formerly French king's eldest son

dav'its *n.pl.* two cranes on a ship's side for lowering and raising life-boats

Davy Jones *n.* (among sailors) the Devil.—**Davy Jones's locker** the grave of those drowned at sea

daw'dle *v.* to waste time, loiter

dawn *n.* daybreak.—*v.* 1. to grow light. 2. to become apparent, as *It at last dawned on him that he was in danger*

day *n.* 1. the time between sunrise and sunset. 2. period of 24 hours. 3. date, time, as *the present day.* 4. daylight.—**day'break, day-spring** the dawn.—**day'dream** absent-minded thoughts.—**day'light saving** altering the clock in summer to make the day appear longer.—**day in day out** daily for a long time.—**to call it a day** to finish work. —**to see daylight** to see the end in sight.—**to win the day** to win the battle

daze *v.* to confuse, bewilder.—**dazed** *adj.*

daz'zle *v.* to blind, confuse with brightness.—*n.*—**dazz'ling** *pres. part.*—**dazz'led** *p.t.* and *p. part.*

dea'con (dee'kon) *n.* 1. the lowest order of the clergy. 2. an official of a Free Church. —**dea'coness** *fem.*

dead (ded) *adj.* 1. no longer alive. 2. without feeling, movement, energy. 3. complete, sure.—*adv.* utterly, as *dead certain.*—**the dead** *n.pl.*—**dead'en** *v.* to reduce (pain, sound, etc.).—**dead'ly** *adv.* fatal.—**dead-beat'**, **dead-tired'** *adj.* utterly exhausted.—**dead-heat'** *n.* race where two competitors finish exactly together.—**dead-lett'er** *n.* 1. a law no longer observed. 2. a letter which post cannot deliver.—**Dead Heart'** *n.* Central Australian desert country.—**dead'line** *n.* the time for a task to be finished.—**dead'-lock** *n.* a stand-still.—**dead'pan** *adj.* without expression.—**dead shot'** *n.* a very good shot

deaf (def) *adj.* unable, or unwilling to hear.—**deaf'en** *v.*—**deaf'ness** *n.*—**deaf mute'** *n.* one both deaf and dumb

deal *n.* fir or pine wood

deal *v.* 1. to give out esp. cards. 2. to do business (with).—**dealt** (delt) *p.t.* and *p. part.*—*n.* 1. a share. 2. a quantity. 3. a bargain.—**deal'er** *n.* trader.—**to deal with** to handle, do business with, be concerned with.—**square deal** a fair bargain

dean *n.* 1. the head of a cathedral chapter. 2. a university official.—**dean'ery** *n.* a dean's house or office

dear *adj.* 1. beloved. 2. expensive.—*n.* beloved one.—*adv.* at a high price, as *His success cost him dear.*—**dear'ly** *adv.*

dearth (derth) *n.* scarcity

death (deth) *n.* 1. the end of life. 2. the end.—**death'less** *adj.* immortal.—**death'ly** *adj.* and *adv.*—**death'-rate** *n.* the number of deaths per year per thousand of the population.—**at death's door** in extreme danger of death.—**death'-bed** the last illness

debar' *v.* to shut out, prevent.—**debar'ring** *pres. part.*—**debarred'** *p.t.* and *p. part.*

debase' *v.* to lower in value, quality, character, esp. coinage by introduction of increased proportion of base metal.—**debas'ing** *pres. part.*—**debased'** *p.t.* and *p. part.*—**debasement** *n.*

debate' *v.* 1. to discuss, argue. 2. to consider.—**deba'ting** *pres. part.*—**deba'ted** *p.t.* and *p. part.*—*n.* discussion.—**deba'table** *adj.*

debauch' *v.* to corrupt.—*n.* a drinking bout.—**debauch'ery** *n.* vice

debil'itate *v.* to weaken.—**debil'ity** *n.* weakness esp. in health

deb'it *n.* book-keeping, entry of sum owed.—*v.* to charge

debonair' *adj.* pleasant, gay

deb'ris (dā'bree) *n. sing.* and *pl.* fragments, rubbish

debt (det) *n.* something owed.—**debt'or** (det'or) *n.* person owing.—**bad debt** a debt which cannot be recovered.—**debt of honour** a debt which need not be paid by law, depending only on the debtor's honour.—**in debt** owing money or goods
Contrast: creditor

dé'but (dā'bū) *n.* a first appearance.—**débutante'** *n.* a young woman first appearing in society, etc.

dec'ade *n.* a period of ten years

dec'adence *n.* decline, decay.—**dec'adent** *adj.*

dec'agon *n.* (geometry) a ten-sided figure

dec'alogue (dek'a-log) *n.* the Ten Commandments

dec'ametre *n.* ten metres in length

decamp' *v.* to make off

decan'ter *n.* a stoppered bottle for wine

decap'itate *v.* to behead.—**decapita'tion** *n.*

decar'bonise *v.* to remove carbon from the pistons and cylinder of an engine

decay' *v.* to rot, waste away.—*n.* waste, loss

decease' (de-sees') *n.* death.—**deceased'** *adj.* dead

deceit' (de-seet') *n.* lying, dishonesty.—**deceit'ful** *adj.*—**deceive'** (de-seev') *v.* to lie, mislead.—**deceiv'ing** *pres. part.*—**deceived'** *p.t.* and *p. part.*

Decem'ber (de-sem'ber) *n.* the twelfth month

de'cency (dee'sen-si) *n.* 1. fit and reasonable behaviour. 2. respectability.—**de'cent** *adj.*
Compare: seemly, decorous, modest, proper

decep'tion (de-sep'shun) *n.* fraud, sham.—**decep'tive** *adj.* misleading

dec'ibel (des'ib-el) *n.* a unit of the loudness of a sound

decide' (de-sīd') *v.* 1. to settle. 2. to determine.—**deci'ding** *pres. part.*—**deci'ded** *p.t.* and *p. part.*—**deci'ded** *adj.* resolute.—**deci'dedly** *adv.*

decid'uous (de-sid'ū-us) *adj.* losing leaves annually, as *An oak is a deciduous tree*

dec'imal (des'i-mal) *adj.* 1. counted by tens or tenths. 2. the point separating units from fractions ($^1/_{10}$ths, $^1/_{100}$ths, etc.) as, 1·57 means $1^{57}/_{100}$.—**decimal system** system of weights, measures, money, etc. based on the number ten

dec'imate (des'i-māt) *v.* to destroy one-tenth, or a great number

dec'imetre *n.* one-tenth of a metre

deci'pher (de-sī'fer) *v.* 1. to decode. 2. to make out the meaning of

decis'ion (de-sizh'un) *n.* 1. settlement, conclusion, as *The decision of the manager is that the sale is to begin next week.* 2. firmness, as *to act with decision.*—**deci'sive** (de-sī'siv) *adj.* definite, as *a decisive victory*

deck *n.* a platform covering a ship's hull.—**deck'-chair** *n.* a folding easy chair.—**deck'-hand** *n.* a sailor working on deck.—**dou'ble-deck'er** *n.* a bus with an upper passenger deck.—**to clear the decks** to get ready for action

deck *v.* to decorate, adorn

declaim' *v.* to recite, make a speech.—**declama'tion** *n.*

declara'tion *n.* announcement, statement, as *The Declaration of American Independence.*—**declare'** *v.* to announce.—**decla'ring** *pres. part.*—**declared'** *p.t.* and *p. part.*

declen'sion *n.* in grammar, the change in

the form of nouns, pronouns and adjectives corresponding to their function in the sentence, as *he, his, him*

decline′ *v.* 1. to go, slope or lean down. 2. to grow weak. 3. to refuse, as *to decline an offer of help.*—**decli′ning** *pres. part.*—**declined′** *p.t.* and *p. part.*—*n.* 1. wasting away. 2. to give the declension of a noun or pronoun

decliv′ity *n.* a slope, an incline

decode′ *v.* to translate a secret code message

decompose′ 1. to separate into elements. 2. to rot.—**decomposi′tion** *n.*

de′cor (dā′kor) *n.* (stage) scenery and furnishings

dec′orate *v.* 1. to adorn, beautify. 2. to give a medal, etc., to. 3. to renew paint and paper.—**dec′orating** *pres. part.*—**dec′orated** *p.t.* and *p. part.*—**decora′tion** *n.* 1. ornament. 2. medal.—**dec′orative** *adj.*—**decora′tor** *n.* a person who paints and papers houses

dec′orous (dek′or-us or dek-or′us) *adj.* behaving properly, dignified.—**dec′orously** *adv.*—**decor′um** *n.* fit and proper behaviour

decoy′ *n.* anything used to entrap others, a bait.—*v.* to entice

decrease′ (dee-krees′) *v.* to make or grow less.—*n.*—**decreas′ing** *pres. part.*—**decreased′** *p.t.* and *p. part.*

decree′ *n.* decision made by a court, order, proclamation.—*v.* to order.—**decree′ing** *pres. part.*—**decreed′** *p.t.* and *p. part.*

decrep′it *adj.* old and feeble, worn out.—**decrep′itude** *n.*

decry′ *v.* to belittle—he **decries′**—**decry′ing** *pres. part.*—**decried′** *p.t.* and *p. part.*

ded′icate *v.* 1. to set apart for some purpose. 2. to devote to God's service. 3. to inscribe a book, etc. to a person.—**dedica′tion** *n.*

deduce′ (de-dūs′) *v.* to reason from facts, infer

deduct′ *v.* to subtract, as *A pound was deducted from each man's wages.*—**deduc′tion** (-shun) *n.* 1. an inference. 2. a subtracting

deed *n.* 1. an act, something done. 2. a legal document

deem *v.* to consider, judge, as *We deemed him worthy of the honour.*—**deem′ster** *n.* in the Isle of Man, a judge

deep *adj.* 1. far down or back. 2. profound, heartfelt. 3. cunning. 4. of colour, dark and rich.—*n.* the sea.—*adv.* far down.—**deep′en** *v.*—**deep′ly** *adv.*—**deep-freeze** refrigeration at a very low temperature.—**deep-fry** to fry by immersing in hot fat.—**deep-litter** a method of rearing poultry on a floor covered with waste.—**deep-rooted, deep-seated** well in, hard to remove.—**in deep water** in difficulties.—**to go off at the deep end** to become very angry

deer *n.* a cud-chewing animal. The male has horns.—**deer** *pl.*—*stag, hart, masc.* of red deer, *buck* of fallow deer.—*hind, fem.* of red deer, *doe* of fallow deer.—*fawn* young fallow deer

deface′ (de-fās) *v.* to disfigure.—**defa′cing** *part.*—**defaced′** *p.t.* and *p. part.*—**deface′ment** *n.*

Compare: mar, spoil, damage

defama′tion (-shun) *n.* slander.—**defame′** *v.* to speak ill of.—**defama′tory** *adj.*

default′ *n.* failure to do, to appear, to pay.—*v.* to fail to do something.—**default′er** *n.*—**default of** in the absence of.—**to win by default** to win because one's opponent fails to arrive

defeat′ *n.* 1. overthrow. 2. lost battle.—*v.* to overcome.—**defeat′ist** *n.* one who accepts defeat easily.—**defeat′ism** *n.* believing in defeat, pessimism

de′fect *n.* fault, imperfection.—**defec′tion** (-shun) *n.* desertion.—**defec′tive** *adj.* faulty.—**defect′** *v.* to desert one's duty or one's country

defence′ *n.* 1. protection. 2. justification, excuse.—**defence′less** *adj.*—**defens′ive** *adj.* serving for defence.—*n.* position or attitude of defence

Compare: 1. cover, shelter, bulwark, guard, safeguard, rampart. 2. apology, plea, vindication. *Contrast:* 1. attack. 2. allegation, accusation, charge

defend′ *v.* to guard, protect.—**defen′dant** *n.* person accused.—**defend′er** *n.*—**defen′sible** *adj.*—**on the defensive** in a position of defence

defer′ *v.* 1. to put off, postpone, as *We will defer consideration of the matter to a later date.* 2. to submit in opinion, as *We deferred to his views on account of his long experience.*—**defer′ring** *pres. part.*—**deferred′** *p.t.* and *p. part.*—**def′erence** *n.* respect.—**deferen′tial** *adj.* respectful.—**defer′ment** *n.* postponement.—**deferred payments** payment by instalments

defiance (de-fī′ans) *n.* resistance, disobedience.—**defi′ant** *adj.*—**defi′antly** *adv.*

defi′ciency (de-fish′en-si) *n.* lack.—**defi′cient** (de-fish′ent) *adj.* not enough.—**def′icit** (def′i-sit) *n.* shortness in sum of money

Note: This word is often followed by *in*, as *The diet of the prisoners was deficient in vitamins*

de′file *n.* a narrow pass.—*v.* to march in file

defile′ *v.* to make dirty or impure.—**defil′ing** *pres. part.*—**defiled′** *p.t.* and *p. part.*—**defile′ment** *n.*

define′ *v.* 1. mark out, fix. 2. to explain.—**defin′able** (dee-fīn′a-bl) *adj.*—**defini′tion** (def-i-ni′shun) *n.* explanation of meaning.—**def′inite** (-it) *adj.* exact.—**def′inite art′icle** in grammar, the word *the*, as contrasted with the *indefinite article, a* or *an*.—**def′initely** *adv.*—**defin′itive** (-iv) *adj.* final

deflate′ *v.* 1. to let air out. 2. to reduce excess of paper money.—**defla′tion** (-shun) *n.*

deflect′ *v.* to turn something aside.—**deflec′tion** *n.*

deforesta′tion *n.* clearing land of trees

deform′ *v.* to spoil the shape of.—**deform′ity** *n.* disfigurement.—**deform′ities** *pl.*

defraud' *v.* to cheat
defray' *v.* to provide money for, as *The expenses of the treat were defrayed by subscriptions*
defrost' *v.* to unfreeze a refrigerator or frozen food
deft *adj.* clever, nimble, esp. with the hands, as *a deft touch.*—**deft'ness** *n.*
defunct' *adj.* dead.—*n.*
defy' *v.* 1. to challenge. 2. to resist, refuse to obey, as *The door defied all our efforts to open it. The disobedient boy defied his mother.*—he **defies'**.—**defy'ing** *pres. part.*—**defied'** *p.t.* and *p. part.*
degen'erate (dee-jen'er-āt) *v.* to grow worse in quality.—*adj.* (deejen'er-at) grown worse.—*n.* a person who has degenerated. —**degenera'tion** (-shun) *n.*
degrada'tion (degradā'shun) *n.* loss of rank or self-respect.—**degrade'** *v.*—**degra'ding** *adj.* lowering
degree' *n.* 1. a step or stage. 2. a rank. 3. university rank, as Bachelor of Arts, etc.
degree' *n.* 1. a step or stage. 2. a rank. 3. 4. unit of measurement of angles and temperature, as *An angle of* 45 *degrees* (45°), *a temperature of* 100 *degrees* (100°). 5. condition, manner. 6. extent.—**by degrees** gradually.—**the third degree** questioning with torture
deifica'tion (dee-i-fi-kā'shun) *n.* making a god of.—**de'ify** *v.*—he de'ifies.—**de'ifying** *pres. part.*—**de'ified** *p.t.* and *p. part.*
deign (dān) *v.* to condescend
De'ity *n.* God.—**de'ity** *n.* a god or goddess.—**de'ities** *pl.*
Note: in this sense the word *Deity* is always preceded by *the*
deject *v.* to cast down, discourage.—**dejec'ted** *adj.*—**dejec'tion** (-shun) *n.* depression
delay' *v.* 1. to hold back, make late, postpone. 2. to linger.—**delay'ing** *pres. part.*—**delayed'** *p.t.* and *p. part.*—*n.* a putting off
delec'table *adj.* delightful.—**delecta'tion** (dee-lek-tā'shun) *n.*
del'egate (del'e-git) *n.* representative.—*v.* (del'ee-gāt) to hand over to a deputy, as *During the headmaster's absence his authority was delegated to the senior master.* —**delega'tion** (-shun) *n.* group of delegates
delete' *v.* to strike out, as a passage from a book.—**dele'ting** *pres. part.*—**dele'ted** *p.t.* and *p. part.*—**dele'tion** *n.*
delib'erate (dee-lib'er-āt) *v.* to consider, debate.—*adj.* (dee-lib'er-it) slow, well-considered, purposed.—**delib'erately** *adv.* —**delibera'tion** (-shun) *n.*
del'icacy *n.* 1. daintiness. 2. choice food. 3. weakness. 4. refinement of feeling, consideration for others.—**del'icacies** *pl.*—**del'icate** *adj.*—**del'icately** *adv.*
delicates'sen *n.pl.* cooked foods
delic'ious (del-ish'us) *adj.* pleasing, delightful.—**delic'iously** *adv.*
delight' (de-līt') *n.* pleasure,joy. —**delight'ful** *adj.*—**delight'fully** *adv.*
delin'eate *v.* 1. to describe. 2. to draw.—**delinea'tion** (-shun) *n.*
delin'quency (de-lin'kwen-si) *n.* offence, fault.—**delin'quent** *n.* offender
deliques'cent (de-lik-wes'ent) *adj.* (chemistry) becoming liquid by absorbing water from the air
delir'ious *adj.* light-headed.—**delir'ium** *n.* fever of the mind
deliv'er *v.* 1. to set free, as *St. George delivered the maiden from the dragon.* 2. to give up, as *The traitors delivered the keys of the city to the enemy.* 3. to distribute, as letters, bills, etc. 4. to pronounce (an opinion or verdict).—**deliv'erance** *n.* release.—**deliv'erer** *n.*—**deliv'ery** *n.* 1. distribution (of letters). 2. handing over. 3. style of speech
dell *n.* a hollow or valley, usually wooded
del'ta *n.* a triangular area of mud deposits at mouth of a river over and about which the river crosses to the sea.—**del'tas** *pl.*
delude' *v.* to mislead.—**delu'ding** *pres. part.*—**delu'ded** *p.t.* and *p. part.*
del'uge (del'ūj) *n.* a flood, a downpour
delu'sion (del-ū'zhun) *n.* a false belief.—**delu'sive** (del-ū'siv) *adj.* misleading
Note: Do not confuse with *illusion*
deluxe' (di-looks') *adj.* very comfortable, luxurious
delve *v.* to dig
dem'agogue (dem'a-gog) *n.* an agitator, a mob leader
demand' *v.* to ask as by right, to claim.—*n.* 1. claim, request, requirement. 2. call for a commodity, as *There is a big demand for ice cream in hot weather.*—**in great demand** sought after by many people
Compare: require, request, order, ask, beseech, beg
You *demand* something to which you think you have a right, or which you are prepared to use force to obtain
You *require* a person to do something when you are enforcing your authority, somewhat in the same way as *ordering* him to do it
Ask and *request* mean much the same—you are simply making your wishes known to someone in the hope that he will fall in with them. When you *beg* or *beseech* or *pray* you are asking for something as a favour
demarca'tion (dee-mar-kā'shun) *n.* a boundary
demean' *v.* (oneself) to degrade oneself
demean'our (dee-meen'or) *n.* behaviour, bearing
demen'ted *adj.* crazy, mad
dem'i at the beginning of a word, means *half*, as in *demi-god*, a being half human, half divine
demise' (dee-mīz') *n.* death

demo'bilise (dee-mō'bil-īz) *v.* to disband (troops).—**demobilisa'tion** (dee-mō-bil-i-zā'shun) *n.*

Note: In common speech this word is sometimes abbreviated to *de'mob n.* and *v.*

democ'racy *n.* 1. government by the people. 2. a state so governed.—**democ'racies** *pl.*—**dem'ocrat** *n.* 1. one who supports democracy. 2. U.S. member of Democratic party in politics (must begin with a capital letter when so used).—**democrat'ic** *adj.* favouring popular rights

demol'ish *v.* to destroy, overthrow.—he **demol'ishes.**—**demolit'ion** *n.* (dem-ol-i'-shun, dee-mol-i'shun)

de'mon (dee'mon) *n.* a devil.—**demo'niac** (-mō') *n.* a mad person

dem'onstrate *v.* 1. to prove by reasoning or experiment. 2. to make a show (of armed force, etc.).—**demonstra'tion** (-shun) *n.* 1. making clear. 2. a display of feeling, or of power.—**demon'strable** *adj.* able to be shown or proved.—**demon'strative** *adj.* 1. conclusive, as *giving demonstrative proof.* 2. showing emotion or feeling.—**dem'onstrator** *n.*

Note: In Grammar there are *demonstrative adjectives,* such as *this, the, that, any, some.* These words are used to point out (demonstrate) other words, as *this man, that woman, etc.* When such words, however, are used as substitutes for other words, they are called *demonstrative pronouns,* as *The climate of Great Britain is more temperate than that of the Continent.* Here the word *that* takes the place of *climate,* so it is a demonstrative pronoun and not a demonstrative adjective

demoralisa'tion (-shun) *n.* loss of courage, lowering of morals.—**demor'alise** *v.* to weaken, corrupt.—**demor'alising** *adj.*

demur' *v.* 1. to hesitate. 2. used with *at,* to raise objections, as *They demurred at the suggestion that they should work on Sundays.*—**demur'ring** *pres. part.*—**demurred'** *p.t.* and *p. part.*—*n.* 1. hesitation. 2. objection

demure' (de-mūr') *adj.* 1. modest, grave. 2. pretending to be modest.—**demure'ly** *adv.*

den *n.* 1. a cave or hole of animal. 2. a small room

de'nary *adj.* (of numbers) reckoned on the base of ten

dene (deen) *n.* 1. a little valley

deni'al (de-nī'al) *n.* 1. a refusal, withholding especially of comforts, gifts, etc. as in *self-denial.* 2. saying something is untrue, especially an accusation. 3. a disowning, as *St. Peter's denial of Christ.*—**deni'able** *adj.*

den'izen *n.* an inhabitant

denom'inate *v.* to give a name to.—**denomina'tion** (-shun) *n.* 1. a name. 2. a religious body, as the Methodist Church, the Roman Catholic Church.—**denomin'ator** *n.* in a fraction, the number written below the line, as in $\frac{3}{4}$, 4 is the *denominator,* because it names the kind of fraction, fourths or quarters

denote' *v.* to show, indicate.—**deno'ting** *pres. part.*—**deno'ted** *p.t.* and *p. part.*

denoue'ment (dā-nōō'mon) *n.* the ending of a play or story

denounce' *v.* 1. to speak or write against, as *The speaker denounced gambling.* 2. to accuse, as *He was denounced as a spy to the police.*—**denoun'cing** *pres. part.*—**denounced'** *p.t.* and *p. part.*

dense *adj.* 1. thick. 2. stupid.—**dens'er** *comp.*—**den'sest** *sup.*—**dense'ly** *adv.*—**den'sity** *n.* 1. closeness. 2. in Science the number of grams of mass in one cubic centimetre of a substance

dent *n.* a hollow, a mark.—*v.*—**den'ted** *adj.*

dent'al *adj.* relating to teeth or dentistry

den'tist *n.* a person who attends to teeth.—**den'tistry** *n.* the work of a dentist.—**den'tifrice** *n.* toothpaste.—**denti'tion** (ti'-shun) *n.* arrangement, number and kind of teeth.—**den'ture** *n.* set of false teeth

denude' *v.* to strip, as *The trees were denuded of their leaves by a swarm of locusts.*—**denuda'tion** (-shun) *n.*

denuncia'tion (de-nun-si-ā'shun) *n.* accusation, condemnation. See **denounce**

deny' (de-nī') *v.* 1. to refuse. 2. to declare untrue. 3. to disown.—he **denies'**—**deny'ing** *pres. part.*—**denied** *p.t.* and *p. part.* See **denial.**—**to deny oneself** to refuse oneself some pleasure

depart' *v.* to start, go away.—**the depar'ted** the dead.—**depar'ture** *n.* 1. going away. 2. new enterprise

depart'ment *n.* a division, a branch.—**departmen'tal** *adj.* **department store** a large store selling many kinds of goods

depend' (on) *v.* 1. to rely on, as *She depends on charity* or *You may depend upon it.* 2. to follow from, as *It all depends on what you do.*—**depen'dable** *adj.* reliable.—**depen'dant** *n.* person relying on another for support.—**depen'dence** *n.* trust, reliance on another's support or commands.—**depen'dency** *n.* country controlled by another.—**depen'dent** *adj.* depending

Note: Do not confuse *dependant* and *dependent*

depict' *v.* to portray, describe

deplete' *v.* to empty, take away, exhaust.—**deple'ting** *pres. part.*—**deple'ted** *p.t.* and *p. part.*—**deple'tion** *n.*

deplore' *v.* to regret, lament, be scandalised by.—**deplor'ing** *pres. part.*—**deplored'** *p.t.* and *p. part.*—**deplor'able** *adj.*

deploy' *v.* to spread out (troops)

depop'ulate *v.* to reduce population.—**depopula'tion** (-shun) *n.*

deport' *v.* to exile, send out of a country.—**deporta'tion** (-shun) *n.*

deport'ment *n.* behaviour, bearing

depose′ (de-pōz′) *v.* 1. to remove from high office. 2. to give evidence.—**depo′sing** *pres. part.*—**deposed′** *p.t.* and *p. part.*—**deposi′tion** (-shun) *n.* 1. dethronement. 2. statement

depos′it (de-poz′it) *n.* 1. to put down, as *He deposited the parcel on the floor.* 2. to put in a safe place (e.g. bank.)—*n.* 1. money paid as a first part payment. 2. money put in a bank.—**depos′itor** *n.* person depositing.—**depos′itory** *n.* a safe place

de′pot (de′pō) *n.* 1. a store-house. 2. a military station

deprave′ *v.* to make bad.—**depra′ving** *pres. part.*—**depraved′** *p.t.* and *p. part.*—**deprav′ity** (dee-prav′i-ti) *n.*

dep′recate *v.* to disapprove of, advise against, as *The king's adviser's deprecated his headstrong actions.*—**depreca′tion** (-shun) *n.*—**depreca′tory** *adj.*

depre′ciate (de-pree′shi-āt) *v.* 1. to lower or become lower in value or price, as *The value of the pound depreciated on the Stock Exchange.* 2. to belittle, as *To depreciate a person's efforts.*—**deprecia′tion** (-shun) *n.* a fall in value

depreda′tion (dep-ree-dā′shun) *n.* plundering

depress′ *v.* 1. to lower, press down. 2. to make weak or sad.—he **depress′es.**—**depress′ing** *adj.*—**depres′sion** (de-presh′un) *n.* 1. hollow. 2. centre of low barometric pressure. 3. low state of spirits, trade, etc.

deprive′ (of) *v.* to take away, as *The boys who had misbehaved were deprived of a half-holiday.*—**depri′ving** *pres. part.*—**deprived′** *p.t.* and *p. part.*—**de′priva′tion** (dee-prīv-ā′shun or de-priv-ā′shun)

depth *n.* 1. deepness. 2. a deep place.—**depth′charge** *n.* bomb for dropping on submerged submarine, exploding at set depth.—**out of one's depth** 1. in water too deep. 2. facing a task which is too difficult

deputa′tion (dep-ū-tā′shun) *n.* persons sent to speak for others.—**depute′** *v.* to send with instructions.—**depu′ting** *pres. part.*—**depu′ted** *p.t.* and *p. part.*—**dep′utise** *v.* to act for another, as *Will you deputise for me?*—**dep′uty** *n.* a substitute.—**dep′uties** *pl.*

derail′ *v.* to cause a train to run off the rails.—**derail′ment** *n.*

derange′ (de-rānj′) *v.* 1. to disturb. 2. to make insane.—**derange′ment** *n.*

der′elict *adj.* abandoned, forsaken.—**derelic′tion** (-shun) *n.*

deride′ *v.* to mock, laugh at.—**deris′ion** (de-rizh′un) *n.* mockery.—**deri′sive** *adj.*

deriva′tion (de-ri-vā′shun) *n.* the tracing from a source.—**deriv′ative** *adj.* coming from.—*n.*—**derive′** (from) *v.* 1. to get. 2. to come from.—**deri′ving** *pres. part.*—**derived′** *p.t.* and *p. part.*

derog′atory *adj.* disparaging

der′rick *n.* a crane

der′vish *n.* a member of a Mohammedan religious sect

des′cant *n.* a sung accompaniment to plainsong

descend′ (de-send′) *v.* 1. to go down. 2. (upon, on) to attack. 3. to spring from (ancestor), as *He is descended from one of the Pilgrim Fathers.*—**descen′dant** *n.* off-spring.—**descent′** *n.* a coming down

describe′ *v.* 1. to tell about, in speech or writing. 2. to draw, as a circle.—**descri′bing** *pres. part.*—**described′** *p.t.* and *p. part.*—**descrip′tion** (-shun) *n.* 1. an account. 2. kind, sort.—**descrip′tive** *adj.*

descry′ *v.* to catch sight of.—he **descries′.**—**descry′ing** *pres. part.*—**descried′** *p.t.* and *p. part.*

des′ecrate *v.* to use (something sacred) improperly.—**desecra′tion** (-shun) *n.*

desert′ (de-zert′) *v.* to abandon, leave.—**deser′ter** *n.* one who runs away from duty.—**deser′tion** (de-zer′shun) *n.*

des′ert (dez′ert) *n.* a large barren region

deserts′ (de-zerts′) *n.pl.* reward or punishment deserved, due

deserve′ (de-serv′) *v.* to be worthy of.—**deser′ving** *pres. part.*—**deserved′** *p.t.* and *p. part.*—**deser′vedly** *adv.* rightly.—**deser′ving** *adj.*, as *a deserving case* meaning a person who *deserves* help. Such a person is said to be *very deserving*

des′iccate *v.* to dry up.—**desicca′tion** (des-i-kā′shun) *n.*

design′ (de-zīn) *v.* 1. to plan, as *An architect designs buildings.* 2. to purpose, intend, as *The blinds were designed to keep out the sun.* 3. to make drawings, decorative patterns.—*n.* 1. a plan. 2. a drawing, pattern. 3. the art of making decorative patterns.—**designs′** *n.pl.* intentions, plots, schemes, as *to have designs on, against any one or anything.*—**design′edly** *adv.* on purpose.—**design′er** *n.* one who draws designs for manufacturers, etc.—**design′ing** *adj.* scheming, artful, cunning

des′ignate (dez′ig-nāt) *v.* to name, appoint.—**designa′tion** *n.* 1. an appointment. 2. a description

desirabil′ity (dee-zīr-a-bil′i-ti) *n.* 1. something to be desired. 2. condition of being desirable.—**desir′able** *adj.*

desire′ (de-zīr′) *v.* 1. to wish for, to want. 2. to ask for.—**desir′ing** *pres. part.*—**desired′** *p.t.* and *p. part.*—*n.* 1. wish. 2. something wanted.—**desir′ous** *adj.*

desist′ (de-zist′) *v.* to stop

desk *n.* a table for writing or reading

des′olate (des′ō-lat) *adj.* 1. neglected, barren. 2. lonely, dismal.—*v.* (des′ōlāt) 1. to lay waste. 2. to make unhappy.—**desola′tion** (des-ō-lā′shun) *n.*, as *There were scenes of desolation after the earthquake*

despair′ *n.* hopelessness.—*v.* to lose all hope

Note: This verb is often followed by *of:* as, *They despaired of ever finding their way back. His life was despaired of*

despatch′ see **dispatch′**

despera'do (-ā-or-ah-) *n.* a reckless man (usually a criminal).—**despera'does**

des'perate (des'per-āt) *adj.* 1. hopeless. 2. reckless, rash, daring, bold.—**des'perately** *adv.*—**despera'tion** (des-per-ā'shun) *n.* reckless despair

des'picable *adj.* mean, contemptible

despise' (des-pīz') *v.* to scorn, look down on. —**despi'sing** *pres. part.*—**despised'** *p.t.* and *p. part.*

despite' *prep.* in spite of

despoil' *v.* to plunder, rob.—**despolia'tion** (des-pō-li-ā'shun) *n.*

despond' *v.* to lose hope.—**despon'dency** *n.*—**despon'dent** *adj.* depressed

des'pot *n.* a tyrant, oppressor, absolute ruler. —**despot'ic** *adj.*—**des'potism** *n.* tyranny, absolute rule

dessert' (de-zert') *n.* fruit and sweets served after dinner.—**dessert'-spoon** *n.* a spoon mid-way in size between a tablespoon and a teaspoon

destina'tion (des-tin-ā'shun) *n.* intended end of a journey

des'tine (des'tin) *n.* 1. to fix beforehand, to be fated, as *He was destined to become a great man.* 2. to set apart, as *He was destined for a business career.*—**des'tiny** *n.* 1. fate. 2. course of events.—**des'tinies** *pl.*

des'titute *adj.* in want, without means of livelihood.—**des'titute of** lacking in, as *The desert was destitute of vegetation.*—**destitu'tion** *n.* need, extreme poverty

destroy' *v.* to ruin, put an end to.—**destroy'er** *n.* 1. one who destroys. 2. a small war-vessel

destruc'tion *n.* ruin, death.—**destruc'tive** *adj.* causing destruction.—**destruc'tible** able to be destroyed, easily destroyed

des'ultory *adj.* without method, off and on

detach' *v.* to unfasten, separate.—he **detach'es.**—**detach'ment** *n.* 1. body of soldiers. 2. aloofness, as *John stood by and watched the quarrel with quiet detachment*

de'tail *n.* 1. an item. 2. a minor or unimportant part.—**in detail** 1. with attention to every small particular. 2. bit by bit.—**detail'** *v.* 1. to relate fully. 2. to appoint for a duty

detain' *v.* 1. to keep waiting, delay. 2. to imprison.—**detain'ee** *n.* a prisoner held without trial

detect' *v.* to find out, discover, as *He detected a smell of gas in the cellar.*—**detec'table** *adj.*—**detec'tion** ('shun) *n.*—**detec'tive** *n.* person employed in detecting criminals.—**detec'tor** *n.* device for detecting, e.g. electric waves, poison gas, etc.

deten'tion (-shun) *n.* being kept back or in, esp. in prison

deter' *v.* to hinder, prevent, discourage, dissuade, as *He was not deterred by danger from making the attempt.*—**deter'ring** *pres. part.*—**deterred'** *p.t.* and *p. part.*—

deter'rent *n.* something that prevents or discourages.—**deter'rent** *adj.* having a preventing or dissuading effect

deter'gent (dit-er'jent) *n.* a powder or liquid for cleaning

dete'riorate (de-tee'ri-or-āt) *v.* to become worse.—**deteriora'tion** (de-tee-ri-or-ā'shun) *n.*

Compare: degenerate, decline, spoil, decay. *Contrast:* ameliorate, improve, recover

determina'tion (de-ter-min-ā'shun) *n.* a resolve.—**deter'mine** ('min) *v.* to decide, fix, as *The date of the next meeting was determined.*—**deter'mined** ('mind) *adj.* firm in purpose, as *The enemy offered a determined resistance*

detest' *v.* to hate.—**detest'able** *adj.*—**detesta'tion** (dee-tes-tā'shun) *n.* hatred

dethrone' *v.* to remove from the throne.—**dethrone'ment** *n.*

det'onate *v.* to explode.—**detona'tion** (det-ō-nā'shun) *n.*—**det'onator** *n.* part of a bomb

de'tour (dee'tōōr) *n.* a roundabout way

detract' *v.* to take away, belittle.—**detrac'tion** *n.*—**detrac'tor** *n.* a slanderer

Note: This word is usually followed by *from*

det'riment *n.* loss, harm.—**detrimen'tal** *adj.* harmful

deuce (dūs) *n.* 1. two at cards or dice. 2. forty-all score in tennis. 3. in exclamatory phrases, the devil

deval'uate *n.* to reduce the value of, esp. money

dev'astate *v.* to lay waste.—**dev'astating** *pres. part.*—**dev'astated** *p.t.* and *p. part.*—**devasta'tion** (dev-as-tā'shun) *n.*

devel'op *v.* 1. to grow, as *His muscles developed.* 2. to make grow, as *He developed his muscles by doing exercises.* 3. to treat (photographic film). 4. to unfold, as *The situation developed unexpectedly.*—**devel'opment** *n.*—**devel'oper** *n.* a chemical for developing films

de'viate (dee'vi-āt) *v.* to turn aside.—**devia'tion** *n.*

Note: This word is often followed by *from*

device' (de-vīs') *n.* 1. an invention, a scheme. 2. a heraldic design

dev'il *n.* 1. the spirit of evil. 2. a very wicked or cruel person.—**dev'ilish** *adj.*—**dev'ilment** *n.* mischievousness.—**dev'ilry** *n.* wickedness.—**between the devil and the deep sea** between two evils.—**devil-may-care** reckless

de'vious (dee'vī-us) *adj.* roundabout, not direct

devise' (de-vīz') *v.* to plan, contrive.—**devi'sing** *pres. part.*—**devised'** *p.t.* and *p. part.*

devoid' *adj.* empty, free from

Note: This word is usually followed by *of*

devolve' *v.* to pass to another

devote' (to) *v.* 1. to set apart, as *This gallery is devoted to works by modern artists.* 2. to give up to, as *She devoted her life to works of charity.* 3. to love deeply, as *He was devoted to his mother.*—**devo'ting** *pres. part.*—**devo'ted** *p.t.* and *p. part.*—**devoted'** *adj.* loyal.—**devotee'** *n.* a person devoted, e.g. to some occupation, belief, etc.—**devo'tion** *n.* piety, loyalty, conscientiousness.—**devo'tional** *adj.* concerned with prayer, religion, etc.

devour' *v.* to eat up, destroy

Compare: consume, absorb, engulf, gobble. See eat

devout' (de-vowt') *adj.* 1. pious, religious. 2. earnest

dew *n.* condensed moisture, esp. deposited from the air night and morning.—**dew'drop** *n.*—**dew'lap** *n.* loose skin on throat of cattle.—**dew'y** *adj.*

dexter'ity *n.* skill.—**dex'terous** *adj.*

dex'trose *n.* a form of glucose

diabol'ic, diabol'ical *adj.* devilish.—**diabol'ically** *adv.*, as *diabolically wicked, diabolically clever*, etc.

di'adem (dī'a-dem) *n*, a crown

di'agnose (dī'ag-nōz) *v.* to discover the nature of a disease, as *The doctor diagnosed the illness as measles.*—**diagno'sis** *n.*

diag'onal (dī-ag'on-al) *n.* a line from corner to corner.—*adj.*—**diag'onally** *adv.*

di'agram *n.* a drawing, illustration, plan.—**diagrammat'ic** *adj.*

di'al *n.* a clock face, meter face, or telephone disc.—*v.* to ring a number on an automatic telephone.—**di'alling** *pres. part.*—**di'alled** *p.t.* and *p. part.*

di'alect *n.* local speech, as *Cockney dialect, Lancashire dialect*, etc.

di'alogue (dī'a-log) *n.* 1. a conversation, esp. between two persons. 2. the spoken words of a play

diam'eter *n.* a straight line through the centre of a circle or sphere to each side.—**diamet'rical** *adj.*—**diamet'rically** *adv.* absolutely, completely, exactly (opposite, opposed, etc.)

di'amond *n.* 1. a precious stone. 2. a lozenge-shaped figure. 3. one of the four suits at cards.—**diamond anniversary, jubilee, wedding** the sixtieth anniversary.—**diamond cut diamond** a clash between two determined men.—**a rough diamond** an ill-mannered but good-hearted person

di'aper *n.* (North America) a small towel round a baby's body, a napkin

di'aphragm (di'a-fram) *n.* 1. a muscle between chest and abdomen. 2. a scientific device consisting of a vibrating sheet or plate

diarrhoe'a (dī-a-ree'a) *n.* excessive looseness of the bowels

di'ary *n.* 1. a daily account of events, etc. 2. book for this.—**di'aries** *pl.*—**di'arist** *n.* one who writes a diary

dice *pl.* of **die**, a game played with dice

dicotyle'don (dī-kot-i-lee'don) *n.* a plant such as a sycamore with two cotyledons or seed-leaves

dic'taphone *n.* an instrument for recording speech

dictate' *v.* 1. to tell what to write. 2. to give commands. 3. to render necessary or inevitable, as *His action was dictated by necessity.*—**dicta'ting** *pres. part.*—**dicta'ted** *p.t.* and *p. part.*—**dic'tate** *n.* command, usually used in the plural, as *the dictates of conscience.*—**dicta'tion** *n.* writing words read or spoken

dicta'tor *n.* a person with absolute power.—**dictator'ial** *adj.*—**dicta'torship** *n.* 1. absolute power. 2. a country ruled by dictator

dic'tion (-shun) *n.* the choice and use of words

dic'tionary *n.* a book explaining words.—**dic'tionaries** *pl.*

dic'tum *n.* a saying.—**dic'ta** *pl.*

dice *n.pl.* (*sing.* **die**) 1. cubes marked on each face with dots used in games of chance. 2. a gambling game.—*v.* 1. to play at dice. 2. to gamble, as *to dice with death.* 3. to chop into small cubes, as *diced vegetables*

did'geridoo *n.* aborigine musical instrument consisting of a long wooden tube which booms when blown

die (dī) *v.* 1. to stop living. 2. to come to an end.—he **dies.**—**dy'ing** *pres. part.*—**died** *p.t.* and *p. part.*—**to die away** to become weaker.—**to die down** to pass away.—**to die out** to become extinct

die *n.* See **dice. the die is cast** there is no turning back

di'et (dī'et) *n.* 1. food. 2. special course of feeding.—**di'etary** *n.* allowance or kind of food.—**dieti'tion** (dī-et-i'shun) *n.* one skilled in dietetics.—**dietet'ics** *n.pl.* the science of diet

di'et *n.* an assembly for making laws

dif'fer *v.* 1. to be unlike. 2. to disagree.—**dif'ference** *n.* 1. being unlike. 2. disagreement.—**dif'ferent** *adj.*

Note: These words must be followed by *from*, not by *to* or *than*

differen'tiate (di-fer-en'shi-āt) *v.* 1. to make or become different. 2. to show or mark a difference. 3. (between) to distinguish between.—**differentia'tion** (dif-er-en-shi-ā'shun) *n.*

dif'ficult *adj.* hard, not easy.—**dif'ficulty** *n.* 1. hardness to be done or understood. 2. a hindrance, obstacle, embarrassment.—**dif'ficulties** *pl.*

dif'fidence *n.* lack of confidence.—**dif'fident** *adj.*—**dif'fidently** *adv.*

diffuse' (di-fūz') *v.* 1. to spread (about), as light, knowledge, etc. 2. to spread and mix gases (and liquids).—**diffu'sing** *pres. part.*—**diffused'** *p.t.* and *p. part.*—**diffuse'**

(di-fūs′) *adj.* wordy.—**diffu′sion** (di-fū′-zhun) *n.*

Compare: (*adj.*) long-winded, prolix, copious. *Contrast:* (*adj.*) concise, pithy, brief

dig *v.* 1. to make a hole with spade, hands, etc. 2. to get by digging.—**dig′ging** *pres. part.*—**dug** *p.t.* and *p. part.*, also **digged,** esp. in poetry and the Bible.—**to dig up** to discover

digest′ (di-jest′) *v.* 1. to absorb food in the stomach. 2. to think over.—**di′gest** (dī′jest) *n.* a summary.—**digest′ible** *adj.* easily digested.—**digest′ion** (di-jes′chon) *n.*

dig′ger *n.* 1. one who digs. 2. (S.A. and Aus.) a miner digging for diamonds, gold. 3. Australian or New Zealander

dig′it (dij′it) *n.* 1. a finger or toe. 2. any of the figures 0—9.—**dig′ital computer** *n.* a calculating machine using numbers as digits on a decimal or binary system

dig′nified *adj.* stately.—**dig′nify** *v.* to give dignity to.—**dig′nifying** *pres. part.*—**dig′nified** *p.t.* and *p. part.*—**dig′nitary** *n.* high official.—**dig′nitaries** *pl.*

dig′nity *n.* 1. claim to respect. 2. honourable position, title. 3. stateliness.—**dig′nities** *pl.* —**to stand on one's dignity** to be very formal and aloof

digress′ *v.* to turn aside, as *Do not let us digress from the subject under discussion.*—he **digress′es.**—**digres′sion** (dī-gresh′un) *n.*—**digres′sive** *adj.*

dilap′idated *adj.* falling into ruin.—**dilapida′tion** (-shun) *n.*

dilate′ *v.* 1. to widen, expand. 2. to talk or write at length

dil′atory *adj.* slow.—**dil′atoriness** *n.*

Compare: sluggish, lagging, lackadaisical, behindhand, slack. *Contrast:* swift, prompt, punctual, energetic

dilem′ma *n.* a difficult position requiring choice between two evils as "*on the horns of a dilemma*"

dilettan′te (diletan′ti) *n*, a dabbler with little knowledge of a subject.—**dilettan′ti** *pl.*

dil′igence (dil′i-jens) *n.* 1. steady work. 2. public stage coach.—**dil′igent** *adj.* industrious, as *He was a diligent student.*—**dil′igently** *adv.*

dil′ly-dally *v.* to waste time

dilute′ *v.* to weaken, usually by adding water, as *The wine was diluted with water.*—**dilu′ting** *pres. part.*—**dilu′ted** *p.t.* and *p. part.*—*adj.* weakened usually by added water.—**dilu′tion** (-shun) *n.*

dim *adj.* 1. faint, not bright, indistinct. 2. (of the eyes) not able to see well.—**dim′mer** *comp.*—**dim′mest** *sup.*—*v.* to make or grow dim.—**dim′ming** *pres. part.*—**dimmed** *p.t.* and *p. part.*—**dim′ly** *adv.*—**dim′ness** *n.*—**dim′mer** *n.* an electrical device for dimming stage lights

dime *n.* (North America) a silver coin equal to ten cents

dimen′sion (-shun) *n.* measurement of length, breadth or depth.—*pl.* size.—**dimen′sional** *adj.*

dimin′ish *v.* to lessen.—he **dimin′ishes.**—**diminu′tion** (′shun) *n.*—**dimin′utive** *adj.* very small.—*n.* word formed from another expressing smallness

Compare: decrease, reduce, curtail, lower. *Contrast:* increase, magnify, elevate, extend

dim′ple *n.* a small hollow (esp. in the cheek). —*v.* to show dimples

din *n.* a confused noise.—*v.* (into) to repeat, stress, as *My father dinned* (*it*) *into me when I was a boy that I should always be punctual.*—**din′ning** *pres. part.*—**dinned** *p.t.* and *p. part.*

dine *v.* 1. to eat dinner. 2. to give dinner to.—**din′ing** *pres. part.*—**dined** *p.t.* and *p. part.*—**di′ner** *n.* 1. a person dining. 2. a restaurant car

din′ghy (ding′gi) *n.* a small boat.—**din′ghies** *pl.*

din′go *n.* an Australian wild dog.—**din′goes** *pl.*

din′gy (din′ji) *adj.* dirty-looking, shabby.—**din′giness** *n.*

Compare: drab, sordid, squalid

din′ner *n.* the chief meal of the day.—**din′ner-jacket** *n.* a black dress jacket

di′nosaur (dī′no-sōr) *n.* a gigantic extinct reptile

dint *n.* 1. a dent. 2. force.—**by dint of** by force of

dio′cesan (di-os′e-san) *adj.* belonging to a diocese.—**di′ocese** (dī′o-seez) *n.* the district of a bishop

diox′ide *n.* (chemistry) an oxide with two atoms of oxygen to one of metal

dip *v.* 1. to put in and out of a liquid. 2. to lower and raise again. 3. to slope, sink —**dip′ping** *pres. part.*—**dipped** *p.t.* and *p. part.*—*n.* 1. dipping. 2. a slope or hollow. 3. a bathe, as *to go for a dip.* 4. a kind of candle, as *tallow dip.*—**dip′per** *n.* a ladle for water

diphthe′ria (dif′thee′ria) *n.* an infectious disease of the throat

diph′thong (dif′thong) *n.* the union of two vowel sounds making one sound (e.g. au, oi, eu)

diplo′ma *n.* a document establishing person's right to a title or degree

diplo′macy (di-plō′ma-si) *n.* 1. the art of conducting international relations. 2. tactful dealing.—**dip′lomat** *n.* person engaged in official diplomacy.—**diplomat′ic** *adj.*—**diplomat′ically** *adv.*

dire, dire′ful *adj.* terrible

direct′ *v.* 1. to aim. 2. to manage, order. 3. to address (a letter).—*adj.* 1. straight, as *a direct path.* 2. immediate, as *a direct result.*—**direc′tion** (-shun) *n.* 1. instruction. 2. control. 3. an address. 4. a course of movement, way, destination.—**direct′ly**

adv.—**direct'ness** *n.*—**direc'tory** *n.* a book of names and addresses.—**direc'tories** *pl.*—**direct current** electric current flowing in one direction only.—**direction indicator** a signal or a flasher on a car showing in which direction it is about to turn.

direc'tor *n.* 1. a controller, manager. 2. the head of a business.—**direc'torship** *n.*

dirge (dirj) *n.* a lament, song of mourning

dir'igible (dir'i-ji-bl) *n.* a balloon or airship that can be steered

dirk *n.* a dagger

dirt *n.* 1. filth, anything that soils. 2. earth, mud.—**dir'tiness** *n.*—**dir'ty** *adj.* 1. unclean. 2. mean, as *a dirty trick*.—**dir'tier** *comp.*—**dir'tiest** *sup.*—*v.* to make dirty.—**dir'tying** *pres. part.*—**dir'tied** *p.t.* and *p. part.*—**dir'tily** *adv.*—**dirt'-track** *n.* a cinder track for motor-cycle racing

dis—is added at the beginning of other words and makes their meaning exactly opposite, e.g. disadvantage, disorder, disloyal. If you are seeking the meaning of any word beginning with *dis-* and do not find it below, find the word to which *dis-* has been added

disabil'ity *n.* a lack of power.—**disa'ble** *v.* 1. to cripple. 2. to disqualify.—**disa'bling** *pres. part.*—**disa'bled** *p.t.* and *p. part.*

disabuse' (dis-a-būz') *v.* to undeceive, set right

disaffec'ted *adj.* discontented, disloyal.—**disaffec'tion** *n.*

disagree' *v.* 1. to differ. 2. to quarrel. 3. not to fit in with, not to suit, as *Your version of the affair disagrees with his. Fruit disagrees with some people.*—**disagreed'** *p.t.* and *p. part.*—**disagree'able** *adj.* unpleasant.—**disagree'ment** *n.*

Note: This word is usually followed by *with*

disappear' *v.* 1. to vanish. 2. to be lost.—**disappear'ance** *n.*

disappoint' *v.* not to satisfy hopes, wishes, etc.—**disappoint'ing** *adj.* not coming up to expectations.—**disappoint'ment** *n.*

disarm' *v.* 1. to take away weapons. 2. to reduce a country's war weapons. 3. to win over, as *He disarmed his opponents by his frankness.*—**disarm'ament** *n.*

disarray' *n.* disorder

disas'ter (diz-as'ter) *n.* sudden misfortune. See **catastrophe**.—**disas'trous** *adj.*

disavow' *v.* to deny knowledge or responsibility

disband' *v.* to dismiss

disbelief' *n.* refusal to believe.—**disbelieve'** *v.*

disbud' *v.* to remove buds from

disburse' *v.* to pay out

disc *n.* a thin circular plate, such as a gramophone record.—**disc'-jockey** *n.* a radio announcer of popular music on records.—**disc'-brakes** *n.pl.* motor-car brakes acting on both sides of a disc attached to one of the wheels

discard' *v.* to give up, reject (cards), cast off (clothing)

discharge' *v.* 1. to unload (a ship, etc.). 2. to fire off, release (a gun). 3. to dismiss (an employee). 4. to perform (duties, etc.).—**dischar'ging** *pres. part.*—**discharged'** *p.t.* and *p. part.*—**dis'charge** *n.*

disci'ple (dis-ī'pl) *n.* a follower, one who takes another as teacher and leader, esp. the Twelve Apostles of Christ.—**disciple'ship** *n.*

discern' (dis-ern') *v.* to distinguish, see.—**discern'ment** *n.* insight.—**discer'nible** *adj.*

dis'cipline (dis'i-plin) *n.* 1. training to obey orders. 2. self-control.—*v.* to train, make obedient or orderly.—**disciplina'rian** (dis-i-plin-ār'i-an) *n.* one who keeps order.—**dis'ciplinary** *adj.*

disclaim' *v.* to disown, deny knowledge of.—**disclaim'er** *n.* denial

disclose' (dis-klōz') *v.* to make known.—**disclo'sing** *pres. part.*—**disclosed'** *p.t.* and *p. part.*—**disclo'sure** (disklō'zher) *n.*

discolora'tion (-shun) *n.* a stain

discom'fit (dis-kum'fit) *v.* to defeat.—**discom'fiture** (dis-kum'fi-cher) *n.* being defeated, upset or annoyed

Note: Do not confuse with *discomfort*

discom'fort (dis-kum'fort) *n.* 1. uneasiness. 2. lack of comfort.—*v.*

disconcert' (dis-kon-sert') *v.* to confuse, disturb

disconnect' *v.* to unfasten, to separate.—disconnect'ed *adj.*

discon'solate *adj.* unhappy, downcast

discontent' *n.* dissatisfaction.—**discontent'ed** *adj.*

dis'cord *n.* 1. conflicting sounds. 2. quarrelling.—**discor'dant** *adj.* harsh

dis'count *n.* a deduction made on payment of bill.—**discount'** *v.* 1. to allow for exaggeration. 2. to give present value of (bill of exchange, etc.). 3. to lessen, detract from

discour'age (dis-kur'ij) *v.* 1. to take away confidence. 2. to disapprove of, try to prevent, as *I have tried to discourage him from biting his nails.*—**discour'aging** *pres. part.*—**discour'aged** *p.t.* and *p. part.*—**discour'agement** *n.*

dis'course *n.* 1. speech, sermon. 2. conversation.—**discourse'** *v.* to speak

discourt'eous (dis-kurt'i-us) *adj.* rude, impolite.—**discourt'esy** rudeness

discov'er (dis-kuv'er) *v.* to find out.—**discov'erer** *n.*—**discov'ery** *n.*—**discov'eries** *pl.*

discred'it *v.* to throw doubt on, refuse to believe, as *The judge discredited the prisoner's story.*—*n.* 1. doubt. 2. disgrace.—**discred'itable** *adj.* disgraceful

discreet' *adj.* careful in speaking or doing.—**discreet'ly** *adv.*

Compare: tactful, diplomatic, cautious, prudent. *Contrast:* indiscreet, tactless

discrep'ancy (-si) *n.* a difference, lack of agreement, as *There was a discrepancy between*

one boy's account of the affair and the other's.—**discrep'ancies** *pl.*
discrete' *adj.* separate, not together
Note: do not confuse with **discreet**
discre'tion (dis-kresh'on) *n.* 1. care in speaking or doing, prudence. 2. ability or right to decide, as *We leave the matter to your discretion.*—**at the discretion of** at the wish of.—**at discretion** unconditionally, as in *to surrender at discretion.*—**years of discretion** age at which one is considered fit to look after oneself
discrim'inate *v.* to see or make differences.—**discrimina'tion** (dis-krim-in-ā'shun) *n.* ability to distinguish, perception.—**discrim'inating** *adj.*
Note: Usually followed by *between*
discur'sive *adj.* rambling, wordy
dis'cus *n.* a heavy disc thrown at sports meetings.—**dis'cuses** *pl.*
discuss' *v.* to exchange opinions on, debate.—**discus'sion** (dis-kush'on) *n.*
disdain' *v.* to scorn.—*n.*—**disdain'ful** *adj.*
disease' (di-zeez') *n.* illness.—**diseased'** *adj.*
disfig'ure (dis-fig'er) *v.* to deface, spoil.—**disfig'urement** *n.*
disgorge' (dis-gorj') *v.* 1. to vomit. 2. to give up
disgrace' *n.* 1. shame. 2. loss of favour.—*v.* 1. to bring shame on, as *He disgraced his family.* 2. to put out of favour, office, etc., as *The king's favourite was disgraced.*—**disgrace'ful** *adj.* shameful.—**disgrace'fully** *adv.*
disgrunt'led *adj.* discontented
disguise' (dis-gīz') *v.* 1. to change the appearance. 2. to hide.—**disgui'sing** *pres. part.*—**disguised'** *p.t.* and *p. part.*—*n.* false appearance
disgust' *n.* violent dislike.—*v.* to fill with distaste.—**disgus'ting** *adj.*
dish *n.* 1. a plate, etc., on which food is served. 2. food served on a dish.—**dish'es** *pl.*—*v.* (up) to serve food.—**dish'washer** *n.* a machine for washing dishes
dishear'ten *v.* to make discouraged and despondent
dishev'el *v.* to make untidy.—**dishev'elled** *adj.* disordered
dishon'est *adj.* deceitful, fraudulent
dishon'our *n.* shame, disgrace
disinfect' *v.* to free from germs.—**disinfec'tion** (-shun) *n.*—**disinfec'tant** *n.* germ-killer
disinher'it *v.* to deprive of inheritance
disin'tegrate *v.* to break up.—**disintegra'tion** (dis-in-ti-grā'shun) *n.*
disint'erested *adj.* 1. not seeking personal advantage. 2. (slang) not interested, bored
Compare: unselfish, impartial, generous.
Contrast: self-seeking. See **interested**
disk see **disc**
dis'locate *v.* 1. to put (a bone) out of place. 2. to put into disorder.—**disloca'tion** (dis-lō-kā'shun) *n.*
dis'mal (diz'mal) *adj.* dreary
disman'tle *v.* to put out of action, to strip (of defences, furniture, etc.) as *The captured fortress was dismantled.*—**disman'tling** *pres. part.*—**disman'tled** *p.t.* and *p. part.*
dismay' *n.* horrified amazement.—*v.* to dishearten, frighten.—**dismayed'** *adj.*
dismem'ber *v.* 1. to cut limb from limb. 2. to divide.—**dismem'berment** *n.*
dismiss' *v.* 1. to send away. 2. to disperse. 3. to discharge from employment. 4. to put out of the mind, as *He dismissed the idea.*—he **dismiss'es**.—**dismiss'al** *n.*
dismount' *v.* to get down from a horse, bicycle etc.
disobe'dient *adj.* not obeying.—**disobe'dience** *n.*
disor'der *n.* confusion, untidiness
disown' *v.* to refuse to recognise or to have anything to do with
dispar'age (dis-par'āj) *v.* to speak poorly of.—**dispar'aging** *adj.*—**dispar'agingly** *adv.*—**dispar'agement** *n.*
dispar'ity *n.* inequality, unlikeness, as *There is a great disparity between his age and hers*
dispas'sionate (dis-pash'on-it) *adj.* calm, impartial
dispatch', despatch' *v.* 1. to send off. 2. to kill. 3. to finish off.—he **dispatch'es**.—*n.* 1. sending off. 2. speed, as *to act with great dispatch.* 3. an official message
dispel' *v.* to clear away, disperse.—**dispel'ling** *pres. part.*—**dispelled'** *p.t.* and *p. part.*
dispense' *v.* 1. to deal out. 2. to make up (a medicine). 3. (with) to do without, as *We must learn to dispense with unnecessary luxuries.*—**dispen'sing** *pres. part.*—**dispensed'** *p.t.* and *p. part.*—**dispen'sary** *n.* where medicine is made up.—**dispensa'tion** *n.* 1. exemption. 2. provision (of nature or providence)
disperse' *v.* to scatter.—**disper'sing** *pres. part.*—**dispersed'** *p.t.* and *p. part.*—**disper'sal** *n.* scattering.—**disper'sion** *n.* being scattered
displace' *v.* to move out of position, to take the place of.—**displace'ment** *n.*
display' *n.* exhibition, show.—*v.* to spread out for show
disport' *v.* to play, gambol
dispose' (dis-pōz') *v.* 1. to arrange. 2. to incline or be inclined, to be willing or prepared, as *I do not feel disposed to do so.*—**to dispose of** to sell, get rid of.—**dispo'sing** *pres. part.*—**disposed'** *p.t.* and *p. part.*—**dispo'sal** *n.*—**disposit'ion** *n.* 1. plan, arrangement. 2. inclination towards. 3. power to arrange or control, as *It is in my disposition to decide what is to be done.* 4. character, as *She had a kind disposition*
dispropor'tion ('shun) *n.* inequality (between), lack of proportion.—**dispropor'tionate** (dis-prō-pōr'shun-āt) *adj.* too much
dis'putant *n.* a person contesting or arguing.—**disputa'tion** (dis-pū-tā'shun) *n.* argument
dispute' *v.* 1. to discuss, argue. 2. to oppose,

as *He disputed my claim.*—**dispu'ting** *pres. part.*—**dispu'ted** *p.t.* and *p. part,*—*n.* quarrel, debate, argument, wrangle

disqual'ify (dis-kwol'i-fī) *v.* to make unfit, to debar or rule out.—he **disqual'ifies.**—**disqual'ifying** *pres. part.*—**disqual'ified** *p.t.* and *p. part.*

disqui'et (dis-kwī'et) *v.* to make uneasy, to disturb.—**disqui'etude** *n.* anxiety

disregard' *v.* to neglect, to take no notice of

disrep'utable *adj.* not respectable

disrobe' *v.* to undress

disrupt' *v.* to split, break in pieces.—**disrup'tion** ('shun) *n.*—**disrup'tive** *adj.*

dissat'isfy *v.* to make discontented.—**dissatisfac'tion** ('shun) *n.*—**dissat'isfied** *adj.*

dissect' *v.* to cut up body, etc., for examination.—**dissec'tion** ('shun) *n.*

dissem'ble *v.* to conceal (feelings).—**dissem'bling** *pres. part.*—**dissem'bled** *p.t.* and *p. part.*

dissent' *v.* to differ, disagree.—*n.* disagreement (esp. with doctrine of established church).—**dissen'sion** ('shun) *n.* disagreement, strife.—**dissen'ter** *n.* non-conformist.—**dissen'tient** (dis-en'shent) *n.* or *adj.* one who disagrees, disagreeing

Note: Dissent is usually followed by *from*

disserta'tion (dis-ser-tā'shun) *n.* learned discourse, lecture or treatise

dissim'ilar *adj.* unlike

dissim'ulate *v.* to pretend.—**dissimula'tion** (dis-sim-ū-lā'shun) *n.*

dis'sipate *v.* 1. to scatter, clear away. 2. to waste, squander.—**dissipa'ting** *pres. part.*—**dis'sipated** *p.t.* and *p. part.*—**dissipa'tion** (dis-i-pā'shun) *n.* 1. wastefulness. 2. frivolous or dissolute way of life

disso'ciate (dis-ō'shi-āt) *v.* to separate from.—**dissocia'tion** (dis-ō-shi-ā'shun) *n.*

dissolu'tion (dis-ō-lū'shun) *n.* 1. change from solid to liquid state. 2. breaking-up. 3. destruction.—**dis'solute** *adj.* given up to evil pleasures

dissolve' *v.* 1. to disappear in fluid. 2. to break up. 3. to put an end to (as of meetings, partnerships, etc.).—**dissol'ving** *pres. part.*—**dissolved'** *p.t.* and *p. part.*

dissuade' (dis-wād') *v.* to advise or persuade against.—**dissua'sion** (dis-wā'zhun) *n.*

Note: This word is often followed by *from.* You dissuade a person *from* something he intended to do

dis'taff *n.* stick to hold wool, etc. for hand-spinning.—**dis'taffs** *pl.*—**the distaff side** the female line of descent

dis'tance *n.* 1. the space between two points. 2. a far away place, as *in the distance.*—**dis'tant** *adj.* 1. far away. 2. reserved, unfriendly, formal.—**dis'tantly** *adv.*—**to keep at a distance** to be aloof, to to treat coolly

Contrast: (*adj.*) 1. near, close, nearby. 2. intimate, cordial, friendly

distaste' *n.* dislike, aversion.—**distaste'ful** *adj.* unpleasant.—**distaste'fully** *adv.*

distem'per *n.* 1. a disorder in mind or body. 2. a disease of dogs. 3. a kind of water paint.—*v.*

distend' *v.* to swell out.—**disten'sion** ('shun) *n.*

distil' *v.* to purify a liquid by turning it into vapour and, by cooling, condensing it back to liquid form.—**distil'ling** *pres. part.*—**distilled'** *p.t.* and *p. part.*—**distilla'tion** (dis-til-ā'shun) *n.*—**dis'tillate** *n.* what is distilled.—**distil'lery** *n.* place where spirit is distilled

distinct' *adj.* 1. clear, definite, as *a distinct sound, a distinct sensation.* 2. separate, different, as *Please keep these specimens distinct from the others.*—**distinc'tion** (dis-tingk'shun) *n.* 1. a difference (between). 2. an honour, as *The D.S.O. is a distinction.* 3. high quality, eminence, as *a person of distinction.*—**distinc'tive** *adj.* original.—**distinct'ly** *adv.*—**distinct'ness** *n.* clearness

distin'guish (dis-ting'gwish) *v.* 1. to make, or notice a difference, as *Gardeners can easily distinguish one variety of rose from another. Can you distinguish between the different kinds?* 2. to see, recognise, as *The coastguard distinguished a vessel on the horizon.*—he **distin'guishes.**—**distin'guishable** *adj.*

distort' *v.* 1. to twist out of shape. 2. to change the truth, garble, misrepresent.—**distor'tion** (dis-tor'shun) *n.*

distract' *v.* 1. to turn aside, as *I tried to distract his mind from his worries.* 2. to bewilder, drive mad.—**distrac'tion** (dis-trak'shun) *n.* 1. inattention. 2. diversion. 3. bewilderment

distrain' *v.* to seize goods for debt.—**distraint** *n.'*

distraught' (dis-trawt') *adj.* distressed, crazy

distress' *n.* 1. trouble, grief. 2. suffering, want. 3. difficulty (*a ship in distress, a distress signal*).—*v.* to give pain.—he **distress'es.**—**distress'ing** *adj.*

distrib'ute *v.* 1. to give out. 2. to spread.—**distrib'uting** *pres. part.*—**distrib'uted** *p.t.* and *p. part.*—**distribu'tion** (distrib-ū'shun) *n.*—**distrib'utor** *n.* 1. one who distributes. 2. (petrol engine) a rotating contact distributing the spark to each cylinder in turn

dis'trict *n.* part of a country, region.—**district nurse'** *n.* a nurse appointed to a particular district

Compare: neighbourhood, locality, area

distrust' *v.* to have no confidence in

disturb' *v.* 1. to trouble, upset. 2. to agitate, make uneasy.—**distur'bance** *n.* disorder

disuse' (dis-ūs') *n.* lack of use.—**disuse'** (dis-ūz') *v.* to stop using

ditch *n.* long narrow trench dug in ground.—**ditch** *v.* 1. to dig a ditch 2. to drive into a ditch. 3. to abandon.

dit'to *n.* same as above (sometimes written ,,)

dit'ty *n.* a simple song.—**dit'ties** *pl.*
diurn'al (dī-urn'al) *adj.* daily
divan' *n.* 1. a couch without back or head. 2. an oriental council
dive (dīv) *v.* 1. to plunge under the surface of water. 2. to disappear.—**di'ving** *pres. part.* —**dived** *p.t.* and *p. part.*—*n.* diving.—**di'ver** *n.*—**div'ing-bell** *n.* a bell-shaped steel chamber in which men work under water
diverge' (dī-verj') *v.* to get farther apart, separate, differ.—**diver'ging** *pres. part.*—**diverged'** *p.t.* and *p. part.*—**diver'gence** *n.* difference.—**diver'gent** *adj.*
Note: This word is usually followed by *from*
di'vers (dī'verz) *adj.* various.—**diverse'** (di-vers' or dī-vers') *adj.* different, varied. —**diverse'ly** *adv.*—**divers'ify** *v.* to introduce differences.—**divers'ity** *n.* variety, unlikeness
diver'sion (di-ver'shun) *n.* 1. turning aside. 2. amusement, pastime
divert' *v.* 1. to turn aside. 2. to amuse.—**divert'ing** *adj.* amusing
Note: This word is often followed by *from*
divest' *v.* 1. to unclothe, strip. 2. to deprive
Note: This word is usually followed by *of*, as *He divested himself of his overcoat*
divide' (di-vīd') *v.* 1. to split into parts. 2. to share out.—**divi'ding** *pres. part.*—**divi'ded** *p.t.* and *p. part.*—*n.* in Canada, Australia, etc. a watershed.—**divi'ders** *n.pl.* compasses with metal points for measuring lines
div'idend *n.* 1. a share of profits. 2. a number to be divided by another number. See **divisor**
divina'tion (div-in-ā'shun) *n.* the art of foretelling
divine' *adj.* belonging to, or due to God, sacred.—*n.*—a clergyman.—*v.* to guess, foretell.—**divi'ner** *n.* prophet.—**divin'ity** *n.* 1. being divine. 2. God (*The Divinity*). 3. a god (*a divinity*). 4. the study of scripture, theology
divis'ible (di-viz'i-bl) *adj.* able to be divided
divis'ion (di-vi'zhun) *n.* 1. a dividing. 2. a barrier. 3. separation, difference of opinion. 4. in arithmetic, finding how many times one number is contained in another. 5. a distinct part. 6. an army unit, consisting of at least two brigades, with artillery, etc.—**divis'ional** *adj.*
divi'sor (div-ī'zor) *n.* a number which divides another (in arithmetic). See **div'idend**
divorce' (di-vōrs') *n.* separation of husband and wife by dissolving the marriage.—*v.* to separate thus
di'vot *n.* a piece of turf on a golf course
divulge' (di-vulj') *v.* to reveal, tell, as *to divulge a secret.*—**divul'ging** *pres. part.*—**divulged'** *p.t.* and *p. part.*
diz'ziness *n.* feeling dizzy.—**diz'zily** *adv.*—
diz'zy *adj.* unsteady, feeling as though going to fall.—**diz'zier** *comp.*—**diz'ziest** *sup.*—*v.* to make unsteady
do (dōō) *v.* to perform, accomplish, act.—he **does** (duz)—he **doth** (old form).—**did** *p.t.*—**done** *p. part.*—**do away with** to get rid of, kill.—**do or die** to succeed or die trying.—**do up** to fasten, repair.—**done in, done out, done up** exhausted.—**do without** to forgo.—**make do** to manage as best one can.—**up and doing** active
Note: This is also an *auxiliary verb* and helps to make the interrogative, negative an emphatic forms of other verbs, e.g. *Did he go? He didn't go. Yes, he did*
Avoid the common mistake of confusing the past participle with the past tense, and saying *He done it* instead of *He did it* or *He has done it*
do'cile (dō'sīl) *adj.* easily taught or led
Compare: tame, meek, tractable, gentle.
Contrast: wild, fierce, stubborn, intractable
dock *n.* 1. basin for loading and repairing ships. 2. place where accused stands in court.—*v.* to put ship into dock.—**dock'-yard** *n.* where ships are repaired
dock *v.* to cut short (as a horse's tail)
dock'et *n.* 1. ticket showing contents of package. 2. a list.—*v.* to endorse document with a summary of its contents
doc'tor *n.* 1. a person qualified to treat diseases. 2. a person with university's highest degree.—*v.* 1. to treat medically. 2. to tamper with.—**doc'torate** *n.* university degree or status of doctor
doc'trine (dok'trin) *n.* 1. what is taught. 2. belief, dogma
doc'ument (dok'ū-ment) *n.* writing containing evidence or information.—**documen'-tary** *n.* a film or broadcast report of facts or events
dodge (doj) *v.* 1. to swerve. 2. to avoid (by a trick).—*n.* a trick.—**dod'ger** *n.*
do'do (dō'dō) *n.* a clumsy bird, now extinct
doe (dō) *n.* a female deer, hare, rabbit
doff *v.* 1. to take off (clothes). 2. lay aside
dog *n.* 1. a familiar domestic animal. 2. male of wolf, fox, etc.—**bitch** *fem.*—**puppy, pup** a young dog. See **hound.**—*v.* to follow closely, as *The detective dogged the criminal's footsteps.*—**dog'ging** *pres. part.*—**dogged** *p.t.* and *p. part.*—**dog'ged** *adj.* persistent.—**dog'ger** *n.* (Aus.) a professional hunter of dingoes.—**dog' collar** *n.* 1. collar for a dog. 2. clergyman's white collar fastening at the back.—**dog'-days** *n.pl.* the hot season.—**dog'-eared** *adj.* (of paper, books) much used, with corners turned down.—**dog'-fight** *n.* fight between fighter planes.—**dog'fish** *n.* a species of small shark.—**dog' rose** *n.* wild rose.—**a dog's life** a wretched existence.—**a dog's chance** little chance.—**being a dog in a manger** not letting others use what you cannot use.—**a lame dog** a helpless person.—**dog-tired** very

tired.—**give a dog a bad name and hang him** a bad reputation sticks.—**hot dog** a sandwich of hot sausage meat.—**to go to the dogs** to go to ruin

dog'gerel (dog'er-el) *n.* poor verse

dog'ma *n.* belief, doctrine.—**dog'mas** *pl.*—**dogmat'ic** *adj.* 1. concerned with dogma. 2. assertive, opinionated, bigoted

doi'ly *n.* a small mat of lace or paper imitation lace

dol'drums *n.pl.* 1. ocean region of calms near Equator. 2. low spirits

dole (dōl) *n.* a charitable gift.—**on the dole** out of work and receiving unemployment relief.—**to dole out** to give in small shares

dole'ful *adj.* sad

doll *n.* child's toy image of a person.—*v.* (up) to dress up in finery

dol'lar *n.* silver coin of U.S., Canada and of Australia, etc., worth 100 cents

dol'orous *adj.* sorrowful

dol'phin (dol'fin) *n.* a large sea-animal

dolt (dōlt) *n.* a stupid person

domain *n.* 1. a dominion. 2. land held or ruled over. 3. a sphere of influence, area, province, as *In the domain of drama Shakespeare stands supreme*

dome (dōm) *n.* a high rounded roof

domes'tic *adj,* 1. belonging to the home. 2. concerning the internal affairs of a country. 3. tame (of animals).—*n.* a servant.—**domes'ticate** *v.*—**domesti'city** (dō-mes-tis'-i-ti) *n.* home life

Contrast: (with 2.) foreign, external

dom'icile (dom'i-sīl) *n.* a home, a permanent residence

dom'inant *adj.* commanding

dom'inate *v.* 1. to rule, control. 2. to overlook (of heights).—**domina'tion** (dom-in-ā'shun) *n.*

domineer' (over) *v.* to tyrannise.—**dominee'-ring** *adj.*

domin'ion *n.* 1. rule. 2. land ruled by a government. 3. self-governing part of British Commonwealth, e.g. Canada

dom'ino *n.* a cloak with a half-mask.—**dom'inoes** *n.pl.* a game played with small flat pieces marked with spots

don *v.* to put on.—**don'ning** *pres. part.*—**donned** *p.t.* and *p. part.*

don *n.* 1. a Spanish gentleman. 2. a university tutor

donate' *v.* to give.—**dona'tion** (dō-nā'shun) *n.* a gift

don'key (dong'ki) *n.* 1. a domesticated animal used as beast of burden, ass. 2. a stupid person.—**don'keys** *pl.*

doom *n.* 1. fate. 2. death. 3. sentence, judgment.—*v.* to condemn.—**dooms'day** *n.* the last judgment

door (dor) *n.* a structure to close the entrance to a room, etc.—**door'way** *n.* entrance

dope *n.* 1. a drug. 2. a kind of varnish.—*v.* to drug

dor'mant *adj.* sleeping, inactive.—**dorm'itory** *n.* a sleeping-room with many beds.—**dor'mitories** *pl.*

dor'mouse *n.* a small animal that sleeps all winter.—**dor'mice** *pl.*

dorp *n.* in South Africa, a village

dor'sal *adj.* of, or on, the back

dose (dōs) *n.* the amount of medicine given at one time.—*v.* to give medicine

dot *n.* a spot or mark

dote *v.* to have the mind impaired, esp. by age.—**to dote on** to be foolishly fond of

doub'le (dub'l) *adj.* 1. of two parts. 2. twice as much or twice as many.—*adv.* twice.—*n.* 1. a person exactly like another. 2. twice the quantity.—*v.* 1. to multiply by two. 2. to fold in two. 3. to turn, get round.—**doub'ly** *adv.*—**at the double** running.—**double-decker** a bus with seats upstairs.—**double-dutch** nonsense talk.—**double-faced** insincere.—**double-dyed** wicked.—**to double back** to go back on one's tracks.—**to double-cross** to cheat, to betray.—**to double up** to fold up

doub'let (dub'let) *n.* man's close-fitting garment

doubloon' (dub-lōōn') *n.* an old Spanish gold coin

doubt (dowt) *n.* uncertainty.—*v.* 1. to hesitate. 2. not to believe.—**doubt'ful** *adj.*—**doubt'-fully** *adv.*—**doubt'less** *adv.* surely.—**beyond doubt, without doubt** completely certain.—**a doubting Thomas** a doubter, a sceptic.—**to give someone the benefit of the doubt** to assume him guiltless

Compare: disbelief, hesitation, incredulity, indecision, irresolution, misgiving, perplexity, unbelief

douche (dōōsh) *n.* a jet of water

dough (dō) *n.* flour or meal mixed with water

dough'ty (dow'ti) *adj.* brave

dour (dōōr) *adj.* grim, stern

dove (duv) *n.* 1. a kind of pigeon. 2. an emblem of peace, gentleness, and grace—**dove'cote** *n.* a house for doves.—**dove'tail** *v.* to fit together exactly.—*n.* a joint in woodwork

dow'ager (dow'a-jer) *n.* a woman with title or property derived from late husband

dow'dy *adj.* shabby, unfashionable

dow'el *n.* a wooden pin

dow'er, dow'ry *n.* the property brought by a wife to her husband at marriage

down *n.* open expanse of high ground

down *n.* soft feathers of young birds.—**down'y** *adj.*

down *adv.* to, in or towards a lower position, less important place, smaller bulk, as *to pull down, to send down* (*from the university*), *to boil down.*—*prep.* downwards along, through or into, as *going down the street.*—*adj.* 1. going downwards, as *the down slope.* 2. depressed, miserable, beaten, as *down and out.* 3. in a low or prone position.—*n.* 1. a prejudice against, as *to have a down on someone.* 2. *pl.* reverses of fortune *ups and downs.*—*v.* to put or knock down.—**down-at-heels** shabby.—**down and out** penniless, destitute.—**downcast** unhappy, depressed,—**downfall** ruin, fall from power.—**downhearted** discouraged.—**downpour** a heavy fall of rain.—**downright** decided,—**downstairs.**—**downtrodden** oppressed, bullied.—**down under** in Australia or New Zealand.—**downward** and *adv.* from a higher to a lower position. **downwards** *adj.*

doxol'ogy (doks-ol'o-ji) *n.* short hymn of praise.—**doxol'ogies** *pl.*

dow'ry see **dow'er**

do'zen (duz'n) *n.* set of twelve.—**baker's dozen** thirteen.—**daily dozen** daily physical exercises

doze (dōz) *v.* to be half asleep.—**do'zing** *pres. part.*—**dozed** *p.t.* and *p. part.*—*n.* a nap

drab *adj.* 1. dull light brown. 2. dull

drachm see **dram**

draft *n.* 1. body of troops. 2. sketch, rough copy.—*v.* 1. to outline, sketch. 2. (Aus. and N.Z.) to separate or sort cattle.—**draf'ter** *n.*—**draf'ting-gate** *n.* a gate used to separate sheep or cattle.—**draf'ting yard** a yard divided into compartments for dividing sheep or cattle into groups

drag *v.* 1. to pull with difficulty. 2. to go slowly. 3. to sweep with a net.—**drag'ging** *pres. part.*—**dragged** *p.t.* and *p. part.*—*n.* anything that checks or is pulled

drag'on *n.* a fabulous fire-breathing monster.—**dragonfly** *n.* a brightly coloured insect with four wings

dragoon' *n.* a horse soldier.—*v.* to oppress

drain *v.* 1. to draw off water, etc. 2. to drink up. 3. to exhaust.—*n.* a pipe for draining.—**drain'age** *n.*

drake *n.* a male duck

dram *n.* 1. one-sixteenth of an ounce avoirdupois weight. 2. one-eighth of an ounce apothecaries weight. 3. a small drink of liquor

dra'ma (drah'ma) *n.* 1. a play. 2. art or literature of plays.—**drama'tic** *adj.* 1. of the drama. 2. sudden, exciting.—**dra'matise** *v.* to make into a drama.—**dra'matist** *n.* a playwright

drank *p.t.* of **drink**

drape *v.* to cover with cloth.—**dra'ping** *pres. part.*—**draped** *p.t.* and *p. part.*—**dra'per** *n.* dealer in cloth, etc.—**dra'pery** *n.* cloth, hangings, flowing ropes.—**dra'peries** *pl.*

dras'tic *adj.* violent, thorough

draught (draft or drahft) *n.* 1. act of drinking. 2. amount drunk at once. 3. a current of air. 4. the fish taken in one net. 5. sketch—*n.pl.* a game played on chess-board.—**draught'horse** a horse for heavy loads.—**draughts'man** *n.* a designer.—**draught'y** *adj.* breezy

draw *v.* 1. to pull, as *The horses drew the wagon.* 2. to attract, as *to draw a crowd.* 3. take out, as *to draw money from the bank, water from the well, a sword from its sheath,* etc. 4. to make a pencil picture. 5. to move towards, as *draw near.*—**drew** *p.t.*—**drawn** *p. part.*—*n.* a tie in games.—**draw'back** *n.* disadvantage.—**draw'bridge** *n.* a bridge that pulls up.—**draw'er** *n.* a sliding box in a table, etc.—**draw'ing** *n.* 1. a pencil sketch. 2. the art of sketching.—**draw'ing-room** *n.* reception-room, main sitting-room.—**drawing board** board to which drawing paper is attached.—**drawing paper** paper suitable for drawing on.—**drawing pin** short pin with large flat head.—**drawing-room** a reception room.—**to draw a blank** to discover nothing.—**to draw the line** to refuse to act further

drawl *n.* affected, slow speech.—*v.*

dray *n.* low wagon or cart.—**dray'man** *n.*

dread (dred) *n.* terror, fear.—*v.* to fear.—*adj.* awful.—**dread'ful** *adj.* terrible.—**dread'fully** *adv.*

Compare: (*adj.*) shocking, awful, horrifying

dream (dreem) *n.* 1. a vision during sleep. 2. a fancy, vision.—*v.* to have dreams, to imagine.—**dreamed** or **dreamt** (dremt) *p.t.* and *p. part.*—**dream'er** *n.*—**dream'land** *n.*—**dream'y** *adj.* vague

drear, drear'y *adj.* dismal, comfortless.—**drear'ily** *adv.*

dredge (drej) *n.* machinery for cleaning rivers, harbours, etc. of mud.—*v.* 1. to clean thus. 2. to sprinkle with flour.—**dred'ger** *n.* 1. ship for dredging. 2. box for dredging flour, etc.

dregs *n.pl.* grounds, sediment

drench *v.* 1. to soak. 2. to make (an animal) take medicine.—he **drench'es**

dress *n.* 1. clothing. 2. a frock.—*v.* 1. to clothe. 2. to prepare. 3. draw up in line (troops). 4. apply (as ointment to a wound, manure to land, etc.).—he **dress'es.**—**dress'ing** *n.* 1. bandage, etc., for wound. 2. manure. 3. seasoning.—**dress'maker** *n.* one who makes dresses.—**dress'ing-room** *n.* a room where one dresses.—**dress'ing table** *n.* a bedroom table with drawers and a mirror.—**dress'ing gown** *n.* a loose robe worn over night clothes.—**dress'-circle** *n.* the first rows of seats upstairs in a theatre.—**to dress up** to wear elaborate clothes

drey, dray *n.* a squirrel's nest

drib'ble *v.* 1. to trickle. 2. to run at the mouth. 3. to move ball over playing field by lightly kicking or hitting.—*v.* trickle, drop

dri'er, dry'er *n.* a machine for drying hair, clothes etc.

drift *n.* 1. a wind-blown mass of snow, etc. 2. being driven by wind, tide, etc. 3. deviation from a course. 4. meaning direction, as *I could not follow the drift of his argument.* 5. aimless motion. 6. (S. Africa) a ford.—*v.* 1. to move aimlessly. 2. to be directed from one's course.

—drift'wood *n.* wood carried by water
drill *n.* 1. a boring tool. 2. military exercise. 3. a narrow furrow in which seeds are planted. 4. cotton material.—*v.* 1. to bore (a hole). 2. exercise, practise
drink (dringk) *v.* 1. to swallow liquid. 2. absorb.—**drank** *p.t.*—**drunk, drun'ken** *p. part.*—*n.* 1. liquid for drinking. 2. alcoholic liquor.—**drin'ker** *n.*
drip *v.* to fall in drops.—**drip'ping** *pres. part.* —**dripped** *p.t.* and *p. part.*—*n.* a dripping. —**drip'ping** *n.* melted fat.—**drip-dry** *adj.* (of fabrics) needing no ironing after being hung up to dry
drive *v.* 1. to urge, guide, direct (animals, a vehicle, etc.). 2. to strike (nails, ball, etc.). 3. to rush, dash, drift fast, as *The vessel drove before the storm.*—**dri'ving** *pres. part.*—**drove, drave** (old form) *p.t.*—**dri'ven** *p. part.*—*n.* 1. a trip in car, etc. 2. road leading to house. 3. great effort. 4. stroke (in cricket, golf, etc.).—**dri'ver** *n.* 1. one who drives. 2. kind of golf club for long strokes.—**to drive home** to impress strongly
driv'el *v.* 1. to dribble. 2. to talk nonsense.—*n.*
driz'zle *n.* fine rain.—*v.*
droll (drōl) *adj.* funny, odd.—**drol'lery** *n.*
drom'edary *n.* a one-humped camel.—**drom'edaries** *pl.*
drone *n.* 1. a male honey-bee. 2. an idler. 3. a humming sound.—*v.* to hum, to talk in a monotonous tone
droop *v.* to hang down.—*n.*
drop *n.* 1. a round spot of liquid. 2. a small drink. 3. a fall, descent.—*v.* 1. to let fall. 2. to lower. 3. to cease, abandon, as *We decided to drop the scheme.*—**drop'ping** *pres. part.*—**dropped** *p.t.* and *p. part.*—**drop'-kick** (rugby) *n.* a kick given to the ball as it rises from the ground after being dropped.—*v.*—**at the drop of a hat** at once.—**to drop a brick** (slang) to make an embarrassing mistake
dross *n.* 1. scum of molten metals. 2. rubbish
drought (drowt) *n.* a lack of rain
drove *p.t.* of drive
drown *v*, 1. to suffocate in water. 2. to overpower (of sound)
drow'sy (drow'zi) *adj.* sleepy.—**drow'sily** *adv.*—**drow'siness** *n.*
drub *v.* to thrash.—**drub'bing** *pres. part.*—**drubbed** *p.t.* and *p. part.*
drudge (druj) *n.* an overworked person.—*v.* to do unpleasant work.—**drudg'ery** *n.* toil
drug *n.* a medical substance.—*v.* to give a drug to.—**drug'gist** *n.* (in North America) one who sells medicines, etc.
dru'id (drōō'id) *n.* an ancient Celtic priest
drum *n.* 1. a musical instrument played by beating with sticks. 2. a part of the ear. 3. a drum-shaped container.—*v.* to play a drum, to tap.—**drum'mer** *n.*
dry *adj.* 1. not wet. 2. without rain. 3. not under water. 4. uninteresting. 5. (wit) quiet but keen. 6. (wine) not sweet.—**dri'er** *comp.*—**dri'est** *sup.*—*v.* to remove moisture.—he **dries.**—**dried** *p.t.* and *p. part.*—**dri'ly** *adv.*—**dry'ness** *n.*—**dry cell** *n.* an electric cell filled with paste instead of acid.—**dry dock** a dock which can be emptied of water, so that ships can be repaired.—**dry ice** solid carbon dioxide
dry'ad *n.* a wood-nymph
du'al *adj.* 1. forming a pair. 2. twofold.—**dual carriageway** two parallel roads, each carrying one-way traffic
dub *v.* 1. to make a person a knight. 2. to name
du'bious (dū'bi-us) *adj.* doubtful
du'cal *adj.* of a duke
duch'ess *n.* the wife or widow of duke.—**duch'esses** *pl.*—**duch'y** *n.* a duke's territory or title.—**duch'ies** *pl.*
duck *n.* a wild or tame swimming-bird.—**drake** *masc.*—*v.* to dive, or dip quickly.—**duck'ling** *n.* a young duck.—**like water off a duck's back** to no effect.—**to take to it like a duck to water** to take part in some activity naturally.—**to play ducks and drakes with money** to squander money
duck *n.* strong linen
duct *n.* a channel or tube for carrying liquid. —**duc'tile** *adj.* easily directed, capable of being drawn out into wire or threads
due *adj.* 1. owing, as *I think an apology is due to him.* 2. fitting, proper, deserved, as *after due consideration; his due punishment* 3. expected (to arrive), as *The train is due now.*—*n.* 1. debt, payment (often used in pl.). 2. person's just right, as *To give him his due, I think he means well.*—*adv.* exactly, as *due south.*—**due to** caused by. as *His success is due to hard work*

Note: **Due** must not be used as an adverb to mean *owing* meaning *on account of*, as *They were unfriendly due to a misunderstanding*. This should be *They were unfriendly owing to a misunderstanding*

du'el (dū'el) *n.* a fight with weapons, between two persons.—*v.* to fight in duels.—**du'ellist** *n.*
du'et *n.* music performed by two people
dug'-out *n.* 1. an underground shelter. 2. hollowed out tree-canoe
duke *n.* 1. a nobleman of highest rank. 2. the ruler of a duchy.—**duch'ess** *fem.*—**duke'dom** *n.*
dul'cet (dul'set) *adj.* sweet
dull *adj.* 1. stupid. 2. not sharp. 3. not bright.—**dul'ly** *adv.*—**dull'ness** *n.*
du'ly (dū'li) *adv.* as expected
dumb (dum) *adj.* unable or unwilling to speak. —**dumbfound'** *v.* to amaze into silence.—**dumb'ly** *adv.*—**dumb'ness** *n.*
dum'my *n.* 1. a tailor's model. 2. an imitation, substitute. 3. a baby's rubber teat.—**dum'mies** *pl.*
dump *n.* 1. a rubbish heap. 2. a storing-place. —*v.* to throw down

dump'ling *n.* 1. a small piece of dough boiled in soup or stew. 2. a shell of dough enclosing fruit or meat

dun *n.* dull brown.—*adj.*

dun *v.* to demand payment.—*n.*

dunce *n.* a stupid person

dune (dūn) *n.* a low hill of wind-blown sand

dung *n.* animal manure

dungarees (dungareez') *n.pl.* overalls

dun'geon (dun'jon) *n.* an underground prisoner's cell

dupe (dūp) *n.* a person easily cheated.—*v.* to deceive

du'plicate (dū'plik-it) *n.* an exact copy.—*v.* (dū'plik-āt) to make an exact copy.—*adj.* exactly like.—**duplica'tion** *n.*—**du'plicator** *n.* a machine for duplicating

dupli'city (dū-pli'si-ti) *n.* double dealing, deceit, cunning

dup'py *n.* Jamaican word for a ghost

durabil'ity (dū-ra-bil'i-ti) *n.* resistance to wear.—**dur'able** *adj.* lasting

dura'tion *n.* the time a thing lasts

duress' *n.* 1. hardship. 2. imprisonment

du'ring *prep.* in the time of

dusk *n.* twilight.—**dusk'y** *adj.* dark

dust *n.* fine, powdery loose earth or other matter.—*v.* 1. to sprinkle. 2. to rid of dust. —**dust'er** *n.* cloth.—**dust'y** *adj.*—**dust'-jacket** *n.* a protective outer wrapper for a book.—**to bite the dust** to fall in combat

Dutch *adj.* belonging to Holland

du'ty (dū'ti) *n.* 1. what one ought to do. 2. a job. 3. a tax.—**du'ties** *pl.*—**du'tiful** *adj.* obedient

dwarf *n.* 1. a man, animal, plant, below usual size.—**dwarfs** *pl.*—*adj.*—*v.* to make seem small.—**dwarf'ish** *adj.*

dwell *v.* 1. to live in. 2. to speak at length (on).—**dwelt, dwelled** (old form) *p.t.* and *p. part.*—**dwel'ling** *n.* house.—**dwel'ler** *n.*

dwin'dle *v.* to shrink, grow less

dye *n.* colouring matter.—*v.* to colour.—**dye'-ing** *pres. part.*—**dyed** (dīd) *p.t.* and *p. part.* —**dy'er** *n.*—**dyed-in-the-wool** unchangeable

dy'ing *adj.* about to die.

Note: do not confuse with dye'ing

dynam'ic (dī-na'mik) *adj.* 1. relating to force. 2. forceful, vigorous.—**dynam'ics** *n.pl.* branch of physics dealing with forces causing motion.—**dy'namite** *n.* powerful explosive

dy'namo *n.* machine for making electricity from mechanical energy

dyn'asty (din'as-ti) *n.* a line, or family of rulers

dyspep'sia *n.* indigestion.—**dyspep'tic** *adj.*

E

each (eech) *adj.* and *pron.* every one taken separately, as (*adj.*) *Each boy has a pen. They have a pen each* (*pron.*). *Each has a pen.*—**each other** each one the other

Note: This is used when only two things are spoken of. When more than two are spoken of say *one another*, as *The two sisters loved each other. The whole family loved one another*

ea'ger (ee'ger) *adj*, keen, impatient.—**ea'gerly** *adv.*—**ea'ger'ness** *n.*

Compare: animated, anxious, ardent, earnest, enthusiastic, fervent, zealous. *Contrast:* apathetic, indifferent, lethargic, lukewarm

ea'gle (ee'gl) *n.* 1. large bird of prey. 2. national symbol of the U.S.—**ea'glet** *n.* young eagle

ear (eer) *n.* 1. the entire organ of hearing. 2. the visible part of that organ. 3. sense of hearing, as *She has a good ear* (for music).—**ear'mark** *v.* to set apart for special purpose.—**ear'ring** *n.* an ornament worn on the lobe of the ear.—**ear'shot** *n.* hearing distance.—**to be all ears** to listen very carefully

ear (eer) *n.* a head of corn

earl (erl) *n.* a nobleman ranking between marquis and viscount.—**coun'tess** *fem.*—**earl'dom** *n.*

ear'ly (er'li) *adj.* and *adv.* soon, in good time, before other things, as (*adj.*) *He caught an early train.* (*adv.*) *He rose early next morning.*—**ear'lier** *comp.*—**ear'liest** *sup.*—**ear'liness** *n.*

earn (ern) *v.* 1. to gain money by work. 2. to get for merit

ear'nest (er'nest) *adj.* serious, determined.—**in earnest** serious, sincere.—**ear'nestly** *adv.*

Compare: eager, grave, sober, strenuous. *Contrast:* capricious, fickle, frivolous

ear'nest *n.* money paid over to bind a bargain, foretaste

earn'ings (ern'ings) *n.pl.* wages

earth (erth) *n.* 1. ground, soil. 2. the planet we live on.—*v.* to make an electrical connection to the earth.—**earth'en** *adj.* of clay.—**earth'enware** *n.* crockery.—**earth'ly** *adj.* of this world.—**earth'quake** *n.* underground disturbance.—**earth'wards, earthward** *adv.* towards the earth.—**earth'work** *n.* fortification.—**to come down to earth** to be practical and realistic.—**to move heaven and earth** to do everything possible

ear'wig *n.* a brown insect with shiny wingcases

ease (eez) *n.* 1. comfort, rest, as *He was taking his ease in an arm-chair.* 2. freedom from care, effort, pain, constraint, as *He did it with ease. She is quite at ease in society.*—*v.* 1. to reduce pain or discomfort. 2. to remove pressure, burden, etc.—**ea'sing** *pres. part.*—**eased** *p.t.* and *p. part.*—**to ease off, ease up** to slacken effort

ea'sel (ee'zel) *n.* a support for picture or blackboard

eas'ily (eez'i-li) *adv.* with ease.—**eas'iness** *n.* comfort

east (eest) *n.* 1. the direction of sunrise. 2. regions towards that.—*adj.* coming from the east.—**east'erly** *adj.*—**east'ern** *adj.*

dwelling in the east.—**east'ward** *adj. adv.* towards the east

East'er (eest'er) *n.* the festival in memory of Christ's Resurrection

eas'y (ee'zi) *adj.* 1. not difficult. 2. comfortable. 3. pleasant.—**eas'ier** *comp.*—**eas'iest** *sup.*—**eas'y-chair** *n.* a comfortable, padded chair

eat (eet) *v.* 1. to chew and swallow. 2. consume, destroy.—**ate** (āt) *p.t.*—**ea'ten** (ee'-ten) *p. part.*—**eat'able** *adj.* See **edible.**—**eat'ables** *n.pl.* food.—**to eat away** 1. to eat heartily. 2. to corrode.—**to eat one's heart out** to brood and pine over some trouble.—**to eat one's words** to take back something one has said

eau-de-cologne (ō-di-kol-ōn') *n.* a well-known perfumed toilet water

eaves (eevz) *n.pl.* the over-hanging edges of a roof.—**eaves'dropper** *n.* person who listens to talk not meant for him

Note: This word has no singular form

ebb *n.* the flowing back of the tide.—*v.* to flow back

eb'onite *n.* vulcanised rubber used as an electrical insulator

eb'ony *n.* hard black wood

ebull'ient *adj.* full of enthusiasm and vitality. **ebull'ience, ebull'iency** *n.*

ebulli'tion (eb-ul-i'shun) *n.* 1. a boiling up. 2. an outburst (of feeling, enthusiasm, etc.)

eccen'tric (ek-sen'trik) *adj.* 1. not having the same centre (referring to circles), opposite of **concentric.** 2. odd, unusual.—**eccentri'city** (ek-sen-tri'si-ti) *n.* strange behaviour, an odd act.—*pl.* peculiarities of behaviour

ecclesias'tic (ek-klee-zi-as'tik) *n.* clergyman. —*adj.* belonging to the church.—**ecclesias'tical** *adj.*

ech'o (ek'o) *n.* 1. repetition of sound. 2. imitation.—**ech'oes** (ek'ōz) *pl.*—*v.* to repeat.—**ech'o-sounder** *n.* apparatus for measuring the depth of the sea by timing echoes from the sea-bed

e'clair *n.* a finger-shaped cream cake often coated with icing or chocolate

e'clat (ā'kla) *n.* splendour, success

eclipse' *n.* the darkening of sun, moon, etc. by the passage of another heavenly body. —*v.* to obscure, surpass

ecol'ogy (e-col'oj-i) *n.* the study of the relations between living things and their environment

econom'ic *adj.* having to do with economics. —**econom'ical** *adj.* saving, thirfty.—**econom'ics** *n.pl.* study of the production and distribution of wealth.—**econ'omise** *v.* to use thriftily.—**econ'omist** *n.* person who understands economics

econ'omy *n.* careful management, saving.—**political economy** *n.* See **economics**

ec'stasy (ek'sta-si) *n.* a state of rapture, joy.—**ecsta'tic** *adj.*—**ecstat'ically** *adv.*

ec'zema *n.* a skin disease

ed'dy *n.* a small whirl of water, smoke, etc.—**ed'dies** *pl.*—*v.* to whirl.—**ed'died** *p.t.* and *p. part.*

edge (ej) *n.* 1. the cutting side of a blade. 2. a border, boundary.—*v.* to move gradually. —**edge'ways, edge'wise** *adv.*—**to have the edge on** to have a slight advantage over.—**to set one's teeth on edge** to cause one's teeth to tingle unpleasantly

ed'ible *adj.* eatable

Compare: wholesome. *Contrast:* inedible, poisonous, uneatable

e'dict (ee'dikt) *n.* a decree, order

edifica'tion (ed-i-fi-kā'shun) *n.* moral improvement

ed'ifice (ed'i-fis) *n.* a building

ed'ify *v.* to improve morally

ed'it *v.* to prepare for publication, to revise. —**edit'ion** (ed-i'shun) *n.* 1. the form in which a book is published. 2. the number of copies printed at one time.—**ed'itor** *n.* a person in charge of a publication.—**edito'rial** *n.* leading article in newspaper.—*adj.* of an editor

ed'ucate (ed'ū-kāt) *v.* 1. to bring up. 2. to teach.—**educa'tion** (ed-ū-kā'shun) *n.* schooling and training.—**educa'tional** *adj.* —**ed'ucator** *n.*

Compare: (with education) breeding, instruction, teaching, tuition, culture, learning. *Contrast:* ignorance, illiteracy

Note: Education describes not merely what goes on in schools, but rather the development of a person's character and abilities that goes on all through life; or it may mean a special system of training. *Breeding, instruction, teaching* and *tuition* are all factors in *education; culture, refinement* and *learning* are amongst its effects

eel *n.* a snake-like fish

ee'rie, ee'ry *adj.* uncanny, strange

efface' (e-fās') *v.* to wipe or rub out.—**effa'cing** *pres. part.*—**effaced'** *p.t.* and *p. part.*—**efface'ment** *n.*

effect' *n.* a result, consequence.—*pl.* property.—*v.* to bring about, as *I hope to effect an improvement.*—**effec'tive** *n.* man, or number of men, fit for (military) service.—*adj.* obtaining results, as *an effective action, an effective speaker.*—**effec'tual** *adj.* completely successful or decisive, as *The firm action of the police put an effectual end to disorder.*—**effec'tually** *adv.*—**to no effect** to no purpose, without result.—**to put into effect** to cause to operate.—**to take effect** to become active, to operate

effem'inate *adj.* unmanly

Contrast: virile, vigorous, manly

effervesce' (ef-er-ves') *v.* to bubble up.—**efferves'cence** *n.*—**efferves'cent** *adj.*

effete' (e-feet') *adj.* worn out

effica'cious (ef-i-kā'shus) *adj.* producing desired result, as *the medicine was an efficacious cure.*—**ef'ficacy** (ef'i-ka-si) *n.*

effic'iency (e-fish'en-si) *n.* the ability to do things well.—**effic'ient** *adj.* capable.—**effic'iently** *adv.*

Efficient is used of persons, *effective, effectual* and *efficacious* of things, although an incapable person might be called *ineffectual*. See **effective, effectual, efficacious** (examples)

ef'figy (ef'i-ji) *n.* an image of a person.—**ef'figies** *pl.*

ef'florescent *adj.* (of crystals) losing water and becoming dry and powdery

ef'fluent *adj.* flowing out.—**ef'fluence** *n.*

ef'fort *n.* exertion, trying hard

effront'ery (e-frun'ter-i) *n.* impudence

efful'gence (e-ful'jens) *n.* splendour.—**efful'gent** *adj.*

effu'sion (e-fū'zhun) *n.* 1. a pouring out. 2. a lack of restraint.—**effu'sive** (e-fū'siv) *adj.* gushing

eft *n.* a small newt

egg *n.* an oval rounded body produced by female of birds, fish, etc. and containing the germ of their young

egg (on) *v.* to instigate, incite, urge. (See **urge**)

e'go *n.* oneself.—**e'goism** *n.* selfishness.—**e'goist** *n.* selfish person.—**egoist'ic** *adj.*—**e'gotism** *n.* self-conceit.—**e'gotist** *n.*—**egotis'tical** *adj.* self-centred

E'gypt *n.* a country of North Africa.—**Egyp'tian** *n.* a native of Egypt

ei'der (ī'der) *n.* a sea-duck found in northern regions.—**ei'der-down** *n.* 1. down of the eider. 2. a bed-covering stuffed with this

eight (āt) *adj.* one above seven.—**eighth** (āt-th) *adj.* one above seventh.—**eighteen'** *adj.* eight and ten.—**eighteenth'** *adj.*—**eighty** *adj.* ten times eight.—**eightieth** *adj.*—**piece of eight** *n.* an old Spanish coin

eistedd'fod *n.* a Welsh festival of poetry and music

either (ī'THer, ee'THer) *adj.* one of two, each, as *on either side of the street.*—*pron.* as *Either will do.*—*adv.* also, as well (used after negative), as *I will not go, and he will not either.*—*conj.* in one of two cases (followed by *or*), as *Either retreat or be captured*

ejac'ulate *v.* to exclaim, say suddenly.—**ejacula'tion** (ee-jak-ū-lā'shun) *n.*

eject' *v.* to throw out.—**ejec'tion** (-shun) *n.*—**ejec'tor** *n.* anything which ejects, such as apparatus for ejecting a pilot from an aeroplane in emergency

eke (out) *v.* to make sufficient with difficulty, contrive to make (a living, etc.)

elab'orate (ee-lab'or-at) *adj.* worked out in detail.—*v.* (ee-lab'or-āt).—**elabora'tion** (ee-lab-or-ā'shun) *n.*

e'land *n.* a South African antelope

elapse' *v.* (of time) to pass by

elas'tic *n.* a rubber tape or band.—*adj.* flexible, springing back into place.—**elasti'city** (ee-las-tis'i-ti) *n.*

elate' *v.* to raise the spirits.—**ela'tion** (ee-lā'shun) *n.* high spirits (usually caused by joy or pride)

el'bow (el'bō) *n.* the joint between upper arm and forearm.—*v.* to thrust.—**el'bow-grease** hard rubbing, hard polishing.—**to rub elbows with** to meet and mix with

el'der *adj.* older, senior (referring to two persons), *comp.* of **old.**—*n.* 1. one who is older. 2. official in some churches.—**el'derly** *adj.* growing old.—**el'dest** *adj.* oldest *sup.* of **old**

el'der *n.* a white-flowered tree

elect' *v.* 1. to choose. 2. to choose by vote.—*adj.* chosen, select.—**elec'tion** *n.* choosing by voting.—**elec'tive** *adj.*—**elec'tor** *n.* a person with the right to vote.—**elec'toral** *adj.*—**elec'torate** *n.* body of voters

elec'tric *adj.* charged with electricity.—**elec'trical** *adj.*—**electri'cian** (e-lek-trish'an) *n.* an expert in the science of electricity.—**electri'city** (e-lek-tri'si-ti) *n.* a force producing light, heat, power.—**elec'trify** *v.* 1. to charge with electricity. 2. to startle.—he **elec'trifies.**—**elec'trifying** *pres. part.*—**elec'trified** *p.t.* and *p. part.*—**electric arc** an electric discharge across the gap between two electrodes.—**electric chair** a chair in which criminals are electrocuted in the U.S.A.—**electric charge** electricity stored in a battery of condenser.—**electric eel** a South American fish which can give a strong electric shock.—**electric ray** a flatfish which gives an electric shock

elec'trocute *v,* to kill by electricity.—**electrocu'tion** (e-lek-trō-kū'shun) *n.*

elec'trode *n.* the terminal point where an electric current enters or leaves a cell, solution or arc

electrol'ysis *n.* a chemical change into simpler elements produced by an electric current.—**elec'trolyte** *n.* a solution of a chemical undergoing electrolysis

electromag'net *n.* a soft iron bar magnetised by a current passing through a coil wrapped round it

elec'tron *n.* one of the particles composing an atom, carrying a negative electric charge.—**electron miscroscope** a very powerful miscroscope operated by electrical means

electron'ics *n. pl.* the science which deals with electrons and their use in vacuum tubes for television, radio, guided missiles, computers, etc.

elec'troplate *v.* to coat with silver.—*n.*

el'egance *n.* good taste, refinement.—**el'egant** *adj.*

el'egy (el'e-ji) *n.* 1. a lament for the dead. 2. a sad poem.—**el'egies** *pl.*

el'ement *n.* 1. an ingredient. 2. a substance which cannot be analysed. 3. surroundings, sphere. 4. electric heating wires.—*pl.* first principles.—**elemen'tary** *adj.* 1. simple. 2. primary.—**in one's element** happy in one's ideal surroundings

el'ephant (el'e-fant) *n.* the biggest four-footed animal.—**elephan'tine** *adj.* huge and clumsy

el'evate *v.* to raise.—**el'evating** *pres. part.*—**el'evated** *p.t.* and *p. part.*—**eleva'tion** (el-e-vā'shun) *n.* height.—**el'evator** *n.* 1. lift. 2. a grain storehouse

elev'en *adj.* and *n.* the number above ten.—*n.* a team of eleven players (football, cricket, hockey, etc.).—**elev'enth** *adj.* one above tenth.—**at the eleventh hour** at the last moment

elf *n.* a small fairy.—**elves** *pl.*—**elf'in, el'fish** *adj.*

elic'it (el-is'it) *v.* to draw out (by reasoning or questioning), as *The detective soon elicited the names of the culprits*

eligibil'ity (el-i-ji-bil'i-ty) *n.* qualifying, being fit.—**eli'gible** *adj.* qualified to be chosen, suitable

elimin'ate *v.* to remove, get rid of.—**elimina'tion** (e-lim-in-ā'shun) *n.*

élite' (ā-leet') *n.* select company

elix'ir *n.* 1. a powerful stimulating drink. 2. a substance which it was once thought could change lead into gold, or prolong life indefinitely

elk *n.* a large deer

ell *n.* an old measure of length

ellipse' *n.* an oval the same at both ends.—**ellip'soid** *n.* a solid figure made by a rotating ellipse

ellip'sis *n.* omission of words needed to complete grammatical sense or construction of sentence.—**ellipses** *pl.*

ellip'tical *adj.* in the form of an ellipse

elm *n.* a deciduous tall tree

elocu'tion (el-o-kū'shun) *n.* voice production, the art of public speaking or reciting—**elocu'tionist** *n.*

e'longate (ee'long-gāt) *v.* to lengthen—**elonga'tion** (ee-long-gā'shun) *n.*

elope' *v.* to run away with a lover.—**elope'ment** *n.*

el'oquence (el'o-kwens) *n.* speech that has ease and force.—**el'oquent** *adj.*

else *adv.* 1. besides, as *someone else, what else.* 2. otherwise, as *Do it properly or else don't do it at all.*—**else'where** *adv.* in another place

elu'cidate (e-lū'si-dāt) *v.* to make clear, explain.—**elucida'tion** *n.*

elude' (e-lōōd', e-lūd') *v.* to escape, avoid.—**elu'ding** *pres. part.*—**elu'ded** *p.t.* and *p. part.*—**elu'sion** (e-lū'zhun) *n.*—**elu'sive** *adj.* difficult to catch

el'ver *n.* a young eel

elves *pl.* of elf

ema'ciate (e-mā'shi-āt) *v.* to make thin.—**emacia'tion** (e-mā-si-ā'shun) *n.* thinness.—**ema'ciated** *adj.*

em'anate *v.* to issue from, come from.—**emana'tion** (em-a-nā'shun) *n.*

Compare: originate, proceed, derive, arise

eman'cipate (e-man'si-pāt) *v.* to set free.—**emancipa'tion** (e-man-si-pā'shun) *n.* release

embalm' (em-bahm') *v.* to preserve (a corpse) with spices, etc.

embank'ment *n.* a raised bank of earth

embar'go *n.* 1. order stopping movement of ships. 2. a ban.—**embar'goes** *pl.*

embark' *v.* to go, or put on board ship.—**to embark' on,** to begin.—**embarka'tion** (em-bar-kā'shun) *n.*

embar'rass *v.* 1. to confuse. 2. to hinder.—**he embar'rasses**—**embar'rassment** *n.*

em'bassy *n.* the work or house of an ambassador.—**em'bassies** *pl.*

embat'tled *adj.* 1. of an army, ready for battle. 2. of a tower or wall, having battlements

embed' *v.* to fix fast in something solid.—**embed'ding** *pres. part.*—**embed'ded** *p.t.* and *p. part.*

embell'ish *v.* to adorn.—**embell'ishment** *n.*

em'ber *n.* a glowing cinder.—**em'ber-days** days of fasting.

embez'zle *v.* to steal money in one's care.—**embez'zlement** *n.*

embit'ter *v.* to make bitter

embla'zon (em-blā'zon) *v.* 1. to adorn, show conspicuously. 2. to adorn with heraldic figures

em'blem *n.* 1. a symbol, sign. 2. a badge, device.—**emblemat'ic** *adj.*

embod'y *v.* 1. to include, as *Several important proposals are embodied in this bill.* 2. to express, as *Your words clearly embody your thoughts.* 3. to represent in bodily form, as *The king embodies the nation.*—**he embod'ies.**—**embod'ying** *pres. part.*—**embod'ied** *p.t.* and *p. part.*—**embod'iment** *n.*

emboss' *v.* to carve or stamp in relief.—**he emboss'es**

embrace' (em-brās') *v.* 1. to clasp in the arms. 2. to seize (an opportunity, etc.). 3. to include.—*n.*—**embra'cing** *pres. part.*—**embraced'** *p.t.* and *p. part.*

embra'sure (em-brā'zhur) *n.* 1. an opening in a wall for cannon. 2. the space made by the slanting of the wall beside a window, etc.

embroca'tion (em-brō-kā'shun) *n.* a lotion for rubbing sprains, etc.

embroi'der *v.* 1. to ornament with stitches. 2. to embellish (a story).—**embroi'dery** *n.*

embroil' *v.* 1. to throw into confusion. 2. (with) to bring into a quarrel

em'bryo (em'bri-ō) *n.* 1. the unborn animal starting to develop in the womb or the egg. 2. the young plant developing in the seed.—*adj.* rudimentary.—**em'bryos** (em'bri-ōz) *pl.*—**embryon'ic** *adj.*

emend' *v.* to correct.—**emenda'tion** (ee-men-dā'shun) *n.*

Note: An editor, scholar, or critic *emends* the words of a document or manuscript, but a meeting may *amend,* i.e. alter, a resolution or motion submitted to it

em'erald *n.* a bright green precious stone.—*adj.*

emerge' (e-merj') *v.* to come up, out.—**emer'ging** *pres. part.*—**emerged'** *p.t.* and *p. part.*—**emer'gence** *n.*—**e'mer'gency** (e-mer'jen-si) *n.* sudden event needing prompt action

em'ery *n.* a hard mineral used for polishing.—**emery paper** paper covered with ground emery

emet'ic *n.* a medicine to cause vomiting

em'igrant *n.* a settler in another country.—**em'igrate** *v.* to go and live abroad.—**emigra'tion** (em-i-grā'shun) *n.*

Note: An *emigrant* is a person leaving his own country for another, whereas an *immigrant* is one entering another country.

em'inence (em'i-nens) *n.* 1. height. 2. distinction. 3. the title of a cardinal.—**em'inent** *adj.* distinguished, prominent.—**em'inently** *adv.* particularly, especially

emir' (e-meer') *n.* an Arabian prince.

em'issary *n.* a person sent on a mission.—**em'issaries** *pl.*—**emis'sion** (e-mish'un) *n.* 1. sending out. 2. giving off.

emit' *v.* to send out, as *The chimney emitted smoke.*—**emit'ting** *pres. part.*—**emit'ted** *p.t.* and *p. part.*

emol'ument *n.* pay, salary

emo'tion (ee-mō'shun) *n.* deep feeling.—**emo'tional** *adj.*

em'peror *n.* the sovereign of an empire.—(**empress** *fem.*)

em'phasis (em'fa-sis) *n.* 1. stress on words or syllables. 2. importance attached, as *The teacher laid special emphasis on the importance of neatness.*—**em'phasise** *v.*—**emphat'ic** *adj.* decided.

em'pire *n.* 1. a group of states under one ruler. 2. a territory ruled by an emperor. 3. wide and supreme power.

emplace'ment *n.* a platform for guns, etc.

employ' *v.* 1. to use. 2. to give work to, to hire for pay.—**employ'ing** *pres. part.*—**employed'** *p.t.* and *p. part.*—**employ'ee** *n.* worker.—**employ'er** *n.*—**employ'ment** *n.* work

empor'ium *n.* a trading centre, a large shop

empow'er *v.* to enable

em'press *n.* 1. *fem.* of emperor. 2. wife of an emperor

emp'ty *adj.* 1. containing nothing. 2. senseless, foolish.—**emp'tier** *comp.*—**emp'tiest** *sup.*—*v.* to take out, pour out contents.—**emp'tying** *pres. part.*—**emp'tied** *p.t.* and *p. part.*—**empty-hand'ed** taking nothing

e'mu (ee'mū) *n.* a large Australian bird resembling an ostrich

em'ulate *v.* to strive to equal or excel, to imitate, as *to emulate the heroes of old.*—**emula'tion** (em-ū-lā'shun) *n.*

emul'sion *n.* fine particles, usually oil or fat, suspended in water or other liquid.—**emul'sify** *v.* to make into an emulsion.—**emul'sifying** *pres. part.*—**emul'sified** *p.t.* and *p. part.*

ena'ble *v.* to make able.—**ena'bling** *pres. part.*—**ena'bled** *p.t.* and *p. part.*

enact' *v.* 1. to make into law. 2. to play, act.—**enact'ment** *n.*

enam'el *n.* 1. a smooth, glossy, hard coating for china, metals, etc. 2. the coating of the teeth.—*v.*

enam'our (en-am'er) *v.* to inspire with love.

Note: This verb is generally used in the passive voice in the expression *to be enamoured of* (*somebody or something*)

encamp' *v.* to settle in a camp.—**encamp'ment** *n.*

enchant' *v.* 1. to bewitch. 2. to delight.—**enchant'er** *n.*—**enchan'tress** *fem.*—**enchant'ment** *n.* spell

encir'cle (en-sir'kl) *v.* to surround.—**encir'cling** *pres. part.*—**encir'cled** *p.t.* and *p. part.*—**encir'clement** *n.*

enclose' (en-klōz') *v.* 1. to shut in. 2. to include (in a letter).—**enclo'sing** *pres. part.*—**enclosed'** *p.t.* and *p. part.*—**enclo'sure** (en-klō'zhur) *n.* 1. an enclosed space. 2. something put in (a letter). 3. a fence

encom'pass (en-kum'pas) *v.* to surround

en'core (ong'kōr) *interj.* again.—*n.* song, etc., repeated or added to a programme

encount'er *n.* 1. a meeting. 2. a battle.—*v.* to meet in battle, or unexpectedly

encour'age (en-kur'ij) *v.* to hearten, cheer.—**encour'aging** *pres. part.*—**encour'aged** *p.t.* and *p. part.*—**encour'agement** *n.*

encroach' (en-krōch') *v.* to intrude, trespass (*on* or *upon*).—**encroach'ment** *n.*

encrust' *v.* 1. to form a crust. 2. to cover with a crust or layer

encum'ber *v.* to burden, hinder.—**encum'brance** *n.*

encycloped'ia, encyclopaed'ia (en-sī-klō-pee'di-a) *n.* book of information on all subjects, arranged alphabetically.—**encyclope'dic, encyclopae'dic** *adj.*

end *n.* 1. a finishing. 2. last part, conclusion. 3. death. 4. purpose, aim.—*v.* to finish.—**end'less** *adj.* without end.—**end'ways** *adv.* on end, upright.—**end-product** *n.* the thing produced by a series of actions or processes.—**at a loose end** with nothing to do.—**to go off at the deep end** to become very angry or excited.—**to hold the wrong end of the stick** to misunderstand something.—**to keep one's end up** to hold one's own against difficulties or attacks.—**to make ends meet** to pay one's way by economising.—**to the bitter end** to the very end

endang'er *v.* to place in danger

endeav'our (en-dev'er) *n.* effort.—*v.* to try.—

Compare: attempt, essay, strive, undertake. *Contrast:* abandon, give up, drop

endorse' *v.* 1. to sign one's name on the back of (a cheque, etc.). 2. to approve.—**endorse'ment** *n.*

endow' *v.* 1. to give a source of income to. 2. to equip.—**endow'ment** *n.* 1. money given. 2. talent

endue' *v.* to endow (with a quality)
endur'able *adj.* 1. bearable. 2. lasting
endur'ance (en-dū'rans) *n.* 1. power to bear. 2. power to last.—**endure'** *v.* 1. to bear, stand. 2. to last.—**endu'ring** *pres. part.*—**endured'** *p.t.* and *p. part.*
en'emy *n.* 1. a person or thing acting against another, adversary. 2. a hostile nation, army or ship. 3. something harmful, as *Rust is an enemy of iron.*—**en'emies** *pl.*
energet'ic (en-er-jet'ik) *adj.* active.—**en'ergise** *v.* fill with energy.
en'ergy (en'er-ji) *n.* vigour, force, activity.—**en'ergies** (en'er-jiz) *pl.*
en'ervate *v.* to weaken, deprive of vigour.—**en'ervating** *adj.*
enfee'ble *v.* to weaken.—**enfee'blement** *n.*
enfold' *v.* 1. to wrap up. 2. to clasp
enforce' *v.* to compel obedience to, as *The regulations were strictly enforced.*—**enforce'ment** *n.*—**enforce'able** *adj.*
enfran'chise (en-fran'chīz) *v.* 1. to set free. 2. to give the right of voting.— **enfranchisement** (en-fran'chiz-ment) *n.*
engage' (en-gāj') *v.* 1. to hire, employ. 2. to promise, as in the expression *engaged* (*to be married*). 3. to take part in, as *to engage in trade*, *to be engaged in business.* 4. to begin to fight, as *Our ships engaged the enemy.*—**enga'ging** *pres. part.*—**engaged'** *p.t.* and *p. part.* occupied, in use.—**engage'ment** *n.* 1. promise. 2. battle.—**enga'ging** *adj.* attractive
engen'der (en-jen'der) *v.* to give rise to, produce.
en'gine (en'jin) *n.* a machine to transmit power.—**engineer'** *n.* 1. one who constructs or tends engines. 2. one who makes bridges, roads, etc.—*v.* to contrive.—**engineer'ing** *n.* science or profession of the engineer.
En'gland *n.* the country in the British Isles south of the Cheviot hills.—**En'glish** *adj.* belonging to England.—*n.* the language of the English and other peoples.—**English Channel** the narrow sea separating England from France
engrain' *v.* to implant firmly
engrave' *v.* 1. to cut lines into metal for printing. 2. to carve. 3. to impress deeply.—**engra'ver** *n.*—**engra'ving** *n.* a print.
engross' (en-grōs') *v.* to interest greatly
engulf' *v.* to swallow up
enhance' (en-hahns') *v.* to add to (value, etc.).—**enhance'ment** *n.*
enig'ma *n.* a riddle, puzzle.—**enig'mas** *pl.*—**enigmat'ic** *adj.* mysterious
enjoin' *v.* to command, to bid
Note: Sometimes followed by *on* or *upon*
enjoy' *v.* 1. to take pleasure in. 2. to have the use of (something pleasant), as *to enjoy privileges, good health, etc.*—**enjoy'able** *adj.* pleasant.—**enjoy'ment** *n.* pleasure.
enlarge' (en-larj') *v.* to grow, or make large.—**to enlarge' on** to talk, or write in detail.—**enlarge'ment** *n.* a large photographic print from a smaller negative
enlight'en (en-līt'en) *v.* to instruct, inform.—**enlight'ened** *adj.* well-informed, broad-minded.—**enlight'enment** *n.*
enlist' *v.* 1. to enrol, to gain interest or assistance, 2. to join the army.—**enlist'ment** *n.*
enli'ven (en-lī'ven) *v.* to cheer, brighten
en'mity *n.* hatred.—**en'mities** *pl.*
enno'ble *v.* 1. to make noble, 2. to make a nobleman of
en'nui (ohn'wee) (French) *n.* boredom
enor'mity *n.* great wickedness, a great offence.—**enor'mous** *adj.* huge
enough' (e-nuf') *n.* a sufficient quantity.—*adj.* as much, or as many as need be.—*adv.* sufficiently.—*interj.* stop!
enquire'. See **inquire.**—**enqui'ry**. See **inquiry**
enrage' (en-rāj') *v.* to make furious
enrap'ture (en-rap'cher) *v.* to fill with delight
enrich' *v.* to add to, make rich.—he **enrich'es.**—**enrich'ment** *n.*
enrol', **en'roll'** (en-rōl) *v.* 1. to enter in a register. 2. to enlist.—**enrol'ment** *n.*—**enrol'ling** *pres. part.*—**enrolled'** *p.t.* and *p. part.*
ensconce' (en-skons) *v.* to settle safely
ensem'ble (ohn-sohm'bl) *n.* (French) 1. the whole, a general effect. 2. a woman's complete outfit
enshrine' *v.* 1. to place in a shrine. 2. to preserve
enshroud' (en-shrowd') *v.* to wrap up, conceal
en'sign (en'sīn) *n.* 1. a naval or military flag. 2. a badge. 3. the lowest commissioned officer in U.S. navy and (before 1871) in British Army
enslave' *v.* to make a slave of
ensnare' *v.* to trap
ensue' *v.* to follow, happen after.—**ensu'ing** *pres. part.*—**ensued'** *p.t.* and *p. part.*
ensure' (en-shōōr') *v.* 1. to make safe. 2. to make certain to happen.—**ensur'ing** *pres. part.*—**ensured'** *p.t.* and *p. part.*
entail' *v.* to have as result, as *Spring cleaning entails a great deal of work*
entan'gle (en-tang'gl) *v.* 1. to get mixed, knotted. 2. to catch.—**entan'glement** *n.*
entente' (ohntohnt') *n.* (French) a friendly understanding (between countries)
en'ter *v.* 1. to go, or come into. 2. to join, as *to enter a monastery*, *to enter for a race.* 3. to write in, *as to enter facts in a notebook.* 4. to put in, as *to enter a horse for a race.*—**to enter into** to take part in.—**to enter upon** to set out to do
en'terprise *n.* 1. a bold attempt, undertaking. 2. willingness to undertake new or risky attempts.—**en'terprising** *adj.*
entertain' *v.* 1. to receive as a guest. 2. to amuse. 3. to consider, as *He refused to entertain the suggestion.*—**entertain'er** *n.*—**entertain'ment** *n.* hospitality, amusement

enthral' (en-thrawl') *v.* to fascinate, charm.—**enthral'ling** *pres. part.*—**enthralled'** *p.t.* and *p. part.*

enthu'siasm (en-thū'zi-azm) *n.* great eagerness.—**enthu'siast** *n.* ardent supporter.—**enthusiasti'c** *adj.*—**enthusiast'ically** *adv.*

entice' (en-tīs') *v.* 1. to attract. 2. to tempt.—**enti'cing** *pres. part.*—**enticed'** *p.t.* and *past.*—**enti'cing** *pres. part.*—**enticed'** *p.t.* and *p. part.*—**entice'ment** *n.*

entire' *adj.* 1. whole, complete. 2. not broken.—**entire'ly** *adv.*—**entire'ty** *n.*—**in its entirety** entirely, as a whole.

Compare: (with *adv.*) utterly, absolutely, perfectly. *Contrast:* partly, partially, somewhat

enti'tle (en-tī'tl) *v.* to give a title or claim to, as *This ticket entitles you to a front seat*

en'tity *n.* 1. existence. 2. something having real existence.

entomol'ogy (en-to-mol'o-ji) *n.* the study of insects.—**entomol'ogist** *n.*

en'trails *n. pl.* the intestines, inner parts

entrain' *v.* to board a train

en'trance *n.* 1. a way in. 2. going in.—**en'trant** *n.* a person entering

entrance' (en-trahns', en-trans') *v.* to delight.—**entran'cing** *adj.* charming

entreat' (en-treet') v. to implore. See **beg.**—**entreat'y** *n.* supplication

en'trée (on'trā) *n.* 1. right of admission. 2. a dish once served between main courses

entrench' *v.* to establish in fortified position, with trenches.—**entrench'ment** *n.*—**to be firmly entrenched** to be in a strong position

entrust' *v.* 1. to confide (to). 2. to put in charge.

Note: A person is *entrusted with* some task or with something to mind. The task or thing is *entrusted to* that person

ent'ry *n.* 1. entrance. 2. an item entered (in account, etc.).—**en'tries** *pl.*

entwine' *v.* to fasten round

enu'merate *v.* to count.—**enumera'tion** (ee-nū-mer-ā'shun) *n.* a listing

enun'ciate (e-nun'si-āt) *v.* to pronounce.—**enuncia'tion** (e-nun-si-ā'shun) *n.*

envel'op *v.* to wrap up, enclose.—**envel'opment** *n.*

en'velope (en've-lōp, ohn've-lōp) *n.* 1. a covering. 2. the folded cover of a letter

enven'om *v.* 1. to poison. 2. to fill with bitterness

en'viable *adj.* to be envied.—**en'vious** *adj.* envying, wanting something belonging to someone else.—**en'viously** *adv.*

envi'ronment, en'virons *n.* surroundings

en'voy *n.* 1. a messenger. 2. a diplomatic official below ambassador

en'vy *n.* 1. a discontented view of someone else's fortune, etc. 2. the object of this feeling, as *His new bicycle was the envy of all his companions.*—*v.* to feel envious.—he **en'vies**—**env'ying** *pres. part.*—**en'vied** *p.t.* and *p. part.*

enwrapped' *adj.* wrapped up in

ep'aulette, *n.* the shoulder-piece of a uniform

ephem'eral (e-fem'er-al) *adj.* lasting only a day, or a short time

ep'ic *n.* 1. a poem (usually long and stately) telling of great deeds, e.g. *The Odyssey.* 2. a long film with adventurous episodes, usually set in historical times.—*adj.* like an epic poem, noble, heroic, glorious

ep'icure *n.* one who loves the best of food and drink

epidem'ic *n.* quick spreading of disease.—*adj.* widespread

epider'mis *n.* the outer layer of skin

ep'igram *n.* a short, witty saying or poem.—**epigrammat'ic** *adj.*

ep'ilepsy *n.* an illness causing fits.—**epilep'tic** *adj.*

ep'ilogue (ep'i-log) *n.* speech at the end of a play, a concluding section

epiph'any (epif'ani) *n.* a festival (6 Jan.) in memory of the showing of Christ to the wise men at Bethlehem

epis'copal *adj.* belonging to, or governed by bishops

ep'isode *n.* 1. an incident. 2. a story

epis'tle (e-pis'l) *n.* a letter

ep'itaph (ep'i-taf) *n.* an inscription on a tomb

ep'ithet *n.* an adjective expressing something distinctive about someone, as *blue-eyed Bill,* where "blue-eyed" is the epithet

epit'ome (ep-it'ō-me) *n.* a summary.—**epit'omise** *v.*

e'poch (ee'pok) *n.* 1. a period marked by special events. 2. the beginning of a period.—**e'poch-making** *adj.* so important as to mark the beginning of an epoch

eq'uable (eek- or ek'wa-bl) *adj.* even, smooth, tranquil.—**eq'uably** *adv.*—**equabil'ity** *n.*

e'qual (ee'kwal) *adj.* 1. the same in number, size, value, etc. 2. fit, qualified, as *He was equal to the situation.*—*n.* one as good as another.—*v.* to be the same as.—**equal'ity** *n.*—**e'qualise** *v.*—**e'qually** *adv.* in equal degree—**equal to the occasion** able to deal with an awkward situation

equanim'ity (eek- or ek-wa-nim'i-ti) *n.* calmness, evenness of mind

equate' (ee-kwāt') *v.* to say things are equal.—**equa'tion** (ee-kwā'shun) *n.* 1. a statement of equality between two mathematical expressions (e.g. $2x+4=7$). 2. (in chemistry) a series of formulas showing the result of a chemical action, as $H_2+Cl_2=2HCl$

equa'tor (ee-kwā'tor) *n.* an imaginary line round the earth at an equal distance from the north and south poles. **equato'rial** (ek-wa-tō'ri-al) *adj.*

eq'uerry (ek'we-ri, i-kwer'i) *n.* a member of the royal household, personal attendant of one of the royal family.—**eq'uerries** *pl.*

eques'trian (e-kwes'trian-) *adj.* 1. concerning horse-riding, as *The circus rider showed his equestrian talents.* 2. mounted on a horse.—*n.*

equian'gular (ee-kwi-ang'gu-lar) *adj.* having equal angles

equilat'eral (ee-kwi-lat'er-al) *adj.* having all sides equal

equilib'rium (ee-kwi-lib'ri-um) *n.* balance.

e'quine (ee'kwīn) *adj.* of a horse

eq'uinox (eek- or ek'wi-noks) *n.* the time when the sun crosses the equator, and day and night are equal, about March 21st and Sept. 23rd.—**equinoc'tial** (ee-kwi-nok'shal) *adj.*

equip' (e-kwip') *v.* to fit out, supply.—**equip'ping** *pres. part.*—**equi'pped** *p.t.* and *p. part.*—**eq'uipage** *n.* carriage, with horses, attendants, etc.—**equip'ment** *n.* outfit

eq'uitable (ek'wi-ta-bl) *adj.* fair, reasonable. —**eq'uity** *n.* fairness, the principles of justice

equiv'alent (e-kwiv'a-lent) *adj.* equal in value, meaning or result (to).—*n.* as *A hundred cents are the equivalent of a dollar*

equiv'ocal (e-kwiv'ō-kal) *adj.* 1. of doubtful meaning. 2. open to suspicion

e'ra (ee'ra) *n.* a period of time

erad'icate *v.* to root out, as *The engineer tried to eradicate the faults in the new machine.*—**eradica'tion** (kās'hun) *n.* elimination.—**erad'icator** *n.*

erase' *v.* to rub out.—**era'sing** *pres. part.*—**erased'** *p.t.* and *p. part.*—**era'ser** *n.*—**era'sure** *n.*

ere (air) *prep.* and *conj.* in literature, before

erect' *v.* to set up, construct. See **build.**—*adj.* upright.—**erec'tion** (-shun) *n.*

er'mine (er'min) *n.* 1. the stoat. 2. its fur, white in winter, with black tail-tips, used to decorate robes of judges and peers

erode' *v.* to wear out, eat away, as *The sea erodes the coast.*—**ero'ding** *pres. part.*—**ero'ded** *p.t.* and *p. part.*—**ero'sion** (e-rō'-zhun) *n.* **ero'sive** *adj.*

err *v.* 1. to make mistakes. 2. to be wrong, to sin.

Compare: stray, go astray, transgress

er'rand *n.* 1. a short journey with a message. 2. the message.—**a fool's errand** a wasted journey

er'rant *adj.* 1. wandering in search of adventure, as *a knight errant.* 2. erring

errat'ic *adj.* irregular in movement or behaviour

errat'um (e-rat'um) *n.* a mistake in printing.—**erra'ta** *pl.*

erro'neous (e-rō'nee-us) *adj.* wrong, mistaken

er'ror (e'ror) *n.* 1. a mistake. 2. a wrong opinion

Erse *n.* 1. the Irish Gaelic language. 2. formerly, also the Gaelic language of West Scotland

er'udite *adj.* learned.—**erudi'tion** (e-ru-di'-shun) *n.*

erupt' *v.* to burst out.—**erup'tion** (-shun) *n.*

es'calator (-lā-) *n.* a moving stairway.

escapade' *n.* a prank, wild behaviour

escape' *v.* 1. to get free. 2. to get off safely or unpunished. 3. to slip out (words, sounds, etc.). 4. to go unnoticed or forgotten, as *It escaped my memory.*—**esca'ping** *pres. part.*—**escaped'** *p.t.* and *p. part.*—*n.* 1. an escaping. 2. a leakage, e.g. of gas

escarp'ment *n.* a steep slope

eschew' *v.* to avoid

es'cort *n* 1. an armed guard. 2. a person accompanying another for protection.—**escort'** *v.* to accompany

escu'do *n.* a Spanish or Portuguese silver coin

escut'cheon (es-cut'chun) *n.* a shield with coat-of-arms

Es'kimo *n.* a member of a race of people in Alaska, North Canada and Greenland.—**Es'kimos** *pl.*

espal'ier *n.* a lattice on which trees are trained

espar'to *n.* a strong grass grown in Spain and Algeria of which paper is made

espe'cial (es-pesh'al) *adj.* more than ordinary, special.—**espe'cially** *adv.*

Esperan'to *n.* a language invented in 1887, intended as a universal language

es'pionage (es'-pee-o-nazh) *n.* 1. spying. 2. the use of spies

esplanade' *n.* a walk or terrace along the sea-front

espouse' (es-powz') *v.* 1. to marry. 2. to take up, to champion, as *He espoused the cause of ill-treated animals*—**espous'al** *n.*

espy' *v.* to catch sight of.—he **espies'**.—**espy'ing** *pres. part.*—**espied'** *p.t.* and *p. part*

esquire' *n.* a title added to a gentleman's name on the address of a letter, instead of Mr., and written "Esq."

es'say *n.* 1. an attempt. 2. a written composition.—*v.* (es-sā') to try, test.—**essay'ing** *pres. part.*—**essayed'** *p.t.* and *p. part.*—**es'sayist** *n.* writer of essays

es'sence (es'ens) *n.* 1. a quality without which something would not be what it is. 2. a distilled extract, perfume

essen'tial (e-sen'shal) *adj.* all-important, necessary, as *Fresh air is essential to good health.*—*n.* as *Food is one of the chief essentials of life*

Note: The opposite of the adj. is *inessential*, but of the noun *non-essential*

estab'lish *v.* 1. to set up. 2. to settle. 3. to prove, as *He established his innocence.*—he **estab'lishes.**—**estab'lishment** *n.* 1. household. 2. house of business. 3. the full number of a regiment

estate' *n.* 1. a landed property. 2. property

left by a person who has died. 3. condition, rank

estate′-car *n.* a station wagon, or car with a special body for carrying both passengers and light goods

esteem′ *v.* 1. to value. 2. to consider.—*n.* good opinion.—**es′timable** *adj.*

es′timate (-māt) *v.* 1. to measure value. 2. to quote price.—*n.* (-mat) 1. opinion. 2. price quoted.—**estima′tion** (es-ti-mā′shun) *n.* 1. esteem. 2. judgment, opinion

estrange′ (es-trānj′) *v.* to make unfriendly.—**estrange′ment** *n.*

est′uary *n.* the wide mouth of a river.—**est′uaries** *pl.*

et cet′era (et set′era) and the rest (written "etc.")

etch *v.* to engrave on metal and eat in the lines with acids.—**etch′ing** *n.* 1. this process. 2. picture so produced

eter′nal *adj.* everlasting, changeless.—**eter′nity** *n.* time without end

e′ther (ee′ther) *n.* 1. a fluid supposed to fill all space. 2. the clear sky. 3. colourless liquid used as an anaesthetic.—**ethe′real** (e-thee′re-al) *adj.* 1. heavenly. 2. light, airy

eth′ical *adj.* moral.—**eth′ically** *adv.*—**eth′ics** *n.pl.* the study of right and wrong

Ethio′pia *n.* Abyssinia, a country in East Africa.—**Ethio′pian** *adj.*

etiquette′ (et-i-ket′) *n.* rules of correct behaviour

etymol′ogy (et-i-mol′o-ji) *n.* study of the origin and history of words.—**etymolog′ical** *adj.*

eucalyp′tus (ū-kal-ip′tus) *n.* an Australian gum-tree, producing oil used as disinfectant

eu′charist (ū′kar-ist) *n.* the sacrament of the Lord's Supper

eu′chre (ū′ker) *v.* (Aus.) to defeat, foil, outwit.—*n.* a card game

eugen′ics (ū-jen′iks) *n.pl.* the science of improving the human race

eu′logy (ū′lo-ji) *n.* high praise.—**eu′logies** *pl.*—**eu′logise** *v.*—**eulogis′tic** *adj.*

eu′phemism *n.* a mild word or expression substituted for a blunt one, e.g. *eccentric* for *mad*

eu′phony (yū′fo-ni) *n.* pleasant sounds.—**eupho′nious** (yū-fō′ni-us) *adj.*

Euras′ian *n.* someone with one European parent and one Asian parent

Eu′rope *n.* one of the five continents.—**Europe′an** *adj.*

evac′uate *v.* to leave, withdraw from, to cause to leave, to clear out.—**evac′uating** *pres. part.*—**evac′uated** *p.t.* and *p. part.*—**evacua′tion** (āshun′) *n.*—**evac′uee** *n.* person evacuated to a place of safety

evade′ *v.* to avoid, escape from.—**eva′ding** *pres. part.*—**eva′ded** *p.t.* and *p. part.*

evanes′cent (ev-an-es′ent) *adj.* fleeting

evan′gel (ev-an′jel) *n.* the gospel of Christ.—**evangel′ical** *adj.*—**evan′gelist** *n.* a preacher or writer of the gospel

evap′orate *v.* to turn into vapour.—**evapora′tion** (-ā′shun) *n.*

eva′sion (e-vā′zhun) *n.* 1. escape, 2. an attempt to avoid (a question, etc.).—**eva′sive** *adj.*—**eva′sively** *adv.*

eve *n.* 1. the evening before. 2. time just before. 3. in literature, evening.—**e′ven, e′ventide** *n.* evening

e′ven *adj.* 1. flat, smooth. 2. equal in amount. 3. divisible by two.—*v.* to make even.—*adv.* 1. just, quite, as *even so.* 2. exactly, as *even as he spoke.* 3. used to emphasize a comparison esp. with something less strong, as *Even if you go, you can do little.* **ev′enness** *n.*—**to be even with** to be revenged on.—**to break even** to show neither profit nor loss

eve′ning *n.* the close of day

event′ *n.* a happening (esp. an important one).—**at all events** in any event, whatever happens.—**in the event of** in case of.—**e′vent′ful** *adj.* full of incidents

even′tual *adj.* 1. happening under certain conditions. 2. resulting, final.—**event′ually** *adv.* in the end.—**eventual′ity** *n.* possible event

ev′er *adv.* 1. always. 2. at any time. 3. by any chance.—**ev′ergreen** *n.* a tree that keeps its leaves in winter.—**everlas′ting** *adj.* endless. —**evermore′** *adv.* forever.—**ever and anon** now and then.—**for ever, for evermore** for all time

ev′ery (ev′ri) *adj.* each of all.—**ev′erybody** *n.*—**ev′eryday** *adj.* used, or happening daily.—**ev′eryone** *n.*—**everything** *n.*—**ev′erywhere** *adv.* all places.—**every bit as good as** quite as good as.—**every man Jack** every single person.—**every other** every second one

evict′ *v.* to turn out (a tenant) by law.—**evic′tion** *n.*

ev′idence (ev′i-dens) *n.* 1. a sign. 2. proof, testimony.—**ev′ident** *adj.* plain, easily seen.—**ev′idently** *adv.*—**to turn king's (or queen's) evidence** to give information against fellow-criminals

e′vil *adj.* bad, harmful, wrong.—**worse** *comp.*—**worst** *sup.*—*n.* 1. what is bad, harmful. 2. sin.—**e′vil-do′er** *n.*—**e′villy** *adv.* —**evil-minded** *adj.* wicked, spiteful

evince′ (e-vins′) *v.* to show, indicate.—**evin′cing** *pres. part.*—**evinced′** *p.t.* and *p. part.*

evoke′ *v.* to call forth.—**evoca′tion** (ā-shun) *n.*

evolu′tion (e-vol-ū′shun) *n.* 1. development. 2. the theory that all living things have developed from some simpler form of life. —**evolu′tionary** *adj.*

evolve′ *v.* to unfold, develop.—**evol′ving** *pres. part.*—**evolved′** *p.t.* and *p. part.*

ewe (yū) *n.* a female sheep

ew'er (yū'er) *n.* a water-jug
ex- (former) as in ex-king, ex-president, etc.
exact' (eg-zakt') *adj.* strictly correct, accurate.—*v.* 1. to demand, e.g. obedience. 2. to compel payment, e.g. of money or a penalty.—**exac'ting** *adj.* making very or too great demands.—**exac'tion** (-shun) *n.* a demand, esp. an excessive one.—**exac'titude** *n.* accuracy.—**exact'ness** *n.*
exag'gerate (eg-zaj'er-āt) *v.* to overstate, make things appear greater than they are. —**exaggera'tion** (ā'-shun) *n.*
exalt' (egz-awlt') *v.* 1. to honour, praise. 2. to raise in rank. 3. to delight, uplift.—**exalta'tion** *n.* 1. praising. 2. rapture
exam'ine (eg-zam'in) *v.* 1. to look at closely. 2. to test.—**examina'tion** (eg-zam-in-ā'-shun) *n.* a test.—**examinee'** *n.* person examined.—**exam'iner** *n.* person examining.—**to cross examine** to put questions to a witness who has already testified in a court of law
exam'ple (eg-zam'pl) *n.* 1. model, pattern, 2. warning.—**to make an example of** to punish someone as a warning to others
exas'perate (eg-zas'per-āt) *v.* to irritate, enrage.—**exas'perating** *adj.*—**exaspera'tion** *n.*
ex'cavate *v.* 1. to hollow out. 2. to unearth.—**excava'tion** (-vā'shun) *n.*—**ex'cavator** *n.* a motor-driven digging machine
exceed' (ek-seed') *v.* 1. to be greater than. 2. to go beyond.—**excee'ding** *adj.* very great.—**excee'dingly** *adv.* very
excel' (ek-sel') *v.* to be better than.—**excel'ling** *pres. part.*—**excelled'** *p.t.* and *p. part.*
ex'cellence *n.* high quality.—**ex'cellency** *n.* title given to ambassadors.—**ex'cellent** *adj.* very good indeed
except' (ek-sept') *v.* to leave or take out.—*prep.* not including.—*conj.* unless.—**excep'ting** *prep.* not including.—**excep'tion** (-shun) *n.* something left out.—**excep'tional** *adj.* unusual.—**excep'tionally** *adv.*—**to take exception to** to object to
ex'cerpt (ek-'serpt) *n.* a passage taken from a book
excess' (ek-ses') *n.* 1. too great an amount. 2. extra.—**exces'sive** *adj.* too great.—**exces'sively** *adv.*
exchange' (eks-chānj') *n.* 1. giving one thing and receiving another. 2. a building where merchants meet for business. 3. a central telephone office.—*v.* to give in return for something.—**exchan'ging** *pres. part.*—**exchanged'** *p.t.* and *p. part.*—**exchange'able** *adj.*
Note: You exchange things *with* a person, but exchange one thing *for* another
excheq'uer (eks-chek'er) *n.* the public treasury.—**Chancellor of the Exchequer** a government minister in charge of the nation's finances
excise' (ek-sīz') *n.* 1. a tax on goods, e.g. cigarettes made or sold in the country. 2. the department administering this tax.—**excise'man** *n.*
Contrast: customs duties, which are collected at sea-ports
excise' (ek-sīz') *v.* to cut out.—**excis'ion** (ek-si'zhun) *n.*
exci'table (ek-sī'ta-bl) *adj.* easily stirred by emotion.—**excitabil'ity** *n.*
excite' (ek-sīt') *v.* to rouse, to set in motion. —**excite'ment** *n.*—**exci'ting** *adj.* rousing
exclaim' *v.* to cry out.—**exclama'tion** (mā'shun) *n.*—**exclama'tion mark** the sign (!) used to indicate an exclamation.—**exclam'atory** *adj.*
exclude' (eks-klōōd') *v.* to shut out.—**exclu'sion** (eks-klōō'zhun) *n.*—**exclu'sive** *adj.* 1. select, as *an exclusive club.* 2. only, sole, as *He had exclusive rights to the invention.* 3. not to be had or seen elsewhere as *an exclusive item of news.* 4. (with *of*) apart from, as *There were* 100 *people in the hotel, exclusive of the staff.*—**exclu'sively** *adv.*
excommu'nicate *v.* to shut out from church membership.—**excommunica'tion** (eks-com-ū-ni-kā'shun) *n.*
ex'crement *n.* waste matter from the body.—**excre'tion** (eks-kree'shun) *n.* a discharge
excur'sion (-shun) *n.* a pleasure-trip
excu'sable (eks-kū'za-bl) *adj.* pardonable
excuse' (eks-kūs') *n.* a reason given.—**excuse'** (eks-kūz') *v.* 1. to overlook, forgive. 2. to let off.—**excu'sing** *pres. part.*—**excused'** *p.t.* and *p. part.*
ex'ecrate *v.* 1. to detest, to express abhorrence. 2. to curse.—**execra'tion** (-krā'shun) *n.*—**ex'ecrable** *adj.* detestable
ex'ecute *v.* 1. to carry out, perform, as *to execute orders or a will.* 2. to put to death. —**execu'tion** (-kyū'shun) *n.* 1. performance (of a task). 2. putting to death.—**execu'tioner** *n.*—**exec'utive** *adj.* having power to enforce laws, etc.—*n.* an official or representative with wide powers—**exec'utor** (egz-) *n.* person appointed to carry out a will.—**exec'utrix** *fem.*
exem'plary *adj.* worthy of imitation.—**exem'plify** *v.* 1. to serve as example. 2. to illustrate.—he **exem'plifies.**—**exem'plifying** *pres. part.*—**exem'plified** *p.t.* and *p. part.*
exempt' (eg-zempt') *v.* to make free from.—*adj.* free from.—**exemp'tion** (-shun) *n.*
ex'ercise (ek'ser-sīz) *n.* 1. use of limbs, brain, etc. 2. practice. 3. a task set.—*v.* to use, train, practise, as *to exercise one's muscles, a horse, etc., to exercise care, patience, etc.,* to carry out, employ, as *He exercised his authority,* to worry, harass, as *he was much exercised about his bad health.*—**ex'ercising** *pres. part.*—**ex'ercised** *p.t.* and *p. part.*
exert' (eg-zert') *v.* to use, put forth, e.g.

energy, authority, etc.—**exer'tion** (-shun) *n.* effort

exhala'tion (-ā'shun) *n.* breathing out.—**exhale'** *v.* to breathe out, give off (vapour)

exhaust' (egz-awst') *v.* 1. to draw off. 2. to use up. 3. to weary.—*n.* passage for engine's waste gases.—**exhaus'tion** (-chun) *n.* extreme fatigue.—**exhaust'ive** *adj.* thorough, as *She made an exhaustive search for the lost purse*

exhib'it *v.* to show, display.—*n.* something shown.—**exhibi'tion** (shun) *n.* 1. a public show. 2. a scholarship.—**exhib'itor** *n.*

exhil'arate *v.* to cheer, enliven.—**exhilara'tion** (-ā'shun) *n.*

exhort' (eg-zort') *v.* to urge, advise.—**exhorta'tion** (tā'shun) *n.*

exhume' *v.* to dig up a buried corpse

exig'ence, exig'ency (ek-sij'en-si) *n.* 1. a pressing need. 2. an emergency.—**exi'gencies** *pl.*—**ex'igent** *adj.*

ex'ile *n.* 1. banishment or long absence from one's country. 2. an exiled person

exist' (eg-zist') *v.* to be, have being, live.—**exis'tence** *n.* life.—**exis'tent** *adj.*

ex'it *n.* 1. a way out. 2. going out, esp. of an actor from the stage

ex'odus (ek'sō-dus) *n.* a general departure

exon'erate *v.* to free from blame.—**exonera'tion** (-ā'shun) *n.*

exor'bitant *adj.* excessive, as *exorbitant demands, charges, etc.*

ex'orcise (ek'sor-sīz) *v.* to cast out (evil spirits) by prayers, etc.—**ex'orcism** (ek'sor-sizm) *n.*

exot'ic *adj.* brought in from abroad, used esp. of plants, fashions, etc.—*n.* an exotic plant

expand' *v.* to spread out, to become larger.—**expanse'** *n.* a wide space.—**expan'sion** (-shun) *n.* increase.—**expan'sive** *adj.* 1. broad. 2. talking freely

Compare: swell, stretch, enlarge, amplify, dilate. *Contrast:* contract, constrict, decrease, diminish

expa'tiate (eks-pā'shi-āt) *v.* to speak or write at length

Note: This word is usually followed by *on* or *upon*, as *He expatiated upon the delights of a camping holiday*

expat'riate *v.* to banish from one's native land

expect' *v.* to look for, await, anticipate.—**expect'ancy** *n.* hope.—**expec'tant** *adj.*—**expecta'tion** (-tā-shun) *n.* 1. awaiting. 2. a prospect of something to come

expe'diency (eks-pee'di-en-si) *n.* convenience.—**expe'dient** *n.* a device.—*adj.* fitting, advisable

ex'pedite *v.* to hasten, help on.—**expedi'tious** (-shus) *adj.* speedy

expedi'tion (-shun) *n.* 1. speed. 2. journey. 3. a warlike enterprise.—**expedi'tionary** *adj.*

expel' *v.* to drive or turn out.—**expel'ling** *pres. part.*—**expelled'** *p.t.* and *p. part.*

expend' *v.* to spend, use up.—**expendi'ture** *n.* spending.—**expense'** *n.* cost, money spent.—**expen'sive** *adj.* costly

expe'rience (eks-pee'ri-ens) *n.* 1. knowledge gained by observation and practice. 2. something which happens to a person, as *a strange experience.*—*v.* to meet with, suffer, as *to experience difficulties.*—**expe'rienced** *adj.* skilful

exper'iment *n.* a test to prove something.—*v.*—**experiment'al** *adj.*

ex'pert *n.* a skilled person.—*adj.* practised, skilful

ex'piate (eks'pee-āt) *v.* to pay the penalty for, as *He expiated his crime by repaying what he had stolen.*—**expia'tion** (-ā'shun) *n.*

expira'tion (-ā'shun) *n.* 1. breathing out. 2. the end, a dying out

expire' *v.* 1. to breathe out. 2. to end. 3. to die.—**expi'ry** *n.* end

explain' *v.* to make clear.—**explana'tion** (-ā'shun) *n.*—**explan'atory** *adj.*—**ex'plicable** *adj.* which can be explained

expli'cit (eks-pli'sit) *adj.* 1. stated clearly, as *explicit instructions.* 2. outspoken, as *His criticism was very explicit*

Compare: 1. positive, definite, precise. 2. candid, frank, unequivocal. *Contrast:* 1. vague, indistinct, hazy. 2. implied, hinted at, suggested

explode' *v.* 1. to burst with a bang. 2. to expose (a theory).—**explo'ding** *pres. part.*—**explo'ded** *p.t.* and *past part.* See **explosion**

ex'ploit *n.* a brilliant deed.—**exploit'** *v.* to use for one's own purpose.—**exploita'tion** (-tā'shun) *n.*

explora'tion (-ā'shun) *n.* travelling for discovery

explore' *v.* 1. to examine, search. 2. to travel for discovery.—**explo'ring** *pres. part.*—**explored'** *p.t.* and *p. part.*—**explo'rer** *n.*

explo'sion (eks-plō'zhun) *n.* a sudden bursting noise.—**explo'sive** *n.* a substance that explodes.—*adj.* See **explode**

expo'nent *n.* 1. one who explains or interprets, as *the coach was an exponent of boxing.* 2. a representative, as *Manchester United, playing for the European Cup, proved worthy exponents of British football*

export' *v.* to send goods abroad to foreign buyers.—**ex'port** *n.* an article exported.—**exporta'tion** (-tā'shun) *n.* sending goods out.—**expor'ter** *n.*

expose' (eks-pōz') *v.* 1. to show. 2. to leave unprotected. 3. to disclose.—**expo'sing** *pres. part.*—**exposed'** *p.t.* and *p. part*

exposi'tion (-shun) *n.* 1. an explanation, description. 2. an exhibition.—**expos'itory** *adj.* explaining

expos'tulate *v.* to protest, reason, remonstrate.—**expostula'tion** (-lā'shun) *n.* a protest

expo'sure (eks-pō'zhur) *n.* 1. being unprotected. 2. making known. 3. taking a photograph, i.e. by exposing the film in the camera to the light image conveyed through the lens

expound' *v.* to explain

express' *v.* to make known by word, look, deed.—he express'es.—*adj.* 1. clearly stated. 2. speedy.—*adv.* 1. on purpose. 2. speedily.—*n.* 1. special messenger. 2. quick train

expres'sion (eks-presh'un) *n.* 1. showing by word, look, deed. 2. look on face. 3. phrase. —**expres'sive** *adj.* showing vividly.—**express'ly** *adv.* 1. plainly. 2. on purpose

expul'sion (-shun) *n.* a forcing out

ex'quisite (eks'kwi-zit) *adj.* very beautiful or delicate.—*n.* a dandy.—**ex'quisitely** *adv.*

ex'tant *adj.* still existing

extem'pore (eks-tem'por-ā) *adj.* without preparation, as *an extempore speech.*—*adv.*, as *He spoke extempore.*—**extem'porise** *v.* to speak extempore

extend' *v.* to stretch out, lengthen.—**exten'sion** (-shun) *n.* enlargement.—**exten'sive** *adj.* large, wide-spreading.—**extent'** *n.* size

exten'uate *v.* to lessen (blame).—**extenua-'tion** *n.*

exte'rior (ekstee'ri-or) *n.* outside.—*adj.* outer

exter'minate *v.* to destroy entirely.—**extermina'tion** *n.*

exter'nal *adj.* outside.—**exter'nally** *adv.*

extinct' *adj.* 1. no longer burning, as *an extinct volcano.* 2. having died out, as *Bears are extinct in Britain.*—**extinc'tion** (-shun) *n.*

extin'guish (eks-ting'guish) *v.* 1. to put out (a fire, light, hope, life, etc.). 2. to destroy, annihilate.—he **extin'guishes.**—**extin'guisher** *n.* device for putting out fire

ex'tirpate *v.* to root out.—**extirpa'tion** (pā'shun) *n.*

extol' *v.* to praise highly.—**extol'ling** *pres. part.*—**extolled'** *p.t.* and *p. part.*

extort' *v.* to get by force or threats.—**extor'tion** (-shun) *n.*—**extor'tionate** *adj.* too great, excessive, as *an extortionate price*

ex'tra *adj.* additional, more than usual, as *an extra day's holiday.*—*adv.* more than usually, as *an extra large size.*—*n.* an extra thing, additional charge

extract' *v.* 1. to take out (by force). 2. to distil.—**ex'tract** *n.* passage from a book.—**extrac'tion** (-shun) *n.* 1. drawing out. 2. origin, as *He was of French extraction*

ex'tradite *v.* to deliver (a foreign prisoner) to his own authorities.—**extradi'tion** (shun) *n.*

extra'neous (eks-trā'ne-us) *adj.* 1. added from outside. 2. not belonging to the main matter, as *The lecture was spoiled by the addition of too much extraneous matter*

extraor'dinary (eks-tror'din-ar-i) *adj.* unusual

extrav'agance *n.* 1. wasteful spending. 2. want of restraint.—**extrav'agant** *adj.*

extreme' *n.* the furthest point.—*n. pl.* 1. excesses. 2. things as different as possible. —*adj.* 1. last, as *the extreme end of the pier.* 2. very great, as *extreme cold.* 3. not moderate.—**extreme'ly** *adv.* very.—**extre'mist** (eks-tree'mist) *n.* one who is extreme in words or actions.—**extrem'ity** *n.* 1. farthest end. 2. great difficulty.—**extrem'ities** *pl.* hands and feet.

ex'tricate *v.* to free from difficulties

exu'berance (eg-zū'ber-ans) *n.* 1. abundant growth. 2. overflowing spirits.—**exu'berant** *adj.*

exude' (ek-sūd') *v.* to ooze out

exult' (eg-zult') *v.* to rejoice, triumph.—**exulta'tion** (-ta'shun) *n.*—**exul'tant** *adj.* triumphant

eye (ī) *n.* 1. the organ of sight. 2. power of sight, perception, as *He has an eye for pictures.* 3. observation, as *He is much in the public eye.*—*v.* observe, watch.—**eye'ball** *n.*—**eye'brow** *n.* fringe of hair above the eye.—**eyeglass** *n.* glass to help sight.—**eye'lash** *n.* hair fringing **eye-lid.**—**eye-opener** *n.* surprising fact.—**eye'sore** *n.* an ugly sight.—**eye'witness** *n.* one who saw something for himself.—**in the mind's eye** in imagination.—**to keep an eye on** to watch.—**to keep one's eyes skinned** to be keenly watchful.—**to see eye to eye with** to agree with.—**to turn a blind eye to** to ignore.—**up to the eyes in** very busy with

ey'rie (ee'ri) *n.* an eagle's nest

F

fa'ble *n.* 1. a tale, legend. 2. a short story with a moral, e.g. *Æsop's Fables*

fab'ric *n.* 1. a structure, framework. 2. a cloth material

fabri'cate *v.* 1. to build. 2. to invent (a lie).—**fabrica'tion** (-kā'shun) *n.* an untruth

fab'ulous *adj.* 1. imaginary. 2. unbelievable. 3. wonderful

façade' (fa-sahd') *n.* 1. the front of a building. 2. appearance presented to the world

face (fās) *n.* 1. the front of the head. 2. front, surface. 3. appearance. 4. grimace, as *to make, pull a face.* 5. reputation, as *to save one's face.*—*adj.* nominal, as *face value.*—*v.* 1. to look towards, as *The house faces south.* 2. to meet bravely, as *to face one's difficulties.*—**fa'cing** *pres. part.*—**faced'** *p.t.* and *p. part.*—**to face the music** to take the consequences of one's actions.—**to face up to** to accept something fearlessly. —**to fly in the face of** to defy.—**to lose face** to be humiliated.—**to pull a long face** to look dismal or disapproving.—**to put a bold face on** to act boldly from a weak position.—**to put a good face on** to take with good grace something unpleasant.—**to set one's face against** to oppose

fa'cet (fa'set) *n.* 1. surface (of a cut gem). 2. a single part

face'tious (fa-see'shus) *adj.* 1. given to joking. 2. humorous

fa'cial (fā'shal) *adj.* of the face

fa'cile (fa'sīl) *adj.* 1. easily done. 2. glib.—**facil'itate** (fa-sil'i-tāt) *v.* to make easy.—**facil'ity** *n.* ease.—**facil'ities** *pl.* opportunities

facsim'ile (fak-sim'-i-li) *n.* an exact copy

fact *n.* something known to be true.—**as a matter of fact** really, in actual fact
Compare: truth, reality, actuality, occurrence, detail, happening, deed, circumstance

facti'tious (fak-tish'us) *adj.* artificial, false

fac'tor *n.* 1. a cause, 2. a business agent. 3. one of the numbers which, multiplied together, give a product, as 5 *and* 3 *are the factors of* 15.—**fac'torise** *v.* to split up (a number) into factors

fac'tory *n.* 1. building where goods are manufactured. 2. trading station in a foreign country.—**fac'tories** *pl.*

facto'tum (-tō') *n.* a handy-man

fac'ulty *n.* 1. ability, aptitude. 2. department of a university.—**fac'ulties** *pl.*

fad *n.* craze, passing fashion, pet idea.—**fad'dy** *adj.*

fade *v.* 1. to wither. 2. to lose colour. 3. to grow dim.—**fa'ding** *pres. part.*—**fa'ded** *p.t.* and *p. part.*

fag *n.* 1. toil, work. 2. a school-boy who waits on a senior.—*v.* to work hard.—**fag'ging** *pres. part.*—**fagged** *p.t.* and *p. part.*

fag'got, fag'ot *n.* 1. bundle of sticks. 2. dish of baked chopped liver, etc.

fah'renheit (fah'ren-hīt) *n.* the name of a scale of temperatures in which 32° and 212° represent the freezing and boiling points of water

fail *v.* 1. to run short, as *Supplies failed.* 2. to lose power, as *His eyesight failed.* 3. to be unsuccessful, as *He failed to pass his examination.* 4. not to support, to disappoint, as *His courage failed him.* 5. to become bankrupt.—**fail'ing** *n.* fault, weakness, as *His chief failing is laziness.*—**fail'ure** *n.* 1. non-success. 2. bankruptcy.—**without fail** certainly

faint *n.* unconscious condition.—*v.* to become suddenly unconscious.—*adj.* weak, pale, dim, slight.—**faint'ly** *adv.*

fair *adj.* 1. beautiful. 2. light (hair or skin). 3. clear. 4. just, honest. 5. up to standard, hence, only just up to standard, not very good. 6. favourable.—*adv.* as *to speak anyone fair.*—**fair'ly** *adv.* 1. justly. 2. rather.—**fair'ness** *n.*—**fair-minded** *adj.* just. —**fair-spoken** *adj.* politely persuasive.—**fair play** equal chances for all

fair *n.* an open market or entertainment.—**fair'way** *n.* in golf, the smooth broad strip of grass between tee and green

fai'ry *n.* a small being with magical powers.—**fai'ries** *pl.* —*adj.* of fairies.—**fai'ryland** *n.*—**fai'ry-tale** *n.*

faith *n.* 1. belief (in religion). 2. trust.—**faith'ful** *adj.* loyal.—**faith'ful** *adv.*—**faith'less** *adj.*—**in good faith** sincerely

fake *n.* fraud.—*v.* to hide defects and deceive

fakir' (fa-keer') *n.* a religious beggar in India

fal'con (fawl'ken) *n.* bird of prey sometimes trained in hawking or **fal'conry**

fall (fawl) *v.* 1. to drop. 2. to hang down. 3. to collapse. 4. to become, happen.—**fell** *p.t.*—**fal'len** *p. part.*—*n.* 1 a falling. 2. becoming less, worse. 3. autumn.—**to fall back** to retreat.—**to fall foul of** to quarrel with.—**to fall in** 1. to take one's place. 2. to agree.—**to fall off** to become less.—**to fall on** to attack.—**to fall out** 1. to leave one's place. 2. to quarrel.—**to fall short** to fail to reach.—**to fall through** to fail to happen.—**to fall to** to begin
Compare: descend, decline, droop, fail, sink, subside. *Contrast:* ascend, rise, mount, climb

fal'lacy (fal'a-si) false idea or statement.—**fallacies** *pl.*—**falla'cious** (fal-ā'shus) *adj.* misleading, mistaken

fal'lible *adj.* liable to error

fall-out *n.* radioactive dust from the explosion of a nuclear bomb

fal'low *adj.* 1. ploughed, but left without crop. 2. uncultivated. 3. pale brown or reddish-yellow.—**fal'low deer** *n.* European deer, about 3 feet high

false (fawls) *adj.* 1. untrue, wrong. 2. faithless. 3. sham.—**false'hood** *n.* a lie.—**false'ly** *adv.*—**false'ness.**—**under false pretences** deliberately deceiving

falset'to (fawl-set'ō) *n.* a voice forced higher than its natural range

fal'sify (fawl-si-fī) *v.* to alter dishonestly.—he **fal'sifies.**—**fal'sifying** *pres. part.*—**fal'sified** *p.t.* and *p. part.*—**falsifica'tion** (-kā'shun) *n.*

fal'ter (fawl'ter) *v.* 1. to hesitate. 2. to stumble. 3. to speak hesitatingly

fame *n.* 1. rumour. 2. being well known.—**famed** *adj.*
Compare: (with 2.) repute, reputation, renown, distinction, celebrity, eminence, honour, glory. **Notoriety** means ill-fame

fami'liar *adj.* 1. known well, common, as *The postman is a familiar figure.* 2. intimate, as *a familiar way of speaking to someone.* 3. knowing well, as *He is familiar with the road.*—**familiar'ity** *n.*—**famil'iarise** *v.* to make familiar

fam'ily *n.* 1. parents and children. 2. household. 3. parents, children and near relatives. 4. a class of similar objects.—**fam'ilies** *pl.*—**family tree** a table showing the relationship between members of a family

fam'ine (fam'in) *n.* starvation—**fam'ish** *v.* to starve.—**fam'ished** *adj.* starved

fa'mous (fā'mus) *adj.* well known.—**fa'mously** *adv.* very well

fan *n.* 1. an instrument for producing current

of air. 1. a keen admirer.—*v.* to cool with a fan.—**fan'ning** *pres. part.*—**fanned** *p.t.* and *p. part.*—**fan-heater** *n.* an electric heater with a fan to blow out hot air.—**fan mail** letters written to a celebrity by admirers.—**fan vaulting** in architecture, a kind of vaulting with ribs from a main beam

fanat'ic *n.* an over-zealous person.—**fanat'ical** *adj.*—**fanat'ically** *adv.*—**fanat'icism** (-sizm) *n.*

fan'cier (fan'si-er) *n.* a breeder of prize animals, birds, etc.

fan'ciful (fan'si-ful) *adj.* 1. imaginative. 2. odd, unreal

fan'cy (fan'si) *n.* 1. the power of imagination. 2. a liking, whim. 3. a mental image, notion. 4. followers of a sport or hobby.—**fan'cies** *pl.*—*adj.* elaborate, highly decorated, extravagant.—*v.* 1. to imagine. 2. to like.—**fan'cying** *pres. part.*—**fan'cied** *p.t.* and *p. part.*—**fancy dress** theatrical dress for a pageant or dance

fan'fare *n.* a flourish of trumpets

fang *n.* 1. an animal's long pointed tooth. 2. snake's poison-tooth

fan'light *n.* a window over a door

fan'tail *n.* a pigeon with a fan-shaped tail

fantas'tic *adj.* odd, unreal, wild.—**fantas'tical** *adj.* 1. fancy. 2. whimsical.—**fan'tasy** *n.* —**fan'tasies** *pl.*

far *adj.* distant, as *It is not far.*—*adv.* 1. a long way as *It is far distant.* 2. very much, as *far better.*—**far'ther, fur'ther** *comp.*—**far'thest, fur'thest** *sup.*—**a far cry** a long way.—**far and away** very much.—**far-fetched** unlikely.—**far-flung** widespread.—**far-sighted** 1. able to see far. 2. prudent, able to see future consequences.—**few and far between** rare.—**the Far East** the countries of eastern Asia

farce (fars) *n.* 1. a play intended to excite laughter. 2. an absurd performance or episode.—**far'cical** *adj.* comical

fare (fãr) *n.* 1. the price of a journey. 2. food. —*v.* to get on, as *How did you fare in your undertaking?*

farewell' *n.* leave-taking.—*interj.* good-bye!

farm *n.* land where crops and animals are raised.—*v.* to cultivate.—**far'mer** *n.* owner or tenant of farm.—**farm'-hand** *n.* a farm labourer.—**farm'house** *n.*—**farm'stead** *n.* farm and buildings.—**farm'yard** *n.*

far'rier *n.* 1. a shoeing smith. 2. a horse-doctor

far'row *n.* a litter of pigs

far'ther *comp.* of **far.**—**far'thest** *sup.* of far

far'thing *n.* a British coin of very little value, no longer in use

fasc'ia (fã'sha) *n.* the instrument panel of a motor car

fas'cinate (fas'in-āt) *v.* to charm.—**fas'cinating** *adj.* attractive.—**fascina'tion** *n.*

fas'cism (fash'izm) *n.* a one-party system of government, suppressing rival parties and unions, and supporting aggressive nationalism and anti-socialism. Italy under Mussolini was a fascist state before World War II.—**fas'cist** *n.* a supporter of fascism

fash'ion (fash'un) *n.* 1. make, style. 2. manner. 3. custom in dress.—*v.* to make.—**fash'ionable** *adj.*—**fash'ionably** *adv.*—**in fashion** up-to-date in style

fast *adj.* 1. firm, steady, as *to make a boat fast to its moorings.* 2. firmly fixed, as *a fast dye.* 3. swift, as *a fast train.* 4. ahead of time, as *The clock is fast.* 5. wild, wayward, as *He has got mixed up with a very fast set of people.*—*adv.* 1. firmly, as *to hold fast.* 2. rapidly, as *to go fast.*—**fas'ter** *comp.*—**fas'test** *sup.*

fast *v.* to eat little or no food.—*n.*

fas'ten (fah'sen) *v.* to tie, fix, secure.—**fas'tener** (fahs'ner) *n.* clasp, etc.

fastid'ious *adj.* hard to please

Compare: dainty, captious, particular, faddy, scrupulous

fast'ness *n.* stronghold

fat *adj.* 1. plump, thick, solid. 2. oily, greasy. 3. fertile, profitable.—**fat'ter** *comp.*—**fat'test** *sup.*—*n.* oil substance in animal bodies.—**fat'ten** *v.*—**to kill the fatted calf** to welcome someone home with a celebration.—**the fat is in the fire** trouble arises

fa'tal (fā'tal) *adj.* 1. ending in death. 2. disastrous.—**fatal'ity** *n.* 1. misfortune, disaster. 2. fatal influence.—**fa'tally** (fā'tal-i) *adv.* to death.

fate *n.* 1. destiny, man's appointed lot. 2. death, destruction.—as *He met his fate while climbing.*—**fate'ful** *adj.* 1. important. 2. prophetic

fa'ther (fah'THer) *n.* 1. male parent.—**mother** *fem.* 2. ancestor. 3. early leader (of movement). 4. a priest.—*v.* to act as father.—**fa'therhood** *n.*—**fa'ther-in-law** *n.* the father of husband or wife.—**fa'therland** *n.* one's native country.—**fa'therliness** *n.*—**fa'therly** *adv.*

fath'om *n.* (at sea) a measure of depth of 6 feet.—*v.* 1. to sound water. 2. to understand.—**fath'omless** *adj.* too deep to fathom

fatigue' (fat-eeg') *n.* weariness.—*v.* to tire.—**fati'guing** (fa-tee'ging) *adj.*

fat'ten *v.* to make or grow fat.—**fat'ty** *adj.* fat

fat'uous *adj.* silly.—**fatu'ity** *n.*

fau'cet *n.* (North America) a water tap

fault *n.* 1. a failing, defect. 2. an offence, wrongdoing. 3. (tennis) ball wrongly served. 4. (geology) break in layers of rock that were originally continuous.—**fault'less** *adj.* perfect.—**fault'lessly** *adv.*—**fault'y** *adj.* imperfect.—**fault'ily** *adv.*—**at, in fault** blameworthy.—**to a fault** excessively.—**to find fault with** to criticise

faun (fawn) *n.* a Roman woodland god with horns and hoofs

fau'na *n.* the animal life of a region or period.—**faun'ae, faun'as** *pl.*

fa'vour *n.* 1. kindness. 2. approval. 3. badge. —*v.* 1. to help, oblige, prefer. 2. to resemble, as *He favours his father* (*in appearance*).—**fa'vourable** *adj.* helpful.—**fa'vourably** *adv.*

fa'vourite (fā'vor-it) *n.* a person or thing liked best.—*adj.* liked best.—**fav'ouritism** *n.* unfair preference

fawn *n.* 1. a young fallow deer. 2. a light yellowish brown.—*adj.*

fawn *v.* to flatter, seek favour, cringe, grovel

fear *n.* alarm, being afraid.—*v.* to be afraid.—**fear'ful** *adj.* 1. terrible. 2. timid.—**fear'fully** *adv.*—**fear'less** *adj.*—**fear'some** *adj. terrible*

fea'sible (fee'zi-bl) *adj.* possible

feast (feest) *n.* 1. a banquet. 2. celebration.—*v.* to eat rich food

feat (feet) *n.* a skilful, daring deed

feath'er (feTH'er) *n.* a bird's plume or quill.—*v.* 1. to line with feathers. 2. to turn an oar sideways on the water.—**feath'er-brained** *adj.* silly.—**feather-stitch** *n.* zigzag embroidery.—**feath'erweight** *adj.* 1. very light. 2. (boxing) between 8 st. 6 lb. and 9 st.—**feath'ery** *adj.* light.—**a feather in one's cap** something to be proud of.—**birds of a feather** people with the same interests.—**to feather one's nest** to be rich at someone else's expense.—**to show the white feather** to show cowardice

fea'ture (fee'cher) *n.* 1. a part of the face. 2. a distinct or important part.—**feat'ureless** *adj.* monotonous

Feb'ruary *n.* the second month

feck'less *adj.* careless, improvident

fec'und *adj.* fruitful.—**fecund'ity** *n.*

fed'eral *adj.* 1. belonging to the central government of the U.S. 2. relating to a league of states

federa'tion (-ā'shun) *n.* 1. an organisation, society. 2. a union of states

fee *n.* 1. payment for services. 2. entrance-money

fee'ble *adj.* weak.—**fee'bleness** *n.*—**fee'bly** *adv.*

feed *v.* 1. to give food to. 2. to supply, support.—**fed** *p.t.* and *p. part.*—*n.* food

feel *v.* 1. to touch. 2. to find or know by touch. 3. to experience—**felt** *p.t.* and *p. part.*—*n.* touch.—**feel'er** *n.* organ of touch in some animals.—**feel'ing** *n.* 1. sensation, emotion. 2. sympathy.—**to feel one's way** to go forward cautiously

feign (fān) *v.* to pretend.—**feint** *n.* a sham attack

feli'citate (fel-i'si-tāt) *v.* to congratulate.—**felicita'tion** (-tā'shun) *n.*—**feli'citous** *adj.* happy.—**feli'city** *n.*

fe'line (fee'līn) *adj.* 1. relating to a cat. 2. cat-like

fell *v.* to knock down, cut down

fell *adj.* fierce, cruel, deadly

fel'low *n.* 1. a companion. 2. one of a pair. 3. a member of learned society. 4. a familiar way of referring to a man or boy. —**fel'lowship** *n.* 1. group 2. friendliness. 3. post-graduate scholarship.—**fellow feeling** understanding and sympathy between persons

fel'on *n.* a criminal.—**fel'ony** *n.* a crime.—**felo'nious** (fel-ō'ni-us) *adj.*

felt *n.* cloth made by rolling and pressing wool.—*adj.*

fe'male (fee'māl) *adj.* of the sex bearing offspring.—*n.*—**male** *masc.*

fem'inine (fem'i-nin) *adj.* relating to women. —**mas'culine** *masc.*

Note: In English Grammar all nouns and pronouns denoting females are in the *feminine gender*, e.g. woman, queen, mother, she. See **masculine, neuter**

fe'mur (fee'mer) *n.* the thigh bone

fen *n.* a marsh, bog

fence (fens) *n.* 1. a hedge or railing. 2. a receiver of stolen goods.—*v.* 1. to enclose. 2. to practise sword-play.—**fen'cing** *n.* 1. fences. 2. sword-play.—**to sit on the fence** not to take sides

fend *v.* 1. to ward off, repel. 2. to provide.—**fen'der** *n.* 1. fire-guard. 2. buffer slung between boat and landing-place

Note: In this sense the word *fend* is usually followed by *for*, as *They were left to fend for themselves*

ferment' *v.* 1. to undergo chemical change producing alcohol. 2. to excite.—**fer'ment** *n.* 1. leaven. 2. excitement.—**fermenta'tion** (-tā'shun) *n.*

fern *n.* a plant with feathery leaves

fero'cious (fer-ō'shus) *adj.* fierce.—**fero'city** (fer-os'i-ti) *n.*

ferret *n.* kind of weasel.—*v.* to hunt out

fer'ric, fer'rous *adj.* containing iron

fer'rule *n.* a metal cap at the end of stick

fer'ry *v.* to take across a river etc.—**fer'rying** *pres. part.*—**fer'ried** *p.t.* and *p. part.*—*n.* 1. crossing-place. 2. ferry-boat

fer'tile *adj.* fruitful, productive.—**fertil'ity** *n.*—**fertilisa'tion** *n.* fertilising.—**fer'tilise** *v.* to make fertile, enrich.—**fer'tiliser** *n.* substance to make soil richer

fer'vent *adj.* passionate, hot.—**fer'vour** *n.* warmth, ardour

Compare: intense, earnest, zealous, glowing, enthusiastic, eager. *Contrast:* indifferent, lukewarm, cool

fer'vid *adj.* passionate, intense

fes'tal *adj.* relating to a feast, gay

fes'ter *v.* 1. to discharge matter. 2. to rankle.—*n.* a sore

fes'tival *n.* 1. a celebration. 2. a holiday,

feast.—**fes'tive** *adj.* gay.—**festiv'ity** *n.* a joyous occasion.—**festiv'ities** *pl.*

festoon' *n.* a chain of flowers, etc., hung between two points.—*v.*

fetch *v.* 1. to bring, go and get. 2. to be sold for, as *The horse fetched a good price.* 3. to deliver (a blow). 4. to draw (breath).—he **fetch'es.**—**fetch'ing** *adj.* attractive

fête (fāt) *n.* a festival, party

fe'tid, foe'tid (fee'tid) *adj.* stinking

fe'tish (fee'tish, fet'ish) *n.* 1. an idol worshipped by savages. 2. something worshipped unreasoningly

fet'lock *n.* a tuft of hair behind a horse's hoof

fetter *n.* a chain for the feet.—*pl.* captivity.—*v.* to chain up

feud (fūd) *n.* a long and bitter quarrel, esp. between families

feu'dal (fū-dal) *adj.* belonging to the **feu'dal sys'tem,** or **feu'dalism** (*n.*) in which barons held land from the king in return for military service, and the peasants from the barons in return for labour service

fe'ver (fee'ver) *n.* 1. an illness with high temperature. 2. excitement.—**fe'verish** *adj.* —**fe'verishly** *adv.*

few (fū) *adj.* not many, as *Few people were told.*—*n.* a small number, as *A few were told.*—**few'ness** *n.*

fez *n.* a Turkish cap with a tassel

fian'cé (fee-ohn'sā) *n.* a betrothed man.—**fian'cée** *fem.*

fias'co *n.* a complete failure.—**fias'cos** *pl.*

fib *n.* a small lie.—*v.* to lie.—**fib'bing** *pres. part.*—**fibbed** *p.t.* and *p. part.*

fi'bre *n.* (fī'ber) 1. a thread. 2. part of plant or animal tissue.—**fi'brous** *adj.*—**fi'breboard** *n.* a stiff board made of wood pulp, etc.—**fi'bre-glass** *n.* a mass of fine glass threads used as insulating material or cemented together for constructional purposes

fib'ula *n.* the shin bone

fic'kle *adj.* changeable.—**fic'kleness** *n.*
Compare: capricious, inconstant, unstable, untrustworthy. *Contrast:* constant, decided, determined, firm, resolute, steadfast. See **firm**

fic'tion (-shun) *n.* 1. an invented story. 2. novels.—**fictit'ious** (fik-tish'us) *adj.* imaginary

fid'dle *n.* 1. a violin. 2. (slang) a dishonest trick or swindle.—*v.* 1. to play the violin. 2. (slang) to cheat. 3. to fidget with one's fingers or fuss over a trifle.—**fidd'ler** *n.* —**fid'dlesticks!** *interj.* nonsense!

fidel'ity *n.* faithfulness

fidg'et (fij'et) *v.* to move restlessly.—**fidg'ety** *adj.*

fief (feef) *n.* land held from a feudal lord in return for services

field (feeld) *n.* 1. an enclosed piece of land. 2. a battle-ground. 3. a range of activity.—*v.* to stop, catch, etc., ball in cricket or baseball.—**field'er** *n.*—**field'glasses** *n.* binoculars.—**field-gun** *n.* a light cannon. —**field-mar'shal** *n.* general of highest rank.—**field sports** *n. pl.* hunting, shooting and fishing

fiend (feend) *n.* a devil.—**fiend'ish** *adj.*

fierce (feers) *adj.* savage, wild, raging.—**fierce'ly** *adv.*—**fierce'ness** *n.*

fi'ery (fī'ri) *adj.* 1. of fire. 2. blazing. 3. spirited, hot-tempered.—**fi'erier** *comp.*—**fi'eriest** *sup.*

fife *n.* a kind of flute.—**fifes** *pl.*

fifteen' *adj.* and *n.* ten and five.—**fifteenth'** *adj.*

fifth *adj.* next after fourth.—**fifth column** traitors ready to help an invading enemy. —**fif'tieth** *adj.* next after forty-ninth.—**fif'ty** *n.* and *adj.* five times ten

fig *n.* a soft pear-shaped fruit

fight (fīt) *n.* 1. a combat, struggle. See **battle.**—*v.* 1. to battle against. 2. to struggle against (poverty, etc.).—**fought** (fawt) *p.t.* and *p. part.*.—**fight'er** *n.* 1. aircraft designed for fighting. 2. one who does not give in.—**prize-fight** *n.* a boxing match.—**to fight shy of** to avoid

fig'ment *n.* an imaginary thing, as *It is a mere figment of his imagination*

fig'urative (-iv) *adj.* (of words) used out of their usual meaning.—**fig'uratively** *adv.*

fig'ure (fig'er) *n.* 1. a form, shape, 2. a space enclosed by lines. 3. an illustration, diagram. 4. a number, amount.—*v.* 1. to illustrate, represent. 2. to calculate. 3. to show, be seen.—**fig'uring** *pres. part.*—**fig'ured** *p.t.* and *p. part.*—**fig'ure-skating** *n.* cutting patterns on ice while skating.—**a figure of fun** an object of fun, a laughing stock

fil'ament *n.* a thread, fibre

fil'bert *n.* the cultivated hazel-nut

filch *v.* to steal

file *n.* a tool for smoothing or rubbing hard substances.—*v.* to smooth, polish.—**fi'ling** *pres. part.*—**filed** *p.t.* and *p. part.*—**fi'lings** *n.pl.* bits removed by file

file *n.* 1. a case, rack or wire for holding papers in order. 2. a row of persons standing one behind another.—*v.* to march in file.—**Indian file** a line of persons one behind another

fil'ial *adj.* relating to a son or daughter

fil'igree *n.* delicate ornamental work of fine wire

fill *v.* 1. to make full. 2. to occupy completely. 3. to satisfy. 4. to occupy, as *a position, one's time, etc.*—*n.*, as *to eat one's fill.*—**to fill in** to complete.—**to fill out** to enlarge, get bigger

fil'let *n.* 1. a hair band. 2. meat or fish boned. —*v.* to remove the bones.—**fil'leting** *pres. part.*—**fil'leted** *p.t.* and *p. part.*

fil'lip *n.* 1. a flick of finger and thumb. 2. something that rouses or revives

fil'ly *n.* a young mare. See **horse.**—**colt** *masc.*—**fil'lies** *pl.*

film *n.* 1. a thin skin or layer. 2. roll used in photography and cinematography. 3. a moving picture.—*v.* 1. to cover with a film. 2. to make a moving picture.—**fil'my** *adj.* thin

fil'ter *n.* 1. a strainer. 2. a device for purifying water, etc.—*v.* 1. to pass through a filter. 2. make way through—**filtra'tion** *n.*—**fil'trate** *n.* clear filtered liquid.—**fil'ter paper** *n.* porous paper used for filtering

filth *n.* 1. loathsome dirt. 2. rubbish.—**fil'thy** *adj.*

fin *n.* a fan-like part of a fish with which it swims

fi'nal (fī'nal) *adj.* last, conclusive.—*n.* game, examination, etc., coming at the end of a series.—**fi'nally** *adv.* at last

final'e (fin-ahl'e) *n.* end of a piece of music

finance' (fi-nans', fī-) *n.* the management of money.—*v.* to find money for.—**finan'cial** (fi-nan'shal, fī-) *adj.*—**finan'cier** (fi-nan'seer, fī-) *n.*

finch *n.* one of a family of singing birds

find (fīnd) *v.* 1. to come across, meet with. 2. to discover, get. 3. to learn. 4. to supply, as *I will find the money for the expenses.* 5. to declare, as *to find guilty.*—**found** *p.t.* and *p. part.*—*n.* something found

fine *n.* money paid as punishment.—*v.* to punish by a fine.—**fi'ning** *pres. part.*—**fined** *p.t.* and *p. part.*

fine *adj.* 1. thin, slender. 2. delicate. 3. good, handsome. 4. pure. 5. rainless.—**fi'ner** *comp.*—**fi'nest** *sup.*—**fine'ly** *adv.*—**fine'ness** *n.*—**fi'nery** *n.* showy dress

finesse *n.* subtle skill

fin'ger (fing'ger) *n.* one of the jointed branches of the hand.—*v.* to touch with the fingers.—**fin'ger-plate** *n.* a flat plate on a door to protect it from fingermarks.—**fin'ger-post** *n.* a sign-post at a cross-roads.—**fin'ger-print** *n.* impression of finger-tip (used for identifying criminals).—**to have a finger in** to share in.—**to twist round one's finger** to influence greatly

fi'nis (fī'nis) *n.* the end

fin'ish *v.* 1. to bring to an end, complete. 2. to perfect.—he **fin'ishes**.—*n.* 1. the end. 2. polish, final appearance.—**fin'ished** *adj.*

fi'nite (fī'nīt) *adj.* limited, bounded

Fin'land *n.* a country in the extreme north of Europe.—**Finn** a native of Finland *n.*—**Fin'nish** *adj.*

fiord, fjord' (fyord, fee-ord') *n.* in Norway a narrow inlet of the sea between steep cliffs

fir *n.* a cone-bearing tree

fire *n.* 1. a burning, flame, glow. 2. enthusiasm.—*v.* 1. to cause to burn. 2. to discharge a gun or rifle.—**fire'-alarm** *n.* a signal giving warning of fire.—**fire'-brand** 1. a burning piece of wood. 2. an agitator.—**fire'-engine** *n.* a machine by which firemen put out fires.—**fire'-escape** *n.* a ladder or stairway for escaping from a burning house.—**fire'-extinguisher** *n.* an apparatus containing chemicals for putting out small fires.—**fire'fly** *n.* an insect with a phosphorescent glow.—**fire'man** 1. a stoker. 2. a man paid to fight fires.—**fire'place** *n.* opening in a room for a fire with a flue above it.—**fire'proof** *adj.* non-inflammable.—**fire'works** *n.pl.* rockets, crackers, etc., producing bangs and coloured flames for amusement.—**to hang fire** to be slow in happening.—**to set the Thames on fire** to perform some marvellous feat

firm *adj.* 1. solid, fixed. 2. determined, settled.—**firm'er** *comp.*—**firm'est** *sup.*—*n.* a business, a commercial house.—**firm'ly** *adv.*—**firm'ness** *n.*

Compare: compact, decided, unyielding, resolute, stable, steadfast, unshaken, rigid. *Contrast:* unstable, shaky, irresolute, vacillating

fir'mament *n.* the heavens, sky

first *adj.* 1. earliest. 2. before everyone or everything.—*adv.* before others.—**first-aid** *n.* help given to an injured person before the doctor's arrival.—**first-born** *n.* eldest.—**first-foot** *n.* the first person to enter a house in the New Year.—**first'fruits** *n.pl.* earliest products.—**first'hand** *adj.* obtained directly.—**first night** *n.* the first performance of a show.—**first'rate** *adj.* excellent

firth *n.* an estuary in Scotland

fis'cal *adj.* of public finance.—*n.* treasurer

fish *n.* 1. a cold-blooded animal with gills, living in water. 2. its flesh.—**fish, fish'es** *pl.*—*v.* to catch fish.—**fish'y** *adj.* 1. of fish. 2. (slang) suspicious.—**fish'erman** *n.*—**fish'ery** *n.* fishing-ground.—**fish'monger** (fish'-mung-ger) *n.* a dealer in fish.—**a pretty kettle of fish** a muddle or trouble.—**to fish in troubled waters** to try to profit from the difficulties of others.—**to have other fish to fry** to have other things to do

fis'sure (fish'er) *n.* a crack, split

fist *n.* the clenched hand

fit *n.* 1. a sudden attack of illness. 2. a mood.—**fit'ful** *adj.* irregular.—**fit'fully** *adv.*

fit *adj.* 1. in good condition. 2. suitable. 3. qualified, worthy.—**fit'ter** *comp.*—**fit'test** *sup.*—*n.* as *That coat is a good fit.*—*v.* 1. to suit. 2. to arrange.—**fit'ter** *n.* 1. person who fits clothes. 2. person who makes or adjusts machinery.—**fit'ting** *pres. part.*—**fit'ted** *p.t.* and *p. part.*—**fit'ness** *n.*—**fit'tings** *n.pl.* fixtures

Note: The verb *to fit* is used in a number of phrases such as *to fit in* or *into*, meaning to occupy a space exactly; *to fit up* or *out*, meaning to furnish or supply; *to fit on*, meaning to fix on or try on

five *adj.* next after four.—**fives** *n.pl.* a wall-game played with a ball in a court

fix *v.* 1. to fasten, make firm. 2. to settle, determine. 3. in photography, to make a film or print insensitive to light.—he **fix'es**.—*n.* difficult position.—**fixed** *adj.*—**fix'edly** *adv.*—**fix'er** *n.* a chemical to make a photograph insensitive to light.—**fix'ture** *n.* 1. thing fixed in position. 2. date fixed for match, etc.

fix'ative *n.* a spray to fix pastel colours on paper, or to keep one's hair in position

fizz *v.* to hiss, splutter.—**fiz'zle** *v.* to splutter weakly

fjord see **fiord**

flab'by *adj.* soft and loose.—**flab'bier** *comp.*—**flab'biest** *sup.*

flac'cid (flak'sid) *adj.* flabby

flag *n.* 1. a water-plant. 2. a flat slab of stone. 3. a banner, standard.—*v.* to droop, fade.—**flag'ging** *pres. part.*—**flagged** *p.t.* and *p. part.*

flagella'tion *n.* flogging

flag'on *n.* a vessel to hold liquor

fla'grant (flā'grant) *adj.* glaring, scandalous, outrageous, notorious.—**fla'grantly** *adv.*

flag'ship *n.* the admiral's ship

flag'stone *n.* a paving-stone

flail *n.* instrument for threshing corn by hand

flair *n.* a natural aptitude, as *He has a flair for anything connected with horses*

flak *n.* anti-aircraft gunfire

flake *n.* a light scale-like piece.—*v.* to come off in flakes.—**fla'ky** *adj.*

flamboy'ance *n.* a showy exaggerated manner.—**flamboy'ant** *adj.*

flame *n.* a tongue of light.—*v.* to blaze.—**fla'ming** *pres. part.*—**flamed** *p.t.* and *p. part.*

flamin'go (flam-ing'gō) *n.* a bird with long neck and legs.—**flamin'goes** *pl.*

flank *n.* the side.—*v.* 1 to attack or defend from the side. 2. to stand beside

flan'nel *n.* a soft woollen material.— **flannelette'** *n.* a cotton imitation of flannel.—**flannel flower** *n.* a perennial plant bearing daisy-like flowers with flannel-like bracts, Australian edelweiss

flap *v.* 1. to hit with something broad. 2. to move (wings) up and down.—**flap'ping** *pres. part.*—**flapped** *p.t.* and *p. part.*—*n.* something hanging loosely

flare *v.* 1. to blaze unsteadily. 2. to burst out angrily. 3. to spread (as a skirt).—**fla'ring** *pres. part.*—**flared** *p.t.* and *p. part.*—*n.* 1. flame. 2. signal-light.—**to flare up** 1. to burst into flame. 2. to show sudden anger

flash *v.* 1. to flame suddenly. 2. to gleam. 3. to appear suddenly.—he **flash'es**.—*n.* 1. sudden burst of light. 2. a moment, as *It was all done in a flash*. 3. a cloth military badge.—**flash'y** *adj.* showy.—**flash'light** *n.* 1. a small torch. 2. a brief flash of light to take a photograph in dim lighting.—**a flash in the pan** something that begins brilliantly but soon ends in failure

flask *n.* 1. flat pocket-bottle. 2. narrow-necked bottle

flat *adj.* 1. level, smooth. 2. dull. 3. below true pitch (in music).—*n.* set of rooms on one floor.—**flat'ter** *comp.*—**flat'test** *sup.*—**flat'ness** *n.*—**flat'ten** *v.* to make or become flat

flat'ter *v.* to praise insincerely.—**flat'terer** *n.*—**flat'tery** *n.*

flaunt *v.* 1. to wave proudly. 2. to show off

flau'tist *n.* a flute-player

fla'vour (flā'ver) *n.* taste.—*v.* to season.—**fla'vouring** *n.* a spice or essence to give flavour

flaw *n.* 1. a crack. 2. a defect, fault.—**flaw'less** *adj.*

flax *n.* a plant from whose fibre linen is made.—**flax'en** *adj.* 1. of flax. 2. pale yellow.—**flax, New Zealand** *n.* a plant in N.Z. yielding strong fibre, growing up to nine feet

flay *v.* to strip off the skin or the hide

flea (flee) *n.* a small jumping insect which feeds on blood

fleck *n.* 1. a spot, freckle. 2. a patch of colour.—*v.* to mark, dapple

fledge (flej) *v.* to cover with feathers.—**fledge'ling, fledg'ling** *n.* a young bird

flee *v.* to run away.—**flee'ing** *pres. part.*—**fled** *p.t.* and *p. part.*
Compare: escape, fly, retreat. *Contrast:* stay, remain, advance, attack

fleece (flees) *n.* a sheep's wool.—*v.* 1. to cut off fleece. 2. to rob.—**flee'cy** *adj.* woolly

fleet *n.* 1. a number of ships, cars, etc. 2. a sea force under one command.—*adj.* swift.—**fleet-footed** *adj.* able to run fast.—**fleet'ness** *n.* swiftness

Flem'ing *n.* a native of Flanders.—**Flem'ish** *adj.*

flesh *n.* 1. the soft part of the body between skin and bone. 2. meat. 3. the soft part of fruit.—**flesh'y** *adj.* plump

flex *n.* a pliable covered wire used in electric fittings.—*v.* to bend.—**flex'ible** *adj.* 1. that can be bent easily. 2. supple, pliable. 3. easily manageable, pliant

flick *n.* 1. a light blow. 2. a jerk.—*v.* to strike lightly

flick'er *v.* to burn unsteadily.—*n.* wavering

fli'er (flī'er) *n.* 1. something that flies. 2. an airman

flight (flīt) *n.* 1. flying. 2. a journey in aircraft. 3. a Royal Air Force unit, part of a squadron. 4. stairs between landings. 5. escape, running away.—**flight'-deck** *n.* the main deck of an aircraft carrier.—**flight-lieuten'ant** (lef-ten'ant) *n.* an Air Force Officer.—**flight'y** *adj.* fickle.—**to put to flight** to rout

flim'sy *adj.* 1. thin, delicate, as *of flimsy construction*. 2. weak, as *a flimsy excuse*.—**flim'sier** *comp.*—**flim'siest** *sup.*

flinch *v.* to shrink, draw back, recoil.—he **flinch'es**

fling *v.* 1. to throw. 2. to rush, as *He flung out of the room in a rage*. 3. to kick, plunge.—**flung** *p.t.* and *p. part.*—*n.* 1. a throw. 2. a vigorous dance, e.g. *a Highland fling*

flint *n.* a hard stone.—**flint'y** *adj.* hard, cruel

flip *n.* 1. a thick, light blow. 2. aeroplane trip.—*v.* to move with a flick

flip'pant *adj.* treating serious matters lightly. —**flip'pancy** *n.*

Compare: frivolous, disrespectful, pert, saucy, impertinent, shallow. *Contrast:* serious, grave, respectful, weighty

flip'per *n.* 1. the fin of a fish. 2. a seal's limb. 3. a webbed rubber foot to help swimmers

flirt *v.* 1. to pretend to make love. 2. to throw with a jerk.—*n.* 1. a quick movement. 2. a girl fond of flirting.—**flirta'tion** *n.*

Note: This verb is often followed by *with,* as *He has flirted with many girls in his time.* One may also *flirt with* (i.e. toy with) an idea or project, not pursuing it seriously

flit *v.* 1. to move lightly and rapidly. 2. to go away, change one's dwelling.—**flit'ting** *pres. part.*—**flit'ted** *p.t.* and *p. part.*

flitch *n.* a side of bacon

float (flō) *v.* 1. to rest or move on the surface of a liquid. 2. to start something floating, to set going, as *to float a company.* —*n.* 1. anything small that floats. 2. low-bodied cart.—**floating rib** a lower rib not attached to the breast-bone

flock *n.* 1. a number of animals of one kind together. 2. a religious congregation. 3. a tuft of wool.—*pl.* wool-waste, for stuffing. —*v.* to gather in a crowd

Note: One speaks of a *flock* of sheep. There are other words for groups of other animals. See **herd, covey, drove, pack, swarm, shoal**

floe (flō) *n.* floating ice

flog *v.* to beat hard.—**flog'ging** *pres. part.*—**flogged** *p.t.* and *p. part.*

flood (flud) *n.* 1. an overflow of water. 2. an outpouring, as a *flood of words, light.*—*v.* to fill with water or light.—**flood'-lighting** *n.* artificial lighting of outside of buildings.—**flood'lit** *adj.*—**flood-tide** *n.* a rising tide—**flash flood** (Aus.) a sudden flood

floor (flōr) *n.* 1. a lower surface of a room. 2. a storey of a house.—*v.* 1. to make or provide a floor. 2. to knock down.—**flooring** *n.* floor covering

flop *v.* 1. to fall in a heap.—**flop'ping** *pres. part.*—**flopped** *p.t.* and *p. part.*—*n.* a fall, failure

flo'ra (flaw'ra) *n.pl.* 1. the plants of a region. 2. a list of them.—**flo'ral** *adj.* of flowers

flo'rid *adj.* 1. flowery, showy, as *a florid style of writing.* 2. ruddy, as *a florid complexion*

flor'in *n.* an English two-shilling piece no longer minted

flor'ist *n.* a grower or seller of flowers

floss *n.* 1. rough silk or cocoon. 2. embroidery silk.—**candy-floss** *n.* a sweet like a mass of floss

flotil'la *n.* a small fleet

flot'sam *n.* floating wreckage

flounce *v.* to move impatiently.—*n.* 1. a fling of the body. 2. gathered border on a dress

floun'der *n.* a flat fish

floun'der *v.* to plunge and struggle, esp. in water or mud

flour *n.* the sifted finer part of meal.—**flour'y** *adj.*

flour'ish (flur'ish) *v.* 1. to thrive, prosper. 2. to wave, display.—**he flour'ishes.**—*n.* 1. an ornamental curve (in writing, etc.). 2. a waving. 3. a blast of trumpets

flout *v.* to mock, defy, as *He flouts all the rules*

Contrast: observe, respect, obey

flow (flō) *v.* 1. to move like water. 2. to move easily, abundantly. 3. to hang loosely, as *flowing robes.*—*n.* 1. rise of tide (opposite of **ebb**). 2. ample supply

flow'er *n.* 1. a blossom, bloom. 2. the choicest part.—*v.* to bloom.—**flow'ery** *adj.* 1. full of flowers. 2. full of fine words

fluc'tuate *v.* to rise and fall, vary.—**fluctua'tion** (ā-shun) *n.*

flue (flōō) *n.* a chimney pipe

flu'ent (flōō'ent) *adj.* flowing, ready (in speech).—**flu'ently** *adv.*—**flu'ency** *n.*

fluff *n.* soft feathery stuff, down.—**fluff'y** *adj.*

flu'id (flōō'id) *n.* a gas or liquid.—*adj.* flowing.—**fluid'ity** *n.*

fluke (flōōk) *n.* 1. the flat triangular point of an anchor. 2. a flatfish

fluke (flōōk) *n.* a lucky stroke

flun'key *n.* 1. a footman. 2. a toady.—**flun'keys** *pl.*

fluoresc'ent *adj.* giving off light with little or no heat

flu'orine (flōō'o-reen) *n.* a chemical element, a yellowish gas.—**flu'oride** *n.* a compound of fluorine.—**fluorida'tion** *n.* adding a fluoride to a town's water supply for medical reasons

flur'ry *n.* 1. a sudden gust. 2. nervous haste.—*v.* to agitate

flush *v.* 1. to flow suddenly. 2. to blush. 3. to cleanse by flow of water.—**he flush'es.**—*n.* 1. rush of water. 2. blush. 3. all cards in one's hand being of the same suit.—*adj.* level

flus'ter *v.* to confuse.—*n.*

flute (flōōt) *n.* 1. a musical wind-instrument like a pipe. 2. a groove (in column, etc.).—**flu'ted** *adj.* grooved.—**flu'ting** *n.* a series of grooves

flut'ter *v.* 1. to flap wings. 2. to move quiveringly. 3. to be excited.—*n.*

flu'vial (flōō'vi-al) *adj.* of rivers

flux *n.* 1. a flow. 2. constant changes

fly *n.* a two-winged insect.—**flies** *pl.*

fly *v.* 1. to move in the air. 2. to wave or show (a flag). 3. to rush, flee.—**he flies.**—**fly'ing**

pres. part.—**flew** *p.t.*—**flown** *p. part.*—**fly-blown** *adj.* maggoty.—**fly'catcher** *n.* 1. an insect-eating bird or plant. 2. a sticky paper to catch flies.—**fly'over** *n.* one road over another.—**fly'past** *n.* a ceremonial flight of aircraft.—**fly'weight** *n.* a boxer weighing 8 st. or less.—**fly'-wheel** *n.* a heavy wheel to regulate a revolving shaft.—**flying buttress** a stone arch supporting a wall.—**Flying Dutchman** a ghostly ship condemned to sail round Cape Horn for ever.—**flying fish** a fish that jumps out of water and glides for a short space.—**flying fox** 1. a very large fruit-eating bat. 2. (Aus.) a wire conveyor for transporting articles across a river or a gully, or up and down hillsides.—**flying saucer** a disc-shaped object said to be seen flying in the sky.—**flying squad** a police patrol in fast cars.—**flying start** a quick start.—**a fly in the ointment** a fault in something good.—**to fly in the face of** to defy.—**to fly off the handle, to fly out at** to be in a rage at

foal (fōl) *n.* a young horse or donkey

foam (fōm) *n.* 1. froth on liquid. 2. fury.—*v.* 1. to froth. 2. to rage.—**foam'y** *adj.*

fob *v.* (followed by *off*) to cheat, palm off.—**fob'bing** *pres. part.*—**fobbed** *p.t.* and *p. part.*

Note: You *fob off* a person *with* a thing but you *fob off* a thing *on* a person

fob *n.* a pocket for a watch

fo'cus (fō'kus) *n.* 1. the point at which rays meet after being reflected or refracted. 2. a centre of interest as *she was the focus of* (*their*) *attention.*—**fo'ci** (fō'sī), **fo'cuses** (fō'kuses) *pl.*—*v.* to bring to a focus.—he **fo'cuses.**—**fo-cus'ing** *pres. part.*—**fo'cused** *p.t.* and *p. part.*

fod'der *n.* dried food for cattle, horses.

foe (fō) *n.* an enemy.—**foe'man** *n.*

fog *n.* thick mist.—*v.* to bewilder, mystify.—**fog'gy** *adj.*—**fog'horn** *n.* warning for ships

fo'gey *n.* a fussy old person

foi'ble *n.* a weak point, failing

foil *n.* 1. a thin sheet of metal. 2. something that sets off another by contrast

foil *n.* a light sword tipped with a button used in fencing

foil *v.* to outwit, defeat

foist *v.* to impose, palm off

Note: Usually followed by *on* or *on to.* You foist an imitation article *on* or *on to* a person as genuine

Compare: fob

fold (fōld) *v.* 1. to double up, bend. 2. to wrap up.—*v.* something folded—**fol'der** *n.* 1. a pamphlet of folded sheets. 2. a portfolio

fold *n.* 1. a sheep-pen. 2. a body of church members

fo'liage (fō'li-āj) *n.* the leaves of a plant

fo'lio *n.* 1. a sheet of paper doubled once. 2. a book made of such sheets.—**fo'lios** *pl.*

folk (fōk) *n.* people—*pl.* relatives,—*adj.* originating with the people, as *folk-dance, folk-tale, folk-song.*—**folk-lore** *n.* legends, traditional beliefs

Compare: nation, community, population, tribe, clan

fol'low (fol'ō) *v.* 1. to go or come after. 2. to obey (instructions). 3. to go along (a road, path). 4. to engage in (a profession). 5. to understand (someone's meaning). 6. to result. 7. to imitate.—**fol'lowing** *adj.* next.—*n.* a group of supporters.—**to follow suit** to imitate.—**to follow up** to continue enquiries

fol'ly *n.* 1. foolishness. 2. a foolish action.—**fol'lies** *pl.*

Compare: absurdity, idiocy, imprudence, lunacy, madness, silliness, stupidity.

Contrast: prudence, sense, wisdom

foment' *v.* 1. to bathe with hot lotions. 2. to stir up (trouble, disorder, dissatisfaction, etc.).—**fomenta'tion** (-tā'shun) *n.*

fond *adj.* 1. loving. 2. foolish.—**fond'ly** *adv.*—**fond'ness** *n.*—**to be fond of** to like

Note: One is *fond of* but has *a fondness for* some person or thing

fond'le *v.* to caress

font *n.* a vessel for baptismal water

food (fōōd) *n.* nourishment, a substance used by a living thing for energy or growth

Compare: diet, fare, fodder, nourishment, nutriment, provender, viands, victuals

fool (fōōl) *n.* 1. a silly person. 2. a jester, clown. 3. stewed and crushed fruit mixed with cream, etc. as *gooseberry fool.*—*v.* 1. to act like a fool. 2. to deceive.—**fool'ery** *n.*—**foolhard'iness** *n.* rashness.—**foolhard'y** *adj.*—**fool'ish** *adj.* unwise.—**fool'ishness** *n.*—**fool'proof** *adj.* safe even from fools.—**fools'cap** *n.* a size of paper.—**All Fools' Day** April 1st.—**a fool's paradise** happiness in ignorance of trouble to come

foot *n.* 1. the part of the leg on which we stand. 2. the lowest part, the base. 3. infantry. 4. a measure of twelve inches. 5. a division in a line of poetry.—**feet** *pl.*—*v.* 1. to tread. 2. to pay, as *I will foot the bill.*—**foot'ball** *n.* 1. a large leather ball. 2. the game played with it.—**foot'brake** *n.* a brake on a vehicle worked by foot.—**foot'fall, foot'step** *n.* the sound made by a foot.—**foot'ing** *n.* 1. firm standing. 2. a position.—**foot'light** *n.* one of a row of lights at the front of a stage.—**foot'note** *n.* a note of explanation at the bottom of a page.—**foot'print** *n.* the mark made by a foot.—**foot'rule** *n.* a ruler twelve inches long.—**cu'bic foot** *n.* a cube with each side one foot long.—**foot'wear** *n.* boots, shoes etc.—**foot and mouth disease** a disease of cattle.—**to find one's feet** to adapt oneself well to a new situation.—**to put one's foot down** to act with decision.—**to put one's best foot forward** to step out at a good pace.—**to put one's foot in it** to make a blunder.

—to put one's feet up to rest after exhaustion

fop *n.* a dandy, a man extremely vain of his appearance and clothes.—**fop'pish** *adj.*

for *prep.* because of, on account of, instead of, toward, during, respecting, in search of, in favour of, in spite of, in payment of. —*conj.* because

for'age (for'ij) *n.* food for cattle and horse.—*v.* to search for food

for'asmuch (as) *conj.* since, because

for'ay *n.* raid.—*v.*

for'bear *n.* an ancestor

forbear' (for-bair') *v.* to refrain, be patient.—**forbore'** *p.t.*—**forborne'** *p. part.*—**forbear'ance** *n.*

Note: You *forbear to do* a thing, or you *forbear from doing it*

forbid' *v.* to refuse to allow, to oppose.—**forbade'** (for-bad') *p.t.*—**forbid'den** *p. part.* —**forbid'ding** *adj.* not inviting

Compare: repulsive, unpleasant, threatening. *Contrast:* attractive, pleasing, enticing

force (fōrs) *n.* 1. strength, power, energy. 2. body of troops, police. 3. compulsion.—*v.* 1. to compel, as *I will force him to tell me.* 2. to break open, as *He forced the lock.*—**for'cing** *pres. part.*—**forced** *p.t.* and *p. part.* —**the Forces** *n.pl.* Navy, Army and Air Force.—**force'ful** *adj.* vigorous.—**for'cible** (for'sib-l) *adj.* active, strong, violent.—**brute force** great strength, violence.—**in force** in operation

for'ceps (for'seps) *n.* small pincers used by surgeons

ford *n.* a place where a stream may be crossed on foot.—*v.*

fore *adj.* in front, forward.—**fur'ther, for'mer** *comp.*—**fur'thest, first, fore'most** *sup.*—*n.* front part, bow of ship.—**to the fore** prominent

fore'arm *n.* the arm between the elbow and wrist

forearm' *v.* to arm beforehand

forebode' *v.* to foretell.—**forebo'ding** *n.* a feeling that something unpleasant is going to happen

fore'cast *n.* an estimate of coming events.—**forecast'** *v.* to prophesy

fore'castle (fō'ksl) *n.* 1. forward part of a ship in the bows. 2. the sailors' quarters

fore'father *n.* an ancestor

fore'finger *n.* the finger next to the thumb

fore'front *n.* the very front

forego' *v.* to precede, go before.—he **foregoes.**—**forewent'** *p.t.*—**foregone'** *p. part.*—**forego'ing** *adj.* coming before.—**foregone'** *adj.* decided beforehand.—**a foregone conclusion** an ending that could be told beforehand

fore'ground *n.* the part of a view nearest the observer

fore'head (for'ed) *n.* the part of the face above the eyebrows

for'eign (for'in) *adj.* 1. belonging to another country or place, as *The man spoke with a foreign accent. A foreign body in one's eye causes pain.* 2. unfamiliar.—**for'eigner** *n.*

fore'man *n.* 1. a man in charge of work. 2. the leader of a jury.—**fore'woman** *fem.*—**fore'men** *pl.*

fore'most *adj.* chief, leading

fore'noon *n.* morning until noon

forerun'ner *n.* a sign of what is to come, as *crocuses are forerunners of Spring*

Compare: harbinger, herald, precursor, predecessor

foresee' *v.* to see beforehand.—**foresaw'** *p.t.* —**foreseen'** *p. part.*

foreshad'ow *v.* to indicate what is to come

fore'shore *n.* the part of the shore between high and low watermarks

fore'sight (for'sīt) *n.* looking ahead

for'est *n.* a large woodland tract.—**for'ester** *n.*—**for'estry** *n.* the management of forests

forestall' *v.* to be beforehand

foretell' *v.* to predict, prophesy.—**foretold'** *p.t.* and *p. part.*

fore'word *n.* an introduction, preface

for'feit (for'fit) *n.* a penalty, fine.—*adj.* lost by crime or fault.—*v.* to lose as a penalty. —**for'feiture** *n.* a fine

forgath'er *v.* to meet, assemble

forge (forj) *n.* a smithy, workshop for melting metal.—*v.* 1. to shape. 2. to make a false imitation (e.g. of money, person's handwriting, etc.).—**for'ger** *n.* person making or writing something in false imitation.—**for'gery** *n.*

forge (forj) *v.* to advance.—**to forge ahead** to make steady progress

forget' *v.* not to remember.—**forget'ting** *pres. part.*—**forgot'** *p.t.*—**forgot'ten** *p. part.*—**forget'ful** *adj.*—**forget'-me-not** *n.* a small blue flower

forgive' (for-giv') *v.* to pardon, excuse.—**forgiv'ing** *pres. part.*—**forgave'** *p.t.*—**forgiv'en** *p. part.*—**forgive'ness** *n.*

forgo' *v.* give up, go without, as *Because they were so busy at the factory the manager decided to forgo his holiday.*—he **forgoes'.**—**forwent'** *p.t.*—**forgone'** *p. part.*

fork *n.* 1. a pronged instrument for holding food. 2. a farm tool for digging or lifting. 3. a division into branches.—*v.* to branch. —**forked** *adj.*

forlorn' *adj.* neglected, friendless.—**forlorn' hope** *n.* a desperate enterprise

form *n.* 1. shape, appearance. 2. visible person or animal. 3. nature, kind. 4. bench. 5. class in a school. 6. a printed document to be completed and signed. 7. behaviour according to rule.—*v.* 1. to shape, organise. 2. to imagine. 3. to make part of.—**for'mal** *adj.* 1. according to rule. 2. stiff.—**formal'ity** *n.* 1. observance required by custom. 2. stiffness of manner.—**forma'tion** (-mā'shun) *n.* 1. structure. 2. arrangement

for'mer *adj.* 1. earlier in time. 2. of past times. 3. first-named.—**for'merly** *adv.* previously

formi'ca *n.* trade name for a kind of heat-resisting plastic

for'midable *adj.* 1. terrible, powerful, as *a formidable enemy*. 2. difficult, as *a formidable task*

form'ula *n.* 1. a set form of words. 2. a recipe. 3. a rule or fact expressed in symbols and figures.—**for'mulae, formulas** *pl.* —**for'mulate** *v.* to express, state.—**formula'tion** (-lā'shun) *n.*

forsake' *v.* 1. to abandon. 2. to give up.—**forsa'king** *pres. part.*—**forsook'** *p.t.*—**forsa'ken** *p. part.*

forsooth' *adv.* indeed, in truth

forswear' *v.* 1. to renounce. 2. to swear falsely

fort (fōrt) *n.* a fortified place

forte (fort) *n.* one's strong point, as *Playing tennis is his forte.*—(fort'i) *adv.* (in music) loudly

forth (fōrth) *adv.* forward, away.—**forthcom'ing** *adj.* 1. approaching. 2. ready when wanted.—**forthwith'** *adv.* immediately

for'tieth *adj.* next after thirty-ninth

fortifica'tion (-kā'shun) *n.* 1. strengthening. 2. defensive walls, etc.

for'tify *v.* 1. to strengthen. 2. to protect with forts, etc.—he **for'tifies.**—**for'tifying** *pres. part.*—**for'tified** *p.t.* and *p. part.*

fort'itude *n.* courage in trouble or pain

fort'night (fort'nīt) *n.* two weeks.—**fort'nightly** *adv.*

fort'ress *n.* a fortified place

fortu'itous (for-tū'i-tus) *adj.* accidental, happening by chance

for'tunate (for'tū-nāt) *adj.* lucky.—**for'tunately** *adv.*

for'tune *n.* 1. chance, luck. 2. wealth, sum of money, as *to inherit a fortune.*—**for'tune-tel'ler** *n.* a person who claims to predict the future

for'ty *adj.* four times ten.—*n.*

fo'rum *n.* 1. a public meeting-place in ancient Rome. 2. a tribunal

for'ward *adj.* 1. lying ahead, as *The regiment occupied a forward position.* 2. onward, as *They took a forward path.* 3. advanced, precocious, pert, as *a forward crop, a forward child.*—*adv.* ahead, as *to go forward.*—*n.* one who plays in an advanced position in football, hockey, etc., team.—*v.* 1. to help, as *I will do all I can to forward your interests.* 2. to send, as *to forward a letter.*—**for'wards** *adv.* to the front

fosse *n.* a ditch, moat

fos'sick (fos'sik) (Aus.) *v.* to prospect for gold especially in abandoned diggings.—**fos'sicker** *n.*

fos'sil *n.* the hardened remains of plants or animals.—**fos'silise** *v.*

fos'ter *v.* 1. to encourage. 2. to rear, cherish. —**fos'ter-brother** *n.* one brought up with another as though related—**fos'ter child**—**fos'ter-father**—**fos'ter-mother**

foul (fowl) *adj.* 1. filthy, loathsome. 2. smelly. —*n.* unfair play.—*v.* to make foul.—**foul'ly** *adv.*—**foul play** 1. murder. 2. in sport, a breaking of rules.—**to fall foul of** to come into conflict with

Compare: unclean, dirty, disgusting, abominable, unfair, wicked, impure. *Contrast:* clean, pure, fair, fresh, unsullied

found *v.* 1. to establish, lay the beginnings of. 2. to base.—**founda'tion** (-dā'shun) *n.* 1. base, groundwork. 2. endowment.—**found'er** *n.* —**found'ress** *fem.*

found *v.* to melt metal and run into mould, to cast.—**found'ry** *n.* 1. casting. 2. works where founding is done.—**foun'dries** *pl.*

found'er *v.* 1. to collapse. 2. of a ship, to sink

fount *n.* 1. fountain. 2. source. 3. set of printing type

foun'tain *n.* 1. spring, source. 2. ornamental jet of water.—**foun'tain-pen** *n.* pen with ink reservoir

four (fōr) *adj.* three and one.—**four'score** *adj.* eighty.—**four'square** *adj.* firm.—**fourteen'** *adj.* four and ten.—**fourteenth'** *adj.*—**fourth** *n.* a quarter—*adj.* next after third.—**on all fours** on hands and knees

fowl *n.* bird.—**cock** *masc.*—**hen** *fem.*—**chick, chick'en** a young bird.—**fowl'er** *n.* hunter of wild birds

fox *n.* 1. a red, bushy-tailed animal. 2. its fur. 3. cunning person.—**vix'en** *fem.*—**cub** *n.* young fox or vixen.—**fox'glove** *n.* a tall flowering plant.—**fox'hound** *n.*—**fox'ter'rier** *n.* a small dog.—**fox'trot** *n.* a ballroom dance

frac'tion (-shun) *n.* 1. a piece, part. 2. (arithmetic) numerical quantity less than a whole number, e.g. $\frac{1}{2}$ is a vulgar fraction. 0·5 is a decimal fraction. See **vulgar, decimal.**—**frac'tional** *adj.* 1. containing a fraction. 2. comparatively small

frac'tious (frak-shus) *adj.* cross, peevish

frac'ture (frak'cher) *n.* 1. a break. 2. the part broken. 3. breaking of a bone.—*v.* to break

frag'ile (fraj'īl) *adj.* easily broken, delicate.—**fragil'ity** *n.*

frag'ment *n.* 1. a piece broken off. 2. a small piece, part.—**frag'mentary** *adj.*

fra'grance (frā'grans) *n.* a sweet smell.—**fra'grant** *adj.*

frail *adj.* 1. weak, delicate. 2. unable to resist temptation.—**frail'ty** *n.*

frame *n.* 1. a construction on which something is built. 2. a border for window, picture, etc.—*v.* 1. to put together, make. 2. to put into a frame.—**frame of mind** mood.—**frame'work** *n.* structure

franc *n.* French, Belgian, Swiss coin

France *n.* a country in western Europe.—**French** *n.* the language of France.—*adj.* belonging to France

fran'chise *n.* 1. the right of voting. 2. citizenship

frank *adj.* outspoken, honest.—**frank'ly** *adv.*—**frank'ness** *n.*
Compare: candid, open, straightforward. *Contrast:* artful, secretive, deceitful

fran'tic *adj.* frenzied, wild with grief, joy, etc.—**fran'tically** *adv.*

frater'nal *adj.* brotherly.—**frater'nity** *n.* brotherhood.—**fra'ternise** *v.* to associate, make friends

fra'tricide (fra'tri-sīd) *n.* the crime of killing one's brother.—**fra'tricidal** *adj.*

fraud *n.* trickery, cheating.—**fraud'ulent** *adj.*

fraught (frawt) *adj* laden, filled, esp. in figurative expressions, e.g. *His words were fraught with meaning*

fray *n.* fight.—*v.* 1. to wear out by rubbing. 2. to ravel out

freak (freek) *n.* something odd, unusual.—**freak'ish** *adj.*

frec'kle *n.* a light-brown spot on the skin.—*v.*

free *adj.* 1. not shut up or bound, loose. 2. at liberty to think and act. 3. without tax.—*v.* to release.—**free'ing** *pres. part.*—**freed** *p.t.* and *p. part.*—**free'ly** *adv.*—**free'booter** *n.* robber.—**free'dom** *n.* liberty.—**a free hand** liberty to act freely.—**free-range** (of hens) able to move freely to scratch and feed.—**free selection** (Aus.) 1. choosing or selecting land under the Land laws. 2. the right to choose.—**Free Trade** trade between countries without import duties

free'hold *n.* land or a house, etc. held free of rent.—*adj.*

free'man *n.* 1. a person not a slave. 2. one admitted to citizenship.—**free'men** *pl.*

freeze *v.* 1. to become ice. 2. to feel very cold.—**free'zing** *pres. part.*—**froze** *p.t.*—**fro'zen** *p. part.*—**free'zing point** *n.* the temperature at which a liquid freezes

freight (frāt) *n.* ship's cargo.—**freight'age** *n.* money charged for transport.—**freight'er** *n.* ship carrying freight

fren'zy *n.* madness, fury.—**fren'zied** *adj.*

fre'quency (free'kwen-si) *n.* 1. common occurrence. 2. rate of occurrence. 3. in Science, the number of vibrations of a wave per second

fre'quent (free'kwent) *adj.* 1. happening often. 2. numerous.—**fre'quently** *adv.*
Compare: common, recurrent, recurring, repeated, usual. *Contrast:* few, occasional, rare, scanty, uncommon

frequent' (free-kwent') *v.* to visit often, as *John frequented the youth club*

fres'co *n.* a painting on fresh plaster.—**fres'coes, fres'cos** *pl.*

fresh *adj.* 1. new, additional. 2. recent. 3. not stale. 4. not tired. 5. cool.—**fresh'en** *v.* to make fresh.—**fresh'ly** *adv.*—**fresh'ness** *n.*

fret *v.* 1. to wear away. 2. to worry, to be vexed.—**fret'ful** *adj.*

fret *n.* an interlaced pattern in metal, stone, or wood.—**fret'saw** *n.*—**fret'work** *n.*

fri'ar *n.* a member of one of the religious begging orders

fric'tion (-shun) *n.* 1. rubbing. 2. resistance caused by rubbing. 3. disagreement

Fri'day *n.* the sixth day of the week.—**Good Friday** *n.* the day of the Crucifixion, the Friday before Easter

friend (frend) *n.* 1. a person knowing and feeling affection for another. 2. a supporter.—**friend'less** *adj.*—**friend'liness** *n.*—**friend'ly** *adj.* kindly disposed.—**friend'ship** *n.*

frieze (freez) *n.* a decorative border on a wall

frig'ate *n.* an old type of fast-sailing warship

fright (frīt) *n.* 1. sudden fear. 2. something ugly.—**fright'en** *v.* to terrify.—**fright'ful** *adj.* dreadful.—**fright'fully** *adv.*
Compare: (with fright 1.) alarm, terror, dismay

frig'id (frij'id) *adj.* 1. cold, icy. 2. stiff, dull. 3. chilling in manner.—**frig'idly** *adv.*—**frigid'ity** *n.*

frill *n.* edging, ruffle.—*v.*

fringe (frinj) *n.* 1. an ornamental border of threads, tassels, etc. 2. hair cut low on forehead.—*v.* to adorn with a fringe

frisk *v.* to frolic, play.—**frisk'y** *adj.*

frit'ter *n.* a piece of fried batter containing fruit or meat

frit'ter (away) *v.* to waste, throw away, as *He frittered his time away when he should have been studying*

frivol'ity *n.* foolish behaviour.—**friv'olous** *adj.* silly, trivial
Compare: vain, petty, flimsy, slight. *Contrast:* grave, sound, substantial, serious

frizz *v.* to crisp, curl up.—**friz'zle** *v.*—**friz'zy** *adj.*

fro *adv.* away from (only in **to and fro**)

frock *n.* 1. female dress. 2. a monk's gown.—**frockcoat** *n.* an old type of man's long coat

frog *n.* a small amphibious animal.—**tad'pole** a young frog.—**frog'man** *n.* a diver in shallow water with underwater suit and flippers

frol'ic *n.* a merry game, play.—*v.* to play gaily.—**frol'icking** *pres. part.*—**frol'icked** *p.t.* and *p. part.*—**frol'icsome** *adj.*

from *prep.* expressing departure, moving away, source, distance, cause, change

frond *n.* a plant organ resembling a leaf (esp. of fern)

front (frunt) *n.* the fore part, advanced position.—*adj.* forward, not at the back.—*v.* to face.—**front'age** *n.* 1. extent of front. 2. in Australia, New Zealand, land on river bank.—**front'al** *adj.* 1. belonging to forehead. 2. on the front.—**to put a bold front on** to face boldly

front'ier (frun'teer) *n.* 1. the boundary between two countries. 2. a borderland

front'ispiece (frunt'is-pees) *n.* an illustration facing the title-page of book

frost *n.* 1. freezing. 2. frozen dew or mist.—*v.* to cover with rime.—**frost'y** *adj.*—**frost'ily** *adv.*—**frost'bite** *n.*

froth *n.* 1. foam, scum. 2. idle talk.—**froth'y** *adj.*—**froth'ily** *adv.*

frown *v.* to wrinkle the brows.—*n.* a look of displeasure or deep thought.—**to frown upon** to disapprove of

frow'zy *adj.* dirty, untidy

fru'gal (frōō'gal) *adj.* sparing, economical.—**frugal'ity** *n.*—**fru'gally** *adv.*

Compare: economical, parsimonious, thrifty, careful, temperate. *Contrast:* extravagant, prodigal, wasteful

fruit (frōōt) *n.* the seed or produce of a plant.—*pl.* 1. vegetable products as, *the fruits of the earth.* 2. produce, result, as *the fruits of one's labours.*—**fruit'erer** *n.* a fruit-seller.—**fruit'ful** *adj.* productive, fertile.—**fruit'fully** *adv.*—**frui'tion** (frōō-i'shun) *n.* attainment of object.—**fruit'less** *adj.* without result.—**fruit'y** *adj.* 1. like fruit. 2. luscious, rich

frustrate' *v.* to defeat, disappoint, as *The police frustrated the plans of the criminals.*—**frustra'tion** (-trā'shun) *n.*

fry *v.* to cook in fat.—he **fries.**—**fry'ing** *pres. part.*—**fried** *p.t.* and *p. part.*—**out of the frying pan into the fire** from a bad situation into one worse

fry *n.* young fishes.—**small fry** unimportant people, small or young children

fuch'sia (fū'sha) *n.* a shrub with drooping flowers

fudge *n.* soft sugar candy

fu'el (fū'el) *n.* material for burning.—*v.* to add fuel.—**fu'elling** *pres. part.*—**fu'elled** *p.t.* and *p. part.*—**to add fuel to the flames** to make someone angrier

fug'itive (fū'ji-tiv) *n.* a person running away.—*adj.* 1. running away. 2. passing quickly, short-lived

fulfil' *v.* 1. to satisfy, accomplish, as *My purpose is now fulfilled. The conditions have been fulfilled.* 2. to obey, as *The slave fulfilled his master's commands.*—**ful'filling** *pres. part.*—**fulfilled'** *p.t.* and *p. part.*—**fulfil'ment** *n.*

full (fōōl) *adj.* 1. unable to hold more. 2. complete, as *a full report, full moon, full dress.* 3. ample as, *a full face.*—**ful'ler** *comp.*—**ful'lest** *sup.*—*adv.* very, quite, as *full well,* used also with many adjs. as **full-blooded, full-blown.**—**full stop** 1. a halt. 2. a punctuation point.—**ful'ly** *adv.*—**full'ness** *n.*

ful'minate *v.* 1. to flash, explode. 2. to thunder out (blame, etc.), as *He fulminated against the policy of the Government.*—**fulmina'tion** (-ā'shun) *n.*

ful'some (fool'sum) *adj.* gushing, as *fulsome praise*

fum'ble *v.* to handle awkwardly, grope about.—**fum'bling** *adj.*

fume (fūm) *n.* smoke.—*v.* 1. to smoke. 2. to be furious.—**fu'ming** *pres. part.*—**fumed** *p.t.* and *p. part.*

fu'migate (fū'mi-gāt) *v.* to smoke out esp. for disinfection.—**fumiga'tion** (-gā'shun) *n.*

fun *n.* sport, amusement, joking.—**to make fun of, to poke fun at** to tease

func'tion (fungk'shun) *n.* 1. proper purpose, use, duty. 2. public occasion.—*v.* to work, as *The machines are all functioning properly.*—**func'tional** *adj.*—**func'tionary** *n.* an official

fund *n.* 1. stock, capital, sum of money. 2. store

fundamen'tal *adj.* 1. essential 2. serving as a base.—*n.* base

fu'neral *n.* burial ceremony.—*adj.* relating to a burial.—**fune'real** (fū-nee're-al) *adj.* gloomy

fun'gus (fung'gus) *n.* one of a class of simple plants containing no chlorophyll, such as mushroom, toadstool, mould, etc.—**fun'gi** (fung'gī, fun'jī), **fun'guses** *pl.*

fun'nel *n.* 1. a cone-shaped vessel ending in a tube, for pouring into a small opening. 2. the chimney of a steamship or engine

fun'ny *adj.* 1. comical. 2. strange, as *I had a funny feeling.*—**fun'nier** *comp.*—**fun'niest** *sup.*—**fun'nily** *adv.*—**funnily enough** strange to say

Compare: 1. humorous, laughable, absurd, ludicrous. 2. odd, queer, peculiar, remarkable

fur *n.* 1. short soft hair of certain animals. 2. clothes made of this. 3. crust or coating.—**fur'ry** *adj.*

fu'rious (fū'ri-us) *adj.* 1. very angry. 2. violent, impetuous, as *We were caught in a furious storm.*—**fu'riously** *adv.*

fur'bish *v.* to clean, polish

furl *v.* to roll up (a sail, umbrella, etc.)

fur'long *n.* an eighth part of a mile, 220 yards

fur'lough (fur'lō) *n.* leave of absence

fur'nace (fur'nis) *n.* 1. a place for melting metals. 2. a closed fireplace

fur'nish *v.* 1. to supply. 2. to fit up with furniture.—**fur'nishings** *n.pl.* fittings

fur'niture (fur'ni-cher) *n.* chairs, tables, etc.

fur'rier *n.* dealer in furs

fur'row (fur'ō) *n.* 1. a trench made by a plough. 2. a wrinkle, groove.—*v.* to make furrows

fur'ther 1. *comp.* of fore and far. 2. more distant, as *on the further bank of the river.* 3. additional, as *He gave further reasons.*—*v.* to help forward, as *to further anyone's plans.*—*adv.* 1. more, as *I cannot help you any further.* 2. at a greater distance, as *to go further.*—**fur'therance** *n.* advancement.—**fur'thermore** *adv.* besides.—**fur'thest** *sup.* of *fore* and *far*

fur'tive *adj.* shy, stealthy.—**fur'tively** *adv.*

fu'ry (fū'ri) *n.* rage, passion.—**fu'ries** *pl.*

furze *n.* an evergreen prickly shrub

fuse (fūz) *n.* 1. a piece of soft wire in an electric circuit which melts when too much current flows. 2. tube or cord for setting light to a bomb, firework, etc.

fuse (fūz) *v.* 1. to melt with heat. 2. to blend by melting

fu'selage (fū'zel-āj) *n.* the body of an aeroplane

fusilier' (fū-zil-eer') *n.* a soldier of certain regiments

fusillade' *n.* discharge of many guns

fu'sion (fū'zhun) *n.* 1. melting. 2. union, blending

fuss *n.* unnecessary bustle or bother.—*v.* to make a fuss.—**fus'sy** *adj.*—**fus'sily** *adv.* —**fus'siness** *n.*

fus'ty *adj.* damp-smelling, mouldy.—**fus'tiness** *n.*

fu'tile (fū'tīl) *adj.* 1. useless, ineffectual. 2. unimportant.—**futil'ity** *n.*

fu'ture *n.* time to come.—*adj.* about to happen.—**futur'ity** *n.*—**future tense** (in Grammar) the form taken by a verb when it refers to an action which has not yet taken place, as *I shall go, he will have done*

fuzz *n.* fluff, down.—**fuz'zy** *adj.* 1. fluffy. 2. indistinct

G

gab'ardine, gab'erdine *n.* a 1. long loose upper garment. 2. a fine cloth

gab'ble *v.* to talk quickly (often without meaning)

ga'ble (gā'bl) *n.* the triangular piece of wall enclosed by a ridged roof

gad *v.* to wander restlessly in search of pleasure (usually followed by *about*).—**gad'ding** *pres. part.*—**gad'ded** *p.t.* and *p. part.*

gad'get *n.* a small appliance

Gaelic *n.* the language of the Scottish Highlands

gaff *n.* 1. a fishing spear. 2. a spar for extending top of sail

gag *n.* 1. something put in the mouth to prevent speech. 2. words inserted by actor in his part. 3. a funny story or phrase.—*v.* 1. to silence. 2. to insert words.—**gag'ging** *pres. part.*—**gagged** *p.t.* and *p. part.*

gage (gāj) *n.* 1. a pledge. 2. a challenge to fight.—*v.* to pledge, wager

gag'gle *n.* a flock of geese

gai'ety *n.* being gay, merriment.—**gai'ly** *adv.* joyously

gain *v.* 1. to obtain, as *He gained his object*. 2. to win, win over, as *He gained a prize. He gained the confidence of the new boy*. 3. to reach, as *He gained the shelter of the porch*. 4. (in) to improve, as *He gained in reputation as a result of his speeches*. 5. to make progress, as *He gained a hundred yards the second time round the course*.—*n.* profit, improvement.—**gain'ings** *n.pl.* profits *Compare:* achieve, attain, get, earn, procure. *Contrast:* lose, miss, surrender

gait *n.* a manner of walking

gai'ters *n.pl.* cloth coverings for the lower legs

ga'la *n.* a festive occasion

gal'ah *n.* (Aus.) 1. a grey, rose-crested cockatoo. 2. a stupid person

gal'axy *n.* 1. a vast cluster of stars, the Milky Way. 2. a brilliant company.—**gal'axies** *pl.*

gale *n.* a strong wind

gall (gawl) *n.* 1. bile. 2. bitterness

gall (gawl) *n.* a growth caused by insects on trees

gall (gawl) *n.* a painful swelling (esp. on a horse).—*v.* to make sore, irritate

gal'lant (or gal-lant') *adj.* 1. fine, brave. 2. gay. 3. very attentive to women.—*n.* 1. a man of fashion. 2. a lover.—**gal'lantly** *adv.*—**gal'lantry** *n.* 1. great courage. 2. polite attentions to ladies

gal'leon *n.* a three-decked sailing-ship of war

gal'lery *n.* 1. a long passage. 2. a balcony overlooking large hall. 3. a place for showing works of art.—**gal'leries** *pl.*

gal'ley *n.* 1. a vessel with sails and oars. 2. a frame used in printing. 3. a ship's kitchen. —**gal'ley-slave** *n.* a slave forced to row in a galley

gal'lon *n.* a liquid measure of four quarts

gal'lop *n.* 1. a horse's fastest pace, with all four feet off the ground together. 2. a ride.—*v.* to ride or go fast

gal'lows *n.pl.* a structure for hanging criminals

galore' *adv.* in plenty, as *He is making money galore at present*

galosh'es, golosh'es *n.pl.* (a pair of) overshoes

gal'vanise *v.* 1. to apply electric current to. 2. to rouse by shock, as *to galvanise a person into activity*

gam'ble *v.* 1. to play for money. 2. to risk much for gain.—*n.*—**gam'bling** *pres. part.*—**gam'bled** *p.t.* and *p. part.*—**gam'bler** *n.*

gam'bol *n.* a leap, caper.—*v.* to frisk.—**gam'bolling** *pres. part.*—**gam'bolled** *p.t.* and *p. part.*

game *n.* 1. sport, play, amusement. 2. animals and birds hunted. 3. their flesh.—*adj.* plucky.—**game'keeper** *n.* man employed to breed game, prevent poaching, etc.—**game'ster** *n.* gambler.—**the game is up** all has failed.—**to make game of** to mock.—**to play the game** to play fairly

gam'mon *n.* the lower end of a bacon-flitch

gam'ut *n.* 1. a whole series of musical notes. 2. the entire range

gan'der *n.* a farmyard bird.—**goose** *fem.*—**gos'ling** young goose or gander

gang *n.* a group of criminals, youths, workmen or slaves acting together

gan'grene (gang'green) *n.* decay of the flesh

gang'ster *n.* a member of a criminal gang

gang'way *n.* 1. a bridge from ship to shore. 2. a passage between rows of seats

gaol (jāl), **jail** *n.* a prison.—**gaol'er, jail'er, jail'or** *n.* a prison warder
gap *n.* 1. opening. 2. empty space
gape *v.* 1. to open wide (esp. the mouth), yawn. 2. to stare.—**ga'ping** *pres. part.*—**gaped** *p.t.* and *p. part.*—*n.* 1. a stare. 2. a yawn
gar'age (gar'ij, gar-ahzh') *n.* 1. a house for motor vehicles. 2. a repair-shop for cars
garb *n.* dress of a distinctive kind, as *he was dressed in clerical garb*
gar'bage (gar'bāj) *n.* rubbish, refuse
gar'bled *adj.* twisted, misrepresented, as *The prisoner gave the police a garbled version of what had happened*
gar'den *n.* ground for growing flowers, fruit or vegetables.—*v.* to cultivate a garden.—**gar'den ci'ty** *n.* a model, planned town in country surroundings.—**gar'dener** *n.*—**gar'den-party** *n.* a social gathering in a large garden.—**to lead up the garden path** to mislead
gargan'tuan *adj.* enormous
gar'gle *v.* to wash the throat without swallowing.—*n.* a throat-wash
gar'goyle *n.* a grotesquely carved water-spout
ga'rish *adj.* showy, glaring
gar'land *n.* a wreath of flowers, leaves, etc.
gar'lic *n.* a strong-smelling plant the bulb of which is used in cooking
gar'ment *n.* any article of dress
gar'ner *n.* a granary, store.—*v.* to store
gar'nish *v.* 1. to adorn. 2. to decorate (food).—*n.*
gar'ret *n.* attic, top floor room
gar'rison (gar'i-son) *n.* troops stationed at a fort.—*v.* to occupy with a garrison
gar'rulous *adj.* talkative.—**garru'lity** *n.*
gar'ter *n.* an elastic band to keep stocking up
gas *n.* 1. any air-like fluid occupying all available space. 2. coalgas (for lighting, heating, etc.). 3. a poisonous mixture used in warfare. 4. a gaseous mixture used as an anaesthetic.—**gas'es** *pl.*—*v.* to poison with gas.—**gas'sing** *pres. part.*—**gassed** *p.t.* and *p. part.*—**gas'eous** *adj.*—**gas'mask** *n.* anti-gas respirator.—**gasom'eter, gas'-holder** *n.* a storage tank for gas
gash *n.* a long, deep cut.—*v*
gas'oline, gas'olene *n.* (U.S.) petrol
gasp *v.* to pant with open mouth.—*n.*
gas'tric *adj.* belonging to the stomach.—**gastri'tis** *n.* a disorder of the stomach
gate *n.* 1. an opening in a wall, with barrier. 2. a barrier.—**gate'way** *n.*
gath'er *v.* 1. to collect, bring together. 2. to deduce, as *I gathered from his conversation that he was a stranger*. 3. to form pus, or matter, as *Some dirt got into the scratch and caused it to gather*.—**gath'ering** *n.* 1. assembly. 2. inflamed swelling
gauche (gōsh) *adj.* clumsy, awkward.—**gau'cherie** (gō'sher-ee) *n.*
gaud'y *adj.* showy.—**gaud'ily** *adv.*
gauge (gāj) *n.* 1. thickness of metal. 2. distance between railway-lines. 3. measure.—*v.* to measure, estimate capacity
gaunt *adj.* 1. lean, bony. 2. grim, desolate
Compare: thin, haggard, emaciated, spare
gaunt'let *n.* 1. an armoured glove worn by knights. 2. a glove with a wide cuff.—**to throw down the gauntlet** to issue a challenge.—**to run the gauntlet** to advance under continuous attack, or criticism
gauze *n.* a very thin fabric of silk, wire, etc.
gawk *n.* an awkward person.—**gawk'y** *adj.*—**gawk'iness** *n.*
gay *adj.* 1. merry, light-hearted. 2. brightly coloured
Compare: cheerful, happy, vivacious, bright, wanton, carefree. *Contrast:* sad, solemn, sober, grave, austere, sombre, serious
gaze *n.* a long fixed look.—*v.*—**ga'zing** *pres. part.*—**gazed** *p.t.* and *p. part.*
gazelle' *n.* a small, soft-eyed antelope
gazette' *n.* 1. a newspaper. 2. an official journal of announcements, promotions, bankruptcies. etc.
gazetteer' *n.* a geographical dictionary
gear (geer) *n.* 1. set of cog-wheels. 2. connection by which motor is brought into work. 3. apparatus, tools. 4. harness, equipment—**gear shift** *n.* the gear lever in a motor car. **in gear** connected to gearing system.—**out of gear** disconnected from gearing system
Gei'ger counter (gī'ger) *n.* an instrument sensitive to radioactive particles
gei'sha (gā'sha) *n.* a Japanese dancing girl
gel'atine, gel'atin (jel'a-teen) *n.* jelly-like substance obtained by boiling bones, etc.—**gelat'inous** *adj.*
gel'ignite (jel'ig-nīt) *n.* a high explosive
gem (jem) *n.* a precious stone, jewel.—*v.* to adorn with gems
gen'darme (zhon'darm) *n.* an armed French policeman
gen'der (jen'der) *n.* classification of nouns into masculine, feminine or neuter. Thus, *man* is *masculine gender; woman* is *feminine; parent* is *common* (i.e. because a parent may be either male or female); house is *neuter* (i.e. neither male nor female). In some languages there is no common or neuter gender
geneal'ogy (jeen-e-al'o-ji) *n.* the study of family history.—**geneal'ogies** *pl.*
gen'era (jen'er-a) *pl.* of **genus**
gen'eral (jen'er-al) *adj.* 1. wide-spread, belonging to many, as *a general impression*. 2. usual, as *the general practice*. 3. not precise, as *a general idea of what happened*.—*n.* the commander of an army.—**generalis'simo** *n.* a supreme commander.—**generalise** *v.* to make general rules or statements.—**general'ity** *n.* the main body.—**gen'erally** *adv.* usually
gen'erate (jen'er-āt) *v.* to produce.—

genera'tion (-ā'shun) *n.* 1. bringing into being. 2. a step in the descent of a family, as *The grandfather, the father and the son belong to three different generations.* 3. people born in the same period. 4. about 30 years.—**gen'erator** *n.* an apparatus for producing (electricity, etc.)

generos'ity (jen-eros'i-ti) *n.* unselfishness, liberality.—**gen'erous** *adj.* 1. noble-minded. 2. giving freely.—**gen'erously** *adv.*

Compare: (with generous) kind, charitable, liberal, hospitable, munificent, open-handed. *Contrast:* mean, parsimonious, stingy, close-fisted

gen'esis (jen'e-sis) *n.* the origin, beginning

ge'nial (jee'ni-al) *adj.* kindly, pleasant, as *a genial smile, the genial warmth of the sun's rays.*—**ge'nially** *adv.*

ge'nie (jee'ni) *n.* in Eastern tales, a demon or goblin.—**ge'nii** *pl.*

ge'nius (jee'ni-us) *n.* 1. exceptional ability. 2. a person with this high ability.—**gen'iuses** *pl.*

genteel' (jen-teel') *adj.* well-bred, polite (often used sarcastically or jokingly to mean excessively polite).—**gentil'ity** *n.*

gen'tile (jen'til) *adj.* not Jewish.—*n.*

gen'tle (jen'tl) *adj.* 1. mild, quiet. 2. polite. 3. well-born.—**gen'tleman** *n.* a well-bred man.—**gen'tleness** *n.*—**gen'tlewoman** *n.* a lady.—**gent'ly** *adv.*—**gent'ry** *n.* the class below nobility

Contrast: harsh, severe, fierce, vigorous, hard

gen'uine (jen'ū-in) *adj.* real, true.—**genuinely** *adv.*—**gen'uineness** *n.*

Contrast: false, spurious, counterfeit, artificial, insincere

gen'us (jen'us) *n.* a race, kind, class.—**gen'era** *pl.*

geog'raphy (jee-og'ra-fi) *n.* the science of the earth's form, physical features, products, peoples, etc.—**geographi'cal** *adj.*

geol'ogy (jee-ol'o-ji) *n.* the science of the earth's crust, the rocks, their layers, etc.—**geolog'ical** *adj.*—**geol'ogist** *n.*

geom'etry (jee-om'e-tri) *n.* the science of dimensions, of lines, surfaces and solids.—**geomet'rical** *adj.*

germ (jerm) *n.* 1. a bud or seed. 2. a beginning 3. a tiny plant or animal causing disease.—**ger'micide** (jer'mi-sīd) *n.* germ-killer

ger'minate *v.* to sprout, shoot.—**germina'tion** (-a'-shun) *n.*

Ger'many *n.* a country in northern Europe.—**Ger'man** *adj.* and *n.*

gestic'ulate (jes-tik'ū-lāt) *v.* to make lively movements to show feelings.—**gesticula'tion** (-a'shun) *n.*

ges'ture (jes'tūr) *n.* a movement to convey an idea or feeling.—*v.*

get *v.* 1. to obtain, fetch, as. *Please get me the book.* 2. to become, as *to get rich.* 3. to persuade, as *I will get him to come.* 4. to reach, as *We were glad when we got there.*—**get'ting** *pres. part.*—**got, gat** (old form) *p.t.*—**got, got'ten** (U.S.) *p. part.*

Note: Get is used for a variety of purposes, and is often an overworked word. It is used, too, in many phrases, such as *get away* (escape), *get on* (manage, succeed, agree,) *get up* (rise from bed). Note the difference between *She has* (i.e. possesses) *a new hat* and *She has got* (i.e. obtained, bought—U.S. *gotten*) *a new hat*

gey'ser (gā'zer, gī'zer) *n.* 1. a hot spring spouting water. 2. apparatus for heating water (often pronounced *gee'zer*)

Gha'na (gah'na) *n.* a country in Africa.—**Ghanai'an** (ga-nā'an) *n.* a native of Ghana

ghast'ly (gahst'li) *adj.* 1. horrible. 2. very pale.—*adv.*—**ghast'lier** *comp.*—**ghast'liest** *sup.*

gher'kin *n.* a small pickled cucumber

ghet'to *n.* 1. the Jewish quarter of a city. 2. slum section of a city exclusively occupied by members of one race

ghost (gōst) *n.* a spirit, apparition.—**ghost'ly** *adj.*

ghoul (gōōl) *n.* a demon

gi'ant (jī'ant) *n.* a huge, or very powerful person.—*adj.* huge

gib'ber (jib'er) *v.* to chatter like a monkey.—**gib'berish** (j- or g-) *n.* senseless talk

gib'ber *n.* (Aus.) a boulder or stone.—**gibber country, gibber plain** an inland area covered with stones

gib'bet (jib'et) *n.* a gallows

gibe, jibe *n.* a sneer, jeer.—*v.* to mock

gid'dy *adj.* 1. dizzy, having a swimming in the head. 2. frivolous.—**gid'diness** *n.*

gift *n.* 1. a thing given, a present. 2. ability, talent, as *To be able to sing well is a gift.*—**gift'ed** *adj.* talented.—**do not look a gift horse in the mouth** do not criticise a gift

gig *n.* 1. light, two-wheeled carriage. 2. a light boat

gig *v.* (Aus.) to provoke, taunt, irritate

gigan'tic (jī-gan'tik) *adj.* huge

gig'gle *v.* to laugh stupidly.—*n.*

gild *v.* to overlay with gold.—**gil'ded** *p.t.*—**gilt, gil'ded** *p. part.*

gild see **guild**

gill (jil) *n.* a measure, one fourth of a pint

gill *n.* a breathing organ in fishes

gilt *n.* gold leaf, gold paint for gilding.—*p. part.* of **gild**

gim'let *n.* a small tool with screw point for boring holes

gim'mick *n.* 1. a gadget, a showy but unnecessary device. 2. a personal characteristic used to attract attention or win publicity

gin (jin) *n.* a snare, trap

gin (jin) *n.* a liquor,

gin (jin) *n.* an Aborigine woman

gin'ger (jin'jer) *n.* a plant with hot-tasting root, used in cooking and candies.—**ginger beer'** *n.* aerated water flavoured with ginger.—**gin'gerbread** *n.* ginger-flavoured cake

gin'gerly (jin'jer-li) *adv.* cautiously

ging'ham (ging'am) *n.* a cotton cloth usually checked

gip'sy (jip'-si) *n.* one of a dark-skinned wandering race.—**gip'sies, gyp'sies** *pl.*

giraffe' (ji-raf') *n.* an African grazing animal with long neck and legs

gird *v.* 1. to put a belt round. 2. to encircle, surround.—**girt, gir'ded** *p.t.* and *p. part.*

gir'dle *n.* a belt.—*v.* to surround

gir'der *n.* a strong beam

girl *n.* 1. a female child. 2. a young woman.—**boy** *masc.*—**girl'hood** *n.*—**girl'ish** *adj.*

girth *n.* 1. a strap fixing a saddle on a horse. 2. the measurement round anything

gist (jist) *n.* the main point (of remarks, etc.)

give *v.* 1. to hand over, offer as a present. 2. to supply. 3. to yield.—**giv'ing** *pres. part.*—**gave** *p.t.*—**giv'en** *p. part.*—**giv'er** *n.*—**to give chase** to pursue.—**to give in** 1. to hand in. 2. to yield.—**to give off** to emit a scent etc. —**to give out** to distribute.—**to give rise to** to cause.—**to give up** to surrender, to abandon.—**to give way** to fall back, to withdraw

Compare: present (*v.*), endow, endue, donate, provide. *Contrast:* take (away), deprive, denude, remove

giz'zard *n.* a bird's second stomach for grinding food

gla'cial (glā'shl) *adj.* icy

gla'cier (glā'si-er) *n.* a slow-moving mass of ice in valleys between high mountains

glad *adj.* happy, pleased.—**glad'den** *v.* to make glad.—**glad'ly** *adv.*—**glad'ness** *n.*

glade *n.* an open space in a wood

glad'iator *n.* a trained fighter in the arenas of ancient Rome

glam'our *n.* magic, charm.—**glam'orous** *adj.*—**glam'orise** *v.* to make attractive

glance (glans) *n.* a brief look.—*v.* 1. to look quickly. 2. to strike at a slant and fly off. —**glan'cing** *pres. part.* and *adj.*—**glanced** *p.t.* and *p. part.*

gland *n.* an organ of the body which separates and absorbs certain substances of the blood.—**glandu'lar** *adj.*

glare (glār) *n.* 1. a blinding light. 2. a fierce stare.—*v.* 1. to shine dazzlingly. 2. to stare.—**gla'ring** *pres. part.*—**glared** *p.t.* and *p. part.*

gla'ring (glā'ring) *adj.* 1. very bright. 2. fierce. 3. conspicuous, evident, flagrant, as *a glaring mistake*

glass *n.* 1. a hard, transparent substance. 2. things made of it. 3. a glass drinking-vessel. 4. a lens, telescope, barometer.—*pl.* spectacles.—**glass'ware** *n.*—**glas'sy** *adj.* —**glass wool** *n.* a mass of fine glass fibres used as insulating material

glaze (glāz) *v.* 1. to furnish with glass. 2. to give a glassy finish.—*n.* a smooth coating. —**gla'zier** *n.* one who fits glass windows

gleam (gleem) *n.* a flash of light.—*v.*

glean *v.* 1. to gather, after reapers, in a corn-field. 2. to pick up (facts).—**glea'ner** *n.*

glee *n.* 1. mirth, delight. 2. part-song, round.—**glee'ful** *adj.*

glen *n.* a narrow river valley

glib *adj.* smooth-tongued, speaking too easily to be sincere, specious, as *He was very glib with his excuses*

glide (glīd) *v.* to move smoothly and continuously.—**gli'ding** *pres. part.*—**gli'ded** *p.t.* and *p. part.*—*n.*—**gli'der** *n.* an aircraft without engine

glim'mer *v.* to shine faintly.—*n.*.—**glim'mering** *n.* 1. a gleam. 2. a faint idea

glimpse *n.* a brief view

glint *v.* to flash, glitter.—*n.*

glis'ten (glis'n) *v.* to glitter, sparkle

glit'ter *v.* to shine brightly with flashes of light, sparkle.—*n.*

gloam'ing *n.* twilight, dusk

gloat (over) *v.* 1. to look at greedily, as *The miser gloated over his money-bags.* 2. to rejoice unpleasantly, as *He gloated over his fallen enemies*

globe *n.* 1. a ball, sphere. 2. the earth.—**glo'bal** *adj.* world wide.—**glob'ular** *adj.*—**glob'ule** *n.* small round particle, drop

gloom *n.* 1. darkness. 2. depression.—**gloom'y** *adj.*—**gloom'ily** *adv.*

Compare: sadness, melancholy, moroseness. *Contrast:* light, brightness, joy, happiness

glo'rify *v.* to exalt, make glorious.—he **glor'ifies.**—**glor'ifying** *pres. part.*—**glor'ified** *p.t.* and *p. part.*—**glorifica'tion** *n.*—**glor'ious** *adj.* 1. full of glory. 2. splendid

Compare: (with glorious) magnificent, grand, noble, illustrious. *Contrast:* inglorious, ignoble, wretched

glo'ry *n.* 1. splendour, brightness. 2. praise. 3. fame.—**glo'ries** *pl.*—*v.* to take pride in. —he **glo'ries.**—**glo'rying** *pres. part.*—**glo'ried** *p.t.* and *p. part.*

gloss *n.* a surface brightness.—**gloss'y** *adj.*

glos'sary *n.* a dictionary or vocabulary of special words.—**glos'saries** *pl.*

glove (gluv) *n.* a covering for the hand.—**glove'fight** *n.* a boxing-match.—**glov'er** *n.* a dealer in gloves.—**to throw down the glove** to challenge.—**hand in glove with** closely associated with

glow (glō) *v.* 1. to give light and heat without flames. 2. to look hot. 3. to burn with emotion, e.g. anger, pride, etc.—*n.* 1. shining heat. 2. ardour.—**glow'worm** *n.* insect, female of which emits green light

glow'er *v.* to look angrily

glu'cose (glōō'kōs) *n.* sugar obtained from fruit

glue (glōō) *n.* a sticky substance obtained from animal tissue.—*v.* to fasten with glue.—**glu'ey** *adj.*

glum *adj.* sullen, dejected

glut *v.* 1. to feed greedily. 2. to overfill.—

n. excess, as *There was such a glut of fruit that the growers did not know what to do with it*

glu'tinous (glōō'-tin-us) *adj.* sticky

glut'ton *n.* 1. a person who overeats. 2. an over-eager person, as *He is a glutton for work.*—**glut'tonous** *adj.*—**glut'tony** *n.*

gly'cerine (glis'er-een) *n.* a thick colourless liquid obtained from oils, used in medicine and in making explosives

gnarled (narld) *adj.* knotty, twisted

gnash (nash) *v.* to grind (the teeth)

gnat (nat) *n.* a small blood-sucking fly

gnaw (naw) *v.* 1. to bite steadily. 2. to wear away

gnome (nōm) a small underground goblin

gnu (nū) *n.* a South African antelope

go *v.* 1. to move, proceed. 2. to depart. 3. to become, as *go mad, go white.* 4. to stop functioning, as *The light bulb has gone.* 5. to make a sound. as *The cow goes "moo."* 6. to be sold for, as *The house went for a very low price.*—he goes (gōz).—**go'ing** *pres. part.*—**went** *p.t.*—**gone** (gawn) *p. part.*—*n.* 1. energy. 2. attempt, as *to have a go.*—**go-ahead'** *adj.* enterprising.—**go'-between** *n.* a middleman acting between two other people.—**go'-car** *n.* a small carriage for a child.—**go'-kart** *n.* a miniature racing car.—**go-slow** organised reduction of output by workers.—**goings-on'** *n.pl.* happenings.—**go-as-you-please** easy-going.—**going concern** a business in working order.—**on the go** active.—**to go bad** to decay.—**to go for** to strive for, to attack.—**to have a go** to try.—**to let oneself** go to be unrestrained

goad (gōd) *n.* a spiked stick for driving cattle. —*v.* to prick, urge on

goal (gōl) *n.* 1. a winning post. 2. purpose, destination, objective. 3. posts between which a football is to be driven

goat (gōt) *n.* a cloven-hooved animal with long hair, horns and beard

gob'ble *v.* to eat quickly and noisily.—**gob'bling** *pres. part.*—**gob'bled** *p.t.* and *p. part.*

gob'let *n.* a drinking-cup

gob'lin *n.* a mischievous spirit

God *n.* the Supreme Being, the Creator.—**god'ly** *adj.* pious, holy.—**god'head** *n.* God.—**god** *n.* idol, heathen deity.—**god'dess** *fem.*

god'child *n.* a baptised child in relation to a **god'parent (god'father, god'mother)**

gog'gle *v.* 1. to roll the eyes 2. to stare stupidly.—*n.pl.* protective spectacles

gold (gōld) *n.* 1. a yellow precious metal. 2. coins of this. 3. wealth.—*adj.* yellow.—**gol'den** *adj.*—**gold'fish** *n.* a Chinese carp —**a golden opportunity** an excellent chance.—**golden wedding** a fiftieth anniversary

golf (or gof) *n.* a game played with ball and clubs on a **golf-course** or **golf-links**

golosh'es see **galosh'es**

gon'dola *n.* a Venetian canal-boat.—**gondolier'** *n.* a gondola boatman

gong *n.* a suspended metal disc which booms when struck

good *n.* 1. well-being, benefit, as *it is for your own good.* 2. (short for goodness) moral excellence, as *good is better than evil.*—*adj.* 1. well-behaved, as *a good dog.* 2. virtuous, as *a good deed.* 3. well done, as *a good piece of work.* 4. suitable, as *this dress is a good fit.* 5. sound, as *a car in good condition.*—**bet'ter** *comp.*—**best** *super.* —*interject.* splendid!—**good'ness** *n.*—**good'ly** *adj.* 1. large. 2. handsome.—**Good Friday** the Friday before Easter Sunday.—**a good many** a fairly large number.—**a good while** a fair length of time.—**all in good time** in due course, at the proper time.—**good-humoured** patient, cheerful.—**good-mannered** polite.—**good-natured** obliging.—**to be good for a number of years** likely to last a number of years.—**to be good for nothing** to be worthless.—**to make good** to succeed after a bad start.—**to be up to no good** to be engaged in something wrong

goods *n.pl.* property, merchandise.—**goods train** a train carrying goods and material only

good'bye *interject.* farewell

goodwill' *n.* 1. kindly feeling, favour. 2. the value of the reputation and popularity of a business or shop, as *When he bought the shop he paid* £500 *for the goodwill*

goo'gly *n.* a ball in cricket which breaks from the off although apparently bowled as a leg-break

goose (gōōs) *n.* 1. a large, web-footed bird. 2. a simpleton.—**gan'der** *masc.*—**geese** *pl.*—**goose'berry** *n.* a soft fruit.—**goose'-flesh** *n.* bristling state of skin due to cold or fright.—**goose'step** *n.* soldier's parade step

gore *n.* 1. blood. 2. a triangular piece stitched into a garment.—*v.* to pierce with horns.—**go'ry** *adj.* bloody

gorge (gorj) *n.* 1. the inside of the throat. 2. a narrow pass between mountains.—*v.* to eat greedily

gor'geous (gor'jus) *adj.* splendid, dazzling
Compare: glorious, brilliant, superb, luxurious, magnificent. *Contrast:* sordid, mean, drab, plain

goril'la *n.* the largest ape

gorse *n.* a thick, prickly, shrub

gos'ling (goz'ling) *n.* a young goose

gos'pel *n.* 1. glad tidings. 2. one of the four Gospels in the New Testament

gos'samer *n.* 1. a filmy substance of spider's web floating loose or spread on grass. 2. a delicate gauze.—*adj.* flimsy

gos'sip *n.* 1. idle talk. 2. a person who spreads false rumours.—*v.* to chatter

Goth *n.* a member of an ancient German tribe.—**Goth'ic** *adj.* a mediaeval style of architecture with long pointed arches

gouge (gowj) *n.* a chisel with curved blade.—*v.* to scoop out

gourd (gōōrd) *n.* 1. a fleshy many-seeded fruit (e.g. melon). 2. its rind used as a vessel

gout (gowt) *n.* a swelling of the joints.—**gout'y** *adj.*

gov'ern (guv'ern) *v.* to rule, control.—**gov'erness** *n.* a woman teacher in a private house.—**gov'ernment** *n.* 1. management. 2. body of persons in charge of the state.—**governmen'tal** *adj.*—**gov'ernor** *n.* ruler.—**gov'ernor-general** *n.* the governor of a dominion

Compare: direct, administer, superintend, command, order, conduct. *Contrast:* obey, comply, submit, be subject to

gown *n.* 1. a dress, robe. 2. a loose robe worn by students, graduates, lawyers, etc.

grab *v.* to snatch, seize.—**grab'bing** *pres. part.*—**grabbed** *p.t.* and *p. part.*—*n.* 1. an excavating bucket hung from a crane. 2. sudden clutch

grace (grās) *n.* 1. charm. 2. favour, kindness. 3. God's blessing. 4. short prayer before or after meals. 5. title of duke, archbishop (addressed as *Your Grace*, and spoken of as *His Grace*).—*v.* to honour, adorn.—**grace'ful** *adj.* pleasing.—**grace'less** *adj.* shameless.—**in the good graces of** held in esteem by.—**in the year of grace** in the christian year.—**with good grace** showing willingness

gra'cious (grā'shus) *adj.* 1. friendly, pleasant. 2. condescending, indulgent.—**gra'cious** *adv.*

grade *n.* 1. step, stage. 2. degree, rank, class. 3. slope.—**grada'tion** (gra-dā'shun) *n.* series of degrees.—**gra'dient** (grā'di-ent) *n.* degree of slope.—**grad'ual** (grad'u-al) *adj.* by degrees.—**grad'ually** *adv.*

grad'uate (grad'ū-āt) *v.* to take a university degree.—*n.* (grad'u-at) the holder of a degree.—**grad'uation** (-ā'shun) *n.*

graft *n.* 1. a shoot of one plant set in a slit of another to grow there. 2. self-advancement or profit by unfair means, political influence, etc. 3. hard work.—*v.* 1. to make a graft. 2. to toil

grain *n.* 1. the seed or fruit of a cereal plant. 2. a small particle. 3. the lie of the fibres in wood.—**grain'ing** *n.* markings on wood

gram'mar *n.* 1. the correct use of words, study of structure and usages of a language. 2. a book on this.—**gramma'rian** (gram-mā'ri-an) *n.* person skilled in grammar.—**gram'mar school** *n.* secondary school.—**grammat'ical** *adj.* 1. of grammar. 2. according to rules of grammar

gramme, gram *n.* a unit of weight in the metric system

gram'ophone *n.* a record player, an instrument reproducing recorded sounds

gran'ary *n.* a storehouse for grain.—**gran'aries** *pl.*

grand *adj.* 1. fine, splendid. 2. chief. 3. final, as *The grand total was £500.*—**grand'child** *n.* child of son or daughter (**grand'son** or **grand'daughter**).—**gran'deur** (gran'dūr) *n.* majesty.—**grand'father** *n.* the father of a parent.—**grand'mother** *fem.*

Compare: august, majestic, great, illustrious, magnificent, superb, stately, sublime, exalted. *Contrast:* lowly, humble, mean, poor

Note: Grand is used in the following phrases and expressions: *grandstand* (principal stand for races, sports, etc.), *grand piano* (horizontal piano), *grand opera* (tragic opera with dialogue set to music throughout)

grandil'oquence *n.* a pompous style of speech or writing.—**grandil'oquent** *adj.*—**grandil'oquently** *adv.*

gran'diose *adj.* 1. imposing. 2. pompously, grand

grange (grānj) *n.* 1. a granary. 2. a country-house with farm buildings

gran'ite (gran'it) *n.* a very hard stone

grant *v.* 1. to allow, as *I grant you are right in your reasoning.* 2. to give, bestow, as *William the Conqueror granted estates to his followers.*—*n.* a gift, allowance

Compare: impart, convey, admit, concede. *Contrast:* deny, refuse, withstand, withhold

gran'ulate *v.* to make into grains.—**gran'ular** *adj.*—**gran'ule** *n.* small grain

grape *n.* the fruit of the vine from which wine is made.—**grape'fruit** *n.* a large yellow citrus fruit.—**grape'shot** *n.* pellets fired in clusters from gun

graph (graf) *n.* a drawing showing symbolically a series of relationships (often used in mathematical demonstrations and drawn on squared paper)

graph'ic (graf'ik) *adj.* 1. related to drawing, painting, writing, etc. 2. vividly descriptive.—**graphi'cally** *adv.*

graph'ite *n.* a form of shiny carbon used in pencils

grap'nel *n.* a kind of anchor

grap'ple *n.* a close grip.—*v.* to seize firmly.—**grap'pling** *pres. part.*—**grap'pled** *p.t.* and *p. part.*

grasp *v.* 1. to seize firmly. 2. to understand.—*n.* 1. hand-grip. 2. possession as *in the enemy's grasp.* 3. understanding, as *He has a complete grasp of the subject.*—**gras'ping** *adj.* greedy

grass *n.* low-lying, green plants that cover fields and lawns.—**grass'hopper** *n.* a jumping insect.—**gras'sy** *adj.*

grate *n.* a fire-place.—**gra'ting** *n.* a framework of crossed bars

grate *v.* 1. to scrape on a rough surface. 2. to scrape into small pieces as *to grate cheese.* 3. to make a harsh sound. 4. to irritate, as *His laughter grates on my nerves.*—**gra'ting** *pres. part.*—**gra'ted** *p.t.* and *p. part.*—**gra'ting** *adj.* harsh

grate'ful *adj.* thankful.—**grate'fully** *adv.*

gratifica'tion (-ā'shun) *n.* satisfaction.—**grat'ify** *v.* to please, satisfy.—he **grat'ifies.** —**grat'ifying** *pres. part.*—**grat'ified** *p.t.* and *p. part.*

gra'tis (grā'tis, grat'is) *adv.* free of charge, as *admission is gratis*

grat'itude *n.* thankfulness

gratu'itous *adj.* 1. given free. 2. uncalled for, as *a gratuitous insult.*—**gratu'ity** *n.* a tip, present.—**gratu'ities** *pl.*

grave *n.* 1. a hole in the ground for burial. 2. death.—**grave'stone** *n.* a carved stone over a grave.—**grave'yard** *n.* a cemetery

grave *adj.* 1. serious. 2. solemn.—**grave'ly** *adv.*

Compare: severe, weighty, important, dangerous. *Contrast:* light, frivolous, unimportant, insignificant

grav'el *n.* small stones, coarse sand.—*v.* 1. to cover with gravel. 2. to puzzle, perplex

gra'ven *adj.* carved

grav'itate *v.* 1. to move by force of attraction. 2. to settle.—**gravita'tion** (-shun) *n.*

grav'ity *n.* 1. a force which draws all bodies to the earth. 2. seriousness, importance.—**specific gravity** the weight of a substance compared with the weight of an equal volume of water

gra'vy (grā'vi) *n.* juice from meat in cooking. —**gra'vies** *pl.*

graze *v.* 1. to feed on growing grass. 2. to touch lightly in passing. 3. to scrape the skin from.—**gra'zing** *pres. part.*—**grazed** *p.t.* and *p. part.*

grease (grees) *n.* animal fat oil.—*v.* to put grease on.—**greas'ing** *pres. part.*—**greased** *p.t.* and *p. part.*—**greas'y** *adj.*

great (grāt) *adj.* 1. large. 2. important. 3. distinguished.—**great'er** *comp.*—**great'est** *sup.*—**great-grand'father** *n.* father of grandparent.—**great-grand'mother** *fem.*—**great'ness** *n.*

Compare: immense, enormous, colossal, grand, serious, mighty, extreme. *Contrast:* small, little, puny, unimportant, insignificant

Greece *n.* a country by the Mediterranean sea.—**Greek** *n.* 1. a native of Greece. 2. the language of Greece.—**Gre'cian** (-shan) *adj.*

greed *n.* wanting too much.—**greed'ily** *adv.*—**greed'iness** *n.*—**greed'y** *adj.* 1. gluttonous. 2. over-eager for food, money, etc.—**greed'ier** *comp.*—**greed'iest** *sup.*

green *adj.* 1. the colour of grass. 2. unripe, inexperienced.—*n.* grass-covered ground. —**green'ish** *adj.*—**green'ness** *n.*—**green belt** an area round a town where building is forbidden.—**green'fly** *n.* a small green insect, an aphis.—**green'gage** *n.* a small green plum.—**green'grocer** *n.* a dealer in vegetables and fruit.—**green'heart** *n.* a variety of hard W. Indian timber.—**green'horn** *n.* a simpleton.—**green'house** *n.* a glasshouse for plants.—**green light** permission to proceed.—**greenstone** a popular name of nephrite, a stone found on the west coast of N.Z., used to make ornaments.—**green room** *n.* a room for actors off-stage

greet *v.* to salute, hail.—**greet'ing** *n.*

grega'rious *adj.* 1. living in flocks. 2. fond of company or crowds

grenade' *n.* a small bomb.—**grenadier'** (-deer) *n.* 1. formerly a soldier who shot or threw grenades. 2. a soldier of the Grenadier Guards

grey *adj.* 1. between black and white in colour. 2. dismal.—**grey'beard** *n.* an old man.—**grey'hound** *n.* a swift slender hound used in coursing and racing.—**grey nurse** a ferocious shark found off E. Australia

grid *n.* 1. a frame of bars. 2. a national network of electric cables. 3. system of numbered squares printed on maps for map reference.—**grid'iron** *n.* a cooking utensil with bars

grief (greef) *n.* deep sorrow.—**griefs** *pl.*

Compare: unhappiness, misery, mourning. *Contrast:* joy, rejoicing, happiness

griev'ance (gree'vans) *n.* a real or imaginary wrong

grieve *v.* 1. to feel sorrow. 2. to cause grief.—**griev'ing** *pres. part.*—**grieved** *p.t.* and *p. part.*—**griev'ous** *adj.* painful, severe

grif'fin, grif'fon, gryph'on *n.* a fabulous monster with eagle's head and wings and lion's body

grill *n.* 1. a gridiron. 2. food cooked on one.—*v.* 1. to cook on a grill. 2. to question very thoroughly

grille *n.* a screen of metal bars

grim *adj.* stern, fierce.—**grim'mer** *comp.*—**grim'mest** *sup.*—**grim'ly** *adv.*

grimace' (grim-ās') *n.* a twisting of the face.—*v.*

grime *n.* dirt.—**gri'my** *adj.*

grin *n.* a broad smile.—*v.* to smile.—**grin'ning** *pres. part.*—**grinned** *p.t.* and *p. part.*

grind (grīnd) *v.* 1. to crush to powder. 2. to oppress (often used with *down*). 3. to sharpen, as *to grind knives, scissors, etc.*—**ground** *p.t.* and *p. part.*—*n.* grinding.—**grind'stone** *n.* a flat round stone with a handle, for grinding knives

grip *n.* 1. grasp, firm hold. 2. mastery. 3. handle, holder. 4. a small suitcase.—*v.* to grasp.—**grip'ping** *pres. part.*—**gripped**

p.t. and *p. part.*—**gripe** *v.* 1. to seize. 2. to oppress

gris'ly (griz'li) *adj.* horrifying, gruesome

grist *n.* 1. corn to be ground. 2. profit

gris'tle (grisl) *n.* hard, elastic tissue in the body.—**gris'tly** (gris'ly) *adj.*

grit *n.* 1. sand, gravel. 2. courage.—*v.* to grind (esp. the teeth).—**grit'ting** *pres. part.*—**grit'ted** *p.t.* and *p. part.*—**grit'ty** *adj.*

griz'zled *adj.* grey-haired.—**griz'zly** *adj.* greyish.—**grizzly bear** a large fierce North American bear

groan *n.* a sound of grief or pain.—*v.*

groat *n.* an old English silver coin no longer in use

gro'cer (grō'ser) *n.* a dealer in tea, sugar, etc.—**gro'cery** *n.* a grocer's shop.—**gro'ceries** *n.pl.* his wares

grog *n.* rum (or whisky) and water

groom *n.* 1. a servant in charge of horses. 2. a bridegroom.—*v.* 1. to tend (a horse). 2. (oneself) to make oneself clean and smart. —**grooms'man** *n.* the "best man" at a wedding

groove *n.* 1. a furrow, channel. 2. rut, routine. —*v.* to cut a groove

grope *v.* to feel about, search blindly.—**gro'ping** *pres. part.*—**groped** *p.t.* and *p. part.*

gro'per *n.* (Aus. and N.Z.) a large edible sea-fish, kind of rock cod

gross (grōs) *adj.* 1. coarse, big. 2. thick, solid. 3. very bad, as *a gross blunder*. 4. total (without any deductions, as distinct from net).—*n.* twelve dozen.—**gross'ly** *adv.*

Compare: rank, overfed, indecent, flagrant. *Contrast:* abstemious, delicate, refined

grotesque' (grō-tesk') *adj.* distorted, odd, absurd.—**grotesque'ly** *adv.*

grot'to *n.* a cave.—**grot'toes** *pl.*

ground (grownd) *n.* 1. the surface of the earth. 2. a piece of land. 3. reason, motive (usually in *pl.*, as *What grounds of complaint have you?*).—*pl.* 1. dregs. 2. the land round a house.—*v.* 1. to instruct thoroughly, as *He was well grounded in Latin.* 2. to run ashore. 3. to compel to stay on the ground as *All aircraft were grounded by fog yesterday.*—**ground'less** *adj.* without reason, as *groundless suspicions.*—**ground' bait** *n.* bait thrown to the bottom of water to attract fish.—**ground'nut** *n.* a peanut.—**ground'sheet** *n.* a waterproof camping sheet.—**ground floor** the floor of a building level with the ground

group (grōōp) *n.* number of persons or things together.—*v.* to place together.—**group captain** *n.* an Air Force officer of equivalent rank to an army colonel

Compare: assembly, party, congregation, crowd, company, flock

grouse (grows) *n.* a game bird.—grouse *pl.*

grouse *v.* to grumble.—*n.*—**grouser** *n.*

grove *n.* a small wood

grov'el *v.* 1. to lie face downwards in fear. 2. to crawl at the feet of, abase oneself.—**grov'elling** *pres. part.*—**grov'elled** *p.t.* and *p. part.*

grow (grō) *v.* 1. to increase in size. 2. to be produced, as *grass grows in fields.* 3. to become, as *We grow older every day.* 4. to raise (crops, etc.).—**grew** (grōō) *p.t.*—**grown** *p. part.*—**grow'er** *n.*

growl *v.* 1. to make an angry sound. 2. to complain.—*n.*

growth (grōth) *n.* 1. development. 2. increase. 3. what has grown or is growing, as *a growth of hair on the chin*

grub *n.* 1. larva of an insect. 2. (slang) food.—*v.* (up) to dig, root out.—**grub'bing** *pres. part.*—**grubbed** *p.t.* and *p. part.*—**grub'by** *adj.* dirty

grudge (gruj) *n.* a feeling of ill-will.—*v.* to give or allow unwillingly.—**grudg'ingly** *adv.*

gru'el *n.* thin boiled oatmeal

grue'some (grōō'sum) *adj.* horrible

Compare: fearful, frightening, frightful, weird, uncanny, shocking, blood-curdling

gruff *adj.* rough and deep in voice and speech, abrupt in manner.—**gruff'ly** *adv.*

grum'ble *v.* to complain, murmur.—*n.* complaint.—**grumb'ling** *n.*

grum'py *adj.* cross, bad-tempered.—**grum'pily** *adv.*

grunt *n.* the noise a pig makes.—*v.*

guarantee' (gar-an-tee') *n.* 1. promise to pay if someone else fails to do so. 2. promise to replace goods if unsatisfactory.—*v.* to answer for, give a guarantee for.—**guarantee'ing** *pres. part.*—**guaranteed'** *p.t.* and *p. part.*—**guar'antor** *n.* person giving guarantee

guard (gard) *n.* 1. defence. 2. watch, sentry. 3. official in charge of train.—*v.* to protect, defend.—**guar'ded** *adj.* cautious.—**guar'dian** *n.* 1. a person in charge of a child. 2. keeper, protector.—**guar'dianship** *n.*—**guard'room** *n.* a room for prisoners.—**guards'man** *n.* a soldier in the Guards

Compare: (with *v.*) keep, retain, maintain, hold. *Contrast:* lose, abandon, betray, relinquish

gueril'la (ger-il'a) *n.* one carrying on irregular warfare as one of a band.—*adj.*

guess (ges) *v.* to form an opinion without knowing.—*n.* a conjecture.—**guess'work** *n.*

guest (gest) *n.* a visitor in a private house or hotel

guffaw' *n.* a loud, ugly laugh.—*v.*

gui'dance (gī'dans) *n.* leadership, showing someone the way

guide (gīd) *n.* a leader, person showing the way.—*v.* to lead, direct.—**gui'ding** *pres. part.*—**gui'ded** *p.t.* and *p. part.*—**guide'book** *n.* a traveller's book of information. —**guided missile** a projectile guided to its target by radio

guild, gild *n.* 1. formerly, a company of

merchants or craftsmen, corporation. 2. a society for some common purpose.—**guildhall'** *n.*

guil'der *n.* a Dutch silver coin

guile (gīl) *n.* cunning, deceit.—**guile'ful** *adj.*—**guile'fully** *adv.*—**guile'less** *adj.* simple

guill'otine (gil'ō-teen) *n.* 1. a machine for beheading. 2. a printer's machine for cutting paper.—*v.* to behead

guilt (gilt) *n.* wrong-doing.—**guilt'less** *adj.* innocent.—**guilt'y** *adj.* deserving punishment.—**guil'tier** *comp.*—**guil'tiest** *sup.*

gui'nea (gin'i) *n.* a British monetary unit no longer in use

guise (gīz) *n.* 1. dress. 2. appearance.

guitar' (gi-tar') *n.* a six-stringed musical instrument, played with the fingers

gulf *n.* 1. a large bay. 2. an abyss.—**gulfs** *pl.*

gull *n.* a long-winged sea-bird.—*v.* to deceive, trick.—**gul'lible** *adj.* easily fooled

gul'let *n.* the food-passage from mouth to stomach

gul'ly *n.* 1. a channel or ravine worn by water. 2. (Carrib.) a watercourse, often artificial. —**gul'lies** *pl.*

gulp *v.* 1. to swallow hastily. 2. to gasp, choke

gum *n.* 1. sticky juice of trees. 2. the flesh in which teeth are set. 3. a fluid for sticking. 4. chewing-gum.—*v.* to stick with gum.—**gum'boots** *n.pl.* rubber boots.—**gum, gum tree** *n.* a popular name for any species of eucalyptus of which there are more than 100 varieties.—**up a gum tree** in a difficult situation.—**gum digger** *n.* (N.Z.) 1. a digger for resinous gum on the sites of ancient kauri forests. 2. a dentist.—**gum spear** *n.* a tapered steel shaft up to six feet long used by gum diggers to locate deposits

gun *n.* a weapon for shooting, as rifle, revolver, cannon, etc.—**gun'ner** *n.*—**gun'nery** *n.* use of big guns.—**gun'boat** *n.* a small warship.—**gun'powder** *n.* explosive mixture of saltpetre, sulphur and charcoal.—**to stick to one's guns** to stand firm

gun *n.* (Aus.) a champion.—*adj.*

gun'yah *n.* Aborigine name for a hut or shelter of boughs and leaves

gun'wale (gun'l) *n.* the upper edge of a ship's side

gur'gle *n.* a bubbling sound.—*v.*

gush *n.* 1. sudden pouring out. 2. over-enthusiastic talk.—*v.* 1. to rush out. 2. to express silly enthusiasm

gus'set *n.* a triangle of material let into a garment

gust *n.* a sudden burst of wind, rain, laughter, etc.—**gust'y** *adj.*

gust'o *n.* enjoyment, zest

gut *n.* 1. an intestine. 2. a string made from guts of animals.—*v.* 1. to destroy the contents of (a house). 2. to remove entrails of fish, rabbits, etc.—**gut'ting** *pres. part.*—**gut'ted** *p.t.* and *p. part.*

gut'ter *n.* 1. a channel for draining off water. 2. part of street below the pavement

gut'tural *adj.* formed in the throat

guy (gī) *n.* 1. a rope or chain to steady or secure something. 2. an effigy of Guy Fawkes. 3. an absurdly-dressed person.—*v.* to ridicule, mimic

guz'zle *v.* to eat or drink greedily.—**guz'zler** *n.*

gymna'sium (jim-nā'zi-um) *n.* a place fitted up for athletic exercises.—**gym'nast** *n.* an expert in gymnastics.—**gymnast'ic** *adj.*—**gymnast'ics** *n.pl.* muscular exercises

gyrate' (jī-rāt') *v.* to revolve, move in a circle. —**gyra'tion** (jī-rā'shun) *n.*

gy'roscope *n.* a heavy rotating fly-wheel used to stabilise ships and monorail cars

H

hab'erdasher *n.* a draper.—**hab'erdashery** *n.* small articles of dress, buttons, etc.

hab'it *n.* 1. a custom, practice. 2. a dress (esp. **ri'ding-hab'it**)

hab'itable *adj.* fit to live in.—**hab'itant** *n.* 1. an inhabitant. 2. (a-bee-tan') a Canadian of French descent.—**hab'itat** *n.* natural home of plant or animal.—**habita'tion** (-ā'shun) *n.* dwelling-place

Compare: abode, home, house

habit'ual *adj.* customary, usual.—**habit'ually** *adv.*—**habit'uate** *v.* to accustom.

Compare: accustomed, common, general, ordinary, regular, wonted, inveterate. *Contrast:* unusual, infrequent, exceptional, rare, occasional

hack *n.* 1. a hired horse. 2. one who does inferior literary work for money.—*v.* to cut roughly, gash

hack'ney *n.* 1. riding-horse. 2. hired carriage. —**hack'neyed** *adj.* commonplace as *a hackneyed expression*

had'dock *n.* a fish of the cod family

haem'orrhage, hem'orrhage (hem'or-ij) *n.* bleeding from blood-vessels

haft *n.* a handle esp. of a knife

hag *n.* 1. an ugly old woman. 2. a witch

hag'gard *adj.* wild-looking, care-worn

hag'gis *n.* a Scottish meat and oatmeal dish cooked in a sheep's stomach bag

hag'gle *v.* to dispute in bargaining

hail *v.* 1. to greet. 2. to call.—*interj.* a greeting. —**to hail from,** to come from

hail *n.* frozen rain.—*v.*—**hail'stone** *n.*

hair *n.* a growth from an animal's skin, e.g. covering of human head.—**hair'iness** *n.*—**hair'less** *adj.*—**hair's breadth** *n.* very small space.—**hair'-splitting** *n.* drawing of over-fine distinctions.—**hair-pin** *n.* a two-pronged pin for hair.—**hair'y** *adj.*—**hair-dresser** *n.* a hair stylist.—**hair'pin bend** a very sharp bend in a road.—**hair'spring** *n.* a fine spring in a watch.—**hair'-raising** *adj.* terrifying.—**not to turn a hair** to show no fear

hak'a *n.* 1. a ceremonial Maori war dance. 2. a similar dance for entertainment or sporting events

hal'berd *n.* a combined spear and battle-axe
hal'cyon (hal'si-on) *adj.* calm, peaceful, esp. **halcyon days**
hale *adj.* strong, healthy, as *The old man was hale and hearty*
half (hahf) *n.* one of two equal parts.—**halves** *pl.*—*adj.* forming a half.—*adv.* equally, in part.—**half'-brother, half'-sister** *n.* brother, sister, by one parent only.—**half'-caste** *n.* person of mixed white and coloured parentage.—**half-crown'** *n.* a British coin worth an eighth of a pound no longer in use.—**half'penny** (hāp'ni) *n.*—**half'-pennies** *pl.*—**half'-back** *n.* a player in a team half way between forwards and backs.—**half-mast'** *n.* the position of a flag of mourning or distress half way down a mast.—**half-hear'ted** *adj.* not very enthusiastic.—**to go halves** to share equally
hal'ibut *n.* an edible flatfish
hall (hawl) *n.* 1. a large room. 2. a large house. 3. entrance passage.—**hall'mark** *n.* a mark used by goldsmiths to show genuineness of gold or silver
hallelu'jah. See **alleluia**
hallo', hello' *interj.* 1. a greeting. 2. exclamation of surprise.—**halloo'** *v.* to shout
hall'ow (hal'ō) *v*, to make holy.—**Hall'oween** *n.* eve of All Saints' Day
hallucina'tion (hal-ōō-sin-ā'shun) *n.* a delusion, imagining what is not there
ha'lo *n.* 1. a circle of light round the sun, moon, etc. 2. a luminous circle round saints' heads in pictures.—**ha'loes** *pl.*
halt *v.* to stop.—*n.*—*adj.* lame, crippled.—**halt'er** *n.* a rope for tying an animal
halve (hahv) *v.* to divide in half, share
hal'yard, hal'liard *n.* a rope for hoisting sails
ham *n.* 1. the back of the thigh. 2. a pig's thigh salted and dried. 3. an amateur radio operator. 4. an actor who overacts.—**ham'string** *n.* a tendon at back of knee.—*v.* 1. to cripple by cutting this. 2. to hinder, impede
ham'burger *n.* a split bread roll filled with sausage
ham'let *n.* a small village
ham'mer *n.* a tool with heavy head at end of handle, for driving nails, etc.—*v.* to strike with hammer.—**hammer and tongs** (to work) with noisy energy
ham'mock *n.* a hanging bed
ham'per *v.* to hinder, obstruct.—*n.* a large covered basket

Compare: impede, embarrass, encumber. *Contrast:* help, hasten, expedite

hand *n.* 1. the end part of the arm, palm and fingers. 2. handwriting, as *He writes a good hand.* 3. worker, as *a factory hand.* 4. measure of four inches, used in measuring height of horses. 5. assistance, as *to lend a hand.*—*v.* 1. to lead with the hand, as *He handed her into the carriage.* 2. to pass, as *He handed out the hymn-books.*—**hand'bag** *n.*—**hand'bill** *n.* a small printed notice.—**hand'cuffs** *n.pl.* bracelets with chain to secure prisoners' hands.—**hand'ful** *n.* small quantity.—**hand'fuls** *pl.*—**at hand** close by.—**to change hands** to pass to someone else.—**from hand to mouth** without foresight.—**hand in glove** intimate.—**hand in hand** holding each other's hand.—**hand-to-hand** close.—**in hand** 1. under control. 2. being done.—**on hand** within reach.—**hand over fist** very quickly.—**old hand** an experienced person.—**show of hands** a vote by raising hands.—**on all hands** everywhere.—**out of hand** out of control.—**to get one's hand in** to get used to.—**to get the upper hand** to get the advantage (over).—**to wash one's hands of** to disown.—**to win hands down** to win easily
hand'icap *n.* 1. allowance, start in a race. 2. disadvantage
hand'icraft *n.* occupation requiring skilful hands
hand'iwork *n.* work done by person himself
hand'kerchief (hang'kerchif) *n.* a small square of cloth carried in pocket for wiping the nose
hand'le *n.* part by which something is held.—*v.* 1. to touch, feel. 2. to deal with, as *He is handling that part of the business.*—**hand'ling** *pres. part.*—**hand'led** *p.t.* and *p. part.*
hand'some (han'sum) *adj.* 1. good-looking esp. used of men and buildings. 2. generous, as *a handsome contribution.*—**hand'somely** *adv.*
hand'y *adj.* convenient, near. **hand'yman** *n.* a man who does odd jobs
hang *v.* 1. to attach to something above, 2. to cling. 3. to bend, droop.—**hung** *p.t.* and *p. part.* 4. to execute by hanging.—**hanged** *p.t.*—**hang'dog** *adj.* ashamed.—**to hang about** to loiter.—**to hang back** to hesitate.—**to hang fire** to be delayed

Note: A picture is *hung*, but a criminal is *hanged*

hang'ar *n.* a shed for aircraft
han'ger *n.* a support from which something hangs, as a *coathanger.*—**hanger-on** *n.* an unwanted follower
hang'i, haang'i *n.* a Maori earth oven
hank (hangk) *n.* a skein
hank'er (hangk'er) (after) *v.* to crave
han'som *n.* a two-wheeled cab with driver's seat high up behind
haphaz'ard *adj.* without method
hap'less *adj.* unlucky
hap'pen *v.* to come about, occur.—**hap'pening** *n.* event
hap'py *adj.* glad, content, fortunate.—**hap'pier** *comp.*—**hap'piest** *sup.*—**hap'pily** *adv.*—**hap'piness** *n.*—**happy-go-lucky** easy-going

Compare: cheerful, gay, merry, blessed, joyful. *Contrast:* unhappy, sad, miserable, melancholy, gloomy, sorrowful, troubled

hapu *n.* a Maori word for a sub-tribe or family

hapuku *n.* (N.Z.) a groper, kind of sea fish

harangue' (har-ang') *n.* a long violent speech. —*v.*

har'ass *v.* 1. to worry, trouble. 2. to attack repeatedly.—he **har'asses**

har'binger (har'bin-jer) *n.* in literature, a messenger

har'bour *n.* 1. a place of shelter for ships. 2. a shelter.—*v.* to give shelter to

hard *adj.* 1. not soft, firm, solid. 2. difficult. 3. harsh, cruel. 4. heavy, as *He was sentenced to hard labour*.—*adv.* 1. with effort. 2. close.—**hard'en** *v.* to make hard.—**hard'ihood** *n.* boldness, vigour.—**hard'iness** *n.* strength.—**hard'ly** *adv.* scarcely.—**hard'ship** *n.* suffering.—**hard'ware** *n.* metal articles.—**hard-head'ed** *adj.* shrewd.— **hard heart'ed** *adj.* pitiless.—**hard'board** *n.* compressed fibreboard.—**hard and fast** strict

Compare: 1. impenetrable, unyielding, stubborn, dense. 2. arduous, exacting, complicated. 3. severe, austere, callous. 4. strenuous, oppressive. *Contrast:* 1. penetrable, fluid. 2. easy, simple, straightforward. 3. lenient, mild, indulgent, meek, tender, kind. 4. light

hard'y *adj.* 1. bold, brave. 2. strong.—**hard'ier** *comp.*—**hard'iest** *sup.*

hare (hair) *n.* a long-eared, short-tailed rodent, noted for speed.—*v.* to run fast.—**hare'brained** *adj.* rash, wild.—**hare' and hounds'** *n.* a paperchase

ha'rem, harem' (hār'em, ha-reem') *n.* women's part of Mohammedan house

har'icot (har'ikō) *n.* a French bean

hark *v.* to listen

har'lequin *n.* a pantomime character

harm *n.* hurt, damage.—*v.*—**harm'ful** *adj.* hurtful.—**harm'fully** *adv.*—**harm'less** *adj.* —**harm'lessly** *adv.*

harmon'ica *n.* a mouth organ

harmo'nious *adj.* agreeing together, not clashing

harmo'nium *n.* keyboard instrument with metal reeds

har'mony *n.* 1. agreement. 2. combination of musical notes to make chords. 3. musical sounds.—**har'monies** *pl.*—**har'monise** *v.* to agree with

har'ness *n.* 1. the equipment of a horse. 2. armour.—*v.* to put in harness

harp *n.* a tall stringed musical instrument, played by the fingers.—**harp'ist** *n.*

harpoon' *n.* a spear, with rope attached, for catching whales.—*v.*—**harpoon' gun** a gun used for throwing a harpoon

harp'sichord (harp'si-kord) *n.* a stringed instrument with keyboard like a piano

harp'y *n.* 1. a mythological monster, half woman, half bird. 2. a cruel, rapacious person.—**harp'ies** *pl.*

har'rier *n.* 1. a hound used in hunting hares. 2. a runner. 3. a kind of hawk

har'row (ha'rō) *n.* a frame with iron teeth for breaking up clods.—*v.* 1. to draw a harrow. 2. to distress, hurt, as *Our feelings were harrowed by a description of their sufferings*.—**har'rowing** *adj.*

har'ry *v.* 1. to ravage. 2. to keep pestering.—he **har'ries**.—**har'rying** *pres. part.*—**har'ried** *p.t.* and *p. part.*

harsh *adj.* 1. rough to touch, taste or hearing. 2. severe, cruel.—**harsh'ly** *adv.*—**harsh'ness** *n.*

hart *n.* stag.—**hind** *fem.*

hart'ebeest (hart'ebeest) *n.* a large African antelope

ha'rum-sca'rum (hā'rum-skā'rum) *adj.* scatter-brained

har'vest *n.* 1. gathering in the grain. 2. harvest-time. 3. the season's crops.—*v.* to gather in.—**har'vester** *n.* a reaping machine

hash *v.* to cut up small.—*n.* 1. dish of hashed meat. 2. a mess

hasp *n.* a clasp, door or window fastening

has'sock *n.* a cushion for kneeling on

haste (hāst) *n.* 1. speed. 2. hurry.—*v.* to hurry.—**ha'sten** (hā'sn) *v.* to hurry.—**ha'sty** *adj.* quick, rash.—**ha'stily** *adv.*

hat *n.* a head-covering usually with a brim.—**hat'trick** *n.* in cricket, the taking of three wickets with successive balls.—**to talk through one's hat** to talk nonsense

hatch *n.* 1. the lower half of a divided door. 2. an opening in ship's deck. 3. a trapdoor. 4. an opening in the wall between kitchen and dining room.—**hatch'es** *pl.*—**hatch'way** *n.* an opening in a deck

hatch *v.* 1. to produce young from eggs. 2. to plot.—*v.* to brood

hat'chet *n.* a small axe.—**to bury the hat'chet** to make peace

hate *v.* to dislike strongly.—*n.*—**ha'ting** *pres. part.*—**ha'ted** *p.t.* and *p. part.*—**hate'ful** *adj.*—**ha'tred** *n.* strong dislike

Compare: (with *n.*) abhorrence, aversion, detestation, ill-will, malevolence, repugnance. *Contrast:* love, liking, admiration, goodwill

hat'ter *n.* a maker or seller of men's hats.—**mad as a hatter** crazy

Note: a *milliner* makes ladies' hats

haugh'ty (haw'ti) *adj.* proud, disdainful.—**haught'ier** *comp.*—**haught'iest** *sup.*—**haught'ily** *adv.*

Hau'hau *n.* 1. the Maori religious movement of the 1860's whose members fought the British in the N.Z. wars. 2. a member of this movement

haul *v.* to pull, drag.—*n.* 1. a good pull. 2. catch of fish.—**haul'age** *n.*

haunch (hawnsh) *n.* the hip and thigh.—**haunch'es** *pl.*

haunt *v.* 1. to visit often. 2. (of ghosts) to appear often in the same place.—*n.* a place visited often

have (hav) *v.* 1. to hold, possess. 2. to be obliged (to do), as *He has to go to school.*

3. to get, obtain, as *He had the puncture mended.* 4. to gain advantage over, trick, as *He had me there.*—**I have, thou hast,** he has, we, you, they **have.**—**hav'ing** *pres. part.*—had *p.t.* and *p. part.*—**had rather**—would prefer (to)

ha'ven *n.* 1. a harbour. 2. a refuge

hav'ersack *n.* a soldier's or hiker's food-bag

hav'oc *n.* destruction, ruin
Compare: waste, devastation, carnage

haw *n.* the berry of the hawthorn

hawk *n.* a bird of prey.—*v.* to carry goods for sale, as a street **hawk'er**

haw'ser (haw'zer) *n.* a large rope or small cable

hay *n.* grass mown and dried.—**hay'cock** *n.* a cone-shaped heap of hay.—**hay'stack** *n.* a large pile of hay.—**to make hay while the sun shines** to use opportunities while one can

haz'ard *n.* 1. chance, risk. 2. danger.—*v.* to risk.—**haz'ardous** *adj.*

haze *n.* mist, thin smoke

ha'zel *n.* a bush bearing hazel-nuts

ha'zy *adj.* 1. misty. 2. vague, as *The boy had a very hazy idea of what the master had tried to explain.*—**ha'zier** *comp.*—**ha'ziest** *sup.*

H-bomb *n.* a hydrogen bomb

he *pron.* Refers to third person (male sex) as subject of a sentence, as *He promised to come. Objective* **him,** *possessive* **his,** *fem.* **she,** *neuter* **it,** *plural* **they**

head (hed) *n.* 1. the top part of the body. 2. top. 3. chief part. 4. leader. 5. section (of speech, book, etc.).—*v.* 1. to lead, as *to head the list.* 2. to provide with a head. —*adj.* chief.—**head'ache** (hed'āk) *n.* pain in the head.—**head'ing** *n.* title.—**head'land** *n.* cape, promontory.—**head'light** *n.* a bright lamp on front of car or at masthead. —**head'line** *n.* most important news, in large type, along the top of a newspaper.—**head'long** *adv.* in a rush.—**head'quarters'** *n.pl.* 1. a place where a commander-in-chief sends out his orders. 2. the centre of operations.—**head'strong** *adj.* self-willed.—**head'way** *n.* progress.—**head'y** *adj.* rash, intoxicating.—**to come to a head** to reach a decisive point.—**to head off** to divert.—**to keep one's head** to remain calm.—**to lose one's head** to panic.—**off one's head** mad

heal *v.* to make well, cure

health (helth) *n.* 1. bodily condition. 2. being well.—**health'iness** *n.*—**health'y** *adj.* well, sound

heap *n.* 1. a pile of things. 2. a great quantity. —*v.* to pile

hear *v.* 1. to perceive with the ear. 2. to listen. 3. to learn.—**hear! hear!** form of cheering to denote agreement.—**heard** (herd) *p.t.* and *p. part.*—**hear'ing** *n.* 1. the sense by which we hear. 2. a chance to be heard, as *The chairman asked the audience to give the speaker a fair hearing.*—**hear'say** *n.* rumour

heark'en (har'ken) *v.* to listen

hearse (hers) *n.* a carriage for a coffin

heart (hart) *n.* 1. the organ in the body which pumps the blood. 2. the centre, chief part, as *The heart of the city.* 3. courage, as *The shipwrecked sailors took heart when they saw a ship approaching.* 4. the centre of the emotions. 5. love, tenderness, warmth of feeling, as *Her heart went out to the lost child.* 6. a symbol representing a heart. 7. one of the four suits in playing-cards.—**heart'en** *v.* to encourage.—**heart'-less** *n.* unfeeling.—**hearty** *adj.* 1. vigorous, 2. friendly.—**heart'ily** *adv.*—**after one's own heart** of the sort one very much likes. —**heart and soul** enthusiastically.—**to eat one's heart out** to pine, to grieve.—**to have at heart** to care about.—**to lose heart** to lose courage.—**to take heart** to become braver

hearth (harth) *n.* a fire-place

heat *n.* 1. hotness, warmth. 2. hot weather. 3. hottest part, as *in the heat of the day.* 4. section of a race, eliminating round, as *The winners of the heats ran in the final.* 5. excitement, anger.—*v.* to make hot.—**heat'er** *n.* a stove, radiator, etc.

heath *n.* 1. a tract of waste land. 2. a moorland plant

heath'en (hee'THen) *n.* a person not Christian, Jew or Mohammedan.—**heath'en, heath-'ens** *pl.*—*adj.* pagan, barbarous.—**heath'en-ish** *adj.*

heath'er (heTH'er) *n.* moorland plant with purple or white flower

heave *v.* 1. to lift with effort. 2. to utter (a sigh). 3. to rise and fall.—*n.*—**heav'ing** *pres. part.*—**heaved, hove** *p.t.*—**heaved** *p. part.*—**to heave to** to stop (of a ship).—**to heave in sight** to come into view.—**heave ho!** a sailor's shout of encouragement

heav'en (hevn) *n.* 1. the sky. 2. the abode of God. 3. God. 4. a place or feeling of bliss. —**heav'enly** *adj.*

heav'y (hev'i) *adj.* 1. difficult to lift, weighty. 2. difficult. 3. abundant, as, *a heavy meal, rain, crop.* 4. dull. 5. sad, as *heavy tidings.* —**heav'ily** *adv.*—**heav'iness** *n.*—**heav'y-weight** *n.* a boxer over 12st 7lb
Compare: burdensome, cumbrous, oppressive, grievous, ponderous, plentiful, stolid, sluggish. *Contrast:* light, lively, buoyant, airy

He'brew *n.* 1. a Jew. 2. the ancient language of the Jews

heck'le *v.* to interrupt with questions.—**heck'ler** *n.*

hec'tic *adj.* feverish

hedge (hej) *n.* a fence of bushes.—*v.* 1. to surround with a hedge. 2. to trim a hedge. 3. to avoid straight answer. 4. to secure oneself against loss by betting on both sides.—**hedg'ing** *pres. part.*—**hedged** *p.t.* and *p. part.*—**hedge'hog** *n.* a small animal covered with spines

heed *v.* to take notice of, consider.—*n.* attention, as *to pay heed, to give heed* (to).—**heed'ful** *adj.*—**heed'less** *adj.*

heel *n.* 1. the back part of the foot. 2. the back part of a shoe.—*v.* to put heel on.—**down at heel** shabby.—**to take to one's heels** to run away

heel (over) *v.* (of a ship) to lean to one side.—*n.*

heg'emony, hegem'ony (-g- or -j-) *n.* leadership or domination (of one country over others)

heif'er (hef'er) *n.* a young cow.—**bull, bul'lock** *masc.*

height (hīt) *n.* 1. measure from base to top. 2. being high. 3. high place, mountain top.—**height'en** *v.* 1. to make higher. 2. to increase

Compare: (with *v.*) raise, enhance, intensify, elevate

hei'nous (hā'nus) *adj.* very bad

Compare: monstrous, enormous, flagrant, atrocious, wicked

heir (ār) *n.* a person with right to inherit property or rank.—**heir'ess** *fem.*—**heir-appar'ent** *n.* successor to the throne.—**heir'loom** *n.* treasured thing in a family for generations

hei-ti'ki (hā-ti'ki) *n.* a Maori greenstone neck ornament

hel'icopter *n.* an aircraft with a large horizontal propeller which can rise vertically

he'liograph (hee'li-ō-graff) *n.* an apparatus for signalling by reflecting sun's rays

he'liotrope (hee'-) *n.* a pale purple colour

he'lium (hee'li-um) *n.* a very light gas used in balloons

hell *n.* 1. the abode of the damned. 2. a place of wickedness, misery or torture.—**hell'ish** *adj.*

Hellen'ic *adj.* Greek

hello' *interjec.* see **hallo'**

helm *n.* a tiller or wheel for turning ship's rudder.—**helms'man** *n.* man who steers ship

hel'met, helm *n.* armoured protection for the head

help *v.* 1. to aid, assist. 2. to serve (food). 3. to prevent, as *He cannot help it.*—*n.* aid.—**help'er** *n.*—**help'ful** *adj.*—**help'ing** *n.* a portion of food.—**help'less** *adj.*—**help'meet** *n.* a companion, husband or wife

Compare: support, sustain, second, abet, succour, foster. *Contrast:* hinder, obstruct, embarrass, hamper, frustrate, stop

hel'ter-skel'ter *adv.* in hurry and disorder.—*n.* fairground tower with spiral chute

hem *n.* 1. a border on a garment made by turning the edge and sewing it down.—*v.* 1. to make a hem. 2. (in) to shut in.—**hem'ming** *pres. part.*—**hemmed** *p.t.* and *p. part.*—**hem'stitch** *n.* ornamental drawn-thread stitch

hem'isphere (hem'i-sfeer) *n.* a half of the earth's surface

hem'lock *n.* a poisonous plant

hemp *n.* a plant of which the fibres are used to make rope.—**hemp'en** *adj.*

hen *n.* the female of domestic fowl and other birds.—**cock** *masc.*

hence (hens) *adv.* 1. from this place, as *Let us go hence.* 2. from this time, as *a hundred years hence.*—**henceforth', hencefor'ward** *adv.* from now on

hench'man *n.* a trusty follower.—**hench'men** *pl.*

hep'tagon *n.* a figure with seven angles.—**heptag'onal** *adj.*

her *pron.* Objective and possessive form of she, as *I told her the news* (object) and *This is her hat* (possessive). When used alone in the possessive *her* becomes *hers,* as *This hat is hers.*—**his** *masc.*—**its** *neuter.*—**their** *pl.*

her'ald *n.* a messenger, announcer.—*v.* to announce, proclaim the approach of.—**heral'dic** *adj.*—**her'aldry** *n.* the science dealing with coats-of-arms

herb *n.* 1. a plant with a soft stem, which dies down after flowering. 2. a plant used in medicine or food.—**herba'ceous** (herb-ā'shus) *adj.*—**herb'age** *n.* pasture, grass.—**herb'alist** *n.* one skilled in the use of herbs

hercule'an *adj.* 1. very strong, as *herculean strength.* 2. requiring great strength, as *a herculean task*

herd *n.* 1. a number of animals feeding or travelling together. 2. a herdsman.—*v.* to crowd together.—**herds'man** *n.*

here *adv.* 1. in this place, as *It is here.* 2. to this place, as *Come here.* 3. *n.* this place, as *It is near here.*—**here!** 1. I am present. 2. come here! or look here!—**hereaf'ter** *adv.* after this.—*n.* the next world.—**hereby'** *adv.* by this means.—**here'tofore** *adv.* formerly.—**herewith'** *adv.* with this.—**neither here nor there** of no importance

hered'itary *adj.* 1. coming by inheritance, as *a hereditary title.* 2. that can be passed from one generation to another, as *a hereditary characteristic*

hered'ity *n.* the passing of qualities of mind and body from parents to children

her'esy *n.* a belief opposed to official doctrines.—**her'esies** *pl.*—**her'etic** *n.*—**heret'ical** *adj.*

her'itage (her'i-tāj) *n.* something handed down, inheritance

hermet'ically *adv.* so as to be airtight, as *This tin of meat is hermetically sealed*

her'mit *n.* a person living retired, by himself.—**her'mitage** *n.* a hermit's dwelling

he'ro (hee'rō) *n.* 1. a brave man or boy. 2. the chief character in a story.—**he'roes** *pl.* **her'oine** *fem.*—**hero'ic** *adj.*—**hero'ically** *adv.*—**her'oism** *n.* courage, boldness.—

hero worship a great admiration for someone

her'on *n.* a long-necked wading bird

her'ring *n.* an edible salt water fish

herself' *pron.* emphatic and reflexive form of she, as *She herself desired it* (emphatic) and *She upset herself badly over it* (reflexive).—**himself** *masc.*—**itself** *neuter.*—**themselves** *pl.*

hes'itancy (hez'i-tan-si) *n.* doubt, wavering.—**hes'itant** *adj.* undecided

Contrast: (with *adj.*) decided, definite, firm, resolved, unwavering, unflinching, determined

hes'itate *v.* 1. to pause before acting. 2. to feel doubtful.—**hes'itating** *pres. part.*—**hes'itated** *p.t.* and *p. part.*—**hesita'tion** (-tā'shun) *n.*

het'erodox *adj.* contrary to general or official belief

Compare: heretical, unorthodox, unconventional. *Contrast:* orthodox, approved, accepted

heteroge'neous (het-er-ō-jeen'e-us) *adj.* made up of different kinds, as *The museum contained a heterogeneous collection of exhibits*

Compare: miscellaneous, mixed, dissimilar. *Contrast:* homogeneous, identical, uniform, similar

hew *v.* to cut or chop with an axe.—**hewed** *p.t.*—**hewn, hewed** *p. part.*—**hew'er** *n.*

hex'agon *n.* a figure having six sides.—**hexag'onal** *adj.*

hey'day (hā'dā) *n.* 1. bloom, prime (of prosperity, vigour, etc.)

hi'bernate *v.* to pass the winter in sleep.—**hiberna'tion** (-ā'shun) *n.*

hic'cup, hic'cough *n.* a catching of the breath in spasms.—*v.*

hide (hīd) *v.* 1. to put out of sight, conceal. 2. to keep secret.—*n.* place of concealment.—**hi'ding** *pres. part.*—**hid** *p.t.*—**hid, hid'den** *p. part.*

Compare: (with *hidden*) concealed, secret, covered, buried, obscure. *Contrast:* discovered, uncovered, revealed, published, advertised, unveiled

hide *n.* the skin of an animal, raw or tanned.

hid'eous *adj.* ugly, horrible.—**hid'eously** *adv.*

Compare: repulsive, ghastly, grim, grisly. *Contrast:* attractive, pleasing, beautiful

hieroglyph'ics (hī-rō-glif'iks) *n.pl.* pictures of objects standing for words or sounds, as used by ancient Egyptians

hig'gler *n.* (Carib.) a pedlar

high (hī) *adj.* 1. far up. 2. of great rank or importance. 3. tainted of (meat). 4. exalted, as *in high spirits, a high opinion.* 5. expensive, as *a high price.* 6. intense, as *high pressure, a high wind.* 7. luxurious, as *high living.* 8. advanced, as *high time, high noon.* 9. shrill, as *a high voice.* 10. angry, as *high words.*—*adv.* far up.—**high'ly** *adv.*—**high'ness** *n.* title given to members of royal family.—**high'brow** *n.* an intellectual person.—**high and dry** stranded.—**high explosive** a powerful explosive.—**the high seas** the open sea far from land

Compare: tall, lofty, eminent. *Contrast:* low, base, deep, inferior, short, stunted

high'-flown (hī'flōn) *adj.* extravagant (in speech)

high-han'ded *adj.* overbearing, acting without consulting others

high'land *n.* mountainous country.—**the Highlands** the mountains of north Scotland

high'spir'ited *adj.* 1. proud, fiery. 2. brave

high'way *n.* a main road.—**high'wayman** *n.* a robber on the highway

hike *v.* to tramp, march.—**hi'king** *pres. part.*—**hiked** *p.t.* and *p. part.*—*n.* a long walk.—**hi'ker** *n.*

hila'rious (hil-ā'ri-us) *adj.* laughing, very funny.—**hila'rity** (hil-a'ri-ti) *n.* noisy mirth

hill *n.* 1. a small mountain. 2. a heap, mound.—**hill'ock** *n.* a small hill.—**hil'ly** *adj.* with many hills.—**hil'lier** *comp.*—**hil'liest** *sup.*

hilt *n.* the handle of a sword

hind (hīnd) *n.* 1. a female deer.—**stag, hart** *masc.* 2. a farm worker

hind (hīnd), **hind'er** *adj.* at the back.—**hind'most** *adj.*

hin'der *v.* 1. to stop, delay. 2. to make difficult.—**hin'drance** *n.*

Compare: impede, interrupt, thwart, arrest, retard, debar, obstruct. *Contrast:* help, facilitate, hasten, promote, assist

Hin'du (dōō) *n.* a native of north India whose religion is **Hin'duism**

hinge (hinj) *n.* the joint on which a door swings.—*v.* 1. to hang on a hinge. 2. to turn on, depend on, as *Our success hinges on your help*

hint *n.* a suggestion, indirect reference.—*v.*

hint'erland *n.* the district lying behind a seaport or coastline

hip *n.* 1. the joint of the thigh. 2. the fruit of the wild rose

hip'podrome *n.* a circus, a course for chariot races

hippopot'amus *n.* a large, thick-skinned animal found in African rivers.—**hippopot'amuses, hippopot'ami** *pl.*

hire *n.* payment, wages.—*v.* to employ, pay for the use of.—**hi'ring** *pres. part.*—**hired** *p.t.* and *p. part.*—**hire'ling** *n.* person working for money.—**hire-pur'chase** purchase by instalments

hir'sute *adj.* hairy

hiss *v.* to make a sharp sound like an angry goose.—**he hiss'es.**—*n.* a sound of disapproval.—**hiss'es** *pl.*

histo'rian *n.* a writer of history.—**histor'ic** *adj.* famous in history.—**histor'ical** *adj.* based on or connected with history.—**his'tor'ically** *adv.*

his'tory *n.* 1. the story of a nation. 2. the study of past events. 3. the story of a person's life.—**his'tories** *pl.*

histrion'ic *adj.* 1. relating to acting and the theatre. 2. melodramatic, insincere. *n.pl.* insincere display of emotion

hit *v.* 1. to strike. 2. (upon) to find, meet, 3. to injure.—**hit'ting** *pres. part.*—**hit** *p.t.* and *p. part.*—*n.* 1. a blow. 2. success.—**to hit it off** to get on well.—**to hit the nail on the head** to say something apt.—**to hit upon** to find by chance

hitch *v.* 1. to fasten with a loop. 2. (up) to move with a jerk.—*n.* 1. a jerk. 2. a fastening, loop. 3. a difficulty.—**hitch'es** *pl.*

hitch'-hike *v.* to travel by asking for lifts.—**hitch'-hiker** *n.*

hith'er *adv.* to this place.—**hitherto'** *adv.* up to now

hive (hīv) *n.* 1. a house for bees. 2. a number of bees.—*v.* to place (bees) in hive

hoard (hōrd) *n.* a store, hidden treasure.—*v.* to store and hide

hoard'ing (hōrd'ing) *n.* wooden fence enclosing ground, often used for posting bills

hoar'frost *n.* white frost

hoarse (hōrs) *adj.* husky, rough-voiced

hoar'y *adj.* white or grey (often with age), *as a hoary-headed old man*

hoax (hōks) *n.* a trick played as a joke.—*v.*

hob *n.* a shelf by a fire-place for keeping things warm

hob'ble *v.* 1. to limp. 2. to tie (horse's) legs together

hob'by *n.* a favourite spare-time occupation. —**hob'bies** *pl.*—**hob'by-horse** *n.* 1. a rocking-horse 2. a favourite idea

hob'nail *n.* a large-headed nail for boots

hob'nob *v.* to chat together

hock *n.* the middle joint of animal's hind leg

hock *n.* a German white wine

hock'ey *n.* a team game played with curved sticks and hard ball

hod *n.* a small trough on long stick for carrying mortar

hoe *n.* a garden tool with small blade, for weeding, breaking ground, etc.—*v.*—**hoe'ing** *pres. part.*—**hoed** (hōd) *p.t.* and *p. part.*

hog *n.* 1. a full-grown pig.—**sow** *fem.* 2. greedy or dirty person.—**hogs'head** *n.* large cask

hog'manay *n.* in Scotland, New Year's eve

hoist *v.* to raise aloft.—*n.*

hold (hōld) *v.* 1. to grasp. 2. to keep. 3. to contain. 4. to be able to contain. 5. to keep back. 6. to organise, as *to hold a meeting*. 7. to withstand.—*n.* 1. grasp. 2. claim. —**hold!** stop!—**hol'der** *n.* anything that holds.—**hol'ding** *n.* a farm, land.—**hold forth** to express one's views.—**hold out** to offer, promise.—**held** *p.t.* and *p. part.* —**to hold over** to postpone.—**hold up** 1. delay, impede. 2. stop and rob

Compare: 1. clasp, grip. 2. maintain, continue. 3. accommodate. 4. retain, resist. *Contrast:* relinquish, let go, let slip

hold (hōld) *n.* a space below a ship's deck, for cargo

hold'all *n.* a roomy case or bag

hole (hōl) *n.* 1. a hollow place. 2. opening.—*v.* 1. to make holes in. 2. to put into hole (esp. golf ball)

hol'iday *n.* 1. a day of rest from work. 2. vacation.—**Bank Holiday**, in England, a general holiday

ho'liness *n.* 1. being holy. 2. a title of the Pope

hol'low (hol'ō) *n.* 1. a hole, cavity. 2. a valley.—*v.* (out) to make a hole.—*adj.* 1. empty. 2. not solid. 3. false, as *His promises proved to be hollow*

hol'ly *n.* an evergreen shrub with prickly leaves and red berries.—**hol'lies** *pl.*

hol'ocaust *n.* 1. a burnt offering. 2. great slaughter by fire

hol'ster (hōl'ster) *n.* a leather pistol-case

ho'ly (hō'li) *adj.* 1. sacred. 2. pure, religious. 3. divine.—**ho'lier** *comp.*—**ho'liest** *sup.*—**the Holy Land** Israel, Palestine.—**ho'ly week** *n.* the week before Easter

Compare: sanctified, virtuous, righteous, good, pious, hallowed. *Contrast:* unholy, wicked, irreligious, sacrilegious, impure, unsanctified, profane, impious, unhallowed

hom'age (hom'āj) *n.* 1. respect. 2. formal acknowledgment by vassal of allegiance to his lord

Compare: allegiance, obeisance, loyalty, fidelity, submission

home (hōm) *n.* 1. the place where one lives. 2. an institution for the sick.—**Home** (N.Z.) Britain *adj.* of home, not foreign.—**home'less** *adj.*—**home'ly** *adj.* plain, familiar, domestic.—**home'sick** *adj.* longing for home.—**home'spun** *adj.* coarse (cloth).—**home'stead** *n.* 1. farmhouse and buildings. 2. (Aus.) the centre of management on a sheep or cattle farm.—**home'wards** *adv.*—**homework** *n.* work to be done by a pupil at home.—**home counties** the counties around London.—**Home Office** the government department dealing with civil affairs.—**home unit** (Aus.) a suite of rooms in a building which is purchased outright by the occupier

Compare: abode, dwelling, domicile, fireside, residence, habitation, house

hom'icide (hom'i-sīd) *n.* 1. killing a human being. 2. the killer.—**homici'dal** *adj.*

hom'ily *n.* a sermon.—**hom'ilies** *pl.*

homoge'neous (hom-ō-jee'ne-us) *adj.* of the same nature.—**homo'genise** *v.* to make homogeneous as, *homogenised milk.* See **heterogeneous**

hone *n.* a stone for sharpening tools.—*v.*

hon'est (on'est) *adj.* 1. upright, fair. 2. truthful.—**hon'estly** *adv.*—**hon'esty** *n.*
Compare: scrupulous, honourable, just, trustworthy, equitable, frank, straightforward, true, upright, trusty, trustworthy, truthful. *Contrast:* unscrupulous, dishonourable, dishonest, unjust, untrustworthy, inequitable, deceitful, false, perfidious, untrue, treacherous

hon'ey (hun'i) *n.* a sweet yellow fluid collected by bees and placed in—**hon'eycomb** *n.* rows of wax cells.—**hon'eysuckle** *n.* a species of fragrant climbing plant.—**hon'eymoon** *n.* a holiday spent by newly-married couple

hong'i (hong'ee) *n.* the Maori term for rubbing noses as a greeting

hon'orary (on'or-a-ri) *adj.* 1. giving services without pay, as *the honorary secretary of a society*. 2. given only as an honour, e.g. an honorary university degree.—**honora'rium** *n.* a reward for services volunteered

hon'our (on'or) *n.* 1. high respect. 2. reputation. 3. sense of right.—*pl.* 1. distinctions, titles. 2. specialised University degree.—*v.* 1. to respect highly. 2. to pay when due, as *He has honoured all his debts.*—**hon'ourable** *adj.*
Compare: 1. admiration, worship, veneration, reverence. 2. glory, fame, repute. 3. honesty, justice, virtue, morality, nobility. *Contrast:* 1. contempt, disregard. 2. disrepute, shame, dishonour. 3. meanness, wickedness, immorality

hood *n.* 1. a covering for head and neck. 2. top of motor-car, carriage, etc. 3. a coloured cloth, showing degree, worn over university graduate's gown.—**hood'wink** *v.* to deceive

hoof *n.* the horny casing of the foot of a horse, etc.—**hoofs, hooves** *pl.*

hook *n.* a bent piece of metal for catching hold or for hanging up.—*v.* to catch or fasten with a hook.—**hooked** *adj.* hook-shaped.—**by hook or by crook** by any means

hoo'ligan *n.* a ruffian.—**hoo'liganism** *n.*

hoop *n.* 1. a flat band in the form of a circle (or semi-circle), e.g. a child's hoop (a toy to be bowled along), the metal hoops round a cask. 2. the metal arch through which the ball is hit in the game of croquet.—*v.* to bind with hoops

hoot (hōōt) *n.* 1. the cry of the owl. 2. a shout of scorn.—*v.* to sound a horn, etc.

hop *v.* 1. to spring on one foot. 2. to jump.—**hop'ping** *pres. part.*—**hopped** *p.t.* and *p. part.*—*n.* a jump.—**hop'scotch** *n.* a child's hopping game

hop *n.* a climbing plant with bitter cones used in beer-making.—**hop'ping** *n.* hop-gathering

hope (hōp) *v.* to expect and desire.—**ho'ping** *pres. part.*—hoped *p.t.* and *p. part.*—*n.* 1. expectation. 2. something that rouses hope.—**hope'ful** *adj.* **hope'fully** *adv.* 1. having hope. 2. full of hope, promising,—**hope'less** *adj.*

horde *n.* 1. a wandering tribe. 2. a gang, crowd

hori'zon (hor-ī'zon) *n.* the distant line where earth and sky seem to meet.—**horizon'tal** *adj.* 1. parallel with the horizon. 2. level.—**horizon'tally** *adv.*

horn *n.* 1. hard pointed growth on heads of cows, etc. 2. the substance of horns. 3. a wind-instrument.—**horned** *adj.* having horns.—**hor'ny** *adj.*

hor'net *n.* a large kind of wasp

horn'pipe *n.* a lively sailor's dance

hor'rible *adj.* dreadful, shocking

hor'rid *adj.* 1. terrible. 2. unpleasant

hor'rify *v.* to fill with horror.—he **hor'rifies.**—**hor'rifying** *pres. part.*—**hor'rified** *p.t.* and *p. part.*

hor'ror *n.* 1. terror. 2. dread, hatred.—**hor'ror-stricken** *adj.* filled with horror
Compare: dismay, consternation, disgust, abomination, fright

horse *n.* 1. an animal used for riding and pulling loads.—**mare** *fem.*, **stallion** *masc.*, **colt** young horse, **filly** young female horse, **foal** very young horse, **pony** horse of a small breed. 2. cavalry. 3. a frame on which to hang clothes, etc.—**horse'back** *n.*—*adv.*—**horse'hair** *n.*—**horse'man** *n.*—**horse'woman** *fem.*—**horse'manship** *n.* skill in riding.—**horse'power** *n.* unit of engine-power.—**horse'shoe** *n.* horse's iron shoe.—**hors'y** *adj.*—**a dark horse** a person whose talents lie hidden.—**straight from the horse's mouth** (of information) from the original source.—**to flog a dead horse** to waste one's energies unnecessarily.—**to put the cart before the horse** to do things in the wrong order

hor'ticulture *n.* the art of gardening.—**horticul'tural** *adj.*—**horticul'turalist** *n.*

hosan'na *n.* a cry of praise to God

hose (hōz) *n.* 1. stockings, socks. 2. a rubber tube for carrying water.—**ho'sier** *n.* a dealer in stockings.—**ho'siery** *n.*

hos'pice (hos'pis) *n.* a travellers' place of shelter kept by monks

hos'pitable *adj.* 1. friendly to strangers. 2. fond of entertaining.—**hos'pitably** *adv.*
Compare: generous, liberal, bountiful. *Contrast:* mean, parsimonious, close-fisted

hos'pital *n.* a place for nursing the sick or wounded

hospital'ity *n.* the friendly reception of strangers or guests

host (hōst) *n.* 1. one who receives another as his guest. 2. an inn-keeper.—**hos'tess** *fem.*

host (hōst) *n.* 1. an army. 2. a large number
Compare: assembly, company, throng

host (hōst) *n.* the bread consecrated in the Eucharist

host'age (host'āj) *n.* a person given or taken as a pledge to an enemy

hos'tel *n.* a house where students, workers or hikers live.—**hos'telry** *n.* an inn

hos'tile *adj.* war-like, unfriendly.—**hostil'ity** *n.* 1. being at war. 2. unfriendliness.—**hostil'ities** *pl.* acts of war

Compare: inimical, adverse, antagonistic, contrary, repugnant. *Contrast:* amicable, favourable, cordial, affable

hot *adj.* 1. very warm, giving heat. 2. highly spiced. 3. angry, as *hot words.* 4. strong, emphatic, as *a hot scent.*—**hot'ter** *comp.*—**hot'test** *sup.*—**hot'bed** *n.* a bed of earth heated by manure, for young plants.—**hot dog'** *n.* a hot sausage sandwich.—**hot'-house** *n.* a heated building for tender plants.—**hot' pot** *n.* a meat and vegetable stew.—**to blow hot and cold** to keep changing first for and then against some plan

Compare: burning, fiery, fervid, violent, ardent. *Contrast:* cold, cool, freezing, lukewarm

hotel' (hō-tel') *n.* a large inn

hound *n.* 1. a hunting-dog.—**bitch** *fem.*—**pup, puppy,** young dog. 2. a mean fellow.—*v.* to hunt, pursue

hour (our) *n.* 1. sixty minutes, the twenty-fourth part of a day. 2. the time of day. 3. a special time.—**hour'glass** *n.* a sand-glass running an hour.—**hour'ly** *adv.*—**at the eleventh hour** at the last moment. —**the small hours** the hours just after midnight

house (hows) *n.* 1. a dwelling, a building to live in. 2. a university college in which students live. 3. a sub-division of a school. 4. the House of Commons or House of Lords. 5. a theatre audience.—*v.* (howz) 1. to find a house for. 2. to give shelter to. —**house'-agent** *n.* a person who arranges the buying or selling of houses.—**house'-boat** *n.* a boat used as a dwelling place.—**house'breaker** *n.* a burglar.—**house'hold** *n.* the people in a house.—**house'keeper** *n.* a woman who manages a house for persons living in it.—**house'wife** *n.* a wife in her home.—**house'wifery** (hows'wif-ri) *n.* the management of a house, the science of the home

Compare: hut, cottage, bungalow, hovel, manor, castle, mansion, palace, inn, hospital, shanty, cabin

ho'vel *n.* a small shabby house

hous'ing (howz'ing) *n.* 1. accommodation. 2. a protective covering.—**hous'ing estate, hous'ing scheme** planned area of houses

hov'er *v.* 1. to hang in the air (of birds, aircraft, etc.). 2. to loiter, as *Several attendants were hovering round.* 3. to hesitate.—**hov'ercraft** *n.* a vehicle moving on a cushion of air over the surface of land or water

how *adv.* 1. in what way, as *This is how it is done.* 2. in what condition, as *How are you?* 3. to what extent, as *How many are there?*—**howev'er** *adv.* 1. in whatever manner, as *however it is done.* 2. to whatever extent, as *however big he is.* 3. all the same, as *I am glad, however*

how'dah *n.* a seat to ride in, on an elephant's back

howit'zer *n.* a short gun firing shells at a high elevation

howl *n.* a long loud cry.—*v.*—**howl'er** *n.* a stupid mistake

hub *n.* 1. the centre of a wheel. 2. a centre of activity

hubb'ub *n.* an uproar, confused noise

hud'dle *v.* to crowd together.—*n.*

hue *n.* colour, tint.—**hue and cry** alarm, outcry, after a criminal

huff *n.* a fit of sulking.—**to take the huff** to take offence.—*v.* (in the game of draughts), to remove (opponent's man) as forfeit.—**huf'fy** *adj.*

hug *v.* 1. to hold tightly in the arms. 2. to keep close to, as *The ship hugged the shore.* —**hug'ging** *pres. part.*—**hugged** *p.t.* and *p. part.*—*n.*

huge (hūj) *adj.* very big.—**huge'ly** *adv.* very much

Compare: enormous, gigantic, colossal, immense, vast. *Contrast:* tiny, minute, little, small, microscopic

hulk *n.* 1. a dismantled ship. 2. a big person. —**hulk'ing** *adj.* clumsy, unwieldy

hull *n.* 1. the frame or body of a ship. 2. a shell, husk.—*v.* to remove husks from

hum *v.* 1. to murmur (like a bee). 2. to sing with closed lips.—**hum'ming** *pres. part.*—**hummed** *p.t.* and *p. part.*—*n.*—**hum'ming bird** *n.* a tiny tropical bird which makes a humming sound by vibrating its wings when hovering

hu'man *adj.* belonging to man or mankind.—*n.*

Contrast: inhuman, subhuman, superhuman

humane' (hū-mān') *adj.* kind.—**human'ity** *n.* 1. the human race. 2. kindliness.—**hu'manly** *adv.*

hum'ble *adj.* 1. modest, unimportant. 2. not proud.—*v.* to bring low.—**hum'bly** *adv.*—**to eat humble pie** to be humiliated, to apologise humbly

hum'bug *n.* sham, nonsense.—*v.* to cheat, deceive.—**humbug'ging** *pres. part.*—**hum'-bugged** *p.t. and p. part.*

hum'drum *adj.* dull, wearisome

hu'mid (hū'mid) *adj.* damp, moist.—**humid'ity** *n.*

humil'iate (hū-mil'i-āt) *v.* to abase, fill with angry shame.—**humilia'tion** (-ā'shun) *n.*

humil'ity *n.* being humble, meekness

hum'mock *n.* a hillock, mound

hu'mour (hū'mer) *n.* 1. state of mind, mood. 2. fun, amusement.—*v.* to indulge, as *the mother humoured her sick child.*—

hu'morist *n.* a person who speaks or writes amusingly.—**hu'morous** *adj.*

hump *n.* a lump, esp. on the back.—**hump'-back** *n.*—*v.* (Aus.) to carry on the back.—**to hump the bluey** to go on the tramp

hum'py *n.* 1. aborigine term for a native hut. 2. any primitive dwelling

hu'mus (hū'mus) *n.* organic matter in soil

hunch *n.* 1. a lump. 2. thick slice. 3. idea, presentiment.—*v.* to bend, as *He hunched his shoulders.*—**hunch'back** *n.* humpback

hun'dred *n. adj.* ten times ten.—**hun'dred'th** *adj.*—**hun'dredweight** *n.* twentieth part of a ton, 112 lbs

Hun'gary *n.* a country in central Europe.—**Hunga'rian** *n.* and *adj.*

hung'er (hung'ger) *n.* 1. discomfort caused by lack of food. 2. strong desire.—*v.* to be hungry.—**hun'gry** (hung'gri) *adj.* —**hun'grily** *adv.*

hunt *v.* 1. to chase wild animals. 2. to search for.—*n.* hunting.—**hunt'er** *n.* a person or horse who hunts.—**hunts'man** *n.* a man in charge of pack of hounds

hur'dle *n.* a movable fence for jumping over. —**hur'dle race** *n.*—**hur'dler** *n.*

hurl *v.* to throw violently.—**hur'ly bur'ly** *n.* tumult

hur'ricane *n.* a violent storm

hur'ry *n.* haste, eagerness.—*v.* 1. to move quickly. 2. to urge to haste.—**hur'rying** *pres. part.*—**hur'ried** *p.t.* and *p. part.*—**hur'riedly** *adv.*

hurt *v.* to cause pain, damage, wound.—**hurt** *p.t.* and *p. part.*—*n.* wound, harm.—**hurt'ful** *adj.*

hurt'le *v.* to rush, dash, hurl.—**hurt'ling** *pres. part.*—**hurt'led** *p.t.* and *p. part.*

hus'band (huz'band) *n.* a married man—wife *fem.*—*v.* to economise, as *to husband one's resources.*—**hus'bandman** *n.* a farmer. —**hus'bandry** *n.* 1. farming. 2. thrift

hush *n.* silence.—*v.* 1. to be silent. 2. to make silent.—he **hush'es.**—*interj.* silence

husk *n.* the outer covering of certain seeds and fruits.—*v.*—**hus'ky** *adj.* 1. rough, harsh (esp. of the voice). 2. strong, burly

hus'ky *n.* an Eskimo dog.—**hus'kies** *pl.*

hus'sar *n.* a light cavalry soldier

hus'sy *n.* an impertinent girl—**hus'sies** *pl.*

hus'tle (hus'l) *v.* 1. to push. 2. to bustle, hurry.—**hus'tling** *pres. part.*—**hus'tled** *p.t.* and *p. part.*

hut *n.* a small, roughly-made wooden house

hutch *n.* a pen for rabbits, etc.—**hutch'es** *pl.*

hy'acinth (hī'a-sinth) *n.* a sweet-smelling spring flower

hyae'na see **hye'na**

hy'brid (hī'brid) *n.* the offspring of two plants or animals of different species.—*adj.* cross-bred

hy'drant (hī'drant) *n.* a water-pipe with a nozzle for a hose

hy'drate *n.* in chemistry, a compound of a substance with water

hydrau'lic (hī-draw'lik) *adj.* worked by force of water or some other liquid, as *a hydraulic lift.*—*pl.* the science of water power

hydrocar'bon *n.* a chemical compound of carbon and hydrogen

hydrochlor'ic *adj.* in chemistry, compounded of hydrogen and chlorine, as *hydrochloric acid*

hydro-elec'tric *adj.* concerning electricity produce by water power, as a *hydro-electric scheme*

hy'drogen (hī'dro-jen) *n.* a colourless gas which combines with oxygen to form water.—**hydrogen bomb** *n.* an atomic bomb of enormous power

hydropho'bia (hī-dro-fō'bi-a) *n.* dislike of water, symptom of madness in dogs

hydrostat'ics *n.* the study of the pressures and forces in liquids

hye'na (hī-ee'na) *n.* a fierce animal like a large dog

hygiene' (hī'jeen) *n.* rules for keeping well.—**hygien'ic** (hī-jeen'ik) *adj.* sanitary.—**hygien'ically** *adv.*

hymn (him) *n.* a song of praise to God.—*v.* to sing praise.—**hym'nal** *n.* book of hymns

hyper'bola *n.* a kind of curve studied in geometry

hyper'bole (hī-per'bol-i) *n.* an exaggeration in expression, e.g. *He was as quick as lightning.*—**hyperbol'ical** *adj.*

Contrast: under-statement

hypercrit'ical *adj.* too critical

Compare: carping, severe, fault-finding. *Contrast:* approving, indulgent, lenient

Note: This word must not be confused with *hypocritical*

hy'phen (hī'fen) *n.* a short line (-) indicating that two words or syllables are to be connected or **hy'phenated** *adj.*, e.g. *over-develop, semi-detached*

hypnot'ic (hip-not'ik) *adj.* causing deep sleep.—**hyp'notism** *n.* condition resembling sleep in which a person acts on suggestions of a—**hyp'notist** *n.*—**hyp'notise** *v.*

hypoc'risy (hip-ok'ri-si) *n.* pretending to be what one is not.—**hyp'ocrite** (hip'ō-krit) *n.*—**hypocrit'ical** *adj.*

Compare: deceit, imposture, cant, humbug, dishonesty. *Contrast:* sincerity, candour, truthfulness, straightforwardness, honesty

Note: Not to be confused with *hypercritical*

hypot'enuse (hī-pot'en-ūs) *n.* the side of a right-angled triangle opposite the right angle

hypoth'esis (hī-poth'esis) *n.* theory, probable explanation.—**hypoth'eses** (-seez) *pl.*—**hypothet'ical** *adj.* supposed

hyste'ria (his-tee'ri-a) *n.* a disturbance of

the nervous system, with lack of self-control.—**hyster'ical** (his-ter'ikal) *adj.*—**hyster'ics** *n.pl.* fit of uncontrolled laughing and crying

I

I *pron.* refers to oneself as the subject of a sentence, as *I am going out.*—*objective* **me,** *possessive* **my, mine,** *plural* **we**

i'bex *n.* a species of wild goat

ice (īs) *n.* frozen water.—*v.* 1. to cover with ice. 2. to cover (cake) with sugar.—**i'cing** *pres. part.*—**iced** *p.t.* and *p. part.*—**ice'berg** *n.* a mass of floating ice.—**ice cream** a frozen sweet.—**i'cy** *adj.* 1. slippery. 2. very cold.—**i'cily** *adv.*

Ice'land *n.* a large island in the north Atlantic ocean.—**Ice'landic** *adj.*

i'cicle (ī'si-kl) *n.* a long, hanging spike of ice

ide'a (ī-dee'a) *n.* 1. a thought or picture formed in the mind. 2. a plan, aim

ide'al *n.* a mind-picture of a perfect thing.—*adj.* perfect.—**ide'alise** *v.* to give ideal form to.—**ide'alist** *n.* one who has ideals.—**ide'ally** *adv.*

iden'tical *adj.* the same.—**iden'tically** *adv.*

identifica'tion (ā'shun) *n.* recognition.—**iden'tify** *v.* 1. to treat or regard as the same. 2. to recognise, prove, as the same, as *The policeman identified him as the thief.*—he **iden'tifies.**—**iden'tifying** *pres. part.*—**iden'tified** *p.t.* and *p. part.*

iden'tity *n.* 1. absolute sameness. 2. who a person is.—**iden'tities** *pl.*

id'iom *n.* 1. an expression of speech. 2. a dialect.—**idiomat'ic** *adj.* characteristic of a language

idiosyn'cracy (id-i-ō-sin'kra-si) *n.* a peculiarity in a person

id'iot *n.* a weak-minded person.—**idiot'ic** *adj.* very stupid

i'dle (ī'dl) *adj.* 1. doing nothing. 2. lazy. 3. useless, vain.—*v.*—**i'dleness** *n.*—**i'dler** *n.* a lazy person.—**i'dly** *adv.*

i'dol *n.* an image set up for worship.—**idol'ater** *n.* an idol-worshipper.—**idol'atrous** *adj.*—**idol'atry** *n.*—**i'dolise** *v.* make an idol of

i'dyll (ī'dil, id'il) *n.* 1. happy and picturesque incident or scene in rural surroundings. 2. a short poem describing such an incident or scene—**idyll'ic** *adj.*

if *conj.* 1. on the condition or supposition that, as *You can go if you pay*, 2. whether, as *I should like to know if he is going*

ig'loo *n.* an Eskimo's snow hut

ig'neous *adj.* resulting from fire

ignite' *v.* to set on fire.—**igni'tion** (ig-ni'shun) *n.* firing explosive mixture in engine

igno'ble *adj.* mean, base.—**igno'bly** *adv.*

ignomin'ious (ig-nō-min'i-us) *adj.* shameful.—**ig'nominy** *n.* disgrace

ignora'mus (-ā-) *n.* an ignorant person.—**ignora'muses** *pl.*

ig'norance (ig'nor-ans) *n.* lack of knowledge.—**ig'norant** *adj.* knowing little.—**ig'norantly** *adv.*

Compare: (with *adj.*) illiterate, uneducated, untaught, ill-informed, unlearned. *Contrast:* educated, knowledgeable, learned, well-informed

ignore' *v.* to disregard, take no notice of.—**ignor'ing** *pres. part.*—**ignored'** *p.t.* and *p. part.*

ill *adj.* 1. not well. 2. evil, bad.—**worse** *comp.*—**worst** *sup.*—*n.* harm, evil.—*adv.* badly.—**ill-advised** *adj.* unwise.—**ill at ease** embarrassed, uncomfortable

ille'gal (il-ee'gal) *adj.* unlawful.—**illegal'ity** *n.*

illeg'ible (il-ej'i-ble) *adj.* not readable

illegitimate (il-ej-it'i-mit) *adj.* 1. not lawful. 2. born out of wedlock

illib'eral *adj.* mean, ungenerous.—**illiberal'ity** *n.*

illi'cit (il-i'sit) *adj.* unlawful, contraband

illim'itable *adj.* boundless, without limit

illit'erate *adj.* unable to read or write, uneducated

ill'ness *n.* sickness, disease

illog'ical (il-oj'i-cal) *adj.* not logical, unreasonable

illu'minate *v.* 1. to light up, make brilliant. 2. to decorate (book) with gold and colours.—**illumina'tion** (-a'shun) *n.* 1. lights. 2. decoration.—**illu'mine** *v.* to light up

Compare: 1. brighten, enlighten. 2. embellish

illu'sion (i-lū'zhun) *n.* false appearance, mistaken belief, as *An optical illusion made equal lines seem unequal.*—**illu'sionist** *n.* a conjurer.—**illu'sive** *adj.*—**illu'sory** (ilū'zor-i) *adj.* misleading

il'lustrate *v.* to explain by pictures, diagrams, examples, etc.—**illustrating** *pres. part.*—**il'lustrated** *p.t.* and *p. part.*—**illustra'tion** (-trā'shun) *n.* picture, explanation.—**il'lustrative** *adj.*—**il'lustrator** *n.*

illus'trious *adj.* famous, distinguished

Compare: eminent, noted, renowned, celebrated. *Contrast:* obscure, unknown, unimportant

ill'will *n.* dislike, unkind feeling

im- *pref.* (used before letters *m, b, p.*) 1. not, as *immobile, impossible.* 2. in, as *imprison, imbibe*

im'age (im'aj) *n.* 1. a statue. 2. a likeness. 3. a reflection (in mirror). 4. (in literature) a simile, metaphor

im'agery (im'aj-er-i) *n.* 1. statues, carving. 2. the metaphors and symbols used by a writer of literature

imag'inable (i-maj'in-a-bl) *adj.* which can be imagined.—**imag'inary** *adj.* not real

imagina'tion (i-maj-in-ā'shun) *n.* 1. the power of forming mind-pictures. 2. creative ability. 3. fancy.—**imag'inative** *adj.* coming from imagination

imag'ine (imaj'in) *v.* to fancy, to form pictures in the mind.—**imag'ining** *pres. part.*—**imag'ined** *p.t.* and *p. part.*

im'becile (im'be-seel) *adj.* weak-minded.—*n.*—**imbecil'ity** *n.*

imbibe' *v.* to drink in.—**imbi'bing** *pres. part.* —**imbibed'** *p.t.* and *p. part.*

imbue' *v.* 1. to soak, dye. 2. to inspire, as *imbued with love of liberty.*—**imbu'ing** *pres. part.*—**imbued'** *p.t.* and *p. part.*

im'itate *v.* to take as model, to copy, mimic.—**im'itating** *pres. part.*—**im'itated** *p.t.* and *p. part.*—**imita'tion** (-tā'shun) *n.* copy, likeness.—**im'itative** *adj.*—**im'itator** *n.*

immac'ulate *adj.* spotless, pure.—**immac'ulately** *adv.*

immate'rial *adj.* of no importance.

Compare: inconsiderable, trifling, insignificant, unessential. *Contrast:* important, significant, momentous, essential, material

immature' *adj.* not mature, unripe, undeveloped

immeas'urable (imezh'ur-a-bl) *adj.* boundless, immense

imme'diate *adj.* 1. near, as *in the immediate future.* 2. present, occurring now, as *My immediate needs are food, clothes and money.* 3. not separated by others, as *He is my immediate neighbour.* 4. instant, as *He demanded an immediate reply.*—**imme'diately** *adv.*

immemo'rial *adj.* beyond memory, very old

immense' *adj.* huge vast., See **big.**—**immense'ly** *adv.*—**immen'sity** *n.*

immerse' *v.* 1. to dip, plunge into a liquid. 2. to absorb (in thought, etc.).—**immer'sing** *pres. part.*—**immersed'** *p.t.* and *p. part.*—**immer'sion** (immer'zhun) *n.*—**immer'sion heater** *n.* an electrical heater acting inside a cylinder of water

im'migrant *n.* a settler.—**imm'igrate** *v.* to come into a country as a settler.—**immigra'tion** (-grā'shun) *n.*

Note: A person coming from another country is an *immigrant*, but a person who leaves a country is an *emigrant*

im'minent *adj.* close at hand, as *in imminent danger.*—**im'minently** *adv.*

Note: Do not confuse this word with *eminent*

immo'bile *adj.* unmovable, unmoving

immod'erate *adj.* extreme, unreasonable

im'molate *v.* to kill in sacrifice.—**immola'tion** (-ā'shun) *n.*

immor'al *adj.* wrong, wicked.—**immoral'ity** *n.*

immor'tal *adj.* undying, everlasting.—*n.* an immortal being.—**immortal'ity** *n.*—**immor'talise** *v.* to make immortal

immo'vable (i-mōō'va-bl) *adj.* fixed, which cannot be moved

immune' *adj.* 1. secure, exempt. 2. proof (against a disease).—**immu'nity** *n.*—**im'munise** *v.* to make immune.—**im'munisation** *n.* making immune

Note: Immune may be followed by *against* or *to* or *from*

immure' *v.* to shut up behind walls, imprison

immu'table *adj.* unchangeable

imp *n.* 1. a little devil. 2. a mischievous child

im'pact *n.* a collision

impair' *v.* to weaken, make worse

impale' *v.* to fix on to something pointed, pierce

impart' *v.* 1. to share, give. 2. to tell

impar'tial (im-par'shal) *adj.* just, fair.—**impartial'ity** (im-par-shi-al'i-ti) *n.*

impas'sable *adj.* which cannot be passed

impas'sioned (im-pash'ond) *adj.* deeply moved, as *He made an impassioned speech*

impas'sive *adj.* unmoved, without feeling

impa'tience (im-pā'shens) *n.* lacking patience —**impa'tient** (im-pā'shent) *adj.* unwilling to bear delay, restless.—**impa'tiently** *adv.*

impeach' *v.* to accuse, call in question.—**impeach'ment** *n.*

impec'cable *adj.* faultless, perfect

impecu'nious *adj.* having no money

impede' *v.* to hinder, obstruct.—**impe'ding** *pres. part.*—**impe'ded** *p.t.* and *p. part,*—**imped'iment** *n.* 1. an obstacle. 2. a speech defect

Compare: embarrass, limit, hamper, retard. *Contrast:* help, facilitate, expedite, promote

impel' *v.* to drive, urge.—**impel'ling** *pres. part.*—**impelled'** *p.t.* and *p. part.*

impend' *v.* to be near.—**impend'ing** *adj.* coming

impen'etrable *adj.* which cannot be pierced or passed

impen'itent *adj.* not penitent, not sorry for sin

imper'ative *adj.* 1. commanding. 2. necessary

Note: In Grammar the imperative mood of a verb is that which gives an order or command. Thus, if you say "*Go away,*" *go* is in the imperative

impercep'tible (im-per-sep'ti-bl) *adj.* too slight to be seen or felt.—**impercep'tibly** *adv.*

imper'fect *adj.* 1. faulty. 2. incomplete.—**imperfec'tion** (-shun) *n.*

impe'rial *adj.* 1. of an empire. 2. of an emperor. 3. majestic.—*n.* 1. a small pointed beard. 2. a size of paper.—**impe'rialism** *n.* belief in policy of empire.—**impe'rialist** *adj.*

imper'il *v.* to bring into danger.—**imper'illing** *pres. part.*—**imper'illed** *p.t.* and *p. part.*

impe'rious *adj.* 1. commanding, arrogant. 2. urgent

imper'ishable *adj.* undying, everlasting

imper'sonal *adj.* not referring to any one person.—**imper'sonally** *adv.*

imper'sonate *v.* to pretend to be another, to deceive or amuse.—**impersona'tion** (-ā'shun) *n.*

imper'tinence *n.* rudeness, impudence.—**imper'tinent** *adj.* rude

impertur'bable *adj.* not excitable, calm

imper'vious *adj.* impenetrable

impet'uous *adj.* 1. hasty, acting without thinking. 2. violent, rushing.—**impet'uously** *adv.*—**impetuos'ity** *n.*

im'petus *n.* 1. a moving force. 2. a driving force

impi'ety (im-pī'e-ti) *n.* lack of reverence, wickedness.—**im'pious** (im'pi-us) *adj.*

implac'able *adj.* relentless, not to be appeased, as *Drake was an implacable foe of Spain*

implant' *v.* to insert into

im'plement *n.* tool, utensil.—*v.* to carry into effect

im'plicate *v.* 1. to include. 2. to entangle.—**implica'tion** (-kā'shun) *n.* suggestion

implic'it (im-plis'it) *adj.* 1. suggested, but not expressed in words. 2. complete, utter, as *I have implicit faith in his promise*

implore' *v.* to beg, entreat. See **beg.**—**implo'ring** *pres. part.*—**implored'** *p.t.* and *p. part.*

imply' *v.* to mean, without saying so in words, as *The fact that you did not object implied that you approved of what was done.*—he **implies'.**—**imply'ing** *pres. part.* **implied'** *p.t.* and *p. part.*

impolite' *adj.* rude, unmannerly

impol'itic *adj.* not wise, not prudent

import' *v.* 1. to bring in from a foreign country. 2. to mean, express, as *What does his action import?* 3. to be of importance, as *It imports us to act quickly.*—**im'port** *n.* 1. something brought from abroad. 2. meaning, importance.—**importa'tion** (tā'shun) *n.*—**impor'ter** *n.*

impor'tance *n.* 1. being important. 2. value, significance.—**impor'tant** *adj.* 1. needing great attention. 2. having value, influence. 3. pompous

impor'tunate *adj.* persistent in asking.—**importune'** *v.* to keep asking for something. —**importu'nity** *n.*

impose' (im-pōz') *v.* 1. to lay (a tax) on. 2. (upon) to take advantage of, deceive.—**impo'sing** *adj.* impressive.—**imposi'tion** (i'shun) *n.* 1. a trick, fraud. 2. punishment. 3. burden (of taxation, etc.)

impos'sible *adj.* which cannot be done, cannot happen.—**impossibil'ity** *n.* something impossible.—**impos'sibly** *adv.*

im'post *n.* a duty, tax

impos'tor *n.* a person who takes a false name or character, deceiver.—**impos'ture** *n.* fraud

im'potence *n.* lack of power.—**im'potent** *adj.* helpless

impound' *v.* 1. to confiscate. 2. (old use) to put cattle into an enclosure

impov'erish *v.* to make poor.—he **impov'erishes.**—**impov'erishment** *n.*

imprac'ticable *adj.* which cannot be done.—**imprac'tical** *adj.* not practical

impreca'tion (-kā'shun) *n.* a curse

impreg'nable *adj.* proof against attack
Compare: invincible, immovable, unassailable, invulnerable

im'pregnate *v.* 1. to fertilise. 2. to fill, saturate, as *The air was impregnated with the smell of roses.*—**impregna'tion** (-nā'shun) *n.*

impress' *v.* 1. to force into service. 2. to imprint, fix. 3. to affect, influence.—he **impress'es.**—**im'press** *n.* mark impressed. —**impress'ible** *adj.*

impres'sion (im-presh'un) *n.* 1. a mark, imprint. 2. a printed copy. 3. an effect on the mind. 4. a belief, idea, as *a false impression, to be under the impression that . . .* —**impres'sionable** *adj.* easily influenced.—**impres'sive** *adj.* solemn, effective

im'print *n.* 1. a mark, stamp. 2. a printer's or publisher's name on title-page of book.—**imprint'** *v.* to stamp, mark

impris'on (im-priz'un) *v.* to put into prison.—**impris'onment** *n.*

improb'able *adj.* unlikely

impromp'tu *adj.* and *adv.* without previous preparation

improp'er *adj.* 1. wrong. 2. not suitable. 3. indecent.—**impropri'ety** *n.* improper behaviour

improve' (im-prōōv') *v.* 1. to make better. 2. to make good use of, as *He improved his opportunities for study.*—**impro'ving** *pres. part.*—**improved** *p.t.* and *p. part.*—**improve'ment** *n.* getting better, gain
Compare: ameliorate, amend. *Contrast:* mar, spoil, injure, deteriorate

improv'idence *n.* lack of forethought, carelessness.—**improv'ident** *adj.* thoughtless for the future
Compare: thriftless, prodigal, extravagant, imprudent. *Contrast:* thrifty, saving, economical

im'provise *v.* 1. to compose (music, etc.) without preparation. 2. to arrange or perform without warning or preparation, as *The shipwrecked sailors had to improvise a shelter for themselves.*—**im'provising** *pres. part.*—**im'provised** *p.t.* and *p. part.*—**improvisa'tion** (-ā'shun) *n.*

impru'dent *adj.* rash, unwise

im'pudence *n.* rudeness, insolence.—**im'pudent** *adj.* saucy, rude, immodest

impugn' (im-pūn') *v.* to call in question, challenge

im'pulse *n.* 1. a sudden driving force. 2. a sudden desire to do something.—**impul'sive** *adj.* hasty, unthinking.—**impul'sively** *adv.*

impu'nity *n.* freedom from punishment or hurtful consequences

impure' *adj.* 1. not pure, dirty, mixed. 2. bad. 3. incorrect.—**impur'ity** *n.*—**impur'ities** *pl.*

impute' *v.* to attribute, as *He imputed his downfall to drink.*—**impu'ting** *pres. part.*—**impu'ted** *p.t.* and *p. part.*—**imputa'tion** (-tā'shun) *n.*

in *prep.* 1. expresses inclusion within limits of space, time, circumstance, etc., as *in England, in my opinion.* 2. made of, as *a painting in water-colours.* 3. dressed in, as "*The Woman in White.*" 4. expressed in, as *written in Latin.*—*adv.* in or into some state, place, etc., as *to go in.*—**ins and outs** details

Note: The comparative *inner* and the superlatives *innermost* and *inmost* are used as *adjectives*

in—is added at the beginning of other words to mean either 1. not, e.g. *incurable* means "not curable" or 2. in, into, upon, e.g. *inside, inject.* Before *l, in* becomes *il-* (e.g. *illegal*), before *r,* it becomes *ir-* (e.g. *irreverent*), and before *b, m* and *p* it becomes *im-* (e.g. *impossible*)

If you are seeking the meaning of any word beginning with *in-* and do not find it below, find the word to which it has been added and put "not" before it. Thus *insincere* means *not sincere.* Look up *sincere*

inadver'tence *n.* carelessness, lack of thought. —**inadver'tent** *adj.* unintentional, not paying attention.—**inadver'tently** *adv.*

Compare: (with *adj.*) inattentive, thoughtless, inconsiderate, negligent. *Contrast:* careful, attentive, wary, watchful

inane' *adj.* foolish, silly.—**inan'ity** *n.* foolishness.—**inani'tion** (-i'shun) *n.* exhaustion

inan'imate *adj.* lifeless, dull

in'asmuch (as) *adv.* since, seeing that

inau'gurate *v.* 1. to admit to office. 2. to begin, with ceremony.—**inau'gural** *adj.*—**inaugura'tion** (-ā'shun) *n.*

in'born *adj.* present at birth, inherited

in'bred *adj.* born in, natural.—**inbree'ding** *n.* breeding animals by crossing similar types

incandes'cent (in-kan-des'ent) *adj.* 1. glowing with heat. 2. of artificial light, produced by a glowing filament

incanta'tion (-tā'shun) *n.* a spell, enchantment

incapac'itate (in-ka-pas'i-tāt) *v.* to disable, make unfit.—**incapac'ity** *n.* unfitness

incar'cerate (in-kar'ser-āt) *v.* to imprison.—**incarcera'tion** (-ā'shun) *n.*

incar'nate *adj.* in human flesh.—**incarna'tion** (-nā'shun) *n.*

incen'diary (in-sen'di-ar-i) *n.* a person who deliberately sets fire to property.—*adj.* 1. inciting to trouble. 2. spreading fire.—**incen'diarism** *n.*

in'cense (in'sens) *n.* 1. a perfume burned in religious ceremonies. 2. flattery

incense' (in-sens') *v.* to make angry

Compare: enrage, provoke, exasperate. *Contrast:* soothe, pacify, mollify

incen'tive (in-sen'tiv) *n.* motive, encouragement.—*adj.*

Compare: spur, stimulus, incitement, inducement. *Contrast:* check, discouragement, prevention

incep'tion (in-sep'shun) *n.* beginning

inces'sant (in-ses'ant) *adj.* unceasing, continual.—**incess'antly** *adv.*

inch *n.* a measure, one-twelfth of a foot.—**by in'ches** *adv.* gradually.—**within an inch** of very nearly.—**every inch** completely

in'cident (in'si-dent) *n.* an event, happening. —**inciden'tal** *adj.* occasional.—**inciden'tally** *adv.* by chance, by the way

incin'erate (in-sin'er-āt) *v.* to burn.—**inciner'ator** *n.* furnace, brazier.—**incinera'tion** (-ā'shun) *n.*

incip'ient *adj.* beginning, in the first stage of

inci'sion (in-si'zhun) *n.* cut, gash.—**inci'sive** (in-sī'siv) *adj.* 1. cutting, sharp. 2. keen, biting, as *incisive remarks.*—**inci'sor** (in-sī'zor) *n.* a sharp tooth

incite' (in-sīt') *v.* to rouse, stir up, as *An agitator incited the natives to revolt.*—**inci'ting** *pres. part.*—**inci'ted** *p.t.* and *p. part.*—**incite'ment** *n.* encouragement

Compare: instigate, goad, urge, stimulate. *Contrast:* dissuade, restrain, discourage, check

inclina'tion (-ā'shun) *n.* 1. a leaning, bending. 2. a slope. 3. a preference, desire

incline' *v.* 1. to bend, turn. 2. to slope. 3. to be disposed.—**incli'ning** *pres. part.*—**inclined'** *p.t.* and *p. part.*—**in'cline** *n.* slope

include' (in-klōōd') *v.* to reckon in, contain. —**inclu'ding** *pres. part.*—**inclu'ded** *p.t.* and *p. part.*—**inclu'sion** (in-klōō'zhun) *n.*—**inclu'sive** (in-klōō'siv) *adj.* 1. including the limits stated. 2. including everything

incog'nito *adj.* unknown, keeping identity hidden, as *The king was travelling incognito.* —*adv.*

incohe'rence (in-kō-hee'rens) *n.* a lack of connection, confusion of speech.—**incohe'rent** *adj.* confused, rambling

in'come *n.* receipts, money coming in from wages, business, etc.—**in'come-tax** *n.* a government tax on personal incomes

incom'parable *adj.* unequalled

incon'gruous *adj.* inappropriate, unsuitable. —**incongru'ity** *n.*

inconve'nience *n.* trouble.—**inconve'nient** *adj.* troublesome

incor'porate *v.* to unite in one body, include. —**incorpora'tion** (-ā'shun) *n.*

incor'rigible (in-kor'i-ji-bl) *adj.* which cannot be corrected, as *He is an incorrigible liar*

increase' (in-krees') *v.* 1. to make greater, add to. 2. to become greater in size, number, etc.—**increas'ing** *pres. part.*—**increased'** *p.t.* and *p. part.*—**in'crease** *n.* growth

Compare: enlarge, enhance, augment, extend, magnify. *Contrast:* decrease, diminish, lessen, decline

incred'ible *adj.* surprising, unbelievable.—**incred'ibly** *adv.*—**incred'ulous** *adj.* not believing easily.—**incredu'lity** *n.* doubt

in'crement *n.* the amount of an increase, as

his salary rose by increments of £50 *a year until it reached a maximum*

incrim'inate *v.* to charge with a crime, involve in accusation

incrusta'tion (-tā'shun) *n.* a hard coating

in'cubate *v.* to hatch (eggs).—**incuba'tion** (-bā'shun) *n.*—**in'cubator** *n.* an apparatus for artificial hatching of eggs or for the care of premature babies

in'culcate *v.* to teach repeatedly, to impress strongly

incum'bent *n.* a clergyman in charge of a church.—*adj.* resting on, esp. on a person as a duty, as *It is incumbent upon us to give him our support*

incur' *v.* to bring on oneself, as *to incur debts, to incur someone's displeasure.*—**incur'ring** *pres. part.*—**incurred'** *p.t.* and *p. part.*

incur'sion (in-kur'shun) *n.* invasion

indebt'ed (in-det'ed) *adj.* owing, in debt, obliged.—**indebt'edness** *n.*

indeed' *adv.* in truth, really

indefat'igable *adj.* untiring.—**indefat'igably** *adv.*

indel'ible *adj.* which cannot be removed, permanent.—**indel'ibly** *adv.*

indem'nify *v.* to compensate for loss or damage.—he **indem'nifies.**—**indem'nifying** *pres. part.*—**indem'nified** *p.t.* and *p. part.*—**indem'nity** *n.* insurance, compensation

indent' *v.* 1. to make notches or holes in. 2. to make out an order (for). 3. to begin a line farther in from margin than the rest of a paragraph.—**inden'ted** *adj.*—**indenta'tion** *n.*

inden'ture *n.* a sealed written agreement, esp. one binding apprentice to master

indepen'dence *n.* 1. self-government. 2. freedom to act.—**indepen'dent** *adj.* 1. free from control or help of others. 2. unconnected.—**indepen'dently** *adv.*

in'dex *n.* 1. the forefinger. 2. anything that points out. 3. an alphabetical list of contents of a book. 4. in Mathematics, a small figure indicating "power," e.g. 2^2 is 2×2; 2^3 is 2×2×2—**in'dexes** plural of meanings 1, 2 and 3.—**in'dices** (in'-di-seez) plural of meaning 4

In'dia *n.* a country in southern Asia.—**In'dian** *n.* and *adj.*—**In'dian file** single file.—**In'dian ink** black waterproof ink.—**In'dian summer** a fine spell of weather in late autumn

in'dia-rubber *n.* rubber used for erasing

in'dicate *v.* to point out, show.—**in'dicating** *pres. part.*—**in'dicated** *p.t.* and *p. part.*—**indica'tion** (-kā'shun) *n.*—**indic'ative** *adj.* showing. The *indicative mood* in Grammar is that in which the verb states, e.g. *I am going; he has eaten.* See **imperative, interrogative.**—**in'dicator** *n.* 1. something which points out. 2. a recording instrument

in'dices see **in'dex**

indict' (in-dīt) *v.* to accuse.—**indict'able** (in-dīt'a-bl) *adj.*—**indict'ment** (in-dīt'ment) *n.* a formal accusation

indif'ference *n.* 1. lack of interest. 2. unimportance.—**indif'ferent** *adj.* 1. not caring, as *I am indifferent whether I go or not.* 2. unimportant, as *It is indifferent to me what you do.* 3. neither good nor bad. 4. moderate, rather poor, as *He gave a very indifferent performance.* 5. impartial, as *A judge should be indifferent.*—**indif'ferent'ly** *adv.*

indig'enous (in-dij'e-nus) *adj.* native born in or natural to a country

in'digent (in'dij-ent) *adj.* poor, in need

indiges'tible (in-di-jes'ti-bl) *adj.* not easily digested.—**indiges'tion** (in-di-jes'chon) *n.* failure to digest food

indig'nant *adj.* angry and injured.—**indigna'tion** (-nā'shun) *n.* anger and sense of injury

Compare: exasperated, wrathful, provoked, incensed, annoyed, cross, resentful. *Contrast:* pacified, satisfied, placated, pleased

indig'nity *n.* an insult, unworthy treatment.—**indig'nities** *pl.*

Compare: affront, outrage, offence, humiliation

in'digo *n.* deep blue dye, obtained from plants.—*adj.* of a deep blue colour.—**in'digos** *pl.*

indispen'sable *adj.* necessary, essential

indispose' *v.* 1. to make unwell. 2. to make disinclined.—**indisposed'** *adj.* 1. unwell. 2. unwilling.—**indisposi'tion** (-zi'shun) *n.* 1. slight illness. 2. disinclination

indite' *v.* to write, compose

individ'ual *n.* a single person, animal or thing.—*adj.* 1. single, separate. 2. belonging to a special person or thing.—**individ'ualism** *n.* independent action by individuals, instead of co-operation.—**individ'ualist** *n.*—**individ'ualistic** *adj.*—**individual'ity** *n.* distinctive character.—**individ'ually** *adv.* separately

Compare: characteristic, peculiar, distinct, particular, separate, insulated. *Contrast:* general, collective, common

in'dolence *n.* laziness.—**in'dolent** *adj.*—**in'dolently** *adv.*

indom'itable *adj.* unconquerable, never giving up, as *the Arctic explorers were men of indomitable character*

Indone'sia *n.* a republic of several islands in the East Indies.—**Indone'sian** *n.* and *adj.*

in'door *adj.* inside a house.—**in'doors** *adv.*

indu'bitable *adj.* undoubted

Compare: indisputable, undeniable, certain

induce' (in-dūs') 1. to persuade. 2. to produce (esp. electricity).—**indu'cing** *pres. part.*—**induced'** *p.t.* and *p. part.*—**induce'ment** *n.* incentive, attraction

induct' *v.* to instal in office.—**induc'tion** (-shun) *n.* 1. introduction. 2. reasoning from particular facts to general truths. 3. production of an electric or magnetic state in a body by its being near an electrified or magnetised body. 4. in an internal combustion engine, that part of the piston's action which draws the gas from the carburettor.—**induc'tive** *adj.*

indulge' (in-dulj') *v.* 1. to humour, give way to. 2. to allow oneself a pleasure.—**indul'ging** *pres. part.*—**indulged** *p.t.* and *p. part.*—**indul'gence** *n.*—**indul'gent** *adj.* kind, making allowances

indus'trial *adj.* belonging to industry.—**indus'trialist** *n.* a powerful man in industry. **indus'trialism** *n.* the factory system.—**indus'trialise** *v.* to make industrial.—**indus'trialised** *p.t.*, *p. part.* and *adj.*

indus'trious *adj.* hard-working

in'dustry *n.* 1. diligence in any employment. 2. manufacture or trade.—**in'dustries** *pl.*

ine'briate *v.* to make drunk.—*n.* a drunkard. —*adj.*—**inebria'tion** (-ā'shun) *n.*

ined'ible *adj.* not fit to eat

inef'fable *adj.* beyond words, indescribable. —**inef'fably** *adv.*

Compare: unutterable, unspeakable

inel'igible *adj.* not qualified, not suitable

inept' *adj.* not fit, foolish.—**inep'titude** *n.* unfitness, foolishness

inert' *adj.* 1. lifeless, not moving. 2. slow, dull.—**iner'tia** (in-er'sh-a) *n.* 1. lack of motion, dullness. 2. (in Science) property by which matter remains at rest or continues in motion in a straight line, unless affected by external force

Compare: inactive, tepid, apathetic, lethargic, sluggish. *Contrast:* active, energetic, lively, volatile

ines'timable *adj.* too great to be measured, as *Bob's clever play was of inestimable value to the team*

inev'itable *adj.* unavoidable, as *Death is inevitable*

inex'orable *adj.* relentless, not yielding to entreaties

inex'plicable *adj.* which cannot be explained

infal'lible *adj.* 1. unfailing, as *an infallible remedy.* 2. incapable of error.—**infallibil'ity** *n.*

in'famous *adj.* having a very bad reputation, disgraceful.—**in'famy** *n.* disgrace, wickedness.—**in'famies** *pl.*

in'fancy *n.* 1. babyhood. 2. early stages.—**in'fant** *n.* 1. a very young child. 2. a person under 21, a minor.—*adj.*—**infant'icide** *n.* 1. the murder of a baby. 2. a person guilty of this.—**in'fantile** *adj.* childish

in'fantry *n.* foot-soldiers.—**in'fantryman** *n.*

infat'uate *v.* to excite a foolish passion.—**infat'uated** *adj.*—**infatua'tion** (-ā'shun) *n.*

infect' *v.* 1. to give disease-germs to, as *The air was infected with microbes.* 2. to spread an influence, as *The people were infected with discontent*, or *they were infected with enthusiasm.*—**infec'tion** (-shun) *n.* spreading disease.—**infec'tious** (in-fek'shus) *adj.* catching

infer' *v.* to deduce by reasoning, as *The detectives inferred from the footprints that the criminal was tall.*—**infer'ring** *pres. part.*—**inferred'** *p.t.* and *p. part.*—**in'ference** *n.* reasoning, deduction

infe'rior (in-fee'ri-or) *adj.* lower in rank or quality.—*n.* a person of lower rank.—**inferior'ity** *n.*—**inferiority complex** a deep-seated lack of self-confidence

infer'nal *adj.* of the lower world, hellish.—**infer'nally** *adv.*—**infer'no** *n.* hell

infest' *v.* to haunt, to swarm in, as *the house was infested with ants*

in'fidel *n.* an unbeliever.—**infidel'ity** *n.* 1. disbelief (in religion). 2. disloyalty

in'filtrate *v.* to trickle through.—**infiltra'tion** (-trā'shun) *n.*

in'finite (in'fin-it) *adj.* boundless, vast.—**the in'finite** *n.* God.—**infinites'imal** *adj.* extremely small.—**infin'ity** *n.* infinite time, or space

infin'itive *n.* (grammar) the verb itself, not expressing persons or time, as *to see, to buy*

infirm' *adj.* 1. weak in body. 2. irresolute.—**infirm'ity** *n.*—**infir'mary** *n.* hospital

inflame' *v.* 1. to set on fire. 2. to excite.—**inflam'mable** *adj.* catching fire easily

inflamma'tion (-mā'shun) *n.* a swelling, with heat, pain, and redness.—**inflam'matory** *adj.* 1. exciting anger, etc. 2. causing inflammation

inflate' *v.* 1. to blow up, swell. 2. to raise (prices) artificially. 3. to increase a country's currency abnormally, thus causing it to fall in value.—**infla'ting** *pres. part.*—**infla'ted** *p.t.* and *p. part.*—**infla'tion** (-flā'shun) *n.*

inflect' *v.* 1. to bend. 2. to change the tone of voice.—**inflec'tion, inflex'ion** (-shun) *n.* 1. bend. 2. change of tone

inflex'ible *adj.* unbending

inflict' *v.* to impose (pain, etc.).—**inflic'tion** (-shun) *n.* burden, pain

in'fluence (in'flōō-ens) *n.* power to affect.—*v.* to have power over.—**in'fluencing** *pres. part.*—**in'fluenced** *p.t.* and *p. part.*—**influen'tial** (-shal) *adj.*

influen'za *n.* a contagious feverish illness

in'flux *n.* a flowing in

inform' *v.* 1. to tell. 2. to inspire.—**infor'mant** *n.* a person giving information.—**informa'tion** (-mā'shun) *n.* knowledge.—**infor'mative** *adj.*—**infor'mer** *n.* one who gives information to the police, against a criminal

Compare: advise, apprise, disclose, impart, notify, teach

inform'al *adj.* casual, friendly

infra-red' *adj.* referring to invisible rays of wavelength just longer than that of red light

infringe' (in-frinj') *v.* 1. to break (the law). 2. to trespass.—**infringe'ment** *n.*

infu'riate *v.* to enrage, make furious.—**infu'riating** *adj.*
infuse' (in-fūz') *v.* 1. to soak, steep, in order to bring out qualities. 2. to pour in, instil. —**infu'sing** *pres. part.*—**infused'** *p.t.* and *p. part.*—**infu'sion** (in-fū'zhun) *n.*
ingen'ious (in-jee'ni-us) *adj.* 1. clever. 2. skilful at inventing.—**ingenu'ity** (in-jen-ū'i-ti) *n.* skill
ingen'uous (in-jen'ū-us) *adj.* open, simple, innocent.—**ingen'uously** *adv.*
in'gle-nook *n.* a chimney corner
in'got (ing'got) *n.* a mass of metal, esp. gold or silver, cast in a mould
ingrain' *v.* to stain, dye.—**ingrained'** *adj.* deeply fixed
in'grate *adj.* ungrateful.—*n.*
ingra'tiate (in-grā'shi-āt) *v.* to get (oneself) into favour (with someone)
ingre'dient *n.* one part of a mixture
in'gress *n.* entrance
inhab'it *v.* to live in.—**inhab'itable** *adj.*—**inhab'itant** *n.* a person living in a place
inhale' *v.* to breathe in.—**inha'ling** *pres. part.*—**inhaled'** *p.t.* and *p. part.*—**inhala'tion** (-ā'shun) *n.* breathing in
inhe'rent (in-hee'rent) *adj.* inborn, inseparable from a person
inher'it *v.* 1. to receive by legal descent, as heir, as *He inherited his uncle's property.* 2. to derive from parents or ancestors, as *He inherits his good looks from his mother.* —**inher'itance** *n.*—**inher'itor** *n.* heir.—**inher'itress, inher'itrix** *fem.*
inhib'it *v.* to repress, restrain.—**inhibi'tion** (i'shun) *n.* restraint, repression
inhu'man *adj.* cruel, brutal.—**inhuman'ity** *n.*
inim'ical *adj.* hostile, unfriendly
iniq'uitous (in-ik'wi-tus) *adj.* unjust, wicked. —**iniq'uity** (in-ik'wi-ti) *n.* a wicked act.—**iniq'uities** *pl.*
ini'tial (in-ish'al) *n.* the first letter of a word, esp. a name.—*v.* to mark with one's initials.—**ini'tialling** *pres. part.*—**ini'tialled** *p.t.* and *p. part.*—*adj.* first, as *The initial expenses will be heavy.*—**ini'tially** *adv.*
ini'tiate (i-nish'i-āt) *v.* 1. to begin, set on foot. 2. to admit (into a society).—**initia'tion** (-ā'shun) *n.*—**ini'tiative** (i-nish'-i-a-tiv) *n.* 1. lead, as *The enemy took the initiative and attacked.* 2. ability to act independently, enterprise, as *Tom showed initiative in forming a football team*
Compare: enterprise, self-reliance
inject' *v.* to force in (esp. with syringe). —**injec'tion** (-shun) *n.*
injunc'tion (-shun) *n.* a command, order
in'jure (in'jur) *v.* to harm, damage.—**injuring** *pres. part.*—**in'jured** *p.t.* and *p. part.*—**injur'ious** (in-jōō'ri-us) *adj.* harmful.—**in'jury** *n.* damage, harm.—**in'juries** *pl.*
Compare: hurt, abuse, wrong, spoil, wound
ink (ingk) *n.* a fluid used for writing.—*v.* to mark with ink.—**ink'pot** *n.*—**ink'stand** *n.*—**ink'well** *n.*—**ink'y** *adj.* smeared with ink
ink'ling *n.* a vague idea, an awareness
inlaid' *p.t.* and *p. part.* of **inlay.**—*adj.* adorned with a design set in the surface
in'land *n.* the interior of a country.—*adj.* not on the coast.—*adv.* towards the interior
in'-law *n.* a relation through marriage, as **sister-in-law, father-in-law**
inlay' *v.* to insert, set in.—**inlay'ing** *pres. part.* —**in'laid** *p.t.* and *p. part.*—*n.* inlaid pattern
in'let *n.* a bay, narrow entrance
in'mate *n.* an occupant, inhabitant (usually of a hospital, prison, institution)
in'most *adj.* furthest in or inside. See **in**
inn *n.* a public house for lodging and refreshment.—**inn'keeper** *n.*
Compare: tavern, hotel, public-house, hostelry, saloon
innate' *adj.* inborn, natural, as *Cats have an innate dislike of dogs*
in'ner *adj.* lying within. See **in.**—**in'nermost.** See **in, inmost**
in'nings *n.pl.* in cricket, the batsman's turn of play, a side's turn of batting
in'nocence (in'o-sens) *n.* 1. freedom from guilt. 2. simplicity.—**in'nocent** *adj.*
innoc'uous *adj.* harmless
in'novate *v.* to introduce something new.—**innova'tion** (-vā'shun) *n.* a change.—**innova'tor** *n.*
innuen'do *n.* a malicious hint, an insinuation —**innuen'does** *pl.*
innu'merable *adj.* countless, very numerous
inoc'ulate *v.* to treat with disease germs (as a protection).—**inocula'tion** (-lā'shun) *n.*
Note: A patient is inoculated *with* a serum *against* a disease
inor'dinate *adj.* too great, excessive, as *an inordinate desire for riches*
inorgan'ic *adj.* concerning lifeless matter. In chemistry, concerning substances which are not carbon compounds
in'quest (in'kwest) *n.* an official inquiry before a jury
inquire', enquire' (in-kwīr') *v.* to ask for information.—**inqui'rer** *n.*—**inqui'ry, in'quiry** *n.* 1. a question. 2. a search for information.—**inqui'ries** *pl.*
inquisi'tion (in-kwi-zish'un) *n.* 1. an official inquiry. 2. a tribunal for the suppression of heresy, e.g. the Spanish Inquisition.—**inquis'itor** *n.*—**inquisito'rial** *adj.*
inquis'itive (in-kwiz'i-tiv) *adj.* curious, prying
Compare: meddlesome, inquiring, peeping, searching. *Contrast:* uninterested, unconcerned, indifferent, heedless
in'road (in'rōd) *n.* an attack, raid
insane' *adj.* of unsound mind, mad.—**insane'ly** *adv.*—**insan'ity** *n.*—madness
insa'tiable (in-sā'sha-bl) *adj.* impossible to satisfy, greedy.—**insa'tiate** (in-sā'shi-āt) *adj.* never satisfied
Compare: ravenous, voracious, unappeasable

inscribe' *v.* 1. to write or engrave words. 2. in geometry, to draw one figure inside another, touching at certain points.—**inscri'bing** *pres. part.*—**inscri'bed** *p.t.* and *p. part.*—**inscrip'tion** (-shun) *n.* words inscribed

inscru'table *adj.* which cannot be understood, mysterious

in'sect *n.* a small animal with body divided into three parts, head, thorax, abdomen, with six legs, and two or four wings.—**insect'icide** *n.* a chemical to kill insects.—**insectiv'orous** *adj.* insect-eating

insen'sate *adj.* meaningless, stupid

insen'sible *adj.* 1. unaware, not able to feel, as *The blow rendered him insensible.* 2. gradual, as *Twilight changed to darkness by insensible stages.*—**insensibil'ity** *n.*—**insen'sibly** *adv.*

insert' *v.* to put in among or between or into, as *to insert a key in a lock, an advertisement in a newspaper, etc.*—**inser'tion** (-shun) *n.*

in'set *n.* an insertion.—*v.* 1. to make an inset. 2. to start writing, printing, etc., some distance in from the margin

in'shore *adj.* and *adv.* towards or close to the shore

inside' *n.* inner part, interior.—*adj.* secret, as *inside information.*—*adv.* within, as *Come inside.*—*prep.* in, as *He is inside the house*

insid'ious *adj.* 1. sly, cunning, stealthy. 2. working slowly (of disease, etc.).—**insid'iously** *adv.*

in'sight (in'sīt) *n.* seeing with understanding

insig'nia *n.pl.* badges of office or honour

insignif'icance *n.* unimportance.—**insignif'icant** *adj.* small, trifling, unimportant

insin'uate *v.* 1. to introduce gradually, as *He insinuated himself into the inner councils of the society.* 2. to hint, as *Do you mean to insinuate that he is a cheat?*—**insin'uating** *adj.*—**insinua'tion** (-shun) *n.*

insip'id *adj.* dull, tasteless.—**insipid'ity** *n.*

insist' *v.* 1. to demand firmly, as *I insist that you come. I insist on your coming.* 2. to maintain strongly, as *He insisted that he had not done it.* 3. to dwell on some point.—**insis'tence** *n.*—**insis'tent** *adj.* urgent

in'solence *n.* offensive rudeness.—**in'solent** *adj.*—**in'solently** *adv.*

insolv'ent *adj.* of a person or firm, bankrupt

insom'nia *n.* sleeplessness

inspect' *v.* to examine closely or officially.—**inspec'tion** (-shun) *n.*—**inspec'tor** *n.* 1. an official appointed to inspect. 2. a police officer

inspira'tion (-ā'shun) *n.* 1. breathing in. 2. a good stimulating influence

inspire' *v.* 1. to breathe in. 2. to arouse a feeling, as *His past record inspires confidence.* 3. to stimulate (esp. thought), as *The poet was inspired by the beauty of the scene.*—**inspi'ring** *adj.*

instabil'ity *n.* lack of firmness

install' (in-stawl') *v.* 1. to place, put in, as *to install machinery in a factory.* 2. to establish (person in office), as *to install a new president.*—**installa'tion** (-ā'shun) *n.* 1. installing. 2. machinery

instal'ment (in-stawl'ment) *n.* 1. payment of part of a debt. as *He paid for the vacuum cleaner in 24 monthly instalments.* 2. one of a series of parts, as *There will be another instalment of this exciting story in our next issue*

in'stance *n.* 1. an example, as *There have been several instances of this kind lately.* 2. a request, suggestion, as *I did it at his instance.*—*v.* to mention as an example.—**for instance** as an example

in'stant *n.* 1. a moment. 2. a day of the current month, e.g. *the* 18th *instant* (*or inst.*) *means the* 18*th of this month.*—*adj.* 1. urgent, pressing. 2. immediate.—**instanta'neous** *adj.* done in an instant.—**in'stantly** *adv.* immediately

instead' (in-sted') *adv.* in place (of)

in'step *n.* the top of the foot between toes and ankle

in'stigate *v.* to urge on, incite.—**instiga'tion** (-gā'shun) *n.*—**in'stigator** *n.*

Compare: stimulate, spur, animate, encourage, actuate, tempt. *Contrast:* deter, dissuade, discourage

instil' *v.* 1. to put in by drops. 2. to put (ideas) in the mind gradually and thoroughly, as *The need for care with machinery was instilled into the minds of the apprentices.*—**instil'ling** *pres. part.*—**instilled'** *p.t.* and *p. part.*—**instilla'tion** (-lā'shun) *n.*

in'stinct *n.* 1. a natural power that guides animals. 2. impulse, unlearned skill.—**instinct'ive** *adj.*

in'stitute *n.* a society.—*v.* to establish, set up.—**institu'tion** (-tū'shun) *n.* 1. an established custom. 2. a society, organisation. 3. a beginning.—**institu'tional** *adj.*

instruct' *v.* 1. to teach. 2. to inform, give directions to.—**instruc'tion** (-shun) *n.* teaching, education.—*pl.* directions, orders.—**instruc'tive** *adj.* helpful, informative.—**instruc'tor** *n.* teacher.—**instruc'tress** *fem.*

in'strument (in'stroo-ment) *n.* 1. a tool, implement. 2. a person or thing made use of. 3. a device for making music.—**instrument'al** *adj.* 1. helpful, as *The boy's uncle was instrumental in finding him a job.* 2. for, of musical instruments.—**instrumen'talist** *n.* player.—**instrumental'ity** *n.* agency, help

insubor'dinate *adj.* disobedient.—**insubordina'tion** (-ā'shun) *n.*

in'sular *adj.* 1. belonging to islands. 2. narrow-minded.—**insular'ity** *n.*

in'sulate *v.* 1. to separate, set apart. 2. to

isolate (electricity) by non-conducting materials.—**insula'tion** (lā'shun) *n.*— **in'sulator** *n.* a non-conductor of electricity
in'sult *n.* a rude speech or action.—**insult'** *v.* to treat with scorn or rudeness.—**insul'ting** *adj.*
insu'perable (in-sū'per-a-bl) *adj.* that cannot be overcome
insu'rance (in-shōōr'ans) *n.* 1. an arrangement for payment in case of accident, fire, death, etc. 2. the amount payable by person who insures. See **premium.** 3. the amount paid to person who has insured.—**insure'** *v.* to secure payment in case of loss. —**insu'ring** *pres. part.*—**insured'** *p.t.* and *p. part.*—**insu'rance policy** the document on which an insurance contract is recorded
insur'gent (in-ser'jent) *adj.* in revolt, rebellious.—*n.*
insurrec'tion (-shun) *n.* a rising, revolt
Compare: sedition, revolution, riot, rebellion, mutiny
intact' *adj.* whole, untouched, undamaged
intan'gible (in-tan'ji-bl) *adj.* 1. that cannot be touched. 2. difficult to grasp or define mentally
in'teger (in'te-jer) *n.* a whole number
in'tegral *adj.* 1. essential to the whole. 2. complete.—**in'tegrate** *v.* combine parts into a whole
integ'rity *n.* 1. honesty. 2. soundness
Compare: probity, rectitude, uprightness, reliability. *Contrast:* dishonesty, trickery, untrustworthiness
in'tellect *n.* reasoning power, mind.—**intellect'ual** *adj.* using, or showing intelligence
intel'ligence (in-tel'i-jens) *n.* 1. quickness of understanding. 2. information, news.—**intel'ligent** *adj.*—**intel'ligently** *adv.*—**intel'ligible** *adj.* easily understood
intend' *v.* 1. to mean. 2. to plan, purpose
intense' *adj.* very strong, very deep.—**intensifica'tion** (-kā'shun) *n.* strengthening.—**inten'sify** *v.* to make more intense.—he **inten'sifies.**—**inten'sifying** *pres. part.*—**inten'sified** *p.t.* and *p. part.*—**inten'sity** *n.*—**inten'sive** *adj.* complete and thorough
Compare: (with intense) severe, strenuous, fervent, violent, extreme, excessive, eager, vivid
intent' *n.* intention.—*adj.* bent on, eager.—**inten'tion** (-shun) *n.* 1. meaning, purpose. 2. plan.—**inten'tional** *adj.* planned
inter' *v.* to bury.—**inter'ring** *pres. part.*—**interred'** *p.t.* and *p. part.*—**inter'ment** *n.* burial
in'ter- *pref.* between one another, among
interact' *v.* to act upon one another
intercede' (in-ter-seed') *v.* to plead for someone
Note: You intercede *with* someone *for* someone else, or *on behalf of* someone else
intercept' (in-ter-sept') *v.* to seize in passing, as *The master intercepted a note that was being passed round the class*
interces'sion (in-ter-sesh'un) *n.* interceding, pleading for others.—**interces'sor** *n.*
in'terchange *n.* exchange.—**interchange'** *v.* to put things in each other's place.—**interchan'ging** *pres. part.*—**interchanged** *p.t.* and *p. part.*—**interchan'geable** *adj.*
in'tercourse *n.* 1. conversation. 2. exchange of ideas, services, etc.
in'terdict *v.* to forbid, prohibit.—*n.* a prohibition.—**interdic'tion** (-shun) *n.*
int'erest *n.* 1. curiosity and attention. 2. advantage, benefit, as *I did it in your interest. It is to his interest to do so.* 3. money paid for borrowing money.—*v.* to stir curiosity.—**in'terested** *adj.* 1. influenced by private considerations. 2. attentive.—**in'teresting** *adj.* holding attention
Compare: absorbing, fascinating, amusing, entertaining. *Contrast:* uninteresting, dull, boring, wearisome, tedious
interfere' *v.* 1. to meddle, as *We should get on better if you did not interfere* (*with what we are doing*). 2. to clash, as *We should not let pleasure interfere with duty.*—**interfe'rence** *n.*
in'terim *n.* the meantime, the period between two stated times
inte'rior *n.* 1. the inside. 2. inland.—*adj.* inner, internal
interject' *v.* to interrupt someone by a sudden remark.—**interjec'tion** (-shun) *n.* 1. interjecting. 2. in Grammar, an exclamation, e.g. Oh! Ah! What! etc.
interlace' (in-ter-lās') *v.* to weave over and under, to join by lacing.—**interla'cing** *pres. part.*—**interlaced'** *p.t.* and *p. part.*
interlock' *v.* to lock, clasp together
in'terloper *n.* an intruder
in'terlude *n.* 1. an entertainment between the acts of a play. 2. something filling an interval. 3. an interval
interme'diary *n.* a go-between.—*adj.* coming between
interme'diate *adj.* coming between two
inter'minable *adj.* endless
intermis'sion (in-ter-mish'un) *n.* an interval, pause
intermit'tent *adj.* stopping for a time
intern' *v.* to make a person live in a prison-camp, or some such place, as *Citizens of enemy countries are interned in war-time.*—*n.* (U.S.) resident assistant doctor in a hospital.—**intern'ment** *n.*
inter'nal *adj.* 1. inside, interior. 2. domestic. —**inter'nally** *adv.*
internat'ional (in-ter-nash'on-al) *adj.* 1. between nations, as *international trade.* 2. belonging to all nations, as *Art is international*
In'terpol *n.* an international police organisation
interpose' *v.* 1. to put between. 2. to come

between.—**interpo'sing** *pres. part.*—**interposed'** *p.t.* and *p. part.*—**interposi'tion** (-shun) *n.*
Compare: (with *v.*) insert, intervene, mediate. *Contrast*: withdraw, avoid, stand aside

inter'pret *v.* 1. to explain. 2. to translate. 3. in music or acting, to represent.—**interpreta'tion** (-tā'shun) *n.*—**inter'preter** *n.* a translator of conversation in a foreign language
Compare: (with *v.*) elucidate, construe, decipher

interreg'num *n.* an interval between reigns

inter'rogate *v.* to question.—**interroga'tion** (-gā'shun) *n.* 1. questioning. 2. question mark (?).—**interrog'ative** *adj.* asking a question
Note: In Grammar the *interrogative mood* means the use of a verb to ask a question, e.g. *Will he go? Are you?*

interrupt' *v.* to break in upon, stop from continuing.—**interrup'tion** (-shun) *n.* stopping

intersect' *v.* to divide by cutting or crossing. —**intersec'tion** (-shun) *n.* crossing

intersperse' *v.* 1. to scatter here and there, as *Songs were interspersed among dances in the programme.* 2. diversify, as *The evening's entertainment was interspersed with songs and dances.*—**intersper'sing** *pres. part.*—**interspersed'** *p.t.* and *p. part.*—**intersper'sion** (-shun) *n.*

inter'stice (in-ter'stis) *n.* a chink, crevice

in'terval *n.* 1. a pause or space between. 2. in music, a difference of pitch

intervene' *v.* 1. to come between, as *Only a short time intervened between one war and another.* 2. to interfere, as *John did not intervene in the other boys' quarrel.*—**interve'ning** *pres. part.*—**intervened'** *p.t.* and *p. part.*—**interven'tion** (-shun) *n.*

in'terview (in'ter-vū) *n.* an arranged meeting. —*v.* to talk with, as *A newspaper reporter is sent to interview a prominent person and publish the results in the paper.*—**interview'er** *n.*

intes'tate *adj.* having made no will

intes'tine (in-tes'tin) *n.* the bowels

in'timacy (in'tim-a-si) *n.* closeness, familiarity.—**in'timacies** *pl.*—**in'timate** *adj.* 1. inmost. 2. familiar, close.—*n.* a close friend

in'timate (in'tim-āt) *v.* to hint, make known, as *It was intimated to him that his presence was no longer desirable.*—**intima'tion** (-ā'shun) *n.* announcement
Compare: suggest, declare, tell, indicate, inform

intim'idate *v.* to frighten by threats.—**intim'idating** *pres. part.*—**intim'idated** *p.t.* and *p. part.*—**intimida'tion** (-dā'shun) *n.*
Compare: daunt, scare, dishearten, dispirit, overawe, bully. *Contrast:* encourage, embolden, hearten

in'to *prep.* 1. expresses motion to a point within, as *Let us go into the garden.* 2. expresses change of condition from one thing to another, as *the cream was churned into butter*

intol'erable *adj.* unbearable.—**intol'erance** *n.* interference with ways or opinions of others.—**intol'erant** *adj.*

intona'tion (-nā'shun) *n.* 1. intoning. 2. rise and fall of the voice.—**intone'** *v.* to recite in a monotone, chant.—**into'ning** *pres. part.*—**intoned'** *p.t.* and *p. part.*

intox'icant *n.* alcoholic drink.—**intox'icate** *v.* 1. to make drunk. 2. to excite madly.—**intox'icating** *pres. part.*—**intox'icated** *p.t.* and *p. part.*—**intoxica'tion** (-kā'shun) *n.*

intran'sitive *n.* in Grammar describes a verb which does not take an object, e.g. *I cannot play* (*play* is intransitive), but *I cannot play the piano* (*play* is transitive)

intrep'id *adj.* fearless, brave.—**intrepid'ity** *n.*

in'tricate *adj.* 1. complicated. 2. difficult to understand.—**in'tricacy** *n.*

in'trigue (in'treeg) *n.* a secret plot.—*v.* (intreeg') 1. (with) to plot. 2. to arouse curiosity, as *I am very intrigued by the peculiar noises next door.*—**intri'guing** *pres. part.*—**intrigued'** *p.t.* and *p. part.*

intrin'sic *adj.* essential.—**intrin'sically** *adv.*

introduce' (in-tro-dūs') *v.* 1. to bring in or forward. 2. to make known, present. 3. to insert.—**introdu'cing** *pres. part.*—**introduced'** *p.t.* and *p. part.*—**introduc'tion** (-shun) *n.* 1. beginning. 2. bringing in. 3. presenting.—**introduc'tory** *adj.*

introspec'tive *adj.* examining one's thoughts and feelings

intrude' (in-trōōd') *v.* to thrust in without invitation.—**intru'ding** *pres. part.*—**intru'ded** *p.t.* and *p. part.*—**intru'der** *n.*—**intru'sion** (in-trōō'zhun) *n.*—**intru'sive** *adj.*

intui'tion (in-tū-ish'un) *n.* insight without reasoning, immediate understanding.—**intu'itive** *adj.*

in'undate *v.* to flood.—**inunda'tion** (dā'shun) *n.*

invade' *v.* 1. to enter a place or country as an enemy. 2. to take possession of.—**inva'ding** *pres. part.*—**inva'ded** *p.t.* and *p. part.*—**inva'der** *n.*

in'valid (in'va-leed) *n.* a sick or disabled person.—*v.* (out) to remove a disabled man from service.—*adj.* ill, weak

inval'id *adj.* not valid, without value.—**inval'idate** *v.* to make invalid

inval'uable *adj.* priceless, of immense value

inva'riable (vā') *adj.* unchanging.—**inva'riably** *adv.* constantly

inva'sion (in-vā'zhun) *n.* invading, attacking by entering

invec'tive *n.* violent, abusive speech
Compare: vituperation, railing, obloquy

invent' *v.* 1. to make up, as *The boy invented an excuse for being late.* 2. to make something new, as *Eli Whitney invented a machine for removing the seeds from cotton.*—**inven'tion** (-shun) *n.*—**inven'tive** *adj.* good at inventing.—**inven'tor** *n.*

Compare: devise, contrive, originate, discover

in'ventory *n.* a detailed list of goods or belongings.—**in'ventories** *pl.*

in'verse *adj.* reversed in position.—**inver'sion** *n.* inverting

invert' *v.* to turn upside down

inver'tebrate *n.* an animal having no backbone.—*adj.*

invest' *v.* 1. to clothe. 2. to endue, as *He was invested with complete control.* 3. to besiege. 4. to lay out money for profit

inves'tigate *v.* to inquire into, examine.—**inves'tigating** *pres. part.*—**inves'tigated** *p.t.* and *p. part.*—**investiga'tion** (-gā'shun) *n.*—**inves'tigator** *n.*

inves'titure *n.* the formal installation of a person in office

invest'ment *n.* 1. laying out money. 2. money invested.—**inves'tor** *n.*

invet'erate *adj.* 1. deep-rooted, as *an inveterate hatred of falsehood.* 2. long established by habit, as *He is an inveterate gambler*

invid'ious *adj.* likely to arouse ill-will or envy

invig'orate *v.* to fill with energy, to refresh.—**invig'orating** *adj.*

invin'cible (in-vin'si-bl) *adj.* unconquerable.—**invincibil'ity** *n.*

invi'olate *adj.* unharmed, unbroken

invis'ible *adj.* not able to be seen.—**invisible ink** ink which only shows when heated or treated with a chemical

invita'tion (-tā'shun) *n.* a polite request.—**invite'** *v.* 1. to request someone to do something or to come somewhere. 2. to attract.—**invi'ting** *adj.* attractive

invoca'tion (-kā'shun) *n.* calling upon, prayer

in'voice *n.* a list of goods sent, with prices.—*v.*

invoke' *v.* 1. to call on, as *The witch doctor invoked the gods of the tribe.* 2. to appeal to, as *The new teacher invoked the authority of the headmaster.*—**invo'king** *pres. part.*—**invoked'** *p.t.* and *p. part.*

invol'untary *adj.* 1. not done willingly. 2. not intentional.—**involuntar'ily** *adv.*

involve' *v.* 1. to entangle. 2. to entail, include.—**invol'ving** *pres. part.*—**involved'** *p.t.* and *p. part.*

invul'nerable *adj.* not able to be harmed

in'ward *adv.* towards the inside, within.—*adj.*

i'odine (-dīn or -dīn) *n.* a non-metallic element used in medicine

i'on *n.* an electrically charged particle

io'ta (ī-ō'ta) *n.* a very small quantity

Iran' (i-rahn') *n.* a country of central Asia, once called Persia.—**Ira'nian** *n.* a native of Iran

Iraq' *n.* a country of south west Asia.—**Iraq'i** *n.* a native of Iraq

iras'cible (i-ras'i-bl) *adj.* irritable, bad-tempered

irate' (ī-rāt') *adj.* angry.—**ire** *n.* anger

Compare: (with *n.*) temper, resentment, choler, exasperation, fury, rage, irritation

Ire'land *n.* a large island to the west of Britain, Eire.—**I'rish** *adj.*

irides'cent (ir-i-des'ent) *adj.* rainbow-coloured, changing colour

i'ris (ī'ris) *n.* the coloured part of the eye containing the pupil

irk *v.* to weary.—**irk'some** *adj.* tiresome

i'ron (īrn) *n.* 1. a metal, the raw material of steel. 2. something made of iron. 3. *pl.* fetters, chains.—*adj.* like iron, made of iron.—*v.* to smooth with a flat iron.—**i'ronmonger** *n.* a dealer in hardware.—**iron lung** an apparatus assisting the breathing of a patient inside it.—**iron rations** emergency rations.—**to have too many irons in the fire** to have many affairs to attend to

iron'ical (ī-ron'i-kl) *adj.* meaning the opposite of what is said (or done).—**iron'ically** *adv.*—**i'rony** *n.* ironical speech

irra'diate *v.* to shine upon, throw light on

irra'tional (i-rash'on-al) *adj.* unreasonable

irreconci'lable (i-rek-on-sī'la-bl) *adj.* who or which cannot be made to agree, as *Your explanation is irreconcilable with the known facts*

irreg'ular *adj.* 1. not regular. 2. uneven, not smooth. 3. not following the rule.—**irregular'ity** *n.*

irrel'evant *adj.* off the point

irrep'arable *adj.* which cannot be repaired or regained

irrepress'ible *adj.* who or which cannot be kept down, as *My desire to yawn was irrepressible*

irreproach'able *adj.* blameless, perfect

irresist'ible *adj.* who or which cannot be resisted

irres'olute *adj.* hesitating, unsure.—**irresolu'tion** (-shun) *n.*

irrespon'sible *adj.* 1. not responsible. 2. unwilling to take responsibility

irretriev'able *adj.* which cannot be recovered

irrev'erent *adj.* without proper respect

irrev'ocable *adj.* which cannot be recalled or undone

ir'rigate *v.* to water by channels or streams.—**ir'rigating** *pres. part.*—**ir'rigated** *p.t.* and *p. part.*—**irriga'tion** (-gā'shun) *n.*

irritabil'ity *n.* bad temper.—**ir'ritable** *adj.* easily annoyed.—**ir'ritant** *n.* something which irritates

ir'ritate *v.* 1. to annoy, anger. 2. to inflame (skin, etc.).—**irrita'ting** *adj.*—**irrita'tion** (-tā'shun) *n.*

irrup'tion (-shun) *n.* bursting in

is *v.* 3rd person sing. present indicative of **to be**

Is'lam (iz'lahm) *n.* the Mohammedan religion

is'land (ī'land) *n.* land surrounded by water. —**is'lander** *n.* a person living on an island

isle (īl) *n.* an island.—**is'let** (ī'let) *n.* a small island

i'sobar *n.* a line on a map connecting places with the same average barometric pressure

i'solate *v.* to separate, place apart.—**i'solating** *pres. part.*—**i'solated** *p.t.* and *p. part.*—**isola'tion** (-lā'shun) *n.*—**isolation hospital** for infectious diseases

isos'celes (ī-sos'e-leez) *adj.* (triangle) having two sides equal

i'sotherm *n.* an imaginary line joining places with same average temperature

Is'rael *n.* a country on the eastern shore of the Mediterranean sea, Palestine.—**Israe'li** (is-rā'li) *n.* a native of Israel.—**Is'raelite** *n.* a Jew of ancient times

is'sue *n.* 1. going out. 2. giving out, e.g. of bank-notes, etc. 3. outlet. 4. result, as *a happy issue.* 5. question, dispute. 6. offspring, children, as *He died without issue.* 7. copies of newspaper, etc.—*v.* 1. to go out, send out. 2. to result in.—**is'suing** *pres. part.*—**is'sued** *p.t.* and *p. part.* —**at issue** in dispute.—**join issue** (with) to argue

Compare: (with *v.*) emerge, flow, circulate, eventuate

isth'mus (is'mus) *n.* a narrow neck of land connecting two large areas of land

it *pron.* Neuter form of **he** and **she.** *It* is used to refer to a thing, as *The cup fell, but it did not break*, and as the subject of impersonal verbs, as *It is going to rain. It* is also used to mean the person in question, as *Who is it? It is the postman.*—**it** *objective*—**its** *possessive.*—**itself** *emphatic* or *reflexive*

ital'ics *n.pl.* sloping type used in printing, often for emphasis, thus *sloping*

It'aly *n.* a country in southern Europe.—**Ital'ian** *n.* and *adj.*

itch *n.* a tickle, irritation of the skin.—*v.*—he **itch'es**

i'tem (ī'tem) *n.* 1. one of a list of things. 2. a detail. 3. an entry

itin'erant (it-in', ī-tin') *adj.* wandering, travelling from place to place.—**itin'erary** *n.* a route, plan of a journey

its *pron.* Possessive form of **it, his** *masc.*—**her, hers** *fem.*—**their, theirs** *pl.*

Note: This should not be confused with it's, which is contraction for *it is*

itself' *pron.* 1. Emphatic form of **it,** as *The car itself was undamaged.* 2. Reflexive form of **it,** as *That dog will kill itself.*—**himself'** *masc.*—**herself'** *fem.*—**themselves'** *pl.*

Note: Two common errors to be avoided are *hisself* and *theirselves* for *himself* and *themselves*

i'vory a hard white bony substance from tusks of elephants, etc.—**i'vories** *pl.*—*adj.* creamy white

i'vy *n.* a climbing evergreen plant.—**i'vies** *pl.*—**i'vied** *adj.* covered with ivy

J

jab *v.* to strike or prick with something pointed.—**jab'bing** *pres. part.*—**jabbed** *p.t.* and *p. part.*

Compare: dig, poke, prod, probe, stab

jab'ber *v.* to talk fast and confusedly.—*n.*—**jab'berer** *n.* chatterer

jack *n.* 1. a device for turning a cooking spit. 2. a machine for lifting, a weight such as the wheel of a car off the ground. 3. a ship's flag.—*v.* (up) to raise with a jack.—**every man Jack** everybody.—**jack of all trades** someone who can do many jobs.—**Union Jack** the British flag

jack'al (jak'awl) *n.* a wild animal like a dog

jack'ass *n.* 1. a male ass. 2. a stupid person.—**laughing jackass,** see **kookaburra**

jack'daw *n.* a glossy black bird

jack'eroo, jack'aroo *n.* an apprentice, originally a young Englishman learning squatting on a sheep station.—**jackeroo'ing** *n.*

jack'et *n.* 1. a short coat. 2. an outer casing

jack'knife (jak'nīf) *n.* a large pocketknife.—**jack'knives** *pl.*

jack o' lan'tern *n.* a will o' the wisp

Jacobe'an (jak-o-bee'an) *adj.* referring to the time of King James 1 of Britain

jade *n.* an ornamental green stone

jade *n.* 1. a worn-out horse. 2. a mean woman.—**ja'ded** *adj.* tired, worn-out

jag *n.* a sharp point.—**jag'ged** *adj.* rough, pointed

jag'uar (jag'ū-ar) *n.* a large South American spotted wild animal resembling a leopard

jail see **gaol.**—**jail'er** see **gaol'er**

jam *n.* 1. fruit preserved by boiling with sugar. 2. a stoppage.—*v.* 1. to squeeze, press. 2. to stick, become unworkable.—**jam'ming** *pres. part.*—**jammed** *p.t., p. part.*

jamb (jam) *n.* the side post of a door or window

jamboree' *n.* a large gathering of Scouts

jam'ma *n.* (Carib.) a work-song

jan'gle (jang'gl) *v.* to sound harshly.—*n.*

jan'itor *n.* a porter, door-keeper

Jan'uary *n.* first month of the year

Japan' *n.* a country in the Far East.—**Jap'anese** *n.* and *adj.*

japan' *n.* a glossy black varnish.—*v.*

jar *n.* an earthenware vessel

jar *v.* 1. to make an unpleasant grating noise. 2. to irritate, shock. 3. to quarrel.—**jar'ring** *pres. part.*—**jarred** *p.t.* and *p. part.*

jar'gon *n.* 1. gabble, confused talk. 2. talk with too many technical terms

jar'rah *n.* a valuable W. Australian timber tree, eucalyptus

jaun'dice (jawn'dis) *n.* an illness which turns the skin yellow.—**jaun'diced** *adj.* soured.

jaunt *n.* a short pleasure-excursion
jaun'ty *adj.* lively, brisk.—**jaunt'ily** *adv.*
jav'elin *n.* a light spear for throwing
jaw *n.* one of the bones in which the teeth are set.—*pl.* mouth
jay *n.* a noisy bird with bright plumage
jay'-walker *n.* a person who crosses roads regardless of traffic
jazz *n.* music of American Negro origin, played in groups and often improvised.—**jaz'zy** *adj.* very brightly patterned.—**jazz up** *v.* to make lively
jeal'ous (jel'us) *adj.* 1. envious, as *He is jealous of your good fortune.* 2. afraid of being displaced from someone's affection, as a *jealous husband.* 3. (of) watchful for, as *He is very jealous of his rights.* 4. requiring loyalty, as *The Lord thy God is a jealous God.*—**jeal'ousy** *n.*
jeans *n.pl.* close fitting trousers of strong cotton fabric
jeep *n.* a small open motor truck
jeer *v.* to mock, make fun of unkindly.—*n.*
Note: Jeer is often followed by *at*
jel'ly *n.* 1. a sweet dish made with gelatine. 2. anything resembling this.—**jel'lies** *pl.*—*v.* to turn into jelly.—**jell** *v.* to set.—**jel'ly-fish** *n.* a sea-animal like a jelly
jem'my *n.* a burglar's crowbar.—**jem'mies** *pl.*
jeop'ardise (jep'ar-dīz) *v.* to endanger.—**jeop'ardy** (jep'ar-di) *n.* danger, as *The enemy's advance placed the whole of our army in jeopardy*
Compare: (with *n.*) peril, hazard, risk, insecurity. *Contrast:* safety, security
jerk *n.* a short sudden pull.—*v.* to move or pull suddenly.—**jer'ky** *adj.*
jer'kin *n.* a close-fitting short coat
jer'sey *n.* 1. a woollen pullover. 2. a breed of cattle
jest *n.* a joke, fun.—*v.* to make fun.—**jest'er** *n.* joker
jet *n.* a hard black mineral.—*adj.* black and shining
jet *n.* 1. a stream of liquid or gas forced from a small opening under pressure. 2. a spout, nozzle. 3. aircraft propelled by a jet engine.—*v.* to shoot out.—**jet engine** engine propelled by a directed stream of gas
jet'sam *n.* cargo thrown out to lighten ship in distress and then washed ashore.—**jet'tison** *v.* to throw overboard
jet'ty *n.* a small pier or landing-place.—**jet'ties** *pl.*
jew'el *n.* 1. a precious stone. 2. an ornament, with precious stones. 3. something very precious.—**jew'eller** *n.*—**jewe'lry, jew'el-lery** *n.* jewels in a metal setting for wearing
jib *n.* a three-cornered sail from ship's foremast.—*v.* to stop and refuse to go on.—**jib'bing** *pres. part.*—**jibbed** *p.t.* and *p. part.*
jig *n.* a lively dance.—*v.* to move up and down.—**jig'saw** *n.* a machine fretsaw
jin'gle (jing-gl) *v.* to clink (like coins being shaken).—*n.*—**jin'gling** *pres. part.*—**jin'gles** *p.t.* and *p. part.*
jin'ker *n.* (Aus.) a two-wheeled bush contrivance for transporting heavy timber
jiu-jit'su, ju-jut'su *n.* the Japanese way of wrestling, using the opponent's weight to his disadvantage
job *n.* 1. a piece of work. 2. an occupation
Compare: task, employment, livelihood, career
jock'ey *n.* a rider of race-horses.—*v.* 1. to jostle (someone). 2. to persuade someone into doing something by crafty means.—**jock'eys** *pl.*
jocose' (jo-kōs') *adj.* humorous, playful.—**joc'ular** *adj.* joking.—**jocular'ity** *n.*
Compare: (with *jocose* and *jocular*) facetious, waggish, funny, droll, sportive
joc'und *adj.* merry, gay, as *the jocund pealing of the church bells*
jodh'purs *n.pl.* riding breeches
jog *v.* 1. to move, or push with a jerk. 2. to move along jerkily.—**jog'ging** *pres. part.*—*n.* a jolt, jerk.—**jog'trot** *n.* a slow, regular trot
join *v.* 1. to put together, fasten. 2. to unite. 3. to become a member of, e.g. a club.—*n.* a joining
Compare: (with *v.*) connect, combine, mix. *Contrast:* separate, disconnect, sever, split, divorce
join'er *n.* a carpenter who does light work.—**join'ery** *n.*
joint *n.* 1. a place where two things fit. 2. a place where two bones fit. 3. a piece of meat.—*adj.* shared by several.—**joint'ly** *adv.* in common
joist *n.* a beam stretching from wall to wall on which to fix a floor or ceiling
joke *n.* 1. something said or done to cause a laugh. 2. something funny.—*v.* to make jokes.—**jo'king** *pres. part.*—**joked** *p.t.* and *p. part.*—**jo'ker** *n.* 1. one who jokes. 2. an odd playing card used in some games.—**practical joke** a trick played on someone to raise a laugh
jol'lity *n.* gaiety, fun.—**jol'lities** *pl.*
jol'ly *adj.* merry, festive.—**jol'lier** *comp.*—**jol'liest** *sup.*
Compare: good-humoured, cheerful, gay, happy, light-hearted, cheery, jovial. *Contrast:* doleful, dispirited, miserable, melancholy, mournful, sad
jolt (jōlt) *n.* a shock, jerks.—*v.*
jos'tle (jos'l) *v.* to push, crowd roughly.—*n.*—**jos'tling** *adj.*
jot *n.* a very small amount.—*v.* (down) to write shortly and quickly.—**jot'ting** *pres. part.*—**jot'ted** *p.t.* and *p. part.*—**jot'ter** *n.* a note-book
jour'nal (jur'nal) *n.* 1. a diary, daily record

2. a daily newspaper.—**jour'nalism** *n.* writing for the Press.—**journ'alist** *n.*

jour'ney (jur'ni) *n.* a trip, travelling to a place.—**jour'neys** *pl.*—*v.* to travel

Compare: travel, voyage, expedition, excursion, trip, pilgrimage

joust *n.* tournament, encounter with lances between mounted knights

jo'vial *adj.* cheery, good-humoured.—**jovial'ity** *n.*

jowl *n.* the jaw, cheek.—**cheek by jowl** close together

joy *n.* 1. delight, pleasure, gladness. 2. something delightful, as *Her dancing was a joy to see.*—**joy'ful** *adj.*—**joy'fully** *adv.*—**joy'ous** *adj.* glad, joyful

ju'bilant *adj.* rejoicing.—**jubila'tion** (-ā'shun) *n.* rejoicing, triumph

ju'bilee *n.* 1. rejoicing, celebration. 2. a joyful celebration of an anniversary.—**silver jubilee** a twenty-fifth anniversary.—**diamond jubilee** a sixtieth anniversary

Ju'daism (jōō'dā-izm) *n.* the Jewish religion

judge (juj) *n.* 1. an officer appointed to try or decide cases in law-courts. 2. one who decides in a dispute.—*v.* to decide, pass judgment.—**judg'ing** *pres. part.*—**judged** *p.t.* and *p. part.*—**judg'ment, judge'ment** *n.* 1. a sentence passed by a judge, retribution. 2. opinion. 3. ability to judge, decide, discriminate or estimate

judi'cial (jōō-dish'al) *adj.* 1. having to do with law and justice. 2. shrewd, discerning, as *The dealer gave the old car a judicial glance*

judi'cious (jōō-dish'us) *adj.* showing good judgment, wise

ju'do (jōō'dō) *n.* modern jiu-jitsu

jug *n.* a deep container for liquids, with spout and handle

jug'gle *v.* 1. to play conjuring tricks. 2. to practise deceit, deceive, as *The swindler juggled with the statement of accounts. He juggled the shareholders out of their share of the profits.*—**jug'gler** *n.*

Ju'goslavia see Yu'goslavia

jug'ular *adj.* belonging to the neck and throat. —**jug'ular vein** *n.*

juice (jōōs) *n.* liquid from fruit or meat

ju'jube *n.* a lozenge of gelatine, sugar, etc.

juke'-box *n.* a record player operated by a coin

July' (jōō-lī') *n.* the seventh month

jum'ble *v.* to mix up, confuse.—*n.* a muddle, confused heap.—**jum'ble-sale** *n.* sale of old clothes, etc.

jum'buck *n.* (Aus.) a sheep

jump *v.* 1. to spring from the ground. 2. to leap over.—*n.* leap, bound, start.—**to jump to conclusions** to form a hasty opinion from little evidence

jump'er *n.* a woman's woollen blouse

junc'tion (-shun) *n.* 1. a meeting-place, joining. 2. a railway station where lines join

junc'ture *n.* 1. joint. 2. state of affairs, time, as *At this juncture the meeting broke up*

June (jōōn) *n.* the sixth month

jun'gle (jung'gl) *n.* thickly overgrown forest

jun'ior (jōōn'ier) *adj.* 1. younger. 2. in a lower position. 3. for young people.—*n.* a younger person

junk (jungk) *n.* rubbish

junk (jungk) *n.* a Chinese sailing-ship

junk'et (jungk'it) *n.* milk curdled and flavoured

jurisdic'tion (shun) *n.* legal authority, administration of justice

ju'ry (jōō'ri) *n.* 1. a body of persons sworn to decide on verdict in court of law. 2. a body of judges in a competition.—**ju'ries** *pl.*—**ju'ror** *n.* one of a jury.—**ju'ryman** *n.*

just *adj.* 1. fair, right. 2. exact.—*adv.* 1. exactly, as *That is just right.* 2. barely, as *He just managed to catch his train.*—**just'ly** *adv.*

jus'tice (jus'tis) *n.* 1. fairness, right. 2. a magistrate. 3. a trial.—**Justice of the Peace** an unpaid local magistrate

justifi'able *adj.* which can be shown to be right.—**justifica'tion** (-kā'shun) *n.* 1. a good reason. 2. being justified

jus'tify *v.* 1. to prove to be right. 2. to defend. 3. to free from blame.—he **jus'tifies.**—**jus'tifying** *pres. part.*—**jus'tified** *p.t., p. part.*

jut *v.* to project, stick out.—**jut'ting** *pres. part.*—**jut'ted** *p.t.* and *p. part.*

jute (jōōt) *n.* a vegetable fibre used in making mats, rope, etc.

ju'venile (jōō'ven-īl) *adj.* 1. young, youthful. 2. for the young.—*n.* a young person

juxtaposi'tion (-shun) *n.* putting side by side

Compare: contact, proximity, nearness.

K

kai (kī) *n.* N.Z., S. Sea Is. and New Guinea word for food. Sometimes **kai-kai**

kaing'a, kaika, kaik (ka-ing'a, kī-ka, kīk) *n.* a Maori settlement, village

kak'a (N.Z.) a brown parrot.—**kak'abill** *n.* a shrub with showy red flowers resembling a parrot's bill

kale, kail *n.* a cabbage with curly leaves

kalei'doscope (ka-lī'dō-skōp) *n.* a tube in which variety of coloured patterns are produced by means of mirrors

kangaroo' (kang-ga-rōō') *n.* the largest of the Australian marsupials (i.e. animal with a pouch to carry its young). It has powerful hind legs for jumping

ka'olin *n.* fine white china clay

ka'pok *n.* a vegetable fibre for stuffing cushions

ka'rri (kā'ree) *n.* a valuable W. Australian timber tree

kau'ri (kow'ree) a N.Z. coniferous pine tree yielding valuable soft wood.—**kauri gum** resin used in making varnish

ka'yak (kī'ak) *n.* an Eskimo canoe made of skins over wooden frame

keel *n.* the bottom of a ship

keen *adj.* 1. sharp, cutting. 2. eager, enthusiastic.—**keen'ly** *adv.*—**keen'ness** *n.*

Note: Often followed by *on* or *about* (the thing or person concerned)

keep *v.* 1. to have for a long time. 2. to take care of, e.g. poultry, etc. 3. to hold back, detain. 4. to continue, as *He kept doing it. He kept away for a time.* 5. to observe or commemorate, as *To keep Christmas.* 6. to be faithful to, as *He kept his word.*—*n.* 1. board and lodging. 2. central tower of a castle.—**keep'er** *n.* person who guards.—**keep'ing** *n.* 1. care. 2. agreement.—**to keep books** means to make records in account-books.—**to keep company** to go with.—**to keep down** to repress, restrain.—**to keep in with** to keep on good terms with.—**to keep on** to continue.—**to keep time.** 1. said of a clock, to go well. 2. to keep on a musical beat

Compare: (with *v.*) retain, preserve, protect, sustain, regulate, defend, withhold, celebrate.—It will be seen that *keep* has many meanings and that the above words compare respectively with some meanings and not others

keep'sake *n.* a thing treasured because of the giver

keg *n.* a small barrel

kelp *n.* large sea-weed. Its burnt ashes yield iodine

kel'pie *n.* 1. an Australian breed of smooth-haired, prick-eared dog used to handle sheep. 2. (Scottish) a water-sprite

ken *v.* to know.—*n.* knowledge, as *That is beyond our ken*

ken'nel *n.* a house for a dog.—*v.* to put in kennel

kerb *n.* a stone pavement edging

Note: do not confuse spelling with *curb*

ker'chief (ker'chif) *n.* a square cloth worn over the head

ker'nel *n.* 1. inner soft part of nut or stone of fruit. 2. centre, or essential part

ker'osene *n.* lamp-oil made from petroleum

ketch *n.* a small two-masted vessel

ket'tle *n.* a metal container with spout and handle, for heating water.—**ket'tle-drum** *n.* copper drum

key (kee) *n.* 1. a metal instrument for unlocking and locking. 2. the answer to a problem. 3. a translation, set of answers. 4. a lever on the key-board of a piano, etc. 5. a set of musical notes.—*v.* 1. to fasten with, or as with, a key. 2. to tighten (up), e.g. the strings of a musical instrument.—**keyed up** excited.—**key'note** *n.* 1. note on which a musical key is based. 2. main idea.—**key'stone** *n.* a central stone supporting an arch

kha'ki (kah'ki) *n.* yellowish-brown cloth used for soldiers' uniforms.—*adj.*

ki'a o'ra (kee'a ō'ra) *interj.* Maori expression meaning *good luck! health to you!* Now also *hello*

kick *v.* 1. to strike with the foot. 2. (in common speech) to object, complain, disobey.—*n.* 1. a blow with the foot. 2. the recoil (of a gun).—**kick'off** the first kick in a football match

kid *n.* 1. a young goat. 2. leather of its skin. 3. a child.—*v.* to hoax, deceive

kid'nap *v.* to steal a child.—**kid'napping** *pres. part.*—**kid'napped** *p.t.* and *p. part.*—**kid'napper** *n.*

kid'ney *n.* 1. one of two organs separating waste matter and water from the blood. 2. nature, kind, as *Those people are all of the same kidney.*—**kid'neys** *pl.*

kill *v.* 1. to put to death. 2. to destroy.—*n.* act of killing.—**kil'ler** *n.*

Compare: slay, dispatch, murder, assassinate, slaughter, butcher, massacre, execute

kiln *n.* furnace, oven for drying

kil'ogramme *n.* a weight of a thousand grammes (about 2·2 English pounds)

kil'ometre *n.* a thousand metres (about $\frac{5}{8}$ of a mile)

kil'owatt *n.* a unit of electricity, a thousand watts

kilt *n.* a short, pleated skirt worn by Scottish Highlanders.—**kil'ted** *adj.*

kimo'no *n.* 1. a loose Japanese robe fastened with a sash. 2. a dressing-gown in this style

kin *n.* family, relatives

kind (kīnd) *n.* sort, class.—*adj.* helpful, friendly.—**in kind** 1. in the same way, as *He repaid the insult in kind* (i.e. *with an insult*). 2. in goods, not money, as *The farmer paid his rent in kind*

Compare: (with *n.*) type, category, quality; (with *adj.*) benevolent, charitable, amiable, pleasant, humane, kindly

kin'dergarten *n.* a school for teaching young children by games, etc.

kin'dle *v.* 1. to set on fire. 2. to catch fire. 3. to rouse.—**kin'dling** *pres. part.*—**kin'dled** *p.t.* and *p. part.*

Compare: ignite, inflame, provoke, incense, rouse, exasperate. *Contrast:* extinguish, smother, stifle, cool, quieten, quell

kind'liness (kīnd'li-nes) *n.* friendliness.—**kind'ly** *adj.* friendly, kind.—*adv.* in a kind way.—**kind'ness** *n.* 1. being kind. 2. a friendly act

kin'dred *n.* 1. family. 2. relationship.—*adj.* related, similar

kine (kīn) *n.pl.* cattle.—*pl.* of cow

kinet'ic *adj.* concerning motion.—**kinetic energy** the energy which a moving body possesses due to its motion

king *n.* a ruler of a country.—**queen** *fem.*—

prince the son of a king.—**princess'** the daughter of a king.—**king'dom** *n.* a country ruled by a king.—**king'ly** *adj.* like a king.—**king'ship** *n.* the office of a king—**king'-pin** *n.* 1. a chief pin in a machine. 2. an indispensable person.—**King Country** the central part of North Island of N.Z., once belonging to the Maori King and at that time therefore closed to Europeans

king'fisher *n.* a small diving bird of bright plumage

kink (kingk) *n.* 1. a bend, twist. 2. a mental twist, peculiarity

kins'folk *n.pl.* relatives.—**kin'ship** *n.* relationship.—**kins'man** *n.* male relative.—**kins'-men** *pl.*—**kins'woman** *fem.*

ki'osk (kee'osk) *n.* 1. an open pavilion. 2. a small open-fronted shop

kip *n.* (Aus.) a wooden bat used for tossing pennies in the game of two-up

kip'per *n.* a salted, dried or smoked herring. —*v.*

kirk *n.* a Scottish church

kis'met (kiz'met) *n.* fate, destiny

kiss *v.* 1. to touch with the lips. 2. to touch gently.—he **kiss'es**.—*n.*

kit *n.* 1. an outfit, traveller's equipment. 2. a plaited basket of N.Z. flax.—**kit'bag** *n.* a soldier's bag for equipment

kit'chen *n.* a room used for cooking.—**kit'chen-gar'den** *n.* vegetable-garden

kite *n.* 1. a kind of hawk. 2. a light frame flown in the wind

kit'ten *n.* a young cat

ki'wi (kee'wee) *n.* 1. a New Zealand tail-less bird. 2. a New Zealander.—**the Kiwis** N.Z. touring teams

kleptoma'nia *n.* an insane desire to steal.—**kleptoma'niac** *n.*

klip *n.* in South Africa, a rock; mountain, cliff

knack (nak) *n.* skill, special talent for doing something easily

knap'sack (nap'sak) *n.* a canvas bag for kit, carried on the back

knave (nāv) *n.* 1. a rogue, rascal. 2. a playing-card.—**kna'very** *n.* dishonesty, tricks.—**kna'vish** *adj.* dishonest

knead (need) *v.* 1. to work into a dough. 2. to work with the hands, massage

knee (nee) *n.* the joint between thigh and lower leg.—**knee'cap** *n.* 1. a bone on the knee. 2. protection for the knee

kneel (neel) *v.* to fall, or rest on one's knees. —**knelt** (nelt), **kneeled** *p.t. and p. part.*

knell (nel) *n.* the sound of a funeral bell

knick'ers *n.pl.* a girl's or woman's under-garment

knick'knack (nik'nak) *n.* a small ornament

knife (nīf) *n.* a cutting blade fastened in a handle.—**knives** (nīvz) *pl.*—*v.* to stab with a knife

knight (nīt) *n.* 1. a person raised to a rank below the baronets, and entitled "Sir." 2. a piece in the game of chess.—**knight-er'rant** *n.* knight (of old) in search of adventure.—**knights-errant** *pl.*—**knight'hood** *n.* rank of knight.—**knight'ly** *adj.* brave, chivalrous

knit (nit) *v.* 1. to make (garment) with wool or silk looped on long needles. 2. to unite. 3. to draw (brows) together.—**knit'ting** *pres. part.*—**knit'ted, knit** *p.t.* and *p. part.*

knob (nob) *n.* 1. a rounded lump. 2. a door-handle.—**knob'by** *adj.*

knock (nok) *v.* to strike, hit.—*n.* a blow.—**knock'er** *n.* a hinged metal piece for knocking on a door.—**knock'kneed** (nok'need) *adj.* having legs bending inward.—**knock'-out** *n.* a finishing blow

knoll (nōl) *n.* a mound, small hill

knot (not) *n.* 1. a tying or twisting in a rope, etc. 2. a bow (of ribbon), 3. a lump in wood. 4. a measure of speed at sea, a nautical mile (6080 feet) per hour.—*v.* to make a tie or twist in a rope etc.—**knot'ting** *pres. part.*—**knot'ted** *p.t.* and *p. part.*—**knot'ty** *adj.* difficult

know (nō) *v.* 1. to be aware of. 2. to be acquainted with, recognise.—**knew** (nū) *p.t.*—**known** (nōn) *p. part.*—**know'ing** *adj.* shrewd, cunning.—**know'ingly** *adv.*

Compare: apprehend, comprehend, understand, realise, recognise

know'ledge (nol'ej) *n.* 1. what one knows. 2. understanding. 3. information.—**know'-ledgeable** *adj.* well-informed

knuck'le (nuk'l) *n.* finger-joint

koa'la (kō-a'la) *n.* an Australian animal like a small bear, tree-dwelling marsupial

ko'ker *n.* (Guyana) a wooden gate to control the flow of water

kop, kop'je (kop'i) *n.* in South Africa, a hill

koran' (kor-ahn') *n.* sacred book of Mohammedan scriptures

kraal *n.* a native village in South Africa. 2. a cattle pen in South Africa

Krem'lin *n.* 1. in Russia, town citadel. 2. the citadel in Moscow, centre of government of Soviet Russia

kumar'a *n.* (N.Z.) the sweet potato

L

la'bel *n.* slip of paper fixed on something to show what it is, etc.—*v.* to put a label on.—**la'belling** *pres. part.*—**la'belled** *p.t.* and *p. part.*

la'bial *adj.* of the lips.—*n.* a sound formed with the lips

labor'atory *n.* a place for scientific work.—**labor'atories** *pl.*

labo'rious *adj.* 1. requiring much work. 2. hard-working.—**labo'riously** *adv.*

la'bour (lā'ber) *n.* 1. work, toil. 2. workmen, as *The factory is short of labour.*—*v.* to work hard.—**la'boured** *adj.* clumsy, done with great effort.—**la'bourer** *n.* workman. —**a labour of love** a task gladly performed

lab'rador *n.* a breed of dog

lab'yrinth *n.* a maze, network of winding passages.—**labyrinth'ine** *n.*
lace (lās) *n.* 1. a cord for drawing edges together. 2. gold or silver braid. 3. fine, open-work fabric.—*v.* to fasten with laces.—**la'cing** *pres. part.*—**laced** *p.t.* and *p. part.*
la'cerate (las'er-āt) *v.* to tear, wound.—**lacera'tion** (-ā'shun) *n.*
lac'hrymose (lak'ri-mōs) *adj.* tearful
lack *n.* want of, deficiency.—*v.* to be without, as *The saucepan lacked a handle*
lackadais'ical *adj.* languid, without energy
lack'ey *n.* 1. a footman. 2. an obsequious person
lacon'ic *adj.* using few words, concise.—**lacon'ically** *adv.*
Compare: terse, pithy, curt. *Contrast:* prolix, wordy, verbose, long-winded
lac'quer (lak'er) *n.* kinds of varnish.—*v.*
lacrosse' *n.* a team-game played with a ball and long-handled rackets
lac'teal *adj.* milky.—**lac'tic** *adj.* of milk, as *lactic acid*
lad *n.* boy—**lass** *fem.*
Compare: youth, boy, fellow, stripling
lad'der *n.* a set of rungs or steps connecting two poles and used for climbing up or down
la'den (lā'den) *adj.* loaded, burdened
la'dle (lā'dl) *n.* a deep, long-handled spoon
la'dy (lā'di) *n.* 1. a well-bred woman—**gen'tleman** *masc.* 2. a title of a woman of rank—**lord** *masc.*—**la'dies** *pl.*—**la'dylike** *adj.*—**la'dyship** *n.* used instead of titled lady's name, e.g. *Your ladyship* when addressing her and *her ladyship* when speaking about her
la'dybird *n.* a small spotted flying beetle
lag *v.* to fall behind, go too slowly.—**lag'ging** *pres. part.*—**lagged** *p.t.* and *p. part.*—**lag'gard** *n.* one who lags.—*adj.* slow
lag *v.* to insulate hot-water pipes or a cylinder with wrappings.—**lag'ging** *pres. part.*—**lagged** *p.t.* and *p. part.*—**lag'ging** *n.* insulating wrappings
lagoon' *n.* a small pond or lake fed by the sea, often enclosed by coral island
laid *p.t.* and *p. part.* of lay
lair *n.* the resting-place of a wild beast, den
la'ity (lā'i-ti) *n.* 1. persons who are not clergy. 2. persons who have no special professional knowledge
lake (lāk) *n.* a large body of water surrounded by land
lam'a (lahm'a) *n.* a Buddhist priest in Mongolia or Tibet
lamb (lam) *n.* 1. young of the sheep. 2. lamb's meat.—*v.* to give birth to lambs
lame (lām) *adj.* 1. limping, having a hurt foot or leg. 2. feeble, as *a lame excuse.*—*v.* to cripple.—**lame'ness** *n.*
lament' *v.* to sorrow for, weep for, mourn.—*n.* 1. an expression of grief. 2. a song or poem of sorrow.—**lam'entable** *adj.* to be regretted.—**lamenta'tion** (-tā'shun) *n.* noisy grief
lam'inated *adj.* in the form of thin sheets
lamp *n.* 1. a vessel holding oil to be burnt at a wick, for lighting. 2. a glass globe enclosing gas or electric light
lampoon' *n.* a bitter personal attack in writing
lam'prey *n.* an eel-like fish with sucker on mouth
lance *n.* a long spear, formerly carried by horsemen.—*v.* 1. to pierce with a lance. 2. to cut with a surgeon's knife.—**lan'cing** *pres. part.*—**lanced** *p.t.* and *p. part.*—**lan'cer** *n.* a soldier armed with a lance.—**lance-cor'poral** *n.* a non-commissioned officer below corporal
lan'cet *n.* a surgeon's knife
land *n.* 1. the solid part of the earth's surface. 2. ground, soil. 3. country. 4. estate.—*v.* to come to land (from aircraft or ship).—**land'ed** *adj.* owning land, as *a landed proprietor.*—**land-fall** *n.* ship's nearing land.—**land'ing** *n.* 1. coming to land. 2. platform between flights of stairs
land'lord *n.* 1. the owner of houses or property let to tenants. 2. the master of an inn.—**land'lady** *fem.*
land'lubber *n.* a person not used to the sea and ships, a landsman
land'mark *n.* 1. a boundary-mark. 2. something easily seen, serving as a guide
land'scape (lan'scāp) *n.* 1. a country view. 2. a picture of country scenery.—**land'scape-pain'ter** *n.*—**land'scape-gar'dening** *n.*
land'slide, land'slip *n.* a fall of earth from a cliff
lane (lān) *n.* 1. a narrow road. 2. one of two or more courses marked on the road for vehicles travelling abreast. 3. a path marked for a competitor in a race
lan'guage (lang'gwij) *n.* 1. speech, written or spoken. 2. speech used by a nation. 3. style of speech
Compare: expression, diction, dialect, idiom, tongue, vernacular
lan'guid (lang'gwid) *adj.* weak, drooping, weary.—**lan'guidly** *adv.*
lan'guish (lang'gwish) *n.* 1. to be weary or faint, to pine, as *The plant languished owing to lack of water.* 2. to assume an air of sentiment, tenderness, etc.—he **lan'guishes.**—**lan'guor** (lang'ger) *n.* faintness.—**lan'guorous** *adj.*
lank (langk) *adj.* 1. tall and thin. 2. long and limp, as *His hair was lank.*—**lan'ky** *adj.* lank (1).—**lan'kier** *comp.*—**lan'kiest** *sup.*
lan'tern *n.* a case to protect a lamp or candle from draughts.—**lan'tern-jawed** *adj.* with long narrow jaws
lan'yard *n.* a short rope or cord
lap *n.* 1. the front part of a woman's skirt, used to hold something. 2. the seat made by the thighs of a person seated. 3. once

round a race-course.—*v.* to wrap round.—**lap'ping** *pres. part.*—**lapped** *p.t.* and *p. part.*—**lap'dog** *n.* very small dog

lap *v.* 1. to drink by licking up with the tongue. 2. to make a lapping sound.—**lap'ping** *pres. part.*—**lapped** *p.t.* and *p. part.*

lapel' *n.* the part of the front of a coat that is folded back

Lap'lander, Lapp *n.* a member of a race of people in northern Scandinavia

lapse *n.* 1. a slip due to forgetfulness or carelessness, mistake. 2. a fall from virtue. 3. the passing of time.—*v.* 1. to end. 2. to fall away.—**lap'sing** *pres. part.*—**lapsed** *p.t.* and *p. part.*

lap'wing *n.* a kind of plover

lar'board *n.* old word for left, or port side of a ship, when facing towards the bows

lar'ceny (lar'se-ni) *n.* theft.—**lar'cenies** *pl.*

larch *n.* a cone-bearing tree.—**larch'es** *pl.*

lard *n.* pig's fat melted down and prepared for cooking.—*v.* 1. to insert strips of bacon. 2. to enrich (speech with strange words, etc.)

lard'er *n.* a store-room for food

large (larj) *adj.* 1. broad in area. 2. big, numerous. 3. generous.—**larg'er** *comp.*—**lar'gest** *sup.*—**large'ly** *adv.*—**largess', largesse'** *n.* gifts.—**at large** free.—**large-hearted** *adj.* generous, sympathetic

lar'go *n.* a piece of slow solemn music

lar'iat *n.* a rope with a noose for catching cattle, lasso

lark *n.* a singing bird

lark *n.* fun, a joke.—*v.* to have fun

lar'rikin *n.* (Aus. and N.Z.) a hoodlum, hooliganism.—**lar'rikinism** *n.*

lar'va *n.* an insect in the grub or caterpillar stage.—**lar'vae** *pl.*

lar'ynx (lar'ingks) *n.* the upper part of the wind-pipe

lash *n.* 1. a stroke with a whip. 2. the part of the whip that is tied to the handle.—**lash'es** *pl.*—*v.* 1. to whip. 2. to beat against. 3. to bind with cord.—he **lash'es**

lass *n.* a girl.—**lass'es** *pl.*—**lad** *masc.*

las'situde *n.* weariness, lack of energy

Compare: exhaustion, prostration, languor, faintness, heaviness. *Contrast:* vigour, strength, power, stamina, energy

lasso' (las-ō', las-ōō') *n.* a rope with a noose for catching cattle.—**lassos', lassoes'** *pl.*—*v.* to catch with a lasso

last *sup.* of **late.**—*adj.* coming at the end, as *the last time.*—*adv.*, as *He came last.*—*n.* last person or thing, as *He was the last to go.*—**last'ly** *adv.* finally (used when summing points in a speech or argument.)—**at last** finally, after a long time.—**the last straw** the unbearable limit of many troubles

last *n.* a model of a foot on which a shoemaker shapes boots, etc.

last *v.* 1. to continue, hold out. 2. to remain in good condition.—**las'ting** *adj.* durable

Compare: endure, persist. *Contrast:* perish, decay, pass away, cease

latch *n.* 1. a fastening for a door, consisting of a bar. a catch for it, and a lever to lift it. 2. a small lock with spring action.—**latch'es** *pl.*—*v.* to fasten with a latch.—he **latch'es**

late (lāt) *adj.* 1. after the proper time. 2. not early. 3. recent. 4. recently dead.—**la'ter, lat'ter** *comp.*—**la'test, last** *sup.*—*adv.* 1. after the proper time. 2. at a late hour.—**late'ly** *adv.* recently

Note: Later is generally used when speaking of time, e.g. *a later date* (*adj.*), to *come later* (*adv.*). *Latter* refers to the second of two persons or things, e.g. *the latter person* (*adj.*)

la'tent (lā'tent) *adj.* 1. hidden, secret. 2. existing, but not active, as *latent possibilities, latent heat*—**la'tent heat** the heat required to change water to steam without a change of temperature

lat'eral *adj.* on, at the side of something

lath *n.* a thin, narrow strip of wood to support plaster in ceilings

lathe (lāTH) *n.* a machine for holding wood or metal, turning rapidly while they are being shaped

lath'er (laTH'er or lahTH'er) *n.* the froth of soap and water.—*v.* to make a froth

Lat'in *n.* the language of the ancient Romans

lat'itude *n.* 1. the distance north and south of the equator measured in degrees. 2. freedom for independent action, as *The father allowed his sons considerable latitude*

lat'ter *n.* the second, or more recently mentioned

lat'tice (lat'is) *n.* strips of wood or metal crossed with spaces between.—**lat'tice-window** *n.*

laud (lawd) *v.* to praise.—**laud'able** *adj.* worthy of praise.—**laud'ably** *adv.*

laugh (lahf) *n.* a sound expressing merriment, amusement or scorn.—*v.*—**laugh'able** *adj.* funny.—**laught'er** *n.* mirth, sound of laughing.—**to laugh at** to make fun of.—**to laugh in one's sleeve** to be amused without showing it.—**laughing jack'ass** *n.* a large Australian bird.—**laugh'ing-stock** *n.* a figure of fun

Compare: chuckle, snigger, titter, guffaw.

launch (lahnch, lawnch) *v.* 1. to throw. 2. to set going. 3. to set afloat.—he **launch'es**

launch (lahnch, lawnch) *n.* 1. a large boat carried by a warship. 2. a pleasure-boat driven by a motor.—**launch'es** *pl.*

laun'der (lawn'der) *v.* to wash and iron clothes.—**laun'dress** *n.* a woman who washes and irons clothes

launderette' *n.* a place where washing machines can be used for payment

laun'dry (lawn'dri) *n.* 1. a place where clothes

are washed and ironed. 2. clothes sent to a laundry.—**laun'dries** *pl.*

laur'eate (lor'i-āt) *adj.* crowned with laurels (a sign of honour).—**po'et laur'eate** *n.* poet chosen to write poems for the Court

laur'el (lor'el) *n.* an evergreen shrub with glossy leaves.—*pl.* wreath of laurel-leaves, sign of victory or high honour.—**to rest on one's laurels** to be satisfied with what one has achieved

lav'a (lahv'a) *n.* melted rock flowing from volcano and becoming solid as it cools

lav'atory *n.* 1. place for washing oneself. 2. water closet.—**lav'atories** *pl.*

lave (lāv) *v.* to bathe, wash.—**la'ving** *pres. part.*—**laved** *p.t.* and *p. part.*

lav'ender *n.* a small shrub with sweet-smelling flowers, the oil of which is used in perfumes

lav'ish *adj.* 1. giving too freely. 2. too abundant.—*v.* to give too freely.—he **lav'ishes.** —**lav'ishly** *adv.*

law *n.* 1. a rule made by a government for all citizens. 2. the system of rules. 3. any rule. —**law'ful** *adj.* allowed by law.—**law'fully** *adv.*—**law'giver** *n.* one who makes laws.—**law'less** *adj.* not obeying the law.—**law'-abiding** *adj.* peaceful, keeping to the law

Compare: command, decree, edict, act, statute, mandate, principle

lawn *n.* a carefully tended piece of turf in gardens. etc.—**lawn'mower** *n.* machine for cutting grass.—**lawn-ten'nis** *n.* tennis played in the open on a grass or hard court

law'suit (law'sōōt) *n.* bringing a case to the law-court

law'yer *n.* a member of the legal profession

lax *adj.* 1. loose, negligent. 2. not strict.—**lax'ity** *n.*—**lax'ative** *n.* a medicine causing the bowels to act

lay *v.* 1. to put down. 2. to place. 3. (of a hen) to give eggs. 4. to prepare (e.g. table, fire, etc.).—**lay'ing** *pres. part.*—**laid** *p.t.* and *p. part.*—**lay'er** *n.* 1. a thickness, fold. 2. one who lays, e.g., bricklayer.—**to lay by** 1. to set aside. 2. (Aus.) to pay for goods in instalments before taking delivery.—*n.* the article on which payments are being made.—**to lay hands on** to seize.—**to lay hold of** to seize.—**to lay on** to supply.—**to lay out** to plan.—**to lay to rest** to bury

Note: Lay must not be confused with *lie.* Care is needed in the use of both present and past tenses of these verbs, and of their participles. Thus, *the hen is laying an egg*, but *he is lying down. The hen laid an egg*, but *he lay* down. *The hen has laid an egg*, but *he has lain down*

lay *adj.* not belonging to the clergy or a profession

lay *n.* 1. a minstrel's song. 2. any poem or song

lay'by *n.* a narrow space at the side of a road in which vehicles may park

lay'er *n.* 1. a thickness, as *a layer of dust.* 2. a fold. 3. a person who lays, as *brick-layer*

lay'man *n.* a person not belonging to a profession or to the clergy.—**lay'men** *pl.*

laze *v.* to idle, be lazy.—**la'zily** *adv.* in a lazy manner.—**la'ziness** *n.*

la'zy *adj.* 1. disliking work. 2. slow-moving. —**la'zier** *comp.*—**la'ziest** *sup.*

Compare: idle, slothful, inert, torpid.
Contrast: active, industrious, diligent

lea (lee) *n.* meadow, grassland

lead (led) *n.* 1. a soft, heavy grey metal 2. a weight on the end of a line to find depth of water. 3. the soft black middle of a pencil.—*adj.* made of lead.—**lead'en** *adj.* heavy

lead (leed) *v.* 1. to guide, show the way. 2. to be used as a way, as *This path leads to the garden.* 3. to be first, as *The grey mare is leading.*—**led** *p.t.* and *p. part.*—*n.* 1. leading. 2. front place.—**lead'er** *n.* 1. one who leads. 2. an article in a newspaper giving editor's views (also **leading article**). —**lead'ership** *n.* being a leader.—**a leading light** a prominent person.—**a leading man (lady)** a principal actor (actress).—**to lead astray** to lead someone to wrongdoing.—**to lead someone a dance** to cause someone much trouble

leaf (leef) *n.* 1. the flat, green part of a plant growing on a stem. 2. two pages of a book. 3. a thin sheet. 4. a movable part of a table-top.—**leaves** *pl.*—**leaf'let** *n.* small leaf.—**leaf'y** *adj.*—**to take a leaf out of someone's book** to imitate him.—**to turn over a new leaf** to reform one's ways

league (leeg) *n.* 1. a union of persons, clubs, or nations formed to help each other. 2. a a number of sports clubs playing each other in championship

league *n.* a measure of distance, about three miles

leak (leek) *n.* a hole or break through which something escapes which is not meant to, as *a leak in the roof.*—*v.* to escape through a hole.—**leak'age** *n.* gradual leaking.—**leak'y** *adj.*

lean (leen) *adj.* 1. thin. 2. poor, not abundant. —*n.* meat without much fat.—**lean'ness** *n.*

Compare: slender, skinny, barren, poor.
Contrast: fat, plump, fleshy, plentiful, rich

lean (leen) *v.* 1. to bend, stand in a sloping position. 2. to be inclined to. 3. to prop (against).—**leaned, leant** (lent) *p.t.* and *p. part.*—**lean-to** *n.* a shed built against the side of a house, with a separate roof.—**leaning** *n.* inclination, taste for

Note: lean is followed by *on, against* or *towards* according to its meaning, as *The old man leans on his stick. Lean the ladder against the walk I lean towards your opinions*

leap (leep) *n.* a spring, jump.—*v.* to jump.—**leapt** (lept), **leaped** *p.t.* and *p. part.*—

leap'frog *n.* a game in which the player leaps over the bent back of another.—**leap-year** *n.* a year with February 29th as an extra day. This happens every four years.—**by leaps and bounds** very quickly.—**to look before you leap** to think before acting

learn (lern) *v.* 1. to gain knowledge or skill. 2. to find out.—**learnt, learned** *p.t.* and *p. part.*—**learn'ed** *adj.* having much knowledge.—**learn'er** *n.* beginner.—**learn'ing** *n.* knowledge gained by study.—**to learn by heart** to learn so as to be able to repeat exactly

Note: learn must not be confused with *teach.* Thus, *I teach him* and *he learns from me*

Compare: (with *adj.*) wise, scholarly, sage, educated. *Contrast:* ignorant, illiterate, uneducated

lease (lees) *n.* the letting of land or property for a certain time for rent.—*v.* to let, or take on lease

leash (leesh) *n.* a thong for holding dogs.—*v.*

least (leest) *adj.* 1. sup. of **little.** 2. smallest.—*n.* the smallest one.—**at least** at any rate

leath'er (leTH'er) *n.* an animal's skin tanned and prepared.—*adj.* made of leather.—**leath'ern** *adj.*—**leath'ery** *adj.* tough

leave (leev) *v.* 1. to go away from. 2. to go without taking, as *He left his books on the table.* 3. to depart. 4. to let stay, as *Leave the door open.* 5. to give by will, as *He left his fortune to his son.*—**leav'ing** *pres. part.*—**left** *p.t.* and *p. part.*—**to leave off** 1. to stop doing. 2. to stop wearing, as *to leave off winter clothes.*—**to leave out,** not to put in

Note: leave **v.** never means *to allow,* but *leave* **n.** can mean *permission*

leave (leev) *n.* 1. permission. 2. permission to be absent.—**to take leave of** to say goodbye to.—**to take French leave** to be absent without permission

leav'en (lev'en) *n.* 1. yeast, or any substance used to make dough rise. 2. a silent influence.—*v.* to raise with leaven

lec'tern *n.* a church reading-desk

lec'ture (lek'cher) *n.* 1. a talk for an audience. 2. a scolding.—*v.*—**lec'turer** *n.*

led *p.t.* and *p. part.* of **lead**

ledge (lej) *n.* 1. a narrow shelf. 2. a ridge of rock

ledg'er (lej'er) *n.* the chief account-book of a business firm

lee *n.* 1. shelter. 2. the side of a ship away from the wind.—*adj.* sheltered from the wind

leech *n.* 1. a blood-sucking worm, formerly used by doctors. 2. formerly, a doctor.—**leech'es** *pl.*

leek *n.* a vegetable akin to an onion

leer *n.* a nasty side-glance.—*v.*

lees (leez) *n.pl.* dregs, sediment

lee'ward (lū'ard) *n.* the side away from the wind.—*adj.*—*adv.*

lee'way *n.* the leeward drift of a ship.—**to make up leeway** to make up time or distance lost

left *n.* the side opposite to the right.—*adj.*—**left-hand** *adj.*—**left-hand'ed** *adj.* using the left hand more readily than the right

left *p.t.* and *p. part.* of **leave**

leg *n.* 1. one of the limbs on which persons or animals walk. 2. a support resembling a leg, as *the leg of the table.* 3. covering for a leg.—**leg-pull** *n.* a trick.—**leg side** (cricket) the left side of a batsman facing the bowler.—**square leg** (cricket) a fielding position left of the batsman.—**with not a leg to stand on** with no defence

leg'acy (leg'a-si) *n.* 1. anything left in a will. 2. something handed down from ancestors.—**leg'acies** *pl.*

le'gal *adj.* 1. of law. 2. allowed by law.—**le'galise** *v.* to make legal.—**le'gally** *adv.*

leg'ate *n.* an ambassador, messenger.—**lega'tion** (-gā'shun) *n.* 1. a legate's official residence. 2. a diplomatic minister and his assistants

leg'end (lej'end) *n.* 1. an ancient tale that is not history. 2. an inscription on a coin, etc.—**leg'endary** *adj.*

leg'ible (lej'i-bl) *adj.* plain, easily read.—**leg'ibly** *adv.*

le'gion (lee'jun) *n.* 1. a large body of foot-soldiers in ancient Roman army. 2. a military body. 3. a very large number.—**le'gionary** *adj.*

leg'islate (lej'is-lāt) *v.* to make laws.—**legisla'tion** (-lā'shun) *n.* making laws.—**leg'islative** *adj.*—**legislator** *n.* a law-maker.—**leg'islature** (-lā-cher) *n.* a group of law-makers

legit'imate (lej-it'i-māt) *adj.* lawful

legu'minous *adj.* belonging to the same family as peas and beans

lei'sure (lezh'ur) *n.* spare time.—*adj.* free.—**lei'surely** *adj.* and *adv.* without haste

lem'on *n.* 1. a pale yellow fruit with acid juice. 2. pale yellow.—**lemonade'** *n.* a drink made from lemon-juice.—**lemon squash** concentrated lemonade.—**lemon-squeezer** N.Z. soldier's peaked hat

lend *v.* 1. to give someone something to use for a time. 2. to let out for hire or interest.—**lent** *p.t.* and *p. part.*—**lend'er** *n.*—**it lends itself to** it is well suited to

length *n.* 1. being long. 2. measurement from end to end, as *the length of a ruler.* 3. a long stretch. 4. a piece of material, as *a dress length.*—**length'en** *v.* to make longer, to become longer.—**length'wise, length'ways** *adj.* and *adv.* in the direction of the length.—**length'y** *adj.* long.—**at full length** with the body stretched out.—**at length** *adv.* 1. lengthily. 2. at last.—**to keep someone at arm's length** to avoid close friendship with someone

le'nience, le'niency *n.* mildness.—**le'nient** *adj.* not severe, mild.—**le'niently** *adv.*
Compare: (with *adj.*) gentle, merciful, tender. *Contrast:* severe, stern, harsh

lens (lenz) *n.* a piece of glass with one or both sides curved, used in cameras, spectacles, telescopes, etc.—**lens'es** *pl.*

Lent *n.* the forty days from Ash Wednesday till Easter

lent'il *n.* a kind of bean

le'onine *adj.* like a lion

leop'ard (lep'ard) *n.* a fierce wild animal with dark-spotted yellow coat.—**leop'ard-ess** *fem.*

lep'er *n.* a person suffering from leprosy.—**lep'rosy** *n.* a skin-disease.—**lep'rous** *adj.*

less *adj.* 1. *comp.* of **little**. 2. not so much, as *We have less butter and more jam.*—*adv.* not so well, not so much, as *It rains less in summer.*—*n.* a smaller amount or number, as *We have less to eat*

les'sen *v.* to grow or make less, decrease

les'ser *adj.* the smaller of two

les'son *n.* 1. a reading from the Bible. 2. something learnt. 3. something taught

lest *conj.* for fear that, as *Lest we forget*
Note: After words expressing *fear, lest* means *that,* as *They feared lest he should fall*

let *v.* 1. to allow, permit, as *Let me help you.* 2. lease, hire out, as *to let rooms.* 3. to allow to escape, as *to let blood.*—**let'ting** *pres. part.*—**let** *p.t.* and *p. part.*—**let down** 1. to lower. 2. to disappoint.—**let go** to loose one's hold of.—**let off** to release.—**let out** 1. to allow to go out. 2. make larger. 3. let for hire
Note: The meaning of this word is altered by the words with it. Thus *let alone* means not meddle with or touch

let *v.* to hinder.—*n.* hindrance. In tennis, a service in which the ball touches the top of the net before falling on the other side, so cancelling the stroke.—**without let or hindrance** without interference, freely

le'thal (lee'thal) *adj.* deadly, fatal

lethar'gic (leth-ar'jik) *adj.* drowsy.—**leth'-argy** *n.* drowsiness, lack of energy

let'ter *n.* 1. one of the signs used in writing words. 2. a written message.—*pl.* literature.—*v.* to mark with letters.—**let'tered** *adj.* well read.—**let'terhead** *n.* words printed at the top of note-paper.—**let'terpress** *n.* printed matter

let'tuce (let'is) *n.* a plant with crisp green leaves used for salad

lev'ee (lev'i) *n.* a sovereign's reception for men only

lev'el *adj.* even, flat.—*n.* 1. a level place. 2. height, as *The river rose to its winter level.*—*v.* to make level.—**lev'elling** *pres. part.*—**lev'elled** *p.t.* and *p. part.*—**lev'el-headed** *adj.* sensible.—**level crossing** a place where a road and railway cross at the same level

le'ver (lee'ver) *n.* a bar for raising a heavy weight at one end by pushing down the other. The bar is supported at a point in between.—**le'verage** *n.* the action, or power of a lever

lev'eret *n.* a young hare

levi'athan *n.* 1. a sea-monster. 2. a huge ship

lev'ity *n.* an inclination to make a joke of serious matters

lev'y *v.* 1. to collect taxes. 2. to collect troops.—he **lev'ies**.—**lev'ying** *pres. part.*—**lev'ied** *p.t.* and *p. part.*—*n.* collecting money or troops.—**lev'ies** *pl.*—**to levy war** to wage war

lewd *adj.* indecent.—**lewd'ness** *n.*

lexi'con *n.* a dictionary

liabil'ity *n.* 1. being liable. 2. a debt. 3. a disadvantage.—**liabil'ities** *pl.*

li'able *adj.* 1. responsible, obliged to pay. 2. likely, inclined to, as *You are liable to slip on snow*

li'ar *n.* a person who tells lies

liba'tion (ā'shun) *n.* a drink poured out as an offering to the gods

li'bel *n.* a written statement harmful to a person's character and usually false.—*v.* to publish a libel.—**li'belling** *pres. part.*—**li'belled** *p.t.* and *p. part.*—**li'bellous** *adj.*
Compare: calumny, defamation, scandal, slander. Note: *libel* is written. *Slander* is spoken

lib'eral *adj.* 1. generous. 2. open-minded.—**liberal'ity** *n.*—**lib'erally** *adv.*—**a liberal education** education on broad lines, not a training for a special occupation

lib'erate *v.* to set free.—**libera'tion** (-ā'shun) *n.*—**lib'erator** *n.*

lib'erty *n.* freedom.—**lib'erties** *pl.*
Compare: freedom, independence, emancipation. *Contrast:* captivity, imprisonment, slavery, necessity, oppression, servitude, serfdom

librar'ian *n.* a person in charge of a library

li'brary *n.* 1. a collection of books. 2. a room or building where the books are kept.—**li'braries** *pl.*

librett'o *n.* the words of an opera.—**librett'os, librett'i** *pl.*

li'cence (lī'sens) *n.* 1. permission. 2. a printed permit, as *a driving licence.* 3. lack of control.—**poetic licence** the freedom from rules of perspective or grammar permitted to the artist or poet

li'cense (lī'sens) *v.* to allow, give a licence to.—**licensee'** *n.* one who has a licence

li'chen (lī'ken) *n.* a small, flowerless plant forming a crust on stones and trees

lick *v.* 1. to pass the tongue over. 2. to play around, as *the flames were licking the petrol-tank.*—*n.* 1. licking. 2. a small amount, as *a lick of paint*

lid *n.* 1. a movable cover. 2. the cover of the eye.—**lid'ded** *adj.* having a lid

li'do (lee'dō) *n.* a pleasure resort by the water-side

lie (lī) *n.* something untrue, a false statement. —*v.* to tell a lie, speak falsely.—**ly'ing** *pres. part.*—**lied** *p.t.* and *p. part.*

lie (lī) *v.* 1. to rest one's body in a flat position on something. 2. to remain, as *to be idle.* 3. to be found.—**ly'ing** *pres. part.*—**lay** *p.t.*—**lain** *p. part.*—*n.* 1. nature, as *the lie of the land.* 2. position, as *the lie of a ball*

Note: To lie is sometimes confused with *to lay,* especially in the past tense. See lay

lief (leef) *adv.* gladly, willingly, as *They would as lief starve as eat rats.*—**lie'fer** *comp.*

liege (leej) *adj.* bound to give service to the liege-lord, in the Middle Ages.—*n.* 1. a vassal. 2. a lord

lieuten'ant (army, lef-ten'ant, navy and U.S., lōō-ten'ant) *n.* 1. an army or navy officer. 2. person acting instead of one above him

life (līf) *n.* 1. being alive. 2. a way of living, as *He leads a lonely life.* 3. the time during which a person is alive, as *a long and useful life.* 4. the story of a person's life. 5. energy, vigour, as *Put more life into your tennis.*—**lives** (līvz) *pl.*—**life'less** *adj.* 1. dead. 2. dull.—**life'like** *adj.* vivid, looking real.—**life'long** *adj.* lasting through life.—**life-belt** *n.* a ring of cork to keep one afloat in water.—**life'-boat** *n.* a boat kept on a ship or on the sea-coast, for saving lives at sea.—**life'-jacket** *n.* a garment like a waistcoat made of cork or inflated to support a person in the water.—**life'-preser'ver** *n.* a short stick with heavily loaded end.—**life'-saver** (Aus.) a beach guard

lift *v.* 1. to raise, pick up, as *He lifts the sack of coal from the cart.* 2. to go up, rise, as *The mist is lifting.*—*n.* 1. lifting, raising. 2. machine for raising, elevator. 3. a free ride. 4. help

lig'ament *n.* a band of tissue joining the bones

light (līt) *n.* 1. what makes things visible, as *The earth receives its light from the sun.* 2. anything that gives light, as *the light of a torch.* 3. brightness. 4. daylight, dawn, as *The farmer gets up before light.* 5. information, as *This book sheds light on a difficult subject.* 6. aspect, as *to look at something in the right light.*—*v.* 1. to fill with light, as *Two windows light the room.* 2. to set burning, as *to light the fire.* 3. to brighten, as *The sky was lit with the flames.*—**light'ed, lit** *p.t.* and *p. part.*—*adj.* 1. bright. 2. pale, not dark, as *light blue.*—**light'-house** *n.* a tower with a light to guide ships.—**light'-ship** *n.* a ship anchored at a dangerous spot, with bright warning light.—**light year** (astronomy) the distance travelled by light in one year.—**in the light of** taking into account

Compare: (with *v.*) blaze, flame, flare, flash, gleam, glimmer, glisten, glow, shine, sparkle, twinkle. *Contrast:* darken, dim, obscure, shade

light (līt) *adj.* 1. not heavy. 2. easy to do, or carry or bear, as *light work.* 3. not important, as *a light remark.* 4. delicate, easy, graceful, as *a light touch.* 5. happy, cheerful, as *light music.*—**light'ly** *adv.*—**light-head'ed** *adj.* 1. thoughtless. 2. giddy. —**light-heart'ed** *adj.* gay.—**light-mind'ed** *adj.* frivolous, thoughtless.—**light'weight** *n.* a boxer weighing between 9 st and 9 st 9 lb.—**to make light of** to treat as of little importance

light'en (lī'ten) *v.* 1. to give light to, to brighten. 2. to flash lightning

light'en (lī'ten) *v.* 1. to make less heavy. 2. to cheer

light'er (lī'ter) *n.* something that lights, as *fire-lighter, cigarette-lighter*

light'er (lī'ter) *n.* a large, flat-bottomed boat used for unloading ships

light'ness (līt'nes) *n.* 1. brightness. 2. paleness

light'ness (līt'nes) *n.* 1. being light, not heavy. 2. cheerfulness. 3. being thoughtless, not serious enough

light'ning (līt'ning) *n.* electricity flashing in the sky.—**light'ning-conduc'tor** *n.* a metal rod fixed on high buildings to conduct electricity into earth or water

li'keable *adj.* pleasing

like (līk) *v.* to find pleasant, to be attracted to.—**li'king** *pres. part.*—**liking** *n.*

like (līk) *prep.* in the manner of, as *He swims like a duck.*—*adj.* 1. similar, resembling, as *in like manner, what is he like?* 2. equal, as *a like amount.*—*adv.* in the right state for, as *I feel like working.* —*n.* equal, as *I have never seen the like.*—**like'lihood** *n.* probability.—**like'ly** *adj.* 1. probably true, as *a likely tale.* 2. hopeful, promising, as *a likely winner in the race.*—*adv.* probably.—**li'ken** *v.* to compare.—**like'ness** *n.* 1. being like. 2. portrait.—**like'wise** *adv.* in like manner.—**and the like** and so on, and similar things

li'lac *n.* shrub with sweet-smelling violet or white flowers.—*adj.* pale violet in colour

lilt *n.* a light, swinging tune

lil'y *n.* one of many kinds of plant growing from a bulb.—**lil'ies** *pl.*

limb (lim) *n.* 1. an arm or leg. 2. branch of a tree

lime *n.* a white substance obtained by burning limestone in a **lime'-kiln.**—**lime'-stone** *n.* rock containing lime

lime *n.* a small acid fruit like a lemon.—**lime'-juice** *n.*

lime *n.* the linden-tree

lime'-light (līm'-līt) *n.* strong light showing up certain actors on theatre-stage.—**in the limelight** prominent, attracting public interest

lim'it *n.* boundary, edge.—*v.* to restrict, keep within limits.—**limita'tion** *n.* being limited.—**lim'ited** *adj.*—**lim'itless** *adj.*—**within limits** moderately

lim'ousine (lim'ōō-zeen) *n.* a large car with a glass screen behind the driving seat

limp *n.* a lame walk.—*v.*

limp *adj.* 1. without firmness or stiffness. 2. without energy

lim'pet *n.* a small shell-fish that sticks tightly to rocks

lim'pid *adj.* clear.—**limpid'ity** *n.*

line *n.* 1. a cord, string or wire. 2. a long, narrow mark, as *a red line under a word.* 3. a row, series, as *a line of cars.* 4. a course, direction, as *work on these lines.* 5. a class of goods, as *a good line of shoes.* 6. a row of words, as *a line of poetry.*—*v.* 1. to mark with lines. 2. to bring into line. 3. to cover inside, as *to line a coat with fur.*—**li'ning** *pres. part.*—**all along the line** at all points.—**in line with** in agreement with.—**to draw the line at** to refuse to do.—**to line up** to form a line or row.—**to read between the lines** to understand more than the words themselves say.—**to toe the line** to obey

lin'eage (lin'i-āj) *n.* 1. direct descent from an ancestor. 2. ancestors, family.—**lin'eal** *adj.* in direct line of descent

lin'ear *adj.* 1. of lines, like a line. 2. of length, as *linear measure*

lin'en *n.* 1. cloth made of flax. 2. articles made of linen, as *household linen*

li'ner *n.* a vessel belonging to a regular line of ships

ling'er (ling'ger) *v.* 1. to delay, be slow. 2. to remain long

Compare: crawl, dawdle, drag, halt, hesitate, lag, loiter, wait. *Contrast:* accelerate, advance, hasten, hurry, speed, press on, depart

lin'gerie (lan'zher-ee) *n.* ladies' underwear

ling'o (ling'go) *n.* a foreign language.—**ling'oes** *pl.*

Note: lingo is generally used contemptuously of a language one does not understand

ling'uist (ling'gwist) *n.* a person speaking several languages.—**linguist'ic** *adj.* of language

lin'iment *n.* healing ointment for rubbing on sprains, etc.

link (lingk) *n.* 1. a ring of a chain. 2. a thing or person that joins or connects.—*v.* to join, connect

links (lingks) *n.pl.* a course where golf is played

li'nocut *n.* 1. a design cut in linoleum-covered block. 2. a print from this

lino'leum *n.* a floor-covering made of canvas with a surface of cork and linseed-oil

li'notype (lī'nō-tīp) *n.* a printing machine casting whole lines of type at a time

lin'seed *n.* the seed of flax.—**linseed-oil'** *n.*

lint *n.* soft material for dressing wounds

lint'el *n.* the top piece of a door or window

li'on *n.* 1. a large fierce animal of the cat family.—**li'oness** *fem.*—**cub** a young lion. 2. a brave person.—**li'onise** *v.* to treat as a celebrity.—**the lion's share** the largest share

lip *n.* 1. either edge of the mouth. 2. a rounded edge as *the lip of a jug.*—**lip-reading** understanding a speaker by watching the movements of his lips

liq'uefy (lik'wi-fī) *v.* to make liquid.—he **liq'uefies.**—**liq'uefying** *pres. part.*—**liq'uefied** *p.t.* and *p. part.*

liq'uid (lik'wid) *n.* a substance that is neither a solid nor a gas, a substance that flows.—*adj.* 1. flowing. 2. melted

liq'uidate (lik'wi-dāt) *v.* 1. to pay off debts. 2. to settle a business.—**liquida'tion** *n.*

liqu'or (lik'er) *n.* 1. a liquid. 2. strong drink

liqu'orice (lik'or-is) *n.* a plant from which a black sweet is made

li'ra (lee'ra) *n.* an Italian silver coin

lisp *v.* to pronounce "s" and "z" as "th."—*n.*

lis'som *adj.* supple, bending easily, lithe

list *n.* 1. an edge of cloth. 2. a series. written down, as *a list of names.*—*v.* to enter in a list.—**lists** *n.pl.* space for tilting, or fighting with lances

list *v.* to tilt on one side (of a ship)

lis'ten (lis'n) *v.* to try to hear, to pay attention.—**lis'tener** *n.*

list'less *adj.* tired, not interested, indifferent, indolent

lit'any *n.* a form of prayers for mercy.—**lit'anies** *pl.*

lit'eracy *n.* being literate

lit'eral *adj.* 1. of letters. 2. following word by word, as *a literal translation.* 3. taking the usual meaning of words.—**lit'erally** *adv.* exactly

lit'erary *adj.* having to do with literature

lit'erate *adj.* able to read and write, educated

lit'erature *n.* 1. books and writings that are valued for their style or thought, as *English literature.* 2. the study of writings

lithe *adj.* supple, bending easily

lit'igate *v.* to go to law.—**litiga'tion** (gā'shun) *n.*

lit'mus *n.* a vegetable dye turned red by acids and blue by alkalis

li'tre (lee'ter) *n.* the measure of capacity in the metric system (about $1\frac{3}{4}$ pints), equal to 1000 cubic cms.

lit'ter *n.* 1. a kind of stretcher for the wounded. 2. straw, etc. as bedding for animals. 3. untidy bits lying about. 4. young animals born at the same time

lit'tle *adj.* 1. small, not much, as *a little mouse.* 2. not great, mean. 3. not important, as *a little quarrel.*—**less, less'er** *comp.*—**least** *sup.*—*n.* only a small amount, as *Will you have a little butter?*—*adv.* not much, slightly, as *He can swim a little.*—**less** *comp.*—**least** *sup.*

Compare: brief, mean, tiny, minute, petty, narrow, short, slender, slight, small, trivial. *Contrast:* big, large, great, huge, immense, vast, wide, broad, extensive, enormous

lit'urgy (lit'ur-ji) *n.* a form of public worship. —**lit'urgies** *pl.*—**litur'gical** *adj.*

live (liv) *v.* 1. to have life, as *We cannot live without air.* 2. to pass one's life. 3. to last, as *His name will live for ever.* 4. to dwell, as *She lives in a small town.* 5. (on) to feed, as *Cows live on grass.*—**liv'ing** *pres. part.*

live (līv) *adj.* 1. living. 2. burning, as *live coals.* 3. carrying electric current, as *a live wire.* 4. energetic.—**livestock,** farm animals.—**live broadcast** events broadcast or televised while they are taking place.—**live cartridge** a cartridge containing a bullet

live'lihood (līv'li-hood) *n.* means of living

live'liness (līv'li-nes) *n.* gaiety, energy

live'long (liv'long) *adj.* whole, as *The livelong day*

live'ly (līv'li) *adj.* active, full of life, bright.—**live'lier** *comp.*—**live'liest** *sup.*

li'ven *v.* to brighten, cheer

liv'er *n.* an organ in the body which makes bile

liv'ery *n.* a uniform worn by men-servants and by members of certain societies.—**liv'eries** *pl.*

liv'id *adj.* of a bluish pale colour, as *the livid mark of a bruise*

liv'ing *n.* 1. being alive. 2. livelihood, means of support. 3. clergyman's position and the income it brings him.—*adj.* 1. alive now. 2. true to life, as *a living portrait.* 3. enough to live on, as *a living wage.* 4. for living in, as *a living-room*

liz'ard *n.* a four-legged reptile

llam'a *n.* a woolly South American animal, like a camel but without a hump

lo *interj.* see! behold!

load (lōd) *n.* 1. burden, weight. 2. amount carried, as *a load of bricks.*—*v.* 1. to put a load on. 2. to put a charge in a gun

load'stone, lode'stone *n.* magnetic iron ore

loaf (lōf) *n.* a lump of bread as baked.—**loaves** (lōvz) *pl.*

loaf (lōf) *v.* to idle, be lazy.—**loaf'er** *n.*

loam (lōm) *n.* rich soil

loan (lōn) *n.* 1. lending. 2. something lent. 3. permission to use.—*v.* to lend

loath, loth *adj.* unwilling. —**nothing loth** not unwilling

loathe (lōTH) *v.* to be disgusted by, to hate.—**loath'ing** *n.* disgust.—**loath'some** *adj.* disgusting

Compare: abhor, detest, despise, scorn, shun. *Contrast:* admire, approve, enjoy, love, esteem

lob *n.* 1. a slow, underhand ball in cricket. 2. in tennis, a shot sent high in the air.—*v.* to send a lob.—**lob'bing** *pres. part.*—**lobbed** *p.t.* and *p. part.*

lob'by *n.* a passage, or entrance-hall.—**lob'bies** *pl.*

lobe (lōb) *n.* 1. the soft lower end of the ear. 2. any rounded flap

lob'ster *n.* a long sea-animal with hard shell and strong claws which turn red when boiled

lo'cal (lo'cal) *adj.* 1. belonging to a place, as *the local doctor.* 2. only in one place, as *a local anaesthetic.*—**local'ity** *n.* place, district.—**lo'calise** *v.* to keep within one place.—**lo'cally** *adv.*

locate' (lō-cāt') *v.* 1. to find the exact position of, as *We located the enemy's guns.* 2. to establish in a place.—**loca'tion** *n.* 1. position. 2. (South Africa) land reserved for natives, native quarter of white towns and cities

loch (loh) *n.* 1. a lake (in Scotland). 2. an arm of the sea

lock *n.* 1. a way of fastening a door or lid, with a key. 2. a part of river or canal within gates, where the level of the water can be changed to let ships pass.—*v.* 1. to fasten with a lock. 2. to join firmly together.—**lock'er** *n.* small cupboard with a lock

lock *n.* a tuft or curl of hair

lock'et *n.* a small case of precious metal for a portrait, etc., worn round the neck

locomo'tion (lō-co-mō'shun) *n.* action or power of moving

locomo'tive *n.* an engine that moves on its own power.—*adj.* having the power to move

lo'cust (lō'cust) *n.* a destructive insect resembling the grasshopper

lodge (loj) *n.* 1. a small country house. 2. a house at the gate of an estate. 3. a meeting-place of a branch of freemasons, the branch.—*v.* 1. to live in for a time. 2. to rent a room in someone's house. 3. to lay before, as *he lodged a protest with the judge.* 4. to stick, get caught, as *He threw up his cap and it lodged in a tree.*—**lodg'er** *n.* a person living in a rented room. —**lodg'ings** *n.pl.* rented rooms.—**lodg'ment** *n.* being lodged

loft *n.* 1. a room under the roof. 2. a gallery in a church

lof'tiness *n.* height

lof'ty *adj.* 1. very high. 2. proud.—**lof'tier** *comp.*—**lof'tiest** *sup.*

log *n.* 1. a large rough piece of wood. 2. a device for measuring the speed of a ship. 3. a daily account of a ship's voyage.—**log-book** *n.*

lo'ganberry (lō') *n.* a plant with dark red fruit, a cross between the blackberry and the raspberry.—**lo'ganberries** *pl.*

log'gerhead *n.* a stupid person.—**at loggerheads** quarrelling, on bad terms

lo'gic (loj'ik) *n.* 1. the science of reasoning. 2. good sense.—**lo'gical** *adj.* 1. having to do with logic. 2. reasonable

loin *n.* the part of the body on either side between rib and hip

loi'ter *v.* to linger, waste time on the way.—**loi'terer** *n.*
loll *v.* 1. to sit or lie lazily. 2. to hang out (the tongue)
loll'ipop *n.* a hard-boiled sweet on a stick
lone (lōn) *adj.* 1. alone. 2. uninhabited.—**lone'liness** *n.* solitude.—**lone'ly** *adj.* 1. alone. 2. feeling sad because alone. 3. without people.—**lone'lier** *comp.*—**lone'liest** *sup.*—**lone'some** *adj.* feeling lonely
long *adj.* 1. taking up much time or length, as *A year is a long time. A long road.* 2. of a certain length, as *two inches long.*—*adv.* 1. for a long time, as *Have you been here long?* 2. during, as *all night long.*—*n.* a long time, as *They were found before long.*—**long'ways** *adv.* lengthways.—**as long as** provided that.—**in the long run** in the end.—**of long standing** having existed for a long time.—**the long and the short** the whole
Compare: tedious, dilatory, lengthy. *Contrast:* short, brief, near, concise, laconic, prompt
long *v.* to wish very much, as *He longs to be in the team*
longev'ity (lon-jev'i-ti) *n.* long life
long'ing *n.* great desire.—*adj.* full of desire
lon'gitude (lon'ji-tūd) *n.* the distance east or west of a given place (usually Greenwich), measured in degrees.—**longitu'dinal** *adj.* 1. in length. 2. of longitude
long-suf'fering *adj.* bearing pain or trouble patiently
long-winded' *adj.* 1. able to run far without being breathless. 2. talking or writing too long
look *v.* 1. to use the eyes, to try to see, as *Look at the rain.* 2. to seem, appear, as *That looks wrong.* 3. to face, as *The house looks south.*—*n.* a glance.—*pl.* appearance, as *good looks.*—**look'ing-glass** *n.* mirror.—**look'out** *n.* 1. a watch. 2. place for watching. 3. prospect.—**to look after** to take care of.—**to look alive** to be quick.—**to look down on** to despise.—**to look for** 1. to seek. 2. to expect.—**to look forward to** to await with pleasure.—**to look sharp** to be quick.—**to look up** to search (in a book).—**to look up to** to respect
Compare: (with *v.* 1.) see, behold, gaze, glance, stare, survey, watch, scan, view
loom *n.* a machine for weaving
loom *v.* to appear dimly (out of darkness or mist)
loop *n.* 1. the shape of a curved rope, etc., crossing itself. 2. in Canada, a lasso.—*v.* to form a loop
loop'hole *n.* 1. a slit in a wall for firing at an enemy. 2. a means of escape
loose (lōōs) *adj.* 1. not tight, or fastened or fixed, as *a loose rope, a loose tooth.* 2. free, as *We set the dog loose.* 3. careless, slack, as *loose ideas, a loose character.*—*v.* 1. to set free, unfasten. 2. to make slack.—**loos'ing** *pres. part.*—**loose'ly** *adv.*—**loos'en** *v.* to make loose.—**loose'ness** *n.*—**a loose-leaf book** a notebook with detachable pages.—**at a loose end** idle, uncertain what to do next
loot (lōōt) *n.* plunder, booty.—*v.*
lop *v.* 1. to cut branches. 2. to chop off.—**lop'ping** *pres. part.*—**lopped** *p.t.* and *p. part.*
lopsi'ded *adj.* with one side lower than the other
lope *v.* to move with long smooth strides
loqua'cious (lō-kwā'shus) *adj.* talkative.—**loquac'ity** (lō'kwas'i-ti) *n.*
lord *n.* 1. a ruler, master. 2. a nobleman of high rank.—**la'dy** *fem.* 3. a title given to a bishop, judge or Lord Mayor.—**lord'ly** *adj.* proud, dignified.—**lord'ship** *n.* 1. power, rule. 2. a title given to a lord. **la'dyship** *fem.*—**The Lord** 1. God. 2. Jesus Christ.—**the House of Lords** the upper chamber of the British Parliament.—**the Lord's Day** Sunday.—**the Lord Rector** the honorary head of a Scottish university.—**to lord it over** to domineer
lore *n.* 1. learning. 2. facts and legends about a subject, as *bird-lore, folk-lore*
lor'ry *n.* a truck, wagon without sides.—**lor'ries** *pl.*
lo'ry, lou'rie, low'rie *n.* several species of parrot
lose (lōōz) *v.* 1. to be unable to find, as *to lose a dog, to lose the way.* 2. to be robbed of (by accident, misfortune, etc.), as *to lose the toss.* 3. to waste, as *to lose time.* 4. to miss, as *to lose a chance.* 5. to be defeated, as *Our team lost.*—**lo'sing** (lōō'zing) *pres. part.*—**lost** *p.t.* and *p. part.*—**lo'ser** (lōō'zer) *n.* one who loses, one who is defeated.—**lo'sing** *adj.*—**to lose ground** to get worse.—**to lose oneself in** to be absorbed in.—**to lose one's head** to panic.—**to lose sight of** to forget
loss *n.* 1. losing. 2. what is lost. 3. harm or damage done by losing.—**loss'es** *pl.*—**at a loss** puzzled, uncertain
lot *n.* 1. something, e.g. a marked, paper used to decide by chance, as *We draw lots for the prize.* 2. share, fate, as *It was his lot to become leader.* 3. one object or a group of several objects to be sold at an auction. 4. a large number or quantity.—**to throw in one's lot with** to share the fortunes of
Note: The expressions *a lot of, lots of,* are vague and should be avoided before words of quality. Use instead *much, many, several, numerous,* etc. before words expressing number
loth see **loath**
lo'tion (lō'shun) *n.* a healing or cleansing liquid for the skin
lot'tery *n.* a scheme by which many tickets are sold, a few of which draw prizes.—**lot'teries** *pl.*

loud (lowd) *adj.* 1. noisy. 2. showy, as *a loud neck-tie.*—*adv.* loudly.—**loud'ly** *adv.* —**loud-speak'er** *n.* 1. an instrument for making sounds audible to many people at once. 2. part of a radio receiver
Compare: noisy, blatant, clamorous. *Contrast:* soft, quiet, mute, silent, still

lounge (lownj) *v.* to move or stand lazily.—**loun'ging** *pres. part.*—*n.* 1. a comfortable room with deep chairs. 2. a couch.—**lounge-suit** *n.* an ordinary suit for daytime wear

lour, lower (low'er) *v.* 1. to frown, scowl. 2. to look dark

louse (lows) *n.* an insect living on animals or persons.—**lice** *pl.*—**lou'sy** (low'zi) *adj.* dirty

lout *n.* a clumsy, ill-mannered fellow

lov'able *adj.* pleasing, attractive

love (luv) *n.* 1. deep affection. 2. person loved. 3. in games, a score of nothing.—*v.* to be very fond of.—**lov'ing** *pres. part,*—loved *adj.*—**lov'er** *n.*—**fall in love** to begin to love.—**no love lost** dislike.—**to play for love** to play without stakes
Contrast: (with loved) hated, disliked, detested

love'liness *n.* beauty

love'ly (luv'li) *adj.* beautiful, delightful.—**love'lier** *comp.*—**love'liest** *sup.*

lov'ing *adj.* affectionate, fond.—**lov'ingly** *adv.*

low (lō) *adj.* 1. not tall or high, as *a low chair, a low moon.* 2. of humble rank. 3. common, vulgar. 4. not loud, as *She spoke in a low voice.* 5. weak, depressed, as *in low spirits.*—*adv.* 1. not high. 2. not loudly.—**low tide** when the sea is lowest on the shore.—**to lie low** to remain in hiding

low (lō) *v.* to moo (as a cow).—*n.*

low'er (lō'er) *v.* 1. to let down. 2. to make less.—*adj.* less high

low'land *n.* low-lying country.—*adj.*—**the Lowlands** the south-eastern part of Scotland

low'liness *n.* meekness, being humble

low'ly (lō'li) *adj.* 1. humble in position, poor. 2. modest.—**low'lier** *comp.*—**low'liest** *sup.*
Compare: meek, mild, gentle, submissive, humble. *Contrast:* proud, haughty, arrogant

loy'al *adj.* 1. faithful, true. 2. faithful to king and country.—**loy'alist** *n.* a faithful supporter.—**loy'ally** *adv.*—**loy'alty** *n.*—**loy'alties** *pl.*

loz'enge (loz'enj) *n.* 1. a diamond-shaped figure. 2. a sweet, or tablet of medicine

lu'bricant *n.* oil or grease used to make parts of machines work smoothly.—**lu'bricate** *v.* to oil or grease machines.—**lubrica'tion** *n.*—**lu'bricator** *n.*

lu'cid (lōō'sid) *adj.* clear, easily understood, as *a lucid explanation.*—**lucid'ity** *n.*

luck *n.* fortune, chance.—**luck'ily** *adv.* by good fortune.—**luck'less** *adj.* unfortunate.—**luck'y** *adj.* having or bringing good luck.—**luck'ier** *comp.*—**luck'iest** *sup.*—**lucky dip** a tub of sawdust from which one may draw a prize

lu'crative *adj.* profitable.—**lu'cre** (lōō'ker) *n.* riches, sordid gain

lu'dicrous (lōō'di-krus) *adj.* absurd, ridiculous

lu'do *n.* a game on a board with counters moved at the throw of a dice

lug *v.* to drag with an effort, to pull hard.—**lug'ging** *pres. part.*—**lugged** *p.t.* and *p. part.*

lug'gage (lug'ij) *n.* traveller's baggage, trunks, suit-cases, etc.

lug'ger *n.* a kind of sailing vessel

lugu'brious (lōō-gōō'bri-us) *adj.* mournful, sad

luke'warm (lōōk'warm) *adj.* 1. tepid, neither hot nor cold. 2. indifferent

lull *v.* 1. to sing to sleep. 2. to calm, make quiet.—*n.* a short time of quiet in storm or pain.—**lull'aby** (lul'a-bī) *n.* a lulling song.—**lull'abies** *pl.*

lum'ber *n.* 1. roughly-cut timber. 2. useless household articles.—*v.* 1. (U.S.) to fell trees and saw them. 2. to move heavily.—**lum'ber-jack, lum'berman** *n.* man who cuts or sells lumber

lu'minary (lōō'min-ar-i) *n.* 1. the sun, moon, or a star. 2. a person noted for his learning.—**lu'minaries** *pl.*

lu'minous (lōō'min-us) *adj.* bright, shining

lump *n.* 1. a shapeless piece. 2. a swelling.—*v.* to throw together in one mass or sum.—**lump'ish** *adj.* clumsy, stupid.—**lump'y** *adj.* full of lumps.—**a lump sum** a single sum of money in payment of several accounts.—**in the lump,** as a whole

lu'nacy (lōō'na-si) *n.* madness

lu'nar (lōō'nar) *adj.* relating to the moon.—**a lunar month** the time between two new moons

lu'natic (lōō'na-tik) *n.* an insane person.—*adj.* crazy, insane, mad

lunch *n.* a light, midday meal.—**lunch'es** *pl.*—**lunch'eon** *n.* lunch

lung *n.* one of the two air-breathing organs

lunge (lunj) *v.* to thrust forward suddenly.—*n.*—**lun'ging** *pres. part.*

lurch *v.* to roll suddenly on one side, to stagger.—*n.*—**to leave in the lurch** to leave in difficulties

lure (lūr) *n.* a bait, attraction.—*v.* to attract by offering something.—**lu'ring** *pres. part.*

lu'rid (lūr'id) *adj.* 1. very pale, ghastly. 2. glaring, fiery

lurk *v.* 1. to lie hidden, to wait for in hiding. 2. to move stealthily

lus'cious (lush'us) *adj.* delicious, rich and sweet

lush *adj.* 1. rich and juicy. 2. (of grass, etc.) growing plentifully

lust *n.* eager desire.—*v.*—**lust'ful** *adj.*

lus'tre (lus'ter) *n.* 1. glitter, brightness. 2. glory, fame, renown.—**lus'trous** *adj.*

lus'ty *adj.* healthy, strong.—**lus'tier** *comp.*—**lust'iest** *sup.*

lute (lōōt) *n.* an ancient stringed musical instrument like a guitar

luxu'riance *n.* rich growth, abundance.—**luxu'riant** *adj.* growing abundantly

luxu'riate *v.* 1. to grow too abundantly. 2. to indulge in, enjoy

luxu'rious (lux-ōō'ri-us) *adj.* 1. fond of expensive and comfortable things. 2. very comfortable.—**luxu'riously** *adv.*

lux'ury (luk'shur-i) *n.* 1. enjoyment of comforts and of expensive things. 2. something enjoyable but not necessary.—**lux'uries** *pl.*

ly'ing *n.* telling a lie.—*adj.* false

lynch (linch) *v.* to put to death without a proper trial

lynx (lingks) *n.* a wild animal of the cat family with keen sight.—**lynx'-eyed** *adj.*

lyre (līr) *n.* an ancient stringed musical instrument like a harp.—**lyre'bird** *n.* species of large, mound-building birds of S.E. Aust., the male having a lyre-shaped tail

lyr'ic (lir'ik) *n.* 1. a poem of the poet's personal feelings. 2. words for a song.—**lyr'ic, lyr'ical** *adj.*

M

macad'am *n.* a road surface of layers of broken stone pressed smooth

macaro'ni *n.* wheaten flour paste made into long hollow tubes for eating

macaroon' *n.* a biscuit of almond and sugar

macaw' *n.* a large showy American parrot

mace (mās) *n.* 1. a spiked war club. 2. a staff, carried as a sign of office

mace (mās) *n.* a spice made from nutmegs

mach'ete (mash-et', mach-ā'ti) *n.* a large chopping knife

machine' (ma-sheen') *n.* 1. an arrangement of several metal parts combining to do special work, as *a sewing-machine*. 2. an organisation. 3. a bicycle, car, etc.—**machine'-gun** *n.* a gun that fires a quick succession of bullets automatically

machin'ery (ma-sheen'er-i) *n.* 1. machines. 2. the parts of a machine. 3. organisation or methods for achieving some end, as *the machinery of government*.—**machi'nist** *n.* a person who makes or works machines

mack'erel *n.* a sea-fish with blue and silver skin.—**a mackerel sky** a sky with small broken clouds

mack'intosh *n.* a water-proof coat

mad *adj.* 1. insane, out of one's mind. 2. foolish, as *a mad scheme*. 3. frenzied, as *mad with terror*.—**mad about** 1. extremely fond of. 2. very angry, as *he was mad (at) about missing the bus*.—**mad'ly** *adv.*

mad'am *n.* 1. a polite title used in addressing women. 2. a woman or girl who likes to order people about.—**sir** *masc.*—**madame'** (ma-dam') *n.* French form of Mrs. or madam.—**mesdames'** (mā-dam') *pl.*

Note: Madam is used 1. as a polite form of address in speaking, as "*Certainly, madam.*" 2. in writing formally, as "*Dear Madam.*" 3. as a title, as *Madam chairman.*

mad'cap *n.* a wild, hasty person

mad'den *v.* to make mad

made *p.t.* and *p. part.* of **make.**—*adj.* produced, prepared, constructed.—**made-up** *adj.* 1. artificial. 2. finished, complete.—**made to measure** made to the customer's requirements

mad'ness *n.* 1. being mad, insanity. 2. folly. 3. rage, fury

madon'na *n.* 1. the Virgin Mary. 2. a picture or statue of her

mad'rigal *n.* 1. a short poem. 2. a part-song for voices only

magazine' (mag-a-zeen') *n.* 1. a storehouse for explosives and other military stores. 2. a cartridge-chamber in a gun. 3. a publication with stories and articles by different writers

magen'ta *n.* a reddish-purple colour.—*adj.*

mag'got *n.* an insect in the earliest grub stage.—**mag'goty** *adj.* full of maggots

ma'gi (mā'jī) *n.pl.* the three "wise men" from the East, who came to honour the infant Jesus

mag'ic (maj'ik) *n.* 1. the art of making things happen by secret powers or witchcraft. 2. something very wonderful.—*adj.* done by magic, wonderful.—**mag'ical** *adj.*—**mag'ically** *adv.*—**magi'cian** (maj-ish'an) *n.* a wizard

magiste'rial (ma-jis-tee'ri-al) *adj.* 1. belonging to a magistrate. 2. over-bearing, masterful

mag'istrate (maj'is-trāt) *n.* 1. a public officer with power to enforce law. 2. a judge

magnanim'ity *n.* generosity of mind, being above meanness.—**magnan'imous** *adj.* noble

mag'nate *n.* a person of wealth and high position

magne'sium (mag-nee'zi-um) *n.* a silvery-white metal which burns with a dazzling light

mag'net *n.* a piece of iron or steel having power to attract pieces of iron or steel, and pointing north and south when hung up.—**magnet'ic** *adj.* 1. having the power of a magnet. 2. very attractive, *as she has a magnetic personality.*—**mag'netism** *n.*—**mag'netise** *v.* to make into a magnet.—**magnet'ic compass** a mounted magnetised needle which always points to the north.—**magnet'ic tape** tape coated with a fine covering of iron, used in a tape-recorder

magne'to (mag-nee'tō) *n.* a small generator used to provide the spark in a petrol engine

magnif'icence (mag-nif'i-sens) *n.* splendour, great wealth.—**magnif'icent** *adj.* grand

mag'nify (mag'ni-fī) *v.* 1. to make something

look larger than it is. 2. to praise, as *My Soul doth magnify the Lord.*—he **mag'nifies.** —**mag'nifying** *pres. part.*—**mag'nified** *p.t.* and *p. part.*

mag'nitude *n.* 1. size. 2. importance

mag'pie *n.* a chattering black and white long-tailed bird

maharaj'ah *n.* a great Indian prince.—**maharan'i** *fem.*

mahog'any *n.* a tree giving hard, reddish-brown wood.—*adj.* reddish-brown

mahom'medan see **moham'medan**

mahout' (ma-howt') *n.* an elephant-driver

maid (mād) *n.* 1. a young unmarried woman, a girl. 2. a woman servant.—**man** *masc.*—**maid of honour** *n.* a bride's attendant.—**maid'en** *n.* a girl, unmarried woman.—*adj.* 1. unmarried. 2. first, as *maiden voyage.* 3. in cricket, of an over during which no runs are scored.—**maid'enhood** *n.*—**maid'enly** *adj.*—**maiden name** a woman's surname before marriage.—**maiden speech** the first speech in Parliament made by a new member

mail *n.* 1. letters. 2. a bag of letters. 3. a system of carrying parcels and letters, as *the letter was sent by air mail.*—*v.* in U.S. to send by post

mail *n.* a chain armour, or plate-armour.—**mailed** *adj.* covered with mail

maim *v.* to cut off or damage a limb, to cripple

main *n.* 1. the open sea. 2. chief gas or water-pipe.—*adj.* 1. chief, most important. 2. full, as *by main force.*—**main'land** *n.* a country without its islands.—**the Mainland** South Island of N.Z.—**main'ly** *adv.* for the most part.—**main'mast** *n.* the chief mast in a ship.—**main'sail** *n.* the lowest sail of a mainmast.—**main'spring** *n.* 1. the chief spring in a watch or clock. 2. chief motive or reason.—**in the main** for the most part, on the whole.—**with might and main** with all one's strength

maintain' *v.* 1. to keep up. 2. to support, defend, as *to maintain a family.* 3. to carry on, preserve, as *to maintain traditions.* 4. to defend an opinion.—**main'tenance** *n.*

maize *n.* Indian corn

majes'tic *adj.* royal, stately, noble.—**majes'tically** *adv.*

Compare: kingly, august, princely, regal, royal. *Contrast:* contemptible, mean, inferior, poor, servile, base

maj'esty *n.* dignity, stateliness.—**his maj'esty** or **her maj'esty** is a title given to kings and queens in referring to them, **Your Majesty** in addressing them.—**maj'esties** *pl.*

ma'jor *n.* 1. an army officer ranking next above captain. 2. a person over 21.—*adj.* greater.—**major'ity** *n.* 1. the greater number. 2. the number by which a winning vote is greater than the other. 3. being a major

make *v.* 1. to build, shape, produce, put together, as *to make a ship, a cake.* 2. to appoint, as *He was made a bishop.* 3. to cause to do something, as *We were made to get up.* 4. to reach, as *The ship made port in safety.* 5. to earn, as *He makes £20 a week.* 6. to perform, do, as *to make a mistake, a journey.* 7. to amount to, as *Two and two make four.* 8. to prepare, as *to make a bed.* —**ma'king** *pres. part.*—**made** *p.t.* and *p. part.*—*n.* 1. style, form, as *A good make of shoe.* 2. kind, as *What make of car is that?*—**ma'ker** *n.*—**make'shift** *n.* something used instead of the right thing.—**ma'king** *n.* make, structure.—*pl.* essential qualities, as *He has the makings of a good bowler.*—**make away with** to get rid of, kill.—**make believe** to pretend.—**make for** to go towards with purpose.—**make fun of** to laugh at.—**make good** to pay for, fulfil.—**make a little of** to treat lightly.—**make much of** to treat as being important.—**make out** 1. to write out, e.g. a cheque. 2. to pretend. 3. to understand. 4. to succeed, get on, as *How did you make out?*—**make over** to hand over.—**make sail** to start out.—**make up** 1. to put together. 2. to invent. 3. to put powder, lipstick etc. on a face. 4. to settle a quarrel.—**make up to** to make friendly approaches to

mal'ady *n.* an illness. disease,—**mal'adies** *pl.*

mala'ria (malār'ia) *n.* a fever due to mosquito bites

mal'content *adj.* discontented.—*n.* a dissatisfied person inclined to rebel

male *n.* a man or boy, male animal.—*adj.* 1. bull, ram, stallion, lion, tiger, boar, etc. are *male animals.* 2. strong, vigorous—**female** *fem.*

maledic'tion (-shun) *n.* a curse

mal'efactor *n.* a criminal, evil-doer

malev'olence *n.* ill-will, spite.—**malev'olent** *adj.* ill-disposed

mal'ice (mal'is) *n.* spiteful action, illwill.—**malic'ious** (mal-ish'us) *adj.* intending unkindness

malign' (ma-līn') *adj.* evil, hurtful.—*v.* to speak evil of.—**malig'nant** *adj.* 1. very evil. 2. very harmful. 3. likely to cause death.—**malig'nity** *n.*

malin'ger (ma-ling'ger) *v.* to pretend to be ill in order to avoid work.—**malin'gerer** *n.*

mal'leable *adj.* which can be hammered into shape without breaking

mal'let *n.* a wooden hammer

malnutri'tion (-tri'shun) *n.* under-feeding, wrong kind of feeding

malt (mawlt) *n.* grain prepared for brewing. —*v.* to make grain into malt

maltreat' *v.* to ill-treat, handle roughly.—**maltreat'ment** *n.*

mamba *n.* 1. a deadly African snake, usually black. 2. a dance

mamma' *n.* mother

mam'mal *n.* an animal that suckles its young

mam'mon *n.* 1. wealth as an evil influence. 2. the god of riches
mam'moth *n.* a huge extinct animal like an elephant.—*adj.* enormous, gigantic
man *n.* 1. a human being, person. 2. the human race. 3. an adult male. 4. a manservant.—**men** *pl.*—**wo'man** *fem.*—**maid'en, maid,** a girl, or young unmarried woman.—*v.* to supply with men, as *to man a ship.*—**man'ning** *pres. part.*—**manned** *p.t.* and *p. part.*—**a man of the world** a man used to the ways of other men.—**the man in the street** the ordinary man
man'a *n.* Maori term for power, influence, authority, prestige
man'acle *n.* a handcuff.—*v.* to handcuff
man'age (man'aj) *v.* 1. to control, conduct, as *to manage a business, a horse, etc.* 2. to succeed in doing, as *They managed to arrive in time.*—**man'aging** *pres. part.*—**man'ageable** *adj.*—**man'agement** *n.* 1. conduct, control. 2. the directors of a business.—**man'ager** *n.* a person in charge of a business, etc.—**manageress'** *fem.*
man'darin *n.* 1. an important Chinese official. 2. a kind of small orange
man'date *n.* 1. a command. 2. a commission given to a nation to control the affairs of another. 3. instruction given by voters to their representative.—**man'datory** *adj.*
man'dolin, man'doline *n.* a kind of guitar
mane *n.* long hair on the neck of a horse, lion, etc.
man'ful *adj.* brave, resolute.—**man'fully** *adv.*
man'ganese *n.* a metallic element
mange (mānj) *n.* a skin disease in animals.—**man'gy** *adj.*
man'ger (mān'jer) *n.* a box fixed in a stable-wall for horses and cattle to feed from
man'gle (mang'gl) *v.* to tear roughly, to hack, spoil.—**man'gling** *pres. part.*
mango *n.* sub tropical fruit
man'hole *n.* an opening through which a man can enter a sewer, etc. for repairs
man'hood *n.* 1. being a man. 2. the men of a country. 3. manly qualities, courage
ma'nia (mā'ni-a) *n.* 1. madness. 2. a craze, unreasonable desire.—**ma'niac** *n.* a madman.—*adj.* insane, crazy
man'icure *n.* care of hands and nails.—*v.* to care for the hands.—**man'icurist** *n.*
man'ifest *adj.* plain, clear.—*v.* to show, make plain.—*n.* a list of a ship's cargo.—**manifesta'tion** (-tā'-shun) *n.* revelation, showing.—**manifes'to** *n.* a public declaration.—**manifes'tos** *pl.*
man'ifold *adj.* many and varied
manip'ulate *v.* 1. to handle. 2. to manage skilfully.—**manipula'tion** (-lā'shun) *n.*
mankind' *n.* 1. the human race. 2. men
man'ly *adj.* like a man, firm, brave.—**man'lier** *comp.*—**man'liest** *sup.*—**man'liness** *n.*
man'na *n.* the food God gave the Israelites in the desert
man'nequin (man'i-kin) *n.* a person employed by dressmakers to wear and show costumes
man'ner *n.* 1. the way something happens or is done. 2. style, sort, custom.—*pl.* behaviour.—**man'nerism** *n.* a habit, trick of speech or behaviour.—**man'nerly** *adj.* well-mannered.—**man'nerliness** *n.*

Compare: method, style, way, practice, mien, appearance, habit, look, aspect, deportment, carriage, fashion

manoeuv're, U.S. maneu'ver (manōō'ver) *n.* 1. a planned movement of troops or ships. 2. a clever move.—*pl.* mock warfare as training. —*v.* to make a clever move
man'or *n.* land belonging to the lord of the manor.—**mano'rial** *adj.*—**man'or-house** *n.*
manse *n.* the house of a Presbyterian minister
man'sion (man'shun) *n.* a large house. See **house**
man'slaughter (man'slaw-ter) *n.* killing a person unintentionally
man'tel *n.* a shelf over a fire-place.—**man'telpiece** *n.*
mantil'la *n.* an ornamental shawl worn over the head by Spanish ladies
mant'le *n.* 1. a loose cloak. 2. a covering. 3. a mesh cap fixed on a gas-jet to give better light.—*v.* to spread over, cover, conceal
man'ual *adj.* done with the hands as *manual work.*—*n.* 1. a hand-book. 2. an organ key-board
manufac'ture *n.* the making of articles or materials in large quantities.—*v.*—**manufac'turer** *n.* an owner of factories, person who manufactures
manure' *n.* anything put in the soil to make it richer.—*v.*
man'uscript *n.* 1. a book or paper written by hand. 2. a copy of matter to be printed. —*adj.*
Manx *adj.* concerning the Isle of Man.—**Manx cat** a tailless cat
man'y (men'i) *adj.* 1. numerous, as *Many children are away to-day.*—**more** *comp.* **most** *superl.*—*n.* a large number, as *Many prefer football to cricket.*—**so many** such a great number

Note: many a, meaning *many,* must be followed by a singular verb, as *Many a man returns richer than he went*

Mao'ri (mow'ree) *n.* 1. N.Z. native. 2. the language of the Maoris.—*adj.* pertaining to the Maoris or their language
map *n.* a flat drawing of the earth or some part of it, showing mountains, rivers, etc. —*v.* 1. to make a map. 2. to plan.—**map'ping** *pres. part.*—**mapped** *p.t.* and *p. part.*
ma'ple *n.* a tree of the sycamore family, one kind of which gives sugar
mar *v.* to spoil, injure.—**mar'ring** *pres. part.* —**marred** *p.t.* and *p. part.*
ma'rae (ma'ri) *n.* the assembly place of any Maori settlement

maraud′ *v.* to raid for plunder.—**maraud′er** *n.* a robber

mar′ble *n.* 1. hard limestone which takes a high polish. 2. a small hard ball in game of marbles.—**mar′bled** *adj.* veined like marble

march *v.* 1. to walk in step as soldiers do. 2. to cause to march, as *He was marched off to bed.*—*n.* 1. distance marched, as *a day's march.* 2. a tune for marching to. 3. progress, as *the march of events.*—**march′es** *pl.*—**march-past** *n.* a ceremonial parade.

march *n.* a border-country, between frontiers. —**march′es** *pl.*

March *n.* the third month

marchioness′ (mar-shon-es′) *n.* the wife or widow of a marquis.—**mar′quis, mar′quess** *masc.*

mare *n.* female of the horse, donkey, etc.—**horse, stal′lion** *masc.*

margarine′ (-jar-een′, -gar-een′) *n.* a butter substitute made from vegetable oils

mar′gin (mar′jin) *n.* 1. an edge, border, as *the margin of the sea.* 2. a blank space round a page. 3. an extra amount, beyond what is necessary, as *Allow a margin of 10 minutes in case of delay.*—**mar′ginal** *adj.*

marine′ (mar-een′) *adj.* of, found or used at sea, as *marine vegetation.*—*n.* 1. shipping, as *the merchant marine.* 2. a soldier serving on a ship.—**mar′iner** *n.* a sailor.—**tell that to the (horse) marines!** an exclamation of disbelief

marionette′ *n.* a doll, or puppet worked with strings

mar′itime (mar′i-tīm) *adj.* 1. bordering on the sea. 2. sea-faring

mark *n.* a German coin

mark *n.* 1. something set up to be aimed at, as *He shot, but missed his mark.* 2. a sign, as *Politeness is a mark of good breeding.* 3. a line, dot, scar or any other impression. 4. a number or letter showing how well work has been done, as *a good mark for a good essay.*—*v.* 1. to make a mark on, write one's name on. 2. to indicate, as *A red light marks danger.* 3. to watch, see, note, as *Mark my words.*—**marked** *adj.* noticeable.—**mark′er** *n.* a person or thing keeping score in a game.—**beside the mark** not to the point.—**to make one's mark** to be successful.—**to mark out** to mark with lines, as *to mark out a tennis-court.*—**to mark time** 1. to move the feet up and down without advancing. 2. to make no progress with one's plans.—**to miss the mark** to fail.—**up to the mark** up to standard

mark′et *n.* 1. an assembly for buying and selling. 2. a place where goods are sold. 3. a demand for goods, as *a brisk market.* 4. a trading-centre, as *Every country seeks new markets.*—*v.* to buy or sell in a market. —**mar′ketable** *adj.* which can be sold.—**mar′ket-place** *n.*

marks′man *n.* one who shoots well.—**marks′manship** *n.*

marmalade′ *n.* a preserve, usually made of oranges

maroon′ *n.* a dull crimson colour.—*adj.*

maroon′ *v.* to leave a person on a desert island—*n.* a West Indian negro fugitive from slavery

maroon′ *n.* a rocket fired with a loud explosion as a signal

marquee′ (mar-kee′) *n.* a large tent

mar′quis, mar′quess *n.* nobleman ranking next below a duke.—**mar′chioness** *fem.*

mar′riage (mar′ij) *n.* 1. being married. 2. marrying. 3. a wedding.—**mar′ried** *adj.* having a husband or wife

mar′row (mar′ō) *n.* 1. a soft substance inside bones. 2. the most important part

mar′ry *v.* 1. to join as husband and wife. 2. to take as husband or wife.—**he mar′ries.** —**mar′rying** *pres. part.*—**mar′ried** *p.t.* and *p. part.*

Mars *n.* 1. the Roman god of war. 2. a planet of similar size to the earth

marsh *n.* low-lying wet land.—**marsh′es** *pl.*—**marsh′y** *adj.*

marsh′al *n.* a high officer of state.—**field-mar′shal** *n.* a military officer of highest rank.—*v.* 1. to arrange in proper order. 2. to conduct with ceremony.—**mar′shalling** *pres. part.*—**mar′shalled** *p.t.* and *p. part.*

marsu′pial *n.* a mammal which carries its young in a pouch

mart *n.* a market, trading-centre

mar′ten *n.* a small animal like a weasel

mar′tial (mar′shl) *adj.* war-like, suited to war.—**mar′tial law,** the taking over of authority by the army in times of trouble

mar′tian (mar′shan) *adj.* belonging to the planet Mars

mar′tin *n.* a kind of swallow

martinet′ *n.* a strict disciplinarian

mar′tyr (mar′ter) *n.* 1. a person put to death, or suffering greatly, for his beliefs. 2. a person in constant suffering, as *He is a martyr to gout.*—*v.* to put a person to death for his beliefs.—**mar′tyrdom** *n.* a martyr's death

mar′vel *n.* a wonderful thing.—*v.* to feel amazement or admiration.—**mar′velling** *pres. part.*—**mar′velled** *p.t.* and *p. part.*—**mar′vellous** *adj.* wonderful, amazing

mas′cot *n.* something supposed to bring good luck

mas′culine (mas′kū-lin) *adj.* 1. male. 2. manly, strong. 3. in grammar, of male gender, as "*he*" *is the masculine pronoun,* "*she*" *the feminine.*—*n.* the male gender, as "*King*" *is the masculine of* "*Queen*"

mash *n.* 1. meal mixed with warm water for horses, etc. 2. any soft mixture.—*v.* to crush into a mash

mask *n.* 1. a covering for the face. 2. a disguise, pretence, as *He hid his rage under a mask of indifference.*—*v.* to hide, disguise
Compare: (with *v.*) cloak, conceal, hide, disguise, dissemble, masquerade, pretend, screen, veil. *Contrast:* betray, disclose, declare, divulge, explain, expose, publish, reveal, show

ma'son *n.* a worker in stone.—**ma'sonry** *n.* stone-work

masquerade' *n.* a masked ball—*v.* to go about in disguise

mass *n.* 1. a quantity of matter, 2. a lump, large amount. 3. the greater part.—**mas'ses** *pl.*—*v.* to make into a mass, collect.—**the masses,** the common people.—**to mass-produce** to manufacture large quantities of an article

mass *n.* Communion service in the Roman Catholic Church

mass'acre (mass'a-ker) *n.* a general slaughter, killing in large numbers.—*v.*

massage' (ma-sahzh') *n.* rubbing and kneading the muscles and joints as a cure.—*v.* to treat with massage.—**masseur'** (mas-sir') *n.* one who practises massage.—**masseuse'** (mas-sihz') *fem.*

mas'sive *adj.* large and heavy

mast *n.* 1. a pole fixed on a ship to support sails and rigging. 2. any tall pole.—**mast-head** *n.* the top of the mast

mas'ter *n.* 1. the man in control. 2. a male teacher. 3. the head of a house, a merchant ship, etc.—**mis'tress** *fem.* 4. an artist, or highly skilled workman. 5. title of a University degree, as *Master of Arts.*—*v.* 1. to overcome, control, as *He mastered his anger.* 2. to become skilful in, as *She has mastered decimals.*—**mas'terful** *adj.* showing authority.—**mas'terly** *adj.* expert, clever.—**mas'terpiece** *n.* 1. work showing great skill. 2. an artist's best work.—**master-stroke** *n.* a very successful plan.—**mas'tery** *n.* 1. control, power, 2. victory
Compare: captain, chief, commander, director, employer, foreman, governor, head, leader, manager, overseer, owner, principal, proprietor, sovereign, teacher

mas'ticate *v.* to chew.—**mastica'tion** (-kā'-shun) *n.*

mas'tiff *n.* a large, powerful dog

mat *n.* 1. a small carpet made of rushes, etc. 2. a piece of material to protect table surface. 3. a thick tangled mass.—*v.* to make into a tangle, as *The rain had matted her hair.*—**mat'ting** *pres. part.*—**mat'ted** *p.t.* and *p. part.*

mat'ador *n.* the man who kills the bull in a bullfight

match *n.* 1. a small stick tipped with a mixture which bursts into flame when rubbed. 2. a fuse for firing an explosive.—**match'es** *pl.*—**match'box** *n.*—**match'wood** *n.* wood which burns very easily

match *n.* 1. person or thing exactly equal or corresponding to another, as *A bicycle is no match for a car. These silks are a good match.* 2. a game, contest, as *a football match.* 3. a marriage.—**match'es** *pl.*—*v.* 1. to be alike, equal in size, colour, etc., as *The cushions match the carpet.* 2. to be equal in strength, skill, etc. 3. to marry. 4. to find a match for.—**match'less** *adj.* without equal.—**match'wood** *n.* 1. thin wood for matches. 2. splintered wood

mate *n.* 1. a companion, friend. 2. a husband or wife. 3. a merchant ship's officer, below captain.—*v.* to marry, to pair.—**ma'ting** *pres. part.*

mate'rial *n.* 1. the stuff from which anything is made, as *woollen material.* 2. something used in construction, as *the material for a book.*—*adj.* 1. important. 2. formed from matter. 3. not concerned with the spirit, as *material comforts.*—**mate'rialise** *v.* to come into being.—**mate'rially** *adv.* considerably

mater'nal *adj.* 1. motherly. 2. related on the mother's side.—**mater'nity** *n.* motherhood

mathemat'ical *adj.* 1. having to do with mathematics. 2. exact

mathemati'cian (math-e-ma-tish'an) *n.* a person skilled in mathematics

mathemat'ics *n.pl.* the science of quantity and number

mat'inee (mat'in-ā) *n.* a morning or afternoon performance

mat'ins *n.pl.* morning prayers

matric'ulate *v.* to be admitted as a student in a university.—**matricula'tion** (-lā'shun) *n.*

mat'rimony *n.* marriage.—**matrimonial** *adj.*

ma'tron *n.* 1. an elderly married woman. 2. a woman in charge of household affairs in a school, hospital, etc.—**ma'tronly** *adj.* 1. elderly. 2. dignified

mat'ter *n.* 1. substance, what a thing is made of. 2. affair, business, as *We have an important matter to decide.* 3. something said or written, considered apart from style, as *The matter of your essay is good.* 4. discharge from a sore, etc.—*v.* to be important, as *It matters a great deal.*—**as a matter of course** naturally.—**as a matter of fact** in truth.—**for that matter** as far as that is concerned.—**what is the matter?** what is wrong?

mat'ting *n.* rush, fibre, etc. used for making mats

mat'tress *n.* a flat case stuffed with hair, etc. and used as a bed or on a bed

mature' *v.* to ripen, develop.—*adj.* 1. ripe, complete. 2. payable, due.—**matu'rity** *n.*

maud'lin *adj.* weakly sentimental

maul *v.* 1. to beat, bruise. 2. to handle roughly

maw *n.* the stomach of animals

mawk'ish *adj.* sickly, sentimental

max'im *n.* a short saying expressing a general

truth, a proverb. "*More haste, less speed*" *is a maxim*

max'imum *n.* the greatest amount.—**max'ima** *pl.*—*adj.* greatest, as *What is his maximum speed?*

may *v.* 1. to have permission, as *You may go.* 2. to be possible, as *It may be fine.* 3. to wish (in exclamations), as *May you win!*—**maybe** *adv.* perhaps

Note: May is used only in the present and past tenses. *I may, thou mayst, he may*, present. *I might, thou mightst, he might*, past

May *n.* the fifth month.—**May'day** *n.* 1st of May.—**may'pole** *n.* a flower-decked pole round which people danced on May Day.—**May'-tree** *n.* hawthorn

mayonnaise' *n.* a salad dressing of egg yolk beaten with oil

mayor (mār) *n.* the head of a town corporation.—**mayor'ess** *n.* 1. the mayor's wife. 2. a lady mayor.—**mayor'alty** *n.* mayor's office

maze *n.* 1. a network of paths or lines. 2. a confused state.—*v.* to confuse, bewilder

mead *n.* meadow.—**mead'ow** (med'ō) *n.* grassland

mea'gre (mee'ger) *adj.* 1. thin. 2. poor, not abundant, as *We had a meagre dinner*

Compare: poor, lean, thin, lank, feeble, skinny, starved. *Contrast:* abundant, fat, plump, hearty, portly, round, stout

meal (meel) *n.* 1. the food taken at one time. 2. grain ground into powder.—**meal'y** *adj.*

mean (meen) *adj.* 1. poor, shabby. 2. not generous, stingy, smallminded, as *a mean trick.*—**mean'ly** *adv.*—**mean'ness** *n.* being mean

mean (meen) *v.* 1. to intend, have in mind, as *What do you mean to do? This letter was meant for you.* 2. to try to express, signify, as *What does this word mean?*—**meant** (ment) *p.t.* and *p. part.*

mean (meen) *adj.* 1. at equal distance from both extremes. 2. average

mean'der (mee-an'der) *v.* 1. to wind about. 2. to wander aimlessly.—*n.* a winding, esp. of a river.

mean'ing *n.* what is intended.—*adj.* expressive.—**mean'ingless** *adj.* senseless

means *n.pl.* 1. that by which something is done, as *he used a ladder as a means of reaching the roof.* 2. wealth, resources, as *a man of means.*—**by means of** because of, with the help of.—**by all means** certainly.—**by no means** certainly not

mean'time, mean'while *n.* the time between one happening and another.—*adv.*

meas'les (meez'lz) *n.pl.* an infectious disease, marked by the appearance of red spots

meas'ure (mezh'ur) *v.* 1. to find out the size or amount, as *We measured the length of the carpet.* 2. to be of a certain size, as *The desk measures* 3 *feet by* 2 *feet.* 3. to test, as *He measured his strength against mine.*—*n.* 1. size or quantity, as *The milkman gives good measure.* 2. something to measure by, as *a tape-measure.* 3. a unit of measure, as *a pint is a liquid measure.* 4. musical or poetical time or rhythm. 5. a bar of music. 6. a plan. 7. a law.—**meas'ured** *adj.* 1. regular. 2. slow, as *He spoke in measured tones.*—**meas'ureless** *adj.* unlimited, immense.—**meas'urement** *n.* 1. way of measuring. 2. size, amount measured

meat (meet) *n.* 1. food. 2. the flesh of animals used as food.—**meat'y** *adj.* 1. full of meat. 2. solid, nourishing

mechan'ic (me-kan'ik) *n.* a workman skilled in using tools.—**mechan'ical** *adj.* 1. made by machinery, having to do with machines. 2. done without thought or attention.—**mechan'ics** *n.pl.* the science of machinery. —**mech'anism** *n.* 1. a piece of machinery. 2. the way in which something works.—**mech'anise** *v.* to make mechanical, to work by machinery

med'al *n.* a piece of metal round or star-shaped, with an inscription, and used as a reward or memento.—**medal'lion** *n.* a large medal, something like a medal used as a decoration or design.—**med'allist** *n.* the winner of a medal

med'dle *v.* to busy oneself with other people's business.—**med'dling** *pres. part.*—**med'dler** *n.*—**med'dlesome** *adj.* interfering

mediae'val, medie'val (-ee') *adj.* belonging to the Middle Ages

me'diate (mee'di-āt) *v.* to act as go between in a dispute in order to settle it.—**media'tion** (-ā'shun) *n.*—**me'diator** *n.*

med'ical *adj.* having to do with doctors and the science of medicine.—**medic'ament** *n.* medicine, a remedy.—**med'icated** *adj.* containing medicine.—**medic'inal** (med-is'-in-al) *adj.* having healing properties.—**medical practitioner** *n.* a doctor

med'icine (med'i-sin) *n.* 1. the art of healing. 2. drugs and anything that restores health

medie'val see **mediæ'val**

medio'cre (mee-di-ō'ker) *adj.* neither bad nor good, ordinary.—**medioc'rity** *n.*

med'itate *v.* to think about, reflect, plan.—**med'itating** *pres. part.*—**medita'tion** (-tā'-shun) *n.* serious thought.—**med'itative** *adj.*

me'dium *n.* 1. a middle condition, at neither extreme. 2. a means, as *A newspaper is a good medium for advertising.*—**me'dia** *pl.*—*adj.* middle, moderate.—**me'dium waves**, in radio, between 100 and 800 metres

med'ley *n.* a mixture of things of different sorts

meek *adj.* humble, gentle.—**meek'ness** *n.* patience

meet *v.* 1. to come face to face with. 2. to come across, as *We met stormy weather.* 3. to go towards someone who is coming.

4. to pay, satisfy, as *We cannot meet your demands.*—**met** *p.t.* and *p. part.*—*n.* a meeting for a hunt.—**meet'ing** *n.* an assembly.—**meet with,** to come across, have, as *He met with opposition.*—**Well met!** welcome!

meet *adj.* fit, proper

meg'aphone (meg'a-fōn) *n.* a horn for carrying the sound of the voice to a distance

mel'ancholy (mel'an-ko-li) *n.* sadness, gloom. —*adj.* low-spirited, dejected

mê'lée (me'lā) *n.* a confused struggle

mel'low *adj.* 1. ripe and soft, as *a mellow pear.* 2. rich, delicate, as *a mellow light.* 3. softened by age or experience.—*v.* to become mellow

melo'dious *adj.* sweet-sounding, musical

mel'odrama *n.* a play full of exciting events and ending happily.—**melodramat'ic** *adj.* sensational

mel'ody *n.* sweet music, a tune.—**mel'odies** *pl.*

mel'on *n.* a large juicy fruit of the gourd family

melt *v.* 1. to become liquid or soft under heat, as *Snow melts in spring.* 2. to disperse, as *The crowd melted away.* 3. to disappear, as *His anger melted.* 4. to make or become tender, as *Her heart melted.*—**melted** *p.t., p. part.*—**molten** *adj.*

mem'ber *n.* 1. a limb. 2. a person belonging to a group.—**mem'bership** *n.* 1. being a member. 2. the members

mem'brane *n.* thin skin or tissue in a plant or animal body

memen'to *n.* something serving as a reminder, as *This tree was planted as a memento of his visit.*—**memen'tos** *pl.*

mem'oir (mem'war) *n.* 1. a record of events. 2. a life-story, reminiscences

mem'orable *adj.* worth remembering

memoran'dum *n.* 1. a note to help the memory 2. a note of a business order. 3. an informal letter.—**memoran'da** *pl.*

memor'ial *n.* something serving to keep in memory a person or event, as *This statue is a memorial to a great man.*—*adj.*

mem'orise *v.* to learn by heart.—**mem'orising** *pres. part.*

mem'ory *n.* 1. the power of calling to mind or keeping in mind. 2. the thing recalled, as *happy memories.*—**mem'ories** *pl.*

men'ace (men'as) *n.* a threat, as *Fire is a great menace in saw-mills.*—*v.* to threaten. —**men'acing** *pres. part.*

menag'erie (men-aj'er-i) *n.* a collection of wild animals kept for show

mend *v.* 1. to repair, correct, put right, as *to mend a wrong, a road, a torn dress.* 2. to improve in health.—*n.* repaired place

menda'cious (men-dā'shus) *adj.* false, untruthful.—**mendac'ity** (men-das'iti) *n.*

men'dicant *n.* a beggar.—*adj.* begging

me'nial (mee'ni-al) *adj.* belonging to a servant.—*n.* a servant given unpleasant jobs

mensura'tion *n.* the measurement of lengths, areas and volumes

ment'al *adj.* belonging to the mind, done in the mind, as *mental arithmetic.*—**mental'ity** *n.* quality of mind.—**men'tally** *adv.* in the mind

men'tion (men'shun) *n.* a remark about something or somebody, as *He made no mention of his accident.*—*v.* to speak about, in passing

men'tor *n.* a wise adviser and friend

men'u *n.* a list of dishes to be served

mer'cantile *adj.* commercial, engaged in trade, as *mercantile marine*

mer'cenary (mer'sen-ar-i) *adj.* influenced simply by money.—*n.* a soldier serving for pay in a foreign army

mer'chandise *n.* things bought and sold, goods

mer'chant *n.* a trader on a big scale.—*adj.* belonging to trade, as *merchant ships.*—**mer'chantman** *n.* a trading ship.—**mer'chant na'vy** *n.* a fleet of trading ships

mer'ciful (mer'si-ful) *adj.* showing mercy, pity.—**mer'cifully** *adv.*—**mer'ciless** *adj.* cruel.—**mer'cilessly** *adv.*

Compare: gentle, forgiving, humane, compassionate, clement, pitiful, pitying, tender-hearted. *Contrast:* cruel, brutal, fierce, inhuman, merciless, pitiless, ruthless, savage, unmerciful

mer'cury *n.* a heavy, white metal, liquid at ordinary temperature, quicksilver.—**mercu'rial** *adj.* changeable, high-spirited

mer'cy (mer'si) *n.* 1. being unwilling to punish or to cause suffering, compassion. 2. a blessing.—**at the mercy of** in the power of

Compare: clemency, compassion, forbearance, forgiveness, grace, kindness, leniency, pardon, pity, tenderness

me're (mee'ree) *n.* a Maori war club

mere *n.* a pool, lake

mere *adj.* not more than, only, as *a mere scratch.*—**mere'ly** *adv.* only. simply

merge (merj) *v.* 1. to absorb, mix. 2. to become absorbed, as *The sky seemed to merge into the sea.*—**mer'ging** *pres. part.*

merid'ian *n.* 1. the position of the sun at noon. 2. the highest point reached by a star. 2. a circle passing through any position on the earth's surface and the north and south poles.—*adj.* belonging to noon

meringue' (me-rang') *n.* a cake made of sugar and white of an egg

mer'it *n.* 1. goodness, value. 2. something deserving praise, as *a medal won for merit.* —*v.* to deserve, as *Good work merits praise.*—**merito'rious** *adj.* deserving praise. —**in order of merit** the best first, the next best second, and so on

Compare: worth, desert, excellence

mer'maid *n.* a sea-creature in fairy-tales,

like a fish from the waist down.—**mer'man** *masc.*
mer'rily *adv.* in a merry way
mer'riment *n.* laughter, fun, gaiety
mer'ry *adj.* gay, joyous, laughing.—**mer'rier** *comp.*—**mer'riest** *sup.*—**mer'ry-go-round** *n.* a circular, revolving machine with toy animals or cars on which children can ride.—**mer'ry-making** *n.* fun
mesh *n.* one of the open spaces of a net.—**mesh'es** *pl.*—**mesh'work** *n.* meshes, network
mes'merise *v.* to hypnotise, influence a person so that he loses his will-power.—**mes'merism** *n.*
me'son (mee'zon) *n.* an atomic particle
mess *n.* 1. a confusion, muddle. 2. a dirty or untidy state, as *The room was in a mess after the party.* 3. a portion of food, as *a mess of pottage.* 4. a group of persons who regularly have meals together, as *officers' mess.* 5. the place where they have meals.—*v.* to make a mess, spoil, soil
mes'sage (mes'ij) *n.* words, spoken or written, sent from one person to another.—**mes'senger** *n.* a person taking a message
Messi'ah *n.* 1. Christ. 2. deliverer expected by the Jewish people
mes'sy *adj.* dirty, untidy.—**mes'sier** *comp.*—**mes'siest** *sup.*
met'al *n.* 1. a hard, bright substance such as gold, silver, copper, iron, lead, tin, etc. 2. broken stones for road-making.—*adj.*—**metal'lic** *adj.*—**met'allurgy** *n.* science of metals
metamor'phosis (met-a-mor'fō-sis) *n.* change of form, substance, character.—**metamor'phoses** *pl.* (-seez)
met'aphor (met'a-for) *n.* a figure of speech by which a vivid comparison is suggested. The difference between *metaphor* and *simile* is that a *metaphor* is not introduced by "like" or "as." *A sea of corn* is a metaphor. *The cornfield is like a sea,* is a simile
mete *v.* to measure, share out
me'teor *n.* a shooting-star.—**meteor'ic** *adj.* brilliant and passing quickly, as *a film star's meteoric career*
meteorolog'ical *adj.* having to do with weather and atmosphere.—**meteorol'ogy** *n.* the science of the weather and atmosphere
me'ter *n.* an instrument for measuring gas, electricity, etc.
me'thane (mee'thān) *n.* an inflammable hydrocarbon gas
meth'od *n.* 1. a way of doing something. 2. system, orderliness.—**method'ical** *adj.* orderly, following a method
Meth'odism *n.* the religious beliefs and practices of the Methodists, the followers of John and Charles Wesley
meth'ylated spirit *n.* a mixture of alcohol and wood spirit used as fuel, originally colourless, but often coloured with a violet dye
metic'ulous *adj.* very careful of small details
me'tre (mee'ter) *n.* 1. a unit of length in the decimal system (39.37 ins). 2. rhythm, arrangement of accents in verse.—**met'ric system,** a decimal system of weights and measures based on the metre.—**met'rical** *adj.* having to do with measurement.—**met'ricate** *v.* to convert weights and measures to the metric system
metrop'olis *n.* the chief city of a state.—**metropol'itan** *adj.*
met'tle *n.* spirit, courage.—**on one's mettle,** ready for effort.—**met'tlesome** *adj.* spirited
Mex'ico *n.* a country on the southern border of the United States.—**Mex'ican** *n.* a native of Mexico
mews *n.pl.* stables
mew *v.* to make a sound like a cat.—*n.*
mi'ca *n.* mineral found in glittering scales or plates
mi'crobe *n.* a minute plant or animal causing disease or fermentation
microm'eter (mī-krom'eter) *n.* an instrument for measuring very small lengths
mi'crophone (mī'kro-fōn) *n.* an instrument for making sounds louder, esp. in radio
microprojec'tor *n.* an instrument for throwing a large picture of a tiny object on to a screen
mi'croscope *n.* an instrument by which minute objects are made visible.—**microscop'ic** *adj.* 1. belonging to a microscope. 2. very small
mid *adj.* middle, as *mid-winter.*—*prep.* among.—**mid'day** *n.* noon.—**mid-off** (cricket) a fielding position in front of the batsman to the left of the bowler.—**mid-on** (cricket) a fielding position in front of the batsman to the right of the bowler
mid'dle *n.* a point at equal distances from each end or side, centre.—*adj.* 1. at the centre, as *the middle boy.* 2. in between, as *a middle size.*—**middle-aged'** *adj.* between 40 and 60.—**Middle Ages** the period of history from about the years 400 A.D. to 1500 A.D.—**middle weight** a boxer whose weight is between 10st 7 lb and 11 st 6 lb
mid'dy *n.* (Aus.) 1. a glass of beer. 2. a ten-ounce container
midge (mij) *n.* a small insect, gnat
mid'get (mi'jit) *n.* a very small person
mid'night (mid'nīt) *n.* twelve o'clock at night
mid'shipman *n.* a naval officer between naval cadet and sub-lieutenant.—**mid'shipmen** *pl.*
midst *n.* middle.—*prep.* among
mid'summer *n.* the longest day of the year
mid'way *n.* half-way.—*adj. adv.*
mien (meen) *n.* a person's look, manner
might (mīt) *n.* power, strength.—**might'ily** *adv.* 1. powerfully. 2. very.—**might'y** *adj.* strong, powerful.—**might'ier** *comp.*—**might'iest** *sup.*
might *p.t.* of may
mi'grant *n.* one that migrates.—*adj.* as *a migrant bird*

migrate′ (mī-grāt′) *v.* to move from one place to another.—**migra′ting** *pres. part.*—**migra′tion** (-grā′shun) *n.*—**migra′tory** *adj.* changing from place to place, according to the season

milch *adj.* giving milk, kept for its milk, as *a milch-cow*

mild (mīld) *adj.* 1. gentle. 2. warm, not severe, as *a mild climate.* 3. not sour or strongly flavoured, as *mild cheese.*—**mild′ly** *adv.*—**mild′ness** *n.*

Compare: gentle, merciful, tender, soft, temperate. *Contrast:* rough, harsh, stormy

mil′dew *n.* a white growth on plants and things exposed to damp.—*v.* to be covered with mildew

mile *n.* a measure of length, 1760 yards.—**mile′age** (mī′laj) *n.* distance in miles.—**mile-post** *n.* a post showing the distance from neighbouring towns.—**mile′stone** *n.*

mil′itant *adj.* engaged in warfare.—*n.*

mil′itarism *n.* support of military force and methods.—**mil′itarist** *n.*

mil′itary *adj.* of soldiers or army or warfare.—*n.* soldiers

mil′itate *v.* to fight, oppose, act against.—**mil′itating** *pres. part.*

mili′tia (mil-ish′a) *n.* a force of citizens trained for home defence

milk *n.* 1. a white fluid with which animals feed their young. 2. cow's milk used as human food.—**milk′bar** *n.* a place where milk-shakes are sold.—**milk′maid** *n.* a dairy worker.—**milk′man** *n.* a man who sells or delivers milk.—**milk′shake** *n.* milk whisked with a flavouring.—**milk′sop** *n.* a cowardly person.—**milk′y** *adj.* mild, containing milk

mill *n.* 1. machinery for grinding corn, etc. 2. a building containing such machinery, 3. a factory, as *a cotton-mill.*—*v.* 1. to grind finely. 2. to cut fine grooves across the edges of a coin

millenn′ium *n.* 1. a period of a thousand years. 2. the thousand years during which some believe Christ will reign on earth

mil′ler *n.* owner of a flour-mill

mil′let *n.* small grain of an Indian cereal plant

mil′ligram, mil′ligramme *n.* one thousandth part of a gramme

mil′limetre *n.* one thousandth part of a metre

mil′liner *n.* a person who makes or sells women's hats.—**millinery** *n.* 1. women's hats. 2. trimming and selling hats

mil′lion *n.* a thousand thousands.—**millionaire′** *n.* owner of a million pounds, dollars etc.

mil′lipede *n.* an insect with many legs

mill′-race *n.* a stream of water driving a mill-wheel

mill′stone *n.* one of a pair of flat round stones used for grinding corn

mime *n.* a kind of play without words, using actions and gestures.—*v.* to act without words, to mimic

mim′ic *n.* a person who imitates to amuse.—*v.* to imitate closely, as *Monkeys love to mimic men.*—**mim′icking** *pres. part.*—**mim′icked** *p.t.* and *p. part.*—*adj.* imitating, not real, as *mimic warfare.*—**mim′icry** *n.*

minaret′ *n.* a tall, slender tower on a Mohammedan mosque

mince (mins) *v.* 1. to chop up small. 2. to walk with very short steps.—**min′cing** *pres. part.*—*n.* meat cut up very small.—**mince′-meat** *n.* a mixture of chopped currants, spices, suet, etc., used in **mince-pies′**

mind (mīnd) *n.* 1. the part of a person which thinks, feels, wishes, etc. 2. intelligence, ability. 3. memory, as *I tried to remember but it went out of my mind.*—*v.* 1. to attend to, as *Mind the baby for me.* 2. to be careful, as *Mind the step.* 3. to object to, as *Would you mind hurrying?*—**mind′ed** *adj.* inclined.—**mind′ful** *adj.* remembering.—**absent-minded** forgetful.—**on one's mind** always in one's thoughts.—**the mind's eye** the imagination.—**to be of one mind** to agree.—**to have a mind to** to think of doing.—**to have in one's mind** to intend doing, to remember.—**to know one's own mind** to know what one wants.—**to make up one's mind** to decide.—**to my mind** in my opinion.—**to set one's mind on** to decide to have

mine (mīn) *pron. possessive form* of I.—**ours** *pl.*

mine *n.* 1. a deep hole for digging out coal, metals, etc. 2. an underground passage in which explosives are placed. 3. a large shell placed in the sea to destroy ships.—*v.* 1. to dig in a mine, make a mine. 2. to lay mines.—**mi′ning** *pres. part.*—**mi′ner** *n.*—**mine′-field** *n.* a part of sea or land where mines are sown.—**mine′-layer** *n.* a ship used for laying mines.—**mine′-sweeper** *n.* a ship used for clearing mines

min′eral *adj.* 1. obtained by mining. 2. not animal or plant.—*n.* a mineral substance.—**mineral′ogy** *n.* science of minerals

min′gle (ming′gl) *v.* to mix.—**min′gling** *pres. part.*

Compare: combine, blend, merge, unite. *Contrast:* separate, clear, disentangle

mini- *pref.* very small, as *mini-car, mini-skirt*

min′iature *n.* 1. a very small painted portrait. 2. a model on a small scale.—*adj.* made on a small scale

min′imise *v.* to bring to the smallest possible amount, as *Doctors do everything possible to minimise the dangers of infection*

min′imum *n.* the smallest possible quantity—**min′ima** *pl.*—*adj.* smallest, least, as *minimum wage*

min′ion *n.* 1. favourite. 2. slavish follower

min′ister *n.* 1. the person in charge of a

State department. 2. person sent abroad to represent his government. 3. a clergyman.—*v.* 1. to serve. 2. to tend, look after. —**ministe'rial** (minis-tee'-ri-al) *adj.*—**ministra'tion** (-trā'shun) *n.* serving

min'istry *n.* 1. ministering. 2. a minister's service. 3. a body of government officials. 4. clergymen.—**min'istries** *pl.*

mink (mingk) *n.* an animal resembling a weasel, with valuable fur

mi'nor (mī'ner) *adj.* smaller, less, as *minor ills.*—*n.* person under 21.—**minor'ity** (min-or'i-ti) *n.* 1. the smaller number, as *Only a minority wanted to stay in. The majority decided to go out.* 2. being under age, as *During the King's minority, a regent ruled*

min'ster *n.* 1. the church of a monastery. 2. a cathedral

min'strel *n.* 1. a singer or musician in the Middle Ages. 2. a performer of negro songs.—**min'strelsy** *n.*

mint *n.* a sweet-smelling plant used in cooking

mint *n.* 1. a place where money is coined. 2. a large amount.—*v.* to coin money

minuet' *n.* a slow graceful dance

min'us (mī'nus) *n.* the sign.—as 5−2=3.—*prep.* less, as *five minus two leaves three.*—*adj.* less than nothing, as *He has no money and owes 6d. so he has minus 6d.*

min'ute (min'it) *n.* 1. a sixtieth part of an hour or degree. 2. a moment.—*pl.* record of what happened at a meeting

minute' (mī-nūt') *adj.* 1. very small. 2. very detailed, exact.—**minute'ly** *adv.*

mir'acle *n.* 1. an event beyond the laws of nature. 2. something very wonderful.—**mirac'ulous** *adj.* marvellous

mirage' (mir-ahzh') *n.* an appearance in the air of objects or scenes not really there, due to atmospheric conditions

mire *n.* soft mud.—**mi'ry** *adj.*

mir'ror *n.* 1. a looking-glass. 2. anything that reflects.—*v.*

mirth *n.* laughter, gaiety.—**mirth'ful** *adj.*—**mirth'less** *adj.*

Compare: jollity, laughter, gaiety, hilarity, glee, cheerfulness. *Contrast:* sadness, sorrow, melancholy, dejection

mis—is added at the beginning of other words and has the meaning "wrongly," e.g. *misapply* means apply wrongly. If you are seeking the meaning of any word beginning with *mis*—and do not find it below, find the word to which *mis-* has been added and put "wrongly" after it. Thus, to find the meaning of *misdirect* say to yourself *direct wrongly*. If you do not know what this means, look up *direct*

misadven'ture *n.* a mishap, unlucky accident

misbehave' (mis-be-hāv') *v.* to behave badly. —**misbeha'viour** (-hāv'yer) *n.*

miscar'ry *v.* to fail, go wrong.—it **miscar'ries.**—**miscar'ried** *p.t.* and *p. part.*—**miscar'riage** *n.* 1. failure. 2. the premature birth of a baby which dies

miscella'neous (mis-el-ā'ne-us) *adj.* mixed, made up of different sorts.—**miscel'lany** (mis-el'an-i, mis'el-ān-i) *n.* 1. a mixture. 2. a collection of assorted writings

mischance' *n.* a mishap, unlucky event

mis'chief (mis'chif) *n.* 1. harm, as *Storms often do much mischief.* 2. troublesome behaviour. 3. teasing.—**mis'chievous** (mis'-chiv-us) *adj.*

miscon'duct *n.* bad behaviour.—**misconduct'** *v.* 1. to behave badly. 2. to manage badly

mis'creant (mis'cri-ant) *n.* a villain

misdeed' *n.* a wicked action

misdemean'our *n.* an offence, wrong deed

mi'ser (mī'zer) *n.* a person who hoards money.—**mi'serly** *adj.* mean, stingy

mis'erable (miz'er-a-bl) *adj.* 1. very unhappy. 2. poor, wretched.—**mis'erably** *adv.*

mis'ery (miz'er-i) *n.* 1. great unhappiness. 2. distress, poverty.—**mis'eries** *pl.*

misfire' *n.* (of a gun or petrol engine) a failure to explode or ignite.—*v.* 1. to fail to explode. 2. (of a plan) to fail to go into action

mis'fit *n.* a bad fit

misfor'tune *n.* bad luck

misgiv'ing *n.* doubt, fear

mis'hap *n.* an unlucky accident

mislead' (mis-leed') *v.* 1. to lead astray. 2. to deceive.—**misled'** *p.t.* and *p. part.*

miss *v.* 1. to fail to hit or reach, or catch, as *He missed a catch.* 2. not to notice, as *I missed him in the crowd.* 3. to be too late for, as *to miss a train.* 4. to omit, as *I have missed a word.* 5. to regret the absence of. —he **miss'es**—*n.* missing

miss *n.* a title given to a girl or an unmarried woman.—**miss'es** *pl.* See **master**

missha'pen *adj.* deformed, badly shaped

mis'sile (mis'īl, mis'il) *n.* something which can be thrown or shot to do damage

mis'sion (mish'un) *n.* 1. special work. 2. persons sent out on some service.—**mis'sionary** *n.* a person on a religious mission.—**mis'sionaries** *pl.*—*adj.* of religious missions

mis'sive *n.* a letter

misspell' *v.* to spell wrongly.—**misspel'ling** *n.*

misspend' *v.* to spend foolishly, waste. —**misspent'** *p.t.* and *p. part.*

misstate' *v.* to state wrongly.—**misstate'ment** *n.*

mist *n.* very fine drops of water in the air.—*v.* 1. to rain mist. 2. to dim.—**mist'y** *adj.* covered with mist, dim.—**mist'ily** *adv.* in a misty manner.—**mist'iness** *n.* cloudy condition

mistake' *n.* an error in thought or action.—*v.* 1. to misunderstand, as *I mistook what you said.* 2. to take a person or thing for another, as *He mistook the toad for a stone.*—**mista'king** *pres. part.*—**mistook**

p.t.—**mista'ken** *p. part.*—**mista'ken** *adj.* wrong

mist'letoe (mis'l-tō) *n.* a plant with white berries, which grows on fruit and other trees

mis'tress *n.* 1. a woman in control of a household. 2. a woman teacher. 3. a woman with complete skill.—**mas'ter** *masc.*

Mrs. is an abreviation of **mistress**

mistrust' *n.* lack of trust, confidence.—*v.* to doubt.—**mistrust'ful** *adj.* suspicious, doubtful

mite *n.* 1. a very small coin. 2. a very small child. 3. a very small insect

mit'igate *v.* to relieve, make less severe, as *The heat was mitigated by a cool breeze.*—**mit'igating** *pres. part.*—**mitiga'tion** (gā'-shun) *n.*

Compare: allay, soothe, subdue, modify, abate. *Contrast:* aggravate, increase

mi'tre *n.* 1. a bishop's ceremonial head-dress. 2. joint between two pieces of wood meeting at right angles

mit'ten *n.* 1. a glove in which the four fingers are covered together. 2. a glove leaving the fingers bare

mix *v.* 1. to put together, blend, as *Mix sugar and butter to make toffee.* 2. to be mixed, unite, as *Oil and water do not mix.*—he **mix'es.**—**mixed** (mixt).—*adj.* made up of different kinds.—**mix'ture** *n.* what has been mixed.—**mix up** 1. mix together. 2. confuse

miz'zen *n.* a sail on the aftermost mast.—**miz'zen mast** *n.* the aftermost mast of a three-masted ship

moan (mōn) *n.* 1. a low murmur of pain. 2. any similar sound.—*v.* to make this sound

moat (mōt) *n.* a deep, wide ditch round a town or building as a protection against enemies

mob *n.* 1. a disorderly crowd of people. 2. (Aus.) a flock of sheep or herd of cattle.—*v.* to attack, ill-treat in a mob.—**mob'bing** *pres. part.*—**mobbed** *p.t.* and *p. part.*

mo'bile (mō'bīl) *adj.* moving easily.—**mobil'ity** *n.*—**mobilisation** (-zā'shun) *n.* calling forces into active military service.—**mo'bilise** *v.* to organise for war.—**mo'bilising** *pres. part.*

moc'casin *n.* a soft leather shoe worn by North American Indians

mock *v.* 1. to make fun of. 2. to disappoint.—*adj.* sham, imitation, as *a mock battle.*—**mock'er** *n.* a scoffer.—**mock'ery** *n.* 1. a bad imitation. 2. making fun of

mode *n.* manner, style, fashion

mod'el *n.* 1. a small copy of an object, as *a model of a ship.* 2. an example to be imitated. 3. a person posing for artists. 4. a person employed by a dress-maker to show off clothes.—*adj.* perfectly behaved, as *a model child.*—*v.* 1. to make, fashion. 2. to display clothes.—**mod'elling** *pres. part.*—**mod'elled** *p.t.* and *p. part.*

mod'erate (mod'er-it) *adj.* 1. not extreme, medium, as *moderate opinions.* 2. fairly good, as *this drawing is only moderate.*—**mod'erate** (mod'er-āt) *v.* to soften, make less violent.—**mod'erating** *pres. part.*—**mod'erately** *adv.* fairly.—**modera'tion** (-ā'-shun) *n.* restraint

mod'ern *adj.* of present or recent times, new.—**mod'ernise** *v.* to bring up to date

mod'est *adj.* 1. not vain or boastful. 2. shy quiet. 3. decent. 4. humble.—**mod'esty** *n.*

modifica'tion (-kā'shun) *n.* changing the form of, toning down.—**mod'ify** *v.* to change, make less severe.—he **mod'ifies.**—**mod'ifying** *pres. part.*—**mod'ified** *p.t.* and *p. part.*

mod'ulate *v.* to soften, to vary the tone, to change from one key in music to another.—**mod'ulating** *pres. part.*—**modula'tion** (-lā'shun) *n.*

moham'medan, mahom'medan *n.* a moslem, a follower of the religious leader Moham'-med

moist *adj.* damp.—**moist'en** (moi'sn) *v.* to make damp.—**mois'ture** *n.* wetness in small drops

mo'ko *n.* a Maori system of tattooing

mo'lar *n.* a tooth for grinding

molass'es *n.* a by-product of sugar

mole *n.* a dark spot on the skin

mole *n.* a small burrowing animal with velvety fur.—**mole'-hill** *n.* earth thrown up by a burrowing mole

mole *n.* a stone breakwater or pier

mol'ecule *n.* the smallest possible part of a substance that possesses all the properties of the substance

molest' *v.* to annoy, interfere with.—**molesta'tion** (-tā'shun) *n.*

mol'lify *v.* to soften, clam down.—he **mol'lifies.**—**mol'lifying** *pres. part.*—**mol'lified** *p.t.* and *p. part.*

mol'lusc *n.* an animal with a soft body and often a hard shell, e.g. snail, oyster, etc.

mol'lycoddle *v.* to pamper

mol'ten *adj.* melted. See **melt**

mo'ment *n.* 1. an instant, short space of time, as *I will be ready in a moment.* 2. importance, as *a matter of great moment.*—**mo'mentary** *adj.* lasting only a moment.—**moment'ous** *adj.* very important

moment'um *n.* 1. the force of a moving body, as *The car gathered momentum down the hill.* 2. (in science) the product of the mass and velocity of a body

mon'arch (mon'ark) *n.* the ruler of a kingdom or empire.—**monarch'ial** *adj.*—**mon'archist** *n.* a supporter of monarchy.—**mon'archy** *n.* 1. a state ruled by a sovereign. 2. his rule.—**mon'archies** *pl.*

mon'astery *n.* a house occupied by a community of monks.—**mon'asteries** *pl.*—**monas'tic** *adj.*

Mon'day (mun'dā) *n.* the day after Sunday
mon'etary *adj.* of money, as *a monetary system, a monetary reward*
mon'ey (mun'i) *n.* 1. coins or paper notes used in buying or selling. 2. wealth.—**mon'eyed** *adj.* wealthy.—**mon'eys** *pl.*
Mongo'lia *n.* an Asiatic country west of China.—**Mongo'lian** *n.* and *adj.*
mon'goose *n.* a small Indian animal like a ferret.—**mon'gooses** *pl.*
mon'grel (mung'grel) *n.* an animal, esp. a dog, of mixed breed.—*adj.* of mixed breed
mon'itor *n.* 1. a pupil in a school, having special duties. 2. an adviser. 3. a small warship.—**mon'itress** *fem.*
monk (mungk) *n.* a man who lives apart, under vows, in a monastery.—**nun** *fem.*
monk'ey (mung'ki) *n.* a mammal of a group ranging from apes to marmosets.—**monk'eys** *pl.*—**mon'key-nut** *n.* a peanut, groundnut
mon'o- *prefix* one
mon'ocle *n.* an eye-glass for one eye
mon'ogram *n.* a person's initials made into one design
mon'ologue (mon'ō-log) *n.* 1. a dramatic composition with only one speaker. 2. a long speech by one actor in a play
monop'olise *v.* to have sole possession or control of something.—**monop'olising** *pres. part.*
monop'oly *n.* sole possession or control of a trade, etc.—**monop'olies** *pl.*
mon'orail *n.* a railway with a single rail on which special cars run
monosyl'lable *n.* a word of one syllable.—**monosyllab'ic** *adj.*
mon'otone *n.* a single tone, style, colour, as *He reads in a dull monotone*
monot'onous *adj.* on one note, dull, wearisome.—**monot'ony** *n.* sameness
monsoon' *n.* a seasonal wind of the Indian ocean, blowing from the south-west in summer and from the north-east in winter
mon'ster *n.* 1. a misshapen animal or plant. 2. a huge animal or thing. 3. a very cruel or wicked person.— **monstros'ity** *n.* something huge and horrible.—**mons'trous** *adj.* 1. huge. 2. unnatural. 3. shocking, horrible
month (munth) *n.* one of the twelve divisions of a year.—**month'ly** *adj.* happening once a month, every month.—*adv.*
mon'ument *n.* anything that preserves the memory of a person or event.—**monument'al** *adj.* 1. serving as a monument. 2. huge
mood (mōōd) *n.* a state of mind and feelings, as *Toothache put him in a bad mood.*—**in the mood** feeling inclined (to do something).—**mood'y** *adj.* changeable, gloomy
moon (mōōn) *n.* a planet revolving round the earth in 28 days and reflecting the sun's light.—**moon'beam** *n.* a ray from the moon.—**moon'light** *n.*—**moon'lit** *adj.*—**moon'-probe** *n.* a rocket fitted with instruments aimed at the moon to explore its surface.—**moon'shine** *n.* nonsense.—**moon'struck** *adj.* crazy
moor *n.* hilly waste land, covered with heather.—**moor'hen** *n.* a water-hen
moor *v.* to fasten a ship with chains or ropes.—**moor'ings** *n.pl.* ropes, etc. fastening a ship
moose *n.* a large North American deer
moot *n.* a meeting.—*v.* to bring for discussion.—**a moot point** a doubtful point
mop *n.* a bundle of cloth, rags, etc. fastened at the end of a handle for cleaning floors.—*v.* to wipe up, clean.—**mop'ping** *pres. part.*—**mopped** *p.t.* and *p. part.*
mope *v.* to be dull, depressed.—**mo'ping** *pres. part.*—**mo'pish** *adj.*
moraine' *n.* a line of stony rubbish left by a glacier
mor'al *n.* a lessen, teaching drawn from a story.—*pl.* conduct, behaviour.—*adj.* 1. concerned with right and wrong. 2. right, good.—**morale'** (mor-ahl') *n.* spirits, courage.—**mor'alise** *v.* to speak about right or wrong.—**mor'alist** *n.*—**moral'ity** *n.* goodness or badness.—**mor'ally** *adv.*—**a moral victory** *n.* an apparent defeat which really gives satisfaction, encouragement or hope
morass' *n.* a marsh, swamp.—**morass'es** *pl.*
mor'bid *adj.* unwholesome, sickly, as *a morbid love of horrors*
mor'dant *adj.* biting, acute, as *mordant sarcasm.*—*n.* a substance that fixes dyes
more *adj.* comparative form of **many** and **much.** *More* is used to form the comparative of many adjectives and adverbs, as *beautiful, more beautiful, beautifully, more beautifully.*—**moreo'ver** *adv.* also, in addition, as *I have no time to go out, moreover, it is too hot*
morn'ing *n.* the early part of the day, before noon
morose' (mor-ōs') *adj.* sullen, sour-tempered
Moroc'co *n.* a country of north Africa.—**Moroc'can** *n.* and *adj.*
mor'row (mor'ō) *n.* the following day
morse *n.* a system of signalling with dots and dashes
mor'sel *n.* 1. a mouthful. 2. a small piece
mor'tal *adj.* 1. that must die, as *All men are mortal.* 2. deadly, causing death, as *a mortal wound.* 3. very great, as *mortal fear.*—*n.* 1. a mortal being. 2. man.—**mortal'ity** *n.* 1. being mortal. 2. loss of life 3. death-rate.—**mor'tally** *adv.* 1. fatally. 2. bitterly
mor'tar *n.* 1. a mixture of lime, sand and water for holding bricks, etc. together. 2. a bowl in which substances are pounded. 3. a short kind of cannon
mort'gage (mor'gij) *n.* a claim on property held, by a lender of money, until the loan is repaid

mortifica'tion (-kā'shun) *n.* 1. shame, humiliation. 2. decay of a limb

mort'ify *v.* 1. to hurt a person's feelings. 2. to overcome desires by suffering. 3. to decay.—he **mort'ifies.—mort'ifying** *pres. part.*—**mort'ified** *p.t.* and *p. part.*

mor'tise (mor'tis) *n.* an opening cut in wood or stone to receive a tenon, in a mortise and tenon joint

mor'tuary *n.* a place where dead bodies may be kept before identification and burial

mosa'ic (mō-zā'ik) *n.* a pattern made up of small bits of glass, stone, etc. inlaid

mos'lem, mus'lim *n.* a follower of Mohammed, a mohammedan

mosque (mosk) *n.* a Mohammedan temple

mosqui'to (mos-kee'tō) *n.* a long thin insect like a gnat.—**mosqui'toes** *pl.*

moss *n.* a small plant growing in masses on moist surfaces.—**moss'es** *pl.*—**mos'sy** *adj.*

most (mōst) *adj.* superlative form of **many** and **much.** *Most* is used to form the superlative of most adjectives and adverbs, as *beautiful, most beautiful, beautifully, most beautifully.*—**most'ly** *adv.* chiefly, for the most part, as *This apple is mostly bad*

mote *n.* a speck of dust

mo'tel *n.* a kind of hotel taking the form of a group of small bungalows for renting to motorists for short periods

moth *n.* an insect like the butterfly, usually flying by night, and with feelers which are not club-shaped.—**moth'y** *adj.*—**moth'-eaten** *adj.* damaged by the grub of the moth, which breeds in fur, wool, etc.—**moth'-ball** *n.* a ball of camphor to repel moths

moth'er (muTHer) *n.* 1. a female parent.—**fa'ther** *masc.* 2. the head of a community of nuns.—*v.* to act as mother.—**moth'erhood** *n.* being a mother.—**moth'erly** *adj.* kind, comforting.—**moth'er-in-law** *n.* the mother of one's husband or wife.—**mo'thers-in-law** *pl.*—**mother-of-pearl'** *n.* a hard, colourful lining of certain shells

mo'tion (mō'shun) *n.* 1. movement, way of moving. 2. proposal in a meeting.—*v.* to direct by a sign, as *I was motioned in.*—**mo'tionless** *adj.* still

mo'tive (mō'tiv) *n.* that which makes a person act, as *What was your motive in hiding this letter?*—*adj.* causing motion, as *motive power of steam*

mot'ley *n.* a jester's dress.—*adj.* 1. of different colours. 2. mixed

mo'tor *n.* 1. a machine supplying power to move. 2. an automobile.—*v.* to travel by motor-car.—*adj.* run by motor.—**mo'torist** *n.* a user of a motor-car.—**mo'tor-boat** *n.*—**mo'tor-cy'cle** *n.*—**mo'torway** *n.* a road specially built for fast motor vehicles

mot'tled *adj.* spotted with different colours

mot'to *n.* a saying adopted as a rule of conduct.—**mot'toes** *pl.*

mould (mōld) *n.* 1. a hollow object into which metal, etc., is poured to shape it. 2. a shape, pattern.—*v.* to shape

mould (mōld) *n.* mildew, a growth caused by dampness.—**mould'er** *v.* to rot, decay

mould (mōld) *n.* loose earth

moul'ding (mōl'ding) *n.* 1. something moulded. 2. ornament along a line in a building

moult (mōlt) *v.* to shed feathers, change plumage

mound *n.* a heap of earth or stones

mount *v.* 1. to go up, as *to mount a hill.* 2. to get on horse-back. 3. to furnish with a horse, as *He was mounted on a grey.* 4. to put in a setting.—*n.* 1. a high hill, as *the Mount of Olives.* 2. a horse. 3. a setting, as *a picture with a white mount*

mount'ain *n.* 1. a very large hill. 2. a heap.—**mountaineer'** *n.* 1. a person living in the mountains. 2. a climber.—**moun'tainous** *adj.*—**mountain devil** (Aus.) 1. a strange-looking lizard. 2. a low-growing shrub

mount'ebank *n.* 1. a buffoon. 2. a quack, a trickster

mourn (mōrn) *v.* to feel sorrow, grieve.—**mourn'er** *n,*—**mourn'ful** *adj.* sad.—**mourn'ing** *n.* 1. grief. 2. outward sign of grief.—*adj.*

Compare: lament, bewail, deplore. *Contrast:* rejoice, exult, make merry

mouse (mows) *n.* small, gnawing long-tailed animal—**mice** (mīs) *pl.*—*v.* to catch mice

moustache' (mus-tahsh') *n.* hair on a man's upper lip

mouth *n.* 1. the opening in the head, for eating, speaking, etc. 2. an opening into anything hollow, as *the mouth of a cave.* 3. an entrance to river, harbour.—**mouth'ful** *n.*—**mouth'piece** *n.* 1. the end of a pipe, musical instrument, etc. placed between lips. 2. one who speaks for others.—**mouth'-organ** *n.* a small musical wind-instrument, a harmonica.—**down in the mouth** sad, gloomy

mov'able (mōōv'a-bl) *adj.* which can be moved.—**mov'ables** *n.pl.* belongings

move (mōōv) *v.* 1. to change the position of, as *Move your chair to the window.* 2. to go somewhere else, as *We are moving to another house.* 3. to take action. 4. to stir, rouse, as *He was moved to anger.*—*n.* 1. a moving. 2. a step towards something.—**move'ment** *n.* 1. moving. 2. effort of a society towards some goal. 3. main division of a piece of music.—**mo'ving** *adj.* stirring, touching.—**to move in (out)** to move one's belongings into (or out of) a new house.—**to move on** to proceed after standing still.—**to get a move on** to hurry

mow (mō) *v.* to cut grass, etc. with a scythe or machine.—**mown** (mōn) *p. part.*—**mow'er** *n.* 1. person mowing. 2. mowing-machine

much *adj.* a great deal of, as *A millionaire has much money.*—*n.* a large amount, as *He*

gives much to the poor. How much have you lost?—*adv.* a great deal, as *This work is much better.*—**more** *comp.*—**most** *super*
muck *n.* manure, dirt.—**muck'y** *adj.*
mud *n.* soft, wet earth.—**mud'guard** *n.* a wheel cover to prevent flying mud
mud'dle *v.* to confuse, to make a mess of, to blunder.—**mud'dling** *pres. part.*—*n.* mess, confusion
mud'dy *adj.* covered with mud.—**mud'dier** *comp.*—**mud'diest** *sup.*
muff *n. v.* to miss a catch, a chance, etc.
muf'fin *n.* a round flat cake eaten hot and buttered
muf'fle *v.* 1. to wrap up. 2. to deaden a sound, as *The snow muffled their steps.*—**muf'fling** *pres. part.*—**muf'fler** *n.* warm scarf
muf'ti *n.* plain clothes, not uniform
mug *n.* a drinking-cup
mulat'to *n* born of a black and a white parent
mul'berry *n.* a tree on the leaves of which silk-worms are fed.—**mul'berries** *pl.*
mule *n.* a mongrel animal, half donkey, half horse.—**muleteer'** *n.* a mule-driver.—**mu'lish** *adj.* stubborn
mul'ga *n.* (Aus.) 1. one of several species of densely-growing acacia, used as fodder. 2. an aborigine shield
mul'lock *n.* refuse from a mine
mul'tiple *adj.* having many parts, as *He received multiple injuries.*—*n.* a quantity which contains another an exact number of times, as *Nine is a multiple of three.*—**multiplica'tion** *n.* multiplying, being multiplied.—**multiplic'ity** (mul-ti-plis'i-ti) *n.* a great number.—**mul'tiplier** *n.* number by which another is multiplied.—**mul'tiply** *v.* 1. to make many, as *Mice multiply very quickly.* 2. to find the sum of a number a given number of times, as *If you multiply* 2 *by* 4 *it makes* 8.—**mul'tiplying** *pres. part.*—**mul'tiplied** *p.t.* and *p. part.*—**lowest common multiple** the lowest number which will contain two or more other numbers an exact number of times
mul'titude *n.* a great number, a great crowd.—**multitu'dinous** *adj.* very numerous
mum'ble *v.* to mutter, speak indistinctly.—*n.*—**mum'bling** *pres. part.*
mum'mer *n.* a person wearing a mask and acting in a kind of play.—**mum'mery** *n.*
mum'my *n.* 1. dead body, embalmed to preserve it. 2. mother—**mum'mies** *pl.*
mumps *n.pl.* contagious disease marked by swelling in the neck
munch *v.* to chew.—he **munch'es**
mund'ane *adj.* belonging to this world
munic'ipal (mū-nis'i-pal) *adj.* having to do with the affairs of a city or town.—**municipal'ity** *n.* 1. a city or town with local self-government. 2. the governing body.—**municipal'ities** *pl.*
munif'icence (mū-nif'i-sens) *n.* great generosity.—**munif'icent** *adj.*
muni'tions (mū-nish'unz) *n.pl.* war-material, e.g. guns, air-craft, etc.
mu'ral *adj.* of a wall, on a wall.—*n.* a painting on a wall
mur'der *n.* the unlawful and planned killing of a human being.—*v.*—**mur'derer** *n.* a killer.—**mur'deress** *fem.*—**mur'derous** *adj.*
murk *n.* thick darkness.—**murk'y** *adj.*
mur'mur *n.* a low, indistinct, unbroken sound.—*v.* 1. to make this sound, as *The trees murmured in the wind.* 2. to complain
mus'cle (mus'l) *n.* a tissue in the body which produces movement by being tightened or loosened.—**mus'cular** (mus'kū-lar) *adj.* 1. of the muscle. 2. strong
muse (mūz) *v.* to be lost in thought.—**mu'sing** *pres. part.*—**Muse** *n.* poetic inspiration
muse'um (mū-zee'um) *n.* a place to show interesting objects
mush'room *n.* a small fungus, or umbrella-shaped plant, which grows very quickly.—*adj.* growing rapidly
mu'sic (mū'zik) *n.* 1. the art of expressing feeling by a pleasing arrangement of sounds. 2. the written or printed signs representing sounds. 3. any pleasant sounds, as *the music of the sea.*—**mu'sical** *adj.*—**mu'sically** *adv.*—**musi'cian** (mū-zish'-an) *n.* a person who sings or plays
musk'et *n.* an old kind of gun.—**musketeer'** *n.* a soldier armed with a musket.—**mus'ketry** *n.*
mus'lim see **mos'lem**
mus'lin (muz'lin) *n.* a fine cotton fabric
mus'sel *n.* a shell-fish with double shell
Mus'sulman *n.* a Mohammedan.—**Mus'sulmans** *pl.*
must *v. aux.* be obliged, be necessary. This is the only form of this verb used in modern English. There is no past tense, past or present participle
must *n.* something which must be done
must'ang *n.* a wild horse of the prairies
must'ard *n.* a powder made from the seeds of the mustard-plant and used for flavouring
must'er *v.* to collect, assemble.—*n.* an assembly, esp. of troops for exercise or inspection
must'y *adj*, mouldy, stale.—**must'ier** *comp.*—**must'iest** *sup.*
mute (mūt) *adj.* dumb, silent.—*n.* 1. a dumb person. 2. a hired mourner. 3. a clip placed on a stringed instrument to soften the tone.—**mute'ly** *adv.* silently
mu'tilate (mū-) *v.* to cut or break off a part, to damage seriously.—**mu'tilating** *pres. part.*—**mutila'tion** (-ā'shun) *n.*
mutineer' (mū-) *n.* a rebel
mu'tinous (mū-) *adj.* rebellious
mu'tiny (mū-) *n.* a rebellion against authority, esp. in the forces.—*v.*—**mu'tinies** *pl.*
mut'ter *v.* to speak with the mouth nearly closed.—*n.*

mut'ton *n.* the flesh of sheep used as food as *roast mutton, mutton-chop*
mu'tual (mū-) *adj.* shared jointly by each of two persons, the one to the other, as *The dog and his master feel mutual affection.*—**mu'tually** *adv.*
muz'zle *n.* 1. the mouth and nose of an animal. 2. straps or wires covering muzzle to prevent biting. 3. the open end of a gun, etc.—*v.* to put a muzzle on, to prevent from speaking
my *poss. adj.* belonging to me.—**my'self** *pron.* I, me
myr'iad (mir'iad) *n.* an endless number.—*adj.* innumerable
myrrh (mir) *n.* a sweet-smelling gummy substance, used in medicines and incense
myr'tle *n.* an evergreen shrub with sweet-smelling white flowers
myste'rious (mis-tee'ri-us) *adj.* full of mystery
mys'tery (mis'ter-i) *n.* 1. a secret. 2. something difficult to understand. 3. a religious rite. 4. a Biblical play.—**mys'teries** *pl.*
mystifica'tion (-kā'shun) *n.* perplexity, being mystified
mys'tify (mist'i-fī) *v.* to puzzle, bewilder.—he **mys'tifies.**—**mys'tifying** *pres. part.*—**mys'tified** *p.t.* and *p. part.*
myth (mith) *n.* 1. a legend, story. 2. an imaginary person or thing.—**myth'ical** *adj.*—**mytholog'ical** (-loj') *adj.* belonging to mythology.—**mythol'ogy** (mith-ol'o-ji) *n.* 1. the study of myths. 2. myths

N

nab *v.* to seize suddenly.—**nab'bing** *pres. part.*—**nabbed** *p.t.* and *p. part.*
na'bob *n.* an Indian prince
nag *n.* a small riding-horse
nag *v.* to worry by constant scolding.—**nag'ging** *pres. part.*—**nagged** *p.t.*, *p. part.*
nail (nāl) *n.* 1. a hard protective layer at the finger-ends. 2. a claw. 3. a small metal spike for fixing together, or to be used as a peg.—*v.* to fix with a nail.—**hard as nails** tough.—**to hit the nail on the head** to describe exactly, to come to the exact point.—**tooth and nail** with violence
naïve' (na-eev') *adj.* innocent, simple
na'ked *adj.* 1. without clothes, bare. 2. uncovered.—**na'kedness** *n.*—**with the naked eye** without glasses, telescope, etc.
name *n.* 1. the word by which a person or thing is spoken about, as *His name is Tom.* 2. reputation, as *He has a name for kindness.*—*v.* 1. to give a name to. 2. to call by a name. 3. to appoint, mention, as *He has been named captain.*—**na'ming** *pres. part.*—**name'less** *adj.*—**name'ly** *adv.* that is to say.—**name'sake** *n.* a person with the same name as another.—**to call names** to insult.—**in the name of** 1. acting for. 2. appealing to the authority of
nan'ny-goat *n.* a she-goat.—**bil'ly-goat** *masc.*
nap *n.* a short sleep—*v.* to take a short sleep—**napping** *pres. part.*—**napped** *p.t.* and *p. part.*
nap *n.* short, woolly surface of cloth
nape *n.* the back of the neck
nap'kin *n.* 1. a square piece of linen used for wiping fingers or lips at table. 2. a small towel, a baby's nappie
napoleon'ic *adj.* like the Emperor Napoleon I, forceful, dominating
narcis'sus (nar-sis'us) *n.* a spring flower
narcot'ic *n.* a drug causing sleep
nark *n.* an envious critic.—*v.* to annoy
narrate' *v.* to relate, tell a story.—**narra'ting** *pres. part.*—**narra'tion** (-rā'shun) *n.* relating.—**nar'rative** *n.* a story.—*adj.* telling a story.—**narra'tor** *n.*
nar'row (nar'ō) *adj.* 1. not wide, as *The narrow stream becomes a broad river.* 2. small, limited, as *a narrow mind, a narrow area.*—*v.* to become narrow.—**nar'rowly** *adv.*—**nar'rowness** *n.*—**nar'row-mind'ed** *adj.* not fair or generous in thought.—**a narrow escape** being nearly caught
na'sal (nā'zal) *adj.* of the nose, pronounced through the nose, as *N is a nasal sound.*—*n.*
nas'tiness *n.* something very unpleasant, dirty, etc.—**nas'tily** *adv.* in a nasty way
nastur'tium (nas-tur'shum) *n.* a plant with gay yellow and red flowers
nas'ty *adj.* unpleasant, dirty.—**nas'tier** *comp.*—**nas'tiest** *sup.*
na'tal *adj.* relating to birth
na'tion (nā'shun) *n.* 1. a people or race with the same language and history. 2. a state.—**nat'ional** (nash'on-al) *adj.* of a nation, as *a national army.*—*n.* citizen of a nation, as *a British national.*—**nat'ionalise** *v.* to take private firms or property into state ownership.—**nat'ionalism** *n.* patriotic feelings.—**nat'ionalist** *n.*—**national'ity** *n.* belonging to a particular nation.—**national'ities** *pl.*—**nat'ional an'them** the official song of a state
na'tive (nā'tiv) *n.* 1. a person belonging to a place by birth. 2. a member of a non-European race, as *the natives of Africa.*—*adj.* 1. produced in a certain place, as *native birds.* 2. inborn, as *a native genius.* 3. belonging by birth, as *my native land.*—**nativ'ity** *n.* birth.—**The Nativ'ity,** the birth of Christ
Compare: natural, indigenous, inborn, innate, inherent. *Contrast:* foreign, alien, strange, acquired, artificial
nat'ty *adj.* neat and smart
nat'ural *adj.* 1. of nature, as *natural history.* 2. not artificial, happening in the ordinary course of things, as *In summer it is natural to wear fewer clothes.* 3. inborn, as *Cats have a natural dislike of water.* 4. in music, neither sharp nor flat.—**nat'uralist** *n.* one who studies plants and animals.—**naturalisa'tion** (zā'shun) *n.* being naturalised.—**nat'uralise** *v.* 1. to admit a foreigner

to citizenship. 2. to accustom to a new climate.—**nat'urally** *adv.*

na'ture *n.* 1. the world, everything in it except what man has made. 2. life. 3. sort, kind, character, as *A cat is cruel by nature.* 4. all the forces, activities, laws in creation.—**na'ture study** simple botany and zoology

naught (nawt) *n.* nothing, zero

naught'ily (nawt'i-li) *adv.* in a naughty way. —**naught'iness** *n.* bad behaviour, mischief

naught'y (nawt'i) *adj.* badly-behaved, mischievous.—**naught'ier** *comp.*—**naught'iest** *sup.*

naus'ea (naw'si-a) *n.* 1. sea-sickness, any sickness of the stomach. 2. disgust.—**naus'eate** *v.* to disgust.—**naus'eous** *adj.* sickening, loathsome

nau'tical *adj.* having to do with ships or seamen

na'val *adj.* having to do with the navy, ships, etc., as *a naval officer*

nave *n.* the body of a church, from the west door to the choir

nav'igable *adj.* 1. offering passage for ships, as *a navigable river.* 2. sea-worthy, as *This boat is too badly damaged to be navigable*

nav'igate *v.* 1. to sail. 2. to steer a ship.—**nav'igating** *pres. part.*—**naviga'tion** (gā'-shun) *n.* 1. navigating. 2. finding a ship's course.—**nav'igator** *n.* 1. a man in charge of navigating a ship. 2. an explorer on the seas. 3. an airman who directs course of aircraft

nav'vy *n.* a labourer working on the making of roads, railways etc.

na'vy *n.* 1. a fleet. 2. the warships of a country, with their crews and organisation.—**na'vies** *pl.*—**navy-blue'** *n.* and *adj.* dark blue

nay *adv.* 1. no. 2. even, also, as *We are ready, nay eager, to help*

neap *adj.* low.—**neap tide** *n.* the low tide at the first and third quarters of the moon

near *adj.* 1. close, not far. 2. closely related, as *a near relative.* 3. in driving, describing the side of the road closest to the vehicle, as *The kerb was on the near side.* 4. mean, stingy.—*v.* to approach, as *The ship was nearing port.*—*adv.* at a short distance, as *Christmas draws near.*—*prep.* close to, as *We live near the church.*—**near'ly** *adv.* almost.—**near'ness** *n.*—**nearby'** *adj.* close at hand.—**near-sight'ed** *adj.* unable to see far.—**a near miss** almost a hit

neat *adj.* 1. clean and tidy, as *a neat desk.* 2. cleverly expressed, as *a neat retort.* 3. pure, not mixed, as *neat whisky.*—**neat'ly** *adv.*—**neat'ness** *n.*

Compare: orderly, trim, spruce, prim, dapper. *Contrast:* dirty, disorderly, dowdy, rough, slovenly, soiled, untidy, negligent

neb'ula *n.* a bright cloudy spot in the night-sky often caused by a cluster of stars.—**neb'ulae** *pl.*—**neb'ulous** *adj.* vague

nec'essary (nes'es-ar-i) *adj.* which must be done, essential.—*n.* something which must be had.—**nec'essaries** *pl.*—**necessar'ily** *adv.*

Compare: compulsory, essential, indispensable, needful, required, unavoidable

neces'sitate (ne-ses'i-tāt) *v.* to make necessary, oblige

necess'ity (ne-ses'i-ti) *n.* 1. need, something without which one cannot live, as *food and air are necessities.* 2. poverty. 3. something forcing one to act.—**necess'ities** *pl.*

neck *n.* 1. the part of the body joining the head to the shoulders. 2. a narrow part, as *the neck of a bottle.*—**neck'lace** *n.* an ornamental string of jewels, etc. worn round the neck.—**neck'tie** *n.*—**neck'wear** *n.* collars, ties, etc.

nec'tar *n.* 1. the drink of the gods. 2. the sugary juice of flowers

née (nā) (French) *adj.* born, a word placed before a married woman's maiden name

need *n.* 1. want, lack, as *We are in need of help.* 2. *necessity,* as *there is no need to be angry.* 3. poverty.—*v.* 1. to require, be in want of, as *They need our help.* 2. ought to, to have to, as *We need to hurry.*—**need'ful** *adj.* necessary

nee'dle *n.* 1. a thin, pointed tool with a hole for thread, used in sewing. 2. a tool for knitting. 3. a pointer (on a compass, etc.). 4. leaf of fir or pine

need'less *adj.* unnecessary.—**needs must** must of necessity.—**need'y** *adj.* very poor

nega'tion (-gā'shun) *n.* 1. denial. 2. opposite

neg'ative *n.* 1. a word or statement that denies, or says no. 2. in photography, a picture in which the lights and shadows are reversed.—*adj.* 1. less than zero, as *a negative quantity.* 2. saying no, as *a negative answer.*—*v.* 1. to deny, contradict. 2. to cancel

neglect' *v.* 1. to leave undone. 2. to take no care of.—*n.* being neglected.—**neglect'ful** *adj.* careless.—**neg'ligence** (neg'-li-jens) *n.* neglect, carelessness.—**neg'ligent** *adj.* careless.—**neg'ligible** *adj.* which can be overlooked

Compare: heedlessness, carelessness, disregard, failure, oversight, slackness, slight

nego'tiate (ne-gō'shi-āt) *v.* 1. to discuss business terms. 2. to arrange. 3. to get over (a difficulty).—**negotia'tion** (-ā'shun) *n.* discussion.—**nego'tiator** *n.*

ne'gro (nee'grō) *n.* a man belonging to the black African race.—**ne'gress** *fem.*—**ne'groes** *pl.*

neigh (nā) *n.* the cry of a horse.—*v.*

neigh'bour (nā'bor) *n.* a person living near another.—**neigh'bourhood** *n.* a district.—**neigh'bouring** *adj.* nearby.—**neigh'bourly** *adj.* friendly

nei'ther (nī'THer, nee'THer) *adj.* not the one

nor the other of two, as *Jack and Jill fell, but neither child was hurt.*—*pron.*, as *Jack and Jill fell, but neither was hurt*

Note: 1. *neither* may be followed by *nor*, but not by *or* (*either* is followed by *or*). 2. *neither* is followed by a singular verb after singular nouns. *Neither* is followed by a plural verb only after plural nouns. Thus, *neither Jack nor Jill was hurt. Neither knives nor forks were on the table.* Note also, *neither of them was hurt*

ne'on *n.* a gas used in **ne'on light** *n.* a brilliant, cheap form of electric light

neph'ew (nef'ū, nev'ū) *n.* a brother's or sister's son.—**niece** *fem.*

Nep'tune *n.* 1. a Greek sea god. 2. a large planet

nerve *n.* 1. a fibre carrying feelings to and from the brain. 2. courage. 3. impudence. —*v.* to give courage to.—**nerv'ing** *pres. part.*—**nerve'less** *adj.* weak.—**ner'vous** *adj.* 1. of the nerves, as *the nervous system.* 2. timid. 3. strong, as *full of nervous energy.*—**ner'vousness** *n.*—**a war of nerves** a campaign of rumour and propaganda which avoids actual fighting.—**to get on someone's nerves** to irritate him

nest *n.* 1. a place where a bird lays and hatches its eggs. 2. an animal's breeding-place, as *a wasp's nest.* 3. a snug place.—*v.* to build or have a nest, as *Larks nest in long grass.*—**nest-egg** *n.* 1. a dummy egg in a hen's nest to encourage laying. 2. money saved up

nes'tle (nes'l) *v.* to settle comfortably and warmly.—**nest'ling** *n.* a bird too young to leave the nest

net *n.* 1. an open-work fabric of string, cord, hair, etc. 2. a piece of this used for catching fish, etc.—*v.* to catch with a net.—**net'ting** *pres. part.*—**net'ted** *p.t.* and *p. part.*—**net'work** *n.* a group of interlinked streets, railways, radio stations etc.

net, nett *adj.* left after all deductions, free of charges, as *a net gain*

net'ball *n.* a game played between two teams in which a ball is thrown into a net hung from a tall post

neth'er (neTH'er) *adj.* lower.—**neth'ermost** *adj.* lowest —**Neth'erlands** *n.* Holland

nett see **net**

net'ting *n.* string or wire net

net'tle *n.* a plant with stinging hairs on the leaves.—*v.* to annoy, irritate

neu'ter (nū'ter) *adj.* neither masculine nor feminine

neu'tral (nū'tral) *adj.* 1. taking neither side in a war or dispute. 2. indefinite in colour, etc. 3. (chemistry) neither acid nor alkaline. 4. (electricity) neither positive nor negative.—*n.* a neutral state.—**neutral'ity** *n.*—**neu'tralise** *v.* 1. to make neutral. 2. to affect in the opposite way, counterbalance.—**neu'tralising** *pres. part.*

neu'tron *n.* an atomic particle bearing no electric charge

nev'er *adv.* at no time.—**nev'er-more'** *adv.* never again.—**nevertheless'** *adv.* for all that

new *adj.* 1. fresh, not existing before, as *a new style.* 2. recently come or made, as *a new hat, a new arrival.* 3. different, another, as *Try a new nib.* 4. unfamiliar, as *She is new to the job.*—**newfan'gled** (nū-fang'gld) *adj.* of new fashion.—**new'ly** *adv.*—**new'ness** *n.*—**new Australian** an immigrant, usually non-British, who seeks or obtains Australian citizenship.—**new moon** the moon in its first quarter.—**the new world** America

Compare: novel, recent, modern, fresh, youthful

Note: New is often used joined to another word, as *new-comer, new-born, new-laid, new-made*

Newfound'land *n.* 1. a province on Canada's eastern seaboard. 2. a large breed of dog

news (nūz) *n.* a report of recent happenings, fresh information.—**news'boy** *n.* a boy who sells newspapers.—**news'paper** *n.* printed sheets of news.—**news'-reel** *n.* a short reel of film showing topical events.—**news'vendor** *n.* a newspaper seller

Note: News has no plural

newt *n.* a small amphibious animal resembling a lizard

next *adj.* 1. nearest, as *the next house.* 2. immediately following, as *the next day.*—*adv.* immediately after, as *What happened next?*—**next-door** 1. in the next house. 2. very near, as *lying is next door to cheating.* —**next-of-kin** *n.* the nearest relative(s)

nib *n.* a pen-point

nib'ble *v.* to take little bites.—*n.*—**nib'bling** *pres. part.*

nice (nīs) *adj.* 1. pleasing, agreeable, kind. 2. hard to please. 3. careful, exact, as *nice habits.* 4. exact, very small, as *a nice distinction.*—**ni'cer** *comp.*—**ni'cest** *super.*—**nice'ly** *adv.*—**ni'cety** *n.* 1. exactness. 2. detail.—**ni'ceties** *pl.*

Compare: choice, fine, neat, tasteful, exact, precise

niche (nich) *n.* a hollow place in a wall for a statue

nick *n.* a notch cut or broken out of something.—*v.*—**in the nick of time** just in time

nick'el *n.* 1. a silver-white metal. 2. in U.S. a five-cent piece

nick'name *n.* a name added to, or replacing a person's real name

nic'otine (teen) *n.* a poison contained in tobacco-leaves

niece (nees) *n.* a brother's or sister's daughter. —**neph'ew** *masc.*

nig'gard *n.* a stingy person.—**nig'gardly** *adj.* and *adv.*

nig'ger *n.* 1. an offensive word for a negro. 2. a dark brown colour

nig'gling *adj.* fussy over small details

nigh (nī) *adj. adv. prep.* near.—**next** *super.*

night (nīt) *n.* 1. the time of darkness between sunset and sunrise. 2. darkness.—**night'fall** *n.* the coming of darkness.—**night'ingale** *n.* a bird which usually sings at night.—**night'ly** *adj.* happening every night.—*adv.* every night.—**night'mare** *n.* a bad dream.—**night-safe** *n.* a safe in the outer wall of a bank which can be used by customers at night

nil *n.* nothing

nim'ble *adj.* quick and active.—**nim'bly** *adv.*

nine (nīn) *n. adj.* one more than eight.—**nine'pins** *n.pl.* skittles.—**nineteen'** *n. adj.* nine and ten.—**nineteenth'** *n. adj.*—**nine'tieth** *adj.*—**nine'ty** *n. adj.* nine times ten.—**ninth** (nīnth) *n. adj.* one more than eighth.—**a nine days' wonder** an event that causes excitement for a short time only

nin'ny *n.* a fool, stupid person.—**nin'nies** *pl.*

nip *v.* 1. to pinch sharply. 2. to check the growth of plants by nipping the buds.—*n.* a sharp pinch.—**nip'ping** *pres. part.*—**nipped** *p.t.* and *p. part.*—**nip'pers** *n.pl.* pincers.—**to nip in the bud** to stop something in its early stages

nip'ple *n.* a teat

ni'trate *n.* a salt formed from nitric acid and an alkali

ni'trogen (nī'tro-jen) *n.* one of the gases making up the air.—**nitrog'enous** (nī-troj'en-us) *adj.*

no *adj.* not any, as *We have no string.*—*adv.* not so, as *Are you ill? No.*—*n.* a vote, or voter, against, as *The noes have won*

nobil'ity *n.* 1. noble character or rank. 2. a group of people holding special rank

no'ble *adj.* 1. of high character, rank or birth. 2. fine, splendid.—*n.* a man of high rank.—**no'bleman** *n.* a noble—**no'blemen** *pl.*—**no'bly** *adv.*

no'body *n.* 1. no person. 2. a person of no importance.—**no'bodies** *pl.*

noctur'nal *adj.* of the night

nod *v.* 1. to bow the head slightly. 2. to let the head droop with sleep.—**nod'ding** *pres. part.*—**nod'ded** *p.t.* and *p. part.*

node *n.* a knot on a root or branch.—**no'dal** *adj.*

nod'ule *n.* a small lump, esp. on a plant stem or root

noise (noiz) *n.* 1. a sound. 2. unpleasant sounds.—*v.* to spread news.—**noise'less** *adj.*—**nois'ily** *adv.* in a noisy way.—**nois'iness** *n.* being noisy

Compare: din, clamour, tumult, uproar, roar, clatter, hubbub, outcry, racket, rattle. *Contrast:* peace, stillness, silence, quiet, calm

noi'some *adj.* disgusting

noi'sy (noi'zi) *adj.* 1. making a noise, as *a noisy form.* 2. full of noise, as *a noisy street.*—**noi'sier** *comp.*—**noi'siest** *sup.*

no'mad *n.* a member of a tribe that wanders from pasture to pasture.—**nomad'ic** *adj.*

nom'inal *adj.* 1. not real, existing only in name, as *They pay a nominal rent of £5 a year.* 2. consisting of names, as *a nominal roll.*—**nom'inally** *adv.*

nom'inate *v.* 1. to name as candidate. 2. to appoint.—**nom'inating** *pres. part.*—**nomina'tion** (-ā'shun) *n.*—**nominee'** *n.* a person nominated

non-com'batant *n.* a person who does not fight in war-time

non-commis'sioned (non-kom-ish'und) *adj.* without a commission.—**non-commissioned officer** a sergeant or corporal

non-commit'tal *adj.* saying neither yes nor no

non-conduc'tor *n.* a substance that does not easily conduct heat, electricity, etc.

nonconform'ist *n.* a person not conforming to the established church.—**nonconform'ity** *n.* refusal to conform

non'descript *adj.* not easily described, indefinite, as *a nondescript colour*

none (nun) *adj.* no, as *none other than the king.*—*pron.* no one, as *We waited, but none came.*—*adv.* in no way, as *He is none the worse for his fall*

nonen'tity *n.* 1. a person of no importance. 2. something which does not exist.—**nonen'tities** *pl.*

nonplussed' *adj.* puzzled

non'sense *n.* foolish words or acts or ideas.—**nonsen'sical** *adj.*

nook *n.* a sheltered corner

noon (nōōn) *n.* midday.—**noon'day** *n.*—*adj.*—**noon'tide** *n. adj.* noon

noose (nōōs) *n.* 1. a running loop which tightens when the rope is pulled. 2. a snare.—*v.*

nor'mal *adj.* usual, regular.—*n.* a line at right angles to another.—**nor'mally** *adv.*

north *n.* 1. the direction to your left as you face the rising sun. 2. the part of the world, of a country, etc., towards this point.—*adj.* towards the north.—*adv.* in the north.—**north-east'** *n. adj. adv.* between north and east.—**north-east'erly** *adj.*—**north'erly** *adj.* towards or from the north.—**north'ern** *adj.*—**north'ward** *adj. adv.* towards the north.—**north-west'** *n. adj. adv.* between north and west.—**north-west'erly** *adj.*—**north-west'ern** *adj.*

nose (nōz) *n.* 1. the part of the face above the mouth. 2. the sense of smell, as *A cat has a good nose for mice.* 3. the prow of a boat.—*v.* to smell, to discover.—**no'sing** *pres. part.*—**nose'dive** *n.* a swift downward plunge by aircraft.—**nose'gay** *n.* a posy.—**no'sey** very inquisitive.—**to pay through the nose** to pay a very high price.—**to turn up one's nose at** to despise

nos'tril *n.* one of the two openings of the nose

not *adv.* *Not* is used in saying "no" and to

express the opposite of the word following as *Do not run, I am not hot*

no'table *adj.* remarkable.—*n.* an important person.—**no'tably** *adv.*

Compare: noted, remarkable, distinguished, prominent, memorable, important. *Contrast:* unknown, common, ordinary

no'tary *n.* a public officer who draws up deeds, etc.—**no'taries** *pl.*

nota'tion (-tā'shun) *n.* signs used to represent numbers, quantities, etc.

notch *n.* a nick, a deep v-shaped cut in a stick etc.—*v.*—**not'ches** *pl.*

note *n.* 1. a sign standing for a musical sound. 2. a single tone. 3. a short letter, as *a note of invitation.* 4. a remark, short explanation, as *We took notes of the speech.* 5. fame, reputation, as *a man of note.*—*v.* 1. to observe. 2. to write down.—**no'ting** *pres. part.*—**no'ted** *adj.* well-known.—**note'worthy** *adj.* remarkable

noth'ing (nuth'ing) *n.* not anything

no'tice (nō'tis) *n.* 1. a warning, as *A visitor arrived at short notice.* 2. an announcement, bill. 3. attention, as *Take no notice of him.*—*v.* 1. to see, observe, as *Have you noticed my new book?* 2. to speak about.—**no'ticing** *pres. part.*—**no'ticeable** *adj.* easily noticed.—**no'ticeably** *adv.*

notifica'tion (-kā'shun) *n.* notice

no'tify *v.* to announce, give notice of, as *We notified the police of the theft.*—**no'tifying** *pres. part.*—**no'tified** *p.t.* and *p. part.*

no'tion (-shun) *n.* 1. an idea, opinion. 2. fancy

notori'ety *n.* bad fame

noto'rious (nō-to'ri-us) *adj.* well-known for something bad, as *a notorious gangster*

notwithstand'ing *adv.* all the same, nevertheless.—*prep.* in spite of, as *We had games notwithstanding the rain*

nou'gat (nōō'gah, nug'at) *n.* a sweet containing nuts

nought (nawt) *n.* 1. nothing, as *Our plans came to nought.* 2. zero

noun (nown) *n.* a word used as a name of a person, an idea, or a thing. *Tom, chair, home, speed, pride* are *nouns*

nour'ish (nur'ish) *v.* 1. to feed. 2. to keep up, maintain.—**nour'ishment** *n.* food

nov'el *adj.* new, strange.—*n.* a long prose story usually about imaginary people and their actions.—**nov'elist** *n.* a writer of novels.—**nov'elty** *n.* newness, something new. —**nov'elties** *pl.*

Compare: strange, recent

Novem'ber *n.* the eleventh month

nov'ice (nov'is) *n.* 1. a beginner, one new to anything. 2. a member of a religious order who has not yet taken full vows. —**novit'iate, novic'iate** (nov-ish'i-āt) *n.* novice's period of trial

now *adv.* 1. at the present time, as *I am now feeling better.* 2. immediately, as *Do it now or it will be too late.*—**just now** a moment ago.—**now'adays** in these times.—**now and again, now and then** sometimes

no'where *adv.* in no place

nox'ious (nok'shus) *adj.* harmful, dangerous

noz'zle *n.* a pointed piece attached to the end of a hose-pipe, etc.

nu'clear (-kli-ar) *adj.* 1. in a nucleus. 2. caused by nuclear fission.—**nu'clear energy** energy released from the nuclei of atoms, atomic energy.—**nu'clear fission** the breaking up of an atom with the release of an enormous amount of energy

nu'cleus *n.* 1. a centre, kernel. 2. a central part around which others gather. 3. (science) the main part of an atom.—**nu'clei** (nū'kli-ī) *pl.*

nude *adj.* naked, bare.—**nu'dity** *n.*

nudge (nuj) *v.* to touch slightly with the elbow.—*n.*—**nudg'ing** *pres. part.*

nug'get *n.* a lump, esp. a rough lump of native gold

nui'sance (nū'sans) *n.* something unpleasant, annoying, troublesome

Compare: offence, plague, pest. *Contrast:* delight, benefit, blessing

null *adj.* of no value, empty.—**nullifica'tion** (-kā'shun) *n.* making null.—**null'ify** *v.* to make of no effect.—**null'ity** *n.* being null

nulla-nulla *n.* 1. an aborigine club. 2. a small marsupial

numb (num) *adj.* without feeling, esp. because of cold.—*v.* to make numb.—**numb'ness** *n.*

num'ber *n.* 1. a word telling how many, as *Two hundred.* 2. a numeral, as 5, 1000. 3. sum, total, as *Our numbers have gone up.* 4. large or small quantity, as *We saw a number of rabbits.* 5. singular or plural. 6. an issue of a magazine, as *The summer number of "Punch."*—*v.* 1. to give a number to, as *The pages are numbered.* 2. to amount to.—**num'berless** *adj.* countless

nu'meral *n.* a figure or sign standing for a number, as *IX, C,* 42, 1.—*adj.* expressing number

nu'merate *v.* to count.—**nu'merator** *n.* the upper number in a fraction.—**numer'ical** *adj.* having to do with numbers

nu'merous *adj.* very many

nun *n.* a woman living in a convent, under religious vows.—**monk** *masc.*—**nun'nery** *n.* a convent of nuns

nup'tial (nup'shal) *adj.* of marriage or a wedding.—*n.pl.* a marriage

nurse *n.* 1. a person trained to take care of the sick. 2. a person who takes care of children.—*v.* 1. to act as nurse. 2. to tend, hold closely.—**nurs'ing** *pres. part.*—**nurse'maid** *n.* a woman who helps to bring up young children.—**nurs'ing-home** *n.* a privately owned building where patients are nursed

nur'sery *n.* 1. a room for children. 2. a place where young plants are grown.—**nur'-**

series *pl.*—**nur'seryman** *n.* a gardener.—**nurse'ling** *n.* a baby.—**nursery school** a school for children aged 2 to 5 years

nur'ture *n.* bringing-up, education.—*v.* to bring up, train

nut *n.* 1. a fruit with a hard shell and a kernel. 2. a small block with a hole to be screwed on a bolt.—**nut crack'er** *n.*

nut'meg *n.* the hard seed of an East Indian tree, used for flavouring

nu'triment *n.* food, nourishment.—**nutri'tion** (nū-trish'un) *n.* food.—**nutri'tious** *adj.* nourishing.—**nu'tritive** *adj.*

nuz'zle *v.* to press with the nose, to nestle.—**nuz'zling** *pres. part.*

ny'lon *n.* a man-made fibre.—**ny'lons** *n.pl.* stockings made of nylon

nymph (nimf) *n.* a maiden, in legends, living in the sea, woods, mountains, etc.

O

oaf (ōf) *n.* a lout, clumsy person.—**oaves** or **oafs** *pl.*—**oaf'ish** *adj.*

oak (ōk) *n.* several kinds of forest tree.—*adj.*—**oak'en** *adj.*

oar (ōr) *n.* a long pole with a blade used in rowing.—*v.* to row.—**oars'man** *n.* a rower

oa'sis *n.* a fertile spot in the desert.—**oa'ses** (ō-ā'seez) *pl.*

oast'-house *n.* a kiln for drying hops

oat (ōt) *n.* a grain used for food.—**oat'en** *adj.*—**oat'meal** *n.* rolled oats

oath (ōth) *n.* 1 a solemn statement of truth, calling on God as witness. 2. a swear word

ob'durate *adj.* stubborn, hard

obe'dience (ō-bee'di-ens) *n.* doing what one is told to do.—**obe'dient** *adj.*—**obe'diently** *adv.*

obei'sance (ō-bā'sans) *n.* 1. a low bow. 2. homage, respect

ob'elisk *n.* a tapering stone shaft, four-sided, with a top like a pyramid

obese' (ō-bees') *adj.* very fat.—**obe'sity** *n.*

obey (ō-bā') *v.* to do what one is told

obit'uary *n.* an announcement of a death in a newspaper with a short biography.—**obit'uaries** *pl.*

ob'ject *n.* 1. a thing, something that can be touched or seen. 2. something or someone towards which feeling or action is directed, as *What is the object of our search?* 3. an end, purpose, as *My object in coming is to return this basket.* 4. in grammar, see *Note.*—**object'** *v.* 1. to oppose, give a reason against. 2. to dislike, as *He objects to noise*

Note: The *object* of a verb or preposition is a noun, pronoun, or sentence to which the action of the verb is directed. In the sentence *I sent a letter to my friend, letter* is the object of *sent,* and *my friend* is the object of *to*

objec'tion (-shun) *n.* 1. a reason against. 2. dislike.—**objec'tionable** *adj.* unpleasant

objec'tive *n.* something aimed at.—*adj.* 1. not personal, existing as an object, outside the mind. 2. for grammatical meaning, see *Note* on *object*

obliga'tion (-gā'shun) *n.* 1. duty, as *Every player is under an obligation to keep the rules.* 2. a promise, 3. a feeling bound to return a favour.—**oblig'atory** *adj.* binding, compulsory

oblige' (ō-blij') *v.* 1. to compel. 2. to do a favour, as *Would you oblige me by holding this door open?*—**obli'ging** *adj.* ready to help

oblique' (o-bleek') *adj.* slanting, indirect.—**oblique'ly** *adv.*—**oblique' ang'le** *n.* any angle other than a right angle

oblit'erate *v.* to blot out, destroy.—**oblitera'tion** (-ā'shun) *n.*

obliv'ion *n.* forgetting, being forgotten.—**obliv'ious** *adj.* forgetful, unaware

ob'long *n.* a figure having four straight sides and angles of 90°, longer than it is broad.—*adj.*

obnox'ious (ob-nok'shus) *adj.* offensive, very unpleasant

o'boe *n.* a wood-wind instrument.—**o'boist** *n.* an oboe player

obscene' (ob-seen') *adj.* indecent, disgusting.—**obscen'ity** (ob-sen'i-ti) *n.*

obscure' *adj.* 1. dim, not clear, vague, as *obscure shapes, an obscure sentence.* 2, unnoticed, not known, as *an obscure writer.*—*v.* to conceal, make dim.—**obscu'ring** *pres. part.*—**obscu'rity** *n.* 1. darkness. 2. being unknown

Compare: (with *adj.*)*:* dark, dim, doubtful, hidden, indistinct, unintelligible, vague

ob'sequies (ob'sek-wiz) *n.pl.* funeral ceremony

obse'quious (ob-see'kwi-us) *adj.* slavishly polite

obser'vable (ob-zer'va-bl) *adj.* to be seen

obser'vance (ob-zer'vans) *n.* keeping a law or custom.

obser'vant *adj.* 1. watchful, quick. 2. careful to keep a law, etc.

observa'tion (ob-zer-vā'shun) *n.* 1. habit of noticing, as *Scientists are trained in observation.* 2. being seen, as *to escape observation.* 3. a remark, as *No one made any observation*

obser'vatory (ob-zer'va-tor-i) *n.* a building for observing the stars.—**obser'vatories** *pl.*

observe' (ob-zerv') *v.* 1. to notice. 2. to watch, study, as *He observes birds.* 3. to keep a custom, etc., as *to observe Sunday.* 4. to remark.—**obser'ving** *pres. part.*—**obser'ver** *n.*

obsess' *v.* to haunt, fill the mind.—**obsess'ion** (-shun) *n.*

ob'solete *adj.* out of date, disused, as *Spears are obsolete weapons*

ob'stacle *n.* a hindrance, something in the way

ob'stinacy *n.* being obstinate.—**ob'stinate** *adj.* 1. stubborn. stupidly firm. 2. difficult to cure, as *an obstinate cold*

obstrep'erous *adj.* noisy, unruly

obstruct' *v.* to hinder, block up.—**obstruc'tion** (-shun) *n.* an obstacle.—**obstruc'tive** *adj.* opposing, hindering

obtain' *v.* 1. to get. 2. to be usual, as *Different laws obtain in different countries.*—**obtain'able** *adj.*

obtrude' (ob-trōōd') *v.* to push in where unwanted.—**obtru'ding** *pres. part.*—**obtru'sion** (ob-trōō'zhun) *n.*—**obtru'sive** *adj.*

obtuse' (ob-tūs') *adj.* 1. not sharp or pointed. 2. stupid, slow.—**obtuse' angle** *n.* an angle greater than a right angle.—**obtuse'ly** *adv.*

ob'verse *n.* the side of a coin or medal with the head or chief design

Compare: reverse

ob'viate *v.* to prevent, to clear away, as *The hole is covered to obviate danger.*—**ob'viating** *pres. part.*

ob'vious *adj.* clear, plain, evident.—**ob'viously** *adv.*

occa'sion (o-kā'zhun) *n.* 1. an opportunity, as *He seized the occasion to score.* 2. reason, cause, as *There is no occasion for a quarrel.* 3. the time when a thing happens. 4. a special event, as *A wedding is a great occasion.*—*v.* to cause.—**occa'sional** *adj.* happening now and then.—**occa'sionally** *adv.* now and then.—**to rise to the occasion** to deal successfully with an emergency

oc'cident (ok'si-dent) *n.* the west

oc'cupant *n.* a person occupying, a person in possession, as *The house has no occupant now*

occupation' (-pā'shun) *n.* 1. occupying, seizing. 2. employment

oc'cupy *v.* 1. to take possession, as *The enemy occupied the village.* 2. to live in, as *They occupy only two rooms.* 3. to hold, as *to occupy a position.* 4. to employ, as *School occupies most of our time.*—he **oc'cupies.**—**oc'cupying** *pres. part.*—**oc'cupied** *p.t.* and *p. part.*—**to occupy oneself with** to be busy with

occur' *v.* 1. to happen. 2. to come to mind. 3. to be found, as *These words occur on the first page.*—**occur'ring** *pres. part.*—**occurred'** *p.t.* and *p. part.*—**occur'rence** *n.* event

o'cean (ō'shun) *n.* 1. the salt water covering nearly three-fourths of the earth's surface. 2. one of the large divisions of this.—**ocean'ic** (ō-she-an'ik) *adj.*

oc'elot (os'ilot) *n.* a South American wild cat

o'chre (ō'ker) *n.* a brownish yellow paint

oct'agon *n.* a plane figure with eight sides and eight angles.—**octag'onal** *adj.*

oc'tave *n.* 1. a sound eight notes higher than another. 2. the eight notes taken together

octa'vo *n.* a size of book in which each sheet is folded into eight leaves

Octo'ber *n.* the tenth month

oc'topus *n.* a soft-bodied sea-animal with eight arms covered with suckers.—**oc'topuses** *pl.*

oc'ular *adj.* of the eye, seen.—**oc'ulist** *n.* a person who treats eye-diseases

odd *adj.* 1. not even, not divisible by two, as *Five is an odd number.* 2. with some left over, as *We number a hundred odd.* 3. not part of a set, as *an odd glove.* 4. strange, queer, 5. casual, unconnected, as *odd jobs.*—**od'dity** *n.* 1. strangeness. 2. a queer person.—**odd'ly** *adv.*

Compare: strange, rare, queer, eccentric, fantastic, peculiar, quaint, uncommon, unusual

odds *n.pl.* 1. difference, balance. 2. the advantage to one of two competitors.—**odds and ends,** bits left over.—**the odds are that,** it is likely that

ode (ōd) *n.* a poem of lofty style and tone

o'dious *adj.* hateful.—**o'dium** *n.* 1. hatred. 2. blame

o'dorous *adj.* giving out a smell

o'dour *n.* a smell

od'yssey *n.* a long adventurous journey

of (ov) *prep.* *Of* has a great variety of meanings. A few are shown in these phrases.—*A book of poems. Tired of work. A yard of silk. The reign of King George. A man of strong will. We know him of old. The death of Caesar. What do you think of this? The top of the tree. One of us*

off *adv.* away, as *We went off quickly.* —*prep.* away from, as *I fell off the tree.*—*adj.* 1. in cricket, on right of batsman, as *the off stump.* 2. of vehicles, animals, etc. on the farther side from the edge of the road, on the right. See near.—**badly off** poor.—**be off!** go away!—**off and on** now and then.—**off colour** not feeling well.—**off shore** not far from the shore.—**off'shore** (as *an offshore wind*) from the shore.—**right off** well away from.—**well off** rich

off'al *n.* 1. waste parts of meat. 2. refuse, scraps

offence' *n.* 1. offending. 2. being angry, hurt. 3. attacking, as *The tank is a weapon of offence.* 4. wrong-doing, as *Stealing is an offence*

offend' *v.* 1. to displease. 2. to do wrong.—**offen'der** *n.*

offen'sive *adj.* 1. unpleasant, disgusting, as *an offensive smell.* 2. attacking.—*n.* an attack

of'fer *v.* 1. to present for acceptance or refusal, as *I offered my services.* 2. to attempt, as *He did not offer to move.* 3. to present itself.—*n.* a bid, offering.—

of'fering *n.* a gift, contribution.—**of'fertory** *n.* a collection in a church service
offhand' *adv.* without thought or preparation. —*adj.* careless
off'ice (of'is) *n.* 1. a public position. 2. a duty, job. 3. a place for conducting business. 4. a form of worship.—*pl.* parts of a house given up to household work.—**of'fice-boy** *n.* a boy doing small jobs in an office
off'icer (of'i-ser) *n.* 1. a person holding public office, as *medical officer*. 2. person in command, in army, navy, or air force
offic'ial (o-fish'al) *n.* a person holding a public office.—*adj.* 1. belonging to an office. 2. having authority.—**offi'cially** *adv.*—**offi'ciate** (o-fish'i-āt) *v.* to perform a duty
offic'ious (o-fish'us) *adj.* meddlesome, too ready with advice
off'ing *n.* the distant part of the sea, seen from the shore.—**in the offing** likely to happen
off'set *n.* 1. side branch. 2. balance. 3. beginning.—*v.* to set off, balance against
off'shoot *n.* a branch, a branching off
off'side *adj.* (football etc.) of a player, in an illegal position on the field of play
off'spring *n.* children, descendants
oft'en *adv.* many times
o'gle *v.* to make eyes at.—*n.*
o'gre (ō'ger) *n.* a man-eating monster.—**o'gress** *fem.*
ohm (ōm) *n.* a unit of electrical resistance
oil *n.* a thick greasy liquid obtained from various plants, animals, substances and minerals.—*v.* to put oil on.—**oil'cloth** *n.* canvas covered with paint, used as floor-covering.—**oil paints** colours mixed with linseed oil.—**oil'skin** *n.* cloth made waterproof with oil.—**oil'y** *adj.*—**to pour oil on troubled waters** to smooth out a quarrel
oint'ment *n.* a greasy substance for healing or softening the skin
O.K. *adv.* correct, all right
ok'ra *n.* an African plant whose pods are used as a vegetable
old (ōld) *adj.* 1. not young, having lived or existed a long time. 2. worn, as *old boots.* 3. former, as *an old pupil.* 4. of age, as *two years old.*—**ol'der, el'der** *comp.*—**ol'dest, el'dest** *sup.* see *Note.*—**ol'den** *adj.* old.—**old'en days** times of long ago.—**old-fash'ioned** *adj.* 1. fond of old ways. 2. out of date

Compare: ancient, antique, aged, olden, venerable, timeworn. *Contrast:* new, modern, novel, recent, young, youthful

Note: In modern English the forms *older, oldest* are used instead of *elder, eldest*, except in special cases, such as *the elder son. Elder* cannot be followed by *than*

ol'igarchy (ol'i-gark-i) *n.* government by a few persons
ol'ive (ol'iv) *n.* an evergreen tree, the fruit of which is used for making olive-oil.—*adj.* grey-green.—**ol'ive branch** *n.* emblem of peace.—**ol'ive oil** oil pressed from olives
Olympic Games *n.pl.* international athletic contests held every four years since 1896
o'mega *n.* the last letter of the Greek alphabet
om'elet, om'elette *n.* a dish made of eggs beaten, seasoned and fried
o'men *n.* a sign of good or bad fortune to come
om'inous *adj.* threatening evil
omis'sion (ō-mish'un) *n.* 1. omitting. 2. something left out
omit' *v.* to leave out, neglect.—**omit'ting** *pres. part.*—**omit'ted** *p.t.* and *p. part.*
om'nibus *n.* a bus, vehicle for taking passengers between stages on a route.—*adj.* containing several things.—**om'nibuses** *pl.*
omni'potence *n.* complete power.—**omni'potent** *adj.* all powerful
omnipres'ent *adj.* present everywhere at once
omnis'cience (om-nish'ens om-ni'si-ens) *n.* knowing everything.—**omnis'cient** *adj.*
omniv'orous *adj.* eating all foods
on *prep.* as *a man on a horse.*—*adv.* as *Put your coat on.*—*adj.* as *the on side*
once (wuns) *adv.* 1. one time, as *Jump once more.* 2. formerly, in the past, as *There was once a wicked king.*—*conj.* as soon as, as *Once you have learned to row, you will like it.*—**at once** 1. immediately, as *Do this at once.* 2. at the same time, as *Both of them spoke at once.*—**all at once** suddenly. —**more than once** often.—**not once** never.—**once and for all** once only.—**once in a while** now and then.—**once upon a time** a time long ago
one (wun) *adj.* 1. a single, as *one shoe.* 2. united, as *one nation with one purpose.* 3. only, as *Tom scored the one goal.*—*n.* the figure 1.—*pron.* a single example, as *one of us.*—**oneself** an emphatic or reflexive form of one.—**one by one** singly. —**one'-sid'ed** *adj.* 1. having one good side. 2. favouring one side rather than another. —**one-way traffic** traffic in one direction only
on'ion (un'iun) *n.* a bulb with a strong smell and taste, used as a vegetable
on'looker *n.* a spectator, person looking on
on'ly (ōn'li) *adj.* one, as *my only brother.*—*adv.* nothing more than, as *I have only sixpence, It is only an owl hooting.*—*conj.* but, as *I would have come, only it rained.*—**if only** I wish, as *if only it would be sunny*
on'set *n.* a violent attack
on'side (games) opposite of **off'side**
on'slaught (on'slawt) *n.* a fierce attack
o'nus (ō'nus) *n.* responsibility, as *the onus for taking care of the puppy falls on me*
on'wards *adv.* 1. forward. 2. in advance
on'yx *n.* a semi-precious stone
ooze *n.* soft mud, slime.—*v.* to pass slowly through.—**oo'zing** *pres. part.*
o'pal *n.* a milky-white and bluish gem with

coloured reflections.—**opales'cent** (ō-pal-es'ent)*adj.*

opaque' (ō-pāk') *adj.* not transparent, which cannot be seen through

o'pen *adj.* 1. not shut or blocked up. 2. without lid or door. 3. spread out, as *an open book*. 4. public, for anyone to attend, as *an open meeting*. 5. prepared to consider as *open to new ideas*. 6. sincere, outspoken.—*v.* 1. to set open, unclose, as *open the window*. 2. to lay bare, disclose. 3. to begin, as *school opens soon*.—*n.* clear space.—**o'pener** *n.*—**o'pening** *n.* 1. hole, gap. 2. beginning. 3. good chance.—**o'penly** *adv.*—**o'penness** *n.* frankness.—**open cheque** an uncrossed cheque.—**open air** outdoors.—**open-handed** open-hearted, generous. —**open-eyed** watchful. —**open-minded** fair, unprejudiced.—**open secret** a secret widely shared.—**to lay open** to disclose.—**to keep open house** to be very hospitable

op'era *n.* a musical drama.—**grand opera** full scale opera with a tragic story.—**light opera** amusing and romantic opera

op'erate *v.* 1. to work, be active. 2. to influence. 3. to perform operations.—**op'erating** *pres. part.*

operat'ic *adj.* of or like opera

opera'tion (-ā'shun) *n.* 1. working, the way a thing works. 2. surgical treatment. 3. a military movement.—**op'erative** *adj.* working.—*n.* a mechanic.—**op'erator** *n.* one who operates

Compare: action, effect, force, performance, result

operet'ta *n.* a short light opera

opin'ion *n.* what one thinks about something, belief, judgment.—**opin'ionated** *adj.* stubborn in holding an opinion

o'pium *n.* a drug used for causing sleep and easing pain

oposs'um *n.* a small American animal which lives in trees and carries its young in a pouch

oppo'nent *n.* an adversary, person on the opposite side in a fight, etc.—*adj.* opposing

Compare: antagonist, adversary, competitor, rival, foe, enemy. *Contrast:* friend, ally, supporter

op'portune *adj.* favourable, convenient.—**opportu'nity** *n.* a favourable time.—**opportu'nities** *pl.*

oppose' (op-ōz') *v.* 1. to act or speak against, resist, as *to oppose an enemy*. 2. to set against. 3. to contrast, as *Kindness is opposed to cruelty*.—**oppo'sing** *pres. part.*—**oppo'ser** *n.*

Compare: check, obstruct, hinder, contend with, resist, defy, repel, dispute, withstand

op'posite (op'o-zit) *adj.* 1. facing, as *The house opposite*. 2. contrary, as *in the opposite direction*.—*n.* contrary thing or person.—**opposi'tion** (-zi'shun) *n.* 1. resistance. 2. the party or parties opposed to the one in power

oppress' *v.* 1. to govern harshly. 2. to weigh down.—he **oppress'es**.—**oppress'ion** *n.* 1. harsh treatment. 2. heaviness.—**oppres'sive** *adj.* 1. heavy. 2. hard to bear.—**oppres'sor** *n.*

opt *v.* to choose.—**to opt out** to decide not to take part

op'tic *adj.* of the eye.—**op'tical** *adj.* of the eye, or sight or optics.—**opti'cian** (op-tish'an) *n.* maker or seller of eye-glasses, etc.—**op'tical illusion** *n.* an illusion deceiving the eye.—**optics** the study of light and sight

op'timism *n.* a disposition to look on the bright side, belief that good will be stronger than evil.—**op'timist** *n.*—**optimist'ic** *adj.*

op'tion (-shun) *n.* 1. choice. 2. the thing chosen.—**op'tional** *adj.* not compulsory

op'ulence *n.* wealth, abundance.—**op'ulent** *adj.* rich

o'pus (ō'pus) *n.* a work, a musical composition

or *conj.* *Or* usually suggests a choice, as *Will you have tea or coffee? Sooner or later*. Sometimes *or* explains, as *an ovum, or egg*. For *either . . . or*, see **either**

or'acle *n.* 1. a place where the gods were consulted. 2. the answers given. 3. a very wise person.—**orac'ular** *adj.* wise and mysterious

or'al *adj.* 1. spoken as *an oral examination*. 2. of the mouth.—**or'ally** *adv.*

or'ange (or'inj) *n.* 1. a reddish-yellow juicy fruit. 2. the tree. 3. its colour when ripe

orangeade' *n.* a sweet drink made from orange juice

ora'tion (-ā'shun) *n.* a formal speech.—**or'ator** *n.* a public speaker.—**orator'ical** *adj.*

orator'io *n.* a religious musical composition.—**orator'ios** *pl.*

or'atory *n.* eloquent public speech

or'atory *n.* a small chapel

orb *n.* 1. a globe, sphere. 2. the eye

orb'it *n* the curving track of a heavenly body or satellite moving round another body.—**or'bital** *adj.*

or'chard *n.* a place where fruit-trees are grown

or'chestra (or'kes-tra) *n.* 1. a group of musicians playing instrumental music. 2. the place they occupy in a theatre, etc.—**orches'tral** *adj.*

or'chid (or'kid) *n.* a flower of unusual shape and colours

or'dain' *v.* 1. to admit to the Christian ministry. 2. to fix, decide

ordeal' (or-deel') *n.* an experience that tests courage

or'der *n.* 1. the way things follow each other, as *alphabetical order*. 2. good arrangement. 3. command, instructions, as *by order of the general.* 4. peaceful condition, as *Order reigned again after the war.* 5. a rank, class, group. 6. a religious or other society.—*v.* 1. to arrange. 2. to command, instruct.—**or'derliness** *n.* being orderly.—**or'derly** *adj.* 1. tidy. 2. well-behaved.—*n.* a soldier following an officer to carry orders.—**in order that** so that, so as to.—**made to order** made as ordered.—**out of order** 1. not working. 2. against the rules

ord'inal *adj.* showing position in a series, as *Third is an ordinal number*
Contrast: cardinal

or'dinance *n.* a rule, decree

or'dinarily *adv.* usually

or'dinary *adj.* 1. usual. 2. commonplace, dull

ordina'tion (-ā'shun) *n.* ordaining, admission as minister to the church

ord'nance *n.* guns, cannon, military stores

ore *n.* a mineral substance containing metal

or'gan *n.* 1. a musical instrument with pipes worked by bellows, and played by keys. 2. part of a plant or animal doing a certain work. 3. a means of action, e.g. a newspaper.—**organ'ic** *adj.* of the bodily organs, having organs.—**or'ganism** *n.* 1. a body made up of organs. 2. a system, a society working together.—**organ'ic chemistry** the chemistry of the carbon compounds

or'gandie *n.* very fine muslin

or'ganist *n.* a person who plays an organ

organisa'tion (-shun) *n.* 1. a group or society working together. 2. an arrangement of separate parts into working order.—**or'ganise** *v.* to arrange in working order.—**organising** *pres. part.*—**or'ganiser** *n.*

or'gy (or'ji) *n.* a drunken revel.—**or'gies** *pl.*

o'rient *n.* the East.—**orient'al** *adj.* eastern

or'ifice (or'i-fis) *n.* an opening, hole

or'igin (or'i-jin) *n.* the beginning, start

or'iginal (or-ij'ina-l) *adj.* 1. first, earliest. 2. new, not copied. 3. thinking or acting for oneself.—*n.* a thing from which another is copied.—**orig'inally** *adv.* in the beginning.—**original'ity** *n.* being original

orig'inate (or-ij'in-āt)) *v.* 1. to begin. 2. to bring into existence.—**orig'inating** *pres. part.*—**orig'inator** *n.*

Or'lon *n.* the trade name for a man-made fibre similar to nylon

or'molu (or'mo-loo) *n.* gilded bronze

or'nament *n.* decoration, something to add beauty.—**ornament'al** *adj.*

ornate' *adj.* richly decorated

ornithol'ogy (-ji) *n.* the study of birds.—**ornithol'ogist** *n.*

or'phan (or'fan) *n.* a child whose parents have died.—*adj.*—**or'phanage** *n.* a home for orphans

or'thodox *adj.* 1. holding generally accepted opinions. 2. conventional, usual.—**or'thodoxy** *n.*

orthopae'dic (-pee') *adj.* concerning the treatment of deformed bones

os'cillate (os'i-lāt) *v.* 1. to swing to and fro. 2. to vary between extremes. 3. in wireless, to set up wave motion.—**os'cilla'tion** (-lā'shun) *n.*

o'sier (ō'zier) *n.* a kind of willow used for basket-making

osmo'sis *n.* the flow of a liquid through a porous membrane

os'sify *v.* to change into bone, to harden

osten'sible *adj.* professed, but not real.—**osten'sibly** *adv.* apparently

ostenta'tion (-tā'shun) *n.* show, a display meant to impress.—**ostenta'tious** (-tā'-shus) *adj.* showing off

ost'ler (os'ler) *n.* a stableman who looks after horses

os'trich *n.* a large, swift-running African bird with valuable tail-feathers

oth'er (uTH'er) *adj.* 1. different, as *There is no other road.* 2. additional, as *Have you other sums to do?* 3. opposite, as *the other bank of the river.*—*pron.* other person or thing, as *Here is one ball, where is the other?* —*adv.* otherwise, as *He cannot do other than volunteer.*—**every other**, every second, as *every other day*

oth'erwise (uTH'erwīz) *adv.* 1. in a different way, as *I could not act otherwise.* 2. in other ways, as *It is cloudy, but otherwise pleasant.*—*conj.* else, or, as *Hurry, otherwise you will miss the bus*

Ot'toman *adj.* of the Turks—*n.* 1. a Turk. 2. a kind of couch

ot'ter *n.* a fish-eating water animal

ought (awt) *v.* thou *oughtest*, he, she, they *ought*. This verb has no past tense, past or present participle. Its only negative form is *ought not*, as *I ought not to do it, I ought not to have done it.* Avoid the common mistakes, *hadn't ought* and *didn't ought*

ounce (owns) *n.* 1. a weight, the twelfth of the troy pound, sixteenth of the avoirdupois pound. 2. an animal resembling the leopard

our *pron.* possessive form of **we**, as in *That is our risk.* When used alone, *our* becomes *ours*, as *The risk is ours.*—**my** *sing.*—

ours, see **our**.—**mine** *sing.*

ourselves' (our-selvz') *pron. emphatic* and *reflexive* form of **we**, as in *We ourselves are to blame* and *We blamed ourselves severely.*—**myself** *sing.*

oust *v.* to put out, drive out

out *adv.* 1. coming from, away, as *We ran out.* 2. not indoors, as *Father is out.* 3. not alight, as *His pipe is out.* 4. open, as *The buds are out.* 5. made known, as *The results are out.*—**out of** *prep.* 1. from among, as *He was chosen out of 20 boys.* 2. away from, as *out of hearing.* 3. without, as *out of money.*—**out of date** not in use any more.—**out of pocket** losing money.—**out of the way** 1. off the general route. 2. unusual

Note: Out is used after many verbs to

express special meanings. Some of these are—*Speak out, call out,* speak clearly, *clear out,* remove rubbish (or go away) *break out,* said of a rash, a rebellion, etc., *find out,* discover, *pick out,* choose, *fight it out,* fight to a finish

out'back *n.* (Aus.) uncultivated remote inland country

out'board *adj.* outside a ship or boat.—**out'board motor** a portable engine driving a boat from over the stern

out'break *n.* 1. a breaking out of war, anger, disease, etc. 2. a riot

out'burst *n.* a bursting forth, esp. of heated words

out'cast *n.* a homeless, friendless person.—*adj.*

out'come *n.* result

out'cry *n.* a loud clamour, sudden crying out. —**out'cries** *pl.*

outdo' *v.* to surpass, do better.—**outdo'ing** *pres. part.*—**outdid'** *p.t*—**outdone'** *p. part.*

out'door *adj.* in the open air.—**out'doors'** *adv.*

out'er *adj.* on the outside, as *the outer door.*—**out'ermost** *sup.*—**out'er space** the distant parts of the universe

out'fit *n.* equipment, everything necessary for a purpose.—**out'fitter** *n.* 1. a seller of outfits. 2. a seller of men's clothes

outflank' *v.* to get beyond the enemy's flank

outgrow' *v.* to grow too big or too old for.—**outgrew'** *p.t.*—**outgrown'** *p. part.*—**out'-growth** *n.* an offshoot

out'ing *n.* a pleasure-trip

outland'ish *adj.* queer, strange

out'law *n.* a person outside the protection of the law, an exile.—*v.* 1. to make into an outlaw. 2. to declare illegal.—**out'lawry** *n.*

out'lay *n.* expenses, money spent

out'let *n.* a way out

out'line *n.* 1. a line showing the shape of an object or figure. 2. a rough plan, sketch.—*v.* to describe or draw in outline

outlive' (-liv) *v.* to live longer than,—**outliv'ing** *pres. part.*

out'look *n.* 1. view. 2. prospect, what is likely to happen

outnum'ber *v.* to be more numerous than

out'patient *n.* a hospital patient who lives at home and goes to hospital for treatment

out'post *n.* a small body of soldiers on guard outside a camp

out'put (-poot) *n.* the amount produced by factories, etc.

out'rage (out'rāj) *n.* a violent offence, a great insult.—*v.* (out-rāj') to insult.—**outra'geous** (out-rā'jus) *adj.*

out'right (out'rīt) *adv.* 1. entirely, completely, as *He was bowled outright.* 2. once for all. —*adj.* direct

outrun' *v.* to run faster than.—**outrun'ning** *pres. part.*—**outran'** *p.t.*—**outrun** *p. part.*

out'set *n.* beginning, start

out'side *n.* not inside, as *the outside of a house.* —*adj.* on the outside, as *an outside wall.*—*adv.* outdoors, as *Take the dog outside.*—*prep.* out of, as *We are now outside enemy country*

out'size *adj.* of clothes, larger than the average sizes

out'skirts *n.pl.* the districts on the edge of a town

outspo'ken *adj.* fearless in speech, frank

outstand'ing *adj.* 1. noticeable, important. 2. of an account, unsettled

out'stay *v.* to stay longer than.—**to outstay one's welcome** to stay too long, until one is no longer welcome

outstretched' *adj.* stretched out

outstrip' *v.* 1. to pass, run faster than. 2. to do better than.—**outstrip'ping** *pres. part.*—**outstripped'** *p.t.* and *p.part.*

out'ward *adj.* 1. directed towards the outside. 2. appearing on the surface.—*adv.* towards the outside.—**out'wardly** *adv.* on the outside.—**out'ward bound** travelling across the sea to a foreign land.—**outward bound school** an adventure school training teenagers in open-air skills and activities

outweigh' (out-wā') *v.* 1. to weigh more than. 2. to be more important than

outwit' *v.* to be too clever for.—**outwit'ting** *pres. part.*—**outwit'ted** *p.t.* and *p. part.*

outworn' *adj.* 1. worn out. 2. out of date

o'val *adj.* egg-shaped.—*n.* an oval figure or thing

o'vary *n.* 1. a female organ producing eggs or ova. 2. the lower end of the pistil of a flower, containing seeds

ova'tion (-vā'shun) *n.* a burst of applause, an enthusiastic welcome

ov'en (uv'n) *n.* the inside part of a stove for baking, etc.

o'ver *adv.* 1. above, as *He flew over.* 2. across, as *jump over.* 3. finished, as *The concert is over.* 4. too much, as *There is money over.* 5. again, as *twice over.*—*prep.* 1. above, as *He flew over the river.* 2. across, as *He lives over the street.* 3. above in rank, etc., as *He is over* 50 *men.* 4. about, as *worried over money matters.*—*n.* in cricket, a series of six balls.—**over and over** again and again.—**to stand over** to wait.—**to throw over** to abandon

Note: over- before a word often means "too much", as **over-careful, over-eat,** and **over-excite**

o'verall (o'ver-awl) *n.* a loose frock to protect a dress.—*n.pl.* loose trousers to protect a suit

overawe' *v.* to overcome with awe

overbal'ance *v.* 1. to fall, lose one's balance. 2. to outweigh.—**overbal'ancing** *pres. part.*

overbear'ing *adj.* inclined to domineer

o'verboard *adv.* from a ship into the water, as *to jump overboard*

overcast' *adj.* dark, cloudy

overcharge' *v.* 1. to charge too high a price. 2. to overload

o'vercoat *n.* a heavy top coat

overcome' *v*, to conquer, get the better of.—**overcom'ing** *pres. part.*—**overcame'** *p.t.*—**overcome'** *p. part.*

overdo' *v.* 1. to do too much. 2. to cook too much. 3. to overact.—**overdid'** *p.t.*—**overdone'** *p. part.*

o'verdraft *n.* money overdrawn from a bank

overdraw' *v.* 1. to draw from a bank more money than one has there. 2. to exaggerate.—**overdrew'** *p.t.*—**overdrawn'** *p. part.*

overdue' *adj.* which should have arrived, or been paid, but has not

overes'timate *v.* to put the amount or value too high

overflow' *v.* to flow over, to flood.—**o'verflow** *n.* what flows over

overhaul' *v.* 1. to catch up. 2. to examine and repair.—**o'verhaul** *n.*

o'verhead *adj.* placed above.—**overhead'** *adv.* above, in the sky.—*n.pl.* the permanent expenses of running a business, apart from the cost of raw materials and manufacturing

overhear' *v.* to hear without the speaker knowing, to hear by accident.—**overheard'** (ō-ver-herd') *p.t.* and *p. part.*

overjoyed' *adj.* delighted

o'verland *v.* (Aus.) to take across country.—**overland'er** *n.* 1. (hist.) a traveller who made long expeditions with stock from one colony to another. 2. now anyone driving stock over long distances

overlap' *v.* to cover in part, as *slates on a roof overlap.*—**overlap'ping** *pres. part.*—**overlapped'** *p.t.* and *p. part.*

overlay' *v.* to cover with a coating.—**overlaid'** *p.t.* and *p. part.*—**o'verlay** *n.* covering

overload' *v.* to load too heavily

overlook' *v.* 1. to see over, have a view from above. 2. not to notice. 3. to pardon, excuse. 4. to supervise

o'vernight (ō'ver-nīt) *adj.* during one night, from one evening to the following morning as *an overnight train.*—*adv.* all night, as *he stayed overnight*

overpow'er *v.* to master, conquer

overrate' *v.* to estimate too highly

overreach' *v.* 1. to reach beyond. 2. to outwit, cheat

overrule' *v.* to cancel a rule or decision by higher authority.—**overru'ling** *pres. part.*

overrun' *v.* to spread over, in numbers, as *The enemy overran the country.*—**overrun'ning** *pres. part.*—**overran'** *p.t.*—**overrun'** *p. part.*

overseas' *adv.* beyond the sea, abroad

o'verseer *n.* one who overlooks work of others

o'versight (ō'ver-sīt) *n.* 1. a mistake, a failing to notice. 2. supervision

overshad'ow *v.* 1. to cast a shadow on. 2. to make a person or thing seem less important

o'verspill *n.* people leaving a district through shortage of housing, for rehousing elsewhere

overt' *adj.* open, not concealed.—**overt'ly** *adv.*

overtake' *v.* to catch up and pass, to come upon.—**overta'king** *pres. part.*—**overtook'** *p.t.*—**overta'ken** *p. part.*

overthrow' *v.* 1. to knock down. 2. to vanquish.—**overthrew'** *p.t.*—**overthrown'** *p. part.*—**o'verthrow** *n.* defeat

Compare: defeat, conquer, subdue, master, overcome, overpower, reduce, surmount, vanquish, beat, crush

o'verture *n.* 1. a proposal. 2. an opening piece played by an orchestra, introducing an opera, etc.

overturn' *v.* 1. to upset, fall over. 2. to overthrow

overwhelm' *v.* to bury, crush utterly.—**overwhelm'ing** *adj.* irresistible

overwork' *v.* to work too hard

overwrought' (o-ver-rawt') *adj.* 1. overexcited, exhausted. 2. too complicated

o'viform *adj.* egg-shaped.—**ovip'arous** *adj.* egg-laying

o'vum *n.* (biology) an unfertilised egg.—**o'va** *pl.*

owe (ō) *v.* to be in debt, as *to owe money.*—**ow'ing** *pres. part.*—**ow'ing to** because of

owl *n.* a night-bird of prey.—**owl'et** *n.* a young owl.—**owl'ish** *adj.* solemn and dull

own (ōn) *v.* 1. to have, possess. 2. to admit, as *I own I was wrong.*—*adj.* belonging to oneself, as *That is her own pen.*—**own'er** *n.*—**own'ership** *n.* possessing.—**on one's own** without help or advice.—**to hold one's own** not to give in

ox *n.* a large horned animal sometimes used for farm-work.—**ox'en** *pl.*

oxal'ic acid *n.* a poisonous acid used in industry

ox'ide *n.* (chemistry) a compound of an element, or some other compound, with oxygen

Ox'bridge *n.* the universities of Oxford and Cambridge.—*adj.* of the universities of Oxford and Cambridge

ox'idise *v.* to combine with oxygen, to rust

ox'ygen (ok'si-jen) *n.* a gas without which plants and animals cannot live. It has neither colour, scent, not taste

oys'ter *n.* a shell-fish with a double shell

o'zone *n.* a form of oxygen with a refreshing smell

P

pa *n.* originally a Maori settlement surrounded by a stockade, a fort, now an unfortified one

pace (pās) *n.* 1. a step. 2. the length of a step, as *ten paces away.* 3. speed, as *a fast pace.*—*v.* to walk with a slow, regular step, as *The policeman paced up and down.*—**pa'cing** *pres. part.*—**pace'maker** *n.*

someone who sets the pace, as in a race.—**to keep pace with** to go as fast as.—**to put someone through his paces** to get him to show what he can do

pacif'ic (pa-sif'ik) *adj.* peaceful.—**pacifica'tion** (-kā'shun) *n.* pacifying.—**pac'ifism** (pas'i-fizm) *n.* belief in possibility of doing away with war.—**pac'ifist** *n.*

pac'ify (pas'i-fī) *v.* to make calm, peaceful.—**pac'ifying** *pres. part.*—**pac'ified** *p.t.* and *p. part.*

pack *n.* 1. a bundle of things, wrapped up to be carried. 2. a set of hounds or wolves. 3. a set of playing-cards. 4. a set, gang, lot, as *a pack of thieves.* 5. a mass of floating ice, as *an ice pack.*—*v.* 1. to put together in a box, trunk, etc. 2. to press or crowd closely together, as *Six men, packed into a small car*

pack'age (pak'ij) *n.* a bundle, parcel.—**pack'et** *n.* 1. a small package. 2. a mailboat.—**pack'-horse** *n.* a horse for carrying goods

pact *n.* an agreement, bargain

pad *n.* 1. soft stuff used as a cushion. 2. sheets of paper fastened together in a block. 3. a shinguard. 4. the foot or sole of a dog, fox, etc.—*v.* to stuff, make soft, protect with a pad, as *a padded seat.*—**pad'ding** *pres. part.*—**pad'ded** *p.t.* and *p. part.*

pad'dle *n.* a short oar with a broad blade at one or each end.—*v.* to move by paddle.—**pad'dle-wheel** *n.* one of two wheels on either side of a ship, with boards in the place of spokes to propel the ship

pad'dle *v.* to walk with bare feet in water.—**pad'dling** *pres. part.*

pad'dock *n.* a small grass field

pad'dy field *n.* a field of rice

pad'lock *n.* a lock with a rounded bar, hinged at one end, which can be fixed on any ring or staple.—*v.*

pa'dre (pah'dray) *n.* a chaplain in the armed services

pæ'an (pee'an) *n.* a song of triumph

pa'gan *adj.* heathen, worshipping false gods.—*n.*—**pa'ganism** *n.*

page (pāj) *n.* one side of a leaf of a book

page (pāj) *n.* 1. a boy servant. 2. a boy attendant on a bride

pa'geant (paj'ent) *n.* a show, a procession of persons in costume, dramatic scenes from history.—**pa'geantry** *n.* show, display

pago'da *n.* a tall, sacred tower found in China or India

pail *n.* an open vessel with a handle, bucket.—**pail'ful** *n.*

pain *n.* 1. suffering in body or mind. 2. punishment, as *on pain of death.*—*v.* to give pain.—**pain'ful** *adj.* hurting.—**pain'fully** *adv.*—**pain'less** *adj.*—**to take pains,** to exercise care.—**pains'taking** *adj.* careful

Compare: ache, agony, discomfort, distress, pang, suffering, torment, torture, trouble

paint *n.* colouring matter prepared for putting on a surface with brushes.—*v.* 1. to cover with paint. 2. to make a picture with paint. 3. to describe.—**paint'er** *n.*—**paint'ing** *n.* a picture in paint

paint'er *n.* a rope fastening a boat to a ship

pair *n.* a set of two, esp. when used, or going together.—*v.* to arrange in pairs

Pakeha (pa-kee-ha) *n.* Maori term for a white man

pal'ace (pal'as) *n.* 1. the official residence of a king or bishop. 2. a fine mansion. See house

pal'atable *adj.* agreeable to eat

pal'ate *n.* 1. the roof of the mouth. 2. taste

pala'tial (-ā'shal) *adj.* spacious, like a palace

pale *n.* 1. a pointed stake used for fences. 2. a boundary, as *beyond the pale*

pale *adj.* without much colour, dim.—*v.* to grow white.—**pale'face** *n.* a North American Indian's name for a white person.—**pale'ness** *n.*

pal'ette *n.* a thin board on which an artist mixes his colours

pal'frey (pawl'fri) *n.* a saddle-horse for a lady

palisade' *n.* a fence of stakes

pall (pawl) *n.* a cloth spread over a coffin

pall (pawl) *v*, to become tasteless or tiresome

pal'let *n.* a straw bed, a poor bed

pal'lid *adj.* pale—**pal'lor** *n.* paleness

palm (pahm) *n.* 1. the inner hand between wrist and fingers. 2. a branchless tree growing in warm climates. 3. a leaf of this as symbol of victory.—*v.* to pass off as something better, as *The pedlar palmed off the brass ring on the countryman as a gold one.*—**Palm' Sun'day** *n.* the Sunday before Easter.—**palm'y** *adj.* flourishing

pal'pable *adj.* 1. that may be touched or felt. 2. easily seen, obvious, as *a palpable blunder.*—**pal'pably** *adv.*

pal'pitate *v.* to beat quickly, throb, tremble.—**pal'pitating** *pres. part.*—**palpita'tion** (-ta'-shun) *n.* violent beating of the heart

pal'sy (pawl'zi) *n.* a disease causing trembling, and then paralysis

pal'try (pawl'tri) *adj.* worthless, petty

pam'pas *n.pl.* the grassy plains of South America

pam'per *v.* to spoil with too much care

pam'phlet (pam'flet) *n.* a thin, paper-covered book

pan *n.* 1. a shallow dish used in cooking, etc. 2. a musical instrument made from steel oil drum used in W. Indian bands.—**pan'cake** *n.* batter fried in a pan.—*v.* to move a cine camera horizontally over a wide view.—**to pan out,** to turn out, as *Our holiday did not pan out well*

pan'da *n.* a black-and-white Himalayan bear

pandemo'nium *n.* confusion and uproar

pan'der *v.* to help others to indulge unworthy desires

pane *n.* a piece of glass in a window or door

pan'el *n.* 1. a piece of wood let into a door or wall, usually below the surrounding piece. 2. a piece of material let into a dress, etc. 3. the members of a jury. 4. a list of National Health Insurance doctors. 5. a group of people taking part in a quiz before an audience.—**pa'nelling** *n.* panel decoration

pang *n.* a sudden pain, as *a pang of toothache*

pan'ic *n.* sudden terror.—*adj.* mad, unreasoning, as *panic fear.*—**pan'icky** *adj.*—**pan'ic-strick'en** *adj.* terrified

Compare: (with panic) fear, fright, horror, terror, dismay, dread

pan'nier *n.* a basket carried by a donkey, etc. slung across its back

pan'oply *n.* full armour

panoram'a (pan-o-rahm'a) *n.* 1. a picture unrolled before a spectator. 2. a wide view.—**panoram'ic** *adj.*

pan'sy (pan'zi) *n.* a flower resembling the violet, but larger.—**pan'sies** *pl.*

pant *v.* to gasp for breath.—*n.*

pantaloon' *n.* a clown in a pantomime

pan'ther *n.* a kind of leopard

pan'tomime *n.* 1. a play in dumb show. 2. a farcical theatre show for the Christmas season

pan'try *n.* a small room for storing food, silver, etc.—**pan'tries** *pl.*

pa'pacy (pā'pa-si) *n.* 1. the office of the Pope. 2. government by popes.—**pa'pal** *adj.* of the Pope

pa'per *n.* 1. a material made by manufacturing wood-pulp, rags, etc., into thin flat sheets. 2. a sheet of paper. 3. a newspaper. 4. an article, essay.—*v.* to cover with paper, as *to paper a room.*—*adj.* made of paper.—**pa'per-chase** *n.* a sport in which runners follow a trail of torn scraps of paper.—**pa'per-clip** *n.* a bent wire clip to fasten papers.—**pa'per-knife** *n.* a blunt knife for opening letters.—**pa'per-weight** *n.* an ornamental weight put on loose papers to prevent scattering

pap'ier-ma'che (pap'yā-ma'shā) *n.* material made of paper pulp and glue, moulded into a shape and then dried

papy'rus (papī'-rus) *n.* writing material of the old Egyptians, made from reeds

par *n.* equality, equal value

par'able *n.* a story told to teach a truth or a lesson

parab'ola *n.* a kind of curve studied in geometry

par'achute (par'a-shoot) *n.* an apparatus, opening like an umbrella, to enable a person to come safely to earth from a great height.—**par'achu'tist** *n.*

parade' *n.* 1. a display, show. 2. a procession. 3. a review of troops. 4. a ground used for review. 5. a public walk, promenade.—*v.* 1. to display, as *He parades his knowledge of cars.* 2. to march.—**para'ding** *pres. part.*

par'adise (par'a-dīs) *n.* 1. the Garden of Eden. 2. Heaven

par'adox *n.* a statement that seems absurd, but is in fact true or founded on truth, as *The child is father to the man* (Wordsworth).—**par'adoxes** *pl.*—**paradox'ical** *adj.*

par'affin *n.*oil distilled from wood, etc.

par'agon *n.* a model of perfection

par'agraph (par'a-graf) *n.* 1. a sentence or several sentences dealing with the same subject. 2. a short notice in a newspaper.—*v.* to arrange in paragraphs

par'akeet *n.* a small long-tailed parrot

par'allel *adj.* 1. at equal distances everywhere, as *Railway lines are parallel.* 2. very similar, as *a parallel case.*—*n.* comparison showing how similar two things are, as *to draw a parallel between two wars.*—*v.* to compare

parallel'ogram *n.* a four-sided figure with opposite sides parallel

par'alyse (par'a-līz) *v.* to cripple, make helpless.—**par'alysing** *pres. part.*—**paral'ysis** (par-al'i-sis) *n.* loss of power or feeling.—**paralyt'ic** *adj. n.*

par'amount *adj.* supreme, chief, greatest, as *of paramount interest*

par'apet *n.* 1. a low wall. 2. a defensive wall on a fort or earth-wall on a trench

parapherna'lia *n.pl.* belongings, odds and end, equipment

par'aphrase (par'a-frāz) *v.* to express the meaning of a passage in other words.—*n.*

par'asite *n.* a plant or animal living on or in another.—**parasit'ic** *adj.* living on others

par'asol *n.* a sunshade

par'cel (par'sel) *n.* 1. things packed in a box or paper. 2. a piece of land.—*v.* 1. to divide. 2. to wrap up.—**par'celling** *pres. part.*—**par'celled** *p.t.* and *p. part.*

parch *v.* 1. to dry by heat. 2. to make, or become hot and dry

parch'ment *n.* skin prepared for writing

pard'on *n.* forgiveness.—*v.* 1. to forgive. 2. to free from punishment.—**par'donable** *adj.* excusable

Compare: (with *v.*) acquit, forgive, excuse, overlook, absolve, remit

pare *v.* to peel, to cut away the edge or outside.—**pa'ring** *pres. part.*

pa'rent (pā'rent) *n.* a father or mother.—**pa'rentage** *n.* ancestry, family.—**parent'al** *adj.*

paren'thesis *n.* 1. a word or sentence inserted in a sentence as an explanation, as *Jane* (*you know her, don't you?*) *is my cousin.* 2. the curved lines used to enclose a parenthesis.—**parenthet'ical** *adj.*

pa'ring (pā'ring) *n.* a piece pared off, rind

par'ish *n.* 1. the district under a clergyman. 2. a division of a county.—**parish'ioner** *n.* member of a parish

park *n.* 1. a public garden, recreation ground. 2. land around a big country house.

3. a space in a camp for army wagons, etc. 4. a space for cars.—*v.* to leave a car in a park

par'ley *n.* a meeting for discussion between opposing chiefs.—*v.*

par'liament (par'li-ment) *n.* 1. an assembly for discussing and passing laws. 2. in the United Kingdom, the House of Commons and the House of Lords.—**parliamenta'rian** *n.* 1. (history) a Roundhead in the Civil War. 2. an experienced member of Parliament.—**parliament'ary** *adj.*

par'lour *n.* a sitting-room

paro'chial (par-ō'ki-al) *adj.* 1. of a parish. 2. narrow-minded

par'ody *n.* a humorous imitation of something written seriously.—**par'odies** *pl.*—*v.* to write a parody

parole' *n.* word of honour, given by prisoner, not to escape, as *The prisoners go out on parole*

par'oxysm *n.* a fit, an emotional crisis

par'quet (par'kā) *n.* flooring of wooden blocks in patterns

par'rot *n.* 1. a bird with bright plumage and hooked beak which can be taught to imitate speaking. 2. someone who repeats without understanding

par'ry *v.* to avoid a blow, question, etc. by turning it aside.—**par'ried** *p.t.* and *p. part.*

parse (parz) *v.* to describe a word, giving its part of speech and its use in the sentence.—**par'sing** *pres. part.*

Par'see *n.* an Indian of Persian descent and religion

parsimo'nious *adj.* stingy, too anxious to save.—**par'simony** *n.*

pars'ley *n.* a small plant used as a garnish for food

par'snip *n.* a plant whose root is used as a vegetable

par'son *n.* a clergyman.—**par'sonage** *n.* a parson's house

part *n.* 1. not the whole, a share, piece. 2. a character in a play, as *the hero's part*. 3. an actor's lines. 4. a place, as *foreign parts*. 5. a side in a quarrel, as *Bob always takes his sister's part*.—*v.* to divide, separate, as *The crowd parted*.—*adj.* not the whole, as *part-time work*.—**for my part** as far as I am concerned.—**for the most part** mostly.—**parts of speech** words classified as nouns, verbs, etc.—**to part company** (of people) to leave, to separate.—**to part with** to sell, to give away.—**to play a part** to pretend to be.—**to take part in** to share in.—**to take someone's part** to support him

Note: You *part* money *into* shares, but you *part* people *from* each other. You *part with* money, but *from* a person

partake' *v.* to have a share.—**parta'king** *pres. part.*—**partook'** *p.t.*—**parta'ken** *p. part.*—**parta'ker** *n.*

par'tial (par'shal) *adj.* 1. incomplete, as *a partial defeat*. 2. favouring one side, not just. 3. fond of, as *partial to cream*.—**partial'ity** (par-shi-al'i-ti) *n.*—**par'tially** *adv.* partly

parti'cipate (par-tis'i-pāt) *v.* to share in, take part.—**parti'cipating** *pres. part.*—**participa'tion** (-pā'shun) *n.*—**parti'cipant** *n.* someone who takes part in

par'ticiple (par'ti-si-pl) *n.* that part of a verb which does the work of an adjective as well as that of a verb, as *a broken window, a raging storm*

par'ticle *n.* a very small bit, as *a particle of dust*

partic'ular *adj.* 1. not general, belonging to one person or thing, as *my particular job*. 2. single, thought of separately. 3. hard to please, exact.—*n.* detail, as *correct in every particular*.—*pl.* an account in detail.—**particular'ity** *n.*—**partic'ularly** *adv.* especially

par'ting *n.* 1. going away, separation. 2. a line along which hair is divided.—*adj.* given, etc., when departing, as *a parting gift*

partisan' (par-ti-zan') *n.* a person supporting a party, etc.—**partisan'ship** *n.* strong feeling of loyalty

parti'tion (par-tish'un) *n.* 1. division. 2. a dividing wall.—*v.* to divide into parts

part'ner *n.* 1. a person sharing in a business. 2. a husband or wife. 3. a person dancing or playing with another.—**part'nership** *n.*

par'tridge (par'trij) *n.* a small game bird of the grouse family

Note: A flock of partridges is called a *covey*

part'-song *n.* a song in which two or more voices blend, singing different parts

part'-time *adj.* (working) for less than the usual hours a week.—**part-time'** *adv.*

par'ty *n.* 1. a group of people with the same political opinions. 2. persons working, travelling or being entertained together. 3. each of the sides in a lawsuit or an agreement.—**par'ties** *pl.*—*adj.* belonging to a party

pas'chal (pas'kal) *adj.* concerning the Jewish Passover, or Easter

pash'a *n.* a Turkish officer or official of high rank

pass *v.* 1. to go by, to be beyond, to go through, as *The years passed. The bus passes the house*. 2. to go beyond, surpass, as *This passes everything*. 3. to move from one to the other, as *Pass on the good news. Pass the salt*. 4. to spend time, as *We passed a jolly evening*. 5. to be successful, as *He has passed his examination*.—**passed, past** *p.t.* and *p. part.*—*n.* 1. a narrow mountain passage. 2. a written permission. 3. a state of affairs, as *This is a pretty pass*. 4. success in an examination.—**pass'able** *adj.* 1. which can be crossed. 2. fairly good.—**pass'ably** *adv.*—**to pass away** to die.—**to pass by** to ignore.—**to pass for** to be taken as.—**to**

pass out to faint.—**to pass over** to overlook
pass'age (pas'ij) *n.* 1. passing. 2. a crossing, voyage. 3. a corridor. 4. part of a book, etc. 5. an exchange of angry words, or blows.—**bird of passage** a migratory bird
pas'senger (pas'en-jer) *n.* a traveller in a train, bus, etc.
passe-partout' (pas-par-too') *n.* adhesive tape for framing pictures
pass'ion (pash'un) *n.* 1. strong feeling. 2. fury, rage. 3. love. 4. suffering.—**The Passion** the sufferings of Christ.—**pass'-ionate** *adj.* having strong feelings
pas'sive *adj.* not resisting, being acted upon
Note: The *passive voice* of a verb is used when the subject is the receiver of the action told by the verb, as *I have been hit*
Contrast: the *active* voice, as I *have hit him*
Pass'over *n.* a Jewish festival
pass'port *n.* a paper or book giving permission to travel in certain countries, a visa
pass'word *n.* a secret word allowing one to pass a sentinel
past *p. part.* of pass.—*adj.* ended, gone by, as *The holidays are past.*—*n.* past time, past life.—*adv.* by as *I saw the train go past.*—*prep.* beyond, as *past understanding*
Note: The *past tense* is the part of a verb used when we speak of something that is over, as *We escaped.* Do not confuse *past with passed.* e.g. I passed him (*p.t.* of pass), I went past him (*p. part.* of pass)
paste (pāst) *n.* 1. a soft mixture, e.g. flour and water. 2. a fine glass to imitate gems.—*v.* to stick with paste.—**pa'sting** *pres. part.*—**paste'board** *n.* a stiff, thick paper
pas'tel *n.* a soft, coloured crayon.—*adj.* soft and pale, as *pastel shades*
pas'teurise (pas'terīz) *v.* to sterilise milk by heating it
pas'tille *n.* a small sweet for coughs and sore throats
pas'time *n.* a sport, recreation, amusement
pas'tor (pahs'tor) *n.* a minister of a congregation.—**pas'toral** *adj.* 1. of a pastor. 2. about shepherds, or country life.—*n.* a pastoral poem.—**pastoral'ist** *n.* (Aus.) a raiser of sheep or cattle, especially in a big way, as distinct from an agriculturalist
pas'try (pās'-tri) *n.* 1. flour-paste mixed with fat and baked. 2. pies, tarts, etc. of pastry.—**pas'tries** *pl.*
pas'turage (pahs'tūr-ij) *n.* pastureland
pas'ture (pahs'tūr) *n.* 1. grass as food for cattle. 2. ground where cattle graze.—*v.* to feed on grass
pas'ty (pahs'ti) *n.* a small meat pie.—**pas'ties** *pl.*
pa'sty (pā'sti) *adj.* pale, unhealthy-looking
pat *n.* a light, quick blow.—*v.* to tap.—**pat'-ting** *pres. part.*—**pat'ted** *p.t.* and *p. part.*
pataka *n.* a Maori term for a storehouse
patch *n.* 1. a piece of cloth, etc., to mend a hole. 2. a spot, stain. 3. a plot of ground.—**patch'es** *pl.*—*v.* to mend.—**patch'work** *n.* odd pieces sewn together.—**patch'y** *adj.* 1. full of patches. 2. irregular
pate *n.* the head, the top of the head
pa'tent *n.* government writing giving a person the sole right to make and sell something.—*v.* to obtain a patent.—*adj.* open, evident, easily seen.—**patent leather** thin very shiny leather.—**patent medicine** medicine ready-made under a trade name.—**patentee'** *n.* the holder of a patent
pater'nal *adj.* 1. of a father, fatherly. 2. related on the father's side, as *paternal grandparents.*—**pater'nity** *n.* fatherhood
path *n.* 1. a way, narrow road. 2. a course of action, as *the path of duty.* 3. the direction followed, as *the path of the sun.*—**path'way** *n.* a footpath
Compare: way, road, lane, alley, track, highway, street, course, channel, route, thoroughfare
pathet'ic *adj.* arousing pity.—**pa'thos** *n.* the quality in speech, music, writing or art which excites a feeling of pity
pathol'ogy *n.* the study of disease
pa'tience (pā'shens) *n.* 1. calm bearing of pain, annoyance, troubles, etc. 2. a card-game.—**pa'tient** (pā'shent) *adj.* having patience.—*n.* a person under doctor's care
Compare: (with *n.* 1.) calmness, endurance, forbearance, fortitude, long-suffering, submission, resignation
pat'io *n.* an inner courtyard
pa'triarch (pā'tri-ark) *n.* the father and ruler of a family, esp. in the Bible.—**patriarch'al** *adj.*
patri'cian (pa-trish'an) *n.* 1. a noble of ancient Rome. 2. a person of noble birth.—*adj.* of noble birth
pa'triot (pā- or pa-) *n.* one who loves and supports his country.—**patriot'ic** *adj.*—**pa'triotism** *n.*
patrol' (pa-trōl') *n.* men, or ships, going round to see that all is well.—*v.* to keep guard.—**patrol'ling** *pres. part.*—**patrolled'** *p.t.* and *p. part.*—**patrol'-car** *n.* a police car for patrolling roads
pa'tron (pā-) *n.* 1. a person who protects and supports another. 2. a guardian saint.—**pa'troness** *fem.*—**pa'tronage** (pā- or pa-) *n.* support.—**pat'ronise** *v.* 1. to support. 2. to treat in a superior manner.—**pat'ronising** *pres. part.*
pat'ter *n.* the quick easy talk of a comedian, conjurer or salesman
pat'ter *v.* to tap in quick succession, as *rain pattering on the window.*—*n.* a tapping sound
pat'tern *n.* 1. a model for imitation. 2. a paper shape from which to cut cloth, etc. 3. a design, as *the pattern of the wallpaper*
pat'ty *n.* a small meat pie
paunch *n.* belly

pau'per *n.* a poor person

pause (pawz) *n.* a stop or rest.—*v.* to stop for a time.—**paus'ing** *pres. part.*

Compare: (with *v.*) halt, desist, cease, be still, stay

pave *v*, 1. to make a surface with stones or bricks. 2. to prepare, as *to pave the way.*—**pa'ving** *pres. part.*—**pave'ment** *n.* a paved way.—**to pave the way for** to make preparations for, to make it easy for

pavil'ion *n.* 1. a large tent. 2. a light building for spectators or players on sports-ground

paw *n.* a foot of an animal.—*v.* 1. to scrape with paws or feet. 2. to handle clumsily

pawl *n.* a catch on a spring, to prevent slipping back

pawn *v.* to leave (goods) as security for borrowed money.—*n.* a piece, of lowest rank, in chess.—**in pawn** left as security.—**pawn'broker** *n.* a person who lends money on goods pawned.—**pawn'shop** *n.*

paw-paw, papau *n.* a tropical fruit

pay (pā) *v.* 1. to give money for goods or for work. 2. to bring in profit, as *It pays to be honest.*—**paid** *p.t.* and *p. part.*—*n.* money, wages.—**pay'able** *adj.* due.—**pay'ment** *n.* 1. paying. 2. amount paid.—**to pay a call** to visit.—**to pay attention to** attend carefully to.—**to pay a compliment** to praise.—**to pay up** to settle a debt

pea (pee) *n.* 1. a plant bearing seed in pods used for food. 2. one of the seeds

peace (pees) *n.* calm, quiet, freedom from war, order.—**peace'able** *adj.* peace-loving.—**peace'ful** *adj.*—**peace'maker** *n.*—**peace'-offering** *n.* a present given to restore friendship

peach *n.* a juicy stone-fruit with delicate flavour.—**peach'es** *pl.*

pea'cock *n.* a bird with brilliant plumage and fan-like tail.—**pea-hen** *fem.*

peak *n.* 1. the sharp top of a mountain. 2. the highest point, as *the peak of success.* 3. the front brim of a cap.—**peaked** *adj.* pointed.—**peak period** a period when a service is working at its maximum

peal (peel) *n.* a loud sound of bells, laughter, thunder, etc.—*v.*

pear (pār) *n.* 1. a tree, giving delicious juicy fruit. 2. its fruit

pearl (purl) *n.* a smooth, whitish gem found in pearl-oysters.—**pearl'y** *adj.*—**to cast pearls before swine** to offer fine things to those unable to value them

peas'ant (pez'ant) *n.* a country labourer.—**peas'antry** *n.* peasants

peat (peet) *n.* turf, dried and used as fuel

peb'ble *n.* a small, rounded stone.—**peb'bly** *adj.*

peck *v.* to pick or strike with the beak.—*n.* a dry measure, one-fourth of a bushel

pecu'liar *adj.* 1. strange, odd, as *It is peculiar to walk backwards.* 2. special, one's own, as *the owl's peculiar hoot.*—**peculiar'ity** *n.* 1. some singular quality found in a person or thing. 2. strangeness.—**peculiar'ities** *pl.*

ped'agogue (ped'a-gog) *n.* a teacher

ped'al *n.* any lever worked by the foot to move any kind of machinery or instrument, as *the pedals of a bicycle, of an organ.*—*v.* to use a pedal.—**ped'alling** *pres. part.*—**ped'alled** *p.t.* and *p. part.*

ped'ant *n.* one who places too much value on rules and details of book-learning.—**pedant'ic** *adj.*—**ped'antry** *n.*

ped'dle *v.* to travel from house to house selling small wares.—**ped'dling** *pres. part.*

ped'estal *n*, the base of a column, lamp, etc.

pedes'trian *n.* a person going on foot.—*adj.* 1. walking. 2. for pedestrians. 3. humdrum

ped'igree *n.* a list of ancestors, as *Our dog has a good pedigree*

ped'lar *n.* one who sells goods from house to house

Note: a *pedlar* goes from house to house, a *hawker* sells from a cart or van

peel *n.* the rind, outer skin of fruit, etc.—*v.* 1. to strip off the skin. 2. to come off.—**peel'ing** a strip of fruit or vegetable skin

peep *v.* to look through a hole, to look quickly or secretly.—*n.*

peep *v.* to cry, as a chick, to chirp.—*n.*

peer *v.* 1. to peep. 2. to look closely, as with short-sighted eyes

peer *n.* 1. one of the same rank, an equal. 2. a nobleman.—**peer'ess** *fem.*—**peer'age** *n.* 1. peer's rank. 2. the peers.—**peer'less** *adj.* without equal

pee'vish *adj.* cross, complaining.—**pee'vishly** *adv.*—**pee'vishness** *n.*

peg *n.* a wooden nail or pin.—*v.* to fasten with pegs.—**peg'ging** *pres. part.*—**pegged** *p.t.* and *p. part.*—**to peg away,** to persevere.—**off the peg** (clothes) ready made.—**a square peg in a round hole** someone doing unsuitable work.—**to peg away** to work steadily at.—**to take someone down a peg** to humiliate him

pe'kinese (pee'kin-eez) *n.* a breed of small dog

pel'ican *n.* a large water-bird with a pouch for storing fish under a large bill

pel'let *n.* 1. a small ball. 2. a pill. 3. small shot

pell-mell' *adv.* in complete confusion

pel'met *n.* a strip of board or cloth above curtains, to hide the runners

pelt *v.* 1. to throw things at, as *The traitor was pelted with stones.* 2. to come down heavily, as *The hail came pelting down*

pelt *n.* an animal's skin before it is tanned

pel'vis *n.* the frame formed by the hip bones of the body

pen *n.* a tool for writing with ink.—*v.* to write.—**pen'ning** *pres. part.*—**penned** *p.t.* and *p. part.*—**pen'manship** *n.* skill in writing.—**ball point pen** a fountain pen with a small ball bearing serving as nib.—**fountain pen** a pen with ink in the barrel.—

pen-friend someone one has not met, with whom one exchanges letters
pen *n.* a small enclosed space for sheep, etc.—*v.* to put in a pen.—**pen'ning** *pres. part.*—**penned** *p.t.* and *p. part.*
pe'nal (pee'nal) *adj.* having to do with punishment, as *penal laws.*—**pe'nalise** *v.* 1. to make something punishable. 2. to punish
pen'alty *n.* the punishment for an offence.—**pen'alties** *pl.*
pen'ance *n.* punishment suffered to show sorrow or penitence for wrong-doing
pence (pens) *n.pl.* pennies
pen'cil (pen'sil) *n.* a tool for writing or drawing.—*v.* to draw, to mark with a pencil.—**pen'cilling** *pres. part.*—**pen'cilled** *p.t.* and *p. part.*
pen'dant *n.* a hanging ornament, usually on a necklace.—**pen'dant** *adj.* hanging
pend'ing *prep.* during, while awaiting, as *The prisoners collected food pending their escape*
pen'dulous *adj.* hanging loosely, swinging
pen'dulum *n.* a weight swinging to and fro from a fixed point, esp. as regulator for a clock.—**pen'dulums** *pl.*
pen'etrate *v.* 1. to enter into, as *Our spies penetrated into the enemy's camp.* 2. to pierce, as *The knife penetrated his hand.*—**pen'etrating** *adj.* acute.—**penetra'tion** (-trā'-shun) *n.* 1. penetrating. 2. insight
pen'guin (peng'gwin) *n.* a swimming sea bird with flippers; it is unable to fly
penicil'lin *n.* a chemical which destroys many kinds of bacteria
penin'sula *n.* a piece of land nearly surrounded by water.—**penin'sular** *adj.*
pen'itence *n.* sorrow for wrong-doing.—**pen'itent** *adj.* sorry for wrong-doing.—*n.* a penitent person, a person doing penance.—**peniten'tial** (pen-iten'shal) *adj.* of penitence.—**peniten'tiary** *n.* prison
pen'knife (pen'nīf) *n.* folding pocket-knife.—**pen'knives** (pen'nīvz) *pl.*
pen'nant *n.* long narrow flag esp. at mast-head of ship
pen'niless *adj.* without money
pen'non *n.* a narrow, triangular flag
pen'ny *n.* a British copper coin.—**pence, pennies** *pl.*—**pen'nyweight** (pen'i-wāt) *n.* twenty-four grains, troy weight.—**pen'ny-wise** *adj.* economical in small things.—**pen'nyworth** *n.* what can be bought for a penny
pen'sion (pen'shun) *n.* 1. money allowance for past services, disablement, special merit, etc. 2. a boarding-house or boarding school on the continent of Europe (pronounced pahn'syon in France and pahn-syōn in Germany).—*v.* to grant a pension to, as *The old servant was pensioned off.*—**pensioner** *n.* a person receiving a pension
pen'sive *adj.* sadly thoughtful
pent, pent-up *adj.* closely shut up
pent'agon *n.* a figure with five sides and five angles.—**pentag'onal** *adj.*
pent'ecost *n.* a Jewish festival, fifty days after the Passover, Whitsunday
pent'house *n.* 1. a shed with sloping roof against a higher wall. 2. a small house or apartment on the flat roof of a building with walking space round it
penult'imate *n.* the last but one
pen'ury *n.* misery, great poverty
peo'ple (pee'pl) *n.* 1. a race, nation, as *the peoples of Europe.* 2. persons, as *The street is full of people.*—*v.* to fill with inhabitants
pep *n.* (slang) energy, vigour
pep'per *n.* the fruit of a plant which gives a very hot spice.—*v.* 1. to sprinkle with pepper. 2. to pelt.—**pep'pery** *adj.* irritable
pep'permint *n.* a plant grown for its strong-tasting oil, used in medicine and in sweets
per *prep.* 1. through, by means of, as *per goods train.* 2. for each, as *five per cent per annum*
peradven'ture *adv.* perhaps
peram'bulate *v.* to walk about.—**peram'-bulating** *pres. part.*—**peram'bulator** *n.* a pram, a small carriage for a child
perceive' (per-seev') *v.* 1. to know, by seeing, hearing, feeling, etc. 2. to understand.—**perceiv'ing** *pres. part.*
Compare: know, understand, comprehend. *Contrast:* miss, lose, ignore, overlook
percent'age (per-sent'ij) *n.* rate or part of each hundred, as *Only a small percentage were absent*
percep'tible (per-sep'ti-bl) *adj.* noticeable, to be perceived.—**percep'tibly** *adv.*
percep'tion (per-sep'shun) *n.* understanding or perceiving, as *a man of keen perception.*—**percep'tive** *adj.* quick to notice
perch *n.* 1. a resting-place for a bird. 2. a measure, five and a half yards.—**perch'es** *pl.* 3. a fresh-water fish.—**perch** *pl.*—*v.* to alight, sit on a perch
perchance' (per-chahns') *adv.* perhaps
per'colate *v.* to drip through small holes, to filter.—**per'colator** *n.* a coffee-making appliance, in which hot water percolates through the coffee
percus'sion (per-kush'on) *n.* 1. striking together, shock, collision. 2. musical instruments played by striking
perdi'tion (per-dish'un) *n.* ruin, death, hell
per'emptory (per'emp-tor-i) *adj.* final, allowing no refusal, as *a peremptory order*
peren'nial *adj.* lasting through the years.—*n.* a plant that lasts more than two years, as *Daisies are perennials*
per'fect *adj.* 1. complete, whole, as *a perfect circle.* 2. without fault, as *a perfect apple.* 3. entire, as *a perfect idiot.*—**perfect'** *v.* to finish, make perfect.—**perfec'tion** (-shun)

n. being perfect, completing.—**per'fectly** *adv.* 1. in a perfect manner. 2. quite

Compare: faultless, correct, finished, ideal, sinless, spotless, unblemished, infallible, undefiled

perfid'ious *adj.* treacherous, deceitful.—**per'fidy** *n.*

per'forate *v.* to pierce, make holes in, as *Most stamps have perforated edges.*—**per'forating** *pres. part.*—**perfora'tion** (-ā'-shun) *n.*

perforce' *adv.* of necessity

perform' *v.* 1. to do, to carry out. 2. to act or play before an audience.—**perform'ance** *n.* 1. doing. 2. a single show, as *the afternoon performance.*—**perform'er** *n.*

per'fume *n.* 1. a pleasant smell. 2. scent.—**perfume'** *v.* to scent.—**perfu'mery** *n.* 1. a place for making or selling scent. 2. scents

perfunc'tory *adj.* careless, indifferent, as *a perfunctory greeting*

perhaps' *adv.* possibly, it may be

per'ianth *n.* the outer part of a flower

per'il *n.* danger.—**per'ilous** *adj.* dangerous

Compare: jeopardy, risk, hazard, insecurity. *Contrast:* safety, protection, shelter, defence, security, safeguard

perim'eter *n.* the outer boundary of a plane figure

pe'riod (pee'ri-od) *n.* 1. the time in which some event happens, as *an exciting period of history.* 2. a complete sentence. 3. a full stop.—**period'ic** *adj.* happening regularly, as *periodic visits to the dentist*

period'ical *adj.* at set intervals.—*n.* a magazine published regularly.—**period'ically** *adv.*

periph'ery *n.* the outer edge, the outskirts

per'iscope *n.* an instrument, used esp. in submarines, for giving a view of objects on a different level

per'ish *v.* to die, wither.—**per'ishable** *adj.* liable to decay

per'iwinkle (per'-i-wing-kl) *n.* 1. a trailing plant with a blue flower. 2. a sea-snail used for food

per'jure (per'jer) *v.* to swear falsely.—**per'jury** *n.*

perm *n.* 1. a permanent hair-wave. 2. a permutation in football pools

permanence *n.* lasting, being permanent.—**per'manent** *adj.* lasting, as *Gypsies have no permanent home.*—**per'manently** *adv.*

per'meate *v.* to soak, to penetrate and spread, as *Smoke permeated the whole house.*—**per'meating** *pres. part.*

permis'sible *adj.* allowable

permis'sion (per-mish'n) *n.* leave, consent, allowing

permit' *v.* to allow let.—**permit'ting** *pres. part.*—**permit'ted** *p.t.* and *p. part.*—**per'mit** *n.* written permission

Compare: authorise, empower, give leave, suffer, tolerate

permuta'tion *n.* (mathematics) the number of ways a given number of objects can be arranged

perni'cious (per-nish'us) *adj.* hurtful, destructive

perox'ide *n.* an oxide containing more than the usual amount of oxygen.—**hydrogen peroxide** a liquid used as a bleach

perpendic'ular *adj.* upright.—*n.* a perpendicular line

per'petrate *v.* to commit, e.g. a crime, trick, etc.—**perpetra'tion** (-trā'shun) *n.*—**per'petrator** *n.*

perpet'ual *adj.* continuous, lasting for ever.—**perpet'ually** *adv.*—**perpet'uate** *v.* to make perpetual, save from being forgotten.—**perpetua'tion** (-ā'shun) *n.*—**perpetu'ity** *n.* the state or quality of lasting forever.—**in perpetu'ity** forever

perplex' *v.* to puzzle.—**perplex'ity** *n.* doubt, confusion

per'secute *v.* 1. to ill-treat. 2. to oppress for holding an opinion.—**per'secuting** *pres. part.*—**persecu'tion** (-shun) *n.* 1. ill-treating. 2. being ill-treated.—**per'secutor** *n.*

persever'ance (per-se-vee'rans) *n.* persistence, going on doing something hard.—**persevere'** *v.* to persist.—**persever'ing** *pres. part.*

Per'sia *n.* Iran, a country in central Asia.—**Per'sian** *n.* and *adj.*

persist' *v.* 1. to continue, to go on in spite of obstacles, as *The rain persisted all day. We persisted over the rough road.* 2. to maintain, keep saying.—**persis'tence** *n.*—**persis'tent** *adj.* lasting, obstinate, as *a persistent beggar*

Compare: last, endure, persevere, remain, stay, insist

per'son *n.* 1. a human being. 2. the body. 3. in grammar, the form of pronoun or verb used to show the speaker, *first person, as I, we, mine;* the person spoken to, *second person,* as *thou, you*; the person or thing spoken about, *third person,* as *he, she, it, they.*—**per'sonable** *adj.* of good appearance.—**per'sonage** *n.* 1. an important person. 2. a character in a play

per'sonal *adj.* 1. private. 2. done by oneself, belonging to oneself, as *a personal visit.* 3. of the body or person, as *personal cleanliness.*—**personal'ity** *n.* the qualities that make one person different from another.—**per'sonally** *adv.* 1. in person. 2. speaking for oneself

personifica'tion (-kā'shun) *n.* 1. representing something as a person. 2. type, as *Florence Nightingale was the personification of dedication to a cause*

person'ify *v.* 1. to represent as a person. 2. to stand for, typify.—**person'ifying** *pres. part.*—**person'ified** *p.t.* and *p. part.*

personnel' *n.* all the persons in a group or organisation

perspec'tive *n.* 1. the art of drawing on a

flat surface to give the effect of distance and size. 2. a view which shows things or events in their right relationship to each other

per'spex *n.* a trade name for a transparent plastic

perspica'cious (per-spik-ā'shus) *adj.* quick to see and understand.—**perspicac'ity** *n.*

perspira'tion (-rā'shun) *n.* sweat.—**perspire'** *v.*—**perspi'ring** *pres. part.*

persuade' (per-swād') *v.* to win over by argument, to make someone ready to do something.—**persua'ding** *pres. part.*—**persua'sion** (per-swā'zhun) *n.* 1. persuading. 2. belief.—**persua'sive** *adj.*

pert *adj.* bold, saucy, as *a pert answer*

pertain' *v.* to belong

pertina'cious (per-tin-ā'shus) *adj.* persistent in holding to an opinion, etc.—**pertinac'ity** (per-tin-as'i-ti) *n.*

per'tinent *adj.* to the point, as *a pertinent remark*

perturb *v.* to make uneasy, to disquiet.—**perturba'tion** (-bā'shun) *n.*

peru'sal (per-ōō'zl) *n.* reading.—**peruse'** (per-ōōz') *v.* to read.—**peru'sing** *pres. part.*

pervade' *v.* to spread through, as *The smell of oranges pervades the room.*—**perva'ding** *pres. part.*—**perva'sive** *adj.*

perverse' *adj.* contrary, obstinate in wrongdoing.—**perver'sion** (-zhun) *n.* wrong use.—**perver'sity** *n.* perverse behaviour

pervert' *v.* to turn to a wrong use, to spoil, corrupt.—**per'vert** *n.* a perverted person

pese'ta (pe-sā'ta) *n.* a Spanish coin

pes'simism *n.* a disposition to look on the dark side of things, a belief that evil will be stronger than good.—**pes'simist** *n.*—**pessimis'tic** *adj.*

pest *n.* a nuisance, troublesome or harmful thing or person, as *Rats are pests*

pest'icide (pest'i-sīd) *n.* a chemical for killing rats or other pests

pest'er *v.* to annoy, trouble, as *We are pestered with flies*

pest'ilence *n.* plague, disease.—**pest'ilent** *adj.* deadly, troublesome.—**pestilen'tial** (-shal) *adj.* infectious, bringing disease

pes'tle (pes'l) *n.* a thick, short rod for pounding things in a mortar

pet *n.* 1. a favourite animal. 2. a person treated with affection.—*v.* to treat with affection.—**pet'ting** *pres. part.*—**pet'ted** *p.t.* and *p. part.*

pet'al *n.* one section of the outer, coloured part of a flower

pet'ard *n.* an explosive bomb, firework

pe'ter (out) *v.* to grow less and then die out

peti'tion (pe-tish'un) *n.* 1. a formal request handed to an authority. 2. a prayer.—*v.* to present a petition.—**peti'tion er** *n.*

pet'rify *v.* 1. to turn into stone. 2. to strike with terror.—**pet'rifying** *pres. part.*—**pet'rified** *p.t.* and *p. part.*

pet'rol *n.* refined petroleum.—**petro'leum** *n.* a mineral oil

pet'ticoat *n.* a woman's underskirt

pet'tiness *n.* being petty, meanness

pet'ty *adj.* 1. unimportant, as *petty details.* 2. small-minded, mean, as *petty about money.*—**petty cash** small amounts of money spent.—**petty officer** in the Navy, a non-commissioned officer

pet'ulance *n.* being cross and peevish.—**pet'ulant** *adj.*

pew *n.* a fixed seat in a church

pew'ter *n.* 1. an alloy of tin and lead. 2. pots, etc., made of this

pfen'nig *n.* a German copper coin

phalan'ger (fal-an'jer) *n.* the scientific name of opossum and some other marsupials

phal'anx (fal'angks) *n.* soldiers, or people, in close formation.—**phalanxes** *pl.*

phan'tom (fan'tom) *n.* a ghost, apparition.—*adj.* unreal, ghostly

pha'raoh (fā'rō) *n.* a king of ancient Egypt

phar'macy (far'ma-si) *n.* 1. preparing and dispensing drugs. 2. a dispenser's shop.—**phar'macies** *pl.*—**phar'macist** *n.*—**pharmaceu'tical** *adj.* engaged in pharmacy, as *a pharmaceutical chemist*

phase (fāz) *n.* 1. a stage in the development of something. 2. a view of the moon or planets at a certain time

pheas'ant (fez'ant) *n.* a game-bird with long tail

phe'nol *n.* carbolic acid

phenom'enon (fen-om'en-on) *n.* 1. a fact or event that can be observed, as *Sunset is a phenomenon.* 2. a remarkable thing or person.—**phenom'ena** *pl.*

phi'al (fī'al) *n.* a small glass bottle

philanthrop'ic (fil-an-throp'ik) *adj.* helpful, charitable

philan'thropist (fil-an'thro-pist) *n.* a person anxious to help his fellow-men.—**philan'thropy** *n.*

philos'opher (fil-os'ō-fer) *n.* a person who studies or possesses wisdom.—**philosoph'ical** *adj.* 1. of philosophy. 2. reasonable. 3. resigned. —**philos'ophy** *n.* the study of wisdom and knowledge, and the causes and laws of the universe

phlegm (flem) *n.* 1. thick matter sent up from the lungs in coughing. 2. calmness, indifference.—**phlegmat'ic** (fleg-mat'ik) *n.* not excitable

pho'bia (fō'bia) *n.* a fear, as **hydrophobia** *is the fear of water*

phoe'nix (fee'niks) *n.* a mythical bird, said to have lived 500 years, to have burned itself and to have risen again from its ashes to live another life

phone (fōn) *n.* short form of *telephone*

phonet'ic (fō-net'ik) *adj.* relating to speech-sounds.—**phonet'ics** *n.pl.* the study of the sounds in speech

pho'nograph (fō'no-graf) *n.* an early instrument for recording and reproducing sounds

phos'phate (fos'fāt) *n.* a salt of an acid containing phosphorus and used in fertilisers

phosphores'cence (fos-for-es'ens) *n.* a faint glow in the dark

phos'phorus (fos'for-us) *n.* a yellowish substance which glows in the dark

pho'to (fō'tō) *n.* short form of *photograph.*—**photo-finish** the close finish of a race in which a photograph decides the winner

pho'to-elec'tric *adj.* relating to electricity generated by light.—**pho'to-electric cell** a device which is sensitive to faint light

pho'tograph (fō'tō-graf) *n.* a picture taken with a camera by means of light on a sensitive film.—**photog'rapher** *n.*—**photograph'ic** *adj.*—**photog'raphy** *n.* taking photographs

pho'tosyn'thesis *n.* the process by which plants make starch or sugar in the presence of sunlight

phrase (frāz) *n.* 1. a group of words containing neither subject nor predicate, as *Arriving at noon.* 2. an expression commonly used.—*v.* to express, as *How shall I phrase my apology?*—**phra'sing** *pres. part.* —**phrase book** a collection of phrases and sayings of a language useful to a traveller.

phy'sic (fiz'ik) *n.* medicine.—*n.pl.* the science dealing with matter and energy, including heat, light electricity, sound, etc.

phys'ical (fiz'i-kal) *adj.* 1. of the body, bodily. 2. according to the laws of nature. —**phy'sically** *adv.*—**phys'ical geog'raphy** *n.* a study of the natural features of the earth, climate, tides, etc.

physi'cian (fiz-ish'an) *n.* a doctor of medicine

physiog'nomy (fiz-i-on'o-mi) *n.* 1. judging character from the face. 2. face, features

physiol'ogy (fiz-i-ol'o-ji) *n.* the science of the nature and functions of living things

physiothe'rapy *n.* the treatment of illness by massage, exercises, etc.

physique (fiz-eek') *n.* the build, form, and development of the body

pi'anist (pee'an-ist) *n.* a person who plays the piano

pian'o, pianofort'e *n.* a large musical instrument with a key-board.—**pian'os** (pian'ōz) *pl.*

pic'ador *n.* a bull-fighter mounted on horseback

pick *n.* a tool with a sharp point for breaking up hard ground.—**pick'axe** *n.* a pick

pick *v.* 1. to gather, as *to pick fruit.* 2. to choose, as *to pick a team.* 3. to break up. 4. to pull out waste parts.—*n.* the best parts. —**to pick a lock** to open without a key.—**to pick a pocket** to steal from someone's pocket.—**to pick holes in** to find fault with. —**to pick out** to choose.—**to pick up** 1. to lift up. 2. to learn, as *to pick up foreign words*

pick'axe *n.* a tool for breaking coal, the ground, etc.

pick'et *n.* 1. a pointed stake. 2. a small body of soldiers on police duty. 3. a striker or group of strikers waiting at a place of employment to dissuade workers from going to work.—*v.* to post as a picket

pick'le *n.* 1. salt water, etc. for preserving vegetables, etc. 2. trouble, difficulty.—*v.* to preserve in salt, vinegar, etc.—*n.pl.* pickled vegetables

pick'pocket *n.* one who steals from another's pocket

pic'nic *n.* a pleasure-trip, with a meal out of doors.—*v.* to take part in a picnic.—**pic'nicking** *pres. part.*—**pic'nicked** *p.t.* and *p. part.*

picto'rial *adj.* 1. having to do with painting or pictures. 2. illustrated with pictures.—**picto'rially** *adv.*

pic'ture (pik'cher) *n.* 1. a painting, drawing, or print. 2. a portrait.—*v.* to represent, to describe, to imagine, as *Picture her delight!*—**picturesque'** (pik-tur-esk') *adj.* 1. interesting enough to make a picture, of charming appearance. 2. (of language) vivid.—**the pictures** *n.pl.* a cinema-show

Compare: photograph, copy, likeness, image, miniature, representation, sketch, cartoon

pie *n.* a dish of meat or fruit covered with pastry

pie'bald (pī'bawld) *adj.* spotted in two colours, usually black and white, as *a piebald horse*

piece (pees) *n.* 1. a bit, part of a whole. 2. a coin. 3. a musical or literary composition. —*v.* to mend, put together, as *to piece a broken doll.*—**pie'cing** *pres. part.*—**piece of eight** an old Spanish coin.—**piece'meal** bit by bit.—**piece'work** work paid for by how much is done, not by the hours worked

pied (pīd) *adj.* piebald, of two or more colours

pier (peer) *n.* 1. a column or support of an arch. 2. a stone wall to break the force of the sea. 3. a landing-place built out into the sea

pierce (peers) *v.* 1. to make a hole in, as *The needle pierced her finger.* 2. to penetrate, as *A cry pierced the night.*—**pier'cing** *pres. part.*—*adj.* sharp, as *a piercing glance*

Compare: bore, stab, puncture, perforate, enter

pi'ety *n.* being pious, godliness, religious conduct

pig *n.* 1. a farm-animal raised for its meat, which is called pork. 2. a young hog. 3. a greedy or dirty person.—**pigs, swine** *pl.*—**boar, hog** *masc.*—**sow** *fem.*—**pig'let** *n.* a young pig.—**pig'gery** *n.* a place where pigs are kept.—**pig'iron** cast iron.—**Pig Islands** New Zealand

pi'geon (pij'un) *n.* a bird with a cooing note. —**pi'geon hole** *n.* 1. a place for pigeon to rest in. 2. a compartment in a desk, for holding papers.—*v.* to put away

pig'ment *n.* colouring matter, paint or dye
pig'my see **pygmy**
pig'sty (pig'stī) *n.* an enclosed place for pigs.—**pig'sties** *pl.*
pig'tail *n.* a plait of hair hanging from the back of the head
pike *n.* 1. a spear formerly used by infantry. 2. a large, fresh-water fish.—**plain as a pike'staff,** easy to see
pil'chard *n.* a small fish like a herring
pile *n.* 1. a heap, as *a pile of books.* 2. a huge building.—*v.* to heap up, as *The leaves pile up in autumn.*—**pi'ling** *pres. part.*
pile *n.* a beam driven into the earth to support a bridge, etc.
pile *n.* short, soft hair on cloth, carpet, etc.
pil'fer *v.* to steal small things.—**pil'ferer** *n.*
pil'grim *n.* a traveller to a holy place.—**pil'grimage** (pil'grim-ij) *n.*—**Pilgrim Fathers** the group of English puritans who settled in New England in 1620
pill *n.* medicine in a small solid ball.—**to sugar the pill** to make something unpleasant seem pleasant
pil'lage (pil'ij) *n.* plunder, robbery with violence.—*v.*
pil'lar *n.* 1. a column. 2. a support.—**pil'lar-box** *n.* letter-box in a short metal pillar.—**from pillar to post** from place to place
pil'lion *n.* a cushion or seat for a passenger behind a motor-cyclist, or pedal-cyclist
pil'lory *n.* a wooden frame with holes for the head and hands in which an offender was locked and exposed to jeering and pelting for punishment.—**pil'lories** *pl.*—*v.* to subject to mockery and ridicule.—**pil'loried** *p.t. and p. part.*
pil'low (pil'ō) *n.* a cushion for the head, in bed.—*v.*
pi'lot *n.* 1. a person who takes charge of ship entering or leaving harbour. 2. one who directs aircraft. 3. a guide.—*v.* to steer, guide.—**pilot-officer** *n.* a British air force officer, equal to an army second-lieutenant in rank
pim'ple *n.* a small swelling on the skin
pin *n.* 1. a short, thin piece of rigid wire with a head and a point, for fastening things together. 2. a peg of wood or metal.—*v.* 1. to fasten with a pin. 2. to seize and hold fast, as *He was pinned by a falling branch.*—**pin'ning** *pres. part.*—**pinned** *p.t.* and *p. part.*—**pin'cushion** *n.* a small cushion to hold pins.—**pin'money** *n.* pocket money.—**pin'prick** *n.* 1. a small hole. 2. a small annoyance.—**pin'-table** *n.* a game of chance, with a ball falling between fixed pins.—**pins and needles** a prickly feeling in a limb that is numb.—**pin-up** a photograph of a film-star, female nude, pinned to a wall
pin'afore *n.* a child's overall
pin'cers (pin'serz) *n.pl.* a tool for gripping, with two hinged jaws
pinch *v.* 1. to squeeze, nip, as *She pinched her finger in the window.*—*n.* 1. a nip. 2. as much as can be taken with finger and thumb, as *a pinch of salt.*—**at a pinch** if necessary.—**to take with a pinch of salt** to be doubtful of
pine *n.* an evergreen, cone-bearing tree.—**pine'-needle** *n.* the spiky leaf of a pine tree
pine *v.* to waste away with grief, etc.—**pi'ning** *pres. part.*
pine'apple *n.* 1. a tropical plant with large juicy fruit. 2. its fruit
pin'ion *n.* a wing.—*v.* to bind the arms to the side
pink (pingk) *n.* 1. a sweet-smelling garden plant. 2. pale red. 3. excellent condition, as *in the pink of health.*—*adj.* pale red
pin'nace (pin'as) *n.* a warship's boat
pin'nacle *n.* 1. a turret, slender tower. 2. the highest point
pin'point *v.* to mark a position exactly
pint (pīnt) *n.* a liquid measure, half a quart.
pioneer' *n.* 1. a person who prepares the way for others to follow. 2. an explorer. 3. a person who starts something new
pi'ous *adj.* religious, godly
pip *n.* a seed in a fruit
pip *n.* 1. a spot on playing-cards, dominoes, dice. 2. a star on an army officer's shoulder
pipe *n.* 1. a tube for carrying water, gas, etc. 2. a musical instrument like a whistle. 3. a bird's note. 4. a tube with a small bowl at the end for smoking tobacco.—*v.* 1. to play on a pipe. 2. to transport through pipes. 3. to make a high-pitched sound.—**pi'ping** *pres. part.*—**pi'per** *n.* pipe-player.—**pipe'-clay** *n.* fine clay used for whitening. **pipe'-dream** *n.* a wishful daydream which cannot be fulfilled
pipette' *n.* a small tube for transferring fluids from one container to another
pi'ping *n.* 1. cord for reinforcing joins and edges. 2. a group of pipes.—*adj.* shrill.—**pi'ping hot** extremely hot
pippin *n.* any of various kinds of apple
pique (peek) *n.* hurt or offended feeling as *She was in a pique at being left out.*—*v.* 1. to irritate, annoy. 2. to arouse curiosity, etc.
pi'racy (pī'ra-si) *n.* robbery at sea
pi'rate (pī'rat) *n.* a sea-robber.—**pirat'ical** *adj.*
pis'til *n.* a part of a flower where seeds are made
pis'tol *n.* a small gun fired with one hand
pis'ton *n.* a plug fitting a cylinder and working backwards and forwards as in a steam-engine
pit *n.* 1. a deep hole, a mineshaft. 2. a hollow hole in a surface. 3. the part of a theatre behind the stalls.—*v.* 1. to mark with small scars. 2. to put to the test as *David pitted his strength against Goliath's.*—**pit'ting** *pres. part.*—**pit'ted** *p.t.* and *p. part.*
pitch *v.* 1. to throw, toss. 2. to set up, e.g.

a tent. 3. to fall headlong, as *He pitched downstairs.* 4. of a ship, to plunge.—*n.* 1. way of throwing. as *Watch the pitch of the ball.* 2. height, degree, as *the pitch of perfection.* 3. slope. 4. a ground for cricket, football, etc. 5. the position of a note in the range of musical sounds

pitch *n.* a sticky substance made from tar or turpentine, tar from **Pitch Lake,** Trinidad. —**pitch dark** completely dark

pitch'er *n.* a large jug

pitch'fork *n.* a large fork for lifting and tossing hay

pit'eous (pit'i-us) *adj.* deserving pity, as *She gave a piteous cry*

pit'fall *n* 1. a covered pit for trapping animals or men. 2. any hidden trap

pith *n.* 1. a spongy substance in the stems of certain plants. 2. the most important part, essence.—**pith'ily** *adv.* concisely.—**pith'y** *adj.* 1. of pith, having pith. 2. concise, short, but full of meaning

pit'iable *adj.* deserving pity

pit'iful *adj.* 1. full of pity. 2. deserving pity. 3. mean, deserving scorn.—**pit'ifully** *adv.*—**pit'iless** *adj.* cruel

pit'tance *n.* a small allowance of food or money

pit'y *n.* 1. sympathy, sorrow for the suffering of others. 2. something to be regretted, as *What a pity you missed the party!*—**pit'ies** *pl.*—*v.* to feel pity for.—**he pit'ies.**—**pit'ying** *pres. part.*—**pit'ied** *p.t.* and *p. part.*

piv'ot *n.* a shaft or pin on which something turns.—*v.* 1. to provide with a pivot. 2. to turn on a pivot.—**piv'oting** *pres. part.*—**piv'oted** *p.t.* and *p. part.*

pix'y, pixie *n.* a fairy.—**pix'ies** *pl.*

plac'ard *n.* a poster, notice for posting up.—*v.* to post placards

placate' *v.* to appease, soothe

place (plās) *n.* 1. a particular part of space, spot. 2. position, as *out of place, in the second place.* 3. town, village, buildings. 4. employment, position, rank. 5. a person's seat, as *She gave up her place.*—*v.* to put in a certain spot.—**pla'cing** *pres. part.*

Compare: space, situation, site, locality, station, part, post.—**place'-kick** *n.* (Rugby) a kick at the goal after a try.—**to take place** to happen

pla'cid (plas'id) *adj.* calm, untroubled.—**placid'ity** *n.*

pla'giarism (plā'jiar-izm) *n.* stealing and using as one's own another's ideas, writings or inventions.—**pla'giarise** *v.*

plague (plāg) *n.* pestilence, terrible disease.—*v.* to pester, annoy

plaice *n.* an edible flat fish.—**plaice** *pl.*

plaid (plād) *n.* 1. a checked woollen cloth used as a wrap by Highlanders. 2. cloth with check pattern

plain *adj.* 1. clear, easy to see or understand, as *plain writing.* 2. simple, homely, as *plain food.* 3. not beautiful, as *a plain face.*—*n.* a stretch of flat country.—*adv.* clearly.—**plain'ly** *adv.*—**plain'ness** *n.*—**plain-spok'en** *adj.* frank.—**plain clothes man** a policeman on duty but in uniform.—**plain dealing** honesty.—**plain sailing** absence of difficulties.—**plain-song** a kind of church music

Note: Do not confuse with *plane*

plaint *n.* 1. complaint, grievance. 2. lament

plaint'iff *n.* a person bringing a grievance to the law-court

plain'tive *adj.* sad, mournful.—**plain'tively** *adv.*

plait (plat) *n.* a braid of hair, straw, etc.—*v.*

plan *n.* 1. a drawing showing how a house, a town, a garden, is arranged, a map. 2. a way of doing things decided on beforehand, as *We stuck to our plan in spite of the rain.*—*v.* 1. to arrange beforehand, as *We have planned our holidays.* 2. to make a plan.—**plan'ning** *pres. part.*—**planned** *p.t.* and *p. part.*

plane *n.* a carpenter's tool for smoothing wood.—*v.*

plane *n.* a tree with broad leaves

plane *n.* 1. a flat level surface. 2. an aeroplane. —*adj.* flat, level.—**plane'-table** *n.* a surveyor's board on a tripod

plan'et *n.* one of nine heavenly bodies moving round our sun.—**plan'etary** *adj.*—**planeta'rium** *n.* a model of the solar system in a domed room

plank (plangk) *n.* a long, flat piece of sawn timber.—**to walk the plank** to be forced by pirates to walk along a plank into the sea

plank'ton (plangk'ton) *n.* minute plants and animals in the sea

plant *n.* 1. a living thing which is not an animal. 2. equipment or machinery needed for manufacture.—*v.* 1. to set in the ground to grow. 2. to set firmly, to place

plan'tain (plan'tin) *n.* 1. a tropical plant like a banana. 2. its fruit. 3. a common weed with broad leaves

planta'tion (-tā'shun) *n.* 1. ground planted with trees. 2. a large estate where rubber, tea, cotton, etc. are grown.—**plan'ter** *n.* a person owning or managing a plantation

plaque (plak) *n.* an inscribed mounted plate

plas'ter *n.* 1. a mixture of lime, sand and water for coating walls, etc. 2. linen, spread with a sticky medicinal substance, for protecting cuts, etc.—*v.* 1. to put plaster on. 2. to spread thickly.—**plas'terer** *n.*—**plaster of Paris** a white powder which sets hard with water

plas'tic *adj.* 1. made of plastic. 2. easily shaped, soft, as *Clay is plastic.* 3. giving form to matter, as *sculpture is a plastic art.*—**plasti'city** (plas-ti'si-ti) *n.*—**plas'tic** *n.* a man-made substance which can be shaped when hot.—**plas'tic surgery** restoring a damaged face or limb by surgery

plate *n.* 1. a shallow, round dish. 2. gold or

silver table utensils. 3. a thin flat sheet of metal, glass, etc. 4. in photography, thin sheet of glass coated with a sensitive emulsion.—*v.* to cover with thin coating of gold, silver,, etc. as *plated spoons*.—**plate-glass'** *n.* thick glass for shop-windows, etc. —**pla'ting** *n.* a thin covering of metal

plat'eau (plat'ō) *n.* a tableland, piece of level high land.—**plat'eaus, plat'eaux** (plat'ōz) *pl.*

plat'form *n.* a raised floor, a stage, landing-stage at railway station

plat'inum *n.* a white, heavy precious metal

plat'itude *n.* a dull, commonplace remark

platoon' *n.* a small body of soldiers

plat'ter *n.* a dish, plate

plat'ypus *n.* duck mole, a furred, duck-billed, egg-laying semi-aquatic mammal

plau'dit *n.* applause

plaus'ible *adj.* seeming fair and reasonable, as *a plausible excuse*

play (plā) *n.* 1. sport, game, amusement, as *They are at play*. 2. a piece acted on the stage. 3. gambling. 4. action, as *The ball is in play*.—*v.* 1. to take part in sport, games, etc. 2. to act, perform, as *to play a trick*. 3. to make music on an instrument. 4. to move lightly, as *Shadows play on the window*.—**play'er** *n.*—**play'ful** *adj.* frolicsome.—**play'ground** *n.*—**play'house** *n.* theatre.—**play'mate** *n.*—**play'thing** *n.* a toy. —**play'wright** *n.* a writer of plays.—**to play down** to make appear to be unimportant. **to play the game** to act fairly.—**to play someone up** to make a fool of him.—**to play up** to play hard.—**to play up to** to flatter someone

plea (plee) *n.* 1. an excuse. 2. a defence offered by accused. 3. a request, as *a plea for pardon*

plead (pleed) *v.* 1. to offer as an excuse, as *to plead poverty*. 2. to beg, ask earnestly, as *to plead for help*. 3. to address a court of law

Compare: entreat, beseech, implore, urge, solicit, press

plea'sant (plez'ant) *adj.* agreeable, friendly, pleasing.—**plea'santly** *adv.*—**plea'santness** *n.*—**plea'santry** *n.* a joke

Compare: attractive, kind, kindly, obliging, delightful. *Contrast:* disagreeable, displeasing, dreary, gloomy, hateful, harsh, grim, ill-natured, unkind, unpleasant

please (pleez) *v.* 1. to be agreeable to. 2. to like, to be willing.—**pleas'ing** *pres. part.* —**pleas'ant** *adj.*—**pleas'urable** (plezh'er-a-bl) *adj.* agreeable

Note: please is also used in polite requests, as *Please be quick*

pleas'ure (plezh'er) *n.* 1. delight, joy. 2. amusement, sport. 3. will, choice, as "*This is our pleasure," said the Queen*

pleat (pleet) *n.* a three-fold band made by folding material on itself.—*v.*

plebe'ian (pleb-ee'an) *adj.* belonging to the common people.—*n.*

pleb'iscite (pleb'i-sīt) *n.* the vote of a whole people, nation or community on one important question

pledge (plej) *n.* 1. a promise. 2. something given as a security. 3. a toast in someone's honour.—*v.* 1. to promise, as *They pledged themselves to secrecy*. 2. to leave as security. 3. to drink the health of.—**pledg'ing** *pres. part.*

plenipoten'tiary (plen-i-po-ten'sha-ri) *n.* an envoy or ambassador with full power to act.—*adj.*

plen'itude *n.* abundance, completeness

plen'teous *adj.* plentiful

plen'tiful *adj.* abundant, more than enough, ample.—**plent'ifully** *adv.*

Compare: plenteous, bounteous, bountiful, copious, full, generous, large, lavish, luxuriant, profuse, rich, overflowing, teeming

plen'ty *n.* 1. abundance. 2. enough, a sufficient quantity

pli'able *adj.* 1. easily bent, flexible. 2. easily influenced

pli'ant *adj.* pliable.—**pli'ancy** *n.*

pli'ers *n.pl.* small pincers

plight (plīt) *n.* difficult condition (esp. poor), as *in a sorry plight*

Plim'soll-line *n.* a loading mark on the side of a ship

plim'solls *n.pl.* rubber-soled canvas shoes

plod *v.* to walk or work with resolution.—**plod'ding** *pres. part.*—**plod'ded** *p.t.* and *p. part.*—**plod'der** *n.* a slow, hard worker

plot *n.* 1. a small piece of land. 2. the plan of a play or story. 3. a secret plan, conspiracy.—*v.* 1. to make a map, as *They plotted their course home*. 2. to plan secretly.—**plot'ting** *pres. part.*—**plot'ted** *p.t.* and *p. part.*—**plot'ter** *n.*

plough (plow) *n.* a heavy instrument for cutting and turning up soil.—*v.* to furrow, turn up with a plough.—**plough'man** *n.*—**plough'share** *n.* the blade of the plough

plov'er (pluv'er) *n.* one of various birds, a lapwing

pluck *v.* 1. to pick, pull off. 2. to strip feathers. 3. to rob.—*n.* courage.—**pluck'y** *adj.* brave.—**to pluck up courage** to try to be brave

plug *n.* 1. anything used to stop up a hole. 2. tobacco pressed hard. 3. an electrical connector with prongs fitting into a socket. —*v.* to stop with a plug.—**plug'ging** *pres. part.*—**plugged** *p.t.* and *p. part.*

plum *n.* 1. soft stone-fruit. 2. something good

plu'mage (plōō'mij) *n.* a bird's feathers

plumb (plum) *n.* a **plumb-line**, a weight on a line to measure depth or find if a wall, etc. is vertical.—*v.* to find the depth of.—*adj.* vertical

plum'ber (plum'er) *n.* a man who repairs

pipes, etc. with lead.—**plumb'ing** *n.* plumber's work

plume (plōōm) *n.* a feather ornament.—*v.* 1. to deck with plumes. 2. to pride oneself, as *She plumes herself on her cooking.*—**plu'ming** *pres. part.*

plump *adj.* rounded, rather fat.—*v.* 1. to sit or fall suddenly. 2. to drop or throw suddenly

plun'der *v.* to rob openly and violently.—*n.* 1. robbery. 2. things robbed.—**plun'derer** *n.*

plunge (plunj) *v.* 1. to drive or thrust into, as *He plunged his hand into the basin.* 2. to throw oneself into, to dive.—**plun'ging** *pres. part.*—*n.* a dive, thrust

plu'ral (plōō'ral) *adj.* when we speak of more than one, we use the *plural* number, as *one man* but *two men*

plus *prep.* in addition to as *Two plus five equals seven.*—*n.* the plus sign (of addition)

plush *n.* cloth with a long, soft nap

plu'tocrat *n.* a man who is powerful because of his wealth

ply *v.* 1. to use steadily, work at, as *The cobbler plies his trade at home.* 2. to supply urgently, as *They plied him with questions.* 3. to go to and fro, as *The ferry-boat plies across the lake.*—he **plies.**—**ply'ing** *pres. part.*—**plied** *p.t.* and *p. part.*

ply *n.* a thickness of cloth, wool or wood, as *three-ply wood.*—**ply'wood** *n.* sheets of wood glued together

pneumati'c (nū-mat'ik) *adj.* 1. worked by or fitted with air. 2. having to do with air

pneumo'nia (nū-mō'ni-a) *n.* inflammation of the lungs

poach (pōch) *v.* to cook an egg by boiling in water without the shell

poach (pōch) *v.* to take game or fish on some-one else's land without permission.—**poach'er** *n.*

pock'et *n.* 1. a small bag sewn into clothes. 2. a small bag. 3. a hollow in the earth containing ore, etc.—*v.* to put into one's pocket.—**pock'et-book** *n.* a wallet for carrying notes, etc.—**pock'et-knife** *n.* a folding knife.—**pock'etful** *n.*—**be out of pock'et,** to have lost money

pod *n.* the long shell in which beans and peas grow their seeds

poddy, poddy calf *n.* (Aus.) a hand-fed calf. Similarly, **poddy foal**

po'em *n.* a composition written in verse, lines in which words are arranged to make rhythm, and where there is beauty of thought and expression

po'et *n.* a writer of poems.—**po'etess** *fem.*—**poet'ic, poet'ical** *adj.* 1. having to do with poetry. 2. having the qualities of poetry

po'etry *n.* the art or work of a poet

poi'gnant (poi'nant) *adj.* sharp, stinging, moving, as *poignant sorrow.*—**poi'gnancy** (poi'nan-si) *n.*

point *n.* 1. a sharp end, as *the pencil's point.* 2. a dot, mark. 3. a certain spot or moment, as *At that point I stopped.* 4. a detail. 5. an essential idea, as *Your remark has point.* 6. a small headland. 7. a railway switch to turn trains on to other lines. 8. a direction on a compass, as *North and South are points of the compass.* 9. degree, as *boiling-point.*—*v.* 1. to sharpen. 2. to fill up joints between stones with mortar. 3. to show direction, as *The arrow points the way.*—**poin'ted** *adj.* sharp.—**poin'ter** *n.* 1. a rod used for pointing. 2. a dog trained to point out game.—**point'-blank'** *adv.* 1. at close range. 2. directly, bluntly.—**point' duty** *n.* duty of policeman to direct traffic at a certain point.—**in point of fact** really

poise (poiz) *n.* balance, as *A steady mind and body give poise.*—*v.* to balance, as *poised on a tight-rope.*—**poi'sing** *pres. part.*

poi'son (poi'zn) *n.* a substance which is very harmful to life and health.—*v.* to kill or injure with poison.—**poi'sonous** *adj.*

poke *v.* to push or stir with the end of a stick, finger, poker, etc.—**poke one's nose into** to pry into other people's business.—**po'king** *pres. part.*—**po'ker** *n.* 1. a gambling card game. 2. a metal rod for poking a fire.—**po'ky** *adj.* small, shut in

Po'land *n.* a European country west of Russia.—**Pole** *n.* a native of Poland.—**Po'lish** *adj.*

po'lar *adj.* near the north or the south pole.—**po'lar bear** *n.* a large white bear living in arctic regions

polder *n.* land reclaimed from the sea

pole *n.* 1. a long, rounded piece of wood. 2. a measure of length, 52 yards

pole *n.* each of the ends of the axis of the earth, or each end of a magnet.—**pole'star** *n.* a star near the North Pole, which often serves as a guide.—**polar'ity** *n.* having ends magnetically opposite, or electrically positive and negative.—**polarised light** light vibrating in one plane only

police' (po-lees') *n.* 1. public order. 2. a body of men who work for the government to keep order and arrest wrong-doers.—*v.* to keep order.—**police'man** *n.* a member of police.—**police'woman** *fem.*—**police state** a state ruled by a dictator whose laws are enforced by secret police

pol'icy (pol'i-si) *n.* 1. a line of action, plan for managing affairs esp. of state, as *It is a good policy not to run into debt.* 2. prudence, care for one's interests. 3. a contract of insurance.—**pol'icies** *pl.*

pol'ish *v.* 1. to make shiny. 2. to refine, as *You must polish your manners.*—*n.* 1. a polished state, shiny surface. 2. a substance used for polishing.—**pol'ishes** *pl.*

polite' *adj.* well-mannered, courteous, thoughtful for others.—**polite'ly** *adv.* **polite'ness** *n.*

pol'itic *adj.* 1. prudent, wise. 2. political

polit'ical *adj.* having to do with the state or its affairs.—**politi'cian** (pol-i-tish'an) *n.* a person engaged in political affairs.—**pol'itics** *n.pl.* management of state affairs

pol'ka *n.* a kind of lively dance

poll (pōl) *n.* 1. the head. 2. a counting of voters or of votes.—*v.* 1. to cut off the top of trees. 2. to vote, to receive votes. 3. to remove the horns of sheep, cattle

pol'len *n.* a fine yellow dust in flowers

pollina'tion (-ā'shun) *n.* carrying of pollen from stamen to stigma

pollute' (pol-ōōt') *v.* to make dirty, impure, as *This stream has been polluted by a dead cat.*—**pollu'ting** *pres. part.*—**pollu'tion** (-shun) *n.*

po'lo *n.* a game like hockey played on horseback with long mallets

poltroon' *n.* a coward.—**poltroon'ery** *n.*

polyes'ter (pol-i-es'ter) *n.* a kind of artificial plastic substance

pol'ygon (pol'i-gon) *n.* a figure with many angles or sides.—**polyg'onal** *adj.*

polytech'nic (pol-i-tek'nik) *adj.* dealing with many arts and crafts.—*n.*

pom'egranate *n.* a fruit with thick rind and many seeds

pom'mel (pum'el) *n.* a knob on a sword-hilt or on a saddle.—*v.* to beat, esp. with fists.—**pommelling** *pres. part.*—**pom'melled** *p.t.* and *p. part.*

pomp *n.* splendid show, ceremony, as *The prince was married with great pomp.*—**pomp'ous** *adj.* 1. showy. 2. self-important

pond *n.* a pool, small lake

pond'er *v.* to think over carefully

Compare: deliberate, meditate, muse, study, consider

pond'erous *adj.* heavy and clumsy, dull, as *a ponderous style*

pont'iff *n.* 1. the Pope. 2. a high priest.—**pontif'ical** *adj.*

pontoon' *n.* 1. a flat-bottomed boat used to support a temporary bridge. 2. a flat-bottomed boat. 3. a gambling card game

po'ny *n.* a horse of a small breed.—**po'nies** *pl.*

poo'dle *n.* a breed of dog with short curly hair

pool *n.* a pond, a deep place in a river

pool *v.* 1. to put money, etc., into a common fund, as *They pooled their pocket-money to buy a dog.*—*n.* 1. a common fund. 2. a system of gambling on football results

poop *n.* the stern of a ship

poor *adj.* 1. having little or no money. 2. feeble, as *a poor speaker*. 3. to be pitied, as *The poor dog is hurt.*—**poor'ly** *adv.*—**poor'ly** *adj.* not well.—**poor'ness** *n.*

pop *n.* a sudden, small explosive sound.—*v.* 1. to make this sound, as *The gun popped.* 2. to come or go suddenly. 3. to put suddenly, as *She popped her head through the window.*—**pop'ping** *pres. part.*—**popped** *p.t.* and *p. part.*—**pop'corn** *n.* Indian corn which bursts open when roasted.—**pop'-music** *n.* very popular modern dance music

Pope *n.* the head of the Roman Catholic Church

pop'lar *n.* a tall, slender tree

pop'lin *n.* a ribbed fabric of cotton and wool

pop'py *n.* a plant with bright flowers.—**pop'pies** *pl.*

pop'ulace *n.* the common people

pop'ular *adj.* 1. of the people, as *popular taste*. 2. liked by most people as *a popular writer.*—**popular'ity** *n.*—**pop'ularize** *v.* to make popular.—**pop'ularly** *adv.*

pop'ulate *v.* to fill with inhabitants, as *a thickly-populated district*

popula'tion (-lā'shun) *n.* 1. the inhabitants. 2. number of inhabitants.—**pop'ulous** *adj.* thickly populated

por'celain (por'slin) *n.* fine earthenware, china

porch *n.* a covered entrance to a building.—**porch'es** *pl.*

por'cupine *n.* an animal covered with long, pointed quills

pore *v.* to fix the eyes or the mind on, as *to pore over a book.*—**por'ing** *pres. part.*

pore *n.* a very small opening esp. in the skin

pork *n.* pig's flesh used for food.—**pork'er** *n.* young pig

por'ous *adj.* full of pores, allowing liquid to soak through, as *A sponge is porous*

por'poise (por'pus) *n.* a large, blunt-nosed, sea-animal

por'ridge (por'ij) *n.* oatmeal boiled in milk or water

port *n.* 1. a harbour. 2. a town with a harbour

port *n.* an opening in the side of a ship.—**port-hole**

port *n.* the left side of a ship, looking towards the bows, larboard

port *n.* a strong, red wine

port'able *adj.* which can be carried, as *a portable wireless-set*

port'age (port'ij) *n.* carrying goods, boats, etc. overland between rivers

port'al *n.* a large door or gate

portcul'lis *n.* a grating to raise or lower in front of a gateway in ancient castles

portend' *v.* to foretell, give warning of.—**por'tent** *n.* a warning, sign.—**porten'tous** *adj.* threatening, solemn

port'er *n.* 1. a door-keeper. 2. a man employed to carry luggage, etc.

portfo'lio *n.* 1. a case for carrying loose papers, etc. 2. the office of a minister of state.—**portfo'lios** *pl.*

port'ico *n.* a porch, covered walk.—**port'icos** *pl.*

por'tion (-shun) *n.* a part, share.—*v.* to divide into shares

port'ly *adj.* stout, bulky

por'trait (port'rit) *n.* a picture of a person

portray' *v.* 1. to paint or draw a likeness. 2. to describe.—**portray'al** *n.*

pose (pōz) *n.* 1. a position of the body, esp. assumed for effect, as *He posed for the sculptor.* 2. affectation, pretence.—*v.*

1. to take up an attitude. 2. to assume a false pose, as *He posed as a rich man.* 3. to put a question to.—**poser** *n.* a difficult question.—**po'sing** *pres. part.*

posi'tion (po-zish'un) *n.* 1. the way a thing is placed, as *The ball is in a difficult position.* 2. a place, as *What is your position on the list?* 3. an attitude. 4. a rank, as *a high position in the army.* 5. job, as *He has just obtained a good position*

pos'itive (poz'i-tiv) *adj.* 1. certain, definite, as *positive information.* 2. confident, too confident. 3. not negative, real, as *He gave positive help, not just promises.*—*n.* in grammar, the simple form of an adjective, contrasted with the *comparative* and *superlative*, as *"Good" is the positive, "better" the comparative*

possess' (po-zes') *v.* 1. to own. 2. to occupy, hold. 3. to control.—he **possess'es**

posses'sion (po-zesh'un) *n.* 1. something owned, property. 2. owning.—**posses'sive** (po-zes'iv) *adj.* 1. wanting to have too much influence on someone. 2. see *Note.*—**posses'sor** *n.* owner

Note: the *possessive* form is used to show the possessor or owner, as *my dog, this is yours, the camel's hump*

possibil'ity *n.* what is possible, possible event.—**possibil'ities** *pl.*

pos'sible *adj.* which can happen, be done, exist, which may be true.—**pos'sibly** *adv.*

pos'sum *n.* short form of **opossum.**—**to play possum** to sham death

post (pōst) *n.* an upright pole fixed firmly, usually as a support.—*v.* to put up a notice

post (pōst) *n.* 1. the official carrying of letters and parcels, mail. 2. a collection or delivery of letters, etc., as *When does the post go?* 3. a station, place of duty, as *Stay at your post.* 4. a place held by body of troops. 5. an office, a job, as *the post of ship's cook.*—*v.* 1. to mail letters, etc. 2. to station someone, as *He was posted on the bridge.*—**post'age** *n.* money paid for sending a letter.—**post'al** *adj.*—**post'al-order** *n.* a money-order which can be sent by post.—**post'card** *n.* a card sent by post.—**post-haste** *adv.* very quickly

post'er *n.* a large advertising notice posted up

poste'rior (pos-tee'ri-or) *adj.* later.—*n.* behind, back

poster'ity *n.* descendants, future generations

pos'tern *n.* a back entrance or door, a small door or gate

post'humous (pos'tū-mus) *adj.* 1. after death. 2. born after the death of the father. 3. published after the author's death.—**post'humously** *adv.*

postil'ion, postill'ion *n.* a man who rides one of a pair of horses drawing a carriage

post'man *n.* a man who carries and delivers the post.—**post'men** *pl.*

post'master *n.* an official in charge of a post-office.—**post'mistress** *fem.*

post-mor'tem *n.* the medical examination of a dead body

postpone' *v.* to put off to a later time.—**postpo'ning** *pres. part.*—**postpone'ment** *n.*

Compare: defer, adjourn, delay, procrastinate

post'script *n.* something written after the end of a letter or book

pos'tulate *v.* to assume, to suppose

pos'ture *n.* a position of the body.—*v.* to pose

po'sy (pō'zi) *n.* a bunch of flowers.—**po'sies** *pl.*

pot *n.* a vessel made of earthenware, glass or metal.—*v.* to put into a pot.—**pot'ting** *pres. part.*—**pot'ted** *p.t.* and *p. part.*

pot'ash *n.* an alkali made from wood ashes.—**caustic potash** potassium hydroxide

pota'to *n.* a vegetable, the swollen underground stems of the plant.—**pota'toes** *pl.*

po'tency (pō'ten-si) *n.* strength, power, as *the potency of a poison.*—**po'tent** *adj.* powerful, influential

po'tentate *n.* a prince, ruler

poten'tial (pō-ten'shal) *adj.* which may act or be, but does not act or exist now, as *The soil is full of potential wealth.*—**potential'ity** *n.* possible power.—**poten'tial, poten'tially** *adv.*—**potential energy** (science) energy waiting to be released

pot'hole *n.* 1. a deep hole or cave in the earth. 2. a hole in the surface of a road.—**pot'-holing** *v.* the exploring of potholes

po'tion (-shun) *n.* a dose of medicine or poison

pot'ter *n.* a maker of earthenware pots and dishes.—**pot'tery** *n.* 1. earthenware. 2. a place where pots are made.—**pot'teries** *pl.*

pot'ter *v.* to move about or work in a casual manner

pouch (powch) *n.* a small bag.—**pouch'es** *pl.*

poul'terer (pōl'ter-er) *n.* a dealer in poultry

poul'tice (pōl'tis) *n.* a soft, moist bag of bread or herbs applied to the skin as a cure

poul'try (pōl'tri) *n.* farmyard birds, fowls, etc.

pounce *v.* to jump on suddenly, to swoop.—*n.*—**poun'cing** *pres. part.*

pound *n.* 1. a weight, sixteen ounces avoirdupois, twelve ounces troy. 2. a unit of money, one hundred pence

pound *v.* 1. to beat heavily. 2. to crush to powder

pound *n.* an enclosed space for stray cattle

poun'dal *n.* (science) a unit of force, the force giving a mass of one pound an acceleration of one foot per second per second

pour (por) *v.* 1. to come out in a stream, as *Water poured through the crack.* 2. to cause to flow, as *Pour the milk into the cup*

pout *v.* to push out the lips, as *She pouted sulkily.*—*n.*

pov'erty *n.* being poor, poorness.—**pov'erty-stricken** *adj.* very poor

pow'der *n.* 1. a solid reduced to fine dry dust.

2. a medicine in powder form. 3. tinted cosmetic in powder form.—*v.* 1. to put powder on, sprinkle, as *The cake is powdered with sugar.* 2. to make into powder.—**pow'dery** *adj.*—**pow'dering** *n.*

pow'er *n.* 1. ability to act, as *He gave all the help in his power.* 2. strength, might, authority, as *the power to arrest offenders.* 3. a mighty nation, as *America and Russia are great powers.*—*v.* to supply power to, as *The engine is powered by electricity.*—**pow'erful** *adj.* strong, mighty.—**pow'erless** *adj.*—**pow'er-house** *n.* a place for generating and distributing electric power.—**power-point** *n.* a wall socket supplying electricity

Compare: capacity, efficiency, energy, force. *Contrast:* weakness, impotence, inability, incapacity, inefficiency, weakness, helplessness

prac'ticable *adj.* which can be done, or used, as *a practicable idea*

prac'tical *adj.* 1. having to do with action rather than ideas, as *a practical mind.* 2. useful, sensible, as *a practical dress.*—**prac'tically** *adv.* 1. really so, though not in name. 2. in a useful way

prac'tice (prak'tis) *n.* 1. doing something often to gain skill, as *football practice.* 2. habit, method, as *It was her practice to bathe before breakfast* 3. the business of a doctor or lawyer

prac'tise *v.* 1. to do usually, as *to practise patience.* 2. to work at, as *to practise batting.* 3. to exercise a profession, as *to practise law.*—**prac'tising** *pres. part.*—**prac'tised** *adj.* skilled

practit'ioner (-shun-er) *n.* lawyer or doctor.—**general practitioner** *n.* a doctor who has not specialised in any branch of medicine

prair'ie *n.* a wide stretch of grassland without trees

praise (prāz) *v.* 1. to speak well of. 2. to worship, honour.—**prai'sing** *pres. part.*—*n.* praising.—**praise'worthy** *adj.*

Compare: (with *n.*) applause, approval, approbation, acclamation, compliment, flattery, plaudit

prance *v.* 1. to jump about on hind legs, of horses. 2. to strut about.—**pran'cing** *pres. part.*

prank (prangk) *n.* a trick, frolic

prate *v.* to chatter, talk idly.—**pra'ting** *pres. part.*

prat'tle *v.* to talk like a child.—*n.* babble

prawn *n.* a shell-fish resembling a shrimp

pray *v.* 1. to offer prayers to God. 2. to beg, ask earnestly.—**prayer** (prār) *n.* 1. an entreaty to God. 2. praying.—**prayer'ful** *adj.*

preach (preech) *v.* 1. to give a talk on a religious subject. 2. to advise strongly, to recommend. 3. to give unwelcome moral advice—he **preach'es.**—**preach'er** *n.*

pream'ble *n.* a preface, introduction

preca'rious (pre-kār'i-us) *adj.* uncertain, dangerous, as *The fisherman earns a precarious living*

Compare: insecure, risky, unsteady, hazardous, perilous

precau'tion (-shun) *n.* care taken beforehand.—**precau'tionary** *adj.*

precede' (pree-seed') *v.* 1. to go before, as *A precedes B in the alphabet.* 2. to be more important.—**prece'ding** *pres. part.*—**prece'dence** *n.* 1. going before. 2. higher position, as *They entered in order of precedence.*—**pre'cedent** (pres'i-dent) *n.* something done or said which will serve as an example.—**prece'ding** *adj.* coming before

pre'cept (pree'sept) *n.* a rule for conduct

pre'cinct (pree'singkt) *n.* ground round a church or official building

pre'cious (presh'us) *adj.* 1. of great value. 2. affected, too refined—**pre'ciousness** *n.*

pre'cipice (pres'i-pis) *n.* a steep cliff

precip'itate (pre-sip'i-tāt) *v.* 1. to throw down violently, hurl. 2. to cause to hasten, as *The accident precipitated his death.*—*adj.* too sudden, rash, as a *precipitate action.*—**precipita'tion** (-tā'shun) *n.*—**precip'itous** *adj.* very steep

pré'cis (prā'see) *n.* a summary

precise' (pre-sīs') *adj.* 1. exact, accurate. 2. careful.—**precise'ly** *adv.*—**precis'ion** (pre-sizh'un) *n.* accuracy

Compare: careful, correct, distinct, perfect, minute, particular, strict, flawless

preclude' (pre-clōōd') *v.* to shut out, prevent

preco'cious (pre-kō'shus) *adj.* developed too soon.—**preco'city** (prekos'i-ti) *n.*

precur'sor *n.* a forerunner

preda'tory *adj.* 1. given to plundering and robbery. 2. given to preying, as *The tiger is a predatory animal*

predeces'sor (pre-di-ses'or) *n.* a person holding a position before another

Contrast: successor

predestina'tion (-ā'shun) *n.* fate, a deciding beforehand on the destiny of man.—**predes'tined** *adj.* ordained beforehand

predic'ament *n.* an unpleasant or difficult situation

pred'icate *n.* the part of a sentence containing what is said about the subject, e.g. *a boy dug a hole.* In this sentence, *dug a hole* is the *predicate*

predict' *v.* to tell beforehand, foretell.—**predic'tion** (-shun) *n.* prophecy.—**predict'able** *adj.*

predilec'tion (-shun) *n.* preference, liking

predom'inant *adj.* chief, most powerful, prevailing, as *a predominant colour, a predominant opinion*

predom'inate *v.* to prevail, to be most powerful.—**predom'inating** *pres. part.*

pre-em'inence (pree-em'in-ens) *n.* being above all others.—**pre-em'inent** *adj.*

preen *v.* 1. (of a bird) to trim feathers with

the beak. 2. (of a person) to show self-satisfaction

pre'-fab *n.* a prefabricated house

prefab'ricate *v.* to make a house, ship, etc. in sections ready for erection later

pref'ace *n.* remarks at the beginning of a book or speech.—**pref'atory** *adj.* introductory

pre'fect *n.* 1. a person in authority. 2. the chief official in a French department. 3. a senior scholar responsible for maintaining discipline

prefer' *v.* 1. to like better, as *He prefers coffee to tea.* 2. to promote.—**prefer'ring** *pres. part.*—**preferred'** *p.t.* and *p. part.*—**pre'ferable** *adj.* better.—**pref'erably** *adv.*

Compare: elect, favour, choose

pref'erence *n.* liking better, choice.—**prefer'ment** *n.* promotion

Compare: pick, alternative, option, election

pre'fix *n.* a syllable or word placed at the beginning of a word, and changing its meaning, as *dislike, insincere, non-combatant*

preg'nant *adj.* 1. bearing a child in the womb. 2. full of ideas or meaning

prehistor'ic *adj.* belonging to the time before written history begins

prejudge' (pree-juj') *v.* to judge before hearing

prej'udice (prej'oo-dis) *n.* 1. opinion formed without enough knowledge or thought. 2. harm, injury, as *She played games to the prejudice of her work.*—*v.* 1. to injure. 2. to have one's mind fixed unfavourably. —**prejudi'cial** (prej-oo-dish'al) *adj.*

prel'ate (prel'at) *n.* a bishop, or clergyman of higher rank

prelim'inary *adj.* introductory, coming before the chief business, as *a preliminary examination.*—*n.*

prel'ude *n.* 1. a performance, or piece of music, serving as introduction. 2. preface, as *Black clouds were the prelude to a fearful storm*

prem'ature *adj.* too soon, happening before the proper time.—**prem'aturely** *adv.*

premed'itate *v.* to plan beforehand.—**premed'itating** *pres. part.*—**premedita'tion** (-tā'shun) *n.*

prem'ier (pre'mi-er) *adj.* chief, first, as *premier duke.*—*n.* the Prime Minister

premiere' (prem-i-ār') *n.* a first performance

prem'ises *n.pl.* house or buildings with its belongings

pre'mium *n.* 1. a reward. 2. money paid for insurance. 3. a bonus, extra payment

premoni'tion (pree-mon-ish'un) *n.* forewarning, feeling of coming evil

preoccupa'tion (-pā'shun) *n.* having one's mind full of a certain subject.—**preoc'cupied** *adj.* absent-minded, abstracted

preoc'cupy *v.* to occupy the mind.—**preoc'cupying** *pres. part.*—**preoc'cupied** *p.t.* and *p. part.*

pre-packed' *adj.* sold in packing put on by the manufacturer

prepara'tion (-ā'shun) *n.* 1. making ready. 2. being ready. 3. work done beforehand for a lesson. 4. medicine

prepar'atory *adj.* introductory, preparing for, as *a preparatory school*

prepare' (pree-pār') *v.* 1. to make ready, as *to prepare food.* 2. to get ready, as *We were prepared for the worst. I am prepared to pay.*—**prepa'ring** *pres. part.*

Compare: arrange, fit, adjust, provide, order, procure

prepay' *v.* to pay in advance.—**prepay'ing** *pres. part.*—**prepaid'** *p.t.* and *p. part.*

prepon'derance *n.* greater weight, numbers, power.—**prepon'derate** *v.* to be the most important

preposi'tion (prep-o-zish'un) *n.* a word put in front of a noun. With the noun it makes a phrase which does the work of either an adj. or an adverb, as *Put it on the table. A boy* with *red hair*

prepossess' (pree-po-zes') *v.* 1. to possess beforehand. 2. to impress, esp. favourably. —**prepossess'ing** *adj.* attractive.—**preposses'sion** (-shun) *n.*

prepos'terous *adj.* absurd, ridiculous

prerog'ative *n.* right, special privilege

pres'age (pres'ij) *n.* an omen, sign of something about to happen.—*v.* (pre-sāj')

Presbyte'rian *n.* a member of the nonconformist Presbyterian church.—**pres'bytery** *n.* 1. the house of a Roman Catholic parish priest. 2. a body of Presbyterian ministers

prescribe' *v.* 1. to order. 2. to order the use of a medicine.—**prescri'bing** *pres. part.*

prescrip'tion (-shun) *n.* 1. an order. 2. a written order for medicine

pre'sence (prez'ens) *n.* 1. being present, as *Your presence is requested.* 2. personal appearance. 3. impressive bearing, as *the actor had great presence.*—**pre'sence of mind** *n.* ability to think and act quickly

pres'ent (prez'ent) *adj.* 1. here. 2. existing now, as *the present mayor.*—*n.* 1. present time. 2. in grammar the *present tense* is used when we speak of something happening now, or just going to happen, as *I am coming*

pres'ent (prez'ent) *n.* a gift

present' (pre-zent') *v.* 1. to show as, *They presented themselves.* 2. to introduce. 3. to offer, give, as *to present a bill.*—**present'able** *adj.* fit to be seen.—**presenta'tion** (-tā'shun) *n.* presenting

present'iment (pre-zen'ti-ment) *n.* foreboding, a sense of coming misfortune

pres'ently *adv.* soon

preserva'tion (prez-er-va'shun) *n.* 1. preserving. 2. being preserved

preser'vative *n.* a substance which protects from decay or injury

preserve' (pre-zerv') *v.* 1. to keep from harm or decay. 2. to keep up.—**preser'ving** *pres. part.*—*n.* 1. jam. 2. a place where game is kept for shooting

preside' (pre-zīd') *v.* 1. to be in charge of a meeting. 2. to control.—**presi'ding** *pres. part.*—**pres'idency** *n.* being president

pres'ident (prez'-ident) *n.* 1. the head of a society, company, etc. 2. the chosen head of a republic.—**presiden'tial** (prez-i-den'-shal) *adj.*

press *v.* 1. to push or squeeze, as *Press the button.* 2. to urge, recommend strongly, as *We pressed our demands.*—*n.* 1. a crowd. 2. a machine for pressing esp. a printing machine. 3. the printing-house. 4. newspapers. 5. journalists

press *v.* to force into military or naval service.—**press'gang** *n.* men formerly employed in pressing men for the navy

press'ing *adj.* urgent

pres'sure (presh'er) *n.* 1. weight. 2. strain, as *the pressure of work.* 3. influence, as *Pressure was brought to bear and at last he consented to do the job.*—**pressure-cooker** *n.* a utensil which cooks food under steam pressure

prestige' (pres-teezh') *n.* reputation and the confidence based on it

presum'ably (pre-zū'ma-bli) *adv.* probably

presume' (pre-zūm') *v.* 1. to suppose that something is true, as *I presume you know the rules.* 2. to venture, as *May I presume to offer advice?* 3. to take liberties, as *Are we presuming on your kindness?*—**presu'ming** *pres. part.*

presump'tion (pre-zump'shun) *n.* 1. something very probable. 2. impudent behaviour.—**presump'tive** *adj.* probable.—**heir presump'tive** *n.* the person who will inherit unless a nearer heir is born.—**presump'tuous** *adj.* impudent

presuppose' (pree-sup-ōz') *v.* to take for granted.—**presupposi'tion** (-shun) *n.*

pretence' *n.* 1. pretending, a false appearance. 2. a false excuse

pretend' *v.* 1. to make believe. 2. to claim.—**pretend'er** *n.* a person claiming a title, etc.

Compare: affect, assume, feign, profess, sham, simulate

preten'tion (-shun) *n.* 1. claim. 2. claim to merit, importance, etc.—**preten'tious** (preten'shus) *adj.* showy, self-important

pre'text *n.* an excuse

Compare: show, disguise, cloak, mask, ruse, semblance, simulation

pret'tily (prit'i-li) *adv.* in a pretty manner

Compare: sweetly, neatly, charmingly, attractively, gracefully, elegantly, delightfully, daintily

pret'tiness *n.* being pretty

pret'ty (prit'i) *adj.* pleasing, charming, as *pretty manners, a pretty hat.*—**pret'tier** *comp.*—**pret'tiest** *sup.*—*adv.* fairly, as *I am pretty sure of it*

prevail' *v.* 1. to succeed, to gain the victory, as *We prevailed on him to speak. Right will prevail over evil.* 2. to be widespread, most usual, as *Old customs still prevail here.*—**prevail'ing** *adj.* usual

prev'alence *n.* being prevalent.—**prev'alent** *adj.* widespread, common, usual, as *a prevalent disease*

prevar'icate (pree-var'i-kāt) *v.* to avoid telling the truth.—**prevar'icating** *pres. part.*—**prevarica'tion** (-shun) *n.*

prevent' *v.* 1. to stop from happening, as *Rain prevented play.* 2. to hinder, as *He will come if nothing prevents him.*—**preven'tion** (-shun) *n.*—**prevent'ive** *n.* something that prevents.—*adj.* hindering, as *to take preventive measures*

pre'view *n.* a private view of pictures, etc. before they are shown in public

pre'vious (pree'vius) *adj.* happening before, former.—**pre'viously** *adv.* before

prey (prā) *n.* 1. an animal hunted and killed by another. 2. a victim.—*v.* (on) 1. to hunt, plunder. 2. to vex. fill with worry

price (prīs) *n.* 1. the cost of buying something. the cost of obtaining something, as *The price of victory.* 2. value, as *stones of great price.*—*v.* to fix a price.—**pri'cing** *pres. part.*—**price'less** *adj.* above price, very valuable

Compare: cost, value, worth, charge, expense

prick *n.* 1. a sharp point. 2. a very small hole, as *a pin-prick.* 3. pain caused by a sharp point.—*v.* to pierce or mark with a sharp point, as *The thorn pricked me.*—**to prick up one's ears,** to listen with sudden attention.—**to prick out** (seedling) to plant out

prick'le *n.* a thorn, spike.—*v.* to feel a tingle.—**prick'ling** *pres. part.*—**prick'ly** *adj.* full of thorns, etc.

pride *n.* 1. too great an opinion of oneself. 2. self-respect, as *She takes pride in her work.* 3. something to be proud, of as *He is his mother's pride.*—**to pride oneself** to be proud of

priest (preest) *n.* 1. a minister of a religion. 2. a servant of a god.—**priest'ess** *fem.*—**priest'hood** *n.* priest's office.—**priest'ly** *adj.*

prig *n.* a self-satisfied person.—**prig'gish** *adj.*

prim *adj.* stiff, proper, formal

pri'ma don'na (pree'ma don'a) *n.* a leading woman singer in an opera.—**pri'ma don'nas** *pl.*

pri'marily *adv.* 1. at first. 2. chiefly

pri'mary *adj.* 1. first in time or importance, as *primary schools.* 2. original.—**pri'mary col'ours** red, yellow and blue which cannot be produced by the mixing of other colours

pri'mate *n.* 1. an archbishop. 2. one of the higher mammals, man, monkey, etc.

prime *adj.* 1. first, chief. 2. excellent.—*n.* the

best part, as *the prime of life.*—*v.* 1. to charge (a gun) with powder. 2. to instruct beforehand.—**Prime Min'ister** *n.* the leader of the government.—**prime number** a number which has no factors

pri'mer *n.* a schoolbook for beginners

prime'val (prī-mee'val) *adj.* belonging to the earliest age of the world, original, as *primeval forests*

prim'itive *adj.* 1. first, living in ancient times, as *primitive man.* 2. simple, undeveloped, as *A pointed stick is a primitive weapon*

prim'rose *n.* 1. a spring flower with pale yellow flowers. 2. pale yellow

prince *n.* 1. a ruler, chief. 2. son of royal birth of a king or queen.—**princ'ess** (prin'ses) *fem.*—**prince'ly** *adj.* 1. noble. 2. magnificent.—**Prince Consort** the husband of a Queen of Britain.—**Prince of Wales** heir to the British throne

prin'cipal (prin'si-pal) *adj.* most important, chief, as *This actor took the principal part.* —*n.* 1. head of a school or college. 2. sum of money bringing in interest.—**prin'cipally** *adv.* mainly

Note: do not confuse *principal* (*adj.*) with *principle*

principal'ity (prin-si-pal'i-ti) *n.* country ruled by a prince.—**principal'ities** *pl.*

prin'ciple (prin'si-pl) *n.* 1. an accepted truth on which other truths are based, as *the principle of government.* 2. rule guiding behaviour. 3. uprightness, as *a man of good principle*

Note: Do not confuse *principle* **n.** with *principal adj.*

print *n.* 1. mark made by pressing on a surface, as *a finger-print.* 2. words, pictures made by inked type, or photography. 3. cotton with a pattern pressed on it.—*v.* 1. to stamp words, etc. on paper. 2. to produce, publish, as *His letter was printed in the paper.*—**print'er** *n.*—**print'ing** *n.*—**printing-press** *n.* a machine used for printing

pri'or *adj.* earlier.—**prior'ity** *n.* 1. being earlier. 2. coming first in importance

pri'or *n.* the head of religious house.—**pri'oress** *fem.*—**pri'ory** *n.* a religious house. —**pri'ories** *pl.*

prise see **prize**

prism (prizm) *n.* 1. a solid with bases or ends of the same shape and size, and parallel to each other. The long sides are parallelograms. 2. a transparent solid of this shape by which light is refracted.—**prismat'ic** *adj.*

pris'on (priz'n) *n.* a place where lawbreakers are locked up.—**pris'oner** *n.* 1. a person kept in prison for breaking the law. 2. a person captured in war

pri'vacy (prī'va-si, priv'asi) *n.* seclusion, being apart from others

pri'vate (prī'vat) *adj.* not public, for one person, or a few only, as *a private road, a private letter.*—*n.* a soldier without rank. —**pri'vately** *adv.* secretly.—**private school** a school not under government control

priva'tion (-vā'shun) *n.* want, hardship, lack of necessities

priv'et *n.* an evergreen shrub much used for hedges

priv'ilege (priv'i-lej) *n.* a special right or favour, as *Senior pupils sometimes have privileges.*—**priv'ileged** *adj.* favoured

priv'y *adj.* secret.—**priv'y coun'cil** *n.* a body of persons appointed by the King

prize *n.* 1. a reward given for success. 2. something worth working for. 3. something taken from the enemy in war.—*v.* to value highly, as *He prizes his stamp-collection.* —**prizefight** *n.* boxing-match for money

prize, prise *v.* to force open

pro- prefix 1. before. 2. in favour of

pro *n.* an argument in favour of.—**pros and cons** arguments for and against

pro (prō) *n.* a professional games player

probabil'ity *n.* being probable, likelihood

prob'able *adj.* 1. likely, to be expected. 2. likely to be true as, *a probable explanation.* —**prob'ably** *adv.*

proba'tion (-bā'shun) *n.* 1. a test of character, behaviour. 2. a period of preparation in a religious order. 3. a system of suspending sentence as long as the offender is of good behaviour and reports regularly to a **probation officer**

probe *v.* to search thoroughly, to examine.—**pro'bing** *pres. part.*—*n.* a surgical instrument for examining wounds

pro'bity *n.* honesty, uprightness

prob'lem *n.* a question or difficulty to be solved.—**problema'tic, problema'tical** *adj.* doubtful, uncertain

probos'cis (prō-bos'is) *n.* 1. elephant's trunk, a snout. 2. sucking tube of certain insects

proce'dure (prō-seed'yer) *n.* a way of doing things, conduct, as *The correct procedure for applying for a motor licence*

proceed' (prō-seed') *v.* 1. to go forward, advance, continue, as *The work is proceeding satsfactorily.* 2. to begin, to set about, as *He proceeded to make himself comfortable.* —**proceed'ing** *n.* action.—*pl.* 1. business done at a meeting. 2. suing in a law-court. —**pro'ceeds** *n.pl.* money gained at a sale

pro'cess (prō'ses) *n.* 1. a state of going on, as *It is in process of manufacture.* 2. a method of making, as *a new process for making steel.* 3. a legal action, summons

proces'sion (prō-sesh'un) *n.* 1. marching forward. 2. orderly progress. 3. persons marching in a certain order.—**proces'sional** *adj.*

proclaim *v.* 1. to announce publicly. 2. to show, as *The apparel oft proclaims the man* (Shakespeare).—**proclama'tion** (-mā'shun) *n.* official announcement

Compare: declare, decree, publish, manifest, reveal

procras'tinate *v.* to put off, delay.—**procras'-tinating** *pres. part.*—**procrastina'tion** (-ā'-shun) *n.*

procur'able (prō-kū'ra-bl) *adj.* obtainable

procure' *v.* to get, obtain.—**procur'ing** *pres. part.*

prod *v.* to poke with something pointed.—**prod'ding** *pres. part.*—**prod'ded** *p.t.* and *p. part.*—*n.* a pointed instrument

prod'igal *adj.* 1. wasteful. 2. lavish.—*n.* a wasteful person, spendthrift.—**prodigal'ity** *n.* extravagance.—**prod'igally** *adv.*

Compare: extravagant, spendthrift, careless, dissipated. *Contrast:* thrifty, careful, prudent

prodig'ious (prō-dij'us) *adj.* 1. enormous. 2. extraordinary.—**prodig'iously** *adv.*—**prod'-igy** (prod'i-ji) *n.* a marvel.—**prod'igies** *pl.*

produce' (pro-dūs') *v.* 1. to show, bring out, as *The conjurer produced a rabbit from the hat.* 2. to make, supply, as *His remark produced no effect. Canada produces wheat.*—**produ'cing** *pres. part.*—**prod'uce** *n.* result, thing produced.—**produ'cer** *n.* 1. one who produces. 2. an organiser of a play or film

Compare: 1. exhibit, display. 2. cause, create, effect, manufacture, originate, engender, yield

prod'uct *n.* 1. what is produced by manufacture or growth. 2. in Mathematics, the result of multiplication.—**produc'tion** (-shun) *n.* 1. manufacture. 2. things produced.—**produc'tive** *adj.* 1. producing. 2. fertile

profana'tion (ā'shun) *n.* showing disrespect for sacred things

profane' *adj.* 1. not sacred. 2. without respect for holy things.—*v.* to treat without reverence.—**profa'ning** *pres. part.*—**profan'-ity** *n.* 1. irreverence. 2. blasphemy, swearing

profess' *v.* 1. to declare. 2. to claim. 3. to have as one's profession.—he **profess'es**

profes'sion (prō-fesh'n) *n.* 1. declaration. 2. an occupation, esp. learned or artistic.—**profes'sional** *adj.* of a profession.—*n.* a paid player at football, golf, etc.—**pro-fes'sionally** *adv.*

profes'sor *n.* a teacher of the highest rank in a University.—**professor'ial** *adj.*—**profes'sorship** *n.*

prof'fer *v.* to offer.—*n.*

profi'ciency (prō-fish'en-si) *n.* ability, skill.—**profi'cient** *adj.* expert, skilful

pro'file (prō'feel, prō'fīl) *n.* an outline seen from the side, e.g. of the face

prof'it *n.* gain, benefit.—*v.* to gain, get advantage.—**prof'itable** *adj.* bringing profit.—**prof'itably** *adv.*—**prof'itless** *adj.*

prof'ligate *n.* a wicked, reckless person.—*adj.*

profound' *adj.* 1. deep. 2. learned, hard to understand.—**profund'ity** *n.*

profuse' (prō-fūs') *adj.* lavish, abundant.—**profu'sion** (pro-fū'zhun) *n.* great abundance

progen'itor (prō-jen'i-tor) *n.* fore-father, ancestor

prog'eny (proj'en-i) *n.* children, descendants

pro'gramme *n.* 1. a list of events. 2. a plan of what is going to be done

pro'gress *n.* going forward, advancing, improvement.—**progress'** *v.* to go forward.—**progres'sion** (prō-gresh'n) *n.*—**pro-gres'sive** *adv.* 1. advancing. 2. favouring progress

Contrast: reaction, decline, decay, retrogression, stoppage

prohib'it *v.* to forbid, to prevent.—**prohibi't-ion** (-shun) *n.* forbidding.—**prohib'itive** *adj.*

Compare: debar, hinder, inhibit, preclude, prevent. *Contrast:* permit, allow, consent, suffer, sanction

proj'ect *n.* a plan.—**project'** *v.* 1. to plan. 2. to throw. 2. to cause to appear on, e.g. a screen. 4. to stick out.—**projec'tile** *n.* a missile, e.g. cannon-ball

projec'tion (-shun) *n.* 1. something that sticks out. 2. throwing.—**projec'tor** *n.* 1. a person who makes business plans. 2. an apparatus for throwing pictures on a screen

proletar'iat(e) (prō-let-ār'i-at) *n.* the working classes, wage-earners

prolif'ic *adj.* fruitful, producing much

pro'logue (prō'log) *n.* a speech introducing a play

prolong' *v.* to make longer, lengthen.—**prolonga'tion** (prō-long-gā'shun) *n.* extension

promenade' (prom-e-nahd') *n.* a place for walking up and down.—*v.* to walk up and down

prom'inence *n.* 1. a part that sticks out. 2. a state of being conspicuous, importance

prom'inent *adv.* eminent, most visible, standing out in full relief

promis'cuous *adj.* mixed, confused

prom'ise (prom'is) *n.* 1. giving one's word to do or not to do something. 2. giving reason for hope, as *His work is full of promise.*—*v.* 1. to give one's word. 2. to give hope.—**prom'ising** *adj.* showing early signs of future success.—**breach of promise** the breaking of an engagement to marry.—**to promise well** to show early signs of future success

prom'ontory *n.* a headland, high land jutting into the sea.—**prom'ontories** *pl.*

promote' *v.* 1. to move up to a higher rank or position, as *The soldier was promoted for his courage.* 2. to help on, *to promote a company.*—**promo'ting** *pres. part.*—**promo'tion** (-mō'shun) *n.*

prompt *adj.* quick, done at once.—*v.* 1. to suggest. 2. to remind, e.g. an actor, of his next words.—**prompt'er** *n.*—**prompt'itude** *n.* readiness.—**prompt'ness** *n.* quickness. —**prompt'ly** *adv.*

prone *adj.* 1. lying face downward. 2. inclined to, as *He is prone to make mistakes in subtraction*

prong *n.* one spike of a fork

pro'noun *n.* a word used instead of a noun, e.g. *he, she, it, who, which, etc.*

pronounce' (pro-nowns') *v.* 1. to speak, utter, sound. 2. to give a decision, pass judgment, as *He pronounced the wine excellent.* —**pronoun'cing** *pres. part.*—**pronounced'** *adj.* strong, decided.—**pronounce'ment** *n.* declaration

pronuncia'tion (pro-nun-si-ā'shun) *n.* the way words are sounded

proof *n.* 1. a way of showing that something is true beyond doubt. 2. a test. 3. a trial copy of printed matter.—*adj.* able to resist, as *proof against temptation, waterproof*

prop *n.* 1. something that supports, holds up. 2. abbreviation of (stage) property.—*v.* to hold up.—**prop'ping** *pres. part.*—**propped** *p.t.* and *p. part.*

propagan'da *n.* any method of making someone believe what you want them to, whether true or false

prop'agate *v.* 1. to produce young, to multiply. 2. to spread.—**prop'agating** *pres. part.* —**propaga'tion** (-gā'shun) *n.*

Compare: promote, extend, diffuse. *Contrast:* eradicate, destroy, exterminate

propel' *v.* to drive forward.—**propel'ling** *pres. part.*—**propelled'** *p.t.* and *p. part.*—**propel'ler** *n.* a revolving shaft with blades for driving a ship or aircraft

prop'er *adj.* 1. right, suitable, fit. 2. handsome, as *a proper man.*—**proper noun** in Grammar, the name of a person, place, etc., e.g. *John, London.*—**proper fraction** in Mathematics, a fraction less in value than a whole number, e.g. $\frac{1}{3}$.—**prop'erly** *adv.* 1. correctly, 2. strictly

prop'erty *n.* 1. a thing owned, possessions. 2. a quality, belonging to something, as *The lecturer described the properties of matter.* 3. an article used on the stage in a play. 4. (Aus.) a land holding, generally of considerable size.—**prop'erties** *pl.*

proph'ecy (prof'es-i) *n.* 1. foretelling the future. 2. a forecast, prediction.—**proph'ecies** *pl.*—**proph'esy** (prof'e-sī) *v.* to foretell.—**proph'esying** *pres. part.*—**proph'esied** *p.t.* and *p. part.*

Note: The difference between *prophecy* (*n.*) and *prophesy* (*v.*)

proph'et (prof'et) *n.* 1. a person who foretells the future. 2. a religious teacher, preacher. —**proph'etess** *fem.*—**prophet'ic** *adj.* foretelling, warning

propit'iate (prō-pish'i-āt) *v.* to appease, to gain the favour of.—**propitia'tion** (-ā'shun) *n.*—**propit'ious** (pro-pish'us) *adj.* favourable

Compare: conciliate, reconcile. *Contrast:* offend, estrange

propor'tion (-shun) *n.* 1. a share. 2. a size or number, compared with another.—*v.* to arrange, so that there is balance.—**propor'tional** *adj.* in the right proportion, corresponding.—**propor'tionate** *adj.* proportional

propo'sal (propō'zl) *n.* 1. a plan, suggestion. 2. an offer of marriage

propose' (pro-pōz') *v.* 1. to suggest, put forward, plan, as *We propose to go for our holidays in August.* 2. to offer marriage. —**propo'sing** *pres. part.*

proposit'ion (prop-o-zish'un) *n.* 1. a statement. 2. an offer, proposal

propound' *v.* to propose, put forward

propri'etary *adj.* holding or held as property

propri'etor *n.* an owner.—**propri'etress** *fem.*—**propri'etorship** *n.* ownership

propri'ety *n.* fitness, proper behaviour.—**propri'eties** *pl.*

Compare: decorum, decency, modesty. *Contrast:* impropriety, indecorum, misbehaviour, misconduct, rudeness

propul'sion (-shun) *n.* driving forword

prosa'ic (prō-zā'ik) *adj.* 1. like prose. 2. ordinary, commonplace

proscribe' *v.* 1. to outlaw, banish. 2. to condemn, speak against.—**proscri'bing** *pres. part.*—**proscrip'tion** (shun) *n.*

prose (prōz) *n.* 1. plain speech or writing, not verse, esp. as literature

pros'ecute *v.* 1. to take legal action against as *Trespassers will be prosecuted.* 2. to carry on, pursue, as *We will prosecute the war until victory has been won*—**pros'ecuting** *pres. part.*—**prosecu'tion** (-kū'shun) *n.* 1. legal proceedings. 2. people bringing proceedings. 3. carrying on.—**pros'ecutor** *n.*

pros'elyte *n.* a person who has changed his religious belief

pros'pect *n.* 1. a view. 2. expectation, outlook. —**prospect'** *v.* to explore, search.—**prospec'tive** *adj.* awaited, expected.—**prospec'tor** *n.* someone who searches for minerals or oil

prospec'tus *n.* a printed notice describing and advertising a company, school, etc.

pros'per *v.* to flourish, succeed, to cause to do well.—**prosper'ity** *n.* good fortune.—**pros'perous** *adj.* fortunate, wealthy

pros'trate *adj.* 1. lying flat on the ground. 2. overcome, helpless.—**prostrate'** *v.* 1. to throw down flat. 2. to overcome.—**prostra'ting** *pres. part.*—**prostra'tion** (-shun) *n.*

pro'sy *adj.* dull, commonplace

protag'onist *n.* a leading character

protect' *v.* to defend, shield.—**protec'tion** (shun) *n.* 1. care, defence. 2. anything that protects, shelter.—**protec'tive** *adj.*—**protec'tor** *n.* defender.—**protec'torate** *n.* a weaker state protected and controlled by a stronger

Compare: guard, preserve, secure. *Contrast:* attack, expose, betray

protégé (prot'ā-zhā) *n.* a person under the care of another.—**prot'égée** *fem.*

pro'tein (-teen) *n.* an organic compound forming essential part of any diet (found in meat, milk, eggs, etc.)

protest' *v.* 1. to declare solemnly. 2. to object, speak against.—**pro'test** *n.* objection

Prot'estant *n.* a member of any of the Christian churches except the Roman Catholic and Greek Orthodox.—**Prot'estantism** *n.*

protesta'tion (-tā'shun) *n.* a solemn declaration

pro'toplasm *n.* a substance which is an essential part of every living cell

pro'ton *n.* part of an atomic nucleus with a positive electrical charge

pro'totype *n.* the first type, a model, pattern

protract' *v.* to draw out, lengthen.—**protrac'tion** (-shun) *n.* 1. extension. 2. drawing to scale.—**protrac'tor** *n.* an instrument for measuring angles

protu'berance *n.* a swelling, bulge.—**protu'berant** *adj.*

protrude' (pro-trōōd') *v.* to stick out, project.—**protru'sion** (-zhun) *n.*

proud *adj.* 1. too satisfied with oneself or one's possessions. 2. haughty, arrogant. 3. self-respecting. 4. stately, dignified. 5. causing pride, as *It was a proud moment for him.*—**proud'ly** *adv.*

prove (prōōv) *v.* 1. to test, as *The exception proves the rule.* 2. to show that something is true, as *He proved that the two triangles were equal.* 3. to turn out to be, as *It proved a great success.*—**pro'ving** *pres. part.*—**proved, pro'ven** (prō', prōō') *p. part.* —**not proven** in Scots law, verdict that there is not enough evidence to decide whether the accused is guilty or not

prov'ender *n.* food for cattle or horses

prov'erb *n.* a short saying in common use, e.g. *A stitch in time saves nine.*—**prover'bial** *adj.* 1. like a proverb. 2. well known.—**prover'bially** *adv.*

provide' *v.* 1. to prepare for. 2. to supply, as *The native chief provided a guide.*—**provi'ding** *pres. part.*—**provi'ded** *conj.* on condition, as *I will do so provided that you do the same*

Compare: arrange, furnish, produce

Note: A soldier is *provided with* weapons. He must *provide against* a surprise attack. All possibilities must be *provided for*

prov'idence *n.* 1. foresight, care for the future. 2. God's kindly care.—**prov'ident** *adj.* showing care and foresight.—**providen'tial** (prov-i-den'shal) *adj.* fortunate

prov'ince *n.* 1. a division of a country. 2. range, division of work or activity.—*pl.* any part of the country outside the capital.

—**provin'cial** (pro-vin'shal) *adj.* 1. of a province. 2. unpolished, narrow-minded

provi'sion (pro-vizh'on) *n.* 1. supply 2. preparation. 3. a condition.—*pl.* food.—**provi'sional** *adj.* for a time, temporary

provi'so (prō-vī'zō) *n.* a condition.—**provi'sos** *pl.*

provoca'tion (-kā'shun) *n.* something that rouses anger.—**provoc'ative** *adj.* exciting anger, laughter, thought, etc.

provoke' *v.* 1. to rouse, irritate, excite.—**provo'king** *pres. part.*

Compare: anger, exasperate, incite, annoy. *Contrast:* pacify, allay, placate, soothe

prov'ost *n.* 1. the mayor of a Scottish town. 2. the head of a college

prow *n.* the pointed fore part of a ship

prow'ess *n.* 1. bravery, valour. 2. a heroic act. 3. fighting or athletic capacity, as *his prowess as a batsman*

Compare: 1. heroism, gallantry, valour, 2. capability, skill

prowl *v.* to roam secretly in search of prey, etc.

proxim'ity *n.* nearness

prox'y *n.* a person authorised to be a substitute for another.—**prox'ies** *pl.*—**by proxy** by means of a person acting as a representative or substitute

prude (prōōd) *n.* a woman who is foolishly proper.—**prud'ery** *n.*—**pru'dish** *adj.*

pru'dence (prōō'dens) *n.* thinking ahead, carefulness in speech or action.—**pru'dent** *adj.* wise, discreet.—**pruden'tial** *adj.* showing prudence

Compare: (with *adj.*) cautious, judicious, discreet, frugal. *Contrast:* imprudent, foolish, rash, prodigal

pru'dish (prōō'dish) *adj.* foolishly proper

prune (prōōn) *n.* a dried plum

prune (prōōn) *v.* to cut out dead parts, useless branches, etc.—**pru'ning-hook** *n.* a knife with a curved blade for pruning trees, etc.

Prus'sia *n.* a province of eastern Germany.—**Prus'sian** *n.* and *adj.*

pry *v.* to peep, look secretly

psalm (sahm) *n.* a sacred song.—*pl.* a book of the Old Testament.—**psalm'ist** *n.* a writer of psalms

psal'ter (sawl'ter) *n.* a psalm-book

pseu'do (sōō'dō, sū'dō) *adj.* 1. false, fake. 2. (in compounds) false, imitation e.g. *pseudo-scientific, pseudo-modern.*—**pseu'donym** (sōō'dō-nim, sū'do-nim) *n.* a name assumed by an author instead of his own, as *Mark Twain was the pseudonym* (or *nom-de-plume*) *of Samuel L. Clemens*

psy'chic (sī'kik) *adj.* 1. of the soul or mind. 2. belonging to what appears to be outside the range of ordinary experience

psycholog'ical (sī-ko-loj'i-kol) *adj.* of the mind.—**psycholog'ically** *adv.*

psychol'ogy (sī-kol'o-ji) *n.* the study of the mind

pub'lic *adj.* 1. belonging to the people,

common to all, as *a public park.* 2. generally known, as *The story was made public.* —*n.* the people.—**public-house'** an inn, tavern.—**pub'lic school** *n.* (England) a large school outside the state education system, often endowed, and with fee-paying pupils who are prepared mainly for the Universities and public services.—**public-spir'ited** *adj.* active for the public good

Compare: open, general, well known, communal. *Contrast:* private, secret, personal, individual

pub'lican *n.* 1. a tax-collector in ancient Rome. 2. innkeeper

publica'tion (-kā'shun) *n.* 1. making generally known. 2. preparing books, etc. for sale. 3. something published

public'ity (pub-lis'i-ti) *n.* 1. being widely known. 2. advertising, seeking public notice

pub'lish *v.* 1. to make generally known. 2. print for sale.—he **pub'lishes.**—**pub'lisher** *n.* a person who brings out books, etc.

puck *n.* 1. a goblin. 2. a flat rubber disc used in ice-hockey

puck'er (up) *v.* to gather into wrinkles.—*n.*

pud'ding (pōōd'ing) *n.* food cooked into a soft, sweetened mass

pud'dle *n.* 1. a small muddy pool. 2. a rough cement

pu'erile (pū'e-rīl) *adj.* childish, trivial

puff *n.* 1. a short blast of breath, wind, smoke, etc. 2. short pastry. 3. small pad for powdering skin.—*v.* 1. to send out in a puff. 2. to pant.—**puf'fy** *adj.* swollen

pug *n.* a small, snub-nosed dog

pu'gilist (pū'ji-list) *n.* a boxer.—**pu'gilism** *n.* boxing

pugna'cious (pug-nā'shus) *adj.* ready to fight, quarrelsome.—**pug'na'city** (pug-nas'-i-ti) *n.*

pull *v.* 1. to draw towards one. 2. to row a boat.—*n.* pulling, effort.—**to pull a face** to make a grimace.—**to pull in** (of a vehicle) to draw to a halt at the side of the road.—**to pull off** to be successful in gaining something.—**to pull oneself together** to regain control of oneself.—**to pull one's punches** to be less harsh or severe than one could be.—**to pull one's weight** to do one's fair share of work.—**to pull out** 1. (of a vehicle) to move into the middle of the road. 2. to leave. 3. to withdraw.—**to pull round** (or **through**) to recover from an illness.—**to pull to pieces** to criticise strongly.—**to pull up** to draw to a halt

pul'let *n.* a young hen

pul'ley *n*, a wheel with a groove in the rim for a cord, used to raise weights by a downward pull.—**pul'leys** *pl.*

Pull'man *n.* a railway carriage specially made for comfort

pull'-over *n.* a kind of jersey or sweater without fastening, to be pulled over the head

pulp *n.* 1. the soft part of fruit. 2. any soft, moist matter.—*v.* to reduce to pulp

pul'pit (pōōl'pit) *n.* 1. a platform for a preacher. 2. preaching

pulsate' *v.* to throb, quiver.—**pulsa'ting** *pres. part.*—**pulsa'tion** (-sā'shun) *n.*

pulse *n.* 1. the throbbing of the arteries, esp. in the wrist. 2. any regular beat.—*v.* to beat, throb

pulse *n.* peas, beans, lentils, as food

pul'verise *v.* to crush to powder, to grind.—**pulverisa'tion** (zā'shun) *n.*

pu'ma *n.* a large tawny American wildcat

pum'ice (pum'is) *n.* a very light porous kind of lava, used for cleaning and polishing

pum'mel *v.* to beat with the fists.—**pum'melling** *pres. part.*—**pum'melled** *p.t.* and *p. part.*

pump *n.* 1. a machine for raising water from a well. 2. a machine for forcing liquids or air in or out.—*v.* to force in or out with a pump

pump *n.* a light shoe

pump'kin *n.* a very large round fruit that grows on a vine

pun *n.* a play on words which sound alike but have a different meaning.—*v.* to make a pun

punch *n.* 1. a tool for making holes or stamping. 2. a blow with the fist.—*v.* 1. to make a hole or stamp. 2. to strike with the fist.—he **punch'es**

punch *n.* a hot drink made of a mixture of sugar, lemon, spices and spirits

punctil'ious *adj.* very careful of small details

Compare: scrupulous, precise, formal, exact

punc'tual *adj.* prompt, in good time.—**punc'tual'ity** *n.*

punctuate *v.* to put in punctuation marks, e.g. full-stops, colons, semi-colons, commas, etc.—**punctua'tion** (ā'shun) *n.*

punc'ture *n.* a small hole made by pricking, pricking.—*v.* to prick a hole.—**punc'turing** *pres. part.*

pun'gency (pun'jen-si) *n.* sharpness, esp. in taste or smell

pun'gent (pun'jent) *adj.* sharp, keen, biting, as *a pungent smell, pungent remarks*

pun'ish *v.* 1. to cause pain or suffering for an offence. 2. to hurt (as in boxing, etc.).—he **pun'ishes**—**pun'ishment** *n.*—**cap'ital pun'ishment** *n.* execution, death

Compare: chastise, chasten, castigate, correct

pu'nitive (pū'ni-tiv) *adj.* intended to punish

pun'net *n.* a small basket for fruit

punt *n.* a flat-bottomed boat propelled by pushing with a pole.—*v.* 1. to use a punt-pole. 2. to kick a ball dropped from the hands before it reaches the ground

pu'ny *adj.* small and weak

pup *n.* a puppy, young dog

pu'pa *n.* a stage in an insect's life when it is

a case or cocoon, chrysalis.—**pu'pae** (pū'pee) *pl.*

pu'pil *n.* 1. a person who is taught. 2. the opening in the middle of the eye

pup'pet *n.* 1. a doll worked by wires from above, and made to act. 2. a person under the control of another

pur'chase *v.* to buy.—**pur'chasing** *pres. part.* —*n.* 1. a thing bought. 2. buying. 3. grip, firm hold.—**pur'chaser** *n.* buyer

pure *adj.* 1. clean, spotless, as *pure white.* 2. unmixed, as *pure imagination.* 3. innocent, without evil.—**pure'ly** *adv.* 1. in a pure way. 2. merely, simply

Compare: 1. unsullied. clear. 2. sheer, mere, unadulterated. 3. chaste, virtuous. *Contrast:* 1. dirty, foul, defiled, tainted. 2. adulterated, mixed, corrupt. 3. impure, wicked

purg'atory *n.* 1. a place where souls are cleansed of sin. 2. a state of trial and suffering

purge *v*, to make clean.—**pur'ging** *pres. part.*

purifica'tion (-kā'shun) *n.* cleansing, purifying

pur'ify *v.* to make pure.—he **pur'ifies.**—**pur'ifying** *pres. part.*—**pur'ified** *p.t.* and *p. part.*

puritan'ical *adj.* like the Puritans in the seventeenth century who were very strict in morals and religion

pu'rity (pū'ri-ti) *n.* 1. being clean. 2. being unmixed. 3. innocence

purl *n.* a stitch in knitting that is the reverse of a plain stitch.—*v.*

purloin' *v.* to steal

pur'ple *n.* 1. a colour between crimson and violet. 2. purple robe, high rank of those who wear such robes.—**pur'plish** *adj.*

pur'port *n.* meaning.—**purport'** *v.* 1. to mean, as *What does this purport?* 2. to profess, as *This dispatch purports to give a true account of what is happening there*

pur'pose (pur'pis) *n.* intention, design, aim.—*v.* to intend, plan.—**pur'posing** *pres. part.*—**pur'posely** *adv.* on purpose, intentionally

Compare: (with *v.*) propose, resolve, mean, determine

purr *n.* the sound a cat makes when pleased. —*v.*

purse *n.* a small bag for carrying money.—*v.* to draw into wrinkles, as *to purse the lips* (*when whistling, etc.*)—**pur'sing** *pres. part.*—**pur'ser** *n.* officer who keeps accounts, etc. on a ship

pursu'ance *n.* carrying out, pursuit, as *in pursuance of our intentions*

pursue' (pur-sū') *v.* 1. to chase, follow, as *The hounds pursued the fox.* 2. to aim at, as *to pursue pleasure.* 3. to carry on, as *to pursue a policy, a profession, etc.*—**pursu'ing** *pres. part.*—**pursu'er** *n.*—**pursuit'** (pur-sūt') *n.* 1. chase. 2. occupation

Compare: 1. hunt. 2. seek. 3. continue, conduct, practise

purvey' (pur-vā') *v.* to supply, especially food. —**purvey'or** *n.*

pus *n.* thick yellowish matter found in sores

push (poosh) *v.* 1. to press against. 2. to make one's way. 3. to urge forward, as *We will push the scheme for all we are worth.*—he **push'es.**—*n.* 1. pushing. 2. a military advance.—**push'ful, push'ing** *adj.* self-assertive, given to pushing oneself forward

Compare: shove, drive, force, impel, press, propel, urge, promote

put (poot) *v.* 1. to place, set, lay, deposit. 2. to express.—**put'ting** *pres. part.*—**put** *p.t.* and *p. part.*—**to put about** 1. to turn back. 2. to let it be known.—**to be put to it** to be hard pressed.—**to put back** to retard.—**to put by** to save.—**to put off** to defer a decision.—**to put up** 1. to erect. 2. to give someone lodging.—**to put up with** to suffer.—**to put to death** to execute.—**to stay put** to remain in one place

pu'trefy (pū'tri-fī) *v.* to rot, decay.—it **pu'trefies**—**pu'trefying** *pres. part.*—**pu'trefied** *p.t.* and *p. part.*—**putrefac'tion** *n.*

pu'trid *adj.* rotten

putt *v.* 1. (golf) to strike a ball gently on the green. 2. (Scottish) to throw (an iron ball called a *shot*) from the shoulder.—*n.* 1. the stroke so made in golf. 2. the throw of the shot

put'ty *n.* a paste made of whiting and oil used for sticking panes of glass, etc.

puz'zle *n.* 1. a problem, difficulty. 2. a toy meant to perplex, a riddle.—*v.* 1. to perplex. 2. to think hard about.—**puz'zling** *pres. part.*

pyg'my pig'my (pig'mi) *n.* a dwarf, elf.—**pyg'mies** *pl.*

pyja'mas (pij-ah'maz), **paja'mas** (U.S.) *n.pl.* a sleeping suit

py'lon (pī'lon) *n.* a tower for suspension of electric cables

pyr'amid (pir'a-mid) *n.* a solid figure on a triangular, square or polygonal base with sloping sides ending in a point, esp. the great stone pyramids in Egypt.—**pyram'idal** *adj.*

pyre (pīr) *n.* a pile of wood for burning a dead body

pyrotech'nics (pī-ro-tek'niks) *n.pl.* fireworks

py'thon (pī'thon) *n.* a large snake that crushes its prey

Q

quack *n.* 1. the cry of the duck. 2. an ignorant and dishonest person who pretends to be a doctor.—*adj.* sham, false

quad'rangle (kwod'rang-gl) *n.* 1. a figure with four sides and four angles. 2. a four-sided court.—**quadran'gular** *adj.*

quad'rant (kwod'rant) *n.* 1. a quarter of a circle. 2. an instrument used in navigation for taking measurements

quadrilat'eral *adj.* having four sides and four angles.—*n.* a four-sided figure

quadrille' (kwod-ril') *n.* 1. a dance for four couples. 2. music for the dance

quad'ruped (kwod'rōō-ped) *n.* a four-footed animal

quad'ruple (kwod'rōō-pl) *adj.* 1. four-fold. 2. made up of four parts. 3. four times greater.—**quad'ruplet** *n.* one of four children born together

quaff (kwahf) *v.* to drink deeply

quag'mire (kwag'mīr) *n.* marshy ground, a bog

quail (kwāl) *n.* a bird of the partridge family

quail (kwāl) *v.* to flinch, show fear

quaint (kwānt) *adj.* odd, old-fashioned in an interesting way.—**quaint'ly** *adv.*

Compare: queer, fanciful, whimsical, curious, antique

quake (kwāk) *v.* to shake, tremble esp. with fear.—**qua'king** *pres. part.*

Quak'er (kwā'ker) *n.* a member of the Society of Friends

qualifica'tion (kwol-i-fi-kā'shun) *n.* 1. what makes a person fit to do a job, special knowledge. 2. something which limits

qual'ified (kwol'i-fīd) *p.t.* and *p. part.* of **qualify**—*adj.* 1. fit, competent. 2. limited

qual'ify (kwol'i-fī) *v.* 1. to make fit for, prepare, as *He has qualified as a doctor.* 2. to limit, as *He qualified his promise with several conditions.*—**qual'ifying** *pres. part.*—**qual'ified** *p.t.* and *p. part.*

Compare: 1. fit, adapt, equip, prepare, enable, 2. restrict, dilute, assuage, modify

qual'ity (kwol'i-ti) *n.* 1. kind, degree, as *of the finest quality.* 2. something which distinguishes a thing from others, as *Hardness is a quality of steel.* 3. goodness, excellence, as *What is needed is quality rather than quantity.*—**qual'ities** *pl.*

qualm (kwahm) *n.* 1. a sick feeling. 2. a misgiving, feeling of doubt

quan'dary (kwon'da-ri) *n.* doubt, uncertainty, as *He was in a quandary, not knowing what he ought to do*

Compare: perplexity, dilemma, difficulty, hesitation

quan'titative *adj.* 1. of quantity. 2. which can be measured

quan'tity (kwon'ti-ti) *n.* 1. size, number, amount. 2. a large amount.—**quan'tities** *pl.*

quar'antine (kwor'an-teen) *n.* keeping a person, ship, etc. away from others to avoid infection.—*v.* to put into quarantine

quar'rel (kwor'el) *n.* 1. an angry dispute. break-up of friendship.—*v.* 1. to fall out with. 2. to find fault with.—**quar'relling** *pres. part.*—**quar'relled** *p.t.* and *p. part.* —**quar'relsome** *adj.* ready to quarrel

Compare: disagreement, controversy, dispute, breach, rupture, misunderstanding, wrangle, squabble, strife, feud. *Contrast:* reconciliation, accord, agreement, harmony, friendship, amity

quar'ry (kwor'i) *n.* a place where stone is cut or blasted out of the ground for building, etc.—*v.*.—**quar'ries** *pl.*

quar'ry (kwor'i) *n.* an animal hunted, prey.—**quar'ries** *pl.*

quart (kwort) *n.* a quarter of a gallon

quar'ter (kwor'ter) *n.* 1. a fourth part. 2. district, place. 3. direction. 4. mercy shown to an enemy.—*pl.* lodgings.—*v.* 1. to divide into quarters. 2. put troops into lodgings.—**quar'terly** *adj.* happening each quarter of the year.—**quar'ter-deck** *n.* officers' deck.—**quar'ter-master** *n.* an army or naval petty officer in charge of stores or signals.—**quar'ter-staff** *n.* a pole used for defence.—**at close quarters** very near

quartette', quartet' (kwor-tet') *n.* 1. a musical piece for four voices or instruments. 2. four singers or players. 3. a group of four

quar'to (kwor'to) *n.* a size of book in which each sheet is folded into four leaves (4to). —**quar'tos** *pl.*—*adj.* of this size

quartz (kworts) *n.* a very hard mineral found in large hexagonal crystals

quash (kwosh) *v.* to wipe out, to put down

qua'ver (kwā'ver) *v.* 1. to tremble, shake. 2. to say or sing in quavering tones.—*n.* 1. a shaking. 2. a musical note half the length of a crotchet

quay (kee) *n.* a solid, fixed landing-stage for ships

queen (kween) *n.* 1. the wife of a king. 2. a woman sovereign.—**king** *masc.* 3. a fertile female bee, wasp, etc.—*v.* to act as queen. —**queen'ly** *adj.*—**queen-mother** *n.* the mother of a king or queen.—**queen it** to behave in an arrogant fashion

queer (kweer) *adj.* odd, strange, unusual.—*v.* to upset.—**to queer someone's pitch** to spoil his plans.—**queer'ly** *adv.*

Compare: curious, peculiar, eccentric, bizarre, fantastic, grotesque, singular

quell (kwel) *v.* to subdue, put down, as *The government quelled a rebellion*

quench (kwench) *v.* 1. to put out, extinguish. 2. to stop, relieve, slake thirst.—he **quench'es.**—**quench'less** *adj.* which cannot be quenched

quer'ulous (kwer'ū-lus) *adj.* complaining, peevish.—**quer'ulousness** *n.*

que'ry (kwee'ri) *n.* 1. a question. 2. a question-mark (?).—*v.* to raise a doubt about. —**que'rying** *pres. part.*—**que'ried** *p.t.* and *p.part.*

quest (kwest) *n.* a search.—*v.* to seek, search

ques'tion (kwes'chn) *n.* 1. a sentence that seeks an answer. 2. a problem, something to be discussed.—*v.* 1. to ask questions. 2. to doubt, dispute.—**ques'tionable** *adj.* doubtful, uncertain.—**ques'tion-mark** *n.* a punctuation mark (?) at the end of a question.—**beyond question** without doubt. —**out of the question** impossible.—**to call in question** to express doubt

questionnaire' (kest-yon-ār') *n.* a printed list of questions

queue (kū) *n.* 1. a plait of hair. 2. a line of waiting persons, cars, etc.—**queue** *v.*—**queueing** *pres. part.*—**queued** *past t.* and *p. part.*

quib'ble (kwib'l) *n.* 1. avoiding the point of an argument by stressing an unimportant aspect. 2. a play on words, pun.—*v.* to twist, distort the truth.—**quib'bling** *pres. part.*

quick (kwik) *adj.* 1. rapid, fast. 2. active, keen. 3. hasty, impatient. 4. living, as *the quick and the dead.*—*n.* the sensitive flesh below toe- or fingernail.—*adv.* quickly.—**quick'en** *v.* 1. to hasten, make quicker. 2. to stir, rouse, as *His interest was quickened.* 3. to come alive, make live.—**cut to the quick** to hurt the feelings of someone very much

quick'lime *n.* a white substance used for making mortar

quick'ness *n.* speed, being quick, keen

quick'sand *n.* soft, deep sand which swallows up animals, people, etc.

quick'silver *n.* mercury

quid (kwid) *n.* 1. lump of tobacco for chewing. 2. (slang) £1

quies'cent (kwī-es'ent) *adj.* at rest, still, quiet

qu'iet (kwī'et) *adj.* 1. without noise. 2. still, without movement. 3. peaceful.—*n.* stillness, peace.—*v.* to soothe, make quiet.—**qui'eten** *v.*—**qui'etly** *adv.*—**qui'etness** *n.*

Compare: silent, calm, pacific. *Contrast:* noisy, loud, turbulent, restless

qui'etude *n.* stillness, rest, peace

quill (kwil) *n.* 1. a strong wing-feather. 2. pen made from a quill. 3. spine of a porcupine

quilt (kwilt) *n.* a padded bed-cover.—*v.* to stitch together two pieces of cloth with padding between

quince (kwins) *n.* a hard, pear-shaped fruit

quinine' (kwi-neen') *n.* a bitter medicine obtained from cinchona bark

quintes'sence (kwint-es'ens) *n.* the purest form, essential part

quintette', quintet' (kwin-tet') *n.* 1. a musical piece for five voices or instruments. 2. five players or singers

quip (kwip) *n.* a smart, witty remark

quire (kwīr) *n.* twenty-four sheets of paper

quit (kwit) *v.* to leave, go away.—**quit'ting** *pres. part.*—**quit'ted** *p.t.* and *p. part.*—*adj.* free, clear

Compare: 1. abandon, abscond. 2. conduct, bear, acquit

quite (kwīt) *adv.* 1. completely, wholly. 2. fairly, to some extent.—*interj.* just so

quits (kwits) *adj.* on even terms by paying back

quiv'er (kwiv'er) *v.* to shake, tremble.—*n.*

quiv'er (kwiv'er) *n.* a case for carrying arrows

quixot'ic (kwik-sot'ik) *adj.* showing enthusiasm for ideals and honour to the neglect of one's own interests, like Don Quixote

quiz (kwiz) *v.* 1. to make fun of. 2. to look at closely, curiously. 3. to question closely.—*n.* 1. a riddle. 2. a competition in which teams or individuals answer a series of questions for entertainment. 3. a series of questions.—**quiz'zing** *pres. part.*—**quizzed** *p.t.* and *p. part.*—**quiz'zical** *adj.* odd, mocking

quoit (koit) *n.* a heavy ring for throwing at a mark in a game of **quoits**

quo'rum (kwō'rum) *n.* the number of members that must be present if business done at a meeting is to be valid

quo'ta (kwō'ta) *n.* a share due, number received at one time

quota'tion (-ta'shun) *n.* 1. a passage copied from a book, etc. 2. words repeated by someone else than the speaker. 3. the stated price of goods

quote (kwōt) *v.* 1. to repeat words, or a passage from a book. 2. to name a price.—**quo'ting** *pres. part.*

quo'tient (kwō'shnt) *n.* the number resulting from dividing one number by another

R

rab'bi (rab'i) *n.* a Jewish doctor of law, minister

rab'bit *n.* 1. a wild or domesticated animal of the hare family. 2. a poor player of a game

rab'ble *n.* a crowd of noisy, vulgar people, a mob

rab'id *adj.* raging, mad, unreasonable

ra'bies (rā'beez) *n.* madness in dogs, hydrophobia

raccoon', racoon' *n.* a furry animal of North America

race (rās) *n.* 1. persons or animals having the same ancestors. 2. people who have something in common. 3. a special breed of animal

race (rās) *n.* 1. a sweeping onward movement. 2. running, sailing, etc. in competition. 3. a strong current of water esp. driving a water-wheel.—*v.* 1. to run swiftly. 2. to compete in contest of speed, etc.—**ra'cing** *pres. part.*—**ra'cer** *n.*—**race'-track** *n.* ground prepared for racing

ra'cial (rā'shal) *adj.* 1. belonging to a race (of people, etc.). 2. of the differences between races. 3. of the relationships between races.—**ra'cialism** (rā'shal-ism) *n.* 1. belief in the superiority of one's own race over others. 2. showing this belief by persecuting the race believed inferior.—**ra'cialist** *n.*—**racial discrimination** showing preference for one's own race to the disadvantage of people of another race

rack *n.* 1. a wooden frame for holding hay, etc. 2. various kinds of frames for holding clothes, plates, tools, luggage, etc. 3. an instrument of torture by stretching.—*v.* 1. to strain, stretch, as *He racked his brains for an answer.* 2. to torture

rack *n.* 1. flying clouds. 2. destruction, as *rack and ruin*

rack'et *n.* 1. a loud noise, din. 2. a dishonest scheme for making money.—**racketeer'** *n.* in U.S. an armed criminal, gangster

rack'et, rac'quet *n.* a bat used in tennis

ra'cy (rā'si) *adj.* 1. having a strong flavour. 2. spirited, lively

ra'dar (rā'dar) *n.* an electronic system of detecting distant objects

ra'diance (rā'di-ans) *n.* brightness, splendour

ra'diant *adj.* 1. bright, shining. 2. giving out rays

ra'diate *v.* 1. to give out rays. 2. to send out from a central point.—**ra'diating** *pres. part.* —**radia'tion** (-ā'shun) *n.*

ra'diator *n.* 1. a heating apparatus for a room. 2. part of an engine for cooling it

rad'ical *adj.* 1. of a root, going to the root. 2. thorough, fundamental, as *The new manager made radical changes.* 3. of extreme opinions

Note: Do not confuse this word with *radicle* (*n.*)

rad'icle *n.* rootlet

ra'dio *n.* 1. wireless telephony. 2. a receiving set.—**ra'dios** *pl.*—**ra'diogram** *n.* 1. a telegram sent by radio. 2. a combined radio receiver and record player.—**ra'diograph** *n.* an X-ray photograph.—**radio tel'escope** *n.* an apparatus for detecting distant invisible stars

rad'ish *n.* a small root with a sharp taste.—**rad'ishes** *pl.*

ra'dium *n.* a rare metal used in the treatment of cancer

ra'dius *n.* any straight line from the centre to the outside, or circumference, of a circle.—**ra'dii** *pl.*

raf'fia *n.* prepared palm fibre for making mats

raf'fle *n.* a gamble in which many tickets or numbers are sold, one of which gets a prize

raft *n.* a floating platform of logs or planks fastened together

raft'er *n.* one of the main beams of a roof

rag *n.* a torn piece of material.—*v.* (popular use) tease, torment, play rough jokes upon. —*adj.* made of rags.—**rag'amuffin** *n.* a ragged person

rage (rāj) *n.* fury, violent anger.—*v.* to speak or act with fury, to storm.—**ra'ging** *pres. part.*

Compare: wrath, temper, wildness, ferocity

rag'ged (rag'ed) *adj.* 1. torn, in rags. 2. wearing rags. 3. rough, shaggy, not smooth. 4. lacking finish or precision, as *The marching of the recruits was very ragged*

rag'-time *n.* early jazz music with much syncopation of a simple melody

raid *n.* a sudden attack.—*v.* to make a raid on. —**raid'er** *n.* person, ship, aircraft, etc. raiding

Compare: foray, invasion, incursion, irruption

rail *n.* a bar, esp. part of a fence, railway-line. —*v.* to enclose with rails

rail *v.* to complain bitterly.—**rail'er** *n.*—**rail'ing** *n.* complaints, jeers

rail'ing *n.* a fence of rails

rail'lery (rāl'er-i) *n.* good-humoured teasing, joking

rail'road *n.* (U.S.) railway

rail'way *n.* a road or track with lines of steel rails on which trains run

rai'ment *n.* clothes

rain *n.* water-drops falling from the clouds.—*v.* 1. to fall as rain. 2. to pour down.—**rain'y** *adj.*—**rain'bow** *n.* an arch of colours in the sky, formed in rain by the sun's rays.—**rain'fall** *n.* the total amount of rain falling on an area in a given period of time.—**rain'-gauge** (rān'gāj) *n.* an instrument for measuring rainfall.—**to rain cats and dogs** to rain heavily.—**a rainy day** a time of need

raise (rāz) *v.* 1. to set up, build. 2. to lift, put up. 3. to bring forward. as *to raise a question.* 4. to cause, as *to raise doubts.* 5. to collect, as *to raise funds.* 6. to end (a siege). 7. to breed, bring up (a family, livestock, etc.).—**rai'sing** *pres. part.*

rai'sin (rā'zin) *n.* a dried grape

raj (rahj) *n.* rule in India, as *The British Raj.* —**raj'ah** (rahj'ah) *n.* an Indian ruler or prince.—**ran'ee** (rahn'ee) *fem.*

rake *n.* 1. a long-handled tool with a bar at the end, set with teeth for drawing together hay, etc. 2. a dissolute person. 3. slope, esp. of a ship.—*v.* 1. to use a rake. 2. to collect, draw together. 3. to search keenly. 4. to sweep with shot.—**ra'king** *pres. part.*—**ra'kish** *adj.* 1. dissolute. 2. sloping. 3. stylish or speedy looking

ral'ly *v.* 1. to bring together, e.g. scattered troops. 2. to regain health or strength.—**ral'lying** *pres. part.*—**ral'lied** *p.t.* and *p. part.*—*n.* a meeting.—**ral'lies** *pl.*

ral'ly *v.* to tease.—**ral'lying** *pres. part.*—**ral'lied** *p.t.* and *p. part.*

ral'ly *n.* (in tennis, etc.) a quick exchange of strokes

ram *n.* 1. male sheep.—**ewe** *fem.* 2. swinging beam with a metal head for battering. 3. a beak projecting from bow of a warship below the water.—*v.* 1. to stuff. 2. to strike with a ram.—**ram'ming** *pres. part.* —**rammed** *p.t.* and *p. part.*

ram'ble *v.* 1. to wander about. 2. to be delirious.—**ram'bling** *pres. part.*—*n.* a walk.—**ram'bler** *n.* 1. one who rambles. 2. a climbing rose

ramifica'tion (-kā'shun) *n.* a branch, development

ram'ify *v.* to divide into parts or branches.—

ram'ifying *pres. part.*—**ram'ified** *p.t.* and *p. part.*
ram'jet *n.* a type of jet engine in aircraft
rampage' *v.* to dash about violently.—*n.*
ramp'ant *adj.* 1. standing on hind legs, as *the lion rampant,* on a coat-of-arms. 2. angry. 3. unchecked, very prevalent, as *Cattle-stealing was rampant in the district*
ram'part *n.* a bank of earth built up as a defence
ram'shackle *adj.* tumble-down, old, falling to pieces
ranch *n.* a Canadian or American farm for the raising of cattle, horses or sheep in large herds. 2. a large farm for a special crop as *a fruit ranch.*—*v.* to manage, to work on a ranch.—**ran'cher, ranch'man**
ran'cid (ran'sid) *adj.* sour, stale.—**rancid'ity** *n.*
ran'cour (rang'kor) *n.* bitter ill-feeling, resentment.—**ran'corous** *adj.* spiteful
ran'dom *adj.* by chance, without purpose.—**at ran'dom** by chance
ra'nee *n.* see raj
range (rānj) *n.* 1. a row, line, as *a range of mountains.* 2. extent, series, as *a range of patterns.* 3. the distance a gun can reach. 4. a place for practising shooting. 5. a cooking-stove.—*v.* 1. to set in a row. 2. to extend. 3. to roam, as *The hunters ranged the mountains.*—**ran'ging** *pres. part.*—**ran'ger** *n.* 1. a forest keeper. 2. a senior Girl Guide.—**range'finder** *n.* an apparatus for finding the distance of a target or an object to be photographed
rank (rangk) *n.* 1. a row, line. 2. a division. 3. social position, class. 4. title, high position.—*n.pl.* common soldiers.—*v.* 1. to draw up in a rank, classify. 2. to have rank or place
rank *adj.* 1. growing too thickly and coarsely. 2. strong-smelling. 3. extreme.—**the rank and file** private soldiers
ran'kle (rang-kl) *v.* 1. to be sore, inflamed. 2. to cause pain, anger (when remembered) as *The insult rankled in his mind.*—**ran'kling** *pres. part.*
ran'sack *v.* to search thoroughly, plunder
ran'som *n.* money paid for the release of a prisoner.—*v.* to pay, demand or accept ransom for
rant *v.* to use violent, high-sounding language, to rave.—**rant'er** *n.*
rap *n.* a smart, slight blow, a sharp knock.—*v.* to tap.—**rap'ping** *pres. part.*—**rapped** *p.t.* and *p. part.*
rapa'cious (ra-pā'shus) *adj.* greedy, grasping, plundering—**rapac'ity** (rapas'i-ti) *n.*
Compare: extortionate, avaricious, ravenous
rape *v.* to carry off by force
rap'id *adj.* quick, swift.—**rapid'ity** *n.* speed.—**rap'ids** *n.pl.* part of river where water rushes swiftly
ra'pier (rā'pi-er) *n.* a light, narrow-bladed sword
rap'ine (rap'in) *n.* plundering
rapt *adj.* lost in thought or joy, absorbed
rap'ture *n.* delight, ecstasy.—**rap'turous** *adj.* enthusiastic, joyful
rare (rār) *adj.* 1. uncommon, unusual. 2. especially good, as *rare fun, rare wines.* 3. thin, as *The atmosphere was very rare at that height.* 4. underdone, nearly raw.—**rare'ly** *adv.* seldom
Compare: 1. infrequent, extraordinary, singular, remarkable. 2. excellent, choice, fine. 3. sparse. *Contrast:* 1. common, frequent, commonplace, general, usual, frequent. 2. poor, inferior, mediocre. 3. dense, thick
ra'refy (rā'ri-fī) *v.* to make thin, become thin or less dense.—**ra'refying** *pres. part.*—**ra'refied** *p.t.* and *p. part.*
ra'rity *n.* 1. something rare. 2. scarcity
ras'cal *n.* a rogue, worthless person.—**rascal'ity** *n.* dishonest behaviour.—**ras'cally** *adj.* bad
rash *adj.* hasty, thoughtless, reckless.—**rash'ly** *adv.*
Compare: headstrong, injudicious, daring, imprudent, ill-considered, venturesome, indiscreet, foolhardy, incautious. *Contrast:* prudent, careful, wary, circumspect, guarded, timid, discreet
rash *n.* inflamed spots or patches on the skin
rash'er *n.* thin slice of bacon or ham
rash'ness *n.* recklessness, being over-daring or indiscreet
rasp *n.* 1. a coarse file. 2. a grating sound.—*v.* 1. to file. 2. to scrape, to make a harsh sound. 3. to irritate
rasp'berry (rahz'ber-i) *n.* a small, soft fruit growing on bushes.—**rasp'berries** *pl.*
rat *n.* a small gnawing animal.—**rat'-race** *n.* fierce competition.—**to smell a rat** to be suspicious
rat'chet *n.* a set of teeth on a bar or wheel allowing movement in one direction only
rate *n.* 1. the proportion between two of things. 2. price. 3. speed. 4. a local tax.—*n. pl.* local taxation.—*v.* 1. to estimate the value of. 2. to decide the amount of tax due.—**ra'ting** *pres. part.*—**rate'-payer** *n.*
rate *v.* to scold, as *The teacher rated him soundly for his careless work*
rath'er (rahTH'er) *adv.* 1. more readily, in preference, as *I would rather, I had rather stay here.* 2. somewhat, to some extent, as *rather big, rather early*
ratifica'tion (-kā'shun) *n.* approval, confirmation
rat'ify *v.* to approve, confirm in writing.—**rat'ifying** *pres. part.*—**rat'ified** *p.t.* and *p. part.*
ra'ting *n.* 1. classification, type esp. of ship. 2. sailor, as *A naval rating.* 3. angry rebuke
ra'tio (rā'shi-ō) *n.* proportion, relation
rat'ion (rash'n) *n.* a fixed allowance of

food.—*v.* 1. to supply with rations. 2. to fix amount of food to be distributed

rat'ional (rash'on-al) *adj.* reasonable, moderate, sane.—**ra'tionally** *adv.*

rat'tle *v.* to give out a number of short, sharp sounds.—**rat'tling** *pres. part.*—*n.* 1. short, sharp sound. 2. a toy or instrument that rattles.—**rat'tle-snake** *n.* a poisonous American snake which makes a rattling sound with its tail

rau'cous *adj.* hoarse, harsh

rav'age (rav'ij) *v.* to lay waste, destroy.—**rav'aging** *pres. part.*—*n.* destruction

rave (rāv) *v.* 1. to talk wildly, too excitedly. 2. to rage, storm.—**ra'ving** *pres. part.*

rav'el *v.* 1. to entangle. 2. to fray out, separate into strands.—**rav'elling** *pres. part.*—**rav'elled** *p.t.* and *p. part.*

ra'ven *n.* a large black bird like a crow

rav'enous *adj.* 1. very hungry. 2. greedy

ravine' (ra-veen') *n.* a deep, narrow valley, gorge

rav'ish *v.* 1. to carry off by force. 2. to delight, as *His exquisite playing of the violin ravished the audience.*—he **rav'ishes.**—**rav'ishing** *adj.* beautiful, delightful.—**rav'ishment** *n.*

raw *adj.* 1. uncooked. 2. not manufactured or prepared. 3. without skin, tender, 4. unpractised, without experience. 5. damp and cold.—**raw'hide** *n.* untanned skin.—**raw'ness** *n.*

ray (rā) *n.* 1. a line or beam of light. 2. something light, a gleam

ray'on *n.* a shiny, silk-like fabric made from wood fibre

raze, rase *v.* to destroy completely, as *The city was razed to the ground by a disastrous fire.*—**ra'zing, ra'sing** *pres. part.*

ra'zor *n.* an instrument used for shaving

re- is added at the beginning of other words and has the meaning "again." e.g. *rejoin* means join again. If you are seeking the meaning of any word beginning with *re-* and do not find it below, find the word to which *re-* has been added and put "again" after it. Thus, to find the meaning of *rekindle*, say to yourself *kindle again.* If you do not know what this means, look up *kindle*

reach *v.* 1. to arrive at, get to, as *to reach one's destination.* 2. to obtain and pass on, as *Reach me the poker, please.* 3. to stretch out, extend as *The floods reach from here to the river.*—he **reach'es.**—*n.* 1. range, capacity, as *out of his reach.* 2. distance, as *within easy reach.* 3. a stretch of river.—**reach'es** *pl.*

react' *v.* 1. to act in return, produce a response. 2. recoil. 3. to act chemically.—**reac'tion** (-shun) *n.*—**reac'tionary** *adj.* favouring a backward movement in politics.—*n.*—**react'or** *n.* an atomic pile

read (reed) *v.* 1. to look at and understand writing or print. 2. to speak aloud written or printed words. 3. to understand. 4. to find mentioned in a book, etc.—**read** (red) *p.t.* and *p. part.*—**read'able** (reed'a-bl) *adj.* interesting.—**read'er** (reed'er) *n.* 1. a person who reads. 2. a school book of passages for reading.—**to read between the lines** to find a hidden meaning in what is read or heard

read'ily (red'i-li) *adv.* promptly, willingly, easily

read'iness (red'i-nes) *n.* 1. being willing, as *readiness to obey.* 2. being ready, as *readiness to start*

Compare: 1. compliance, willingness. 2. alertness, aptitude, promptitude

read'ing (reed'ing) *n.* 1. study, or perusal, of written or printed matter. 2. a public entertainment at which something is read. 3. an interpretation, way of explaining, as *My reading of his intentions is different from yours*

read'y (red'i) *adj.* 1. prepared, as *ready to go.* 2. prompt, willing, as *ready to obey.* 3. about to, in condition to, as *The fruit is ready to be gathered.* 4. quick, facile, as *a ready wit.* 5. available, actual, as *ready money.*—*adv.* completed beforehand, as *ready-made.*—**read'ier** *comp.*—**read'iest** *sup.*—**read'y-made** *adj.* not made to order

re'al *adj.* actual, true, existing in fact.—**real estate, real property** land, buildings, etc. (not money or goods).—**re'alism** *n.* 1. in art and literature, showing things as they are in real life. 2. practical or unprejudiced attitude, one without delusions.—**re'alist** *n.*—**re'alist'ic** *adj.* 1. like-life. 2. practical

Compare: genuine, veritable, authentic, sure. *Contrast:* imaginary, ideal, theoretical, false

real'ity (ree-al'it-i) *n.* 1. real existence. 2. truth, true facts.—**real'ities** *pl.*

realisa'tion (-zā'shun) *n.* 1. understanding. 2. making real, fulfilment

re'alise *v.* 1. to understand, as *Now I realise what he meant.* 2. to make real, being about, as *All his hopes were realised.* 3. to change into money, as *He realised some of his shares.* 4. to bring in money, as *The sale of his horses realised enough money to pay his debts.*—**re'alising** *pres. part.*

re'ally *adv.* truly, in fact

Note: This word (followed by a question-mark) may be used to mean *Is that so?* It may also be used (followed by an exclamation mark, and acting as an *interjection*) to mean *Indeed!*

realm (relm) *n.* 1. a kingdom. 2. a region, sphere

ream *n.* twenty quires, 480 sheets of paper

reap *v.* 1. to cut grain. 2. to bring in the harvest from the field. 3. to bring in a reward, to receive the consequences of some act.—**reap'er** *n.* 1. one who reaps. 2. a reaping-machine

rear *v.* 1. to raise, build. 2. to bring up, as *The hen reared a brood of ducklings.* 3. to rise on the hind legs

rear *n.* the back part.—*adj.* at the back.—**rear-ad'miral** *n.* an officer below vice-admiral.—**rear'-guard** *n.* troops protecting the rear of an army

rea'son (ree'zon) *n.* 1. cause, explanation. 2. ability to think. 3. sensible thought.—*v.* to discuss or debate reasonably.—**rea'sonable** *adj.* 1. sensible. 2. fair, moderate.—**rea'sonably** *adv.*—**rea'soning** *n.* thinking out from facts given.—**to stand to reason** to be obvious

reassure' (ree-a-shoor') *v.* to banish fears, restore confidence, as *He reassured us that he had no more claims to make.*—**reassu'ring** *pres. part.*

re'bate *n.* a discount, amount taken off price.—**rebate'** *v.* to give as discount

reb'el *n.* a person who resists authority.—*adj.* defiant, resisting.—**rebel'** *v.* to rise up against authority.—**rebel'ling** *pres. part.*—**rebel'lion** *n.* revolt, rising.—**rebel'lious** *adj.*

rebound' *v.* to spring back.—**re'bound** *n.* springing back

rebuff' *n.* an unfriendly check, refusal.—*v.* to repulse, refuse to accept

rebuke' *v.* to reprove, find fault with.—*n.*—**rebu'king** *pres. part.*

Compare: reprimand, reprehend, censure, chide, upbraid, scold, reprove. *Contrast:* commend, praise, applaud

rebut' *v.* to disprove.—**rebut'ting** *pres. part.*—**rebut'ted** *p.t.* and *p. part.*

recal'citrant (ree-kal'sit-trant) *adj.* rebellious, refractory

recall' (re-kawl') *v.* 1. to call back. 2. to remember. 3. to withdraw.—*n.* an order to return

recant' *v.* to take back an opinion, etc.—**recanta'tion** (-tā'shun) *n.*

recapit'ulate *v.* to sum up, to repeat the main points.—**recapit'ulating** *pres. part.*—**recapitula'tion** (-lā'shun) *n.*

recede' (re-seed') *v.* 1. to go back, withdraw. 2. to slope backwards.—**rece'ding** *pres. part.*

receipt' (re-seet') *n.* 1. a written statement showing that money, etc. has been received. 2. receiving, as *He acknowledged his receipt of the letter.*—*n.pl.* money received

receive' (re-seev') *v.* 1. to take, accept, get. 2. to welcome, entertain.—**receiv'ing** *pres. part.*—receiv'er *n.* 1. a person who takes stolen goods. 2. an officer appointed to take public money. 3. an apparatus for receiving wireless messages. 4. a telephone ear-piece

re'cent (ree'sent) *adj.* new, modern, that has lately happened.—**re'cently** *adv.*

recep'tacle (re-sep'ta-kl) *n.* a place to hold things, container

recep'tion (re-sep'shun) *n.* 1. receiving. 2. being received. 3. welcome, as *a warm reception.* 4. a formal kind of party or entertainment, as *a wedding reception.*—**recep'tionist** *n.* someone who receives and attends to hotel guests, clients, etc.

recep'tive (re-sep'tiv) *adj.* quick to receive, esp. ideas

recess' (re-ses') *n.* 1. an interval during which work stops. 2. a hollow in a wall, alcove. 3. a secret, inner place.—**recess'es** *pl.*—**reces'sion** (re-sesh'un) *n.* withdrawal.—**reces'sive** *adj.* receding

re'cipe (res'i-pe) *n.* 1. directions for cooking a dish. 2. a prescription

recip'ient (re-sip'i-ent) *n.* a person who receives

recip'rocal (re-sip'rō-kal) *adj.* in return, mutual, done by each for the other.—**recip'rocally** *adv.*

recip'rocate (re-sip'rō-kāt) *v.* to give in return, to interchange, as *I reciprocate your good wishes.*—**reciproca'tion** (kā'shun) *n.*—**recipro'city** (res-i-pros'i-ti) *n.* giving and receiving

reci'tal (re-sī'tal) *n.* 1. the telling of a story, etc. 2. a musical entertainment

recita'tion (res-i-tā'tion) *n.* repeating from memory a piece of poetry or prose

recite' (re-sīt') *v.* 1. to repeat aloud. 2. to tell one by one.—**reci'ting** *pres. part.*

reck *v.* to care, heed.—**reck'less** *adj.* very careless, too daring.—**reck'lessness** *n.*

reck'on *v.* 1. to count. 2. to consider. 3. to rely on.—**reck'oning** *n.* 1. calculation. 2. account, settlement of bill.—**reck'oner, ready-reck'oner** *n.* a book of calculations

Compare: 1. compute, calculate. 2. think, suppose, deem. 3. depend on, count on

reclaim' *v.* 1. to bring back from wrong, reform. 2. to make fit for cultivation

reclama'tion (-mā'shun) *n.* reclaiming, restoring to a good condition

recline' *v.* to lean back, rest.—**recli'ning** *pres. part.*

recluse' (re-klōōs') *n.* a person who lives apart from the world, hermit.—*adj.*

recogni'tion (rek-og-nish'un) *n.* 1. recognising, knowing again. 2. acknowledgment, favourable attention

rec'ognise *v.* 1. to know again. 2. to notice. 3. admit, acknowledge, as *to recognise a person's rights.*—**rec'ognising** *pres. part.*

recoil' *v.* 1. to draw back in horror. 2. to spring back, rebound.—*n.*

recollect' *v.* to remember.—**recollec'tion** (-shun) *n.* memory, remembrance

recommend' *v.* 1. to advise, suggest, as *The doctor recommended a change of air.* 2. to speak favourably about, as *I can recommend this hotel.* 3. to hand over to the care of, as *He recommended his nephew to my care.*—**recommenda'tion** (-dā'shun) *n.* 1. advice. 2. praise

rec'ompense *v.* to reward, to pay for, to make up for loss.—**rec'ompensing** *pres. part.* —*n.* reward, compensation

rec'oncile (rek'on-sīl) *v.* 1. to make friendly again. 2. to settle a quarrel. 3. to bring into agreement, as *I cannot reconcile your statement with the facts.*—**reconci'ling** *pres. part.*—**reconcilia'tion** (-ā'shun) *n.*

rec'ondite (or **recon'dite**) *adj.* 1. (of subjects) little known, abstruse. 2. (of authors) difficult, very learned

Compare: deep, occult, unfathomable, obscure. *Contrast:* plain, clear, easy, obvious, evident

recon'naissance (rek-on'is-ans) *n.* an examination of enemy positions

reconnoi'tre (rek-on-oi'ter) *v.* to observe and get information about, esp. enemy's movements

record' *v.* to put down in writing.—**rec'ord** *n.* 1. what has been recorded. 2. a disc bearing recorded music, song, etc. 3. the best recorded performance.—*adj.* best so far.—**rec'ord-player** *n.* a machine for playing records

record'er *n.* 1. the chief legal officer in some cities. 2. a large flute, played vertically

recount' *v.* 1. to count again. 2. to tell in detail

re'count (ree'kownt) *n.* a second count (of votes)

recoup' (re-kōōp') *v.* to recover, compensate, as *to recoup one's losses, to recoup oneself*

recourse' (re-kōrs') *n.* 1. resorting to, as *He had recourse to the law as a remedy for his wrongs.* 2. thing resorted to, expedient, as *When accused, his usual recourse is lying*

recov'er (re-kuv'er) *v.* 1. to get back, as *He recovered his suit-case from the lost property office.* 2. to get well, as *She has quite recovered from her illness.*—**recov'ery** *n.*

Compare: 1. retrieve, regain, reclaim. 2. amend, recuperate, be cured. *Contrast:* 1. lose. 2. die, fail, sink

rec'reant *adj.* cowardly, false.—*n.* traitor, coward

recrea'tion (-ā'shun) *n.* amusement, play, pleasant, occupation.—**recrea'tional** (rek-ree-ā'shon-al *adj.*

recrimina'tion (-ā'shun) *n.* accusing in return, counter-charge

recruit' (re-krōōt') *n.* 1. a newly enlisted soldier. 2. a new member of a society.—*v.* 1. to get recruits. 2. to recover health and strength

rec'tangle (rek'tang-gl) *n.* a four-sided figure with four right angles.—**rectan'gular** *adj.*

rec'tify *v.* to put right, correct.—**rec'tifying** *pres. part.*—**rec'tified** *p.t.* and *p. part.*—**rec'tifier** *n.* an apparatus for converting alternating electric current to direct current

rectilin'ear, rectilin'eal *adj.* 1. forming a straight line. 2. made up of straight lines

rec'titude *n.* honesty, uprightness

rec'tor *n.* 1. a clergyman in charge of a parish. 2. the head of a Scottish university or high school.—**rec'tory** *n.*a rector's house

recum'bent *adj.* lying down

recu'perate (-kū') *v.* to recover from illness, loss, etc.—**recu'perating** *pres. part.*—**recupera'tion** (-ā'shun) *n.*

recur' *v.* 1. to go back in speech or thought, as *The speaker constantly recurred to what the Chairman has said.* 2. to happen again, be repeated, as *If this recurs the consequences will be serious.*—**recur'ring** *pres. part.*—**recurred'** *p.t.* and *p. part.*—**recur'rence** *n.* repetition.—**recur'rent** *adj.* repeated

red *n.* 1. the colour of blood, rubies, etc. 2. a Communist, extreme socialist.—*adj.* —**red'der** *comparative.*—**red'dest** *superlative.*—**red'breast** *n.* robin.—**red'coat** *n.* British soldier.—**red'den** *v.* to turn red, blush.—**red'dish** *adj.* rather red.—**Red Cross** *n.* an international organisation to relieve sufferings caused by war.—**red en'sign** *n.* flag of British merchant ships.—**red-hand'ed** *adj.* in the very act of crime.—**red-her'ring** *n.* something which misleads.—**red-hot'** *adj.* 1. red with heat. 2. furious, excited.—**red-letter day** a memorable day.—**red tape** tape for tying documents, a symbol of officialdom.—**to see red** to become very angry

redeem' *v.* 1. to buy back. 2. to set free. 3. to free from sin. 4. to make up for.—The Redeem'er *n.* Jesus Christ

redemp'tion (-shun) *n.* 1. buying back. 2. setting free. 3. salvation.—**beyond redemption** impossible to reform

red'olent *adj.* 1. smelling strongly of. 2. bringing to one's mind, suggestive

Compare: odorous, aromatic, fragrant

redoub'le (re-dub'l) *v.* to increase, as *The attackers redoubled their efforts.*—**redoub'ling** *pres. part.*

redoubt' (re-dowt') *n.* a small fort, detached outwork

redoubt'able (re-dowt'a-bl) *adj.* formidable, to be feared

redound' *v.* to contribute, turn to (one's advantage, credit, etc.)

redress' *v.* to set right, as *to redress a person's wrongs.*—*n.* relief, compensation

red'skin *n.* a North American Indian

reduce' (re-dūs') *v.* 1. to make less, decrease. 2. to weaken, lower. 3. to change into another state, as *to reduce to powder.* 4. to capture (a fortress, city, etc.). 5. to bring back to normal position, as *to reduce a fracture, dislocation,* etc.—**redu'cing** *pres. part.*—**redu'cible** *adj.* which can be reduced. —**in reduced circumstances** living on a low income

Compare: 1. abate, lessen, relax, diminish, contract. 2. degrade, dilute. 3. transform, concentrate. 4. take, storm, conquer. 5. restore, alleviate

reduc'tion (-shun) *n.* 1. reducing. 2. being reduced

redun'dancy *n.* more than is necessary.—**redun'dant** *adj.*

reed *n.* 1. a tall, hollow grass growing in marshy places. 2. a pipe to blow on. 3. the vibrating part of some musical instruments.—**reed'y** *adj.* 1. with many reeds. 2. making a thin sharp sound.—**a broken reed** someone who cannot be relied upon in an emergency

reef *n.* 1. narrow ridge of rock near the surface of the sea. 2. (S.A.) gold-bearing quartz vein.—**reefs** *pl.*

reef *n.* the part of a sail which can be taken in or let out.—*v.* to take in a reef

reek *n.* a strong smell, smoke.—*v.* to give off smoke or a strong smell

reel *n.* 1. an apparatus for winding rope, etc. 2. a spool for winding cotton, films, etc. 3. a Scottish dance.—*v.* 1. to wind on a reel. 2. to sway, stagger. 3. to be dizzy

refec'tory *n.* a room for meals, esp. in a monastery, or college

refer' *v.* 1. to consult for information, as *to refer to a dictionary*. 2. to send a person to another (for a decision), as *The clerk referred me to the manager*. 3. to speak about, as *He referred to you several times.* 4. to ascribe to, as *He referred his success to hard work.*—**refer'ring** *pres. part.*—**referred'** *p.t.* and *p. part.*

referee' *n.* 1. an umpire, person who decides points in a game or sport. 2. a person to whom something is referred.—*v.* to act as umpire

ref'erence (ref'er-ens) *n.* 1. the act of referring. 2. the act of directing attention to some information. 3. mention, allusion. 4. a person who can be asked about another person's character, etc. 5. a certificate of character.—**reference library** a library of books to be studied in the library only

referen'dum *n.* putting an important question to the direct vote of a whole nation.—**referen'da** *pl.*

refine' *v.* 1. to make pure, purify. 2. to make finer, more polished.—**refined'** *adj.* polite, genteel.—**refine'ment** *n.* fineness of feelings, taste, manners.—**refi'nery** *n.* place where sugar, petroleum, etc. is refined.—**refi'neries** *pl.*

reflect' *v.* 1. to throw back, esp. rays of light. 2. to give back an image, to mirror. 3. to throw blame or discredit on, as *The untidiness of the classroom reflects on the class.* 4. to think over, meditate.—**reflec'tion** (-shun) *n.* 1. reflected light, heat, image. 2. thought.—**reflec'tive** *adj.* thoughtful

reflec'tor *n.* a polished surface for reflecting light, heat, sound, etc.

re'flex *adj.* 1. reflected, bent back. 2. involuntary, not controlled, by the will

reflex'ive *adj.* in Grammar, denoting the agent's acting upon himself, e.g. *He hurt himself. Hurt* is a *reflexive verb, himself* a *reflexive pronoun*

reform' *v.* to make better, improve.—*n.* improvement.—**reforma'tion** (-mā'shun) *n.* a change for the better.—**refor'matory** *n.* (formerly) a place where young offenders were taught to be law-abiding.—**refor'matories** *pl.*—**refor'mer** *n.* leader of reform

Compare: reconstruct, remodel, amend, correct

refract' *v.* to break the course of light as it passes from one medium (e.g. air) to another (e.g. water or glass).—**refrac'tion** (-shun) *n.*—**angle of refraction** (science) the angle between a ray of light and a line perpendicular to the medium it passes through

refrac'tory *adj.* 1. difficult to manage, disobedient. 2. stubborn

refrain' *n.* a line or phrase repeated in a song or poem

refrain' *v.* to hold back, check oneself, as *He refrained from saying what he thought*

refresh' *v.* to cheer, revive, make fresh.—**refresh'ment** *n.* 1. being refreshed, rest. 2. food, drink

refrig'erator (re-frij'er-ā-tor) *n.* a very cold cabinet in which food is kept to preserve it

ref'uge (ref'ūj) *n.* shelter from danger or trouble.—**refugee'** (ref-ū-jee') *n.* a person taking refuge from persecution or war

Compare: retreat, asylum, cover, stronghold, sanctuary, protection

refund' (ree-fund') *v.* to pay back.—**re'fund** *n.*

refu'sal (re-fū'zl) *n.* the act of rejecting, saying no

refuse' (re-fūz') *v.* to reject, say "no" to a request.—**refu'sing** *pres. part.*

Compare: repel, rebuff, repudiate, deny. *Contrast:* agree, accept, receive, welcome, embrace

ref'use *n.* rubbish

refuta'tion (-tā'shun) *n.* disproving, showing an argument or claim to be false

refute' *v.* to disprove, show an argument or claim to be incorrect.—**refu'ting** *pres. part.*

re'gal *adj.* royal, fit for a king.—**re'gally** *adv.*

regale' *v.* to entertain, feast.—**rega'ling** *pres. part.*

rega'lia *n.pl.* 1. the emblems of royalty as used at a coronation. 2. emblems of certain societies and orders

regard' *v.* 1. to look at. 2. to consider, as *I regard that as a silly thing to do.* 3. to respect.—*n.* 1. a look. 2. respect, esteem.—*pl.* good wishes.—**as regards, with regard to.**—concerning, with reference to. **regard'ful** *adj.* careful, mindful.—**regard'ing** *prep.* about, concerning.—**regard'less** *adj.* not caring, as *Preparations were made regardless of expense*

Compare: 1. behold, view. 2. think. 3. esteem, honour, admire, love

regat'ta *n.* a boat or yacht race

re'gency (ree'jen-si) *n.* 1. a regent's office. 2. government by regents

regen'erate (ree-jen'er-āt) *v.* to give new and better life to.—**regen'erate** (ree-jen'er-it) *adj.* reformed, born anew.—**regenera'tion** (-ā'shun) *n.*

re'gent (ree'jent) *n.* one who rules a kingdom during the absence, minority or illness of its king

reg'icide (rej'i-sīd) *n.* 1. one who kills a king. 2. the crime of killing a king

regime' (rā-zheem') *n.* system of government or management

reg'iment (rej'i-ment) *n.* a body of soldiers under the command of a colonel.—**regiment'al** *adj.* belonging to a regiment.—**regiment'als** *n.pl.* uniform

Regi'na (rej-ī'na) *n.* the title of a reigning queen

re'gion (ree'jn) *n.* a place, district, large area.—**re'gional** *adj.* belonging to a particular region

Compare: land, territory, space, neighbourhood

reg'ister (rej'is-ter) *n.* 1. a list, record. 2. a range of voice or instrument. 3. a machine for recording.—*v.* 1. to enter in a list. 2. to write down

reg'istrar (rej'is-trar) *n.* an official who keeps a register, e.g. of births, deaths, marriages

registra'tion (rej-is-trā'shun) *n.* registering

reg'istry (rej'is-tri) *n.* 1. registering. 2. a place where a register is kept.—**reg'istries** *pl.*

regret' *n.* sorrow for something lost or done or left undone.—*v.* to grieve, be sorry.—**regret'ting** *pres. part.*—**regret'ted** *p.t.* and *p. part.*—**regret'ful** *adj.* sorry.—**regret'table** *adj.*

reg'ular *adj.* 1. usual, habitual. 2. fixed by rule. 3. even, not varying. 4. correct.—*n.* a soldier belonging to the standing army.—**regular'ity** *n.* order, being regular.—**reg'ularly** *adv.*

Compare: normal, orderly, methodical, systematic, invariable. *Contrast:* irregular, disorderly, unsystematic, variable

reg'ulate *v.* to make regular, control, set right.—**reg'ulating** *pres. part.*—**regula'tion** (-lā'shun) *n.* 1. rule, law. 2. control, adjustment.—**reg'ulator** *n.* person or device that regulates

rehabil'itate *v.* 1. to restore to a former position or reputation, as *He was rehabilitated in the public favour.* 2. to help a person to recover his normal capacities (lost through illness etc.).—**rehabilita'tion** (-tā'shun) *n.*

rehear'sal (re-hers'al) *n.* practice for a public performance

rehearse' (re-hers') *v.* 1. to practise beforehand. 2. to repeat, as *They rehearsed their grievances to the king.*—**rehears'ing** *pres. part.*

reign (rān) *n.* 1. royal power. 2. period of a sovereign's rule.—*v.* to rule

reimburse' (ree-im-burs') *v.* to pay back, as *The Good Samaritan promised to reimburse the innkeeper.*—reimburs'ing *pres. part.*—reimburse'ment *n.*

rein (rān) *n.* 1. a narrow strap attached to the bit to check or guide a horse. 2. control.—*v.* to control

rein'deer (rān'deer) *n.* a large deer living in cold regions

reinforce' *v.* to strengthen with new materials or fresh men.—**reinforc'ing** *pres. part.*—**reinforce'ment** *n.* something to strengthen.—*pl.* fresh troops, ships, etc.

reinstate' *v.* to replace, restore to a former position, as *When his innocence was proved he was reinstated in his post.*—**reinsta'ting** *pres. part.*—**reinstate'ment** *n.*

reit'erate *v.* to repeat again and again.—**reit'erating** *pres. part.*—**reitera'tion** (-ā'shun) *n.*

reject' *v.* to refuse to have, to throw aside.—**rejec'tion** *n.*

Compare: repel, discard, decline. *Contrast:* accept, acknowledge, retain, uphold, maintain

rejoice' *v.* 1. to be glad, as *I rejoice to see you again.* 2. to make glad, as *It rejoices me to see you looking so well.*—**rejoi'cing** *pres. part.*

rejoin' *v.* 1. join again. 2. to say in answer.—**rejoin'der** *n.* answer, retort

reju'venate *v.* to make young again.—**reju'venating** *pres. part.*—**reju'venation** (-ā'shun) *n.*

relapse' *v.* to fall back into illness, silence, evil, etc.—*n.*. **relap'sing** *pres. part.*

relate' *v.* 1. to tell, recount. 2. to connect in thought, think of together.—**rela'ting** *pres. part.*—**rela'ted** *adj.* connected by family

rela'tion (-shun) *n.* 1. an account, story. 2. a connection between persons or things. 3. a member of the same family.—**rela'tionship** *n.* connection

rel'ative *n.* a member of the same family, as *All his relatives came to visit him.*—*adj.* in relationship or comparison with something else, not absolute or complete, as *relative success.*—**relative pronoun** a pronoun referring to a noun or pronoun mentioned or implied before; as, in *The dog which you bought, which* is a relative pronoun.—**relative adverb** e.g. *where* in *The street where you live.*—**rel'atively** *adv.* comparatively

relax' *v.* 1. to make loose, ease. 2. to become loose, slacken. 3. to become less strict.—**relaxa'tion** *n.* 1. loosening. 2. amusement, recreation

relay' *n.* 1. fresh set or supply. 2. in wireless, a programme received from another station and transmitted.—*v.* to pass on.—**relay race** team race in which a baton is passed from one member to another.—**relay'ing** *pres. part.*—**relayed'** *p.t.* and *p. part.*

release' *v.* to let go, set free.—**releas'ing** *pres. part.*—*n.* 1. freedom, relief. 2. a mechanical device to catch hold and let go

rel'egate *v.* 1. to send away. 2. to put down as *The football team was relegated from the first to the second division.*—**rel'egating** *pres. part.*—**relega'tion** (-gā'shun) *n.*

relent' *v.* to become less severe, to feel more merciful.—**relent'less** *adj.* harsh, cruel

Compare: pitiless, merciless, severe, unrelenting, vengeful, implacable. *Contrast:* pitiful, merciful, lenient, forgiving, compassionate

rel'evance, rel'evancy *n.* being to the point.—**rel'evant** *adj.* connected with the subject in hand

reliabil'ity *n.* being trustworthy, dependable

reli'able *adj.* trustworthy, to be depended on

reli'ance *n.* trust, confidence.—**reli'ant** *adj.* trusting

rel'ic *n.* 1. something left from the past. 2. something kept as a memorial of a saint.—*pl.* a dead body

relief' (re-leef') *n.* 1. the end of pain, trouble, difficulty. 2. help. 3. release from duty. 4. a person releasing another from duty. 5. a carved design standing out from a surface. 6. distinctness.—**relief map** *n.* a map showing heights and hollows.—**to throw into relief** to make clearer, more distinct

relieve' (re-leev') *v.* 1. to lessen pain, trouble, etc. 2. to bring help. 3. to take someone's place on duty. 4. (of) take from, as *I relieved him of his burden.*—**reliev'ing** *pres. part.*

Compare: 1. alleviate, mitigate, allay, ease. 2. succour. 3. release

relig'ion (re-lij'n) *n.* 1. ordered beliefs and worship. 2. belief in God.—**relig'ious** (re-lij'us) *adj.* 1. connected with religion. 2. deeply interested in religion. 3. belonging to a religious order

Compare: faith, doctrine, cult, piety, worship, godliness, theology, morality

relin'quish (re-ling'kwish) *v.* to give up, as *He has relinquished the position of secretary.*—he **relin'quishes**

rel'ish *n.* 1. taste, flavour. 2. enjoyment. 3. sauce or other savoury flavouring.—*v.* to enjoy, like.—he **rel'ishes**

reluc'tance *n.* unwillingness.—**reluc'tant** *adj.* unwilling

Compare: averse, disinclined, indisposed, slow, loath. *Contrast:* eager, disposed, desirous, inclined, willing

rely' (on) *v.* to depend on, trust, as *I know that I can rely on* (*or upon*) *your discretion.*—he **relies'**—**rely'ing** *pres. part.*—**relied** *p.t.* and *p. part.*

remain' *v.* 1. to stay, as *to remain at home, to remain a bachelor.* 2. to be left, as *They gathered up the fragments that remained.*—**remain'der** *n.* what is left.—**remains** *n.pl.* 1. remainder. 2. a dead body

remand' (re-mahnd') *v.* to send back, an accused person to custody for further enquiries

remark *v.* 1. to notice, observe. 2. to say.—*n.* something said, observation.—**remark'able** *adj.* unusual, noticeable.—**remark'ably** *adv.*

reme'dial (re-mee'di-al) *adj.* healing, helping to cure

rem'edy *n.* a way of curing or relieving disease, trouble, wrong, etc.—**rem'edies** *pl.*—*v.* to put right.—**rem'edying** *pres. part.*—**rem'edied** *p.t.* and *p. part.*

remem'ber *v.* 1. not to forget, to keep in mind. 2. to have in mind. 3. to send greetings from.—**remem'brance** *n.* 1. memory. 2. keepsake.—*pl.* greetings

remind' *v.* to make one remember, bring to mind.—**remind'er** *n.*

reminis'cence (rem-inis'ens) *n.* 1. remembering. 2. telling what one remembers, recollection.—**reminis'cent** *adj.* recalling past events

remiss' *adj.* careless, slack.—**remiss'ness** *n.* carelessness

Compare: heedless, neglectful, inattentive, dilatory. *Contrast:* careful, mindful, attentive, painstaking

remis'sion (re-mish'un) *n.* 1. forgiveness, pardon. 2. release

remit' *v.* 1. to forgive sins. 2. to make less, slacken, as *Do not remit your efforts to improve.* 3. to send money.—**remit'ting** *pres. part.*—**remit'ted** *p.t.* and *p. part.*—**remit'tance** *n.* money sent

rem'nant *n.* a small remaining amount or piece, as *a remnant of cloth*

remons'trance *n.* protest

rem'onstrate *v.* to protest, object, give reasons against.—**rem'onstrating** *pres. part.*

Note: You remonstrate *with* a person *about* or concerning something that displeases you

remorse' *n.* regret after wrong-doing or neglect.—**remorse'ful** *adj.*—**remorse'fully** *adv.*—**remorse'less** *adj.* pitiless, having no regret

remote' *adj.* 1. far away, as *They live in a remote part of the country.* 2. slight, as *I think that the chances of its being found are very remote.*—**remote'ly** *adv.*

remo'val (re-mōō'val) *n.* 1. taking or going away. 2. dismissal

remove' (re-mōōv') *v.* 1. to take off or away. 2. to go away. 3. to dismiss from a post.—**remov'ing** *pres. part.*—*n.* 1. a step, stage. 2. a moving to a higher form in school

remu'nerate *v.* to reward. pay.—**remu'nerating** *pres. part.*—**remunera'tion** (-ā'shun) *n.* pay.—**remu'nerative** *adj.* profitable

Compare: (with *n.*) salary, stipend, wages

renaiss'ance, renas'cence (re-nā'sens) *n.* 1. great revival of learning in the fourteenth to sixteenth centuries. 2. a revival of arts and letters

rend *v.* to tear violently.—**rent** *p.t.* and *p. part.*

ren'der *v.* 1. to pay back, give back, as *to render good for evil.* 2. to deliver, present, as *Render unto Caesar the things that are Caesar's.* 3. to translate, as *to render into English.* 4. to melt down and purify, e.g. lard.—**ren'dering** *n.* 1. translation. 2. presentation so as to show the meaning

ren'dezvous (ron'dā-vōō) *n.* meeting-place, appointment

ren'egade *n.* 1. one who deserts from his party or his religious beliefs. 2. a traitor.—*adj.* disloyal

renew' *v.* 1. to make new, revive. 2. to begin again. 3. to patch, replace. 4. to grow again.—**renew'al** *n.* a beginning again

Compare: renovate, recommence, repeat, repair, change

ren'net *n.* juice from a cow's stomach used to curdle milk (in making cheese, curds)

renounce' *v.* 1. to give up. 2. to disown, reject. —**renouncing** *pres. part.*

ren'ovate *v.* to restore, repair, make like new. —**ren'ovating** *pres. part.*—**renova'tion** (-vā'-shun) *n.*

renown' *n.* fame.—**renowned'** *adj.* famous

Compare: reputation, honour, glory

rent *n.* regular payment for the use of land, buildings, rooms, etc.—*v.* 1. to hold as a tenant. 2. to let.—**rent'al** *n.* money paid for rent

rent *n.* a tear, hole

renuncia'tion (re-nun-si-ā'shun) *n.* renouncing, giving up, self-denial

repair' *v.* to mend, restore, renovate.—*n.* 1. mending. 2. good condition.—**repair'able** *adj.* which can be repaired

repair' *v.* to go to

rep'arable *adj.* which can be put right

repara'tion (-rā'shun) *n.* compensation for injury done

repartee' *n.* a smart, witty reply

repast' *n.* a meal, food

repa'triate *n.* to send back to one's country. —**repatria'tion** (-ā'shun) *n.*

repay' *v.* 1. to pay back. 2. return, reward.—**repay'ing** *pres. part.*—**repaid** *p.t.* and *p. part.*—**repay'ment** *n.*

repeal' *v.* to withdraw, cancel, do away with, as *Sir Robert Peel repealed the Corn Laws in* 1846.—*n.* abolition, withdrawal

Compare: rescind, revoke, annul, abolish

repeat' *v.* 1. to do again, occur again. 2. to say again. 3. to recite.—**repeat'edly** *adv.* again and again.—**repeat'er** *n.* 1. a watch that strikes the hours. 2. a quick-firing gun

repel' *v.* 1. to drive back, as *The attack was repelled.* 2. to disgust, cause to dislike, as *I was repelled by his sinister appearance.*—**repel'ling** *pres. part.*—**repell'ed** *p.t.* and *p. part.*—**repel'lent** *adj.* unpleasant

repent' *v.* 1. to be sorry, to regret. 2. to regret wrong-doing.—**repent'ance** *n.*—**repent'ant** *adj.* sorry for wrong-doing

repercus'sion (ree-per-kush'n) *n.* 1. bounding back, recoil. 2. echo, effect, as *This act will have repercussions all over the world*

rep'ertoire (rep'er-twar) *n.* the list of pieces that a singer, actor, etc. is prepared to perform.—**rep'ertory** *n.* a store, repertoire. —*adj.*—**repertory theatre** theatre in which a permanent company of actors perform different plays at different times

repeti'tion (rep-e-tish'un) *n.* 1. act of repeating. 2. something repeated, done again. 3. poetry, etc. learned by heart.—**repeti'tious** *adj.* having many repetitions

replace' (ree-plās') *v.* 1. to put back, as *He replaced the book on the shelf.* 2. to take the place of, as *Smith has replaced Brown at the top of the class.*—**repla'cing** *pres. part.*—**replace'ment** *n.* 1. replacing. 2. substitute, something put in place of another

replen'ish *v.* to fill up again, as *The storm replenished the empty water-tank.*—**replen'ishment** *n.*

replete' *adj.* filled, stuffed.—**reple'tion** (-shun) *n.* fullness

Compare: gorged, stocked, crammed, full, abounding

rep'lica *n.* an exact copy of a work, made by the artist

reply' *n.* an answer.—**replies** *pl.*—*v.* to answer. —**reply'ing** *pres. part.*—**replied'** *p.t.* and *p. part.*

Compare: (with *v.*) respond, rejoin, retort

report' *v.* 1. to tell, give views of. 2. to give an account of. 3. to give information against.—*n.* 1. a rumour. 2. an account, statement. 3. a bang.—**report'er** *n.* a person who collects news for a newspaper

Compare: (with report *n.*) description, narrative, recital, tale, relation

repose' (re-pōz') *v.* 1. to rest. 2. to lay to rest. —**repo'sing** *pres. part.*—*n.* 1. rest, sleep. 2. calm, quietness

repos'itory (re-poz'i-tor-i) *n.* a place for storing things

reprehend' *v.* to blame, reprove

reprehen'sible *adj.* deserving blame

represent' *v.* 1. to describe, picture, as *This tapestry represents episodes in the Norman Conquest.* 2. to act the part of, as *She represented Britannia in the pageant.* 3. to stand for, speak for, as *He represents a constituency in Parliament.* On the map, *One inch represents a mile.* 4. to state (in argument, etc.), as *He represented the necessity of acting at once*

representa'tion (-tā'shun) *n.* 1. a description, portrait. 2. being represented, e.g. in Parliament

represen'tative *n.* 1. a person appointed to speak and act for others. 2. an example, type.—*adj.* 1. typical, like others of the same kind. 2. made up of representatives

repress' *v.* to crush, keep under, check.—he **repress'es.**—**repres'sion** (represh'un) *n.* restraint.—**repres'sive** *adj.*

Compare: oppress, curb, put down, subdue, overpower, suppress

reprieve' (re-preev') *v.* to suspend, put off the execution of a condemned person.—*n.*

rep'rimand *v.* to rebuke sharply. (See rebuke.)—*n.*

repri'sal (re-prī'zal) *n.* the act of paying back an injury by another injury, retaliation

reproach' *n.* 1. blame. 2. disgrace.—*v.* to blame, scold, as *He reproached him with his treachery.*—he **reproach'es.**—**reproach'ful** *adj.* full of reproach

rep'robate *n.* a wicked person.—*adj.* sinful.—**reproba'tion** (-bā'shun) *n.* blame, disapproval

reproduce' (ree-pro-dūs') *v.* 1. to produce again. 2. to make a copy of. 3. to produce offspring.—**reprodu'cing** *pres. part.*—**reproduc'tion** (-shun) *n.* 1. reproducing. 2. a copy. 3. breeding.—**reproduc'tive** *adj.*

reproof' *n.* blame, reproach

reprove' (re-proov') *v.* to reproach, blame, express disapproval. (See **rebuke.**)—**reprov'ing** *pres. part.*

rep'tile *n.* a crawling animal such as a snake, lizard, tortoise, etc.

repub'lic *n.* a democratic state not ruled by a king, e.g. the U.S.A.—**repub'lican** *adj.* 1. of a republic. 2. believing in republican government. 3. of one of the two main political parties in the U.S.—*n.*

repu'diate *v.* to reject, disown, refuse to accept, as *He repudiated his wife's debts.*—**repu'diating** *pres. part.*—**repudia'tion** (-ā'-shun) *n.*

repug'nance *n.* distaste, aversion, strong, dislike.—**repug'nant** *adj.* distasteful, unpleasant

repulse' *v.* 1. to drive back. 2. to refuse, reject, as *My offer of friendship was rudely repulsed.*—**repul'sing** *pres. part.*—*n.* defeat, rejection, refusal.—**repul'sion** (-shun) *n.* aversion, strong dislike.—**repul'sive** *adj.* offensive, very unpleasant

rep'utable *adj.* of good character, well thought of

reputa'tion (- ā'shun) *n.* 1. what is generally thought or said about a person or thing. 2. good name

repute' *n.* 1. reputation. 2. esteem, as *held in high repute.*—*v.* to consider, regard as.—**repu'ted** *adj.* supposed

request' (re-kwest') *n.* 1. act of asking. 2. something asked for, demand.—*v.* to ask, invite

Compare: (with *v.*) pray, solicit, entreat

req'uiem (rek'wee-em) *n.* 1. mass for the dead. 2. music for it

require' (re-kwīr') *v.* 1. to need, as *The joint will require a lot of cooking.* 2. to order, bid, request, as *I require a room for the night, please.*—**requi'ring** *pres. part.*—**require'ment** *n.* condition, need

re'quisite (rek'wi-zit) *adj.* needed, necessary.—*n.* a thing needed, necessity

requisi'tion (rek-wi-zish'un) *n.* 1. demand, esp. written. 2. a list of things required.—*v.* to demand, to press into service, as *The government has requisitioned this house for the soldiers*

Compare: commandeer, seize, take over

requite' (re-kwīt') *v.* to pay back, reward or avenge, return.—**requi'ting** *pres. part.*

Compare: recompense, reciprocate, retaliate

Note: You *requite* a person *with* something *for* something else, or you *requite* something *for* something else, e.g. *He requited me with evil for good. Requite good for evil*

rescind' (re-sind') *v.* to cancel, do away with (a law, decree, resolution, etc.)

rescue *v.* to save, deliver.—**res'cuing** *pres. part.*—saving.—**res'cuer** *n.*

research' (re-serch') *n.* careful study in search of facts, investigation

resem'blance (re-zem'blans) *n.* likeness, similarity, being alike

resem'ble (re-zem'bl) *v.* to be like, as *He resembles his father.*—**resem'bling** *pres. part.*

resent' (re-zent') *v.* to feel angry, indignation at, as *He resents being treated as a child.*—**resent'ful** *adj.* bitter, injured.—**resent'ment** *n.*

reserva'tion (rez-er-vā'shun) *n.* 1. holding back, setting apart. 2. seat or accommodation booked. 3. doubt. 4. in N. America, area of land set aside for native Indians or wild animals

reserve' (re-zerv') *v.* to hold back, set apart, keep for further use.—**reser'ving** *pres. part.*—*n.* 1. store, something kept back. 2. self-restraint, a silent manner. 3. an area of land reserved for a particular purpose, as *a game reserve,* in S.A. more especially for native habitation.—*pl.* part of an army only called out in emergency.—**reserved'** *adj.* not making friends easily, self-restrained.—**in reserve** ready for use

Compare: cold, constrained, reticent, shy, taciturn

res'ervoir (rez'ervwar) *n.* 1. a place for collecting and storing water. 2. a store

reside' (re-zīd') *v.* to live, dwell.—**resi'ding** *pres. part.*—**res'idence** (rez'idens) *n.* 1. a house, home. 2. living, dwelling.—**res'ident** *n.* a person living in a place.—*adj.* living in, not visiting only.—**residen'tial** (rez-i-den'shal) *adj.* with houses only

res'idue (rez'i-dū) *n.* remainder, what is left.—**resid'ual** *adj.* left over

resign' (re-zīn') *v.* 1. to give up (esp. an office, position). 2. to submit, as *They resigned themselves to their fate.*—**resigna'tion** (rez-ig-na'shun) *n.* 1. resigning. 2. submission.—**resigned'** (re-zīnd') *adj.* uncomplaining, patient

resil'ience (re-zil'iens) *n.* power of springing

back, elasticity.—**resil'ient** *adj.* 1. rebounding. 2. able to recover quickly

res'in (rez'in) *n.* a sticky substance formed in some trees, esp. firs and pines.—**res'inous** (-us) *adj.*

resist' (re-zist') *v.* to oppose, to stand or act against, as *to resist the enemy, to resist a proposal.*—**resis'tance** *n.* 1. opposition. 2. (electricity) non-conductivity.—**resis'tant** *adj.*—**resist'less** *adj.* which cannot be resisted.—**line of least resistance** the easiest course to take.—**passive resistance** protest made without violence

Compare: withstand, confront, combat. *Contrast:* yield, give in, surrender withdraw, agree, comply

res'olute (rez'o-lūt) *adj.* determined, firm, bold.—**resolu'tion** (-shun) *n.* 1. firmness. 2. something decided on, decision. 3. breaking up into parts

resolve' (re-zolv') fixed purpose, resolution. —*v.* 1. to decide firmly. 2. to break up into parts, analyse. 3. pass away, into another state, as *This question resolves itself into one of ways and means.*—**resol'ving** *pres. part.*—**resolved'** *adj.* determined, decided

res'onance (rez'o-nans) *n.* an echoing, resounding quality.—**res'onant** *adj.*

resort' (to) (re-zort') *v.* 1. to visit, go often, frequent. 2. to turn to for help, as *He resorted to money-lenders.*—*n.* 1. place often visited, esp. a holiday place. 2. help, recourse.—**in the last resort** when all else has failed

resound' (re-zound') *v.* 1. to ring, echo, fill with sound. 2. to be talked about widely.—**a resounding success** a great success

resource' (re-sōrs') *n.* skill, quick wit in getting out of difficulties.—*pl.* supplies, means of help.—**resource'ful** *adj.* quick-witted.—**resource'fulness** *n.*

respect' *n.* esteem, regard.—*pl.* greetings, as *Father sends his best respects to you.*—*v.* 1. to honour, feel regard for, as *The boys respect the headmaster.* 2. to treat with consideration, as *I respect your feelings in the matter.*—**to pay one's respects** to visit someone as a mark of respect

Compare: honour, admiration, veneration, reverence, obedience, good-will, consideration. *Contrast:* contempt, disregard, disrespect

respect' *n.* way, manner, as *in that respect, in all respects.*—**respect'ing** *adj.* regarding. —**with respect to** concerning.—**in respect of** on account of, for

respectabil'ity *n.* the quality of being socially respectable

respec'table *adj.* 1. worthy of respect, decent. 2. fairly good

respect'ful *adj.* polite, considerate.—**respect'fully** *adv.*

respec'tive *adj.* belonging to each, own, separate, as *They went their respective ways* (i.e. *each went his own way.*)—**respec'tively** *adv.* severally, each separately, as *Uncle Jim gave a train and a doll to Fred and Mary respectively* (i.e. *the train to Fred and the doll to Mary*)

respira'tion (-ā'shun) *n.* breathing.—**res'pirator** *n.* an instrument to help breathing. —**res'piratory** *adj.* having to do with breathing

respire' *v.* to breathe.—**respi'ring** *pres. part.*

res'pite (res'pīt) *n.* 1. a temporary time of rest or relief. 2. delay in carrying out a punishment, reprieve.—*v.*

resplen'dent *adj.* brilliant, radiant, glorious

respond' *v.* 1. to answer. (See **reply.**) 2. to act in answer, as *The aeroplane responded easily to the controls*

response' *n.* an answer, reply, by word or action

responsibil'ity *n.* 1. being responsible, obligation. 2. trust, charge.—**responsibil'ities** *pl.*

respon'sible *adj.* 1. expected to answer for. 2. reliable, trustworthy

Note: You are responsible *for* your duties *to* your superior

respon'sive *adj.* willing to respond

rest *n.* 1. sleep, being quiet. 2. freedom from tiredness, trouble, pain, work. 3. a pause in reading or music. 4. a support.—*v.* 1. to be quiet, to lie still. 2. to be supported, as *The arch rested on two pillars.* 3. to lie down, remain, as *to rest under an imputation. It rests with you to decide.*—**rest'ful** *adj.* peaceful.—**rest'less** *adj.* not resting, uneasy

Compare: ease, calm, peace, tranquillity, repose, sleep, slumber, recreation. *Contrast:* activity, work, labour, toil, strife, discomfort, anxiety, struggle

rest *n.* the others, what is left, the remainder

rest'aurant (rest'ōr-ong) *n.* a place where meals may be bought

restitu'tion (-shun) *n.* the act of giving back, or making up for something lost or taken, reparation

rest'ive *adj.* impatient, restless, resisting control

restora'tion (-ā'shun) *n.* 1. putting back in place, as *the restoration of Charles II to the throne.* 2. recovery of health or of something lost or damaged

restor'ative *n.* something that restores health. —*adj.*

restore' *v.* 1. to bring or put back. 2. to repair, renew.—**resto'ring** *pres. part.*

restrain' *v.* to keep back, check.—**restraint'** *n.* 1. restraining. 2. being restrained. 3. self-control

restrict' *v.* to limit, keep within bounds.—**restrict'ed** *adj.* limited.—**restric'tion** (-shun) *n.* a rule or condition which restricts.—**restrict'ive** *adj.*

result' (re-zult') *n.* 1. an effect that follows because of something. 2. the total of examination marks, final score in a game, answer to a sum.—*v.* to follow, to have as a result, as *The match resulted in a win for the home team.*—**resul'tant** *adj.*

Compare: outcome, total, conclusion, end, finish, consequence, product

resume' (re'zūm') *v.* 1. to begin again as *The concert was resumed after the interval.* 2. to occupy again, as *They resumed their seats.*—**resu'ming** *pres. part.*—**rés'umé** (rā'-zōō-mā) *n.* summary

resump'tion (re-zump'shun) *n.* act of beginning again, taking up again

resurg'ence *n.* revival, renewal

resurrect' (rez-ur-rekt') *v.* to bring back to life

resurrec'tion (rez-u-rek'shun) *n.* a rising again.—**the Resurrection,** the rising of Christ from the dead

resus'citate (re-sus'i-tāt) *v.* to revive, bring back to life.—**resuscita'tion** (-tā'shun) *n.*

re'tail (ree'tāl) *n.* sale in small quantities.—*adj.*—**retail'** *v.* 1. to sell goods in small quantities. 2. to pass on, tell (gossip, etc.).—**retail'er** *n.*

retain' *v.* 1. to keep. 2. to pay for the services of, as *He retained the ablest lawyer he could find.*—**retain'er** *n.* 1. a nobleman's servant. 2. a fee paid for a e.g. lawyer's services

Compare: 1. detain, hold, secure, engage, hire. *Contrast:* 1. loose, let go, abandon, discard, give up, relinquish, surrender. 2. dismiss, discharge

retal'iate *v.* to pay back evil with evil.—**retal'iating** *pres. part.*—**retalia'tion** (-ā'-shun) *n.* the act of returning like for like.—**retalia'tory** *adj.*

retard' *v.* to make slow or late, to delay, hinder.—**retar'ded** *adj.* backward educationally or mentally

Contrast: hasten, accelerate, advance

reten'tion (-shun) *n.* the act of retaining, keeping, being kept.—**reten'tive** *adj.* able to keep, able to remember

ret'icence (ret'i-sens) *n.* reserve in speech, keeping silent.—**ret'icent** *adj.*

ret'ina *n.* the cells at the back of the eye, which receive the image of things seen.—*pl.*—**ret'inas, ret'inae** (-nee)

ret'inue *n.* attendants on a personage, following

retire' *v.* 1. to go back, retreat, withdraw. 2. to go to bed. 3. to give up business, work, etc.—**retir'ing** *pres. part.*—*adj.* shy, reserved.—**retire'ment** *n.* 1. giving up work. 2. retreat

retort' *v.* to reply, esp. sharply.—*n.* a sharp reply

retort' *n.* a vessel with a narrowing neck set at an angle, used for distilling, etc.

retouch' (ree-tuch') *v.* to improve, e.g. a photograph, by new touches

retrace' (ree-trās') *v.* to go over again, as *We had to retrace our footsteps back to the main road.*—**retra'cing** *pres. part.*

retract' *v.* to draw back or in, take back what has been said.—**retrac'tion** (-shun) *n.*

retreat' *n.* 1. going back, withdrawal, 2. a quiet or safe place. 3. retirement for prayer and contemplation.—*v.* to withdraw, go back before an enemy

Compare: refuge, seclusion, asylum, shelter, haunt

retrench' *v.* to cut down expenses, economise.—**retrench'ment** *n.*

retribu'tion (-shun) *n.* punishment deserved, revenge

retrieve' (re-treev') *v.* 1. to recover, regain, as *He retrieved his hat from the river.* 2. to rescue from a bad state, as *to retrieve from ruin.* 3. to set right, as *to retrieve a bad start.* 4. to bring in a game-bird.—**retriev'ing** *pres. part.*—**retriev'er** *n.* a dog trained to retrieve game

ret'rograde *adj.* going backward, getting worse

retrogres'sion (re-tro-gresh'n) *n.* moving backward, getting worse.—**retrogres'sive** *adj.*

ret'rospect *n.* looking backward.—**retrospec'tion** (-shun) *n.*—**retrospec'tive** *adj.*

return' *v.* 1. to go back, to come back. 2. to give or send back. 3. to pay back. (See **requite.**) 4. to elect, as *He was returned unopposed.*—*n.* 1. returning, being returned. 2. profits. 3. an official report

reu'nion (ree-ū'nion) *n.* a meeting or joining together again

reveal' *v.* to show, make known

Compare: disclose, uncover, discover, divulge, uncover. *Contrast:* hide, conceal, cloak

reveill'e (ree-val'i) *n.* a morning bugle-call to waken soldiers

rev'el *n.* merry-making, noisy feasting.—*v.* to make merry, to enjoy.—**rev'elling** *pres. part.*—**rev'elled** *p.t.* and *p. part.*—**revel in** enjoy keenly.—**re'veller** *n.* one who revels.—**re'velry** *n.* merrymaking

Compare: carousal, jollification, carnival, rout

revela'tion (-ā'shun) *n.* 1. the act of disclosing. making known. 2. a surprising disclosure

revenge' (re-venj') *v.* to punish for a wrong done, to return evil for evil.—**reveng'ing** *pres. part.*—*n.* harmful return, vengeance

Note: You *revenge* yourself *on* someone, you *have* your *revenge* or you are *revenged*; but you *avenge* an insult or a wrong. (See **avenge.**)—**revenge'ful** *adj.* spiteful

rev'enue *n.* income, money coming in yearly.—**in'land rev'enue** *n.* a country's yearly income from taxes, etc.

rever'berate *v.* to re-echo, resound. **reverbera'tion** (-ā'shun) *n.* echo

revere' *v.* to respect deeply, to honour.—**rever'ing** *pres. part.*—**rev'erence** *n.* 1.

honour, respect. (See **respect**.) 2. a bow, curtsey. 3. a title given to an Irish priest, as *your reverence, his reverence*

rev'erend *adj.* 1. deserving respect. 2. used as title in front of clergyman's name

Note 1: One writes or says *Rev. J. Smith* or *Rev. Mr. Smith*, but not *Rev. Smith*

Note 2: Do not confuse *reverend* and *reverent*

rev'erent *adj.* full of reverence.—**reveren'tial** (-shal) *adj.* expressing reverence

rev'erie *n.* a day-dream

revers'al *n.* a change round, reversing, being reversed

reverse' *v.* 1. to change completely. 2. to turn upside down, or the other way round. 3. to make (a car) go backwards.—*n.* 1. the side opposite, as *The coin has a figure of Britannia on the reverse.* 2. a defeat, as *The enemy has suffered a reverse.—adj.* opposite, contrary, as *This is the reverse of true.*—**revers'ible** *adj.* which can be reversed.—**revers'ing** *pres. part.*

rever'sion (re-ver'shun) *n.* turning back, return to a former state

revert' *v.* 1. to turn back, return to a former state. 2. to come back to a subject

review' (re-vū') *n.* 1. an inspection of soldiers. 2. a critic's opinion of a book. 3. a magazine in which books are reviewed.—*v.* 1. to view again. 2. to look back on. 3. to inspect troops. 4. to write a review of a book.—**review'er** *n.*

revile' *v.* to abuse, call by ill names.—**revi'ling** *pres. part.*

revise' (re-vīz') *v.* 1. to look over and correct. 2. to reconsider and change, as *I have revised my opinion of the affair.* 3. to go over again to refresh one's memory.—**revis'ing** *pres. part.*—**revis'ion** (re-vizh'n) *n.* 1. revising. 2. a revised form

revi'val *n.* 1. a bringing back to life, restoring to vigour. 2. a religious awakening. 3. a new production of an old play

revive' *v.* 1. to restore to life, vigour, to refresh. 2. to come back to life or use.—**revi'ving** *pres. part.*

revoke' *v.* 1. to withdraw, cancel, repeal, e.g. a law. 2. (in cards) not to follow suit when able to do so.—**revo'king** *pres. part.*

revolt (re-vōlt') *v.* 1. to rebel, to rise against. 2. to be disgusted *at* or *by*.—*n.* a rising, rebellion.—**revol'ting** *adj.* disgusting

revolu'tion (rev-o-lōō'shun) *n.* 1. a complete turn or spin, as *of a wheel.* 2. a great change, as *a revolution in design*, etc. 3. a violent overthrow of a government, as *The French Revolution of* 1789.—**revolu'tionary** *adj.* bringing great changes.—*n.* revolutionist.—**revolu'tionist** *n.* a person helping to make revolution.—**revolu'tionise** *v.* to change completely

revolve' *v.* 1. to turn round, rotate. 2. to move round a point. 3. to turn over in one's mind.—**revol'ving** *pres. part.*

revol'ver *n.* a repeating pistol with a revolving cartridge-magazine

revue' (rev-ū') *n.* a variety entertainment

revul'sion (-shun) *n.* sudden violent change of feeling

reward' *n.* recompense for something done, as *A reward was offered for the return of the lost dog.*—*v.* to pay for, give reward, as *For his services the King rewarded him with a medal*

Rex *n.* title of a reigning king

rhap'sody (rap'so-di) *n.* an enthusiastic or extravagant musical composition or speech

rhe'ostat (ree'ō-stat) *n.* a variable electrical resistance for regulating current

rhet'oric (ret'or-ik) *n.* 1. the art of using words with effect. 2. exaggerated language. **rhetori'cian** (ret-ori'shun) *n.* person skilled in rhetoric.—**rhetor'ical** *adj.*—**rhetorical question** a question asked in order to create an effect and not expecting an answer

rheumat'ic (rōō-mat'ik) *adj.* of rheumatism, subject to rheumatism

rheu'matism (rōō'mat-izm) *n.* painful inflammation of joints and muscles

rhino'ceros (rī-nos'er-os) *n.* a large, thick-skinned animal with one, or two, horns on its snout.—*pl.* **rhino'ceroses**

rhi'zome (ri'zōm) *n.* a thick underground stem sending out shoots and roots

rhododen'dron (rō-dō-den'dron) *n.* evergreen shrub with clusters of showy flowers

rhomb, rhom'bus (rom'bus) *n.* parallelogram with equal sides but no right angles

rhu'barb (rōō'barb) *n.* plant with fleshy leaf-stalks, used for food

rhyme, rime (rīm) *n.* 1. similarity of sound at ends of lines of verse from last accented syllable, e.g. *go* and *so*, *father* and *rather* are *rhymes*. 2. verse marked by rhyme.—*v.* —**without rhyme or reason** utter nonsense

rhyth'm (riTH'm) *n.* a measured beat or flow in words, music, movement.—**rhyth'mic, rhyth'mical** *adj.* having rhythm

rib *n.* 1. one of the curved bones coming from the spine and making the framework of the upper part of the body. 2. a curved timber in the framework of a boat. 3. a ridge on cloth.—**ribbed** *adj.*

rib'ald *adj.* coarsely humorous.—*n.* **rib'aldry** coarse humour

rib'bon, rib'and *n.* 1. narrow band or strip of material. 2. anything resembling this.—**ribbon development** building houses in rows along both sides of a main road

rice (rīs) *n.* the starchy, white seeds of an Eastern plant, used as food

rich *adj.* 1. having much money or property. 2. fertile, abundant, as *rich pasture-land.* 3. valuable, as *a rich reward.* 4. splendid, costly, as *rich attire.* 5. (of food) containing much fat or sugar.—**rich'es** (rich'iz) *n.pl.* (no *sing.* form) wealth.—**rich'ly** *adv.*—**rich'ness** *n.* rich quality

Note: A richly deserved punishment means a thoroughly deserved punishment

Compare: 1. wealthy, opulent. 2. luxuriant, ample. 3. precious. 4. sumptuous, luxurious. 5. luscious, succulent. *Contrast:* 1. poor, indigent. 2. sterile, meagre. 3. worthless. 4. cheap, mean, humble. 5. plain

rick *n.* a stack of hay, or corn

rick'ets *n.* a disease of children resulting in softening of the bones.—**rick'ety** *adj.* 1. suffering from rickets. 2. unsteady, shaky

rick'shaw *n.* a Japanese light carriage drawn by a man

ric'ochet (rik'ō-shā) *v.* to glance off, as a stone on the surface of water, or a bullet off a rock.—*n.*—**ricochet'ing, ricochett'ing** (rik-o-shā'ing) *pres. part.*—**ricochet'ed, ricochetted'** (rik-o-shād') *p.t.* and *p. part.*

rid *v.* to clear off, make free from.—**rid'ding** *pres. part.*—**rid'ded, rid** *p.t.*—**rid** *p. part.*—**get rid of** dismiss, clear away, abolish.—**rid'dance** *n.* a clearing away.—**good riddance!** exclamation approving of the removal of someone or something

rid'dle *n.* a question, puzzle, enigma.—*v.* to make riddles, to speak in riddles

rid'dle *n.* a coarse sieve.—*v.* 1. to pass through a sieve. 2. to pierce with many holes, as *riddled with bullets*

ride *v.* 1. to go on horse-back, bicycle, train, etc. 2. to control a horse. 3. to lie at anchor. 4. to float lightly.—**ri'ding** *pres. part.*—**rode** *p.t.*—**rid'den** *p. part.*—*n.* 1. a journey on horse-back, bicycle, etc. 2. road for riding on horseback.—**to ride for a fall** to act in a way that will lead to trouble.—**to ride out a storm** to come safely through it

ri'der *n.* 1. a person who rides. 2. something added to a document or statement after it was completed. 3. an exercise based on a geometrical theorem

ridge (rij) *n.* 1. the line where two sloping surfaces meet. 2. a long narrow hill. 3. any narrow raised strip.—**ridged** *adj.*

rid'icule *v.* to laugh at, make fun of.—**rid'iculing** *pres. part.*—*n.* mockery

ridic'ulous *adj.* absurd, foolish, deserving to be laughed at

Compare: silly, nonsensical, ludicrous, preposterous, comical, farcical, funny, grotesque, outrageous, stupid. *Contrast:* serious, imposing, important, clever, wise, majestic

ri'ding *n.* one of three administrative divisions of Yorkshire (e.g. the West Riding) or New Zealand

rife *adj.* common, numerous, as *Rumours were rife*

riff'-raff *n.* rabble, worthless people

ri'fle *n.* a gun with grooves in its barrel.—*v.* 1. to make grooves in gun-barrel. 2. to search and rob.—**ri'fleman** *n.* a soldier armed with rifle.—**rifle-range** *n.* a place for shooting practice

rift *n.* a crack, split, break

rig *v.* 1. to fit a ship with spars, ropes, etc. 2. to fix up in a makeshift way (usually followed by *up*). 3. to fit out, equip (usually followed by *out*). 4. to conduct or manage dishonestly.—**rig'ging** *pres. part.*—**rigged** *p.t.* and *p. part.*—*n.* the way a ship's masts and sails are arranged.—**rig'ging** *n.* a ship's ropes and spars.—**rig'ger** *n.* a fitter employed on a ship or aircraft

right (rīt) *adj.* 1. correct, proper. 2. just, good, true. 3. on the right side.—*n.* what is just, true.—*pl.* fair treatment, as *to stand up for one's rights.*—*v.* 1. to correct. 2. to make straight.—*adv.* 1. straight, exactly. 2. completely, thoroughly. 3. on or to the right.—*interj.* agreed, ready, go.—**rightly** *adv.*—**right of way** 1. a public path over private land. 2. (N.Z.) a lane, track.—**right angle** an angle of 90°.—**to be in one's right mind** to be sane.—**to get on the right side of someone** to get into good favour with him.—**to put right** to correct, repair.—**to put to rights** to repair, to make in good condition

right'eous (rī'chus) *adj.* good, honest, just.—**right'eousness** *n.* virtue, uprightness

right'ful (rīt'ful) *adj.* just, proper, according to law.—**right'fully** *adv.*

right'-hand (rīt'hand) *adj.* on the side of a person which is to the east when he faces north, the opposite of left

rig'id (rij'id) *adj.* 1. stiff, unbending. 2. strict. —**rigid'ity** *n.*

rig'marole *n.* foolish words without meaning

rig'our *n.* harshness, severity, strictness.—**rig'orous** *adj.*—**rig'orously** *adv.*

rill *n.* a small stream, brook

rim *n.* 1. the outer ring of a wheel. 2. an edge, border.—**rim'less** *adj.*

rime *n.* white frost, hoar frost.—**ri'my** *adj.*

rind (rīnd) *n.* peel, bark, outer crust

ring *n.* 1. a small circle of gold, silver, etc., esp. as worn on the finger, 2. any circle. 3. an enclosed space.—*v.* to fit with a ring.—**ring'ing** *pres. part.*—**ringed** *p.t.* and *p. part.* —**ring-road** *n.* a road round a town bypassing the centre.—**ringer** *n.* (Aus.) a champion shearer.—**to run rings round** to defeat easily

ring *v.* 1. to sound. 2. to cause a bell to sound. 3. to resound, re-echo.—**rang** *p.t.* — **rung** *p. part.*—*n.* sound of a bell.—**ring'er** *n.* —**to ring the changes on** to use several items in different ways.—**to ring down the curtain** to bring to an end.—**to ring true** to appear true or sincere.—**to ring up** to telephone

ring'leader *n.* a person who leads others into mischief or rebellion

ring'let *n.* a curly lock of hair

rink (ringk) *n.* 1. a sheet of ice for skating on. 2. a floor for roller-skating

rinse *v.* 1. to wash in clean water. 2. to wash

lightly.—**rin'sing** *pres. part.*—*n.* a rinsing

ri'ot *n.* disorder, tumult, violent confusion.—*v.* to make a riot.—**ri'oter** *n.*—**ri'otous** *adj.* disorderly, unruly.—**to run riot** to throw off restraint.—**to read the Riot Act** to warn against bad behaviour

rip *v.* to tear, slash, cut away.—**rip'ping** *pres. part.*—**ripped** *p.t.* and *p. part.*—*n.* a tear, rent.—**rip-cord** *n.* a cord to open out a parachute.—**rip-saw** *n.* a saw to saw along the grain of wood.—**let rip** to behave in an unrestrained way

ripe *adj.* 1. fit to be gathered and eaten. 2. ready, mature.—**ri'pen** *v.* to grow ripe.—**ripe'ness** *n.*

Compare: mellow, luscious, seasoned, perfect, finished. *Contrast:* green, sour, undeveloped, imperfect, immature, crude, callow

rip'ple *v.* 1. to flow in little waves. 2. to form little waves on.—**rip'pling.** *pres. part.*—*n.* a small wave

rise (rīz) *v.* 1. to get up, stand up. 2. to go up, move upward. 3. to increase, as *The sound of the wind rose and fell.* 4. to begin, as *the Thames rises in the Cotswolds.* 5. to revolt, as *The tribes rose in revolt.*—**ri'sing** *pres. part.*—**rose** *p.t.*—**ris'en** *p. part.*—*n.* 1. a slope. 2. increase. 3. beginning.—**ri'sing** *n.* 1. upward move. 2. revolt.—**to give rise to** to cause.—**to take a rise out of someone** to tease him and make him angry or look foolish.—**to rise to the occasion** to cope in a crisis

risk *n.* danger, chance of loss or harm.—*v.* 1. to venture. 2. to expose to the chance of loss.—**risk'y** *adj.* dangerous.—**risk'ier** *comp.*—**risk'iest** *sup.*

rissole *n.* a fried cake of minced meat, etc.

rite (rīt) *n.* a solemn ceremony, esp. religious

rit'ual *adj.* concerning rites, done as a rite.—*n.* rites, set order of religious service

ri'val *n.* a person in pursuit of the same object as another, competitor.—*v.* to compete with, vie with, as *Jack now rivals Harry as the best player in the team.*—**ri'valling** *pres. part.*—**ri'valled** *p.t.* and *p. part.*—*adj.* competing.—**ri'valry** *n.* competition.—**rivalries** *pl.*

rive *v.* to split, tear.—**ri'ving** *pres. part.*—**rived** *p.t.*—**rived, riv'en** *p. part.*

riv'er *n.* a large stream of water.—**riv'erside** *n.*—**river basin** *n.* land drained by a river and its tributaries.—**riv'er bed** *n.* the ground over which a river flows.—**to sell down the river** to betray

Compare: stream, watercourse, estuary, creek, brook, rill, rivulet

riv'et *n.* a bolt for fastening plates of metal together, each end being hammered flat.—*v.* 1. to fasten with rivets. 2. to fix.—**riv'eting** *pres. part.*—**riv'eted** *p.t.* and *p. part.*

riv'ulet *n.* a small river

roach *n.* a freshwater fish

road (rōd) *n.* 1. a way with a surface suitable for vehicles. 2. a way.—*pl.* water near the shore where ships may anchor.—**road' block** *n.* a barrier set up by police or army to halt traffic.—**road' hog** *n.* a driver who disregards the safety of other road-users.—**road'man** *n.* one who repairs roads.—**road'side** *n.*—**road'stead** *n.* water near the shore.—**road'way** *n.*—**road'worthy** *adj.* safe to use on a road

Compare: way, passage, path, course, route, highway, thoroughfare, lane, street

A *way* to a place consists of a *passage* or *path* to it, and one's *course* or *route* follows that *road.* It may be a main *road* (*highway* or *thoroughfare*) or may be along a *lane* (narrow road). If it is in a town or city it will probably lie through *streets* (town *roads*)

roam (rōm) *v.* to wander, to ramble.—**roam'er** *n.*

roan (rōn) *adj.* bay or dark colour mixed with grey or white.—*n.* a roan horse

roar (rōr) *n.* a loud, deep, hoarse sound.—*v.*

roast (rōst) *v.* to cook before an open fire or in an oven.—*n.* roast meat.—*adj.* roasted

rob *v.* to steal, take away, plunder.—**rob'bing** *pres. part.*—**robbed** *p.t.* and *p. part.*—**rob'ber** *n.* thief.—**rob'bery** *n.* theft with violence.—**rob'beries** *pl.*

Compare: (with robber) burglar, footpad, highwayman, bandit, pirate, buccaneer

A *burglar* is a *robber* of houses, banks, etc. A *footpad* or *highwayman* holds up people on the road to rob them. *Bandits* work in bands or gangs. *Pirates* and *buccaneers* are robbers on the sea

robe *n.* 1. a long, loose dress. 2. a garment worn as a sign of office or profession.—*v.* to dress.—**ro'bing** *pres. part.*

rob'in *n.* a small bird with yellowish-red breast.—**rob'in red'breast**

ro'bot (rō'bot) *n.* a man-like machine

robust' *adj.* strong and healthy, sturdy

Compare: hearty, vigorous, powerful, stout, stalwart, muscular, sturdy, lusty. *Contrast:* sickly, weak, puny, feeble

rock *n.* 1. a mass of stone. 2. a stone. 3. kind of hard sweet

rock *v.* to move to and fro, to sway.—**rock'ing-chair** *n.* a chair which rocks.—**rock'ing-horse** *n.* a wooden horse which rocks.—**ro'cker** curved piece of wood on which chair or cradle rocks.—**rock'n'roll** *n.* 1. very acrobatic kind of dance. 2. music for this dance

rock'ery *n.* a bank of earth and stones for plants in a garden

rock'et *n.* 1. a projectile shot into the air or into space by the recoil of hot gases. 2. a firework on a stick that can be shot high into the air for signalling or for amusement

rock'y *adj.* made of rock, rugged, full of rocks

rod *n.* 1. a thin, straight, rounded bar or stick. 2. a cane, birch. 3. a measure, 5½ yards
ro'dent *n.* a gnawing animal.—*adj.* gnawing
rode'o (rō-dā'ō) *n.* (U.S.) 1. a round-up of cattle. 2. an exhibition of cowboy's skill
roe (rō) *n.* a small kind of deer.—**roe'buck** *masc.*
roe (rō) *n.* fish's eggs
rogue (rōg) *n.* 1. a rascal, dishonest person. 2. a mischievous person. 3. a wild animal of savage temper living apart from its herd, as *a rogue elephant.*—**ro'guery** (rō'ger-i) *n.*—**ro'guish** (rō'gish) *adj.* 1. cheating. 2. playful
role (rōl) *n.* 1. an actor's part. 2. a part taken on in real life
roll (rōl) *v.* 1. to move by turning over and over. 2. to wind round. 3. to smooth out. 4. to swing from side to side. 5. to make a deep sound.—*n.* 1. anything rolled, as paper, meat, cake. 2. bread in small rounded shapes. 3. a list. 4. the beat of a drum.—**roll-call** *n.* calling over names from a list.—**roll'er** *n.* a cylinder of wood, stone, metal, etc. used for pressing or crushing, etc.—**roll'er-skate** *n.* skate mounted on rollers.—**roll'ing -pin** *n.* roller for smoothing out dough.—**rolling-stock** *n.* railway engines, carriages and goods vans.—**roll'-top** *adj.* (desk) having a sliding top made of movable narrow strips of wood
Ro'man *adj.* belonging to Rome.—*n.* a citizen of Rome.—**Roman Catholic** pertaining to the Roman Catholic Church, the head of which is the Pope.—**Roman numerals** letters used (originally by the ancient Romans) as figures, e.g. V for 5, X for 10, C for 100, etc.
romance' (rō-mans') *n.* 1. a story of adventures in love and war. 2. love and adventure. 3. an exaggerated story.—*v.* to exaggerate.—**roman'cer** *n.* 1. writer of romances. 2. person who makes up fanciful stories
roman'tic *adj.* belonging to romance, fanciful, having ideas suited to romance
romp *v.* to play roughly.—*n.* 1. a frolic. 2. a child who likes romping.—**romp'ers** *n.pl.* loose trousers for a young child
rood *n.* 1. the Cross of Christ, a crucifix. 2. forty square poles, the fourth part of an acre
roof *n.* 1. the outside top covering of a building. 2. something resembling this.—roofs *pl.*—*v.* to put a roof on.—**roof'ing** *n.* material for roofs.—**roof'less** *adj.* 1. without a roof. 2. homeless.—**roof of the mouth** palate
rook *n.* 1. a kind of crow. 2. a cheat, dishonest gambler. 3. one of the pieces in a game of chess (also called the castle).—**rook'ery** *n.* colony of rooks and their nesting-place. —**rook'eries** *pl.*
room *n.* 1. space. 2. opportunity, occasion as *room for improvement, room for doubt.* 3. a division of a house.—*v.* to occupy a room.—**room'ful** *n.*—**room'iness** *n.* plenty of space.—**room'y** *adj.*

Compare: 1. place, 2. absence, vacancy, accommodation. 3. apartment, chamber
roost *n.* a perch for fowls, a hen-house.—*v.* to perch.—**roost'er** *n.* a cock
root *n.* 1. the underground part of a plant which fixes it and supplies it with water and mineral salts. 2. source, origin, as *the root of the trouble.*—*v.* 1. to cause to take root. 2. to pull up. 3. to fix firmly, as *It was rooted in his mind. He had a rooted objection to it.*—**to root around** to grope, to search.—**to root out** to remove completely, to destroy
rope *n.* a thick cord.—*v.* to tie, or mark off with a rope.—**ropeable, ropable** *adj.* (Aus.) 1. of cattle, controllable only by roping. 2. angry.—**rope'-ladder** *n.* a ladder made of rope.—**to give someone rope** to give him more freedom to act.—**to know the ropes** to be familiar with usual procedure
ro'sary (rō'zar-i) *n.* 1. a series of prayers. 2. a string of beads for keeping count of these prayers. 3. a rose-garden.—**ro'saries** *pl.*
rose (rōz) *n.* 1. a beautiful flower with thorny stems. 2. nose-piece for a watering-can. hose-pipe, etc.—*adj.* rose-pink.—**ro'seate** (rō'ze-at) *adj.* rose-coloured, rosy.—**rose-coloured spectacles** unfounded optimism
rosette' (rō-zet') *n.* an ornament of ribbon, or of stone, shaped like a rose
ros'ter *n.* a list of duties to be taken by different people in order.—see **rota**
ros'trum *n.* a platform used during public speaking.—**ros'tra, ros'trums** *pl.*
ro'sy (rō'zi) *adj.* 1. rose-coloured, ruddy. 2. hopeful, as *Your prospects of success are rosy.*—**ro'sier** *comp.*—**ro'siest** *sup.*
rot *v.* to decay, spoil.—**rot'ting** *pres. part.*—**rot'ted** *p.t.* and *p. part.*—*n.* 1. decay, going bad. 2. a sheep disease. 3. (in common speech) nonsense
ro'ta (rō'ta) *n.* a list showing duties to be taken by different people in order.—*see* **ros'ter**
ro'tary *adj.* turning like a wheel
rotate' *v.* 1. to move round a centre, to revolve. 2. to take turns in a certain order. —**rota'ting** *pres. part.*—**rota'tion** (-tā'shun) *n.* turning, revolving.—**in rota'tion** in turn.—**rota'tory** *adj.*
ro'tor (rō'tor) *n.* a rotating part of a machine
rot'ten *adj.* 1. decayed, corrupt, bad. 2. worthless, dishonest.—**rot'tenness** *n.*
rotund' *adj.* round, plump.—**rotund'ity** *n.*
rou'ble (rōō'bl) *n.* a Russian silver coin
rouge (rōōzh) *n.* red colouring matter for cheeks or lips.—*v.* to colour with rouge
rough (ruf) *adj.* 1. not smooth, uneven. 2. violent, ill-mannered, coarse. 3. stormy, wild, as *rough weather*. 4. without comforts. 5. unfinished, as *a rough sketch.* 6. makeshift. 7. approximate, as *a rough guess.*—

n. 1. a violent person. 2. (golf) uncut grass. —*v.* to make rough.—**rough'en.**—*v.*—**rough'ly** *adv.*—**rough and ready** makeshift. —**a rough diamond** a good-hearted but uncouth man.—**a rough house, a rough and tumble** a general fight among a group of men.—**to ride roughshod over** to act in a dominating pitiless way

Compare: jagged, unpolished, turbulent, disorderly, brutal, incomplete. *Contrast:* smooth, gentle, polished, courteous, calm, level, even

rough'cast (ruf'kast) *n.* a mixture of lime and gravel for the surface of outside walls

round *adj.* 1. shaped like a circle or a ball or a roller. 2. roughly correct, as *in round figures.* 3. large, plain, as *written in a good round hand.*—*n.* 1. something round in shape. 2. movement in a circle. 3. duty, regular course, as *the daily round, a milkman's round.* 4. a stage in a game or sport, as *a ten-round boxing contest.* 5. part-song. —*v.* to make rounded to get round.—**round up** to herd (cattle) together.—*n.*—*adv.* 1. in a circle. 2. by a longer road.—*prep.* 1. about. 2. on all sides of.—**a round number** an approximate number.—**a round trip** a journey to and from a place.—**to go the rounds** to visit several people or places in turn.—**to round off** to complete.—**in the round** (theatre) having the audience on at least three sides of the stage

roundabout *n.* 1. a merry-go-round. 2. an obstacle at cross-roads forcing drivers to slow down by preventing them from driving in a straight line.—*adj.* indirect

roun'ders *n.* a children's game like a simple form of baseball

round'ly *adv.* thoroughly, plainly

roun'delay (rown'de-lā) *n.* a simple song with a refrain

rouse (rowz) *v.* 1. to wake up, stir up. 2. to waken.—**rous'ing** *pres. part.*

rouse'about *n.* (Aus. and N.Z.) an odd job man on a station, especially in a shearing shed

rout *n.* 1. a retreat in disorder. 2. a company of revellers, mob.—*v.* 1. to defeat and put to flight. 2. (out) fetch out, get out

route (rōōt) *n.* a road, way

routine' (rōōteen') *n.* a regular way of doing things

rove *v.* to wander, roam.—**ro'ving** *pres. part.* —**ro'ver** *n.* 1. a wanderer. 2. a pirate. 3. a senior Scout

row (rō) *n.* a number of things in a straight line

row (rō) *v.* to move by using oars.—*n.* a ride in a rowing-boat

row *n.* a noisy quarrel, a disturbance

row'dy *adj.* rough, noisy

row'an (row'an) *n.* a mountain ash

row'el *n.* a small, pointed wheel on a horseman's spur

row'lock (rul'uk) *n.* the pins between which oars work

roy'al *adj.* 1. of kings and queens. 2. fit for a king, regal, splendid.—**roy'ally** *adv.*

roy'alist *n.* a supporter of monarchy.—*adj.*

roy'alty *n.* 1. being royal, royal power. 2. the royal family. 3. payment to an inventor, etc. for use of his invention. 4. payment to an author depending on sale of his book —**roy'alties** *pl.*

rub *v.* 1. to move one thing to and fro against another. 2. to clean, polish by rubbing. 3. to become worn by rubbing.—**rub'bing** *pres. part.*—**rubbed** *p.t.* and *p. part.*—*n.* difficulty.—**to rub someone the wrong way** to irritate him by some thoughtless words or action

rub'ber *n.* 1. person or thing that rubs. 2. strong elastic substance. 3. indiarubber, for erasing pencil-marks

rub'bish *n.* 1. useless stuff, waste. 2. nonsense. —**rub'bishy** *adj.*

rub'ble *n.* rough stones, broken bricks, etc.

Ru'bicon (rōō'bikon) *n.* a stream in Italy.—**to cross the Rubicon** to make some decisive action

ru'bicund (rōō'bi-kund) *adj.* ruddy, red

ru'bric (rōō'brik) *n.* 1. the title of a chapter. 2. directions for conduct of the church service

ru'by (rōō'bi) *n.* a red, precious stone.—**ru'bies** *pl.*—*adj.* red

ruck *n.* 1. a crease, fold. 2. main body (of competitors in a race, etc.) 3. (Rugby) loose scrum.—*v.* to wrinkle, crease

ruck'sack (rŏŏk'sack) *n.* a bag slung by straps on back of walker, climber, etc.

rud'der *n.* a flat piece hinged to the stern of a ship or boat for steering it

rud'dy *adj.* of a fresh, healthy red.—**rud'dier** *comp.*—**rud'diest** *sup.*

rude (rōōd) *adj.* 1. rough, as **a rude hut** or **rude fare.** 2. bad-mannered, impolite. 3. vulgar, not decent. 4. robust, strong, as *he was a picture of rude health.*—**rude'ly** *adv.*—**rude'ness** *n.*—**a rude awakening** an unpleasant discovery which spoils an illusion

ru'diment (rōō'di-ment) *n.* the beginning, early stage.—**rudiment'ary** *adj.* elementary, undeveloped

rue (rōō) *v.* to regret, to repent.—*n.* repentance, sorrow.—**rue'ful** *adj.* sorrowful.—**rue'ful** *adv.*

ruff *n.* 1. a starched and pleated collar or frill, worn in the 16th century. 2. a collar of feathers or hairs standing out on the neck of a bird or animal

ruf'fian *n.* a rough, brutal fellow.—**ruf'fianly** *adj.*

ruf'fle *v.* 1. to disturb something smooth. 2. to annoy.—**ruf'fling** *pres. part.*—*n.* a frilled cuff

rug *n.* 1. a thick, heavy floor-covering. 2. a thick woollen wrap

Rug'by *n.* a kind of football named after the school where it was first played, with 15

or 13 players on a side, and with an oval ball which can be handled

rug'ged *adj.* rough, uneven, as *a rugged coastline, rugged features, rugged kindness*

ru'in (rōō'in) *n.* 1. destruction. 2. downfall.—*pl.* remains of damaged buildings.—*v.* to spoil, to bring to destruction.—**ruina'tion** (-ā'shun) *n.* destruction, downfall.—**ru'inous** *adj.* bringing ruin, in a state of ruin

rule (rōōl) *n.* 1. a strip of wood or metal for measuring length. 2. a guide for action or conduct. 3. what is usual. 4. government.—*v.* 1. to govern. 2. to decide authoritatively.—**ru'ling** *pres. part.*—**as a rule** usually.—**a golden rule** a valuable guide to action.—**rule of thumb** a rule found to work from practice.—**slide rule** a ruler with a sliding scale for making rapid calculations.—**work to rule** carefully obey all rules in order to slow rate of production

Compare: order, regulation, system, law

ru'ler (rōō'ler) *n.* 1. a person who governs. 2. a strip of wood or metal for measuring

rum *n.* a spirit made from sugar-cane

rum *adj.* (in common use) odd, peculiar

rum'ba, rhum'ba *n.* a ballroom dance

rum'ble *v.* to make a deep, hollow sound like thunder.—*n.* **rum'bling** *pres. part.*

ru'minant (rōō'min-ant) *n.* an animal that chews the cud

ru'minate (rōō'min-āt) *v.* 1. to chew the cud. 2. to think over, ponder.—**rumina'tion** (-ā'shun) *n.* 1. chewing the cud. 2. reflection

rum'mage (rum'ij) *v.* to search thoroughly, to ransack.—*n.* 1. a search. 2. odds and ends, old clothing

Note: You *rummage about* or you *rummage in* a drawer

rum'my *n.* a card game.—*adj.* queer

ru'mour (rōō'mer) *n.* general talk, doubtful news that is spread.—*v.* to spread news

rump *n.* 1. the back part of an animal's body. 2. a remnant, esp. of a parliament, e.g. *The Rump Parliament*, 1648-53

rum'ple *v.* to crease, crumple, to make untidy.—**rum'pling** *pres. part.*

rum'pus *n.* in common talk, a disturbance, noisy confusion

run *v.* 1. to move very quickly. 2. to flow. 3. to compete in a race, enter a candidate. 4. to go, keep going. 5. to cause to run. 6. to force, as *to run a needle into one's finger*. 7. to evade, as *to run the blockade*. 8. to manage, as *to run a business*.—**run'ning** *pres. part.*—**ran** *p.t.*—**run** *p. part.*—*n.* 1. running, moving quickly. 2. a course. 3. enclosed space for animals. 4. a ride. 5. a rash, sudden demand, as *a run on the bank*. 6. a series, as *a run of success*. 7. (in cricket) point scored by batsman.—**a running battle** a fight while one side pursues the other.—**a running jump** a jump taken after a short run.—**in the long run** eventually.—**in the running** with a chance of winning.—**on the run** to be fleeing from enemies.—**to be run down** to be ill and depressed.—**to run amok** (amuck') to rush about attacking those around.—**to run down** 1. to run over. 2. to cease to go. 3. to talk against others.—**to run over** 1. to knock down with a car. 2. to read or say quickly.—**to run out of** to use up supplies.—**to run through** 1. to use up. 2. to penetrate. 3. to read or say rapidly.—**to run up** to make quickly.—**to run up against** to meet

rung *n.* 1. one of the rounds or bars in a ladder. 2. a crossbar joining legs of a chair

run'nel *n.* 1. a small stream. 2. a channel for water, gutter

run'ner *n.* 1. a messenger, a racer. 2. a curved piece of wood on which a sleigh slides. 3. a slender stem coming from the main stem and taking root.—**runner-up** *n.* the one next behind the winner

run'way *n.* a concrete space for an aeroplane to take off from or land on

ru'pee (roo'pee) *n.* an Indian silver coin

rup'ture *n.* 1. a break. 2. a quarrel.—*v.* to break, burst

ru'ral (rōō'ral) *adj.* of the country, rustic

ruse (rōōz) *n.* a trick, device

rush *v.* 1. to carry along violently and rapidly, as *They rushed him off to hospital*. 2. to dash, to hurry. 3. to attack violently, as *The besiegers tried to rush the drawbridge*.—he **rush'es**.—*n.* 1. the act of rushing, a dash. 2. a sudden demand. 3. a gathering of miners at a place where gold, diamonds, etc. have been discovered, a race of miners to peg out claims for development.—**rush-hour** *n.* the time of day when most people are travelling home from work

Compare: impel, drive, push, hasten, force, capture

rush *n.* a marsh-plant with a slender, hollow stem used in basket-making, etc.—**rush'es** *pl.*

rus'set *adj.* reddish-brown

Rus'sia *n.* a large country partly in Europe and partly in Asia, the U.S.S.R.—*n.* **Rus'sian** a native of Russia.—*adj.*

rust *n.* 1. the reddish-brown coating formed on iron when exposed to air or damp. 2. a disease of plants.—*v.* to become rusty

rus'tic *adj.* 1. belonging to the country, rural. 2. simple, unpolished. 3. roughly made.—*n.* a countryman.—**rustic'ity** (rus-tis'i-ti) *n.*

rus'tle (rus'l) *v.* 1. to make a sound as of blown dead leaves. 2. in U.S. to steal cattle.—**rus'tler** *n.*—**rus'tling** *pres. part.*—*n.* a rustling sound

rus'ty *adj.* 1. covered with rust. 2. rust-coloured.—**rus'tier** *comp.*—**rus'tiest** *sup.*

rut *n.* 1. a track made by wheels. 2. a fixed habit, a groove

ruth'less (rōōth'less) *adj.* pitiless, cruel. See **relentless**.—**ruth'lessly** *adv.*

rye *n.* a grain used for cattle-feeding, or to make coarse, black bread

rye-grass *n.* a kind of grass grown for cattle food

S

Sab'bath *n.* the seventh day, Jewish day of rest. Sunday is the Christian Sabbath

sa'ble *n.* a small animal with valuable dark fur, the fur from this animal.—*adj.* black, gloomy

sa'bot (sab'ō) *n.* a wooden shoe carved from a solid piece of wood

sab'otage (sab'ot-ahzh) *n.* wilful damage done by workmen to machinery, etc.

sa'bre (sā'ber) *n.* a cavalry sword

sac *n.* (biology) a pouch or small cavity

sacc'harine (sak'ar-in) *n.* a very sweet substance.—*adj.* like sugar

sach'et (sash'ā) *n.* a scented pad or bag

sack *n.* 1. a large bag of some coarse material. 2. the plundering of a captured town. 3. (in common speech) dismissal from a job. —*v.* 1. to plunder, pillage. 2. (in common speech) dismiss from job.—**sack'cloth** *n.* coarse, cloth, sacking

sac'rament *n.* a solemn religious ceremony, esp. baptism and the Eucharist.—**sacrament'al** *adj.*

sa'cred *adj.* 1. holy, religious. 2. which must not be injured

sac'rifice (sak'ri-fīs) *n.* 1. an offering made to God. 2. the giving up of something for the sake of something else.—*v.* 1. to offer as a sacrifice. 2. to give up, as *He sacrificed his holiday to help in his brother's business.* —**sacrifi'cial** (sak-ri-fish'al) *adj.*

sac'rilege (sak'ri-lij) *n.* disrespect or injury to sacred things.—**sacrile'gious** (sak-ri-li'-jus) *adj.*

sac'rosanct *n.* 1. sacred. 2. not to be broken or dishonoured

sad *adj.* 1. sorrowful. 2. dull, sober, incorrigible. 3. mischievous, troublesome, as *a sad tease, a sad coward.*—**sad'der** *comp.*—**sad'dest** *sup.*—**sad'den** *v.* to make sad.—**sad'ly** *adv.*

Compare: unhappy, miserable, downcast, gloomy, depressed, disconsolate, dreary, pitiful, mournful

Contrast: See **happy**

sad'dle *n.* 1. a rider's seat to fasten on a horse, or form part of a bicycle. 2. a ridge between mountains.—*v.* 1. to put a saddle on. 2. to burden, as *Now he is saddled with more responsibilities.*—**sad'dler** *n.* maker or seller of saddles

safar'i *n.* a hunting expedition in Africa.—**safar'i suit** *n.* shorts and bush shirt worn by men in hot weather

safar'i (safah'ri) *n.* in Africa, a hunting expedition

safe *adj.* 1. free from danger or harm, harmless, as *He is safe and well. Is it safe to eat?* 2. careful, cautious, as *a safe driver.* 3. sure, unlikely to prove wrong, as *It is safe to say that.*—*n.* 1. a strong box for valuables. 2. a cool cupboard for food, as a *meat-safe.*—**safes** *pl.*—**safe con'duct** a pass or permission granted to enable a person to go unharmed through a district. —**safe'guard** *v.* to keep safe, protect.—*n.* protection.—**safe'ty** *n.* the condition of being safe.—**safe'ty-belt** *n.* a belt to secure one to the seat of a car or plane.—**safe'ty-curtain** *n.* in a theatre, a fireproof curtain on the stage.—**safe'ty lamp** *n.* a miner's oil lamp which will not ignite surrounding gases.—**safe'ty pin** *n.* a bent pin with a guarded point.—**safe'ty valve** *n.* a valve to let off steam pressure

Compare: 1. secure, protected, unharmed. 2. prudent, moderate. 3. certain, undoubted. *Contrast:* 1. unsafe, risky, dangerous. 2. rash, impetuous, extreme. 3. doubtful, uncertain

saf'fron *n.* 1. orange colouring matter obtained from the autumn crocus. 2. flavouring matter from the same.—*adj.*yellow

sag *v.* to sink in the middle, to hang sideways under pressure, to droop.—**sag'ging** *pres. part.*—**sagged** *p.t.* and *p. part.*

sa'ga (sah'ga) *n.* an ancient story of Norse heroes

saga'cious (sa-gā'shus) *adj.* 1. wise, shrewd, having sound judgment. 2. (of animals) unusually intelligent.—**sagac'ity** (sa-gas'i-ti) *n.*

sage (sāj) *adj.* wise.—*n.* a wise man

Compare: sagacious, learned, clever, experienced, prudent, serious, profound, far-seeing

sage (sāj) *n.* a herb whose leaves are used for seasoning

sa'go (sā'gō) *n.* a starchy food obtained from a tropical plant

sa'hib (sah'ib) *n.* an Indian title, "sir"

sail *n.* 1. a piece of canvas stretched to catch the wind and make a ship move. 2. a ship, ships. 3. a trip in a sailing-boat.—*v.* 1. to travel by water. 2. to begin a voyage. 3. to manage a boat.—**sail'or** *n.* a seaman.—**plain sailing** a straightforward task.—**to set sail** to start a voyage.—**to sail near the wind** to act so as to nearly break the law

saint *n.* 1. a holy person. 2. one of the blessed in heaven.—**saint'liness** *n.* holiness.—**saint'ly** *adj.* like a saint, holy.—**saint'lier** *comp.*—**saint'liest** *sup.*

sake *n.* end, purpose, cause, account, as *for the sake of peace, for my sake, for goodness' sake*

sal *n.* (chemistry) salt.—**sal ammoniac** ammonium chloride.—**sal volat'ile** (vol-at'i-li) *n.* smelling salts

sal'ad *n.* vegetables or fruit served cold with a dressing

salaman'der *n.* 1. an animal resembling the lizard and supposed to live in fire. 2. a kind of lizard

sal'ary *n.* fixed payment for services, wages. —**sal'aries** *pl.*

sale *n.* 1. act of selling, exchanging goods for money. 2. selling at specially low prices.—**sales'man** *n.* person who sells, traveller.—**sales'woman** *fem.*—**sales'manship** *n.* the art of selling

sa'leable *adj.* fit to be sold, easy to sell

sa'lient *adj.* prominent, easily seen, striking. —*n.* a bulge in a line of defence

sa'line *adj.* salty, containing salt

sali'va *n.* the liquid which forms in the mouth

sal'low *adj.* of a sickly yellow colour or complexion

sal'ly *n.* 1. a rushing out, esp. from a fort. 2. a witty remark.—**sal'lies** *pl.*—*v.* to rush, to set (*out* or *forth*).—**sal'lying** *pres. part.*—**sal'lied** *p.t.* and *p. part.*

sal'mon (sam'on) *n.* large fish with pink flesh

saloon' *n.* 1. a large reception-room. 2. a public dining-room. 3. a large cabin in a ship. 4. in U.S. a drinking-bar

salt *n.* 1. a white substance found in sea-water and in the earth and used for seasoning food. 2. a chemical compound of an acid and a metal. 3. in common talk, a sailor.—*v.* to season or preserve with salt.—*adj.* tasting of salt, full of salt.—**salt'y** *adj.*

salt pan *n.* a land depression where a layer of salt collects due to evaporation.—**the salt of the earth** worthy people.—**to take with a pinch of salt** to accept (a story) with some disbelief.—**not worth his salt** useless

saltpe'tre (sawlt-pee'ter) *n.* potassium nitrate used in making gunpowder

salu'brious (sal-ōō'bri-us) *adj.* healthy

sal'utary *adj.* wholesome, resulting in good, as *The warning had a salutary effect*

saluta'tion *n.* a greeting

salute' (sal-ōōt') *v.* 1. to greet with words or a bow, or a kiss. 2. to raise the hand to the head in military salute.—**salu'ting** *pres. part.*—*n.* 1. a greeting. 2. saluting in military style

sal'vage (sal'vij) *n.* 1. the saving of a ship or other property from loss at sea or by fire. 2. payment made for salvaging. 3. property saved.—*v.* to save property

salva'tion (-ā'shun) *n.* 1. act of saving, being saved. 2. act of saving the soul from sin.—**Salvation Army** the Chritisian missionary and welfare organisation founded by "General" Bramwell Booth

salve (sahv, salv) *n.* a healing ointment.—*v.* to soothe, to heal

sal'ver *n.* a small tray

sal'vo *n.* 1. a discharge of guns as a salute. 2. a round of cheers or applause.—**sal'voes** *pl.*

sam'ba *n.* a South American ballroom dance

same *adj.* identical, not different. *pron.* as *I told him the same. He did the same as I did.*—**all the same** not withstanding, nevertheless.—**same'ness** *n.* being the same, monotony

Samoyed' (sam-o-yed') *n.* 1. a member of a north European Mongolian race. 2. a kind of dog

sam'ple *n.* 1. a specimen, example. 2. a part to show what the rest is like.—*v.* 1. to select. 2. to test, to try.—**sam'pling** *pres. part.*

sam'pler *n.* piece of embroidery to show variety of stitches

sanator'ium *n.* 1. a place for the treatment of invalids. 2. a health resort.—**sanator'ia** *pl.*

sanctifica'tion *n.* making holy, consecration

sanc'tify (sangk'ti-fī) *v.* 1. to make holy, to consecrate. 2. to free from sin.—**sanc'tifying** *pres. part.*—**sanc'tified** *p.t.* and *p. part.*

sanctimo'nious *adj.* making a show of being holy.—**sanc'timony** *n.*

sanc'tion (sangk'shun) *n.* 1. permission, authority, as *The headmaster gave his sanction to the scheme.* 2. enforcement of authority. 3. reward (or punishment).—*v.* to allow, give permission

sanc'tity (sangk'ti-ti) *n.* 1. holiness, purity. 2. sacredness

sanc'tuary *n.* 1. a holy place. 2. a place of safety for a fugitive. 3. refuge, protection. —**sanc'tuaries** *pl.*

sanc'tum (sangk'tum) *n.* 1. a sacred place, shrine. 2. a private room

sand *n.* tiny grains made by the wearing down of rock.—*pl.* the sea-shore formed of stretches of sand.—*v.* to cover or mix with sand.—**sand'y** *adj.*

sand'al *n.* an open shoe without a heel

sand'bank *n.* a ridge of sand under the sea

sand'-dune *n.* a ridge of sand beside the sea

sand'paper *n.* paper with sand stuck on it, for scraping or polishing

sand'stone *n.* rock formed mostly of sand

sand'wich *n.* two slices of bread with meat or some other filling between.—*v.* to insert between two things, as *We had two Geography lessons with a short break sandwiched between them.*—**sand'wichman** a man carrying notice boards back and front

sane *adj.* 1. healthy in mind, sound. 2. sensible, as *a sane outlook on life*

Compare: normal, rational, lucid. *Contrast:* insane, mad, deranged, crazy, abnormal

sang'-froid' (sohng'frwa') (French) *n.* coolness in the face of difficulty or danger

san'guinary (sang'gwin-a-ri) *adj.* bloodthirsty, with much bloodshed

san'guine (sang'gwin) *adj.* 1. hopeful, confident. 2. ruddy, healthy in colour

san'itary *adj.* 1. of health. 2. helping the protection of health against dirt.—**sanita'tion** (-tā'shun) *n.* carrying out sanitary measures

san'ity *n.* 1. soundness of mind, being sane. 2. good sense

sap *n.* the life-giving juice of plants
sap *n.* a covered trench leading to enemy trenches.—*v.* 1. to dig under the foundations. 2. to determine, wear away, as *His strength was sapped by illness.*—**sap'ping** *pres. part.*—**sapped** *p.t.* and *p. part.*
sap'ling *n.* a young tree
sap'phire (saf'īr) *n.* a bright-blue precious stone.—*adj.* bright blue
sar'casm *n.* 1. a bitter remark made to hurt someone's feelings. 2. ironical wit.—**sarcas'tic** *adj.* sneering, biting, ironical
sarcoph'agus (sar-kof'a-gus) *n.* an ornamental stone coffin
sardine' (sar-deen') *n.* a kind of small herring (preserved in oil for food)
sardon'ic *adj.* bitterly humorous, mocking, scornful.—**sardon'ically** *adv.*
Compare: sarcastic, sneering, ironical, satirical
sarong' *n.* a knee-length cloth wrapped round the waist, worn in the East Indies
sartor'ial *adj.* of tailors or tailoring
sash *n.* a scarf worn round the waist or across one shoulder.—**sash'es** *pl.*
sash *n.* a window-frame.—**sash'es** *pl.*
Sa'tan *n.* the devil
satan'ic *adj.* devilish, wicked
sat'chel *n.* 1. a leather bag. 2. a bag for school-books
sate *v.* 1. to satisfy the appetite. 2. to glut, to have too much
sateen' *n.* a cotton or woollen imitation of satin
sat'ellite *n.* 1. a small planet revolving round a larger, a moon. 2. a projectile fired high enough into space to orbit round the earth.—*adj.* smaller in importance, as *a satellite firm*
sa'tiate (sā'shi-āt) *v.* to satisfy completely, to surfeit
sati'ety (sat-ī'et-i) *n.* overfed feeling, disgust
sat'in *n.* silk cloth with one shiny side.—*adj.*
sat'ire (sat'īr) *n.* 1. ridicule, sarcasm, irony, used to attack folly or wickedness. 2. writing, or a play, attacking in this way, e.g. *Gulliver's Travels is a satire on human nature.*—**sati'rical** *adj.* containing satire.—**sat'irist** *n.* writer of satire.—**sat'irise** *v.* to attack with satire
satisfac'tion (-shun) *n.* 1. being satisfied, contented. 2. something that satisfies
satisfac'tory *adj.* pleasing, giving satisfaction, sufficiently good.—**satisfac'torily** *adv.*
sat'isfy *v.* 1. to content, to meet the wishes of. 2. to convince.—he **sat'isfies.**—**sat'isfying** *pres. part.*—**sat'isfied** *p.t.* and *p. part.*
Compare: (with satisfied) contented, filled, surfeited, satiated, glutted, replete
sat'urate *v.* 1. to fill with moisture, to soak. 2. (chemistry) to dissolve as much as possible.—**sat'urating** *pres. part.*—**sat'ura'tion** (-rā'shun) *n.*
Sat'urday *n.* the seventh day of the week
Sat'urn *n.* a planet surrounded by rings
sat'urnine *adj.* gloomy-looking, frowning
sat'yr (sat'er) *n.* a woodland god, half-man, half-beast
sauce *n.* 1. a liquid, served with food to improve the taste. 2. (slang) impudence.—**sauce'pan** *n.* a cooking utensil with lid and handle
sau'cer (saw'ser) *n.* a curved shallow plate to put under a cup
sau'cy (saw'si) *adj.* cheeky, impudent
saun'ter *v.* to stroll, to walk slowly along.—*n.* (See **walk**)
saus'age (sos'ij) *n.* minced meat in a skin
sav'age (sav'ij) *adj.* 1. uncivilised. 2. fierce, cruel.—*n.* a member of a savage tribe, a barbarian.—*v.* to attack by trampling and biting.—**sav'agely** *adv.*—**sav'agery** *n.* 1. savage state. 2. cruelty
Compare: ferocious, barbarous, wild, furious, brutal, untamed. *Contrast:* civilised, tame, gentle, domesticated
savan'na, savan'nah *n.* treeless grasslands
sav'ant (sav'ant, sav'ong) *n.* a learned man
save *v.* 1. to make safe, to rescue from harm, danger, etc. as *He saved my life. He saved me from drowning.* 2. to keep for the future, store up, as *to save money.* 3. to prevent, as *That will save a lot of trouble.*—**sa'ving** *pres. part.*—*n.* as *The goalkeeper made a fine save.*—*prep.* except, as *All the players save one have arrived.*—*conj.* but, as *The car was undamaged save that some paint was chipped off.*—**to save one's face** keep up appearances.—**sa'ver** *n.*
Compare: 1. deliver, preserve. 2. hoard, store, collect. 3. obviate, avoid, avert
sa'ving *adj.* 1. economical, avoiding waste. 2. redeeming, as *A sense of humour is a saving grace.*—*n.* something saved.—*pl.* money saved.—*prep.* except
sa'viour (sāv'yer) *n.* one who saves.—**Sa'viour** Jesus Christ
sa'vour *n.* taste, flavour.—*v.* 1. to taste or smell. 2. (of) to suggest, as *Your attitude savours of unwillingness.*—**sa'voury** *adj.* pleasant to taste or smell
saw *n.* an old saying, maxim
saw *n.* a tool with sharp teeth for cutting wood, metal, etc.—to cut with a saw.—**saw'ing** *pres. part.*—**sawed** *p.t.*—**sawed, sawn** *p. part.*—**saw'dust** *n.* fine wood-fragments made in sawing.—**saw'mill** *n.* a place where wood is sawn by machinery.—**saw'yer** *n.* a man who saws
Sax'on *n.* 1. a native of Saxony in Germany. 2. one of the invaders of England in the years 400 to 600 A.D.
sax'ophone *n.* a musical wind instrument
say (sā) *v.* 1. to state. 2. to tell, express. 3. to repeat. 4. to suppose, as *Say that it costs £100. The cost will be, say, £100.*—he **says** (sez) he **saith** (seth) (old form).—**say'ing** *pres. part.*—**said** (sed) *p.t.* and *p. part.*—*n.* what is said, as *Let him have his say.*—**say, I say** (*interj.*) listen

Compare: utter, announce, speak, recite

scab *n.* 1. a crust formed over a wound. 2. a skin-disease in animals

scab'bard *n.* a case for the blade of a sword, sheath

scaf'fold *n.* 1. a temporary platform for workmen. 2. a platform used during the execution of criminals.—**scaf'folding** *n.* a framework of poles and platforms for workmen

scald (skawld) *v.* 1. to burn with boiling liquid or steam. 2. to rinse with boiling water.—*n.* injury by scalding

scale (skāl) *n.* 1. a balance for weighing. 2. one pan of a balance.—*v.* to weigh.—**to turn the scale** to be a deciding factor.—**to turn the scale at** to weigh (a certain amount)

scale *n.* 1. one of the thin, hard plates forming the outer covering of fishes and reptiles. 2. a thin layer.—*v.* to remove the scales from

scale *n.* 1. a series of musical notes arranged in order of pitch. 2. marks on a measuring instrument. 3. instrument for measuring. 4. size of, e.g. a map compared with actual distances, as 1 *inch* to 1 *mile*. 5. size, as *business on a large scale*.—*v.* 1. to climb. 2. to measure.—**sca'ling** *pres. part.*—**scale up** to make bigger.—**scale down** to make smaller.—**on a large scale** grandly.—**on a small scale** in miniature

scale, scale a ride *v.* (Aus.) to ride on a train, bus or other vehicle without paying.—**scaler**

sca'lene (skā'leen) *adj.* of a triangle, having the three sides unequal

scal'lop, scol'lop *n.* 1. a shell-fish. 2. edging in small curves.—*v.* to shape in small curves

scalp *n.* the skin and hair of the top of the head.—*v.* to cut off the scalp

scamp *n.* rascal, lazy fellow.—*v.* to do a job carelessly

scam'per *v.* to run quickly.—*n.*

scamp'i *n.* (Italian) fried prawns

scan' *v.* 1. to examine, to look closely. 2. (of poetry) to examine the metre.—**scan'ning** *pres. part.*—**scanned** *p.t.* and *p. part.*

scan'dal *n.* 1. disgrace, action offending public opinion. 2. evil gossip.—**scan'dalise** *v.* to shock, offend.—**scan'dalmonger** *n.* a person who spreads gossip.—**scan'dalous** *adj.* disgraceful

Scandina'via *n.* Norway and Sweden considered together.—*n.* **Scandina'vian** a native of Scandinavia

scant *adj.* scarcely enough.—*v.* to stint, to limit

scan'tily *adv.* in a scanty manner.—**scan'tiness** *n.* lack, being scanty

scan'ty *adj.* not enough, insufficient, of small amount.—**scan'tier** *comp.*—**scan'tiest** *sup.*

scape'goat *n.* a person bearing the blame for others

scape'grace (skāp'grās) *n.* a worthless person, scamp

scar *n.* a mark left by a wound that has healed.—*v.* to mark with a scar.—**scar'ring** *pres. part.*—**scarred** *p.t.* and *p. part.*

scarce (skārs) *adj.* hard to find, not plentiful. (See **rare**.) **scarce'ly** *adv.* hardly.—**scar'city** (skār'si-ti) *n.* lack

scare *v.* to frighten, to startle.—*n.* fright, panic.—**scare'crow** (skār'krō) *n.* something to frighten birds away from crops

scarf *n.* 1. a long strip of material worn about the neck and shoulders. 2. a loose necktie.—**scarfs, scarves** *pl.*

scar'let *n.* 1. a brilliant red. 2. cloth of this colour.—**scar'let fe'ver** *n.* an infectious fever with a scarlet rash.—**scar'let runner** *n.* a bean with scarlet flowers

scarp *n.* a steep hill

sca'thing *adj.* severe, biting, as *The master made some scathing remarks about the boy's writing*

scat'ter *v.* 1. to throw, to sprinkle. 2. to disperse, drive off

scav'enger (skav'en-jer) *n.* a street cleaner, a person employed to remove refuse

scene (seen) *n.* 1. the place of any happening, as *the scene of the accident*. 2. place of action of a play or story, as *The scene of the chapter was West Africa*. 3. division of a play, as *Scene III*. 4. a view, as *a delightful scene*. 5. a display of temper, as *There was a terrible scene when his father found out*. 6. an incident, as *scenes from real life*. 7. stage scenery.—**behind the scenes** working unseen by the public.—**on the scene** present

sce'nery (see'ner-i) *n.* 1. painted hangings, etc. on a stage. 2. landscape, view.—**sce'nic** (see'nik) *adj.* belonging to natural or stage scenery

scent (sent) *n.* 1. smell, perfume. 2. sense of smell.—*v.* 1. to detect, to track by smell. 2. to make fragrant

scep'tic (skep'tic) *n.* a person who does not accept as true religious doctrines or generally accepted views.—**scep'tical** *adj.* doubting.—**scep'ticism** (skep'ti-sizm) *n.*

scep'tre (sep'ter) *n.* the staff borne by kings as a symbol of sovereignty

sched'ule (shed'ūl) *n.* a list of details or items.—*v.* to make a schedule.—**behind schedule** not keeping up to the time planned

scheme (skeem) *n.* 1. a plan, 2. an outline, syllabus. 3. a plan of action.—*v.* to plot, plan a trick.—**sche'ming** *adj.* crafty

Compare: project, design, system, arrangement, device

scher'zo (skārts'ō) *n.* a lively piece of music

schism (sizm) *n.* a division, difference of opinion in a church.—**schismat'ic** *adj.* causing discord

schnor'kel (shn-) *n.* a tube through which an underwater submarine or swimmer can take in air. See **snorkel.**

schol'ar (skol'ar) *n.* 1. pupil at school. 2. a learned person. 3. a person holding a scholarship.—**schol'arly** *adj.* learned

schol'arship *n.* 1. learning. 2. help given to a student as a result of competitive examination

scholas'tic (skol-as'tik) *adj.* of schools, or education, or scholars

school (skōōl) *n.* 1. a place for teaching the young. 2. a group of thinkers, artists, etc. with the same methods or opinions, as *The Post Impressionist School.* 3. a department of a University, faculty, as *The School of Medicine.* 4. shoal (of whales, porpoises, etc.) 5. clique, esp. of gamblers. —*adj.* belonging to school, as **school'-master, school'mistress.**—*v.* to train, accustom, as *The dog was schooled to obedience*

schoon'er (skōō'ner) *n.* 1. a ship with fore and aft sails. 2. a measure of beer

sci'ence (sī'ens) *n.* 1. knowledge of facts arranged in a system. 2. a branch of systematic knowledge, e.g. a natural science, a social science.—**science fiction** stories about fantastic adventures in the future, on other planets, with new inventions

scientif'ic (sī-en-tif'ik) *adj.* using the laws of science.—**scientif'ically** *adv.*

sci'entist (sī'en-tist) *n.* a person who knows much about science

scim'itar (sim'i-tar) *n.* a short, curved, Oriental sword

scin'tillate (sin'til-āt) *v.* to flash, sparkle.—**scintilla'tion** (-lā'shun) *n.*

sci'on (sī'on) *n.* 1. a shoot, twig for grafting. 2. a descendant, heir

scis'sors (siz'erz) *n.pl.* a cutting instrument of two blades fastened so that the edges work toward each other

scoff (at) *v.* to jeer, mock.—**scof'fer** *n.* scorner, mocker

scold (skōld) *v.* to find fault with, to blame angrily.—*n.* a scolding woman, nag

sconce (skons) *n.* a wall bracket for a candle, etc.

scone (skon) *n.* a small cake baked on a griddle or in an oven

scoop *n.* 1. a kind of ladle or shovel. 2. a tool for hollowing out.—*v.* 1. to ladle out. 2. to hollow out, to rake in

scoot'er *n.* a lightweight motor-cycle

scope (skōp) *n.* 1. range of the mind, amount that the mind can understand. 2. opportunity, as *His new job will give him plenty of scope*

scorch *v.* 1. to burn the surface of. 2. to dry up, wither.—he **scor'ches**

score *n.* 1. a set of twenty. 2. a cut, mark, line. 3. a record of points in a game. 4. a written, or printed piece of orchestral music. 5. reason, as *You need have no doubts on that score.* 6. debt, account.—*v.* 1. to mark. 2. to win points in a game. 3. to keep a record of points.—**sco'ring** *pres. part.*

scorn *n.* contempt, feeling that something is mean.—*v.* to despise.—**scorn'ful** *adj.* contemptuous.—**scornfully** *adv.*

scor'pion *n.* a small animal with a sting in its tail

scotch *v.* 1. to disable, as *We have scotch'd the snake, not killed it.* 2. to put an end to, as *The scheme was scotched*

scot free' *adj.* unharmed, unpunished

Scot'land *n.* a country in the north of Britain. —**Scot, Scotsman'** *n.* a native of Scotland. —**Scot'tish, Scots, Scotch** *adjs.*

scoun'drel *n.* a villain, wicked person

scour (skowr) *v.* to clean or polish by rubbing

scour (skowr) *v.* to move quickly in search of something, to range, as *The police scoured the country for the escaped prisoners*

scourge (skurj) *n.* 1. a whip, lash. 2. a punishment. 3. plague, pestilence.—*v.* to flog.—**scour'ging** *pres. part.*

scout *n.* 1. a man sent out to observe the enemy. 2. a member of the Scout organisation.—*v.* to reconnoitre, act as scout

scout *v.* to dismiss an idea as absurd, to reject

scowl *v.* to frown angrily.—*n.* a sullen look, frown

scrag *n.* 1. a bony person or animal. 2. the lean end of a neck of mutton.—**scrag'gy** *adj.* skinny, thin

scram'ble *v.* 1. to move by climbing or crawling. 2. to fight for something. 3. to cook eggs by stirring them in the pan.—**scramb'ling** *pres. part.*—*n.* 1. a rough walk. 2. a struggle

scrap *n.* 1. a little bit, piece. 2. something thrown away.—*adj.* as *scrap iron.*—*v.* to break up, throw away.—**scrap'ping** *pres. part.*—**scrapped** *p.t.* and *p. part.*—**scrap'-book** *n.* a book in which pictures, cuttings, etc. are kept

scrape *v.* 1. to rub with something sharp. 2. to clean by scraping. 3. to make a harsh noise.—**scra'ping** *pres. part.*—*n.* 1. a scraping. 2. an awkward position, trouble, as *He got himself into a scrape.*—**scra'per** *n.* tool for scraping

scrap'py *adj.* unfinished, not well put together

scratch *v.* 1. to mark with something pointed. 2. to make a thin surface wound. 3. to rub to relieve itching. 4. to strike off a list, withdraw.—*n.* 1. a wound or mark. 2. a sound made by scratching. 3. a starting-point in a race.—*adj.* 1. starting from scratch. 2. got together hurriedly, as *a scratch team.*—scratch'es *pl.*—**to come up to scratch** to be of a good standard.—**to start from scratch** to start from the beginning with no advantage

scrawl *v.* to write or draw untidily, to scribble. —*n.* careless, hasty writing

scream *v.* 1. to make a loud, piercing cry. 2. to speak too loudly.—*n.* a shrill cry
Compare: squeal, yell, shriek, shout, screech

screech *v.* to scream piercingly.—*n.* a shrill scream

screed *n.* a long, tiresome piece of writing

screen *n.* 1. a covered frame to protect from heat, light or observation. 2. anything like this. 3. a sheet on which films are shown. 4. a wooden or stone partition in a church. 5. a kind of sieve (for coal, etc.)—*v.* 1. to shelter, to hide. 2. to show a film

screw (skrōō) *n.* 1. a nail with a spiral groove twisting round it. 2. a ship's propeller. 3. a twist. 4. a miser. 5. a wretched horse.—*v.* 1. to fasten with a screw. 2. to oppress, to extort from.—**screw'driver** *n.* tool for turning screws

scrib'ble *v.* 1. to write or draw carelessly. 2. to make meaningless marks.—*n.* something scribbled.—**scrib'bler** *n.*

scribe *n.* 1. a person paid to write. 2. a Jewish doctor of the law

scrim'mage (skrim'ij) *n.* a confused struggle

script *n.* 1. handwriting, written letters or signs. 2. a style of printing that imitates handwriting. 3. text of a play, film, etc.

scrip'tural *adj.* according to the Bible

scrip'ture *n.* 1. the Bible. 2. a sacred book

scroll (skrōl) *n.* 1. a roll of parchment or paper. 2. an ornament shaped like a roll

scrounge *v.* (slang) to cadge, to steal small articles

scrub *v.* 1. to clean by rubbing hard, esp. with a brush and water. 2. to reject, erase.—*n.*—**scrub'bing** *pres. part.*—**scrubbed** *p.t.* and *p. part.*

scrub *n.* 1. a stunted tree, brushwood. 2. country overgrown with thick bushes. 3. an undersized person.—**scrub'by** *adj.* stunted

scruff *n.* the back of the neck

scrum *n.* (Rugby football) a struggle between the forwards of two teams for the ball passed between them.—**scrum-half** *n.* the half-back who passes the ball into the scrum.—**scrum'mage** *n.* a scrum

scru'ple (skrōō'pl) *n.* a feeling of doubt and uneasiness about doing something.—*v.* to hesitate, doubt.—**scru'pulous** *adj.* careful to do the right thing, conscientious
Compare: misgiving, qualm, uncertainty

scru'tinise (skrōō'tin-īz) *v.* to examine closely.—**scru'tinising** *pres. part.*

scru'tiny (skrōō'tin-i) *n.* 1. close inspection. 2. an official examination of votes

scud *v.* to move swiftly, to skim along.—**scud'ding** *pres. part.*—**scud'ded** *p.t.* and *p. part.*—*n.* flying clouds of spray

scuf'fle *v.* to struggle roughly, to push about.—*n.*—**scuf'fling** *pres. part.*

scull *n.* 1. a short oar. 2. an oar at the stern for propelling a boat.—*v.* to use a scull

scul'lery *n.* a place where dishes are washed, etc.—**scul'leries** *pl.*

scul'lion *n.* a kitchen under-servant

sculp'tor *n.* a person who carves in stone or metal.—**sculp'tress** *fem.*

sculp'ture *n.* 1. the art of carving or modelling. 2. a piece of sculpture, a statue.—**sculpt, sculp'ture** *v.* to carve, to model

scum *n.* 1. froth, etc. on the surface of a liquid. 2. the worst part, worthless people

scup'per *n.* a hole in the side of a ship for running water off the deck

scurf *n.* dry flakes on the skin, dandruff.—**scurf'y** *adj.*

scurril'ity *n.* offensive, coarse, abusive (language, writing, etc.)—**scur'rilous** *adj.*

scur'ry *v.* to hurry, to scamper.—*n.*—he **scur'ries.**—**scur'rying** *pres. part.*—**scur'ried** *p.t.* and *p. part.*

scur'vy *adj.* mean, low.—*n.* a disease caused by lack of fresh food

scut'cheon (skuch'on) *n.* a shield with a coat of arms

scut'tle *n.* a coal-bucket

scut'tle *n.* a hole with a lid, in the side or deck of a ship.—*v.* to make a hole in a ship in order to sink it.—**scut'tling** *pres. part.*

scut'tle *v.* to run away, scamper, scurry.—**scut'tling** *pres. part.*

scythe (sɪᴛʜ) *n.* a long curved blade swung by a handle held in both hands, for mowing grass, etc.—*v.*

sea *n.* 1. the mass of salt water covering most of the earth. 2. a part of this. 3. a broad stretch, as *a sea of corn.* 4. large waves, the swell, as *a heavy sea.*—**sea'-board** *n.* the coast.—**sea'-dog** *n.* an old sailor.—**sea'-faring** (-fār-ing) *adj.* working on the sea.—**sea'girt** *adj.* surrounded by the sea.—**sea'-gull** *n.* a large sea-bird.—**sea'horse** *n.* a small fish with head shaped like a horse's.—**sea'ward** *adj.* and *adv.* towards the sea.—**all at sea** bewildered.—**to put to sea** to start a voyage

seal *n.* a sea-animal with flippers, hunted for its fur.—**seal'skin**

seal *n.* 1. a metal or stone stamp engraved with design for making an impression on wax. 2. an impression made in this way.—*v.* 1. to fix a seal on. 2. to confirm, to decide. 3. to close tightly.—**seal'ing-wax** *n.* wax which, when heated, becomes soft and takes impression

seal'yham *n.* a breed of small dog

seam *n.* 1. a line formed by sewing together two pieces of cloth, etc. 2. a line where edges join. 3. a thin layer, e.g. of coal.—*v.* 1. to join by sewing. 2. to mark, as *His brow was seamed with care*

sea'man *n.* a sailor.—**sea'men** *pl.*—**sea'manship** *n.* skill in navigating

seam'stress, semp'stress (sem'stres) *n.* a woman who earns her living by sewing

seam'y *adj.* unpleasant, sordid, as *The seamy side of life*

sear *v.* 1. to wither, dry up. 2. to scorch, burn

search (serch) *v.* 1. to look for, to look through in order to find. 2. to examine.—he **search'es.**—*n.* searching, seeking.—**search'ing** *adj.* piercing, sharp.—**search'-light** *n.* an electric arc-light which throws a powerful beam in any direction.—**search'-warrant** *n.* a magistrate's permit for police to enter private premises

Compare: seek, explore, investigate, hunt, scrutinise

seas'on (seez'n) *n.* 1. one of the four divisions of the year, spring, summer, autumn, winter. 2. a period during which something happens every year.—*v.* 1. to flavour with salt, etc. 2. to make sound or fit.—**sea'sonable** *adj.* suitable for the season, timely.—**sea'sonal** *adj.* depending on seasons.—**sea'soning** *n.* flavouring.—**sea'son-ticket** *n.* 1. a ticket enabling the holder to make unlimited journeys on a bus or train route for a certain time. 2. a ticket of entry to a series of shows (at a cheaper rate)

seat *n.* 1. something to sit on. 2. a right to sit, as a *seat in Parliament.* 3. a manner of sitting, as *He has a good seat on a horse.* 4. the part of the body on which one sits. 5. a country house, residence. 6. the part of a garment on which one sits.—*v.* 1. to place on a seat. 2. to have enough seats for, as *The hall seats* 500. 3. to become stretched (of garments) through sitting

sea'worthy *adj.* in a fit condition to put to sea

se'cant (see'kant) *n.* (geometry) a straight line cutting a circle or curve

secede' (se-seed') *v.* to withdraw, esp. from a church.—**seces'sion** (se-sesh'n) *n.*

seclude' (si-klōōd') *v.* to shut off, keep apart.—**seclu'sion** (si-klōō'zhun) *n.* retirement, solitude

sec'ond (sek'und) *adj.* 1. next after the first. 2. another.—*n.* 1. person or thing coming second. 2. person supporting or helping. 3. the sixtieth part of a minute.—*v.* to support.—**sec'ondly** *adv.*—**second-hand'** *adj.* 1. bought after use by a former owner. 2. not original.—**second na'ture** *n.* an instinctive habit.—**second-rate'** *adj.* of inferior quality.—**second-sight'** *n.* an ability to foresee coming events by supernatural means

sec'ondary (sek'un-dar-i) *adj.* 1. following the first. 2. coming after the primary stage of education. 3. of less importance.—**sec'ondary school** *n.* a school for children over 11 years of age

se'crecy (see'kre-si) *n.* 1. being secret. 2. ability to keep secrets

se'cret (see'kret) *adj.* hidden, kept from general knowledge.—*n.* something kept secret, a mystery.—**secret ser'vice** *n.* a country's organisation of spies

secretar'ial (-tār'-al) *adj.* of a secretary

sec'retary *n.* 1. a person employed to write letters, keep records, etc. 2. a person in charge of a government department.—**sec'retaries** *pl.*

secrete' (se-kreet') *v.* 1. to hide, conceal. 2. collect, to produce, as *The liver secretes bile.*—**secre'ting** *pres. part.*—**secre'tion** (-shun) *n.*

se'cretive (see'kre-tiv) *adj.* making a habit of keeping things secret, not frank

sect *n.* a group of people holding certain opinions or religious beliefs, denomination.—**sectar'ian** (-tār'i-an) *adj.* 1. belonging to a sect, denominational. 2. narrow-minded

sec'tion (-shun) *n.* 1. separation by cutting. 2. a piece cut off, division, slice. 3. a part of a book.—**sec'tional** *adj.*

sec'tor *n.* 1. the part of a circle enclosed by two radii and the arc which they cut off. 2. part of a front occupied by an enemy

sec'ular *adj.* 1. not religious, worldly. 2. living in the world, not in a monastery

secure' *adj.* 1. safe, free from care. 2. firmly fixed, safe from attack, escape, etc. (See safe).—*v.* 1. to make safe, as *The general secured his communications.* 2. to fix, make firm, as *He secured it with a nail.* 3. to obtain, get, as *I secured his help.*—**secu'ring** *pres. part.*—**secure'ly** *adv.*

secu'rity *n.* 1. condition of being secure, safe. 2. protection. 3. something given as a bond or pledge

sedan' *n.* a covered chair on poles for carrying a passenger

sedate' *adj.* calm, serious.—**sedate'ly** *adv.*

Compare: dignified, stately, staid, serene, unhurried, unruffled, sober, grave. *Contrast:* agitated, frolicsome, lively, excited, flurried, flighty

sed'ative *adj.* soothing.—*n.* soothing medicine

sed'entary *adj.* 1. sitting much, as *A clerk in an office leads a sedentary life.* 2. done while sitting

sedge (sej) *n.* a grass-like plant growing in swampy places

sed'iment *n.* matter which settles to the bottom of liquid.—**sediment'ary** *adj.*

sedit'ion (sed-ish'un) *n.* talk or action exciting discontent or rebellion.—**sedit'ious** (sed-ish'us) *adj.*

seduce' (se-dūs') *v.* to persuade someone to do wrong, to lead astray.—**sedu'cing** *pres. part.*—**seduc'tion** (-shun) *n.*—**seduc'tive** *adj.* attractive, charming

see *v.* 1. to look at and be aware of. 2. to find out, as *I will see what can be done.* 3. to understand, as *I see what you mean.* 4. to make sure, as *I will see that it is done.*—**see'ing** *pres. part.*—**saw** *p.t.*—**seen** *p. part.*—**let me see** give me time to consider.—**to see something through** to continue until it is finished.—**to see through something**

not to be deceived by outward appearances. **—to see red** to be extremely angry.**—to see someone off** to say goodbye at the station, quayside, etc.

Compare: perceive, observe, notice, behold, ascertain, comprehend, ensure.

see *n.* 1. a bishop's diocese. 2. a bishop's authority or office

seed *n.* 1. the part of a plant from which a new plant grows. 2. a single grain of this. 3. children, descendants. 4. one of the best players in a tennis tournament.—*v.* 1. to sow seeds. 2. to remove seeds. 3. to arrange the draw in a tennis tournament so that the best players do not meet in the early rounds.**—seed'ling** *n.* a plant grown from a seed.**—seeds'man** *n.* a dealer in seeds.**—seed'y** *adj.* 1. gone to seed. 2. shabby. 3. ill. **—to run to seed** 1. to produce seeds and no more flowers. 2. to become stale and worn

see'ing *conj.* since

seek *v.* 1. to look for, to try to find or get. (See **search.**) 2. to try.**—seek'ing** *pres. part.***—sought** (sawt) *p.t.* and *p. part.*

seem *v.* to appear to be.**—seem'ingly** *adv.* apparently

seem'liness *n.* fitness, suitable behaviour.**—seem'ly** *adj.* proper

seep *v.* to trickle, ooze

seer *n.* a prophet, a person who has visions

seer'sucker *n.* a thin ridged cotton or linen fabric

see'saw *n.* 1. up and down movement. 2. a plank resting on support and moving up and down.—*v.* to move up and down

seethe *v.* 1. to bubble, boil. 2. to be agitated, as *Seething with discontent.***—see'thing** *pres. part.***—seethed** *p.t.***—seethed, sod'den** (old form) *p. part.*

seg'ment *n.* 1. piece cut off, division, section. 2. (geometry) the part of a circle cut off by a chord

seg'regate *v.* to set apart, to separate from others.**—seg'regating** *pres. part.***—segrega'tion** (gā'shun) *n.*

seis'mograph (sīz'mo-graf) *n.* an instrument for recording earthquakes

seize (seez) *v.* 1. to grasp, lay hold of. 2. to take possession. 3. to understand quickly. **—seiz'ing** *pres. part.***—seiz'ure** (see'zher) *n.* 1. seizing. 2. a sudden attack of illness.**—to seize up** (of a machine) to jam, to be stuck

Compare: clasp, snatch, grab, grip

sel'dom *adv.* rarely, not often

select' *v.* to pick out, choose.—*adj.* choice, picked.**—selec'tion** (-shun) *n.* 1. choice. 2. (Aus.) a piece of Crown land taken up under system of free selection.**—selector** *n.* one who takes up a selection of Crown land.**—selec'tive** *adj.* having power to select

sele'nium (se-lee'ni-um) *n.* a non-metallic element whose electrical conductivity changes with exposure to light

self *n.* 1. a person's or thing's own individuality, as *Love of self is not a quality to cultivate.* 2. used reflexively or emphatically, esp. in compounds such as *myself,* etc.**—selves** *pl.***—self-asser'tion** *n.* putting forward one's own opinions, wishes, etc.**—self-con'scious** *adj.* unable to forget oneself.**—self-contained** *adj.* 1. reserved. 2. complete in itself.**—self-evident** obvious.**—self-indulgent** pampering oneself.**—self-made** *adj.* successful by one's own effort.**—self-possessed'** *adj.* cool, master of oneself. **—self'same** *adj.* identical.**—self-ser'vice** *adj.* (of stores, restaurants) with goods set out for customers to pick up for themselves, paying at a cash desk.**—self-suffi'cient** *adj.* independent

sel'fish *adj.* thinking of oneself first, inconsiderate of others.**—sel'fishly** *adv.***—sel'fishness** *n.* self-interest

sell *v.* 1. to hand over for money or other payment. 2. to have for sale. 3. to betray.**—sold** (sōld) *p.t.* and *p. part.***—sel'ler** *n.*

sel'vage, sel'vedge (sel'vej) *n.* an edge of cloth finished to prevent fraying out

sem'aphore (sem'a-fōr) *n.* 1. a post with movable arm for signalling. 2. a system of signalling.—*v.*

sem'blance (sem'blans) *n.* appearance, likeness

sem'icircle (sem'i-sir-kl) *n.* a half-circle.**—semicir'cular** *adj.*

semico'lon *n.* a punctuation mark (;) denoting a longer pause than a comma, but shorter than a colon

semi-detached *n.* one of two houses built together in one structure

sem'inary *n.* a college, training-school for priesthood

Sem'ite *n.* one of a race of peoples including Jews and Arabs.—*adj.* **Se-mit'ic**

sen'ate *n.* 1. the upper council of state in ancient Rome. 2. a governing body, usually the upper house (as in the Congress of the U.S.A.).**—sen'ator** *n.* a member of a senate.**—senator'ial** *adj.*

send *v.* 1. to cause to go somewhere. 2. to cause a messenger to go.**—sent** *p.t.* and *p. part.***—send'-off** *n.* friendly greetings on departure.**—send down** to expel from university.**—send on** to readdress and repost.**—send word** to send a written or spoken message

se'nile (see'nīl) *adj.* showing the weakness of old age.**—senil'ity** *n.*

se'nior (see'nior) *adj.* 1. older, as *senior pupils.* 2. of higher rank or standing, as *the senior master.*—*n.* an older person, person of higher standing.**—senior'ity** *n.*

sensa'tion (-sā'shun) *n.* 1. feeling. 2. action of the senses. 3. a state of excitement.**—sensa'tional** *adj.* exciting

sense *n.* 1. one of the five senses, sight, hearing, smell, taste, touch. 2. understanding, judgment. 3. meaning, as *I want you to get the general sense of the passage.* 4. feeling, as *a sense of responsibility.*—*v.* to feel, to be aware.—**sen'sing** *pres. part.*—**sense'less** *adj.* 1. stupid. 2. unconscious.—**common sense** practical everyday wisdom. —**sixth sense** an instinctive awareness of danger, etc.

Compare: 1. perception. 2. intelligence. reason, discrimination. 3. purport. 4. awareness

sensibil'ity *n.* 1. ability to feel, act of being sensitive. 2. condition of feeling hurt or offended too easily

sen'sible *adj.* 1. reasonable, wise. 2. aware. 3. noticeable, considerable.—**sen'sibly** *adv.*

sen'sitive *adj.* 1. (to) easily affected, e.g. by heat, light, etc. 2. easily hurt.—**sen'sitiveness** *n.*

sen'sual *adj.* relating to the bodily senses, as *Gluttony is sensual.*—**sensual'ity** *n.* self-indulgence.—**sen'suous** *adj.* affecting the senses, as *sensuous music, poetry, etc.*

sent'ence (sent'ens) *n.* 1. judgment on a criminal. 2. (in Grammar) set of words, complete in itself, usually containing a finite verb, expressing statement, question or command

senten'tious (sen-ten'shus) *adj.* 1. saying much in a few words. 2. speaking in a heavy, important way

sent'iment *n.* 1. feeling and thought. 2. a thought expressed in words

sentiment'al *adj.* 1. having too much soft feeling. 2. acting from feelings rather than thought or reason. 3. dependent on sentiment.—**senti-mental'ity** *n.*

sent'inel *n.* a soldier placed on guard.—**sent'ry** *n.* sentinel.—**sent'ries** *pl.*

sep'al *n.* the part of the outer green cup or calyx of the flower, which protects the bud

sep'arate (sep'a-rit) *adj.* apart, not connected or joined.—**sep'arate** (sep'ar-āt) *v.* 1. to put apart, divide. 2. to go apart, become parted.—**sep'arating** *pres. part.*—**sep'arately** *adv.* one at a time

Compare: (with *v.*) disconnect, detach, split, sunder, sever, divorce, part. *Contrast:* mix, mingle, amalgamate, join, connect, unite

separa'tion *n.* 1. dividing. 2. being apart.—**sep'arator** *n.* an apparatus for separating cream from milk

se'pia (see'pia) *n.* a brown colouring made from fluid secreted by cuttlefish

se'poy *n.* an Indian soldier in the former British Indian Army

Septem'ber *n.* the ninth month

sep'tic *adj.* poisoned, infected

sep'ulchre (sep'ul-ker) *n.* tomb, grave.—**sepul'chral** *adj.* 1. of the grave. 2. gloomy. —**sep'ulture** *n.* burial

se'quel (see'kwel) *n.* 1. what follows as a result of something. 2. a continuation

se'quence (see'kwens) *n.* an orderly series, succession

se'quin (see'kwin) *n.* a small, round metal ornament used as a decoration for dresses

ser'aph (ser'af) *n.* one of the highest of the order of angels.—**ser'aphs, ser'aphim** *pl.*—**seraph'ic** *adj.* angelic

sere *adj.* withered, dried up

serenade' (ser-en-ād') *n.* music sung or played at night, esp. by a lover below his lady's window.—*v.* to give a serenade

serene' (ser-een') *adj.* calm, peaceful, clear.—**serene'ly** *adv.*—**seren'ity** *n.* peace

serf *n.* a slave who is passed from one owner to the next with the land he works on.—**serf'dom** *n.* serf's condition

serge (serj) *n.* a kind of twilled cloth

ser'geant (sar'jent) *n.* 1. a non-commissioned officer next above a corporal. 2. a police officer.—**ser'geant-ma'jor** *n.* the highest non-commissioned officer in a regiment

se'rial (see'ri-al) *n.* a story published in sections.—*adj.* forming a series

se'ries (see'riz) *n.* a succession, a set of similar things or events.—**se'ries** *pl.*

se'rious (see'ri-us) *adj.* 1. thoughtful. 2. not joking, in earnest. 3. important as *a serious matter.* 4. dangerous, as *a serious crime.*—**se'riousness** *n.*

Compare: grave, earnest, sober, solemn, sedate, weighty, momentous. *Contrast:* trivial, unimportant, light, joking

ser'mon *n.* 1. a talk on a religious subject from the pulpit. 2. a warning and serious talk.—**ser'monise** *v.* to talk like a preacher

ser'pent *n.* 1. a snake. 2. a cunning person.—**ser'pentine** *adj.* 1. shaped like a snake, winding. 2. treacherous

ser'ried (ser'id) *adj.* close, crowded

se'rum *n.* a watery animal fluid, esp. a thin part of blood used for inoculation

ser'vant *n.* 1. a person employed to do housework. 2. a person in employment, e.g. **civil servant** a government employee

Compare: 1. maid, domestic charwoman, cook, butler, footman, help. 2. employee, functionary

serve *v.* 1. to work for someone. 2. to be a member of the Forces. 3. to be useful or suitable. 4. to wait at table. 5. to supply, deliver, hand round. 6. (tennis) to put the ball in play. 7. to treat, as *You served him badly.* 8. to assist priest in Eucharist. 9. to do the work (of), as *It serves a double purpose.*—**ser'ving** *pres. part.*—**ser'ver** *n.* 1. a tray for plates, etc. 2. a priest's assistant at Eucharist.—**it serves him right** he has got what he deserves (especially of punishment)

ser'vice (ser'vis) *n.* 1. employment as servant. 2. work done for another. 3. a department of public employment. 4. persons in government employment, as *the Civil Service.* 5. use, help, advantage, as *He was of great service.* 6. a meeting for worship, a religious ceremony. 7. a set of dishes, as *a dinner service.* 8. a manner of serving at tennis.—**ser'viceable** *adj.*—**service hatch** *n.* an opening for food to be passed from kitchen to dining room.—**at your service** ready to help you

serviette' *n.* a table-napkin

ser'vile (ser'vīl) *adj.* 1. like a slave. 2. without spirit or independence.—**servil'ity** *n.* slavish bahaviour

ser'vitude *n.* slavery, bondage

ses'sion (sesh'un) *n.* 1. a meeting of a court or parliament. 2. a series of these meetings

set *v.* 1. to place, put in place. 2. to arrange. 3. to fix, to become fixed or hard. 4. to sink (of the sun).—**set'ting** *pres. part.*—**set** *p.t.* and *p. part.*—*n.* 1. a setting, arrangement. 2. a direction. 3. a number of things used together. 4. an attack, as *He made a dead set at me.* 5. (tennis) a group of games.—*adj.* 1. formal, arranged beforehand. 2. fixed in place.—**set'back** *n.* check.—**set'-to** *n.* a fight.—**to set to** to start work.—**to set about** 1. to make a start. 2. to attack.—**to set aside** to put on one side.—**to set down** to write down.—**to set eyes on** to see, to meet.—**to set forth** 1. to start out. 2. to write, to state.—**to set free** to release.—**to set sail** to start sailing.—**to set off** 1. to start a journey. 2. to explode (a firework).—**to set one's hand to** to begin work on.—**to set one's heart on** to long for.—**to set one's teeth** to become determined.—**to set on fire** to burn.—**to set upon** to attack

set'-square *n.* a triangular instrument for drawing a line at an angle

settee' *n.* a couch with a back

set'ter 1. a person who sets, e.g. printing-type, jewels, etc. 2. a dog trained to scent game

set'ting *n.* 1. the music of a song. 2. the mounting of a jewel, etc. 3. scenery, background

set'tle *v.* 1. to put in order, as *The lawyer has settled the matter.* 2. to decide, as *I have settled what to do.* 3. to pay, as *to settle a bill.* 4. to come to rest, establish oneself, as *The bee settled on the flower.* 5. to come to an agreement, as *We have settled our differences.*—**set'tling** *pres. part.*

Compare: 1. adjust, compose, regulate. 2. determine. 3. liquidate. 4. alight, repose. 5. arrange

set'tle *n.* a bench with a high back

set'tlement *n.* 1. conditions for settling property on someone. 2. payment. 3. a colony.—**set'tler** *n.* colonist

sev'en *n.* one more than six.—*adj.*—**sev'enteen'** *n.* seven and ten.—**sev'enteenth'** *adj.* next after sixteenth.—**sev'enth** *adj.* next after sixth.—**sev'entieth** *adj.*—**sev'enty** *n.* seven times ten.—**seventh heaven** extreme joy.—**the seven seas** all the oceans

sev'er *v.* to cut off, separate.—**sev'erance** *n*

sev'eral *adj.* 1. some, a few. 2. separate, various.—*pron.* a few.—**sev'erally** *adv.*

severe' (si-veer') *adj.* 1. strict, stern. 2. serious, as *a severe attack of influenza.* 3. hard, rigorous, as *a severe climate.* 4. plain, unadorned, as *a severe style of hair-dressing.*—**sev'erely** *adv.*—**sever'ity** *n.*

sew (sō) *v.* to join with needle and thread.—**sew'ing** *pres. part.*—**sewed** (sōd) *p.t.*—**sewed, sewn** *p. part.*—**sew'ing machine** *n.* a machine for sewing cloth

sew'age (sū'ij) *n.* refuse carried away in sewers.—**sew'er** *n.* a drain for refuse.—**sew'erage** *n.* drainage by sewers

sex *n.* 1. the physical difference characterising male or female. 2. male persons, female persons.—**sex'ual** *adj.* to do with sex.—**sex'y** *adj.* sexually attractive

sex'tant *n.* an instrument for measuring angles, altitude of a heavenly body, etc.

sextet' *n.* a group of six singers or players

sex'ton *n.* a church care-taker, gravedigger

shab'by *adj.* 1. wearing old clothes, ragged. 2. mean, ungenerous, as *a shabby trick.*—**shab'bier** *comp.*—**shab'biest** *sup.*—**shab'bily** *adv.*—**shab'biness** *n.*

shack *n.* a hut, cabin

shack'le *v.* a link joining two pieces of chain for fastening wrists or ankles of a prisoner.—*pl.* handcuffs.—*v.* to fetter, fasten with shackles

shade *n.* 1. a rather dark place. 2. a place out of sunlight, sheltered spot. 3. depth of colour. 4. a ghost. 5. (U.S.) a window-blind.—*v.* 1. to screen, to protect. 2. to darken.—**sha'ding** *pres. part.*

shad'ow (shad'ō) *n.* 1. a patch of shade. 2. the shade thrown by a person or thing standing in the light. 3. something unreal, without substance.—*v.* 1. to protect from light. 2. to follow very closely, as *The burglar was shadowed by detectives.*—**shad'owy** *adj.* 1. shady. 2. dim

sha'dy *adj.* 1. dim, protected from light. 2. of doubtful honesty.—**sha'dier** *comp.*—**sha'diest** *sup.*

shaft *n.* 1. the long stem of a spear, arrow, etc. 2. one of two poles between which a horse is harnessed. 3. a rod connecting parts of a machine. 4. deep passage leading down to a mine. 5. the main part of a column

Note: We speak figuratively of a *shaft* of light (i.e. a beam), a *shaft* of wit or sarcasm (i.e. a sharp, pointed remark)

shag'gy (shag'i) *adj.* rough, hairy

Compare: unkempt, fuzzy, shock-headed

shah *n.* the ruler of Persia

shake *v.* 1. to move violently up and down or backwards and forwards. 2. to wave, brandish. 3. to tremble, rock. 4. to weaken, as *Nothing could shake his determination.*—**sha'king** *pres. part.*—**shook** *p.t.*—**sha'ken** *p. part.*—*n.* 1. a shak-

ing, jerk, shock. 2. a dance.—**sha'ky** *adj.* 1. trembling, 2. weak.—**shake' down** to make a rough bed.—**shake off** to get rid of. —**shake up** to disturb, rouse from idleness
Compare: agitate, vibrate, quiver, shudder, flap

shale *n.* clay rock like slate but softer

shall *v. auxiliary* helps to form tenses of other verbs. *I shall, thou shalt, he, we, etc. shall*
Note: I shall go, you will go, he will go expresses simply future action, but *I will go, you shall go, he shall go* express intention, or command.—*should, p.t.*

shal'low *adj.* not deep.—*n.pl.* an area of shallow water

sham *n.* an imitation, fraud, pretence.—*v.* to pretend.—**sham'ming** *pres. part.*—**shammed** *p.t.* and *p. part.*—*adj.* false, pretended

sham'ble *v.* to walk with dragging, shuffling feet.—*n.*—**sham'bling** *pres. part.*

sham'bles *n.pl.* 1. a slaughter-house. 2. a state of utter confusion

shame *n.* 1. a guilty feeling of having done something wrong or silly. 2. disgrace. 3. something to regret.—*v.* 1. to disgracc. 2. to cause to feel shame.—**sha'ming** *pres. part.*—**shame'faced** *adj.* ashamed of oneself.—**shame'ful** *adj.* disgraceful.—**shame'fully** *adv.*—**shame'less** *adj.* impudent

shampoo' *v.* to wash the hair.—*n.* the act of shampooing, a hair-wash

sham'rock *n.* a small plant with three small leaves; the national emblem of Ireland

shang'hai (shang'hī) *n.* (Aus.) a boy's catapult.—(-hī') *v.* to kidnap with violence

shank *n.* a leg, esp. between knee and ankle

shan'ty *n.* 1. a rough cabin, hut. 2. a sailor's song.—**shan'ties** *pl.*—**shan'ty town** a town or district with small shabby, roughly-built houses

shape *n.* 1. form, appearance. 2. order, pattern.—*v.* 1. to give form to, to fashion, make. 2. to take shape.—**sha'ping** *pres. part.*—**shape'less** *adj.*—**shape'ly** *adj.* well-formed, pleasing

share *n.* a portion, part belonging to one person.—*v.* 1. to give a share, to take a share. 2. to have in common.—**sha'ring** *pres. part.*—**share'holder** *n.* someone who owns shares in a company.—**the lion's share** the largest part

shark *n.* 1. a large, fierce sea-fish. 2. a swindler, dishonest person

sharp *adj.* 1. having a keen edge or fine sharp point. 2. distinct, clear-cut. 3. biting, harsh, as *a sharp frost.* 4. fierce, as *a sharp struggle.* 5. brisk, quick, as *He went for a sharp walk.* 6. quick-witted, watchful. 7. unscrupulous, as *sharp practice.*—**look sharp** hurry, waste no time.—*n.* in music, a note half a tone above the natural pitch. —*adv.* punctually, as *At* 2.30 *sharp.*—**sharp'en** *v.* to make sharp.—**sharp'er** *n.* a swindler.—**sharpness** *n.*—**sharp'-set** *adj.* hungry.—**sharp'shooter** *n.* a marksman

sharp'ener *n.* a small machine for sharpening pencils, knifes, etc.

shat'ter *v.* 1. to break in pieces. 2. to destroy
Compare: smash, crush, shiver

shave *v.* 1. to cut close, esp. hair of the face or head. 2. to graze past.—**sha'ving** *pres. part.*—**shaved** *p.t.*—**shaved, sha'ven** *p. part.*—*n.* the act of shaving, being shaved. —**sha'vings** *n.pl.* thin slices of wood planed off.—**a close shave** a narrow escape

shawl *n.* a square piece of material worn esp. round shoulders

she *pron.* nominative feminine of 3rd person pronoun.—*objective, her—possessive, her, hers.—masc., he.—neuter, it.—adj.* of the female sex, as *a she cat*

sheaf *n.* a bundle, esp. of corn.—**sheaves** (sheevz) *pl.*

shear (sheer) *v.* 1. to cut closely with shears or scissors. 2. to clip the wool or fleece.—**sheared, shorn** *p. part.*—**shears** *n.pl.* large scissors for clipping

sheath (sheeth) *n.* a covering, esp. for knife or sword, scabbard.—**sheathe** *v.* to put into a sheath

shed *v.* 1. let fall, as *to shed leaves.* 2. to throw off, as *to shed one's coat.* 3. to pour out, to cause to flow, as *to shed tears.*—**shed'ding** *pres. part.*—**shed** *p.t.* and *p. part.*

shed *n.* a shelter used as store or workshop

sheen *n.* gloss, brightness

sheep *n.* 1. a timid animal valued for its heavy coat of wool. 2. a timid, stupid person.—**sheep** *pl.*—**ram** *masc.*—**ewe** *fem.* —**lamb** young sheep.—**sheep'cote** *n.* a shelter for sheep.—**sheep'fold** *n.* a sheep-pen.—**sheep'ish** *adj.* bashful, stupidly shy. —**the black sheep of a family** a member who has disgraced himself
Note: A group of sheep is called a *flock*

sheer *adj.* 1. complete, absolute, as *sheer nonsense.* 2. steep, perpendicular, as *a sheer drop of* 100 *feet.* 3. almost transparent (fabrics, stockings, etc.).—*adv.* directly.—*v.* 1. to deviate from course (esp. of a ship). 2. (off) to depart—*n.* the upward slope of a ship's lines fore and aft

sheet *n.* 1. a large linen or cotton covering for inside of bed. 2. a thin, flat piece of anything. 3. a complete piece of paper. 4. a wide expanse, esp. of water.—**a clean sheet** an unspoiled record of good character

sheet *n.* a rope fastened in the corner of a sail.—**sheet-an'chor** *n.* a specially large anchor

sheik (shāk, sheek) *n.* an Arab chief

shek'el *n.* an ancient Jewish silver coin

shelf *n.* a thin board fixed on a wall, etc. on which to hold things.—**shelves** *pl.*

shell *n.* 1. a hard, outside covering or case of an animal, fruit, etc. 2. an explosive. 3. frame-work.—*v.* 1. to remove the shell.

2. to fire at with shells.—**shell-fish** *n.* a water-animal with a hard shell

shel'lac *n.* a resin used to make a varnish

shel'ter *n.* 1. something that gives protection from danger, weather, attack, etc. 2. protection.—*v.* to protect, to find shelter. See **protect**

shelve *v.* 1. to put on a shelf. 2. to put aside, as *The question was shelved for the time being.*—**shel'ving** *pres. part.*

shelve *v.* to slope gently.—**shel'ving** *pres. part.*

shep'herd (shep'erd) *n.* a man who tends sheep.—**shep'herdess** *fem.*—*v.* 1. to drive sheep. 2. to guide, conduct

sher'iff *n.* the chief official in a county

sher'ry *n.* a Spanish wine

shield (sheeld) *n.* 1. plate of armour carried on the left arm. 2. anything serving to protect.—*v.* to protect, to defend

shift *v.* 1. to move from one position to another. 2. to remove.—*n.* 1. group of workmen relieving others. 2. the time during which a group works. 3. a means to an end, trick. 4. a woman's waistless dress.—**shift'less** *adj.* lazy, incapable.—**shift'y** *adj.* not to be trusted, tricky

Compare: move, convey, transfer, transport, displace, change. *Contrast:* stay, remain, retain

shil'ling *n.* an old silver coin

shilly-shal'ly *v.* to waver, hesitate, to be undecided

shim'mer *v.* to gleam.—*n*

shin *n.* the front part of the leg below the knee

shine *v.* 1. to give out light, to gleam. 2. to polish. 3. to excel, to be good at.—**shi'ning** *pres. part.*—**shone, shined** *p.t.* and *p. part.* —*n.* 1. light, brightness. 2. gleam, polish

shin'gle (shing'gl) *n.* wooden roof-tile.—*v.* to cut the hair short.—**shin'gling** *pres. part.*

shin'gle *n.* pebbles on the sea-shore

shi'ny *adj.* bright, shining.—**shi'nier** *comp.*—**shi'niest** *sup.*

ship *n.* a large, sea-going vessel.—*v.* 1. to put goods on board. 2. to embark, as passenger or sailor.—**ship'ping** *pres. part.* —**shipped** *p.t.* and *p. part.*—**ship'mate** *n.* a fellow sailor.—**ship'ment** *n.* 1. shipping goods. 2. goods shipped.—**ship'ping** *n.* the ships of a country.—**ship'shape** *adj.* orderly.—**ship'yard** *n.* a place where ships are built or repaired.—**when my ship comes home** when I become rich

Note: A group of ships is called a *fleet* or (a small group) a *flotilla.* A country's ships of war make up its *navy*

There are many kinds of *craft,* as *ships* are sometimes called, from the small *rowing-boat* to the *warship* (which may be a *battleship,* a *cruiser,* a *destroyer,* a *submarine,* a *corvette* or a *sloop*), or the great passenger *liner* owned by a company. There are *steamships* and *sailing-ships* (such as *clippers, barques, schooners, yachts, frigates*). There are *life-boats, lightships, fishing-smacks* and *tramp steamers*

shire *n.* a county

shirk *v.* to try to avoid work, duty, etc.—**shirk'er** *n.*

shirt *n.* a man's undergarment

shiv'er *v.* to tremble with cold or fear.—*n.*

shiv'er *v.* to break in pieces

shoal (shōl) *n.* a large number of fish swimming together

shoal *n.* 1. a shallow place. 2. a sandbank under water

shock *n.* 1. a sudden disturbance, a violent shaking. 2. an attack of illness.—*v.* to fill with horror, disgust, painful surprise.—**shock'ing** *adj.* disgusting, very bad

shock *n.* an untidy mass of hair

shod'dy *n.* cloth made of mixed old and new wool.—*adj.* second-rate, made of poor material

shoe (shōō) *n.* 1. a covering for the foot. 2. a curved bar put on a horse's hoof.—*v.* to fit with shoes.—**shoe'ing** *pres. part.*—**shod** *p.t.* and *p. part.*—**shoe'horn** *n.* a piece of metal to help in putting on a shoe.—**shoe'maker** *n.*

shoot *v.* 1. to move swiftly and suddenly. 2. to let off a gun, etc. 3. to kill or wound with a gun. 4. to grow quickly. 5. to take a shot at goal.—**shot** *p.t.* and *p. part.*—*n.* 1. act of shooting. 2. young branch.—**to shoot ahead** to progress very quickly.—**to have shot one's bolt** to have made every effort.—**shooting star** a small meteorite, white hot, in the earth's atmosphere

shop *n.* 1. a place where goods are bought and sold. 2. a place where things are made or repaired, workshop.—*v.* to visit shops.—**shop'ping** *pres. part.*—**shopped** *p.t.* and *p. part.*—**shop'keeper** *n.* one who owns a shop.—**shop'lifter** *n.* one who steals from a shop.—**shop'per** *n.* one who buys in a shop.—**shop'soiled** *adj.* faded or dirty through being in a shop.—**to talk shop** to talk about one's own business or occupation

Compare: store, emporium, bazaar, market

shore *n.* the edge of a sea or large lake

shore *n.* a prop.—*v.*

short *adj.* 1. not long. 2. not tall. 3. soon finished. 4. curt, angry, as *He was very short with me. Short-tempered.* 5. of pastry, crumbling. 6. not reaching a certain measure or quality, as *The shopkeeper gave short weight.*—*adv.* suddenly, as *to stop short.*—**short'age** *n.* lack.—**shortbread, short'cake** *n.* rich kind of biscuit.—**short cir'cuit** *n.* the accidental touching of electrical contacts, causing a powerful surge of current.—**short'coming** *n.* defect, fault.—**shortcut** *n.* a quick way to a place. —**short-sighted** 1. unable to see clearly distant objects. 2. lacking foresight

short'en *v.* 1. to make short. 2. to grow short

short'hand *n.* a method of rapid writing by signs and contractions

short'ly *adv.* 1. briefly, using few words. 2. soon

shot *n.* 1. shooting. 2. a small ball of lead for a gun. 3. firing a gun, etc. 4. a person shooting, as *He is a good shot.* 5. a try, attempt, esp. at hitting.—**shot, shots** *pl.* —**a dead shot** an accurate shooter.—**a shot in the dark** a guess

shot *adj.* of changing colour, as *shot silk*

should (shood) *p.t.* of **shall**

Note: Should is used as an auxiliary to form compounds expressing condition, e.g. *I should go if I were you. Should you go, I will go too,* and also obligation, e.g. *You should do as you are told. I should go, you would go, he would go* express condition or wish, but *I would go, you should go, he should go* express intention, obligation, necessity

shoul'der (shōl'der) *n.* 1. the part of a body to which an arm or foreleg is attached.—*v.* 1. to put on one's shoulder, to bear, as *to shoulder responsibility.* 2. to push.—**shoul'der-blade** *n.* flat shoulder-bone.—**to give someone the cold shoulder** to snub him

shout *n.* a loud call or cry.—*v.* to call loudly

shove (shuv) *n.* a push.—*v.* to push.—**shov'ing** *pres. part.*

shov'el (shuv'el) *n.* a kind of spade.—*v.* to lift or move with a shovel.—**shov'elling** *pres. part.*—**shov'elled** *p.t.* and *p. part.*

show (shō) *v.* 1. to point out, to let be seen, as *to show the way.* 2. to explain, as *to show how it was done.* 3. to give, accord, as *to show anyone a kindness.* 4. to be visible, as *The house shows through the trees.* 5. to demonstrate, as *That shows the kind of man he is.*—**show'ing** *pres. part.* —**showed** *p.t.*—**shown, showed** (shewn, shewed) *p. part.*—*n.* 1. something shown, a display. 2. appearance.—**show'room** *n.* a large room where goods (e.g. cars) are for sale.—**to give the show away** to reveal hidden secrets or faults.—**to show off** to try to make an impression.—**to show up** 1. to demonstrate. 2. to unmask.—**to show willing** to be willing.—**to steal the show** to draw most attention

show'er *n.* 1. a short fall of rain. 2. anything like a fall of rain.—*v.* to rain.—**show'ery** *adj.*—**shower-bath** *n.* a bath in water sprayed from an overhead tap

show'y (shō'i) *adj.* 1. making a show, bright and attractive. 2. too bright, conspicuous. —**show'ily** *adv.*

shrank *p.t.* of **shrink**

shrap'nel *n.* a shell filled with bullets which explode in a shower

shred *n.* a small piece torn off, strip.—*v.* to tear into small pieces.—**shred'ding** *pres. part.*—**shred'ded** *p.t.* and *p. part.*

shrew (shrōō) *n.* 1. a kind of long-snouted mouse. 2. a bad-tempered woman

shrewd (shrōōd) *adj.* keen, clever.—**shrewd'ly** *adv.*—**shrewd'ness** *n.*

shrew'ish *adj.* sharp-tongued, scolding

shriek (shreek) *n.* a scream.—*v.*

shrift *n.* a confession made to a priest, absolution.—**to give short shrift** to punish any one quickly

shrill *adj.* sharp, piercing.—**shril'ly** *adv.*

shrimp *n.* a small shell-fish shaped like a lobster.—*v.* to catch shrimps

shrine *n.* 1. a case with relics of a saint. 2. a chapel for this. 3. a sacred place

shrink (shringk) *v.* 1. to become smaller. 2. to flinch, draw back in fear, etc.—*v.* to make smaller.—**shrank** *p.t.*—**shrunk'en, shrunk** *p. part.*—**shrink'age** *n.*

shriv'el *v.* to dry up, to shrink.—**shriv'elling** *pres. part.*—**shriv'elled** *p.t.* and *p. part.*

shroud *n.* a covering-sheet for the dead.—*pl.* ropes from a mast to the side of a ship. —*v.* to hide, veil, as *shrouded in mystery*

Shrove Tuesday *n.* the day before Ash Wednesday (which is the first day of Lent)

shrub *n.* a bush, low tree.—**shrub'bery** *n.* place planted with shrubs

shrug *v.* to raise the shoulders as a sign of impatience, scorn, etc.—**shrug'ging** *pres. part.*—**shrugged** *p.t.* and *p. part.*

shrunken (shrungk'en) *adj.* 1. reduced in size. 2. shrivelled, as *He had shrunken cheeks.* See **shrunk**

shud'der *v.* to tremble with horror, cold, etc.—*n.*

shuf'fle *v.* 1. to drag the feet, to move without lifting the feet. 2. to mix, esp. cards in a pack. 3. to try to deceive.—**shuf'fling** *pres. part.*—*n.* shuffling

shun *v.* to avoid, to keep clear of.—**shun'ning** *pres. part.*—**shunned** *p.t.* and *p. part.*

shunt *v.* 1. to move a train from one line to another. 2. to push aside

shut *v.* to close.—**shut'ting** *pres, part.*— **shut** *p.t.* and *p. part.*—**to shut down** to close. —**to shut in** to enclose.—**to shut out** to keep from entering.—**to shut up** to close, (slang) to keep one's mouth closed, keep quiet

shut'ter *n.* 1. a wooden screen for a window 2. a cover for a camera lens which opens when the press button is used.

shut'tle *n.* 1. an instrument used in weaving to carry the thread from one side of the web to the other. 2. an instrument for winding thread.—*v.* to go backwards and forwards.—**shuttle service** transport service with only one vehicle

shut'tlecock *n.* a cork with a fan of feathers stuck in it for use with a small racket or battledore

shy (of) *adj.* timid, awkward.—**shy'er** *comp.* —**shy'est** *sup.*—*v.* 1. (at) to start back in alarm. 2. (in common speech) to throw.—*n.*—**shy'ing** *pres. part.*—**shied** (shīd) *p.t.* and *p. part.*—**shy'ly** *adv.* timid-ly.—**shy'ness** *n.*—**fight shy of** to avoid

Compare: bashful, reserved, coy, modest, retiring, diffident, elusive. *Contrast:* self-confident, forward, bold, brazen

shy'ster *n.* (Aus.) a crook, imposter

Siam' (sī-am') *n.* a country in south-east Asia, Thailand.—**Siamese'** *adj.* belonging to Siam.—**Siamese cat** a breed of cat with a dark head and light body

Sibe'ria (sī-bee'ri-a) *n.* a part of the U.S.S.R. east of the Ural mountains.—*adj.* **Sibe'rian**

sib'ilant *adj.* having a hissing sound

sick *adj.* 1. ill. 2. inclined to vomit. 3. tired, disgusted.—**sick'en** *v.* to make sick, to become sick.—**sick at heart** very downcast. —**sick from, sick with** sick because of.—**sick to death of** very tired of

sick'le *n.* a curved blade on a short handle, used when reaping

sick'ly *adj.* 1. unhealthy, weak, pale. 2. producing nausea, as *a sickly smell.*—**sick'lier** *comp.*—**sick'liest** *sup.*

Compare: delicate, ailing, weakly, pallid, faint, languid, feeble. *Contrast:* healthy, strong, robust, hearty

sick'ness *n.* 1. illness. 2. vomiting

side *n.* 1. one of the surfaces of an object. 2. either surface of a thing having only two. 3. part of the body to the right or left. 4. a region, direction. 5. one of two parties or groups.—*v.* to take sides (with).—*adj.* at one side, towards one side, etc. as *a side road.*—**side'board** *n.* kind of cupboard in a dining-room.—**side'long** *adj.* towards one side.—**side'-track** *n.* siding.—*v.* to turn aside.—**side'walk** *n.* (U.S.) pavement, footpath.—**side'ways** *adv.*—**to put on side** to act in a conceited way.—**to take sides (with)** to join with.—**to side-step** to avoid

si'ding *n.* a track added to the side of a railway

si'dle *v.* to move sideways

sides'man *n.* a churchwarden's helper

siege (seej) *n.* the surrounding of a town or fortified place by an army, a besieging

sier'ra *n.* a mountain range

sies'ta *n.* a midday rest in hot countries

sieve (siv) *n.* 1. a utensil with a mesh for separating large pieces from fine, or solids from liquids

sift *v.* 1. to separate with a sieve. 2. to examine carefully.—**sif'ter** *n.*

sigh (sī) *v.* to let out a long, deep breath of relief, tiredness, etc.—*n.*

sight (sīt) *n.* 1. the power of seeing. 2. something seen, scene, a view as *It was a fine sight.* 3. a device on a rifle for guiding the eye.—*adj.* (slang) much, great deal.—*v.* 1. to see. 2. to adjust sight of gun, etc.—**sight'less** *adj.* blind.—**sight'ly** *adj.* pleasing. —**sight'seer** *n.* a tourist seeing the places of interest in a town or country

sign (sīn) *n.* a mark, movement, or anything that shows or means something.—*v.* 1. to make a sign. 2. to write one's name (on).—**to sign off** to finish.—**to sign on** to sign an agreement for employment.—**to sign up** to enlist

Compare: indication, emblem, symbol, token, symptom, gesture, manifestation

sig'nal *n.* a sign giving an order or message.—*v.* to make signals to.—**sig'nalling** *pres. part.*—**sig'nalled** *p.t.* and *p. part.*—*adj.* remarkable.—**sig'nally** *adv.*

sig'nature *n.* 1. a person's name written by himself. 2. signing

sig'net *n.* a small seal.—**sig'net ring** *n.* a finger ring set with a seal

signif'icance *n.* 1. meaning, as *What is the significance of his words?* 2. importance, as *The author is of great significance.*—**signif'icant** *adj.* 1. meaning something. 2. important.—**significa'tion** (kā'shun) *n.* meaning.—**sig'nify** *v.* 1. to mean. 2. to express. 3. to be of importance.—**he sig'nifies.** —**sig'nifying** *pres. part.*—**sig'nified** *p.t.* and *p. part.*

sign'post *n.* a post at a crossroads showing directions

Sikh (seek) *n.* a member of a Hindu community

si'lage (sī'lij) *n.* cattle fodder preserved in a silo

si'lence (sī'lens) *n.* 1. absence of noise. 2. the act of keeping silent.—*v.* to make silent.—**si'lent** *adj.* 1. saying nothing. 2. quiet, without noise.—**si'lently** *adv.*

Compare: quiet, quietness, hush, stillness, secrecy. *Contrast:* See **noise**

silhouette' (sil-ōō-et') *n.* 1. a portrait cut from black paper or painted in black on white. 2. an outline seen against the light. —*v.*

sil'ica *n.* a hard mineral, silicon oxide. Sand is a form of silica

sil'icon *n.* a non-metallic element

silk *n.* 1. fine thread spun by silkworms. 2. material made from this.—*adj.* made of silk.—**silk'en** *adj.* of silk.—**silk'y** *adj.* smooth, soft.—**silk'ier** *comp.*—**silk'iest** *sup.*

silk'worm *n.* a caterpillar that spins silk and makes a cocoon

sill *n.* a piece of wood or stone at the bottom of a door or window

sil'liness *n.* the act of being silly

sil'ly *adj.* foolish. without sense.—**sil'lier** *comp.*—**sil'liest** *sup.*—*n.*

Compare: fatuous, absurd, ridiculous, senseless, nonsensical, imbecile, stupid, brainless, simple. *Contrast:* intelligent, wise, sensible, clever, shrewd

si'lo (sī'lō) *n.* an airtight tower or pit in which green stuff is stored for animal fodder

silt *n.* mud, sand, etc. deposited by water.—*v.* (up) to fill with silt

sil'van, syl'van *adj.* of the woods, rural

sil'ver *n.* 1. a white, precious metal. 2. coins

made of silver. 3. things made of silver.—*adj.* made of, or of the colour of silver.—*v.* to coat with silver.—**sil'versmith** *n.* worker in silver.—**sil'very** *adj.*—**silver paper** thin tinfoil.—**silver wedding** **a** twenty-fifth wedding anniversary

sim'ian *adj.* like an ape

sim'ilar *adj.* like, resembling, as *The two dresses are similar. This one is similar to that.*—**similar'ity** *n.* resemblance

sim'ile *n.* a figure of speech making a comparison, e.g. *The night is as black as pitch.* See **metaphor**

simil'itude *n.* 1. outward likeness. 2. simile

sim'mer *v.* 1. to keep boiling gently. 2. to be on the point of bursting out into anger, laughter, etc. as *simmering with suppressed anger*

sim'per *v.* to smile in a silly, affected manner. —*n.*

sim'ple *adj.* 1. of one kind, not compound or complex, as *a simple sentence* (i.e. *one without subordinate clauses*). 2. plain, not adorned, as *a simple frock.* 3. easy, as *This kind of sum is quite simple.* 4. natural, unaffected, as *a simple life.* 5. humble, as *simple folks.* 6. weak-minded, as *Simple Simon.* 7. pure, absolute, as *It is simple madness to attempt it.*—**sim'ply** *adv.*

sim'pleton *n.* a silly person

simplic'ity (sim-plis'i-ti) *n.* the act of being simple

simplifica'tion (-kā'shun) *n.* making plain, simple

sim'plify *v.* to make, simple, to make easier. —he **sim'plifies.**—**sim'plifying** *pres. part.* —**sim'plified** *p.t.* and *p. part.*

sim'ulate *v.* 1. to pretend. 2. to imitate.—**sim'ulating** *pres. part.*—**simula'tion** (-lā'shun) *n.* 1. pretence. 2. imitation

simulta'neous *adj.* happening at the same time.—**simulta'neously** *adv.*

sin *n.* wrong-doing, breaking the laws of God.—*v.* to do wrong.—**sin'ning** *pres. part.* —**sinned** *p.t.* and *p. part.*

since (sins) *adv.* after past time or happening, as *He has not been since.*—*prep.* as *He has not been since Tuesday.*—*conj.* because, as *Since you did not come I thought you had gone away*

sincere' (sin-seer') *adj.* true, genuine, honest, unaffected.—**sincere'ly** *adv.*—**sincer'ity** (sin-se'ri-ti) *n.*

Contrast: false, underhanded, hypocritical, treacherous

sin'ew (sin'ū) *n.* tough tissue joining muscle to bone.—*pl.* strength, power.—**sin'ew** *adj.* strong

sin'ful *adj.* wicked

sing *v.* 1. to make a musical sound with the voice. 2. to celebrate in song or poetry. 3. to hum, whistle, etc. 4. (out) to shout.—**sing'ing** *pres. part.*—**sang** *p.t.*—**sung** *p. part.*—**sing'er** *n.*

singe (sinj) *v.* to burn the surface of.—**singe'ing** *pres. part.*—**singed** (sinjd) *p.t.* and *p. part.*

sing'le (sing'gl) *adj.* 1. one only. 2. alone, separate. 3. unmarried. 4. formed of only one part, fold, etc.—*v.* to pick out.—**sing'ly** *adv.*—**sing'le-handed** *adj.* without help.—**sing'le-heart'ed** *adj.* sincere.—**sing'le-minded** *adj.* true to one purpose

sing'ular (sing'gū-lar) *adj.* 1. odd, remarkable. 2. in Grammar, relating to one, e.g. *man is singular, men is plural.*—**singular'ity** *n.* oneness, oddness

sin'ister *adj.* 1. evil-looking, unlucky. 2. in heraldry, on the left side

sink (singk) *v.* 1. to fall slowly, to go under or lower. 2. to cause to go under water. 3. to dig.—**sink'ing** *pres. part.*—**sank** *p.t.*—**sunk'en, sunk** *p. part.*—*n.* a basin with a pipe for carrying away water

sin'ner *n.* one who sins, wrong-doer

sin'uous *adj.* curving, winding

sip *v.* to drink in very small portions, to taste.—*n.*—**sip'ping** *pres. part.*—**sipped** *p.t.* and *p. part.*

si'phon (sī'fon) *n.* 1. a bent tube for drawing off liquids. 2. a bottle with a tap through which liquid is forced by pressure of the gas inside.—*v.* (off), to draw off liquid through a tube

sir *n.* 1. a title of respect.—**mad'am** *fem.* 2. title of a knight or baronet.—**la'dy** *fem.*

sire *n.* 1. a father. 2. an animal's male parent. —**dam** *fem.* 3. a title used in addressing a king

si'ren *n.* 1. a long, piercing whistle used as a signal or warning. 2. a beautiful legendary maiden who enticed men to their doom by sweet singing

sir'loin *n.* the upper part of a loin of beef

siroc'co *n.* a hot, dry, wind from N. Africa

sis'ter *n.* 1. the daughter of the same parents as another child.—**bro'ther** *masc.* 2. a nun, member of a sisterhood. 3. a nurse in position of authority.—**sister-in-law** *n.* 1. the sister of a husband or wife. 2. a brother's wife.—**sis'ters-in-law** *pl.*—**sis'terly** *adj.* like a sister.—**sis'terhood** *n.* 1. women living together under religious vows. 2. relationship between sisters

sit *v.* 1. to rest, e.g. on a chair, to be seated. 2. to hold a session. 3. to be member of an assembly. 4. (birds) to cover eggs and hatch them.—**sit'ting** *pres. part.*—**sat,** sate (old spelling) *p.t.* and *p. part.*—**to make someone sit up** to shock him.—**to sit tight** to take no action, to remain unmoving in the face of danger.—**sitdown strike** work stoppage by workmen who do not leave the factory

site *n.* a place, situation, plot of ground for a building.—*v.*

sit'ting *n.* 1. a meeting, session. 2. the time during which a person sits.—*v. pres. part.* of sit

sit'uated *adj.* placed

Compare: located, sited, circumstanced

situa'tion (-ā'shun) *n.* 1. place, position. 2. employment, post. 3. case, state of affairs, *An awkward situation arose*

six *adj.* one more than five.—**six'pence** *n.* a silver coin worth six pennies.—**sixteen'** *adj.* six and ten.—**sixteenth'** *adj.* one more than fifteenth.—**sixth** *adj.* one more than fifth.—**six'ty** *adj.* six times ten.—**six'tieth** *adj.*

size *n.* 1. bigness, dimensions. 2. a kind of glue.—*v.* 1. to arrange in sizes. 2. (up), to assess

siz'zle *v.* to make a hissing sound.—*n.*

skate *n.* 1. a steel blade with a framework for attaching to a shoe and used for gliding over ice. 2. a flat-bodied fish.—*v.* to glide on ice.—**ska'ting** *pres. part.*—**ska'ter** *n.*—**to skate on thin ice** to deal with a difficult situation carefully and tactfully.—**to skate round a subject** to avoid talking about it directly

skein (skān) *n.* 1. a flight of wild geese or swans. 2. a loose knot of wool, etc.

skel'eton *n.* 1. the bones of a body kept in their natural positions. 2. a frame, outline.—**skel'eton-key** *n.* a key made to fit most locks.—**a skeleton in the cupboard** a shameful or embarrassing secret

sketch *n.* 1. a rough, drawing, outline. 2. a short play or story.—*v.* to draw roughly.—he **sketch'es**.—**sketch'-book** *n.*—**sketch'y** *adj.* unfinished

skew'er *n.* a long pin to fasten meat together.—*v.*

ski (skee, shee) *n.* a long, wooden or metal runner fastened to the foot for gliding over snow.—**skis** *pl.*—*v.* to glide on skis.—**ski'ing** *pres. part.*—**skied** *p.t.* and *p. part.*

skid *n.* something to prevent a wheel from going round.—*v.* to slip sideways, of a wheel, to slip without revolving.—**skid'ding** *pres. part.*—**skid'ded** *p.t.* and *p. part.*

skiff *n.* a small boat

skil'ful *adj.* showing skill, clever, expert.—**skil'fully** *adv.*

skill *n.* ability coming from practice or experience.—**skilled** *adj.* trained

Compare: (with *adj.*) proficient, expert, adept, practised, experienced, skilful. *Contrast:* unskilled, inexpert, inept, inexperienced, untrained, unpractised, amateurish

skim *v.* 1. to take off the top of a liquid. 2. to read carelessly. 3. to glide over.—**skim'ming** *pres. part.*—**skimmed** *p.t.* and *p. part.*

skimp *v.* 1. to give short measure, to be saving. 2. to do something carelessly

skin *n.* 1. the outer covering of the body. 2. peel, rind.—*v.* to take off the skin, to peel.—**skin'ning** *pres. part.*—**skinned** *p.t.* and *p. part.*—**skin-deep'** *adj.* only on the surface.—**skin'-flint** *n.* a mean person.—**skin'ny** *adj.* thin.—**skin'-diving** *n.* sport of underwater swimming with oxygen cylinders and mask but no diving suit.—**by the skin of one's teeth** very nearly, only just.—**to be thin (thick) skinned** to be sensitive (insensitive).—**to save one's skin** to escape safely

skip *v.* 1. to jump lightly, spring. 2. to pass over, as *He skipped several chapters.*—*n.*—**skip'ping** *pres. part.*—**skipped** *p.t.* and *p. part.*

skip'per *n.* the captain of a ship

skir'mish *n.* a fight between small groups.—*v.* to engage in a skirmish

skirt *n.* 1. the lower part of a woman's dress. 2. a woman's garment fitted to and hanging from the waist.—*v.* to go along the edge of.—**skirting-board** *n.* one of the boards running round the foot of the walls of a room

skit *n.* a short, humorous sketch or satire

skite *v.* (N.Z.) to boast.—*n.*

skit'tish *adj.* frisky

skit'tles *n.pl.* a game resembling ninepins

skulk *v.* to hide, to lurk, to sneak

skull *n.* the bones enclosing the brain.—**skull'-cap** *n.* close-fitting cap

skunk *n.* 1. small, strong-smelling N. American animal valued for its fur. 2. (slang) a contemptible person

sky *n.* the open space above the world, as seen from the ground.—**skies** (skīz) *pl.*—**sky'light** *n.* window in a roof.—**sky'-scraper** *n.* a very tall building

slab *n.* a thick, broad piece

slack *adj.* 1. loose. 2. slow, dull, as *Business is slack.* 3. careless.—*n.* small coal.—*pl.* loose trousers.—*v.* to be lazy.—**slack off** to become less intense or active.—**slack'en** *v.* 1. to become slower. 2. to loosen.—**slack'ly** *adv.*—**slack'ness** *n.*

slag *n.* waste left from melted metal

slake *v.* to satisfy thirst, to quench.—**sla'king** *pres. part.*

slam *v.* 1. to shut noisily, to bang. 2. to throw down violently.—*n.*—**slam'ming** *pres. part.*—**slammed** *p.t.* and *p. part.*

slan'der *n.* a false statement about a person intended to do harm.—*v.*—**slan'derous** *adj.*

Compare: defamation, scandal, libel, aspersion, backbiting, detraction

slang *n.* words used in conversation though not accepted as good language.—**slang'y** *adj.*

slant *v.* to slope.—*n.*—**slant'wise** *adv.* obliquely, slanting

slap *n.* a blow with the open hand, smack.—*v.* to smack.—**slap'ping** *pres. part.*—**slapped** *p.t.* and *p. part.*—**slap'dash** *adj.* careless, random

slash *v.* 1. to cut violently, to gash. 2. to cut into long strips.—*n.* a cutting stroke, gash

slat *n.* a narrow strip of wood or metal

slate *n.* 1. a bluish-grey stone that splits into smooth layers. 2. a piece of this for covering roof or writing on.—*v.* 1. to cover with slates. 2. (in common speech) to criticise severely, scold

slat'tern *n.* a dirty, untidy woman, slut.—**slat'ternly** *adj.*

slaugh'ter (slaw'ter) *v.* to kill.—*n.* butchery, massacre, carnage.—**slaugh'terous** *adj.* murderous

Slav *n.* a member of one of the races of eastern Europe.—*adj.* **Slavon'ic**

slave *n.* 1. a person who can be bought and sold. 2. a person who works without proper payment.—*v.* to work hard.—**sla'very** *n.*—**sla'vish** *adj.* mean, base

slay *v.* to kill. (See **kill**).—**slay'ing** *pres. part.* —**slew** *p.t.*—**slain** *p. part.*—**slay'er** *n.*

sledge (slej), **sled, sleigh** (slā) *n.* a carriage on runners for sliding on snow

sledge, sledge'-hammer *n.* a heavy, blacksmith's hammer

sleek *adj.* glossy and smooth

sleep *v.* to rest with closed eyes and unconscious mind, to slumber.—*n.*—**sleep'ing** *pres. part.*—**slept** *p.t.* and *p. part.*—**sleep'er** *n.* 1. one who sleeps. 2. a beam supporting a railway line.—**sleep'ily** *adv.*—**sleep'iness** *n.* being sleepy.—**sleep'y** *adj.* drowsy.—**sleep'ier** *comp.*—**sleep'iest** *sup.*

sleep'out *n.* (Aus.) an enclosed or partly enclosed verandah used for additional sleeping accommodation

sleet *n.* rain and snow or hail falling together. —*v.*

sleeve *n.* the part of a garment which covers the arm.—**to have a card up one's sleeve** to have a secret plan in reserve.—**to laugh up one's sleeve** to be amused secretly.—**to wear one's heart on one's sleeve** to show one's feelings openly

sleight (slīt) *n.* skill.—**sleight of hand** *n.* conjuring, juggling

slen'der *adj.* 1. slim, thin. 2. small, as *slender chances of success.*—**slen'derness** *n.*

sleuth (slūth) *n.* a detective

slew, slue (slū) *v.* to swing round

slew *p.t.* of **slay**

slice (slīs) *n.* a thin, flat piece cut off.—*v.* to cut into slices.—**slic'ing** *pres. part.*

slick *adj.* 1. smooth. 2. smooth-tongued, smart, tricky.—*n.* oil deposit left on the surface of road or sea

slide *v.* 1. to slip smoothly along. 2. to move quietly and quickly, as *He slid the letter under the door.* 3. to pass without taking action, as *He let the matter slide.*—**sli'ding** *pres. part.*—**slid** *p.t.* and *p. part.*—*n.* 1. smooth track for sliding. 2. glass plate (as in magic-lantern, etc.). 3. a flat brooch to keep hair tidy.—**slide'-rule** *n.* a ruler with a sliding part for making rapid calculations

slight (slīt) *adj.* 1. slim, slender. 2. trivial, as *a slight headache.*—*v.* to neglect, to offend. —*n.* slighting treatment, as *I consider it a slight not to have been invited.*—**slight'ly** *adv.* little

slim *adj.* thin, slender, small.—*v.* to reduce one's weight by diet.—**slim'mer** *comp.*—**slim'mest** *sup.*

slime *n.* sticky mud.—**sli'my** *adj.*

sling *n.* 1. a strap with a string attached at each end for hurling a stone. 2. a hanging bandage for a wounded arm. 3. a rope for hoisting or carrying.—*v.* to throw, to hoist, swing.—**sling'ing** *pres. part.*—**slung** *p.t.* and *p. part.*

slink *v.* to creep, to sneak in a guilty manner **slink'ing** *pres. part.*—**slunk** *p.t.* and *p. part.*

slip *v.* 1. to move smoothly. 2. to lose one's balance. 3. to make a mistake. 4. to escape from, as *It slipped my mind.*—**slip'ping** *pres. part.*—**slipped** *p.t.* and *p. part.*—*n.* 1. a slipping. 2. a slight mistake. 3. a twig cut for planting or grafting. 4. (cricket) a position on the off-side, behind the wicket. 5. a pillow-case. 6. a petticoat.—**slip'rails** *n.pl.* (Aus.) panels of fence which can be removed to serve as a gate.—**to give someone the slip** to escape in a quick clever way.—**there's many a slip twixt cup and lip** (proverb) something often goes wrong when a plan is being carried out

Compare: fall, slide, lapse, glide, escape, unleash

slip'per *n.* a light indoor shoe

slip'pery *adj.* 1. smooth enough to slip on. 2. difficult to catch, tricky

slip'shod *adj.* untidy, careless

slip'stream *n.* the air thrown back by the jet or propeller of an aeroplane

slit *v.* to cut open, to make a long cut.—**slit'ting** *pres. part.*—**slit** *p.t.* and *p. part.*—*n.* a long, narrow cut

slob'ber *v.* 1. to let saliva run out of the mouth. 2. to be weak and silly

sloe (slō) *n.* 1. the blackthorn. 2. its small, purple fruit

slog *v.* 1. to hit hard, esp. at cricket. 2. to work hard.—**slog'ging** *pres. part.*—**slogged** *p.t.* and *p. part.*

slo'gan *n.* 1. a Highland war-cry. 2. a catchword, or phrase used by a party or business, e.g. *Eat more fruit. It's quicker by rail*

sloop *n.* a one-masted sailing ship

slop *v.* to splash, to spill carelessly.—**slop'ping** *pres. part.*—**slopped** *p.t.* and *p. part.*—*n.* dirty water

slope *n.* 1. gently-rising ground. 2. slant, angle.—*v.* 1. to go up or down. 2. to place in slanting position.—**slo'ping** *pres. part.*

slop'py *adj.* 1. wet, muddy. 2. careless, untidy. 3. weak, silly

slot *n.* a narrow opening, slit.—*v.*—**slot machine** *n.* a machine which delivers goods when a coin is inserted in a slot

sloth (slōth) *n.* 1. laziness, slowness. 2. a slow-moving South American animal.—**sloth'ful** *adj.* See **lazy**

slouch *n.* a careless, stooping walk.—*v.* —**slouch'ing** *adj.*

slough (slow) *n.* a muddy place, bog
slough (sluf) *n.* skin shed by a snake.—*v.*
slov'en (sluv'n) *n.* a dirty, untidy person.—**slov'enliness** *n.*—**slov'enly** *adj.* untidy
slow (slō) *adj.* 1. taking a long time. 2. of a clock, behind time. 3. dull, stupid.—*v.* to slacken speed (often followed by *up* or *down*).—**slow'ly** *adv.*—**slow'ness** *n.*
Compare: sluggish, tardy, lingering. *Contrast:* quick, rapid, speedy, lively
slow'worm *n.* a small lizard
sludge *n.* a sticky mud, melting snow or dirty oil
slug *n.* 1. a small snail without a shell. 2. an air gun bullet.—**slug'gard** *n.* a lazy person.—**slug'gish** *adj.* slow-moving
sluice (slōōs) *n.* a gate or door to control the flow of water in a canal, etc.—*v.* to flood, to drench
slum *n.* over-crowded dirty part of a town.—**slum'my** *adj.*—**slum-clearance** *n.* the replacement of slum houses by new houses
slum'ber *n.* sleep.—*v.*—**slum'berous, slum'brous** *adj.* peaceful
slump *n.* a sudden, heavy fall in prices.—*v.* 1. to fall suddenly. 2. to sit down heavily
slung *p.t.* and *p. part.* of **sling**
slunk *p.t.* of **slink**
slur *v.* to pass over lightly, to run sounds into one in singing, speaking.—**slur'ring** *pres. part.*—**slurred** *p.t.* and *p. part.*—*n.* 1. slurring. 2. a slight, insult
slush *n.* melting snow, mud.—**slush'y** *adj.*
slut *n.* a dirty, untidy woman.—**slut'tish** *adj.*
sly *adj.* liking to do things secretly, underhand, cunning. (See **deceitful.**)—**sly'ly** *adv.*—**sly'ness** *n.*—**sly grog** (Aus.) liquor sold illegally
smack *n.* a taste, slight flavour, trace.—*v.* as *This smacks of treachery*
smack *v.* 1. to open the lips with a loud sound. 2. to slap.—*n.* a smacking, a slap
smack *n.* a small fishing vessel
small (smawl) *adj.* 1. little, not large or big. 2. mean. (See **little, big.**)—**small'ness** *n.*—**small arms** rifles and revolvers.—**small change** coins of small value.—**small-pox** *n.* a dangerous infectious disease.—**small hours** early morning.—**small-talk** trivial conversation.—**to feel small** to feel humbled
smart *adj.* 1. sharp, keen, quick, as *He gave the door a smart tap.* 2. clever, quick-witted, as *a smart business man.* 3. well-dressed, fashionable, as *smart clothes.*—*v.* to be painful, to feel pain, as *the wound smarted.*—*n.* sharp pain.—**smart'en** *v.* to make smarter.—**smart'ly** *adv.*—**smart'ness** *n.*
smash *v.* 1. to break into pieces. 2. to destroy utterly.—he **smash'es.**—*n.* 1. a heavy blow. 2. a violent collision. 3. a disaster.—**smashing** *adj.* 1. crushing. 2. excellent
smat'tering *n.* slight knowledge, as *He had only a smattering of French*
smear *v.* to rub with something dirty or sticky.—*n.* a dirty mark
smell *v.* 1. to be aware of through the nose. 2. to breathe in (an odour). 3. to give out an odour.—**smelt, smelled** *p.t.* and *p. part.*—*n.* 1. act of smelling, the sense of smell. 2. odour.—**smel'ly** *adj.* having a strong smell.—**to smell a rat** to be suspicious
smelt *v.* to melt ore in order to obtain metal.—*n.* a small salmon-like fish
smile *v.* to look pleased, amused. scornful, etc. by curving the lips up or down.—*n.* (See **laughter**).—**smi'ling** *adj.*
smirch *v.* to make dirty, to disgrace
smirk *v.* to smile in a silly, affected way.—*n.*
smite *v.* to strike, hit.—**smi'ting** *pres. part.*—**smote** *p.t.*—**smit'ten** *p. part.*
smith *n.* a worker in iron, gold, etc.—**smith'y** *n.* forge, blacksmith's workshop
smock *n.* a loose outer garment with upper part gathered by stitching
smog *n.* fog mixed with smoke or dirt
smoke *n.* 1. the cloud that rises from anything burning. 2. smoking tobacco.—*v.* 1. to give off smoke. 2. to draw in smoke from a cigarette, etc. and puff it out. 3. to dry food by smoking.—**smok'ing** *pres. part.*—**smo'ker** *n.*—**smo'ky** *adj.*
smooth *adj.* 1. even, not rough. 2. easy, pleasant. (See **rough**).—*v.* to make smooth.—**smooth'ly** *adv.*—**smooth'ness** *n.*—**smooth-tongued** *adj.* flattering, polite
smoth'er (SMUTH'er) *v.* 1. to suffocate, to stifle, kill by excluding air. 2. to hush up, keep down
smoul'der (smōl'der) *v.* to burn without a flame
smudge (smuj) *n.* a dirty mark, smear.—*v.*—**smudg'y** *adj.*
smug *adj.* self-satisfied
smug'gle *v.* to bring in or take out secretly (esp. without paying customs duties, etc.).—**smu'ggling** *pres. part.*—**smug'gler** *n.*
smut *n.* 1. soot, dirt. 2. a disease which attacks corn.—*v.* to blacken, smudge.—**smut'ty** *adj.*
snack *n.* a light meal.—**snack'-bar** *n.* a small café
snag *n.* 1. a stump, esp. a tree-trunk in a river. 2. an obstacle, an unexpected fault. 3. a pulled thread in a nylon stocking
snail *n.* a small, soft, slow-moving animal often with a shell on its back
snake *n.* a long, crawling reptile.—**sna'ky** *adj.*—**a snake in the grass** a treacherous enemy
snap *v.* 1. to make a quick bite or snatch, to seize quickly (sometimes followed by *at* or *up*, as *to snap at the chance, to snap up a bargain*). 2. to break suddenly. 3. to photograph by snapshot. 4. to make, or cause, to make, a sharp sound, as *to snap one's fingers.*—**snap'ping** *pres. part.*—**snapped** *p.t.* and *p. part.*—*n.* 1. a quick, sharp sound. 2. a bite. 3. a clasp or catch.

4. a card game.—*adj.* sudden.—**snap'py** *adj.* 1. ill-tempered. 2. speedy.—**snap'shot** *n.* a quickly-taken photograph

snare *n.* a trap with a noose.—*v.* to catch in a snare

snarl *v.* to growl with bared teeth.—*n.*

snatch *v.* to seize suddenly, to grab. (See **seize**).—*n.* 1. a grab. 2. a short time, small amount, as *a snatch of sleep, snatches of conversation.*—**snatch'es** *pl.*

sneak *v.* 1. to move secretly, to slink. 2. to tell tales, make mischief.—*n.* a mean, sly person

sneer *v.* to smile or speak scornfully.—*n.*

sneeze *v.* to make a sudden explosive sound through the nose.—*n.*—**snee'zing** *pres. part.*—**not to be sneezed at** not to be despised

sniff *v.* 1. to draw in breath through the nose with a hissing sound. 2. to smell.—*n.*

snig'ger *v.* to giggle, to laugh secretly

snip *v.* to cut, to cut bits off.—**snip'ping** *pres. part.*—**snip'ped** *p.t.* and *p. part.*—*n.* 1. a bit cut off. 2. (slang) a bargain.—**snip'pet** *n.* a small piece

snipe *n.* a long-billed marsh bird.—*v.* to shoot at enemy soldiers from cover.—**sni'per** *n.*

sniv'el *v.* 1. to sniff. 2. to cry, whine with pretended grief.—**sniv'elling** *pres. part.*—**sniv'elled** *p.t.* and *p. part.*

snob *n.* one who thinks too highly of wealth, social position, etc.—**snob'bery** *n.*—**snob'-bish** *adj.*

snook'er *n.* a game played with coloured balls on a billiard table

snooze *v.* to doze, to be half asleep

snore *v.* to make noises with the breath while asleep.—*n.*—**snor'ing** *pres. part.*

snor'kel *n.* a device for underwater breathing consisting of two vertical tubes (or one tube with two passages) for taking in and blowing out air. See **schnorkel.**

snort *v.* to make a noise by driving breath through the nostrils.—*n.*

snout *n.* the nose and mouth of an animal

snow (snō) *n.* frozen vapour falling in white flakes.—*v.* to fall in snow, or like snow.—**snow'ball** *n.*—**snow'drift** *n.* a bank of snow piled up.—**snow'drop** *n.* a white, early spring flower.—**snow'fall** *n.*—**snow'flake** *n.*—**snow'-plough** *n.* a machine for clearing snow.—**snow'storm** *n.*—**snow'y** *adj.*

snub *v.* to treat in a cold, unfriendly way.—**snub'bing** *pres. part.*—**snubbed** *p.t.* and *p. part.*—*n.* a snubbing, rebuff.—*adj.* of a nose, turned up

snuff *n.* 1. to breathe in through the nose. 2. to clean a candle-wick.—*n.* powdered tobacco taken into the nose.—**snuff'box** *n.*—**snuff out** to extinguish

snuf'fle *v.* 1. to sniff, snivel. 2. to speak through the nose.—*n.*

snug *adj.* comfortable and warm.—**snug'gle** *v.* to nestle

so *adv.* 1. to the extent that, as *Be so good as to . . .* 2. in such manner, as *He did so.* 3. thus, as *So he said. So did you.* 4. to such an extent, as *It hurts so.*—*conj.* therefore, accordingly, as *He is ill, so (that) he cannot come.*—*interj.* Oh! Indeed!—**so and so** unspecified person(s) or thing(s).—**or so** or thereabouts.—**so forth,** so on, etcetera. —**so much** a certain amount

Note: so is often followed (in comparisons) by *as* or *that*, as *I am not so old as he is. It went so fast that we could not catch it*

soak (sōk) *v.* 1. to leave in liquid. 2. to wet thoroughly, to drench. 3. (in) to absorb.—*n.* 1. a soaking. 2. also **soakage** (Aus.) a depression holding water after rain, low lying land where water lies

soap (sōp) *n.* a substance made of fat and soda used for washing.—*v.* to rub with soap.—**soap'y** *adj.*—**soap'suds** *n.pl.* soapy lather

soar (sōr) *v.* to fly high.—**soar'ing** *n.* rising high on wings or in thought

sob *v.* to catch the breath while crying.—*n.*—**sob'bing** *pres. part.*—**sobbed** *p.t.* and *p. part.*

so'ber (sō'ber) *adj.* 1. not drunk. 2. calm, sensible.—*v.* to make sober, to become sober.—**so'berly** *adv.*

sobri'ety *n.* soberness

soc'cer *n.* Association football

sociabil'ity (sō-sha-bil'i-ti) *n.* being friendly, fond of company

so'ciable (sō'sha-bl) *adj.* friendly, liking company.—**so'ciably** *adv.*

so'cial (sō'shal) *adj.* 1. friendly. 2. living with others, as *The bee is a social insect.* 3. connected with the way people live, as *social problems.*—*n.* a friendly party.—**so'cialism** *n.* a political plan for state ownership, distribution of wealth, etc.—**so'cialist** *n.*

soci'ety (sō-sī'et-i) *n.* 1. company, as *I find this society very pleasant.* 2. living with others. 3. people and their customs. 4. fashionable life or people. 5. a club, group.—**soci'eties** *pl.*

sociol'ogy *n.* the study of human groups and societies

sock *n.* 1. a short stocking. 2. an inner sole

sock'et *n.* a hole into which something is fitted

sod *n.* a flat piece of earth with grass

so'da *n.* one of the compounds of sodium.—**bicar'bonate of so'da** *n.* a powder used in baking.—**washing so'da** *n.* sodium carbonate.—**so'da-water** *n.* water full of carbon dioxide gas

sod'den *adj.* 1. soaked, wet through. 2. moist and heavy

so'dium *n.* a white, metallic element

so'fa *n.* a long padded seat with a back

soft *adj.* 1. not hard. 2. smooth, pleasant, as *A soft answer turneth away wrath.* 3. not loud, as *soft music.* 4. mild, gentle, as *a soft shower of rain.* 5. kind, as *soft-hearted.* 6. weak, silly. 7. (of drinks) not intoxicating.—*adv.* quietly.—**sof'ten** (sof'n) *v.* to make soft or easy.—**soft'ly** *adv.*—**soft'ness** *n.*

Compare: (with *v.*) allay, alleviate, temper, moderate. *Contrast:* harden, aggravate. *Compare:* (with *adv.*) gently, mildly, delicately, slowly. *Contrast:* roughly, fiercely, hurriedly, loudly

sog'gy *adj.* damp and heavy

soil *n.* earth, ground

soil *v.* to make dirty, to stain.—*n.* dirt

so'journ (sō'jurn) *v.* to stay for a time.—*n.*—**soj'ourner** *n.*

Compare: live, dwell, abide, reside

sol'ace (sol'is) *n.* comfort, consolation.—*v.* to cheer

so'lar *adj.* of the sun.—**so'lar sys'tem** *n.* the sun and its planets

sol'der (sol'der) *n.* an easily-melted metal used for joining or mending metal objects. —*v.*

sol'dier (sōl'jer) *n.* 1. a man serving in an army. 2. a man expert in warfare.—*v.* to serve as a soldier.—**sol'dierly** *adj.*—**sol'diery** *n.* soldiers

Note: a large assembly of soldiers composes an *army*, which is subdivided into *divisions*. The usual unit of organisations is a *regiment*, subdivided into *companies*, and further into *platoons*. Two or more regiments working together form a brigade

sole *n.* 1. a kind of flat fish. 2. the under part of a foot. 3. the under part of a shoe, etc. —*v.* to put a sole on the shoe, etc.—**so'ling** *pres. part.*

sole *adj.* single, only.—**sole'ly** *adv.* alone

sol'ecism (sōl'e-sizm) *n.* a breaking of the rules in grammar or manners

sol'emn (sol'em) *adj.* 1. serious. 2. done with ceremony, formal. (See **serious.**)—**solem'nity** *n.* seriousness.—**sol'emnise** *v.* to perform a ceremony, to celebrate, observe, as *to solemnise a marriage*

solic'it (sol-is'it) *v.* to ask urgently, to appeal, invite. (See **beg.**)—**solicitation** (-tā'shun) *n.*

solic'itor (so-lis'i-tor) *n.* 1. a lawyer, legal adviser

solic'itous (so-lis'i-tus) *adj.* anxious.—**soli'citude** *n.* concern, anxiety

sol'id *adj.* 1. not hollow. 2. hard, firm. 3. whole, undivided, as *Public opinion is solid on this question.* 4. reliable. 5. having length, breadth and thickness.—*n.* a solid body.—*pl.* food that is more solid than liquid.—**sol'idly** *adv.*—**solid'ity** *n.* a feeling of being united.—**solid'ify** *v.* to make solid, to become solid.—**solid'ity** *n.*

solil'oquy (sō-lil'ō-kwi) *n.* a speech made to oneself.—**solil'oquies** *pl.*—**solil'oquise** *v.*

sol'itary *adj.* 1. alone, single. 2. lonely, retired, as *He leads a solitary life*

Compare: separate, lone, secluded

sol'itude *n.* 1. a condition of being alone. 2. a lonely spot

so'lo *n.* a piece of music for a single instrument or voice.—**solos** *pl.*—**so'loist** *n.* performer of solo

sol'stice (sol'stis) *n.* the time of the year when the sun is farthest from the equator

solubil'ity *n.* 1. act of dissolving easily. 2. the extent to which a substance will dissolve in a liquid

sol'uble *adj.* 1. which can dissolve. 2. which can be solved

solu'tion (sol-ōō'shun) *n.* 1. the answer to a problem. 2. an explanation. 3. a gas or a solid dissolved in a liquid

solve *v.* to find an answer, to explain.—**sol'ving** *pres. part.*

sol'vent *adj.* able to pay all debts.—*n.* a liquid which can dissolve other substances

som'bre (som'ber) *adj.* dark, gloomy

sombre'ro *n.* a wide-brimmed felt hat

some (sum) *adj.* 1. of uncertain number or quantity, as *He bought some marbles.* 2. indefinite, unspecified, as *Some boy has spilt the ink.* 3. (U.S.) remarkable, nothing like, as *Some chicken! Some neck!*—*adv.* approximately, as *Some five hundred men.* —*pron.* as *I have bought some.*—**some'body** 1. some person. 2. an important person.—**some'one.**—**some'how** in some way

som'ersault (sum'er-sawlt) *n.* turning head over heels.—*v.*

some'thing (sum'thing) *n.* a thing not named or known

some'time (sum'tīm) *adv.* any time, as *Come and see me sometime.*—*adj.* former, as *The sometime ruler of Spain.*—**some'times** at times, now and then

some'what (sum'whot) *n.* something,—*adv.* to some extent, as *somewhat cold*

some'where (sum'whār) *adv.* in, at or to some place

somnam'bulist *n.* a person who walks in his sleep

som'nolent *adj.* sleepy.—*n.* **som'nolence**

son (sun) *n.* a boy child.—**daughter** *fem.*—**son'-in-law** *n.* a daughter's husband

sonat'a (so-naht'a) *n.* a piece of music in several movements for one or two players

song *n.* 1. that which is sung. 2. a poem for singing.—**song'ster** *n.* 1. a singer. 2. a singing-bird.—**song'stress** *fem.*—**to buy something for a song** to pay little for it

Compare: 1. strain, melody, music. 2. air, chant, ditty, lay, anthem, hymn, lyric, psalm

son'ic *adj.* relating to sound

son'net *n.* a poem of fourteen lines with a fixed arrangement of rhymes

sono'rous (sō-nō'rus) *adj.* having a full, deep sound

soon (sōōn) *adv.* 1. before long, as *They will soon be here.* 2. early, as *Come as soon as possible.* 3. willingly, as *I would as soon do it as . . .*

soot *n.* a black substance formed by burning

soothe (sōōth) *v.* to calm, comfort, soften. See **allay.—sooth'ing** *pres. part.*

sooth'sayer *n.* a person who claims to foretell the future

sop *n.* 1. a piece of bread soaked in liquid. 2. something given to soothe, a bribe.—*v.* to soak.—**sop'ping** *pres. part.*—**sopped** *p.t.* and *p. part.*

sophis'ticated (so-fis'ti-kā-ted) *adj.* experienced, artificial, worldly-wise.—**sophis'tication** (-kā'shun) *n.*

Contrast: unsophisticated, ingenuous, artless, callow, inexperienced, simple

soph'omore *n.* (U.S.A.) a second-year university student

so'porific *adj.* causing sleep

sop'py *adj.* very wet, soaking

sopra'no (so-prah'no) *n.* 1. the highest voice in women or boys. 2. a singer with this voice.—**sopra'nos** *pl.*

sor'cerer (sōr'se-rer) *n.* an evil magician, wizard.—**sor'ceress** *fem.*—**sor'cery** *n.* evil magic

sor'did *adj.* 1. dirty, squalid, as *a sordid slum.* 2. mean, base, as *a sordid love of money.*—**sor'didly** *adv.*

sore *adj.* 1. painful. 2. offended, feeling hurt. —*n.* a sore place.—**sore'ly** *adv.* sadly, greatly.—**sore'ness** *n.* pain.—**like a bear with a sore head** bad-tempered.—**a sight for sore eyes** a beautiful sight.—**sore point** a topic that causes offence or disagreement

sor'rel *n.* 1. a reddish-brown colour. 2. a horse of this colour

sor'row (sor'ō) *n.* grief, sadness.—*v.* to grieve, to be sad.—**sor'rowful** *adj.* See **sad.—sor'rowfully** *adv.*

Compare: trouble, mourning, distress, repentance, unhappiness. *Contrast:* joy, rejoicing, happiness, gaiety, jubilation

sor'ry *adj.* 1. feeling regret, pity, etc. 2. mean, poor, as *He was driving a sorry horse.* 3. regrettable, pitiable, as *a sorry sight.*—**sor'rier** *comp.*—**sor'riest** *sup.*

sort *n.* kind, class.—*v.* to arrange in order, separate.—**sort'er** *n.*—**out of sorts** not well

sort'ie (sort'ee) *n.* a sudden rushing out of troops from a besieged place

sot *n.* a drunkard.—**sot'tish** *adj.* stupid

sough (sow, suf) *n.* the sighing of the wind. —*v.*

sought (sawt) *p.t.* and *p. part.* of seek

soul (sōl) *n.* 1. the spiritual part of a human being. 2. a person, as *There were a hundred souls on board.*—**soul'ful** *adj.* showing deep feeling.—**soul'less** *adj.*

sound *n.* what can be heard, noise.—*v.* 1. to make a sound. 2. to cause to sound, as *to sound the alarm.* 3. to pronounce, as *This sounds the doom of tyranny.* 4. to seem, as *It sounds very unlikely.*—**sound'-proof** *adj.* made to keep out sound.—**to break the sound barrier** to fly faster than sound, i.e. faster than 760 miles per hour

sound *adj.* 1. healthy, in good condition, whole. 2. safe. 3. reasonable, sensible, as *a sound scheme.* 4. deep, hearty, as *a sound thrashing.*—**sound'ly** *adv.* thoroughly —**sound'ness** *n.*

sound *v.* 1. to find the depth of, e.g. water by using a line and plummet. 2. to test, examine

sound *n.* a strait, a narrow strip of sea

soup (sōōp) *n.* liquid food made, e.g. by boiling meat and vegetables.—**in the soup** in trouble

sour *adj.* 1. tasting like lemon, acid. 2. fermented. 3. bad-tempered.—*v.* to turn sour.—**sour'ly** *adv.*—**sour'ness** *n.*—**sour grapes** something one pretends to dislike because one cannot have it

source (sōrs) *n.* 1. a spring, fountain. 2. a beginning, place from which something comes

souse (sowz) *v.* 1. to put in brine or vinegar. 2. to soak

south *n.* the cardinal point opposite to the north.—*adj.* facing towards the south.—*adv.* towards the south.—**south-east'** *n.* half-way between south and east.—**south'erly** (sUTH'er-li) *adj.*—**south'ern** (sUTH'ern) *adj.*—**south'wards** *adv.* towards the south.—**south-west'** *n.* half-way between south and west.—**south'west'erly** *adj.*—**south-west'ern** *adj.*

souvenir' (sōō-ven-eer') *n.* something given or kept in remembrance

sou'west'er *n.* a waterproof hat with a flap to protect the neck

sov'ereign (sov'rin) *n.* 1. a supreme ruler, monarch. See **king.** 2. a British gold coin, worth twenty shillings.—*adj.* 1. supreme, greatest, as *a sovereign remedy.* 2. independent, as *a sovereign state.*—**sov'ereignty** *n.* supreme authority

soviet' *n.* a council, an assembly forming part of the Russian government.—**Soviet Union** the modern name for Russia

sow *n.* a female pig.—**boar, hog, swine** *masc.*

sow (sō) *v.* 1. to scatter seed. 2. to spread abroad.—**sow'ing** *pres. part.*—**sowed** *p.t.*—**sowed, sown** *p. part.*—**sow'er** *n.*—**to sow one's wild oats** to act foolishly when young

soy'a *n.* a bean, grown in Asia, used in making oil cattle food, flour and sauce

spa (spah) *n.* 1. a mineral spring. 2. a place where there is one

space (spās) *n.* 1. room, place. 2. distance. 3. length of time. 4. the expanse of the universe.—*v.* to place at intervals, to separate (often followed by *out*).—**spa'cing** *pres. part.*—**space'man** *n.* a traveller in space.—**space'ship** *n.* a rocket or vehicle travelling in space.—**outer space** space beyond the solar system

spa'cious (spā'shus) *adj.* vast, ample, roomy

spade *n.* a tool used for digging

spaghet'ti (spa-get'i) *n.* long, thin tubes of flour paste used for food

Spain *n.* a country of south-western Europe.

—**Span'iard** *n.* a native of Spain.—*adj.* **Span'ish**

span *n.* 1. the space from thumb to little finger-tip when the hand is extended, nine inches. 2. a space of time, as *Seventy years is man's span of life.* 3. distance across an arch, or from wing-tip to wing-tip. 4. a team of oxen.—*v.* 1. to stretch over, as *The bridge spans the stream.* 2. to measure with the hand.—**span'ning** *pres. part.*—**spanned** *p.t.* and *p. part.*

span'gle (spang'gl) *n.* a small piece of glittering metal used as ornament.—*v.* to glitter

span'iel *n.* a dog with long-drooping ears and silky hair

spank (spangk) *v.* to smack.—*n.*

span'ner *n.* a tool for gripping nut of a screw, etc.

spar *n.* a pole, esp. as part of a ship's rigging

spar *v.* 1. to box, to make motions as though boxing. 2. (with) to dispute, esp. in fun.—**spar'ring** *pres. part.*—**sparred** *p.t.* and *p. part.*

spare *v.* 1. to save, do without, as *Spare the rod and spoil the child.* 2. to save from hurt, as *The enemy spared the inhabitants of the town.* 3. to lend, give, as *Please spare a copper.*—**spa'ring** *pres. part.*—*adj.* 1. extra, not in use, as *a spare part.* 2. thin, frugal.—**spa'ring** *adj.* saving, economical.—**spa'ringly** *adv.*—**spare part** extra part kept as a replacement for a part in an engine.—**spare time** leisure

spark *n.* 1. a small, burning bit, e.g. of wood. 2. a trace.—*v.* to send out sparks.—**spark'ing plug** *n.* a part fitted into a petrol engine to ignite the mixture of petrol and air

spark'le *n.* 1. a glitter, twinkle. 2. gaiety, liveliness. *v.* 1. to emit small sparks, to glitter. 2. to be witty and lively

spar'row (spar'ō) *n.* a small, brown bird, common in towns

sparse *adj.* thinly scattered

spar'tan *adj.* suffering hardship or pain without flinching

spasm (spazm) *n.* 1. a sudden, muscular movement, twitching. 2. a short spell of pain, energy, temper, etc.—**spasmod'ic** *adj.* sudden and irregular

spat *n.* a short, cloth gaiter

spate *n.* a sudden flood in a river

spa'tial (spā'shal) *adj.* of space

spat'ter *v.* 1. to splash. 2. to fall in drops.—*n.*

spat'ula *n.* a tool with a broad, flat blade for mixing or spreading

spawn *n.* eggs of frogs, fishes, etc.—*v.* to produce eggs

speak (speek) *v.* 1. to talk, say something. 2. to converse. 3. to make a speech. See say—**speak'ing** *pres. part.*—**spoke, spake** (old form), **spo'ken** *p. part.*—**speak'er** *n.* 1. a person who speaks. 2. a chairman, president.—**to speak up** to speak loudly and clearly.—**roughly speaking** in general. —**on speaking terms** friendly

spear *n.* a long, pointed weapon.—*v.* to pierce with a spear

spec'ial (spesh'al) *adj.* 1. unusual. 2. of a particular kind. 3. for a particular person or purpose.—**spec'ialist** *n.* a person who gives himself up to a particular subject.—**spec'ialise** *v.* to be a specialist.—**spec'ially** *adv.* particularly.—**spec'ialty** (spe'shi-alti) *n.* a special product, study, etc.

spe'cies (spee'sheez) *n.* 1. a class of animals or plants having certain characteristics in common. 2. a kind, sort.—**spe'cies** *pl.*

specif'ic (spe-sif'ik) *adj.* 1. definite. 2. peculiar to.—*n.* a cure for a particular disease. —**specif'ically** *adv.*

specifica'tion (spes-i-fi-kā'shun) *n.* a detailed description

spec'ify (spes'-ifī) *v.* to mention definitely, to give details.—**spec'ifying** *pres. part.*—**spe'cified** *p.t.* and *p. part.*

spe'cimen (spes'i-men) *n.* a sample, part used to show the quality of the whole

spe'cious (spee'shus) *adj.* having an appearance of right, plausible, as *specious excuses*

speck *n.* 1. a small spot, mark. 2. a particle, small bit.—*v.* to mark with specks.—**speck'led** *adj.* spotted, with specks

spec'tacle *n.* a show, a public exhibition.—*pl.* glasses to correct a person's sight.—**spectac'ular** *adj.* showy

specta'tor *n.* one who looks on

spec'tre *n.* a ghost.—**spec'tral** *adj.*

spec'troscope *n.* an instrument for breaking up light and examining its spectrum

spec'trum *n.* the coloured band into which a beam of light can be broken up.—*pl.* **spec'tra**

spec'ulate *v.* 1. to wonder and guess about something, to reflect. 2. to buy or sell at a risk, in the hope of big profits.—**spec'ulating** *pres. part.*—**specula'tion** (-lā'shun) *n.* —**spec'ulative** *adj.*—**spec'ulator** *n.* a person speculating in business

Compare: 1. conjecture, ponder, theorise. 2. gamble, venture, risk

speech 1. the power of speaking. 2. speaking, talk, formal address, as *The Prime Minister made a speech.* 3. a manner of speaking. 4. a language.—**speech'es** *pl.*—**speech'ify** *v.* to make speeches.—**speech'less** *adj.* unable to speak

Note: a group of people listening to a *speech* is called the *audience*

speed *n.* 1. swift movement, rapidity. 2. pace. —*v.* 1. to go fast. 2. to wish or give success to, as *God speed the plough.* 3. to see off (on a journey).—**sped** *p. part.* and *p.t.*—**speed'ily** *adv.* soon.—**speed'boat** *n.* a fast motor-boat.—**speedom'eter** *n.* an instrument to showspeed.—**speed'way** *n.* a track for fast driving.—**speed'y** *adj.* quick

spell *v.* 1. to write or say the letters of a word. 2. to spell correctly. 3. to imply, mean, as *This spells his ruin.*—**spel'ling**

pres. part.—**spelt, spelled** *p.t.* and *p. part.*—*n.* 1. words having magic power. 2. charm, fascination, as *to cast a spell over someone, under her spell.* 3. (Aus.) a period of rest from work, as *to have a spell.*—**spell'-bound** *adj.* fascinated.—**spel'ling** *n.* the way a word is spelt

spell *n.* 1. a short period of time or work. 2. in Australia, a rest during work

spend *v.* 1. to pay out money. 2. to use up, as *to spend one's time.*—**spent** *p.t.* and *p. part.*—**spend'thrift** *n.* person who wastes money

spew *v.* to vomit

sphere (sfeer) *n.* 1. a round body, ball, globe. 2. the place in which a person works, has influence, etc.—**spher'ical** (sfer'i-kal) *adj.* round.—**spher'oid** *n.* a body which is nearly a sphere

sphinx (sfingks) *n.* 1. a monster in ancient fables, half woman, half lion. 2. a statue of this, esp. one in Egypt. 3. a mysterious person

spice (spīs) *n.* 1. a vegetable substance used in flavouring, e.g. ginger, cloves, cinnamon, etc. 2. a trace.—*v.* to season with spices.—**spi'cy** *adj.*

spick-and-span' *adj.* very clean

spi'der *n.* a small animal with eight legs, which spins a web.—*adj.* **spi'dery** very thin

spiel (speel) *n.* 1. set advice. 2. a wordy explanation.—*v.* to talk plausibly or glibly.—**spiel'er** one who lives on his wits

spike *n.* 1. a sharp point. 2. a nail. 3. an ear of corn, long flower-cluster.—*v.* 1. to put spikes on. 2. to pierce.—**spi'ky** *adj.*

spill *v.* 1. to let liquid run out, to pour out. 2. to upset, let fall. 3. to flow over.—**spil'ling** *pres. part.*—**split, spilled** *p.t.* and *p. part.*—*n.* an accident, mishap

spill *n.* a strip of wood or twist of paper for lighting candles, etc.

spin *v.* 1. to twist wool, cotton, flax, etc. into thread. 2. to turn like a top.—**spin'ning** *pres. part.*—**span, spun** *p.t.*—**spun** *p. part.*—*n.* a spinning, as *The aeroplane got into a spin*

spin'ach *n.* a plant whose leaves can be eaten

spi'nal *adj.* belonging to the spine

spin'dle *n.* 1. the rod on which spun thread is wound. 2. a thin shaft about which something revolves

spin-drier *n.* a machine that dries washed clothes as it whirls them round

spin'drift *n.* spray blown from the sea's surface

spine *n.* 1. the backbone. 2. a thorn, prickle.—**spine'less** *adj.* weak

spin'et *n.* a musical instrument like a harpsichord

spin'ney *n.* a small wood, copse. See **coppice**

spin'ster *n.* an unmarried woman.—**bach'elor** *masc.*

spi'ny (spī'nī) *adj.* covered with spines or thorns

spi'ral *adj.* coiled, like the thread of a screw.—*n.* a continuous coil—**spi'rally** *adv.*

spire *n.* 1. the pointed part of a steeple. 2. a pointed stem

spir'it *n.* 1. soul. 2. a ghost. 3. essential meaning, as *We must keep the spirit as well as the letter of the agreement.* 4. courage, energy. 5. a rousing influence. 6. alcoholic liquor.—*v.* to carry away secretly (usually followed by *away* or *off*).—**spir'ited** *adj.* lively, courageous.—**spir'itless** *adj.* depressed, without energy.—**good spirits** cheerfulness.—**low spirits, poor spirits** unhappiness, despondency.—**spir'it-level** *n.* an instrument which shows a horizontal level by an air-bubble in alcohol (or oil)

spir'itual *adj.* 1. of the soul or spirit. 2. caring for things of the soul. 3. sacred, religious.—*n.* a negro religious song

spir'itualism *n.* a belief that the spirits of the dead can give messages to the living.—**spir'itualist** *n.* believer in spiritualism

spir'ituous *adj.* of the nature of or containing alcohol

spit *n.* 1. a pointed rod on which meat is roasted over a fire. 2. a point of land running into the sea.—*v.* to run through with a sword

spit *v.* 1. to throw out saliva from the mouth. 2. to make a sound like spitting.—**spit'ting** *pres. part.*—**spat** *p.t.* and *p. part.*—*n.* saliva.—**to be the dead spit of** to be exactly like

spite *n.* ill will, a wish to hurt.—*v.* to thwart.—**spite'ful** *adj.*—**in spite of** notwithstanding—**to cut off one's nose to spite one's face** to injure oneself in order to hurt someone else

Compare: enmity, hatred, malice, uncharitableness, grudge

spit'tle *n.* saliva, spit

splash *v.* to scatter water, mud, etc.—*n.* 1. splashing, the sound it makes. 2. a patch, spot.—**splash'es** *pl.*—**splash'down** *n.* landing in the sea of a spacecraft

splay *v.* 1. to spread out. 2. to make slanting.—*n.* a slanting surface.—*adj.* spread, slanting, as *splay-footed*

spleen *n.* 1. a gland in the stomach. 2. bad temper, low spirits, spite

splen'did *adj.* 1. brilliant, magnificent. 2. fine, excellent.—**splen'didly** *adv.*

splen'dour *n.* 1. brilliance, great brightness, as *the spendour of the sunset.* 2. glory, magnificence, pomp, as *The coronation was a scene of great splendour*

splice (splīs) *v.* 1. to join ropes by weaving together the untwisted ends. 2. to join wood by overlapping.—**spli'cing** *pres. part.*

splint *n.* a thin piece of wood to hold a broken limb in position

splint'er *n.* a chip, small pointed piece of wood, glass, etc.—*v.* to break, or to be broken into splinters

split *v.* to divide, to break or cut through.—**split'ting** *pres. part.*—**split** *p.t.* and *p. part.* —*n.* a crack or tear.—**to split the difference** to settle a disagreement by each side giving way equally.—**to split hairs** to argue about trifling differences

splutter *v.* 1. to talk excitedly with spitting sounds. 2. to make popping sounds

spoil *v.* 1. to damage, ruin. 2. to plunder, rob, as *The Israelites spoiled the Egyptians.* —**spoils** *n. pl.* booty, plunder.—**spoil'ing** *pres. part.*—**spoilt, spoiled** *p.t.* and *p. part.* —**to be spoiling for** to be eager for

spoke *n.* one of the bars joining the centre of a wheel to the rim.—**to put a spoke in someone's wheel** to interfere with his plans

spoke'shave *n.* a small plane with a handle at either end

spokes'man (spōks'man) *n.* a person who speaks for others

spolia'tion (spō-li-ā'shun) *n.* robbery, plunder, destruction

sponge (spunj) *n.* 1. a kind of sea-animal. 2. its framework used for cleaning. 3. any porous substance resembling this, e.g. *sponge-cake.*—*v.* 1. to wipe or wash with a sponge. 2. (on) to live at someone else's expense, to impose on the generosity of others.—**spon'ging** (spun'jing) *pres. part.*—**spon'gy** *adj.* soft and full of holes.—**to throw up the sponge** to admit defeat

spon'sor *n.* 1. a person who is responsible for another. 2. a godfather, godmother.—*v.* to answer for, support, as *He sponsored his brother's application for membership of the club*

spontane'ity *n.* being spontaneous, without compulsion

sponta'neous *adj.* 1. natural, without being compelled. 2. acting from its own energy

Compare: instinctive, involuntary, voluntary, willing

spool *n.* a bobbin, reel

spoon *n.* an instrument consisting of a shallow bowl on the end of a handle, used in taking food.—**spoon'ful** *n.* what a spoon can hold.—**spoon'fuls** *pl.*

spoor *n.* the track or trail of a wild animal

sporad'ic *adj.* occurring now and then, separate.—**sporad'ically** *adv.*

spore *n.* a plant germ, seed

spor'ran *n.* a pouch worn in front of a kilt

sport *n.* 1. fun, amusement. 2. outdoor games, hunting, etc. 3. joking, ridicule, as *to make sport of anyone or anything.* 4. a good-humoured person, one who does not mind being teased or losing a game. 5. a plant or animal varying from the normal type, a freak.—*v.* 1. to play. 2. to display, as *to sport a new hat.*—**sport'ive** *adj.* playful.—**sports'man** *n.* 1. a person who hunts, etc. 2. one who loses cheerfully, or is ready to take a chance.—**sports'men** *pl.*

spot *n.* 1. mark, speck, stain. 2. place.—*v.* 1. to become spotted. 2. to make spots on. 3. notice, identify.—**spot'ting** *pres. part.*—**spot'ted** *p.t.* and *p. part.*—**spot'less** *adj.*—**spot'lessly** *adv.*—**spot'light** *n.* 1. a strong light thrown on a person, e.g. on the stage. 2. a lamp used to throw light.—**spot'ted** *adj.* marked with spots.—**spot'ty** *adj.* spotted.—**to put on a spot** to put in an unpleasant position

spouse (spowz) *n.* a husband or wife

spout *v.* to pour out in a stream or spray.—*n.* 1. a lip or tube for pouring liquid. 2. a stream, jet

sprain *v.* to twist a muscle.—*n.*

sprat *n.* a small fish

sprawl *v.* to lie with the limbs spread out.—*n.*

spray *n.* 1. a branch with its flowers or leaves. 2. a sprinkle of flung liquid. 3. an instrument for spraying.—*v.* to sprinkle.—**spray'er** *n.*

spread (spred) *v.* 1. to stretch out, as *to spread a tablecloth.* 2. to scatter, as *to spread news.* 3. to smear, put a layer on a surface, as *to spread butter on bread.* 4. to become scattered.—**spread** *p.t.* and *p. part.*—*n.* 1. extent. 2. (slang) a good meal

spree *n.* fun, frolic

sprig *n.* a twig, small branch

spright'ly (sprīt'li) *adj.* lively, brisk.—**spright'lier** *comp.*—**spright'liest** *sup.*

Compare: blithe, airy, active. *Contrast:* heavy, clumsy, slow, sluggish

spring *v.* 1. to jump, leap. 2. to burst out. 3. to rise, to be descended from.—**sprang** *p.t.*—**sprung** *p. part.*—*n.* 1. a leap, jump. 2. a place where water comes from the earth. 3. beginning, cause. 4. coiled metal with elastic force. 5. the season after winter.—**spring'-balance** *n.* a spring with a scale for measuring weights.—**spring'-board** *n.* a diving board.—**spring'tide** *n.* 1. spring-time. 2. a high tide at new or full moon.—**to spring'-clean** to clean a house thoroughly, usually in spring.—**spring'-time** *n.*—**spring'y** *adj.* elastic

spring'bok *n.* an African antelope

sprin'kle (spring'kl) *v.* to scatter small drops or bits.—*n.*—**sprink'ling** *pres. part.* —*n.* a small quantity

sprint *v.* to run a short distance at great speed.—*n.*—**sprint'er** *n.*

sprite *n.* an elf, fairy

sprock'et *n.* a cog on a wheel

sprout *v.* to put out shoots, begin to grow.—*n.*

spruce (sprōōs) *n.* a kind of fir-tree

spruce (sprōōs) *adj.* neat in dress

spry *adj.* lively, nimble

spume *n.* spray, foam

spur *n.* 1. a pricking instrument on a horseman's heel. 2. anything that urges one on. 3. a point sticking out.—*v*, to urge on, to excite, incite.—**spur'ring** *pres. part.*—**spurred** *p.t.* and *p. part.*—**on the spur of the moment** suddenly.—**to win one's spurs** to win fame

spu'rious (spū'ri-us) *adj.* sham, false

spurn *v.* to push away with scorn, to reject, as *They have spurned our offered friendship*

spurt, spirt *n.* 1. a jet, stream. 2. a short, sudden effort.—*v.* to rush out, squirt

sput'nik *n.* an artificial satellite launched by Russia in 1957

spy *n.* a person who secretly gets information from the enemy.—**spies** *pl.*—*v.* 1. to find out by watching. 2. to see.—**spy'ing** *pres. part.*—**spied** *p.t.* and *p. part.*—**spy'-glass** *n.* a small telescope

squab'ble (skwob'l) *v.* to quarrel noisily.—**squab'bling** *pres. part.*

squad (skwod) *n.* a small party of soldiers

squad'ron (skwod'ron) *n.* a division of a cavalry regiment, fleet or air force.—**squad'ron-lead'er** *n.* an R.A.F. officer above Flight-Lieutenant and below Wing-Commander

squal'id (skwol'id) *adj.* dirty, wretched

squall (skwawl) *v.* to scream, cry.—*n.* a sudden violent storm.—**squal'ly** *adj.*

squal'or (skwol'or) *n.* filth, misery

squan'der (skwon'der) *v.* to waste, to spend wastefully

square (skwār) *n.* 1. a figure having four equal sides and four right angles. 2. an open space in a town. 3. the product of a number multiplied by itself. 4. an instrument for drawing right angles.—*adj.* 1. square in form. 2. honest, fair, as *a square deal*. 3. ample, as *a square meal*.—*v.* to agree with, as *His story seems to square with the facts*.—**squa'ring** *pres. part.*—**square'ness** *n.*—**all square** both sides equal in a game.—**square dance** a dance for groups of four dancers.—**square foot** (inch, etc.) the area of a square each side of which is a foot (inch, etc.).—**square root** of a number which when multiplied by itself gives the original number. e.g. 4 *is the square root of* 16

squash (skwosh) *v.* 1. to crush flat, to press.—*n.* 1. something squashed, a crowd. 2. a game played with rackets and soft balls

squat (skwot) *v.* 1. to sit on the heels, or with knees drawn up. 2. to settle on land without leave.—**squat'ting** *pres. part.*—**squat'ted** *p.t.* and *p. part.*—*adj.* short and thick.—**squat'ter** *n.* 1. a person who settles on land without leave. 2. (Aus.) a tenant of the Crown renting large areas for pasturage. 3. (Aus.) any other owner of large pastoral property

squaw *n.* a North American Indian wife or woman

squawk (skwawk) *v.* to make a harsh, frightened sound.—*n.*

squeak (skweek) *v.* to make a small, shrill sound.—*n.*

squeal (skweel) *v.* to make a shrill cry.—*n.*

squeam'ish *adj.* 1. easily made sick. 2. easily shocked

Compare: fastidious, scrupulous

squeeze (skweez) *v.* 1. to press, crush. 2. to force out.—**squee'zing** *pres. part.*

squib *n.* 1. a small firework. 2. (Aus.) a coward

squint *v.* to have the eyes turned in different directions.—*n.*

squire (skwīr) *n.* 1. a country gentleman. 2. a lady's escort.—*v.*

squirm *v.* to twist, to wriggle

squir'rel (skwir'el) *n.* a small animal living in trees, and having a long, bushy tail

squirt *v.* to force out liquid in a jet.—*n.* an instrument for squirting

stab *v.* to pierce with a pointed weapon.—**stab'bing** *pres. part.*—**stabbed** *p.t.* and *p. part.*—*n.* a blow or wound made with a pointed weapon

stabil'ity *n.* firmness, being likely to last.—**sta'bilise** *v.* to make steady, firm.—**stabilisation'** (-zā'shun) *n.*—**sta'biliser** *n.* a fin or instrument to make a ship or aeroplane steady

sta'ble *n.* a building where horses are kept.—*v.* to put into a stable.—**sta'bling** *pres. part.*

sta'ble *adj.* firm, steady, resolute

Compare: durable, lasting, constant, permanent. *Contrast:* unstable, changeable, irresolute, infirm, unsteady

stack *n.* 1. a pile or heap, esp. of hay or straw. 2. a tall chimney.—*v.* to pile into a stack

sta'dium *n.* a sports ground with seats all round for spectators.—**sta'dia, sta'diums** *pl.*

staff (stahf) *n.* 1. a stick, pole.—**staffs, staves** *pl.* 2. a group of assistants in office, school, etc.—**staffs** *pl.* 3. the five lines on which music is written.—**staves** *pl.*

stag *n.* a male deer.—**hind** *fem.*

stage (stāj) *n.* 1. a platform. 2. a platform in a theatre. 3. actors, the drama. 4. a scene of action. 5. a stopping-place, distance between stops. 6. degree, step, period, as *The battle had reached a critical stage.*—*v.* to produce (a play, etc.)—**stage-coach** *n.* passenger-coach following a regular route.—**stage'-fright** *n.* nervousness in front of an audience.—**stage'struck** *adj.* eagerly wanting to become an actor or actress

stagg'er *v.* 1. to walk unsteadily, to sway reel, totter. 2. to shake, shock

stag'nant *adj.* 1. not flowing, standing still, as *stagnant waters*. 2. dull, not changing.—**stagnate'** *v.* to be stagnant.—**stagna'tion** (-nā'shun) *n.*

staid *adj.* of sober and quiet character

Compare: grave, serious, regular, composed. *Contrast:* flighty, lively, frolicsome

stain *n.* 1. a spot, mark. 2. a colouring substance.—*v.* 1. to soil, mark. 2. to spoil by disgrace.—**stain'less** *adj.*

stair *n.* 1. a set of steps in a house. 2. one step.—**stair'case** *n.* a flight of steps.—**stair'way** *n.* stairs

stake *n.* 1. a pointed stick or post. 2. money

risked on the result of a race, etc.—*v.* 1. to mark off with stakes. 2. to risk money on a result

stal'actite *n.* a lime-formation, shaped like an icicle, hanging from the roof of a cave

stal'agmite *n.* a lime-formation, cone-shaped, formed on the floor of a cave

stale *adj.* not fresh, old.—**stale'mate** *n.* a position in chess in which no move can be made

Compare: hackneyed, trite, weary, overdone, musty. *Contrast:* new, unusual, sparkling

stalk (stawk) *n.* the stem of a plant or flower

stalk (stawk) *v.* 1. to approach game stealthily in order to catch or kill. 2. to walk stiffly or haughtily

stall (stawl) *n.* 1. a space in a stable for one animal. 2. a stand for selling things in a market, etc. 3. a seat in the chancel of church. 4. the front seat in theatre.—*v.* 1. to put in a stall. 2. to stick fast (esp. of machinery). 3. (of an aeroplane) to lose flying speed and become uncontrollable. 4. to delay deliberately.

stal'lion *n.* a male horse.—**mare** *fem.*

stal'wart (stawl'wart) *adj.* sturdy, brave, strong, firm.—*n.*

Compare: brawny, robust, burly, dependable, bold. *Contrast:* puny, feeble, weak, pale, timid

sta'men *n.* the part of the flower that holds the pollen

stam'ina *n.* strength, endurance

stam'mer *v.* to speak hesitatingly, to stutter. —*n.*

stamp *v.* 1. to put down a foot with force. 2. to make a mark on. 3. to fix a postage stamp on.—*n.* 1. a stamping of the foot. 2. a mark. 3. a piece of gummed paper printed with a design to show postage has been paid

stampede' (stam-peed') *n.* a sudden rush of terrified people or animals.—*v.* to rush madly

stance *n.* the way a player stands before striking a golf or cricket ball

stand *v.* 1. to be on one's feet, erect. 2. to rise to one's feet. 3. to place, set, as *Stand the lamp on the table.* 4. to take up a position, as *He was told to stand in front of the class.* 5. to bear, endure, as *I can't stand it any longer.* 6. to halt, stop.—**stood** *p.t.* and *p. part.*—*n.* 1. a stop, halt. 2. resistance. 3. something to stand things on or in. 4. raised wooden seats, esp. *grand-stand.* —**stand'-by** *n.* something kept for emergency.—**stand'-in** *n.* someone who acts in place of another.—**to stand by** 1. to support (someone). 2. to hold firmly to what one has said.—**to stand for** to signify.—**to stand one's ground** to be firm.—**to stand well with someone** to be thought well of by him.—**to stand to win** to be in a position to win.—**to stand the test** to prove reliable. —**to stand up for** to defend.—**to stand in good stead** to be good in emergency.—**to make a stand** to resist firmly.—**it stands to reason** it is reasonable

stan'dard *n.* 1. a flag, symbol. 2. a test or measure by which things are compared, as *This work is not up to your usual standard.* 3. an upright support.—*adj.* according to rule.—**stan'dardise** *v.* to make all alike in size, weight, shape, etc.

stand'ing *adj.* 1. erect, upright. 2. lasting, permanent, as *The master's absent-mindedness was a standing source of amusement to the boys.* 3. stagnant.—*n.* 1. duration, as *a quarrel of many years' standing.* 2. reputation, as *a man of standing in the town*

stand'pipe *n.* an upright pipe serving as a hydrant

stand'point *n.* point of view, opinion

stand'still *n.* a state of stopping

stan'za *n.* a group of lines of poetry.—**stan'zas** *pl.*

sta'ple *n.* 1. a U-shaped piece of metal with pointed ends to drive into wood. 2. the most important article grown or manufactured in a place. 3. cotton or wool fibre. —*adj.* chief, as *The staple diet of the Chinese is rice.*—**stapler** *n.* a device for fastening papers together with small metal clips.—*v.* **to staple** to fasten paper with a stapler

star *n.* 1. a heavenly body seen as a twinkling point of light. 2. a sign, asterisk. 3. a famous player, actor, etc. 4. something shaped with five points.—*v.* 1. to mark with a star. 2. to take chief part (in film, play, etc.).—**star'ring** *pres. part.*—**starred** *p.t.* and *p. part.*

star'board (star'bōrd) *n.* the right-hand side of a ship, looking forward.—*adj.*

starch *n.* a substance found in potatoes, rice, etc. and used for stiffening linen.—*v.*—**starch'y** *adj.* 1. containing starch. 2. stiff. 3. formal, prim

star'dom *n.* being a star actor or actress

stare *v.* to look fixedly, with eyes wide open. —*n.*—**sta'ring** *pres. part.*

Compare: gaze, peer, look, scan

stark *adj.* 1. stiff. 2. bleak. 3. downright, absolute, as *stark nonsense, madness,* etc.—*adv.* completely, as *stark mad, stark naked*

star'ry *adj.* 1. full of stars. 2. shining

start *v.* 1. to make a sudden movement. 2. to begin a journey, etc. 3. to set going.—*n.* 1. a sudden movement. 2. a beginning. 3. a departure of competitors in race.—**start'er** *n.* person giving signal for start.—**by fits and starts** on and off, erratically

Compare: (with *n.*) commencement, outset, initiation, source, inauguration, inception, outset. *Contrast:* finish, end, conclusion, termination

start'le *v.* to surprise, give a fright to.—**start'ling** *pres. part.*

starva'tion (-vā'shun) *n.* starving

starve *v.* 1. to die of hunger. 2. to suffer from cold or hunger. 3. to keep without food.—**star'ving** *pres. part.*—**starve'ling** *n.* a starving person

state *n.* 1. condition, as *in a state of decay.* 2. a political, self-governing body, as *In some countries the railways are owned by the state.* (See **nation, government.**) 3. ceremony, as *the king rode in state.* 4. rank, as *the ambassador was received with ceremony befitting his state.*—*v.* to express in words, say definitely.—**sta'ting** *pres. part.*

state'ly *adj.* dignified, imposing, regal.—**state'lier** *comp.*—**state'liest** *sup.*

state'ment *n.* a declaration, account, report

states'man *n.* man skilled in managing the affairs of a state.—**states'men** *pl.*—**states'manship** *n.*

stat'ic *adj.* 1. standing still. 2. about bodies at rest or balancing each other.—**stat'ic** *n.* (radio) a sharp, jarring noise made by electrical disturbances, such as thunderstorms, in the air.—**static electricity** an electric charge on a body, not moving as an electric current

sta'tion (stā'shun) *n.* 1. a place where something or someone stands. 2. a position in life. 3. a stopping-place for railway trains. 4. a post for fireman, soldiers, police, etc. 5. (Aus.) originally the homestead and outbuildings on a squatter's property; now, the whole property.—*v.* to place

sta'tionary (stā'shun-ar-i) *adj.* standing still, not changing

Note: Do not confuse this word with **stationery**

sta'tioner (stā'shun-er) *n.* person who sells stationery.—**sta'tionery** *n.* writing materials, ink, paper, pencils, etc.

Note: Do not confuse this word with **stationary**

statis'tics *n.pl.* 1. facts and numbers collected and arranged. 2. the study of these

stat'uary *n.* statues

stat'ue *n.* an image carved or cast to represent a person or animal.—**statuesque'** *adj.* like a statue, calm, dignified.—**statuette'** *n.* a small statue

stat'ure *n.* the height of a person

sta'tus (stā'tus) *n.* position, standing, rank

stat'ute *n.* a law.—**stat'utory** *adj.*

staunch, stanch (stawnch, stahnch) *v.* to stop a flow of blood.—*adj.* strong, loyal

stave *n.* 1. one of the curved pieces forming a cask, tub, etc. 2. a verse of a song. 3. a cudgel, staff.—*v.* to break a hole in.—**to stave off** to delay a difficulty.—**sta'ving** *pres. part.*—**stove, staved** *p.t.* and *p. part.*

stay *v.* 1. to remain. 2. to stop. 3. to reside for a time (*with* someone or *at* some place). 4. to delay.—**stayed** *p.t.* and *p. part.*—*n.* time spent somewhere.—**to stay put** to remain unmoving

Compare: 1. abide, rest, wait. 2. prevent. 3. sojourn. 4. hinder, suspend

stay *n.* 1. a support. 2. a rope supporting a mast, etc.—*v.* to support

stead (sted) *n.* place, as *I went in his stead.*—**to stand in good stead** to be useful in emergency

stead'fast (sted'fahst) *adj.* firm, unchanging

Compare: resolute, unswerving, constant, staunch, unshaken, determined. *Contrast:* irresolute, untrustworthy, changeable, vacillating, fickle, capricious

stead'ily (sted'i-li) *adv.* in a steady way, firmly.—**stead'iness** *n.* being steady

stead'y (sted'i) *adj.* 1. firm. 2. regular, even. 3. sober, reliable.—**stead'ier** *comp.*—**stead'iest** *sup.*—*v.* to make steady, to check

steak (stāk) *n.* a slice of meat or fish for frying

steal (steel) *v.* 1. to take something that belongs to someone else, to rob. 2. to move secretly, as *He stole out of the room when no one was looking.*—**stole** *p.t.*—**sto'len** *p. part.*—**to steal a march on someone** to gain an advantage by acting quickly

stealth (stelth) *n.* secretly, stealthy action.—**stealth'y** *adj.* sly, secret.—**stealth'ily** *adv.*

steam *n.* vapour from boiling water.—*v.* 1. to give off steam. 2. to cook with steam. 3. to move by steam.—**steam'boat** *n.*—**steam engine** *n.*—**steam'er** *n.* 1. a steamship. 2. a container for cooking by steam.—**steam'y** *adj.*

steed *n.* (poetry) a horse, a war horse

steel *n.* 1. a hard metal made by mixing carbon in iron. 2. a tool or weapon of steel.—*v.* to harden.—*adj.* made of steel.—**steel'y** *adj.*—**steel wool** *n.* a pad of steel shavings used for scouring.—**steel'yard** *n.* a balance with a sliding weight used for weighing

steep *adj.* sloping sharply.—**steep'ly** *adv.*

steep *v.* to soak

steep'le *n.* a church tower with a spire.—**steep'le-chase** *n.* a cross-country horse-race.—**steep'le-jack** *n.* a man who repairs steeples, chimneys, etc.

steer *n.* a young mule or bullock

steer *v.* 1. to guide a ship, car, etc. 2. to direct one's course.—**steer'age** *n.* 1. steering. 2. part of a ship occupied by passengers paying the lowest fares.—**steers'-man** *n.* a man who steers ship

stel'lar *adj.* of stars

stem *n.* 1. the part of a plant which bears leaves. 2. something resembling this. 3. the front end of a ship

stem *v.* to stop, check, resist, as *They tried to stem the tide of failure.*—**stem'ming** *pres. part.*—**stemmed** *p.t.* and *p. part.*

stench *n.* a bad smell

sten'cil (sten'sil) *n.* a thin sheet of metal or waxed sheet with letters or a design cut out, used for painting, duplicating etc.—

v. to use a stencil.—**sten'cilling** *pres. part.* —**sten'cilled** *p.t.* and *p. part.*

stenog'rapher *n.* a person whose work is shorthand writing.—**stenog'raphy** *n.* shorthand writing

stento'rian *adj.* very loud (of voice)

step *v.* 1. to move and set down a foot. 2. to measure by stepping.—**step'ping** *pres. part.* —**stepped** *p.t.* and *p. part.*—*n.* 1. one movement of the leg in walking, etc. 2. a foot-print. 3. sound of someone walking. 4. stair, rung, etc. 5. action, as *What steps have been taken in the matter?* 6. a degree in a scale.—**step'child** *n.* child of husband or wife, by a former marriage.—**step'brother** *n.*—**step'daugh'ter** *n.*—**step'father** *n.*—**step'mother** *n.*—**step'sister** *n.* —**step'son** *n.*—**to step out** to walk fast.—**to step up** to increase.—**to take steps** to take action

steppe *n.* a vast, treeless plain in Russia

stereophon'ic *adj.* (of sound) coming through separate channels to give greater realism

stereoscop'ic *adj.* (of pictures) having a three-dimensional effect

ster'eotyped *adj.* fixed, unchanging

ster'ile *adj.* 1. barren, not productive. 2. free from germs.—**steril'ity** *n.* barrenness. —**ster'ilise** *v.* 1. to make unproductive. 2. to free from germs.—**ster'ilisa'tion** (-zā'shun) *n.*

ster'ling *adj.* 1. of British coin. 2. genuine. 3. of good character.—**Sterling Area** those countries of the world whose currency is connected with British money standards

stern *adj.* 1. severe, strict. 2. determined, as *a stern resolve.*—**stern'ness** *n.*

Compare: 1. hard, grim, austere, forbidding. 2. resolute, unyielding, firm

stern *n.* the hind part of a ship

steth'oscope *n.* a doctor's instrument for listening to heart beats

steve'dore *n.* a man who loads or unloads ships

stew *v.* to cook by boiling slowly.—*n.* food cooked in this way

stew'ard *n.* 1. a man who manages the property of another. 2. an attendant on a ship's passengers.—**stew'ardess** *fem.* 3. official in charge of a race-meeting, etc.—**stew'ardship** *n.* steward's position or work

stick *n.* 1. a thin, rounded piece of wood. 2. something resembling this

stick *v.* 1. to stab, fix, fasten. 2. to attach, to be fastened. 3. to hold fast. 4. to come to a stop.—**stuck** *p.t.* and *p. part.*—**stick'y** *adj.* which sticks.—**stick'ier** *comp.*—**stick'iest** *sup.*—**stick'er** *n.* a gummed label.—**to stick at** to work hard at.—**to stick at nothing** to go to any extremes.—**to stick in one's throat** to be hard to accept.—**to stick it** to bear it to the end.—**to stick out for** to insist on having.—**to stick to someone** to continue to help him

stick'leback *n.* a small, spiny fish

stick'ler *n.* one who insists on trifles of procedure, authority, etc.

stiff *adj.* 1. hard to bend, or move. 2. difficult, as *a stiff examination.* 3. firm. 4. cold, formal, awkward. 5. strong, as *a stiff breeze, a stiff whisky.* 6. high, as *a stiff price.*—**stiff'en** *v.* to become stiff, to make stiff.—**stiff'ly** *adv.*—**stiff'necked** *adj.* obstinate

Compare: rigid, hard, inflexible, constrained. *Contrast:* pliable, limp, easy

sti'fle *v.* 1. to make breathing difficult, smother. 2. to check, keep back, as *to stifle a yawn.*—**sti'fling** *pres. part.*

stig'ma *n.* 1. a brand, mark of disgrace. 2. that part of the pistil of a flower which receives the pollen.—*pl.* **stig'mas.**—**stig'mata** *n.pl.* marks resembling the five wounds of Christ miraculously appearing on the bodies of certain saints.—**stig'matise** *v.* to mark out as bad, to reproach

stile *n.* steps for climbing a wall or fence

stilet'to *n.* 1. a small dagger. 2. a pointed tool for making eyelet-holes.—**stilet'tos** *pl.*

still *adj.* without movement, quiet.—*v.* to calm, make quiet.—*adv.* 1. for all that, as *Still, why does he do it?* 2. yet, as *He is still doing it.* 3. even, as *We had still further to go.* 4. (in poetry) always.—**still'ness** *n.* quiet.—**still'-born** *adj.* born lifeless.—**still'-life** *n.* a painting or arrangement of lifeless objects, such as flowers or fruit

still *n.* an apparatus for distilling

stilt *n.* one of a pair of poles with foot-rests for walking raised from the ground.—**stil'ted** *adj.* stiff, pompous

stim'ulant *n.* drug or food which increases energy.—*adj.* exciting, stimulating

stim'ulate *v.* to rouse, excite, as *The master tried to stimulate an interest in the subject.* —**stim'ulating** *pres. part.*—**stimula'tion** (-lā'shun) *n.*

stim'ulus *n.* something that rouses to activity. —**stim'uli** *pl.*

sting *n.* 1. a prick, wound caused by an insect, nettle, etc. 2. a sharp pain.—*v.* to cause sharp pain, to hurt.—**stung** *p.t.* and *p. part.*

stin'gy (stin'ji) *adj.* mean, miserly.—**stin'gier** *comp.*—**stin'giest** *sup.*

Contrast: See **generous**

stink (stingk) *n.* a strong, bad smell.—*v.* to give out a bad smell.—**stank** *p.t.*—**stunk** *p. part.*

stint *v.* to limit, to be very saving.—*n.* a fixed amount of work

sti'pend (stī'pend) *n.* salary, pay. (See **wages**)

stip'ulate *v.* to insist, make a condition in an agreement.—**stip'ulating** *pres. part.*—**stipula'tion** (-lā'shun) *n.* condition

stir *v.* 1. to move. 2. to mix, e.g. with a spoon. 3. to excite.—**stir'ring** *pres. part.*—**stirred** *p.t.* and *p. part.*—*n.* excitement

stir'rup *n.* a rider's foot-rest hung from saddle

stitch *n.* 1. a complete movement of needle in sewing, knitting, etc. 2. sudden, sharp pain.—**stitch'es** *pl.*—*v.* to sew.—**a stitch in time saves nine** a small piece of work done early enough saves more work later

stoat (stōt) *n.* a kind of weasel, ermine

stock *n.* 1. a stump, post. 2. a race, family. 3. the wooden part of a gun to which the mechanisms of the gun are attached. 4. farm animals, as *livestock.* 5. supply. 6. money invested in a company. 7. a trader's goods, etc. 8. stiff neckband. 9. liquor from meat, etc. used in preparing soups. 10. a flowering plant.—*v.* to supply, to keep a supply.—*adj.* usual, standard, as *I take a stock size in gloves.*—**the stocks** *n.pl.* 1. a frame with holes for the feet of offenders. 2. the frame on which a ship is constructed.—**stock'-broker** *n.* one who deals in stocks and shares.—**stock'rider** (Aus.) man employed to look after cattle, often on unfenced station.—**stock'route** (Aus.) a passage through property required by law to be left for travelling stock.—**stock'man** a man employed in handling, raising or selling cattle.—**stock'whip** whip for driving cattle.—**stock-in-trade** goods for selling.—**stock-still** quite still.—**to take stock** 1. to make a list of goods. 2. to size up a situation or person

stockade' *n.* fence or enclosure of stakes

stock'ing *n.* a close-fitting covering for foot and leg

stock'y *adj.* thick-set, sturdy

stodg'y (stoj'i) *adj.* heavy, dull

stoep (stōōp) *n.* in U.S. and S. Africa, a porch, verandah

sto'ic *n.* 1. a person who is indifferent to pleasure or pain. 2. a person with great self-control.—**stoic, sto'ical** *adj.*—**sto'icism** (-sizm) *n.*

stoke *v.* to feed a fire.—**sto'king** *pres. part.*—**sto'ker** *n.* man who tends a furnace

stole *p.t.* of **steal**

stole *n.* 1. long, narrow band worn by clergymen. 2. a fur worn round the shoulders by ladies

stol'id *adj.* hard to rouse, slow, dull.—**stol'idly** *adv.*—**stolid'ity** *n.*

Compare: heavy, obtuse, lethargic, phlegmatic. *Contrast:* active, acute, susceptible, quick-witted, lively, volatile

sto'ma (stō'ma) *n.* a plant pore.—*pl.* **sto-ma'ta**

stom'ach (stum'ak) *n.* 1. the bag in the body which receives and digests food. 2. appetite, inclination.—*v.* to put up with

stone *n.* 1. a piece of rock, pebble. 2. a gem, 3. a hard case containing seed of fruit. 4. fourteen pounds weight.—*v.* 1. to throw stones at. 2. to remove stones.—**sto'ning** *pres. part.*—*adj.* made of stone.—**sto'ny** *adj.* 1. full of stones. 2. hard.—**stone-blind'** *adj.* completely blind.—**stone-cold'** *adj.* very cold.—**stone-deaf'** *adj.* completely deaf.—**stony-heart'ed** *adj.* merciless

stook *n.* a stack of corn-sheaves.—*v.*

stool *n.* a chair without back or arms

stoop *v.* to bend forward.—*n.* a stooping manner of walking, or sitting

Note: To stoop to some action is to demean onself to do it, e.g. *to stoop to deceit, to telling untruths,* etc.

stop *v.* 1. to fill up, as *He stopped the hole.* 2. to prevent, check, as *I will stop the train.* 3. to remain, as *to stop at home.* 4. to come to an end, to cease, as *The music stopped.* 5. to bring to an end, as *Please stop that noise.*—**stop'ping** *pres. part.*—**stopped** *p.t.* and *p. part.*—*n.* 1. a stopping, being stopped. 2. a punctuation mark.—**stop'-page** *n.*—**stop'per** *n.* cork, etc.—**stop-press'** *n.* very late news printed at the last moment in a newspaper.—**stop'-watch** *n.* a watch which can be started and stopped immediately, for use in timing races, etc.

stor'age (stōr'aj) *n.* storing, place for storing

store *n.* 1. supply, stock. 2. a place for keeping goods. 3. (See **shop.**)—*v.* to keep, put away.—**sto'ring** *pres. part.*—**store'-house** *n.*—**to set store by** to think highly of

sto'rey, sto'ry *n.* a floor, a set of rooms in a house, on the same level.—**sto'reys** *pl.*

stork *n.* a large bird with long neck, legs and bill

storm *n.* 1. strong wind or thunder and rain. 2. a violent disturbance. 3. an attack on a fortified place, as *The citadel was taken by storm.*—*v.* 1. to rage. 2. to attack.—**storm'y** *adj.*—**a storm in a teacup** a fuss about a trifle

Compare: tempest, gale, squall, hurricane, tornado, blizzard

sto'ry *n.* a tale, account.—**sto'ries** *pl.*—**sto'ry-teller** *n.*

Compare: narrative, anecdote, recital, report

stout *adj.* 1. bold, vigorous, strong. (See **stalwart.**) 2. too fat.—*n.* a kind of beer.—**stout'ly** *adv.*—**stout'ness** *n.*

stove *n.* an apparatus for cooking, heating

stow (stō) *v.* to pack away.—**stow'away** *n.* a person who hides on a ship to escape, or to get a free passage

strad'dle *v.* 1. to stand or sit astride of. 2. (of bombs from aircraft) to fall in a line across the target.—**strad'dling** *pres. part.*

strag'gle *v.* to stray, wander, to lag behind.—**strag'gler** *n.*

straight (strāt) *adj.* 1. not bent or curved. 2. honest. 3. level. 4. in order.—*adv.* direct, in a straight line.—**straight'en** *v.* 1. to make straight. 2. to tidy.—**straightfor'ward** *adj.* 1. honest. 2. direct.—**a straight face** an unsmiling expressionless face

straight'way (strāt'wā) *adv.* at once

strain *v.* 1. to stretch. 2. injure, esp. muscles. 3. to make a great effort. 4. to press through, filter.—*n.* 1. stretching force. 2.

violent effort. 3. sprain, injury. 4. tone of speaking or writing, as *I will write to him in the strain you suggest.* 5. part of a tune, as *He heard the strains of a band in the distance.*—**strained** *adj.* not natural.—**strain'er** *n.* sieve, filter, etc.

strain *n.* 1. a breed, race. 2. a streak, trace, as *There is an unpleasant strain of cruelty in his character*

strait *n.* a narrow channel of water connecting two larger areas.—*pl.* difficulty, as *The widow was in sore straits.*—*adj.* narrow, strict.—**strait'en** *v.* to limit.—**strait-laced** *adj.* very strict

strand *n.* shore.—*v.* to run aground.—**strand'ed** *adj.* left helpless, without means of transport

strand *n.* a thread or wire making up a rope when twisted

strange (strānj) *adj.* 1. unfamiliar, not known. 2. unusual, surprising.—**strange'ly** *adv.*—**strange'ness** *n.*

Compare: 1. foreign, alien, rare. 2. odd, queer, extraordinary

stran'ger (strān'jer) *n.* 1. an unknown person. 2. a foreigner. 3. a person new to a place

strang'le (strang'gl) *v.* 1. to kill by choking. 2. to suppress.—**strang'ling** *pres. part.*—**strang'ler** *n.*—**strangula'tion** (-lā'shun) *n.*

strap *n.* a strip of leather, etc. serving as a band.—*v.* 1. to fasten with a strap. 2. to beat with a strap.—**strap'ping** *pres. part.*—**strapped** *p.t.* and *p. part.*—**strap'ping** *adj.* tall and strong

stra'ta (strā'ta, straht'a) *pl.* of **stra'tum**

strat'agem (strat'a-jem) *n.* a trick, clever plan for deceiving an enemy

strate'gic (strat-ee'jik) *adj.* important in strategy.—**strat'egist** *n.* an expert in strategy

strat'egy (strat'e-ji) *n.* generalship, esp. planning military movements on a large scale

Contrast: tactics

strat'osphere *n.* the upper atmosphere above six miles beyond the earth's surface

stra'tum (strā'tum, strah'tum) *n.* a layer forming part of the earth's crust.—**stra'ta** *pl.*

straw *n.* dried stalks of corn, a single stalk.—**straw'board** *n.* cardboard made of straw.—**a straw in the wind** a small sign indicating something important

straw'berry *n.* a creeping plant with red fruit.—**straw'berries** *pl.*

stray *v.* to wander, get lost.—*n.* strayed animal.—*adj.* 1. lost. 2. scattered

streak *n.* 1. a line, stripe, layer. 2. a strain in the character, as *He has a nasty streak.*—*v.* to mark with streaks.—**streak'y** *adj.*

stream *n.* 1. a small river, brook. 2. a flow of liquid. 3. a moving crowd.—*v.* 1. to flow 2. to move.—**stream'er** *n.* ribbon, pennon.—**stream'let** *n.*—**stream'-lined** *adj.* shaped to offer least resistance to air; effective

street *n.* a road in a town with houses on both sides. See **road**

strength *n.* being strong, power.—**strength'en** *v.* to make stronger

Compare: force, vigour, might, toughness, intensity, potency

stren'uous *adj.* 1. active, energetic. 2. requiring much effort.—**stren'uously** *adv.*

Compare: 1. earnest, zealous, ardent, energetic. 2. busy, exacting, laborious

stress *n.* 1. force, pressure, as *We were compelled to act as we did by the stress of circumstances.* 2. importance, accent, as *In the word "father" the stress is on the first syllable.*—*v.* to call into special notice, as *The teacher stressed the importance of neatness.*—he **stress'es**

stretch *v.* 1. to draw out, to hold out. 2. to extend, to spread.—*n.* extent, expanse.—**stretch'es** *pl.*—**stretch'er** *n.* a frame for carrying the sick, wounded, etc.—**to stretch one's legs** to walk about

strew (strōō) *v.* to scatter over a surface, to sprinkle.—**strewed, strowed** *p.t.*—**strewn, strown, strewed,** *p. part.*

strick'en *adj.* struck down with trouble illness, etc. (See **strike**)

strict *adj.* 1. exact. 2. severe, harsh, demanding obedience.—**strict'ly** *adv.*—**strict'ness** *n.*

Contrast: lenient, lax, easy-going

stric'ture *n.* a rebuke, criticism

stride *v.* 1. to walk with long steps. 2. to pass over with one step. (See **walk**).—**stri'ding** *pres. part.*—**strode** *p.t.*—**strid'den** *p. part.*—*n.* a long step.—**to take something in one's stride** to do it without effort

stri'dent *adj.* harsh, shrill

strife *n.* conflict, fighting

strike *v.* 1. to hit, to come sharply against. 2. to make a coin, etc. 3. to come into the mind, as *It strikes me that it must be getting late.* 4. to sound. 5. to stop work because of a grievance. 6. to find gold, etc.—**stri'king** *pres. part.*—**struck** *p.t.* and *p. part.*—**strike out** 1. to make a start esp. in swimming. 2. to cross out.—**strick'en** *p. part.* is now only used as an adjective.—*n.* 1. a stoppage of work. 2. the discovery of mineral resources, as *an oil strike.*—**stri'ker** *n.* worker on strike.—**stri'king** *adj.* remarkable.—**stri'kingly** *adv.*—**to strike cuttings** to make them take root.—**to strike up** to begin to sing or play music

string *n.* 1. a fine cord, thin rope. 2. row, series. 3. a cord used in musical instruments.—*v.* 1. to put on a string. 2. to tie with string.—**strung** *p.t.* and *p. part.*—**stringed** *adj.* having strings.—**strings** *pl.* the stringed instruments in an orchestra.—**highly strung** *adj.* excitable.—**to pull strings** to use the iufluence of someone in order to gain something

strin'gent (strin'jent) *adj.* severe, strict

strip *v.* 1. to make bare, uncover, take away.

2. to undress. 3. (of machinery, etc.) to take to pieces.—**strip'ping** *pres. part.*—**stripped** *p.t.* and *p. part.*—*n.* a long narrow piece

stripe *n.* 1. a narrow mark or band. 2. a stroke with a whip.—*v.* to mark with stripes.—**striped** *adj.*

strip'ling *n.* a youth

strive *v.* 1. to try hard. 2. to struggle.—**stri'ving** *pres. part.*—**strove** *p.t.*—**striv'en** *p. part.*

stroke *n.* 1. a blow. 2. a sudden attack of illness. 3. a completed movement in a series. 4. the mark of a pen. 5. the rower sitting nearest the stern.—*v.* to caress, pass the hand over.—**stro'king** *pres. part.*—**to stroke someone the wrong way** to annoy him

stroll (strōl) *v.* to walk without hurry. (See **walk.**)—*n.* a leisurely walk.—**strol'ler** *n.*

strong *adj.* 1. having force, power. 2. able to resist, firm.—**strong'er** (strong'ger) *comp.*—**strong'est** (strong'gest) *sup.*—**strong'ly** *adv.*—**strong'hold** *n.* a fortress.—**strong drink** alcoholic drink, spirits.—**strong language** swearing.—**strong-box** *n.* an iron chest for valuables.—**strong-room** *n.* a burglar-proof room for valuables.—**strong-minded** *adj.* having firm convictions.—**a strong verb** a verb which changes its stem for the past tense. e.g. sing, sang; sit, sat.—**going strong** continuing actively
Compare: powerful, mighty, forceful, vigorous, muscular, hardy, robust, violent, potent, zealous, convincing. *Contrast:* weak, puny, delicate, feeble, frail

strong'hold *n.* a fort

strop *n.* a strip of leather for sharpening razors.—*v.* to sharpen a razor.—**strop'ping** *pres. part.*—**stropped** *p.t.* and *p. part.*

struc'tural *adj.* of a building, used in building

struc'ture *n.* 1. a way of building. 2. a building. 3. something made up of parts

strug'gle *v.* to make a great effort, to fight against.—(See **strive**)—**strug'gling** *pres. part.*—*n.* effort, fight

strum *v.* to play a stringed instrument without care or skill.—**strum'ming** *pres. part.*—**strummed** *p.t.* and *p. part.*

strut *v.* 1. to walk pompously. (See **walk.**) 2. to support with struts.—**strut'ting** *pres. part.*—**strut'ted** *p.t.* and *p. part.*—*n.* 1. a strutting walk. 2. a support for strengthening, e.g. a rafter

strych'nine (strik'neen) *n.* a poisonous-drug

stub *n.* 1. the stump of a tree. 2. a small piece of pencil, cigarette, etc.—*v.* to strike, e.g. one's toes, against.—**stub'bing** *pres. part.*—**stubbed** *p.t.* and *p. part.*

stub'ble *n.* 1. stumps of straw left after reaping. 2. unshaven bristly hair.—**stub'bly** *adj.* short and stiff

stub'born *adj.* obstinate, hard to persuade.—**stub'bornly** *adv.*

stuc'co (stuk'o) *n.* fine plaster for covering walls

stud *n.* 1. a large nail-head, knob. 2. a kind of movable button.—*v.* to set with studs.—**stud'ding** *pres. part.*—**stud'ded** *p.t.* and *p. part.*

stud *n.* a set of horses kept for breeding.—**stud'-farm** *n.*

stu'dent *n.* a person who studies, esp. at a university or college

stud'ied *p.t.* and *p. part.* of **study.**—*adj.* deliberate, planned

stu'dio (stū'di-ō) *n.* 1. the work-room of an artist. 2. a place where film plays are photographed.—**stu'dios** *pl.*

stu'dious *adj.* 1. fond of study. 2. thoughtful, careful

stud'y *n.* 1. gaining knowledge by learning or application, esp. from books. 2. something studied. 3. a room used for studying. 4. an artistic composition, esp. in music or painting. 5. absent-mindedness, contemplation. 6. endeavour, care.—*v.* 1. to try to learn. 2. to examine, as *He studied the map.* 3. to consider. 4. to take care of, as *He studied his employer's interests.*—**stud'ying** *pres. part.*—**stud'ied** *p.t.* and *p. part.*—*adj.* deliberate.—**in a brown study** in deep thought

stuff *n.* material, substance.—*v.* 1. to pack, fill. 2. to eat greedily

stuf'fing *n.* 1. seasoning for stuffing a fowl, etc. 2. padding

stuff *n.* material, substance.—*v.* 1. to pack, fill. 2. to eat greedily.—**stuf'fy** *adj.* close, without fresh air

stum'ble *v.* to trip and nearly fall.—**stum'bling** *pres. part.*—**stum'ble on** to come on by chance.—**stum'bling-block** *n.* obstacle hindrance

stump *n.* 1. a part of a fallen tree remaining in the ground. 2. what is left after the main part has gone. 3. one of the uprights of the wicket in cricket.—*v.* 1. to walk noisily. 2. (in cricket) to put out batsman, who is out of his ground, by knocking off bails, with ball held in hand. 3. to puzzle.—**stump'er** *n.* (cricket) a wicket-keeper.—**stump'y** *adj.* short and thick

stun *v.* to knock senseless, to shock.—**stun'ning** *pres. part.*—**stunned** *p.t.* and *p. part.*

stunt *v.* to check the growth of.—**stunt'ed** *adj.* small, undersized

stunt *n.* a sensational feat or campaign

stupefac'tion (-shun) *n.* amazement, dazed, condition

stu'pefy (stū'pe-fī) *v.* to make stupid, to daze.—he **stu'pefies.**—**stu'pefying** *pres. part.*—**stu'pefied** *p.t.* and *p. part.*

stupen'dous *adj.* amazing, vast
Compare: astounding, gigantic, tremendous, overwhelming, enormous

stu'pid *adj.* dull, not intelligent.—**stu'pidly** *adv.*—**stupid'ity** *n.*

stu'por *n.* a dazed state

stur'diness *n.* strength

stur'dy *adj.* robust, strongly-built. (See **stalwart, strong.**)—**stur'dier** *comp.*—**stur'diest** *sup.*

stur'geon (stur'jin) *n.* a large fish, whose eggs are eaten as caviare

stut'ter *v.* to stammer, speak with difficulty. —*n.*

sty *n.* a pen for pigs.—**sties** *pl.*

sty, stye *n.* a small sore spot on the eyelid, —**sties** *pl.*

style *n.* 1. a manner of writing, doing, etc. as *The batsman had a beautiful style.* 2. fashion, as *the latest style.* 3. title, name, as *A member of the Privy Council is entitled to the style of "Right Honourable."* 4. a pointed tool for writing on waxed tablets. 5. distinction, quality, superior manner, as *They travelled in style.*—*v.* to describe.—**sty'lish** *adj.* fashionable, smart. —**sty'list** *n.* a master of style

sty'lus *n.* a pointed diamond, sapphire, etc. at the end of a record-player's pick-up arm

sty'mie *n.* (golf) a position where the opponent's ball lies between the player and the hole.—**to be stymied** to find an obstacle in the way

suave (swāv) *adj.* smoothly polite.—**sua'vity** (swav'it-i) *n.*

sub *prep.* under. Used as prefix, e.g. **subscribe** to write underneath, **submarine** craft which goes under water, **sublieutenant** rank below lieutenant in navy

sub'altern *n.* an army officer below the rank of captain

subcon'scious (sub-kon'shus) *adj.* 1. partly conscious. 2. referring to the *subconscious mind,* i.e. that part of the mind, the workings of which are not realised by the individual concerned

sub'divide *v.* to divide again.—**subdivis'ion** *n.*

subdue' *v.* to conquer, overcome as *The rebellion was subdued.*—**subdued'** *p.t.* and *p. part.* —*adj.* softened, as *in a subdued light.*—**subdu'ing** *pres. part.*

sub'ject *n.* 1. a person under control of others. 2. something spoken about, read, etc. topic, theme, as *an interesting subject, the subject of a book, play, etc.* 3. (in Grammar) that part of the sentence, noun or pronoun with which the verb agrees in number and person. 4. a person having a certain tendency as *He is a bilious subject.* —*adj.* 1. obliged to obey. 2. liable to, as *subject to headaches.* 3. on condition of, as *subject to your approval*

subject' *v.* 1. to subdue. 2. to expose, cause to suffer.—**subjec'tion** (shun) *n.* 1. conquering. 2. being controlled

sub'jugate *v.* to overcome, conquer.—**subjuga'tion** (-gā'shun) *n.*

sublet' *v.* to let property already rented from the owner

sub'limate *v.* (chemistry) to purify certain solids, such as iodine, by heating to a vapour and then condensing to a solid

sublime' *adj.* noble, grand, awe-inspiring.—**sublime'ly** *adv.*—**sublim'ity** *n.*—**from the sublime to the ridiculous** from a noble thought or action to one which is absurd

Compare: elevated, lofty, stately, dignified, majestic, magnificent. *Contrast:* mean, petty, ridiculous, trivial, little, base

sub'marine (sub'mar-een) *adj.* below the surface of the sea.—*n.* a war-vessel that can go under water

submerge' (sub-merj') *v.* 1. to put under water. 2. to sink, plunge under water.—**submer'ging** *pres. part.*—**submer'gence** *n.*

submer'sion (-shun) *n.* being submerged

submis'sion (sub-mish'un) *n.* 1. surrender, obedience. 2. presentation for consideration or examination.—**submiss'ive** *adj.* humble, obedient

submit' *v.* 1. to give in, surrender. 2. to put forward for consideration, as *to submit evidence.*—**submit'ting** *pres. part.*—**submit'ted** *p.t.* and *p. part.*

Note: a person *submits* himself *to* authority. Evidence is *submitted for* consideration

subord'inate *adj.* of lower rank or importance. —*n.* one under the orders of another.—**subord'inate** (sub-ord'ināt) *v.* to treat as subordinate.—**subordina'tion** (-ā'shun) *n.*

suborn' *v.* to bribe to do evil or commit perjury

subscribe' *v.* 1. to sign one's name beneath. 2. to pay a contribution. 3. to express agreement, as *I subscribe to those opinions.* —**subscri'bing** *pres. part.*—**subscri'ber** *n.*—**subscrip'tion** ('shun) *n.* money paid or raised

sub'sequent *adj.* later, coming after.—**sub'sequently** *adv.* afterwards

subser'vient *adj.* 1. servile. 2. serving a purpose

subside' *v.* to sink, settle, grow less.—**subsi'ding** *pres. part.*—**sub'sidence** *n.*

subsid'iary *adj.* helping to complete.—*n.* a helper

sub'sidise *v.* to support with money

sub'sidy *n.* a sum of money granted.—**sub'sidies** *pl.*

subsist' *v.* to exist, live on.—**subsis'tence** *n.* living

sub'soil *n.* a layer of earth under the surface

sub'stance *n.* 1. the most important part. 2. matter, what a thing is made of. 3. wealth, as *a man of substance*

substan'tial (sub-stan'shl) *adj.* 1. real, true. 2. strong, solid. 3. important.—**substan'tially** *adv.*

substan'tiate (sub-stan'shi-āt) *v.* to prove.—**substantia'tion** (-ā'shun) *n.*

sub'stantive (sub'stan-tiv) *n.* (grammar) a noun.—*adj.* having a separate and real existence

sub'stitute *n.* a thing or person put in place of another.—*v.* to put in exchange for.—**sub'stituting** *pres. par.*—**substitu'tion** (-shun) *n.*

sub'tend *v.* (geometry) to be opposite to, as *each side of an equilateral triangle subtends an angle of* 60 *degrees*

sub'terfuge (sub'ter-fūj) *n.* a trick, excuse to avoid something

subterra'nean *adj.* underground

subt'le (sut'l) *adj.* 1. clever. 2. fine, faint, as *There is a subtle difference between one flavour and the other.* 3. sly.—**subt'ly** *adv.*—**subt'lety** (sut'l-ti) *n.*

subtract' *v.* to take away.—**subtrac'tion** (-shun) *n.*

sub'urb *n.* a district just outside a city.—**suburb'an** *adj.* 1. in or like a suburb. 2. conventional.—**suburb'ia** *n.* suburbs and their inhabitants

subver'sion (-shun) *n.* overthrow, ruin.—**subver'sive** *adj.* causing overthrow, esp. of principles, government, etc.

subvert' *v.* to overthrow, destroy

sub'way *n.* an underground electric railway

succeed' (suk-seed') *v.* 1. to follow, take the place of, as *Queen Victoria succeeded William IV.* 2. to obtain a good result, to do well, as *He succeeded in passing his examination*

success' (suk-ses') *n.* 1. good result, good fortune. 2. a person or thing having success.—**success'ful** *adj.* fortunate.—**success'fully** *adv.*

succes'sion (suk-sesh'un) *n.* 1. a following one after another, series. 2. the right to succeed, e.g. to a throne.—**succes'sive** *adj.* following in order.—**success'or** *n.* one who follows another

succinct' (suk-sint') *adj.* in few words, brief

Compare: concise, pithy, terse, laconic.
Contrast: wordy, verbose, long-winded

suc'cour *n.* help.—*v.*

suc'culence (suk'ū-lens) *n.* juiciness.—**suc'culent** *adj.* juicy

succumb' (suk-um') *v.* 1. to give way, yield. 2. to die, as *He succumbed to his injuries*

such *adj.* 1. of that kind, as *Such men are dangerous.* 2. so great, so good, etc. as *They had such a good time.*—*pron.* that, those (already referred to or suggested), as *Such was not my wish.*

suck *v.* 1. to draw into the mouth. 2. to roll in the mouth. 3. to drink in, absorb.—*n.* sucking.—**suck'er** *n.* 1. that which sucks. 2. a new shoot rising from a plant root. 3. a round disc which sticks to a surface by suction. 4. (slang) a foolish person easily taken in by a trick

suck'le *v.* to nurse at the breast.—**suck'ling** *pres. part.*—**suck'ling** *n.* a very young child

su'crose (sōō'crōz) *n.* cane-sugar

suc'tion (-shun) *n.* 1. sucking. 2. making two things stick together by removing the air in the space between

sud'den *adj.* unexpected, quick.—**all of a sudden** suddenly.—**sud'denly** *adv.*—**sud'denness** *n.*

Compare: (with *adv.*) rapidly, hastily, hurriedly, swiftly, impetuously, rashly

suds *n.pl.* froth of soap and water

sue (sū) *v.* 1. to prosecute, take action against. 2. to beg, entreat, as *to sue for mercy.*—**su'ing** *pres. part.*—**sued** *p.t.* and *p. part.*

suede (swād) *n.* soft kid leather.—*adj.*

su'et (sōō'it) *n.* hard animal fat for cooking

suf'fer *v.* 1. to feel pain, grief, etc. 2. to allow, permit, as *Suffer the little children to come unto me.* 3. undergo, as *to suffer the death penalty.*—**suf'ferance** *n.* permission.—**suf'ferer** *n.*—**suf'fering** *n.* pain, distress

suffice' (suf-īs') *v.* to be enough, to satisfy.—**suffi'cing** *pres. part.*—**suffi'ciency** (suf-ish'en-si) *n.* a large enough amount

suffi'cient (suf-ish'ent) *adj.* enough

Compare: adequate, ample, satisfactory.
Contrast: insufficient, inadequate, scanty

suf'fix *n.* a letter or word added to the end of a word (e.g. *-tion* is a *noun suffix* because it changes verbs like *suggest, direct* into nouns like *suggestion, direction. -Ess* and *-ine* are *feminine suffixes,* as in *lioness, heroine*)

suf'focate *v.* to choke, to kill by stopping the breathing.—**suffoca'tion** (-kā'shun) *n.*

suf'frage (suf'rij) *n.* the right of voting.—**suffragette', suf'fragist** *n.* a supporter of women's claim to the vote

suffuse' (suf-ūz') *v.* to spread over, as *a blush suffused her countenance.*—**suffu'sing** *pres. part.*—**suffu'sion** (zhun) *n.* 1. suffusing. 2. flush

su'gar (shōō'gar) *n.* a sweet substance made from sugar-beet or sugar-cane.—*v.* to sweeten with sugar.—**su'gary** *adj.*—**su'gar-beet, su'gar-cane** *ns.* plants from which sugar is obtained

suggest' (su-jest') *v.* 1. to put an idea into someone's mind, to hint. 2. to show indirectly, as *The man's appearance suggested poverty.* 3. to propose, as *He suggested a game of chess.*—**sugges'tion** (chun) *n.* a hint, proposal.—**sugges'tible** *adj.* easily influenced.—**sugges'tive** *adj.* hinting at more than is obvious

suici'dal (sū-i-sī'dal) *adj.* causing suicide, disastrous

su'icide (sū'i-sīd) *n.* 1. killing oneself deliberately. 2. the ruin of one's own interests. 3. a person who commits suicide

suit (sūt) *n.* 1. action at law, suing. 2. a request. 3. a set of clothes or armour, worn together. 4. one of four sets in a pack of cards.—*v.* 1. to go with, fit, as *That hat suits you.* 2. to please, satisfy, as *The arrangement suits me perfectly.*—**suit'-case** *n.* flat travelling-case.—**to follow suit** to imitate someone's action.—**to suit oneself** to do as one pleases

suit'able (sūt'a-bl) *adj.* fitting, right for the purpose.—**suit'ably** *adv.*—**suitabil'ity** *n.*

suite (sweet) *n.* 1. attendants on a high personage. 2. a set of rooms, furniture, tunes. 3. a series of musical pieces

suit'or (sūt'or) *n.* 1. one who sues in law-court. 2. a wooer

sulk *v.* to be silent and bad-tempered.—**sulk'y** *adj.* sullen.—**sul'kier** *comp.*—**sul'kiest** *sup.*—**sul'kily** *adv.*

sul'len *adj.* 1. injured and angry. 2. gloomy.—**sul'lenly** *adv.*—**sul'lenness** *n.*

sul'ly *v.* to soil, stain.—he **sul'lies.**—**sul'lying** *pres. part.*—**sul'lied** *p.t.* and *p. part.*

sul'phate *n.* a salt of sulphuric acid

sul'phide *n.* a chemical compound of sulphur and another element

sul'phite *n.* a salt of sulphurous acid

sul'phur (sul'fer) *n.* a yellow substance that burns with a blue flame.—**sulphur'ic acid** *n.* a strong acid, oil of vitriol.—**sulphur'ous acid** *n.* a weak acid, formed when sulphur dioxide dissolves in water

sul'tan *n.* a Mohammedan prince.—**sultan'a** (sul-tah'na) *n.* 1. a sultan's wife. 2. a kind of raisin

sul'triness *n.* oppressive heat

sul'try *adj.* hot and close.—**sul'trier** *comp.*—**sul'triest** *sup.*

sum *n.* 1. the total of numbers or things added together. 2. a problem in arithmetic. 3. an amount of money.—*v.* 1. to add up. 2. (up) to go over the main points in an argument, lawsuit, speech, etc.—**sum'ming** *pres. part.*—**summed** *p.t.* and *p. part.*—**summing-up** *n.* a summary, as made by a judge at the end of a law-suit

su'mac (shōō'mak, sū'mak) *n.* 1. a Canadian shrub whose leaves turn red in autumn. 2. the dried leaves and roots of the sumac used in tanning and dyeing

sum'marily *adv.* 1. briefly. 2. instantly

sum'marise *v.* to make a summary, to say briefly

sum'mary *n.* a short statement of chief points.—**sum'maries** *pl.*—*adj.* done without delay

sum'mer *n.* the hot season.—*v.* to pass the summer.—**sum'mery** *adj.*

sum'mit *n.* the highest point, top

sum'mon *v.* 1. to send for. 2. to gather up, e.g. strength

sum'mons *n.* a demand for one to appear in court.—*v.* **sum'mons**

sump *n.* 1. an oil-reservoir under a car-engine. 2. a cavity in a mine where water collects

sump'tuous *adj.* costly, rich.—**sump'tuously** *adv.*—**sump'tuousness** *n.* magnificence

sun *n.* 1. the heavenly body from which we receive light and warmth. 2. the sun's rays.—*v.* to place in sunlight.—**sun'ning** *pres. part.*—**sunned** *p.t.* and *p. part.*—**sun'bathe** *v.* to expose one's body deliberately to the sun.—**sun'beam** *n.*—**sun'burn** *n.*—**sun'downer** *n.* (Aus.) a tramp who takes care to arrive at a station at sundown, so that, without doing any work, he may be provided with food and shelter.—**sun'light** (sun'līt) *n.* the light of the sun.—**sun'lit** *adj.* lighted by the sun.—**sun'rise** (sun'rīz) *n.* the rising of the sun.—**sun'set** *n.* the going down of the sun.—**sun'shade** *n.* an umbrella, or a blind, used as protection against the sun.—**sun'shine** *n.*—**sun'stroke** *n.* illness caused by too much heat.—**sun'tan** *n.* browning of the skin by exposure to the sun

sun'dae (sun'dā) *n.* an ice-cream with crushed fruit and nuts on top

Sun'day *n.* the first day of the week

sun'der *v.* to separate

sun'dial (sun'dīl) *n.* an instrument for telling the time, using shadows made by the sun on a clock-face

sun'dries *n.pl.* odds and ends

sun'dry *adj.* various, several

sunk'en *adj.* sunk, as *with sunken cheeks, a sunken ship.* (See **sink**)

sun'ny *adj.* 1. full of sunlight. 2. cheerful, bright.—**sun'nier** *comp.*—**sun'niest** *sup.*
Compare: bright, cheerful, warm, genial, cheery, happy, *Contrast:* dark, gloomy, chilly, dull, overcast

sup *v.* to sip.—*n.* a mouthful

sup *v.* to have supper.—**sup'ping** *pres. part.*—**supped** *p.t.* and *p. part.*

su'per (sū'per) *pref.* over or beyond, used in many compounds, such as **super-abundance** meaning more than an abundance, **super-fine** of extra quality, **super-human** above human.—*adj.* first-rate

superan'nuate *v.* to cause to retire (esp. on a pension) because of age or illness.—**superannua'tion** (-ā'shun) *n.* 1. pension of a superannuated person. 2. regular contribution made by employee towards pension

superb' *adj.* splendid, grand, majestic.—**superb'ly** *adv.*

su'percharge *v.* to force an extra amount of mixture into the cylinder of a petrol engine

supercil'ious (sū-per-sil'i-us) *adj.* proud, haughty and indifferent

superfic'ial (sū-per-fish'al) *adj.* 1. on the surface, as a *superficial wound.* 2. shallow, without depth, as *a superficial mind, character.*—**superficial'ity** *n.*

su'perfine *adj.* very fine

superflu'ity *n.* too great an abundance

super'fluous *adj.* not needed, more than necessary

superhu'man *adj.* more than human, beyond human power

superimpose' *v.* to place over something else

superintend' *v.* to have charge of, manage, direct.—**superintend'ence** *n.*—**superintend'ent** *n.* 1. person in charge. 2. a police officer above a chief inspector in rank

supe'rior *adj.* 1. higher, better. 2. proud.—*n.*

a person superior in rank.—**superior'ity** *n.*

super'lative *adj.* of the highest kind.—*n.* in Grammar the *superlative* of an adjective or adverb is that which expresses the highest degree of the quality, e.g. *tallest* is the *superlative of tall*, *most intensely* of *intensely*

su'permarket *n.* a large self-service store selling many kinds of goods

supernat'ural *adj.* miraculous, beyond the forces of nature

superscrip'tion (-shun) *n.* something written above or on

supersede' *v.* to take the place of, as *Smith has superseded Brown as our goalkeeper.*—**superse'ding** *pres. part.*

superson'ic *adj.* 1. (of aeroplanes) moving faster than sound. 2. (of sound waves) of very high frequency, inaudible to human ears

superstit'ion (sū-per-stish'un) *n.* 1. unreasonable fear of what is unknown. 2. a belief based on fear or magic.—**superstit'ious** (-shus) *adj.*

su'pertax *n.* an additional tax on large incomes

supervene' *v.* to happen as an addition, or immediately after, as *The patient seemed to be recovering, when heart failure supervened, and he died.*—**superve'ning** *pres. part.*—**superven'tion** (-shun) *n.*

su'pervise *v.* to direct, manage.—**su'pervising** *pres. part.*—**supervis'ion** (sū-per-vizh'un) *n.*—**su'pervisor** *n.*

Compare: superintend, control, overlook, inspect

su'pine *adj.* 1. lying on the back. 2. lazy, idle

Compare: 1. prone, recumbent, 2. neglectful, dormant, careless. *Contrast:* 1. upright, erect. 2. energetic, watchful, alert

sup'per *n.* the last meal of the day

supplant' *v.* to take the place of, esp. unfairly, as *The dictator was supplanted by his enemy*

sup'ple *adj.* bending, easily, pliable

Compare: flexible, lithe, compliant. *Contrast:* stiff, rigid, inflexible, stubborn

sup'plement *n.* an extra part, added to complete, e.g. a book.—**supplement'** *v.* to add to.—**supplement'ary** *adj.* additional

sup'pliant *adj.* asking humbly.—*n.* a person asking humbly

sup'plicate *v.* to implore, pray.—**supplica'tion** (-kā'shun) *n.* humble entreaty, prayer

supply' (sup-l'ī) *v.* 1. to provide, as *The baker supplies our bread. He supplies us with bread.* 2. to make up for, as *Extra cheese will supply the lack of meat.*—**supply'ing** *pres. part.*—**supplied'** *p.t.* and *p. part.*—*n.* 1. store, stock. 2. supplying, substitute.—**suppli'er** *n.*—**supplies'** *pl.*

support' *v.* 1. to hold up, to assist. 2. to provide for, as *She supports her widowed mother.* 3. to help, speak in favour of, as *I will support your application.* 4. to endure, bear, as *to support suffering.*—*n.* a help, prop.—**support'er** *n.* a person who supports

Compare: sustain, maintain, bear, uphold

suppose' (su-pōz') *v.* 1. to accept as possible. 2. to think, imagine.—**suppo'sing** *pres. part.*—**suppo'sedly** *adv.*—**supposit'ion** (-ō-zish'un) *n.* a thing supposed, supposing

suppress' *v.* 1. to crush, put down. 2. to check, hold back.—he **suppress'es**—**suppres'sion** (sup-resh'un) *n.*

suppress'or *n.* 1. one who suppresses. 2. a device on electrical apparatus to prevent interference to radio or television reception

suprem'acy (su-prem'a-si) *n.* highest authority or power

supreme' *adj.* highest in power or authority, greatest.—**supreme'ly** *adv.*

sur'charge (sur'charj) *n.* extra charge.—**surcharge'** *v.* 1. to charge extra. 2. to overload

sure (shōōr) *adj.* 1. certain. 2. trustworthy, reliable.—**sur'er** *comp.*—**sur'est** *sup.*—**sure'ly** *adv.* 1. certainly. 2. firmly.—**sure'-footed** *adj.* not liable to trip or fall

Compare: (with *adj.*) assured, indisputable, positive, actual, real, secure. *Contrast:* uncertain, unsure, doubtful, insecure

sure'ty (shōōr'ti) *n.* 1. certainty. 2. security against loss, etc. 3. a person responsible for appearance in court, etc. of another.—**sure'ties** *pl.*

surf *n.* the foam of waves breaking on the shore.—**surf'-riding** *n.* the sport of balancing on a narrow **surf board** while being swept over water by surf

sur'face (sur'fis) *n.* 1. the outside. 2. the top visible side. 3. outward appearance

sur'feit (sur'fit) *n.* too much, esp. of food

surge (surj) *v.* to move in waves.—*n.* waves

sur'geon (sur'jn) *n.* a doctor who performs operations.—**sur'gery** *n.* 1. treatment by operation. 2. a doctor's consulting room.—**sur'gical** *adj.*

sur'ly *adj.* rude, ill-natured. (See **rude**).—**sur'lier** *comp.*—**sur'liest** *sup.*

surmise' (sur-mīz') *v.* to guess.—*n.*

Compare: (with *n.*) conjecture, suspicion, inference, supposition

surmount' *v.* 1. to get over, overcome. 2. to be on top of

sur'name *n.* a family name.—*v.* to give a name

surpass' *v.* to do better, to excel.—he **surpass'es**

sur'plice (sur'plis) *n.* a loose white robe worn by clergymen and choir

sur'plus *n.* an amount left over, beyond what is needed.—*adj.*

surprise' (sur-prīz') *v.* 1. to catch someone unprepared, to come upon, as *The enemy* *was surprised by a night attack.* 2. to astonish, as *I was surprised to see you there.*—**surpri'sing** *pres. part.*—*n.* 1. act of coming upon without warning. 2. astonishment. 3. something unexpected, as *What a surprise!*

surren'der *v.* to give up, to yield.—*n.* a surrendering

surrepti'tious (sur-ep-tish'us) *adj.* secret, stealthy.—**surrepti'tiously** *adv.*

surround' *v.* 1. to be all round. 2. to come all round.—**surround'ings** *n.pl.* neighbourhood, scenery, environment

sur'tax *n.* an additional tax on incomes

survey' (sur-vā') *v.* 1. to look at, to view. (See **look**). 2. to measure land and make a map of it.—**sur'vey** *n.* 1. a view, inspection. 2. a plan, map.—**survey'or** *n.* 1. an inspector. 2. a person whose profession is surveying

survi'val *n.* 1. continuation of life. 2. an object, person, belief, etc. still existing from earlier time, as *The village stocks are a picturesque survival*

survive' *v.* 1. to remain alive, as *In a struggle for existence only the fittest will survive. He survived the shipwreck.* 2. to outlive, as *She survived her husband by ten years.*—**survi'ving** *pres. part.*—**survi'vor** *n.* person left alive when others have died

susceptibil'ity (sus-ep-ti-bil'i-ti) *n.* being easily influenced, sensitiveness

suscep'tible (sus-ep'ti-bl) *adj.* 1. (to) easily moved or influenced, sensitive, as *She is very susceptible to flattery.* 2. (of) capable of, as *The facts are susceptible of more than one interpretation*

suspect' *v.* 1. to think likely. 2. to believe guilty or false.—**sus'pect** *n.* person thought guilty.—*adj.* suspected

suspend' *v.* 1. to hang up, to attach to something above. 2. to stop for a time, as *The rule was suspended for a month. The secretary was suspended while inquiries were made.*—**suspend'ers** *n.pl.* 1. straps for holding up stockings. 2. in U.S., braces

suspense' *n.* uncertainty, anxiety

suspen'sion (sus-pen'shon) *n.* 1. condition of being held up. 2. being suspended.—**suspen'sion bridge** *n.* a bridge held up by cables attached to a tower at each end

suspi'cion (sus-pish'n) *n.* 1. the feeling of one who suspects, doubt. 2. a small amount, suggestion, as *The flavour is improved by a suspicion of garlic.*—**suspi'cious** (sus-pish'us) *adj.* 1. suspecting, feeling doubtful. 2. causing suspicion

Compare: (with *n.* 1.) mistrust, distrust, apprehension, jealousy, misgiving

sustain' *v.* 1. to keep up, hold up. (See **support.**) 2. to endure, bear. 3. to confirm, as *His innocence was sustained at the trial*

sus'tenance *n.* support, food

swab (swob) *n.* 1. a mop. 2. a small pad of cotton-wool, lint, etc.—*v.* to clean with a swab.—**swab'bing** *pres. part.*—**swabbed** *p.t.* and *p. part.*

swad'dle (swod'l) *v.* to wrap a baby tightly in **swaddling clothes** or **bands**

swag *n.* (Aus.) a tramp's bundle, wrapped in a blanket.—**swag'man** *n.* a tramp, travelling on foot through the bush

swag'ger (swag'er) *n.* to strut, to walk or act boastfully or insolently.—*n.* a boastful walk or manner

swain *n.* 1. a young countryman. 2. a lover

swal'low (swol'ō) *v.* 1. to take in down one's throat. 2. to engulf.—*n.* swallowing

swal'low (swol'ō) *n.* a fork-tailed migratory bird

swamp (swomp) *n.* a marsh, bog, wet soft land.—*v.* 1. to flood, soak. 2. to overwhelm.—**swamp'y** *adj.*

swan (swon) *n.* a large water-bird with a graceful curved neck.—**swan'-song** *n.* the last work or performance of a writer, actor, etc.

Note: A young swan is called a **cygnet**

sward (sword) *n.* turf. short grass

swarm (sworm) *n.* 1. a large number of animals or insects. 2. a cluster of bees. 3. a crowd.—*v.* 1. (of bees) to form a cluster. 2. to crowd

swarm (sworm) *v.* (up) to climb by gripping with hands and knees

swar'thy (swor'TH-i) *adj.* dark-complexioned, sunburnt

swash'buckler *n.* a swaggering bully

swas'tika *n.* a cross with four equal arms, each bent at a right angle

swat (swot) *n.* to kill (an insect) by striking it.—**swat'ting** *pres. tense*—**swat'ted** *p.t.* and *p. part.*

swathe (swāTH) *v.* to wrap in bandages.—*n.* a bandage

sway *v.* 1. to swing unsteadily. 2. to cause to swing, as *The wind swayed the sign-board.* 3. to influence, govern, as *He is swayed by various motives.*—*n.* 1. swaying, motion. 2. influence, government

swear (swār) *v.* 1. to make a solemn promise. 2. to bind by a promise. 3. to curse.—**swore,** *p.t.*—**sworn** *p. part.*

sweat (swet) *n.* 1. moisture coming from the pores in the skin. 2. a sweating state.—*v.* 1. to give out sweat. 2. to toil. 3. to underpay workers.—**sweat, sweated** *p.t.* and *p. part.*—**sweat'er** *n.* a thick woollen jersey

swede *n.* 1. a turnip. 2. a native of Sweden

Swe'den *n.* a country in northern Europe.—**Swede** *n.* a native of Sweden.—**Swe'dish** *adj.*

sweep *v.* 1. to pass quickly or majestically, as *She swept out of the room.* 2. to clean with a broom, to brush. 3. to move in a long curve, as *The road sweeps round the mountain.* 4. to carry away, as *The tree trunk was swept away by the stream.*—**swept** *p.t.* and *p. part.*

—*n.* 1. a sweeping, removing. 2. a wide curve. 3. range, stretch. 4. long oar. 5. one who cleans chimneys.—**sweep'ings** *n.pl.* dust, rubbish.—**sweep'stake** *n.* gamble in which the winner takes all the money contributed.—**to sweep the board** to win everything

sweet *adj.* 1. tasting like sugar. 2. pleasant. 3. fresh, in good condition, not sour. 4. gentle, pretty.—*n.* 1. a dessert course. 2. candy.—**sweet-bri'ar** *n.* a wild rose.—**sweet'en** *v.* to make sweet.—**sweet'heart** *n.* a lover.—**sweet'ness** *n.*—**sweet'ly** *adv.* —**sweet-pea'** *n.* a garden plant with bright, scented flowers

swell *v.* 1. to grow bigger. 2. to grow louder, to make louder. 3. to rise. 4. to bulge.—**swelled** *p.t.*—**swol'len** *p. part.*—*n.* 1. swelling, being swollen. 2. long, heaving waves.—**swel'ling** *n.* a sore, swollen, spot

Compare: expand, distend, inflate, enlarge, increase. *Contrast:* shrink, shrivel, contract, decrease, dwindle, wither

swel'ter *v.* to sweat, to suffer from too much heat

swerve *v.* to turn aside.—*n.*—**swer'ving** *pres. part.*

swift *adj.* quick, fast-moving, ready.—*n.* a long-winged bird.—**swift'ly** *adv.*—**swift'-ness** *n.* speed

Compare: rapid, speedy, fleet. *Contrast:* slow, sluggish, dilatory

swill *v.* 1. to pour liquid over. 2. to drink greedily.—*n.* 1. rinsing. 2. liquid food for pigs

swim *v.* 1. to move along in water. 2. to float. 3. to be flooded. 4. to cross by swimming. 5. to feel dizzy, as *His head was swimming.*—**swim'ming** *pres. part.*—**swam** *p.t.*—**swum** *p. part.*—*n.* act of swimming.—**swim'mer** *n.*—**in the swim** 1. playing an active part. 2. up-to-date

swin'dle *v.* to cheat.—**swind'ling** *pres. part.*—*n.* a trick, fraud.—**swind'ler** *n.*

swine *n.* 1. a pig, hog. 2. a coarse, brutal person.—**boar, hog** *masc.*—**sow** *fem.*—**swine** *pl.*—**swine'herd** *n.* a person who looks after pigs.—**swi'nish** *adj.*

swing *v.* 1. to move to and fro, to sway. 2. to move round. 3. to walk with arms swinging.—**swung** *p.t.* and *p. part.*—*n.* 1. swinging. 2. a seat hung from ropes. 3. syncopated music.—**in full swing** very active

swipe *v.* to hit with a sweeping stroke.—*n.*

swirl *v.* to whirl, to move round swiftly.—*n.*

swish *v.* 1. to swing a rod, etc. with a hissing sound. 2. to cane.—he **swish'es**.—*n.* a hissing sound

Swiss *adj.* belonging to Switzerland

switch *n.* 1. an easily bent twig or stick. 2. a movable rail at junctions. 3. a device for making and breaking electric circuit.—*v.* 1. to strike with a switch. 2. to turn an electric current on or off. 3. to turn, to change quickly.—he **switch'es**.—**switch'-back** *n.* a railway with many ups and downs at amusement fairs.—**switch'board** *n.* a panel with many plugs or switches, as in a telephone exchange

Swit'zerland *n.* a country in central Europe.—**Swiss** *n.* a native of Switzerland.—*pl.* **Swiss.**—*adj.* belonging to Switzerland

swiv'el *n.* a fastener or link in two parts which can revolve the one on the other.—*v.* to turn on a swivel.—**swiv'elling** *pres. part.*—**swiv'elled** *p.t.* and *p. part.*

swol'len *p.t.* and *p. part.* of **swell.**—**swollen-headed** conceited

swoon *v.* to faint.—*n.*

swoop *v.* to rush down on and seize.—*n.* a swift downward sweep, attack.—**at one fell swoop** at one attempt

sword (sord) *n.* a weapon with a long blade.—**to draw the sword** to go to war—**to sheathe the sword** to make peace.—**to put to the sword** to slaughter.—**swords'man** *n.* a person skilled in using a sword.—**swords'-manship** *n.*—**to cross swords** (with) to fight or argue (with)

Compare: cutlass, sabre, rapier, foil, scimitar

swot *v.* to study hard.—**swot'ting** *pres. part.*—**swot'ted** *p.t.* and *p. part.*

syc'amore (sik'a-mōr) *n.* a tree, resembling the plane, with broad leaves

syc'ophant (sĭk'ō-fant) *n.* a flatterer.—**sycophan'tic** *adj.*

syl'lable *n.* a division of a word as a unit for pronunciation

syl'labus (sil'a-bus) *n.* an outline of a course of study, etc. programme.—**syl'labi, syl'-labuses** *pl.*

sylph (silf) *n.* a spirit of the air

syl'van (sil'van) *adj.* wooded, rustic

sym'bol (sim'bol) *n.* a sign, something that stands for something else, as *The Cross is the symbol of Christianity. The signs* + and — *are mathematical symbols.*—**symbol'ic, symbol'ical** *adj.* used as a symbol.—**sym'bolise** *v.* to stand for

symmet'rical *adj.* well-balanced, regular, having both sides alike.—**sym'metry** (sim'e-tri) *n.* a well-balanced arrangement

Compare: (with *n.*) balance, harmony, grace, proportion, beauty

sympathet'ic (sim-path-et'ik) *adj.* 1. feeling sympathy, kind. 2. agreeing.—**sympathet'-ically** *adv.*

sym'pathise *v.* to feel or express sympathy.—**sym'pathising** *pres. part.*

sym'pathy *n.* 1. feeling for another in pain or trouble. 2. agreement, as *I am in complete sympathy wiih the scheme.* 3. sharing one another's tastes and feelings.—**sym'-pathies** *pl.*

Compare: 1. compassion, commiseration, pity. 2. concurrence, approval. 3. affinity

Note: You feel *sympathy with* a person's

feelings or opinions, but you have *sympathy for* their sufferings or afflictions

sym'phony (sim'fo-ni) *n.* 1. a harmony of sounds. 2. a composition for a full orchestra.—**sym'phonies** *pl.*

symp'ton *n.* 1. a sign that something exists. 2. an indication of disease.—**symptomat'ic** *adj.*

syn'agogue (sin'a-gog) *n.* a Jewish congregation or meeting-place

syn'chromesh (sin'kro-mesh) *n.* a device on a motor vehicle to enable gears to turn at the same speed, and so engage easily

syn'chronise (sin'kron-īz) *v.* to happen at the same time, or at the same pace.—**syn'chronising** *pres. part.*—**syn'chronous** *adj.*

syn'copate *v.* 1. to shorten a word by leaving out letters from the middle, e.g. *can't* for *cannot.* 2. in music, to begin on an unaccented beat.—**syncopa'tion** (-pā'shun) *n.*

syn'dicate *n.* a company of persons combining for a particular enterprise

syn'od (sin'od) *n.* a church assembly, council

syn'nonym (sin'ō-nim) *n.* a word having the same meaning as another, as *compassion* and *pity.*—**synon'ymous** *adj.* meaning the same

Note: there are many synonyms in this dictionary, introduced by the word *Compare*

synop'sis *n.* summary.—**synop'ses** *pl.*

syn'tax *n.* the part of grammar dealing with arrangement of words in sentences

syn'thesis *n.* a putting together, combination.—**syn'theses** *pl.*—**synthet'ic** *adj.* 1. resulting from synthesis. 2. artificial

Compare: (with *adj.*) spurious, sham, substitute. *Contrast:* analytic, analytical

sy'phon *n.* see **si'phon**

Syr'ia *n.* a country in western Asia.—**Syr'ian.** *adj.*—*n.* a native of Syria

syringe' (sir-inj') *n.* an instrument for drawing in liquid and forcing it out in a stream or spray, a squirt.—**hypoderm'ic syringe** *n.* a syringe fitted with a hollow needle for injections.—*v.*

syr'up (si'rup) *n.* 1. sugar boiled in water. 2. sugar-cane juice thickened into a sweet, heavy liquid.—**syr'upy** *adj.*

sys'tem *n.* 1. a set of things making together a whole, as *The solar system.* 2. an organisation, as *a railway system.* 3. a regular order, method, as *He has a system of study.*—**systemat'ic** *adj.* according to a plan.—**systemat'ically** *adv.*—**sys'tematise** *v.* to arrange into a system

Compare: combination, mode, manner, order, regularity

T

tab *n.* 1. a small strap or loop. 2. a label

tab'ard *n.* a herald's short sleeveless coat

tab'by *n.* 1. a brown or grey cat with black stripes. 2. a female cat.—**tab'bies** *pl.*

tab'ernacle *n.* 1. a tent used as a place of worship by the Israelites. 2. a place of worship

ta'ble *n.* 1. a piece of furniture with a flat top supported by legs. 2. a tablet. 3. food, as *He keeps a very good table.* 4. a list, a set of figures, giving information briefly.—*v.* to put on a table.—**table-d'hôte'** (tabl-dōt)' *adj.* (of a meal) at a fixed price with limited choice of courses.—**table'spoon** *n.* a large spoon, larger than a dessert spoon.—**table-ten'nis** *n.* a form of tennis played indoors on a table, with light bats and a celluloid ball.—**to turn the tables** (on someone) to gain a victory from what seems to be defeat

tab'leau (tab'lō) *n.* 1. a dramatic scene. 2. representation of a scene by a group of persons.—**tab'leaux** (tab'lōz) *pl.*

tab'let *n.* 1. a small, flat surface of stone, wood, paper, etc. for writing on. 2. a small, flat pellet of medicine

tab'loid *adj.* (of newspaper) presenting news in a simplified form.—*n.* tablet of medicine

taboo' *adj.* forbidden.—*n.* a setting apart of something or someone as sacred or accursed, a ban.—*v.* to put under a taboo

ta'bor *n.* a small drum

tab'ular *adj.* 1. arranged in lists. 2. shaped like a table

tab'ulate *v.* to arrange in tables or lists.—**tab'ulating** *pres. part.*—**tabula'tion** (-lā'shun) *n.*

tac'it (tas'it) *adj.* 1. implied but not expressed, as *Since he did not forbid it, I suppose we have his tacit consent.* 2. silent, as *a tacit spectator.*—**tac'itly** *adv.*

Compare: understood, inferred, speechless. *Contrast:* spoken, explicit, manifest, declared

tac'iturn (tas'i-turn) *adj.* speaking little, habitually silent.—**tacitur'nity** *n.*

tack *n.* 1. a small nail. 2. a long, loose stitch. 3. course of a ship against the wind.—*v.* 1. to nail with tacks. 2. to stitch lightly. 3. to sail against the wind in zigzag course.—**to get down to brass tacks** to face the real facts of a situation

tack'le *n.* equipment, apparatus, esp. for lifting.—*v.* 1. to seize, esp. as in football. 2. to deal with, as *to tackle difficulties.*—**tack'ling** *pres. part.*

tack'y *adj.* sticky

tact *n.* skill in saying and doing the right thing, and in dealing with people.—**tact'ful** *adj.*—**tact'fully** *adv.*—**tact'less** *adj.* without tact, clumsy

Compare: adroitness, diplomacy, discernment, perception. *Contrast:* tactlessness, indiscretion

tac'tical *adj.* of tactics, concerning the handling of troops or ships in battle

tac'tics *n.pl.* the art of handling troops or ships in battle. (See **strategy**)

tad'pole *n.* a young frog or toad with a tail

taf′feta *n.* a stiff, silk fabric
taff′rail *n.* the rail round the stern of a ship
taf′fy *n.* 1. (Canada) candy made from brown sugar or molasses and butter. 2. (U.S.) flattery
tag *n.* 1. a small, loose end. 2. a metal end, e.g. on shoe-lace. 3. a label. 4. a stock phrase or quotation.—*v.* to fasten on
tail *n.* 1. the part of the spine which projects from the back of animals. 2. any hind part.—*v.* (off) to get smaller.—**tail′-board** *n.* movable back of cart.—**tail-end′** *n.* the last part.—**tail′-light** *n.* a light at back of vehicle.—**to tail away** to fall behind, to become less.—*adj.* **tail′less** without a tail
tail′or *n.* a maker of outer clothing, esp. for men.—*v.* to work as a tailor
taint *n.* a stain, corruption, disgrace.—*v.* 1. to spoil, stain. 2. to infect
take *v.* 1. to lay hold of, to get, receive, as *to take a prize.* 2. to seize, to catch, as *to take prisoner.* 3. to require, as *It takes a lot of doing.* 4. to hire, as *to take a cab.* 5. to understand, as *to take something for granted.* 6. to choose, as *to take a partner.*—**tak′ing** *pres. part.*—**took** *p.t.*—**ta′ken** *p. part.*—**ta′king** *adj.* 1. attractive. 2. infectious.—**ta′kings** *pl.* money taken.—**to take after** (someone) to resemble.—**to take down** 1. to pull down. 2. to write down.—**to take in** 1. to include. 2. to deceive (someone). 3. to understand. 4. to give lodging to.—**to take no notice** to pay no attention.—**to take off** 1. to remove. 2. to imitate (someone). 3. (of an aeroplane) to set out.—**to take on** 1. to undertake. 2. to engage (someone). 3. to show strong feelings. 4. to accept as an opponent.—**to take out** 1. to deduct. 2. to remove (a stain). 3. to obtain (a library book, licence, etc.)—**to take over** to assume control of.—**to take to** to form a liking for.—**to take up** 1. to raise. 2. to occupy. 3. to absorb. 4. to engage in.—**to take a back seat** to observe without taking part.—**to take in hand** to assume control of.—**to take the chair** to preside over a meeting.—**to be taken aback** to be surprised.—**to take it upon oneself** to take over control.— **to take it out of someone** to punish him.—**to take someone up** 1. to make a friend of him. 2. to reprove him.—**to take to one's bed** to go to bed ill.—**to take to one's heels** to flee
tal′cum, talc *n.* toilet-powder made from a soft mineral
tale *n.* 1. a story (See **story**.) 2. number, count.—**tale′-bearer** *n.* one who tells gossip.—**to tell tales** to spread gossip
tal′ent *n.* 1. special skill, ability. 2. an ancient weight or money.—**tal′ented** *adj.* gifted, having natural ability
Compare: aptitude, genius, endowments, parts, cleverness
tal′isman *n.* an object supposed to have magical powers, a charm.—**tal′ismans** *pl.*
talk (tawk) *v.* 1. to speak. 2. to express, e.g. by signs. 3. to discuss, as *to talk things over.*—*n.* 1. speech, conversation. 2. rumour, gossip.—**talk′ative** *adj.* fond of talking.—**talk′er** *n.*—**small talk** talk about trifles.—**to talk big** to boast.—**to talk down** to browbeat someone by constant talk.—**to talk down to** to speak in a patronising way to.—**to talk into** to persuade.—**to talk round** to persuade by talking.—**to talk shop** to speak about one's work.—**to talk over** to discuss
tall (tawl) *adj.* high, above average bodily height.—**tall′er** *comp.*—**tall′est** *sup.*—**tall story** a story difficult to believe
tal′low (tal′ō) *n.* animal-fat prepared for making candles
tal′ly *n.* 1. a stick with notches cut for keeping accounts. 2. account, reckoning.—**tal′lies** *pl.*—*v.* to fit, correspond with.—it **tal′lies.** —**tal′lying** *pres. part.*—**tal′lied** *p.t.* and *p. part.*
tal′ly-ho *n.* a huntsman's cry
tal′on *n.* a claw of a bird of prey
tamarack′ *n.* a N. American larch tree
tambourine′ (tam-bor-een′) *n.* a flat half-drum with jingling discs of metal attached
tame *adj.* 1. not wild, domesticated. 2. dull, not exciting, as *It was a poor circus, and the performance was very tame.*—*v.* to make tame.—**ta′ming** *pres. part.*—**tame′ly** *adv.*—**ta′mer** *n.*—**tame′able** *adj.*
tam′per *v.* 1. to interfere improperly, to meddle, as *Someone has been tampering with the works.* 2. to corrupt, to influence improperly, as *The witnesses had been tampered with*
tan *v.* 1. to make hide into leather. 2. to make brown.—**tan′ning** *pres. part.*—**tanned** *p.t.* and *p. part.*—*n.* 1. oak-bark used in tanning hide. 2. yellowish-brown. 3. browning of the skin from exposure to the sun—*adj.*
tan′dem *n.* 1. bicycle for two riders, one behind the other. 2. a carriage with two horses one behind the other
tang *n.* strong taste or flavour
tan′gent (tan′jent) *n.* straight line touching a curve at a point
tan′gi (tang′ee) *n.* 1. Maori word for lamentation. 2. a celebration
tan′gible (tan′ji-bl) 1. which can be felt by touching. 2. real
Compare: palpable, material, positive.
Contrast: impalpable, vague, intangible
tan′gle (tang′gl) *n.* a confused heap.—*v.* to twist into a confused heap.—**tang′ling** *pres. part.*
tank (tangk) *n.* 1. a large container for storing water, etc. 2. an armoured car on caterpillar wheels
tank′ard (tang′kard) *n.* a large, metal drinking-cup with lid
tank′er (tang′ker) *n.* a ship fitted with tanks for carrying oil

tani'wha (tā-nee'whā) *n.* a mythical Maori monster

tan'ner *n.* a person who tans hides.—**tan'nery** *n.* a place where hides are tanned.—**tan'neries** *pl.*

tan'talise *v.* to torment by offering and then putting out of reach.—**tan'talising** *pres. part.*

tant'amount *adj.* equal, as *The king's wishes were tantamount to commands in those days*

tan'trum *n.* a fit of bad temper

tap *n.* 1. a hollow plug for drawing off liquid. 2. a device for turning liquid on or off.—*v.* 1. to put a tap in. 2. to draw off.—**tap'ping** *pres. part.*—**tapped** *p.t.* and *p. part.*—**tap'-root** *n.* the main root of a plant

tap *v.* to strike lightly, to knock gently.—**tap'ping** *pres. part.*—**tapped** *p.t.* and *p. part.* —*n.* a slight blow

tape *n.* a long, narrow strip of linen, paper, etc.—**tape-meas'ure** *n.* a tape marked for measuring.—**tape'-recorder** *n.* an apparatus for recording sounds on magnetic tape

ta'per *n.* a very thin wax candle.—*v.* to become thinner at one end

tap'estry *n.* woven wall hangings with designs in colours.—**tap'estries** *pl.*

tap'u (tap'ōō) *adj.* Maori word meaning prohibited, banned. (See **taboo**)

tar *n.* a thick, black substance obtained from coal or wood.—*v.* to cover with tar.—**tar'ring** *pres. part.*—**tarred** *p.t.* and *p. part.* —**tarred with the same brush** having the same faults.—**to spoil the ship for a ha'porth of tar** to spoil a good thing for lack of some detail

tar'dily *adv.* late, slowly

tar'diness *n.* lateness, slowness

tar'dy *adj.* slow, behind time.—**tar'dier** *comp.* —**tar'diest** *sup.*

Compare: late, dilatory, sluggish. *Contrast:* punctual, fast, quick

tare *n.* 1. a weed. 2. a plant of the vetch family

tare *n.* allowance made for weight of box, cart, etc. when goods are weighed therein

tar'get *n.* 1. a mark to aim at in shooting. 2. a small shield

tar'iff *n.* 1. duty to be paid on goods. 2. a list of charges

tar'-macadam *n.* road material of tar and stones

tarn *n.* a small mountain-lake

tar'nish *v.* 1. to dim the brightness, esp. of metal. 2. to lose brightness.—**it tar'nishes.** —*n.* dimness, dullness

Compare: stain, darken, obscure, taint
Contrast: brighten, cleanse, polish, restore

tarpau'lin *n.* canvas treated with tar or oil to make it waterproof.—*adj.*

tar'ry (ta'ri) *v.* to stay, to linger, to wait.—he **tar'ries.**—**tar'rying** *pres. part.*—**tar'ried** *p.t.* and *p. part.*

tar'ry (tar'i) *adj.* covered with tar

tart *adj.* sour, sharp

tart *n.* a small fruit pie

tar'tan *n.* woollen cloth woven with colours in a check pattern

tar'tar *n.* 1. a crust that forms on the teeth. 2. substance deposited on wine-casks. 3. a native of Tartary. 4. a cruel violent-tempered person

task *n.* a piece of work to be done.—*v.* to put work on, to burden.—**task'master** *n.* —**to take to task** to find fault with.—**task force** *n.* (U.S.) a military force sent to carry out a specific operation

Compare: labour, job, toil, assignment

tas'sel *n.* an ornament consisting of a bunch of threads on a knob.—**tas'selled** *adj.*

taste *n.* 1. flavour. 2. the sense by which flavour is observed. 3. a small quantity. 4. liking, as *to have a taste for music.* 5. the ability to decide what is beautiful, as *She has very good taste in dress.* 6. style, sense of what is fitting or proper, manner, as *Such behaviour shows very bad taste.*—*v.* 1. to perceive the flavour of. 2. to eat or drink. 3. to have a certain flavour, as *It tastes nasty. It tastes of onions.*—**ta'sting** *pres. part.*—**taste'ful** *adj.* showing good taste.—**taste'fully** *adv.*—**taste'less** *adj.* 1. insipid. 2. showing bad taste.—**ta'sty** *adj.* pleasantly flavoured

tat'ter *n.* a rag.—*v.* to tear into rags

tat'tle *v.* to gossip.—*n.* foolish talk.—**tat'tling** *pres. part.*

tattoo' *n.* 1. a drum-beat, a bugle-call. 2. a military display

tattoo' *v.* to mark patterns on the skin by pricking and rubbing in inks

taunt *n.* a remark intended to hurt, insult.—*v.* to scoff at, to mock

Compare: sneer, jeer, jibe, mockery, ridicule

taut *adj.* drawn, tight, fully stretched, tense.—**taut'en** *v.* to make tense

tav'ern *n.* an inn, ale-house

taw'dry *adj.* cheap and showy

taw'ny *adj.* yellowish-brown

tax *n.* charge made by government on goods, income, property, etc.—**tax'es** *pl.*—*v.* 1. to put a tax on. 2. to burden, strain, as *the climb taxed his strength.* 3. to accuse, as *He taxed me with breaking my promise.* —he **tax'es.**—**taxa'tion** (-ā'shun) *n.*

tax'i *n.* a car for hire with driver.—*pl.* **tax'is.**—**tax'i-truck** *n.* (Aus.) a light truck available for casual hire as a taxi.—*v.* 1. to go in a taxi. 2. of air-craft, to run along surface.—**tax'ying** *pres. part.*—**tax'imeter** *n.* instrument in taxi for showing fare

tax'idermist *n.* a man who stuffs dead animals.—**tax'idermy** *n.* the act of stuffing dead animals

tea *n.* 1. dried leaves of a plant cultivated in China, India, Japan, etc. 2. a drink made from this. 3. an afternoon meal

teach *v.* 1. to give lessons. 2. to show how to do something.—he **teach'es**—**taught** *p.t.* and *p. part.*—**teach'er** *n.*—**teach'ing** *n.* 1. teacher's work. 2. what is taught.—**teach'able** *adj.*

Compare: instruct, educate, train, tutor, enlighten, inform, school

Note: Do not confuse this verb with **learn**

teak *n.* an East Indian tree giving very hard wood

team *n.* 1. two or more animals harnessed together. 2. a company of workers, players in a game.—**team'ster** *n.* the driver of a team.—**team-spir'it** *n.* working for the general good.—**team'-work** *n.* concerted effort

tear (tair) *v.* 1. to pull apart. 2. to make a hole in. 3. to become torn. 4. to rush.—**tore** *p.t.*—**torn** *p. part.*—*n.* a hole, torn place

Compare: rend, slit, split, rip

tear (teer) *n.* a drop of water falling from the eye.—**tear'ful** *adj.* weeping.—**tear-stained** *adj.*—**tear'-gas** *n.* a gas causing watering of the eyes and temporary blindness

tease (teez) *v.* 1. to annoy, torment. 2. to comb out wool, etc.—**tea'sing** *pres. part.*—*n.* a person who teases

Compare: vex, plague, provoke, tantalise. *Contrast:* conciliate, please, content, mollify

teas'el *n.* 1. a plant bearing a prickly burr. 2. a hooked brush used to *tease* cloth

tea'spoon *n.* a small spoon for stirring tea.—**tea'spoonful** *n.*—**tea'spoon'fuls** *pl.*

teat *n.* the part of breast or udder from which milk is sucked

tea'-tree *n.* (Aus. and N.Z.) any one of several trees and shrubs whose leaves were used by early settlers as substitutes for tea

tech'nical (tek'ni-kal) *adj.* 1. belonging to a mechanical art, or to a craft. 2. belonging to a special art or science.—**tech'nically** *adv.*—**technical'ity** *n.* technical detail, word, etc.

technic'ian (tek-nish'an) *n.* someone engaged in a mechanical skill

technique' (tek-neek') *n.* a method of performance, skill in an art

technol'ogy (tek-nol'o-ji) *n.* the science of industrial arts

te'dious (tee'di-us) *adj.* tiring, dull.—**te'diously** *adv.*—**te'dium** *n.* dreariness

Compare: wearisome, boring, slow, dreary, monotonous. *Contrast:* interesting, lively, bright

tee *n.* a small heap of sand or small wooden support on which golfer's ball is placed for a drive

teem *v.* 1. to swarm, abound, as *The water teemed with fish.* 2. to pour (with rain)

teen'ager *n.* someone aged between thirteen and twenty

teens *n.pl.* years of life between thirteen and twenty

teethe (teeTH) *v.* to cut teeth.—**teeth'ing** *pres. part.*

teeto'tal *adj.* not drinking intoxicants.—**teeto'taller** *n.* a person who never drinks intoxicants

tel'egram *n.* a message sent by telegraph

tel'egraph *n.* a way of sending messages by electricity or signals.—**telegraph'ic** *adj.*—**teleg'raphist** *n.* a person who works a telegraph.—**teleg'raphy** *n.*

telep'athy *n.* the supposed communication of thoughts and feelings between people at a distance

tel'ephone (tel'e-fōn) *n.* an instrument for sending sounds or speech to distant hearer.—*v.* to send a message by telephone.—**telephon'ic** *adj.*—**teleph'onist** *n.* a person who works on a telephone.—**teleph'ony** *n.*

tel'escope *n.* an instrument with lenses for making distant objects seem larger and nearer.—*v.* 1. to force into one another, like the parts of a telescope (which slide into each other). 2. to compress.—**telescop'ic** *adj.*

televis'ion (tel-e-vizh'un) *n.* a machine for seeing distant objects by use of wireless transmission

tell *v.* 1. to say, to relate, as *to tell a story* 2. to make known, to inform against (often followed by *of* or *on*). 3. to order, as *I told him to go.* 4. to count, as *The shepherd was telling his sheep.* 5. to produce an effect, as *That will tell against him.*—**told** *p.t.* and *p. part.* 6. to ascertain, as *to tell the time, I can't tell who it is.*—**tel'ler** *n.* 1. a person who tells. 2. a person who counts.—**tel'ling** *adj.* striking, remarkable.—**tell off** to upbraid, reproach

Compare: 1. speak, relate, publish, utter, narrate. 2. betray, give away. 3. bid, command. 4. reckon, enumerate. 5. count, have influence. 6. see, find out

temer'ity *n.* rashness, boldness

tem'per *v.* 1. to harden. 2. to moderate, to tone down.—*n.* 1. degree of hardness of steel, etc. 2. disposition. 3. a burst of anger.—**to lose one's temper** to become angry

temp'erament *n.* a person's natural disposition.—**temperament'al** *adj.* 1. due to temperament. 2. moody, capricious, sensitive

temp'erance *n.* 1. self-restraint, moderation. 2. moderation in drinking intoxicants

tem'perate *adj.* moderate, sober, as *a temperate climate, temperate habits.*—**tem'perately** *adv.*

Compare: calm, cool, equable, frugal, abstemious. *Contrast:* intemperate, violent, immoderate, passionate, extravagant, extreme

tem'perature *n.* degree of heat or cold

tem'pest *n.* violent storm.—**tempes'tuous** *adj.* stormy, violent

tem'ple *n.* a building for worship
Compare: church, chapel, cathedral, shrine, synagogue, mosque
tem'ple *n.* the flat part of the head between forehead and ear
tem'po *n.* 1. in music, time, rate. 2. rate of movement
temp'oral *adj.* 1. of time. 2. of this life or world. 3. not spiritual, worldly
Contrast: eternal, spiritual, divine
temporar'ily *adv.* for a time
tem'porary *adv.* lasting only for a time, as *After the school was burned down we had to move into temporary premises*
Contrast: permanent, lasting, perpetual
tem'porise *v.* to delay, to gain time, to avoid immediate action.—**tem'porising** *pres. part.*
tempt *v.* 1. to try, to test. 2. to persuade, esp. to do evil. 3. to attract.—**tempta'tion** (-tā'shun) *n.*—**temp'ter** *n.*—**temp'tress** *fem.*
ten *adj.* one more than nine
ten'able *adj.* which can be held or defended, as *He won a scholarship tenable at the grammar school. When the enemy outflanked us our position was no longer tenable*
tena'cious (ten-ā'shus) *adj.* holding fast, as *tenacious of one's rights.*—**tenac'ity** (ten-as'i-ti) *n.* firmness
Compare: stubbornness, resolution, retentiveness
ten'ancy (ten'an-si) *n.* 1. being a tenant. 2. property rented
ten'ant *n.* a person who pays rent.—**ten'antry** *n.* the tenants on an estate
tend *v.* 1. to incline, to move in a certain direction. 2. to have the effect of
Note: This verb is generally followed by *to* or *towards*, as *His opinions tend towards Socialism. It tends to get cold in the evenings*
tend *v.* to take care of, as *The shepherd tends his sheep.*—**tend on** or **upon** to wait on, attend
ten'dency (ten'den-si) *n.* inclination, bent.—**ten'dencies** *pl.*
tend'er *n.* 1. a ship attending larger ones with stores, etc. 2. a truck behind an engine, carrying coal, etc.
tend'er *v.* to offer.—*n.* an offer to do certain work for a certain payment
tend'er *adj.* 1. soft, not tough, as *tender meat.* 2. delicate, as *a tender plant.* 3. gentle, loving, as *tender care.*—**tend'erheart'ed** *adj.* kind.—**tender'ly** *adv.*—**tend'erness** *n.*
tend'on *n.* a cord of fibres joining a muscle to a bone
ten'dril *n.* thin, sensitive part of leaf or stem which attaches itself to anything
ten'ement *n.* a house, esp. divided into cheap apartments
ten'et *n.* an opinion, belief held to be true
Compare: dogma, creed, maxim, doctrine, principle
ten'fold *adj.* ten times as many.—*n.*
ten'nis *n.* a game played by two or four players with rackets and balls
ten'or *n.* 1. course, direction, as *They continued on an even tenor.* 2. general meaning, as *That was the tenor of his remarks.* 3. a male voice between alto and bass. 4. a singer with this voice
tense *adj.* 1. stretched tight, taut, 2. strained
tense *n.* in Grammar, the change of form of a verb to show the time of the action, e.g. *I go, am going* are *Present Tenses: I shall go, shall be going, shall have gone* are *Future Tenses: I went, have gone, was going, had gone, have been going, had been going* are *Past Tenses* of the verb *to go*
ten'sile *adj.* which can be stretched
ten'sion (ten'shun) *n.* 1. stretching, strain when stretched. 2. strain, excitement
tent *n.* a movable canvas shelter supported by poles
tent'acle *n.* a feeler on certain animals' heads
ten'tative *adj.* experimental, done as a trial.—**ten'tatively** *adv.*
ten'terhook *n.* a hooked nail used in stretching cloth.—**on tenterhooks** in suspense, anxiously waiting
tenth *adj.* next after ninth
ten'uous *adj.* thin, fine
ten'ure *n.* conditions or period of holding land, an office, etc.
te'pee (tee'pee) *n.* a North American Indian wigwam
tep'id *adj.* fairly warm, lukewarm.—**tepid'ity** *n.*
tercente'nary (ter-sen-tee'nar-i) *n.* a three-hundredth anniversary.—*adj.*
term *n.* 1. limit, end. 2. fixed time during which courts sit, schools are open, etc. 3. a word or expression.—*v.* to name.—**terms** *n.pl.* 1. conditions. 2. relationship, as *to be on good terms with someone.*—**to come to terms** to reach agreement
ter'minal *adj.* 1. at the end, forming an end.—*n.* an end, esp. a point of connection in electrical apparatus
ter'minate *v.* to end, put an end to.—**terminating** *pres. part.*—**termina'tion** (-ā'shun) *n.*
terminol'ogy (ter-min-ol'o-ji) *n.* special terms used in a science, profession, etc.
ter'minus *n.* 1. end. 2. a station at the end of a railway.—**ter'mini** *pl.*
ter'mite *n.* an ant-like insect living in communities
ter'race (te'ras) *n.* 1. a raised, flat piece of ground, shelf cut out of a hill. 2. a row of houses
ter'ra-cot'ta *n.* hard, unglazed pottery.—*adj.* brownish-red
terres'trial *adj.* of the earth, of land
Contrast: aerial, aquatic, celestial
ter'rible *adj.* causing fear. (See **dreadful.**)—**ter'ribly** *adv.*
Note: In common speech *terribly* is

often loosely used, to mean very, as *I am terribly sorry*

ter'rier *n.* a small, active dog fond of burrowing for rabbits, etc.

terrif'ic *adj.* terrible, dreadful.—**terrif'ically** *adv.*

ter'rify *v.* to frighten.—he **ter'rifies.**—**ter'rifying** *pres. part.*—**ter'rified** *p.t.* and *p. part.*

Compare: alarm, dismay, scare, intimidate, appal, affright, daunt, cow

territo'rial *adj.* of territory.—*n.* a volunteer soldier for home defence, a member of the **Territorial Army.**—**territorial waters** the rivers of a country and the sea bordering it

ter'ritory *n.* land, region under a ruler.—**ter'ritories** *pl.*

Compare: district, province, state, domain, area

ter'ror *n.* great fear, horror. (See **fear**).—**ter'rorise** *v.* to force by fear.—**ter'rorist** *n.*

terse (ters) *adj.* short and to the point, concise.—**terse'ly** *adv.*

test *n.* an examination to decide fitness or quality.—*v.* to try, put to a test.—**test'-match** *n.* a cricket match between two countries.—**test'-pilot** *n.* someone who tests new aeroplanes.—**test'-tube** *n.* a glass tube, closed at one end, used in scientific experiments

test'ament *n.* a will.—**Old Test'ament, New Test'ament** *n.* the two divisions of the Bible

testa'tor *n.* one who makes a will.—**testa'trix** *fem.*

test'ify *v.* to bear witness, to declare.—he **test'ifies.**—**test'ifying** *pres. part.*—**test'ified** *p.t.* and *p. part.*

testimo'nial *n.* 1. a certificate of character, ability, qualifications, etc. 2. a gift showing gratitude, regard, etc.

test'imony *n.* evidence, statement proving something.—**test'imonies** *pl.*

tête-a-tête (tāt-ah-tāt) *n.* a private conversation for two persons.—*adj.*—*adv.*

teth'er (teTH'er) *v.* to tie up an animal with a rope.—*n.* a rope or chain for fastening grazing animal

Teu'ton *n.* a member of a German tribe.—**Teuton'ic** *adj.*

text *n.* 1. the actual words of a book, etc. 2. the main body of a book. 3. a verse from the Bible as subject of a discussion.—**text'ual** *adj.*—**text-book** *n.* study-book for pupils

tex'tile *adj.* woven, which can be woven.—*n.pl.* woven goods

tex'ture *n.* 1. the quality and arrangement of weaving in a material. 2. structure, make-up

than *prep.* and *conj.* used to introduce second part of a comparison, as *I am older than my sister*

Note: When you say *I am older than she* (*is*), *than* is a conjunction. When you say, *I am older than her, than* is a preposition

thane *n.* a nobleman in Anglo-Saxon times

thank *v.* to express gratitude.—**thank'ful** *adj.* grateful, pleased.—**thank'fully** *adv.*—**thank'less** *adj.* 1. bringing no thanks, as a *thankless task.* 2. ungrateful, as *a thankless child.*—**thanks** *n.pl.* words of gratitude.—**thank'-offering** *n.* a gift to show thanks.—**thanksgiv'ing** *n.* giving thanks to God

that *adj.* is used to point out some person or thing, usually at a distance, as *That boy is my brother. I do not like that thing.*—*pron.* as *This is better than that.*—*pl.* **those.** —*pron. relative* which, as *This is the house that Jack built.*—*conj.* used to introduce subordinate noun clauses, as *Please tell him that I am coming. adv.* to such a degree or extent, so, as *I have done that much*

thatch *n.* straw or rushes used for roofing a house or stack.—*v.* to make a straw roof

thaw *v.* to melt ice, snow, etc.—*n.*

the the definite article, used to indicate special person, persons, thing or things, as contrasted with the indefinite article *a.*

the'atre *n.* 1. a place where plays are performed. 2. a room of similar shape for lectures, operations, etc. 3. drama. 4. an area where a war is fought.—**theat'rical** *adj.* 1. of the theatre. 2. showy, spectacular.—**theat'ricals** *n.pl.* amateur dramatic performances

thee *pron.* objective form of *thou,* as *I bid thee farewell.*—**you** *pl.*

theft *n.* the act of stealing

their *adj.* possessive form of *they,* as *We came in their car.* When used alone *their* becomes *theirs,* as *The car is theirs.*—**his** *masc. sing.*—**her** (hers) *fem. sing.*—**its** *neuter sing.*

them *pron.* objective form of *they,* as *I will send them.*—**him** *masc. sing.*—**her** *fem. sing.*—**it** *neuter sing.*

theme *n.* 1. the subject matter of writing or discussion. 2. a short composition. 3. a melody repeated with variations in a piece of music

themselves' *pron. pl.* 1. emphatic and 2. reflexive form of *they,* as *They themselves said so. They hurt themselves.*—**himself'** *masc. sing.*—**herself'** *fem. sing.*—**itself'** *neuter sing.*

then *adv.* 1. at that time, as *He was then a schoolboy.* 2. next, as *Mix the ingredients well and then bake in a quick oven.*—*conj.* therefore, so, as *Then you didn't mean what you said.*—*adj.* existing at that time, as *The then secretary.*—*n.* that time, as *It will be too late by then.*—**now and then** occasionally.—**every now and then** from time to time

thence *adv.* from that place, as *They departed thence.*—**thence'forth** *adv.* from that time on.—**thencefor'ward** *adv.* from then on

theod'olite *n.* a surveyor's instrument for measuring angles

theolo'gian (thee-o-lō'jan) *n.* a person skilled in theology.—**theolog'ical** (thee-o-loj'i-kal) *adj.* of theology

theol'ogy (thee-ol'o-ji) *n.* the study of God and religious truth.—**theol'ogies** *pl.*

the'orem *n.* a mathematical statement which has to be proved

theoret'ical *adj.* based on theory, not on fact or experience.—**theoret'ically** *adv.*—**the'orise** *v.* to form theories

the'ory *n.* 1. an idea suggested to explain something, based on reasoning. 2. a system of rules, as opposed to practice.—**the'ories** *pl.*

there *adv.* 1. in, at or to that place, as *He lives there. We will go there.* 2. used to introduce a statement, as *There are many ways of doing it.*—*n.* that place, as *He lives near there.*—*interj.* 1. Lo! Behold! as *There! What did I tell you!* 2. Never mind (to a child), as *There! There! You'll soon be better*

Note: Do not confuse *there* with *their*

There is used to make many other words, such as:—**thereabout'** near there.—**there'abouts** approximately.—**thereaf'ter** after that.—**thereat'** at which, at that.—**there'by** by which, by that.—**there'fore** thus, accordingly.—**therein'** in that.—**thereof'** of that.—**thereon'** on that.—**thereto'** to that.—**there'upon** upon that, at that moment.—**therewith'** with that

therm *n.* 1. a unit of heat equal to 100,000 British Thermal Units, used in measuring coal gas. 2. (in science) the amount of heat required to heat one gramme of water one degree Centigrade.—**British Thermal Unit** the amount of heat required to raise one pound of water one degree Fahrenheit

therm'al *adj.* 1. of heat. 2. of hot springs

thermom'eter *n.* an instrument for measuring temperature

ther'mos, ther'mos flask *n.* a vacuum flask for keeping liquids hot, or cold

ther'mostat *n.* an automatic device for keeping temperature even in electrical equipment

the'sis *n.* 1. a subject for discussion. 2. an essay in support of a statement.—**the'ses** (thee'seez) *pl.*

they *pron. pl.* plural form of *he, she,* or *it,* as *John and Mary set out together and they soon caught us up.*—**them** *objective.*—**their, theirs** *possessive.*—**themselves'** *emphatic and reflexive*

thick *adj.* 1. not thin, wide. 2. dense, crowded. 3. foggy. 4. stiff.—*n.* the densest part.—*adv.* thickly.—**thick'en** *v.* to make thick.—**thick'et** *n.* dense shrubs.—**thick'ly** *adv.*—**thick'ness** *n.*—**thick'est** *adj.* sturdy, solid.—**in the thick of** in the midst of.—**thick-skinned'** *adj.* not sensitive to criticism

Compare: (with thicket) bush, undergrowth, jungle

thief (theef) *n.* a person who steals.—**thieves** *pl.* (See **robber**)

thieve (theev) *v.* to steal.—**thiev'ing** *pres. part.*—**thiev'ish** *adj.*

thigh (thī) *n.* the leg above the knee

thim'ble *n.* a metal cap to protect the fingertip when sewing

thin *adj.* 1. of little thickness, not fat. 2. not abundant. 3. not closely packed. 4. lean, slight.—**thin'ner** *comp.*—**thin'nest** *sup.* (See **fat.**)—*v.* to make thin, to become thin.—**thin'ning** *pres. part.*—**thinned** *p.t.* and *p. part.*—**thin'ness** *n.*

thine *adj.* and *pron.* possessive form of *thou* used by itself or before a vowel, as *It is thine. Lift up thine eyes.* (See **thy.**)—**your, yours** *pl.*

thing *n.* any object that can be thought about, touched, smelt, heard, seen or tasted

think (thingk) *v.* 1. to use one's mind. 2. to believe. 3. to have in mind.—**thought** *p.t.* and *p. part.*—**to think better of** to reconsider a hasty judgment.—**to think much of** to like greatly.—**to think nothing of** to have a poor opinion of.—**to think over** to consider at length

Compare: cogitate, consider, muse, ponder, suppose

third *adj.* next after second.—*n.* one of three equal parts.—**third-degree'** *n.* rough treatment of a prisoner to obtain a confession.—**third-rate'** *adj.* of poor quality

thirst *n.* 1. a parched feeling in the throat caused by desire to drink. 2. a strong desire.—*v.* to suffer from thirst.—**thirst'y** *adj.*—**thirst'ier** *comp.*—**thirst'iest** *sup.*—**thirst'ily** *adv.*

Note: The verb *thirst* is sometimes followed by *after,* as *to hunger and thirst after righteousness*

thirteen' *adj.* three and ten.—*n.*—**thirteenth'** *adj.* one more than twelfth

thir'tieth *adj.* next after twenty-ninth

thir'ty *adj.* three times ten.—*n.*

this *adj.* used to indicate some person or thing, usually close to the speaker, as *I will take this seat.*—*pron.* as *Will you take this?*—**these** *pl.*

this'tle (this'l) *n.* a prickly plant.—**this'tledown** *n.* seeds of the thistle

thith'er (thiTH'er) *adv.* to that place, there

thong *n.* a narrow strip of leather

tho'rax *n.* 1. the chest. 2. the second section of an insect's body

thorn *n.* 1. a prickle on a plant. 2. a prickly plant.—**thorn'y** *adj.* 1. full of thorns. 2. troublesome

thor'ough (thur'a) *adj.* 1. complete, entire, as *She gave the house a thorough cleaning.* 2. accurate, careful, not superficial, as *His work is very thorough.*—**thor'oughly** *adv.*—**thor'oughbred** *adj.* of pure breed.—*n.* a pure-bred animal.—**thor'oughfare** *n.*

1. a road open at both ends. 2. a right of way.—**thor'oughness** *n.*

those *pl.* of **that**

thou *pron.* old form of the second person pronoun (singular) when regarded as the subject of the sentence, as *Thou canst not say I did it*.—**thee** *objective*.—**thy, thine** *possessive*.—**thyself** *reflexive and emphatic*.—**ye, you** *pl.*

though (thō) *conj.* in spite of the fact that, as *Though in great danger, he showed no fear*. (See **although**.)—*adv.* for all that, however, as *I don't like it, though*.—**as though** as if

thought (thawt) *p.t.* and *p. part.* of **think**.—*n.* 1. an idea. 2. thinking, using one's brain.—**thought'ful** *adj.* 1. thinking. 2. careful, considerate.—**thought'less** *adj.* careless

thou'sand (thou'zand) *adj.* ten hundred.—*n.*—**thou'sandth** *adj.*

thral'dom (thrawl'dom) *n.* bondage, slavery

thrash *v.* 1. to beat, whip. 2. See **thresh**.—he **thrash'es**

thread (thred) *n.* 1. a fine cord. 2. the ridge cut on a screw. 3. an idea connecting parts of a story, etc.—*v.* 1. to pass thread through. 2. to put on a thread. 3. to pick one's way.—**thread'bare** *adj.* worn-out, shabby

threat (thret) *n.* 1. an announcement of intention to punish or hurt. 2. a sign of coming evil.—**threat'en** *v.* 1. to use a threat. 2. to menace

three *adj.* two and one.—*n.*—**three'fold** *adj.* having three parts, three times.—**three'pence** (threp'ens) *n.*—**three'score** *adj.* sixty

thresh *v.* to beat out grain from wheat, to thrash.—he **thresh'es**.—**thresh'er** *n.* a threshing-machine

thresh'old (thresh'hōld) *n.* 1. a plank or stone under a door. 2. a doorway, entrance. 3. a beginning, as *on the threshold of a new career*

thrice (thrīs) *adv.* three times

thrift *n.* 1. saving, economy. 2. the sea-pink.—**thrift'ily** *adv.*—**thrift'less** *adj.* wasteful. careless.—**thrift'y** *adj.* saving, careful.—**thrift'ier** *comp.*—**thrift'iest** *sup.*

Compare: gain, frugality, profit, parsimony, prudence. *Contrast:* extravagance, prodigality, wastefulness

thrill *n.* an excited feeling.—*v.* 1. to feel or cause to feel excited. 2. to tremble.—**thril'ling** *adj.* exciting.—**thril'ler** *n.* an exciting story or film

thrive *v.* to grow well, to flourish, prosper.—**thri'ving** *pres. part.*—**throve** *p.t.*—**thriv'en** *p. part.*

throat *n.* 1. the front of the neck. 2. the passages going through the neck

throb *v.* to beat strongly, to palpitate.—**throb'bing** *pres. part.*—**throbbed** *p.t.* and *p. part.*—*n.* a throbbing

throe (thrō) *n.* extreme pain, agony.—**in the throes of** struggling with some difficulty

throne *n.* a chair of state for kings, queens, bishops.—*v.* to enthrone, place on throne

throng *n.* a crowd.—*v.*

throt'tle *v.* 1. to choke. 2. to suffocate.—**throt'tling** *pres. part.*—*n.* a valve regulating supply of petrol or steam to an engine

through (thrōō) *prep.* 1. from end to end, from side to side, between. 2. because of, by means of, as *He won through sheer determination*.—*adv.* as *to go through*.—*adj.* 1. without a stop, as *a through train*. 2. from end to end, etc., as *a through passage*.—**throughout'** *prep.* and *adv.* right through

throw (thrō) *v.* 1. to fling into the air. 2. to cause to fall.—**threw** *p.t.*—**thrown** *p. part.*—*n.* throwing, being thrown.—**to throw in the sponge** to admit defeat

Compare: hurl, cast, heave, pitch, project, toss

thrush *n.* a song-bird

thrust *v.* 1. to push, stab, drive. 2. to push one's way.—**thrust** *p.t.* and *p. part.*—*n.* a stab, a push

thud *n.* a dull, heavy sound.—*v.* to make a thud.—**thud'ding** *pres. part.*—**thud'ded** *p.t.* and *p. part.*

thug *n.* a murderous robber

thumb (thum) *n.* the short, thick finger.—*v.* to dirty, or handle with the thumb

thump *v.* to strike heavily, to pound.—*n.* a dull, heavy blow

thun'der *n.* 1. the loud noise that follows lightning. 2. any loud noise.—*v.* to sound loudly.—**thun'derbolt** *n.* a destructive lightning-flash.—**thun'derclap** *n.* a crash of thunder.—**thun'derous** *adj.*—**thun'derstruck** *adj.* amazed

Thurs'day *n.* the fifth day of the week

thus *adv.* 1. in this way. 2. therefore

thwart *v.* to prevent from doing something, to defeat.—*adv.* across.—*n.* a seat across a boat

thy *pron.* possessive form of *thou*, as *Thy voice is sweet*. When used alone *thy* becomes *thine*, as *a sweet voice is thine*. In poetry *thine* is used instead of *thy before a* vowel, e.g. *thine eyes*.—**your** *pl.*

thyme (tīm) *n.* a sweet-smelling herb

thy'roid *n.* a large gland in the throat

thy'self *pron.* emphatic or reflexive form of *thou*, as (1) *Thou thyself has said it*, or (2) *Thou hast betrayed thyself*.—**yourselves** *pl.*

tia'ra (tee-ah'ra) *n.* 1. a jewelled band as head-ornament. 2. the Pope's crown

tib'ia *n.* the shin-bone

tick *n.* 1. the sound of a watch or clock. 2. a small mark.—*v.* 1. to make a sound like a clock. 2. to make a mark

tick *n.* a small insect living in hair or fur

tick *n.* a mattress-cover

tick'et *n.* 1. a card or paper to admit the holder. 2. a label.—**ticket-of-leave'** *n.* (Aus.) a certificate issued to a convict allowing him restricted freedom and permission

to work for himself.—*v.* to mark with a ticket
tick'le *v.* 1. to touch, lightly causing laughter. 2. to amuse.—**tick'ling** *pres. part.*—*n.* an itch, tickling.—**tick'lish** *adj.* 1. easily tickled. 2. difficult to manage
ti'dal *adj.* of tides, caused by the tide.—**ti'dal-wave** *n.* a great ocean-wave usually caused by an earthquake
tide *n.* 1. the rise and fall of the sea happening about every twelve hours. 2. time, season. —**to tide over** to help
ti'diness *n.* being tidy, neatness
ti'dings *n.pl.* news
ti'dy *adj.* neat, orderly.—**ti'dier** *comp.*—**ti'diest** *sup.*—*v.* to put in order.—he **tid'ies.**—**ti'dying** *pres. part.*—**ti'died** *p.t.* and *p. part.*
tie (tī) *v.* 1. to fasten, bind. 2. to form into a knot. 3. to have equal points in game or race.—**ty'ing** *pres. part.*—**tied** *p.t.* and *p. part.*—*n.* 1. a necktie. 2. something that connects or unites. 3. a drawn game, equal score
tier (teer) *n.* a row, e.g. of seats or houses arranged one above the other
tiff *n.* a slight quarrel
ti'ger *n.* a large, fierce wild animal with dark stripes.—**ti'gress** *fem.*
tight (tīt) *adj.* 1. firm. 2. stretched. 3. close, fitting closely. 4. (slang) drunk.—*adv.* closely.—**tight'en** *v.* to make tight.—**tights** *n.pl.* close-fitting costume worn by acrobats
ti'ki (tī'kee) *n.* (N.Z.) greenstone ornament. —**Ti'ki** mythological figure held in some stories to be the first man
tile *n.* a thin piece of stone or baked clay for covering roofs, etc.—*v.*
till *n.* a money-drawer in a shop
till *v.* to cultivate land.—**till'age** *n.*
till *prep.* until, up to the time of, as *Wait till this afternoon.*—*conj.* to the time that, as *Wait till I come back*
til'ler *n.* a bar to move the rudder of a boat
tilt *v* 1. to slope, slant. 2. to fight on horseback with a lance, as *Don Quixote tilted at windmills.*—*n.* 1. slope. 2. combat with lances, a thrust
tim'ber *n.* 1. wood for building, carpentry, etc. 2. trees suitable for felling.—**tim'bered** *adj.* 1. made of wood. 2. wooded
tim'bre (tam'ber) *n.* the quality of sound distinguishing voices or instruments
time *n.* 1. the whole of the past, present and future divided into periods. 2. one of these periods. 3. hour. 4. a point in time. 5. occasion. 6. rhythm, speed. 7. time allowed. —*v.* to choose or note the time of.—**ti'ming** *pres. part.*—*n.* ability to arrange the order in which events should happen. —**time'ly** *adj.* happening at the right time. —**time'-hon'oured** *adj.* respected because it is old.—**time'-signal** *n.* a radio signal giving the time.—**time'-switch** *n.* a switch starting an appliance working at a set time.—**time'-table** *n.* plan showing hours of work, times of arrival and departure, etc.—**all in good time** at the right time.—**from time to time** now and then.—**in time** 1. soon enough. 2. after some time.—**on time** punctual
tim'id *adj.* shy, easily scared.—**timid'ity** *n.*—**tim'idly** *adv.*
Compare: frightened, fearful nervous, timorous. *Contrast:* See **bold, brave**
tim'orous *adj.* timid, very shy
tim'pani (*pl.* of **tim'panō**) *n.pl.* set of orchestral kettle drums
tin *v.* 1. a soft, white metal. 2. a container made of, or coated with tin.—*v.* 1. to coat with tin. 2. to put in a tin for preserving.—**tin'ning** *pres. part.*—**tinned** *p.t.* and *p. part.* —**tin'-foil** *n.* a thin wrapping sheet of an alloy of lead and tin.—**tin'plate** *n.* sheet iron coated with tin
tinc'ture *n.* 1. medical substance mixed with alcohol. 2. colour, trace.—*v.* to colour
tin'der *n.* 1. material used to catch a spark from flint and steel. 2. anything easily set on fire
tinge (tinj) *v.* 1. to colour or flavour slightly. —**tinge'ing, ting'ing** *pres. part.*—*n.* slight colour, trace
ting'le (ting'gl) *v.* to thrill, to have a prickly feeling.—**ting'ling** *pres. part.*
tin'ker (ting'ker) *n.* a mender of pots and pans.—*v.* to work in a clumsy way
tin'kle (ting'kl) *v.* to make sounds like a small bell.—**tin'kling** *pres. part.*—*n.* a light, ringing sound
tin'sel *n.* 1. glittering metal foil used for decorations. 2. anything cheap and showy
tint *n.* 1. a shade of colour. 2. a slight colour. —*v.* to colour, tinge
ti'ny *adj.* very small. See **little.**—**ti'nier** *comp.* —**ti'niest** *sup.*
tip *n.* 1. the slender, or pointed end of anything. 2. something put to protect an end, e.g. of a billiard cue. 3. a small present of money. 4. a slight push. 5. a (useful) hint.—*v.* 1. to put a tip (1.) on. 2. to give a tip (2.) to. 3. to upset, to slant.—**tip'ping** *pres. part.*—**tipped** *p.t.* and *p. part.*—**tip'ster** *n.* one who sells tips (see 5) about horse races.—**tip'toe** *n.*—*v.*—**tiptop'** *adj.* of the very best
tip'sy *adj.* slightly drunk
tirade' (tī-rād') *n.* a long, ranting speech
tire *v.* to weary, to become tired.—**ti'ring** *pres. part.*—**tired** *p. t.* and *p. part.*—*adj.* wearied.—**tired of** bored by.—**tire'less** *adj.* —energetic, not easily tired.—**tire'some** *adj.* annoying
tire, tyre *n.* a rim of metal, rubber, etc. round a wheel
tis'sue (tis'ū, tish'ōō) *n.* 1. a fine, woven material. 2. a substance of which parts of plants and animals are composed. 3. collection, as *His story was a tissue of lies.* —**tis'sue-paper** *n.* very soft, thin paper

tit *n.* a kind of small bird, titmouse, tomtit
titan'ic *adj.* huge, gigantic
tit'bit *n.* a nice bit of food or news
tithe (tīTH) *n.* 1. a tenth part, esp. of agricultural produce, once paid as a tax to the Church
ti'tle *n.* 1. a heading, name of a book, etc. 2. a name showing rank, etc. 3. a legal right to property.—**ti'tle-page** *n.* the page of a book, showing the title.—**ti'tled** *adj.* of noble rank
tit'mouse *n.* a small bird.—**tit'mice** *pl.*
tit'ter *v.* to laugh secretly, to giggle
tit'tle *n* 1 a small mark. 2. something very small, the least bit.—**tit'tle-tat'tle** idle gossip
tit'ular *adj.* in name or title only
to *prep.* 1. towards, in the direction of. 2. as far as. 3. used to introduce a comparison, as *As two is to four, so is four to eight. This is superior to that.* 4. used to introduce the infinitive mood of verbs, e.g. *to go, to be*—*adv.* to the required or normal state or position, as *come to, fall to, heave to.*—**to and fro** backwards and forwards
toad (tōd) *n.* a frog-like amphibian with warty body.—**toad'stool** *n.* a poisonous mushroom.—**toad'y** *n.* a person who flatters basely.—*v.*
toast (tōst) *v.* 1. to brown at the fire. 2. to warm. 3. to drink the health of.—*n.* 1. slice of bread browned at the fire. 2. drinking the health of. 3. person whose health is proposed.—**toast'er** *n.* an electric appliance for toasting bread.—**toast'master** *n.* an announcer of toasts at banquets
tobac'co *n.* a plant of which the leaves, when prepared, are used for smoking.—**tobac'cos** *pl.*—**tobac'conist** *n.* a dealer in tobacco
tobog'gan *n.* a kind of long flat sledge without runners, curving up at the front, used in winter sports.—*v.*—**tobog'ganing** *pres. part.*
today', to-day' *n.* this day.—*adv.* 1. on this day. 2. at the present time
tod'dle *v.* to walk with unsteady, short steps.—*n.*—**tod'dling** *pres. part.*—**tod'dler** *n.* small child
toe (tō) *n.* one of the five members at the end of a foot.—*v.* to reach or touch with the toe
tof'fee *n.* a sweet made of boiled sugar and butter
to'ga *n.* a loose, outer garment worn by ancient Romans.—**to'gas** *pl.*
togeth'er *adv.* 1. with each other, in company. 2. at the same time
tohung'a *n.* a Maori word for a wise man, a magician
toil *v.* to work hard.—*n.* heavy work, labour. See **work**.—**toil'er** *n.*—**toil'some** *adj.* hard.—**toil'worn** *adj.*
toil'et *n.* 1. the process of dressing. 2. dress, style of dress. 3. a lavatory.—*adj.* used for the toilet
to'ken *n.* a sign, something serving as a symbol, keepsake, or guarantee
Compare: indication, evidence, pledge, mark
tol'erable *adj.* 1. bearable. 2. fairly good, moderate.—**tol'erably** *adv.*
tol'erance *n.* 1. patience with beliefs or opinions different from one's own. 2. (in engineering, etc.) allowance for variation.—**tol'erant** *adj.*
tol'erate *v.* to put up with endure.—**tol'erating** *pres. part.*—**tolera'tion** (-ā'shun) *n.* not interfering with the beliefs of others, as *In civilised countries a policy of religious toleration is followed*
Compare: tolerance, broad-mindedness, indulgence. *Contrast:* bigotry, intolerance, rancour, persecution
toll (tōl) *v.* to ring a bell slowly at regular intervals.—*n.*
toll (tōl) *n.* a tax, esp. for the use of a bridge or road
tom'ahawk *n.* a fighting axe used by American Indians
toma'to (tō-mah'tō) *n.* 1. a plant bearing juicy red or yellow fruit. 2. the fruit.—**tomat'oes** *pl.*
tomb (tōōm) *n.* a grave.—**tomb'stone** *n.* a stone or monument marking a grave
tome *n.* a large book, volume
tombo'la (tombō'la) *n.* a kind of lottery in which prizes are awarded for numbers drawn from a drum
tomor'row, to-mor'row (too-mo'rō) *n.* the day after to-day.—*adv.* on the day after this one
tom'tit *n.* a blue tit
tom'tom *n.* a drum used by savages
ton (tun) *n.* 1. a British measure of weight, 20 cwt. or 2240 lbs. 2. (U.S.A.) a weight of 2000 lbs.—**metric ton** a weight of 1000 kg.
tone *n.* 1. sound, quality of musical sound. 2. healthy condition. 3. style, general character, as *The tone of the letter was quite friendly.* 4. a shade of colour.—*v.* 1. to harmonise. 2. to give tone to.—**to'ning** *pres. part.*—**to tone down** to soften
tongs *n.pl.* large pincers, esp. for handling coal
tongue (tung) *n.* 1. the organ in the mouth used in tasting, speaking, etc. 2. speech, way of speaking. 3. a language. 4. something shaped like a tongue.—**tongue'-tied** *adj.* slow in speech, shy.—**to give tongue** to bark.—**to hold one's tongue** to keep silent.—**with tongue in cheek** insincerely
ton'ic *n.* 1. anything that braces, medicine. 2. in music, the key note of a scale.—*adj.* 1. relating to tone. 2. strength-giving
tonight', to-night' (too-nīt') *n.* this night.—*adv.* on the night of this day
ton'nage (tun'aj) *n.* 1. carrying capacity of a ship. 2. ships. 3. a tax paid by a ship in port according to its size
ton'sils *n.pl.* two glands at the back of the

mouth.—**tonsilli'tis** *n.* inflammation of the tonsils

ton'sure (ton'sher) *n.* the shaven crown of a priest's head

too *adv.* 1. to a greater degree than is necessary or desirable, as *too large, too many, too much.* 2. also, as *He came too*

tool *n.* 1. something used in doing work with the hands. 2. a person used by another for his own purposes.—*v.* to use a tool on

Compare: implement, instrument, appliance, mechanism, agent

toot *n.* the sound of a horn.—*v.*

tooth (tōōth) *n.* 1. any of the bone-like parts rooted in the jaws and used for biting. 2. something like this.—**teeth** *pl.*—**tooth'-ache** (tōōth'-āk) *n.*—**tooth'-brush** *n.* brush for cleaning teeth.—**tooth'some** *adj.* good to eat.—**armed to the teeth** fully armed.—**by the skin of one's teeth** only just.—**in the teeth of** against the fury of.—**to fight tooth and nail** to fight fiercely with any weapon.—**to set one's teeth on edge** to offend one greatly (esp. harsh noises)

top *n.* 1. the highest part. 2. the highest rank, as *at the top of the class.* 3. a platform on ship's mast.—*adj.* highest.—*v.* 1. to cover the top. 2. to be at the top. 3. to cut off the top. 4. (in golf, etc.) to strike the top half of the ball.—**top'ping** *pres. part.*—**topped** *p.t.* and *p. part.*—**top-boots** *n.pl.*—**top-coat** *n.* an overcoat.—**top-hat** *n.* high silk hat.—**the big top** a circus tent.—**from top to toe** from head to foot.—**to be top dog** to be the victor

Compare: summit, apex, peak, climax, acme, pinnacle, crown. *Contrast:* bottom, base

top *n.* a spinning top

to'paz *n.* a precious stone, usually yellow

top'ic *n.* a subject of conversation or discussion.—**top'ical** *adj.* 1. of a topic. 2. about events of the day

top'most *adj.* highest

topog'raphy (top-og'ra-fi) *n.* a detailed description of the geographical features of a place

top'ple *v.* to fall over.—**top'pling** *pres. part.*

top'sy-tur'vy *adv.* upside down, in confusion.—*adj.*

tor *n.* a pointed, rocky hill-top

torch *n.* 1. a lighted stick or rope to be carried about. 2. a small portable electric light.—**torch'es** *pl.*—**torch'bearer** *n.*—**torch'-light** *n.*

tor'eador *n.* a Spanish bull-fighter

tor'ment *n.* great suffering of body or mind.—**torment'** *v.* 1. to distress. 2. to tease, annoy.—**torment'or** *n.*

Compare: anguish, torture, pain, agony

torna'do (tawr-nā'dō) *n.* a violent storm, whirlwind.—**torna'does** *pl.*

torpe'do (tor-pee'do) *n.* a long cigar-shaped self-propelled shell to be aimed underwater at an enemy ship.—**torpe'does** *pl.*—*v.* to hit with a torpedo

tor'pid *adj.* sluggish, dull, inactive.—**torpid'ity** *n.*—**tor'por** *n.* apathy, lack of feeling

tor'rent *n.* a rushing stream, flood.—**torren'tial** (tor-en'shal) *adj.*

tor'rid *adj.* very hot.—**tor'rid zone** *n.* the earth's zone between the tropics

tor'sion *n.* twisting

tor'toise (tor'tus) *n.* a four-footed reptile covered with hard shell.—**tor'toise-shell** *n.* an outer shell or scale of some sea turtles used for making combs, etc.

tor'tuous *adj.* 1. crooked, winding. 2. deceitful

tor'ture *n.* very severe pain.—*v.* to subject to torture.—**tor'turing** *pres. part.*—**tor'turer** *n.*

toss *v.* 1. to throw about, to fling. 2. to throw in the air.—he **toss'es.**—*n.* a tossing, being tossed

tot *n.* 1. a small child. 2. a small quantity

to'tal *adj.* complete, entire.—*n.* the whole amount, sum.—**to'tally** *adv.* completely.—*v.* 1. to add up. 2. to amount to.—**to'talling** *pres. part.*—**to'talled** *p.t.* and *p. part.*

to'tem *n.* an animal, plant or object worshipped as emblem of a tribe.—**to'tem pole** large carved pole bearing carved totem

tot'ter *v.* to walk unsteadily, to begin to fall

tou'can (tōō'kan) *n.* a bright coloured American bird with huge beak

touch (tuch) *v.* 1. to put one's hand on, to feel. 2. to come against. 3. to move, affect (the emotions). 4. (on) to speak about in passing. 5. (up) to improve.—he **touch'es.**—*n.* 1. touching, being touched. 2. sense of feeling. 3. style. 4. small amount, as *a touch of colour.*—**touched** *adj.* (slang) somewhat insane.—**touch'ing** *adj.* moving (to the emotions).—*prep.* about.—**touch'-line** *n.* a side-line on football-field.—**touch'stone** *n.* 1. a stone used for testing gold. 2. a test.—**touch'y** *adj.* irritable, easily offended.—**touch'-down** *v,* 1. (of aircraft) to land. 2. (Rugby football) to score by touching the ground behind the goal posts with the ball.—**in touch with** in communication with.—**to touch up** to repair or improve slightly.—**to touch-type** to typewrite without looking at the keys.—**touch-and-go** uncertain, risky

tough (tuf) *adj.* 1. able to resist, strong. 2. difficult. 3. difficult to bite. 4. (slang) rough and bad.—*n.*—**tough'en** *v.* to make tough.—**tough'ness** *n.*

Contrast: tender, delicate, gentle, soft

tour (tōōr) *n.* a journey from place to place.—*v.* to travel through.—**tour'ist** *n.* a person travelling for pleasure

tour'nament (tōōr'na-ment) *n.* 1. a contest between knights on horseback. 2. a sports competition

tour'niquet (tōōr'ni-kā) *n.* a device for stopping bleeding by pressure on artery

tou'sled (tou'zld) *adj.* untidy, dishevelled

tout *v.* to seek information or custom in underhand way.—*n.*

Note: This verb is usually followed by *for*

tow (tō) *v.* to pull by a rope.—*n.* 1. towing, being towed. 2. vessel in tow

tow (tō) *n.* coarse fibres of flax or hemp used to make ropes

towards', toward' (tōrdz, to-wordz') *prep.* in the direction of

tow'el *n.* cloth for drying something wet.—**tow'elling** *n.* material used for towels

tow'er *n.* 1. a tall square or round building or part of a building. 2. a fortress.—*v.* to stand high, as *He towered above everyone else in the room.*—**tow'ering** *adj.* 1. very tall. 2. very fierce (rage, anger)

town *n.* 1. a collection of houses, etc. larger than a village. (See **village.**) 2. the people in a town.—**town-clerk'** *n.* an official who supervises the administration of a town.—**town-coun'cil** *n.* people elected to govern a town.—**town-hall'** *n.* a place where town business is done.—**town'-ship** *n.* 1. division of a large parish containing a village or town 2. (Aus.) any small town, village or settlement

tox'ic *adj.* caused by poison.—**tox'in** *n.* a poison

toy *n.* a plaything.—*v.* (with) to play with, to trifle

trace (trās) *n.* 1. a mark left, indication. 2. a small amount. 3. a strap by which a horse pulls a vehicle.—*v*, 1. to follow a course. 2. to find out. 3. to copy, to draw a plan.—**tra'cing** *pres. part.*—*n.* a drawing.—**tra'cery** *n.* finely-drawn ornamental pattern of lines.—**to kick over the traces** to act in a wild way

Compare: (with trace *n.*) vestige, remains, remnant, trail, track, mark

track *n.* 1. a mark or line of marks left by something. 2. a road, path. 3. a course prepared for racing. 4. in U.S. a railway line.—*v.* to follow the track of.—**off the beaten track** unusual, not often done or visited.—**to keep track of** to keep in touch with.—**to make tracks for** to go towards.—**to track down** to discover after a search

tract *n.* 1. a region, stretch of land or water. 2. a little book, esp. on a religious subject

trac'table *adj.* easily managed. (See **docile**)

trac'tion (trak'shun) *n.* hauling or drawing, being drawn or pulled.—**trac'tion-en'gine** *n.* a steam engine for pulling loads along a road.—**trac'tor** *n.* a motor-driven engine for drawing ploughs, etc.

trade *n.* 1. buying and selling; commerce. 2. business, commercial work. 3. people in the same trade.—*v.* to deal, to do business.—**tra'ding** *pres. part.*—**tra'der** *n.*—**trade'-mark** *n.* an identifying mark used by a manufacturer on his goods.—**trades'-man** *n.* 1. a shopkeeper. 2. a skilled workman.—**trades'men** *pl.*—**trade'-name** *n.* 1. name under which an article is sold. 2. name by which article is known to traders.—**trade-u'nion** *n.* a society of workers in a trade, to protect their interests.—**trade'-wind** *n.* a wind blowing constantly towards the Equator from north or south

tradi'tion (tra-dish'un) *n.* handing down knowledge, customs, etc. from one generation to the next.—*pl.* customs, memories, etc. handed down, as *We must uphold the fine traditions of the regiment.*—**tradi'tional** *adj.* customary, handed down by tradition.—**tradi'tionally** *adv.*

traduce' (tra-dūs') *v.* to speak ill of, to slander

Compare: calumniate, vilify, disparage, detract, depreciate, decry, defame. *Contrast:* commend, extol, praise, eulogise

traf'fic *n.* 1. trade, commerce. 2. passing to and fro of people, vehicles, etc.—*v.* to trade.—**traf'ficking** *pres. part.*—**traf'ficked** *p.t.* and *p. part.*—**traf'fic lights** *n.pl.* automatic electric lights signalling to traffic at a crossroads

traf'ficator *n.* a winking light on a vehicle about to change course

trage'dian (tra-jee'di-an) *n.* 1. an author of a tragedy. 2. an actor in a tragedy.—**tragedienne'** *fem.*

trag'edy (traj'e-di) *n.* 1. a serious play ending in death and disaster, e.g. *Hamlet.* 2. a terrible event, disaster.—**trag'edies** *pl.*—**trag'ic** *adj.* 1. of tragedy. 2. terrible.—**trag'ical** *adj.* in the style or manner of tragedy.—**trag'ically** *adv.*

trail *v.* 1. to drag behind. 2. to follow, track down. 3. to hang loosely, as *Her long skirt trailed on the ground.* 4. to walk wearily.—*n.* 1. track, smell. 2. a rough road. 3. something trailing, as ***a trail of smoke.***—**hot on the trail** closely following.—**to blaze a trail** to find a way, to lead in a new venture.—**to trail one's coat** to act in a provocative way

trail'er *n.* 1. a person or animal following a trail. 2. a creeper, trailing plant. 3. a truck, etc. pulled behind vehicle. 4. part of a film shown in advance as an advertisement

train *n.* 1. a line of railway coaches joined to locomotive. 2. the part of a gown which trails on the ground. 3. a group of attendants. 4. a trail of gunpowder. 5. a series, procession, as ***a train of events.***—*v.* 1. to bring up, teach. (See **teach.**) 2. to direct, cause to grow. 3. to exercise, to make fit. 4. to point, e.g. a gun.—**train'ing** *n.* 1. education for a special occupation. 2. exercise to make one fit and skilful.—**trainee'** *n.* one who is being trained.—**in training** physically fit

trait (trā, trāt) *n.* a feature or habit characteristic of someone

Compare: characteristic, peculiarity, idiosyncrasy, feature

trait'or *n.* a person who betrays, a faithless, disloyal person.—**trai'tress** *fem.*—**trai'torous** *adj.*

trajec'tory *n.* the path of a missile or object thrown through the air

tram *n.* 1. a passenger-car running on rails through a street. 2. a truck used in a coalmine.—**tram'car** *n.*—**tram'way** *n.*

tram'mel *v.* 1. to hinder, to hamper.—**tram'melling** *pres. part.*—**tram'melled** *p.t.* and *p. part.*—*n.* 1. a net. 2. anything that hinders

Compare: impede, obstruct, embarrass

tramp *v.* 1. to walk heavily. 2. to travel on foot.—*n.* 1. sound of heavy steps. 2. walk, tramping. 3. vagabond, beggar. 4. ship that takes cargo wherever wanted

tram'ple *v.* to tread on, crush under foot.—*n.* —**tram'pling** *pres. part.*

tram'poline *n.* canvas attached by elastic to a frame on which gymnasts make jumps and somersaults

trance (trahns) *n.* state in which a person is unaware of the things around and anything he does is done unconsciously

tran'quil (trang'kwil) *adj.* quiet, calm, peaceful.—**tranquil'lity** *n.*—**tran'quil'ly** *adv.*

Compare: still, serene, unruffled. *Contrast:* troubled, disturbed, stormy, turbulent, excited

trans- *pref.* over, beyond

transact' *v.* to carry on business, to manage. —**transac'tion** (-shun) *n.* business done.—*pl.* proceedings, e.g. of a society.

transatlan'tic *adj.* 1. on the other side of the Atlantic. 2. crossing the Atlantic

transcend' (tran-send') *v.* to surpass, to be above, greater.—**transcen'dence** *n.*—**transcend'ent** *adj.* supreme

transcribe' *v.* to copy in writing.—**transcri'bing** *pres. part.*—**trans'cript** *n.* copy.—**transcrip'tion** (-shun) *n.*

tran'sept *n.* the part of a cross-shaped church that branches off at right angles to the nave

transfer' *v.* to move from one place or person to another, to hand over, as *He transferred his business to another city.*—**transfer'ring** *pres. part.*—**transferred'** *p.t.* and *p. part.*—**trans'fer** *n.* 1. transferring. 2. being transferred. 3. a design which can be transferred to another surface.—**trans'ferable** *adj.*—**trans'ference** *n.*

transfigura'tion (-ā'shun) *n.* 1. a change in appearance. 2. the change in the aspect of Christ on the mountain

transfig'ure (trans-fig'er) *v.* 1. to change the appearance of. 2. to glorify, exalt.—**transfig'uring** *pres. part.*

transfix' *v.* 1. to pierce through. 2. to render motionless, as *transfixed with fear.*—he **transfix'es**

transform' *v.* to change the shape or character of.—**transforma'tion** (mā'shun) *n.* change of form.

Compare: transmute, convert, metamorphose

transform'er *n.* an electrical apparatus for changing the voltage of alternating current

transfuse' (trans-fūz') *v.* 1. to pour from one vessel to another. 2. to transfer blood from one person to another.—**transfu'sing** *pres. part.*—**transfu'sion** (trans-fū'zhun) *n.* transference of blood

transgress' *v.* 1. to go beyond. 2. to break a law, to sin.—he **transgress'es.**—**transgres'sion** (trans-gresh'un) *n.* sin—**transgres'sor** *n.*

Compare: exceed, violate, infringe, overstep. *Contrast:* observe, keep, obey

tran'sient (tran'zi-ent) *adj.* not lasting, fleeting, as *transient feelings*

Compare: brief, ephemeral, momentary. *Contrast:* lasting, permanent, eternal

transis'tor (tran-zis'tor) 1. a very small electrical device acting as a radio valve to amplify small currents. 2. a small portable radio containing transistors

tran'sit *n.* passing through, a passage, crossing, as *The goods were damaged in transit*

transit'ion (tran-zish'un) *n.* a change from one state, thing, to another.—**transi'tional** *adj.*

trans'itive *adj.* in Grammar, a *transitive verb* is one which takes a direct object, e.g. *eat* in *The boys eat apples.* When the verb does not take a direct object (e.g. *run* in *He runs well*) it is said to be *intransitive.*—**trans'itively** *adv.*

trans'itory *adj.* not lasting, passing quickly, as *Youth is transitory*

translate' *v.* 1. to give the meaning in another language. 2. to move from one place to another.—**transla'ting** *pres. part.*—**transla'tion** (-la'shun) *n.*—**transla'tor** *n.*

translu'cent (trans-lōō'sent) *adj.* letting some light through, as *Stained glass windows are translucent*

transmigra'tion (-grā'shun) *n.* 1. passing from one country to settle in another. 2. passing of a soul into another body

transmis'sion (tranz-mish'un) *n.* passing on, sending, on transmitting

transmit' *v.* to pass on, to send along.—**transmit'ting** *pres. part.*—**transmit'ted** *p.t.* and *p. part.*—**transmit'ter** *n.* apparatus for sending on wireless signals.—**transmit'ting-sta'tion** *n.* a station sending out messages by wireless

transmute' *v.* to change from one nature, form or substance to another, as *In olden times alchemists tried to transmute base metals into gold.*—**transmu'ting** *pres. part.* —*n.* **transmuta'tion**

transpa'rence, transpa'rency (-pār) *n.* transparent quality

transpa'rent *adj.* that can be seen through

distinctly, as *transparent glass, transparent excuses*

Compare: translucent. *Contrast:* opaque

transpire' *v.* 1. to pass vapour through pores, leaves, etc. 2. to become known. 3. (in popular speech) to happen.—**transpi'ring** *pres. part.*—*n.* **transpira'tion**

transplant' *v.* to move and plant in a different place

transport' *v.* 1. to carry to another place. 2. to banish, as *He was sentenced to be transported for seven years.* 3. to carry away by great emotion, as *transported with joy.*—**trans'port** *n.* 1. a conveyance, carrying, 2. a ship used to carry men, supplies, etc. 3. strong feelings.—**transporta'tion** (-tā'shun) *n.*

transpose' (trans-pōz') *v.* 1. to change the place or order of. 2. in music, to put into another key.—**transpo'sing** *pres. part.*—**transposit'ion** (zi'shun) *n.*

transubstantia'tion (-shi-ā'shun) *n.* the belief in the Roman Catholic Church, that the bread and wine in the Eucharist become the body and blood of Christ

transverse' *adj.* lying across, at right angles

trap *n.* 1. a way of catching animals, snare. 2. a trick for catching someone. 3. a two-wheeled carriage.—*v.* to catch.—**trap'ping** *pres. part.*—**trapped** *p.t.* and *p. part.*—**trap'-door** *n.* door in a floor or roof

trapeze' (tra-peez') *n.* a horizontal bar suspended from two ropes, used in a gymnasium and circus

trape'zium *n.* a quadrilateral with two sides parallel

trap'per *n.* a man who traps wild animals for their fur

trap'pings *n.pl.* 1. ornamental coverings for horses in processions, etc. 2. ornaments

trash *n.* 1. rubbish. 2. nonsense.—**trash'y** *adj.*

trav'ail *n.* labour, hardship

trav'el *v.* to go from place to place, to journey,—*n.*—**trav'elling** *pres. part.*—**trav'elled** *p.t.* and *p. part.*—**trav'eller** *n.* 1. a person who travels. 2. a travelling salesman

trav'erse (*or* tra-vers') *v.* 1. to cross, to travel across, as *The pioneers traversed vast deserts.* 2. to oppose, as *He sought to traverse my arguments.* 3. to lie across.—*n.* something crossing another

trav'esty *n.* imitation of something serious making it look ridiculous, a parody, as *a travesty of justice.*—**trav'esties** *pl.*—*v.* to parody

trawl *n.* a large net dragged along the bottom of the sea.—*v.* to fish with a trawl.—**traw'ler** *n.* trawling-boat

tray *n.* a flat, shallow holder for carrying small things

treach'erous (trech'er-us) *adj.* deceitful, faithless, disloyal, not to be trusted.—**treach'erously** *adv.*—**treach'ery** *n.* treason, betrayal, falseness

Compare: traitorous, perfidious, untrustworthy. *Contrast:* loyal, faithful, honourable, true, trustworthy

trea'cle (tree'kl) *n.* thick syrup, molasses.—**trea'cly** *adj.* like treacle, sticky

tread (tred) *v.* 1. to step, to set foot on. 2. to trample, crush.—**trod** *p.t.*—**trod'den, trod** *p. part.*—*n.* 1. treading. 2. a way of walking. 3. the top surface of stair or tire

tread'le (tred'l) *n.* a lever worked by the foot to turn a wheel.—*v.*

tread'mill (tred'mil) *n.* 1. a wheel turned by treading on steps. 2. any dull, tiring work

trea'son (tree'zun) *n.* treachery to one's king and country, disloyalty.—**trea'sonable** *adj.* involving treason.—**high treason** treason directed against the crown

treas'ure (trezh'ur) *n.* riches, stored wealth, valuables.—*v.* 1. to collect, store. 2. to prize, value highly.—**treas'uring** *pres. part.*—**treas'urer** *n.* person in charge of money—**treas'ure-trove** *n.* money or valuables found hidden in the ground, etc.

treas'ury (trezh'er-i) *n.* 1. a place where treasure is kept. 2. a government department controlling public money.—**treas'uries** *pl.*

treat *v.* 1. to act towards someone or something in a particular way, to deal with, as *to treat well, to treat woodwork with a preservative, to treat with scorn. The doctor treated him for measles.* 2. to discuss, make terms as *Messengers were sent to treat with the advancing enemy.* 3. to entertain, esp. with food or drink, as *He treated me to a bottle of wine.*—*n.* entertainment, pleasure, as *a Sunday School treat*

treat'ise (tree'tis) *n.* a book or writing discussing a subject in a scholarly way

treat'ment *n.* a way of acting towards a person or thing, dealing with

trea'ty *n.* an agreement between states.—**trea'ties** *pl.*

treb'le *adj.* three times.—*v.* to make three times greater.—*n.* 1. soprano voice in a young person. 2. music for a soprano.—**treb'ly** *adv.* three times

tree *n.* 1. a large plant with woody trunk. 2. a piece of wood, beam.—**a family tree** a table showing the descent of the members of a family from a common ancestor

trek *v.* 1. in South Africa, to draw an ox-wagon. 2. to travel by ox-wagon. 3. to travel, migrate.—**trek'king** *pres. part.*—**trekked** *p.t.* and *p. part.*—*n.* a march, journey

trel'lis *n.* a frame of light bars fixed crosswise

trem'ble *v.* to shake, to quiver.—*n.*—**trem'bling** *pres. part.*

tremen'dous *adj.* 1. awful, overpowering. 2. vast, immense, huge.—**tremen'dously** *adv.*

Compare: astonishing, formidable, appalling, enormous, terrific, colossal

trem'or *n.* a trembling

trem'ulous *adj.* trembling, frightened, shy, as *She replied in a tremulous whisper*

trench *n.* 1. a ditch. 2. a long narrow ditch as shelter in war.—**trench'es** *pl.*—*v.* to dig into trenches

trench'ant *adj.* cutting, sharp, as *his trenchant sword, a trenchant speech*

trench'er *n.* a wooden plate, esp. for cutting bread on.—**trench'erman** *n.* person who eats (usually a large amount).

trend *n.* direction, tendency, as *We follow the trend of events by reading the newspapers.*—*v.* to tend, to run in a certain direction

trepida'tion (dā'shun) *n.* fear, alarm

tres'pass *v.* 1. to go on someone's property without permission. 2. to do wrong.—*n.* 1. trespassing on property. 2. wrongdoing.—**tres'passes** *pl.*—**tres'passer** *n.*

tress *n.* a curl, lock of hair.—**tress'es** *pl.*

tres'tle (tres'l) *n.* a frame or stand for supporting tables, etc.

tri'al *n.* 1. a test, trying. 2. hardship. 3. examination of a case before a judge.—**trial and error** trying several methods to find the best

Compare: 1. proof, verification, experiment, attempt. 2. application, misfortune, tribulation, endeavour

tri'angle (trī'ang-gl) *n.* 1. a three-sided figure with three angles. 2. a musical instrument made of triangular steel rod.—**trian'gular** *adj.* three-cornered

tri'bal *adj.* of a tribe

tribe *n.* 1. a group of people united under the same chief. 2. a set of people, animals, etc.

tribula'tion (-lā'shun) *n.* trouble, misery. (See **trial**)

tribu'nal *n.* a court of justice

trib'une *n.* a raised platform, dais

trib'utary *n.* 1. a stream flowing into a greater one. 2. a person or state paying tribute.—**trib'utaries** *pl.*—*adj.* paying tribute

trib'ute *n.* 1. a tax paid by one state to another. 2. something given or said to show admiration or respect, as *The chairman paid a tribute to the secretary's work*

trice (trīs) *n.* a moment.—**in a trice** in an instant

trick *n.* 1. something done to deceive, a cunning device. 2. a clever act. 3. a habit as *He had the peculiar trick of shutting his eyes when singing.* 4. the cards played in one round.—*v.* to cheat, deceive.—**trick'ery** cheating.—**trick out (with or in)** to adorn, embellish

Compare: (with *n.*) 1. artifice, stratagem, deceit, fraud, swindle, prank, deed. 2. feat, performance

trick'le *v.* to flow in a gentle stream.—*n.*—**trick'ling** *pres. part.*

tri'cycle (trī'sikl) a three-wheeled cycle

tri'dent *n.* a spear with three prongs

trien'nial *adj.* 1. happening every three years. 2. lasting three years

tri'fle *n.* 1. something with little value or importance. 2. a cold sweet of sponge-cake, cream, etc.—*v.* 1. to speak or act lightly. 2. (with) to treat lightly, without seriousness.—**tri'fler** *n.*—**tri'fling** *adj.* of little importance

Compare: bauble, toy, bagatelle

trig'ger *n.* a catch which, when released, fires a gun, etc.

trigonom'etry *n.* a branch of mathematics dealing with sides and angles of triangles

trill *v.* to sing or pronounce with a quavering sound.—*n.*

trill'ium *n.* a North American plant with three leaves surrounding a large three-petalled flower

trim *v.* 1. to make tidy by cutting, to clip. 2. to decorate. 3. to arrange (sails of a boat).—**trim'ming** *pres. part.*—**trimmed** *p.t.* and *p. part.*—*n.* order, being trimmed.—*adj.* neat, tidy

Compare: (with *adj.*) orderly, compact, spruce, smart, jaunty. *Contrast:* slovenly, untidy, disorderly, unkempt, sloppy

trin'ity *n.* the state of being threefold.—**the Trin'ity** the three persons of the Godhead, the Father, Son and Holy Ghost

trin'ket (tring'ket) *n.* a small piece of jewellery

tri'o (tree'o) *n.* 1. music for three voices or instruments. 2. a group of three.—**tri'os** *pl.*

trip *v.* 1. to walk lightly and quickly, as *She tripped across the stage.* 2. to stumble, as *He tripped over a fallen branch.* 3. to cause someone to fall, as *It is against the rules to trip up an opponent at football.*—**trip'ping** *pres. part.*—**tripped** *p.t.* and *p. part.*—*n.* 1. a stumble. 2. an excursion, journey.

tripe *n.* the stomach of a cow, sheep, etc. prepared for food

trip'le *adj.* having three parts.—**trip'let** *n.* a set of three, esp. rhyming verses.—**trip'lets** *n.pl.* three children born at one birth

tri'pod *n.* a stool or stand with three legs

trip'per *n.* a person going on a day-excursion.—**trip'perish** *adj.* much visited by trippers

trite *adj.* stale, commonplace, as *a trite remark*

Compare: stereotyped, hackneyed. *Contrast:* original, striking, fresh, new, vivid

tri'umph (trī'umf) *n.* 1. a great success, victory. 2. a procession of victory in ancient Rome.—*v.* to be victorious, to succeed.—**trium'phal** *adj.* of triumph.—**trium'phant** *adj.* victorious

triv'ial *adj.* unimportant, trifling.—**trivial'ity** *n.* trifle.—**trivial'ities** *pl.*

Compare: slight, insignificant, ordinary, petty, light. *Contrast:* important, weighty, serious, considerable, momentous

Tro'jan *n.* a native of Troy.—**to work like a Trojan** to work hard

troll (trōl) *v.* 1. to sing a catch. 2. to fish by dragging a line along

troll (trōl) *n.* a supernatural being, giant or dwarf

trol'ley *n.* 1. a truck. 2. a pole by which tramcar collects electric power from an overhead wire. 3. (U.S.) an electric street-car.—**trol'leys** *pl.*

trom'bone *n.* a kind of long trumpet with sliding stem

troop *n.* 1. a group of persons or animals. 2. a cavalry unit.—*pl.* soldiers.—*v.* to move in a crowd, as *The audience trooped out.*—**troop'er** *n.* cavalry soldier

tro'phy (trō'fi) *n.* something set up, or kept as a prize, in memory of a victory.—**tro'phies** *pl.*

trop'ic *n.* one of two circles round the earth, the **Tropic of Cancer** north of the equator, and the **Tropic of Capricorn** south of the equator.—**the tropics** the very hot regions between these two circles.—**trop'ical** *adj.*

trot *v.* 1. of a horse, to move at a moderate pace, lifting the right fore-foot and the left hind foot at the same time. 2. to run gently.—**trot'ting** *pres. part.*—**trot'ted** *p.t.* and *p. part.*—*n.* trotting

trou'badour (trōō'ba-dōōr) *n.* a romantic poet of the Middle Ages in France

trou'ble (trub'l) *v.* 1. to disturb. 2. to be distressed, disturbed.—**troub'ling** *pres. part.*—*n.* 1. worry, distress, difficulty. 2. work, effort, care.—**troub'lesome** *adj.* causing trouble,—**troub'lous** *adj.* disturbed, agitated.—**troub'lemaker** *n.* troublesome person.—**troub'leshooter** *n.* one who cures trouble in an organisation.—**ask for trouble** to behave so as to bring trouble to oneself.—**take trouble** to do a thing with care

Compare: (with *n.*) grief, affliction, perplexity, annoyance, anxiety

trough (trawf, trof, trōf) *n.* 1. a long, narrow vessel for holding water, etc. 2. a channel

trounce *v.* to beat, thrash,—**troun'cing** *pres. part.*

troupe (trōōp) *n.* a band, company, esp. of actors, acrobats, etc.

trou'sers (trow'zerz) *n.pl.* two-legged outer garment reaching from waist to ankles

Compare: knickerbockers, knickers, pantaloons, breeches, pants

trous'seau (trōō'sō) *n.* a bride's outfit

trout *n.* a fresh-water fish

trow'el *n.* a small tool for lifting plants, spreading mortar, etc.

troy, troy-weight *n.* British weights used for gold and silver

tru'ant (trōō'ant) *n.* 1. a child absent from school without leave. 2. an idler—*n.* **tru'ancy** playing truant

truce (trōōs) *n.* a short peace by agreement between enemies

truck *n.* 1. an open vehicle for heavy goods or cattle. 2. a motor-lorry. 3. a kind of barrow. 4. payment in goods instead of money, barter.—**to have (no) truck with** to have (no) dealings with

truck'le *v.* to flatter, to give in tamely, as *He refused to truckle to the bully's threats.*—**truck'ling** *pres. part.*

truc'ulent *adj.* ready to fight, aggressive, fierce

Compare: pugnacious, quarrelsome, warlike, violent, savage, cruel. *Contrast:* gentle, peaceable, kind, merciful

trudge (truj) *v.* to walk wearily.—*n.*—(See **walk.**)—**trudg'ing** *pres. part.*

true (trōō) *adj.* 1. exact, correct, 2. loyal, faithful. 3. real, genuine.—**tru'er** *comp.*—**tru'est** *sup.*—**tru'ism** *n.* an obvious truth.—**tru'ly** *adv.* 1. exactly. 2. really. 3. faithfully

trump *n.* 1. a card of a suit ranking above others for one game. 2. (poetical) trumpet, as *The Last Trump*, the sound of the trumpet signifying the end of the world.—*v.* to play the trump card, to take with a trump.—**trumped-up'** *adj.* made up, invented, as *a trumped-up accusation*

trump'ery *adj.* showy but worthless.—*n.* worthless finery

Compare: shoddy, tawdry

trum'pet *n.* 1. a metal wind-instrument with loud, clear tone. 2. something shaped like one.—*v.* 1. to blow a trumpet. 2. to announce loudly, proclaim.—**trump'eter** *n.*

trun'cheon (trun'chun) *n.* a short thick club or baton

trun'dle *v.* to roll along on little wheels.—**trund'ling** *pres. part.*

trunk (trungk) *n.* 1. the main stem of a tree. 2. a person's body without head or limbs. 3. a large box for holding clothes, etc. 4. an elephant's long nose.—**trunks** *n.pl.* shorts worn by swimmers.—**trunk'-call** *n.* a long-distance telephone call

truss *v.* to fasten up, tie (often followed by *up*).—*n.* 1. a support. 2. bundle of hay, etc.—**truss'es** *pl.*

trust *n.* 1. confidence, firm belief. 2. a person or thing entrusted. 3. property held for another. 4. credit. 5. a combination of business firms.—*v.* 1. to rely on, believe in. 2. to hand over to the care of.—**trustee'** *n.* a person entrusted with property of another.—**trust'ful** *adj.* trusting.—**trust'-worthy** *adj.* reliable.—**trust'y** *adj.* faithful.—**trus'tier** *comp.*—**trus'tiest** *sup.*

truth (trōōth) *n.* 1. that which is true. 2. a correct statement. 3. honesty, sincerity.—**truth'ful** *adj.* speaking the truth.—**truth'-fully** *adv.*

Compare: (with *n.* 1 and 2) reality, actuality, fact. 3. veracity. *Contrast:* (1. and 2.) untruth, lie, falsehood. 3. untruthfulness, mendacity

try *v.* 1. to test, as *I want to try my new bicycle.* 2. to attempt, to make an effort, as *Always try hard.* 3. to strain, as *Reading* *in a poor light tries the eyes.* 4. to examine in a law-court.—he **tries.—try'ing** *pres. part.*—**tried** *p.t.* and *p. part.*—*n.* attempt.—**tries** *pl.*—*n.* 1. an attempt. 2. in Rugby football, touching the ball down behind opponent's goal-line, thus scoring three points.—**try'ing** *adj.* annoying, hard to bear.—**to try it on** to count on someone's patience while doing something forbidden. —**to try on** to put on clothing to see if it suits.—**to try out** to test

try'-square *n.* a square used by joiners for marking wood

tryst (trĭst) *n.* 1. an appointment. 2. a place of meeting

tsar *n.* see **czar**

tub *n.* a large, open wooden vessel, bath.—**tub'bing** *pres. part.*—**tubbed** *p.t.* and *p. part.*

tu'ba (tū'ba) *n.* a large brass wind-instrument

tube *n.* 1. a long pipe of rubber, metal, etc. 2. a small metal container for paint, etc. 3. an underground railway.—**tu'bing** *n.* a length of tube

tu'ber *n.* a thick underground stem of certain plants, e.g. potato

tuberculo'sis *n.* a disease of the lungs

tu'bular *adj.* shaped like a tube

tuck *v.* 1. to gather or sew into folds. 2. to gather, roll, fold. 3. to put, stow (often followed by *away, up* or *in*).—*n.* 1. a gather, fold. 2. (slang) food, delicacies.—**tuck'-shop** a school sweet shop.—**to tuck in** to eat heartily

Tu'dor *n.* the family name of English monarchs from 1485 to 1603

Tues'day (tūz'dā) *n.* the third day of the week

tuft *n.* a bunch of hair, grass, etc. growing together, a clump.—**tuf'ted** *adj.*

tug *v.* to pull hard or violently.—**tug'ging** *pres. part.*—**tugged** *p.t.* and *p. part.*—*n.* 1. a violent pull, jerk. 2. a steamship used to tow other vessels.—**tug-of-war'** *n.* a contest between two teams pulling against each other on a rope

tui'tion (tū-ish'un) *n.* teaching, instruction

tu'lip *n.* a spring flower in various showy colours

tum'ble *v.* 1. to fall. 2. to throw down, to toss about. 3. to turn somersaults.—**tum'bling** *pres. part.*—*n.* 1. a fall. 2. disorder.—**tum'bler** *n.* 1. an acrobat. 2. a drinking-glass.—**tumble to** to realize

tum'bril, tum'brel *n.* a rough, two-wheeled cart in which prisoners were taken to the guillotine during the French Revolution

tu'mour *n.* diseased growth, swelling

tu'mult *n.* uproar, violent disorder, riot.—**tumul'tuous** *adj.* noisy, rough

Compare: noise, commotion, turmoil, disturbance, uproar, turbulence. *Contrast:* calm, quietness, peace, repose, tranquillity

tu'mulous *n.* an ancient burial mound.—**tu'muli** *pl.*

tun *n.* 1. a large cask. 2. a measure for liquids

tu'na (tū'na) *n.* the tunny fish of the Californian coast

tun'dra *n.* vast marshy plains in Arctic regions

tune *n.* 1. the music of a song, air, melody. 2. correct pitch in music.—*v.* 1. to put in tune. 2. to adjust a motor car engine to make it go faster.—**tu'ning** *pres. part.*—**tu'ner** *n.*—**tune'ful** *adj.*—**in tune** (music) in correct pitch.—**out of tune** out of pitch.—**to change one's tune** to alter one's way of talking.—**to the tune of** to the amount of.—**to tune in** to adjust a radio set to receive a programme.—**to tune up** to adjust orchestral instruments before playing

tung'sten *n.* a metallic element wolfram, used in alloys and electric lamp filaments

tu'nic *n.* 1. a short, military coat. 2. a loose sleeveless outer garment

tun'nel *n.* an underground passage.—*v.* to make a tunnel.—**tun'nelling** *pres. part.*—**tun'nelled** *p.t.* and *p. part.*

tun'ny *n.* a very large sea-fish used for food

tur'ban *n.* an Oriental man's head-dress made of scarf wound round head or cap

tur'bid *adj.* muddy, thick.—**turbid'ity** *n.*

tur'bine *n.* an engine driven by water, steam, air, etc. passing through a wheel

tur'bo-jet *n.* (aircraft) a jet engine turning a turbine.—**tur'bo-prop** *n.* a jet engine turning a propeller

tur'bot *n.* a large flat seafish

tur'bulence *n.* disorder, commotion. (See **tumult.**)

tur'bulent *adj.* violent, riotous

tureen' (tū-reen') *n.* a covered dish for soup

turf *n.* 1. short grass and the soil in which it grows. 2. a sod.—*pl.* **turfs, turves.**—*v.* to lay with turf.—**the turf** *n.* 1. horse-racing. 2. the race-course

tur'gid (tur'jid) *adj.* 1. swollen. 2. pompous, using long, heavy words

tur'key *n.* a large bird reared for food

Turk'ey *n.* a country in south-western Asia. —*n.* **Turk** a native of Turkey

tur'moil *n.* confusion, disturbance. (See **tumult.**)

turn *v.* 1. to move round, rotate. 2. to change the position of. 3. to change, as *to turn colour.* 4. to change direction. 5. to become sour, as *The heat of the sun caused the milk to turn.* 6. to shape (on a lathe). 7. to send, put, as *to turn out, adrift, off, over, on, etc.*—*n.* 1. rotation, 2. turning. 3. road, walk. 4. performance. 5. action, office, function, as *to do someone a good turn. This coat has served its turn.* 6. shape, manner, disposition, as *of an inquiring turn of mind.* 7. chance, opportunity, as *It's your turn next.*—**turn'coat** *n.* a person who changes his party.—**turn'out** *n.* a gathering of people for some event.—**to turn against** to become hostile to.—**to**

turn down 1. to fold down. 2. to refuse to accept an offer. 3. to go round a corner, as *to turn down a lane.*—**to turn in** 1. to fold inwards. 2. (slang) to go to bed.—**to turn out** 1. to extinguish. 2. to go out of doors. 3. to dismiss. 4. to prove to be, as *It turned out well.*—**to turn up** 1. to fold upwards. 2. to arrive. 3. to happen, to chance.—**to turn someone's head** to unsettle him.—**to turn someone's brain** to make him mad.—**to turn the corner** to overcome a difficulty.—**to turn something to account** to profit from it.—**to turn the tables on someone** to place him suddenly at a disadvantage.—**to turn over a new leaf** to make a fresh start.—**to turn tail** to run away.—**to turn turtle** to capsize

turn'er *n.* someone who works with a lathe

tur'nip *n.* a plant with big round root used as vegetables or fodder

turn'key *n.* a gaoler

turn'out *n.* 1. an outfit. 2. a crowd of spectators. 3. a quantity of produce

turn'over *n.* the amount of money taken in a business

turn'pike *n.* 1. a gate across a road where a toll is paid. 2. the road

turn'stile *n.* a revolving gate for controlling admission of people

turn'table *n.* a circular revolving platform, as on a record-player or for turning railway carriages

turp'entine *n.* oil made from the resin of certain cone-bearing trees

tur'quoise (tur'koiz, tur'kwoiz) *n.* a blue semi-precious stone

tur'ret *n.* 1. a small tower in a building. 2. a revolving tower for gun in ship, tank, etc.

tur'tle *n.* a sea-tortoise

tusk *n.* a long, pointed, tooth projecting from, e.g. elephant's mouth.—**tusk'er** *n.* a fully-grown elephant or boar

tus'sle *n.* struggle, scuffle.—*v.*

tuss'ock *n.* native grass which once covered much open country in N.Z.—**tus'socker** a tramp

tu'telage *n.* guardianship, being under a guardian

tu'tor *n.* 1. a private teacher. 2. a college instructor who directs studies. 3. a guardian

tuxe'do (tuk-see'dō) *n.* (U.S.) a dinner jacket

twad'dle (twod'l) *n.* idle talk, nonsense.—*v.*

twain *adj.* two.—*n.* two persons

twang *n.* 1. the ringing sound like a tone of a banjo. 2. a nasal tone.—*v.* to make a twang

tweak *v.* to seize and twist sharply.—*n.*

tweed *n.* a cloth with a rough surface

twee'zers *n.pl.* small pincers

twelfth *adj.* next to eleventh.—*n.* one of twelve equal parts

twelve *adj.* two more than ten.—*n.*—**twelve'month** *n.* a year

twen'tieth *adj.* one more than nineteenth

twen'ty *adj.* twice ten.—*n.*—**twen'ties** *pl.*

twice *adv.* two times

twid'dle *v.* to twirl, to twist idly.—**twid'dling** *pres. part.*

twig *n.* a small branch

twi'light (twī'līt) *n.* the half light after sunset or before dawn

twill *n.* a material woven in diagonal ribs

twin *n.* one of two children born together.—*adj.* 1. being a twin. 2. very similar

twine *n.* 1. string, strong thread. 2. a twist.—*v.* to wind, twist, coil.—**twi'ning** *pres. part.*

Compare: interlacing, spinning, entwining, intertwining, winding, twisting, meandering, wreathing

twinge (twinj) *n.* a short, sharp pain

twin'kle (twing'kl) *v.* to shine with a dancing light.—**twink'ling** *pres. part.*—*n.* a gleam, flash.—**twink'ling** *n.* 1. gleam. 2. instant

twirl *v.* to turn, twist, spin.—*n.*

twist *v.* 1. to wind, turn. 2. to curve. 3. to distort, make crooked.—*n.* 1. twisting. 2. twisted piece of bread, tobacco, etc.

twitch *v.* to pull sharply jerk.—*n.* a sudden jerk.—**twitch'es** *pl.*

twit'ter *v.* to chirp like a bird.—*n.*

two (tōō) *adj.* one more than one.—*n.*—**two'fold** *adv.* double.—**two'pence** (tup'ens) *n.*—**two-penny** (tup'ni) *adj.* costing two pence.—**two-faced** *adj.* deceitful.—**two-step** *n.* a kind of dance.—**to put two and two together** to sift evidence and form an opinion from it.—**two-up** (Aus.) a gambling game, two pennies being tossed in the air, and bets being made on the result, two heads or two tails

type *n.* 1. a class, group, as *This engine is one of a new type.* 2. an example, symbol, as *He is the type of man to imitate.* 3. a block with letters used for printing.—*v.* to print with a typewriter.—**ty'ping** *pres. part.*—**type'writer** *n.* writing machine with keys.—**type'writing** *n.*—**type'written** *adj.*

ty'phoid (tī'foid) *n.* a dangerous and infectious fever

typhoon' (tī-fōōn') *n.* a violent hurricane

typ'ical (tip'i-kal) *adj.* true to type, serving as a type, characteristic, as *This weather is typical of what we have here. He was a typical country squire.*—**typ'ically** *adv.*

typ'ify (tip'i-fī) *v.* to serve as a type or model.—he **typ'ifies.**—**typ'ifying** *pres. part.*—**typ'ified** *p.t.* and *p. part.*

ty'pist *n.* a person who uses type-writer esp. as a regular occupation

tyran'nical (ti-ran'i-kal) *adj.* like a tyrant, cruel and harsh.—**tyr'annise** *v.* to treat cruelly, to oppress (usually followed by *over*).—**tyr'annising** *pres. part.*—**tyr'annous** *adj.* tyrannical

tyr'anny (ti'ran-i) *n.* cruel and harsh use of power.—**ty'rannies** *pl.*

Compare: despotism, absolutism, dictatorship, oppression, severity

ty'rant (tī'rant) *n.* 1. an absolute ruler, despot. 2. a cruel ruler

tyre see tire
ty'ro, ti'ro *n.* a beginner
tzar see czar

U

U-boat *n.* a German submarine
ud'der *n.* the milk-bag of a cow or goat
Ugan'da *n.* a country in central Africa
ug'liness *n.* the state of being ugly
ug'ly *adj.* 1. unpleasant to look at. 2. bad, unpleasant, as *an ugly wound.* 3. dangerous, threatening, as *an ugly situation arose.*—**ug'lier** *comp.*—**ug'liest** *sup.*
Compare: unsightly, plain, ill-favoured, distasteful, repulsive, revolting. *Contrast:* See **beautiful**
ukele'le (ū-ke-lā'li) *n.* a small four-stringed Hawaiian musical instrument like a guitar
ul'cer (ul'ser) *n.* an open sore.—**ul'cerated** *adj.* having ulcers
ulte'rior *adj.* 1. situated beyond. 2. hidden, beyond what can be seen, as *an ulterior motive*
ul'timate *adj.* furthest, last, final.—**ul'timately** *adv.*—**ultima'tum** *n.* statement of final conditions, as *The enemy's ultimatum demanded that we should surrender immediately*
ul'tra *adj.* beyond what is usual, extreme.—**ul'tra-mod'ern** *adj.*—**ul'tra-marine'** *adj.* blue.—**ultra-violet light** invisible rays of shorter wavelength than violet light
umbrel'la *n.* a light, folding cover on a handle, carried as protection against rain
um'pire *n.* 1. a person chosen to decide disputes. 2. a person chosen to make decisions in a game.—*v.* to act as umpire
un is added at the beginning of nouns and adjectives and has the meaning "not" e.g. *unarmed* means not armed. Added at the beginning of verbs, *un-* means "the opposite of," e.g. *unfasten* means the opposite of to fasten, i.e. to loosen. If you are seeking the meaning of any word beginning with *un-* and do not find it below, find the word to which *un-* has been added, and put "not" or "the opposite of" before it. Thus, to find the meaning of *unfinished,* say to yourself *not finished.* If you do not know what this means, look up *finished*
unabashed' *adj.* not embarrassed, without losing any composure
unaba'ted *adj.* in full force
unaccoun'table *adj.* which cannot be explained
unaccus'tomed *adj.* 1. not accustomed, as *I am unaccustomed to so much excitement* 2. unusual, as *It is an unaccustomed pleasure to see you here*
unadvi'sedly *adv.* rashly
unaffec'ted *adj.* 1. sincere, as *She had a simple, unaffected manner.* 2. not disturbed by, as *I am unaffected by the new arrangements*
unanim'ity *n.* agreement
unan'imous (ū-nan'i-mus) *adj.* of one mind, in complete agreement.
unassu'ming *adj.* modest, not boastful
unavail'ing *adj.* useless, as *Our protests and appeals were unavailing*
Compare: ineffective, fruitless
unaware' *adj.* not aware, unconscious, as *I was unaware that there was anyone else in the room.*—**unawares'** *adv.* by surprise, unexpectedly, as *he was caught unawares*
unbal'anced *adj.* of the mind, disordered, not steady
unbeknown' (un-bi-nōn') *adv.* not known. as *The arrangement was made unbeknown to me*
unbelief' *n.* lack of faith.—**unbeliev'er** *n.* person who does not believe in God
Compare: infidelity, incredulity, disbelief, sceptisicm, distrust. *Contrast:* faith, belief, credulity, confidence
unbend' *v.* 1. to straighten. 2. to relax, become less severe or formal.—**unbent'** *p.t.* and *p. part.*
unbi'ased (un-bī'ast) *adj.* fair, just
unbound'ed *adj.* boundless, vast, infinite
unbri'dled *adj.* violent, unrestrained, as *an unbridled temper*
unbro'ken *adj.* not broken, uninterrupted, continuous, as *an unbroken run of successes*
unbur'den *v.* 1. to relieve from a burden. 2. to relieve one's mind by confession, etc.
uncalled'-for *adj.* 1. unnecessary. 2. impertinent
uncan'ny *adj.* mysterious, weird,
Compare: eerie, strange, supernatural, unearthly
uncared'-for *adj.* neglected, shabby
uncer'tain (un-ser'tin) *adj.* 1. doubtful, not sure, as *It is uncertain whether they will come.* 2. unreliable, as *uncertain weather.* 3. vague, not accurate, as *You seem very uncertain about the details.*—**uncer'tainty** *n.*
unchar'itable *adj.* unkind, selfish
unchart'ed *adj.* unexplored, unknown
un'cle (ung'kl) *n.* 1. a brother of one's mother or father. 2. an aunt's husband.—**aunt** *fem.*
unconcern' (un-kon-sern') *n.* indifference, lack of interest or anxiety.—**unconcerned'** *adj.* indifferent
uncon'scious (un-kon'shus) *adj.* 1. not conscious. 2. not aware. 3. not meant, as *The performance was full of unconscious humour.*—**uncon'sciously** *adv.*—**uncon'sciousness** *n.*
uncouth' (un-kōōth') *adj.* clumsy, awkward, without polish
Compare: crude, unpolished, unmannerly, rough, rude, unseemly, boorish. *Contrast:* polished, polite, civilised, refined, mannerly, courteous
uncov'er *v.* 1. to take cover off. 2. to make known, expose. 3. to take one's hat off
unc'tion (ungk'shun) *n.* 1. anointing with oil. 2. ointment, oil. 3. soothing words or tone.—**unc'tuous** *adj.* 1. oily, greasy. 2.

too smooth, hypocritical, as *The villain protested his innocence in an unctuous voice*

undaun'ted *adj.* fearless. (See **bold, brave**)

undeceive' (un-de-seev') *v.* to free from error

undeni'able *adj.* certain, which cannot be denied.—**undeni'ably** *adv.*

un'der *prep.* 1. below, beneath, as *under the bed.* 2. found by, included in, as *under that heading.* 3. in the time of, as *under the Stuarts.*—*adv.* in a lower place or condition, as *You should keep your dog under.*—*adj.* lower, subordinate, as *the under-gardener.*—**under age** too young to buy alcohol, drive a car, vote, etc.—**under cover** concealed.—**under way** (on water) moving off.—**down under** Australia or New Zealand

Note: Under is used to make up several words, the meaning of which can be seen by adding the meaning of *under* to the meaning of the other part of the word, e.g. *undercurrent, undercharge, underestimate, underclothes, underwear*

un'dercarriage (un'der-car-ij) *n.* the landing gear of aircraft

un'dercut *v.* to sell more cheaply than competitors

underdevel'oped *adj.* 1. not fully developed. 2. backward. 3. (countries) not using their resources

un'der dog (the) *n.* one who is unfortunate in a struggle, or very poor

underes'timate *v.* to form too low an idea of the value of something.—*n.*

undergo' *v.* to suffer, endure, as *to undergo an operation.*—he **undergoes'**—**undergo'ing** *pres. part.*—**underwent'** *p.t.*—**undergone'** *p. part.*

undergrad'uate *n.* a university student who has not taken his first degree

un'derground *adj.* 1. below ground. 2. secret. —*n.* an underground railway

un'dergrowth *n.* shrubs, small trees growing under large ones

un'derhand *adj.* sly, secretly, dishonest.—*adv.*

underline' *v.* 1. to draw a line under. 2. to draw attention to.—**underli'ning** *pres. part.*

un'derling *n.* a person of lower position, an inferior

undermine' *v.* 1. to dig under. 2. to injure or weaken.—**undermi'ning** *pres. part.*

underneath' *adv.* beneath, below, as *The fastening is underneath.*—*prep.*, as *Look underneath the table*

underrate' *v.* to underestimate

understand' *v.* 1. to get the meaning of. 2. to know. 3. to hear, to believe. 4. to supply a word that is not expressed, as *In the sentence, "That is the one I want," the word "which" is understood.*—**understood'** *p.t.* and *p. part.*

Compare: comprehend, apprehend, perceive

understan'ding *n.* 1. intelligence, ability. 2. knowledge. 3. agreement, as *The two rival firms came to an understanding.*—*adj.* intelligent

un'derstudy *n.* an actor or actress who learns another's part to act in place of him if required

undertake' *v.* to agree to do, to set about, to take in hand.—**underta'king** *pres. part.*—**undertook'** *p.t.*—**underta'ken** *p. part.*—**un'dertaker** *n.* a person who manages funerals.—**un'dertaking** *n.* 1. an enterprise. 2. a promise. 3. the management of funerals

un'dertone *n.* 1. a low voice. 2. a subdued colour

undo' (un-dōō') *v.* 1. to unfasten. 2. to cancel, destroy. 3. to ruin.—he **undoes'** (un-duz') —**undo'ing** *pres. part.*—**undid'** *p.t.*—**undone'** (un-dun') *p. part.*—**undo'ing** *n.* ruin, destruction

undue' *adj.* too great, disproportionate—**undu'ly** *adv.*

un'dulate *v.* 1. to move in waves. 2. to wave.—**un'dulating** *pres. part.*—**undula'tion** (-lā'-shun) *n.* 1. a wave. 2. a rise and fall

unearth' *v.* to dig up, to discover.—**unearth'ly** *adj.* ghostly, weird

uneas'y (un-eez'i) *adj.* 1. uncomfortable. 2. restless, worried

uned'ifying *adj.* vulgar, degrading

uner'ring *adj.* accurate, making no mistake

unfeel'ing *adj.* harsh, hard-hearted. (See **callous**)

unfeigned' (un-fānd') *adj.* sincere, without pretence

unfit' *adj.* 1. unsuitable. 2. not in good health

unfold' *v.* 1. to spread out. 2. to reveal, explain, as *He unfolded his plans.* 3. to develop, as *The story gradually unfolded*

unfoun'ded *adj.* without grounds, unreasonable

ungain'ly *adj.* clumsy, awkward

ungod'ly *adj.* wicked

unguar'ded (un-gar'ded) *adj.* careless

ung'uent (ung'gwent) *n.* ointment

unheard'-of *adj.* extraordinary

u'nicorn *n.* an imaginary animal resembling a horse but with one horn in the middle of its forehead

unifica'tion (-kā'shun) *n.* 1. making one, union. 2. making alike

u'niform *adj.* unchanging, regular, keeping to one rule.—*n.* a similar dress worn by members of same body, e.g. soldiers, etc.—**u'niformly** *adv.*—**uniform'ity** *n.* sameness, regularity

Compare: similar, constant, unvarying, alike, consistent. *Contrast:* variable, varying, various, dissimilar

u'nify *v.* to make one, unite.—he **u'nifies**—**u'nifying** *pres. part.*—**u'nified** *p.t.* and *p. part.*

u'nion *n.* 1. uniting, joining into one. 2. alliance. 3. harmony. 4. a group of workers combining to protect their interests.—**u'nionist** *n.* member of trades-union.—**U'nion Jack** *n.* the national flag of Great Britain

Compare: association, federation, combination, marriage, coalition, unification

unique' (ū-neek') *adj.* being the only one of its kind

Compare: sole, single, solitary

Note: You cannot say that anything is *rather unique* or *very unique*. It is either *unique* or it is not

u'nison (ū'ni-zun) *n.* 1. agreement, harmony. 2. in music, sounding at the same pitch

u'nit *n.* 1. a single thing or person. 2. a standard quantity, as *a unit of electricity*

unite' *v.* 1. to join into one. 2. to become one, combine.—**uni'ting** *pres. part.*—**uni'ted** *adj.* joined together.—**Uni'ted King'dom** *n.* Great Britain and Northern Ireland.—**Uni'ted States** *n.pl.* the federation of states under one government in North America

univer'sal *adj.* 1. general, belonging to everyone. 2. widespread. 3. whole, entire.—**univer'sally** *adv.* generally.—**univer'sal joint** *n.* a joint which allows movement in all directions

Compare: widespread, total, whole, unlimited, all-embracing, common

u'niverse *n.* the whole of creation, all things

univer'sity *n.* an institution for advanced studies, with the power of conferring degrees on students after examination.—**univer'sities** *pl.*

unkempt' *adj.* untidy, neglected, as *The tramp had a very unkempt appearance*

unleav'ened (un-lev'nd) *adj.* of bread, made without yeast

unless' *conj.* if not, except when

unlet'tered *adj.* unable to read or write, ignorant

Compare: illiterate, unlearned, untaught. (See **ignorant.**) *Contrast:* scholarly, educated, cultured, learned

unloose' *v.* to untie, set free.—**unloos'ing** *pres. part.*

unman' *v.* to weaken, deprive, of courage.—**unman'ning** *pres. part.*—**unmanned'** *p.t.* and *p. part.*—**unman'ly** *adj.* weak, cowardly

unman'nerly *adj.* rude, impolite

unmask' *v.* 1. to remove a disguise. 2. to expose, show up

unmista'kable *adj.* evident, clear, which cannot be mistaken.—**unmista'kably** *adv.*

unmoved' (un-mōōvd') *adj.* 1. firm. 2. not caring

unnec'essary *adj.* not needed

unno'ticed *adj.* not noticed

unnum'bered *adj.* countless

unpar'alleled (-leld) *adj.* having no equal, matchless

unpre'cedented (un-pres'e-dent-ed) *adj.* never known or done before

unprin'cipled (un-prin'si-pld) *adj.* without principles, bad

Compare: wicked, unscrupulous, immoral. *Contrast:* conscientious, virtuous, good, moral

unrav'el *v.* 1. to separate the threads, disentangle. 2. to solve, as *The mystery was unravelled.*—**unrav'elling** *pres. part.*—**unrav'elled** *p.t.* and *p. part.*

unrelen'ting *adj.* merciless, cruel

unremit'ting *adj.* not stopping, ceaseless, steady, as *unremitting efforts*

unreserved' *adj.* 1. frank, open. 2. full, unlimited.—**unreser'vedly** *adv.*

unri'valled *adj.* without an equal, matchless

unru'ly *adj.* hard to control, badly behaved

unsa'voury *adj.* 1. unpleasant, offensive (esp. in taste or smell). 2. tasteless. 3. of bad character, as *The district had an unsavoury reputation for crime*

unscathed' *adj.* uninjured, without hurt

unscru'pulous *adj.* not caring for right and wrong, wicked

unseat' *v.* 1. to throw out of office, as *He was unseated at the next election.* 2. to throw off a horse, etc.

unfit' *adj.* 1. unsuitable. 2. not in good health

unset'tle *v.* to disturb, to make uncertain.—**unset'tling** *pres. part.*—**unset'tled** *adj.* 1. uncertain, disturbed. 2. not paid, as *unsettled debts*

unsight'ly (un-sīt'li) *adj.* ugly. (See **ugly**)

unsophis'ticated *adj.* simple, without worldly experience

unspeak'able *adj.* 1. which cannot be expressed, as *unspeakable joy.* 2. very bad, as *an unspeakable crime.*—**unspeak'ably** *adv.* extremely

until' *prep.* and *conj.* (See **till**)

untime'ly *adj.* 1. unseasonable, at the wrong time, as *I am afraid our visit is untimely.* 2. too soon, as *His untimely death was due to an accident*

un'to *prep.* to

untold' *adj.* 1. not told, as *The story had to remain untold.* 2. countless, very great, as *untold wealth*

unto'ward (un-tō'ard) *adj.* to be regretted, awkward

unveil' (un-vāl') *v.* 1. to reveal, disclose. 2. to uncover

unwept' *adj.* not mourned for

unwiel'dy *adj.* clumsy, hard to manage, cumbersome

unwit'ting *adj.* unaware.—**unwit'tingly** *adv.* without being aware

unwon'ted (un-wōn'ted) *adj.* unusual

up *adv.* 1. to or in a higher or more important position, place, amount, value, etc. as *It is hanging up.* 2. out of bed, in an upright position, as *to get up in the morning.* —*adj.* going upwards, as *the up train.*—*prep.* to a higher point, in an upward direction as *He climbed up the tree.*—*n.* rise, as *the ups and downs of fortune.*—*up* is often used to make up words such as *uphill, upstairs, upstream, upland,* the meaning of which can easily be seen by adding the meaning of *up* to that of the other part of the word.—**it's up to you** it is for you to act.—**up in arms** indignant. —**up to** capable of.—**up-to-date** knowing or using the latest fashions or developments.—**up to mischief** playing pranks.—**up train** the train going to a city or town—**well up in** (a subject) very knowledgable

upbraid′ *v.* to scold, reproach

upheav′al *n.* 1. a lifting, e.g. of the earth's crust. 2. a violent disturbance

up′hill *adj.* difficult.—**uphill′** *adv.* upward

uphold′ *v.* to support.—**upheld′** *p.t.* and *p. part.*

uphol′ster (up-hōl′ster) *v.* 1. to put covers, etc. on furniture. 2. to furnish a house.—**uphol′sterer** *n.*—**uphol′stery** *n.* carpets, curtains, furniture covers, etc.

up′keep *n.* keeping in repair, maintenance

up′lands *n.pl.* the higher lands of a region

up′lift *n.* joy, enthusiasm

upon′ *prep.* on

up′per *adj. comp.* of **up,** as *the upper classes, to have the upper hand.*—*n.* upper part of boot or shoe.—**up′permost** *adj. sup.* of **up.**—**upper-class′** *adj.* of the highest social class.—**upper-cut′** *n.* an upward blow in boxing.—**to have the upper hand** to have the mastery

Compare: higher, superior, above. *Contrast:* lower, inferior, under

up′right (up′rīt) *adj.* 1. standing straight, erect. 2. honest.—*n.* a post, etc. standing upright.—**up′rightness** *n.*

up′roar *n.* noise, disturbance, confusion

uproot′ *v.* to tear up by the roots

upset′ *v.* 1. to overturn, knock over. 2. to disturb, to distress.—**upset′ting** *pres. part.*—**upset′** *p.t.* and *p. part.*—**up′set** *n.* trouble

up′shot *n.* result, end

upstairs′ *adv.* on a higher floor.—**up′stairs** *adj.*

up′start *n.* person who has suddenly become rich or powerful.—*adj.*

up′ward 1. *adv.* towards a higher place, as *Look upward to the skies.* 2. *adj.* as *an upward glance.*—**up′wards** *adv.*

ura′nium *n.* a radioactive element

ur′ban *adj.* belonging to a town or city

Contrast: rural, countrified, rustic

urbane′ *adj.* courteous, polished, elegant.—**urban′ity** *n.* civility

Compare: suave, refined, polite, civil. *Contrast:* boorish, uncivil, rustic, unmannerly, blunt

ur′chin *n.* an untidy or ragged boy

urge (urj) *v.* 1. to drive on, to press. 2. to beg, entreat, to recommend.—**ur′ging** *pres. part.*

ur′gency *n.* immediate, pressing need.—**ur′gent** *adj.* needing immediate attention.—**ur′gently** *adv.*

u′rine *n.* a yellow liquid secreted by the kidneys.—**u′rea** *n.* a white crystalline compound found in urine

urn *n.* 1. an ornamental vase with a foot or pedestal. 2. a large tea-pot with a tap instead of a spout

U′ruguay *n.* a country in South America.—**Uruguay′an** *adj.* belonging to Uruguay

us *pron.* objective form of *we,* as *She liked us very much.*—**me** *sing.*

u′sage (ū′zaj) *n.* 1. way of using, treatment. 2. custom, practice

use (ūz) *v.* 1. to do something with. 2. to make the most of. 3. to treat, as *to use anyone badly.*—**u′sing** *pres. part.*—**used** (ūzd) *p.t.* and *p. part.*—**used to** (ūst) 1. accustomed to, as *used to hardship.* 2. was in the habit of, as in *she used to do it.*—**use** (ūs) *n.* 1. using. 2. custom. 3. employment. 4. value, worth.—**use′ful** *adj.* of use.—**use′fulness** *n.*—**use′fully** *adv.*—**use′less** *adj.* worthless.—**u′ser** (ū′zer) *n.* one who uses.—**out of use** no longer used

Compare: employ, utilise, exercise, practise

ush′er *n.* 1. a door-keeper. 2. a person showing people to their seats. 3. formerly, a teacher's assistant.—**usherette′** *fem.*—*v.* (in, into) to announce, introduce

u′sual (ū′zhu-al) *adj.* ordinary, common.—**u′sually** *adv.* generally

Compare: accustomed, customary, normal, general, frequent, habitual. *Contrast:* unusual, unaccustomed, exceptional, rare, infrequent, extraordinary, uncommon, singular, strange

u′surer (ū′zū-rer) *n.* a person who lends money at a very high rate of interest

usurp′ (ū-zurp′) *v.* to seize power or authority by force and wrongfully.—**usurpa′tion** (-pā′shun) *n.*—**usur′per** *n.* one who usurps

u′sury (ū′zū-ri) *n.* lending money at an unlawfully high rate of interest

uten′sil *n.* something used for a common, practical purpose, esp. in the kitchen

util′ity *n.* 1. usefulness. 2. a useful thing.—*adj.*

u′tilise *v.* to make use of.—**u′tilising** *pres. part.*—**utilisa′tion** (-zā′shun) *n.*

ut′most *adj.* extreme, furthest, as *The teacher took the utmost trouble to explain.*—*n.* the most extreme degree, distance, effort, etc., as *He did his utmost*

uto′pia *n.* an imaginary, ideal state with perfect laws.—**uto′pian** *adj.* ideal but impossible

ut′ter *adj.* complete, absolute.—**ut′termost** *sup.*—**ut′terly** *adv.* totally

ut′ter *v.* 1. to speak. (See say.) 2. to express.—**ut′terance** *n.* 1. words, speech. 2. expression

u′tu (ōō′tōō) *n.* Maori word for reward, payment, compensation

V

va′cancy *n.* 1. emptiness. 2. an unoccupied post, room, etc. as *I have a vacancy for a junior clerk.*—**va′cancies** *pl.*

va′cant *adj.* 1. empty. 2. not occupied. 3. without thought, stupid, as *He had a very vacant expression in his face.*—**va′cantly** *adv.*

vacate' (vāk-āt') *v.* to leave empty.—**vaca'ting** *pres. part.*—**vaca'tion** (vakā'shun, U.S. vā-kā'shun) *n.* 1. vacating. 2. a holiday

vac'cinate (vak'sin-āt) *v.* to inject vaccine as protection against smallpox.—**vac'cinating** *pres. part.*—**vaccina'tion** (-ā'shun) *n.*—**vaccine'** (vakseen') *n.* poison used in vaccination

vac'illate (vas'i-lāt) *v.* to be undecided, to waver.—**vac'illating** *pres. part.*—**vacilla'tion** (-lā'shun) *n.* hesitation

vac'uum *n.* space completely empty even of air.—**vac'uum-clean'er** *n.* apparatus for sucking in dust.—**vac'uum flask'** *n.* a thermos flask, for keeping liquids hot (or cold) for a long time

vag'abond *n.* 1. a wanderer, tramp, 2. rogue.—*adj.* wandering

va'gary (vā'gar-i vag-ā'ri,) *n.* a whim, fanciful idea.—**vagar'ies** *pl.*

va'grant *n.* a tramp, wanderer.—*adj.* wandering

vague (vāg) *adj.* not clear, indefinite, uncertain.—**vague'ly** *adv.*

Compare: dim, doubtful, obscure, indistinct, unsettled. *Contrast:* clear, definite, unmistakable, distinct, plain

vain *adj.* 1. worthless, useless. 2. conceited.—**vainglor'ious** *adj.* boastful.—**vain'ly** *adv.* without success.—**in vain** 1. without success. 2. unauthorised use of, as *You have been taking my name in vain*

val'ance *n.* a short curtain round a bedstead, etc.

vale *n.* valley

val'entine *n.* a card sent anonymously to a sweetheart on St. Valentine's day, February 14th

val'et (val'et, val'ā) *n.* a manservant looking after his master's clothes, etc.

val'iant *adj.* brave. (See **brave**)

val'id *adj.* sound, good, right, as *Your argument is valid only if your facts are correct.*—**valid'ity** *n.* soundness, esp. before the law

val'ley *n.* low land between hills.—**val'leys** *pl.*

val'orous *adj.* brave

val'our *n.* courage

val'uable *adj.* of great value, worth much.—*n.pl.* valuable things

valua'tion (-ā'shun) *n.* 1. fixing the value of something. 2. estimated worth

val'ue *n.* worth, importance, price.—*v.* 1. to think highly of, to prize. 2. to estimate the value of.—**val'uing** *pres. part.*—**val'uer** *n.* a person who estimates the value of property, etc.

Compare: (with *v.*) appreciate, cherish, esteem

valve *n.* 1. a device to control the passage of a liquid or gas through a pipe. 2. something working in a similar way, as a radio valve controls the passage of electric currents in a radio set.—**val'vular** *adj.*

vam'pire *n.* 1. a blood-sucking ghost. 2. a large South American bat

van *n.* a covered vehicle for carrying goods

Compare: lorry, waggon, truck, cart

van'dal *n.* one who wilfully destroys or defaces works of art, buildings, the countryside etc.—**van'dalism** *n.*

vane *n.* 1. a weather-cock. 2. a blade of a ship's propeller

van'guard (van'gard) *n.* the front part of an army

vanil'la *n.* a tropical plant, the bean of which is used to make a flavouring essence

van'ish *v.* to disappear.—he **van'ishes**

van'ity *n.* 1. vain pride, conceit. 2. worthless display.—**van'ities** *pl.*

van'quish (vang'kwish) *v.* to conquer, defeat.—he **van'quishes.**—**van'quisher** *n.*

van'tage *n.* advantage, better situation

vap'id *adj.* dull, flat, insipid.—**vapid'ity** *n.*

va'porise *v.* to change into vapour

va'pour *n.* 1. a gas formed from a substance more familiar as liquid or solid. 2. steam, mist

va'riable (vā'ri-a-bl) *adj.* changeable, uncertain

va'riance (vā'ri-ans) *n.* difference, disagreement

va'riant *adj.* different.—*n.* a different form or spelling of the same word

varia'tion (vār-i-ā'shun) *n.* difference, change

va'ried (vā'rid) *p.t.* and *p. part.* of **vary.**—*adj.* of different kinds, assorted

Compare: miscellaneous, various, mixed, dissimilar

va'riegated *adj.* of different colours

vari'ety *n.* 1. difference, absence of sameness, as *The reason he travels so much is that he likes variety.* 2. a varied collection, as *There was a variety of people present.* 3. a kind, sort, as *a new variety of roses.* 4. varied entertainment in a theatre.—**vari'eties** *pl.*

va'rious *adj.* 1. of different kinds, diverse. 2. several

Compare: variegated, many, heterogeneous

var'let *n.* 1. formerly a servant. 2. in literature, a rascal

var'nish *n.* a substance put on a surface to make it hard and shiny.—*v.* to put varnish on.—he **var'nishes**

va'ry (vā'ri) *v.* 1. to change, alter. 2. to be different.—he **va'ries.**—**va'rying** *pres. part.*—**va'ried** *p.t.* and *p. part.*

vase (vahz) *n.* an ornamental jar for holding flowers, etc.

vas'sal *n.* in feudal times, a man who held land from a superior to whom he rendered service in return.—**vas'salage** *n.* 1. being a vassal. 2. homage. 3. servitude

vast (vahst) *adj.* huge, very great.—**vast'ly** *adv.*—**vast'ness** *n.* great size

Compare: immense, great, spacious, enormous

vat *n.* a large tub, tank

Vat'ican *n.* the Pope's palace in Rome

vault *n.* 1. an arched roof. 2. a cellar, underground tomb. 3. a leap.—*v.* to leap over something by resting the hands on it
vaunt *v.* to boast, brag about.—*n.* **veal** *n.* calf flesh
veer *v.* 1. of wind, to change direction. 2. to change one's opinion
veg'etable (vej'ta-bl) *n.* a plant used for food.—*adj.* of plants, from plants
vegetar'ian (vej-e-tār'i-an) *n.* a person who does not eat meat.—*adj.* containing vegetables but no meat.—**vegeta'rianism** *n.*
veg'etate (vej'e-tāt) *v.* to live the life of a plant.—**veg'etating** *pres. part.*—**vegata'tion** (-tā'shun) *n.* plant life.—**veg'etative** *adj.*
ve'hemence (vee'i-mens) *n.* violence, passion. —**ve'hement** *adj.* vigorous, as *He made a vehement speech defending himself.*—**ve'hemently** *adv.*
Compare: (with *adj.*) forceful, powerful, energetic, violent, furious, ardent, hot
ve'hicle (vee'ikl) *n.* a carriage, truck, car, sledge or other land conveyance.—**vehic'ular** *adj.*
veil (vāl) *n.* 1. a piece of thin material to cover the face. 2. a cover, pretext.—*v.* to cover, hide
vein (vān) *n.* 1. a tube in the body taking blood to the heart. 2. a rib of a leaf. 3. a crack in a rock filled with ore, etc. 4. a streak. 5. a mood, manner, style, as *He spoke in a humorous vein.*—*v.* to mark with streaks
veldt, veld (velt, felt) *n.* (S.A.) a grassland
vel'lum *n.* parchment of calf-skin prepared for writing on or bookbinding
veloc'ity (vel-os'i-ti) *n.* speed, rate of motion
velours' (vel-ōōr') *n.* a thick velvety fabric
vel'vet *n.* a silk fabric with a thick, short pile.—**vel'vety** *adj.* soft and smooth.—**velveteen'** *n.* a cotton fabric resembling velvet
ve'nal *adj.* prepared to take bribes, corrupt.—**venal'ity** *n.*
vend *v.* to sell.—*n.* **vend'or** a seller
vendet'ta *n.* a private war between families, blood-feud
veneer' *v.* to cover with a thin layer of finer wood.—*n.* a thin layer
ven'erable *adj.* deserving respect, very old
ven'erate *v.* to revere, to respect deeply.—**venera'tion** (-ā'shun) *v.*
Compare: adoration, awe, dread, reverence, worship
Vene'tian (ven-ee'shan) *n.* a citizen of Venice. —**vene'tian blind** *n.* a window blind with adjustable slats
ven'geance (venj'ens) *n.* revenge, punishment for a wrong.—**venge'ful** *adj.* spiteful.—**venge'fully** *adv.*
ve'nial *adj.* (of sins) excusable, unimportant
Compare: slight, trivial, trifling. *Contrast:* serious, grave, inexcusable, unpardonable, mortal
ven'ison (or ven'zon) *n.* the flesh of deer
ven'om *n.* 1. poison of snakes, etc. 2. spite.—**ven'omous** *adj.* 1. poisonous. 2. spiteful
vent *n.* a small opening, outlet for air, etc.—*v.* to pour out, let out, express, as *to vent one's spite on someone.*—**to give vent to (one's feelings)** to express openly and fully
vent'ilate *v.* 1. to change the air, to admit fresh air. 2. to discuss freely, make known, as *The speaker ventilated the men's grievances.*—**ven'tilating** *pres. part.*—**ventila'tion** (-lā'shun) *n.*—**ven'tilator** *n.* a device for ventilating a room
ventril'oquist (ven-tril'o-kwist) *n.* a person who can make his voice seem to come from some other person or place
ven'ture (ven'cher) *n.* a risky undertaking.—*v.* 1. to risk, to dare. 2. to have the courage to do something.—**ven'turing** *pres. part.*—**ven'turesome** *adj.* daring.—**ven'turous** *adj.* bold
ven'ue *n.* a meeting place
vera'cious (ver-ā'shus) *adj.* truthful.—**verac'ity** (ver-as'i-ti) *n.* truth
Compare: (with *n.*) honesty, candour, truthfulness, reality, verity, accuracy. *Contrast:* mendacity, falsehood, untruthfulness, fabrication, error, lie, untruth, deceit
veran'dah, veran'da *n.* a covered platform along the side of a house
verb *n.* the part of speech which asserts or declares, e.g. *is* in **it is cold**, *shines* in **the sun shines**, *like* and *to play* in **children like to play**
verb'al *adj.* 1. expressed in words, spoken. 2. of a verb.—**ver'bally** *adv.*
verba'tim (ver-bā'tim) *adv.* word for word, as *The newspaper gave a verbatim report of the speech*
verbose' (ver-bōs') *adj.* using more words than is necessary, wordy. (See **garrulous.**) —**verbos'ity** *n.*
ver'dant *adj.* green with vegetation
ver'dict *n.* 1. a decision of a jury. 2. a decision, judgment after examination
ver'digris (ver'di-grees) *n.* green rust on copper
ver'dure *n.* fresh green growth of plants, etc. greenness
verge (verj) *n.* the edge, brink.—*v.* to incline towards, to border on, as *He is verging on a nervous breakdown*—**ver'ging** *pres. part.*
ver'ger (ver'jer) *n.* 1. the bearer of a bishop's staff. 2. an official who looks after the interior of a church
verifica'tion (-kā'shun) *n.* proof, confirmation
ver'ify *v.* to prove to be true, to confirm.—he **ver'ifies.**—**ver'ifying** *pres. part.*—**ver'ified** *p.t.* and *p. part.*
ver'ily *adv.* in truth, truly
ver'itable *adj.* real, true
Compare: genuine, authentic, complete
ver'ity *n.* truth, a true fact. (See **veracity**)

vermil'ion *n.* a bright red colour.—*adj.*
ver'min *n.* a small, destructive or harmful creature.—**ver'min** *pl.*—**ver'minous** *adj.* containing vermin
vernac'ular *n.* **1.** the language of one's own country. **2.** homely speech.—*adj.*
ver'nal *adj.* belonging to spring
ver'nier *n.* a movable scale for making very small measurements
ver'satile *adj.* able to do many different things well.—**versatil'ity** *n.*
verse *n.* **1.** poetry. **2.** a line of poetry. **3.** a stanza. **4.** a short division in the Bible.—**versed** (verst) *adj.* skilled, familiar with, as *He was well versed in classical literature*
ver'sion (ver'shun) *n.* **1.** a translation from another language, as *The Authorised Version of the Bible.* **2.** a description, account, as *Please give me your version of what happened*
ver'sus *prep.* against
ver'tebra *n.* one of the bones of the spinal column.—**ver'tebrae** (ver'te-bree) *pl.*—**ver'-tebral** *adj.*—**ver'tebrate** *adj.* having a backbone
ver'tex *n.* the highest point.—**ver'tices** (ver'ti-seez) *pl.*
ver'tical *adj.* upright, perpendicular.—**ver'-tically** *adv.*
ver'y *adv.* to a great extent, as *I am very glad.*—*adj.* **1.** real, true, as *Very God of Very God.* **2.** identical, actual, as *This is the very spot where it happened.* **3.** mere, as *The very idea was enough to scare them.*—**ve'riest** *sup.* as *The veriest beginner knows that you must not do that*
ves'pers *n.pl.* evening service in church
ves'sel *n.* **1.** a container, esp. for liquids. **2.** a ship. (See **ship**)
Compare: (with *n.* 1) barrel, tub, tank, cask, vat, cistern, bucket, pail, jug, beaker, glass, cup, tankard, goblet, mug, bottle, decanter, jar, pan
vest *n.* an under-garment.—*v.* to endow (with authority, property, etc.) as *The authority was vested in a committee*—**vest'ed** *adj.* **1.** robed in church garments. **2.** concerned with property, wealth, etc., as *As a shareholder in a railway company he has a vested interest in transport*
vest'ibule *n.* an entrance-hall
ves'tige (ves'tij) *n.* a trace, mark, as *there is not a vestige of truth in the story*
Compare: remains, sign, indication, evidence
vest'ment *n.* a robe, official garment, esp. worn by clergyman or priest
vest'ry *n.* **1.** a room in a church for keeping vestments, holding meetings, etc. **2.** a parish meeting.—**vest'ries** *pl.*
vest'ure (ves'cher) *n.* dress, garments
vet *n.* (slang) short for *veterinary surgeon.*—*v.* to examine carefully
vet'eran *n.* a person who has served a long time, esp. an old soldier.—*adj.*
vet'erinary *adj.* relating to the medical treatment of animals.—**vet'erinary surge'on** *n.* a doctor qualified to treat animal diseases
ve'to (vee'tō) *n.* **1.** the right to prevent a bill from becoming law. **2.** any forbidding, prohibition.—**ve'toes** *pl.*—*v.* to forbid
vex *v.* to annoy.—he **vex'es.**—**vexa'tion** (-ā'shun) *n.*—**vexa'tious** (-ā'shus) *adj.* annoying.—**vexed** *adj.* cross, angry
Compare: displease, anger, provoke, irritate, afflict, agitate, trouble, pester. *Contrast:* please, soothe, assuage, placate, pacify
vi'a *prep.* by way of
vi'aduct *n.* a bridge over a valley for road or railway
vi'al *n.* a small glass bottle
vi'ands *n.pl.* food
vi'brant *adj.* vibrating, resonant
vibrate' *v.* **1.** to move to and fro rapidly, to quiver. **2.** to throb, thrill, **3.** to resound (in the ear, etc.).—**vibra'tion** (vī-brā'shun) *n.* vibrating, tremor.—**vibra'tory** *adj.*
vic'ar *n.* a clergyman in charge of a parish.—**vic'arage** *n.* a vicar's house
vice (vīs) *n.* wickedness, evil habits
vice, vise (vīs) *n.* an instrument with a screw jaw for holding things while working on them
vice- *pref.* acting as deputy for, as *vice-admiral, vice-chairman,* etc.
vice'roy (vīs'roi) *n.* a ruler acting for a king in a province.—**vice'reine** (vīs'rān) *n.* a viceroy's wife
vi'ce ver'sa (vī'si-ver'sa) *adv.* the other way round
vicin'ity (vi-sin'i-ti) *n.* **1.** neighbourhood. (See **district**). **2.** nearness
vic'ious (vish'us) *adj.* **1.** wicked, full of vice. **2.** spiteful. **3.** faulty, corrupt (in style, reasoning, etc.).—**vi'ciously** *adv.*
viciss'itude (vis-) *n.* change of fortune
vic'tim *n.* **1.** a person or animal killed as a sacrifice. **2.** a person suffering as a result of an accident, deceit, fraud, etc.—**vic'timise** *v.* to persecute
vic'tor *n.* **1.** a conqueror. **2.** a winner
victor'ious *adj.* conquering, winning
vic'tory *n.* **1.** winning a battle, war, etc. **2.** success.—**vic'tories** *pl.*
Compare: achievement, conquest, mastery, supremacy, triumph. *Contrast:* defeat, failure, disaster, rout, overthrow
vic'tual (vit'l) *v.* to supply with food.—**vic'tualling** *pres. part.*—**vic'tualled** *p.t.* and *p. part,*—**vic'tualler** *n.* an innkeeper.—**vic'tuals** *n.pl.* food
vie (vī) *v.* to complete, to try to do better than another, as *The competitors in the race vied with each other for the prize.*—**vy'ing** *pres. part.*—**vied** *p.t.* and *p. part.*
view (vū) *n.* **1.** sight, seeing, as *They came into view.* **2.** a scene, picture. **3.** an opinion, idea, as *What are your views on the matter?*

4. intention, as *with a view to doing something.*—*v.* to look at, examine.—**view'less** *adj.* invisible.—**view'point** *n.* 1. a place from which view can be seen. 2. an attitude, way of looking at.—**view'-finder** *n.* part of a camera showing the view to be taken. —**in view of** considering.—**with a view to** intending

vig'il (vij'il) *n.* 1. a keeping awake, watch. 2. the night before a religious festival.—**vig'ilance** *n.* watchfulness.—**vig'ilant** *adj.* alert, wide awake

vig'orous *adj.* full of vigour.—**vig'orously** *adv.*
Compare: forceful, energetic, strong, active, brisk, healthy, powerful, vivid. *Contrast:* feeble, weak, sickly, lethargic, half-hearted, indolent

vig'our *n.* strength, energy, power, force

vi'king (vī'king) a Scandinavian sea-pirate of the eighth to tenth centuries

vile *adj.* 1. base, mean, bad, as *a vile deed.* (See **wicked.**) 2. foul, disgusting, as *a vile stench.*—**vi'ler** *comp.*—**vi'lest** *sup.*

vil'ify *v.* to slander, speak evil of.—**he vil'ifies.** —**vil'ifying** *pres. part.*—**vil'ified** *p.t.* and *p. part.*

vil'la *n.* 1. a house in the country, a detached house in the suburbs. (See **house.**) 2. a Roman house (with its estate)

vil'lage (vil'aj) *n.* a group of houses in the country.—**vil'lager** *n.* a person living in a village
Compare: (with village) hamlet, parish, town, township, city

vil'lain (vil'an) *n.* 1. a wicked person. 2. a serf under the feudal system (more usually **vil'lein**).—**vil'lainous** *adj.*—**vil'lainy** *n.* wickedness, crime
Compare: scoundrel, rascal, criminal, knave, rogue

vim *n.* energy, vigour

vin'dicate *v.* to defend an action, etc. against attack, to justify.—**vin'dicating** *pres. part.* —**vindica'tion** (-kā'shun) *n.* defence
Compare: uphold, support, assert, maintain. *Contrast:* denounce, condemn

vindic'tive *adj.* spiteful, revengeful.—**vindic'tiveness** *n.*

vine *n.* the climbing plant which bears grapes.—**vi'nery** *n.* a greenhouse for grapes

vin'egar *n.* a sour liquid made from wine, etc. and used for flavouring and preserving food

vine'yard (vin'yard) *n.* a plantation of grapevines

vin'tage (vin'taj) *n.* 1. the gathering of the grapes. 2. a wine of a particular year.—**vintage car** one dating from before 1930

vio'la (vi-ō'la) *n.* 1. a tenor violin. 2. (vī'ol-a) a single-coloured pansy, violet

vi'olate *v.* 1. to use violence against. 2. to break a promise, rule, etc. 3. to disturb, as *Germany violated the neutrality of Belgium.* 4. to desecrate, as *The sanctity of the church was violated by the enemy's soldiers.* —**vi'olating** *pres. part.*—**viola'tion** (-lā'shun) *n.*
Compare: outrage, profane, infringe. *Contrast:* respect, regard, observe, honour

vi'olence (vī'o-lens) *n.* 1. force, roughness. 2. rough treatment.—**vi'olent** *adj.* 1. strong, rough. 2. extreme, as *a violent dislike.*—**vi'olently** *adv.*
Compare: fierce, boisterous, passionate. *Contrast:* calm, mild, gentle, moderate

vi'olet *n.* a plant with a small purple or white flower.—*adj.* bluish-purple

violin' *n.* a musical instrument with four strings played with a bow.—**violin'ist** *n.* a violin-player

violoncel'lo (vī-o-lon-chel'o) *n.* a large stringed instrument, a bass violin (usually called **cello**).—**violoncel'los** *pl.*

vi'per *n.* an adder, a poisonous British snake

vir'gin (vir'jin) *n.* a maiden.—*adj.* pure.—**vir'ginal** *adj.*—**virgin'ity** *n.* maidenhood

vir'ile *adj.* manly, strong.—**viril'ity** *n.*

vir'tual *adj.* not in name, but really so, as *The generals, not the ministers, were the virtual rulers of the country.*—**vir'tually** *adv.* in fact

vir'tue *n.* 1. moral goodness. 2. a good quality. 3. power.—**vir'tuous** *adj.* morally good, pure.—**by virtue of** because of

vir'ulence *n.* 1. a poisonous quality. 2. bitterness, hatred.—**virulent** *adj.* 1. poisonous. 2. bitter, spiteful

vir'us *n.* a poisonous matter produced by infectious disease

vis'age (viz'aj) *n.* the face
Compare: countenance, aspect, physiognomy

vis'count (vī'kount) *n.* nobleman of rank above a baron and below an earl.—**viscount'ess** *fem.*

vis'cous (vis'kus) *adj.* sticky and thick

visibil'ity *n.* the condition of the atmosphere for seeing distant objects

vis'ible (viz'i-bl) *adj.* that can be seen.—**vis'ibly** *adv.*

vi'sion (vizh'un) *n.* 1. ability to see, sight. 2. imagination, foresight. 3. a dream, apparition.—**vis'ionary** *adj.* 1. belonging to, or seen in a vision. 2. unpractical, dreamy.—*n.* one who sees visions

vis'it (viz'it) *v.* 1. to go to see, as *to visit a museum.* 2. to stay with, as *to visit relatives.* 3. to punish (for), as *to visit the sins of the fathers upon the children.*—*n.* visiting.—**vis'itant** *n.* a visitor.—**visita'tion** (-tā'shun) *n.* 1. visit of inspection. 2. punishment from God.—**vis'itor** *n.* a person visiting, guest

vi'sor, vi'zor (vī'zor) *n.* the front part of a helmet made to move up and down before the face

vis'ta *n.* a view, esp. a distant view between rows of trees

vis'ual (viz'u-al) *adj.* of sight, used in seeing. —**vis'ualise** *v.* 1. to make visible, describe, as *Let me visualise the scene for you.* 2. to form a mental, image of, as *Can you visualise the future?*—**vis'ualising** *pres. part.*

vi'tal *adj.* 1. necessary to life, having to do with life. 2. very important, as *It is absolutely vital that this position should be held.*—**vital'ity** *n.* vital force, strength.—**vi'tally** *adv.*—**vi'tals** *n.pl.* vital organs of the body

vi'tamin (vit'a-min, vīt'a-min) *n.* a substance necessary to health, found in certain foods, e.g. fruit, vegetables, butter, milk

vi'tiate (vish'i-āt) *v.* 1. to spoil. corrupt, as *The air was vitiated by smoke.* 2. to make ineffective, as *The effects of a good upbringing were vitiated by the young man's bad companions.*—**vi'tiating** *pres. part.*—**vitia'tion** (-ā'shun) *n.*

vit'reous *adj.* 1. glassy, like glass. 2. made of glass

vit'riol *n.* sulphuric acid.—**vitriol'ic** *adj.* bitter, burning

vitu'perate *v.* to speak harshly and abusively, to revile.—**vitu'perating** *pres. part.*—**vitupera'tion** (-ā'shun) *n.*

Compare: abuse, denunciation, scolding, blame, railing, defamation

viva'cious (vi-vā'shus) *adj.* lively, gay, animated.—**viva'city** (vi-vas'i-ti) *n.*

viva'rium *n.* place where live animals are kept

viv'id *adj.* 1. bright, clear, as *a vivid gleam of light.* 2. lively, graphic, as *a vivid description.*—**viv'idly** *adv.*

viv'ify *v.* to give life to, to animate.—he **viv'ifies.**—**viv'ifying** *pres. part.*—**viv'ified** *p.t.* and *p. part.*

vivisec'tion (-shun) *n.* experiments on living animals for scientific purposes

vix'en *n.* 1. a she-fox.—**fox** *masc.*—**cub** young fox. 2. a bad-tempered woman

viz'ier (viz'eer) *n.* a minister of state in a Mohammedan country

vi'zor See **visor**

vocab'ulary *n.* 1. a list of words arranged alphabetically, with meanings. 2. the stock of words used by a person or group of persons.—**vocab'ularies** *pl.*

vo'cal *adj.* of the voice, with the voice.—**vo'calist** *n.* singer.—**vo'cally** *adv.*

voca'tion (-kā'shun) *n.* 1. occupation, profession, trade, etc. 2. a feeling that one has a calling for some special kind of life or work, e.g. to be a missionary, nun, etc.—**voca'tional** *adj.* for an occupation

vogue (vōg) *n.* fashion

voice (vois) *n.* 1. the sound given out through the mouth. 2. an expressed opinion. 3. the right to give an opinion, as *They will not do so if I have any voice in the matter.*—*v.* to express, as *to voice one's opinions.*—**voic'ing** *pres. part.*—**voice'less** *adj.* dumb, silent.—**to have a voice in** to have the right to express an opinion on.—**with one voice** unanimously

void *adj.* 1. empty. 2. without force or effect, as *The will was declared null and void.* 3. lacking, as *void of meaning.*—*n.* empty space.—*v.* to empty out

voile *n.* a thin veil-like material

vol'atile *adj.* 1. evaporating quickly, as *Petrol is volatile.* 2. lively and changeable.—**volatil'ity** *n.*

Compare: (with 2) airy, gay, flighty, fickle

volcan'ic *adj.* like a volcano, produced by a volcano

volca'no *n.* a mountain, with a hole through which lava, ashes, smoke are periodically thrown up.—**volca'noes** *pl.*

vole *n.* a kind of field-mouse

voli'tion (vol-ish'un) *n.* 1. the act of willing. 2. the power of willing

vol'ley *n.* 1. the discharge of many guns, etc. at once. 2. a shower of stones, hard words, etc. 3. in tennis, a return before the ball touches the ground.—*v.* to send a volley

volt (vōlt) *n.* the unit of electro-motive force.—**volt'age** *n.* electro-motive force expressed in volts.—**volt'meter** *n.* an instrument for measuring force in volts

volubil'ity *n.* 1. talking a great deal. 2. a ceaseless flow of words.—**vol'uble** *adj.* very talkative. (See **garrulous.**)—**vol'ubly** *adv.* using many words

vol'ume *n.* 1. a book, part of a book. 2. amount, mass. 3. space occupied.—**volu'minous** *adj.* bulky, ample

vol'untarily *adj.* freely, from choice

vol'untary *adj.* not forced, done freely, as *The expenses were defrayed by the voluntary contributions of well-wishers.*—*n.* an organ solo in a church service

Compare: unconstrained, gratuitous, willing. *Contrast:* compulsory, forced, constrained

volunteer' *v.* 1. to offer to do something. 2. join a military force freely.—*n.* a person who volunteers

volup'tuous *adj.* 1. pleasing to the senses. 2. too pleasure-loving.—**volup'tuousness** *n.*

vom'it *v.* to throw up food, etc. through the mouth.—*n.* matter vomited

vora'cious (vor-ā'shus) *adj.* greedy, very hungry, as *sharks are voracious.*—**vora'city** (vor-as'i-ti) *n.*

vor'tex *n.* a whirlpool, a whirling movement.—**vor'tices** (vor'ti-seez) *pl.*

vote *n.* 1. a wish or choice expressed formally, e.g. by ballot, show of hands, etc. 2. the right to express choice thus. 3. the result of a vote.—*v.* to give a vote. to grant by vote.—**vo'ting** *pres. part.*—**vo'ter** *n.*

vouch (for) *v.* to guarantee, answer for, as *I will vouch for his good character.*—he **vouch'es.**—**vouch'er** *n.* a paper proving the correctness of an item in accounts

vouchsafe' *v.* to condescend to grant, to give

vow *n.* a solemn promise.—*v.* to promise

vow'el *n.* one of the five sounds in the language denoted by the letters a, e, i, o, and u

voy'age (voi'aj) *n.* a journey by water.—*v.* to travel by water.—**voy'aging** *pres. part.*—**voy'ager** *n.*

vul'canite *n.* rubber hardened by being vulcanised.—**vul'canise** *v.* to treat rubber with sulphur at a high temperature

vul'gar *adj.* 1. coarse, rude, offensive. 2. of the common people, as *vulgar superstitions, the vulgar tongue* (i.e. the language of the people, not of the learned, which used to be Latin).—**vulgar'ity** *n.*—**vul'garise** *v.* to make vulgar, to make too common.—**vulgarisation** (-zā'shun) *n.*—**vulgar fraction** a fraction expressed by numerator above, and denominator below a line, e.g. $\frac{3}{8}$

Compare: common, low, ill-mannered, gross, inelegant, ill-bred, plebeian. *Contrast:* refined, cultivated, elegant, well-bred, polite, aristocratic

vul'nerable *adj.* 1. open to attack, easily injured. 2. sensitive to ridicule, etc.

vul'ture *n.* a large bird of prey which feeds on dead animals

vy'ing *pres. part.* of **vie**, competing

W

wad (wod) *n.* a small pad used to hold something in place.—*v.* to stuff with a wad.—**wad'ding** *pres. part.*—**wad'ded** *p.t.* and *p. part.*—**wad'ding** *n.* soft stuffing

wad'dle (wod'l) *v.* to walk like a duck.—*n.*—**wad'dling** *pres. part.*

wade *v.* to walk through water.—**wa'ding** *pres. part.*—**wa'der** *n.* 1. a waterbird. 2. a high waterproof boot

wa'fer *n.* 1. a thin cake or biscuit. 2. a round piece of sticky paper used as a seal

waf'fle (wof'l) *n.* a flat cake of batter cooked in an iron mould, and eaten with syrup

waft (wahft) *v.* to carry through the air or over water.—*n.* a breath, whiff

wag *v.* to move up and down or to and fro.—**wag'ging** *pres. part.*—**wagged** *p.t.* and *p. part.*

wag *n.* a person who likes making jokes

wage (wāj) *n.* payment for work done (often used in *pl.*).—*v.* to carry on, as *to wage war.*—**wa'ging** *pres. part.*

Compare: pay, salary, stipend, emoluments

wa'ger (wā'jer) *n.* a bet.—*v.* to bet

wag'gish *adj.* liking to make jokes, funny

wag'on, wag'gon *n.* a four-wheeled vehicle for heavy loads. (See **van.**)—**wag'(g)oner** *n.* the driver of a wagon.—**wag(g)onette'** *n.* a four-wheeled open carriage with side seats

waif *n.* a homeless child

wail *n.* a long cry of pain or grief.—*v.* to mourn, lament, cry aloud

Compare: howl, moan, scream

wains'cot *n.* wooden lining of panelling of the walls of a room.—*v.* to line with panelling.—**wains'cotting** *pers. part.*—**wains'cotted** *p.t.* and *p. part.*

waist *n.* 1. the middle part of the body, between hips and ribs. 2. the middle part.—**waist'coat** *n.* a sleeveless garment worn under a coat.—**waist'line** *n.*

wait *v.* 1. to stop until someone comes or something happens, as *We will wait for you. We will wait dinner for him.* 2. to expect, as *to wait for news.* 3. to serve at table. 4. (upon) to attend upon. 5. (upon) to call on formally, as *We will elect a small committee to wait upon the mayor and present our petition.*—*n.* waiting, time of waiting.—**wait'er** *n.* a man who serves at table in hotel or restaurant.—**wait'ress** *fem.*—**waits** *n.pl.* carol-singers or musicians.—**to lie in wait for** to prepare an ambush for

Compare: (with 1) stay, delay, linger, postpone, defer

Waitangi Day *n.* Feb. 6, N.Z.'s national day, commemorating the signing in 1840 of the Treaty of Waitangi, at Waitangi, between the British Crown and Maori chiefs

waive *v.* to give up the right to something, to do without.—**wai'ving** *pres. part.*

wake *v.* 1. to stop sleeping. 2. to rouse from sleep. 3. to stir, to be active.—**wa'king** *pres. part.*—**woke, waked** *p.t.*—**waked, wo'ken** *p. part.*—*n.* watch vigil.—**wake'ful** *adj.* unable to sleep, watchful.—**wake'fulness** *n.*

wake *n.* the track left by a ship.—**in the wake of** behind

wa'ken *v.* to wake

Wales *n.* a country lying on the west of the United Kingdom of Britain

walk (wawk) *v.* 1. to move on foot at an ordinary pace. 2. to cross by walking.—*n.* 1. walking. 2. a stroll. 3. distance on foot. 4. way of walking. 5. for place walking. 6. occupation, as *in various walks of life.*—**walk'er** *n.*—**walk'ing-stick** *n.*—**walk'over** *n.* easy victory.—**walk'about** *n.* wandering (of aborigines) in the bush, especially in the phrase **to go walkabout.**—**walkie-talkie** *n.* a portable radio receiver and transmitter

Compare: proceed, march, dawdle, hasten, stride, strut, slouch, slink, swagger, saunter, stalk, sidle, toddle, waddle, trudge, tramp

wall (wawl) *n.* something built of stone, brick, etc. and serving as the side of a building, a fence, defence of a town, etc.—*v.* to block up with a wall.—**wall'-paper** *n.* a covering for walls of a room.—**with backs to the wall** in a desperate situation.—**to go to the wall** to fail, to be defeated

wall'aby (wol'a-bi) *n.* a small Australian kangaroo

wall'aroo *n.* a large Australian kangaroo

wal'let (wol'et) *n.* a pocketbook for banknotes

wal'low (wol'ō) *v.* to roll about, esp. *in mud or water*
wal'nut (wawl'nut) *n.* 1. a nut with a crinkled shell in two halves. 2. the tree, wood of this tree
wal'rus (wol'rus, wawl'rus) *n.* a large sea-animal with long tusks
waltz (wawls) *n.* a smoothly whirling dance for partners, in three-four time.—*v.* to dance the waltz
wan (won) *adj.* pale, tired-looking
wand (wond) *n.* a slender, straight stick
wand'er (wond'er) *v.* to roam, stray, ramble. —**wand'erer** *n.*
wane *v.* to grow smaller, to decrease in importance, strength, power, as *The moon wanes.*—**wa'ning** *pres. part.*—*n.* decrease, decline, as *His power is on the wane*
Compare: (with *n.*) diminish, decline, fade. *Contrast:* wax, increase
want (wont) *n.* 1. being without, need, lack, as *out of order for want of a screw.* 2. poverty. 3. things needed (often used in plural), as *My wants are satisfied.*—*v.* 1. to need, to be without. 2. to wish for, desire.—**want'ing** *adj.* lacking.—*prep.* without
wan'ton (won'ton) *adj.* 1. reckless, thoughtless. 2. playful, unrestrained.—*v.* to frolic, play.—*n.* a wanton person.—**wan'tonness** *n.*
war *n.* 1. fighting between nations. 2. state of war.—*v.* to make war, to fight.—**war'ring** *pres. part.*—**warred** *p.t.* and *p. part.*—**war'-cry** *n.* a battle slogan shouted as an encouragement.—**war'monger** *n.* someone who urges war.—**civil war** war between two groups of peoples of the same nation. —**cold war** hostility between nations without actual fighting.—**war of nerves** repeated attempts to undermine enemy morale without actual fighting
Compare: conflict, strife, hostilities, warfare
Note: This verb is usually followed by *with* or *against*
war'atah (wor'a-ta) a small shrub with large crimson flower, often used as the Australian emblem
war'ble (wor'bl) *v.* to sing like a bird. *n.*—**war'bling** *pres. part.*—**war'bler** *n.* a song-bird
ward (word) *n.* 1. guardianship, care. 2. a minor under care of a guardian. 3. a division of a city or hospital. 4. indentations of head of key, or lock.—*v.* to guard, to turn aside a blow, etc., as *to ward off attack*
war'den *n.* 1. a guard, watchman. 2. a governor of a prison
ward'er *n.* a prison keeper, jailer.—**ward'ress** *fem.*
ward'robe *n.* 1. a cupboard for holding clothes. 2. a stock of clothes
ward'room *n.* an officers' mess on a warship
ware *n.* goods, manufactured articles esp. in pottery or metal.—**ware'house** *n.* storehouse
war'fare *n.* war, fighting
war'head *n.* an explosive charge in a guided missile
war'ily (wair'i-li) *adv.* cautiously
war'like *adj.* 1. ready to fight, bellicose. 2. military
warm (worm) *adj.* 1. fairly hot. 2. giving warmth. 3. hearty, enthusiastic. (See **hot.**)—*v.* to make warm (often followed by *up*).—**warm'ly** *adv.*—**warmth** *n.* being warm.—**warm-blood'ed** (of animals) having warm blood, not cold-blooded as snakes. —**warm-heart'ed** kind, sympathetic
warn (worn) *v.* to put on guard, to inform beforehand.—**warn'ing** *n.* 1. a notice of danger, of intention to leave, etc. 2. a caution, something said or done to warn
warp (worp) *n.* 1. the lengthwise threads in a loom. 2. a rope.—*v.* 1. to twist out of shape, to become twisted. 2. to move by a rope fastened to a buoy
war'rant (wor'ant) *n.* 1. right, authority, as *What warrant have you for saying that?* 2. a document giving authority, as *A warrant is out for his arrest.*—*v.* to guarantee, promise.—**war'rant off'icer** *n.* officer above N.C.O.s but below commissioned officers.—**war'ranty** *n.* authority
war'ranty *n.* a guarantee
war'ren (wor'en) *n.* ground occupied by rabbits
war'rior (wor'i-er) *n.* a soldier of experience, fighter
wart (wort) *n.* a hard growth on the skin
wa'ry *adj.* cautious, careful.—**wa'rily** *adv.*
wash (wosh) *v.* 1. to clean with water. 2. to wash oneself. 3. (of moving liquid) to carry along.—he **wash'es.**—*n.* 1. a washing. 2. sweep of water. 3. clothes washed at one time. 4. a thin coat of colour.—**wash'er** *n.* 1. a person or machine that washes. 2. a ring put on tap or nut to make it fit tightly.—**wash'y** *adj.* watery.—**wash'-leather** *n.* chamois leather.—**to wash dirty linen in public** to quarrel in front of others. —**to wash one's hands of** to refuse any further responsibility for
wasp (wosp) *n.* a striped insect with a powerful sting.—**wasp'ish** *adj.* irritable
was'sail (wos'l, was'l) *n.* a drinking feast.—**was'sailing** *n.* singing carols at houses
was'tage (wās'tij) *n.* loss by waste
waste *v.* 1. to use carelessly, to throw away. 2. to destroy, ruin. 3. to wear away, decay. —**wa'sting** *pres. part.*—*n.* 1. wasting. 2. what is wasted. 3. desert land, wilderness. —*adj.* 1. desert. 2. useless.—**lay waste** to damage, destroy.—**waste'ful** *adj.* using too much.—**waste'fully** *adv.*—**wa'ster, wa'strel** *n.* extravagant, useless person
watch (wotch) *n.* 1. looking out for, attention.

2. a guard. 3. a spell of duty, esp. on board ship. 4. something for telling the time, worn on wrist or in pocket.—**watch'es** *pl.*—*v.* 1. to look at closely. 2. to keep guard. 3. to stay awake.—he **watch'es.**—**watch'ful** *adj.*—**watch'maker** *n.* one who makes clocks, etc.—**watch'man** *n.* a man set on guard.—**watch'tower** *n.* a look-out post.—**watch'word** *n.* password —**to watch one's time** to wait for the right moment.—**to watch one's words (tongue)** to be careful what one says

Compare: (with watchful) vigilant, attentive, heedful, cautious, wary

wa'ter (waw'ter) *n.* the liquid found in the sea, rivers, lakes, etc.—*v.* 1. to put water on, as *to water the garden.* 2. to supply with water, as *to water horses.* 3. to dilute with water, as *to water (down) the mixture.*—**wa'tery** *adj.*—**wa'ter bag** *n.* a canvas bag for holding water.—**wa'ter col'our** *n.* 1. paint to be mixed with water. 2. a painting of water colours.—**wa'ter course** *n.* a river.—**wa'ter cress** *n.* a creeping herb growing in water, used in salads.—**wa'terfall** *n.* a river falling over a steep place.—**wa'ter fowl** *n.* water birds.—**wa'ter-line** *n.* the line on a ship's side where water reaches.—**wa'terlogged** *adj.* unable to float because full of water.—**wa'termark** *n.* the faint mark on paper made during manufacture.—**wa'terproof** *adj.* not letting water through.—*n.* a waterproof garment. —**wa'tershed** *n.* a ridge separating two rivers.—**wa'terski** *n.* the sport of remaining upright on water while being towed by a motor boat.—*v.*—**wa'terspout** *n.* a column of water sucked up from the sea by a whirlwind.—**wa'tertight** *adj.* not allowing water to pass in or out.—**wa'terworks** *n.* the public water supply.—**wat'ering-place** *n.* a seaside or health resort.—**in hot water** in trouble.—**of the finest, first water** (of a jewel) of finest quality.—**to throw cold water on** to discourage

watt (wot) *n.* a unit of electric power.—**wat'tage** *n.* power in watts

wat'tle (wot'l) *n.* 1. sticks interlaced with twigs to make a fence or hut. 2. any one of more than 300 species of acacia with yellow blossoms, national flower of Australia.—*v.* to interlace twigs, etc.

wave *v.* 1. to move to and fro, to sway. 2. to shape in curves, to give this shape to. 3. to hold up and shake one's hand.—**wa'ving** *pres. part.*—*n.* 1. a swell on water. 2. waving. 3. curve. 4. vibration of electric forces,—**wa'vy** *adj.* having curves.—**wave'band** *n.* a range of wavelengths.—**wave'length** *n.* the distance between two successive crests or troughs in a succession of waves

wa'ver *v.* 1. to hesitate. 2. to weaken, to falter

wax *v.* to grow, increase.—he **wax'es**

wax *n.* 1. a yellow substance made by bees. 2. a similar substance used for making candles, sealing wax, etc.—*v.* to put wax on.—**wax'en** *adj.* made of wax

way *n.* 1. path, road, as *the straight and narrow way.* (See **road.**) 2. manner, method, plan, as *That is the way to do it.* 3. direction, as *Please show me the way to the village.* 4. habit, as *I am used to his ways.*—**way'farer** *n.* a traveller on foot.—**waylay'** *v.* to lie in wait for, accost.—**waylay'ing** *pres. part.*—**waylaid'** *p.t.* and *p. part.*—**way'side** *n.* the edge of the road.—*adj.*—**by the way** incidentally.—**in a bad way** seriously ill or at a disadvantage.—**out of the way** unusual.—**out-of-the-way** remote. —**right of way** a legal right to pass. —**to have a way with one** to be persuasive in a charming way.—**under way** (of a ship) moving.—**ways and means** various methods or resources

way'ward *adj.* disobedient, wilful.—**way'wardness** *n.*

we *pron. pl.* of I.—*obj.* *us.*—*possessive our, ours.*—*emphatic and reflexive ourself, ourselves*

Note: Kings and queens say *we* instead of *I*, and so sometimes do editors or writers of unsigned articles in newspapers, etc.

weak *adj.* 1. not strong, feeble. (See **strong.**) 2. not powerful, easily overcome. 3. having little flavour, diluted as *weak tea.* 4. few in numbers.—**weak'en** *v.* to make weaker.—**weak'ly** *adj.* delicate.—**weak'ness** *n.* 1. being weak. 2. a fault. 3. (for) fondness for, as *I have a weakness for strawberry jam.*—**weak'ling** *n.* a weak person.—**weak-kneed'** *adj.* timid.—**weak-willed'** lacking courage and resolution

weal *n.* well being, happiness

weal *n.* scar made by a stick or lash

weald *n.* 1. forest. 2. wold, open country

wealth (welth) *n.* 1. riches, great possessions. 2. abundance, as *He gave a wealth of examples.* 3. things having use or value.—**wealth'y** *adj.* rich.—**weal'thier** *comp.*—**weal'thiest** *sup.*

Compare: plenty, affluence, opulence, goods, possessions, property

wean *v.* 1. to accustom a baby to food other than mother's milk. 2. to break off from a habit

weap'on (wep'on) *n.* anything used to fight with

wear (wār) *v.* 1. to have on, to be dressed in. 2. to show, as *to wear a cheerful expression* 3. to use, to damage by use. 4. to last long. 5. to tire.—**wore** *p.t.*—**worn** *p. part.*—*n.* 1. dress, clothing. 2. service, use.—**wear'er** *n.*—**to wear away** to disintegrate by wear. —**to wear down** to lessen by wear, to overcome resistance.—**to wear off** to disappear gradually.—**to wear out** to damage by wear, to exhaust

Note: The meaning of this verb is

changed by the prepositions which follow it, e.g. *wear out* (tire, damage by use), *wear on* (go on, go forward, as *The time is wearing on*)

wear'ily (wee'ri-li) *adv.* in a weary way

wear'iness *n.* tiredness

wear'isome *adj.* tiring

wear'y *adj.* 1. tired. 2. tiring.—**wear'ier** *comp.*—**wear'iest** *sup.*—*v.* to make weary. —he **wear'ies.**—**wear'ying** *pres. part.*—**wear'ied** *p.t.* and *p. part.*

Compare: fatigued, worn out, vexed, troubled. *Contrast:* rested, fresh, soothed, roused

wea'sel (weez'l) *n.* a small animal with long slender body, which preys on other animals

weath'er (weTH'er) *n.* condition of the atmosphere, as regards rain, wind, temperature, etc.—*v.* 1. to expose to the air, to season. 2. to endure, resist, as *to weather the storm.*—**weath'er-beaten** *adj.*—**weath'er-cock, weath'er-vane** *n.* something to show which way the wind blows.—**weath'er forecast** an estimate of future weather.—**weath'er glass** a barometer.—**to keep a weather eye open** to be alert.—**to make heavy weather of** to have a troubled time with.—**under the weather** ill, out of sorts

weave *v.* to make cloth, etc. by interlacing threads.—**weav'ing** *pres. part.*—**wove** *p.t.*—**wo'ven** *p. part.*—**weav'er** *n.*

web *n.* 1. something woven. 2. a spider's net. 3. a membrane between the toes of a duck, etc.—**webbed** *adj.* having a web, web-footed.—**web-foot'ed** *adj.* having web between toes.—**web'bing** *n.* strong, coarse material used for straps, etc.

wed *v.* 1. to marry. 2. to unite closely.—**wed'ding** *pres. part.*—**wed'ded** *p.t.* and *p. part.*—**wed'ding** *n.* marriage ceremony

wedge (wej) *n.* a piece of wood or metal, thin at one end and growing thicker.—*v.* 1. to fasten or keep open with a wedge. 2. to pack tightly among other things.—**wedg'ing** *pres. part.*—**thin end of the wedge** the first small step leading to an important result

wed'lock *n.* marriage

Wednes'day (wenz'dā, wed'inz-dā) *n.* the fourth day of the week—**Ash Wednesday** the first day of Lent

wee *adj.* very small, tiny

weed *n.* a wild plant growing where it is not wanted.—*v.* to get rid of weeds.—**weed'y** *adj.* 1. full of weeds. 2. tall and weak

weeds *n.pl.* a widow's mourning clothes

week *n.* 1. a period of seven days. 2. the work-days. Monday to Saturday.—**week'-day** *n.* any day except Saturday and Sunday.—**week'-end** *n.* from Friday or Saturday to Monday.—**week-end'er** *n.* (Aus.) a small holiday cottage.—**week'ly** *adj.* happening once a week.—*adv.* once a week, every week.—**this day week** a week from today.—**week in week out** week after week, continuously

weep *v.* 1. to cry, to shed tears. 2. to lament.—**weep'ing** *pres. part.*—**wept** *p.t.* and *p. part.*

wee'vil *n.* a small beetle which does much damage to grain, etc.

weft *n.* cross threads in weaving, woof

weigh (wā) *v.* 1. to find the weight of, as *to weigh cheese.* 2. to have weight, as *The cheese weighed* 28 *lbs.* 3. to be important, as *That is an argument that weighs heavily with me.* 4. to press on, as *weighed down with care.*—**weigh'bridge** *n.* a platform on which loaded vehicles are weighed.—**to weigh anchor** to raise anchor before sailing away.—**to weigh down** to press heavily on. —**to weigh up** to judge carefully

weight (wāt) *n.* 1. heaviness, the quality which draws everything towards the centre of the earth. 2. something used in weighing on scales. 3. something heavy, a load. 4. importance.—*v.* to burden.—**weight'y** *adj.* 1. heavy. 2. important

weir (weer) *n.* a dam across a river

weird (weerd) *adj.* unearthly, queer. (See **uncanny**)

wel'come (wel'kum) *n.* a kind reception.—*v.* to receive with pleasure.—**wel'coming** *pres. part.*—*adj.* received gladly, as *welcome news*, a *welcome guest*

weld *v.* to join together hot metal by hammering while soft.—*n.* a welded joint.—**weld'er** *n.*

wel'fare *n.* happiness, well-being.—**Welfare State** *n.* a state that takes special measures for the social security of its people

well *n.* a spring, a deep hole sunk in the ground for water or oil.—*v.* to flow out, to gush up

well *adv.* 1. in good manner or degree, as *You have done well to get top of the class.* 2. to a considerable extent, as *It is well past the time.* 3. thoroughly, as *Beat the eggs well.*—*adj.* 1. in good health, as *We are all safe and well.* 2. satisfactory, as *All's well.*—*interj.* 1. as, *Well, to be sure.* 2. or on starting or resuming a conversation.—*comp.* of *adj.* and *adv.* **better**, *sup.* **best.**—**well-advis'ed** prudent.—**well-appoint'ed** fully equipped.—**well-bal'anced** sensible.—**well-being** comfort.—**well-bred** of good manners, of good stock.—**well-dispos'ed** friendly—**well'doer** someone who does good.—**well-informed'** with a good fund of knowledge.—**well-knit'** strongly built.—**well-known'** widely known.—**well-lined'** (of a purse) full of money.—**well-mean'ing** of good intentions.—**well'nigh** nearly.—**well-off'** rich.—**well-read'** with a wide knowledge of books.—**well-spoken,** courteous, with a cultured accent.—**well-to-do'** rich.—**well-tried'** often used with success.—**well' wisher** a friendly person.—**well-worn'** hackneyed, stale.—**as well** also.—**to be well out of** to escape without loss.—**to stand**

well with someone to be in his good graces

Compare: (with *adj.*) healthy, robust, fit, sound

well'ingtons *n.pl.* boots up to the knees

Welsh *n.* the people or language of Wales.—**Welsh rabbit (rarebit)** toasted cheese

welt *n.* 1. the rim of leather between the upper part and sole of a shoe. 2. a deep mark made by a stick or whip.—*v.* 1. to thrash. 2. to fit with a welt

welt'er *v.* to roll about, wallow.—*n.* confusion, mass.—**wel'terweight** *n.* 1. extra weight carried by a racehorse. 2. (boxing) the weight above light-weight and below middle-weight.—*n.*

wench *n.* a girl, young woman.—**wench'es** *pl.*

wend *v.* to go

were *v.* 1. *p.t.* plural of **be.** 2. conditional (or subjunctive) sing. and plural of **be,** as *If it were not for the expense I should travel more than I do*

west *n.* 1. the part of the horizon where the sun sets. 2. part of a country lying to this side.—*adj.* towards the west.—*adv.* to the west.—**west'erly** *adj.* from the west, to the west.—**west'ern** *adj.* of the west, toward the west.—**west'ward** *adj. adv. n.*

wet *adj.* 1. soaked in water or any other liquid, having water, etc. on it. 2. rainy,—**wet'ter** *comp.*—**wet'test** *sup.*—*n.* wetness, water, rain.—*v.* to make wet.—**wet'ting** *pres. part.*—**wet'ted, wet** *p.t.* and *p. part.*

Compare: moist, watery, saturated, fluid, liquid. *Contrast:* dry, solid

weth'er (weᴛʜ'er) *n.* a male sheep.—**ewe** *fem.*

whack *n.* a hit, esp. with a stick.—*v.*

whale (hwāl) *n.* a large sea-animal shaped like a fish, and hunted for its oil and whalebone.—**wha'ler** *n.* a man or ship used for hunting whales

wharf (hwawrf) *n.* a quay or pier for loading and unloading ships.—**wharves, wharfs** *pl.*

what (hwot) *adj.* 1. used to point out amount, number or kind, as *Let me know what time to come.* 2. used in asking questions, as *What time is it?*

Note: What differs from *which* in this use because *which* selects one from a definite number, *what* from an indefinite number, e.g. the difference between *Which would you like?* and *What would you like?*

3. used as an exclamation to mean how great, strange, etc., as *What weather!*—*pron.* that which, as *Tell me what you want.*—*adv.* to what an extent, in what way, as *What good is it? What?*—*interj.* to indicate surprise, etc. as *What!*—**whate'ver whate'er'** (hwot-âr'), **whatsoev'er** *adj. pron.* or *adv.* any (thing) which, of whatever kind, extent, etc. it may be

Note: Avoid the common mistake of using *what as a* relative pronoun instead of *which* e.g. *This is the one what I want* instead of *This is the one which I want*

wheat (hweet) *n.* the corn from which flour is made.—**wheat'en** *adj.* made of wheat

whee'dle *v.* to coax, to persuade by flattery.—**whee'dling** *pres. part.*

wheel *n.* 1. a round frame with spokes, turning on an axle at the centre. 2. anything resembling a wheel.—*v.* 1. to turn, to move on wheels. 2. to revolve, to change direction.—**wheel'-barrow** *n.* a small cart with one wheel, two legs and handles for pushing.—**wheel'wright** *n.* one who makes and repairs wheels.—**to put a spoke in someone's wheel** to spoil his plans.—**wheels within wheels** hidden influences

wheeze *v.* to breathe loudly and with difficulty.—*n.*—**whee'zy** *adj.*

whelk *n.* shell-fish used for food

whelp *n.* a pup, cub, young of a dog, lion, wolf, etc.—*v.* to produce whelps

when *adv.* 1. at what time, as *When did you arrive?* 2. (relative) at which time, while, as *I shall be there when you arrive. He reads when travelling.*—*conj.* whereas, although, as *It's not fair that you should have two when I have none.*—*pron.* what time, which time, as *Till when does this last?*

whence *adv.* 1. from what place. 2. from which, thus, as *Whence it can be seen that...*

whenev'er, whensoev'er *conj.* when, as soon as.—*adv.* every time that

where (hwār) *adv.* 1. at what place, in what direction, as *Where are you going?* 2. (relative) at or to which, as *This is the place where he lives. conj.* whereas, as *You gain where I lose over this deal.*—*pron.* the place at or in, as *This is where he lives.*—**where'abouts** *adv.* in what place *n.* place where someone or something is.—**whereas'** *conj.* considering that, although.—**wherev'er, wheresoe'er, wheresoev'er** emphatic forms of **where.**—**where'fore** *adv.* for which reason.—*n.* reason, as *The whys and wherefores.*—**where'with** *adv.* with which, with what.—*n.* that with which, as *He has wherewith to pay his debts.*—**where'withal**

Note: Where is used in many words, the meaning of which can be seen by adding the meaning of *where* (or sometimes *which*) to the second part of the word, e.g. **whereat'** (*adv.*), **whereby'** (*adv.*), **whereof'** (*adv.*), **whereto'** (*adv.*), **whereun'der** (*adv.*), **whereun'to** (*adv.*), **whereupon'** (*adv.*)

whet *v.* 1. to sharpen. 2. to make keen.—**whetting** *pres. part.*—**whet'ted** *p.t.* and *p. part.*—**whet'stone** *n.* stone for sharpening tools

wheth'er (hweᴛʜ'er) *conj.* used to introduce the first of two alternatives, the second of which may be stated or suggested, as *He* *asked me whether I was going* (*or not*).—*pron.* which of two

whey (hwā) *n.* watery liquid left when milk forms curds

which *adj.* 1. asks for a selection from alternatives, as *Which one will you have?* See notes on **what**. 2. used relatively to refer to something previously referred to, as *Which orders you must strictly obey.*—*pron.* 1. used relatively to refer to thing previously mentioned, as *He found the purse which his mother had lost.* See notes on **what**. 2. used to ask a question calling for a selection, as *Which will you have?*—**whichev'er**, **whichsoev'er** *pron.* and *adj.* emphatic forms of **which**

whiff *n.* a puff of smoke, wind, etc.—*v.* to blow lightly, to puff

while *n.* a space of time, as *in a little while.*—*v.* (away) to pass the time.—*conj.* during the time that.—**whilst** whereas, although, as *While I am sorry for you, I'm afraid I can't do anything.*—**between whiles** in the intervals.—**once in a while** occasionally.—**to be worth one's while** to be to one's advantage

whim *n.* a sudden idea, fancy

whim'per *v.* to whine, to cry feebly and plaintively.—*n.*

whim'sical *adj.* full of whims, fanciful, odd.—**whimsical'ity** *n.*

whine *n.* a long, thin cry, a wail, complaint.—*v.*

whinge, **winge** *v.* (Aus.) to complain at length, whine.—*n.*

whin'ny *v.* to neigh joyfully.—he **whin'nies**.—**whin'nying** *pres. part.*—**whin'nied** *p.t.* and *p. part.*—*n.* the cry of a horse

whip *n.* a lash tied to a stick for beating or urging.—*v.* 1. to beat, thrash. 2. to move suddenly, to snatch.—**whip'ping** *pres. part.*—**whipped** *p.t.* and *p. part.*—**whip'hand** *n.* advantage, control over another.—**whip round** a collection for a present, or for someone in misfortune

whip'pet *n.* a dog like a small greyhound

whir *v.* to move with a buzzing sound, like an engine.—**whir'ring** *pres. part.*—**whirred** *p.t.* and *p. part.*—*n.* a buzzing, whizzing sound

whirl *v.* to swing rapidly round, to spin.—*n.* a whirling movement.—**whirl'igig** *n.* a spinning toy, merry-go-round.—**whirl'pool** *n.* a whirling current of water, eddy.—**whirl'wind** *n.* a violent wind whirling and moving forward

whisk *v.* 1. to sweep or beat briskly. 2. to move lightly and quickly.—*n.* 1. a brush. 2. instrument for beating eggs. 3. quick movement

whisk'er *n.* 1. hair on a man's face. 2. long, stiff hairs on face of cat, etc.—**whisk'ered** *adj.*

whis'ky, (Scotch) **whis'key** (Irish) *n.* a strong liquor made from grain or potatoes

whis'per *v.* 1. to speak very softly. 2. to rustle, murmur. 3. to tell secretly.—*n.* murmur, soft sound

whist *n.* a card-game for four persons

whis'tle (hwis'l) *v.* 1. to make a loud, shrill sound through rounded lips, or with an instrument.—**whis'tling** *pres. part.*—*n.* 1. a clear, shrill, sound. 2. an instrument for whistling

whit *n.* a very little bit, a jot

Whit, **Whitsun** *n.* the weekend including Whit Sunday.—**Whit Sunday** the seventh Sunday after Easter

white *adj.* 1. of the colour of snow. 2. pale. 3. light in colour.—**whi'ter** *comp.*—**whi'test** *sup.*—*n.* 1. white colour. 2. white part.—**whi'ten** *v.* to make white.—**whi'tish** *adj.*—**white collar worker** a non-manual worker.—**white elephant** an expensive but unwanted present.—**white feather** symbol of cowardice.—**white flag** sign of surrender.—**white lie** a small, harmless lie

white'wash *n.* a liquid mixture for whitening walls, etc.—*v.* 1. to cover with whitewash. 2. to try to cover up faults or mistakes

whith'er *adj.* which way? to what place?

whit'tle *v.* 1. to cut or shape wood with a knife. 2. (down) to reduce

whiz, **whizz** *v.* to move with a humming or rushing sound.—**whiz'zing** *pres. part.*—**whizzed** *p.t.* and *p. part.*—*n.* violent, hissing sound

who (hōō) *pron.* 1. which or what person, as *Who is there?* 2. used relatively to refer to person already mentioned, as *the boy who lives next door.* (See **that**.)—*obj.* **whom**, *possessive* **whose**.—**who'so**, **whosoev'er**, **whoe'er'**, **whosoe'er'**, **whomev'er**, **whomsoev'er** emphatic and old forms

Note: Whose may be used to mean *of which* as well as *of whom*

whole (hōl) *adj.* 1. complete, entire. 2. in good health, uninjured.—*n.* 1. sum, total. 2. something complete, not broken.—**whol'ly** *adv.*—**whole-heart'ed** *adj.* enthusiastic

whole'meal (hōl'meel) *adj.* made of flour which contains the whole of the grain

whole'sale (hōl'sāl) *n.* sale of goods by large quantities.—*adj.* 1. in large quantities. 2. selling on wholesale plan.—**wholesa'ler** *n.*

whole'some (hōl'sum) *adj.* good for the health, healthy

Compare: sound, beneficial, pure, nutritious. *Contrast:* unwholesome, unhealthy, corrupt, tainted, impure

whol'ly (hō'li) *adv.* entirely, completely

whoop, **hoop** (hōōp) *n.* a loud, high shout, a war cry.—*v.*—**whoop'ing-cough** *n.* infectious disease with a noisy cough

whorl (hworl) *n.* 1. one turn of a spiral. 2. a ring of leaves round the stem

whor'tleberry *n.* a small plant with purple edible fruit, bilberry

why (whī) *adv.* 1. for what cause, as *Why did*

you do it? 2. (relatively), as *I will tell you why I did so.*—*n.* reasons, as *the whys and wherefores.*—*interj.* to express surprise, protest, etc.

wick *n.* cord in a candle or oil-lamp which burns when lighted

wick'ed *adj.* 1. bad, sinful. 2. playful, mischievous.—**wick'edly** *adv.*—**wick'edness** *n.* sin, evil

Compare: depraved, immoral, vicious, infamous. *Contrast:* righteous, virtuous, good, holy

wick'er *n.* twigs, osier, etc. woven together.—*adj.*—**wick'er work** *n.* basket-work

wick'et *n.* 1. a small gate or door. 2. in cricket, a set of three stumps and bails at which a bowler bowls, or the playing pitch.—**wicket-keeper** *n.* (cricket) the fieldsman behind the batsman's wicket

wide *adj.* 1. broad. 2. open as far as possible. 3. far from the mark.—**wi'der** *comp.*—**wi'dest** *sup.*—*adv.* 1. at many points, as *far and wide*, 2. with a wide opening, as *It was wide open.*—**wide'ly** *adv.* greatly.—**wi'den** *v.* to make wide.—**wide-awake'** *adj.* alert.—**wide'-spread** *adj.* 1. spread widely. 2. general

wid'ow (wid'ō) *n.* a woman whose husband is dead.—**wid'ower** *n.* a man whose wife is dead.—**wid'owhood** *n.* being a widow

width *n.* breadth, distance from side to side

wield (weeld) *v.* to hold and use, as *The labourer wields a pickaxe*

wife *n.* a married woman.—**wives** *pl.*—**hus'band** *masc.*—**wife'hood** *n.*—**wife'ly** *adj.* like a wife

wig *n.* a head of artificial hair

wig'wag *v.* (Canada) 1. to move back and forth. 2. to signal with flags or lights moved according to a code

wig'wam *n.* a tent of poles covered with skins, etc. made by North American Indians

wild (wīld) *adj.* 1. not tamed, as *wild animals.* 2. not cultivated, as *wild strawberries.* 3. excited, violent, unrestrained, as *wild excitement, wild weather.*—**wild'ly** *adv.*—**the wilds** desert, uninhabited country.—**wildcat** *adj.* impetuous.—**wildcat strike** a sudden unauthorised strike.—**wild-goose chase** a search for something that cannot be found, a foolish undertaking

wil'derness *n.* waste land, desert

wile *n.* a trick, cunning deceit

wil'ful *adj.* 1. done on purpose, intended, as *wilful murder*. 2. obstinate, perverse, as *wilful disobedience, a wilful child.*—**wil'fully** *adv.*—**wil'fulness** *n.*

wi'liness *n.* slyness, craft

will *n.* 1. the power to choose and decide. 2. wish, purpose. 3. written statement of a person's wishes about disposal of property after death.—*v.* 1. to have a wish, to intend. 2. to oblige by willing. 3. to leave in one's will.—**willed** *p.t.* and *p. part.* used as an *auxiliary* to make up tenses of other verbs, e.g. *they will go.*—*p.t.* **would.** (See **shall**)

wil'ling *adj.* ready and cheerful.—**wil'lingly** *adv.*—**wil'lingness** *n.* readiness

will-o-the-wisp' *n.* 1. a phosphorescent light flitting over marshes. 2. an elusive person or hope

wil'low (wil'ō) *n.* a tree with very pliable wood used for making cricket-bats, etc.—**willowy** *adj.* slender and graceful

wil'ly-nil'ly *adv.* willing or not, compulsorily

wilt *v.* to droop, to fade

wi'ly *adj.* cunning, sly.—**wi'lier** *comp.*—**wi'liest** *sup.*

win *v.* 1. to gain by work or effort. 2. to be successful. 3. to reach, as *to win the shore.* 4. to persuade, as *I hope to win him* (*over*) *to my point of view.*—**win'ning** *pres. part.*—**won** *p.t.* and *p. part.*—*n.* a victory.—**to win hands down** to win easily

Compare: succeed, gain, triumph, achieve, overcome, obtain, procure, attain, conquer. *Contrast:* lose, fail

wince (wins) *v.* to flinch, to draw back from pain, etc.—*n.*—**win'cing** *pres. part.*

winceyette' (win-si-et') *n.* a kind of light cotton cloth

winch *n.* a machine with a handle for winding a rope which pulls or lifts a heavy weight, windlass

win'chester *n.* 1. a repeating rifle. 2. a large bottle

wind *n.* 1. air moving quickly. 2. breath.—*v*, 1. to smell. 2. to put out of breath.—**to get wind of** to hear a rumour about.—**to sail close to the wind** to be near to breaking the law

wind (wīnd) *v.* 1. to turn, to twist, to change direction. 2. to wrap. 3. to tighten a spring or coil.—**wound** *p.t.* and *p. part.*

wind'fall *n.* 1. a fallen fruit. 2. a piece of good luck

wind'jammer *n.* a large sailing ship

wind'lass *n.* a machine for pulling, a winch

wind'mill *n.* a mill with sails worked by wind

wind'ow (wind'ō) *n.* a hole in a wall to let in light or air.—**wind'ow-pane** *n.* glass in a window

wind'pipe *n.* the passage from throat to lungs

wind'-screen (U.S. **wind'shield**) *n.* the sheet of glass at the front of a motor car

wind'-sock *n.* a canvas tube on an aerodrome mast to show the wind's direction

wind'-tunnel *n.* a passage through which air is blown to test the effect on model aircraft, streamlined car bodies, etc.

wind'-vane *n.* an instrument which points the direction of the wind

wind'ward *n.* the side towards the wind.—*adj.*

wind'y *adj.* with much wind, stormy.—**wind'ier** *comp.*—**wind'iest** *sup.*

wine *n.* 1. the fermented juice of the grape. 2. drink made from other fruits.—**wine'-**

glass *n.*—**wine'-press** *n.* machine for pressing grapes

wing *n.* 1. the part used by a bird or insect in flying. 2. something similar in shape or use. 3. a side of a building extending from the main body. 4. one of the sides of a stage. 5. the flank position, e.g. in football, etc. or in an army. 6. division of R.A.F. composed of two or more squadrons.—*v.* 1. to fly. 2. to wound in the wing.—**winged** *adj.* 1. swift. 2. wounded.—**wing-comman'der** *n.* in R.A.F. officer ranking next below Group Captain

wink (wingk) *v.* 1. to close and open one eye as a hint, to blink. 2. to pretend not to notice, as *His behaviour was winked at.*—*n.* winking.—**forty winks** a short nap

win'kle (wing'kl) *n.* a small edible shellfish.—**to winkle out** to prise out

win'ner *n.* one that wins

win'ning *pres. part.* of **win.**—*adj.* attractive, pleasant.—**win'nings** *n.pl.* what has been won

win'now (win'ō) *v.* 1. to separate the grain from the chaff by blowing. 2. to sift, separate, as *to winnow truth from falsehood*

win'some (win'sum) *adj.* charming

win'ter *n.* the fourth, and coldest season.—*v.* to spend the winter.—**win'try** *adj.* like winter

wipe *v.* to rub with something soft, in order to clean or dry.—*n.*—**wi'ping** *pres. part.*—**wi'per** *n.* something that wipes.—**to wipe out** to destroy

wire *n.* 1. metal drawn into the form of a cord. 2. a telegram.—*v.* 1. to fasten with wire. 2. to send a telegram.—**wi'ring** *pres. part.*—**wire'less** *n.* 1. telegraphy or telephony without connecting wires, radio. 2. a radio receiving set.—**wi'ry** *adj.* strong, tough.—**wire-wool'** *n.* a pad of fine wires for scouring pans.—**live wire** 1. an electrified wire. 2. a go-ahead person

wis'dom (wiz'dom) *n.* 1. knowledge of truth and beauty. 2. good judgment, being wise. 3. prudence, experience

wise (wīz) *adj.* showing knowledge, intelligence and good judgment.—**wi'ser** *comp.*—**wi'sest** *sup.*—**wise'acre** (wīz'ā-ker) *n.* someone who pretends to know everything

Compare: clever, prudent, judicious, sagacious, learned, intelligent, sage. *Contrast:* unwise, foolish, silly, ignorant, thoughtless, injudicious

wise (wīz) *n.* manner, way

wish *v.* 1. to want, to desire.—**he wishes'.**—*n.* a desire.—**wish'es** *pl.*—**wish'ful** *adj.* desirous.—**wishful thinking** believing a thing true because one would like it to be true

wisp *n.* 1. a handful of straw, etc. 2. a twist of hair

wist'ful *adj.* thoughtful, longing.—**wist'fully** *adv.*—**wist'fulness** *n.*

wit *n.* 1. intelligence, understanding, sense. 2. clever and unusual ideas amusingly expressed. 3. a clever and amusing person.—*pl.* sense.—**to wit,** namely.—**at one's wits end** not knowing what to do next.—**to live by one's wits** to live by trickery, avoiding work

witch *n.* woman supposed to use magic, sorceress.—**wiz'ard** *masc.*—**witch'es** *pl.*—**witch'craft** *n.* magic powers, sorcery.—**witch'ery** *n.* 1. witchcraft. 2. charm

with *prep.* 1. in company or possession of, as *Come with me, a man with a dog.* 2. by means of, because of, as *filled with water, ill with measles.* 3. in relation to, concerning, as *I made a bargain with him.* 4. used to show separation, as *to part with, to dispense with.* 5. notwithstanding, as *With all his money, he is not happy*

withal' (wiTH-awl') *adv.* besides

withdraw' *v.* 1. to draw back, retire. 2. to take back, draw away, remove.—**with-drew'** *p.t.*—**withdrawn'** *p. part.*—**with-draw'al** *n.*

with'er (wiTH'er) *v.* 1. to fade, to shrivel. 2. to cause to fade, to blight. 3. to snub

withhold' *v.* to keep back.—**withheld'** *p.t.* and *p. part.*

Compare: keep, retain, restrain, refrain, suspend

within' *adv.* inside, as *The rest of the family are within.*—*prep.* in, inside, as *It is within two miles of here.*—*n.* the inside, as *a view from within*

without' *adv.* outside, as *He waits without.*—*prep.* 1. lacking, as *without food.* 2. outside, beyond, as *without the city walls.*—*conj.* unless (old usage), as *I will not go without you tell me.*—*n.* the outside, as *from without.*—**it goes without saying** it is obvious

withstand' *v.* to oppose, to stand up against.—**withstood'** *p.t.* and *p. part.*

Compare: resist, endure, thwart, confront, face. *Contrast:* yield, give in, give up, accede to

wit'ness *n.* 1. proof, evidence. 2. a person who can give evidence from his own experience. 3. a person who gives evidence in a law-court.—**wit'nesses** *pl.*—*v.* 1. to give evidence. 2. to see. 3. to sign a document as witness.—he **wit'nesses**

wit'ticism (wit'i-sizm) *n.* a witty remark.—**wit'tily** *adv.* in a witty way

wit'tingly *adv.* knowing what one is doing, on purpose

wit'ty *adj.* clever and amusing.—**wit'tier** *comp.*—**wit'tiest** *sup.*

wiz'ard *n.* a sorcerer, a man possessing magic powers.—**witch** *fem.*—**wiz'ardry** *n.*

wiz'ened *adj.* withered, shrivelled

woad (wōd) *n.* a blue dye used by the ancient Britons

wob'ble *v.* to move unsteadily, to sway from side to side.—**wob'bling** *pres. part.*—**wob'bly** *adj.* shaky

woe (wō) *n.* misery, grief, distress.—**woe'be-**

gone *adj.* sorrowful.—**woe'ful** *adj.* unhappy, sad.—**woe'fully** *adv.*

Compare: (with woeful) doleful, miserable, pitiful, calamitous

wold (wōld) *n.* a down; bare, rolling country

wolf (woolf) *n.* a wild animal rather like a dog.—**wolves** *pl.*—**wolf'ish** *adj.* savage, cruel.—**to keep the wolf from the door** to keep hunger away.—**to cry wolf** to raise false alarms until one is not believed

wol'fram *n.* a metallic element used in electric lamp filaments. See **tungsten**

wo'man (woo'man) *n.* a female grown-up person.—**man** *masc.*—**wo'men** (wim'en) *pl.*—**wom'anhood** *n.*—**wom'anish** *adj.* weak.—**woman'kind** *n.* women.—**wom'anliness** *n.* women's qualities.—**wom'anly** *adj.* like a woman

womb (wōōm) *n.* part of the female body that holds the young before birth

wom'bat *n.* an Australian pouched mammal

won'der (wun'der) *n.* 1. marvel, surprising thing or happening. 2. feeling of surprise. —*v.* 1. to be surprised, as *I wonder that he dared to do it.* 2. to want to know, as *I wonder where he is now.*—**won'derful** *adj.* remarkable, fine.—**won'derfully** *adv.*—**won'drous** *adj.* wonderful.—**a nine days' wonder** something that arouses interest for a short time

Compare: (with wonderful) marvellous, amazing, surprising, extraordinary, astonishing, unusual. *Contrast:* ordinary, commonplace, usual, customary

wont (wōnt) *n.* custom, habit, as *It was his wont to go for a walk every evening.*—*adj.* accustomed, as *Nelson was wont to pray before a battle.*—**wont'ed** *adj.* usual

woo *v.* to make love to.—**woo'er** *n.* suitor

wood *n.* 1. a large number of trees growing together. 2. timber, the substance from which the trees are made.—**wood'craft** *n.* knowledge of life in a forest.—**wood'cutter** *n.*—**wood'ed** *adj.* covered with trees.—**wood'en** *adj.* 1. made of wood. 2. stiff.—**wood'land** *n.* wooded country.—**wood'man, woods'man** *n.* a man who lives and works in a forest.—**wood'work** *n.* 1. things made of wood. 2. making things from wood.—**wood'-pulp** *n.* a pulp of wood fibres used in paper-making.—**wood'wind** *n.* (collective) the wooden wind-instruments of an orchestra.—**not to see the wood for the trees** not to see the essential thing in a mass of details.—**out of the wood** out of a difficult situation

Compare: (with wood 1) thicket, brake, coppice, spinney, copse, forest. All these are kinds of *woods*, mentioned in order of increasing size, All are smaller than a *wood*, except *forest*, which is larger

woof *n.* weft, threads that cross the warp in weaving

wool *n.* 1. soft hair of the sheep and certain other animals. 2. material, or clothes made of wool.—**wool'len** *adj.* 1. made of wool. 2. having to do with wool.—**wool'ly** *adj.* of wool, like wool.—**wool'lier** *comp.*—**wool'liest** *sup.*—**wool'sack** *n.* Lord Chancellor's seat in House of Lords.—**wool'-classer** (Aus.) a grader of wool.—**wool'clip** (Aus.) the annual amount of wool shorn.—**wool'shed** (Aus.) building or buildings used for shearing, packing or storing wool.—**wool'gathering** *adj.* absent-minded. —**dyed in the wool** absolute, deep-rooted. —**to pull the wool over someone's eyes** to deceive him

word (wurd) *n.* 1. a sound or group of sounds, spoken or written, expressing an idea and forming part of a sentence. 2. speech, talk, as *I want a word with you.* 3. news, information, message, as *Please send word how you get on.* 4. a promise, as *She gave her word.*—*v.* to express in words.—**word'ing** *n.* choice of words.—**word'y** *adj.* using too many words.—**a word in season** advice given at the right moment.—**as good as one's word** keeping one's promise.—**to eat one's words** to take back what one has said.—**word for word** exactly as spoken

work (wurk) *n.* 1. doing something that needs effort. 2. a task, labours, occupation. 3. something made, as *a work of art.*—*pl.* factory, working parts of a machine.—*v.* 1. to do work, to labour. 2. to act, to cause something or someone to act. 3. to have an occupation.—**worked, wrought** *p.t.* and *p. part.*—**work'-bag, work'-box** *n.* something to hold sewing-materials.—**work'er** *n.*—**work'man, work'ing-man'** *n.* a man who works with his hands.—**work'manlike** *adj.* well done.—**work'manship** *n.* skill, art. —**work'shop** *n.* a place where things are made.—**work'-shy** lazy.—**to work to rule** to waste time deliberately by observing rules with extreme care

Compare: action, effort, employment, business, task, toil, drudgery. *Contrast:* ease, leisure, rest, holiday, vacation, unemployment, idleness, repose

world *n.* 1. the universe, all creation. 2. the earth. 3. mankind. 4. society, the public, everyone. 5. sphere, as *the world of sport.*—**world'liness** *n.* worldly ways.—**world'ly** *adj.* caring for the things of this world, esp. wealth and pleasure.—**the old world** Europe, Africa, Asia.—**the new world** America.—**for all the world like** exactly like.—**out of this world** marvellous.—**to think the world of** to cherish very highly

worm *n.* 1. a small, crawling animal without backbone or legs. 2. the thread of a screw. —*v.* 1. to crawl. 2. to get by sly and secret ways.—**worm'eaten** *adj.* full of small holes

worm'wood *n.* a bitter herb used in medicine

worn *p. part.* of wear.—*adj.* 1. used until damaged. 2. tired, weary.—**worn-out** *adj.* unfit for further use

wor'ry (wur'i) *v.* 1. to seize and shake with

the teeth. 2. to torment, vex, trouble. (See vex.) 3. to feel uneasy.—he **wor'ries.**—**wor'rying** *pres. part.*—**wor'ried** *p.t.* and *p. part.*—*n.* care, anxiety. (See **trouble.**)—**wor'ries** *pl.*

worse (wurs) *comp.* of **bad** and **badly** (also of **ill** and **evil**).—*adv.* 1. in worse health. 2. in worse condition.—*n.* something less good.—**wors'en** *v.* to get worse

wor'ship (wur'ship) *n.* 1. respect, reverence. 2. religious service. 3. a title of respect for a mayor, etc.—*v.* 1. to honour with religious service. 2. to adore. (See **adore.**)—**wor'shipping** *pres. part.*—**wor'shipped** *p.t.* and *p. part.*—**wor'shipper** *n.*

Note: a mayor is addressed as *Your Worship* and spoken of as *His Worship*

worst (wurst) *sup.* of **bad** and **badly** (also of **ill** and **evil**)—*n.* the worst part.—*v.* to defeat.—**if the worst comes to the worst** if things prove as bad as they possibly can be

wor'sted (woos'ted) *n.* woollen yarn.—*adj.* made of woollen yarn

worth (wurth) *n.* merit, importance, value.—*adj.* 1. having value enough for, good enough for. 2. of equal value to.—**worth'ily** *adv.* in a worthy way.—**worth'less** *adj.* useless.—**worth-while** *adj.* worth time and trouble.—**for all one is worth** making every effort

worth'y (wur'thi) *adj.* 1. having worth. 2. deserving, as *worthy of respect, worthy to be respected.*—**worth'ier** *comp.*—**worth'iest** *sup.*—*n.* a person of merit.—**worth'ies** *pl.*

wound (wōōnd) *n.* 1. hurt caused by cutting, shooting, etc. 2. hurt to reputation or feelings.—*v.* to injure by cutting, etc.

wove *p.t.* of **weave.**—*p. part.* **woven**

wow'ser *n.* (Aus.) a narrow-minded, prudish person, a kill-joy.—**wow'serism** *n.*—**wow'serish, wow'seristic** *adj.*

wrack (rak) *n.* 1. sea-weed cast ashore. 2. wreckage, ruin, in the phrase *to go to (w)rack and ruin*

wraith (rāth) *n.* a ghost

wrang'le (rang'gl) *v.* to quarrel noisily.—**wrang'ling** *pres. part.*—*n.* noisy, quarrel (See **quarrel**)

wrap (rap) *v.* to cover by putting something round, to enfold.—**wrap'ping** *pres. part.*—**wrapped** *p.t.* and *p. part.*—*n.* a loose covering.—**wrap'per** *n.* 1. a cover. 2. a dressing-gown.—**wrapped up in** absorbed in

wrath (rawth) *n.* anger. (See **rage.**)—**wrath'ful** *adj.* furious

wreak (reek) *v.* 1. to inflict vengeance, etc. on. 2. to give vent to

wreath (reeth) *n.* 1. a ring of flowers, leaves, etc., a garland. 2. a ring, curl, e.g. of smoke.—**wreathe** (reeTH) *v.* 1. to surround, encircle. 2. to curl, twist.—**wreath'ing** *pres. part.*

wreck (rek) *n.* 1. ruin, destruction. 2. destruction of a ship. 3. something ruined.—*v.* to destroy, damage badly.—**wreck'age** *n.* wrecked remains.—**wreck'er** *n.* 1. a person who wrecks. 2. a person who plunders wrecked ships

wren (ren) *n.* a very small song-bird

wrench (rench) *n.* 1. a violent twist. 2. an adjustable spanner for turning nuts.—*v.* to twist and pull violently.—he **wrench'es**

wrest (rest) *v.* 1. to take by force, to pull away. 2. to twist violently, to distort, as *You wrest my words from their meaning*

wres'tle (res'l) *v.* 1. to try to throw an opponent to the ground. 2. to struggle.—**wrest'ling** *pres. part.*—*n.* wrestling.—**wrest'ler** *n.*

Note: You *wrestle with* an opponent, or *with* difficulties. You *wrestle with* or *against* a temptation

wretch (rech) *n.* 1. a miserable person. 2. a worthless person. (See **villain.**)—**wretch'es** *pl.*—**wretch'ed** *adj.* 1. very unhappy, miserable, as *The prisoners looked thoroughly wretched.* 2. bad, poor, as *a wretched hovel.*—**wretch'edly** *adv.*—**wretch'edness** *n.*

Compare: (with *adj.*) 1. dejected, sad, pitiable, woebegone, 2. base, vile, contemptible, mean, pitiful

wrig'gle (rig'l) *v.* to twist and turn.—*n.*—**wrig'gling** *pres. part.*

wright (rīt) *n.* someone who makes something, as a playwright, wheelwright, shipwright

wring (ring) *v.* 1. to twist and squeeze, as *to wring out washing, to wring one's hands.* 2. to extort, as *to wring money out of someone.*—**wrung** *p.t.* and *p. part.*—**wring'er** *n.* a machine for wringing clothes

wrin'kle (ring'kl) *n.* 1. small crease, fold. 2. hint, clever idea.—*v.* 1. to make wrinkles in. 2. to become wrinkled.—**wrink'ling** *pres. part.*

wrist (rist) *n.* the joint between hand and arm.—**wrist'band** *n.* band of shirt-sleeve.—**wrist'let** *n.* band worn on wrist.—**wrist'watch** *n.*

writ (rit) *n.* 1. something written. 2. a written order from a law-court.—**holy writ** the Bible

write (rīt) *v.* 1. to mark paper with letters or words. 2. to send a letter. 3. to compose a book. 4. to state in writing.—**wri'ting** *pres. part.*—**wrote** *p.t.*—**writ'ten** *p. part.*—**wri'ter** *n.* author.—**wri'ting** *n.* 1. something written, a book, etc. 2. handwriting

writhe (rīTH) *v.* to twist about, esp. in pain.—**wri'thing** *pres. part.*

wrong (rong) *adj.* 1. not right, bad. 2. incorrect; untrue. 3. out of order. 4. mistaken.—*n.* injustice, harm, injury.—*v.* to harm, to do injustice to.—*adv.* badly.—**wrong'ful** *adj.* wrong, unjust.—**wrong'fully** *adv.*—**wrong'ly** *adv.* incorrectly.—**wrong'doer** *n.* someone who breaks the law.—

wrong'headed *adj.* obstinately awkward.—**to get on the wrong side of someone** to antagonise him.—**to hold the wrong end of the stick** to misunderstand something

wrought (rawt) *p.t.* and *p. part.* of **work**.—**wrought iron**, iron made tough by forging

wry (rī) *adj.* crooked, twisted

X

Xmas contraction for **Christmas**

x-rays *n.* rays which can penetrate substances that do not let in ordinary light, used in medicine to examine broken bones, etc.

xy'lophone (zī'lō-fōn) *n.* a musical instrument made of wooden bars which vibrate when struck by small wooden hammers

Y

yacht (yot) *n.* a boat for racing or pleasure. (See **ship**.)—**yachts'man** *n.*

yak *n.* the wild ox of Central Asia

yam *n.* a tropical plant grown for its fleshy, edible root, a kind of potato

yard *n.* a piece of enclosed ground near a building.—**Scotland Yard** the headquarters of the London Metropolitan Police

yard *n.* 1. a measure of length, three feet, thirty-six inches. 2. a spar slung across ship's mast to extend sails.—**yard'arm** *n.* a pole supporting sail.—**yard'stick** *n.* 1. a yard-measure. 2. a standard for comparing things

yarn *n.* 1. spun thread, esp. when prepared for weaving or knitting. 2. a story, tale.—**to spin a yarn** to tell a story

yash'mak *n.* a Moslem woman's veil

yawl *n.* 1. a ship's boat. 2. sailing-boat

yawn *v.* 1. to open the mouth widely because of sleepiness or boredom. 2. to open wide, to gape, as *The abyss yawned at our feet*

yea (yā) *adv.* old form of **yes**

year *n.* the time taken by the earth to revolve round the sun; twelve months; three hundred and sixty-five days and a quarter.—**year'ling** *n.* animal one year old.—**year'ly** *adv.* 1. every year. 2. once a year.—*adj.* happening once a year.—**leap year** a year of 366 days, occurring every four years.—**year in year out** happening year after year, continuously

yearn (yern) *v.* 1. to long for, to desire, as *to yearn for rest.* 2. to feel compassion, tenderness, etc. (followed by *over, to, towards*)

yeast *n.* a substance obtained from fermenting malt and used in making bread.—**yea'sty** (yee'sti) *adj.* frothy, foaming

yell *v.* to shout loudly.—*n.*

yel'low (yel'ō) *adj.* of the colour of lemons, gold, etc.—*n.*—**yellow fever** a tropical disease.—**yellow streak** a cowardly side of someone's character

yen *n.* a Japanese dollar.—*pl.* **yen**

yelp *n.* dog's quick shrill cry.—*v.*

yeo'man (yō'man) *n.* a man owning and farming a small estate.—**yeo'manry** *n.* volunteer cavalry force.—**Yeoman of the Guard** a warder or beefeater of the Tower of London

yes *adv.* 1. signifies agreement or affirmation. 2. as a question, meaning *Is that so?*—*n.*

yes'terday *n.* the day before today.—*adv.* during yesterday.—**yes'ternight** *n.* last night

yet *adv.* 1. by now, as *Is he here yet?* 2. still, as *Yet another day passed.* 3. by that time, in the near future, before the end, as *He will succeed yet.* 4. either (used with *nor*), as *He will not do it for his father, nor yet for his mother.*—*conj.* but, at the same time, as *A stern, yet not unkindly face.*—**as yet** so far, up to now

yew *n.* an ever-green tree with dark leaves, its wood

Yid'dish *n.* a dialect of German, Hebrew and Slavonic used by some Jews

yield (yeeld) *v.* 1. to produce, as *The farm yielded excellent crops.* 2. to give up, surrender.—*n.* produce, result, return

Compare: 1. bring forth, bear. 2. suffer, grant, concede, give in, permit, consent. *Contrast:* withold, withstand, keep, retain, oppose

yo'del *v.* to sing with sudden changes to a high falsetto, as do Swiss mountaineers.—**yo'delling** *pres. part.*—**yo'delled** *p.t.* and *p. part.*

yo'ga *n.* a Hindu system of meditation.—*n.* **yo'gi** someone who practises yoga

yog'hurt (yog'urt) *n.* thick clotted milk

yoke *n.* 1. a wooden bar across the necks of two animals working together. 2. something shaped or used as a yoke. 3. part of a garment round the neck and shoulders. 4. a bond, tie, servitude.—*v.* 1. to put a yoke on. 2. to unite

yo'kel *n.* a country fellow

yolk (yōk) *n.* the yellow part of an egg

yon, yon'der *adv.* over there.—*adj.* that, those over there

yore *n.* the past, long ago

you (yōō) *pron. pl.* of **thou** and **thee**. (See **ye**.) *You* is now used in the singular instead of *thee* and *thou.* It is also used impersonally to mean *one,* as *You never know what may happen*

young (yung) *adj.* not yet old, not fully developed or grown.—*n.* young ones.—**young'ster** *n.* child

Compare: (with *adj.*) youthful, immature, fresh, new. *Contrast:* See **old**

your (yōōr) *adj.* possessive form of the *prons.* **you** and **ye** as *This is your job.*—*sing.* **thy**. When used alone *your* becomes **yours**, as *The job is yours.*—*sing.* **thine**

yourself *pron.* emphatic (as *You yourself said so*) and reflexive (as *You have hurt* *yourself*) form of **you.**—*sing*. **thyself'** *pl.*—**your'selves**

youth (yōōth) *n.* 1. being young. 2. time between childhood and manhood. 3. a young man. 4. young people.—**youthful** *adj.* young

Yu'goslavia, Ju'goslavia *n.* a country of Central Europe.—**Yu'goslav** *n.* a native of Yugoslavia

Yule *n.* Christmas.—**yule log** *n.* —**yule'tide** *n.* the Christmas season

Z

zeal *n.* keenness, enthusiasm. (See **enthusiasm.**)—**zeal'ot** (zel'ot) *n.* a fanatic, over-zealous person.—**zeal'ous** (zel'us) *adj.* eager, conscientious.—**zeal'ously** *adv.*

ze'bra *n.* a wild animal like a horse but with white coat striped with black.—**ze'bra-crossing** *n.* a pedestrian crossing painted with white stripes

zen'ith *n.* 1. the point in the heavens immediately overhead. 2. the highest point, as *He was now at the zenith of his fame*

zeph'yr (zef'er) 1. the west wind. 2. a gentle breeze

ze'ro *n.* 1. nought. 2. nothing. 3. the point on a thermometer from which reckonings are made.—**ze'ro-hour** *n.* the moment at which something is planned to begin.—**ze'ros** *pl.*

zest *n.* 1. enthusiasm, enjoyment. 2. something added to give flavour

Compare: 1. appetite, keenness, heartiness. 2. relish, flavouring, sauce

zig'zag *n.* a line bent into short, sharp turns. —*v.* to move in a zig-zag course.—**zig'zagging** *pres. part.*—**zig'zagged** *p.t.* and *p. part.*—*adj.* forming a zigzag

zinc *n.* a white metal used as a coating for iron, and as a mixture in paint and in medicine

Zi'on *n.* 1. Jerusalem. 2. a place of worship. 3. the home of the saintly after death

zip, zip-fastener, zip'per *n.* a fastener for openings in clothes, made of two rows of interlocking teeth.—*v.* to fasten with a zip

zith'er *n.* a musical stringed instrument

zo'diac *n.* a belt of the heavens outside which the sun, moon, and planets do not pass, and divided into twelve areas called *signs of the Zodiac*, each named after a constellation

zone *n.* 1. an encircling band. 2. a division of the earth made by the arctic and antartic circles and the tropics.—*adj.* **zo'nal**

zoo *n.* contraction for **zoological gardens** a place where wild animals are kept for show.—**zoolog'ical** (zō-ō-loj'i-kal) *adj.* having to do with animals or zoology.—**zool'ogist** *n.* a person skilled in the natural history of animals.—**zool'ogy** (zō-ol'o-ji) *n.* the study of animal life

zoom *v.* 1. to move with a buzzing noise. 2. to rise sharply, as *prices zoomed.*—**zoom lens** (cinematography) a lens which can be altered while filming, causing distant objects to appear to move towards the viewer

zu'lu *n.* a member of a South African tribe